The New Lexicon
RAND McNALLY

ATLAS
of the WORLD

The New Lexicon
RAND M^cNALLY

ATLAS
of the WORLD

LEXICON PUBLICATIONS, INC.
DANBURY, CT

THE NEW LEXICON RAND M^cNALLY ATLAS OF THE WORLD

Copyright © 1992 by Rand McNally & Company.

ISBN 0-7172-4638-8

Printed and manufactured in the United States of America.

CONTENTS

USING THE ATLAS . . . . **I•7 – I•8**

FLAGS OF THE WORLD . . . . **I•9 – I•15**

WORLD TIME ZONES . . . . **I•16**

REFERENCE MAPS . . . . **1 – 128**
Map Symbols and Index Map 1
World . . . . .2 – 3

Europe . . . . **4 – 5**
Scandinavia 6
British Isles 7
Central Europe .8 – 9
France and the Alps . . . . .10 – 11
Spain and Portugal . . . . .12 – 13
Italy . . . . .14 – 15
Southeastern Europe . . . . .16 – 17
Baltic and Moscow Regions . . . . .18 – 19

Asia . . . . **20 – 21**
Northwest Asia . . . . .22 – 23
Northeast Asia . . . . .24 – 25
China, Japan, and Korea . . . . .26 – 27
Eastern and
      Southeastern China . . . . .28 – 29
Japan . . . . .30 – 31
Southeastern Asia . . . . .32 – 33
Burma, Thailand, and
      Indochina . . . . .34 – 35
India and Pakistan 36
Southern India and Sri Lanka 37
Northern India and Pakistan . . . . . . .38 – 39
Eastern Mediterranean Lands 40

Africa **41**
Northern Africa . . . . .42 – 43
Southern Africa . . . . .44 – 45
Eastern Africa and Middle East 46

Antarctica **47**

Pacific Ocean . . . . **48 – 49**

Australia . . . . **50 – 51**
New Zealand 52

South America . . . . : **53**
Northern South America . . . . .54 – 55
Southern South America 56
Southeastern Brazil 57
Colombia, Ecuador, Venezuela,
      and Guyana . . . . .58 – 59

Atlantic Ocean **60**

North America **61**
Mexico . . . . .62 – 63
Central America
      and the Caribbean . . . . .64 – 65

Canada . . . . **66 – 67**
Alberta 68
British Columbia 69
Manitoba 70
New Brunswick, Nova Scotia,
      and Prince Edward Island 71
Newfoundland 72
Ontario 73
Quebec 74
Saskatchewan 75

United States of America . . . . **76 – 77**
Alabama 78
Alaska 79
Arizona 80
Arkansas 81
California 82
Colorado 83
Connecticut 84
Delaware 85
Florida 86
Georgia 87
Hawaii 88
Idaho 89
Illinois 90
Indiana 91
Iowa 92
Kansas 93
Kentucky 94
Louisiana 95
Maine 96
Maryland 97
Massachusetts 98
Michigan 99
Minnesota 100
Mississippi 101
Missouri 102
Montana 103
Nebraska 104
Nevada 105
New Hampshire 106
New Jersey 107
New Mexico 108
New York 109
North Carolina .110

USING THE ATLAS

Maps and Atlases

Satellite images of the world (figure 1) constantly give us views of the shape and size of the earth. It is hard, therefore, to imagine how difficult it once was to ascertain the look of our planet. Yet from early history we have evidence of humans trying to work out what the world actually looked like.

Twenty-five hundred years ago, on a tiny clay tablet the size of a hand, the Babylonians inscribed the earth as a flat disk (figure 2) with Babylon at the center. The section of the Cantino map of 1502 (figure 3) is an example of a *portolan* chart used by mariners to chart the newly discovered Americas. The maps

in this atlas, show the detail and accuracy that cartographers are now able to achieve.

In 1589 Gerardus Mercator used the word *atlas* to describe a collection of maps. Atlases now bring together not only a variety of maps, but an assortment of tables and other reference material as well. They have become a unique and indispensable reference for graphically defining the world and answering the question *where*. With them routes between places can be traced, trips planned, distances measured, places imagined, and our earth visualized.

FIGURE 1

FIGURE 2

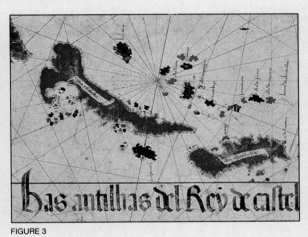
FIGURE 3

Sequence of the Maps

The world is made up of seven major landmasses: the continents of Europe, Asia, Africa, Antarctica, Australia, South America, and North America. The maps in this atlas follow this continental sequence. To allow for the inclusion of detail, each continent is broken down into a series of maps, and this grouping is arranged so that as consecutive pages are turned, a continuous successive part of the continent is shown. Larger-scale maps are used for regions of greater detail or for areas of global significance.

Getting the Information

To realize the potential of an atlas the user must be able to:
1. Find places on the maps
2. Measure distances
3. Determine directions
4. Understand map symbols

Finding Places

One of the most common and important tasks facilitated by an atlas is finding the location of a place in the world. A river's name in a book, a city mentioned in the news, or a vacation spot may prompt your need to know where the place is located. The illustrations and text below explain how to find Yangon (Rangoon), Burma.

Yancheng, China	**B9**	28
Yandoon, Burma	**F3**	34
Yangjiang, China	**G9**	26
Yangon (Rangoon), Burma	**B2**	32
Yangquan, China	**D9**	26
Yangtze see Chang, stm., China	**E10**	26
Yangzhou, China	**C8**	28

FIGURE 4

1. Look up the place-name in the index at the back of the atlas. Yangon, Burma can be found on the map on page 32, and it can be located on the map by the letter-number key *B2* (figure 4). If you know the general area in which a place is found, you may turn directly to the appropriate map and use the special marginal index.

2. Turn to the map of Southeastern Asia found on page 32. Note that the letters *A* through *H* and the numbers *1* through *11* appear in the margins of the map.

3. To find Yangon, on the map, place your left index finger on *B* and your right index finger on *2*. Move your left finger across the map and your right finger down the map. Your fingers will meet in the area in which Yangon is located (figure 5).

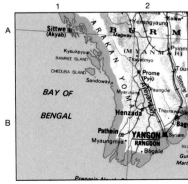
FIGURE 5

Measuring Distances

In planning trips, determining the distance between two places is essential, and an atlas can help in travel preparation. For instance, to determine the approximate distance between Paris and Rouen, France, follow these three steps:

1. Lay a slip of paper on the map on page 10 so that its edge touches the two cities. Adjust the paper so one corner touches Rouen. Mark the paper directly at the spot where Paris is located (figure 6).

FIGURE 6

2. Place the paper along the scale of miles beneath the map. Position the corner at 0 and line up the edge of the paper along the scale. The pencil mark on the paper indicates Rouen is between 50 and 100 miles from Paris (figure 7).

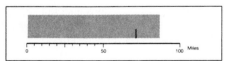

FIGURE 7

3. To find the exact distance, move the paper to the left so that the pencil mark is at 100 on the scale. The corner of the paper stands on the fourth 5-mile unit on the scale. This means that the two towns are 50 plus 20, or 70 miles apart (figure 8).

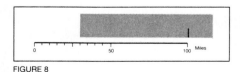

FIGURE 8

Determining Directions

Most of the maps in the atlas are drawn so that when oriented for normal reading, north is at the top of the map, south is at the bottom, west is at the left, and east is at the right. Most maps have a series of lines drawn across them–the lines of *latitude* and *longitude*. Lines of latitude, or *parallels* of latitude, are drawn east and west. Lines of longitude, or *meridians* of longitude, are drawn north and south (figure 9).

Parallels and meridians appear as either curved or straight lines. For example, in the section of the map of Europe (figure 10) the parallels of latitude appear as curved lines. The meridians of longitude are straight lines that come together toward the top of the map. Latitude and longitude lines help locate places on maps. Parallels of latitude are numbered in degrees north and south of the *Equator*. Meridians of longitude are numbered in degrees east and west of a line called the *Prime Meridian*, running through Greenwich, England, near London. Any place on earth can be located by the latitude and longitude lines running through it.

To determine directions or locations on the map, you must use the parallels and meridians. For example, suppose you want to know which is farther north, Bergen, Norway, or Stockholm, Sweden. The map (figure 10) shows that Stockholm is south of the 60° parallel of latitude and Bergen is north of it. Bergen is farther north than Stockholm. By looking at the meridians of longitude, you can determine which city is farther east. Bergen is approximately 5° east of the 0° meridian (Prime Meridian), and Stockholm is almost 20° east of it. Stockholm is farther east than Bergen.

FIGURE 10

Understanding Map Symbols

In a very real sense, the whole map is a symbol, representing the world or a part of it. It is a reduced representation of the earth; each of the world's features–cities, rivers, etc.–is represented on the map by a symbol. Map symbols may take the form of points, such as dots or squares (often used for cities, capital cities, or points of interest), or lines (roads, railroads, rivers). Symbols may also occupy an area, showing extent of coverage (terrain, forests, deserts). They seldom look like the feature they represent and therefore must be identified and interpreted. For instance, the maps in this atlas define political units by a colored line depicting their boundaries. Neither the colors nor the boundary lines are actually found on the surface of the earth, but because countries and states are such important political components of the world, strong symbols are used to represent them. The Map Symbols page in this atlas identifies the symbols used on the maps.

FIGURE 9

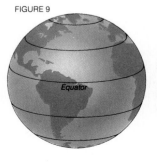

FLAGS OF THE WORLD

A simple piece of colored fabric, usually rectangular in shape, a flag embodies the fundamental human values of community and group identity. As symbols of a political entity, institution, office, or ideology, flags publicly communicate powerful messages and emotions: unity, loyalty, pride, honor, victory, submission, challenge, hope, and resolve.

The most important flags of the modern world are those that identify sovereign nations. Patriots express their love of country by hoisting flags; victorious armies humiliate their enemies by displaying captured flags; dictators use flags to help mold public opinion; insults to the flag may lead to punishment or, if the desecrators are foreign, to an international incident.

History of Flags

The date of the earliest flag is not known, but the first vexilloids (flaglike objects) came into use when people began to live in cities and to organize regular military forces. Archaeological records from the ancient Middle East, Egypt, China, and the Americas suggest that the use of flags was nearly universal among early civilizations. These first flags frequently consisted of a carved emblem—a sacred animal or some natural object—at the top of a pole, sometimes with ribbons attached below. Cloth flags may have been a Chinese invention, since woven silk was developed very early in the Far East.

The beginnings of modern flag design—the combination of colors and forms on cloth to convey certain ideas—may be seen in the development of heraldry during the 12th century in Europe and slightly later in Japan. Heraldry was the design of coats of arms to distinguish individuals, families, and institutions.

One of the most important developments in flag history has been the proliferation of national flags, which began in the late 18th century and continues today. The American and French revolutions of 1775 and 1789, respectively, associated specific designs and colors with the concepts of liberty, independence, democracy, nationalism, and mobilization of the masses. Since then, most of the great multinational empires have vanished. The organization of the world on the basis of countries characterized by a single nationality and ideology has spread from Europe to Latin America, Asia, Africa, the Pacific, and, most recently, the former Soviet Union and Yugoslavia. The old standard of a monarch or imperial regime representing many different peoples has given way to the national flag of a distinctive people with its own language, culture, territory, and aspirations.

Flag Symbolism

The design of each nation's flag carries unique symbolic meaning. Most flags feature such symbols as stripes, stars, animals, crosses, or other emblems. Even the colors chosen for a flag represent some geographic, ideological, or historical feature.

For example, the Union Jack of the United Kingdom combines the crosses of St. George, St. Andrew, and St. Patrick, the patron saints of England, Scotland, and Ireland, respectively. The five points of the star in the national flag of Somalia represent a claim to the five territories in which the Somalis live. The yellow-blue-red flag of Venezuela symbolizes the wealth of the New World (yellow) separated from Spain (red) by the blue ocean. The red of revolution and communism serves as the background for the national flag of China; its five gold stars reflect not only the old Chinese imperial color but also the five largest ethnic groups and "nationalities" (the largest representing the majority Han, the four others representing subnationalities).

As different as the national flags of the world are, cross-cultural borrowing of designs is very common. The red, white, and blue of the U.S. flag clearly were derived from British sources; the Continental Colors of 1776 featured the Union Jack in the top left quadrant. Even today, former French colonies in Africa fly flags similar to the French tricolor.

The evolution of some flag designs is a study in political history. For example, those who struggled against Spanish rule in Latin America achieved one of their early successes in Argentina. The blue-and-white flag adopted by that country (then called the United Provinces of La Plata) in 1816 was also flown by privateers who harassed Spanish ports and ships along the coasts of South and Central America. The same flag was adopted by the leaders of Central America after Spanish rule was thrown off in 1821. As individual republics emerged from the Central American federation (1825-38), they modified the flag but still retained its basic colors. The Revolutions of 1848 in Europe inspired Costa Rica to add a stripe of red through the center of the blue-and-white; Guatemala changed to vertical stripes; and Honduras, Nicaragua, and El Salvador added distinctive emblems on the central white stripe.

The struggle of the Arab countries for independence and unity is also represented in their flags. The first national flag (1947-51) of Cyrenaica was that of the conservative Sanusi religious sect; it was black with a white star and a crescent in the center. Stripes of red and green, symbolizing the Fezzan and Tripolitania, were added when they joined Cyrenaica as the independent country of Libya in 1951. A revolution there in 1969 replaced the monarchy, and the flag was altered to red-white-black, the recognized "Arab liberation colors." In 1971, Libya joined Egypt and Syria in the Confederation of Arab Republics and added its own emblem, the gold hawk of the Quraish tribe, to the center stripe. In 1977, angered by attempts of Egypt's President Anwar Sadat to negotiate peace with Israel, Libya again changed its flag. It chose a field of plain green, the fourth traditional Islamic color.

The flags of the world, shown in the following pages, thus form a kind of map of its sovereign states, political systems, peoples, and history.

Afghanistan

Albania

Algeria

Andorra

Angola

Antigua and Barbuda

Argentina

Armenia

Australia

Austria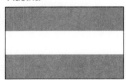

Azerbaijan

Bahamas

Bahrain

Bangladesh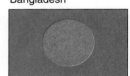

Barbados

Belarus

Belgium

Belize

Benin

Bhutan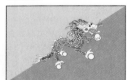

Bolivia

Bosnia and Hercegovina

Botswana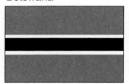

Brazil

Brunei

Bulgaria

Burkina Faso

Burma (Myanmar)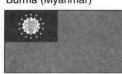

Burundi

Cambodia

Cameroon

Canada

Cape Verde

Central African Republic

Chad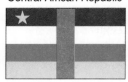

Chile

China

Colombia

Comoros

Congo

Costa Rica

Croatia

Cuba

Cyprus

Czechoslovakia

Denmark
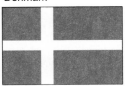

Djibouti

Dominica
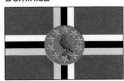

Dominican Republic

Ecuador

Egypt

El Salvador

Equatorial Guinea

Estonia
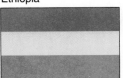

Ethiopia

Fiji

Finland

France
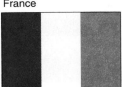

Gabon
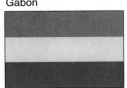

Gambia
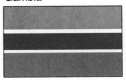

Georgia

Germany

Ghana

Greece

Grenada

Guatemala

Guinea
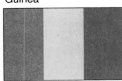

Guinea-Bissau

Guyana
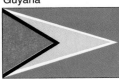

Haiti

Honduras

Hungary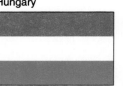

Iceland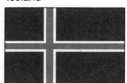

India

Indonesia

Iran

Iraq

Ireland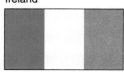

Israel

Italy

Ivory Coast

Jamaica

Japan

Jordan

Kazakhstan

Kenya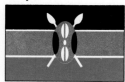

Kiribati

Korea, North

Korea, South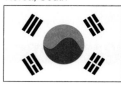

Kuwait

Kyrgyzstan

Laos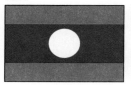

Latvia

Lebanon

Lesotho

Liberia

Libya

Liechtenstein

Lithuania

Luxembourg

Macedonia

Madagascar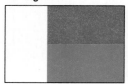

Malawi

Malaysia

Maldives

Mali

Malta

Marshall Islands

Mauritania

Mauritius

Mexico

Micronesia, Federated States of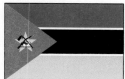

Moldova

Monaco

Mongolia

Morocco

Mozambique

Namibia

Nauru

Nepal

Netherlands

New Zealand

Nicaragua

Niger

Nigeria

Northern Mariana Islands

Norway

Oman

Pakistan

Palau

Panama

Papua New Guinea

Paraguay

Peru

Philippines

Poland

Portugal

Qatar

Romania

Russia

Rwanda

St. Kitts and Nevis

St. Lucia

St. Vincent and the Grenadines

San Marino

Sao Tome and Principe

Saudi Arabia

Senegal

Seychelles
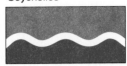

Sierra Leone

Singapore

Slovenia

Solomon Islands

Somalia

South Africa

Spain

Sri Lanka

Sudan

Suriname

Swaziland

Sweden

Switzerland

Syria

Taiwan

Tajikistan

Tanzania

Thailand

Togo

Tonga

Trinidad and Tobago

Tunisia

Turkey

Turkmenistan

Tuvalu

Uganda

Ukraine

United Arab Emirates

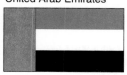

United Kingdom

United States

Uruguay

Uzbekistan

Vanuatu

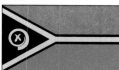

Vatican City

Venezuela

Vietnam

Western Samoa

Yemen

Yugoslavia

Zaire

Zambia

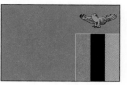

Zimbabwe

United Nations

Organization of American States

Council of Europe

Organization of African Unity

Olympics

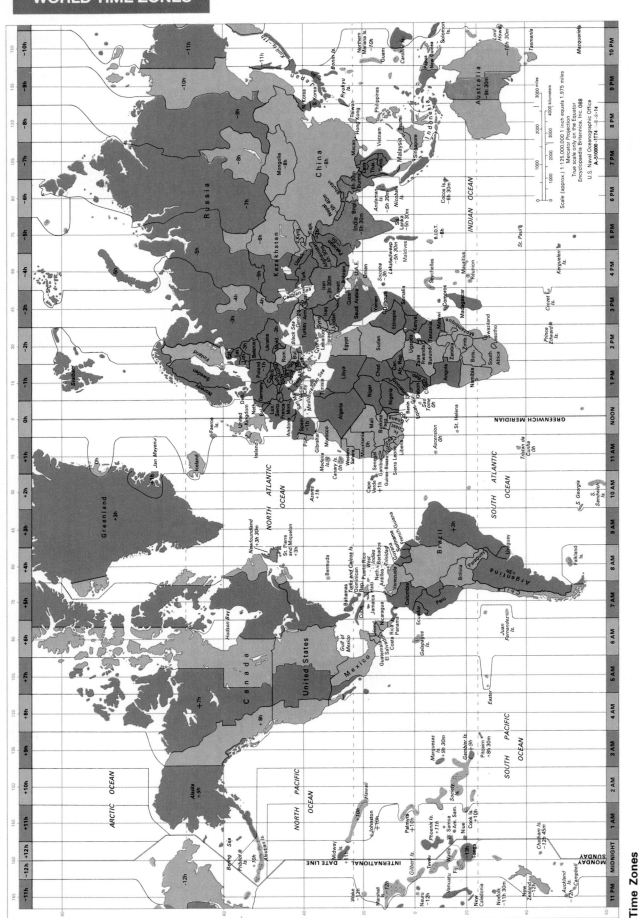

The standard time zone system, fixed by international agreement and by law in each country, is based on a theoretical division of the globe into 24 zones of 15° longitude each. The mid-meridian of each zone fixes the hour for the entire zone. The zero time zone extends 7½° east and 7½° west of the Greenwich meridian, 0° longitude. Since the earth rotates toward the east, time zones to the west of Greenwich are earlier, to the east, later. Plus and minus hours at the top of the map are added to or subtracted from local time to find Greenwich time. Local standard time can be determined for any area in the world by adding one hour for each time zone counted in an easterly direction from

one's own, or by subtracting one hour for each zone counted in a westerly direction. To separate one day from the next, the 180th meridian has been designated as the international date line. On both sides of the line the time of day is the same, but west of the line it is one day later than it is to the east. Countries that adhere to the international zone system adopt the zone applicable to their location. Some countries, however, establish time zones based on political boundaries, or adopt the time zone of a neighboring unit. For all or part of the year some countries also advance their time by one hour, thereby utilizing more daylight hours each day.

Scale (approx.) 1:125,000,000 1 inch equals 1,975 miles
Mercator Projection
True scale only on the Equator
Encyclopaedia Britannica, Inc. 088
U.S. Naval Oceanographic Office
A-510000-1T74   --8--9-14

Time Zones

☐ Standard time zone of even-numbered hours from Greenwich time

☐ Standard time zone of odd-numbered hours from Greenwich time

☐ Time varies from the standard time zone by half an hour

☐ Time varies from the standard time zone by other than half an hour

[h m]   hours, minutes

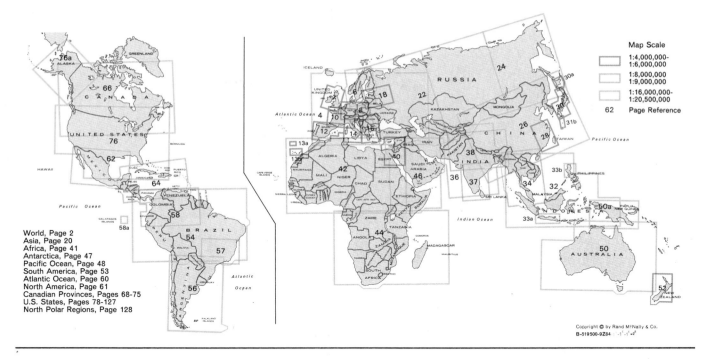

World, Page 2
Asia, Page 20
Africa, Page 41
Antarctica, Page 47
Pacific Ocean, Page 48
South America, Page 53
Atlantic Ocean, Page 60
North America, Page 61
Canadian Provinces, Pages 68-75
U.S. States, Pages 78-127
North Polar Regions, Page 128

Map Scale

☐	1:4,000,000- 1:6,000,000
☐	1:8,000,000 1:9,000,000
☐	1:16,000,000- 1:20,500,000
62	Page Reference

World Maps Symbols

Inhabited Localities

The size of type indicates the relative economic and political importance of the locality

Écommoy Lisieux **Rouen**

Trouville **Orléans** **PARIS**

Bi'r Safājah ° Oasis

Alternate Names

MOSKVA
MOSCOW English or second official language names are shown in reduced size lettering

Basel
Bâle

Volgograd Historical or other alternates in the local language are shown in
(Stalingrad) parentheses

☐ Urban Area (Area of continuous industrial, commercial, and residential development)

Capitals of Political Units

BUDAPEST Independent Nation

Cayenne Dependency (Colony, protectorate, etc.)

Recife State, Province, County, Oblast, etc.

Political Boundaries

International (First-order political unit)

— ·· — ·· — Demarcated and Undemarcated

— · — · — Disputed de jure

▨▨▨▨ Indefinite or Undefined

— — — — — Demarcation Line

Internal

———— State, Province, etc. (Second-order political unit)

MURCIA Historical Region (No boundaries indicated)

GALAPAGOS
(Ecuador) Administering Country

Transportation

———— Primary Road

———— Secondary Road

- - - - - Minor Road, Trail

—+—+— Railway

Canal du Midi Navigable Canal

⟲ Bridge

—⟶ - - - ⟵— Tunnel

TO MALMÖ Ferry

Hydrographic Features

———— Shoreline

~~~~~ Undefined or Fluctuating Shoreline

Amur River, Stream

———— Intermittent Stream

<<<< Rapids, Falls

———— Irrigation or Drainage Canal

~~~~~ Reef

The Everglades Swamp

RIMO GLACIER Glacier

L. Victoria Lake, Reservoir

Tuz Gölü Salt Lake

Intermittent Lake, Reservoir

Dry Lake Bed

(395) Lake Surface Elevation

Topographic Features

Matterhorn △
4478 Elevation Above Sea Level

76 ▽ Elevation Below Sea Level

Mount Cook ▲
3764 Highest Elevation in Country

133 ▼ Lowest Elevation in Country

Khyber Pass ≍
1067 Mountain Pass

Elevations are given in meters.
The highest and lowest elevations in a continent are underlined

Sand Area

Lava

Salt Flat

State, Province Maps Symbols

◉ Capital

◦ County Seat

▲ Military Installation

△ Point of Interest

+ Mountain Peak

— ·· — ·· — International Boundary

— · — · — State, Province Boundary

- - - - - County Boundary

———— Railroad

———— Road

Urban Area

World

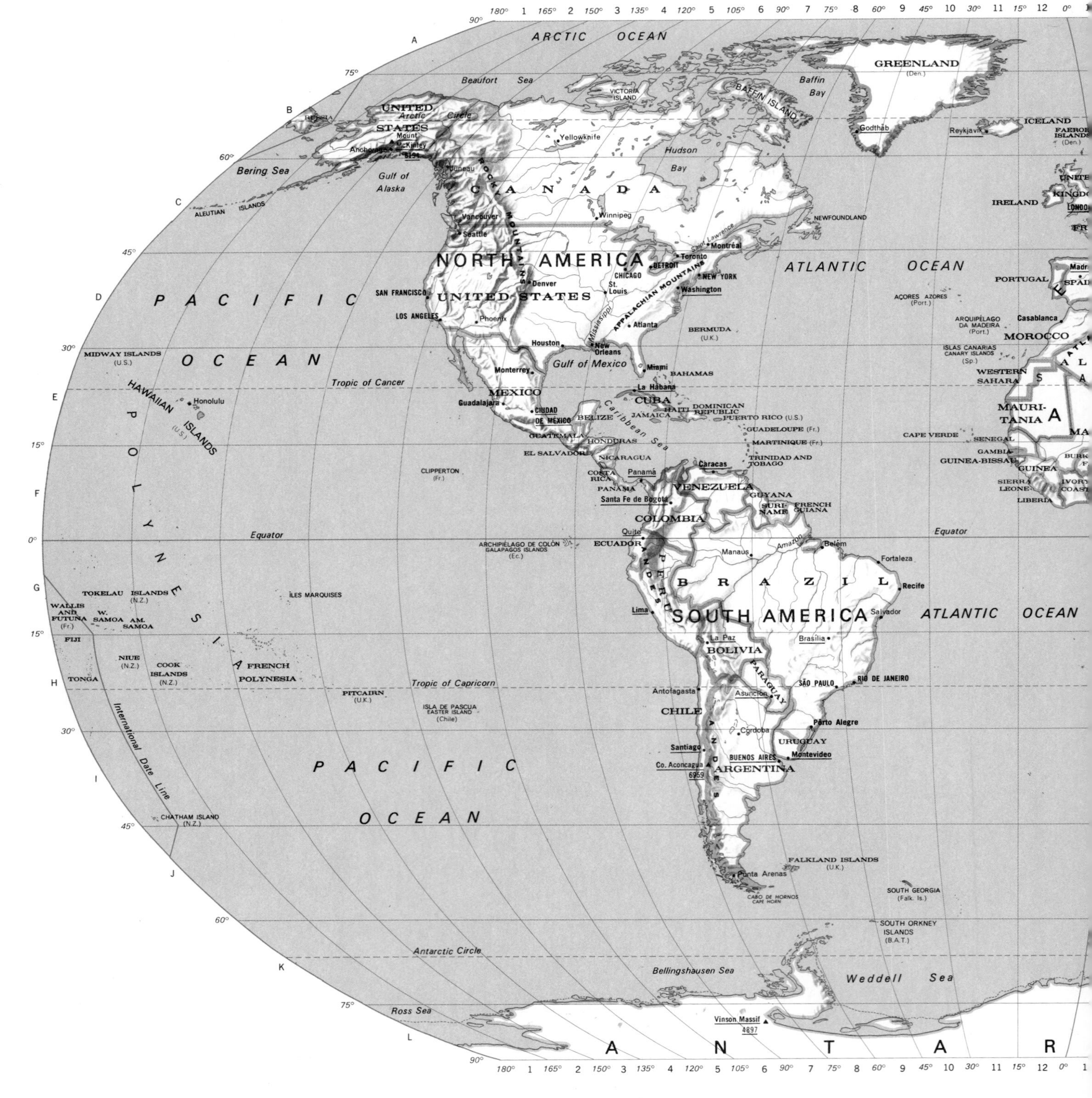
ARCTIC OCEAN
Beaufort Sea
GREENLAND
(Den.)
VICTORIA ISLAND
BAFFIN ISLAND
Baffin Bay
UNITED STATES
Arctic Circle
Mount McKinley
6194
Anchorage
Yellowknife
Godthåb
Reykjavík
ICELAND
Bering Sea
Gulf of Alaska
Juneau
ROCKY MOUNTAINS
Hudson Bay
CANADA
ALEUTIAN ISLANDS
Vancouver
Seattle
Winnipeg
NEWFOUNDLAND
IRELAND
Saint Lawrence
Montréal
Toronto
NORTH AMERICA
DETROIT
CHICAGO
NEW YORK
Washington
ATLANTIC OCEAN
PORTUGAL
SAN FRANCISCO
Denver
St. Louis
UNITED STATES
APPALACHIAN MOUNTAINS
Mississippi
LOS ANGELES
Phoenix
Atlanta
PACIFIC OCEAN
AÇORES AZORES
(Port.)
ARQUIPÉLAGO DA MADEIRA
(Port.)
Casablanca
MOROCCO
BERMUDA
(U.K.)
MIDWAY ISLANDS
(U.S.)
Houston
New Orleans
ISLAS CANARIAS CANARY ISLANDS
(Sp.)
Monterrey
Gulf of Mexico
Miami
BAHAMAS
WESTERN SAHARA
Tropic of Cancer
HAWAIIAN ISLANDS
(U.S.)
Honolulu
MEXICO
La Habana
CUBA
Guadalajara
CIUDAD DE MÉXICO
BELIZE
JAMAICA
HAITI
DOMINICAN REPUBLIC
PUERTO RICO (U.S.)
MAURITANIA
Caribbean Sea
GUADELOUPE (Fr.)
MARTINIQUE (Fr.)
CAPE VERDE
SENEGAL
GUATEMALA
HONDURAS
EL SALVADOR
NICARAGUA
GAMBIA
GUINEA-BISSAU
GUINEA
CLIPPERTON
(Fr.)
COSTA RICA
Panamá
PANAMA
Caracas
TRINIDAD AND TOBAGO
SIERRA LEONE
LIBERIA
VENEZUELA
GUYANA
Santa Fe de Bogotá
SURINAME
FRENCH GUIANA
COLOMBIA
POLYNESIA
Equator
Quito
ARCHIPIÉLAGO DE COLÓN
GALAPAGOS ISLANDS
(Ec.)
ECUADOR
Amazon
Belém
Manaus
Fortaleza
PERU
ANDES
BRAZIL
Recife
TOKELAU ISLANDS
(N.Z.)
ÎLES MARQUISES
WALLIS AND FUTUNA
(Fr.)
W. SAMOA
AM. SAMOA
Lima
SOUTH AMERICA
Salvador
ATLANTIC OCEAN
FIJI
La Paz
Brasília
BOLIVIA
NIUE
(N.Z.)
COOK ISLANDS
(N.Z.)
FRENCH POLYNESIA
TONGA
PARAGUAY
SÃO PAULO
RIO DE JANEIRO
Tropic of Capricorn
PITCAIRN
(U.K.)
Antofagasta
Asunción
ISLA DE PASCUA
EASTER ISLAND
(Chile)
CHILE
Pôrto Alegre
International Date Line
Córdoba
URUGUAY
Santiago
BUENOS AIRES
Montevideo
Co. Aconcagua
6959
ARGENTINA
PACIFIC OCEAN
CHATHAM ISLAND
(N.Z.)
FALKLAND ISLANDS
(U.K.)
Punta Arenas
SOUTH GEORGIA
(Falk. Is.)
CABO DE HORNOS
CAPE HORN
SOUTH ORKNEY ISLANDS
(B.A.T.)
Antarctic Circle
Bellingshausen Sea
Weddell Sea
Ross Sea
Vinson Massif
4897
ANTAR

Europe

ALBANIA.................G11
Amsterdam, 6,965,000
  ('89) (1,860,000★) ....E 8
ANDORRA................G 8
Antwerpen, 497,748 ('87)
  (1,100,000★) ....E 8
Athínai (Athens), 885,737
  ('81) (3,027,331★) ...H12
AUSTRIA.................F10
Barcelona, 1,714,355 ('88)
  (4,040,000★) ....G 8
BELARUS................E13
Belfast, 303,800 ('87)
  (685,000★) ....E 6
BELGIUM................E 8
Beograd (Belgrade),
  1,130,000 ('87)
  (1,400,000★) G12
Berlin, 3,352,848 ('89)
  (3,825,000★) E10
Bern, 134,393 ('90)
  (298,800★) ....F 9
Birmingham, 1,013,995
  ('81) (2,675,000★) ....E 7
Bonn, 282,190 ('89)
  (570,000★) ....E 9
BOSNIA AND
  HERCEGOVINA.......G11
Bremen, 535,058 ('89)
  (800,000★) ....E 9
Bruxelles, 136,920 ('87)
  (2,385,000★) ....E 8
Bucureşti, 1,989,823 ('86)
  (2,275,000★) G13
Budapest, 2,016,132 ('90)
  (2,565,000★) F11
BULGARIA...............G12
Cardiff, 262,313 ('81)
  (625,000★) ....E 7
Char'kov (Kharkov),
  1,611,000 ('89)
  (1,940,000★) F15
CROATIA................F11
CZECHOSLOVAKIA....F11
DENMARK...............D 9
Dnepropetrovsk,
  1,179,000 ('89)
  (1,600,000★) F14
Doneck, 1,110,000 ('89)
  (2,200,000★) F15
Dresden, 518,057 ('89)
  (670,000★) E10
Dublin, 502,749 ('86)
  (1,140,000★) ....E 6
Düsseldorf, 569,641 ('89)
  (1,190,000★) ....E 9
Edinburgh, 433,200 ('89)
  (630,000★) ....D 7
Essen, 620,594 ('89)
  (4,950,000★) ....E 9
ESTONIA................D12
FAEROE ISLANDS......C 6
FINLAND................C13
Firenze, 425,835 ('87)
  (640,000★) G10
FRANCE..................F 8
Frankfurt, 625,258 ('89)
  (1,855,000★) ....E 9
Gdańsk, 461,500 ('89)
  (909,000★) E11
Genève (Geneva), 165,404
  ('90) (460,000★).......F 9
Genova, 727,427 ('87)
  (805,000★) ....G 9
GERMANY...............E10
Gibraltar, 30,077 ('88). H 6
Glasgow, 695,630 ('89)
  (1,800,000★) ....D 7
Göteborg, 431,840 ('90)
  (710,894★) D10
GREECE.................H12
GUERNSEY..............F 7
Hamburg, 1,603,070 ('89)
  (2,225,000★) ....E 9
Helsinki, 490,034 ('88)
  (1,040,000★) C12
HUNGARY................F11
ICELAND.................B 4
IRELAND.................E 6
ISLE OF MAN...........E 7
İstanbul, 6,748,435 ('90)
  (7,000,000★) G13
ITALY....................G10
JERSEY..................F 7
Katowice, 365,800 ('89)
  (2,778,000★) E11
Kazan', 1,094,000 ('89)
  (1,140,000★) D17
Kijev (Kiev), 2,587,000
  ('89) (2,900,000★) ...E14
København, 466,723 ('90)
  (1,685,000★) D10
Köln, 937,482 ('89)
  (1,760,000★) ....E 9
Kraków, 743,700 ('89)
  (828,000★) E11
LATVIA...................D12
Leipzig, 545,307 ('89)
  (700,000★) E10
Leningrad see Sankt-
  Peterburg................D14
LIECHTENSTEIN........F 9
Ljubljana, 233,200 ('87)
  (316,607★) F10

★ Population of metropolitan
  area, including suburbs.

4

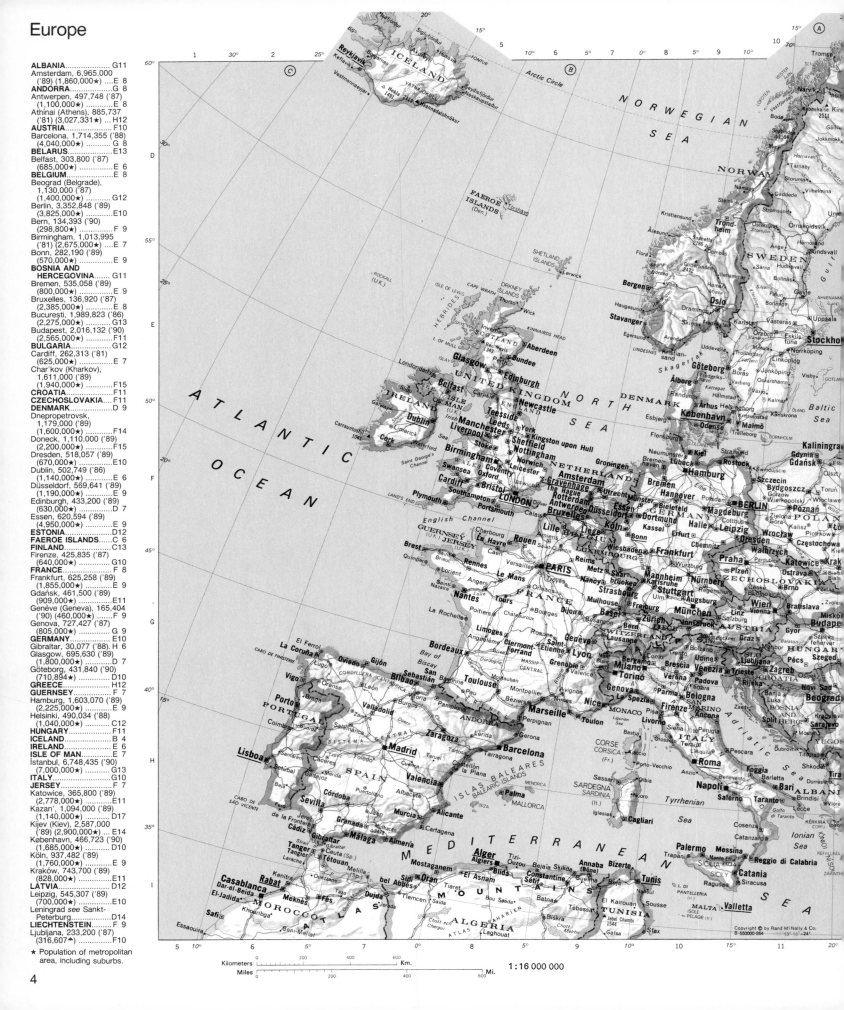

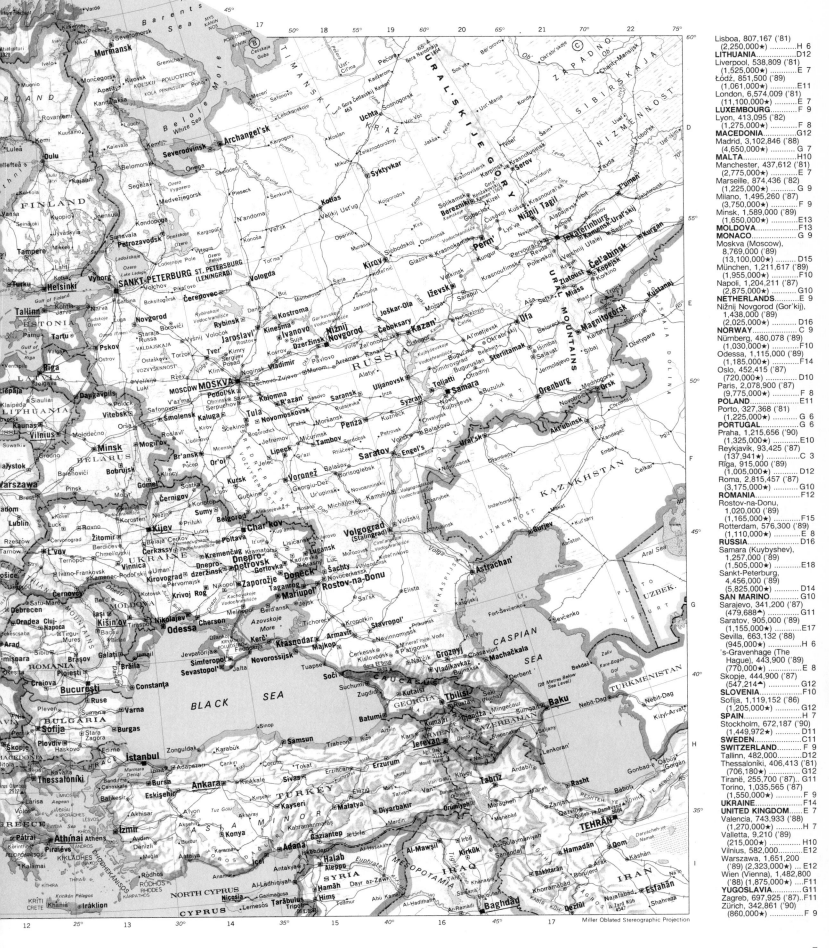

Lisboa, 807,167 ('81)
(2,250,000★)..........H 6
LITHUANIA..............D12
Liverpool, 538,809 ('81)
(1,525,000★)..........E 7
Łódź, 851,500 ('89)
(1,061,000★)..........E11
London, 6,574,009 ('81)
(11,100,000★)..........E 7
LUXEMBOURG..........F 9
Lyon, 413,095 ('82)
(1,275,000★)..........F 8
MACEDONIA..............G12
Madrid, 3,102,846 ('88)
(4,650,000★)..........G 7
MALTA..................H10
Manchester, 437,612 ('81)
(2,775,000★)..........E 7
Marseille, 874,436 ('82)
(1,225,000★)..........G 9
Milano, 1,495,260 ('87)
(3,750,000★)..........F 9
Minsk, 1,589,000 ('89)
(1,650,000★)..........E13
MOLDOVA................F13
MONACO..................G 9
Moskva (Moscow),
8,769,000 ('89)
(13,100,000★)..........D15
München, 1,211,617 ('89)
(1,955,000★)..........F10
Napoli, 1,204,211 ('87)
(2,875,000★)..........G10
NETHERLANDS..........E 9
Nižnij Novgorod (Gor'kij),
1,438,000 ('89)
(2,025,000★)..........D16
NORWAY..................C 9
Nürnberg, 480,078 ('89)
(1,030,000★)..........F10
Odessa, 1,115,000 ('89)
(1,185,000★)..........F14
Oslo, 452,415 ('87)
(720,000★)..........D10
Paris, 2,078,900 ('87)
(9,775,000★)..........F 8
POLAND..................E11
Porto, 327,368 ('81)
(1,225,000★)..........G 6
PORTUGAL..............G 6
Praha, 1,215,656 ('90)
(1,325,000★)..........E10
Reykjavík, 93,425 ('87)
(137,941★)..........C 3
Riga, 915,000 ('89)
(1,005,000★)..........D12
Roma, 2,815,457 ('87)
(3,175,000★)..........G10
ROMANIA................F12
Rostov-na-Donu,
1,020,000 ('89)
(1,165,000★)..........F15
Rotterdam, 576,300 ('89)
(1,110,000★)..........E 8
RUSSIA..................D16
Samara (Kuybyshev),
1,257,000 ('89)
(1,505,000★)..........E18
Sankt-Peterburg,
4,456,000 ('89)
(5,825,000★)..........D14
SAN MARINO............G10
Sarajevo, 341,200 ('87)
(479,688▲)..........G11
Saratov, 905,000 ('89)
(1,155,000★)..........E17
Sevilla, 663,132 ('88)
(945,000★)..........H 6
's-Gravenhage (The
Hague), 443,900 ('89)
(770,000★)..........E 8
Skopje, 444,900 ('87)
(547,214▲)..........G12
SLOVENIA................F10
Sofija, 1,119,152 ('86)
(1,205,000★)..........G12
SPAIN..................H 7
Stockholm, 672,187 ('90)
(1,449,972★)..........D11
SWEDEN..................C11
SWITZERLAND..........F 9
Tallinn, 482,000..........D12
Thessaloníki, 406,413 ('81)
(706,180★)..........G12
Tiranë, 255,700 ('87)..G11
Torino, 1,035,565 ('87)
(1,550,000★)..........F 9
UKRAINE................F14
UNITED KINGDOM...E 7
Valencia, 743,933 ('88)
(1,270,000★)..........H 7
Valletta, 9,210 ('89)
(215,000★)..........H10
Vilnius, 582,000..........E12
Warszawa, 1,651,200
('89) (2,323,000★)..E12
Wien (Vienna), 1,482,800
('88) (1,875,000★)...F11
YUGOSLAVIA............G11
Zagreb, 697,925 ('87)..F11
Zürich, 342,861 ('90)
(860,000★)..........F 9

Miller Oblated Stereographic Projection

5

Scandinavia

Denmark
1990 ESTIMATE

Ålborg, 114,000
 (155,019▲) . . . . H 7
Århus, 202,300
 (261,437▲) . . . . H 8
Copenhagen see
 København . . . . I 9
København (Copenhagen),
 466,723
 (1,685,000★) . . . . . . I 9
Odense, 140,100
 (176,133▲) . . . . I 8

Finland
1988 ESTIMATE

Helsinki (Helsingfors),
 490,034
 (1,040,000★) F15
Lahti, 74,300
 (108,000★) F15
Oulu, 98,582
 (121,000★) D15
Tampere, 170,533
 (241,000★) D14
Turku (Åbo), 160,456
 (228,000★) F14

Norway
1987 ESTIMATE

Bergen, 209,320
 (239,000★) . . . . F 5
Hammerfest,
 7,208('83) A14
Oslo, 452,415
 (720,000★) . . . . G 8
Stavanger, 94,200
 (132,000★)('85) . . . G 5
Trondheim, 135,010 . . E 8

Sweden
1990 ESTIMATE

Göteborg (Gothenburg),
 431,840 (710,894★) . H 8
Helsingborg, 108,359 . H 9
Jönköping, 110,860 . . H10
Linköping, 120,562 . . G10

Malmö, 232,908
 (445,000★) . . . . I 9
Norrköping, 119,921 . G11
Örebro, 120,353 . . . G10
Stockholm, 672,187
 (1,449,972★) G12
Uppsala, 164,754 . . . G11
Västerås, 118,386 . . G11

★ Population of metropolitan area, including suburbs.
▲ Population of entire district, including rural area.

6

Lambert Conformal Conic Projection

Kilometers 0   100   200   300 Km.

Miles 0   100   200   300 Mi.

1 : 8 000 000

Ireland

1986 CENSUS

Cork, 133,271
(173,694★) . . . . . J 4
Dublin (Baile Átha Cliath),
502,749
(1,140,000★) . . . . H 6
Galway, 47,104 . . H 3
Limerick, 56,279
(76,557★) . . . . I 4
Waterford, 39,529
(41,054★) . . . . I 5

Isle of Man

1986 CENSUS

Douglas, 20,368
(28,500★) . . . . . . G 8

United Kingdom

England

1981 CENSUS

Birmingham, 1,013,995
(2,675,000★) I11
Blackpool, 146,297
(280,000★) . . . . H 9
Bournemouth, 142,829
(315,000★) K11
Bradford, 293,336 . . H11
Brighton, 134,581
(420,000★) K12
Bristol, 413,861
(630,000★) J10
Coventry, 318,718
(645,000★) I11
Derby, 218,026
(275,000★) I11
Kingston upon Hull,
322,144 (350,000★) H12
Leeds, 445,242
(1,540,000★) H11
Leicester, 324,394
(495,000★) I11
Liverpool, 538,809
(1,525,000★) H10
London, 6,574,009
(11,100,000★) J12
Manchester, 437,612
(2,775,000★) H10
Newcastle upon Tyne,
199,064
(1,300,000★) G11
Nottingham, 273,300
(655,000★) I11
Oxford, 113,847
(230,000★) J11
Plymouth, 238,583
(290,000★) . . . . K 8
Portsmouth, 174,218
(485,000★) K11
Preston, 166,675
(250,000★) H10
Reading, 194,727
(200,000★) J12
Sheffield, 470,685
(710,000★) H11
Southampton, 211,321
(415,000★) K11
Southend-on-Sea,
155,720 . . . . . . J13
Stoke-on-Trent, 272,446
(440,000★) H10
Sunderland, 195,064 G11
Teesside, 158,516
(580,000★) G11
Wolverhampton,
263,501 . . . . . . I10

Northern Ireland

1987 ESTIMATE

Bangor, 70,700 . . . . G 7
Belfast, 303,800
(685,000★) . . . . . . G 7
Londonderry, 97,500
(97,200★) . . . . . . G 5
Newtownabbey,
72,300 . . . . . . G 7

Scotland

1989 ESTIMATE

Aberdeen, 210,700 . . D10
Dundee, 172,540 . . E 9
Edinburgh, 433,200
(630,000★) . . . . F 9
Glasgow, 695,630
(1,800,000★) . . . . F 8
Greenock, 58,436
(101,000★) ('81) . . F 8
Inverness, 38,204 ('81) D 8
Paisley, 84,330 ('81) . F 8

Wales

1981 CENSUS

Cardiff, 262,313
(625,000★) . . . . . . J 9
Newport, 115,896
(310,000★) . . . . . . J 9
Swansea, 172,433
(275,000★) . . . . . . J 9

★ Population of metropolitan
area, including suburbs.

Copyright © by Rand McNally & Co.
B-553600-264

Conic Projection, Two Standard Parallels

Kilometers
Miles
1:5 000 000

Central Europe

★ Population of metropolitan
area, including suburbs.

8

Kilometers 0 50 100 150 Km.

Miles 0 50 100 150 Mi.

1 : 4 000 000

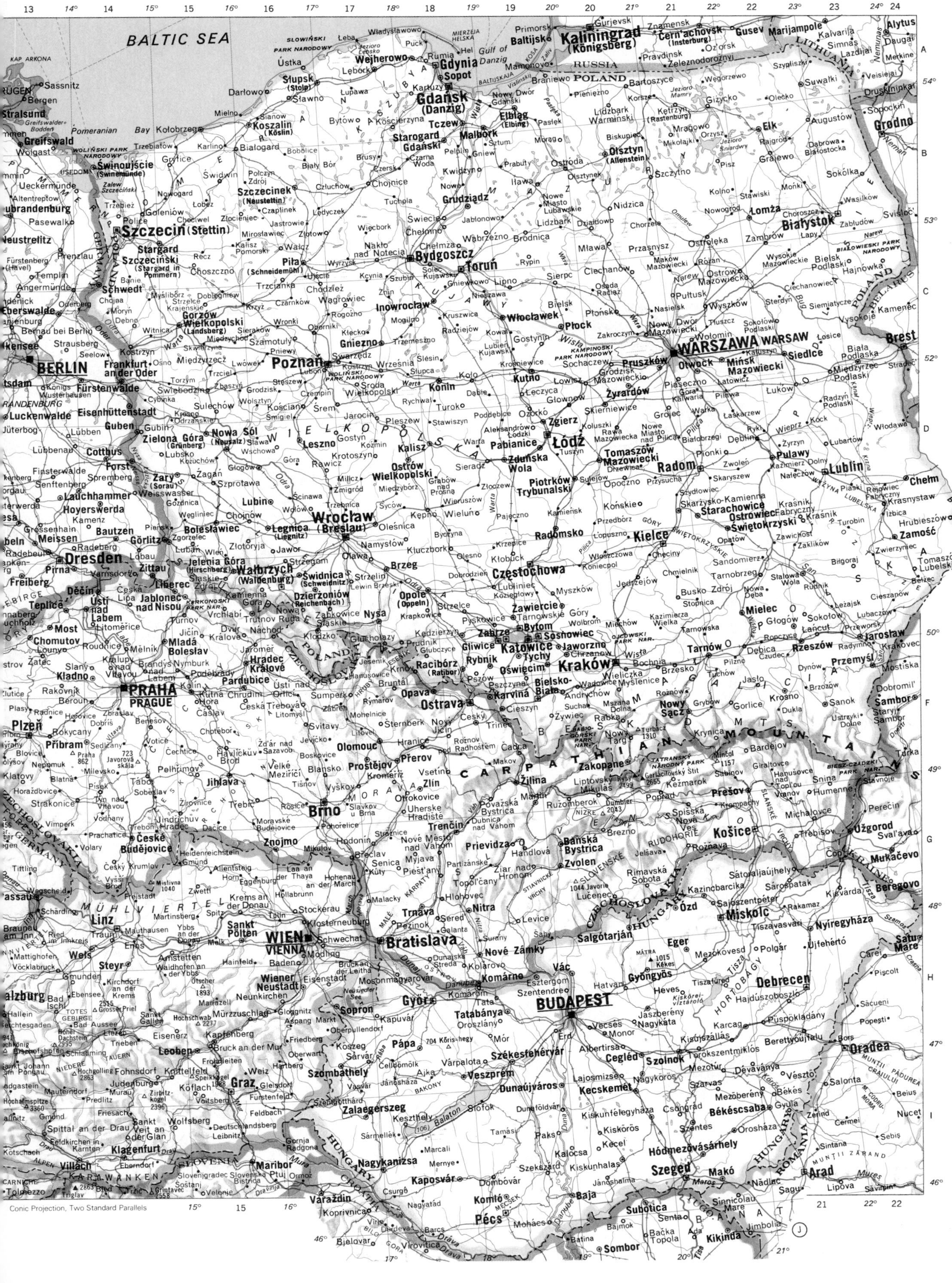

Magdeburg, 290,579 (400,000★) C11
Mannheim, 300,468 (1,400,000★) . . . . . . F 8
Mönchengladbach, 252,910 (410,000★) D 6
München (Munich), 1,211,617 (1,955,000★) G11
Münster, 248,919 . . . . D 7
Nürnberg, 480,078 (1,030,000★) F11
Potsdam, 142,862 . . C13
Rostock, 253,990 . . . . A12
Saarbrücken, 188,467 (385,000★) . . . . F 6
Stuttgart, 562,658 (1,925,000★) . . . . . . G 9
Wiesbaden, 254,209 (795,000★) . . . . E 8
Wuppertal, 371,283 (830,000★) . . . . D 7

Hungary

1990 ESTIMATE

Budapest, 2,016,132 (2,565,000★) H19
Debrecen, 212,247 . . H21
Győr, 129,356 . . . . . . H 7
Miskolc, 196,449 . . . . G20
Pécs, 170,119 . . . . . . I18
Szeged, 175,338 . . . . I20
Szombathely, 85,418 H16

Liechtenstein

1990 ESTIMATE

Vaduz, 4,874 . . . . . . H 9

Luxembourg

1985 ESTIMATE

Luxembourg, 76,130 (136,000★) . . . . F 6

Netherlands

1989 ESTIMATE

Amsterdam, 6,965,000 (1,860,000★) . . . . . . C 4
Eindhoven, 190,700 (379,377★) . . . . D 5
Groningen, 167,800 (206,781★) . . . . B 6
Nijmegen, 145,400 (240,085★) . . . . D 5
Rotterdam, 576,300 (1,110,000★) . . . . . . D 4
's-Gravenhage (The Hague), 443,900 (770,000★) . . . . C 4
Tilburg, 155,100 (224,934★) . . . . D 5
Utrecht, 230,700 (518,779★) . . . . C 5

Poland

1989 ESTIMATE

Białystok, 263,900 . . B23
Bydgoszcz, 377,900 B18
Częstochowa, 254,600 . . . . E19
Gdańsk (Danzig), 461,500 (909,000★) A18
Gdynia, 250,200 . . . . A18
Katowice, 365,800 (2,778,000★) E19
Kielce, 211,100 . . . . . . E20
Kraków, 743,700 (828,000★) E19
łódź, 851,500 (1,061,000★) D19
Lublin, 339,500 (389,000★) D22
Poznań, 586,500 (672,000★) C16
Radom, 223,600 . . . . D21
Szczecin (Stettin), 409,500 (449,000★) B14
Toruń, 199,600 . . . . . . B18
Wałbrzych (Waldenburg), 141,400 (207,000★) E16
Warszawa (Warsaw), 1,651,200 (2,323,000★) C21
Wrocław (Breslau), 637,400 . . . . D17

France and the Alps

France

1982 CENSUS
Aix-en-Provence, 121,327
  (126,552★) I12
Alès, 43,268
  (70,180★) H11
Amiens, 131,332
  (154,498★) . . . . C 9
Angers, 136,038
  (195,859★) . . . . E 6
Angoulême, 46,197
  (103,552★) . . . . G 7
Bayonne, 41,381
  (127,477★) . . . . I 5
Belfort, 51,206
  (76,221★) E13
Besançon, 113,283
  (120,772★) E13
Béziers, 76,647
  (81,347★) I10
Bordeaux, 208,159
  (640,012★) . . . . H 6
Boulogne-Billancourt,
  102,582 . . . . D 9
Boulogne-sur-Mer, 47,653
  (98,566★) . . . . B 8
Brest, 156,060
  (201,145★) . . . . D 2
Brive-la-Gaillarde, 51,511
  (64,301★) . . . . G 8
Caen, 114,068
  (183,526★) . . . . C 6
Calais, 76,527
  (100,823★) . . . . B 8
Cannes, 72,259
  (295,525★) I14
Chalon-sur-Saône, 56,194
  (78,064★) F11
Chambéry, 53,427
  (96,163★) G12
Cherbourg, 28,442
  (85,485★) . . . . C 5
Cholet, 55,524 . . . . . . E 6
Clermont-Ferrand,
  147,361 (256,189★) G10
Compiègne, 40,384
  (62,778★) . . . . C 9
Creil, 34,709
  (82,505★) . . . . C 9
Dieppe, 35,957
  (41,812★) . . . . C 8
Dijon, 140,942
  (215,865★) E12
Douai, 42,576
  (202,366★) B10
Dunkerque, 73,120
  (195,705★) . . . . A 9
Fontainebleau, 15,679
  (35,629★) . . . . D 9
Grenoble, 156,637
  (392,021★) G12
La Rochelle, 75,840
  (102,143★) . . . . F 5
Laval, 50,360
  (55,984★) . . . . D 6
Le Havre, 199,388
  (254,595★) . . . . C 7
Le Mans, 147,697
  (191,080★) . . . . D 7
Lens, 38,244
  (327,383★) . . . . B 9
Lille, 168,424
  (1,020,000★) B10
Limoges, 140,400
  (171,689★) . . . . G 8
Lorient, 62,554
  (104,025★) . . . . E 3
Lourdes, 17,425 . . . . . . I 6
Lyon, 413,095
  (1,275,000★) G11
Mâcon, 38,404
  (47,274★) F11
Marseille, 874,436
  (1,225,000★) J12
Maubeuge, 36,061
  (105,714★) B10
Meaux, 45,005
  (55,797★) . . . . D 9
Melun, 35,005
  (82,479★) . . . . D 9
Metz, 114,232
  (186,437★) C13
Montbéliard, 31,836
  (128,194★) E13
Montluçon, 49,912
  (67,963★) . . . . F 9
Montpellier, 197,231
  (221,307★) I10
Mulhouse, 112,157
  (220,613★) E14
Nancy, 96,317
  (306,982★) D13
Nantes, 240,539
  (464,857★) . . . . E 5
Nevers, 43,013
  (59,274★) E10
Nice, 337,085
  (449,496★) I14
Nîmes, 124,220
  (132,343★) I11
Niort, 58,203
  (61,959★) . . . . F 6

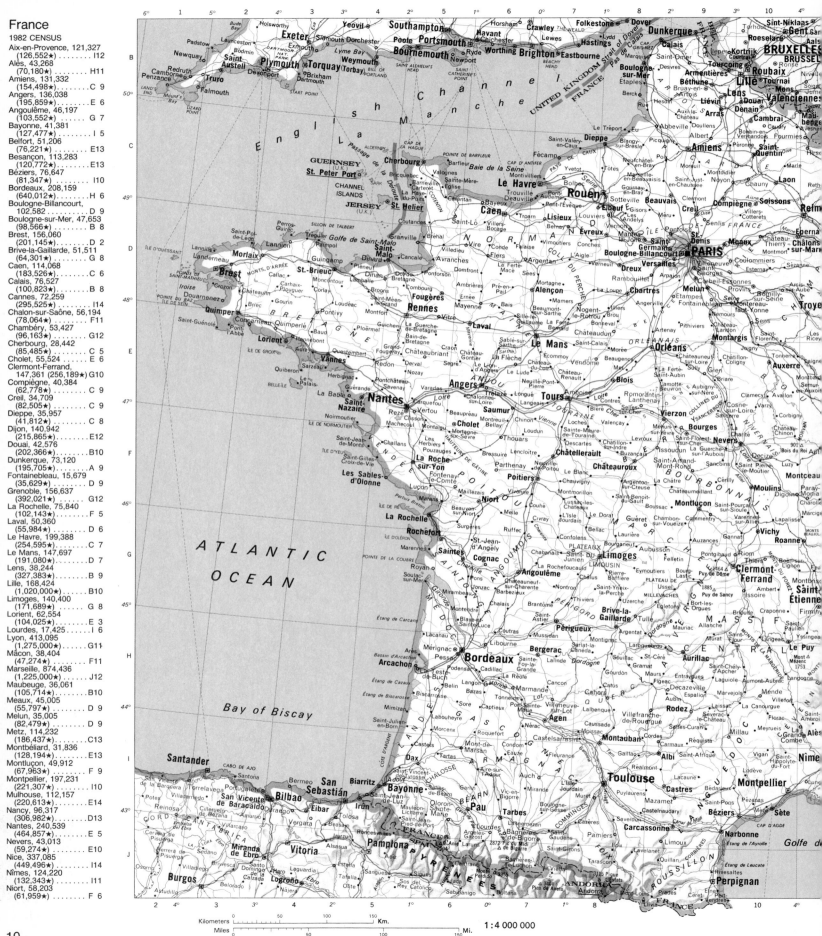

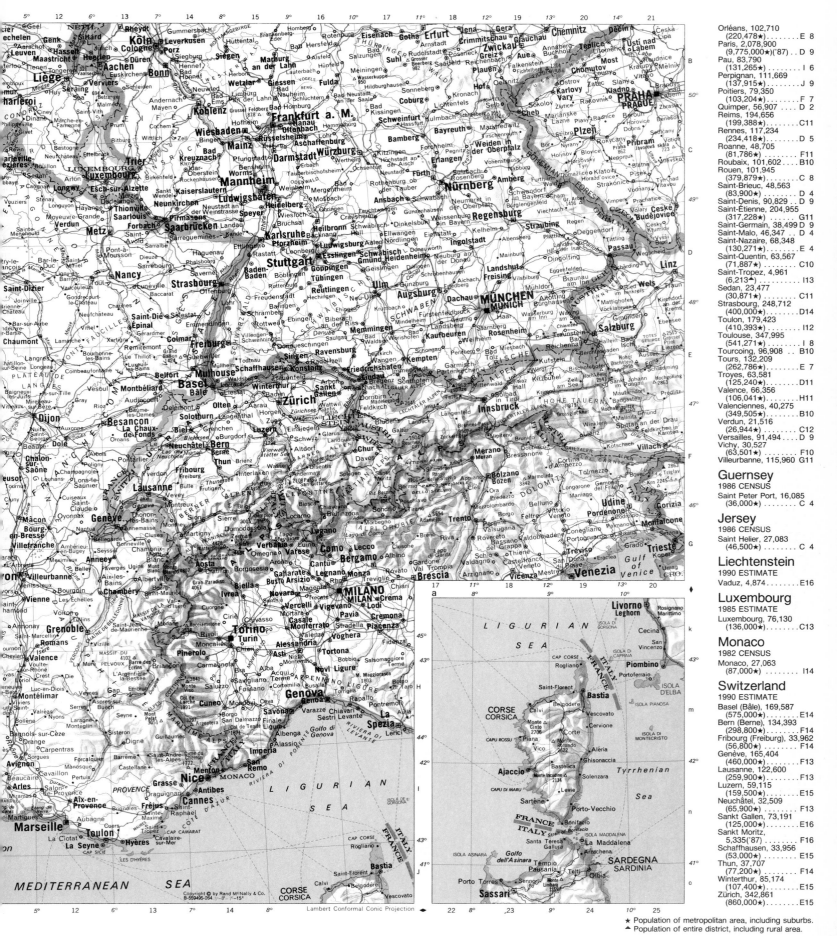

Orléans, 102,710
(220,478★) . . . . E 8
Paris, 2,078,900
(9,775,000★)('87) . . D 9
Pau, 83,790
(131,265★) . . . . I 6
Perpignan, 111,669
(137,915★) . . . . J 9
Poitiers, 79,350
(103,204★) . . . . F 7
Quimper, 56,907 . . . . D 2
Reims, 194,656
(199,388★) C11
Rennes, 117,234
(234,418★) . . . . D 5
Roanne, 48,705
(81,786★) F11
Roubaix, 101,602 . . . .B10
Rouen, 101,945
(379,879★) . . . . C 8
Saint-Brieuc, 48,563
(83,900★) . . . . D 4
Saint-Denis, 90,829 . . D 9
Saint-Étienne, 204,955
(317,228★) G11
Saint-Germain, 38,499 D 9
Saint-Malo, 46,347 . . D 4
Saint-Nazaire, 68,348
(130,271★) . . . . E 4
Saint-Quentin, 63,567
(71,887★) C10
Saint-Tropez, 4,961
(6,213★) I13
Sedan, 23,477
(30,871★) C11
Strasbourg, 248,712
(400,000★) D14
Toulon, 179,423
(410,393★) I12
Toulouse, 347,995
(541,271★) . . . . I 8
Tourcoing, 96,908 . . B10
Tours, 132,209
(262,786★) . . . . E 7
Troyes, 63,581
(125,240★) D11
Valence, 66,356
(106,041★) H11
Valenciennes, 40,275
(349,505★) B10
Verdun, 21,516
(26,944★) C12
Versailles, 91,494 . . . .D 9
Vichy, 30,527
(63,501★) F10
Villeurbanne, 115,960 G11

Guernsey
1986 CENSUS
Saint Peter Port, 16,085
(36,000★) . . . . C 4

Jersey
1986 CENSUS
Saint Helier, 27,083
(46,500★) . . . . C 4

Liechtenstein
1990 ESTIMATE
Vaduz, 4,874 . . . . . . .E16

Luxembourg
1985 ESTIMATE
Luxembourg, 76,130
(136,000★) C13

Monaco
1982 CENSUS
Monaco, 27,063
(87,000★) I14

Switzerland
1990 ESTIMATE
Basel (Bâle), 169,587
(575,000★) E14
Bern (Berne), 134,393
(298,800★) F14
Fribourg (Freiburg), 33,962
(56,800★) F14
Genève, 165,404
(460,000★) F13
Lausanne, 122,600
(259,900★) F13
Luzern, 59,115
(159,500★) E15
Neuchâtel, 32,509
(65,900★) F13
Sankt Gallen, 73,191
(125,000★) E16
Sankt Moritz,
5,335('87) F16
Schaffhausen, 33,956
(53,000★) E15
Thun, 37,707
(77,200★) F14
Winterthur, 85,174
(107,400★) E15
Zürich, 342,861
(860,000★) E15

★ Population of metropolitan area, including suburbs.
▲ Population of entire district, including rural area.

11

Spain and Portugal

Andorra
1986 CENSUS
Andorra, 18,463 .... C13

Gibraltar
1988 ESTIMATE
Gibraltar, 30,077 .... I 6

Portugal
1981 CENSUS
Almada, 42,607 .... G 2
Barreiro, 50,863 .... G 2
Beja, 19,643 .... G 4
Braga, 63,033 .... D 3
Coimbra, 74,616 .... E 3
Covilhã, 21,807 .... E 4
Évora, 34,851 .... G 4
Faro, 27,974 .... H 4
Funchal, 44,111 .... m21
Guimarães, 21,947 .... D 3
Lisboa (Lisbon), 807,167
   (2,250,000★) .... G 2
Montijo, 23,017 .... G 3
Porto, 327,368
   (1,225,000★) .... D 3
Póvoa de Varzim,
   23,729 .... D 3
Santarém, 19,761 .... F 3
Setúbal, 77,885 .... G 3
Vila do Conde, 20,613 D 3
Vila Nova de Gaia,
   62,469 .... D 3

Spain
1988 ESTIMATE
Albacete, 125,997 .. G10
Alcalá de Guadaira,
   50,935 .... H 6
Alcalá de Henares,
   150,021 .... E 8
Alcantarilla, 28,279 .. H10
Alcázar de San Juan,
   26,258 .... F 8
Alcira, 40,575 .... F11
Alcoy, 66,074 .... G11
Algeciras, 99,528 .. I 6
Alicante, 261,051 .... G11
Almendralejo, 25,352 G 5
Almería, 157,644 .... I 9
Andújar, 32,300
   (37,020▲) .... G 7
Antequera, 32,200
   (41,284▲) .... H 7
Aranjuez, 37,694 .... E 8
Arcos de la Frontera,
   19,600 (27,311▲) .. I 6
Arrecife, 36,297 .... p27
Ávila, 45,092 .... E 7
Avilés, 87,811
   (131,000★) .... B 6
Badajoz, 106,400
   (122,407▲) .... G 5
Badalona, 225,229 .. D14
Barcelona, 1,714,355
   (4,040,000★) .. D14
Baza, 20,910 .... H 9
Bilbao, 384,733
   (985,000★) .... B 9
Burgos, 160,561 .... C 8
Burjasot, 35,011 .... F11
Cáceres, 71,598 .... F 5
Cádiz, 156,591
   (240,000★) .... I 5
Cartagena, 70,000
   (172,710▲) H11
Castellón de la Plana,
   131,809 .... F11
Chiclana de la Frontera,
   43,157 .... I 5
Ciudad Real, 56,300 G 8
Córdoba, 302,301 .. H 7
Coria del Río, 21,844 H 5
Cuenca, 42,222 .... E 9
Don Benito, 24,500
   (29,324▲) .... G 6
Durango, 27,425 .... B 9
Écija, 30,900
   (35,836▲) .... H 6
Éibar, 34,355 .... B 9
Elche, 158,300
   (180,256▲) G11
Elda, 56,756 .... G11
El Ferrol del Caudillo,
   86,503 (129,000★) B 3
El Puerto de Santa María,
   49,900 (62,285▲) .. I 5
Gandía, 46,100
   (52,646▲) G11
Gavá, 34,613 .... D14
Gerona, 30,900
   (68,902▲) D14
Getafe, 135,367 .... E 8
Gijón, 262,156 .... B 6
Granada, 263,334 .... H 8
Granollers, 49,045 .. D14
Guadalajara, 61,309 .. E 8
Hospitalet, 278,449 .. D14
Huelva, 137,826 .... H 5
Huesca, 41,841 .... C11
Irún, 54,886 .... B10
Jaén, 106,435 .... H 8

★ Population of metropolitan area, including suburbs.
▲ Population of entire district, including rural area.

12

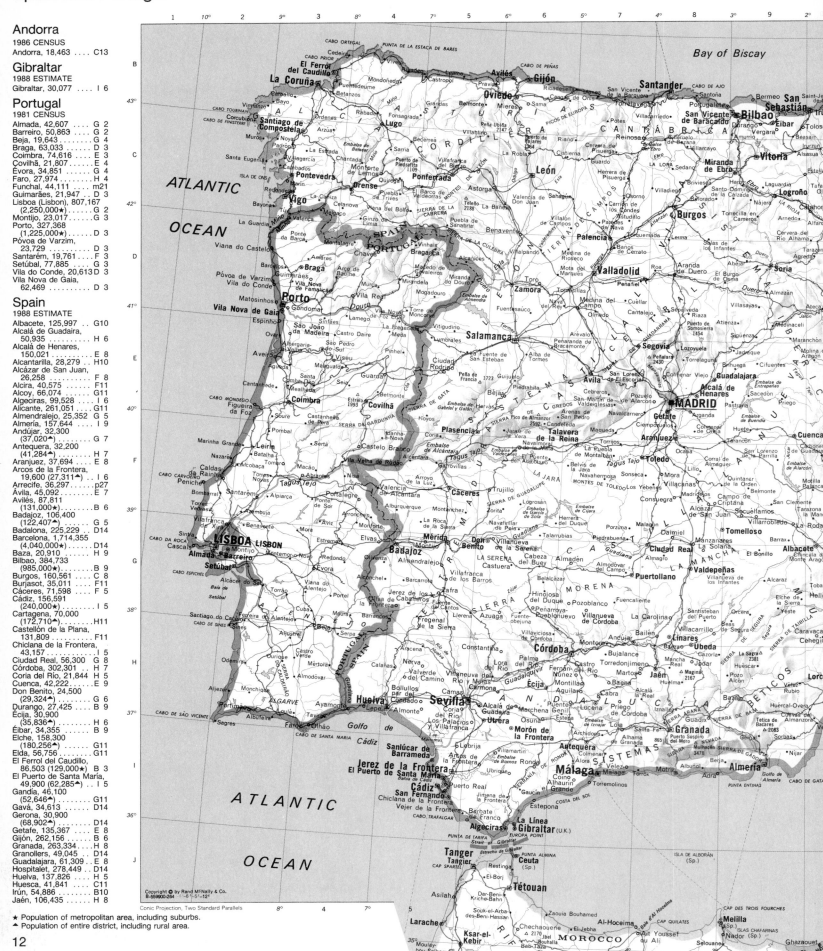

Copyright © by Rand McNally & Co.
B-559900-264

Conic Projection, Two Standard Parallels

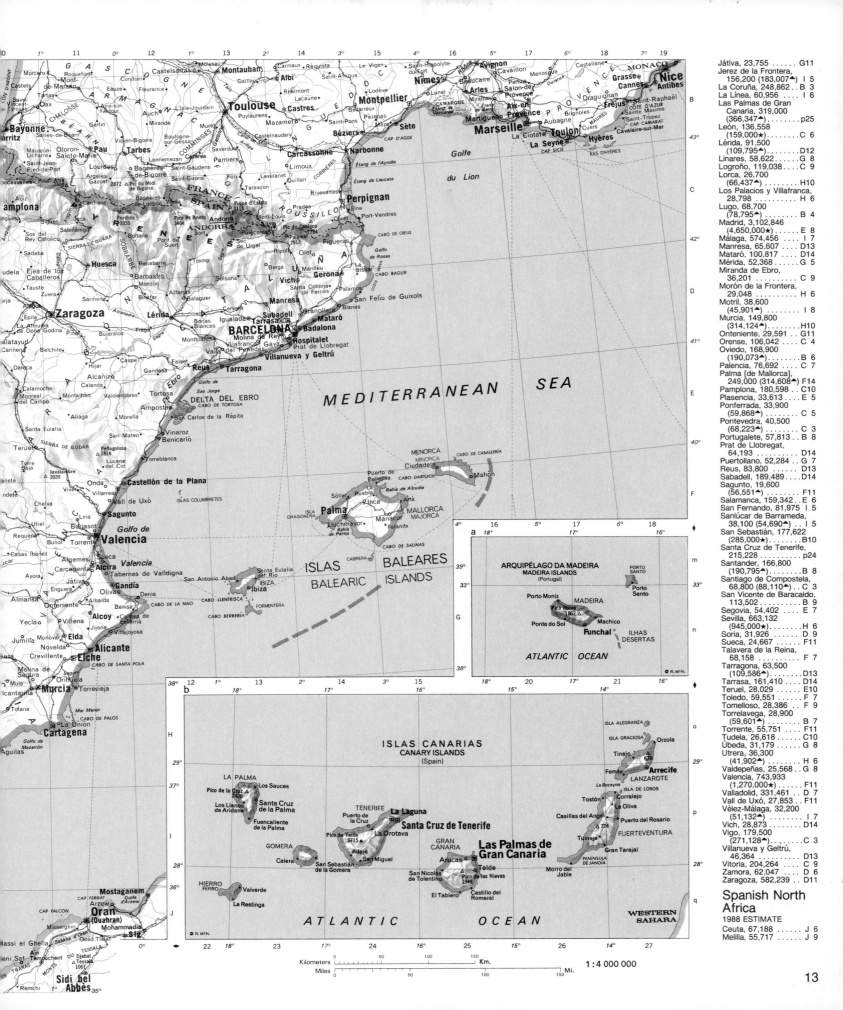

Játiva, 23,755 . . . . . . G11
Jerez de la Frontera,
  156,200 (183,007▲) I 5
La Coruña, 248,862 . . B 3
La Línea, 60,956 . . . . I 6
Las Palmas de Gran
  Canaria, 319,000
  (366,347▲) p25
León, 136,558
  (159,000★) . . . . C 6
Lérida, 91,500
  (109,795▲) D12
Linares, 58,622 . . . . G 8
Logroño, 119,038 . . . C 9
Lorca, 26,700
  (66,437▲) H10
Los Palacios y Villafranca,
  28,798 . . . . H 6
Lugo, 68,700
  (78,795▲) . . . . B 4
Madrid, 3,102,846
  (4,650,000★) . . . . . E 8
Málaga, 574,456 . . . . I 7
Manresa, 65,607 . . . . D13
Mataró, 100,817 . . . . D14
Mérida, 52,368 . . . . G 5
Miranda de Ebro,
  36,201 . . . . C 9
Morón de la Frontera,
  29,048 . . . . H 6
Motril, 38,600
  (45,901▲) . . . . I 8
Murcia, 149,800
  (314,124▲) H10
Onteniente, 29,591 . . G11
Orense, 106,042 . . . . C 4
Oviedo, 168,900
  (190,073▲) . . . . B 6
Palencia, 76,692 . . . . C 7
Palma [de Mallorca],
  249,000 (314,608▲) . F14
Pamplona, 180,598 . . C10
Plasencia, 33,613 . . . E 5
Ponferrada, 33,900
  (59,868▲) . . . . C 5
Pontevedra, 40,500
  (68,223▲) . . . . C 3
Portugalete, 57,813 . . B 8
Prat de Llobregat,
  64,193 . . . . D14
Puertollano, 52,284 . . G 7
Reus, 83,800 . . . . . . D13
Sabadell, 189,489 . . . .D14
Sagunto, 19,600
  (56,551▲) F11
Salamanca, 159,342 . . E 6
San Fernando, 81,975 I 5
Sanlúcar de Barrameda,
  38,100 (54,690▲) . . I 5
San Sebastián, 177,622
  (285,000★) B10
Santa Cruz de Tenerife,
  215,228 . . . . p24
Santander, 166,800
  (190,795▲) . . . . B 8
Santiago de Compostela,
  68,800 (88,110▲) . . C 3
San Vicente de Baracaldo,
  113,502 . . . . B 9
Segovia, 54,402 . . . . E 7
Sevilla, 663,132
  (945,000★) . . . . . . .H 6
Soria, 31,926 . . . . . . D 9
Sueca, 24,667 . . . . . F11
Talavera de la Reina,
  68,158 . . . . F 7
Tarragona, 63,500
  (109,586▲) D13
Tarrasa, 161,410 . . . . D14
Teruel, 28,029 . . . . . E10
Toledo, 59,551 . . . . . F 7
Tomelloso, 28,386 . . F 9
Torrelavega, 28,900
  (59,601▲) . . . . B 7
Torrente, 55,751 . . . . F11
Tudela, 26,618 . . . . . C10
Úbeda, 31,179 . . . . . G 8
Utrera, 36,300
  (41,902▲) . . . . H 6
Valdepeñas, 25,568 . . G 8
Valencia, 743,933
  (1,270,000★) F11
Valladolid, 331,461 . . D 7
Vall de Uxó, 27,853 . . F11
Vélez-Málaga, 32,200
  (51,132▲) . . . . I 7
Vich, 28,873 . . . . . . D14
Vigo, 179,500
  (271,128▲) . . . . C 3
Villanueva y Geltrú,
  46,364 . . . . D13
Vitoria, 204,264 . . . . C 9
Zamora, 62,047 . . . . D 6
Zaragoza, 582,239 . . D11

Spanish North Africa

1988 ESTIMATE
Ceuta, 67,188 . . . . . . J 6
Melilla, 55,717 . . . . . J 9

13

Italy

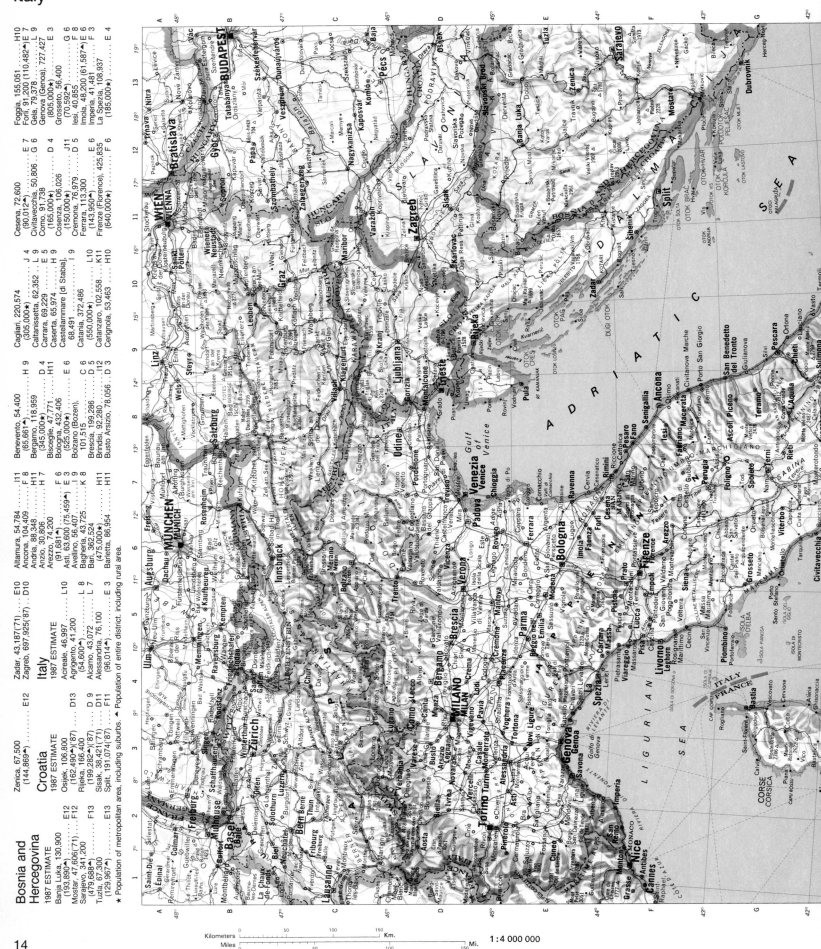

Bosnia and Hercegovina
1987 ESTIMATE
Banja Luka, 130,900
  (193,890▲) E12
Mostar, 47,606(71) F12
Sarajevo, 341,200
  (479,688▲) F13
Tuzla, 67,300 .... E13

Croatia
1987 ESTIMATE
Osijek, 106,800
  (162,490▲)('87) D13
Rijeka, 166,400
  (199,282▲)('87) .... D 9
Sisak, 38,421(71) D11
Split, 191,074('87) F11

Zenica, 67,500
  (144,869▲) E12
Zadar, 43,187(71) E10
Zagreb, 697,925('87) D10

Italy
1987 ESTIMATE
Acireale, 46,997 .... L10
Agrigento, 41,200
  (54,600★) .... L 8
Alcamo, 43,072 .... L 7
Alessandria, 76,100
  (96,014★) .... E 3

Altamura, 54,784 .... I11
Ancona, 104,409 .... F 8
Andria, 88,348 .... H11
Anzio, 30,806 .... H 7
Arezzo, 74,200
  (91,681▲) .... F 6
Asti, 63,600 (75,459▲) .... E 3
Avellino, 56,407 .... I 9
Bagheria, 43,725 .... K 8
Bari, 362,524 .... L 7
Barletta, 86,954 .... H11

Benevento, 54,400
  (65,661▲) .... H 9
Bergamo, 118,959
  (345,000★) .... D 4
Bisceglie, 47,771 .... H11
Bologna, 432,406
  (525,000★) .... E 6
Bolzano (Bozen),
  101,515 .... D 5
Brescia, 199,286 .... D 5
Brindisi, 92,280 .... J12
Busto Arsizio, 78,056 .... D 3

Cagliari, 220,574
  (305,000★) .... L 9
Caltanissetta, 62,352 .... L 9
Carrara, 69,229 .... E 5
Caserta, 65,974 .... H 9
Castellammare (di Stabia),
  68,491 ....
Catania, 372,486
  (550,000★) L10
Catanzaro, 102,558 .... K11
Cerignola, 53,463 .... H10

Cesena, 72,600
  (90,012▲) .... E 7
Civitavecchia, 50,806 .... G 6
Como, 91,738 .... D 4
Cosenza, 106,026
  (150,000★) J11
Cremona, 76,979
  (54,600★) .... D 5
Ferrara, 113,300
  (143,950▲) .... E 6
Firenze (Florence),
  (640,000★) H10

Foggia, 155,051 .... H10
Forlì, 91,200 (110,482▲)... E 7
Gela, 79,378 .... L 9
Genova (Genoa), 727,427
  (805,000★) .... E 3
Grosseto, 56,400
  (70,592▲) .... F 6
Iesi, 40,855 .... F 8
Imola, 48,200 (61,587▲)... E 6
Imperia, 41,481 .... F 3
La Spezia, 108,937
  (185,000★) .... E 4

★ Population of metropolitan area, including suburbs. ▲ Population of entire district, including rural area.

Kilometers 0 50 100 150 Km.
Miles 0 50 100 150 Mi.
1:4 000 000

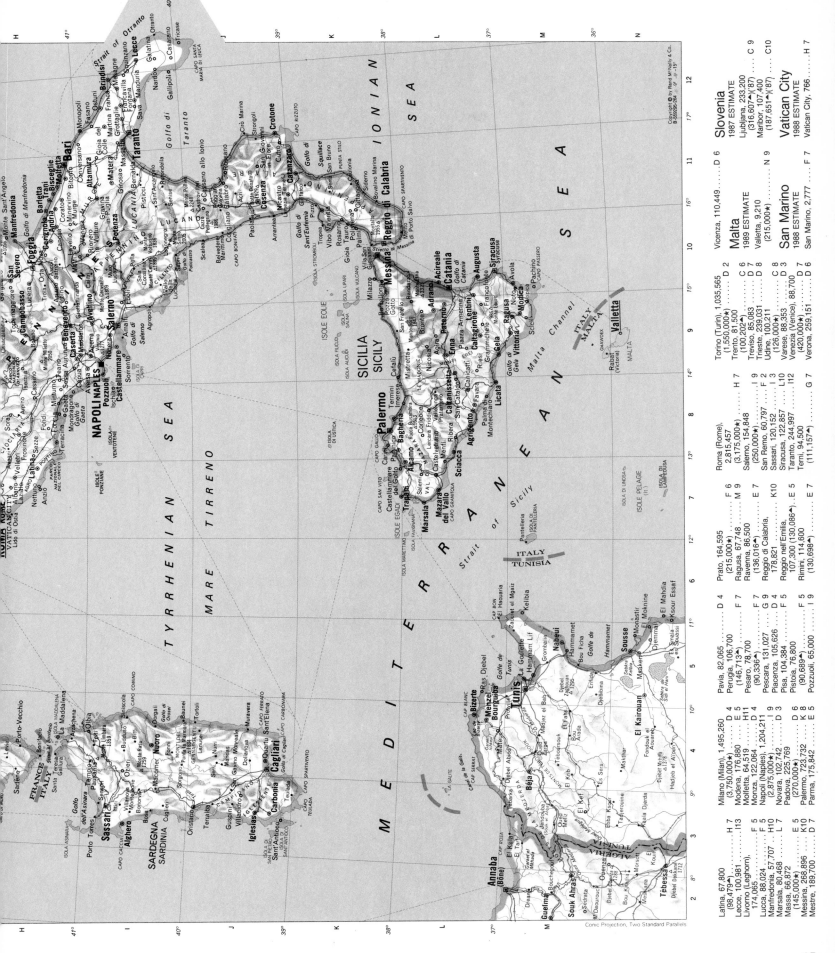

Conic Projection, Two Standard Parallels

15

Southeastern Europe

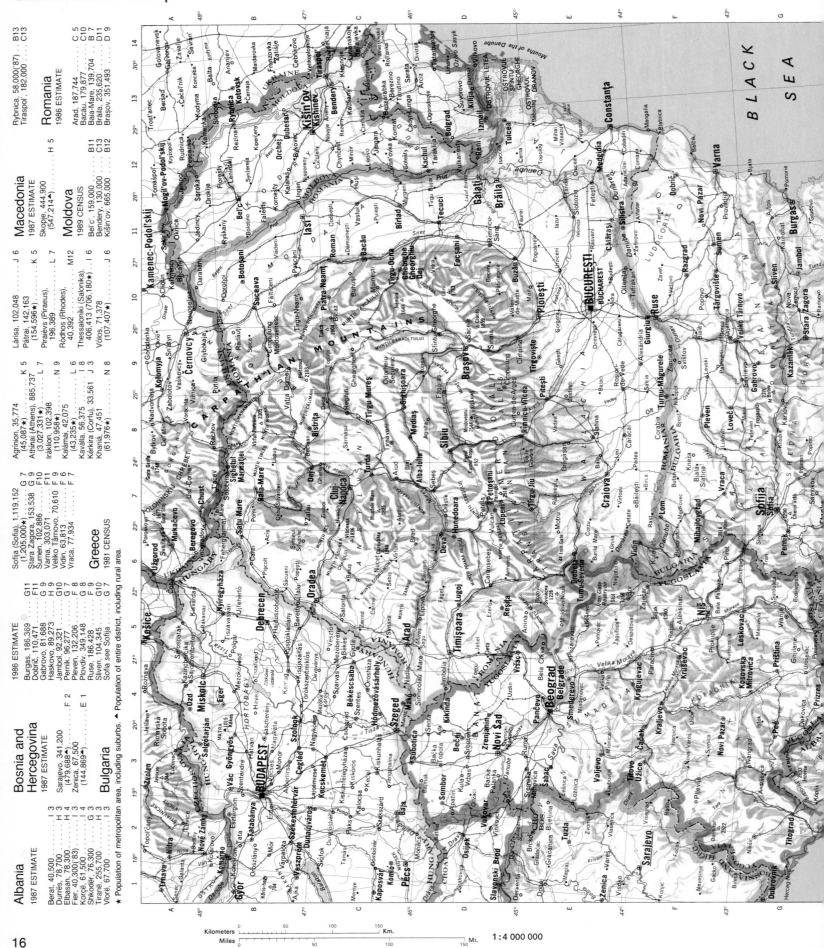

Albania
1987 ESTIMATE

Berat, 40,500	I 3
Durrës, 78,300	H 3
Elbasan, 78,300	H 4
Fier, 40,300(83)	I 4
Korçë, 61,500	I 4
Shkodër, 76,300	G 3
Tiranë, 255,700	H 3
Vlorë, 67,700	I 3

Bosnia and Hercegovina
1987 ESTIMATE

Sarajevo, 341,200	
(479,688▲)	F 2
Zenica, 67,500	
(144,869▲)	E 1

Bulgaria

Burgas, 186,369	G11
Dobrič, 110,471	F11
Gabrovo, 81,688	G 9
Haskovo, 92,321	H 9
Jambol, 89,273	G10
Pernik, 96,277	G 7
Pleven, 132,206	F 8
Plovdiv, 349,148	G 8
Ruse, 186,428	F 9
Sliven, 104,345	G10
Sofia see Sofija	

Sofija (Sofia), 1,119,152	
(1,205,000★)	G 7
Štara Zagora, 153,538	G 9
Šumen, 102,886	F10
Varna, 303,071	F11
Veliko Tárnovo, 70,610	F 9
Vidin, 63,813	F 6
Vraca, 77,934	F 7

Greece
1981 CENSUS

Agrínion, 35,774	
(45,087★)	K 5
Athínai (Athens), 885,737	
(3,027,331★)	L 7
Piraiévs (Piraeus),	
196,389	L 7
Iráklion, 102,398	N 9
Kalámai, 42,075	
(43,235★)	L 6
Kavála, 56,375	I 8
Kérkira (Corfu), 33,561	J 3
Vólos, 71,378	
(107,407★)	K 6
Lárisa, 102,048	J 6
Pátrai, 142,163	
(154,596★)	K 5
Praiévs (Piraeus),	
Rhódhos (Rhodes),	
40,392	
Thessaloníki (Salonika),	
406,413 (706,180★)	I 6
Khaniá, 47,451	
(61,976★)	N 8

Macedonia
1987 ESTIMATE

Skopje, 444,900	
(547,214★)	H 5

Moldova
1989 CENSUS

Bel'c', 159,000	B11
Bendery, 130,000	C13
Kišin ov, 665,000	B12

Romania
1986 ESTIMATE

Arad, 187,744	C 5
Bacău, 179,877	C10
Baia-Mare, 139,704	B 7
Brăila, 235,620	D11
Brașov, 351,493	D 9

Rybnica, 58,000('87)	B13
Tiraspol, 182,000	C13

★ Population of metropolitan area, including suburbs. ▲ Population of entire district, including rural area.

Kilometers

Miles

1 : 4 000 000

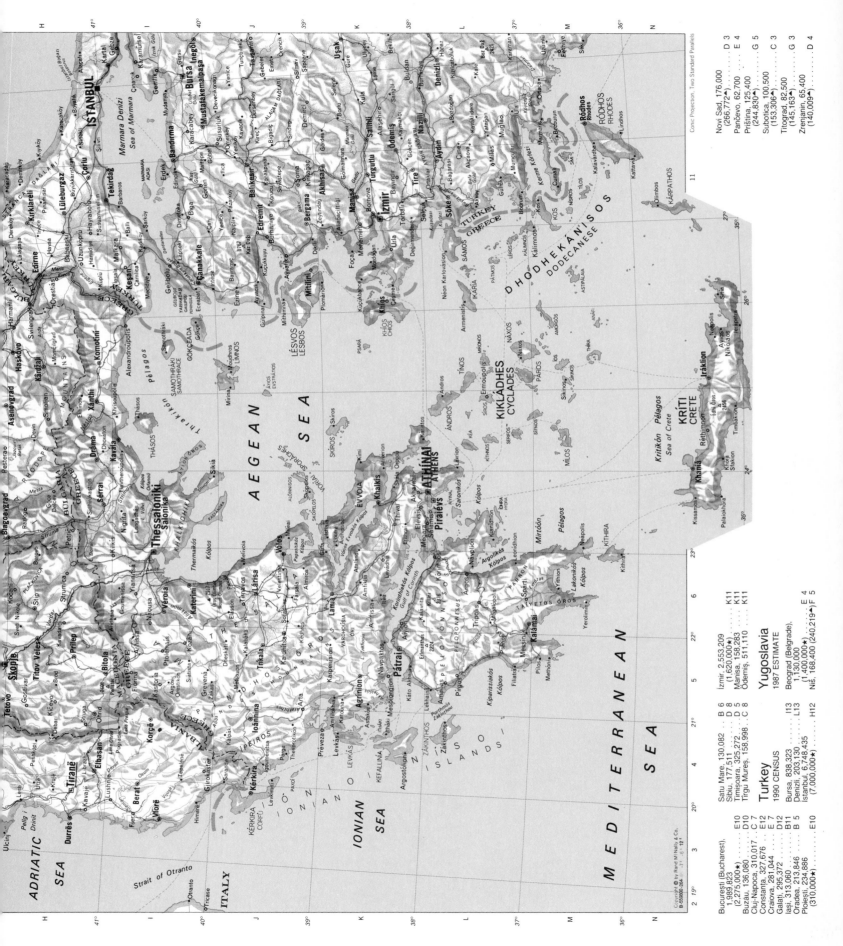

Conic Projection, Two Standard Parallels

Baltic and Moscow Regions

Belarus
1989 CENSUS

Baranoviči, 159,000 . . H 9
Bobrujsk, 223,000 . . H12
Borisov, 144,000 . . . G11
Brest, 258,000 . . . . . I 6
Gomel', 500,000 . . . . . I14
Grodno, 270,000 . . . H 6
Lida, 81,000('87) . . . . H 8
Minsk, 1,589,000
 (1,650,000★) H10
Mogil'ov, 356,000 . . . H13
Molodečno,
 87,000('87) . . . . . . G 9
Novopolock,
 90,000('87) F11
Orša, 123,000 . . . . G13
Pinsk, 119,000 . . . . . I 9
Polock, 80,000('87) . . F11
Rečica, 71,000('87) . . I13
Sluck, 55,000('87) . . H10
Svetlogorsk,
 68,000('87) . . . . . . G 3
Vitebsk, 350,000 . . . F13
Žlobin, 52,000('87) . . I13

Estonia
1989 CENSUS

Kohtla-Järve,
 78,000('87) B10
Narva, 81,000('87) . . B11
Pärnu, 53,000('87) . . C 7
Tallinn, 482,000 . . . B 7
Tartu, 114,000 . . . . . . C 9

Latvia
1989 CENSUS

Daugavpils, 127,000 . . F 9
Jelgava, 72,000('87) . . E 6
Jūrmala, 65,000('87) . . E 6
Liepāja, 114,000 . . . . E 4
Rēzekne, 35,620('79) E10
Rīga, 915,000
 (1,005,000★) . . . . . . E 7
Ventspils, 52,000('87) D 4

Lithuania
1989 CENSUS

Kaunas, 423,000 . . . . G 6
Klaipėda (Memel),
 204,000 . . . . F 4
Panevėžys, 126,000 . . F 7
Šiauliai, 145,000 . . . . F 6
Vilnius, 582,000 . . . . G 8

Russia
1989 CENSUS

Aleksandrov,
 66,000('87) E21
Aleksin, 72,000('87) . . G20
Balachna, 35,359('79) E26

Balašicha, 136,000 . . F20
Bežeck, 30,711('79) . . D19
Bor, 65,000('87) E27
Boroviči, 64,000('87) . C16
Br'ansk, 452,000 . . . . H17
Čechov, 57,000('87) . . F20
Čerepovec, 310,000 . . B20
Čern'achovsk,
 36,361('79) . . . . . . G 4
Chimki, 133,000 . . . . F20
Dmitrov, 64,000('87) . E20
Domodedovo,
 51,000('87) F20
Dubna, 64,000('87) . . E20
Dzeržinsk, 285,000 . . E26
Elektrostal', 153,000 . F21
Furmanov, 44,430('79)D24
Gatčina, 81,000('87) . . B13
Gorki see Nižnij
 Novgorod E27
Gr'azi, 41,082('79) . . I22
Gus'-Chrustal'nyj,
 75,000('87) F23
Ivanovo, 481,000 . . . D23
Jarcevo, 40,908('79) . F15
Jaroslavl', 633,000 . . D22
Jefremov, 58,000('87) H21
Jegorjevsk,
 73,000('87) F22

★ Population of metropolitan
 area, including suburbs.

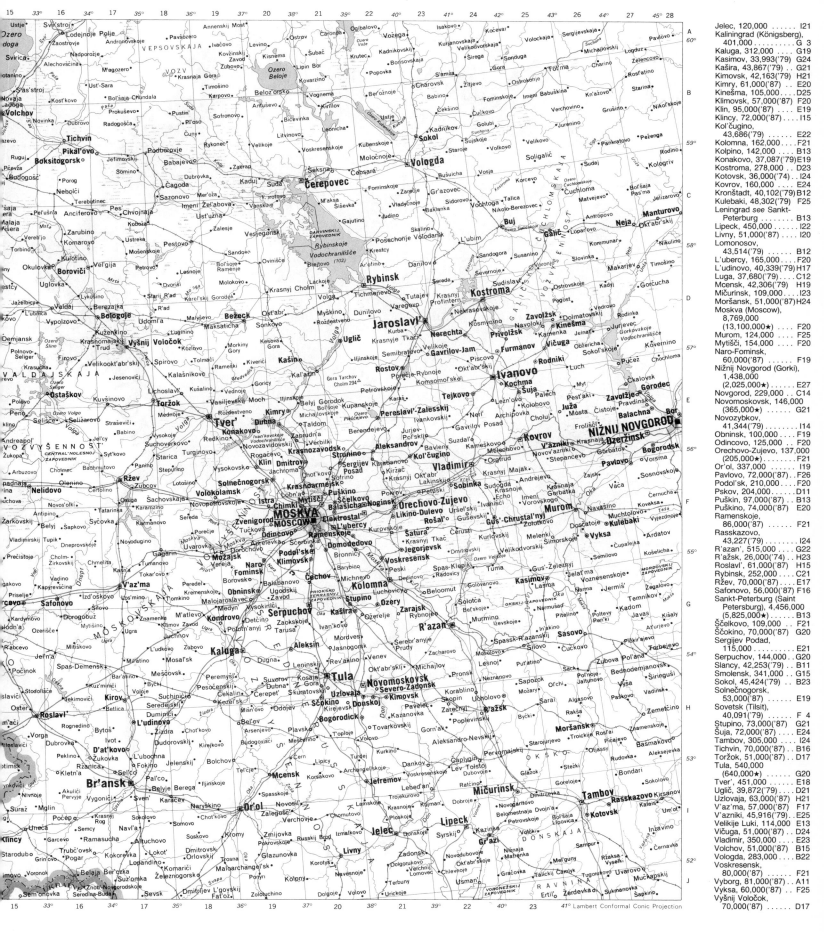

Jelec, 120,000 ...... I21
Kaliningrad (Königsberg),
   401,000 .... G 3
Kaluga, 312,000 ... G19
Kasimov, 33,993('79) G24
Kašira, 43,867('79) .. G21
Kimovsk, 42,163('79) H21
Kimry, 61,000('87) .. E20
Kinešma, 105,000 ... D25
Klimovsk, 57,000('87) F20
Klin, 95,000('87) E19
Klincy, 72,000('87) I15
Kol'čugino,
   43,686('79) E22
Kolomna, 162,000 .... F21
Kolpino, 142,000 ... B13
Konakovo, 37,087('79)E19
Kostroma, 278,000 .. D23
Kotovsk, 36,000('74) .. I24
Kovrov, 160,000 .... E24
Kronštadt, 40,102('79) B12
Kulebaki, 48,302('79) F25
Leningrad see Sankt-
   Peterburg B13
Lipeck, 450,000 .... I22
Livny, 51,000('87) I20
Lomonosov,
   43,514('79) B12
L'ubercy, 165,000 ... F20
L'udinovo, 40,339('79) H17
Luga, 37,680('79) ... C12
Mcensk, 42,306('79) H19
Mičurinsk, 109,000 .... I23
Moršansk, 51,000('87) H24
Moskva (Moscow),
   8,769,000
   (13,100,000★) ... F20
Murom, 124,000 .... F25
Mytišči, 154,000 .... F20
Naro-Fominsk,
   60,000('87) F19
Nižnij Novgorod (Gorki),
   1,438,000
   (2,025,000★) ... E27
Novgorod, 229,000 .. C14
Novomoskovsk, 146,000
   (365,000★) G21
Novozybkov,
   41,344('79) I14
Obninsk, 100,000 .... F19
Odincovo, 125,000 ... F20
Orechovo-Zujevo, 137,000
   (205,000★) F21
Or'ol, 337,000 .... I19
Pavlovo, 72,000('87) .. F26
Podol'sk, 210,000 .... F20
Pskov, 204,000 ...D11
Puškin, 97,000('87) .. B13
Puškino, 74,000('87) .. E20
Ramenskoje,
   86,000('87) F21
Rasskazovo,
   43,227('79) I24
R'azan', 515,000 ... G22
R'ažsk, 26,000('74) .. H23
Roslavl', 61,000('87) H15
Rybinsk, 252,000 .... C21
Ržev, 70,000('87) .. E17
Safonovo, 56,000('87) F16
Sankt-Peterburg (Saint
   Petersburg), 4,456,000
   (5,825,000★) ... B13
Ščelkovo, 109,000 .. F21
Ščokino, 70,000('87) G20
Sergijev Podad,
   115,000 .... E21
Serpuchov, 144,000 .. G20
Slancy, 42,253('79) .. B11
Smolensk, 341,000 .. G15
Sokol, 45,424('79) .. B23
Solnečnogorsk,
   53,000('87) E19
Sovetsk (Tilsit),
   40,091('79) ...... F 4
Stupino, 73,000('87) G21
Šuja, 72,000('87) .. E24
Tambov, 305,000 .. I24
Tichvin, 70,000('87) .. B16
Toržok, 51,000('87) .. D17
Tula, 540,000
   (640,000★) G20
Tver', 451,000 .... E18
Uglič, 39,872('79) .. D24
Uzlovaja, 63,000('87) H21
V'az'ma, 57,000('87) F17
V'azniki, 45,916('79) .. E25
Velikije Luki, 114,000 E13
Vičuga, 51,000('87) .. D24
Vladimir, 350,000 .. E23
Volchov, 51,000('87) B15
Vologda, 283,000 .. B22
Voskresensk,
   80,000('87) F21
Vyborg, 81,000('87) .. A11
Vyksa, 60,000('87) .. F25
Vyšnij Voločok,
   70,000('87) D17

Asia

'Adan, 176,100 ('84)
  (318,000★) ....H 7
AFGHANISTAN...........F 9
Ahmadābād, 2,059,725
  ('81) (2,400,000★) ..G10
Al Baṣrah, 616,700
  ('85).........................F 7
Al-Kuwayt, 44,335 ('85)
  (1,375,000★) ....G 7
Alma-Ata,
  1,128,000 ('89)
  (1,190,000★) E10
Al-Madīnah, 290,000
  ('80).........................G 6
'Ammān, 936,300 ('89)
  (1,450,000★) ....F 6
Ankara, 2,553,209 ('90)
  (2,670,000★) ....F 6
ARMENIA..................F 7
Ar-Riyāḍ, 1,250,000
  ('80).........................G 7
Aschabad, 398,000
  ('89).........................F 8
AZERBAIJAN...............E 7
Baghdād, 3,841,268
  ('87).........................F 7
Baku, 1,150,000 ('89)
  (2,020,000★) ....E 7
Bangalore,
  2,476,355 ('81)
  (2,950,000★) H10
Bangkok see Krung
  Thep H13
BANGLADESH............G12
Batumi, 136,000 ('89)..E 7
Bayrūt, 509,000 ('82)
  (1,675,000★) ....F 6
Beijing (Peking),
  6,710,000 ('88)
  (6,450,000★) F14
BHUTAN...................G12
Biškek, 616,000 ('89)..E10
Bombay, 8,243,405 ('81)
  (9,950,000★) H10
BRUNEI....................I14
BURMA.....................G12
Calcutta, 3,305,006 ('81)
  (11,100,000★) H11
CAMBODIA................H13
Canton see
  Guangzhou G14
Celinograd, 277,000
  ('89).........................D10
Chabarovsk, 601,000
  ('89).........................E16
Changchun, 1,822,000
  ('88) (2,000,000▲) ...E15
Changsha, 1,230,000
  ('88).........................G14
Chengdu, 1,884,000 ('88)
  (2,960,000▲) F13
CHINA.......................F12
Chongqing (Chungking),
  2,502,000 ('88)
  (2,890,000▲) G13
Čita, 366,000 ('89)......D14
Colombo, 683,000 ('86)
  (2,050,000★) I10
CYPRUS....................F 6
CYPRUS, NORTH........F 6
Dacca see Dhaka G12
Dalian, 2,280,000 ('88) F15
Damascus see
  Dimashq ....F 6
Da Nang, 318,653
  ('79).........................H13
Delhi, 4,884,234 ('81)
  (7,200,000★) G10
Dhaka (Dacca), 2,365,695
  ('81) (3,430,312★) ..G12

Dimashq (Damascus),
  1,326,000 ('88)
  (1,950,000★) ....F 6
Dušanbe, 595,000
  ('89).........................F 9
Eṣfahān, 986,753 ('86)
  (1,175,000★) ....F 8
Frunze see Biškek E10
Fukuoka, 1,160,440 ('85)
  (1,750,000★) F16
Fuzhou, 910,000 ('88)
  (1,240,000▲) G14
George Town, 248,241
  ('80) (495,000★) I13
GEORGIA..................E 7
Guangzhou (Canton),
  3,100,000 ('88)
  (3,420,000▲) G14
Hakodate, 319,194
  ('85).........................E17
Ha Noi, 1,089,000 ('89)
  (1,500,000★) G13
Harbin, 2,710,000
  ('88).........................E15
Herāt, 177,300 ('88)....F 9
Hiroshima,
  1,044,118 ('85)
  (1,575,000★) F16
HONG KONG.............G14
Hyderābād, 2,187,262
  ('81) (2,750,000★) ..H10
INDIA.......................G10
INDONESIA................I13
IRAN........................F 8
IRAQ........................F 7
Irkutsk, 626,000 ('89)..D13
Islāmābād, 204,364
  ('81).........................F10
ISRAEL.....................F 6
izmir, 2,553,209 ('90)
  (1,620,000★) ....F 5
Jakutsk,
  187,000 ('89)...........C15
JAPAN......................F16
Jekateringbug,
  1,367,000 ('89)
  (1,620,000★) ....D 9
Jerevan, 1,199,000 ('89)
  (1,315,000★) ....E 7
Jerusalem see
  Yerushalayim ....F 6
Jiddah, 1,300,000
  ('80).........................G 6
Jinan, 1,546,000 ('88)
  (2,140,000▲) F14
JORDAN....................F 6
Kābol (Kabul), 1,424,400
  ('88).........................F 9
Kānpur, 1,481,789 ('81)
  (1,875,000★) G11
Karāchi, 4,901,627 ('81)
  (5,300,000★) ....G 9
Kashi, 146,300 ('86)
  (194,500▲) F10
Kaṭhmāndāu, 235,160
  ('81) (320,000★) G11
KAZAKHSTAN............E 9
Kermān,
  257,284 ('86)...........F 8
Konsomol'sk-na-Amure,
  315,000 ('89)...........D16
KOREA, NORTH..........E15
KOREA, SOUTH..........F15
Krasnojarsk, 912,000
  ('89).........................D12
Krung Thep (Bangkok),
  5,716,779 ('88)
  (6,450,000★) H13
Kuala Lumpur, 919,610
  ('80) (1,475,000★) I13
Kuching, 72,555 ('80)...I14

Copyright © by Rand McNally & Co.

A-519695-286

Kunming, 1,310,000 ('88)
(1,550,000▲) G13
KUWAIT.................... G 7
Kyōto,
1,479,218 ('85).........F16
KYRGYZSTAN............. E10
Kyzyl, 80,000 ('87)....D12
Lahore, 2,707,215 ('81)
(3,025,000★) F10
Lanzhou, 1,297,000 ('88)
(1,420,000▲) F13
LAOS........................ H13
LEBANON................... F 6
Lhasa, 84,400 ('86)
(107,700▲) G12
MACAU...................... G14
Madras, 3,276,622 ('81)
(4,475,000★) H11
Makkah,
550,000 ('80).......... G 6
MALAYSIA.................. I13
MALDIVES.................. I10
Mandalay, 532,949
('83) G12
Manila, 1,587,000 ('90)
(6,800,000★) H15
Mashhad, 1,463,508
('86)........................ F 8
Masqat, 50,000 ('81)...G 8
Mawlamyine, 219,961
('83) H12
MONGOLIA................. E13
Nāgpur, 1,219,461 ('81)
(1,302,066★) G10
Nanjing, 2,390,000
('88) F14
NEPAL....................... G11
New Delhi, 273,036
('81).......................G10
Novosibirsk, 1,436,000
('89) (1,600,000★) ...D11
Ochotsk, 9,000...........D17
OMAN........................ G 8
Omsk, 1,148,000 ('89)
(1,175,000★) D10
Ōsaka, 2,636,249 ('85)
(1,645,000★) F16
PAKISTAN.................. G 9
Patna, 776,371 ('81)
(1,025,000★) G11
Peking see Beijing F14
Peshāwar, 506,896 ('81)
(566,248★) F10
Petropavlovsk-Kamčatskij,
269,000 ('89)..........D18
PHILIPPINES...............H15
Phnum Penh, 700,000
('86) H13
Pyŏngyang, 1,283,000
('81) (1,600,000★) ...F15
QATAR....................... G 8
Qingdao (Tsingtao),
1,300,000 ('88)........F15
Quetta, 244,842 ('81)
(285,719▲) .... F 9
Quezon City, 1,632,000
('90)........................ H15
Rangoon see
Yangon H12
Rāwalpindi, 457,091 ('81)
(1,040,000★) F10
RUSSIA...................... D10
Saigon see Thanh Pho Ho
Chi Minh H13
Samarkand, 366,000
('89)........................ F 9
San'ā', 427,150 ('86)...H 7
SAUDI ARABIA.......... G 7
Semipalatinsk, 334,000
('89)........................ D11

Sendai, 700,254 ('85)
(1,175,000★) F17
Shanghai,
7,220,000 ('88)
(9,300,000★) F15
Shenyang (Mukden),
3,910,000 ('88)
(4,370,000★) E15
Shīrāz, 848,289 ('86)...G 8
SINGAPORE.................I13
Sŏul, 10,522,000 ('89)
(15,850,000★) F15
SRI LANKA..................I11
Srīnagar, 594,775 ('81)
(606,002★) F10
SYRIA........................ F 6
Tabrīz, 971,482 ('86).... F 7
T'aipei, 2,637,100 ('88)
(6,130,000★) G15
TAIWAN......................G15
Taiyuan, 1,700,000 ('88)
(1,980,000▲) F14
TAJIKISTAN................ F10
Taškent, 2,073,000 ('89)
(2,325,000★) .... E 9
Tbilisi, 1,260,000 ('89)
(1,460,000★) .... E 7
Tehrān, 6,042,584 ('86)
(7,500,000★) .... F 8
THAILAND.................. H13
Thanh Pho Ho Chi Minh
(Saigon), 3,169,000 ('89)
(3,100,000★) H13
Tianjin (Tientsin),
4,950,000 ('88)
(5,540,000▲) F14
Tobol'sk,
82,000 ('87)........... D 9
Tōkyō, 8,354,615 ('85)
(27,700,000★) F16
Tomsk, 502,000 ('89)...D11
TURKEY...................... F 6
TURKMENISTAN........ F 9
Ulaanbaatar, 548,400
('89).......................E13
**UNITED ARAB
EMIRATES**............ G 8
Ürümqi, 1,060,000
('88).......................E11
UZBEKISTAN.............. E 9
Vārānasi, 708,647 ('81)
(925,000★) G11
Verchojansk, 1,400....C16
Viangchan, 377,409
('85)....................... H13
VIETNAM................... H13
Vladivostok, 648,000
('89).......................E16
Wuhan, 3,570,000
('88).......................F14
Xiamen, 343,700 ('86)
(546,400▲) G14
Xi'an, 2,210,000 ('88)
(2,580,000▲) F13
Yangon (Rangoon),
2,705,039 ('83)
(2,800,000★) H12
YEMEN....................... H 7
Yerevan see Jerevan ..E 7
Yerushalayim (Jerusalem),
493,500 ('89)
(530,000★) .... F 6
Yokohama, 2,992,926
('85).......................F16
Zhangjiakou,
500,000 ('88)
(640,000▲) E14

★ Population of metropolitan area, including suburbs.
▲ Population of entire district, including rural area.

Lambert Azimuthal Equal Area Projection

21

Northwest Asia

Armenia
1989 CENSUS

Jerevan, 1,199,000
(1,315,000★) . . . . . . I 6

Azerbaijan
1989 CENSUS

Baku, 1,150,000
(2,020,000★) . . . . I 7
Gjandža, 278,000 . . . . I 7
Sumgait, 231,000 . . . . I 7

Belarus
1989 CENSUS

Brest, 258,000 . . . . . . G 2
Gomel', 500,000 . . . . . G 4
Grodno, 270,000 . . . . . G 2
Minsk, 1,589,000
(1,650,000★) . . . . . G 3
Mogil'ov, 356,000 . . . G 4
Vitebsk, 350,000 . . . . F 4

Estonia
1989 CENSUS

Tallinn, 482,000 . . . . . F 2

Georgia
1989 CENSUS

Kutaisi, 235,000 . . . . . I 6
Tbilisi, 1,260,000
(1,460,000★) . . . . . . I 6

Kazakhstan
1989 CENSUS

Akt'ubinsk, 253,000 . . G 9
Alma-Ata, 1,128,000
(1,190,000★) I13
Čelinograd, 277,000 . . G12
Čimkent, 393,000 . . . . I11
Džambul, 307,000 . . . . I12
Karaganda, 614,000 . . H12
Pavlodar, 331,000 . . . G13
Petropavlovsk,
241,000 . . . . G11
Semipalatinsk,
334,000 . . . . G14
Temirtau, 212,000 . . . G12
Ural'sk, 200,000 . . . . G 8
Ust'-Kamenogorsk,
324,000 . . . . H14

Kyrgyzstan
1989 CENSUS

Biškek, 616,000 . . . . . I12
Oš, 213,000 . . . . I12

Latvia
1989 CENSUS

Rīga, 915,000
(1,005,000★) . . . . . . F 2

Lithuania
1989 CENSUS

Kaunas, 423,000 . . . . G 2
Klaipėda, 204,000 . . . F 2
Vilnius, 582,000 . . . . . F 3

Moldova
1989 CENSUS

Bel'c', 131,000('81) . . H 3
Kišin'ov, 665,000 . . . . H 3
Tiraspol', 182,000 . . . H 3

Russia
1989 CENSUS

Archangel'sk, 416,000 E 6
Astrachan', 509,000 . . H 7
Belgorod, 300,000 . . . G 5
Br'ansk, 452,000 . . . . G 4
Čeboksary, 420,000 . . F 7
Čel'abinsk, 1,143,000
(1,325,000★) F10
Čerepovec, 310,000 . . F 5
Gor'kij see Nižnij
Novgorod . . . . F 6
Groznyj, 401,000 . . . . I 7
Ivanovo, 481,000 . . . . F 6
Iževsk, 635,000 . . . . . F 8
Jaroslavl', 633,000 . . . F 5
Jekaterinburg
(Sverdlovsk), 1,367,000
(1,620,000★) F10
Kaliningrad, 401,000 . G 2
Kaluga, 312,000 . . . . G 5
Kazan', 1,094,000
(1,140,000★) . . . . . F 7
Kirov, 441,000 . . . . . . F 7
Krasnodar, 620,000 . . H 5
Kurgan, 356,000 . . . . F11
Kursk, 424,000 . . . . . G 5
Leningrad see
Sankt-Peterburg . . F 4
Lipeck, 450,000 . . . . . G 5
Machačkala, 315,000 . . I 7
Magnitogorsk,
440,000 . . . . G 9

★ Population of metropolitan
area, including suburbs.

22

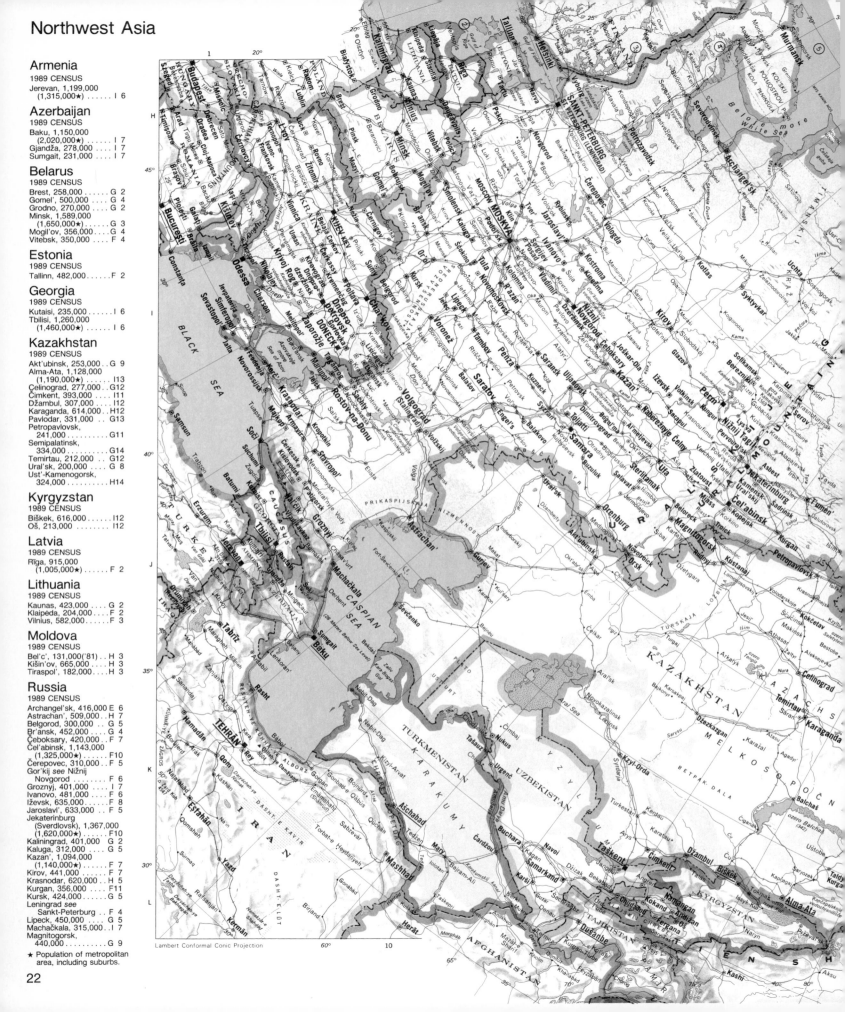

Moskva (Moscow),
    8,769,000
    (13,100,000★) .... F 5
Murmansk, 468,000 . . D 4
Naberežnyje Čelny,
    501,000 . . . . F 8
Nižnij Novgorod (Gor'kij),
    1,438,000
    (2,025,000★) . . . . F 6
Nižnij Tagil, 440,000 . . F 9
Orenburg, 547,000 . . G 9
Or'ol, 337,000 . . . . . G 5
Orsk, 271,000 . . . . . G 9
Penza, 543,000 . . . . G 7
Perm', 1,091,000
    (1,160,000★) . . . . . F 9
Petrozavodsk,
    270,000 . . . . E 4
R'azan', 515,000 . . . . G 5
Rostov-na-Donu,
    1,020,000
    (1,165,000★) . . . . . . H 5
Samara, 1,257,000
    (1,505,000★) . . . . . . G 8
Sankt-Peterburg (St.
    Petersburg), 4,456,000
    (5,825,000★) . . . . . . F 4
Saransk, 312,000 . . . G 7
Saratov, 905,000
    (1,155,000★) . . . . . . G 7
Smolensk, 341,000 . . G 4
Soči, 337,000 . . . . . . I 5
Stalingrad see
    Volgograd . . . . H 6
Stavropol', 318,000 . . H 6
Sverdlovsk see
    Jekaterinburg F10
Syktyvkar, 233,000 . . E 8
Taganrog, 291,000 . . H 5
Tambov, 305,000 . . . G 6
Toljatti, 630,000
    (640,000★) . . . . . . G 7
Tula, 540,000
    (640,000★) . . . . G 5
Tver' (Kalinin),
    451,000 . . . . F 5
Ufa, 1,083,000
    (1,100,000★) . . . . . G 9
Uljanovsk, 625,000 . . G 7
Vladikavkaz, 300,000 . . I 6
Vladimir, 350,000 . . . F 6
Volgograd (Stalingrad),
    999,000
    (1,360,000★) . . . . . H 6
Vologda, 283,000 . . . . F 5
Volžskij, 269,000 . . . . H 6
Voronež, 887,000 . . . G 6

Tajikistan
1989 CENSUS
Dušanbe, 595,000 . . . . J11

Turkmenistan
1989 CENSUS
Aščhabad, 398,000 . . J 9

Ukraine
1989 CENSUS
Čerkassy, 290,000 . . H 4
Černigov, 296,000 . . G 4
Char'kov, 1,611,000
    (1,940,000★) . . . . . G 5
Cherson, 355,000 . . . . H 4
Dneprodzeržinsk,
    282,000 . . . . H 4
Dnepropetrovsk,
    1,179,000
    (1,600,000★) . . . . . H 4
Doneck, 1,110,000
    (2,200,000★) . . . . . . H 5
Gorlovka, 337,000
    (710,000★) . . . . . . H 5
Jalta, 89,000('87) . . I 4
Kijev (Kiev), 2,587,000
    (2,900,000★) . . . . . G 4
Krivoj Rog, 713,000 . . H 4
Lugansk, 497,000 . . . . H 5
L'vov, 790,000 . . . . . H 2
Mariupol' (Ždanov),
    517,000 . . . . H 5
Nikolajev, 503,000 . . H 4
Odessa, 1,115,000
    (1,185,000★) . . . . . H 4
Poltava, 315,000 . . . H 4
Sevastopol', 356,000 . . I 4
Simferopol', 344,000 . . I 4
Sumy, 291,000 . . . . . H 4
Vinnica, 374,000 . . . H 3
Yalta see Jalta . . . . I 4
Zaporožje, 884,000 . . H 5
Žitomir, 292,000 . . . . G 3

Uzbekistan
1989 CENSUS
Andižan, 293,000 . . . . I12
Buchara, 224,000 . . . . J10
Fergana, 200,000 . . . I12
Namangan, 308,000 . . I12
Samarkand, 366,000 . . J11
Taškent, 2,073,000
    (2,325,000★) I11

23

Northeast Asia

Russia
1989 CENSUS

Abakan, 154,000 .... G12
Ačinsk, 122,000 .... F12
Alapajevsk,
  51,000('87) .... F 6
Aldan, 20,000('74) .. F19
Alejsk, 31,390('79) .. G10
Aleksandrovsk-
  Sachalinskij,
  20,000('74) G22
Angarsk, 266,000....G14
Anžero-Sudžensk,
  108,000......... F11
Arsenjev, 67,000('87). .I20
Art'om, 73,000('87) .. I20
Art'omovsk,
  17,000('79) G12
Asbest, 83,000('87).. F 6
Asino, 31,329('79) ..F11
Balej, 25,000('79)... G17
Barabinsk, 35,035('79)F 9
Barnaul, 602,000
  (665,000★) G10
Belogorsk,
  71,000('87) G19
Belovo, 118,000('87) G11
Berdsk 59,000('87). .G10
Berezniki, 201,000.. F 5
Bijsk, 233,000 .... G11
Bikin, 18,000('79) ..H20
Birobidžan,
  82,000('87) H20
Blagoveščensk,
  206,000......... G19
Bogotol, 29,000('79) F11
Bolotnoje, 20,000('79) F10
Bratsk, 255,000 .... F14
Čel'abinsk, 1,143,000
  (1,325,000★) ..... F 6

Čeremchovo,
  73,000('87) G14
Černogorsk,
  80,000('87) G12
Chabarovsk, 601,000 H21
Chanty-Mansijsk,
  27,961('79) ...... E 7
Cholmsk, 50,000('87) H22
Čita, 366,000 ..... G16
Čusovoj, 59,000('87) F 5
Dudinka, 23,000('74) D11
Gorno-Altajsk,
  39,917('79) G11
Gubacha, 32,461('79) F 5
Gusinoozersk,
  18,000('79) G15
Igarka, 16,918('79) . D11
Inta, 58,000('87) .... D 6
Irbit, 53,000('87) ... F 6
Irkutsk, 626,000 ... G14
Iskitim, 69,000('87). G10
Issyk-Kul', 64,000('87) I 9
Jakutsk, 187,000 ... E19
Jekaterinburg, 1,367,000
  (1,620,000★) ..... F 6
Jenisejsk, 22,000('79) F12
Jurga, 92,000('87) .. F10
Južno-Sachalinsk,
  157,000......... H22
Kamen'-na-Obi,
  40,684('79) G10
Kamensk-Ural'skij,
  209,000......... F 6
Kansk, 110,000 ....F13
Karpinsk, 36,569('79) F 6
Kemerovo, 520,000 . F11
Kirensk, 16,000('74) .F15
Kisel'ovsk, 128,000 . G11
Kizel, 40,157('79) ... F 5
Kolpaševo,
  27,000('79) F10
Komsomol'sk-na-Amure,
  315,000......... G21
Kopejsk, 99,000('87) F 6
Korkino, 63,000('81) G 6
Korsakov, 43,348('79) H22
Krasnojarsk, 912,000 F12

★ Population of metropolitan
  area, including suburbs.

24

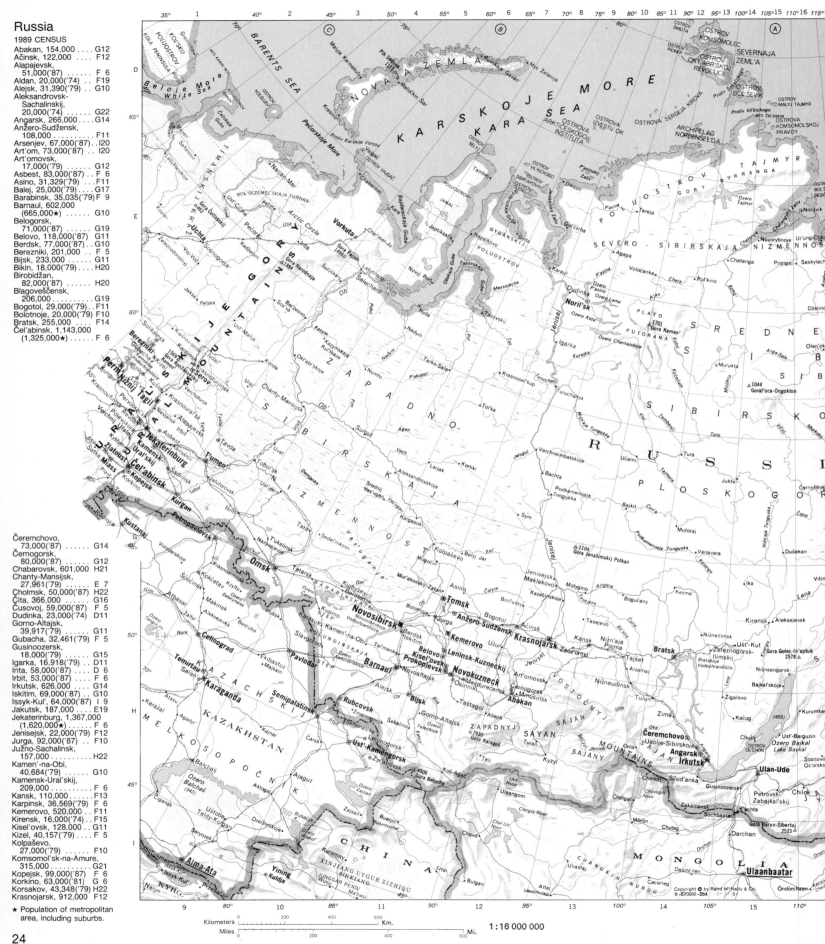

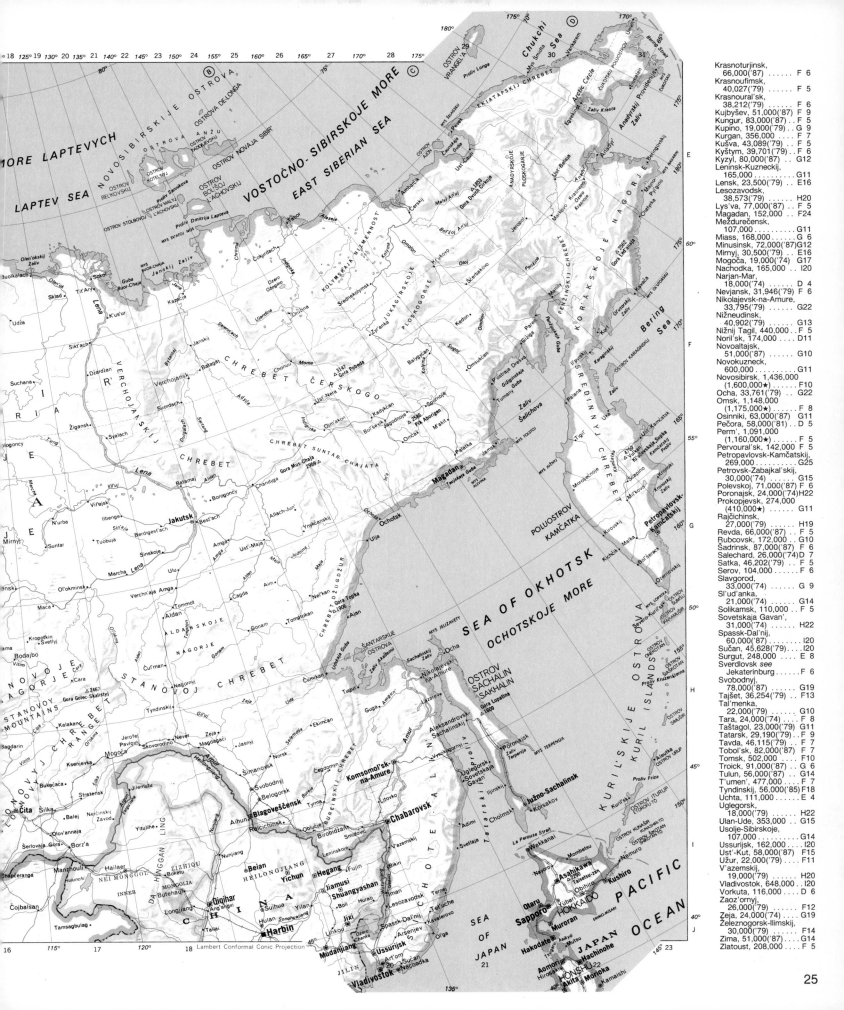

Krasnoturjinsk,
  66,000('87) ..... F 6
Krasnoufimsk,
  40,027('79) ..... F 5
Krasnoural'sk,
  38,212('79) ..... F 6
Kujbyšev, 51,000('87) F 9
Kungur, 83,000('87) .. F 5
Kupino, 19,000('79) . . G 9
Kurgan, 356,000 ..... F 7
Kušva, 43,089('79) . . F 5
Kyštym, 39,701('79) .. F 6
Kyzyl, 80,000('87) .. G12
Leninsk-Kuzneckij,
  165,000 .... G11
Lensk, 23,500('79) .. E16
Lesozavodsk,
  38,573('79) H20
Lys'va, 77,000('87) .. F 5
Magadan, 152,000 .. F24
Meždurečensk,
  107,000 .... G11
Miass, 168,000 ...... G 6
Minusinsk, 72,000('87) G12
Mirnyj, 30,500('79) .. E16
Mogoča, 19,000('74) . G17
Nachodka, 165,000 .. I20
Narjan-Mar,
  18,000('74) ...... D 4
Nevjansk, 31,946('79) F 6
Nikolajevsk-na-Amure,
  33,795('79) G22
Nižneudinsk,
  40,902('79) G13
Nižnij Tagil, 440,000 .. F 5
Noril'sk, 174,000 ... D11
Novoaltajsk,
  51,000('87) G10
Novokuzneck,
  600,000 .... G11
Novosibirsk, 1,436,000
  (1,600,000★) F10
Ocha, 33,761('79) .. G22
Omsk, 1,148,000
  (1,175,000★) ...... F 8
Osinniki, 63,000('87) . G11
Pečora, 58,000('81) .. D 5
Perm', 1,091,000
  (1,160,000★) ...... F 5
Pervoural'sk, 142,000 F 5
Petropavlovsk-Kamčatskij,
  269,000 .... G25
Petrovsk-Zabajkal'skij,
  30,000('74) G15
Polevskoj, 71,000('87) F 6
Poronajsk, 24,000('74) H22
Prokopjevsk, 274,000
  (410,000★) G11
Rajčichinsk,
  27,000('79) H19
Revda, 66,000('87) .. F 5
Rubcovsk, 172,000 . . G10
Šadrinsk, 87,000('87) F 6
Salechard, 26,000('74) D 7
Satka, 46,202('79) .. F 5
Serov, 104,000 ...... F 6
Slavgorod,
  33,000('74) ...... G 9
Sl'ud'anka,
  21,000('74) G14
Solikamsk, 110,000 . . F 5
Sovetskaja Gavan',
  31,000('74) H22
Spassk-Dal'nij,
  60,000('87) I20
Sučan, 45,628('79) ... I20
Surgut, 248,000 ..... E 8
Sverdlovsk see
  Jekaterinburg ...... F 6
Svobodnyj,
  78,000('87) G19
Tajšet, 36,254('79) .. F13
Tal'menka,
  22,000('79) G10
Tara, 24,000('74) .... F 8
Taštagol, 23,000('79) G11
Tatarsk, 29,190('79) . F 9
Tavda, 46,115('79) ... F 7
Tobol'sk, 82,000('87) F 7
Tomsk, 502,000 ..... F10
Troick, 91,000('87) . . G 6
Tulun, 56,000('74) . . G14
T'umen', 477,000 .... F 7
Tyndinskij, 56,000('85) F18
Uchta, 111,000 ...... E 4
Uglegorsk,
  18,000('79) H22
Ulan-Ude, 353,000 . . G15
Usolje-Sibirskoje,
  107,000 .... G14
Ussurijsk, 162,000 ... I20
Ust'-Kut, 58,000('87) F15
Užur, 22,000('79) F11
V'azemskij,
  19,000('79) H20
Vladivostok, 648,000 . I20
Vorkuta, 116,000 .... D 6
Zaoz'ornyj,
  26,000('79) F12
Zeja, 24,000('74) G19
Železnogorsk-Ilimskij,
  30,000('79) F14
Zima, 51,000('87) ... G14
Zlatoust, 208,000 .... F 5

China, Japan, and Korea

Bhutan

1982 ESTIMATE

Thimphu, 12,000 .... F 4

China

1988 ESTIMATE

Andong, 579,800('86) C11
Anshan, 1,330,000 .. C11
Bangbu, 403,900
  (612,600▲)('86) E10
Baoding, 423,200
  (535,100▲)('86) D10
Baotou, 1,130,000 .. C 8
Beijing (Peking), 6,710,000
  (6,450,000★) D10
Benxi, 860,000 ..... C11
Canton see
  Guangzhou ...... G 9
Changchun, 1,822,000
  (2,000,000▲) C12
Changsha, 1,230,000 F 9
Changzhou,
  522,700('86) E10
Chengdu, 1,884,000
  (2,960,000▲) ..... E 7
Chongqing, 2,502,000
  (2,890,000▲) ..... F 8
Dalian, 2,280,000 .... D11
Datong, 810,000
  (1,040,000▲) ..... C 9
Fushun, 1,290,000 .. C11
Fuzhou, 910,000
  (1,240,000▲) F10
Guangzhou (Canton),
  3,100,000
  (3,420,000▲) ...... G 9
Guiyang, 1,030,000
  (1,430,000▲) ..... F 8
Handan, 870,000
  (1,030,000▲) ..... D 9
Hanzhou, 1,290,000 E 11
Harbin, 2,710,000 .. B12
Hefei, 740,000
  (930,000▲) E10
Hegang, 588,300('86) B13
Hengyang, 419,200
  (601,300▲)('86) .... F 9
Hohhot, 670,000
  (830,000▲) ..... C 9
Huainan, 700,000
  (1,110,000▲) E10
Huangshi,
  451,900('86) E10
Jilin, 1,200,000 ...... C12
Jinan (Tsinan), 1,546,000
  (2,140,000▲) D10
Jinzhou, 710,000
  (810,000▲) C11
Jixi, 700,000
  (820,000▲) B13
Kaifeng, 458,800
  (629,100▲)('86) .... E 9
Kunming, 1,310,000
  (1,550,000▲) ..... F 7
Lanzhou, 1,297,000
  (1,420,000▲) ..... D 7
Lasa (Lhasa), 84,400
  (107,700▲)('86) .... F 5
Liuzhou, 680,000 .... G 8
Luoyang, 760,000
  (1,090,000▲) ..... E 9
Mudanjiang, 650,000 C12
Nanchang, 1,090,000
  (1,260,000▲) .. F10
Nanjing, 2,390,000 .. E10
Nanning, 720,000
  (1,000,000▲) ..... G 8
Ningbo, 570,000
  (1,050,000▲) F11
Peking see Beijing .. D10
Qingdao (Tsingtao),
  1,300,000 ...... D11
Shanghai, 7,220,000
  (9,300,000▲) E11
Shantou (Swatow),
  560,000 (790,000▲) G10
Shenyang (Mukden),
  3,910,000
  (4,370,000★) C11
Shijiazhuang,
  1,220,000 ..... D 9
Suzhou, 740,000 .... E11
Taiyuan, 1,700,000
  (1,980,000▲) ..... D 9
Tangshan, 1,080,000
  (1,440,000▲) D10
Tianjin (Tientsin),
  4,950,000
  (5,540,000▲) D10
Ürümqi, 1,060,000 .. C 4
Wenzhou, 372,200
  (530,600▲)('86) F11
Wuhan, 3,570,000 .. E 9
Wuhu, 396,000
  (502,200▲)('86) .. E10
Wuxi, 880,000 ...... E11
Xi'an (Sian), 2,210,000
  (2,580,000▲) ..... E 8
Xining, 620,000 ..... D 7
Xuzhou, 860,000 .... E10
Zhangjiakou (Kalgan),
  500,000 (640,000▲) C 9

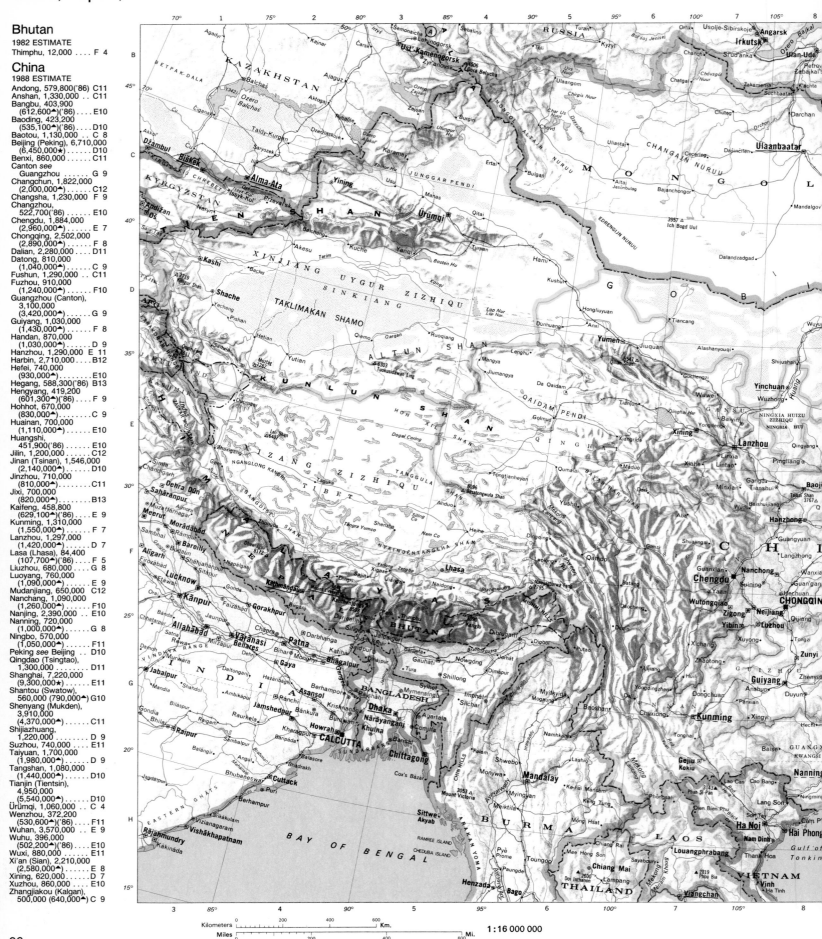

26

Kilometers

Km.

Miles

1:16 000 000

Zhengzhou, 1,150,000
  (1,580,000▲) ..... E 9
Zibo, 840,000
  (2,370,000▲) D10

Hong Kong
1986 CENSUS

Kowloon (Jiulong),
  774,781 .... G 9
Victoria (Xianggang),
  1,175,860
  (4,770,000★) ..... G 9

Japan
1985 CENSUS

Asahikawa, 363,631 ..C15
Chiba, 788,930 ...... D15
Fukuoka, 1,160,440
  (1,750,000★) E13
Hakodate, 319,194 .. C15
Hamamatsu, 514,118 E14
Himeji, 452,917
  (660,000★) E13
Hiroshima, 1,044,118
  (1,575,000★) E13
Kagoshima, 530,502.. E13
Kanazawa, 430,481 .. D14
Kitakyūshū, 1,056,402
  (1,525,000★) E13
Kōbe, 1,410,834 .... E14
Kumamoto, 555,719.. E13
Kurashiki, 413,632 .. E13
Kyōto, 1,479,218 .... D14
Matsuyama, 426,658 E13
Nagasaki, 449,382 .. E12
Nagoya, 2,116,381
  (4,800,000★) D14
Niigata, 475,630 .... D14
Okayama, 572,479 .. E13
Ōsaka, 2,636,249
  (16,450,000★) E14
Sapporo, 1,542,979
  (1,900,000★) C15
Sendai, 700,254
  (1,175,000★) D15
Shizuoka, 468,362
  (975,000★) E14
Tōkyō, 8,354,615
  (27,700,000★) D14
Utsunomiya, 405,375 D14
Yokohama, 2,992,926 D14

Korea, North
1981 ESTIMATE

Ch'ŏngjin, 490,000 .. C12
Kaesŏng, 259,000 .. D12
Namp'o, 241,000 .. D12
P'yŏngyang, 1,283,000
  (1,600,000★) D12
Sinŭiju, 305,000 .. C11
Wŏnsan, 398,000 .. D12

Korea, South
1989 ESTIMATE

Chŏnju, 426,473('85) D12
Inch'ŏn, 1,628,000 .. D12
Kwangju, 1,165,000 .. D12
Masan, 448,746
  (625,000★)('85) D12
Pusan, 3,773,000
  (3,800,000★) D12
Soŭl (Seoul), 10,522,000
  (15,850,000★) D12
Taegu, 2,207,000 .... D12
Taejŏn, 1,041,000 .. D12

Macau
1987 ESTIMATE

Macau (Aomen),
  429,000 .... G 9

Mongolia
1989 ESTIMATE

Ulaanbaatar (Ulan Bator),
  548,400 .... B 8

Nepal
1981 CENSUS

Kāthmāndaū
  (Kathmandu), 235,160
  (320,000★) .... F 4

Taiwan
1988 ESTIMATE

Kaohsiung, 1,342,797
  (1,845,000★) G11
T'aichung, 715,107 .. G11
T'ainan, 656,927 .... G11
T'aipei, 2,637,100
  (6,130,000★) F11

★ Population of metropolitan area, including suburbs.
▲ Population of entire district, including rural area.

27

Eastern and Southeastern China

★ Population of metropolitan area, including suburbs.   ▲ Population of entire district, including rural area.

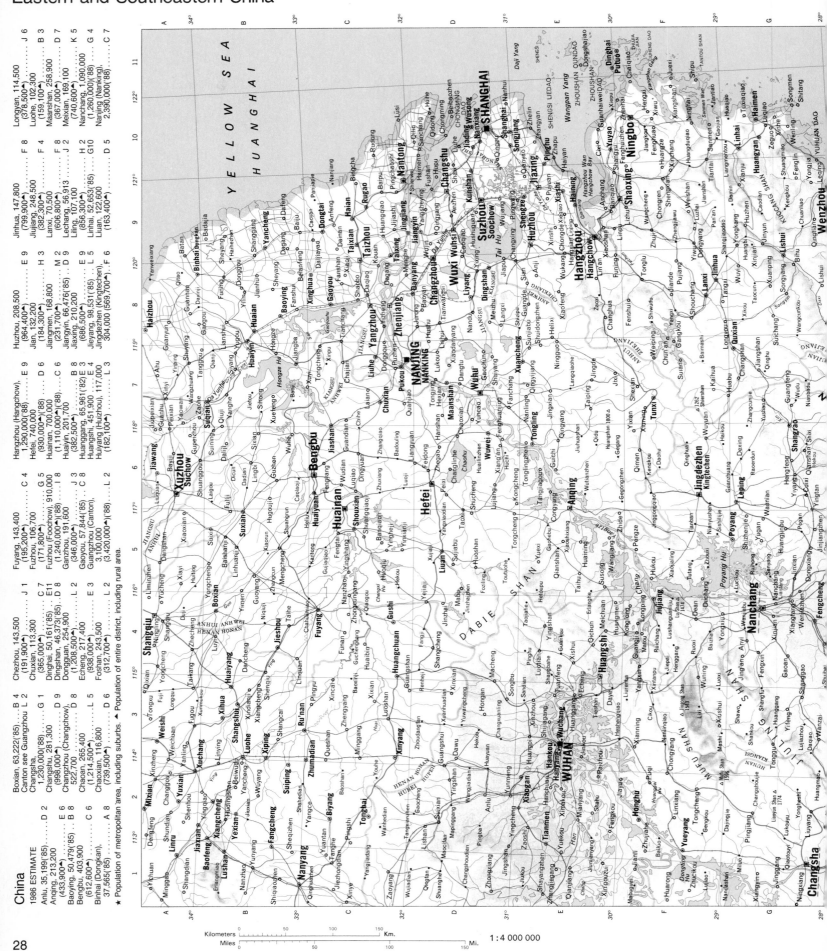

Kilometers 0 | 50 | 100 | 150 Km.
Miles 0 | 50 | 100 | 150 Mi.
1 : 4 000 000

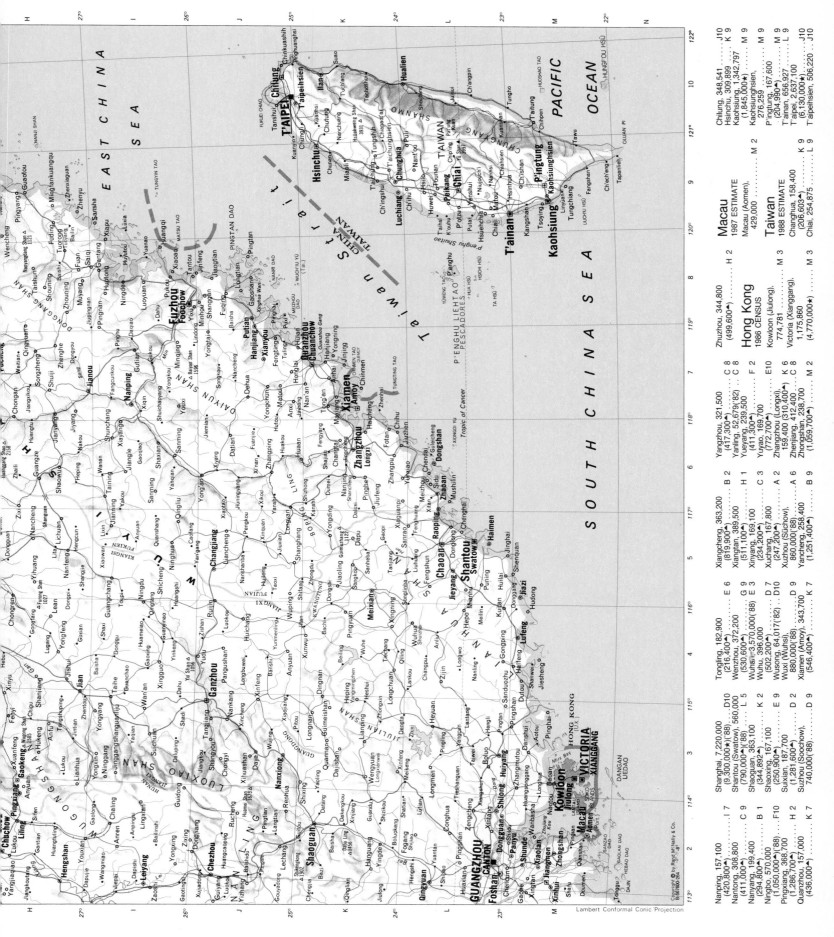

Nanping, 157,100 .... I 7
(420,800▲)
Nantong, 308,800 .... C 9
(411,000★)
Nanyang, 199,400 .... B 1
(294,800▲)
Ningbo, 570,000 .... F10
(1,050,000★)('88)
Pingxiang, 368,700 .... H 2
(1,286,700▲)
Quanzhou, 157,000 .... K 7
(436,000▲)

Shanghai, 7,220,000 .... D10
(9,300,000★)('88)
Shantou (Swatow), 560,000 .... L 5
(790,000★)('88)
Shaoguan, 363,100 .... K 2
(344,892▲)
Shaoxing, 167,100 .... E 9
(250,900▲)
Suixian, 187,700 .... D 2
(1,281,600▲)
Suzhou (Soochow), 157,000 .... K 7
(740,000▲)

Tongling, 182,900 .... E 6
(216,400▲)
Wenzhou, 372,200 .... G 9
(530,600▲)
Wuhan, 3,570,000('88) .... E 3
Wuhu, 396,000 .... D 7
(502,200▲)
Wusong, 64,017('82) D10
(247,200▲)
Wuxi (Wuhsi), 880,000('88) .... D 9
Xiamen (Amoy), 343,700 .... K 7
(546,400▲)

Xiangcheng, 363,200 .... B 2
(819,900▲)
Xiangtan, 389,500 .... H 1
(511,100▲)
Xinyang, 169,100 .... C 3
(234,200▲)
Xuchang, 167,800 .... A 2
(247,200▲)
Xuzhou (Süchow), 860,000('88) .... A 6
Yancheng, 258,400 .... B 9
(1,251,400▲)

Yangzhou, 321,500 .... C 8
(417,300▲)
Yanling, 52,679('82) .... C 8
Yueyang, 239,500 .... F 2
(411,300▲)
Yuyao, 169,700 .... E10
(772,700▲)
Zhangzhou (Longxi), 159,400 .... K 6
(310,400▲)
Zhenjiang, 412,400 .... C 8
Zhongshan, 238,400 .... M 2
(1,059,700★)

Zhuzhou, 344,800 .... H 2
(499,600▲)

Hong Kong
1986 CENSUS
Kowloon (Jiulong), 774,781
Victoria (Xianggang), 1,175,860

Macau
1987 ESTIMATE
Macau (Aomen), 429,000

Taiwan
1988 ESTIMATE
Changhua, 158,400 .... L 9
(206,603▲)
Chiai, 254,875 .... J10

Chilung, 348,541 .... J10
Hsinchu, 309,899 .... K 9
Kaohsiung, 1,342,797 .... M 9
(1,845,000★)
Kaohsiunghsien, 276,259 .... M 9
P'ingtung, 167,600 .... M 9
(204,990▲)
T'ainan, 656,927 .... L 9
T'aipei, 2,637,100 .... L 9
(6,130,000★)
T'aipeihsien, 506,220 .... J10

Lambert Conformal Conic Projection

Copyright © by Rand McNally & Co.
B-967600-264

29

Japan

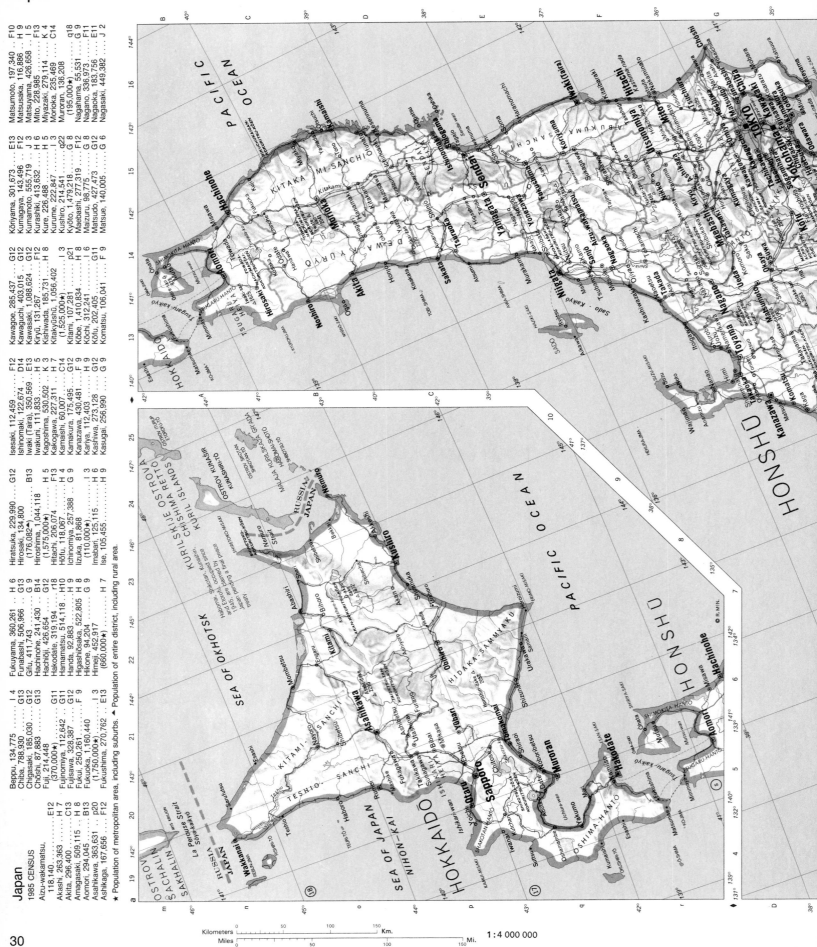

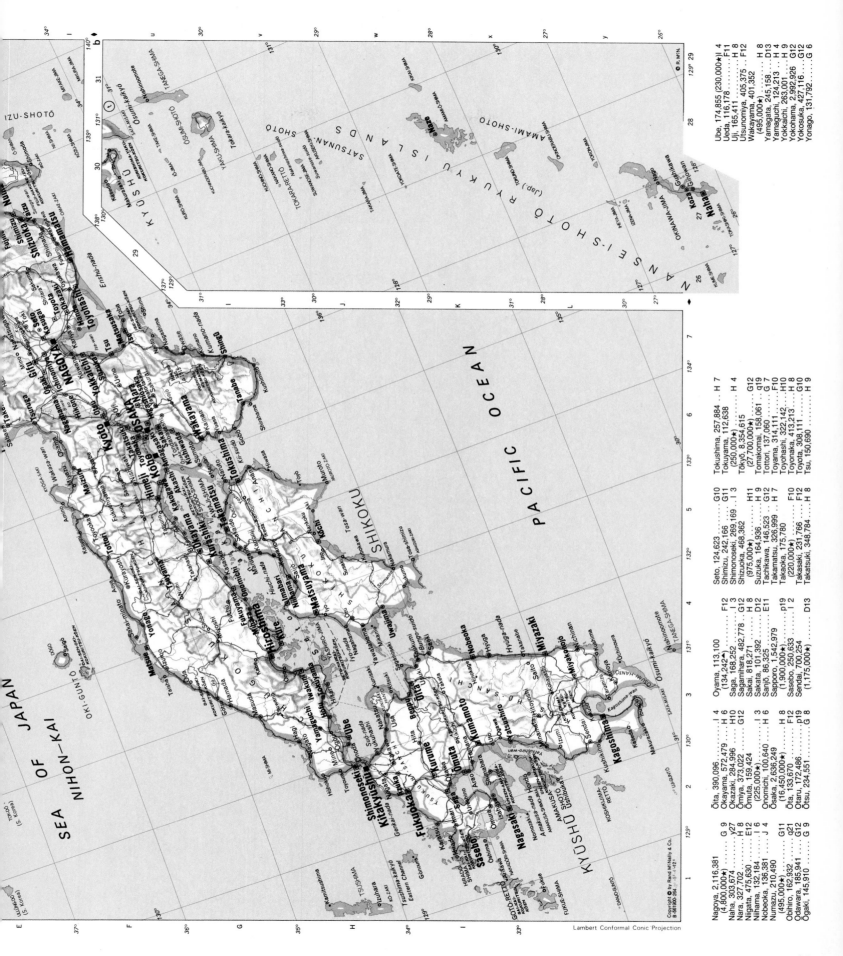

SEA OF JAPAN
NIHON-KAI

PACIFIC OCEAN

KYŪSHŪ

SHIKOKU

NANSEI-SHOTŌ RYUKYU ISLANDS

SATSUNAN-SHOTŌ

AMAMI-SHOTŌ

IZU-SHOTŌ

Nagoya, 2,116,381 . . . . G 9
(4,800,000★) y27
Naha, 303,674 . . . . H10
Niigata, 475,630 . . . . E12
Niihama, 132,184 . . . . I 6
Nobeoka, 136,381 . . . . . . J 4
Numazu, 210,490 . . . . G11
(495,000★) q21
Obihiro, 162,932 . . . . p19
Odawara, 185,941 . . . . . . G12
Ōgaki, 145,910 . . . . G 9

Ōita, 390,096 . . . . I 4
Okayama, 572,479 . . . . . . H 6
Okazaki, 284,996 . . . . . . H10
Ōmiya, 373,022 . . . . G12
Ōmuta, 159,424 . . . . I 3
(225,000★) . . . . I 3
Onomichi, 100,640 . . . . . . H 6
Ōsaka, 2,636,249 . . . . H 8
(16,450,000★) F12
Ōtaru, 172,486 . . . . p19
Ōtsu, 234,551 . . . . G 8

Oyama, 113,100 . . . . F12
(134,242★) . . . . I 3
Saga, 168,252 . . . . G12
Sagamihara, 482,778 . . . . G12
Sakai, 818,271 . . . . H 8
Sakata, 101,392 . . . . D12
Sanjō, 86,325 . . . . E11
Sapporo, 1,542,979 . . . . . p19
(1,900,000★) p19
Sasebo, 250,633 . . . . I 2
Sendai, 700,254 . . . . D13
(1,175,000★) D13

Seto, 124,623 . . . . G10
Shimizu, 242,166 . . . . . . G11
Shimonoseki, 269,169 . . . . I 3
Shizuoka, 468,362 . . . . . . G12
(975,000★) G12
Suzuka, 164,936 . . . . H 9
Tachikawa, 146,523 . . . . . G12
Takamatsu, 326,999 . . . . . H 7
Takaoka, 175,780 . . . . . . F10
(220,000★) F10
Takasaki, 231,766 . . . . . . F12
Takatsuki, 348,784 . . . . . H 8

Tokushima, 257,884 . . . . . H 7
Tokuyama, 112,638 . . . . . I 3
(250,000★) . . . . I 3
Tōkyō, 8,354,615 . . . . G12
(27,700,000★) G12
Tomakomai, 158,061 . . . . . q19
Tottori, 137,060 . . . . G 7
Toyama, 314,111 . . . . F10
Toyohashi, 322,142 . . . . . H10
Toyonaka, 413,213 . . . . . . H 8
Toyota, 308,111 . . . . G10
Tsu, 150,690 . . . . H 9

Ube, 174,855 (230,000★) . . I 4
Ueda, 116,178 . . . . F11
Uji, 165,411 . . . . H 8
Utsunomiya, 405,375 . . . . F12
Wakayama, 401,352 . . . . . H 8
(495,000★) . . . .
Yamagata, 245,158 . . . . . . D13
Yamaguchi, 124,213 . . . . . H 4
Yokkaichi, 263,001 . . . . . . H 9
Yokohama, 2,992,926 . . . . G12
Yokosuka, 427,116 . . . . . . G12
Yonago, 131,792 . . . . G 6

31

Southeastern Asia

Brunei
1981 CENSUS
Bandar Seri Begawan,
22,777 (64,000★) . . E 5

Burma
1983 CENSUS
Bago, 150,528 . . . . . B 2
Henzada, 82,005 . . . . . B 2
Mandalay, 532,949 . . A 2
Mawlamyine, 219,961 B 2
Monywa, 106,843 . . . . A 2
Pathein, 144,096 . . . . B 1
Pyè (Prome), 83,332 . . B 2
Sittwe (Akyab),
107,621 . . . . A 1
Yangon (Rangoon),
2,705,039
(2,800,000★) . . . . . . B 2

Cambodia
1986 ESTIMATE
Phnum Pénh, 700,000 C 3

Indonesia
1980 CENSUS
Ambon, 111,914
(207,702★) . . . . F 8
Balikpapan, 208,040
(279,852▲) . . . . F 6
Bandung, 1,633,000
(1,800,000★)('85) . . m13
Banjarmasin,
424,000('83) . . . . F 5
Banjuwangi, 90,378 . . n17
Blitar, 78,503
(100,000★) n16
Bogor, 246,946
(560,000★) m13
Cilacap, 127,017 . . . . m14
Cirebon, 223,504
(275,000★) m14
Denpasar, 159,233 . . G 6
Dili, 6,890 (67,039★) . G 8
Garut, 145,624 . . . . . m13
Jakarta, 9,200,000
(10,000,000★)('89) m13
Jambi, 155,761
(230,046★) . . . . . . F 3
Jember, 171,284 . . . . n16
Kediri, 176,261
(221,830▲) m16
Kudus, 154,478 . . . . m15
Kupang, 84,587 . . . . H 7
Madiun, 150,562
(180,000★) m15
Magelang, 123,358
(160,000★) m15
Malang, 547,000('83) m16
Manado, 217,091 . . . E 7
Medan, 2,110,000('85) E 2
Padang, 405,600
(657,000★)('83) . . . F 3
Pakanbaru, 186,199 . . E 3
Palembang,
874,000('83) . . . . . F 3
Pangkalpinang, 90,078 F 4
Pasuruan, 95,864
(125,000★) m16
Pekalongan, 132,413
(260,000★) m14
Pemalang, 72,663 . . m14
Pematangsiantar, 150,296
(175,000★) . . . . . . E 2
Pontianak,
343,000('83) . . . F 4
Probolinggo, 100,296 m16
Purwokerto, 143,787 m14
Salatiga, 85,740 . . . m15
Samarinda, 182,473
(264,012▲) . . . . . . F 6
Semarang,
1,206,000('83) m15
Sukabumi, 109,898
(225,000★) m13
Surabaya,
2,345,000('85) m16
Surakarta, 491,000
(575,000★)('83) m15
Tanjungkarang-
Telukbetung, 284,167
(375,000★) k12
Tasikmalaya, 192,267 m14
Tegal, 131,440
(340,000★) m14
Tual, 7,833 . . . . G 9
Tulungagung, 91,585 . n15
Ujungpandang,
841,000('83) . . . . G 6
Yogyakarta, 421,000
(510,000★)('83) m15

Laos
1975 ESTIMATE
Louangphrabang,
46,000 . . . . B 3
Paksé, 47,000 . . . . . B 4
Savannakhet, 53,000 . B 3
Viangchan,
377,409('85) . . . . . B 3

32

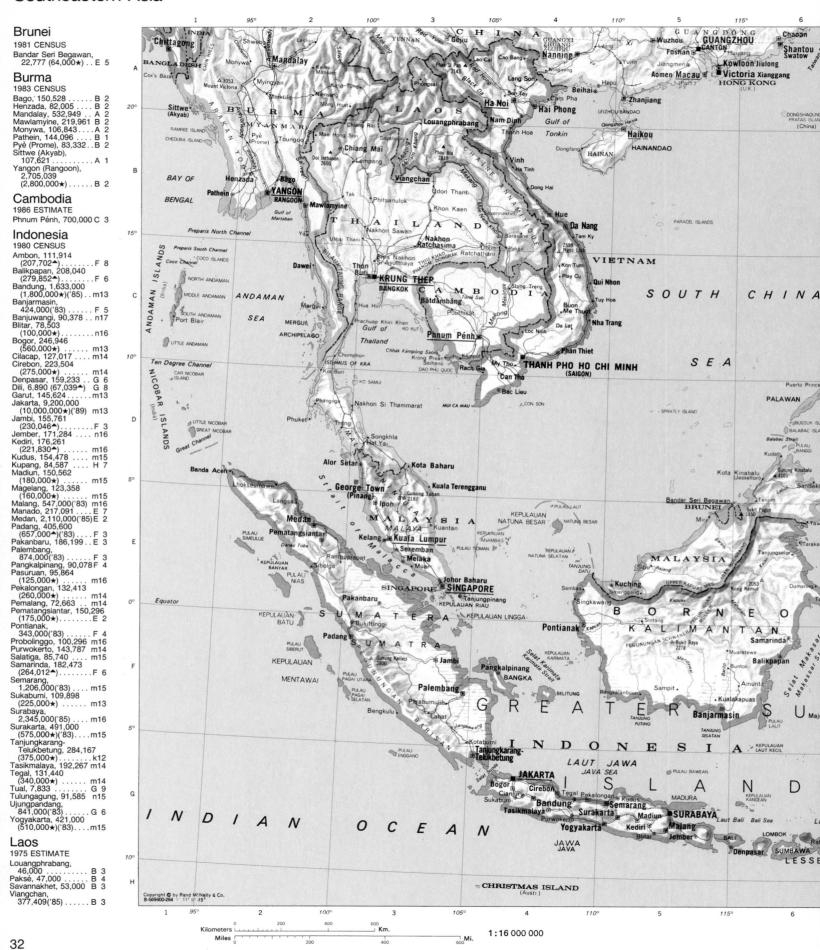

Malaysia
1980 CENSUS

Alor Setar, 69,435 .. D 3
George Town (Pinang),
  248,241 (495,000★) D 3
Ipoh, 293,849 .... E 3
Johor Baharu,
  246,395 .... E 3
Kelang, 192,080 .... E 3
Kota Baharu, 167,872 D 3
Kuala Lumpur, 919,610
  (1,475,000★) ..... E 3
Kuala Terengganu,
  180,296 .... D 3
Kuantan, 131,547 .... E 3
Kuching, 72,555 .... E 5
Melaka, 87,494 ...... E 3
Sandakan, 70,420 .. D 6
Seremban, 132,911 .. E 3
Sibu, 85,231 .... E 5

Philippines
1990 CENSUS

Angeles, 236,000 .... q19
Bacolod, 364,000 ... C 7
Baguio, 183,000 ... p19
Batangas, 31,600
  (184,000★) r19
Cabanatuan, 75,700
  (173,000★) q19
Cavite, 92,000
  (175,000★) q19
Cebu, 610,000
  (720,000★) ...... C 7
Cotabato, 127,000 .. D 7
Dagupan, 122,000 .. p19
Davao, 569,300
  (850,000★) ...... D 8
Dumaguete, 80,000 .. D 7
Iloilo, 311,000 ... C 7
Legaspi, 63,000
  (121,000★) r20
Lipa, 30,000
  (160,000★) r19
Lucena, 151,000 ... r19
Malolos, 95,699('80) .. q19
Manila, 1,587,000
  (6,800,000★) q19
Naga, 115,000 ..... r20
Pasig, 318,853('84) . q19
Puerto Princesa, 52,000
  (92,000▲) ...... D 6
Quezon City,
  1,632,000 .... q19
San Fernando,
  110,891('80) q19
San Pablo, 83,900
  (161,000★) q19
Tarlac, 38,205
  (175,691▲)('80) .. q19
Zamboanga, 107,000
  (444,000▲) ...... D 7

Singapore
1989 ESTIMATE

Singapore, 2,685,400
  (3,025,000★) ..... E 3

Thailand
1988 ESTIMATE

Bangkok see Krung
  Thep .... C 3
Chiang Mai, 164,030 . B 2
Hat Yai, 138,046 .... D 3
Khon Kaen, 131,340 . B 3
Krung Thep (Bangkok),
  5,716,779
  (6,450,000★) .... C 3
Nakhon Ratchasima,
  204,982 .... C 3
Nakhon Sawan,
  105,220 .... C 3
Nakhon Si Thammarat,
  72,407 .... D 2
Phitsanulok, 77,675 . B 3
Songkhla, 84,433 .... D 3
Ubon Ratchathani,
  100,374 .... B 3
Udon Thani, 81,202 . B 3

Vietnam
1979 CENSUS

Can Tho, 182,856 .. C 4
Da Nang, 318,653 .. B 4
Hai Phong, 456,000
  (1,279,067)('89) .. A 4
Ha Noi, 1,089,000
  (1,500,000★)('89) . A 4
Hue, 165,710 ...... B 4
My Tho, 101,493 .... C 4
Nam Dinh, 160,179 .. A 4
Nha Trang, 172,663 . C 4
Phan Thiet, 75,241 .. C 4
Qui Nhon, 127,211 .. C 4
Rach Gia, 81,075 ... C 4
Saigon see Thanh Pho Ho
  Chi Minh .... C 4
Thanh Pho Ho Chi Minh
  (Saigon), 3,169,000
  (3,300,000★)('89) .. C 4
Vinh, 159,753 ...... B 4

★ Population of metropolitan area, including suburbs.
▲ Population of entire district, including rural area.

Lambert Conformal Conic Projection

Burma, Thailand, and Indochina

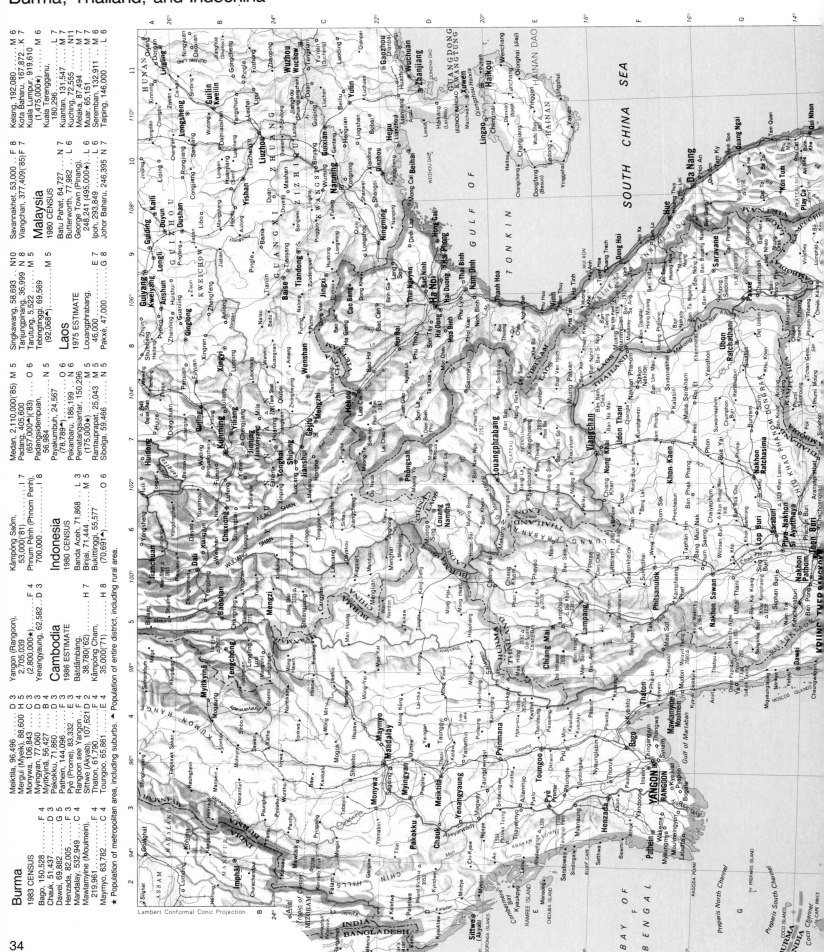

Burma
1983 CENSUS
Bago, 150,528 .... F 4
Chauk, 51,437 .... D 3
Dawei, 69,882 .... G 5
Henzada, 82,005 .... F 3
Mandalay, 532,949 .... E 3
Mawlamyine (Moulmein),
219,961 .... F 4
Maymyo, 63,782 .... E 4

Meiktila, 96,496 .... D 3
Mergui (Myeik), 88,600 .... H 5
Monywa, 106,843 .... C 3
Myingyan, 77,060 .... D 3
Myitkyinā, 56,427 .... B 4
Pakokku, 71,860 .... D 3
Pathein, 144,096 .... F 3
Pyè (Prome), 83,332 .... E 3
Rangoon see Yangon
Sittwe (Akyab), 107,621 .... D 2
Thaton, 61,790 .... F 4
Toungoo, 65,861 .... E 4

Yangon (Rangoon),
2,705,039 .... F 4
(2,800,000★) ....
Yenangyaung, 62,582 .... D 3

Cambodia
1986 ESTIMATE
Bătdâmbâng,
38,780('62) ....
Kâmpóng Cham,
35,000('71) .... O 6

Kâmpóng Saôm,
53,000('81) .... I 7
Phnom Pénh (Phnom Penh),
700,000 .... I 8

Indonesia
1980 CENSUS
Banda Aceh, 71,868 .... L 3
Binjai, 71,444 .... M 5
Bukittinggi, 55,577 ....

Medan, 2,110,000('85) .... F 8
Padang, 405,600
(657,000★)('83) .... F 7
Padangsidempuan,
56,984 ....
Payakumbuh, 24,567
(78,789★) .... O 6
Pekanbaru, 186,199 .... N 6
Pematangsiantar, 150,296
(175,000★) .... L 6
Rantauprapat, 25,043 .... M 5
Sibolga, 59,466 .... G 8

Savannakhet, 53,000 .... F 8
Viangchan, 377,409('85) F 7

Malaysia
1980 CENSUS
Batu Pahat, 64,727 .... N 7
Butterworth, 77,982 .... L 6
George Town (Pinang),
248,241 (495,000★) .... L 6
Ipoh, 293,849 .... L 6
Johor Baharu, 246,395 .... N 7

Singkawang, 58,693 .... N10
Tanjungpinang, 36,999 .... N 8
Tarutung, 5,522 .... M 5
Tebingtinggi, 69,569
(92,068★) .... M 5

Laos
1975 ESTIMATE
Louangphrabang,
46,000 .... E 7
Paksé, 47,000 .... G 8

Kelang, 192,080 .... M 6
Kota Baharu, 167,872 .... K 7
Kuala Lumpur, 919,610
(1,475,000★) .... M 6
Kuala Terengganu,
180,296 ....
Kuantan, 131,547 .... M 7
Kuching, 72,555 .... N11
Melaka, 87,494 .... M 7
Muar, 65,151 .... M 7
Seremban, 132,911 .... M 6
Taiping, 146,000 .... L 6

★ Population of metropolitan area, including suburbs. ▲ Population of entire district, including rural area.

Lambert Conformal Conic Projection

34

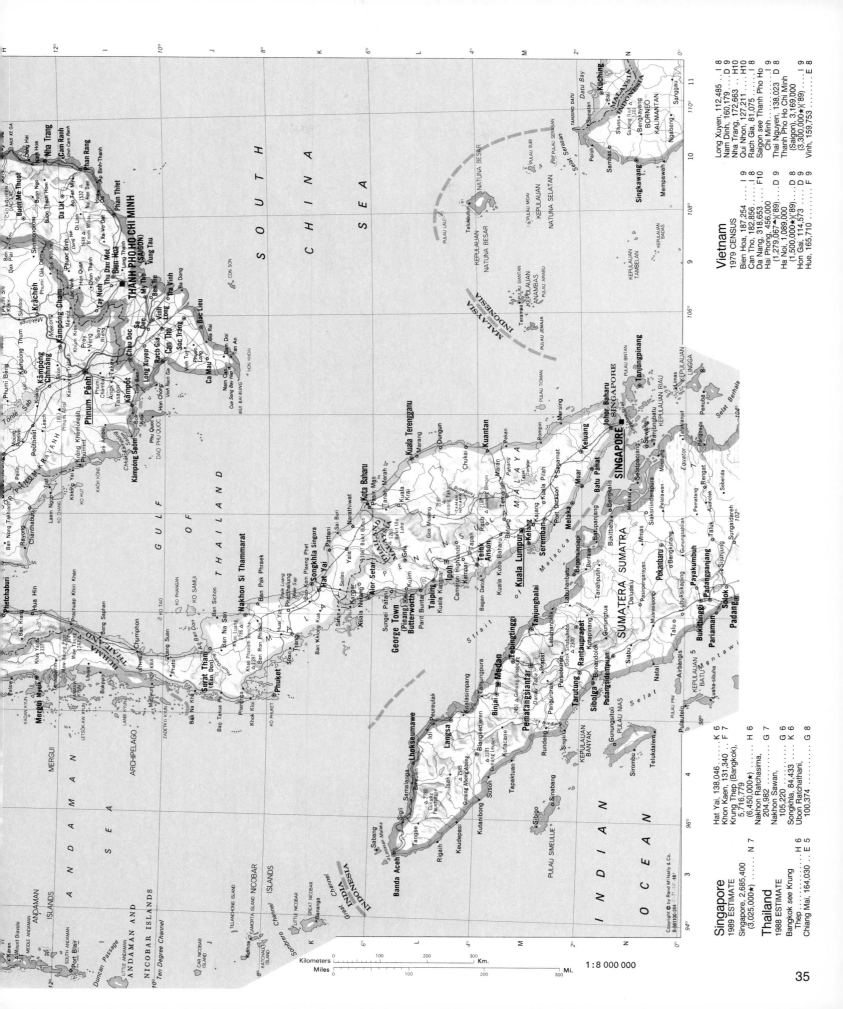

Singapore

1989 ESTIMATE

Singapore, 2,685,400
(3,025,000★) .... N 7

Thailand

1988 ESTIMATE

Bangkok see Krung
  Thep .... H 6
Chiang Mai, 164,030 ... E 5

Hat Yai, 138,046 .... K 6
Khon Kaen, 131,340 ... F 7
Krung Thep (Bangkok),
  5,716,779
  (6,450,000★) .... H 6
Nakhon Ratchasima,
  204,982 .... G 7
Nakhon Sawan,
  105,220 .... G 6
Songkhla, 84,433 ...... K 6
Ubon Ratchathani,
  100,374 .... G 8

Vietnam

1979 CENSUS

Bien Hoa, 187,254 .... I 9
Can Tho, 182,856 .... I 8
Da Nang, 318,653 ...... F10
Hai Phong, 456,000
  (1,279,067▲)('89) .... D 9
Ha Noi, 1,089,000
  (1,500,000★)('89) .... D 8
Hon Gai, 114,573 .... D 8
Hue, 165,710 .... F 9

Long Xuyen, 112,485 ... I 8
Nam Dinh, 160,179 ..... D 9
Nha Trang, 172,663 ...H10
Rach Gia, 81,075 .... I 8
Saigon see Thanh Pho Ho
  Chi Minh
Thai Nguyen, 138,023 .. D 8
Thanh Pho Ho Chi Minh
  (Saigon), 3,169,000
  (3,300,000★)('89) .... I 9
Vinh, 159,753 .... E 8

1:8 000 000

Kilometers
Miles

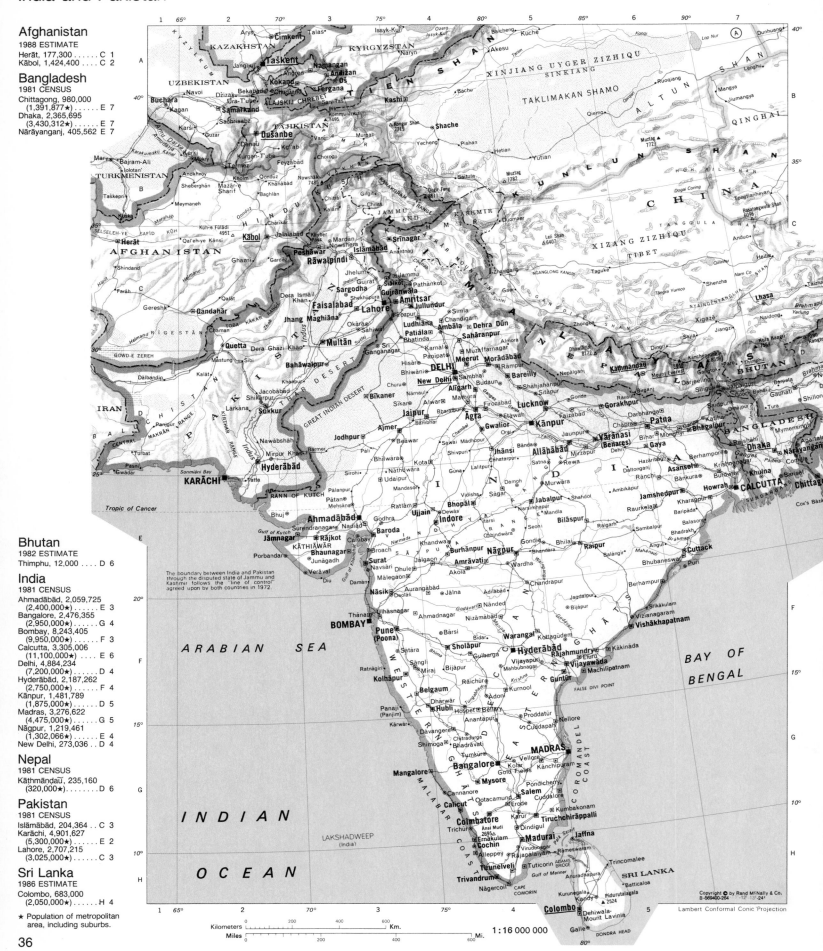

India and Pakistan

Afghanistan
1988 ESTIMATE
Herāt, 177,300 . . . . . C 1
Kābol, 1,424,400 . . . . C 2

Bangladesh
1981 CENSUS
Chittagong, 980,000
(1,391,877★) . . . . . . E 7
Dhaka, 2,365,695
(3,430,312★) . . . . . E 7
Nārāyanganj, 405,562 E 7

Bhutan
1982 ESTIMATE
Thimphu, 12,000 . . . . D 6

India
1981 CENSUS
Ahmadābād, 2,059,725
(2,400,000★) . . . . . . E 3
Bangalore, 2,476,355
(2,950,000★) . . . . . . G 4
Bombay, 8,243,405
(9,950,000★) . . . . . . F 3
Calcutta, 3,305,006
(11,100,000★) . . . . E 6
Delhi, 4,884,234
(7,200,000★) . . . . . . D 4
Hyderābād, 2,187,262
(2,750,000★) . . . . . . F 4
Kānpur, 1,481,789
(1,875,000★) . . . . . . D 5
Madras, 3,276,622
(4,475,000★) . . . . . . G 5
Nāgpur, 1,219,461
(1,302,066★) . . . . . . E 4
New Delhi, 273,036 . . D 4

Nepal
1981 CENSUS
Kāthmāndaū, 235,160
(320,000★) . . . . D 6

Pakistan
1981 CENSUS
Islāmābād, 204,364 . . C 3
Karāchi, 4,901,627
(5,300,000★) . . . . . . E 2
Lahore, 2,707,215
(3,025,000★) . . . . . . C 3

Sri Lanka
1986 ESTIMATE
Colombo, 683,000
(2,050,000★) . . . . . . H 4

★ Population of metropolitan
area, including suburbs.

36

The boundary between India and Pakistan
through the disputed state of Jammu and
Kashmir follows the "line of control"
agreed upon by both countries in 1972.

Copyright © by Rand McNally & Co.
B-569400-264

Lambert Conformal Conic Projection

Kilometers
Km.
Miles
Mi.
1:16 000 000

India

1981 CENSUS

Akola, 225,412	B 4
Amrāvati, 261,404	B 4
Aurangābād, 284,607	
(316,421★)	C 3
Bangalore, 2,476,355	
(2,950,000★)	F 4
Baroda, 734,473	
(744,881★)	A 2
Belgaum, 274,430	
(300,372★)	E 3
Bhāvnagar, 307,121	
(308,642★)	B 2
Bhilai, 290,090	
(490,214★)	B 6
Bhubaneswar,	
219,211	B 8
Bombay, 8,243,405	
(9,950,000★)	C 2
Calicut, 394,447	
(546,058★)	G 3
Cochin, 513,249	
(685,836★)	H 4
Coimbatore, 704,514	
(965,000★)	G 4
Cuttack, 269,950	
(327,412★)	B 8
Dhule, 210,759	B 3
Gulbarga, 221,325	D 4
Guntūr, 367,699	D 6
Hubli, 527,108	E 3
Hyderābād, 2,187,262	
(2,750,000★)	D 5
Indore, 829,327	
(850,000★)	A 3
Kolhāpur, 340,625	
(351,392★)	D 3
Madras, 3,276,622	
(4,475,000★)	F 6
Madurai, 820,891	
(960,000★)	H 5
Mālegaon, 245,883	B 3
Mysore, 441,754	
(479,081★)	F 4
Nāgpur, 1,219,461	
(1,302,066★)	B 5
Nāsik, 262,428	
(429,034★)	C 2
Nellore, 237,065	E 5
Pondicherry, 162,636	
(251,420★)	G 5
Pune (Poona), 1,203,351	
(1,775,000★)	C 2
Raipur, 338,245	B 6
Salem, 361,394	
(518,615★)	G 5
Sholāpur, 511,103	
(514,860★)	D 3
Surat, 776,583	
(913,806★)	B 2
Thāna, 309,897	C 2
Tiruchchirāppalli, 362,045	
(609,548★)	G 5
Trivandrum, 483,086	
(520,125★)	H 4
Ulhāsnagar, 273,668	C 2
Vijayawāda, 454,577	
(543,008★)	D 6
Vishākhapatnam, 565,321	
(603,630★)	D 7
Warangal, 335,150	C 5

Sri Lanka

1986 ESTIMATE

Colombo, 683,000	
(2,050,000★)	I 5
Dehiwala-Mount Lavinia,	
191,000	I 5
Kandy, 130,000	I 6
Kotte, 104,000	I 5

★ Population of metropolitan area, including suburbs.

37

Northern India and Pakistan

Afghanistan
1981 ESTIMATE
Baghlān, 41,000('82) . . B 3
Ghaznī, 31,196 . . . . . . D 3
Jalālābād, 58,000('82) C 4
Kābol, 1,424,400('88) C 3
Khānābād, 27,482 . . . B 3
Kholm, 28,788 . . . . . . B 2
Mazār-e Sharīf,
   130,600('88) . . . . . B 2
Meymaneh, 39,218 . . C 1
Qandahār,
   225,500('88) . . . . . E 1
Sheberghān, 19,475 . . B 1

Bangladesh
1981 CENSUS
Barisāl, 172,905 . . . . . . I14
Brāhmanbāria, 87,570 I14
Chittagong, 980,000
   (1,391,877★) I14
Comilla, 184,132 . . . . I14
Dhaka, 2,365,695
   (3,430,312★) I14
Jessore, 148,927 . . . . I13
Khulna, 648,359 . . . . . I13
Mymensingh, 190,991 H14
Nārāyanganj, 405,562 I14
Pābna, 109,065 . . . . . H13
Rājshāhi, 253,740 . . . . H13
Rangpur, 153,174 . . . . H13
Saidpur, 126,608 . . . . H13
Sirājganj, 106,774 . . . H13
Sylhet, 168,371 . . . . . H14

Bhutan
1982 ESTIMATE
Thimphu, 12,000 . . . . G13

India
1981 CENSUS
Āgra, 694,191
   (747,318★) . . . . . . G 8
Ahmadābād, 2,059,725
   (2,400,000★) . . . . . I 5
Ajmer, 375,593 . . . . . G 6
Alīgarh, 320,861 . . . . G 8
Allāhābād, 616,051
   (650,070★) . . . . . . H 9
Alwar, 145,795 . . . . . G 7
Amritsar, 594,844 . . . . E 6
Asansol, 183,375
   (1,050,000★) I12
Bareilly, 386,734
   (449,425★) . . . . . . F 8
Baroda, 734,473
   (744,881★) . . . . . . I 5
Bhāgalpur, 225,062 . . H12
Bhātpāra, 260,761 . . . I13
Bhāvnagar, 307,121
   (308,642★) . . . . . . J 5
Bhilai, 290,090
   (490,214★) . . . . . . J 9
Bhopāl, 671,018 . . . . . I 7
Bhubaneswar, 219,211 J11
Bīkaner, 253,174
   (287,712★) . . . . . . F 5
Calcutta, 3,305,006
   (11,100,000★) I13
Chandīgarh, 373,789
   (422,841★) . . . . . . E 7
Cuttack, 269,950
   (327,412★) J11
Dehra Dūn, 211,416
   (293,010★) . . . . . . E 8
Delhi, 4,884,234
   (7,200,000★) . . . . . F 7
Durgāpur, 311,798 . . . . I12
Gaya, 247,075 . . . . . . H11
Ghāziābād, 271,730
   (287,170★) . . . . . . F 7
Gorakhpur, 290,814
   (307,501★) G10
Gwalior, 539,015
   (555,862★) . . . . . . G 8
Howrah, 744,429 . . . . I13
Indore, 829,327
   (850,000★) . . . . . . I 6
Jabalpur, 614,162
   (757,303★) . . . . . . I 8
Jaipur, 977,165
   (1,025,000★) . . . . . G 6
Jammu, 206,135
   (223,361★) . . . . . . D 6
Jāmnagar, 277,615
   (317,362★) . . . . . . I 4
Jamshedpur, 438,385
   (669,580★) I12
Jhānsi, 246,172
   (284,141★) . . . . . . H 8
Jodhpur, 506,345 . . . . G 5
Jullundur, 408,186
   (441,552★) . . . . . . E 6
Kānpur, 1,481,789
   (1,875,000★) . . . . . G 9
Kota, 358,241 . . . . . . H 6
Lucknow, 895,721
   (1,060,000★) . . . . . G 9
Ludhiāna, 607,052 . . . E 6
Mathura, 147,493
   (160,995★) . . . . . . G 7

★ Population of metropolitan
   area, including suburbs.

38

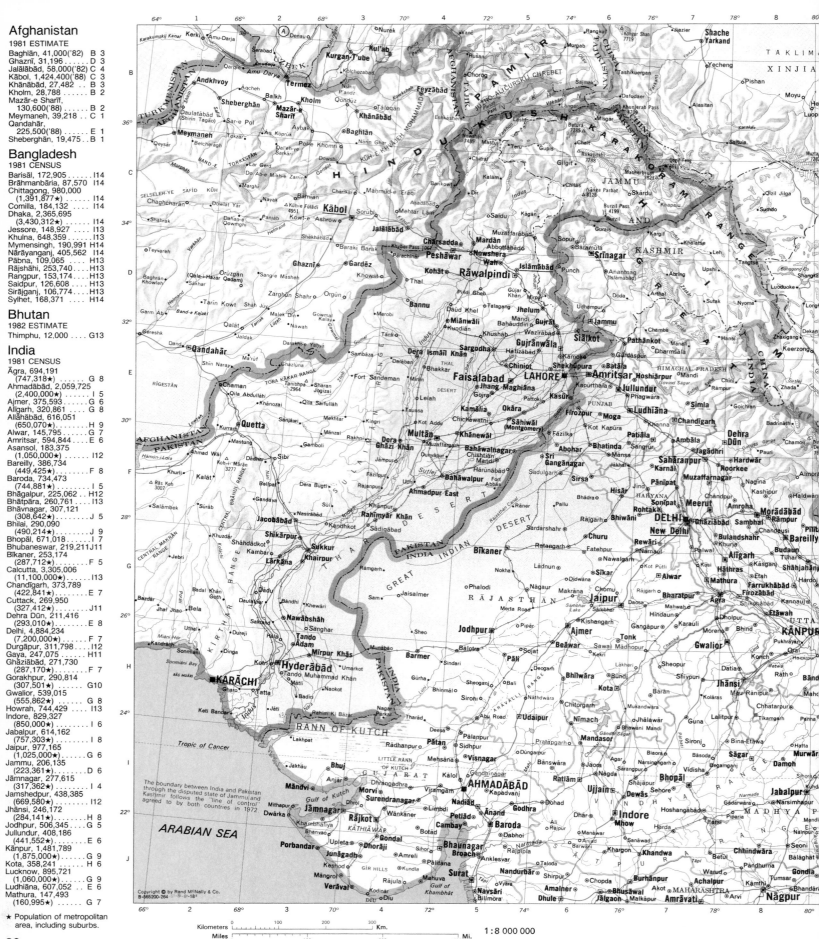

The boundary between India and Pakistan
through the disputed state of Jammu and
Kashmir follows the "line of control"
agreed to by both countries in 1972

Kilometers
Miles

1 : 8 000 000

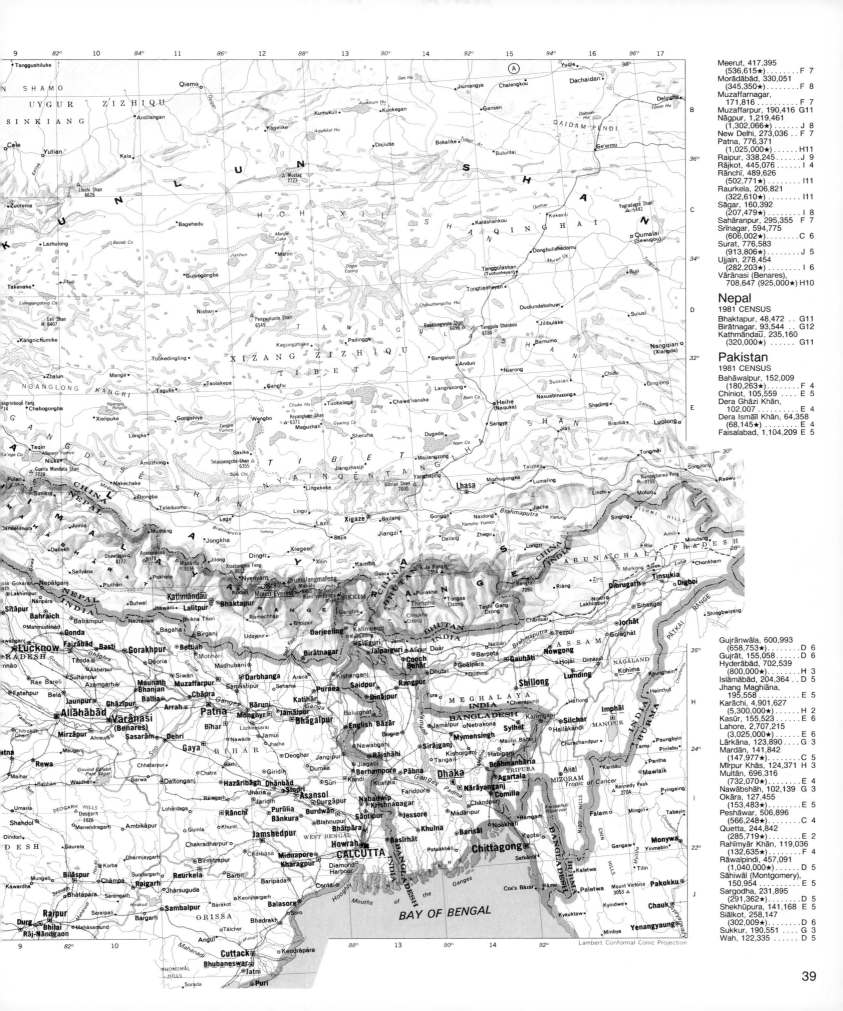

Meerut, 417,395
(536,615★) . . . . F 7
Morādābād, 330,051
(345,350★) . . . . F 8
Muzaffarnagar,
171,816 . . . . F 7
Muzaffarpur, 190,416 G11
Nāgpur, 1,219,461
(1,302,066★) . . . . . . J 8
New Delhi, 273,036 . . F 7
Patna, 776,371
(1,025,000★) H11
Raipur, 338,245 . . . . J 9
Rājkot, 445,076 . . . . . I 4
Rānchī, 489,626
(502,771★) I11
Raurkela, 206,821
(322,610★) I11
Sāgar, 160,392
(207,479★) . . . . I 8
Sahāranpur, 295,355 F 7
Srīnagar, 594,775
(606,002★) . . . . C 6
Surat, 776,583
(913,806★) . . . . J 5
Ujjain, 278,454
(282,203★) . . . . I 6
Vārānasi (Benares),
708,647 (925,000★) H10

Nepal
1981 CENSUS

Bhaktapur, 48,472 . . G11
Birātnagar, 93,544 . . G12
Kathmāndau, 235,160
(320,000★) G11

Pakistan
1981 CENSUS

Bahāwalpur, 152,009
(180,263★) . . . . F 4
Chiniot, 105,559 . . . E 5
Dera Ghāzi Khān,
102,007 . . . . E 4
Dera Ismāīl Khān, 64,358
(68,145★) . . . . E 4
Faisalabad, 1,104,209 E 5

Gujrānwāla, 600,993
(658,753★) . . . . D 6
Gujrāt, 155,058 . . . . . D 6
Hyderābād, 702,539
(800,000★) . . . . H 3
Islāmābād, 204,364 . . D 5
Jhang Maghiāna,
195,558 . . . . E 5
Karāchi, 4,901,627
(5,300,000★) . . . . . H 2
Kasūr, 155,523 . . . . . E 6
Lahore, 2,707,215
(3,025,000★) . . . . . E 6
Lārkāna, 123,890 . . . . G 3
Mardān, 141,842
(147,977★) . . . . C 5
Mīrpur Khās, 124,371 H 3
Multān, 696,316
(732,070★) . . . . E 4
Nawābshāh, 102,139 G 3
Okāra, 127,455
(153,483★) . . . . E 5
Peshāwar, 506,896
(566,248★) . . . . C 4
Quetta, 244,842
(285,719★) . . . . E 2
Rahīmyār Khān, 119,036
(132,635★) . . . . F 4
Rāwalpindi, 457,091
(1,040,000★) . . . . . D 5
Sāhiwāl (Montgomery),
150,954 . . . . E 5
Sargodha, 231,895
(291,362★) . . . . E 5
Shekhūpura, 141,168 E 5
Siālkot, 258,147
(302,009★) . . . . D 6
Sukkur, 190,551 . . . . G 3
Wah, 122,335 . . . . . . D 5

Lambert Conformal Conic Projection

39

Eastern Mediterranean Lands

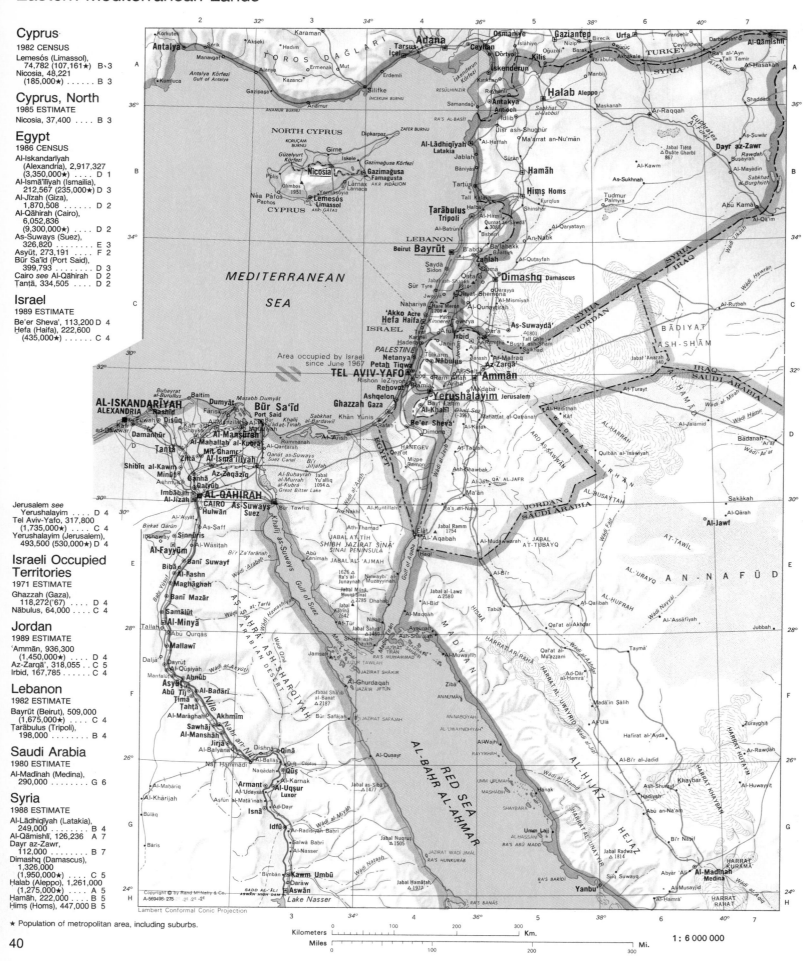

Cyprus
1982 CENSUS
Lemesós (Limassol),
74,782 (107,161★) . . B 3
Nicosia, 48,221
(185,000★) . . . . . B 3

Cyprus, North
1985 ESTIMATE
Nicosia, 37,400 . . . . B 3

Egypt
1986 CENSUS
Al-Iskandarīyah
(Alexandria), 2,917,327
(3,350,000★) . . . D 1
Al-Ismā'īlīyah (Ismailia),
212,567 (235,000★) D 3
Al-Jīzah (Giza),
1,870,508 . . . . . D 2
Al-Qāhirah (Cairo),
6,052,836
(9,300,000★) . . . D 2
As-Suways (Suez),
326,820 . . . . . . E 3
Asyūṭ, 273,191 . . . F 2
Būr Sa'īd (Port Said),
399,793 . . . . . . D 3
Cairo see Al-Qāhirah . D 2
Ṭanṭā, 334,505 . . . D 2

Israel
1989 ESTIMATE
Be'er Sheva', 113,200 D 4
Ḥefa (Haifa), 222,600
(435,000★) . . . . . C 4

Jerusalem see
Yerushalayim . . . . D 4
Tel Aviv-Yafo, 317,800
(1,735,000★) . . . . C 4
Yerushalayim (Jerusalem),
493,500 (530,000★) D 4

**Israeli Occupied
Territories**
1971 ESTIMATE
Ghazzah (Gaza),
118,272 ('67) . . . D 4
Nābulus, 64,000 . . . C 4

Jordan
1989 ESTIMATE
'Ammān, 936,300
(1,450,000★) . . . D 4
Az-Zarqā', 318,055 . C 5
Irbid, 167,785 . . . . . C 4

Lebanon
1982 ESTIMATE
Bayrūt (Beirut), 509,000
(1,675,000★) . . . . C 4
Ṭarābulus (Tripoli),
198,000 . . . . . . B 4

Saudi Arabia
1980 ESTIMATE
Al-Madīnah (Medina),
290,000 . . . . G 6

Syria
1988 ESTIMATE
Al-Lādhiqīyah (Latakia),
249,000 . . . . . . B 4
Al-Qāmishlī, 126,236 . A 7
Dayr az-Zawr,
112,000 . . . . . . B 7
Dimashq (Damascus),
1,326,000
(1,950,000★) . . . C 5
Halab (Aleppo), 1,261,000
(1,275,000★) . . . . A 5
Ḥamāh, 222,000 . . B 5
Ḥimṣ (Homs), 447,000 B 5

★ Population of metropolitan area, including suburbs.

40

Lambert Conformal Conic Projection

Kilometers

Km.

Miles

Mi.

1 : 6 000 000

Copyright © by Rand McNally & Co.
A-569498-275

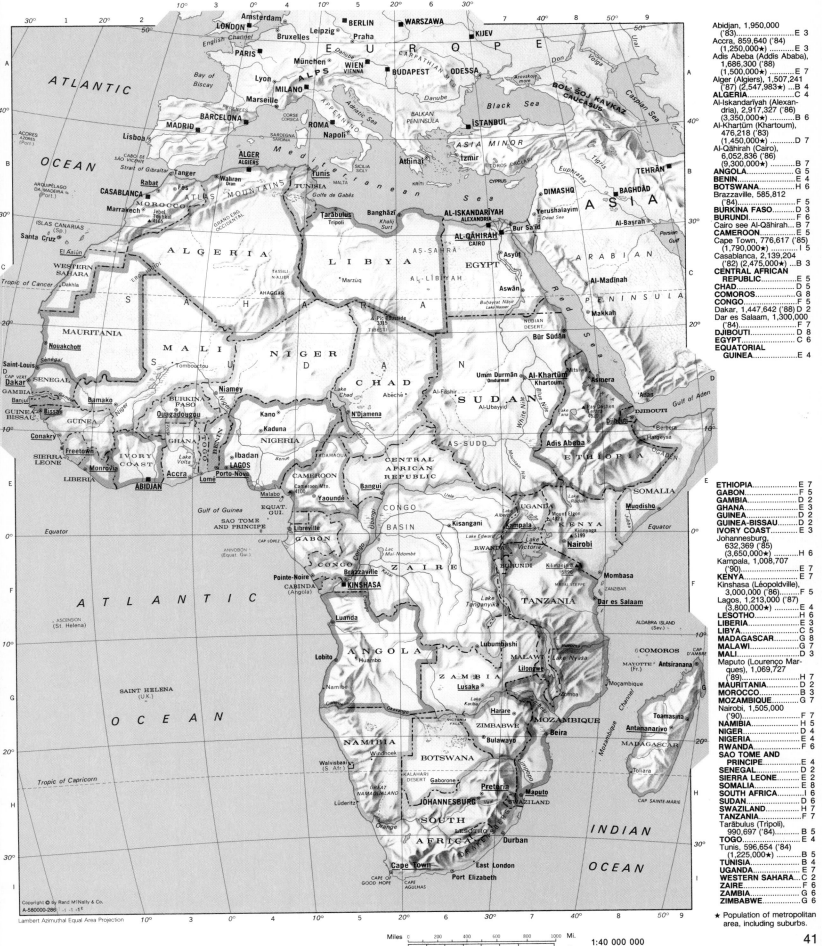

Africa

Abidjan, 1,950,000
  ('83)..................E 3
Accra, 859,640 ('84)
  (1,250,000★)........E 3
Adis Abeba (Addis Ababa),
  1,686,300 ('88)
  (1,500,000★)........E 7
Alger (Algiers), 1,507,241
  ('87) (2,547,983★)...B 4
ALGERIA................C 4
Al-Iskandarīyah (Alexan-
  dria), 2,917,327 ('86)
  (3,350,000★)........B 6
Al-Khartūm (Khartoum),
  476,218 ('83)
  (1,450,000★)........D 7
Al-Qāhirah (Cairo),
  6,052,836 ('86)
  (9,300,000★)........B 7
ANGOLA.................G 5
BENIN...................E 4
BOTSWANA...............H 6
Brazzaville, 585,812
  ('84)..................F 5
BURKINA FASO...........D 3
BURUNDI................F 6
Cairo see Al-Qāhirah...B 7
CAMEROON...............E 5
Cape Town, 776,617 ('85)
  (1,790,000★) ...I 5
Casablanca, 2,139,204
  ('82) (2,475,000★)..B 3
CENTRAL AFRICAN
  REPUBLIC.............E 5
CHAD...................D 5
COMOROS................G 8
CONGO..................F 5
Dakar, 1,447,642 ('88)D 2
Dar es Salaam, 1,300,000
  ('84)..................F 7
DJIBOUTI...............D 8
EGYPT..................C 6
EQUATORIAL
  GUINEA...............E 4

ETHIOPIA...............E 7
GABON..................F 5
GAMBIA.................D 2
GHANA..................E 3
GUINEA.................D 2
GUINEA-BISSAU..........D 2
IVORY COAST............E 3
Johannesburg,
  632,369 ('85)
  (3,650,000★) ....H 6
Kampala, 1,008,707
  ('90)..................E 7
KENYA..................E 7
Kinshasa (Léopoldville),
  3,000,000 ('86).......F 5
Lagos, 1,213,000 ('87)
  (3,800,000★)........E 4
LESOTHO................H 6
LIBERIA................E 3
LIBYA..................C 5
MADAGASCAR.............G 8
MALAWI.................G 7
MALI...................D 3
Maputo (Lourenço Mar-
  ques), 1,069,727
  ('89)..................H 7
MAURITANIA.............D 2
MOROCCO................B 3
MOZAMBIQUE.............G 7
Nairobi, 1,505,000
  ('90)..................F 7
NAMIBIA................H 5
NIGER..................D 4
NIGERIA................E 4
RWANDA.................F 6
SAO TOME AND
  PRINCIPE.............E 4
SENEGAL................D 2
SIERRA LEONE..........E 2
SOMALIA................E 8
SOUTH AFRICA..........I 6
SUDAN..................D 6
SWAZILAND.............H 7
TANZANIA..............F 7
Tarābulus (Tripoli),
  990,697 ('84)........B 5
TOGO...................E 4
Tunis, 596,654 ('84)
  (1,225,000★) ....B 5
TUNISIA................B 4
UGANDA.................E 7
WESTERN SAHARA........C 2
ZAIRE..................F 6
ZAMBIA.................G 6
ZIMBABWE...............G 6

★ Population of metropolitan
  area, including suburbs.

Copyright © by Rand McNally & Co.
A-580000-286 -1 -1 -1ᴱ
Lambert Azimuthal Equal Area Projection

Miles 0   200   400   600   800   1000 Mi.
Kilometers 0   400   800   1200 1600 Km.
1:40 000 000

41

Northern Africa

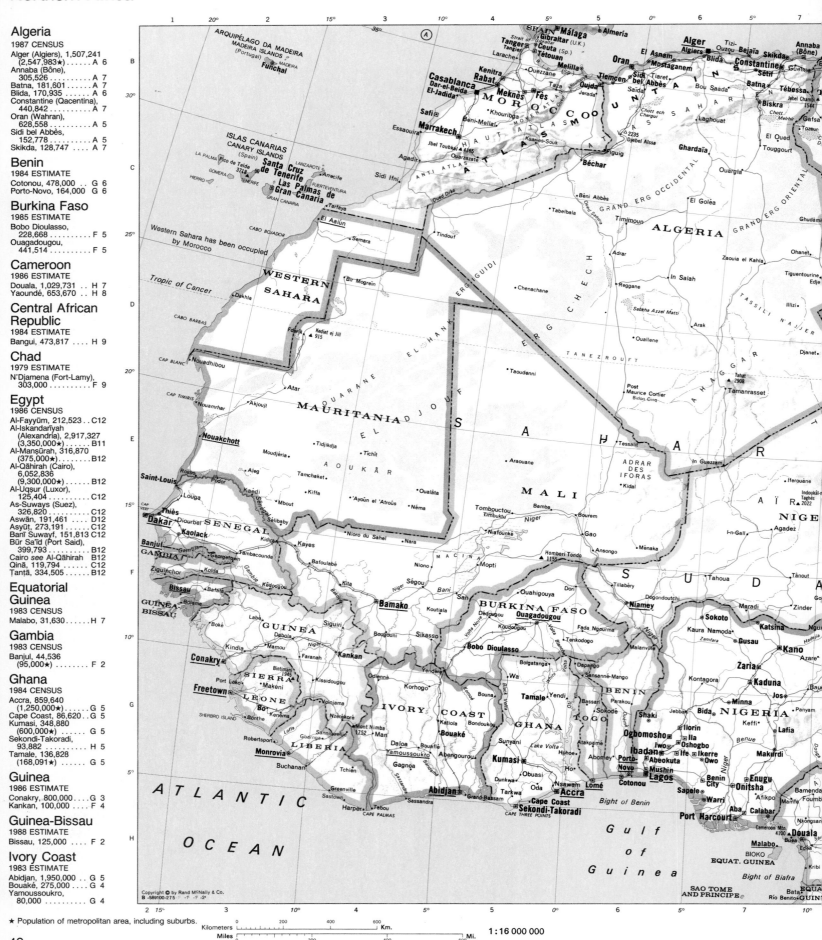

Algeria
1987 CENSUS
Alger (Algiers), 1,507,241
(2,547,983★) ...... A 6
Annaba (Bône),
305,526 .... A 7
Batna, 181,601 ...... A 7
Blida, 170,935 ...... A 6
Constantine (Qacentina),
440,842 .... A 7
Oran (Wahran),
628,558 .... A 5
Sidi bel Abbès,
152,778 .... A 5
Skikda, 128,747 ..... A 7

Benin
1984 ESTIMATE
Cotonou, 478,000 .. G 6
Porto-Novo, 164,000 G 6

Burkina Faso
1985 ESTIMATE
Bobo Dioulasso,
228,668 .... F 5
Ouagadougou,
441,514 .... F 5

Cameroon
1986 ESTIMATE
Douala, 1,029,731 .. H 7
Yaoundé, 653,670 .. H 8

Central African Republic
1984 ESTIMATE
Bangui, 473,817 .... H 9

Chad
1979 ESTIMATE
N'Djamena (Fort-Lamy),
303,000 .... F 9

Egypt
1986 CENSUS
Al-Fayyūm, 212,523 ..C12
Al-Iskandarīyah
(Alexandria), 2,917,327
(3,350,000★) B11
Al-Manşūrah, 316,870
(375,000★) B12
Al-Qāhirah (Cairo),
6,052,836
(9,300,000★) B12
Al-Uqşur (Luxor),
125,404 ....C12
As-Suways (Suez),
326,820 ....C12
Aswān, 191,461 ....D12
Asyūţ, 273,191 .....C12
Banī Suwayf, 151,813 C12
Būr Sa'īd (Port Said),
399,793 ....B12
Cairo see Al-Qāhirah B12
Qinā, 119,794 ......C12
Ţanţā, 334,505 .....B12

Equatorial Guinea
1983 CENSUS
Malabo, 31,630 ......H 7

Gambia
1983 CENSUS
Banjul, 44,536
(95,000★) .... F 2

Ghana
1984 CENSUS
Accra, 859,640
(1,250,000★) ..... G 5
Cape Coast, 86,620 . G 5
Kumasi, 348,880
(600,000★) ...... G 5
Sekondi-Takoradi,
93,882 .... H 5
Tamale, 136,828
(168,091★) ...... G 5

Guinea
1986 ESTIMATE
Conakry, 800,000 ...G 3
Kankan, 100,000 ....F 4

Guinea-Bissau
1988 ESTIMATE
Bissau, 125,000 .... F 2

Ivory Coast
1983 ESTIMATE
Abidjan, 1,950,000 .. G 5
Bouaké, 275,000 ... G 4
Yamoussoukro,
80,000 .... G 4

★ Population of metropolitan area, including suburbs.

42

1:16 000 000

Kilometers
Miles

Copyright © by Rand McNally & Co.
B -589100-275

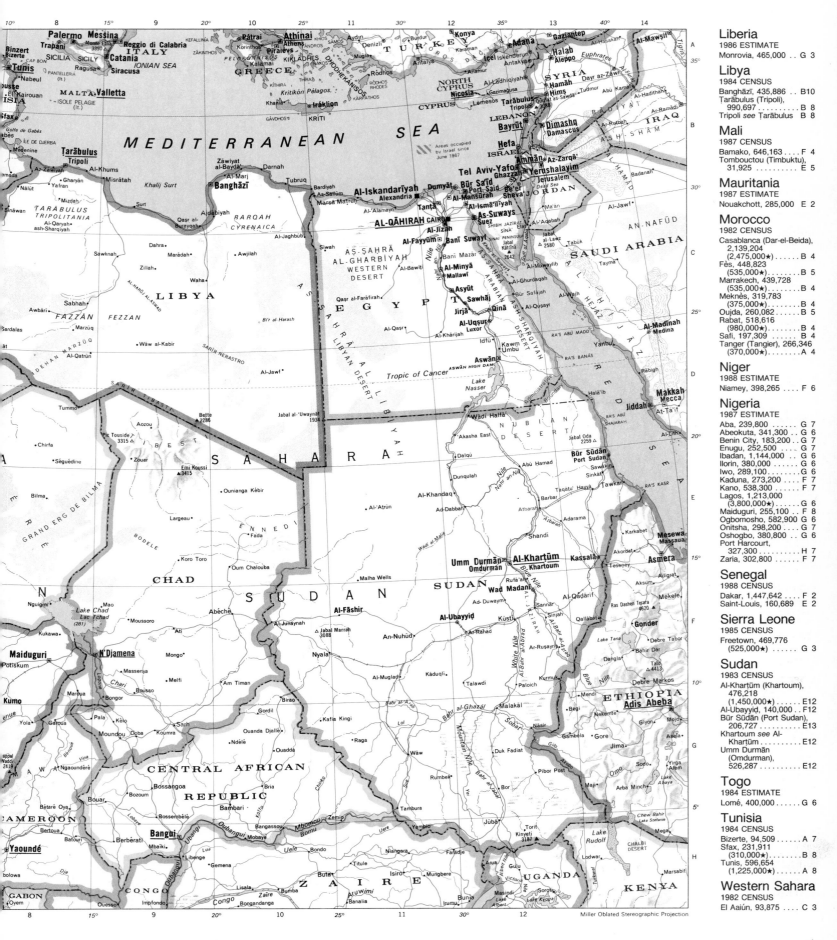

Liberia
1986 ESTIMATE
Monrovia, 465,000 . . G 3

Libya
1984 CENSUS
Banghāzī, 435,886 . . B 10
Ṭarābulus (Tripoli),
  990,697 . . . . B 8
Tripoli see Ṭarābulus   B 8

Mali
1987 CENSUS
Bamako, 646,163 . . . . F 4
Tombouctou (Timbuktu),
  31,925 . . . . E 5

Mauritania
1987 ESTIMATE
Nouakchott, 285,000 E 2

Morocco
1982 CENSUS
Casablanca (Dar-el-Beida),
  2,139,204
  (2,475,000★) . . . . . B 4
Fès, 448,823
  (535,000★) . . . . . . B 5
Marrakech, 439,728
  (535,000★) . . . . . . B 4
Meknès, 319,783
  (375,000★) . . . . . . B 4
Oujda, 260,082 . . . . . . B 5
Rabat, 518,616
  (980,000★) . . . . . . B 4
Safi, 197,309 . . . . . . B 4
Tanger (Tangier), 266,346
  (370,000★) . . . . . . A 4

Niger
1988 ESTIMATE
Niamey, 398,265 . . . . F 6

Nigeria
1987 ESTIMATE
Aba, 239,800 . . . . . G 7
Abeokuta, 341,300 . . G 7
Benin City, 183,200 . . G 7
Enugu, 252,500 . . . . G 7
Ibadan, 1,144,000 . . . G 6
Ilorin, 380,000 . . . . . . G 6
Iwo, 289,100 . . . . G 6
Kaduna, 273,200 . . . . F 7
Kano, 538,300 . . . . . F 7
Lagos, 1,213,000
  (3,800,000★) . . . . . G 6
Maiduguri, 255,100 . . F 8
Ogbomosho, 582,900 G 6
Onitsha, 298,200 . . . G 7
Oshogbo, 380,800 . . G 6
Port Harcourt,
  327,300 . . . . H 7
Zaria, 302,800 . . . . . F 7

Senegal
1988 CENSUS
Dakar, 1,447,642 . . . . F 2
Saint-Louis, 160,689 . E 2

Sierra Leone
1985 CENSUS
Freetown, 469,776
  (525,000★) . . . . . . G 3

Sudan
1983 CENSUS
Al-Kharṭūm (Khartoum),
  476,218
  (1,450,000★) . . . . . E 12
Al-Ubayyid, 140,000 . F 12
Būr Sūdān (Port Sudan),
  206,727 . . . . E 13
Khartoum see Al-
  Kharṭūm . . . . E 12
Umm Durmān
  (Omdurman),
  526,287 . . . . E 12

Togo
1984 ESTIMATE
Lomé, 400,000 . . . . . . G 6

Tunisia
1984 CENSUS
Bizerte, 94,509 . . . . . A 7
Sfax, 231,911
  (310,000★) . . . . B 8
Tunis, 596,654
  (1,225,000★) . . . . . A 8

Western Sahara
1982 CENSUS
El Aaiún, 93,875 . . . . C 3

Southern Africa

Angola
1983 ESTIMATE
Benguela, 155,000 . . D 2
Huambo, 203,000 . . . D 3
Lobito, 150,000 . . . . D 2
Luanda,
1,459,900('89) . . . . C 2
Namibe, 100,000('81) E 2

Botswana
1987 ESTIMATE
Gaborone, 107,677 . . F 5

Burundi
1986 ESTIMATE
Bujumbura, 273,000 . B 5

Comoros
1990 ESTIMATE
Moroni, 23,432 . . . . D 8

Congo
1984 CENSUS
Brazzaville, 585,812 . B 3
Pointe-Noire, 294,203 B 2

Gabon
1985 ESTIMATE
Libreville, 235,700 . . A 1
Port-Gentil, 124,400 . . B 1

Kenya
1990 ESTIMATE
Mombasa, 537,000 . . B 7
Nairobi, 1,505,000 . . B 7
Nakuru, 101,700('84) . B 7

Lesotho
1986 CENSUS
Maseru, 109,382 . . . G 5

Madagascar
1984 ESTIMATE
Antananarivo,
663,000('85) . . . . E 9
Antsiranana, 100,000 D 9
Fianarantsoa, 130,000 F 9
Mahajanga, 85,000 . . E 9
Toamasina, 100,000 . E 9

Malawi
1987 CENSUS
Blantyre, 331,588 . . E 7
Lilongwe, 233,973 . . D 6
Zomba, 42,878 . . . . E 7

Mauritius
1987 ESTIMATE
Port Louis, 139,730
(420,000★) F11

Mayotte
1985 ESTIMATE
Dzaoudzi, 5,865
(6,979★) . . . . D 9

Mozambique
1989 ESTIMATE
Beira, 291,604 . . . . E 6
Maputo (Lourenço
Marques),
1,069,727 . . . . . . G 6
Xai-Xai, 51,620('86) . . G 6

Namibia
1988 ESTIMATE
Windhoek, 114,500 . . F 3

Reunion
1982 CENSUS
Saint-Denis, 84,400
(109,072▲) F11

Rwanda
1983 ESTIMATE
Kigali, 181,600 . . . . B 6

Sao Tome and
Principe
1970 CENSUS
São Tomé, 17,380 . . A 1

Seychelles
1984 ESTIMATE
Victoria, 23,000 . . . . B11

★ Population of metropolitan area, including suburbs.
▲ Population of entire district, including rural area.

44

Miller Oblated Stereographic Projection

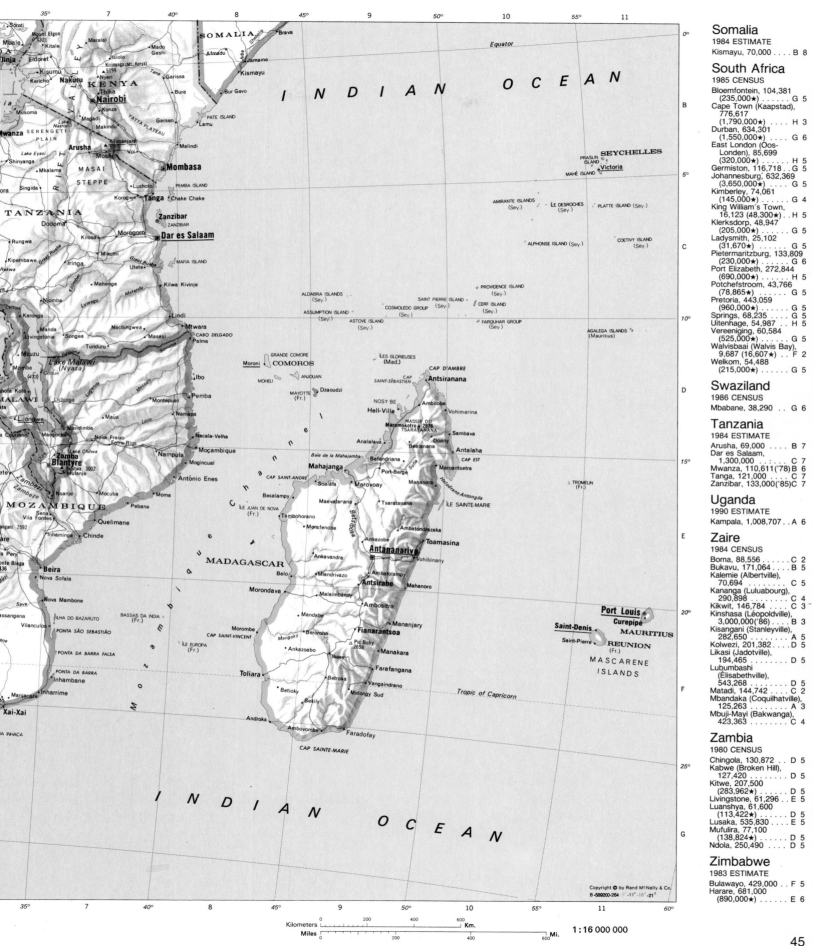

INDIAN OCEAN

Equator

0°

SOMALIA

KENYA

Nairobi

Mombasa

TANZANIA

Dar es Salaam

Zanzibar

SEYCHELLES

Victoria

MAHÉ ISLAND

AMIRANTE ISLANDS (Sey.)

ÎLE DESROCHES (Sey.)

PLATTE ISLAND (Sey.)

5°

ALPHONSE ISLAND (Sey.)

COETIVY ISLAND (Sey.)

PROVIDENCE ISLAND (Sey.)

ALDABRA ISLANDS (Sey.)

SAINT PIERRE ISLAND (Sey.)

CERF ISLAND (Sey.)

ASSUMPTION ISLAND (Sey.)

COSMOLEDO GROUP (Sey.)

ASTOVE ISLAND (Sey.)

FARQUHAR GROUP (Sey.)

10°

MALAWI

Lake Malawi (Nyasa)

Blantyre

MOZAMBIQUE

Beira

GRANDE COMORE

Moroni COMOROS

MOHELI

ANJOUAN

MAYOTTE (Fr.)

Dzaoudzi

ÎLES GLORIEUSES (Mad.)

NOSY BE

Hell-Ville

CAP D'AMBRE

Antsiranana

CAP SAINT-SÉBASTIEN

AGALEGA ISLANDS (Mauritius)

MASSIF DU TSARATANANA

Maromokotro 2876

Mahajanga

Baie de la Mahajamba

CAP SAINT-ANDRE

CAP EST

15°

TROMELIN (Fr.)

ÎLE JUAN DE NOVA (Fr.)

MADAGASCAR

Antananarivo

Antsirabe

ÎLE SAINTE-MARIE

Toamasina

BASSAS DA INDIA (Fr.)

ÎLE EUROPA (Fr.)

Fianarantsoa

Pic Boby 2658

Port Louis
Curepipe
MAURITIUS

Saint-Denis

Saint-Pierre REUNION (Fr.)

MASCARENE ISLANDS

20°

Toliara

Tropic of Capricorn

F

CAP SAINTE-MARIE

25°

INDIAN OCEAN

Kilometers

Km.

Miles

Mi.

1:16 000 000

Copyright © by Rand McNally & Co.

B-589200-264

Somalia
1984 ESTIMATE

Kismayu, 70,000 . . . . B 8

South Africa
1985 CENSUS

Bloemfontein, 104,381 (235,000★) . . . . . . G 5
Cape Town (Kaapstad), 776,617 (1,790,000★) . . . . H 3
Durban, 634,301 (1,550,000★) . . . . G 6
East London (Oos- Londen), 85,699 (320,000★) . . . . . . H 5
Germiston, 116,718 . . G 5
Johannesburg, 632,369 (3,650,000★) . . . . . G 5
Kimberley, 74,061 (145,000★) . . . . . . G 4
King William's Town, 16,123 (48,300★) . . H 5
Klerksdorp, 48,947 (205,000★) . . . . . . G 5
Ladysmith, 25,102 (31,670★) . . . . . . G 5
Pietermaritzburg, 133,809 (230,000★) . . . . . . G 6
Port Elizabeth, 272,844 (690,000★) . . . . . . H 5
Potchefstroom, 43,766 (78,865★) . . . . . . G 5
Pretoria, 443,059 (960,000★) . . . . . . G 5
Springs, 68,235 . . . . . G 5
Uitenhage, 54,987 . . H 5
Vereeniging, 60,584 (525,000★) . . . . . . G 5
Walvisbaai (Walvis Bay), 9,687 (16,607★) . . F 2
Welkom, 54,488 (215,000★) . . . . . . G 5

Swaziland
1986 CENSUS

Mbabane, 38,290 . . G 6

Tanzania
1984 ESTIMATE

Arusha, 69,000 . . . . B 7
Dar es Salaam, 1,300,000 . . . . . . C 7
Mwanza, 110,611('78) B 6
Tanga, 121,000 . . . . C 7
Zanzibar, 133,000('85)C 7

Uganda
1990 ESTIMATE

Kampala, 1,008,707 . . A 6

Zaire
1984 CENSUS

Boma, 88,556 . . . . . . C 2
Bukavu, 171,064 . . . B 5
Kalemie (Albertville), 70,694 . . . . C 5
Kananga (Luluabourg), 290,898 . . . . . . C 4
Kikwit, 146,784 . . . . . C 3
Kinshasa (Léopoldville), 3,000,000('86) . . . B 3
Kisangani (Stanleyville), 282,650 . . . . . . A 5
Kolwezi, 201,382 . . . . D 5
Likasi (Jadotville), 194,465 . . . . D 5
Lubumbashi (Elisabethville), 543,268 . . . . . . D 5
Matadi, 144,742 . . . . C 2
Mbandaka (Coquilhatville), 125,263 . . . . . . A 3
Mbuji-Mayi (Bakwanga), 423,363 . . . . C 4

Zambia
1980 CENSUS

Chingola, 130,872 . . D 5
Kabwe (Broken Hill), 127,420 . . . . . . D 5
Kitwe, 207,500 (283,962★) . . . . . D 5
Livingstone, 61,296 . . E 5
Luanshya, 61,600 (113,422★) . . . . . . D 5
Lusaka, 535,830 . . . E 5
Mufulira, 77,100 (138,824★) . . . . . . D 5
Ndola, 250,490 . . . . D 5

Zimbabwe
1983 ESTIMATE

Bulawayo, 429,000 . . F 5
Harare, 681,000 (890,000★) . . . . . E 6

Eastern Africa and Middle East

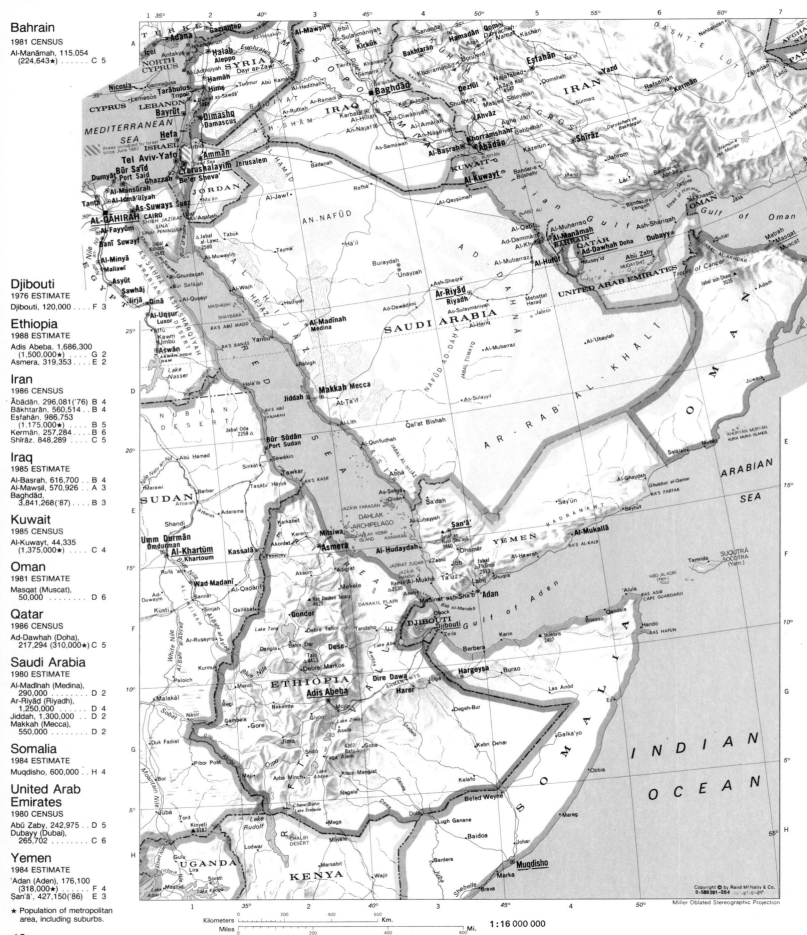

Bahrain
1981 CENSUS

Al-Manāmah, 115,054
(224,643★) ...... C 5

Djibouti
1976 ESTIMATE

Djibouti, 120,000 .... F 3

Ethiopia
1988 ESTIMATE

Adis Abeba, 1,686,300
(1,500,000★) ... G 2
Asmera, 319,353 .... E 2

Iran
1986 CENSUS

Ābādān, 296,081('76) B 4
Bākhtarān, 560,514 .. B 4
Esfahān, 986,753
(1,175,000★) ... B 5
Kermān, 257,284 ... B 6
Shīrāz, 848,289 ... C 5

Iraq
1985 ESTIMATE

Al-Baṣrah, 616,700 .. B 4
Al-Mawsil, 570,926 .. A 3
Baghdād,
3,841,268('87) .... B 3

Kuwait
1985 CENSUS

Al-Kuwayt, 44,335
(1,375,000★) .... C 4

Oman
1981 ESTIMATE

Masqat (Muscat),
50,000 .... D 6

Qatar
1986 CENSUS

Ad-Dawhah (Doha),
217,294 (310,000★) C 5

Saudi Arabia
1980 ESTIMATE

Al-Madīnah (Medina),
290,000 ...... D 2
Ar-Riyāḍ (Riyadh),
1,250,000 ...... D 4
Jiddah, 1,300,000 .. D 2
Makkah (Mecca),
550,000 .... D 2

Somalia
1984 ESTIMATE

Muqdisho, 600,000 .. H 4

United Arab Emirates
1980 CENSUS

Abū Zaby, 242,975 .. D 5
Dubayy (Dubai),
265,702 ...... C 6

Yemen
1984 ESTIMATE

'Adan (Aden), 176,100
(318,000★) ...... F 4
San'ā', 427,150('86) E 3

★ Population of metropolitan
area, including suburbs.

46

Kilometers
Miles
1:16 000 000

Miller Oblated Stereographic Projection

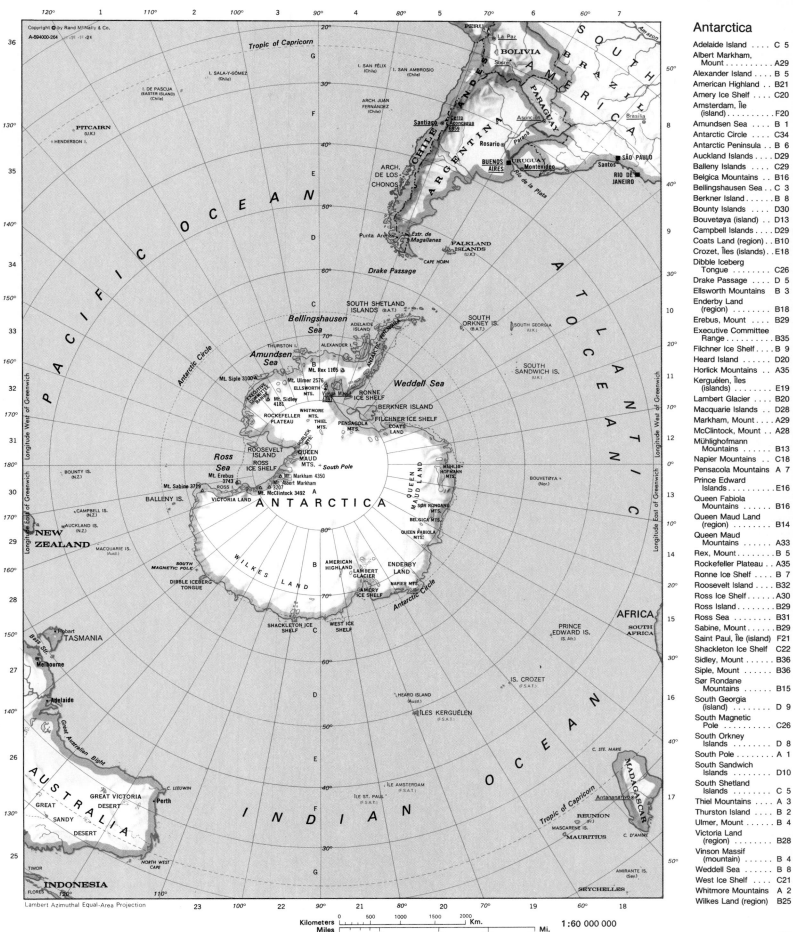

Antarctica

Antarctica

Adelaide Island . . . . C 5
Albert Markham,
    Mount A29
Alexander Island . . . . B 5
American Highland . . B21
Amery Ice Shelf C20
Amsterdam, Île
    (island) F20
Amundsen Sea . . . B 1
Antarctic Circle C34
Antarctic Peninsula . . B 6
Auckland Islands D29
Balleny Islands C29
Belgica Mountains . . B16
Bellingshausen Sea . . C 3
Berkner Island . . . . B 8
Bounty Islands D30
Bouvetøya (island) . . D13
Campbell Islands . . . D29
Coats Land (region) . . B10
Crozet, Îles (islands) . . E18
Dibble Iceberg
    Tongue C26
Drake Passage . . . . D 5
Ellsworth Mountains   B 3
Enderby Land
    (region) B18
Erebus, Mount B29
Executive Committee
    Range B35
Filchner Ice Shelf . . . . B 9
Heard Island D20
Horlick Mountains . . A35
Kerguélen, Îles
    (islands) E19
Lambert Glacier B20
Macquarie Islands . . D28
Markham, Mount A29
McClintock, Mount . . A28
Mühlighofmann
    Mountains B13
Napier Mountains . . . C18
Pensacola Mountains A 7
Prince Edward
    Islands E16
Queen Fabiola
    Mountains B16
Queen Maud Land
    (region) B14
Queen Maud
    Mountains A33
Rex, Mount . . . . . . B 5
Rockefeller Plateau . . A35
Ronne Ice Shelf . . . . B 7
Roosevelt Island B32
Ross Ice Shelf A30
Ross Island B29
Ross Sea B31
Sabine, Mount B29
Saint Paul, Île (island) F21
Shackleton Ice Shelf   C22
Sidley, Mount B36
Siple, Mount B36
Sør Rondane
    Mountains B15
South Georgia
    (island) . . . . D 9
South Magnetic
    Pole C26
South Orkney
    Islands . . . . D 8
South Pole . . . . A 1
South Sandwich
    Islands D10
South Shetland
    Islands . . . . C 5
Thiel Mountains . . . A 3
Thurston Island . . . . B 2
Ulmer, Mount . . . . . . B 4
Victoria Land
    (region) B28
Vinson Massif
    (mountain) . . . . . B 4
Weddell Sea . . . . . . B 8
West Ice Shelf C21
Whitmore Mountains   A 2
Wilkes Land (region) B25

Pacific Ocean

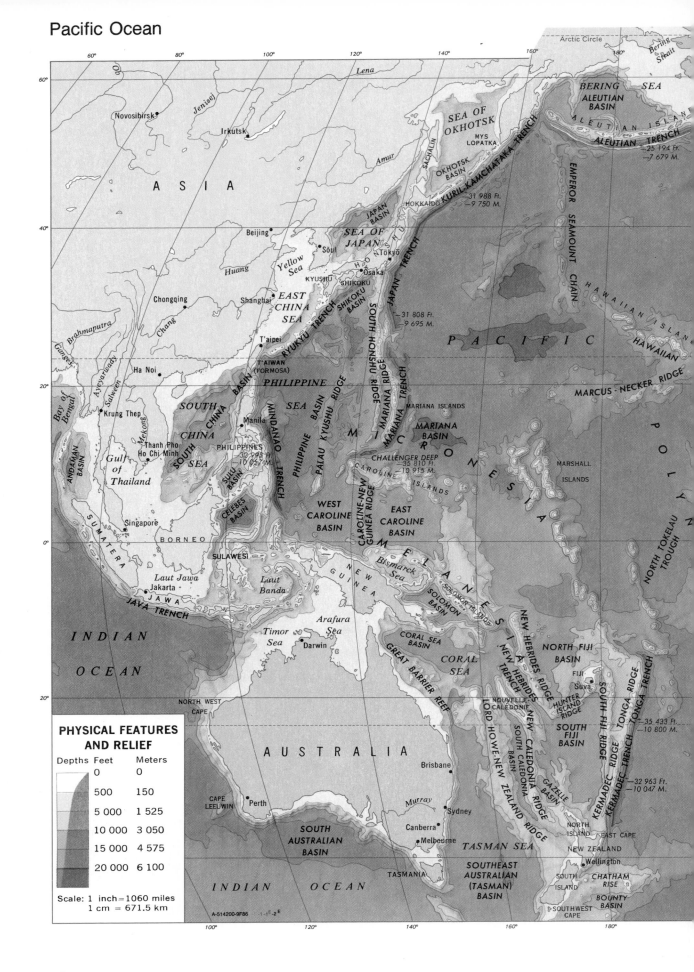

PHYSICAL FEATURES AND RELIEF

Depths Feet	Meters
0	0
500	150
5 000	1 525
10 000	3 050
15 000	4 575
20 000	6 100

Scale: 1 inch = 1060 miles
1 cm = 671.5 km

A-514200-9F86   -1-1ᴱ-2ᴱ

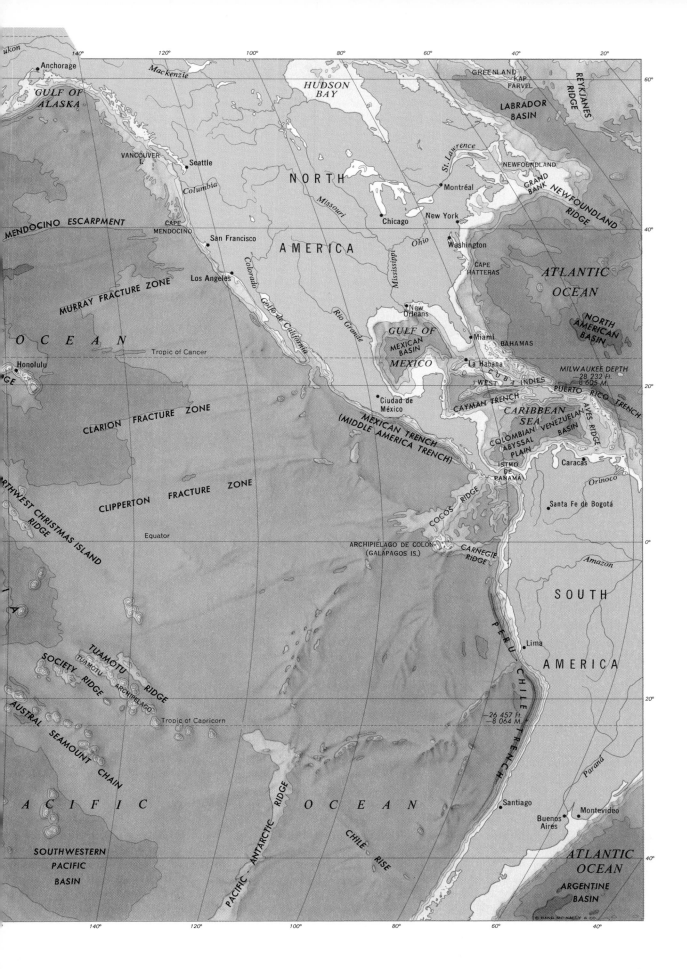

GULF OF ALASKA
Anchorage
Mackenzie
Yukon

GREENLAND
KAP FARVEL
REYKJANES RIDGE

HUDSON BAY

LABRADOR BASIN

NORTH

VANCOUVER I.
Seattle
Columbia
CAPE MENDOCINO
San Francisco

St. Lawrence
NEWFOUNDLAND
Montréal
GRAND BANK
NEWFOUNDLAND RIDGE

MENDOCINO ESCARPMENT

Missouri
Chicago
New York

AMERICA

Los Angeles
Ohio
Washington
Mississippi
CAPE HATTERAS

ATLANTIC OCEAN

MURRAY FRACTURE ZONE
Colorado
Rio Grande
Golfo de California

New Orleans

NORTH AMERICAN BASIN

O C E A N

Tropic of Cancer

GULF OF
MEXICAN BASIN
MEXICO
Miami
BAHAMAS

Honolulu

La Habana
MILWAUKEE DEPTH
−28,232 Ft.
−8,605 M.

CLARION FRACTURE ZONE
Ciudad de México

CUBA
WEST INDIES
PUERTO RICO TRENCH

CAYMAN TRENCH
CARIBBEAN SEA
AVES RIDGE

CLIPPERTON FRACTURE ZONE

MEXICAN TRENCH
(MIDDLE AMERICA TRENCH)

COLOMBIAN ABYSSAL PLAIN
VENEZUELAN BASIN
Caracas

NORTHWEST CHRISTMAS ISLAND RIDGE

COCOS RIDGE
ISTMO DE PANAMÁ
Orinoco

Santa Fe de Bogotá

Equator
ARCHIPIÉLAGO DE COLON
(GALÁPAGOS IS.)
CARNEGIE RIDGE

Amazon

SOUTH

TUAMOTU RIDGE
SOCIETY RIDGE
TUAMOTU
TUAMOTU ARCHIPELAGO

AMERICA

Lima

AUSTRAL SEAMOUNT CHAIN

Tropic of Capricorn

PERU-CHILE TRENCH

−26,457 Ft.
−8,064 M.

Paraná

P A C I F I C
O C E A N

Santiago
Montevideo

PACIFIC-ANTARCTIC RIDGE

CHILE RISE

Buenos Aires

ATLANTIC OCEAN

SOUTHWESTERN PACIFIC BASIN

ARGENTINE BASIN

© RAND McNALLY & CO.

49

Australia

Australia

1989 ESTIMATE
Adelaide, 12,340
  (1,036,747★) . . . . . . F 7
Albany, 14,958 . . . . . . G 3
Albury, 40,730
  (66,530★) . . . . G 9
Alice Springs,
  23,600 . . . . D 6
Ararat, 8,015('86) . . G 8
Armidale, 21,600 . . . . F10
Augusta, 933('86) . . . F 3
Ballarat, 36,680
  (80,090★) . . . . G 8
Barcaldine,
  1,427('86) . . . . D 9
Bendigo, 32,050
  (67,920★) . . . . G 8
Blackall, 1,497('86) . . D 9
Bombala, 1,458('86) . . G 9
Bordertown,
  2,318('86) . . . . G 8
Bourke, 3,018('86) . . F 9
Bowen, 7,705('86) . . C 9
Brisbane, 744,828
  (1,273,511★) E10
Broken Hill, 22,550 . . F 8
Broome, 5,778('86) . . C 4
Bunbury, 26,398 . . . . F 3
Bundaberg, 33,024
  (45,161★) D10
Burketown,
  232('86) . . . . C 7
Burnie, 20,665('86) . . H 9
Busselton,
  7,784('86) . . . . F 3
Cairns, 42,839
  (80,875★) . . . . C 9
Camooweal,
  315('86) . . . . C 7
Canberra, 247,194
  (271,362★)('86) . . . G 9
Carnarvon,
  6,847('86) . . . . D 2
Ceduna, 2,877('86) . . F 6
Cessnock, 43,870 . . . . F10
Charleville,
  3,588('86) . . . . E 9
Charters Towers,
  7,208('86) . . . . D 9
Cloncurry,
  2,297('86) . . . . D 8
Coffs Harbour,
  47,890 . . . . F10
Cooktown, 964('86) . . C 9
Coolgardie, 989('86) . . F 4
Cooma, 7,406('86) . . G 9
Croydon, 229('86) . . C 8
Cunnamulla,
  1,697('86) . . . . E 9
Dampier, 2,201('86) . . D 3
Darwin, 63,900
  (72,937★) . . . . B 6
Derby, 3,258('86) . . . . C 4
Devonport, 25,370 . . H 9
Dongara, 1,496('86) . . E 2
Dubbo, 32,230 . . . . . . F 9
Elizabeth, 29,998 . . . . F 7
Emerald, 5,982('86) . . D 9
Esperance,
  6,440('86) . . . . F 4
Geelong, 13,190
  (148,980★) . . . . . . G 8
Geraldton, 20,968 . . . . E 2
Gladstone,
  22,033('86) D10
Glen Innes,
  5,971('86) E10
Goondiwindi,
  4,103('86) E10
Goulburn, 21,580 . . . . F 9
Grafton, 15,890 . . . . . . E10
Griffith, 13,630('86) . . F 9
Gympie, 10,772('86) . . E10
Halls Creek,
  1,182('86) . . . . C 5
Hay, 2,961('86) . . . . . . F 8
Hobart, 47,280
  (181,210★) . . . . H 9
Home Hill,
  3,286('86) . . . . C 9
Horsham, 12,850 . . . . G 8
Hughenden,
  1,791('86) . . . . D 8
Ingham, 5,202('86) . . C 9
Inverell, 9,693('86) . . E10
Ipswich, 75,283 . . . . . . E10
Kalgoorlie, 26,813 . . . . F 4
Kingaroy, 6,362('86) . . E10
Launceston, 32,150
  (92,350★) . . . . H 9
Leonora, 1,004('86) . . E 4
Lismore, 39,450 . . . . E10
Longreach,
  3,159('86) . . . . D 8
Mackay, 22,583
  (50,885★) . . . . D 9
Maitland, 47,280 . . . . F10
Marble Bar, 332('86) . . D 3
Mareeba, 6,614('86) . . C 9
Marree, 300('76) . . . . E 7
Meekatharra,
  1,018('86) . . . . E 3

★ Population of metropolitan
  area, including suburbs.

50

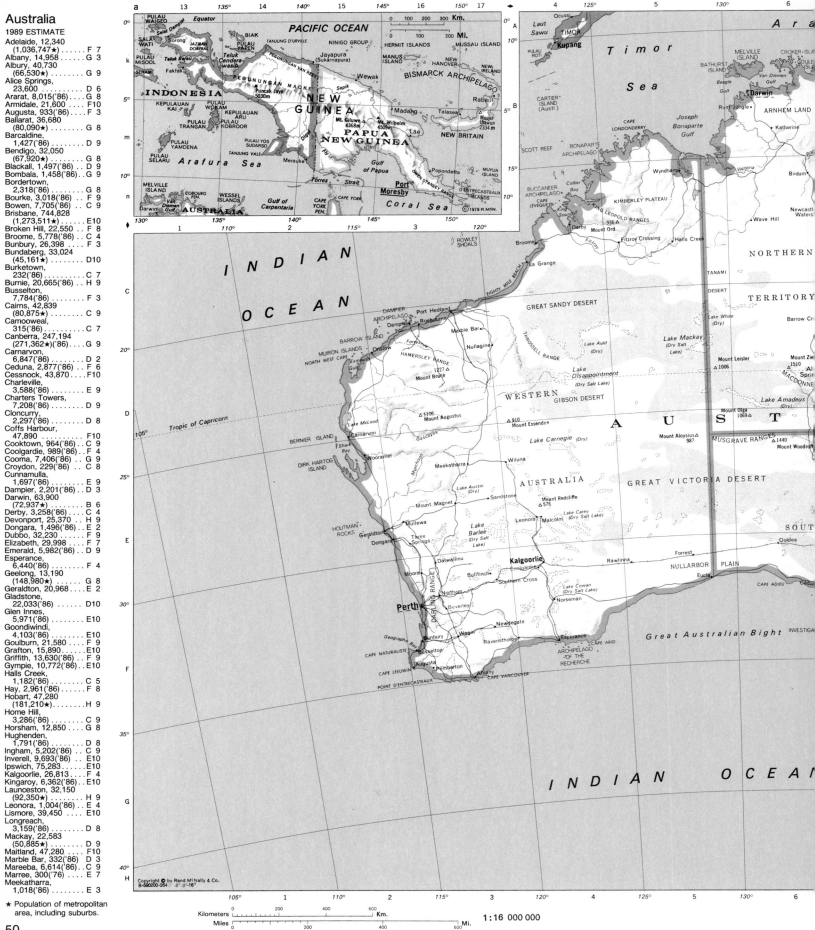

Melbourne, 55,300
    (3,039,100★) ...... G 8
Mildura, 20,512('86) .. F 8
Mitchell, 1,212('86) .. E 9
Moora, 1,469('86) .... F 3
Moree, 10,215('86) .. E 9
Morwell, 16,880 .... G 9
Mount Gambier, 22,194
    (27,228★) .... G 8
Mount Isa, 24,023 .. D 7
Mount Magnet,
    1,000('86) .... E 3
Mullewa, 758('86) .... E 3
Murwillumbah,
    7,678('86) E10
Nambour, 9,579('86) E10
Naracoorte,
    4,636('86) .... G 8
Newcastle, 130,940
    (425,610★) F10
New Norfolk,
    6,152('86) .... H 9
Normanton,
    1,109('86) .... C 8
Norseman,
    1,775('86) .... F 4
Northam, 6,377('86) . F 3
Nyngan, 2,502('86) . F 9
Onslow, 750('86) .... D 3
Oodnadatta, 200('76) E 7
Orange, 32,980 ..... F 9
Pemberton, 802('86) . F 3
Perth, 82,413
    (1,158,387★) ...... F 3
Peterborough,
    2,239('86) .... F 7
Port Augusta,
    15,752 .... F 7
Port Hedland,
    13,069('86) ...... D 3
Port Lincoln, 12,941 . F 7
Port Macquarie,
    22,884('86) F10
Port Pirie, 15,210 .... F 7
Quilpie, 780('86) .... E 8
Ravensthorpe,
    299('86) .... F 3
Richmond, 704('86) .. D 8
Rockhampton, 58,890
    (61,694★) D10
Roebourne,
    1,269('86) .... D 3
Roma, 6,069('86) .... E 9
Saint George,
    2,323('86) .... E 9
Sale, 13,800 .... G 9
Shepparton, 26,420
    (39,700★) .... G 9
Smithton, 3,414('86).. H 9
Southern Cross,
    898('86) .... F 3
Swan Hill,
    8,831('86) .... G 8
Sydney, 9,800
    (3,623,550★) F10
Tamworth, 34,430 .. F10
Taree, 38,760 ..... F10
Tennant Creek,
    3,503('86) .... C 6
Tenterfield,
    3,370('86) E10
Theodore, 576('86) .. D10
Toowoomba,
    81,071 .... E10
Townsville, 83,339
    (111,972★) .... C 9
Wagga Wagga,
    52,180 .... G 9
Walgett, 2,151('86) .. E 9
Wangaratta, 16,320 .. G 9
Warrnambool,
    24,480 .... G 8
Weipa, 2,406('86) ... B 8
Whyalla, 26,706 .... F 7
Wilcannia, 1,048('86) F 8
Wiluna, 279('86) .... E 4
Winton, 1,281('86) .. D 8
Wollongong, 174,770
    (236,690★) F10
Woomera,
    1,805('86) .... F 7
Wyndham,
    1,329('86) .... C 5

Indonesia
1980 CENSUS

Jayapura, 60,641 .... k15
Kupang, 84,587 .... B 4
Sorong, 52,041 ...... k13

Papua New Guinea
1987 ESTIMATE

Lae, 79,600 .... m16
Madang, 24,700 .... m16
Port Moresby,
    152,100.......... m16
Rabaul, 14,954('80) .. k17
Wewak, 23,200 ...... k15

51

New Zealand

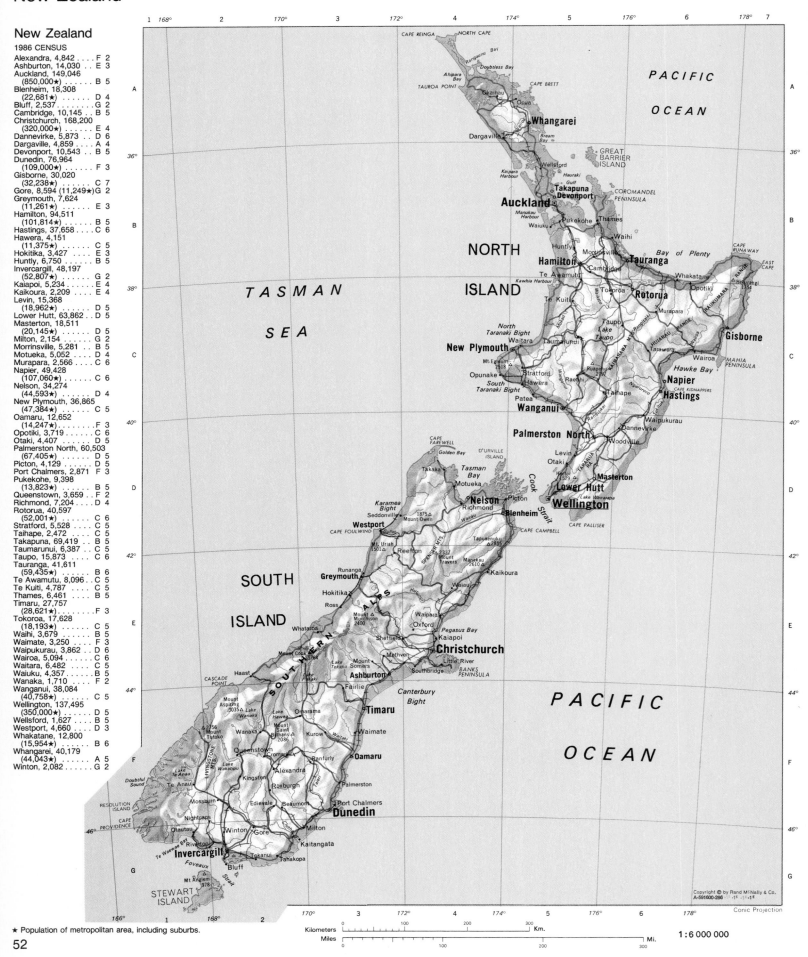

New Zealand

1986 CENSUS

Alexandra, 4,842 . . . . . F 2
Ashburton, 14,030 . . . E 3
Auckland, 149,046
  (850,000★) . . . . B 5
Blenheim, 18,308
  (22,681★) . . . . D 4
Bluff, 2,537 . . . . G 2
Cambridge, 10,145 . . B 5
Christchurch, 168,200
  (320,000★) . . . . . . E 4
Dannevirke, 5,873 . . D 6
Dargaville, 4,859 . . . . A 4
Devonport, 10,543 . . B 5
Dunedin, 76,964
  (109,000★) . . . . . . F 3
Gisborne, 30,020
  (32,238★) . . . . C 7
Gore, 8,594 (11,249★) G 2
Greymouth, 7,624
  (11,261★) . . . . E 3
Hamilton, 94,511
  (101,814★) . . . . . . B 5
Hastings, 37,658 . . . . C 6
Hawera, 4,151
  (11,375★) . . . . C 5
Hokitika, 3,427 . . . . . E 3
Huntly, 6,750 . . . . . . B 5
Invercargill, 48,197
  (52,807★) . . . . G 2
Kaiapoi, 5,234 . . . . . E 4
Kaikoura, 2,209 . . . . E 4
Levin, 15,368
  (18,962★) . . . . D 5
Lower Hutt, 63,862 . . D 5
Masterton, 18,511
  (20,145★) . . . . D 5
Milton, 2,154 . . . . . . G 2
Morrinsville, 5,281 . . B 5
Motueka, 5,052 . . . . D 4
Murapara, 2,566 . . . C 6
Napier, 49,428
  (107,060★) . . . . . . C 6
Nelson, 34,274
  (44,593★) . . . . D 4
New Plymouth, 36,865
  (47,384★) . . . . C 5
Oamaru, 12,652
  (14,247★) . . . . F 3
Opotiki, 3,719 . . . . . C 6
Otaki, 4,407 . . . . . . D 5
Palmerston North, 60,503
  (67,405★) . . . . D 5
Picton, 4,129 . . . . . . D 4
Port Chalmers, 2,871 F 3
Pukekohe, 9,398
  (13,823★) . . . . B 5
Queenstown, 3,659 . . F 2
Richmond, 7,204 . . . D 4
Rotorua, 40,597
  (52,001★) . . . . C 6
Stratford, 5,528 . . . . C 5
Taihape, 2,472 . . . . . C 5
Takapuna, 69,419 . . . B 5
Taumarunui, 6,387 . . C 5
Taupo, 15,873 . . . . . C 6
Tauranga, 41,611
  (59,435★) . . . . B 6
Te Awamutu, 8,096 . . C 5
Te Kuiti, 4,787 . . . . . C 5
Thames, 6,461 . . . . . B 5
Timaru, 27,757
  (28,621★) . . . . F 3
Tokoroa, 17,628
  (18,193★) . . . . C 5
Waihi, 3,679 . . . . . . B 5
Waimate, 3,250 . . . . F 3
Waipukurau, 3,862 . . D 6
Wairoa, 5,094 . . . . . C 6
Waitara, 6,482 . . . . . C 5
Waiuku, 4,357 . . . . . B 5
Wanaka, 1,710 . . . . . F 2
Wanganui, 38,084
  (40,758★) . . . . C 5
Wellington, 137,495
  (350,000★) . . . . . . D 5
Wellsford, 1,627 . . . . B 5
Westport, 4,660 . . . . D 3
Whakatane, 12,800
  (15,954★) . . . . B 6
Whangarei, 40,179
  (44,043★) . . . . A 5
Winton, 2,082 . . . . . . G 2

★ Population of metropolitan area, including suburbs.

52

Conic Projection

Kilometers
Miles

1 : 6 000 000

Copyright © by Rand McNally & Co.
A-591600-286

South America

Antofagasta, 185,486
('82)..................... F 3
Arequipa, 108,023 ('81)
(446,942★)............ E 3
ARGENTINA.............. G 4
Asunción, 477,100 ('85)
(700,000★)............ F 5
Barranquilla, 899,781 ('85)
(1,140,000★) .... B 3
Belém, 1,116,578 ('85)
(1,200,000★) ....D 6
Belo Horizonte, 2,114,429
('85) (2,950,000★) ...E 6
Bogotá *see* Santa Fe de
Bogotá..................C 3
BOLIVIA................ E 4
Brasília, 1,567,709
('85)...................... E 6
BRAZIL................ E 5
Buenos Aires, 2,922,829
('80) (10,750,000★) . G 5
Caracas, 1,816,901 ('81)
(3,600,000★) ....B 4
Cartagena, 531,426
('85)...................... B 3
Cayenne, 38,091 ('82)..C 5
Chiclayo, 213,095 ('81)
(279,527★)............ D 3
CHILE.................G 3
Ciudad Bolívar, 182,941
('81)......................C 4
COLOMBIA............ C 3
Concepción, 267,891 ('82)
(675,000★)............ G 3
Cuzco, 89,563 ('81)
(184,550★)............ E 3
ECUADOR............. D 3
FALKLAND ISLANDS... I 5
Fortaleza, 1,582,414 ('85)
(1,825,000★)..........D 7
FRENCH GUIANA...... C 5
Georgetown, 78,500 ('83)
(188,000★)............ C 5
Guayaquil, 1,572,615 ('87)
(1,580,000★)..........D 3
GUYANA............... C 5
Iquitos, 178,738 ('81)..D 3
João Pessoa, 348,500
('85) (550,000★) .....D 7
La Paz, 992,592 ('85)..E 4
La Plata, 477,175
('80).....................G 5
Lima, 371,122 ('81)
(4,608,010★)..........E 3
Maceió, 482,195 ('85). D 7
Manaus, 809,914 ('85) D 5
Maracaibo, 890,643
('81)...................... B 3
Medellín, 1,468,089 ('85)
(2,095,000★)..........C 3
Mendoza, 119,088 ('80)
(650,000★)............ G 4
Montevideo, 1,251,647
('85) (1,550,000★) .. G 5
Natal, 510,106 ('85).....D 7
PARAGUAY............. F 5
Paramaribo, 241,000 ('88)
(296,000★)............ C 5
PERU.................. E 3
Porto Alegre, 1,272,121
('85) (2,600,000★) ..G 5
Quito, 1,137,705 ('87)
(1,300,000★) ....D 3
Recife, 1,287,623 ('85)
(2,625,000★)..........D 7
Rio Branco, 109,800 ('85)
(145,486▲)............ D 4
Rio de Janeiro, 5,603,388
('85) (10,150,000★) . F 6
Rosario, 938,120 ('80)
(1,045,000★)..........G 4
Salta, 260,744 ('80).....F 4
Salvador, 1,804,438 ('85)
(2,050,000★)..........E 7
San Miguel de Tucumán,
392,888 ('80)
(525,000★)............ F 4
Santa Fe, 292,165
('80).....................G 4
Santa Fe de Bogotá,
3,982,941 ('85)
(4,260,000★)..........C 3
Santiago, 232,667 ('82)
(4,100,000★)..........G 3
Santos, 460,100 ('85)
(1,065,000★) ....F 6
São Luís, 227,900 ('85)
(600,000★)............ D 6
São Paulo, 10,063,110
('85) (15,175,000★) . F 6
Stanley, 1,200 ('86)......I 5
Sucre, 86,609 ('85).....E 4
SURINAME............. C 5
Teresina, 425,300 ('85)
(525,000★)............ D 6
Trujillo, 202,469 ('81)
(354,301★)............ D 3
URUGUAY.............. G 5
Valparaíso, 265,355 ('82)
(675,000★)............ G 3
VENEZUELA............ C 4
Vitória, 201,500 ('85)
(735,000★)............ F 6

★ Population of metropolitan area, including suburbs.
▲ Population of entire district, including rural area.

1:40 000 000

53

Northern South America

Bolivia
1985 ESTIMATE
Cochabamba, 317,251G 5
La Paz, 992,592 . . . . G 5
Oruro, 178,393 . . . . . G 5
Potosí, 113,380 . . . . G 5
Santa Cruz, 441,717 G 6
Sucre, 86,609 . . . . . . G 5

Brazil
1985 ESTIMATE
Anápolis, 225,840 . . G 9
Aracaju, 360,013 . . F11
Araçatuba, 129,304 . . H 8
Bauru, 220,105 . . . . H 9
Belém, 1,116,578
  (1,200,000★) . . . . . D 9
Belo Horizonte, 2,114,429
  (2,950,000★) G10
Brasília, 1,567,709 . . G 9
Campina Grande,
  279,929 . . . . E11
Campinas, 841,016
  (1,125,000★) . . . . . H 9
Campo Grande,
  384,398 . . . . H 8
Campos, 187,900
  (366,716▲) H10
Caruaru, 152,100
  (190,794▲) E11
Cuiabá, 220,400
  (279,651▲) . . . . . . G 7
Feira de Santana, 278,600
  (355,201▲) F11
Fortaleza, 1,582,414
  (1,825,000★) . . . D11
Goiânia, 923,333
  (990,000★) . . . . . G 9
Governador Valadares,
  192,300 (216,957▲) G10
João Pessoa, 348,500
  (550,000★) E12
Juàzeiro do Norte,
  159,806 . . . . E11
Juiz de Fora, 349,720 H10
Jundiaí, 268,900
  (313,652▲) . . . . . .H 9
Maceió, 482,195 . . . E11
Manaus, 809,914 . . . . D 6
Montes Claros, 183,500
  (214,472▲) G10
Natal, 510,106 . . . . . . E11
Niterói, 441,684 . . . . . H10
Petrolina, 92,100
  (225,000★) E10
Petrópolis, 170,300 . . H10
Piracicaba, 211,000
  (252,079▲) . . . . . .H 9
Porto Velho, 152,700
  (202,011▲) . . . . . . E 6
Presidente Prudente,
  155,883 . . . . H 8
Recife, 1,287,623
  (2,625,000★) E12
Ribeirão Prêto,
  383,125 . . . . H 9
Rio de Janeiro, 5,603,388
  (10,150,000★) H10
Salvador, 1,804,438
  (2,050,000★) F11
Santarém, 120,800
  (226,618▲) . . . . . . .D 8
Santos, 460,100
  (1,065,000★) . . . . . .H 9
São Carlos, 140,383 . H 9
São José do Rio Prêto,
  229,221 . . . . H 9
São Luís, 227,900
  (600,000★) D10
São Paulo, 10,063,110
  (15,175,000★) . . . . H 9
Sorocaba, 327,468 . . . H 9
Teresina, 425,300
  (525,000★) E10
Uberaba, 244,875 . . . . G 9
Uberlândia, 312,024 . . G 9
Vitória, 201,500
  (735,000★) H10
Vitória da Conquista,
  145,800 (198,150▲) F10
Volta Redonda, 219,267
  (375,000★) H10

Colombia
1985 CENSUS
Armenia, 187,130 . . . . C 3
Barrancabermeja,
  137,406 . . . . B 4
Barranquilla, 899,781
  (1,140,000★) . . . . . A 4
Bogotá see Santa Fe de
  Bogotá . . . . C 4
Bucaramanga, 352,326
  (550,000★) . . . . . . .B 4
Buenaventura,
  160,342 . . . . .C 3
Buga, 82,992 . . . . C 3
Cali, 1,350,565
  (1,400,000★) . . . . . C 3
Cartagena, 531,426 . . A 3
Cúcuta, 379,478
  (445,000★) . . . . . . .B 4

Ibagué, 292,965 . . . . . C 3
Manizales, 299,352
  (330,000★) . . . . B 3
Medellín, 1,468,089
  (2,095,000★) . . . . . B 3
Montería, 157,466 . . . . B 3
Neiva, 194,556 . . . . . . C 3
Palmira, 175,186 . . . . C 3
Pasto, 197,407 . . . . . . C 3
Pereira, 233,271
  (390,000★) . . . . C 3
Popayán, 141,964 . . C 3
Santa Fe de Bogotá,
  3,982,941
  (4,260,000★) . . . . . . C 4
Santa Marta, 177,922 A 4
Tuluá, 99,721 . . . . . . C 3
Valledupar, 142,771 . . A 4
Villavicencio, 178,685 C 4

Ecuador
1987 ESTIMATE
Ambato, 126,067 . . . . D 3
Cuenca, 201,490 . . . . D 3
Guayaquil, 1,572,615
  (1,580,000★) . . . . . D 3
Machala, 144,396 . . . D 3
Manta, 135,990 . . . . . D 2
Portoviejo, 141,568 . . D 2
Quito, 1,137,705
  (1,300,000★) . . . . . . D 3

French Guiana
1982 CENSUS
Cayenne, 38,091 . . . . C 8

Guyana
1983 ESTIMATE
Georgetown, 78,500
  (188,000★) . . . . B 7

Peru
1981 CENSUS
Arequipa, 108,023
  (446,942★) . . . . . . G 4
Ayacucho, 57,432
  (69,533★) . . . . F 4
Cajamarca, 62,259 . . E 3
Callao, 264,133 . . . . . F 3
Cerro de Pasco, 55,597
  (66,373★) . . . . F 3

Chiclayo, 213,095
  (279,527★) . . . . . E 3
Chimbote, 223,341 . . E 3
Cuzco, 89,563
  (184,550★) . . . . . . F 4
Huancayo, 84,845
  (164,954★) . . . . . . F 3
Huánuco, 61,812 . . . E 3
Ica, 114,786 . . . . F 3
Iquitos, 178,738 . . . . D 4
Lima, 371,122
  (4,608,010★) . . . . . F 3
Piura, 144,609
  (207,934★) . . . . . . E 2
Sullana, 89,037 . . . . D 2
Tacna, 97,173 . . . . . . G 4
Trujillo, 202,469
  (354,301★) . . . . . . E 3
Tumbes, 47,936 . . . . D 2
Vitarte, 145,504 . . . . F 3

Suriname
1988 ESTIMATE
Paramaribo, 241,000
  (296,000★) . . . . B 7

Venezuela
1981 CENSUS
Acarigua, 91,662 . . . . B 5
Barinas, 110,462 . . . . B 4
Barquisimeto, 497,635 A 5
Cabimas, 140,435 . . A 4
Calabozo, 61,995 . . . B 5
Caracas, 1,816,901
  (3,600,000★) . . . . . A 5
Ciudad Bolívar,
  182,941 . . . . B 6
Ciudad Guayana,
  314,497 . . . . B 6
Ciudad Ojeda, 83,565 A 4
Cumaná, 179,814 . . . A 6
El Tigre, 73,595 . . . . B 6
Maracaibo, 890,643 . . A 4
Maracay, 322,560 . . . A 5
Maturín, 154,976 . . . . B 6
Mérida, 143,209 . . . . B 4
Puerto Cabello,
  71,759 . . . . A 5
Punto Fijo, 71,114 . . A 4
San Cristóbal,
  198,793 . . . . B 4
Valencia, 616,224 . . . A 5
Valera, 102,068 . . . . B 4

★ Population of metropolitan area, including suburbs.
▲ Population of entire district, including rural area.

55

Southern South America

Argentina
1980 CENSUS

Avellaneda, 334,145..C 5
Bahía Blanca, 223,818D 4
Buenos Aires, 2,922,829
  (10,750,000★)......C 5
Catamarca, 78,799
  (90,000★)........B 3
Comodoro Rivadavia,
  96,817............F 3
Concordia, 94,222...C 5
Córdoba, 993,055
  (1,070,000★)......C 4
Corrientes, 180,612..B 5
La Plata, 477,175....C 5
Mar del Plata,
  414,696..........D 5
Mendoza, 119,088
  (650,000★).......C 3
Paraná, 161,638....C 4
Posadas, 143,889...B 5
Río Cuarto, 110,254..C 4
Rosario, 938,120
  (1,045,000★)......C 4
Salta, 260,744......A 3
San Isidro, 289,170..C 5
San Juan, 118,046
  (300,000★)......C 3
San Miguel de Tucumán,
  392,888 (525,000★)B 3
Santa Fe, 292,165...C 4
Santiago del Estero,
  148,758 (200,000★)B 4

Brazil
1985 ESTIMATE

Bauru, 220,105......A 7
Blumenau, 192,074..B 7
Campinas, 841,016
  (1,125,000★)......A 7
Caxias do Sul,
  266,809.........B 6
Curitiba, 1,279,205
  (1,700,000★)......B 7
Florianópolis, 178,400
  (365,000★)......B 7
Joinvile, 302,877...B 7
Jundiaí, 268,900
  (313,652▲)......A 7
Londrina, 296,400
  (346,676▲)......A 6
Maringá, 196,871...A 6
Pelotas, 210,300
  (277,730▲)......C 6
Piracicaba, 211,000
  (252,079▲)......A 7
Ponta Grossa,
  223,154.........B 6
Porto Alegre, 1,272,121
  (2,600,000★)......C 6
Presidente Prudente,
  155,883.........A 6
Ribeirão Prêto,
  383,125.........A 7
Rio Grande, 164,221 C 6
Santa Maria, 163,900
  (196,827▲)......B 6
Santos, 460,100
  (1,065,000★)......A 7
São Carlos, 140,383 A 7
São Paulo, 10,063,110
  (15,175,000★)....A 7
Sorocaba, 327,468 ..A 7

Chile
1982 CENSUS

Antofagasta, 185,486 A 2
Chillán, 118,163 .....D 2
Concepción, 267,891
  (675,000★).......D 2
Osorno, 95,286......E 2
Punta Arenas, 95,332 G 2
Rancagua, 139,925 .C 2
Santiago, 232,667
  (4,100,000★)......C 2
Talca, 128,544 ......D 2
Talcahuano, 202,368 D 2
Temuco, 157,297 ...D 2
Valdivia, 100,046 ...D 2
Valparaíso, 265,355
  (675,000★).......C 2
Viña del Mar, 244,899 C 2

Falkland Islands
1986 ESTIMATE

Stanley, 1,200 ......G 5

Paraguay
1985 ESTIMATE

Asunción, 477,100
  (700,000★).......B 5

Uruguay
1985 CENSUS

Montevideo, 1,251,647
  (1,550,000★)......C 5
Paysandú, 76,191....C 5
Salto, 80,823 ....C 5

★ Population of metropolitan area, including suburbs.
▲ Population of entire district, including rural area.

56

Copyright © by Rand McNally & Co.
B-549200-264

Oblique Conic Conformal Projection

Kilometers 0 200 400 600 Km.
Miles 0 200 400 600 Mi.

1:16 000 000

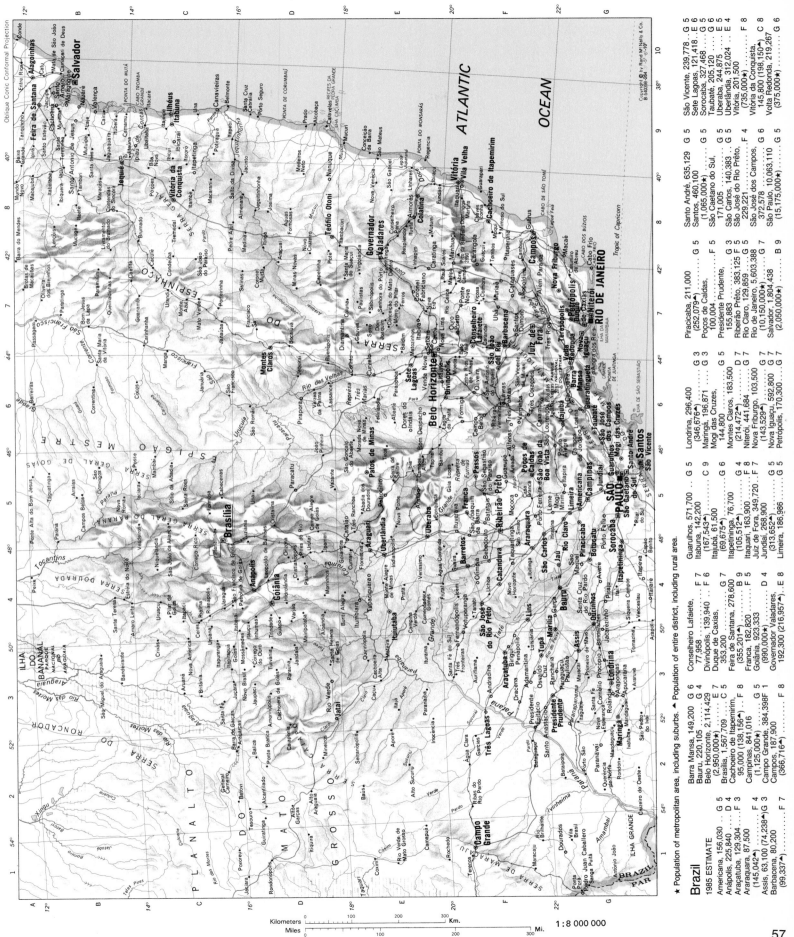

★ Population of metropolitan area, including suburbs. ▲ Population of entire district, including rural area.

Brazil
1985 ESTIMATE

Americana, 156,030 ..... G 5	Conselheiro Lafaiete, 77,958 ..... F 7	Piracicaba, 211,000 (252,079▲) ..... G 5
Anápolis, 225,840 ..... D 4	Divinópolis, 139,940 ..... F 6	Poços de Caldas, 100,004 ..... F 5
Aracatuba, 129,304 ..... F 3	Duque de Caxias, 353,200 ..... G 7	Presidente Prudente, 155,883 ..... G 3
Araraquara, 87,500 ..... F 4	Feira de Santana, 278,600 (355,201▲) ..... B 9	Ribeirão Prêto, 383,125 ..F 5
Assis, 63,100 (74,238▲)G 3	Franca, 182,820 ..... F 5	Rio Claro, 129,859 ..... G 5
Barbacena, 80,200 ..... F 7	Goiânia, 841,016 (1,125,000★) ..... D 4	Rio de Janeiro, 5,603,388 (10,150,000★) ..... G 7
Barra Mansa, 149,200 .. G 6	Governador Valadares, 192,300 (216,957▲)..E 8	Salvador, 1,804,438 (2,050,000★) ..... B 9
Bauru, 220,105 ..... G 4	Guarulhos, 571,700 ..... G 5	Santo André, 635,129 ... G 5
Belo Horizonte, 2,114,429 (2,950,000★) ..... E 7	Itabuna, 142,200 (167,543▲) ..... C 9	Santos, 460,100 (1,065,000★) ..... G 5
Brasília, 1,567,709 (2,950,000★)	Itajubá, 61,500 ..... G 6	São Caetano do Sul, 171,005 ..... G 5
Cachoeiro de Itapemirim, 95,000 (138,156▲) .. F 8	Itapetininga, 76,700 (105,512▲) ..... G 4	São Carlos, 140,383 .... G 5
Campinas, 841,016 (1,125,000★) ..... G 5	Itaquari, 163,900 ..... F 8	São José do Rio Prêto, 229,221 ..... F 4
Campo Grande, 384,398F 1	Juiz de Fora, 349,720 .. F 7	Vitória da Conquista, 145,800 (198,150▲) .. C 8
Campos, 187,900 (366,716▲) ..... F 7	Jundiaí, 268,900 (313,652▲) ..... G 5	São Vicente, 239,778 ... G 5
	Limeira, 186,986 ..... G 5	Sete Lagoas, 121,418 ... E 6
	Londrina, 296,400 (346,676▲) ..... G 5	Sorocaba, 327,468 ..... G 6
	Maringá, 196,871 ..... G 3	Taubaté, 205,120 ..... G 5
	Mogi das Cruzes, 144,800 ..... G 6	Uberaba, 244,875 ..... E 5
	Montes Claros, 183,500 (214,472▲) ..... D 7	Uberlândia, 312,024 ... E 4
	Niterói, 441,684 ..... G 7	Vitória, 201,500 (735,000★) ..... F 8
	Nova Friburgo, 103,500 (143,529▲) ..... G 7	Volta Redonda, 219,267 (375,000★) ..... G 6
	Nova Iguaçu, 592,800 ... G 5	
	Petrópolis, 170,300..... G 7	

Kilometers 0 100 200 300 Km.
Miles 0 100 200 300 Mi.

1:8 000 000

Colombia, Ecuador, Venezuela, and Guyana

Aruba
1987 ESTIMATE
Oranjestad, 19,800 . . A 7

Colombia
1985 CENSUS
Armenia, 187,130 . . . . E 5
Barrancabermeja,
  137,406 . . . . D 6
Barranquilla, 899,781
  (1,140,000★) . . . . . B 5
Bello, 212,861 . . . . . . D 5
Bogotá see Santa Fe de
  Bogotá . . . . E 5
Bucaramanga, 352,326
  (550,000★) . . . . . . D 6
Buenaventura,
  160,342 . . . . F 4
Buga, 82,992 . . . . F 4
Cali, 1,350,565
  (1,400,000★) . . . . . F 4
Cartagena, 531,426 . . B 5
Cartago, 97,791 . . . . . E 5
Ciénaga, 56,860 . . . . . B 5
Cúcuta, 379,478
  (445,000★) . . . . D 6
Duitama, 56,390 . . . . E 6
Envigado, 91,391 . . . . D 5
Espinal, 37,563 . . . . . E 5
Facatativá, 44,331 . . . E 5
Florencia, 66,430 . . . . G 5
Florida, 30,040 . . . . . F 4
Floridablanca,
  143,824 . . . . D 6
Girardot, 70,078 . . . . E 5
Ibagué, 292,965 . . . . E 5
Ipiales, 45,419 . . . . . . G 4
Itagüí, 137,623 . . . . . D 5
La Dorada, 48,572 . . . E 5
Magangué, 49,160 . . . C 5
Manizales, 299,352
  (330,000★) . . . . E 5
Medellín, 1,468,089
  (2,095,000★) . . . . . D 5
Montería, 157,466 . . . C 5
Neiva, 194,556 . . . . . F 5
Ocaña, 51,443 . . . . . . C 6
Palmira, 175,186 . . . . F 4
Pamplona, 34,213 . . . D 6
Pasto, 197,407 . . . . . G 4
Pereira, 233,271
  (390,000★) . . . . E 5
Planeta Rica, 24,238 . C 5
Popayán, 141,964 . . . F 4
Puerto Berrío, 21,414 D 5
Quibdó, 47,950 . . . . . D 4
Ríohacha, 46,667 . . . . B 6
Santa Fe de Bogotá,
  3,982,941
  (4,260,000★) . . . . . E 5
Santa Marta,
  177,922 . . . . B 5
Santa Rosa de Cabal,
  37,112 . . . . E 5
Sincelejo, 120,537 . . . C 5
Sogamoso, 64,437 . . . E 6
Soledad, 165,791 . . . B 5
Tuluá, 99,721 . . . . . . E 4
Tumaco, 45,456 . . . . G 3
Tunja, 93,792 . . . . . . E 6
Valledupar, 142,771 . . B 6
Villavicencio, 178,685 E 6
Zipaquirá, 45,676 . . . . E 5

Ecuador
1987 ESTIMATE
Alfaro, 51,023('82) . . . I 3
Ambato, 126,067 . . . . H 3
Babahoyo,
  42,266('82) . . . . . . H 3
Chone, 33,839('82) . . H 2
Cuenca, 201,490 . . . . I 3
Esmeraldas, 120,387 G 3
Guayaquil, 1,572,615
  (1,580,000★) . . . . . I 3
Ibarra, 53,428('82) . . H 3
Jipijapa, 27,146('82) . H 2
Latacunga,
  28,764('82) . . . . . . H 3
Loja, 71,652('82) . . . . J 3
Machala, 144,396 . . . I 3
Manta, 135,990 . . . . . H 2
Milagro, 102,884 . . . . I 3
Portoviejo, 141,568 . . H 2
Quevedo,
  67,023('82) . . . . . . H 3
Quito, 1,137,705
  (1,300,000★) . . . . . . H 3
Riobamba,
  75,455('82) . . . . . . H 3
Santo Domingo de los
  Colorados, 104,059 H 3
Tulcán, 30,985('82) . . G 4

Guyana
1983 ESTIMATE
Georgetown, 78,500
  (188,000★) D13
New Amsterdam,
  20,000('82) D14

★ Population of metropolitan
  area, including suburbs.

58

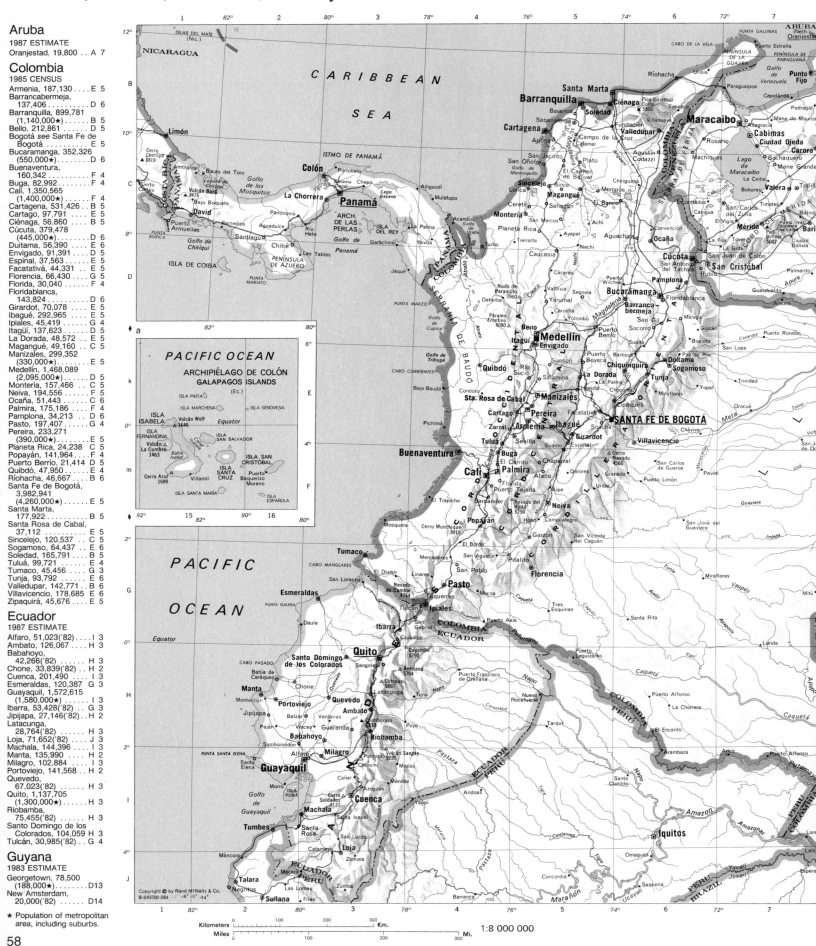

PACIFIC OCEAN
ARCHIPIÉLAGO DE COLÓN
GALAPAGOS ISLANDS
(Ec.)

Copyright © by Rand McNally & Co.
B-549700-264

Kilometers
Miles
1:8 000 000

Netherlands Antilles
1981 CENSUS

Willemstad, 31,883
(130,000★) . . . . A 8

Panama
1990 CENSUS

Colón, 54,469
(96,000★) . . . . . . C 3
David, 65,635 . . . . . . C 1
La Chorrera, 44,110 . . C 3
Panamá, 411,549
(770,000★) . . . . C 3
Puerto Armuelles,
12,562('80) . . . . . . C 1
Santiago, 43,678 . . . . C 2

Trinidad and Tobago
1990 CENSUS

Arima, 29,695 . . . . . . B12
Point Fortin,
6,538('80) B12
Port of Spain, 50,878
(370,000★) B12
San Fernando, 30,092
(75,000★) B12
Scarborough,
6,089('80) B12

Venezuela
1981 CENSUS

Acarigua, 91,662 . . . . C 8
Altagracia de Orituco,
31,582 . . . . C 9
Anaco, 43,607 . . . . . . C10
Araure, 41,747 . . . . . . C 8
Barcelona, 156,461 . . . B10
Barinas, 110,462 . . . . C 7
Barquisimeto,
497,635 . . . . B 8
Cabimas, 140,435 . . . B 7
Calabozo, 61,995 . . . . C 9
Cantaura, 21,236 . . . . C10
Caracas, 1,816,901
(3,600,000★) . . . . . . B 9
Caripito, 18,172 . . . . . B11
Carora, 58,694 . . . . . . B 7
Carúpano, 64,579 . . . . B11
Ciudad Bolívar,
182,941 . . . . C11
Ciudad Guayana,
314,497 . . . . C11
Ciudad Ojeda (Lagunillas),
83,565 . . . . B 7
Coro, 96,339 . . . . B 8
Cumaná, 179,814 . . . . B10
El Tigre, 73,595 . . . . C10
El Tocuyo, 22,854 . . C 8
Guanare, 64,025 . . . . C 8
La Guaira, 21,815 . . . B 9
Los Teques, 112,857 B 9
Machiques, 27,242 . . B 6
Maiquetía, 66,056 . . . B 9
Maracaibo, 890,643 . . B 7
Maracay, 322,560 . . . B 9
Maturín, 154,976 . . . C11
Mérida, 143,209 . . . C 7
Ocumare del Tuy,
40,666 . . . . B 9
Porlamar, 51,079 . . . . B11
Puerto Ayacucho,
28,248 . . . . E 9
Puerto Cabello,
71,759 . . . . B 8
Puerto la Cruz,
53,881 . . . . B10
Punto Fijo, 71,114 . . B 7
Rosario, 23,914 . . . . B 6
San Carlos, 37,892 . . C 8
San Carlos del Zulia,
31,437 . . . . C 7
San Cristóbal,
198,793 . . . . D 6
San Felipe, 57,526 . . B 8
San Fernando de Apure,
57,308 . . . . D 9
San José de Guanipa,
35,689 . . . . C10
San Juan de Colón,
23,447 . . . . C 6
San Juan de los Morros,
57,219 . . . . C 9
Tinaquillo, 28,168 . . . . C 8
Trujillo, 31,774 . . . . . C 7
Tucupita, 27,299 . . . . C11
Upata, 33,238 . . . . . . C11
Valencia, 616,224 . . . . C 8
Valera, 102,068 . . . . C 7
Valle de la Pascua,
55,761 . . . . C 9
Yaritagua, 31,936 . . . . B 8
Zaraza, 24,562 . . . . . . C10

Atlantic Ocean

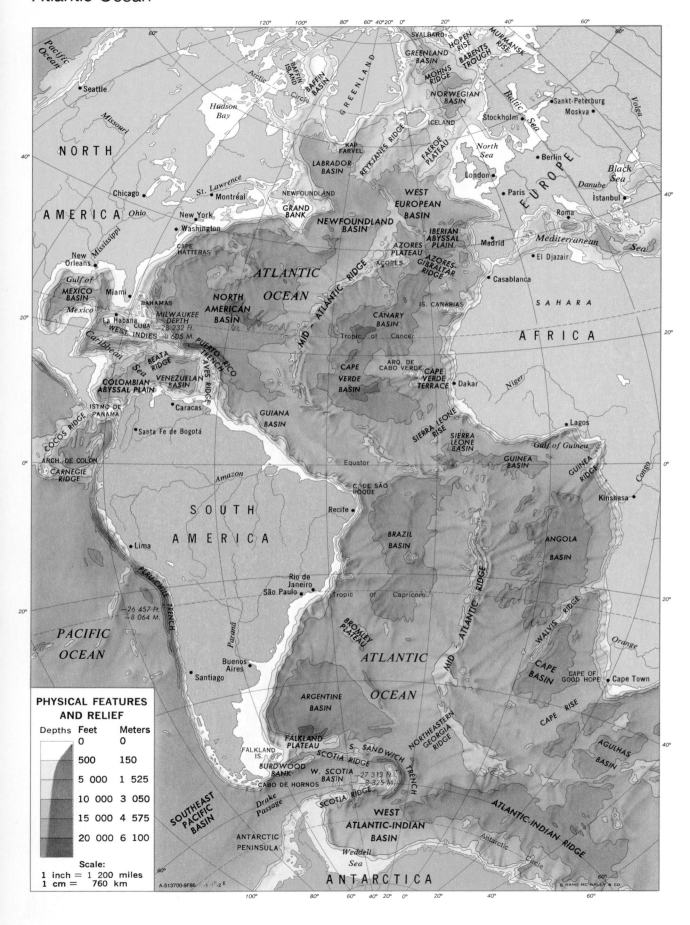

PACIFIC Ocean

•Seattle

NORTH

AMERICA

Hudson Bay

Missouri

Chicago•

New York•

•Washington

CAPE HATTERAS

New Orleans•

Gulf of Mexico BASIN

Miami•

Mexico•

BAHAMAS

La Habana• CUBA

MILWAUKEE DEPTH
28 232 Ft.
−8 605 M.

WEST INDIES

Caribbean Sea

BEATA RIDGE

COLOMBIAN ABYSSAL PLAIN

VENEZUELAN BASIN

AVES RIDGE

Caracas•

ISTMO DE PANAMA

•Santa Fe de Bogotá

COCOS RIDGE

ARCH. DE COLON

CARNEGIE RIDGE

Amazon

SOUTH

AMERICA

•Lima

PERU-CHILE TRENCH

−26 457 Ft.
−8 064 M.

PACIFIC OCEAN

Santiago•

Parana

SOUTHEAST PACIFIC BASIN

ANTARCTIC PENINSULA

Buenos Aires•

FALKLAND IS.

FALKLAND PLATEAU

BURDWOOD BANK

CABO DE HORNOS

Drake Passage

SCOTIA RIDGE

W. SCOTIA BASIN

S. SANDWICH

ARCTIC Circle

BAFFIN ISLAND

BAFFIN BASIN

St. Lawrence

Montréal•

NEWFOUNDLAND

GRAND BANK

Ohio

Mississippi

GREENLAND

KAP FARVEL

LABRADOR BASIN

NEWFOUNDLAND BASIN

ATLANTIC

OCEAN

NORTH AMERICAN BASIN

NORTH AMERICAN BASIN

Tropic of Cancer

MID-ATLANTIC RIDGE

CAPE VERDE BASIN

GUIANA BASIN

Equator

C. DE SÃO ROQUE

Recife•

BRAZIL BASIN

Rio de Janeiro•
São Paulo•

Tropic of Capricorn

BROMLEY PLATEAU

ATLANTIC

OCEAN

ARGENTINE BASIN

MID-ATLANTIC RIDGE

NORTHEASTERN GEORGIA RIDGE

SCOTIA RIDGE

−27 313 Ft.
−8 325 M.

S. SANDWICH TRENCH

WEST ATLANTIC-INDIAN BASIN

Weddell Sea

Antarctic Circle

ANTARCTICA

SVALBARD

HOPEN RISE

GREENLAND BASIN

MOHNS RIDGE

NORWEGIAN BASIN

ICELAND

REYKJANES RIDGE

FAEROE PLATEAU

MURMANSK RISE

BARENTS TROUGH

•Sankt-Peterburg

Moskva•

Volga

Stockholm•

Baltic Sea

North Sea

•Berlin

London•

EUROPE

Black Sea

WEST EUROPEAN BASIN

Paris•

Danube

•İstanbul

Roma•

IBERIAN ABYSSAL PLAIN

AZORES PLATEAU

AÇORES

AZORES-GIBRALTAR RIDGE

Madrid•

Mediterranean Sea

•El Djazair

•Casablanca

IS. CANARIAS

CANARY BASIN

SAHARA

AFRICA

ARQ. DE CABO VERDE

CAPE VERDE TERRACE

•Dakar

Niger

SIERRA LEONE RISE

SIERRA LEONE BASIN

•Lagos

Gulf of Guinea

GUINEA BASIN

GUINEA RIDGE

Congo

•Kinshasa

ANGOLA BASIN

WALVIS RIDGE

Orange

CAPE BASIN

CAPE OF GOOD HOPE

•Cape Town

CAPE RISE

AGULHAS BASIN

ATLANTIC-INDIAN RIDGE

PHYSICAL FEATURES AND RELIEF

Depths	Feet	Meters
	0	0
	500	150
	5 000	1 525
	10 000	3 050
	15 000	4 575
	20 000	6 100

Scale:
1 inch = 1 200 miles
1 cm = 760 km

A-513700-9F86 -1-¹⁻-2ᴱ

© RAND MCNALLY & CO.

60

North America

Atlanta, 394,017 ('90)..F12
BAHAMAS...................G13
Baltimore, 736,014
('90).......................F13
BARBADOS................H14
BELIZE.......................H12
Boston, 574,283 ('90)..E13
Calgary, 636,104 ('86)
(671,326★) ....D 9
CANADA....................D11
Chicago, 2,783,726
('90)........................E12
Ciudad de México (Mexico
City), 8,831,079 ('80)
(14,100,000★) H11
COSTA RICA.............H12
CUBA.........................G13
Dallas, 1,006,877 ('90)..F11
Denver, 467,610 ('90)..F10
Detroit, 1,027,974
('90)........................E12
**DOMINICAN
REPUBLIC**..............H13
EL SALVADOR..........H12
GREENLAND..............B16
Guadalajara, 1,626,152
('80) (2,325,000★) .. H10
GUATEMALA..............H11
HAITI..........................H13
HONDURAS................H12
Houston, 1,630,553
('90)........................G11
JAMAICA....................H13
Kansas City, 435,146
('90)........................F11
La Habana (Havana),
2,036,800 ('87)
(2,125,000★) G12
Los Angeles, 3,485,398
('90).........................F 9
Memphis, 610,337
('90)........................F11
MEXICO......................G10
Miami, 358,548 ('90)..G12
Milwaukee, 628,088
('90)........................E12
Minneapolis, 368,383
('90)........................E11
Montréal, 1,015,420 ('86)
(2,921,357★) E13
New Orleans, 496,938
('90)........................G11
New York, 7,322,564
('90)........................E13
NICARAGUA...............H12
Ottawa, 300,763 ('86)
(819,263★) E13
PANAMA.....................I13
Philadelphia, 1,585,577
('90)........................F13
Phoenix, 900,013 ('90) F 9
PUERTO RICO...........H14
San Antonio, 935,933
('90)........................G11
San Francisco, 723,959
('90).........................F 8
Santo Domingo, 1,313,172
('81).......................H13
Seattle, 516,259 ('90)..E 8
Toronto, 612,289 ('86)
(3,427,168★) E13
**TRINIDAD AND
TOBAGO**..................H14
UNITED STATES.........F11
Washington, 606,900
('90)........................F13

★ Population of metropolitan
area, including suburbs.

Copyright ⓒ by Rand McNally & Co.
A-520000-286   -1 -1 -2 ᴱ

Lambert Azimuthal Equal Area Projection

Miles 0 200 400 600 800 1000 Mi.
Kilometers 0 400 800 1200 1600 Km.

1:40 000 000

61

Mexico

Mexico

1980 CENSUS

Acámbaro, 38,224 . . . G 9
Acapulco [de Juárez],
  301,902 . . . . I10
Aguascalientes,
  293,152 . . . . G 8
Ameca, 25,946 . . . G 7
Apatzingán [de la
  Constitución],
  55,522 . . . . H 8
Apizaco, 30,498 . . . . H10
Caborca, 33,696 . . . B 3
Campeche, 128,434 . H14
Celaya, 141,675 . . . G 9
Chihuahua, 385,603 . C 6
Chilpancingo [de los
  Bravos], 67,498 . . . I10
Ciudad Acuña, 38,898 C 9
Ciudad Chetumal,
  56,709 . . . . H15
Ciudad del Carmen,
  72,489 . . . . H14
Ciudad de México (Mexico
  City), 8,831,079
  (14,100,000★) . . . H10
Ciudad de Valles,
  65,609 . . . . G10
Ciudad Guzmán,
  60,938 . . . . H 8
Ciudad Hidalgo,
  32,311 . . . . H 9
Ciudad Juárez,
  544,496 . . . . B 6
Ciudad Madero,
  132,444 . . . . F11
Ciudad Mante, 70,647 F10
Ciudad Obregón,
  165,572 . . . . D 5
Ciudad Victoria,
  140,161 . . . . F10
Coatzacoalcos,
  127,170 . . . . H12
Colima, 86,044 . . . . H 8
Córdoba, 99,972 . . . H11
Cuernavaca, 192,770 H10
Culiacán, 304,826 . . E 6
Delicias, 65,504 . . . C 7
Durango, 257,915 . . E 7
Empalme, 31,555 . . D 4
Ensenada, 120,483 . B 1
Fresnillo, 56,066 . . . F 8
Gómez Palacio,
  116,967 . . . . E 8
Guadalajara, 1,626,152
  (2,325,000★) . . . . G 8
Guadalupe, 370,524 . E 9
Guanajuato, 48,981 . G 9
Guaymas, 54,826 . . D 4
Hermosillo, 297,175 . C 4
Hidalgo del Parral,
  75,590 . . . . D 7
Iguala, 66,005 . . . . H10
Irapuato, 170,138 . . G 9
Jalapa Enríquez,
  204,594 . . . . H11
Juchitán [de Zaragoza],
  38,801 . . . . I12
La Barca, 20,889 . . G 8
Lagos de Moreno,
  44,223 . . . . G 9
La Paz, 91,453 . . . . E 4
La Piedad [Cavadas],
  47,441 . . . . G 8
León [de los Aldamas],
  593,002 . . . . G 9
Los Mochis, 122,531 E 5
Manzanillo, 39,088 . H 7
Matamoros, 188,745 E11
Matehuala, 41,550 . F 9
Mazatlán, 199,830 . . F 6
Mérida, 400,142 . . . G15
Mexicali, 341,559
  (365,000★) . . . . . A 2
Mexico City see Ciudad
  de México H10
Minatitlán, 106,765 . I12
Monclova, 115,786 . D 9
Montemorelos, 28,342 E10
Monterrey, 1,090,009
  (2,015,000★) . . . . E 9
Morelia, 297,544 . . . H 9
Navojoa, 62,901 . . . D 5
Nogales, 65,603 . . . B 4
Nueva Casas Grandes,
  28,514 . . . . B 6
Nueva Rosita, 33,121 D 9
Nuevo Laredo,
  201,731 . . . . D10
Oaxaca [de Juárez],
  154,223 . . . . I11
Ocotlán, 48,931 . . . G 8
Orizaba, 114,848
  (215,000★) H11
Pachuca [de Soto],
  110,351 . . . . G10
Papantla [de Olarte],
  43,935 . . . . G11
Pátzcuaro, 32,902 . . H 9
Piedras Negras,
  67,455 . . . . C 9
Poza Rica de Hidalgo,
  166,799 . . . . G11

★ Population of metropolitan
  area, including suburbs.

62

PACIFIC OCEAN

ISLAS REVILLAGIGEDO (Mex.)

Tropic of Cancer

Copyright © by Rand McNally & Co.
B-531600-264 -4° -6° -14°

Kilometers 0 100 200 300 Km.
Miles 0 100 200 300 Mi.

1 : 8 000 000

63

Central America and the Caribbean

Antigua and Barbuda
1977 ESTIMATE
Saint Johns, 24,359 . . F17

Bahamas
1982 ESTIMATE
Nassau, 135,000 . . . . B 9

Barbados
1980 CENSUS
Bridgetown, 7,466
  (115,000★) H18

Belize
1985 ESTIMATE
Belize City, 47,000 . . F 3
Belmopan, 4,500 . . . . F 3

Cayman Islands
1988 ESTIMATE
Georgetown, 13,700 E 7

Costa Rica
1988 ESTIMATE
Limón, 40,400
  (62,600▲) . . . . . . I 6
San José, 278,600
  (670,000★) . . . . . . J 5

Cuba
1987 ESTIMATE
Camagüey, 265,588 . . D 9
Guantánamo, 179,091 D10
Havana see La
  Habana . . . . C 6
Holguín, 199,861 . . . . D 9
La Habana (Havana),
  2,036,800
  (2,125,000★) . . . . . C 6
Santa Clara, 182,349 C 8
Santiago de Cuba,
  364,554 . . . . D10

Dominican Republic
1981 CENSUS
Santiago, 278,638 . . E 12
Santo Domingo,
  1,313,172 . . . . . . E 13

El Salvador
1985 ESTIMATE
San Salvador, 462,652
  (920,000★) . . . . . . H 3
Santa Ana, 137,879 . . H 3

Guadeloupe
1982 CENSUS
Basse-Terre, 13,656
  (26,600★) F17

Guatemala
1989 ESTIMATE
Guatemala, 1,057,210
  (1,400,000★) . . . . G 2

★ Population of metropolitan
  area, including suburbs.

Copyright © by Rand McNally & Co.
B-530100-264

1:9 000 000

Haiti
1987 ESTIMATE
Port-au-Prince, 797,000
(880,000★) E11

Honduras
1988 CENSUS
San Pedro Sula,
279,356 .... G 4
Tegucigalpa, 551,606 G 4

Jamaica
1987 ESTIMATE
Kingston, 646,400
(770,000★) ..... E 9
Montego Bay,
70,265('82) ...... E 9

Martinique
1982 CENSUS
Fort-de-France, 99,844
(116,017★) G17

Netherlands Antilles
1981 CENSUS
Willemstad, 31,883
(130,000★) ..... H 13

Nicaragua
1985 ESTIMATE
León, 101,000 ..... H 4
Managua, 682,000 .. H 4

Panama
1990 CENSUS
Colón, 54,469
(96,000★) .... J 8
Panamá, 411,549
(770,000★) ..... J 8

Puerto Rico
1980 CENSUS
Ponce, 161,739
(232,551★) E14
San Juan, 424,600
(1,775,260★) E14

Saint Lucia
1987 ESTIMATE
Castries, 53,933 .... G17

Saint Vincent and the Grenadines
1987 ESTIMATE
Kingstown, 19,028
(28,936★) H17

Trinidad and Tobago
1988 ESTIMATE
Port of Spain, 59,200
(370,000★) I17

Lambert Conformal Conic Projection

Canada

ALBERTA.................F10
Alma, 25,923 ('86)
  (29,977★)................G18
Baie-Comeau, 26,244 ('86)
  (33,047★)................G19
Banff, 4,208 ('81)........F 9
Barrie, 48,287 ('86)
  (67,703★)................H17
Bathurst, 14,683 ('86)
  (34,895★)................G19
Belleville, 36,041 ('86)
  (87,530★)................H17
Brandon, 38,708 ('86).G13
BRITISH COLUMBIA...F 8
Brockville, 20,880 ('86)
  (37,115★)................H17
Calgary, 636,104 ('86)
  (671,326★)................F10
Cambridge, 79,920
  ('86)........................H16
Campbell River, 15,370
  ('81)........................F 7
Campbellton, 9,077 ('86)
  (17,418★)................G19
CANADA....................D13
Charlottetown, 15,776
  ('86) (53,868★)........G20
Chatham, 42,211 ('86).H16
Chicoutimi, 61,083 ('86)
  (158,468★)................G18
Chilliwack, 41,337 ('86)
  (50,288★)................G 8
Churchill, 1,186 ('81)..E14
Corner Brook, 22,719
  ('86) (33,730★)........G21
Cornwall, 46,425 ('86)
  (51,719★)................G18
Dartmouth, 65,243
  ('86)........................H20
Dawson Creek, 10,544
  ('86)........................E 8
Dolbeau, 8,554 ('86)
  (15,288★)................G18
Drummondville, 36,020
  ('86) (56,283★)........G18
Edmonton, 573,982 ('86)
  (785,465★)................F10
Edmundston, 11,497 ('86)
  (22,614★)................G19
Eskimo Point, 1,189
  ('86)........................D14
Flin Flon, 7,591 ('86)
  (9,211★)................F12
Fort McMurray, 34,949
  ('86) (48,497★)........E10
Fort Saint John, 13,355
  ('86)........................E 8
Fredericton, 44,352 ('86)
  (65,768★)................G19
Gander, 10,207 ('86)
  (10,899★)................G22
Gaspé, 17,350 ('86)...G20
Granby, 38,508 ('86)
  (51,176★)................G18
Grande-Prairie, 26,471
  ('86)........................E 9
Grand Falls, 9,121 ('86)
  (25,612★)................G21
Guelph, 78,235 ('86)
  (85,962★)................H16
Halifax, 113,577 ('86)
  (295,990★)................H20
Hamilton, 306,728 ('86)
  (557,029★)................H17
Happy Valley-Goose Bay,
  7,248 ('86)..............F20
Hull, 58,722 ('86)........G17
Inuvik, 3,389 ('86)......C 6
Jasper, 3,269 ('81)......F 9
Joliette, 16,845 ('86)
  (34,897★)................G18
Jonquière, 58,467
  ('86)........................G18
Kamloops, 61,773
  ('86)........................F 8
Kelowna, 61,213 ('86)
  (89,730★)................G 9
Kenora, 9,621 ('86)
  (15,456★)................G14
Kirkland Lake, 11,604
  ('86)........................H16
Kitchener, 150,604 ('86)
  (311,195★)................H16
Kitimat, 11,196 ('86)...F 7
Labrador City, 8,664 ('86)
  (11,301★)................F19
La Tuque, 10,723 ('86)
  (13,468★)................G18
Laval, 284,164 ('86)....G18
Lethbridge, 58,841
  ('86)........................G10
Lloydminster, 17,356
  ('86)........................F11
London, 269,140 ('86)
  (342,302★)................H16
MANITOBA..................F13
Matane, 13,243 ('86)
  (15,361★)................G19
Medicine Hat, 41,804 ('86)
  (50,734★)................F10
Midland, 12,092 ('86)
  (35,003★)................H17
Moncton, 55,468 ('86)
  (102,084★)................G20

★ Population of metropolitan
  area, including suburbs.

66

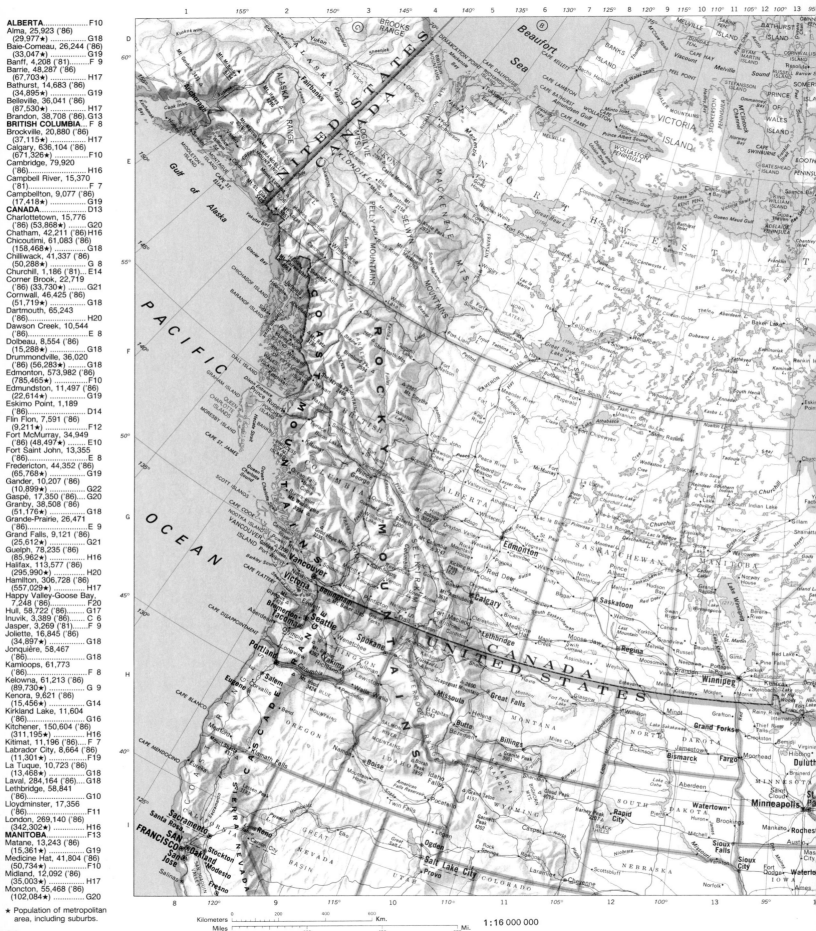

Montréal, 1,015,420 ('86)
(2,921,357★) G18
Moose Jaw, 35,073 ('86)
(37,219★) F11
Nanaimo, 49,029 ('86)
(60,420★) .... G 8
NEW BRUNSWICK..... G19
NEWFOUNDLAND...... F21
New Glasgow, 10,022
('86) (38,737★) G20
Niagara Falls, 72,107
('86) H17
North Bay, 50,623 ('86)
(57,422★) G17
**NORTHWEST
TERRITORIES**........ C13
NOVA SCOTIA.......... G20
ONTARIO................ G16
Orillia, 24,077 ('86)
(31,252★) H17
Oshawa, 123,651 ('86)
(203,543★) H17
Ottawa, 300,763 ('86)
(819,263★) G17
Owen Sound, 19,804 ('86)
(27,364★) H16
Pembroke, 14,131 ('86)
(22,560★) G17
Penticton, 23,588 ('86)
(38,966★) .... G 9
Peterborough, 61,049
('86) (87,083★) H17
Portage-la-Prairie, 13,198
('86)...................... G13
Port Alberni, 18,241
('86)...................... G 8
Prince Albert, 33,686 ('86)
(40,841★) F11
**PRINCE EDWARD
ISLAND**................ G20
Prince George, 67,621
('86)...................... F 8
Prince Rupert, 15,755
('86) (17,581★) .... F 6
QUÉBEC.................. F18
Québec, 164,580 ('86)
(603,267★) G18
Rankin Inlet, 1,374
('86)...................... D14
Red Deer, 54,425 ('86)F10
Regina, 175,064 ('86)
(186,521★) F12
Saint-Hyacinthe, 38,603
('86) (48,303★) G18
Saint-Jérôme, 23,316 ('86)
(44,048★) G18
Saint John, 76,831 ('86)
(121,265★) G19
Saint John's, 96,216 ('86)
(161,901★) G22
Sarnia, 49,033 ('86)
(85,700★) H16
SASKATCHEWAN...... F11
Saskatoon, 177,641 ('86)
(200,665★) F11
Sault Sainte Marie, 80,905
('86) (84,617★) G16
Selkirk, 10,013 ('86).... F13
Sept-Îles (Seven Islands),
25,637 ('86)
(28,050★) F19
Shawinigan, 21,470 ('86)
(61,965★) G18
Sherbrooke, 74,438 ('86)
(129,960★) G18
Sorel, 19,522 ('86)
(46,096★) G18
Sudbury, 88,717 ('86)
(148,877★) G16
Summerside, 8,020 ('86)
(15,614★) G20
Swift Current, 15,666
('86)...................... F11
Sydney Mines, 8,063
('86)...................... G20
Thetford Mines, 18,561
('86) (31,940★) G18
Thunder Bay, 112,272
('86) (122,217★) G15
Timmins, 46,657 ('86). G16
Toronto, 612,289 ('86)
(3,427,168★) H17
Trail, 7,948 ('86)
(20,257★) .... G 9
Trois-Rivières, 50,122
('86) (128,888★) G18
Truro, 12,124 ('86)
(41,516★) G20
Val-d'Or, 22,252 ('86)
(27,178★) G17
Vancouver, 431,147 ('86)
(1,380,729★) .... G 8
Victoria, 66,303 ('86)
(255,547★) .... G 8
Whitehorse, 15,199
('86)...................... D 5
Windsor, 193,111 ('86)
(253,988★) H16
Winnipeg, 594,551 ('86)
(625,304★) G13
Yellowknife, 11,753
('86)...................... D10
YUKON.................... D 5

Copyright © by Rand McNally & Co.
B-520200-264

Lambert Conformal Conic Projection

67

Alberta

Alberta

1986 CENSUS

Airdrie, 10,390 . . . . . . D 3
Athabasca, 1,970 . . . . . B 4
Banff . . . . D 3
Barrhead, 3,991 . . . . . B 3
Beaumont, 3,944 . . . . . C 4
Beaverlodge, 1,808 . . B 1
Blackfalds, 1,688 . . . . C 4
Bonnyville, 5,470 . . . . B 5
Bow Island, 1,650 . . . E 5
Brooks, 9,464 . . . . D 5
Calgary, 636,104
  (671,326★) . . . . . . D 3
Camrose, 12,968 . . . . C 4
Canmore, 4,182 . . . . . D 3
Cardston, 3,497 . . . . . E 4
Carstairs, 1,629 . . . . . D 3
Claresholm, 3,382 . . . D 4
Coaldale, 4,796 . . . . . E 4
Cochrane, 4,190 . . . . . D 3
Cold Lake, 3,195 . . . . B 5
Coronation, 1,310 . . . C 5
Crowsnest Pass,
  6,912 . . . . E 3
Devon, 3,691 . . . . . . C 4
Didsbury, 3,184 . . . . D 3
Drayton Valley, 5,290 C 3
Drumheller, 6,366 . . . D 4
Edmonton, 573,982
  (785,465★) . . . . . . C 4
Edson, 7,323 . . . . . . C 2
Fairview, 2,998 . . . . . A 1
Fort Chipewyan, 922 . f 6
Fort Macleod, 3,123 . E 4
Fort McMurray, 34,949
  (48,497★) . . . . . . A 5
Fort Saskatchewan,
  11,983 . . . . C 4
Fox Creek, 2,068 . . . . B 2
Gibbons, 2,335 . . . . C 4
Grand Centre, 3,655 . B 5
Grande Cache, 3,646 C 1
Grande Prairie,
  26,471 . . . . B 1
Grimshaw, 2,579 . . . . A 2
Hanna, 3,017 . . . . . . D 5
High Level, 3,004 . . . F 7
High Prairie, 2,817 . . C 2
High River, 5,096 . . . D 4
Hinton, 8,629 . . . . . . C 2
Innisfail, 5,535 . . . . . C 4
Jasper . . . . C 1
Lac La Biche, 2,553 . B 5
Lacombe, 6,080 . . . . C 4
La Crete, 689 . . . . . . f 7
Lake Louise, 688 . . . D 2
Lamont, 1,576 . . . . . C 4
Leduc, 13,126 . . . . . C 4
Lethbridge, 58,841 . . E 4
Lloydminster, 17,354 C 5
Magrath, 1,637 . . . . E 4
Medicine Hat, 41,804
  (50,734★) . . . . . . D 5
Morinville, 5,364 . . . C 4
Nordegg, 53 . . . . . . C 2
Okotoks, 5,214 . . . . D 4
Olds, 4,871 . . . . D 3
Peace River, 6,288 . . A 2
Penhold, 1,580 . . . . C 4
Picture Butte, 1,576 . E 4
Pincher Creek, 3,800 E 4
Ponoka, 5,473 . . . . . C 4
Provost, 1,725 . . . . . C 5
Raymond, 2,957 . . . . E 4
Redcliff, 3,834 . . . . . D 5
Red Deer, 54,425 . . . C 4
Redwater, 1,982 . . . . C 4
Rimbey, 1,786 . . . . . C 4
Rocky Mountain House,
  5,182 . . . . C 3
Saint Albert, 36,710 . C 4
Saint Paul, 5,030 . . . B 5
Sherwood Park . . . . C 4
Slave Lake, 5,429 . . . B 3
Smith, 251 . . . . B 3
Spruce Grove, 11,918 C 4
Stettler, 5,147 . . . . . C 4
Stony Plain, 5,802 . . C 3
Strathmore, 3,544 . . . D 4
Sundre, 1,712 . . . . . D 3
Swan Hills, 2,403 . . . B 3
Sylvan Lake, 3,937 . . C 3
Taber, 6,382 . . . . . . E 4
Three Hills, 2,528 . . D 4
Valleyview, 1,987 . . . B 2
Vegreville, 5,276 . . . C 4
Vermilion, 3,879 . . . . C 5
Vulcan, 1,420 . . . . . D 4
Wainwright, 4,665 . . C 5
Westlock, 4,532 . . . . B 4
Wetaskiwin, 10,071 . C 4
Whitecourt, 5,737 . . . B 3

★ Population of metropolitan
  area, including suburbs.

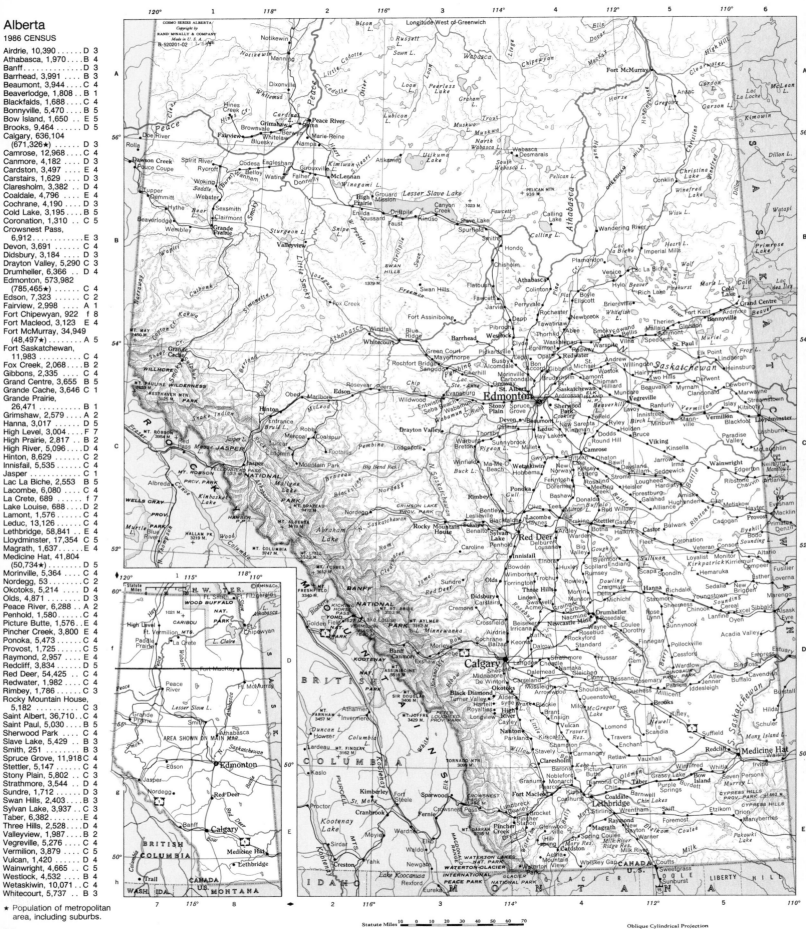

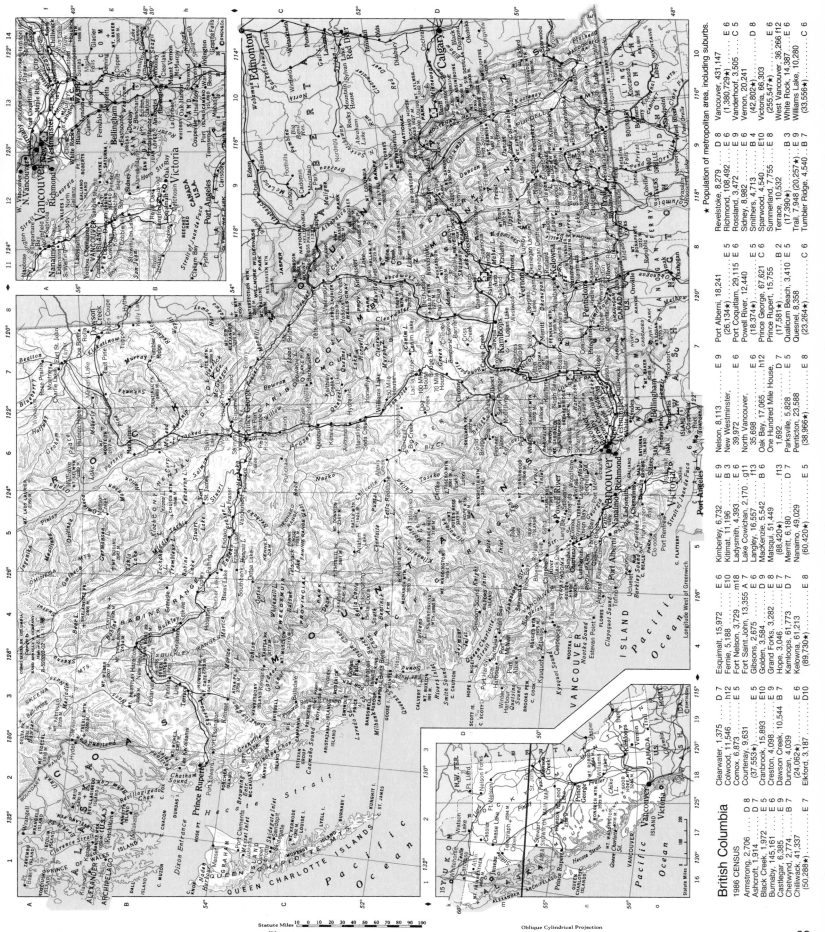

British Columbia

British Columbia
1986 CENSUS

Armstrong, 2,706	D 8	Clearwater, 1,375	D 7
Ashcroft, 1,914	D 7	Colwood, 11,546	h12
Black Creek, 1,972	E 5	Comox, 6,873	E 5
Burnaby, 145,161	E 6	Courtenay, 9,631	E 5
Castlegar, 6,385	E 9	Cranbrook, 15,893	E10
Chetwynd, 2,774	B 7	Creston, 4,098	E 9
Chilliwack, 41,337	E 7	Dawson Creek, 10,544	B 7
(50,288★)		Duncan, 4,039	E 7
		Elkford, 3,187	D10

Esquimalt, 15,972	E 6	Kimberley, 6,732	E 9
Fernie, 5,188	E10	Kitimat, 11,196	B 3
Fort Nelson, 3,729	m18	Ladysmith, 4,393	E 6
Fort Saint John, 13,355	A 7	Lake Cowichan, 2,170	g11
Gibsons, 2,675	E 6	Langley, 16,557	f13
Golden, 3,584	D 9	MacKenzie, 5,542	B 6
Grand Forks, 3,282	E 8	Matsqui, 51,449	E 7
Hope, 3,046	E 7	(88,420★)	
Kamloops, 61,773	D 7	Merritt, 6,180	D 7
(89,730★)		Nanaimo, 49,029	E 6
Kelowna, 61,213	E 8	(60,420★)	

Nelson, 8,113	E 9	Port Alberni, 18,241	E 5
New Westminster, 39,972	E 6	(26,134★)	
North Vancouver, 35,698	E 6	Port Coquitlam, 29,115	E 6
		Powell River, 12,440	E 6
Oak Bay, 17,065	h12	(18,374★)	
One Hundred Mile House, 1,692	D 7	Prince George, 67,621	C 6
		Prince Rupert, 15,755	C 6
Parksville, 5,828	E 5	Summerland, 7,755	E 8
Penticton, 23,588	E 8	Terrace, 10,532	B 2
(38,966★)			

Qualicum Beach, 3,410	E 5	Revelstoke, 8,279	D 8
Quesnel, 23,588	C 6	Richmond, 108,492	E 6
(23,264★)		Rossland, 3,472	E 9
Vancouver, 431,147	E 6	Sidney, 8,982	E 6
(1,380,729★)		Smithers, 4,713	B 4
Vanderhoof, 3,505	C 5	Sparwood, 4,540	E10
Vernon, 20,241	D 8	Summerland, 7,755	E 8
(42,802★)			
Victoria, 66,303	E 8		
(255,547★)			
West Vancouver, 36,266	f12		
White Rock, 14,387	E 6		
Williams Lake, 10,280	C 6		
(33,556★)			

★ Population of metropolitan area, including suburbs.

Statute Miles

Kilometers

Oblique Cylindrical Projection

69

Manitoba

Manitoba
1986 CENSUS

Altona, 2,958 . . . . . . E 3
Arborg, 1,018 . . . . . . D 3
Ashern, 620 . . . . D 2
Beausejour, 2,535 . . D 3
Birch River, 509 . . . . C 1
Birtle, 850 . . . . D 1
Boissevain, 1,572 . . . . E 1
Brandon, 38,708 . . . . E 2
Camperville, 588 . . . . D 1
Carberry, 1,544 . . . . . E 2
Carman, 2,500 . . . . . E 2
Churchill, 1,109 . . . . f 9
Cranberry Portage,
  849 . . . . B 1
Cross Lake, 580 . . . . B 3
Crystal City, 487 . . . . E 2
Dauphin, 8,875 . . . . . D 1
Deloraine, 1,134 . . . . E 1
Duck Bay, 559 . . . . . C 1
Easterville, 675 . . . . . C 2
East Selkirk, 572 . . . D 3
Elkhorn, 534 . . . . . . E 1
Emerson, 725 . . . . . E 3
Erickson, 565 . . . . . . D 2
Flin Flon, 7,591
  (9,211★) . . . . . . B 1
Gilbert Plains, 816 . . D 1
Gillam, 1,909 . . . . . . A 4
Gimli, 1,681 . . . . D 3
Gladstone, 951 . . . . . D 2
Glenboro, 719 . . . . . E 2
Grandview, 941 . . . . D 1
Gretna, 503 . . . . E 3
Grunthal, 639 . . . . . . E 3
Hamiota, 815 . . . . . . D 1
Hartney, 523 . . . . . . E 1
Killarney, 2,318 . . . . E 2
Lac du Bonnet, 1,021 D 3
Leaf Rapids, 1,950 . . A 1
Lorette, 1,169 . . . . . E 3
Lundar, 562 . . . . D 2
MacGregor, 854 . . . . E 2
Manitou, 856 . . . . . . E 2
McCreary, 578 . . . . . D 2
Melita, 1,239 . . . . . . E 1
Minitonas, 559 . . . . . C 1
Minnedosa, 2,520 . . D 2
Moose Lake, 541 . . . C 1
Morden, 5,004 . . . . . E 2
Morris, 1,613 . . . . . . E 3
Neepawa, 3,314 . . . . D 2
Niverville, 1,452 . . . . E 3
Norway House, 633 . . C 3
Notre Dame de Lourdes,
  628 . . . . E 2
Pilot Mound, 819 . . . E 2
Pine Falls, 831 . . . . . D 3
Plum Coulee, 677 . . . E 3
Portage la Prairie,
  13,198 . . . . E 2
Powerview, 724 . . . . D 3
Reston, 616 . . . . E 1
Rivers, 1,157 . . . . . . D 1
Riverton, 635 . . . . . . D 3
Roblin, 1,913 . . . . . . D 1
Rossburn, 664 . . . . . D 1
Russell, 1,669 . . . . . D 1
Saint Adolphe, 1,059 E 3
Sainte Anne-des-Chênes,
  1,402 . . . . E 3
Saint Claude, 610 . . . E 2
Saint Jean Baptiste,
  571 . . . . E 3
Saint Malo, 742 . . . . E 3
Saint Pierre-Jolys,
  912 . . . . E 3
Sainte Rose du Lac,
  1,030 . . . . D 2
Selkirk, 10,013 . . . . D 3
Shoal Lake, 832 . . . . D 1
Snow Lake, 1,837 . . B 1
Somerset, 534 . . . . . E 2
Souris, 1,751 . . . . . . E 1
South Indian Lake,
  743 . . . . A 2
Steinbach, 7,473 . . . E 3
Stonewall, 2,349 . . . D 3
Swan River, 3,946 . . C 1
Teulon, 953 . . . . D 3
The Pas, 6,283 . . . . C 1
Thompson, 14,701 . . B 3
Treherne, 762 . . . . . E 2
Virden, 3,054 . . . . . . E 1
Wabowden, 571 . . . . B 2
Wawanesa, 502 . . . . E 2
Winkler, 5,926 . . . . . E 3
Winnipeg, 594,551
  (625,304★) . . . . . E 3
Winnipeg Beach, 548 D 3
Winnipegosis, 832 . . D 2

★ Population of metropolitan
  area, including suburbs.

70

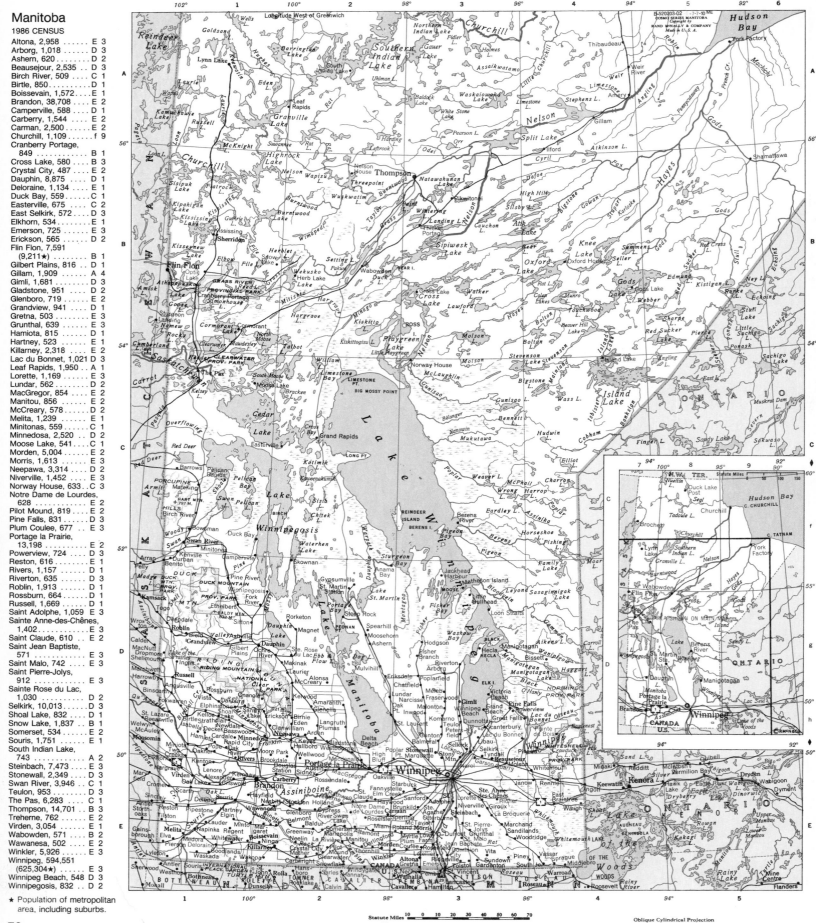

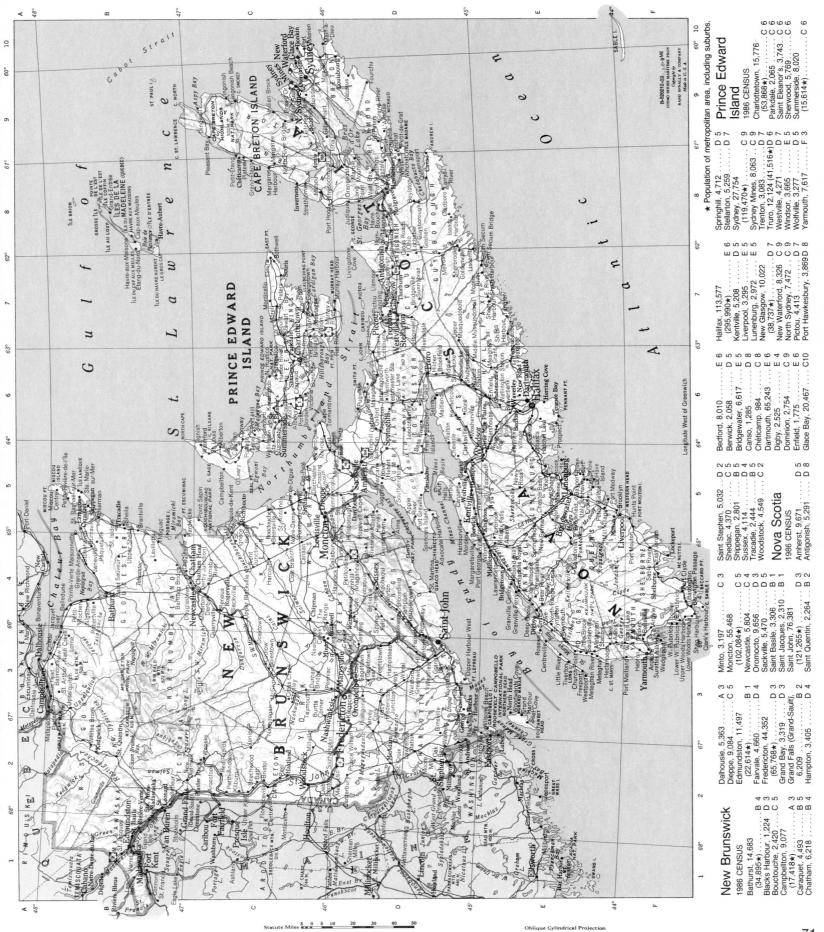

Prince Edward Island

B-502012-02 - 89-9ME
OSMG SERIES MARITIME PROV
Copyright by
RAND M°NALLY & COMPANY
Made in U.S.A.

★ Population of metropolitan area, including suburbs.

1986 CENSUS

Charlottetown, 15,776 (53,868★)	C 6
Parkdale, 2,065	C 6
Saint Eleanor's, 3,743	C 6
Sherwood, 5,769	C 6
Summerside, 8,020	C 6

New Brunswick

1986 CENSUS

Bathurst, 14,683 (34,895★)	B 4
Blacks Harbour, 1,224	D 3
Bouctouche, 2,420	C 5
Campbellton, 9,077 (17,418★)	A 3
Caraquet, 4,493	B 5
Chatham, 6,218	B 4
Dalhousie, 5,363	A 3
Dieppe, 9,084	C 5
Edmundston, 11,497 (22,614★)	B 1
Fairvale, 4,660	D 4
Fredericton, 44,352 (65,768★)	D 3
Grand Bay, 3,319	D 3
Grand Falls (Grand-Sault), 6,209	B 2
Hampton, 3,405	D 4
Minto, 3,197	C 3
Moncton, 55,468 (102,084★)	C 5
Newcastle, 5,804	B 4
Oromocto, 9,656	D 3
Sackville, 5,470	D 5
Saint Basile, 3,306	B 1
Saint Jacques, 2,310	B 1
Saint John, 76,381 (121,265★)	D 3
Saint Quentin, 2,264	B 2
Saint Stephen, 5,032	C 3
Shediac, 4,370	C 5
Shippegan, 2,801	B 5
Sussex, 4,114	C 4
Tracadie, 2,444	B 5
Woodstock, 4,549	C 2

Nova Scotia

1986 CENSUS

Amherst, 9,671	D 5
Antigonish, 5,291	D 8
Bedford, 8,010	E 6
Berwick, 2,058	D 5
Bridgewater, 6,617	E 5
Canso, 1,285	D 8
Chéticamp, 984	C 8
Dartmouth, 65,243	E 6
Digby, 2,525	E 4
Dominion, 2,754	C 9
Enfield, 1,775	E 6
Glace Bay, 20,467	C10
Halifax, 113,577 (295,990★)	E 6
Kentville, 5,208	D 5
Liverpool, 3,295	E 5
Lunenburg, 2,972	E 5
New Glasgow, 10,022	D 7
New Waterford, 8,326	C 9
North Sydney, 7,472	C 9
Pictou, 4,413	D 7
Port Hawkesbury, 3,869	D 8
Springhill, 4,712	D 5
Stellarton, 5,259	D 7
Sydney, 27,754 (119,470★)	C 9
Sydney Mines, 8,063	C 9
Trenton, 3,083	D 7
Truro, 12,124 (41,516★)	D 6
Westville, 4,271	D 7
Windsor, 3,665	E 5
Wolfville, 3,277	D 5
Yarmouth, 7,617	F 3

Statute Miles 5 0 5 10 20 30 40 50
Kilometers 5 0 5 15 25 35 45 55 65 75

Oblique Cylindrical Projection

Newfoundland

Newfoundland and Labrador

1986 CENSUS

Arnold's Cove, 1,117 . . . E 4
Badger, 1,151 . . . . . D 3
Baie Verte, 2,049 . . . . D 3
Bay Bulls, 1,114 . . . . . E 5
Bay Roberts, 4,446 . . . E 5
Bishop's Falls, 4,213 . . . D 4
Bonavista, 4,605 . . . . D 5
Botwood, 3,916 . . . . D 4
Buchans, 1,281 . . . . D 3
Burgeo, 2,582 . . . . . E 3
Burin, 2,892 . . . . . . E 4
Burnt Islands, 1,042 . . E 2
Carbonear, 5,337
 (13,082★) . . . . . . E 5
Carmanville, 987 . . . . D 4
Cartwright, 674 . . . . B 3
Catalina, 1,211 . . . . D 5
Channel-Port-aux-
 Basques, 5,901 . . . E 2
Clarenville, 2,967 . . . D 4
Conception Bay South,
 15,531 . . . . E 5
Corner Brook, 22,719
 (33,730★) . . . . . D 3
Cox's Cove, 999 . . . . D 2
Deer Lake, 4,233 . . . . D 3
Dunville, 1,833 . . . . . E 4
Durrell, 1,060 . . . . . D 4
Englee, 1,012 . . . . . C 3
Fogo, 1,153 . . . . . . D 4
Fortune, 2,370 . . . . . E 4
Gambo, 2,723 . . . . . D 4
Gander, 10,207 . . . . D 4
Glenwood, 1,038 . . . . D 4
Glovertown, 2,184 . . . D 4
Grand Bank, 3,732 . . . E 4
Grand Falls, 9,121
 (25,612★) . . . . . D 4
Hampden, 875 . . . . . D 3
Happy Valley-Goose Bay,
 7,248 . . . . B 1
Harbour Breton,
 2,432 . . . . E 4
Harbour Grace, 3,053 . E 5
Hare Bay, 1,436 . . . . D 4
Hermitage, 831 . . . . . E 4
Isle-aux-Morts, 1,203 . E 2
Joe Batt's Arm [-Barr'd
 Islands-Shoal Bay],
 1,232 . . . . D 4
King's Point, 923 . . . D 3
Labrador City, 8,664
 (11,301★) . . . . . . h 8
Lark Harbour, 829 . . D 2
La Scie, 1,429 . . . . . D 4
Lawn, 1,015 . . . . . . E 4
Lewisporte, 3,978 . . . D 4
Lourdes, 937 . . . . . D 2
Marystown, 6,660 . . . E 4
Milltown [-Head of Bay
 d'Espoir], 1,276 . . E 4
Mount Pearl, 20,293 . E 5
Musgrave Harbour,
 1,527 . . . . D 5
Nain, 1,018 . . . . g 9
New Harbour, 957 . . . D 4
Norris Arm, 1,127 . . . D 4
Norris Point, 1,010 . . . D 3
Pasadena, 3,268 . . . . D 3
Placentia, 2,016 . . . . E 5
Point Leamington,
 850 . . . . D 4
Port au Port [West-
 Aguathuna-Felix Cove],
 842 . . . . D 2
Pouch Cove, 1,576 . . E 5
Ramea, 1,380 . . . . . E 3
Robert's Arm, 1,111 . . D 4
Rocky Harbour, 1,268 D 3
Roddickton, 1,223 . . . C 3
Rose-Blanche [-Harbour le
 Cou], 967 . . . . . . E 2
Saint Alban's, 1,780 . . E 4
Saint Anthony, 3,182 . C 4
Saint George's, 1,852 . D 2
Saint John's, 96,216
 (161,901★) . . . . . E 5
Saint Lawrence,
 1,841 . . . . E 4
Shoal Harbour, 1,049 . D 4
Spaniard's Bay, 2,190 . E 5
Springdale, 3,555 . . . D 3
Stephenville, 7,994 . . D 2
Stephenville Crossing,
 2,252 . . . . D 2
Summerford, 1,169 . . D 4
Torbay, 3,730 . . . . . E 5
Trepassey, 1,460 . . . E 5
Twillingate, 1,506 . . . D 4
Upper Island Cove,
 2,055 . . . . E 5
Victoria, 1,895 . . . . . E 5
Wabana (Bell Island),
 4,057 . . . . E 5
Wabush, 2,637 . . . . . h 8
Wesleyville, 1,208 . . . D 5
Whitbourne, 1,151 . . . E 5
Windsor, 5,545 . . . . D 4
Witless Bay, 1,022 . . E 5

★ Population of metropolitan
 area, including suburbs.

Statute Miles 5 0 5 10 20 30 40 50 60
Kilometers 5 0 5 10 20 30 40 50 60 70 80

Lambert Conformal Conic Projection

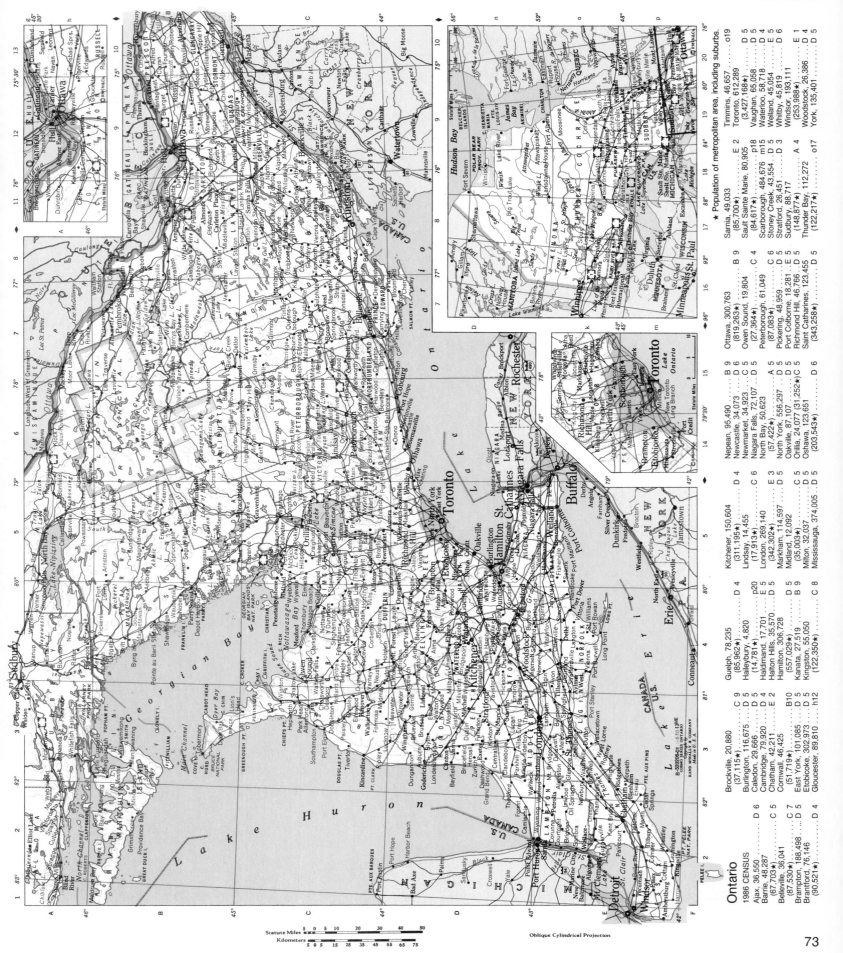

★ Population of metropolitan area, including suburbs.

Timmins, 46,657 .... o19		D 5
Toronto, 612,289		D 6
(3,427,168★) .... D 5		
Vaughan, 84,617★ p18		D 4
Waterloo, 58,718 .... m15		E 5
Waterloo, 65,058		D 6
Whitby, 45,451		E 5
Whitby, 26,451 .... D 3		
Windsor, 193,111		E 1
(253,988★)		
Woodstock, 26,386 .... D 4		
York, 135,401★		D 5

Sarnia, 49,033
(85,700★) .... E 2
Sault Sainte Marie, 80,905
(84,617★) .... C 4
Scarborough, 484,676 m15
Stoney Creek, 61,049
(57,422★) p18
Stratford, 26,451 .... D 3
Sudbury, 88,717
(148,877★) .... A 4
Thunder Bay, 112,272
(122,217★) o17

Nepean, 95,490		B 9
(311,195★) .... D 4		
Newcastle, 34,073 .... C 5		
Newmarket, 34,923 .... C 5		
Niagara Falls, 72,107		
(84,677★)		
North Bay, 50,623		A 5
(57,422★) .... E 3		
North York, 556,297 .... D 5		
Oakville, 87,107		
Orillia, 27,519 .... D 5		
Oshawa, 123,651		

Ottawa, 300,763
(819,263★) .... B 9
Owen Sound, 19,804
(27,364★) .... C 4
Peterborough, 61,049
(57,083★) .... D 6
Pickering, 48,959 .... D 5
Port Colborne, 18,281 .... E 5
Richmond Hill, 46,766 .... D 5
Saint Catharines, 123,455
(343,258★) .... D 5

Guelph, 78,235		D 4
(85,962★) .... D 5		
Haileybury, 4,820		
(14,781★)		
Haldimand, 17,701		
Halton Hills, 35,570		
Hamilton, 306,728		E 2
(557,029★) .... D 5		
Kanata, 27,519 .... B 9		
Kingston, 55,050 .... D 5		

Kitchener, 150,604
(311,195★) .... D 4
Lindsay, 14,455
(17,913★) .... C 6
London, 269,140
(342,302★) .... E 3
Markham, 114,597 .... D 5
Midland, 12,092 ....
Milton, 32,037 .... D 5
Mississauga, 374,005 .... D 5

1986 CENSUS

Ajax, 36,550		D 6
Barrie, 48,287		C 5
(67,703★)		
Belleville, 36,041		C 7
Brampton, 188,498 .... D 5		
Brantford, 76,146		D 4

Brockville, 20,880
(37,115★) .... C 9
Burlington, 116,675 .... D 5
Caledon, 29,666 .... D 4
Cambridge, 79,920 .... E 2
Chatham, 42,211 ....
Cornwall, 46,425 ....
(51,719★) ....
East York, 101,085 .... D 5
Etobicoke, 302,973 .... D 5
Gloucester, 89,810 .... h12

B-500206-01 -6-10.13ME
RAND MCNALLY & COMPANY
Made in U.S.A.

Statute Miles
Kilometers

Oblique Cylindrical Projection

73

Quebec

★ Population of metropolitan area, including suburbs.

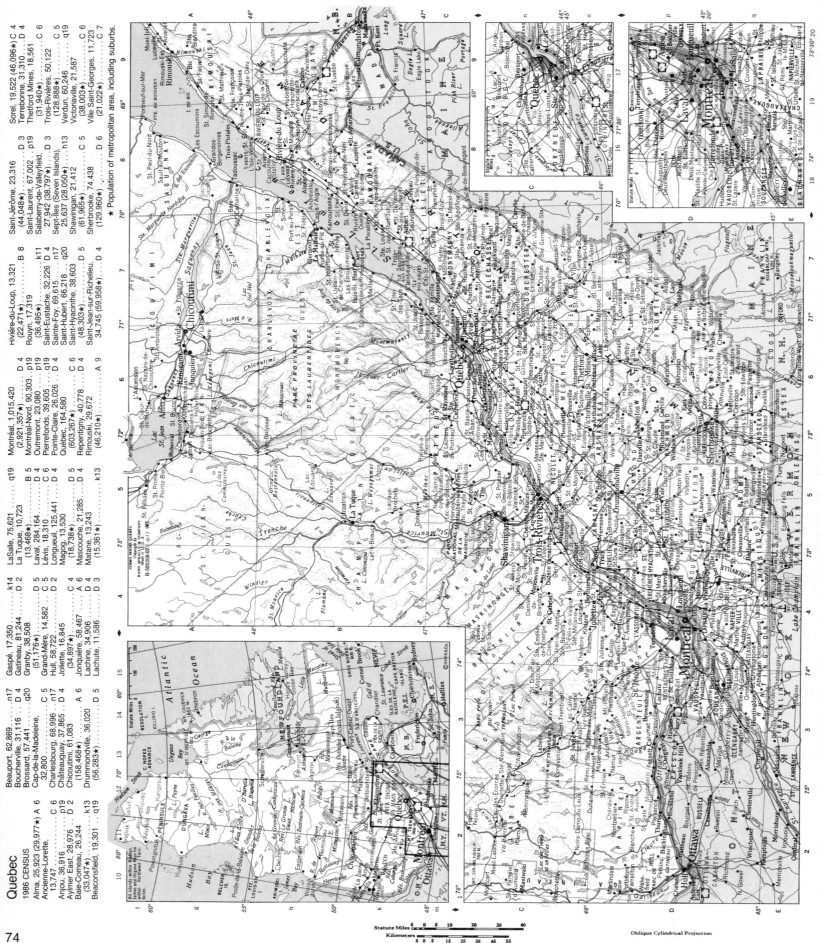

Statute Miles

Kilometers

Oblique Cylindrical Projection

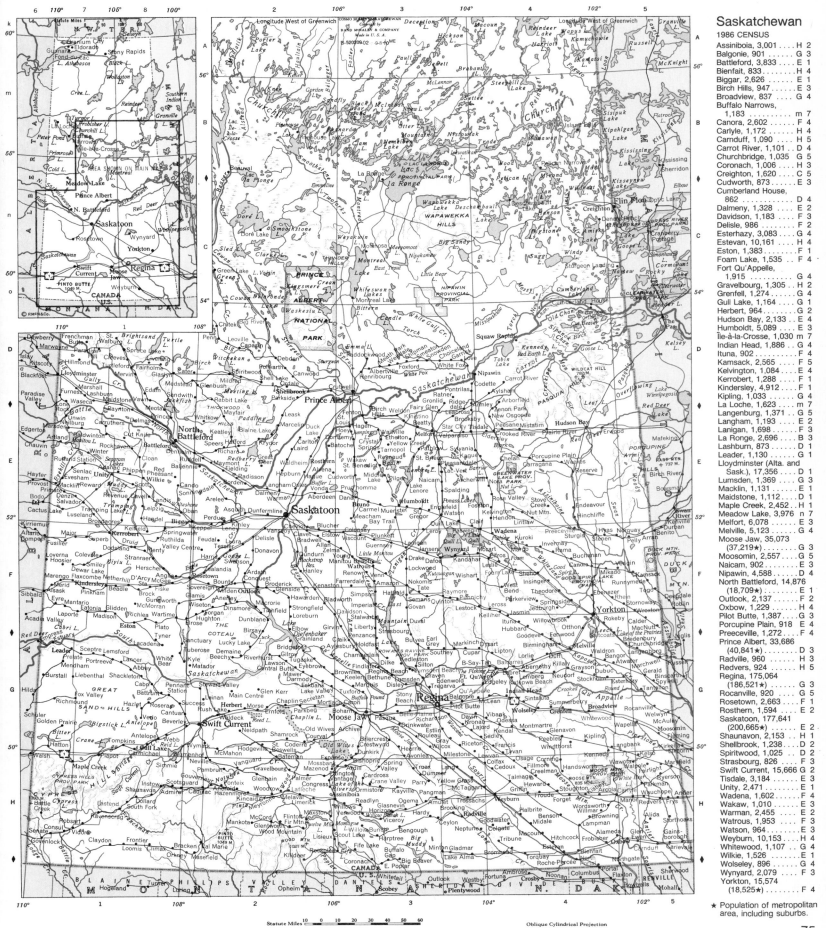

Saskatchewan

1986 CENSUS

Assiniboia, 3,001 . . . . H 2
Balgonie, 901 . . . . . . G 3
Battleford, 3,833 . . . . E 1
Bienfait, 833 . . . . . . H 4
Biggar, 2,626 . . . . . . E 1
Birch Hills, 947 . . . . . E 3
Broadview, 837 . . . . . G 4
Buffalo Narrows,
  1,183 . . . . m 7
Canora, 2,602 . . . . . F 4
Carlyle, 1,172 . . . . . H 4
Carnduff, 1,090 . . . . H 4
Carrot River, 1,101 . . D 4
Churchbridge, 1,035 . G 5
Coronach, 1,006 . . . H 3
Creighton, 1,620 . . . C 5
Cudworth, 873 . . . . E 3
Cumberland House,
  862 . . . . D 4
Dalmeny, 1,328 . . . E 2
Davidson, 1,183 . . . F 3
Delisle, 986 . . . . . F 2
Esterhazy, 3,083 . . . G 4
Estevan, 10,161 . . . H 4
Eston, 1,383 . . . . . F 1
Foam Lake, 1,535 . . F 4
Fort Qu'Appelle,
  1,915 . . . . G 4
Gravelbourg, 1,305 . . H 2
Grenfell, 1,274 . . . . G 4
Gull Lake, 1,164 . . . G 1
Herbert, 1,383 . . . . G 2
Hudson Bay, 2,133 . . E 4
Humboldt, 5,089 . . . E 3
Île-à-la-Crosse, 1,030 m 7
Indian Head, 1,886 . . G 4
Ituna, 902 . . . . . . F 4
Kamsack, 2,565 . . . F 5
Kelvington, 1,084 . . E 4
Kerrobert, 1,288 . . . F 1
Kindersley, 4,912 . . . F 1
Kipling, 1,033 . . . . G 4
La Loche, 1,623 . . . m 7
Langenburg, 1,371 . . G 5
Langham, 1,193 . . . E 2
Lanigan, 1,698 . . . . F 3
La Ronge, 2,696 . . . B 3
Lashburn, 873 . . . . D 1
Leader, 1,130 . . . . G 1
Lloydminster (Alta. and
  Sask.), 17,356 . . . D 1
Lumsden, 1,369 . . . G 3
Macklin, 1,131 . . . . E 1
Maidstone, 1,112 . . . D 1
Maple Creek, 2,452 . . H 1
Meadow Lake, 3,976 . m 7
Melfort, 6,078 . . . . E 3
Melville, 5,123 . . . . G 4
Moose Jaw, 35,073
  (37,219★) . . . . . . G 3
Moosomin, 2,557 . . . G 5
Naicam, 902 . . . . . E 3
Nipawin, 4,588 . . . . D 4
North Battleford, 14,876
  (18,709★) . . . . . . E 1
Outlook, 2,137 . . . . F 2
Oxbow, 1,229 . . . . H 4
Pilot Butte, 1,387 . . . G 3
Porcupine Plain, 918 . E 4
Preeceville, 1,272 . . . F 4
Prince Albert, 33,686
  (40,841★) . . . . . . D 3
Radville, 960 . . . . . H 3
Redvers, 924 . . . . . H 5
Regina, 175,064
  (186,521★) . . . . . . G 3
Rocanville, 920 . . . . G 5
Rosetown, 2,663 . . . F 2
Rosthern, 1,594 . . . . E 2
Saskatoon, 177,641
  (200,665★) . . . . . . E 2
Shaunavon, 2,153 . . . H 1
Shellbrook, 1,238 . . . D 2
Spiritwood, 1,025 . . . D 2
Strasbourg, 826 . . . . F 3
Swift Current, 15,666 . G 2
Tisdale, 3,184 . . . . . E 4
Unity, 2,471 . . . . . . E 1
Wadena, 1,602 . . . . F 4
Wakaw, 1,010 . . . . . E 3
Warman, 2,455 . . . . E 2
Watrous, 1,953 . . . . F 3
Watson, 964 . . . . . . E 3
Weyburn, 10,153 . . . H 4
Whitewood, 1,107 . . . G 4
Wilkie, 1,526 . . . . . E 1
Wolseley, 896 . . . . . G 4
Wynyard, 2,079 . . . . F 3
Yorkton, 15,574
  (18,525★) . . . . . . F 4

★ Population of metropolitan
  area, including suburbs.

United States of America

Akron, 223,019 ('90)...C10
ALABAMA..................E 9
ALASKA.....................M19
Albany, 101,082 ('90)..C12
Albuquerque, 384,736
　('90).....................D 5
Amarillo, 157,615 ('90)D 6
Anchorage, 226,338
　('90).....................M20
Annapolis, 33,187
　('90).....................D11
ARIZONA..................E 4
ARKANSAS...............E 8
Atlanta, 394,017 ('90)..E10
Augusta, 21,325 ('90)..C13
Austin, 465,622 ('90)...E 7
Baltimore, 736,014
　('90).....................D11
Baton Rouge, 219,531
　('90).....................E 8
Billings, 81,151 ('90)...B 5
Birmingham, 265,968
　('90).....................E 9
Bismarck, 49,256 ('90).B 6
Boise, 125,738 ('90)....C 3
Boston, 574,283 ('90)..C12
Buffalo, 328,123 ('90).C11
CALIFORNIA.............D 2
Carson City, 40,443
　('90).....................D 3
Charleston, 57,287
　('90).....................D10
Charleston, 80,414
　('90).....................E11
Charlotte, 395,934
　('90).....................D10
Chattanooga, 152,466
　('90).....................D 9
Cheyenne, 50,008
　('90).....................C 6
Chicago, 2,783,726
　('90).....................C 9
Cincinnati, 364,040
　('90).....................D10
Cleveland, 505,616
　('90).....................C10
COLORADO...............D 5
Colorado Springs, 281,140
　('90).....................D 6
Columbia, 98,052 ('90)E10
Columbus, 178,681
　('90).....................E10
Columbus, 632,910
　('90).....................D10
Concord, 36,006 ('90).C12
CONNECTICUT..........C12
Dallas, 1,006,877 ('90) E 7
DELAWARE...............D11
Denver, 467,610 ('90).D 6
Des Moines, 193,187
　('90).....................C 8
Detroit, 1,027,974
　('90).....................C10
Dover, 27,630 ('90)....D11
El Paso, 515,342 ('90).E 5
FLORIDA..................F10
Fort Wayne, 173,072
　('90).....................C 9
Fort Worth, 447,619
　('90).....................E 7
Frankfort, 25,968 ('90)D10
Fresno, 354,202 ('90)..D 3
GEORGIA..................E10
Grand Rapids, 189,126
　('90).....................C 9
Harrisburg, 52,376
　('90).....................C11
Hartford, 139,739
　('90).....................C12
Helena, 24,569 ('90)....B 4
Houston, 1,630,553
　('90).....................F 7
IDAHO......................C 4
ILLINOIS..................C 9
INDIANA..................C 9
Indianapolis, 731,327
　('90).....................D 9
IOWA.......................C 8
Jackson, 196,637 ('90)E 8
Jacksonville, 635,230
　('90).....................E10
Jefferson City, 35,481
　('90).....................D 8
Juneau, 26,751 ('90)...N21
KANSAS....................D 7
Kansas City, 435,146
　('90).....................D 8
KENTUCKY................D 9
Knoxville, 165,121
　('90).....................D10
Las Vegas, 258,295
　('90).....................D 3
Lincoln, 191,972 ('90).C 7
Little Rock, 175,795
　('90).....................E 8
Los Angeles, 3,485,398
　('90).....................E 3
LOUISIANA...............E 8
Louisville, 269,063
　('90).....................D 9
Madison, 191,262
　('90).....................C 9
MAINE......................B13
MARYLAND...............D11

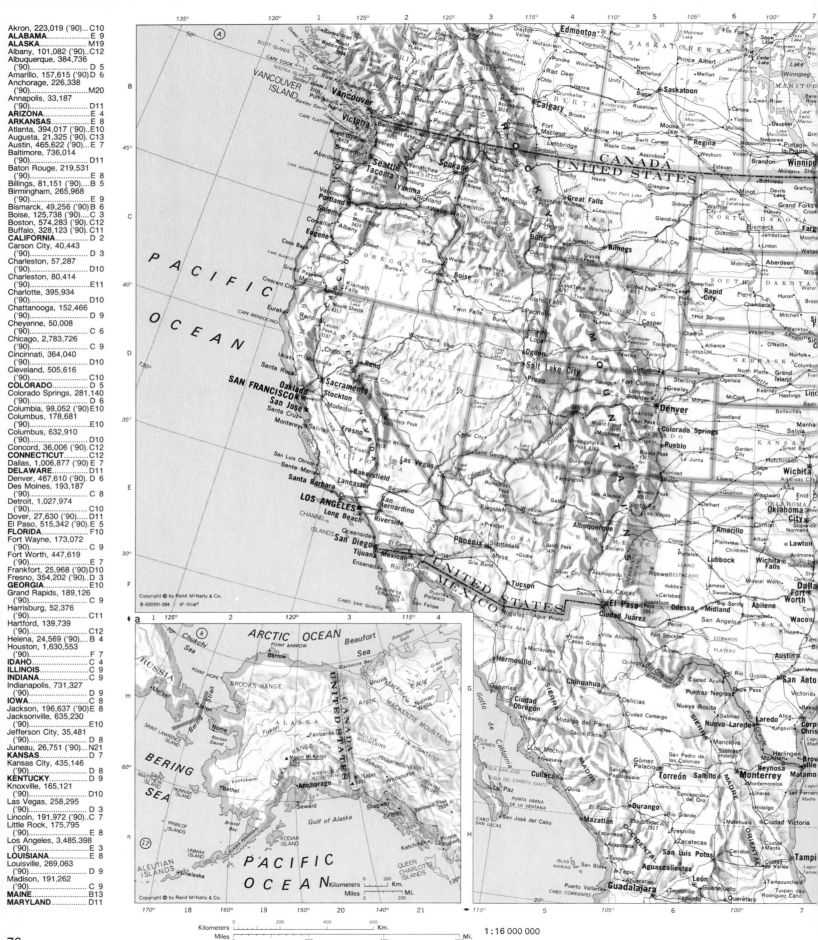

1:16 000 000

MASSACHUSETTS.....C12
Memphis, 610,337
('90)........... D 8
Miami, 358,548 ('90)...C10
MICHIGAN........... F10
Milwaukee, 628,088
('90)........... C 9
Minneapolis, 368,383
('90)........... C 8
MINNESOTA........ B 8
MISSISSIPPI......... E 9
MISSOURI......... D 8
Mobile, 196,278 ('90)...E 9
MONTANA......... B 5
Montgomery, 187,106
('90)........... E 9
Montpelier, 8,247 ('90)C12
Nashville, 487,969
('90)........... D 9
NEBRASKA......... C 7
NEVADA........... D 3
Newark, 275,221 ('90)C12
NEW HAMPSHIRE......C12
NEW JERSEY.........C12
NEW MEXICO........ E 5
New Orleans, 496,938
('90)........... F 8
NEW YORK.........C11
New York, 7,322,564
('90)...........C12
Norfolk, 261,229 ('90).D11
NORTH CAROLINA.....D11
NORTH DAKOTA...... B 6
Oakland, 372,242 ('90)D 2
OHIO............C10
OKLAHOMA......... D 7
Oklahoma City, 444,719
('90)........... D 7
Olympia, 33,840 ('90)..B 2
Omaha, 335,795 ('90). C 7
OREGON........... C 2
PENNSYLVANIA......C11
Philadelphia, 1,585,577
('90)...........D11
Phoenix, 900,013 ('90) E 4
Pierre, 12,906 ('90).... C 6
Pittsburgh, 369,879
('90)...........C11
Portland, 64,358 ('90).C12
Providence, 160,728
('90)...........C12
Raleigh, 207,951 ('90).D11
Rapid City, 54,523
('90)........... C 6
Reno, 133,850 ('90)... D 3
RHODE ISLAND.......C12
Richmond, 203,056
('90)...........D11
Rochester, 231,636
('90)...........C11
Sacramento, 369,365
('90)........... D 2
Saint Louis, 396,685
('90)........... D 8
Saint Paul, 272,235
('90)........... C 8
Saint Petersburg, 238,629
('90)...........F10
Salem, 107,786 ('90)...C 2
Salt Lake City, 159,936
('90)........... C 4
San Antonio, 935,933
('90)........... F 7
San Diego, 1,110,549
('90)........... E 3
San Francisco, 723,959
('90)........... D 2
San Jose, 782,248
('90)........... D 2
Santa Fe, 55,859 ('90) D 5
Savannah, 137,560
('90)...........E10
Seattle, 516,259 ('90)..B 2
Shreveport, 198,525
('90)........... E 8
SOUTH CAROLINA.....E10
SOUTH DAKOTA..... C 7
Spokane, 177,196
('90)........... B 3
Springfield, 105,227
('90)........... D 9
Syracuse, 163,860
('90)...........C11
Tacoma, 176,664 ('90) B 2
Tallahassee, 124,773
('90)...........E10
Tampa, 280,015 ('90)..F10
TENNESSEE........ D 9
TEXAS........... E 7
Toledo, 332,943 ('90)..C10
Topeka, 119,883 ('90).D 7
Trenton, 88,675 ('90)..C12
Tulsa, 367,302 ('90)... D 7
UNITED STATES..... D 7
UTAH........... D 4
VERMONT.........C12
VIRGINIA.........D11
WASHINGTON.........B 2
Washington, 606,900
('90)...........D11
WEST VIRGINIA......D10
Wichita, 304,011 ('90).D 7
WISCONSIN......... C 9
WYOMING...........C 5

Albers Conical Equal-Area Projection

Alabama

Alabama
1990 CENSUS

Alabaster, 14,732 .. B 3
Albertville, 14,507 .. A 3
Alexander City,
　14,917 .... C 4
Andalusia, 9,269 .... D 3
Anniston, 26,623 .... B 4
Arab, 6,321 .... A 3
Athens, 16,901 ..... A 3
Atmore, 8,046 ...... D 2
Attalla, 6,859 ...... A 3
Auburn, 33,830 ..... C 4
Bay Minette, 7,168 .. E 2
Bessemer, 33,497 ... B 3
Birmingham, 265,968 B 3
Bluff Park, 8,000('85) . g 7
Boaz, 6,928 .... A 3
Brewton, 5,885 .... D 2
Center Point,
　22,000('85) ...... f 7
Chickasaw, 6,649 .. E 1
Childersburg, 4,579 . B 3
Clanton, 7,669 ..... C 3
Cullman, 13,367 ... A 3
Decatur, 48,761 .... A 3
Demopolis, 7,512 ... C 2
Dothan, 53,589 .... D 4
Enterprise, 20,123 .. D 4
Eufaula, 13,220 .... D 4
Fairfield, 12,200 ... B 3
Fairhope, 8,485 .... E 2
Fayette, 4,909 ..... B 2
Florence, 36,426 ... A 2
Fort Payne, 11,838 .. A 4
Frisco City, 1,581 .. D 2
Fultondale, 6,400 .. f 7
Gadsden, 42,523 ... A 3
Gardendale, 9,251 . B 3
Geneva, 4,681 .... D 4
Greenville, 7,492 .. D 3
Guntersville, 7,038 . A 3
Haleyville, 4,452 ... A 2
Hamilton, 5,787 .... A 2
Hartselle, 10,795 ... A 3
Homewood, 22,922 . g 7
Hueytown, 15,280 .. g 6
Huntsville, 159,789 . A 3
Irondale, 9,454 .... f 7
Jackson, 5,819 .... D 2
Jacksonville, 10,283 . B 4
Jasper, 13,553 .... B 2
Lanett, 8,985 ..... C 4
Leeds, 9,946 ..... B 3
Millbrook, 6,050 ... C 3
Mobile, 196,278 ... E 1
Monroeville, 6,993 . D 2
Montgomery, 187,106 C 3
Moundville, 1,348 .. C 2
Mountain Brook,
　19,810 .... g 7
Muscle Shoals, 9,611 A 2
Northport, 17,366 .. B 2
Oneonta, 4,844 ... B 3
Opelika, 22,122 ... C 4
Opp, 6,985 .... D 3
Oxford, 9,362 .... B 4
Ozark, 12,922 .... D 4
Pelham, 9,765 .... B 3
Pell City, 8,118 ... B 3
Phenix City, 25,312 . C 4
Piedmont, 5,288 ... B 4
Pleasant Grove, 8,458 g 7
Prattville, 19,587 .. C 3
Prichard, 34,311 ... E 1
Rainbow City, 7,673 . A 3
Roanoke, 6,362 ... B 4
Russellville, 7,812 .. A 2
Saraland, 11,751 ... E 1
Scottsboro, 13,786 .. A 3
Selma, 23,755 ..... C 2
Sheffield, 10,380 ... A 2
Spanish Fort,
　3,415('80) .... E 2
Sylacauga, 12,520 .. B 3
Talladega, 18,175 .. B 3
Tallassee, 5,112 ... C 4
Tarrant, 8,046 ..... B 3
Theodore, 6,392('80) E 1
Tillmans Corner,
　5,000('85) ...... E 1
Troy, 13,051 ..... D 4
Tuscaloosa, 77,759 . B 2
Tuscumbia, 8,413 .. A 2
Tuskegee, 12,257 .. C 4
Vestavia Hills, 19,749 g 7
Warrior, 3,280 .... B 3
Wetumpka, 4,670 .. C 3

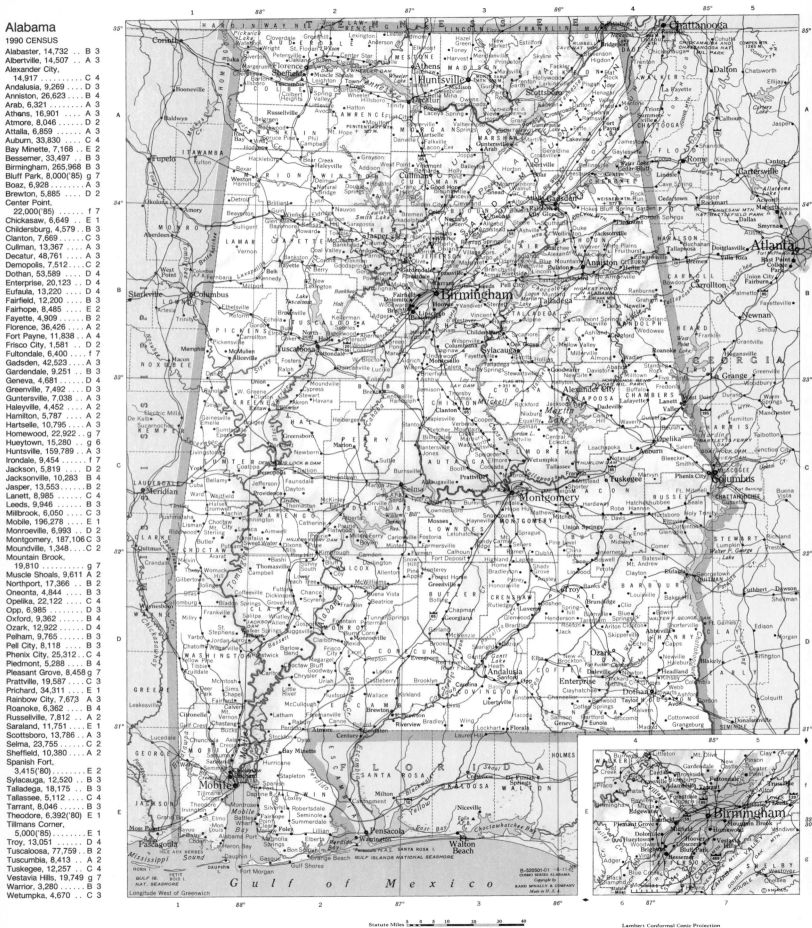

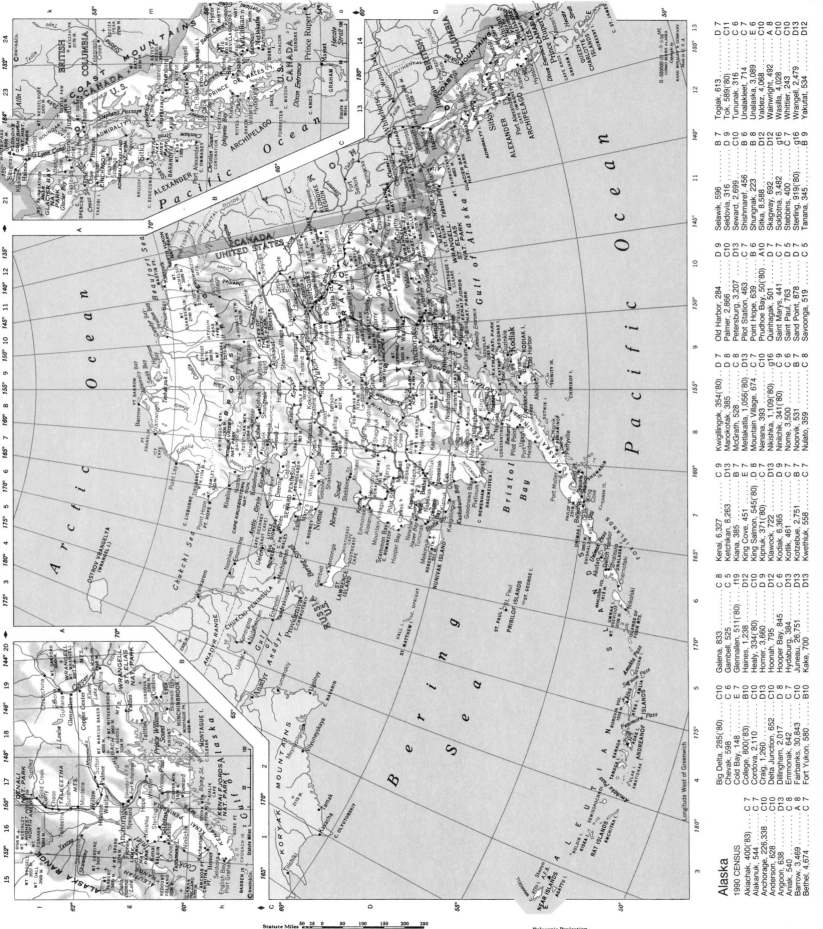

Arizona

Arizona

1990 CENSUS

Ajo, 5,189('80) .... E 3
Apache Junction,
  18,100 .... m 9
Avondale, 16,169 ...... D 3
Bagdad, 2,331('80) .... C 2
Benson, 3,824 .... F 5
Bisbee, 6,288 .... F 6
Black Canyon City,
  850('86) .... C 3
Buckeye, 5,038 .... D 3
Bullhead City, 21,951 . B 1
Camp Verde, 6,243 .... C 4
Casa Grande, 19,082 .. E 4
Casas Adobes,
  12,155('86) .... E 5
Cashion, 3,014('80) .. m 8
Cave Creek, 2,925 .... D 4
Chandler, 90,533 ..... D 4
Chinle, 2,815('80) ... A 6
Chino Valley, 4,837 .. C 3
Claypool, 2,362('80) . D 5
Clifton, 2,840 .... D 6
Coolidge, 6,927 ...... E 4
Cottonwood, 5,918 .... C 3
Crane, 2,650('86) .... E 1
Douglas, 12,822 ...... F 6
Eagar, 4,025 .... C 6
El Mirage, 5,001 ..... k 8
Eloy, 7,211 .... E 4
Flagstaff, 45,857 .... B 4
Florence, 7,510 ...... D 4
Fort Defiance,
  3,431('80) .... B 6
Ganado, 3,400('86) ... B 6
Gila Bend, 1,747 ..... E 3
Gilbert, 29,188 ...... D 4
Glendale, 148,134 .... D 3
Globe, 6,062 .... D 5
Goodyear, 6,258 ...... D 3
Grand Canyon,
  1,348('80) .... A 3
Green Valley,
  7,999('80) .... F 5
Guadalupe, 5,458 .... m 9
Holbrook, 4,686 ...... C 5
Huachuca City, 1,782 . F 5
Kayenta, 3,343('80) .. A 5
Kearny, 2,262 .... D 5
Kingman, 12,722 ...... B 1
Lake Havasu City,
  24,363 .... C 1
Lakeside-Pinetop,
  2,422 .... C 6
Litchfield Park, 3,303 m 8
Mammoth, 1,845 ...... E 5
Mesa, 288,091 .... D 4
Miami, 2,018 .... D 5
Nogales, 19,489 ...... F 5
Oracle, 2,484('80) ... E 5
Page, 6,598 .... A 4
Paradise Valley,
  11,671 .... k 9
Parker, 2,897 .... C 1
Payson, 8,377 .... C 4
Peoria, 50,618 .... D 3
Phoenix, 900,013 ..... D 3
Prescott, 26,455 ..... C 3
Sacaton, 1,951('80) .. D 4
Safford, 7,359 .... E 6
Saint Johns, 3,294 ... C 6
San Carlos,
  2,668('80) .... D 5
San Luis, 70('86) .... E 3
San Manuel,
  5,443('80) .... E 5
Scottsdale, 130,069 .. D 4
Sedona, 7,720 .... C 4
Sells, 1,864('80) .... F 4
Show Low, 5,019 ...... C 5
Sierra Vista, 32,983 . F 5
Snowflake, 3,679 ..... C 5
Somerton, 5,282 ...... E 1
South Tucson, 5,093 .. E 5
Sun City, 57,000 ..... k 8
Superior, 3,468 ...... D 4
Surprise, 7,122 ...... k 8
Taylor, 2,418 .... C 5
Tempe, 141,865 .... D 4
Thatcher, 3,763 ...... E 6
Tolleson, 4,434 ...... m 8
Tombstone, 1,220 ..... F 5
Tuba City, 5,045('80) A 4
Tucson, 405,390 ...... E 5
Twin Knolls,
  5,210('86) .... m 9
Wickenburg, 4,515 .... D 3
Willcox, 3,122 .... E 6
Williams, 2,532 ...... B 3
Window Rock,
  2,230('80) .... B 6
Winslow, 8,190 .... C 5
Youngtown, 2,542 ..... k 8
Yuma, 54,923 .... E 1

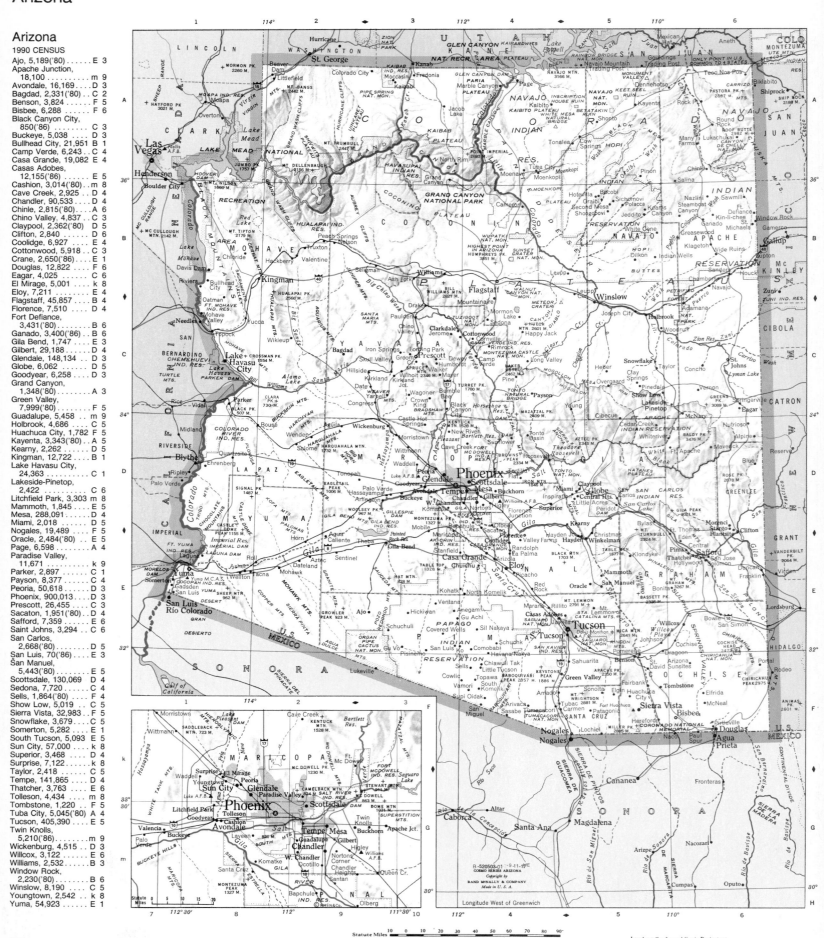

Arkansas

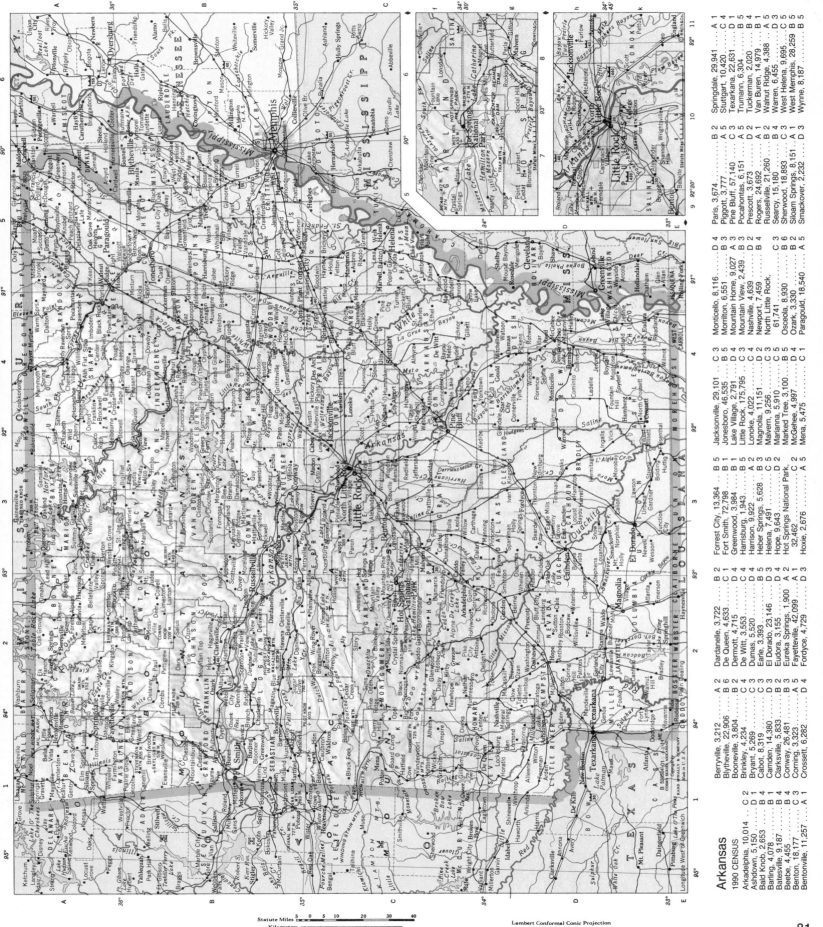

Arkansas

1990 CENSUS

Arkadelphia, 10,014	C 2	
Ashdown, 5,150	D 1	
Bald Knob, 2,653	B 4	
Barling, 4,078	B 4	
Batesville, 9,187	B 4	
Beebe, 4,455	C 3	
Benton, 18,177	C 3	
Bentonville, 11,257	A 1	
Berryville, 3,212	A 2	
Blytheville, 22,906	B 6	
Booneville, 3,804	B 2	
Brinkley, 4,234	C 4	
Bryant, 5,269	C 3	
Cabot, 8,319	C 3	
Camden, 14,380	D 2	
Clarksville, 5,833	B 2	
Conway, 26,481	C 3	
Corning, 3,323	A 5	
Crossett, 6,282	D 4	
Dardanelle, 3,722	B 2	
De Queen, 4,633	C 1	
Dermott, 4,715	D 4	
De Witt, 3,553	C 4	
Dumas, 5,520	C 4	
Earle, 3,393	B 5	
El Dorado, 23,146	D 3	
Eudora, 3,155	D 4	
Eureka Springs, 1,900	A 2	
Fayetteville, 42,099	A 1	
Fordyce, 4,729	D 3	
Forrest City, 13,364	B 5	
Fort Smith, 72,798	B 1	
Greenwood, 3,984	B 1	
Harrisburg, 1,943	B 5	
Harrison, 9,922	A 2	
Heber Springs, 5,628	B 3	
Helena, 7,491	C 5	
Hope, 9,643	D 2	
Hot Springs National Park, 32,462	C 2	
Hoxie, 2,676	A 5	
Jacksonville, 29,101	C 3	
Jonesboro, 46,535	B 5	
Lake Village, 2,791	D 4	
Little Rock, 175,795	C 3	
Lonoke, 4,022	C 4	
Magnolia, 11,151	D 2	
Malvern, 9,256	C 3	
Marianna, 5,910	C 5	
Marked Tree, 3,100	B 5	
McGehee, 4,997	D 4	
Mena, 5,475	C 1	
Monticello, 8,116	D 4	
Morrilton, 6,551	B 3	
Mountain Home, 9,027	A 3	
Mountain View, 2,439	B 3	
Nashville, 4,639	D 2	
Newport, 7,459	B 4	
North Little Rock, 61,741	C 3	
Osceola, 8,930	B 6	
Ozark, 3,330	B 2	
Paragould, 18,540	A 5	
Paris, 3,674	D 4	
Piggott, 3,777	A 5	
Pine Bluff, 57,140	C 3	
Pocahontas, 6,151	A 5	
Prescott, 3,673	D 2	
Rogers, 24,692	A 1	
Russellville, 21,260	B 2	
Searcy, 15,180	C 3	
Sherwood, 18,893	C 3	
Siloam Springs, 8,151	A 1	
Smackover, 2,232	D 3	
Springdale, 29,941	A 1	
Stuttgart, 10,420	C 4	
Texarkana, 22,631	D 1	
Trumann, 6,304	B 5	
Tuckerman, 2,020	B 4	
Van Buren, 14,979	A 1	
Walnut Ridge, 4,388	A 5	
Warren, 6,455	D 3	
West Helena, 9,695	C 5	
West Memphis, 28,259	B 5	
Wynne, 8,187	B 5	

Statute Miles
Kilometers

Lambert Conformal Conic Projection

California

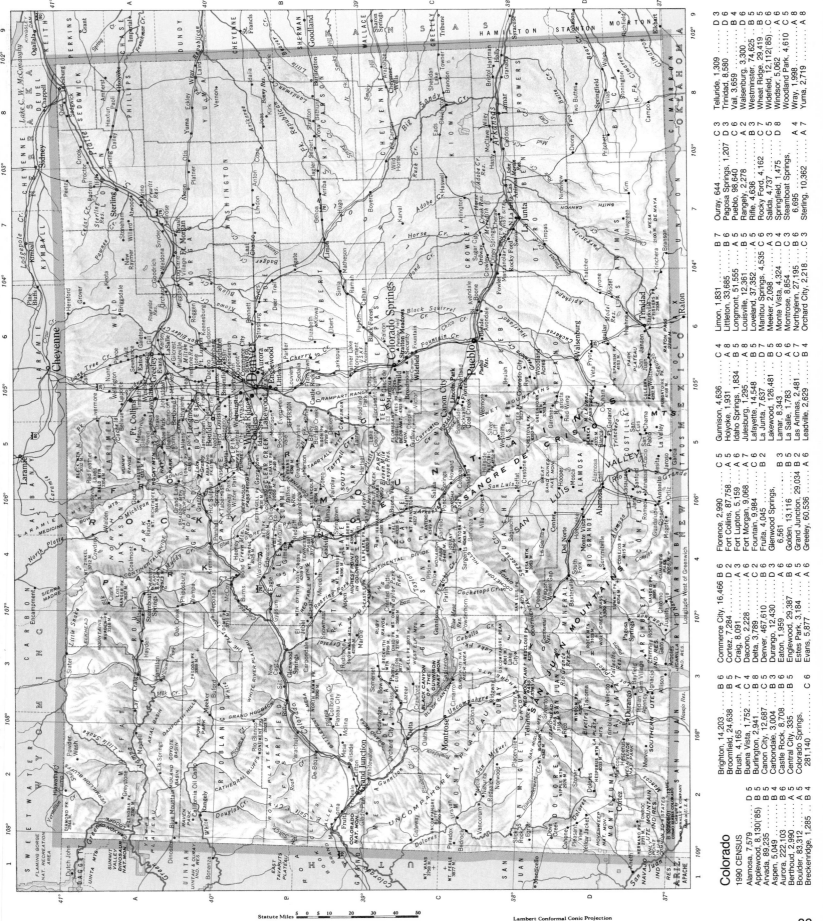

Statute Miles 5 0 5 10 20 30 40 50

Kilometers 5 0 5 15 25 35 45 55 65 75

Lambert Conformal Conic Projection

Colorado

1990 CENSUS

Alamosa, 7,579	D 5	
Applewood, 8,130('85)	B 5	
Arvada, 89,235	B 5	
Aspen, 5,049	C 4	
Aurora, 222,103	B 6	
Berthoud, 2,990	A 5	
Boulder, 83,312	A 5	
Breckenridge, 1,285	B 4	

Brighton, 14,203	B 6	
Broomfield, 24,638	D 2	
Brush, 4,165	A 7	
Buena Vista, 1,752	C 4	
Burlington, 2,941	B 8	
Canon City, 12,687	C 5	
Carbondale, 3,004	B 3	
Castle Rock, 8,708	B 5	
Central City, 335	A 5	
Colorado Springs,		
281,140	C 6	

Commerce City, 16,466	C 5	
Cortez, 7,284	D 2	
Craig, 8,091	A 3	
Dacono, 2,228	A 6	
Delta, 3,789	C 2	
Denver, 467,610	B 5	
Durango, 12,430	D 3	
Eaton, 1,959	A 6	
Englewood, 29,387	B 6	
Estes Park, 3,184	A 5	
Evans, 5,877	A 6	

Florence, 2,990	C 5	
Fort Collins, 87,758	A 5	
Fort Lupton, 5,159	A 6	
Julesburg, 1,295	A 8	
Lafayette, 14,548	D 7	
La Junta, 7,637	B 5	
Lakewood, 126,481	B 5	
Lamar, 8,343	C 8	
La Salle, 1,783	A 6	
Las Animas, 2,481	C 7	
Leadville, 2,629	B 4	

Gunnison, 4,636	C 3	
Holyoke, 1,931	A 8	
Idaho Springs, 1,834	B 5	
Lafayette, 14,548		
Loveland, 37,352	A 5	
Manitou Springs, 4,535	C 6	
Meeker, 2,098	A 3	
Monte Vista, 4,324	D 4	
Montrose, 8,854	C 3	
Northglenn, 27,195	B 6	
Orchard City, 2,218	C 3	

Limon, 1,831	C 4	
Littleton, 33,685	A 8	
Longmont, 51,555	B 5	
Louisville, 12,361	A 5	
Loveland, 37,352		
La Junta, 7,637		
Lakewood, 126,481		
Monte Vista, 4,324		

Ouray, 644	B 7	
Pagosa Springs, 1,207	B 6	
Pueblo, 98,640	A 5	
Rangely, 2,278	B 3	
Rifle, 4,636	A 5	
Rocky Ford, 4,162	C 7	
Salida, 4,737	C 5	
Springfield, 1,475	D 8	
Steamboat Springs,		
6,695	A 4	
Sterling, 10,362	A 7	

Telluride, 1,309	D 3	
Trinidad, 8,580	D 6	
Vail, 3,659	B 4	
Walsenburg, 3,300	D 6	
Westminster, 74,625	B 5	
Wheat Ridge, 29,419	C 6	
Widefield, 12,112('85)	C 6	
Windsor, 5,062	A 6	
Woodland Park, 4,610	C 5	
Wray, 1,998	A 8	
Yuma, 2,719	A 8	

Connecticut

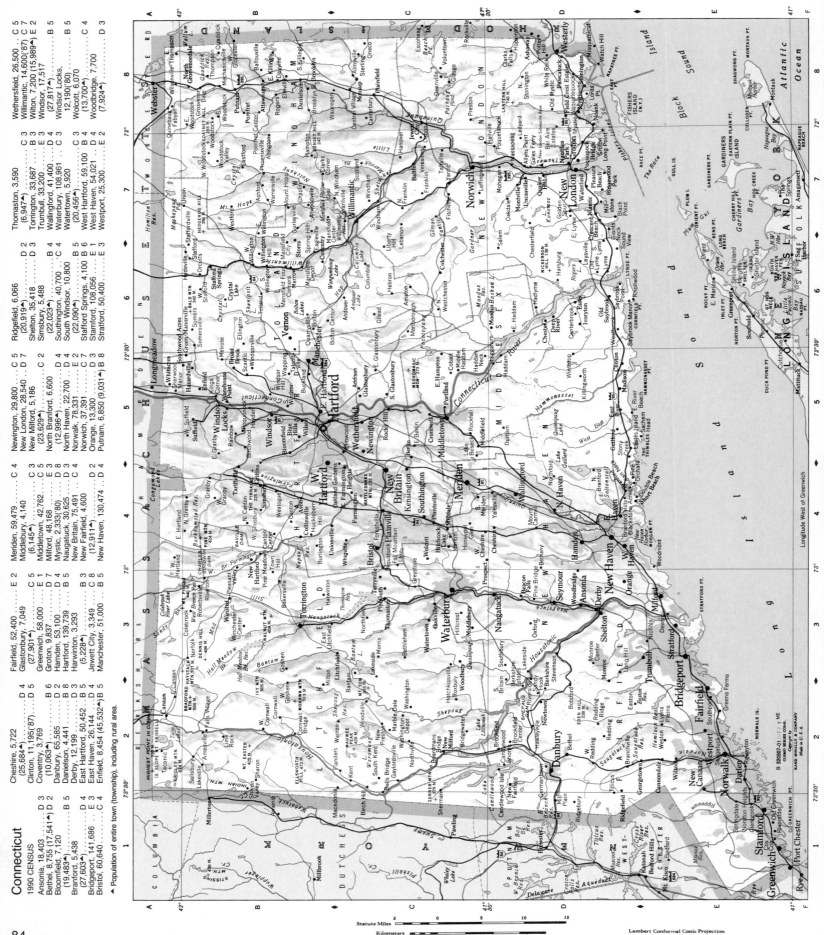

Connecticut

1990 CENSUS

Ansonia, 18,403		D 4
Bethel, 8,755 (17,541▲)		D 2
Bloomfield, 7,120		B 5
Branford, 5,438		D 4
Bristol, 60,640		C 4
Cheshire, 5,722		D 4
(25,684▲)		D 4
Clinton, 11,195('87)		D 5
Coventry, 3,769		C 2
(10,063▲)		B 6
Danbury, 65,585		D 2
Danielson, 4,441		B 8
Derby, 12,199		D 3
East Hartford, 50,452		B 5
(27,603▲)		D 4
East Haven, 26,144		E 3
(5,228▲)		C 8
Enfield, 8,454 (45,532▲)		B 5

Fairfield, 52,400		E 2
Glastonbury, 7,049		C 5
(27,901▲)		C 5
Greenwich, 58,000		E 1
Groton, 10,063		D 7
North Branford, 6,600		D 4
Hamden, 53,100		D 4
Hartford, 139,739		B 5
Hartwinton, 3,293		C 4
Jewett City, 3,349		C 7
Manchester, 51,000		B 5

Newington, 29,800		C 5
New London, 28,540		D 7
New Milford, 5,186		C 2
(23,629▲)		C 2
Middletown, 42,762		C 5
North Branford, 6,600		D 4
(12,996▲)		D 4
Mystic, 2,333('80)		C 4
Naugatuck, 30,625		D 3
South Windsor, 10,800		B 5
New Britain, 75,491		C 4
Norwalk, 78,331		E 2
(22,090▲)		E 2
Norwich, 37,391		C 7
Orange, 13,300		D 4
(12,911▲)		D 2
Putnam, 6,850 (9,031▲)		B 8

Ridgefield, 6,066		D 2
(20,919▲)		D 3
Shelton, 35,418		D 3
Simsbury, 5,488		B 5
(22,023▲)		C 4
Southington, 40,700		C 4
Stafford Springs, 4,100		B 7
(20,456▲)		A 7
Stamford, 108,056		E 1
Stratford, 50,400		E 3

Thomaston, 3,590		C 5
(6,947▲)		C 7
Torrington, 33,687		B 3
Trumbull, 33,200		E 3
Wallingford, 41,400		D 4
Waterbury, 108,961		C 3
Watertown, 5,920		C 3
West Hartford, 59,100		C 5
West Haven, 54,021		D 4
Westport, 25,300		E 2

Wethersfield, 26,500		C 5
Willimantic, 14,600('87)		C 7
Wilton, 7,200 (15,989▲)		E 2
Windsor, 17,517		B 5
(27,817▲)		B 5
Windsor Locks,		B 5
12,190('80)		
Wolcott, 6,070		C 4
(13,700▲)		D 3
Woodbridge, 7,700		
(7,924▲)		

▲ Population of entire town (township), including rural area.

84

Lambert Conformal Conic Projection

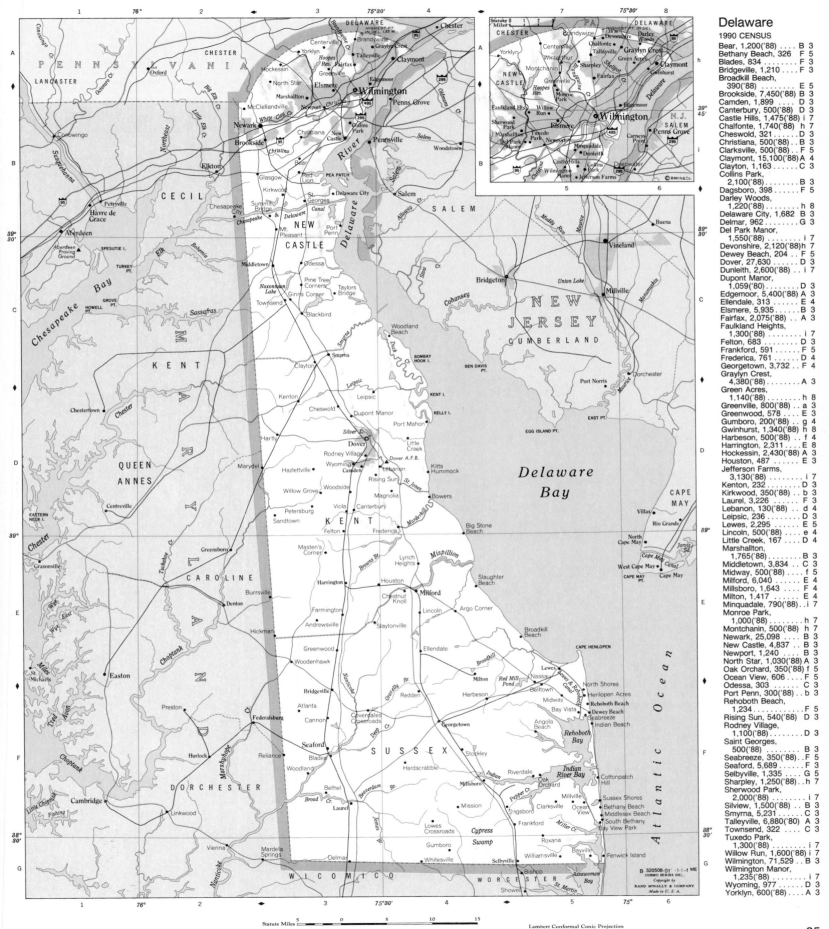

Delaware

1990 CENSUS

Bear, 1,200('88) .... B 3
Bethany Beach, 326 .. F 5
Blades, 834 .... F 3
Bridgeville, 1,210 .... F 3
Broadkill Beach,
  390('88) .... E 5
Brookside, 7,450('88) B 3
Camden, 1,899 ..... D 3
Canterbury, 500('88) . D 3
Castle Hills, 1,475('88) i 7
Chalfonte, 1,740('88) . h 7
Cheswold, 321 ...... D 3
Christiana, 500('88) .. B 3
Clarksville, 500('88) .. F 5
Claymont, 15,100('88) A 3
Clayton, 1,163 ..... C 3
Collins Park,
  2,100('88) .... B 3
Dagsboro, 398 ...... F 5
Darley Woods,
  1,220('88) .... h 8
Delaware City, 1,682 D 3
Delmar, 962 .... G 3
Del Park Manor,
  1,550('88) .... i 7
Devonshire, 2,120('88) h 7
Dewey Beach, 204 .. F 5
Dover, 27,630 ..... D 3
Dunleith, 2,600('88) .. i 7
Dupont Manor,
  1,059('80) .... D 3
Edgemoor, 5,400('88) A 3
Ellendale, 313 ..... E 4
Elsmere, 5,935 .... B 3
Fairfax, 2,075('88) .. A 3
Faulkland Heights,
  1,300('88) .... i 7
Felton, 683 .... D 3
Frankford, 591 ..... F 5
Frederica, 761 ..... D 4
Georgetown, 3,732 .. F 4
Graylyn Crest,
  4,380('88) .... A 3
Green Acres,
  1,140('88) .... h 8
Greenville, 800('88) .. a 3
Greenwood, 578 .... E 3
Gumboro, 200('88) .. g 4
Gwinhurst, 1,340('88) h 8
Harbeson, 500('88) .. f 4
Harrington, 2,311 .... E 8
Hockessin, 2,430('88) A 3
Houston, 487 ...... E 3
Jefferson Farms,
  3,130('88) .... i 7
Kenton, 232 .... D 3
Kirkwood, 350('88) .. b 3
Laurel, 3,226 ...... F 3
Lebanon, 130('88) .. d 4
Leipsic, 236 .... D 3
Lewes, 2,295 ...... E 5
Lincoln, 500('88) ... e 4
Little Creek, 167 ... D 4
Marshallton,
  1,765('88) .... B 3
Middletown, 3,834 .. C 3
Midway, 500('88) ... f 5
Milford, 6,040 ..... E 4
Millsboro, 1,643 .... F 4
Milton, 1,417 ...... E 4
Minquadale, 790('88) . i 7
Monroe Park,
  1,000('88) .... h 7
Montchanin, 500('88) h 7
Newark, 25,098 .... B 3
New Castle, 4,837 .. B 3
Newport, 1,240 .... B 3
North Star, 1,030('88) A 3
Oak Orchard, 350('88) f 5
Ocean View, 606 ... F 5
Odessa, 303 ...... C 3
Port Penn, 300('88) .. b 3
Rehoboth Beach,
  1,234 .... F 5
Rising Sun, 540('88) D 3
Rodney Village,
  1,100('88) .... D 3
Saint Georges,
  500('88) .... B 3
Seabreeze, 350('88) . F 5
Seaford, 5,689 ..... F 3
Selbyville, 1,335 ... G 5
Sharpley, 1,250('88) . h 7
Sherwood Park,
  2,000('88) .... i 7
Silview, 1,500('88) .. B 3
Smyrna, 5,231 ..... D 3
Talleyville, 6,880('80) A 3
Townsend, 322 ..... C 3
Tuxedo Park,
  1,300('88) .... i 7
Willow Run, 1,600('88) i 7
Wilmington, 71,529 .. B 3
Wilmington Manor,
  1,235('88) .... i 7
Wyoming, 977 ..... D 3
Yorklyn, 600('88) .... A 3

Florida

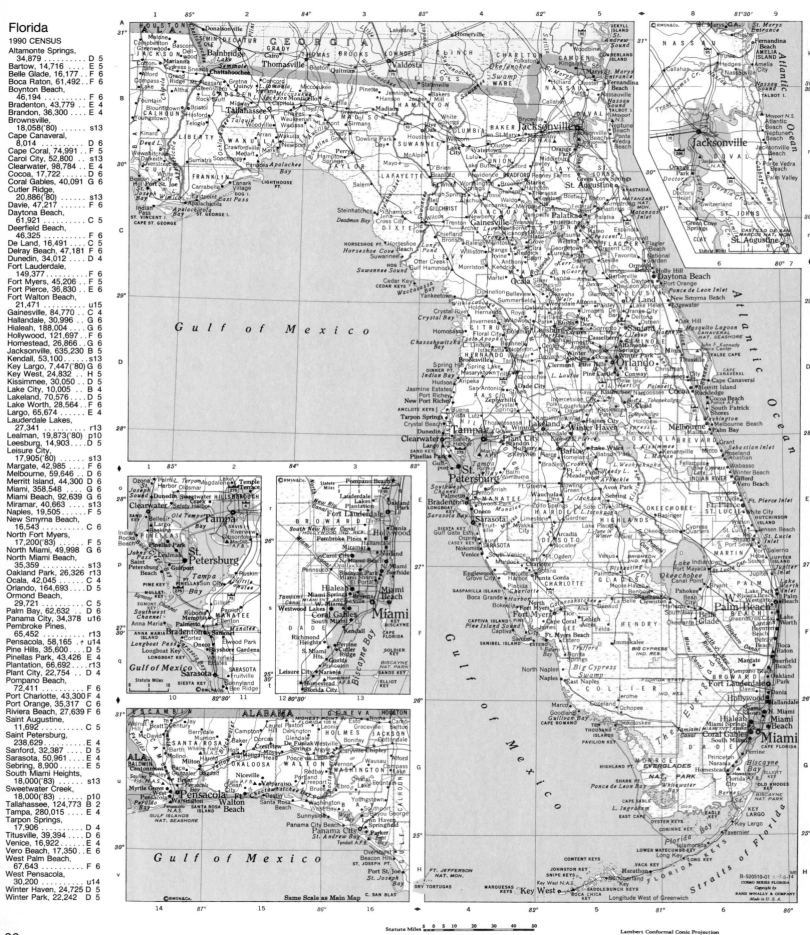

Florida

1990 CENSUS

Altamonte Springs,
34,879 . . . . D 5
Bartow, 14,716 . . . . . . E 5
Belle Glade, 16,177 . . F 6
Boca Raton, 61,492 . . F 6
Boynton Beach,
46,194 . . . . F 6
Bradenton, 43,779 . . . E 4
Brandon, 36,300 . . . . E 4
Brownsville,
18,058('80) s13
Cape Canaveral,
8,014 . . . . D 6
Cape Coral, 74,991 . . F 5
Carol City, 52,800 . . . s13
Clearwater, 98,784 . . E 4
Cocoa, 17,722 . . . . . . D 6
Coral Gables, 40,091 . G 6
Cutler Ridge,
20,886('80) s13
Davie, 47,217 . . . . . . F 6
Daytona Beach,
61,921 . . . . C 5
Deerfield Beach,
46,325 . . . . F 6
De Land, 16,491 . . . . C 5
Delray Beach, 47,181 . F 6
Dunedin, 34,012 . . . . D 4
Fort Lauderdale,
149,377 . . . . F 6
Fort Myers, 45,206 . . F 5
Fort Pierce, 36,830 . . E 6
Fort Walton Beach,
21,471 . . . . u15
Gainesville, 84,770 . . C 5
Hallandale, 30,996 . . G 6
Hialeah, 188,004 . . . . G 6
Hollywood, 121,697 . . F 6
Homestead, 26,866 . . G 6
Jacksonville, 635,230 B 5
Kendall, 53,100 . . . . . s13
Key Largo, 7,447('80) G 6
Key West, 24,832 . . . H 5
Kissimmee, 30,050 . . D 5
Lake City, 10,005 . . . B 4
Lakeland, 70,576 . . . . D 5
Lake Worth, 28,564 . . F 6
Largo, 65,674 . . . . . . E 4
Lauderdale Lakes,
27,341 . . . . r13
Lealman, 19,873('80) p10
Leesburg, 14,903 . . . D 5
Leisure City,
17,905('80) s13
Margate, 42,985 . . . . F 6
Melbourne, 59,646 . . D 6
Merritt Island, 44,300 D 6
Miami, 358,548 . . . . . G 6
Miami Beach, 92,639 G 6
Miramar, 40,663 . . . . s13
Naples, 19,505 . . . . . F 5
New Smyrna Beach,
16,543 . . . . C 6
North Fort Myers,
17,200('83) . . . . . . F 5
North Miami, 49,998 . G 6
North Miami Beach,
35,359 . . . . s13
Oakland Park, 26,326 r13
Ocala, 42,045 . . . . . . C 4
Orlando, 164,693 . . . D 5
Ormond Beach,
29,721 . . . . C 5
Palm Bay, 62,632 . . . D 6
Panama City, 34,378 u16
Pembroke Pines,
65,452 . . . . r13
Pensacola, 58,165 . + u14
Pine Hills, 35,600 . . . D 5
Pinellas Park, 43,426 E 4
Plantation, 66,692 . . . r13
Plant City, 22,754 . . . D 4
Pompano Beach,
72,411 . . . . F 6
Port Charlotte, 43,300 F 4
Port Orange, 35,317 . C 6
Riviera Beach, 27,639 F 6
Saint Augustine,
11,692 . . . . C 5
Saint Petersburg,
238,629 . . . . E 4
Sanford, 32,387 . . . . D 5
Sarasota, 50,961 . . . E 4
Sebring, 8,900 . . . . . E 5
South Miami Heights,
18,000('83) s13
Sweetwater Creek,
18,000('83) p10
Tallahassee, 124,773 B 2
Tampa, 280,015 . . . . E 4
Tarpon Springs,
17,906 . . . . D 4
Titusville, 39,394 . . . D 6
Venice, 16,922 . . . . . E 4
Vero Beach, 17,350 . . E 6
West Palm Beach,
67,643 . . . . F 6
West Pensacola,
30,200 . . . . u14
Winter Haven, 24,725 D 5
Winter Park, 22,242 . D 5

86

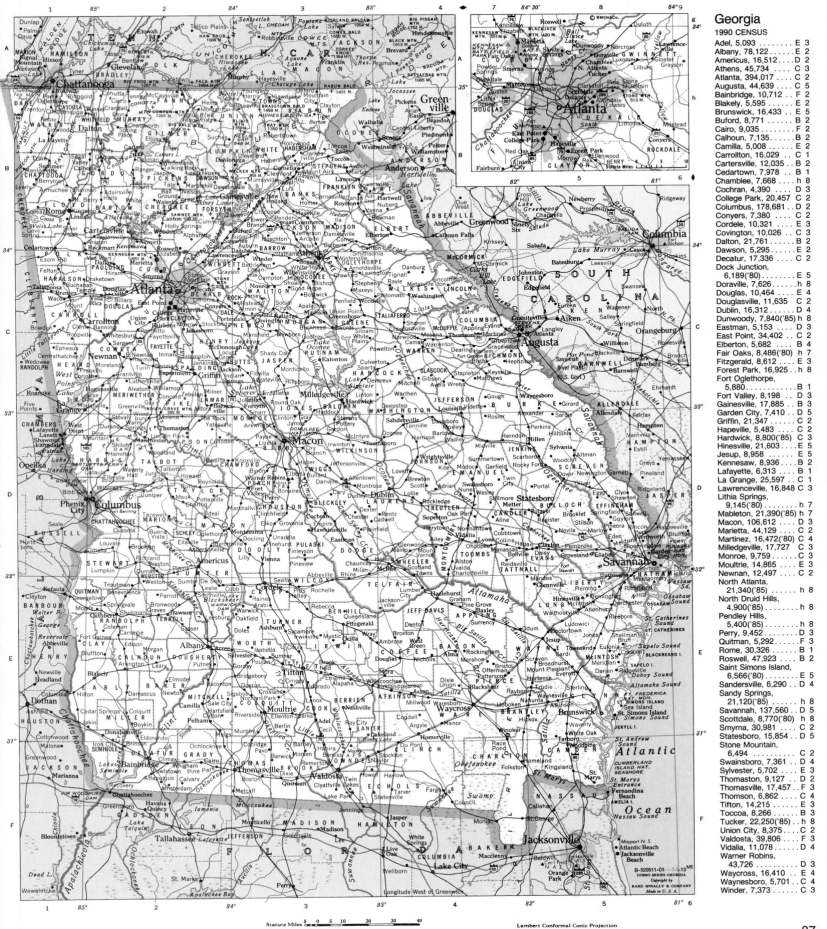

Georgia

1990 CENSUS

Adel, 5,093 . . . . E 3
Albany, 78,122 . . . . . . E 2
Americus, 16,512 . . . . D 2
Athens, 45,734 . . . . . C 3
Atlanta, 394,017 . . . . C 2
Augusta, 44,639 . . . . C 5
Bainbridge, 10,712 . . F 2
Blakely, 5,595 . . . . . . E 2
Brunswick, 16,433 . . E 5
Buford, 8,771 . . . . . . B 2
Cairo, 9,035 . . . . F 2
Calhoun, 7,135 . . . . . B 2
Camilla, 5,008 . . . . . E 2
Carrollton, 16,029 . . C 1
Cartersville, 12,035 . . B 2
Cedartown, 7,978 . . B 1
Chamblee, 7,668 . . . h 8
Cochran, 4,390 . . . . D 3
College Park, 20,457 . C 2
Columbus, 178,681 . . D 2
Conyers, 7,380 . . . . . C 2
Cordele, 10,321 . . . . E 3
Covington, 10,026 . . C 3
Dalton, 21,761 . . . . . B 2
Dawson, 5,295 . . . . . E 2
Decatur, 17,336 . . . . C 2
Dock Junction,
6,189('80) . . . . . E 5
Doraville, 7,626 . . . . h 8
Douglas, 10,464 . . . E 4
Douglasville, 11,635 . C 2
Dublin, 16,312 . . . . . D 3
Dunwoody, 7,840('85) h 8
Eastman, 5,153 . . . . D 3
East Point, 34,402 . . C 2
Elberton, 5,682 . . . . B 4
Fair Oaks, 8,486('80) h 7
Fitzgerald, 8,612 . . . E 3
Forest Park, 16,925 . h 8
Fort Oglethorpe,
5,880 . . . . B 1
Fort Valley, 8,198 . . D 3
Gainesville, 17,885 . B 3
Garden City, 7,410 . D 5
Griffin, 21,347 . . . . C 2
Hapeville, 5,483 . . . C 2
Hardwick, 8,800('85) C 3
Hinesville, 21,603 . . E 5
Jesup, 8,958 . . . . . . E 5
Kennesaw, 8,936 . . B 2
Lafayette, 6,313 . . . B 1
La Grange, 25,597 . . C 1
Lawrenceville, 16,848 C 2
Lithia Springs,
9,145('80) . . . . . . h 7
Mableton, 21,390('85) h 7
Macon, 106,612 . . . . D 3
Marietta, 44,129 . . . C 2
Martinez, 16,472('80) C 4
Milledgeville, 17,727 . C 3
Monroe, 9,759 . . . . . C 3
Moultrie, 14,865 . . . E 3
Newnan, 12,497 . . . C 2
North Atlanta,
21,340('85) . . . . . h 8
North Druid Hills,
4,900('85) . . . . . . h 8
Pendley Hills,
5,400('85) . . . . . . h 8
Perry, 9,452 . . . . . . D 3
Quitman, 5,292 . . . . F 3
Rome, 30,326 . . . . . B 1
Roswell, 47,923 . . . . B 2
Saint Simons Island,
6,566('80) . . . . . . E 5
Sandersville, 6,290 . D 4
Sandy Springs,
21,120('85) . . . . . h 8
Savannah, 137,560 . D 5
Scottdale, 8,770('80) h 8
Smyrna, 30,981 . . . . C 2
Statesboro, 15,854 . D 5
Stone Mountain,
6,494 . . . . C 2
Swainsboro, 7,361 . . D 4
Sylvester, 5,702 . . . E 3
Thomaston, 9,127 . . D 2
Thomasville, 17,457 . F 3
Thomson, 6,862 . . . C 4
Tifton, 14,215 . . . . . E 3
Toccoa, 8,266 . . . . . B 3
Tucker, 22,250('85) . h 8
Union City, 8,375 . . C 2
Valdosta, 39,806 . . . F 3
Vidalia, 11,078 . . . . D 4
Warner Robins,
43,726 . . . . D 3
Waycross, 16,410 . . E 4
Waynesboro, 5,701 . C 4
Winder, 7,373 . . . . . C 3

Hawaii

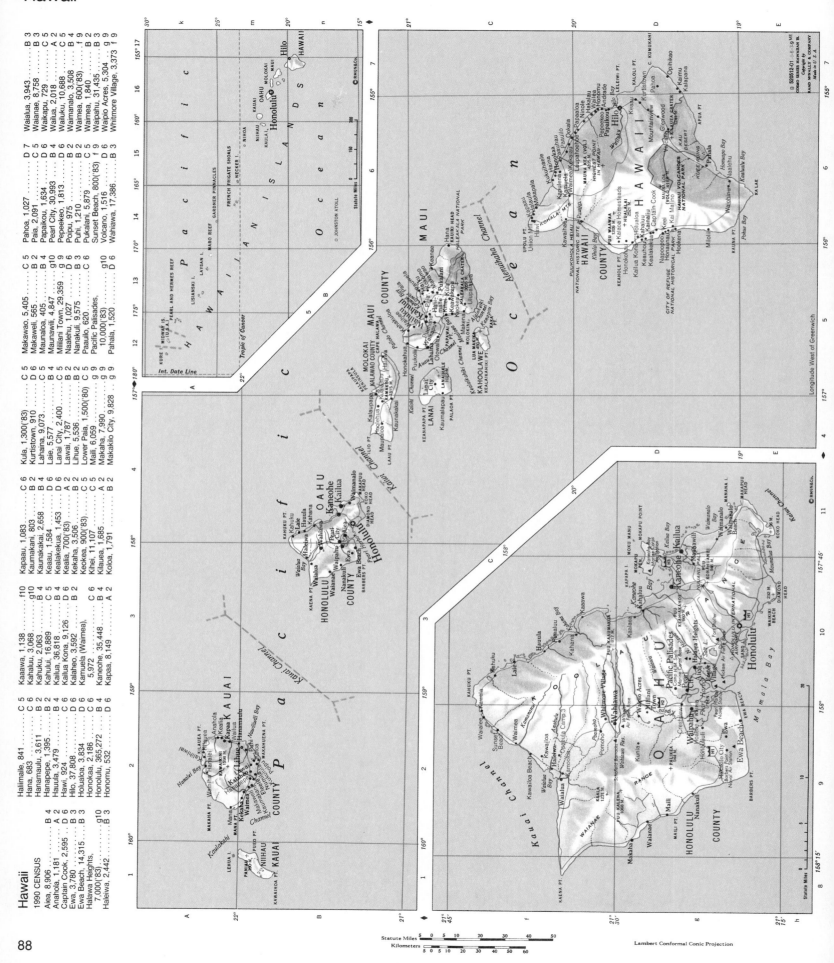

1990 CENSUS

Aiea, 8,906 ... B 4
Anahola, 1,181 ... A 2
Captain Cook, 2,595 ... D 6
Ewa, 3,780 ... B 3
Ewa Beach, 14,315 ... B 3
Halawa Heights, 7,000('83) ... g10
Haleiwa, 2,442 ... B 3
Halimaile, 841 ... C 5
Hana, 683 ... C 6
Hanamaulu, 3,611 ... B 2
Hanapepe, 1,395 ... B 4
Hauula, 3,479 ... B 3
Hawi, 924 ... C 6
Hilo, 37,808 ... D 6
Holualoa, 3,834 ... D 6
Honokaa, 2,186 ... C 6
Honolulu, 365,272 ... B 3
Honomu, 532 ... D 6
Kaaawa, 1,138 ... C 5
Kahaluu, 3,068 ... D 6
Kahuku, 2,063 ... B 4
Kahului, 16,889 ... C 5
Kailua, 36,818 ... B 3
Kailua Kona, 9,126 ... D 6
Kealia, 700('83) ... A 2
Kekaha, 3,506 ... B 2
Kamuela (Waimea), 5,972 ... C 6
Kapaau, 1,083 ... C 6
Kaumakani, 803 ... B 2
Kaunakakai, 2,658 ... B 4
Keaau, 1,584 ... D 6
Kealakekua, 1,453 ... D 6
Kealia, 1,027 ... A 2
Kekaha, 3,506 ... B 2
Keokea, 900('83) ... C 5
Kihei, 11,107 ... C 5
Kilauea, 1,685 ... A 2
Koloa, 1,791 ... B 2
Kula, 1,300('83) ... C 5
Kurtistown, 910 ... D 6
Lahaina, 9,073 ... B 4
Laie, 5,577 ... B 3
Lanai City, 2,400 ... C 5
Lawai, 1,787 ... B 4
Lihue, 5,536 ... B 2
Lower Paia, 1,500('80) ... C 5
Maili, 6,059 ... B 3
Makaha, 7,990 ... B 3
Makakilo City, 9,828 ... B 3
Makawao, 5,405 ... C 5
Makaweli, 565 ... B 2
Maunaloa, 405 ... B 4
Maunawili, 4,847 ... B 3
Mililani Town, 29,359 ... B 3
Naalehu, 1,027 ... D 7
Nanakuli, 9,575 ... B 3
Paauilo, 620 ... C 6
Pacific Palisades, 10,000('83) ... B 3
Pahala, 1,520 ... D 6
Pahoa, 1,027 ... D 7
Paia, 2,091 ... C 5
Papaikou, 1,634 ... D 6
Pearl City, 30,993 ... B 3
Pepeekeo, 1,813 ... D 6
Poipu, 975 ... B 2
Puhi, 1,210 ... B 2
Pukalani, 5,879 ... C 5
Sunset Beach, 800('83) ... f 9
Volcano, 1,516 ... D 6
Wahiawa, 17,386 ... B 3
Waialua, 3,943 ... B 3
Waianae, 8,758 ... B 3
Waikapu, 729 ... C 5
Wailua, 2,018 ... A 2
Wailuku, 10,688 ... C 5
Waimanalo, 3,508 ... B 4
Waimanalo, 600('83) ... f 9
Waimea, 1,840 ... B 3
Waipahu, 31,435 ... B 3
Waipio Acres, 5,304 ... g 9
Whitmore Village, 3,373 ... f 9

Lambert Conformal Conic Projection

88

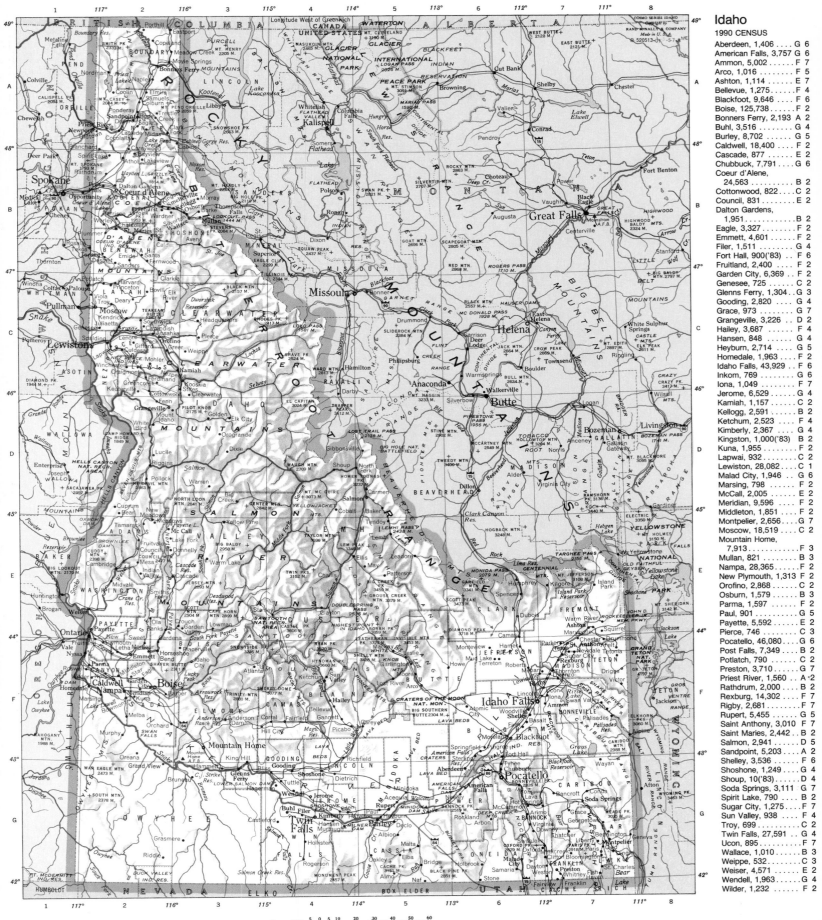

Idaho

1990 CENSUS

Aberdeen, 1,406 .... G 6
American Falls, 3,757 G 6
Ammon, 5,002 ...... F 7
Arco, 1,016 .... F 5
Ashton, 1,114 ..... E 7
Bellevue, 1,275 .... F 4
Blackfoot, 9,646 ... F 6
Boise, 125,738 ...... F 2
Bonners Ferry, 2,193 A 2
Buhl, 3,516 ...... G 4
Burley, 8,702 ...... G 5
Caldwell, 18,400 .... F 2
Cascade, 877 ...... E 2
Chubbuck, 7,791 ... G 6
Coeur d'Alene,
   24,563 ...... B 2
Cottonwood, 822 .... C 2
Council, 831 .... E 2
Dalton Gardens,
   1,951 .... B 2
Eagle, 3,327 ...... F 2
Emmett, 4,601 ..... F 2
Filer, 1,511 .... G 4
Fort Hall, 900('83) .. F 6
Fruitland, 2,400 .... F 2
Garden City, 6,369 .. F 2
Genesee, 725 ..... C 2
Glenns Ferry, 1,304 . G 3
Gooding, 2,820 .... G 4
Grace, 973 .... G 7
Grangeville, 3,226 .. D 2
Hailey, 3,687 ..... F 4
Hansen, 848 ...... G 4
Heyburn, 2,714 .... G 5
Homedale, 1,963 ... F 2
Idaho Falls, 43,929 . F 6
Inkom, 769 .... G 6
Iona, 1,049 .... F 7
Jerome, 6,529 ..... G 4
Kamiah, 1,157 .... C 2
Kellogg, 2,591 .... B 2
Ketchum, 2,523 ... F 4
Kimberly, 2,367 .... G 4
Kingston, 1,000('83) B 2
Kuna, 1,955 ...... F 2
Lapwai, 932 ...... C 2
Lewiston, 28,082 ... C 1
Malad City, 1,946 .. G 6
Marsing, 798 ..... F 2
McCall, 2,005 ..... E 2
Meridian, 9,596 ... F 2
Middleton, 1,851 ... F 2
Montpelier, 2,656 .. G 7
Moscow, 18,519 ... C 2
Mountain Home,
   7,913 .... F 3
Mullan, 821 ...... B 3
Nampa, 28,365 .... F 2
New Plymouth, 1,313 F 2
Orofino, 2,868 .... C 2
Osburn, 1,579 .... B 3
Parma, 1,597 ..... F 2
Paul, 901 .... G 5
Payette, 5,592 .... E 2
Pierce, 746 .... C 3
Pocatello, 46,080 .. G 6
Post Falls, 7,349 ... B 2
Potlatch, 790 ..... C 2
Preston, 3,710 .... G 7
Priest River, 1,560 . A 2
Rathdrum, 2,000 ... B 2
Rexburg, 14,302 ... F 7
Rigby, 2,681 ...... F 7
Rupert, 5,455 ..... G 5
Saint Anthony, 3,010 F 7
Saint Maries, 2,442 . B 2
Salmon, 2,941 .... D 5
Sandpoint, 5,203 .. A 2
Shelley, 3,536 .... F 6
Shoshone, 1,249 .. G 4
Shoup, 10('83) ..... D 4
Soda Springs, 3,111 G 7
Spirit Lake, 790 ... B 2
Sugar City, 1,275 .. F 7
Sun Valley, 938 ... F 7
Troy, 699 .... C 2
Twin Falls, 27,591 . G 4
Ucon, 895 .... F 7
Wallace, 1,010 .... B 3
Weippe, 532 ...... C 3
Weiser, 4,571 ..... E 2
Wendell, 1,963 .... G 4
Wilder, 1,232 ..... F 2

Statute Miles

Kilometers

Lambert Conformal Conic Projection

Illinois

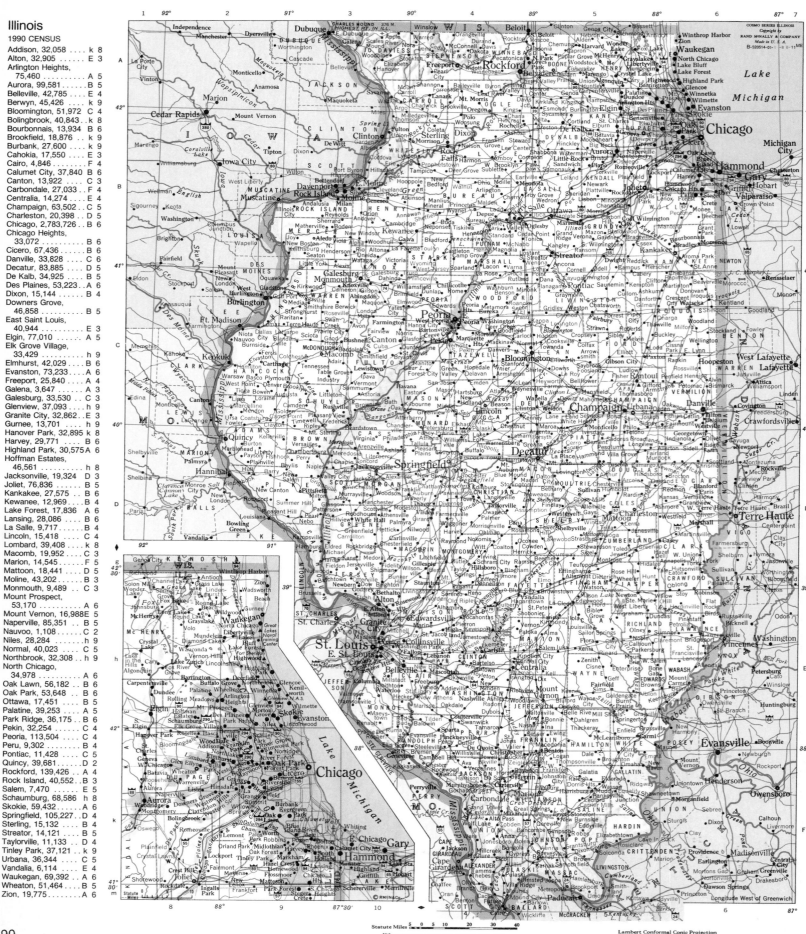

Illinois

1990 CENSUS

Addison, 32,058 .... k 8
Alton, 32,905 ...... E 3
Arlington Heights,
  75,460 .... A 5
Aurora, 99,581 ..... B 5
Belleville, 42,785 ... E 4
Berwyn, 45,426 .... k 9
Bloomington, 51,972 C 4
Bolingbrook, 40,843 . k 8
Bourbonnais, 13,934 B 6
Brookfield, 18,876 .. k 9
Burbank, 27,600 .... k 9
Cahokia, 17,550 .... E 3
Cairo, 4,846 .... F 4
Calumet City, 37,840 B 6
Canton, 13,922 ..... C 3
Carbondale, 27,033 . F 4
Centralia, 14,274 ... E 4
Champaign, 63,502 . C 5
Charleston, 20,398 . D 5
Chicago, 2,783,726 . B 6
Chicago Heights,
  33,072 .... B 6
Cicero, 67,436 ..... B 6
Danville, 33,828 .... C 6
Decatur, 83,885 .... D 5
De Kalb, 34,925 .... B 5
Des Plaines, 53,223 . A 6
Dixon, 15,144 ...... B 4
Downers Grove,
  46,858 .... B 5
East Saint Louis,
  40,944 .... E 3
Elgin, 77,010 ...... A 5
Elk Grove Village,
  33,429 .... h 9
Elmhurst, 42,029 ... B 6
Evanston, 73,233 ... A 6
Freeport, 25,840 ... A 4
Galena, 3,647 ...... A 3
Galesburg, 33,530 .. C 3
Glenview, 37,093 ... h 9
Granite City, 32,862 . E 3
Gurnee, 13,701 .... h 9
Hanover Park, 32,895 k 8
Harvey, 29,771 .... B 6
Highland Park, 30,575 A 6
Hoffman Estates,
  46,561 .... h 8
Jacksonville, 19,324 D 3
Joliet, 76,836 ..... B 5
Kankakee, 27,575 .. B 6
Kewanee, 12,969 ... B 4
Lake Forest, 17,836 A 6
Lansing, 28,086 .... B 6
La Salle, 9,717 .... B 4
Lincoln, 15,418 .... C 4
Lombard, 39,408 ... k 8
Macomb, 19,952 ... C 3
Marion, 14,545 .... F 5
Mattoon, 18,441 ... D 5
Moline, 43,202 .... B 3
Monmouth, 9,489 .. C 3
Mount Prospect,
  53,170 .... A 6
Mount Vernon, 16,988 E 5
Naperville, 85,351 .. B 5
Nauvoo, 1,108 ..... C 2
Niles, 28,284 ..... h 9
Normal, 40,023 .... C 4
Northbrook, 32,308 . h 9
North Chicago,
  34,978 .... A 6
Oak Lawn, 56,182 .. B 6
Oak Park, 53,648 .. B 6
Ottawa, 17,451 .... B 5
Palatine, 39,253 ... A 5
Park Ridge, 36,175 . B 6
Pekin, 32,254 ..... C 4
Peoria, 113,504 .... C 4
Peru, 9,302 .... B 4
Pontiac, 11,428 .... C 5
Quincy, 39,681 .... D 2
Rockford, 139,426 .. A 4
Rock Island, 40,552 . B 3
Salem, 7,470 ...... E 5
Schaumburg, 68,586 h 8
Skokie, 59,432 .... A 6
Springfield, 105,227 . D 4
Sterling, 15,132 ... B 4
Streator, 14,121 ... C 4
Taylorville, 11,133 . D 4
Tinley Park, 37,121 . k 8
Urbana, 36,344 .... C 5
Vandalia, 6,114 .... E 4
Waukegan, 69,392 . A 6
Wheaton, 51,464 ... B 5
Zion, 19,775 ...... A 6

90

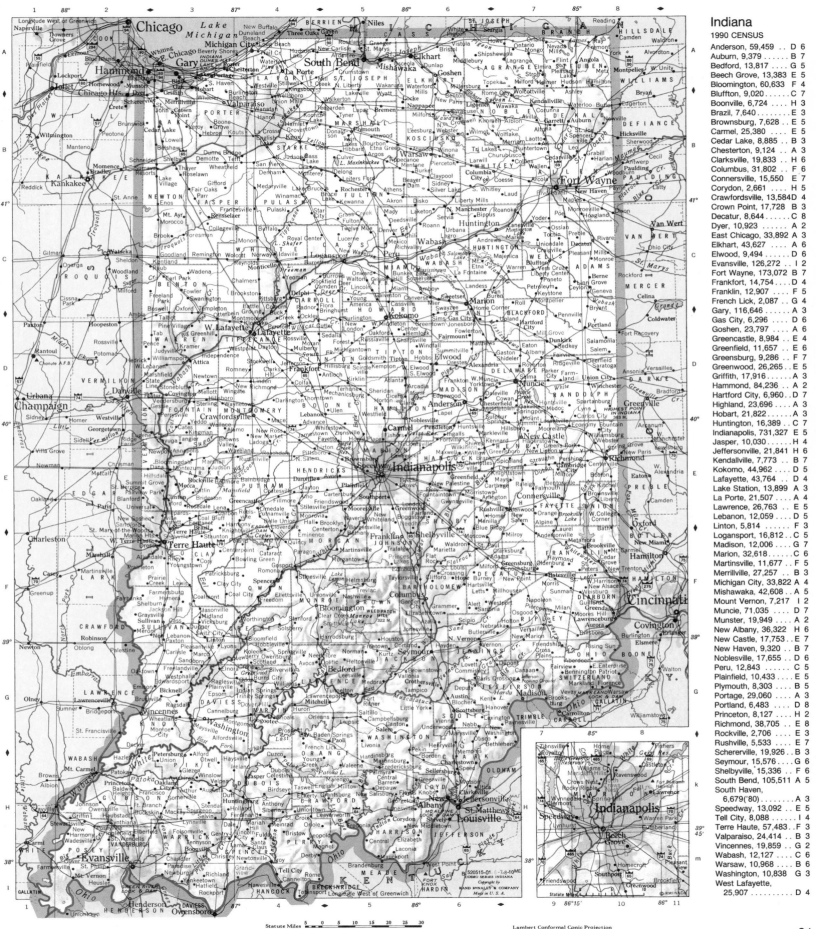

Indiana

1990 CENSUS

Anderson, 59,459 . . D 6
Auburn, 9,379 . . . . . B 7
Bedford, 13,817 . . . . . G 5
Beech Grove, 13,383 . E 5
Bloomington, 60,633 . F 4
Bluffton, 9,020 . . . . . . C 7
Boonville, 6,724 . . . . H 3
Brazil, 7,640 . . . . E 3
Brownsburg, 7,628 . . E 5
Carmel, 25,380 . . . . E 5
Cedar Lake, 8,885 . . B 3
Chesterton, 9,124 . . A 3
Clarksville, 19,833 . . H 6
Columbus, 31,802 . . F 6
Connersville, 15,550 . E 7
Corydon, 2,661 . . . . H 5
Crawfordsville, 13,584 D 4
Crown Point, 17,728 . B 3
Decatur, 8,644 . . . . . C 8
Dyer, 10,923 . . . . A 2
East Chicago, 33,892 A 3
Elkhart, 43,627 . . . . A 6
Elwood, 9,494 . . . . . D 6
Evansville, 126,272 . . I 2
Fort Wayne, 173,072 B 7
Frankfort, 14,754 . . . D 4
Franklin, 12,907 . . . F 5
French Lick, 2,087 . . G 4
Gary, 116,646 . . . . . A 3
Gas City, 6,296 . . . . D 6
Goshen, 23,797 . . . . A 6
Greencastle, 8,984 . . E 4
Greenfield, 11,657 . . E 6
Greensburg, 9,286 . . F 7
Greenwood, 26,265 . . E 5
Griffith, 17,916 . . . . A 2
Hammond, 84,236 . . A 2
Hartford City, 6,960 . D 7
Highland, 23,696 . . . A 3
Hobart, 21,822 . . . . A 3
Huntington, 16,389 . . C 7
Indianapolis, 731,327 E 5
Jasper, 10,030 . . . . . H 4
Jeffersonville, 21,841 H 6
Kendallville, 7,773 . . B 7
Kokomo, 44,962 . . . . D 5
Lafayette, 43,764 . . . D 4
Lake Station, 13,899 . A 3
La Porte, 21,507 . . . A 4
Lawrence, 26,763 . . . E 5
Lebanon, 12,059 . . . D 5
Linton, 5,814 . . . . . . F 3
Logansport, 16,812 . . C 5
Madison, 12,006 . . . G 7
Marion, 32,618 . . . . C 6
Martinsville, 11,677 . F 5
Merrillville, 27,257 . . B 3
Michigan City, 33,822 A 4
Mishawaka, 42,608 . . A 5
Mount Vernon, 7,217 . I 2
Muncie, 71,035 . . . . D 7
Munster, 19,949 . . . A 2
New Albany, 36,322 . H 6
New Castle, 17,753 . . E 7
New Haven, 9,320 . . B 7
Noblesville, 17,655 . . D 6
Peru, 12,843 . . . . . . C 5
Plainfield, 10,433 . . . E 5
Plymouth, 8,303 . . . B 5
Portage, 29,060 . . . . A 3
Portland, 6,483 . . . . D 8
Princeton, 8,127 . . . H 2
Richmond, 38,705 . . E 8
Rockville, 2,706 . . . . E 3
Rushville, 5,533 . . . . E 7
Schererville, 19,926 . . B 3
Seymour, 15,576 . . . G 6
Shelbyville, 15,336 . . F 6
South Bend, 105,511 A 5
South Haven,
  6,679('80) . . . . A 3
Speedway, 13,092 . . E 5
Tell City, 8,088 . . . . I 4
Terre Haute, 57,483 . E 3
Valparaiso, 24,414 . . B 3
Vincennes, 19,859 . . G 2
Wabash, 12,127 . . . . C 6
Warsaw, 10,968 . . . . B 6
Washington, 10,838 . G 3
West Lafayette,
  25,907 . . . . D 4

91

Iowa

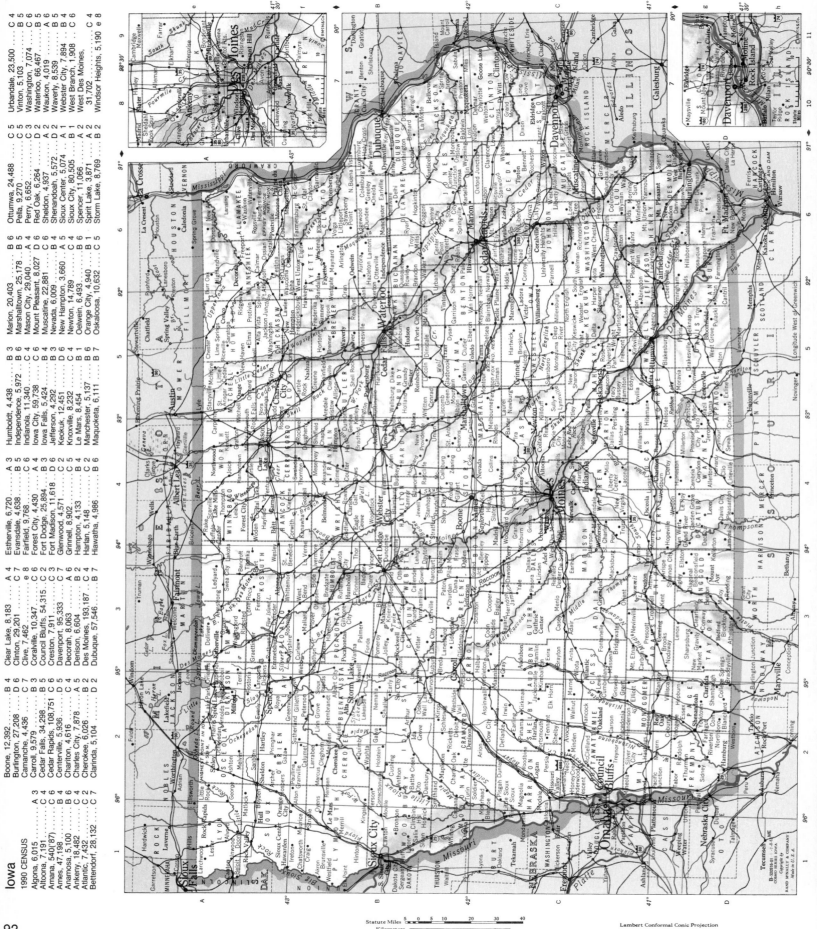

1990 CENSUS

Algona, 6,015 ... A 3
Altoona, 7,191 ... C 4
Amana, 540('87) ... C 6
Ames, 47,198 ... B 4
Anamosa, 5,100 ... B 6
Ankeny, 18,482 ... C 4
Atlantic, 7,432 ... C 2
Bettendorf, 28,132 ... C 7
Boone, 12,392 ... B 4
Burlington, 27,208 ... D 6
Camanche, 4,436 ... B 7
Carroll, 9,579 ... B 3
Cedar Falls, 34,298 ... B 5
Cedar Rapids, 108,751 ... C 6
Centerville, 5,936 ... D 5
Chariton, 4,616 ... C 5
Charles City, 7,878 ... A 5
Cherokee, 6,026 ... B 2
Clarinda, 5,104 ... D 2
Clear Lake, 8,183 ... A 4
Clinton, 29,201 ... B 7
Clive, 7,462 ... e 8
Coralville, 10,347 ... C 6
Council Bluffs, 54,315 ... C 2
Creston, 7,911 ... C 3
Davenport, 95,333 ... C 7
Decorah, 8,063 ... A 5
Denison, 6,604 ... C 2
Des Moines, 193,187 ... C 4
Dubuque, 57,546 ... B 7
Estherville, 6,720 ... A 3
Evansdale, 4,638 ... B 5
Fairfield, 9,768 ... C 6
Forest City, 4,430 ... A 4
Fort Dodge, 25,894 ... B 3
Fort Madison, 11,618 ... D 6
Glenwood, 4,571 ... C 2
Grinnell, 8,902 ... C 5
Hampton, 4,133 ... B 4
Harlan, 5,148 ... C 2
Hiawatha, 4,986 ... B 6
Humboldt, 4,438 ... B 3
Independence, 5,972 ... B 6
Indianola, 11,340 ... C 4
Iowa City, 59,738 ... C 6
Iowa Falls, 5,424 ... B 4
Jefferson, 4,292 ... C 3
Keokuk, 12,451 ... D 6
Knoxville, 8,232 ... C 5
Le Mars, 8,454 ... B 1
Manchester, 5,137 ... B 6
Maquoketa, 6,111 ... B 7
Marion, 20,403 ... B 6
Marshalltown, 25,178 ... B 5
Mason City, 29,040 ... A 4
Mount Pleasant, 8,027 ... C 6
Muscatine, 22,881 ... C 6
Nevada, 6,009 ... B 4
New Hampton, 3,660 ... A 5
Newton, 14,789 ... C 5
Oelwein, 6,493 ... B 5
Orange City, 4,940 ... A 1
Oskaloosa, 10,632 ... C 5
Ottumwa, 24,488 ... C 5
Pella, 9,270 ... C 5
Perry, 6,652 ... C 3
Red Oak, 6,264 ... D 2
Sheldon, 4,937 ... A 2
Shenandoah, 5,572 ... D 2
Sioux Center, 5,074 ... A 1
Sioux City, 80,505 ... B 1
Spencer, 11,066 ... A 2
Spirit Lake, 3,871 ... A 2
Storm Lake, 8,769 ... B 2
Urbandale, 23,500 ... C 4
Vinton, 5,103 ... B 5
Waterloo, 66,467 ... B 5
Waukon, 4,019 ... A 6
Waverly, 8,539 ... B 4
Webster City, 7,894 ... B 4
West Branch, 1,908 ... C 6
West Des Moines, 31,702 ... C 4
Windsor Heights, 5,190 ... e 8

Statute Miles
Kilometers

Lambert Conformal Conic Projection

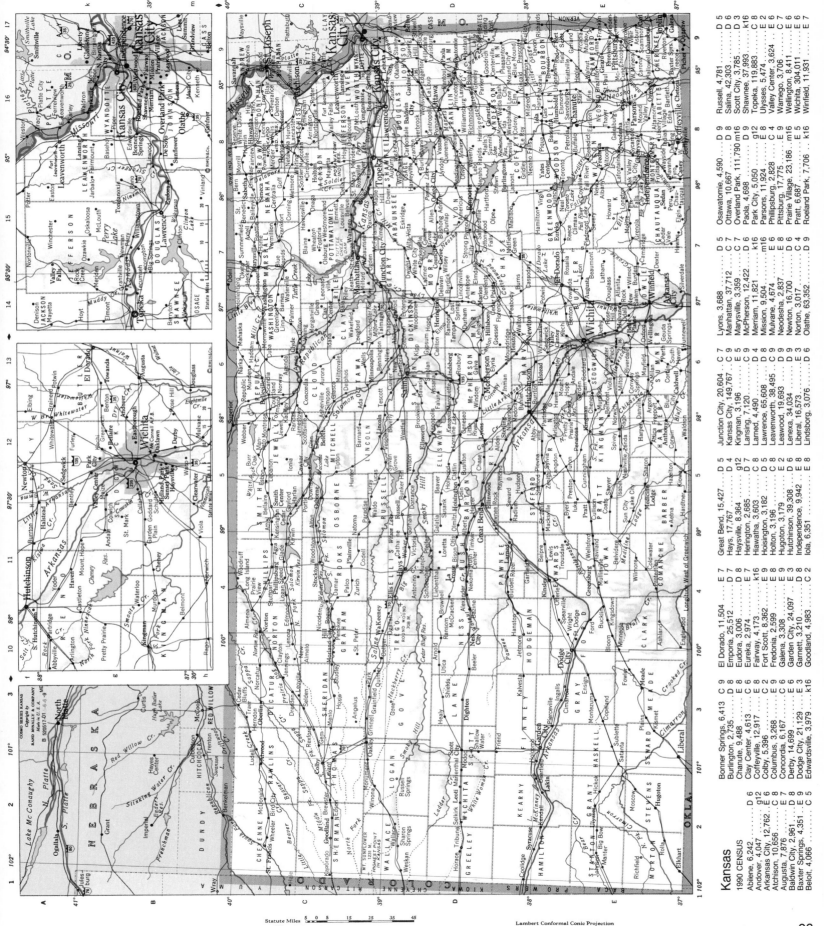

Kansas

1990 CENSUS

Abilene, 6,242	D 6	Lyons, 3,688	C 7
Andover, 4,047	g12	Manhattan, 37,712	C 7
Arkansas City, 12,762	E 6	Marysville, 3,359	C 9
Atchison, 10,656	C 8	McPherson, 12,422	D 6
Augusta, 7,876	E 7	Merriam, 11,821	k16
Baldwin City, 2,961	D 8	Mission, 9,504	D 8
Baxter Springs, 4,351	E 9	Mulvane, 4,674	D 8
Beloit, 4,066	C 5	Neodesha, 2,837	E 9
Bonner Springs, 6,413	C 9	Newton, 16,700	E 6
Burlington, 2,735	D 8	Norton, 3,017	C 4
Chanute, 9,488	E 8	Olathe, 63,352	D 9
Clay Center, 4,613	C 6	Osawatomie, 4,590	D 5
Coffeyville, 12,917	E 9	Ottawa, 10,667	D 8
Colby, 5,396	C 2	Overland Park, 111,790	m16
Columbus, 3,268	E 9	Paola, 4,698	D 9
Concordia, 6,167	C 6	Park City, 5,050	g12
Derby, 14,699	E 7	Parsons, 11,924	E 8
Dodge City, 21,129	E 3	Phillipsburg, 2,775	C 4
Edwardsville, 3,979	k16	Pittsburg, 17,775	E 9
El Dorado, 11,504	E 7	Prairie Village, 23,186	m16
Emporia, 25,512	D 7	Pratt, 6,687	E 5
Eudora, 3,006	C 9	Roeland Park, 7,706	k16
Eureka, 2,974	E 7	Russell, 4,781	D 5
Fairway, 4,173	k16	Salina, 42,303	D 6
Fort Scott, 8,362	E 9	Scott City, 3,785	D 3
Fredonia, 2,599	E 8	Shawnee, 37,993	k16
Galena, 3,308	E 9	Topeka, 119,883	C 8
Garden City, 24,097	E 3	Ulysses, 5,474	E 4
Garnett, 3,210	D 8	Valley Center, 3,624	E 6
Goodland, 4,983	C 2	Wamego, 3,706	C 7
Great Bend, 15,427	D 5	Wellington, 8,411	E 6
Hays, 17,767	D 4	Wichita, 304,011	E 7
Haysville, 8,364	E 7	Winfield, 11,931	E 7
Herington, 2,685	D 7		
Hiawatha, 3,603	C 9		
Hoisington, 3,182	D 5		
Holton, 3,196	C 8		
Hugoton, 3,179	E 2		
Hutchinson, 39,308	D 6		
Independence, 9,942	E 8		
Iola, 6,351	E 8		
Junction City, 20,604	C 7		
Kansas City, 149,767	C 9		
Kingman, 3,196	g12		
Lansing, 7,120	C 9		
Larned, 4,490	D 5		
Lawrence, 65,608	D 8		
Leavenworth, 38,495	C 9		
Leawood, 19,693	D 8		
Lenexa, 34,034	E 2		
Liberal, 16,573	D 6		
Lindsborg, 3,076	E 8		

Statute Miles 5 0 5   15   25   35   45
Kilometers 5 0 5   15   25   35   45   55   65

Lambert Conformal Conic Projection

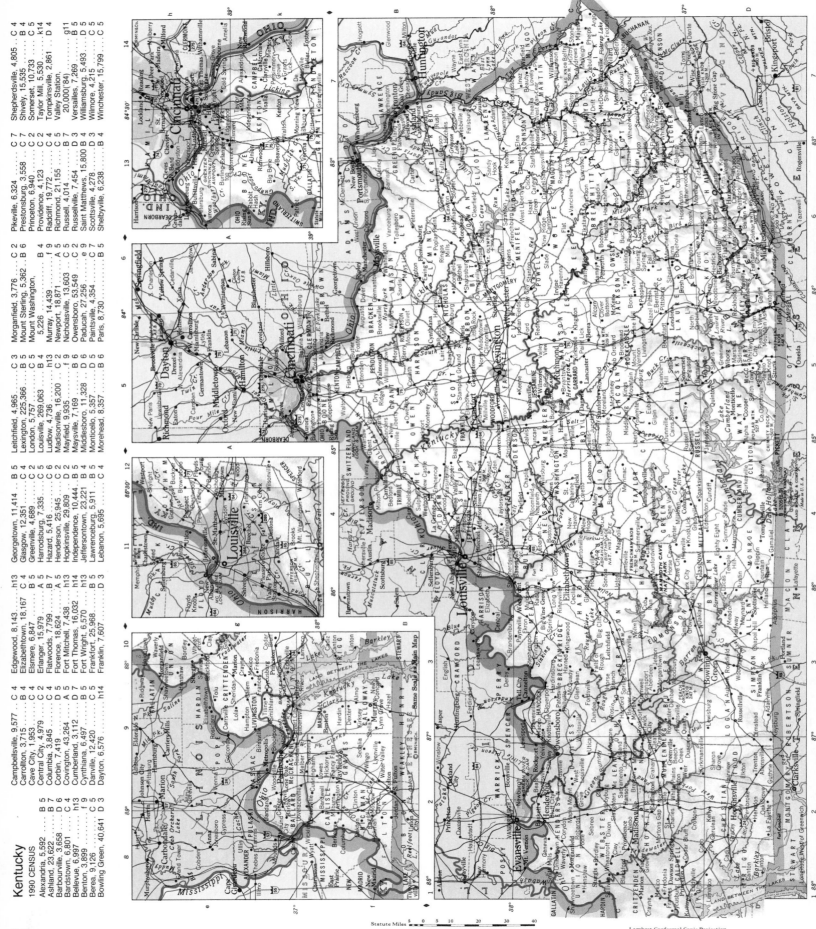

Statute Miles

Kilometers

Lambert Conformal Conic Projection

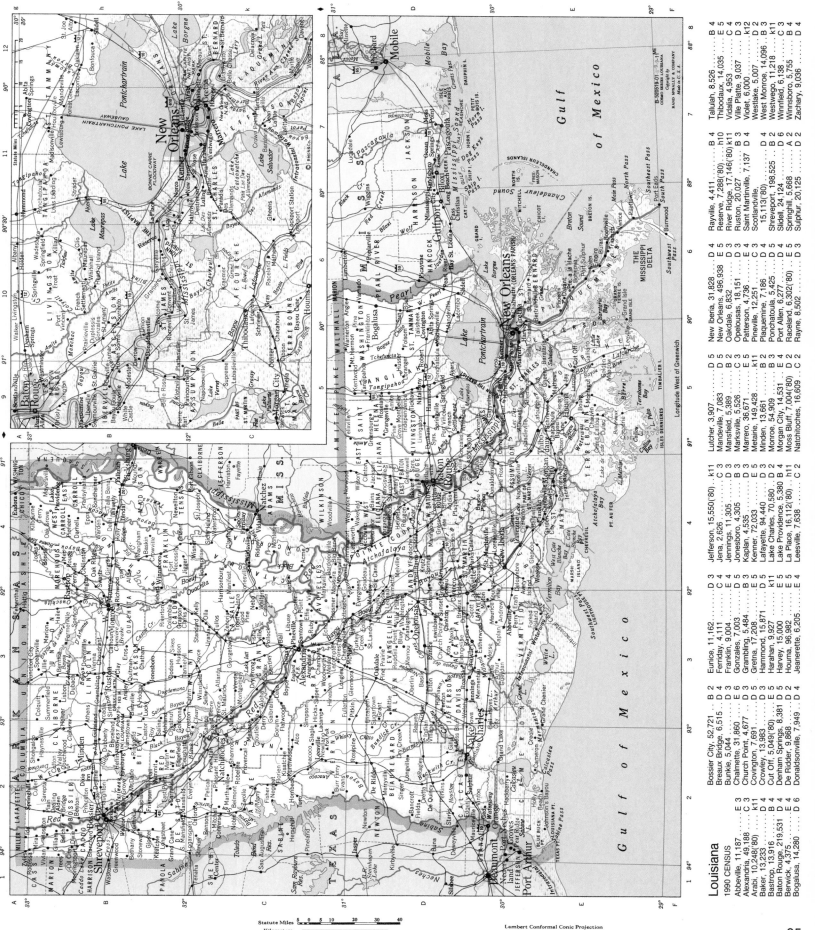

Louisiana

Louisiana
1990 CENSUS

Abbeville, 11,187 ... E 3
Alexandria, 49,188 ... C 3
Arabi, 10,248('80) ... k11
Baker, 13,233 ... D 4
Bastrop, 13,916 ... B 4
Baton Rouge, 219,531 ... D 4
Berwick, 4,375 ... E 4
Bogalusa, 14,280 ... D 6

Bossier City, 52,721 ... B 2
Breaux Bridge, 6,515 ... D 4
Bunkie, 5,044 ... D 3
Chalmette, 31,860 ... E 6
Church Point, 4,677 ... D 3
Covington, 7,691 ... D 5
Crowley, 13,983 ... D 3
Cut Off, 5,049('80) ... E 5
Denham Springs, 8,381 ... D 5
De Ridder, 9,868 ... D 2
Donaldsonville, 7,949 ... D 4

Eunice, 11,162 ... D 3
Ferriday, 4,111 ... C 4
Franklin, 9,004 ... E 4
Gonzales, 7,003 ... D 5
Gretna, 17,208 ... E 5
Hammond, 15,871 ... D 5
Harahan, 9,927 ... k11
Harvey, 15,000 ... E 5
Houma, 96,982 ... E 5
Jeanerette, 6,205 ... E 4

Jefferson, 15,550('80) ... k11
Jena, 2,626 ... C 3
Jennings, 11,305 ... D 3
Jonesboro, 4,305 ... B 3
Kaplan, 4,535 ... E 4
Kenner, 72,033 ... E 5
Lafayette, 94,440 ... D 3
Lake Charles, 70,580 ... D 2
Lake Providence, 5,380 ... B 4
La Place, 16,112('80) ... h11
Leesville, 7,638 ... C 2

Lutcher, 3,907 ... D 5
Mandeville, 7,083 ... D 5
Mansfield, 5,389 ... B 2
Marksville, 5,526 ... C 3
Marrero, 36,671 ... E 5
Metairie, 149,428 ... k11
Minden, 13,661 ... B 2
Monroe, 54,909 ... B 3
Morgan City, 14,531 ... E 4
Moss Bluff, 7,004('80) ... D 3
Natchitoches, 16,609 ... C 2

New Iberia, 31,828 ... D 5
New Orleans, 496,938 ... E 5
Oakdale, 6,832 ... D 3
Opelousas, 18,151 ... D 4
Patterson, 4,736 ... E 4
Pineville, 12,251 ... C 3
Plaquemine, 7,186 ... D 4
Ponchatoula, 5,425 ... D 5
Port Allen, 6,277 ... D 4
Raceland, 6,302('80) ... E 5
Rayne, 8,502 ... D 3

Rayville, 4,411 ... B 4
Reserve, 7,288('80) ... h10
River Ridge, 17,146('80) ... k11
Ruston, 20,027 ... B 3
Saint Martinville, 7,137 ... D 4
Scotlandville,
  15,113('80) ... D 4
Shreveport, 198,525 ... B 2
Slidell, 24,124 ... D 6
Springhill, 5,668 ... A 2
Sulphur, 20,125 ... D 4

Tallulah, 8,526 ... B 4
Thibodaux, 14,035 ... E 5
Vidalia, 4,953 ... C 4
Ville Platte, 9,037 ... D 3
Violet, 6,000 ... k12
Westlake, 5,007 ... D 3
West Monroe, 14,096 ... B 3
Westwego, 11,218 ... k11
Winnfield, 6,138 ... C 3
Winnsboro, 5,755 ... B 4
Zachary, 9,036 ... D 4

Statute Miles
Kilometers

Lambert Conformal Conic Projection

Maine

Maine
1990 CENSUS

Auburn, 24,309 .... D 2
Augusta, 21,325 .... D 3
Bangor, 33,181 ..... D 4
Bar Harbor, 2,685
  (4,443) .... D 4
Bath, 9,799 .... E 3
Belfast, 6,355 ..... D 3
Berwick, 2,378
  (5,995▲) .... E 2
Biddeford, 20,710 .. E 2
Brewer, 9,021 ..... D 4
Bridgton, 1,639
  (4,307▲) .... D 2
Brunswick, 10,990
  (20,906▲) ...... E 3
Bucksport, 2,853
  (4,825▲) .... D 4
Calais, 3,963 ...... C 5
Camden, 3,743
  (5,060▲) .... D 3
Caribou, 9,415 ..... B 5
Dexter, 3,118
  (4,419▲) .... C 3
Dixfield, 1,725
  (2,574▲) .... D 2
Dover-Foxcroft, 2,974
  (4,657▲) .... C 3
Eastport, 1,965 .... D 6
Ellsworth, 5,975 ... D 4
Fairfield, 3,169
  (6,718▲) .... D 3
Farmingdale, 2,014
  (2,918▲) .... D 3
Farmington, 3,583
  (7,436▲) .... D 2
Fort Fairfield, 2,282
  (3,998▲) .... B 5
Fort Kent, 2,375
  (4,268▲) .... A 4
Fryeburg, 1,644
  (2,968▲) .... D 2
Gardiner, 6,746 .... D 3
Gorham, 4,052
  (11,856▲) ...... E 2
Hallowell, 2,534 ... D 3
Hampden, 2,300
  (5,974▲) .... D 4
Houlton, 5,730
  (6,613▲) .... B 5
Kennebunk, 3,294
  (8,004▲) .... E 2
Kennebunkport, 1,685
  (3,356▲) .... E 2
Kittery, 5,465
  (9,372▲) .... E 2
Lewiston, 39,757 ... D 2
Lincoln, 3,524
  (5,587▲) .... C 4
Livermore Falls, 2,441
  (3,455▲) .... D 2
Madawaska, 4,165
  (4,803▲) .... A 4
Madison, 2,788
  (4,725▲) .... D 3
Mexico, 3,207
  (3,344▲) .... D 2
Milford, 1,688
  (2,884▲) .... D 4
Milo, 2,255 (2,600▲) C 4
Newport, 1,748
  (3,036▲) .... D 3
Norway, 2,653
  (4,754▲) .... D 2
Oakland, 3,387
  (5,595▲) .... D 3
Old Town, 8,317 ... D 4
Pittsfield, 3,117
  (4,190▲) .... D 3
Portland, 64,358 ... E 2
Presque Isle, 10,550 B 5
Richmond, 1,578
  (3,072▲) .... D 3
Rockland, 7,972 ... D 3
Rumford, 6,256
  (7,078▲) .... D 2
Saco, 15,181 ...... E 2
Sanford, 10,268
  (20,463▲) ...... E 2
Scarborough, 2,280
  (12,518▲) ...... E 2
Skowhegan, 6,517
  (8,725▲) .... D 3
South Berwick, 2,120
  (5,877▲) .... E 2
South Portland,
  23,163 .... E 2
Thomaston, 2,348
  (3,306▲) .... D 3
Topsham, 4,657
  (8,746▲) .... E 3
Waterville, 17,173 . D 3
Westbrook, 16,121 . E 2
Wilton, 2,262
  (4,242▲) .... D 2
Winslow, 5,903
  (7,997▲) .... D 3
Winthrop, 3,264
  (5,968▲) .... D 3
Yarmouth, 2,981
  (7,862▲) .... E 2
Durham, ... E 2
York, 3,130 (9,818▲) E 2

▲ Population of entire town (township), including rural area.

96

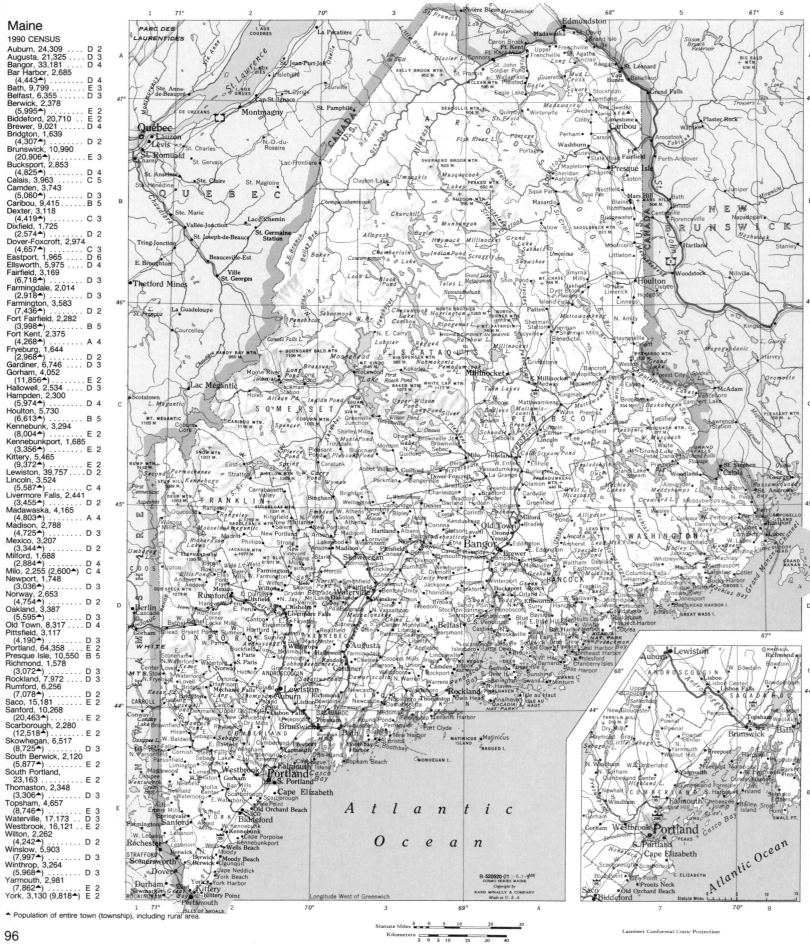

B-520520-01 ..6-7-9ME
COSMO SERIES MAINE
Copyright by
Rand McNally & Company
Made in U.S.A.

Statute Miles
Kilometers

Lambert Conformal Conic Projection

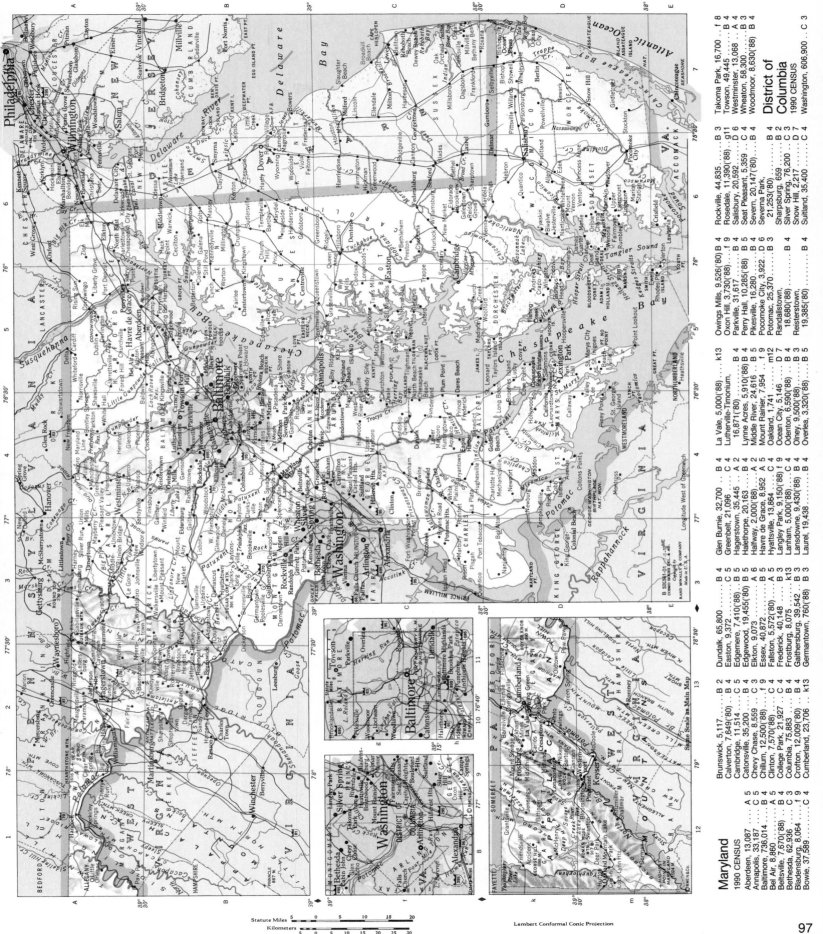

Statute Miles

Kilometers

Lambert Conformal Conic Projection

Maryland
1990 CENSUS

Aberdeen, 13,087	A 5	
Annapolis, 33,187	C 5	
Baltimore, 736,014	B 4	
Bel Air, 8,860	A 5	
Beltsville, 7,670(88)	C 3	
Bethesda, 62,936	C 3	
Bladensburg, 8,064	f 9	
Bowie, 37,589	C 4	

Brunswick, 5,117	B 2	
Calverton, 7,649('80)	B 4	
Cambridge, 11,514	C 5	
Catonsville, 35,200	B 4	
Chevy Chase, 8,559	C 3	
Chillum, 12,500(88)	f 9	
Clinton, 7,570(88)	C 4	
College Park, 21,927	C 4	
Columbia, 75,883	B 4	
Crofton, 12,009('80)	B 4	
Cumberland, 23,706	C 4	

Dundalk, 65,800	B 4	
Easton, 9,372	C 5	
Edgemere, 7,410(88)	B 5	
Edgewood, 19,455('80)	A 5	
Elkton, 9,073	A 6	
Essex, 40,872	B 5	
Fallston, 5,572('80)	A 5	
Frederick, 40,148	C 4	
Frostburg, 8,075	k13	
Gaithersburg, 39,542	B 3	
Germantown, 760(88)	B 3	

Glen Burnie, 32,700	B 4	
Greenbelt, 21,096	C 4	
Hagerstown, 35,445	A 2	
Halethorpe, 20,163	B 4	
Halfway, 2,000(88)	A 2	
Havre de Grace, 8,952	A 5	
Hyattsville, 13,864	C 4	
Langley Park, 9,150(88)	f 9	
Lanham, 5,000(88)	k13	
Lansdowne, 9,430(88)	B 4	
Laurel, 19,438	B 4	

La Vale, 5,000(88)	B 4	
Lutherville-Timonium, 16,871('80)	B 4	
Lynne Acres, 5,910(88)	B 4	
Middle River, 16,280	B 5	
Mount Rainier, 7,954	f 9	
Oakland, 1,741	C 4	
Ocean City, 5,146	D 7	
Odenton, 6,590(88)	B 4	
Olney, 9,500(88)	B 3	
Overlea, 3,320(88)	B 5	

Owings Mills, 9,526('80)	B 4	
Oxon Hill, 3,730('88)	f 9	
Parkville, 31,617	B 4	
Perry Hall, 10,285('88)	B 5	
Pikesville, 16,280	B 4	
Pocomoke City, 3,922	D 6	
Potomac, 25,370	B 3	
Randallstown, 18,680('88)	B 4	
Reisterstown, 19,385('80)	B 4	

Rockville, 44,835	B 3	
Rosedale, 11,390('88)	g11	
Salisbury, 20,592	D 6	
Seat Pleasant, 5,359	C 4	
Severn, 20,147('80)	B 4	
Severna Park, 21,253('80)	B 4	
Sharpsburg, 659	B 2	
Silver Spring, 76,200	C 3	
Snow Hill, 2,217	D 7	
Suitland, 35,400	C 4	

Takoma Park, 16,700	f 8	
Towson, 49,445	B 4	
Westminster, 13,068	A 4	
Wheaton, 58,300	B 3	
Woodmoor, 8,630('88)	B 4	

District of Columbia
1990 CENSUS

Washington, 606,900 . . . . C 3

Massachusetts

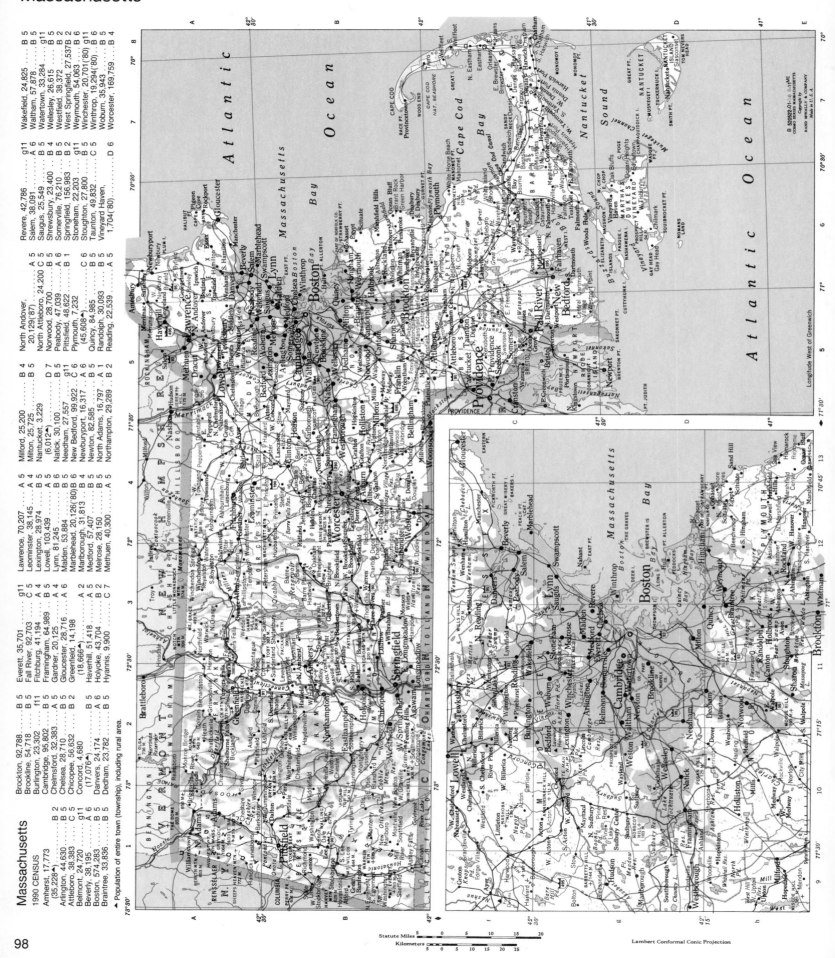

1990 CENSUS

Amherst, 17,773 .... B 5
 (35,228▲)
Arlington, 44,630 .... A 5
Attleboro, 38,383 .... C 5
Belmont, 24,720 .... A 6
 (17,076▲)
Beverly, 38,195 .... A 6
Boston, 574,283 .... B 5
Braintree, 33,836 ...... B 5

Brockton, 92,788 .... B 5
Brookline, 54,718 ...... B 5
Burlington, 23,302 ..... f11
Cambridge, 95,802 ...... A 5
Chelmsford, 32,383 ..... A 5
Chelsea, 28,710 .... B 5
Chicopee, 56,632 .... B 2
Concord, 4,680
 (18,666▲)
Danvers, 24,174 .... A 6
Dedham, 23,782 .... B 5

Everett, 35,701 .... B 5
Fall River, 92,703 .... B 5
Fitchburg, 41,194 ...... A 5
Framingham, 64,989 ..... B 5
Gardner, 20,125 .... A 4
Gloucester, 28,716 ..... A 6
Greenfield, 14,198 ..... A 4
Haverhill, 51,418 ...... A 5
Holyoke, 43,704 .... B 2
Hyannis, 9,900 .... C 7

Lawrence, 70,207 .... A 5
Leominster, 38,145 ..... A 4
Lexington, 28,974 ...... B 5
Lowell, 103,439 .... A 5
Lynn, 81,245 .... B 6
Malden, 53,884 .... B 5
Marblehead, 20,126('80) B 6
Marlborough, 31,813 .... B 5
Medford, 57,407 .... B 5
Melrose, 28,150 .... B 5
Methuen, 40,300 .... A 5

Milford, 25,200 .... B 4
Milton, 25,725 .... B 5
Nantucket, 3,229 .... D 7
 (6,012▲)
Natick, 30,100 .... B 6
Needham, 27,557 .... g11
New Bedford, 99,922 .... B 6
Newburyport, 16,317 .... A 6
Newton, 82,585 .... C 5
North Adams, 16,797 .... A 1
Northampton, 29,289 .... B 2

North Andover,
 20,129('87) .... A 6
North Attleboro, 24,200 C 5
Norwood, 28,700 .... B 5
Peabody, 47,039 .... A 6
Pittsfield, 48,622 ..... B 1
Plymouth, 7,232
 (45,608▲) .... C 6
Quincy, 84,985 .... B 5
Randolph, 30,093 .... B 5
Reading, 22,539 .... A 5

Revere, 42,786 .... B 5
Salem, 38,091 .... A 6
Saugus, 25,549 .... B 5
Shrewsbury, 23,460 ..... B 4
Somerville, 76,210 ..... B 5
Springfield, 156,983 ... B 2
Stoneham, 22,203 .... g11
Taunton, 49,832 .... B 5
Vineyard Haven,
 1,704('80) .... D 4

Wakefield, 24,825 ...... B 5
Waltham, 57,878 .... A 5
Watertown, 33,284 ...... g11
Wellesley, 26,615 ...... B 5
Westfield, 38,372 ...... B 2
West Springfield, 27,537 B 2
Weymouth, 54,063 .... B 5
Winchester, 20,701('80) g11
Winthrop, 19,294('80) .. B 6
Woburn, 35,943 .... B 5
Worcester, 169,759 ..... B 4

▲ Population of entire town (township), including rural area.

98

Statute Miles
Kilometers

Lambert Conformal Conic Projection

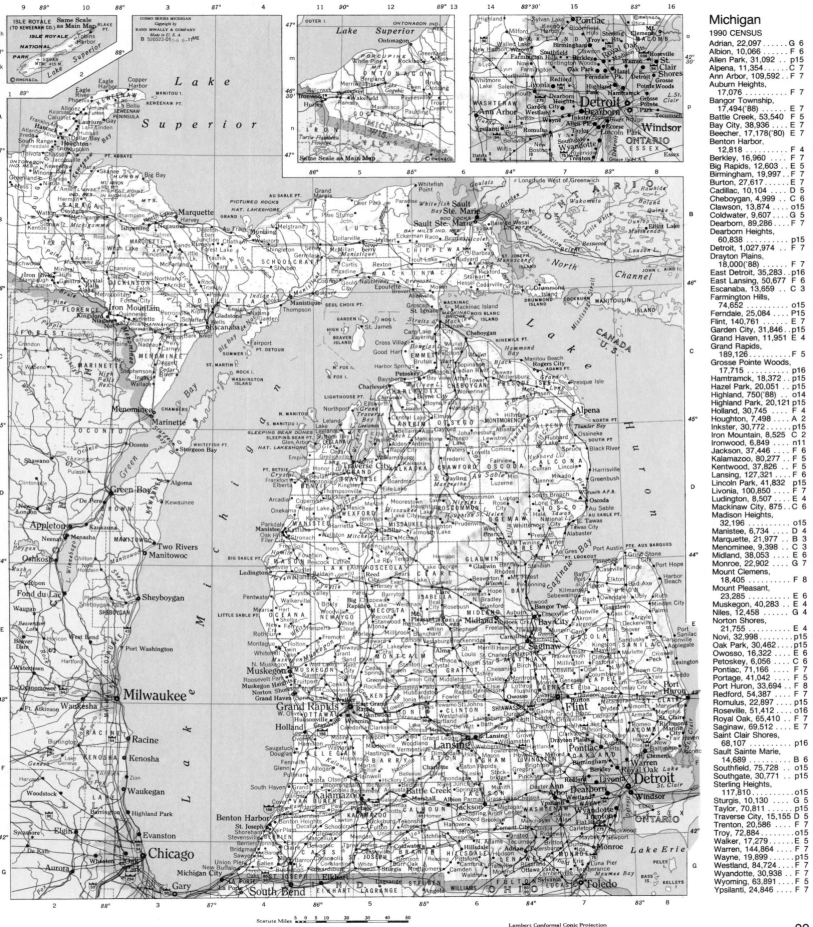

Michigan

1990 CENSUS

Adrian, 22,097 . . . . . . G 6
Albion, 10,066 . . . . . . F 6
Allen Park, 31,092 . . . p15
Alpena, 11,354 . . . . . C 7
Ann Arbor, 109,592 . . F 7
Auburn Heights,
  17,076 . . . . F 7
Bangor Township,
  17,494('88) . . . . . . E 7
Battle Creek, 53,540 . . F 5
Bay City, 38,936 . . . . E 7
Beecher, 17,178('80) . E 7
Benton Harbor,
  12,818 . . . . F 4
Berkley, 16,960 . . . . . F 7
Big Rapids, 12,603 . . . E 5
Birmingham, 19,997 . . F 7
Burton, 27,617 . . . . . E 7
Cadillac, 10,104 . . . . D 5
Cheboygan, 4,999 . . . C 6
Clawson, 13,874 . . . . o15
Coldwater, 9,607 . . . . G 5
Dearborn, 89,286 . . . . F 7
Dearborn Heights,
  60,838 . . . . p15
Detroit, 1,027,974 . . F 7
Drayton Plains,
  18,000('88) . . . . . F 7
East Detroit, 35,283 . . p16
East Lansing, 50,677 . . F 6
Escanaba, 13,659 . . C 3
Farmington Hills,
  74,652 . . . . o15
Ferndale, 25,084 . . P15
Flint, 140,761 . . . . . E 7
Garden City, 31,846 . . p15
Grand Haven, 11,951 E 4
Grand Rapids,
  189,126 . . . . F 5
Grosse Pointe Woods,
  17,715 . . . . p16
Hamtramck, 18,372 . . F 7
Hazel Park, 20,051 . . p15
Highland, 750('88) . . o14
Highland Park, 20,121 p15
Holland, 30,745 . . . . F 4
Houghton, 7,498 . . . A 2
Inkster, 30,772 . . . . . F 7
Iron Mountain, 8,525 C 2
Ironwood, 6,849 . . . n11
Jackson, 37,446 . . . . F 6
Kalamazoo, 80,277 . . F 5
Kentwood, 37,826 . . . F 5
Lansing, 127,321 . . . . F 6
Lincoln Park, 41,832 p15
Livonia, 100,850 . . . . F 7
Ludington, 8,507 . . . . E 4
Mackinaw City, 875 . . C 6
Madison Heights,
  32,196 . . . . o15
Manistee, 6,734 . . . . D 4
Marquette, 21,977 . . . B 3
Menominee, 9,398 . . . C 3
Midland, 38,053 . . . . E 6
Monroe, 22,902 . . . . G 7
Mount Clemens,
  18,405 . . . . F 8
Mount Pleasant,
  23,285 . . . . E 6
Muskegon, 40,283 . . E 4
Niles, 12,458 . . . . . G 4
Norton Shores,
  21,755 . . . . E 4
Novi, 32,998 . . . . . . p15
Oak Park, 30,462 . . . . F 7
Owosso, 16,322 . . . . E 6
Petoskey, 6,056 . . . . C 6
Pontiac, 71,166 . . . . F 7
Portage, 41,042 . . . . F 5
Port Huron, 33,694 . . F 8
Redford, 54,387 . . . . F 7
Romulus, 22,897 . . . p15
Roseville, 51,412 . . . o16
Royal Oak, 65,410 . . F 7
Saginaw, 69,512 . . . E 7
Saint Clair Shores,
  68,107 . . . . p16
Sault Sainte Marie,
  14,689 . . . . B 6
Southfield, 75,728 . . o15
Southgate, 30,771 . . p15
Sterling Heights,
  117,810 . . . . o15
Sturgis, 10,130 . . . . G 5
Taylor, 70,811 . . . . p15
Traverse City, 15,155 D 5
Trenton, 20,586 . . . . F 7
Troy, 72,884 . . . . . o15
Walker, 17,279 . . . . F 5
Warren, 144,864 . . . . F 7
Wayne, 19,899 . . . . p15
Westland, 84,724 . . . F 7
Wyandotte, 30,938 . . F 7
Wyoming, 63,891 . . . F 5
Ypsilanti, 24,846 . . . . F 7

Minnesota

Minnesota

1990 CENSUS

Albert Lea, 18,310 .. G 5
Alexandria, 7,838 .... E 3
Andover, 15,216 .. m12
Anoka, 17,192 .... E 5
Apple Valley, 34,598 .. n12
Austin, 21,907 .... G 6
Bemidji, 11,245 .... C 4
Blaine, 38,975 ..... m12
Bloomington, 86,335 F 5
Brainerd, 12,353 .... D 4
Brooklyn Center,
28,887 .... E 5
Brooklyn Park,
56,381 .... m12
Burnsville, 51,288 ... F 5
Champlin, 16,849 .. m12
Chisholm, 5,290 .... C 6
Cloquet, 10,885 .... D 6
Columbia Heights,
18,910 .... E 5
Coon Rapids, 52,978 E 5
Cottage Grove,
22,935 .... n13
Crookston, 8,119 .... C 2
Crystal, 23,788 .... m12
Detroit Lakes, 6,635 . D 3
Duluth, 85,493 ..... D 6
Eagan, 47,409 ..... n12
East Bethel, 8,050 .. E 5
East Grand Forks,
8,658 .... C 2
Eden Prairie, 39,311 . n12
Edina, 46,070 ..... n12
Ely, 3,968 .... C 7
Fairmont, 11,265 ... G 4
Faribault, 17,085 ... F 5
Fergus Falls, 12,362 . D 2
Fridley, 28,335 .... m12
Golden Valley, 20,971 n12
Grand Marais, 1,171 . k 9
Grand Rapids, 7,976 . C 5
Hastings, 15,445 ... F 6
Hibbing, 18,046 ... C 6
Hopkins, 16,534 ... n12
Hutchinson, 11,523 . F 4
International Falls,
8,325 .... B 5
Inver Grove Heights,
22,477 .... n12
Lakeville, 24,854 ... F 5
Litchfield, 6,041 ... E 4
Little Falls, 7,232 .. E 4
Mankato, 31,477 ... F 5
Maple Grove, 38,736 m12
Maplewood, 30,954 . n12
Marshall, 12,023 ... F 3
Minneapolis, 368,383 F 5
Minnetonka, 48,370 . n12
Montevideo, 5,499 .. F 3
Moorhead, 32,295 .. D 2
Morris, 5,613 ..... E 3
Mound, 9,634 ..... n11
Mounds View, 12,541 m12
New Brighton, 22,207 m12
New Hope, 21,853 .. m12
New Ulm, 13,132 ... F 4
Northfield, 14,684 .. F 5
North Mankato,
10,164 .... F 4
North Saint Paul,
12,376 .... m13
Owatonna, 19,386 . F 5
Pipestone, 4,554 .. G 2
Plymouth, 50,889 .. m12
Prior Lake, 11,482 . F 5
Ramsey, 12,408 ... E 5
Red Wing, 15,134 .. F 6
Redwood Falls, 4,859 F 3
Richfield, 35,710 ... F 5
Robbinsdale, 14,396 m12
Rochester, 70,745 . F 6
Roseville, 33,485 ... m12
Saint Cloud, 48,812 . E 4
Saint Louis Park,
43,787 .... n12
Saint Paul, 272,235 . F 5
Saint Peter, 9,421 .. F 5
Shakopee, 11,739 .. F 5
Shoreview, 24,587 .. m12
South Saint Paul,
20,197 .... n12
Stillwater, 13,882 .. E 6
Thief River Falls,
8,010 .... B 2
Virginia, 9,410 .... C 6
Waseca, 8,385 .... F 5
West Saint Paul,
19,248 .... n12
White Bear Lake,
24,704 .... E 5
Willmar, 17,531 ... E 3
Winona, 25,399 ... F 7
Woodbury, 20,075 . F 6
Worthington, 9,977 . G 3

Statute Miles 5 0 10 20 30 40 50
Kilometers 5 0 15 25 35 45 55 65

Lambert Conformal Conic Projection

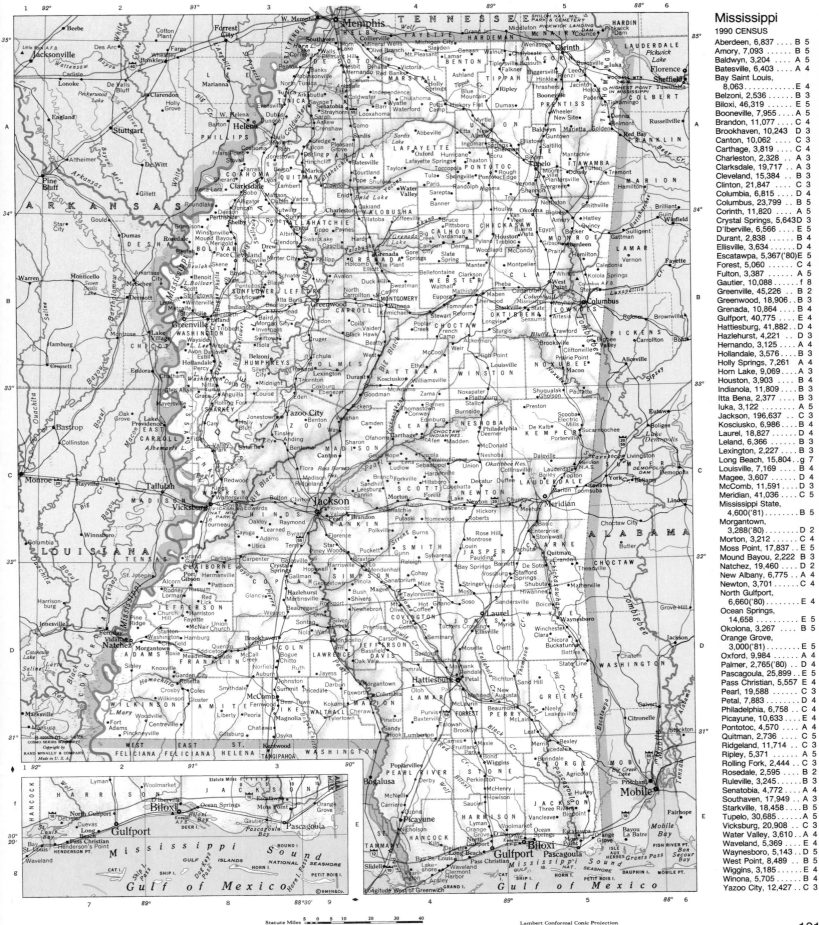

Mississippi

1990 CENSUS

Aberdeen, 6,837 . . . . B 5
Amory, 7,093 . . . . . B 5
Baldwyn, 3,204 . . . . A 5
Batesville, 6,403 . . . . . A 4
Bay Saint Louis,
8,063 . . . . E 4
Belzoni, 2,536 . . . . . B 3
Biloxi, 46,319 . . . . . E 5
Booneville, 7,955 . . . . A 5
Brandon, 11,077 . . . . C 4
Brookhaven, 10,243 . . D 3
Canton, 10,062 . . . . C 4
Carthage, 3,819 . . . . C 4
Charleston, 2,328 . . . A 3
Clarksdale, 19,717 . . . A 3
Cleveland, 15,384 . . . B 3
Clinton, 21,847 . . . . C 3
Columbia, 6,815 . . . . D 4
Columbus, 23,799 . . . B 5
Corinth, 11,820 . . . . A 5
Crystal Springs, 5,643 D 3
D'Iberville, 6,566 . . . E 5
Durant, 2,838 . . . . B 4
Ellisville, 3,634 . . . . D 4
Escatawpa, 5,367('80) E 5
Forest, 5,060 . . . . . C 4
Fulton, 3,387 . . . . . A 5
Gautier, 10,088 . . . . f 8
Greenville, 45,226 . . B 2
Greenwood, 18,906 . . B 3
Grenada, 10,864 . . . B 4
Gulfport, 40,775 . . . E 4
Hattiesburg, 41,882 . . D 4
Hazlehurst, 4,221 . . . D 3
Hernando, 3,125 . . . . A 4
Hollandale, 3,576 . . . B 3
Holly Springs, 7,261 . A 4
Horn Lake, 9,069 . . . A 4
Houston, 3,903 . . . . B 4
Indianola, 11,809 . . . B 3
Itta Bena, 2,377 . . . B 3
Iuka, 3,122 . . . . . . A 5
Jackson, 196,637 . . C 3
Kosciusko, 6,986 . . . C 4
Laurel, 18,827 . . . . D 4
Leland, 6,366 . . . . B 3
Lexington, 2,227 . . . B 3
Long Beach, 15,804 . . g 7
Louisville, 7,169 . . . B 4
Magee, 3,607 . . . . D 4
McComb, 11,591 . . . . D 3
Meridian, 41,036 . . . C 5
Mississippi State,
4,600('81) . . . . . . B 5
Morgantown,
3,288('80) . . . . D 2
Morton, 3,212 . . . . C 4
Moss Point, 17,837 . . E 5
Mound Bayou, 2,222 B 3
Natchez, 19,460 . . . D 3
New Albany, 6,775 . . A 4
Newton, 3,701 . . . . . C 4
North Gulfport,
6,660('80) . . . . . . E 4
Ocean Springs,
14,658 . . . . E 5
Okolona, 3,267 . . . . B 5
Orange Grove,
3,000('81) . . . . . E 5
Oxford, 9,984 . . . . . A 4
Palmer, 2,765('80) . . D 4
Pascagoula, 25,899 . . E 5
Pass Christian, 5,557 E 4
Pearl, 19,588 . . . . C 3
Petal, 7,883 . . . . . D 4
Philadelphia, 6,758 . . C 4
Picayune, 10,633 . . D 4
Pontotoc, 4,570 . . . A 4
Quitman, 2,736 . . . C 5
Ridgeland, 11,714 . . C 3
Ripley, 5,371 . . . . A 5
Rolling Fork, 2,444 . . C 3
Rosedale, 2,595 . . . B 2
Ruleville, 3,245 . . . . B 3
Senatobia, 4,772 . . . A 4
Southaven, 17,949 . . A 3
Starkville, 18,458 . . . B 5
Tupelo, 30,685 . . . . A 5
Vicksburg, 20,908 . . C 3
Water Valley, 3,610 . . A 4
Waveland, 5,369 . . . E 4
Waynesboro, 5,143 . . D 5
West Point, 8,489 . . B 5
Wiggins, 3,185 . . . . E 4
Winona, 5,705 . . . . . B 4
Yazoo City, 12,427 . . C 3

Missouri

Missouri
1990 CENSUS

Arnold, 18,828	C 7
Aurora, 6,459	E 4
Ballwin, 21,816	f12
Belton, 18,150	C 3
Berkeley, 12,450	f13
Blue Springs, 40,153	h11
Bolivar, 6,845	D 4
Boonville, 7,095	C 5

Brentwood, 8,150	f13
Bridgeton, 17,779	C 7
Brookfield, 4,888	B 4
Cape Girardeau, 34,438	D 8
Carthage, 10,747	E 3
Caruthersville, 7,389	E 8
Charleston, 5,085	E 8
Chillicothe, 8,804	B 4
Clayton, 13,874	C 7
Clinton, 8,703	C 4
Columbia, 69,101	C 5

De Soto, 5,993	C 7
Des Peres, 8,395	f13
Dexter, 7,559	E 8
Ellisville, 7,545	f12
Eureka, 4,683	C 7
Excelsior Springs, 10,354	B 3
Farmington, 11,598	D 7
Ferguson, 22,286	C 7
Festus, 8,105	C 7
Florissant, 51,206	f13

Fulton, 10,033	C 6
Gladstone, 26,243	h10
Grandview, 24,967	C 3
Hannibal, 18,004	B 6
Harrisonville, 7,683	C 3
Independence, 112,301	B 3
Jackson, 9,256	D 8
Jefferson City, 35,481	C 5
Jennings, 15,905	f13
Joplin, 40,961	E 3
Kansas City, 435,146	B 3

Kennett, 10,941	E 8
Kirksville, 17,152	A 5
Kirkwood, 27,291	C 7
Lebanon, 9,983	D 5
Lees Summit, 46,418	C 3
Liberty, 20,459	B 3
Macon, 5,571	B 5
Malden, 4,801	E 8
Manchester, 6,542	f12
Maplewood, 9,962	f13
Marshall, 12,711	B 4

Maryland Heights, 25,407	f12
Maryville, 10,663	A 3
Mexico, 11,290	B 6
Moberly, 12,839	B 5
Monett, 6,529	E 4
Neosho, 9,254	E 3
Nevada, 8,597	D 3
O'Fallon, 18,698	f12
Overland, 17,987	f13
Perryville, 6,933	D 8

Pine Lawn, 5,092	f13
Poplar Bluff, 16,996	E 7
Raytown, 30,601	h11
Richmond Heights, 10,448	f13
Rolla, 14,090	D 6
Saint Charles, 54,555	C 7
Sainte Genevieve, 4,411	D 7
Saint Joseph, 71,852	B 3
Saint Louis, 396,685	C 7
Saint Peters, 45,779	E 6

Sedalia, 19,800	C 4
Sikeston, 17,641	E 8
Springfield, 140,494	D 4
Sullivan, 5,661	A 4
Trenton, 6,129	A 4
University City, 40,087	C 7
Warrensburg, 15,244	C 4
Washington, 10,704	C 6
Webb City, 7,449	D 3
Webster Groves, 22,987	f13
West Plains, 8,913	E 6

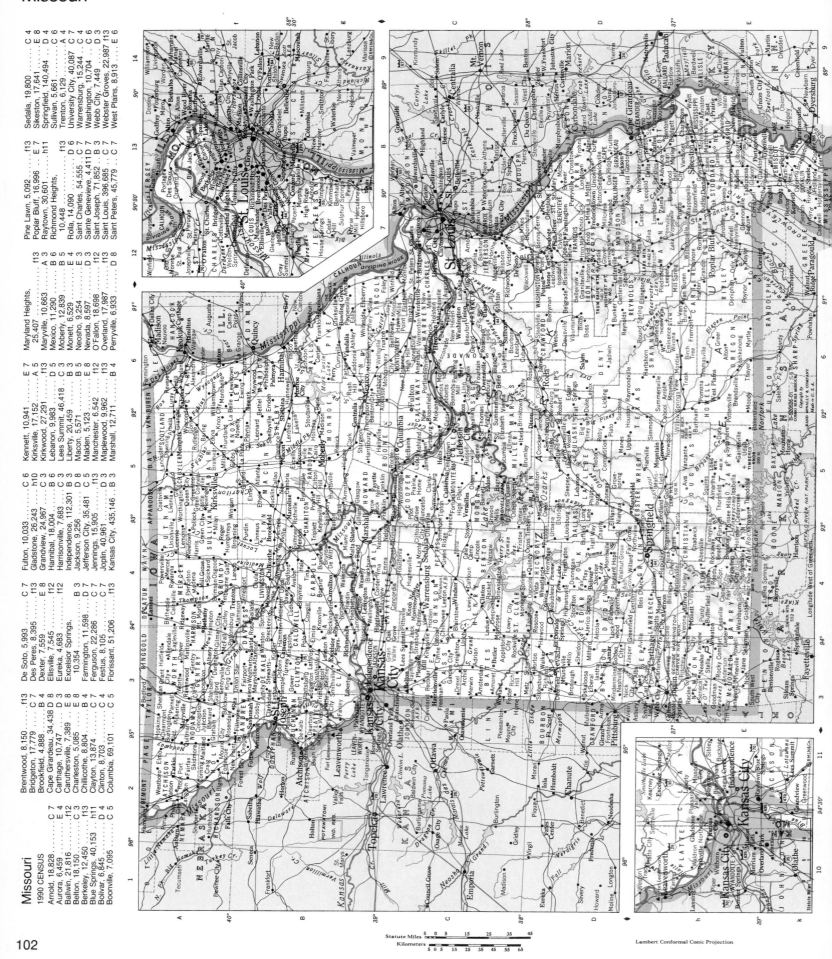

Statute Miles

Kilometers

Lambert Conformal Conic Projection

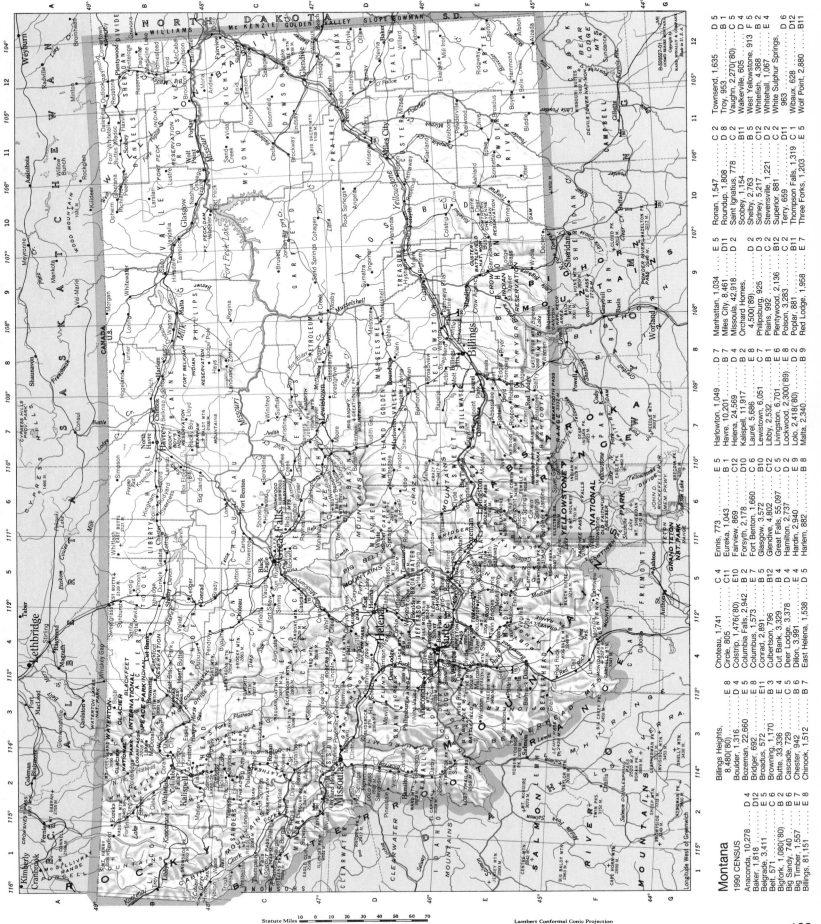

Montana

1990 CENSUS

Anaconda, 10,278	D 4	
Baker, 1,818	D12	
Belgrade, 3,411	C 6	
Belt, 571	C 5	
Bigfork, 1,080('80)	B 2	
Big Sandy, 740	B 6	
Big Timber, 1,557	E 7	
Billings, 81,151	E 8	
Billings Heights, 8,460('80)		
Boulder, 1,316	D 4	
Bozeman, 22,660	D 5	
Bridger, 692	E 8	
Broadus, 572	E11	
Browning, 1,170	B 3	
Butte, 33,336	D 4	
Cascade, 729	C 5	
Chester, 942	B 6	
Chinook, 1,512	B 7	

Choteau, 1,741	C 4	
Circle, 805	C11	
Colstrip, 1,476('80)	E10	
Columbia Falls, 2,942	B 2	
Columbus, 1,573	E 7	
Conrad, 2,891	B 4	
Culbertson, 796	B12	
Cut Bank, 3,329	B 4	
Deer Lodge, 3,378	D 4	
Dillon, 3,991	E 4	
East Helena, 1,538	D 5	

Ennis, 773	E 5	
Eureka, 1,043	B 1	
Fairview, 869	C12	
Forsyth, 2,178	D10	
Fort Benton, 1,660	C 6	
Glasgow, 3,572	B10	
Glendive, 4,802	C12	
Great Falls, 55,097	C 5	
Hamilton, 2,737	D 2	
Hardin, 2,940	E 9	
Harlem, 882	B 8	

Harlowton, 1,049	D 7	
Havre, 10,201	B 7	
Helena, 24,569	D 4	
Kalispell, 11,917	B 2	
Laurel, 5,686	E 8	
Lewistown, 6,051	C 7	
Libby, 2,532	B 1	
Livingston, 6,701	E 6	
Lockwood, 2,300('89)	E 8	
Lolo, 2,418('80)	D 2	
Malta, 2,340	B 8	

Manhattan, 1,034	D 2	
Miles City, 8,461	D11	
Missoula, 42,918	D 2	
Orchard Homes, 4,500('89)	D 2	
Philipsburg, 925	D 3	
Plains, 992	C 2	
Plentywood, 2,136	B12	
Polson, 3,283	C 2	
Poplar, 881	B11	
Red Lodge, 1,958	E 7	

Ronan, 1,547	C 2	
Roundup, 1,808	D 8	
Saint Ignatius, 778	C 2	
Scobey, 1,154	B11	
Shelby, 2,763	B 5	
Sidney, 5,217	C12	
Stevensville, 1,221	D 2	
Superior, 881	C 1	
Terry, 659	D11	
Thompson Falls, 1,319	C 1	
Three Forks, 1,203	E 5	

Townsend, 1,635	D 5	
Troy, 953	B 1	
Vaughn, 2,270('80)	C 5	
Walkerville, 605	D 4	
West Yellowstone, 913	F 5	
Whitefish, 4,368	B 2	
Whitehall, 1,067	E 4	
White Sulphur Springs, 963	D 6	
Wibaux, 628	D12	
Wolf Point, 2,880	B11	

Statute Miles 0 10 20 30 40 50 60 70
Kilometers 0 10 30 50 70 90

Lambert Conformal Conic Projection

103

Nebraska

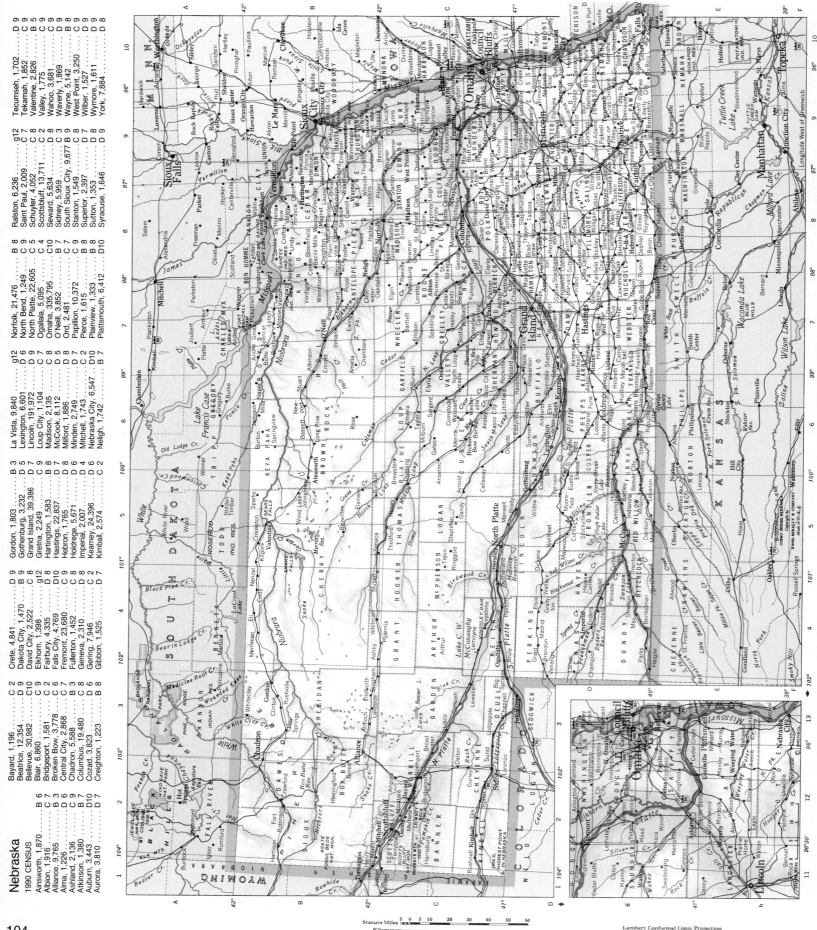

Statute Miles

Kilometers

Lambert Conformal Conic Projection

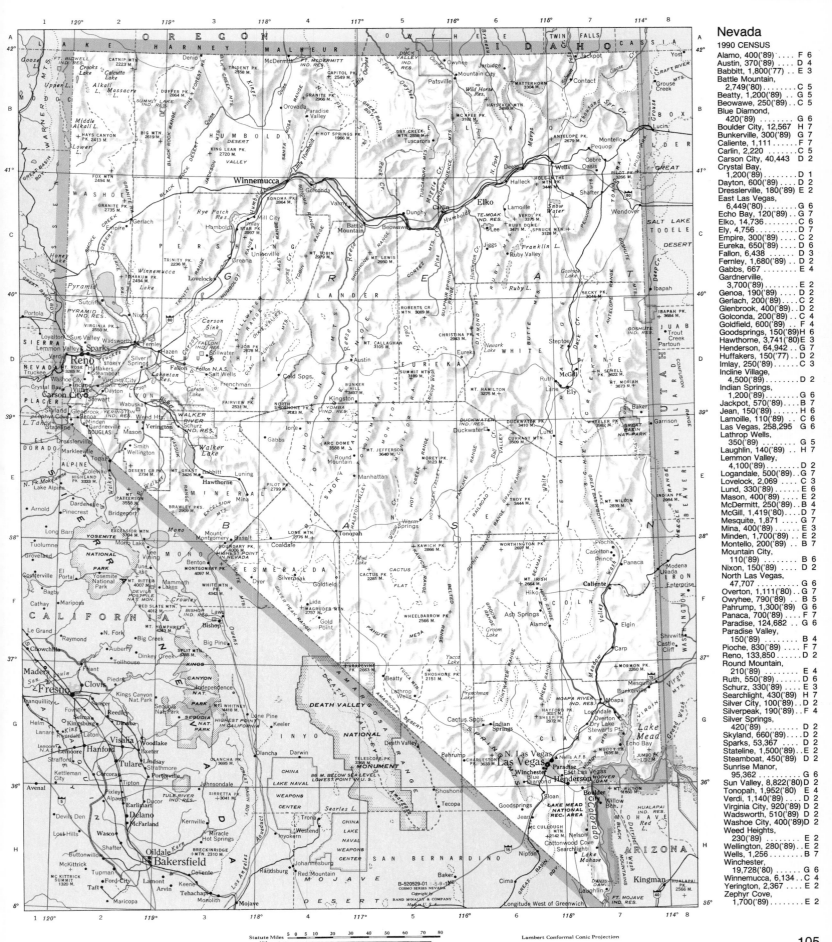

Nevada

1990 CENSUS

Alamo, 400('89) .... F 6
Austin, 370('89) .... D 4
Babbitt, 1,800('77) .. E 3
Battle Mountain,
  2,749('80) .... C 5
Beatty, 1,200('89) ... G 5
Beowawe, 250('89) .. C 5
Blue Diamond,
  420('89) .... G 6
Boulder City, 12,567 . H 7
Bunkerville, 300('89) . G 7
Caliente, 1,111 ...... F 7
Carlin, 2,220 .... C 5
Carson City, 40,443 .. D 2
Crystal Bay,
  1,200('89) .... D 1
Dayton, 600('89) .... D 2
Dresslerville, 180('89) E 2
East Las Vegas,
  6,449('80) .... G 6
Echo Bay, 120('89) .. G 7
Elko, 14,736 .... C 6
Ely, 4,756 .... D 7
Empire, 300('89) .... C 2
Eureka, 650('89) .... D 6
Fallon, 6,438 .... D 3
Fernley, 1,680('89) .. D 2
Gabbs, 667 .... E 4
Gardnerville,
  3,700('89) .... E 2
Genoa, 190('89) .... D 2
Gerlach, 200('89) .... C 2
Glenbrook, 400('89) . D 2
Golconda, 200('89) .. C 4
Goldfield, 600('89) .. F 4
Goodsprings, 150('89) H 6
Hawthorne, 3,741('80) E 3
Henderson, 64,942 .. G 7
Huffakers, 150('77) .. C 3
Imlay, 250('89) ..... C 3
Incline Village,
  4,500('89) .... D 2
Indian Springs,
  1,200('89) .... G 6
Jackpot, 570('89) ... B 7
Jean, 150('89) ...... H 6
Lamoille, 110('89) ... C 6
Las Vegas, 258,295 .. G 6
Lathrop Wells,
  350('89) .... G 5
Laughlin, 140('89) ... H 7
Lemmon Valley,
  4,100('89) .... D 2
Logandale, 500('89) . G 7
Lovelock, 2,069 ..... C 3
Lund, 330('89) ...... E 6
Mason, 400('89) .... E 2
McDermitt, 250('89) . B 4
McGill, 1,419('80) ... D 7
Mesquite, 1,871 ..... G 7
Mina, 150('89) ...... E 3
Minden, 1,700('89) .. E 2
Montello, 200('89) .. B 7
Mountain City,
  110('89) .... B 6
Nixon, 150('89) ..... D 2
North Las Vegas,
  47,707 .... G 6
Overton, 1,111('80) . G 7
Owyhee, 790('89) .. B 5
Pahrump, 1,300('89) G 6
Panaca, 700('89) .... F 7
Paradise, 124,682 ... G 6
Paradise Valley,
  150('89) .... B 4
Pioche, 830('89) .... F 7
Reno, 133,850 ...... D 2
Round Mountain,
  210('89) .... E 4
Ruth, 550('89) ...... D 6
Schurz, 330('89) .... E 3
Searchlight, 430('89) H 7
Silver City, 100('89) . D 2
Silverpeak, 190('89) . F 4
Silver Springs,
  420('89) .... D 2
Skyland, 660('89) ... D 2
Sparks, 53,367 ...... D 2
Stateline, 1,500('89) . E 2
Steamboat, 450('89) . D 2
Sunrise Manor,
  95,362 .... G 6
Sun Valley, 8,822('80) D 2
Tonopah, 1,952('80) . E 4
Verdi, 1,140('89) .... D 2
Virginia City, 920('89) D 2
Wadsworth, 510('89) D 2
Washoe City, 400('89) D 2
Weed Heights,
  230('89) .... E 2
Wellington, 280('89) . E 2
Wells, 1,256 .... B 7
Winchester,
  19,728('80) .... G 6
Winnemucca, 6,134 .. C 4
Yerington, 2,367 .... E 2
Zephyr Cove,
  1,700('89) .... E 2

New Hampshire
1990 CENSUS
Alton, 975 (3,286▲) ... D 4
Amherst, 850
  (9,068▲) .... E 3
Antrim, 1,142
  (2,360▲) .... D 3
Ashland, 1,479
  (1,915▲) .... C 3
Bedford, 1,400
  (12,563▲) ...... E 3
Berlin, 11,824 ..... B 4
Bristol, 1,258
  (2,537▲) .... C 3
Charlestown, 1,294
  (4,630▲) .... D 2
Claremont, 13,902 .. D 2
Colebrook, 1,131
  (2,444▲) .... g 7
Concord, 36,006 .... D 3
Conway, 1,781
  (7,940▲) .... C 4
Derry, 12,248
  (29,603▲) ...... E 4
Dover, 25,042 ...... D 5
Durham, 8,448
  (11,818▲) ...... D 5
Enfield, 1,581
  (3,979▲) .... C 2
Epping, 1,384
  (5,162▲) .... D 4
Exeter, 8,947
  (12,481▲) ...... E 5
Farmington, 3,284
  (5,739▲) .... D 4
Franklin, 8,304 .... D 3
Goffstown, 2,700
  (14,621▲) ...... D 3
Gorham, 2,180
  (3,173▲) .... B 4
Greenville, 1,447
  (2,231▲) .... E 3
Hampton, 6,779
  (12,278▲) ...... E 5
Hanover, 6,861
  (9,212▲) .... C 2
Henniker, 1,538
  (4,151▲) .... D 3
Hinsdale, 1,546
  (3,936▲) .... E 2
Hooksett, 1,868
  (8,767▲) .... D 4
Hudson, 6,248
  (19,530▲) ...... E 4
Jaffrey, 2,684
  (5,361▲) .... E 2
Keene, 22,430 ...... E 2
Laconia, 15,743 .... C 4
Lancaster, 2,134
  (3,522▲) .... B 3
Lebanon, 12,183 .... C 2
Lisbon, 1,151
  (1,664▲) .... B 3
Littleton, 4,480
  (5,827▲) .... B 3
Manchester, 99,567 .. E 4
Marlborough, 1,184
  (1,927▲) .... E 2
Meredith, 1,202
  (4,837▲) .... C 3
Merrimack, 1,300
  (22,156▲) ...... E 4
Milford, 6,269
  (11,795▲) ...... E 3
Milton, 1,000 (3,691▲) D 5
Nashua, 79,662 ..... E 4
New London, 1,335
  (3,180▲) .... D 3
Newmarket, 3,749
  (7,157▲) .... D 5
Newport, 4,388
  (6,110▲) .... D 2
Northfield, 1,375
  (4,263▲) .... D 3
North Hampton, 1,000
  (3,637▲) .... E 5
Peterborough, 2,100
  (5,239▲) .... E 3
Pittsfield, 1,584
  (3,701▲) .... D 4
Plaistow, 1,850
  (7,316▲) .... E 4
Plymouth, 3,628
  (5,811▲) .... C 3
Portsmouth, 25,925 .. D 5
Raymond, 1,192
  (8,713▲) .... D 4
Rochester, 26,630 .. D 5
Rollinsford, 1,173
  (2,645▲) .... D 5
Rye, 835 (4,612▲) .. D 5
Salem, 12,000
  (25,746▲) ...... E 4
Somersworth, 11,249 D 5
Tilton, 1,380 (3,240▲) D 3
Troy, 1,318 (2,097▲) E 2
Whitefield, 1,005
  (1,909▲) .... B 3
Winchester, 1,732
  (4,038▲) .... E 2
Wolfeboro, 2,000
  (4,807▲) .... C 4

▲ Population of entire town (township), including rural area.

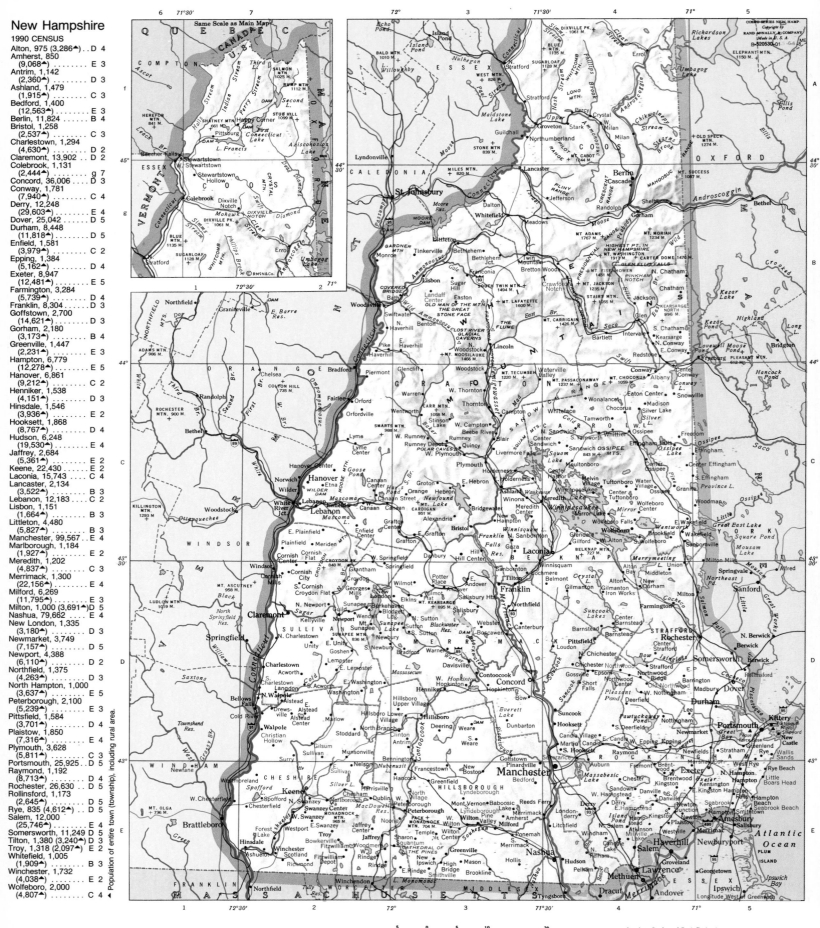

Statute Miles

Kilometers

Lambert Conformal Conic Projection

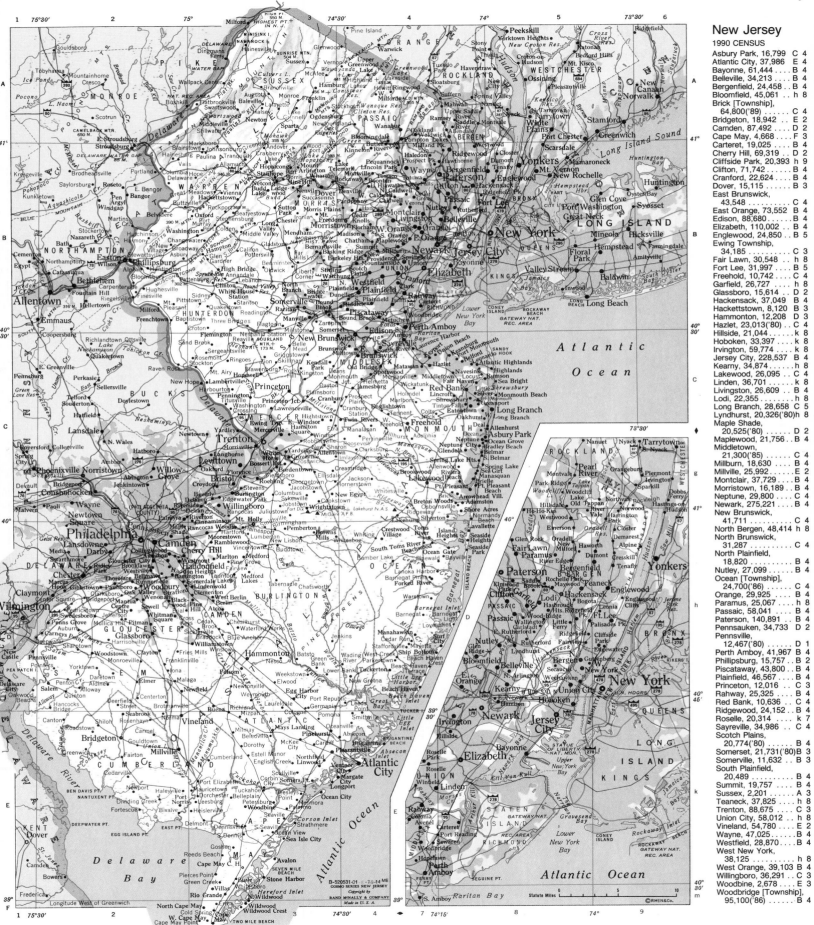

New Jersey

1990 CENSUS

Asbury Park, 16,799 . . . . C 4
Atlantic City, 37,986 . . . E 4
Bayonne, 61,444 . . . . . . B 4
Belleville, 34,213 . . . . B 4
Bergenfield, 24,458 . . B 4
Bloomfield, 45,061 . . . h 8
Brick [Township],
  64,800('89) . . . . C 4
Bridgeton, 18,942 . . E 2
Camden, 87,492 . . . . D 2
Cape May, 4,668 . . . . . F 3
Carteret, 19,025 . . . . B 4
Cherry Hill, 69,319 . . . D 2
Cliffside Park, 20,393 . h 9
Clifton, 71,742 . . . . . . B 4
Cranford, 22,624 . . . . B 4
Dover, 15,115 . . . . B 3
East Brunswick,
  43,548 . . . . C 4
East Orange, 73,552 . . B 4
Edison, 88,680 . . . . . . B 4
Elizabeth, 110,002 . . B 4
Englewood, 24,850 . . B 5
Ewing Township,
  34,185 . . . . C 3
Fair Lawn, 30,548 . . h 8
Fort Lee, 31,997 . . . . B 5
Freehold, 10,742 . . . . C 4
Garfield, 26,727 . . . . h 8
Glassboro, 15,614 . . . D 2
Hackensack, 37,049 . . B 4
Hackettstown, 8,120 . B 3
Hammonton, 12,208 . D 3
Hazlet, 23,013('80) . . . C 4
Hillside, 21,044 . . . . . k 8
Hoboken, 33,397 . . . . k 8
Irvington, 59,774 . . . k 8
Jersey City, 228,537 B 4
Kearny, 34,874 . . . . . h 8
Lakewood, 26,095 . . C 4
Linden, 36,701 . . . . . k 8
Livingston, 26,609 . . B 4
Lodi, 22,355 . . . . h 8
Long Branch, 28,658 C 5
Lyndhurst, 20,326('80)h 8
Maple Shade,
  20,525('80) . . . . . . D 2
Maplewood, 21,756 . . B 4
Middletown,
  21,300('85) . . . . . . C 4
Millburn, 18,630 . . . . B 4
Millville, 25,992 . . . . E 2
Montclair, 37,729 . . . B 4
Morristown, 16,189 . . B 4
Neptune, 29,800 . . . . C 4
Newark, 275,221 . . . . B 4
New Brunswick,
  41,711 . . . . C 4
North Bergen, 48,414 h 8
North Brunswick,
  31,287 . . . . C 4
North Plainfield,
  18,820 . . . . B 4
Nutley, 27,099 . . . . . . B 4
Ocean [Township],
  24,700('86) . . . . . . C 4
Orange, 29,925 . . . . . B 4
Paramus, 25,067 . . . h 8
Passaic, 58,041 . . . . . B 4
Paterson, 140,891 . . B 4
Pennsauken, 34,733 . D 2
Pennsville,
  12,467('80) . . . . . . D 1
Perth Amboy, 41,967 B 4
Phillipsburg, 15,757 . . B 2
Piscataway, 43,800 . . C 4
Plainfield, 46,567 . . . B 4
Princeton, 12,016 . . . C 3
Rahway, 25,325 . . . . B 4
Red Bank, 10,636 . . . C 4
Ridgewood, 24,152 . . B 4
Roselle, 20,314 . . . . . k 7
Sayreville, 34,986 . . . C 4
Scotch Plains,
  20,774('80) . . . . . . B 4
Somerset, 21,731('80) B 3
Somerville, 11,632 . . B 3
South Plainfield,
  20,489 . . . . B 4
Summit, 19,757 . . . . B 4
Sussex, 2,201 . . . . . . A 3
Teaneck, 37,825 . . . h 8
Trenton, 88,675 . . . . C 3
Union City, 58,012 . . h 8
Vineland, 54,780 . . . E 2
Wayne, 47,025 . . . . . B 4
Westfield, 28,870 . . . B 4
West New York,
  38,125 . . . . h 8
West Orange, 39,103 B 4
Willingboro, 36,291 . . C 3
Woodbine, 2,678 . . . E 3
Woodbridge [Township],
  95,100('86) . . . . . . B 4

New Mexico

New Mexico
1990 CENSUS

Alameda, 5,900('87) . . . . . B 3
Alamogordo, 27,596 . . . . E 4
Albuquerque, 384,736 B 3
Anthony, 3,285('80) . . F 3
Armijo, 14,600('87) . . . . k 7
Artesia, 10,610 . . . . . . E 5
Aztec, 5,479 . . . . A 2
Bayard, 2,598 . . . . . . E 1
Belen, 6,547 . . . . C 3
Bernalillo, 5,960 . . . . . B 3
Bloomfield, 5,214 . . . . A 2
Carlsbad, 24,952 . . . . E 5
Carrizozo, 1,075 . . . . . D 4
Cedar Crest,
   1,200('87) . . . . k 8
Central, 1,835 . . . . . . E 1
Chama, 1,048 . . . . . . A 4
Chimayo, 1,993('80) . . A 4
Clayton, 2,484 . . . . . A 6
Clovis, 30,954 . . . . . . C 6
Crownpoint,
   1,134('80) . . . . B 2
Deming, 10,970 . . . . . E 2
Dona Ana, 950('87) . . E 3
Dulce, 1,648('80) . . . . A 2
Espanola, 8,389 . . . . . B 3
Eunice, 2,676 . . . . . . E 6
Farmington, 33,997 . . A 1
Five Points,
   4,200('87) . . . . B 3
Fort Sumner, 1,269 . . C 5
Fort Wingate,
   950('87) . . . . B 1
Gallup, 19,154 . . . . . . B 1
Grants, 8,626 . . . . . . B 2
Hagerman, 961 . . . . . D 5
Hatch, 1,136 . . . . E 2
Hobbs, 29,115 . . . . . . E 6
Hurley, 1,534 . . . . . . E 1
Isleta, 1,246('80) . . . . C 3
Jal, 2,156 . . . . E 6
Jemez Pueblo,
   1,503('80) . . . . B 3
Kirtland, 2,358('80) . . A 1
La Luz, 1,194('80) . . . D 4
La Mesa, 900('87) . . . E 3
Las Cruces, 62,126 . . E 3
Las Vegas, 14,753 . . . B 4
Lordsburg, 2,951 . . . . E 1
Los Alamos,
   11,039('80) . . . . . . B 3
Los Lunas, 6,013 . . . . C 3
Los Ranchos de
   Albuquerque, 3,955 B 3
Loving, 1,243 . . . . . . E 5
Lovington, 9,322 . . . . E 6
Magdalena, 861 . . . . . C 2
Mescalero, 1,259('80) D 4
Mesilla, 1,975 . . . . . . E 3
Milan, 1,911 . . . . B 2
Moriarty, 1,399 . . . . . C 3
Mountainair, 926 . . . . C 3
Mountain View,
   2,300('87) . . . . C 3
Paradise Hills,
   5,096('80) . . . . B 3
Portales, 10,690 . . . . C 6
Questa, 1,707 . . . . . . A 4
Ranchos de Taos,
   1,411('80) . . . . A 4
Raton, 7,372 . . . . . . A 5
Rio Rancho, 32,505 . . B 3
Roswell, 44,654 . . . . D 5
Ruidoso, 4,600 . . . . . D 4
Ruidoso Downs, 920 D 4
San Felipe Pueblo,
   1,465('80) . . . . B 3
Santa Cruz, 975('87) . B 3
Santa Fe, 55,859 . . . . B 4
Santa Rosa, 2,263 . . . C 5
Santo Domingo Pueblo,
   2,082('80) . . . . B 3
Shiprock, 7,237('80) . A 1
Silver City, 10,683 . . . E 1
Socorro, 8,159 . . . . . C 3
Springer, 1,262 . . . . . A 5
Sunland Park, 8,179 . F 3
Taos, 4,065 . . . . A 4
Taos Pueblo,
   1,030('87) . . . . A 4
Tesuque, 1,014('80) . . B 4
Texico, 966 . . . . C 6
Thoreau, 1,099('80) . . B 1
Tierra Amarilla,
   900('87) . . . . A 3
Tohatchi, 1,011('80) . . B 1
Truth or Consequences
   (Hot Springs), 6,221 D 2
Tucumcari, 6,831 . . . B 6
Tularosa, 2,615 . . . . . D 4
Tyrone, 950('87) . . . . E 1
University Park,
   4,353('80) . . . . E 3
Zuni, 5,551('80) . . . . B 1

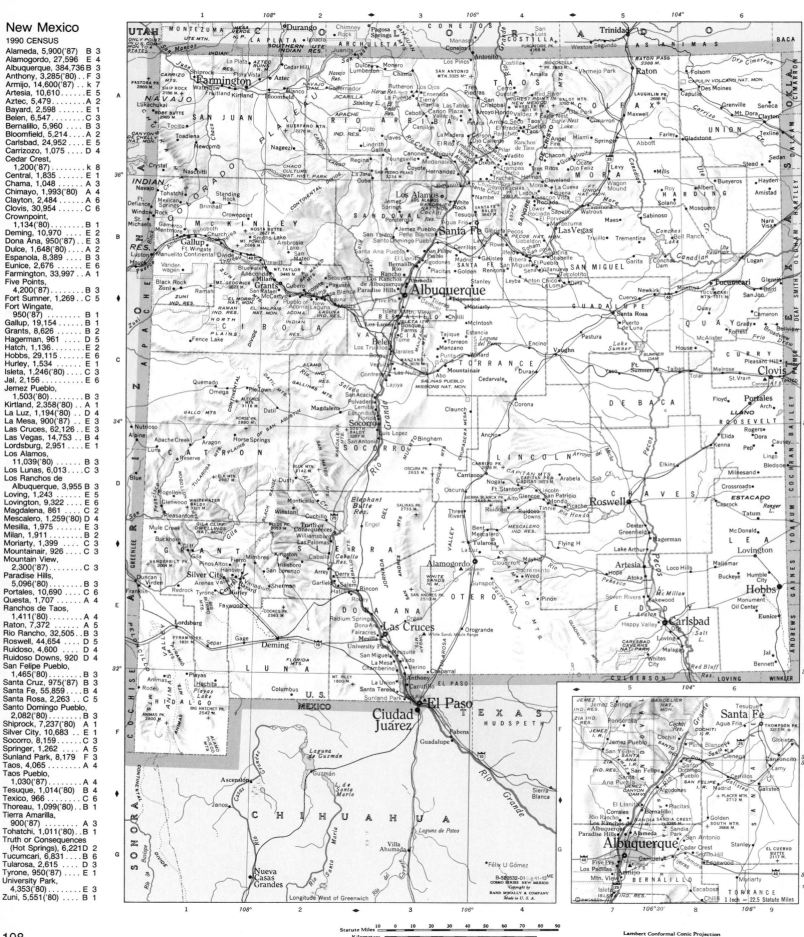

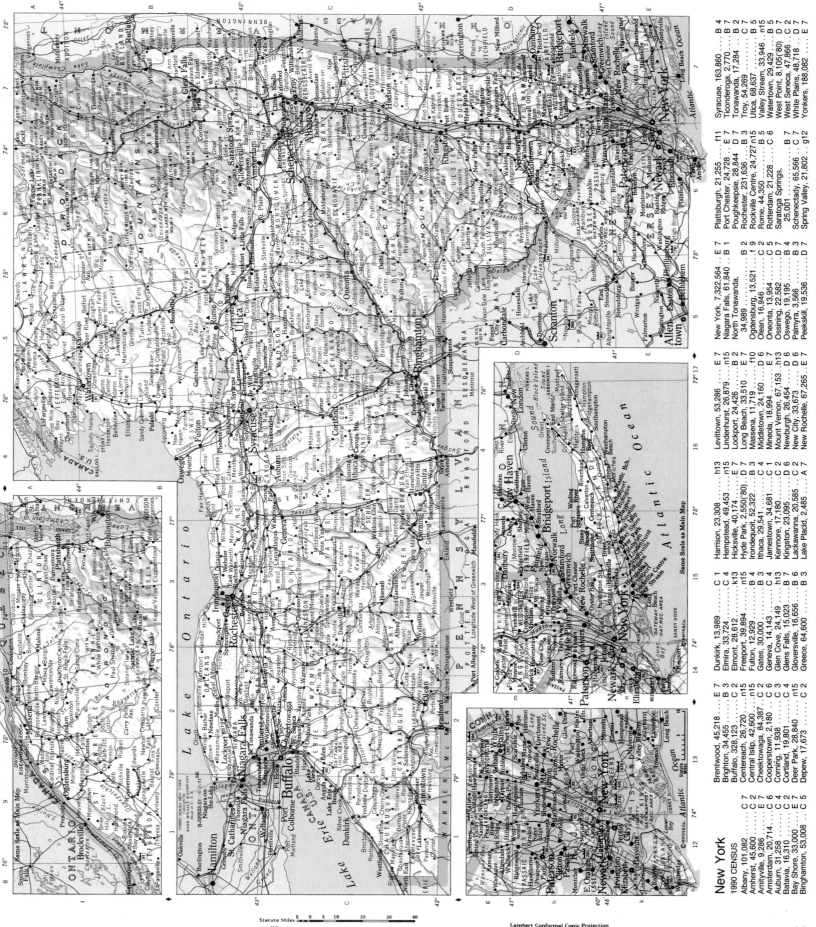

Statute Miles
Kilometers

Lambert Conformal Conic Projection

109

North Carolina

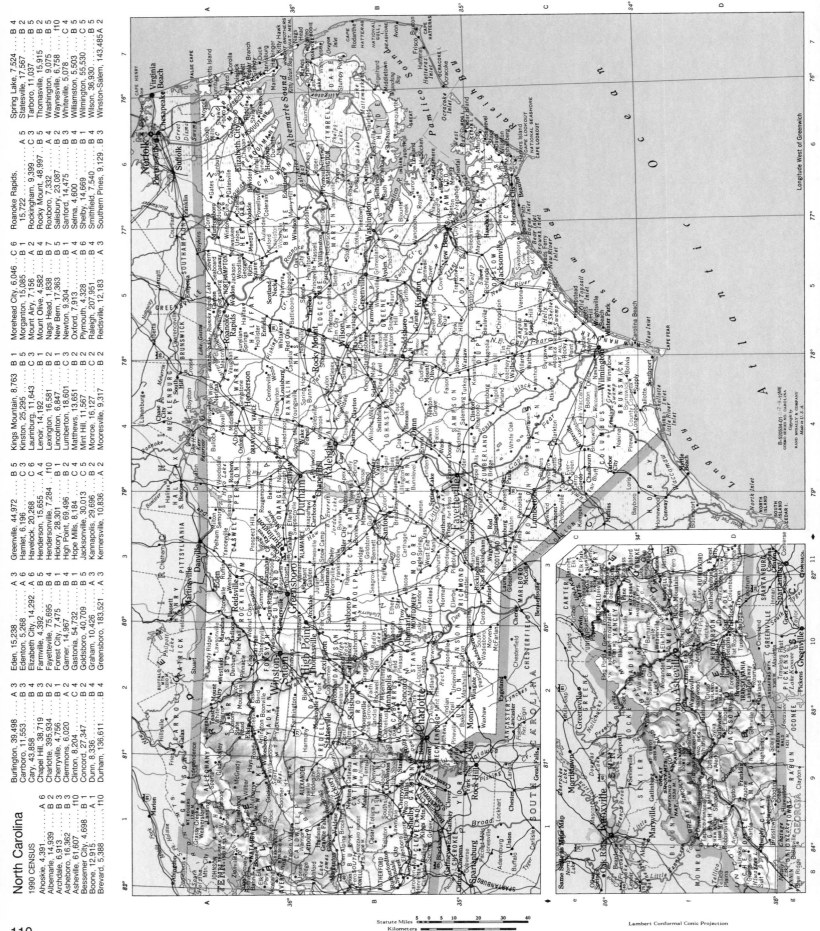

North Carolina
1990 CENSUS

Ahoskie, 4,391 ..... A 6
Albemarle, 14,939 ..... B 3
Archdale, 6,913 ..... B 3
Asheboro, 16,362 ..... B 3
Asheville, 61,607 ..... f10
Bessemer City, 4,698 ..... B 1
Boone, 12,915 ..... A 1
Brevard, 5,388 ..... f10

Burlington, 39,498 ..... A 3
Carrboro, 11,553 ..... B 3
Cary, 43,858 ..... B 3
Chapel Hill, 38,719 ..... B 3
Charlotte, 395,934 ..... B 2
Cherryville, 4,756 ..... B 1
Clemmons, 6,020 ..... A 2
Clinton, 8,204 ..... C 4
Concord, 27,347 ..... B 2
Durham, 136,611 ..... B 4

Eden, 15,238 ..... A 3
Edenton, 5,268 ..... A 6
Elizabeth City, 14,292 ..... A 6
Farmville, 4,392 ..... B 5
Fayetteville, 75,695 ..... B 4
Forest City, 7,475 ..... B 1
Garner, 14,967 ..... B 4
Gastonia, 54,732 ..... B 1
Goldsboro, 40,709 ..... B 5
Graham, 10,426 ..... A 3
Greensboro, 183,521 ..... A 2

Greenville, 44,972 ..... B 5
Hamlet, 6,196 ..... C 3
Havelock, 20,268 ..... C 6
Henderson, 15,655 ..... A 4
Hendersonville, 7,284 ..... f10
Hickory, 28,301 ..... B 1
High Point, 69,496 ..... B 2
Hope Mills, 8,184 ..... B 4
Jacksonville, 30,013 ..... C 5
Kannapolis, 29,696 ..... B 2
Kernersville, 10,836 ..... A 2

Kings Mountain, 8,763 ..... B 1
Kinston, 25,295 ..... B 5
Laurinburg, 11,643 ..... C 3
Lenoir, 14,192 ..... B 1
Lexington, 16,581 ..... B 2
Lincolnton, 6,847 ..... B 1
Lumberton, 18,601 ..... C 4
Matthews, 13,651 ..... B 2
Mint Hill, 11,567 ..... B 2
Monroe, 16,127 ..... C 2
Mooresville, 9,317 ..... B 2

Morehead City, 6,046 ..... C 6
Morganton, 15,085 ..... B 1
Mount Airy, 7,156 ..... A 2
Mount Olive, 4,582 ..... B 5
Nags Head, 1,838 ..... B 7
New Bern, 17,363 ..... B 5
Newton, 9,304 ..... B 1
Oxford, 7,913 ..... A 4
Plymouth, 4,328 ..... B 6
Raleigh, 207,951 ..... B 4
Reidsville, 12,183 ..... A 3

Roanoke Rapids, 15,722 ..... A 5
Rockingham, 9,399 ..... C 3
Rocky Mount, 48,997 ..... B 5
Roxboro, 7,332 ..... A 4
Salisbury, 23,087 ..... B 2
Sanford, 14,475 ..... B 3
Selma, 4,600 ..... B 4
Shelby, 14,669 ..... B 1
Smithfield, 7,540 ..... B 4
Southern Pines, 9,129 ..... B 3

Spring Lake, 7,524 ..... B 4
Statesville, 17,567 ..... B 2
Tarboro, 11,037 ..... B 5
Thomasville, 15,915 ..... B 2
Washington, 9,075 ..... B 5
Waynesville, 6,758 ..... f10
Whiteville, 5,078 ..... C 4
Williamston, 5,503 ..... B 5
Wilmington, 55,530 ..... C 5
Wilson, 36,930 ..... B 4
Winston-Salem, 143,485 ..... A 2

Statute Miles
Kilometers

Lambert Conformal Conic Projection

North Dakota

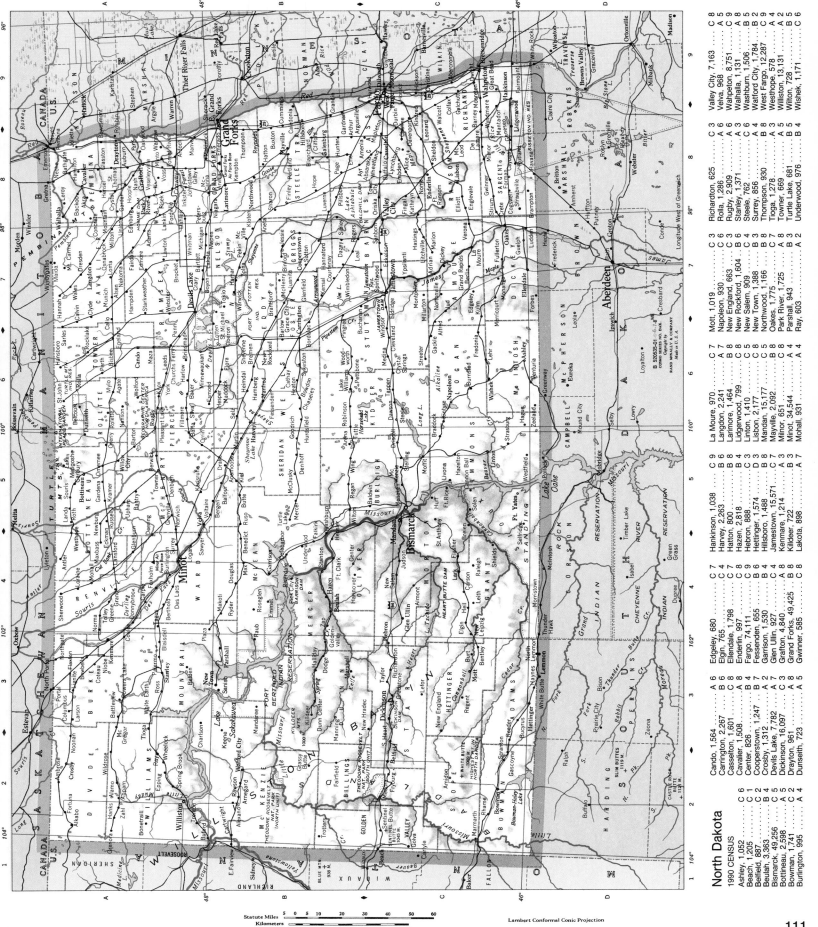

Statute Miles 5 0 5 10 20 30 40 50 60

Kilometers 5 0 5 15 25 35 45 55 65 75

Lambert Conformal Conic Projection

111

Ohio

1990 CENSUS

Akron, 223,019 ..... A 4
Alliance, 23,376 ..... B 4
Bowling Green, 28,176 ..... A 2
Brook Park, 22,865 ..... h 9
Brunswick, 28,230 ..... A 4
Canton, 84,161 ..... B 4
Chillicothe, 21,923 ..... C 3
Cincinnati, 364,040 ..... C 1
Athens, 21,265 ..... C 3
Austintown, 23,300 ..... A 5
Barberton, 27,623 ..... A 4
Beavercreek, 33,626 ..... C 1

Bellefontaine, 12,142 ..... B 2
Boardman, 38,596 ..... A 5
Bowling Green, 28,176 ..... A 2
Brook Park, 22,865 ..... h 9
Brunswick, 28,230 ..... A 4
Canton, 84,161 ..... B 4
Chillicothe, 21,923 ..... C 3
Cincinnati, 364,040 ..... C 1
Cleveland, 505,616 ..... A 4
Cleveland Heights,
    54,052 ..... C 1

Columbus, 632,910 ..... C 2
Cuyahoga Falls, 48,950 ..... A 4
Dayton, 182,044 ..... C 1
Defiance, 16,768 ..... A 1
Delaware, 20,030 ..... B 2
East Cleveland, 33,096 ..... g 9
East Liverpool, 13,654 ..... B 5
Eastlake, 21,161 ..... A 4
Elyria, 56,746 ..... A 3
Euclid, 54,875 ..... A 4
Fairborn, 31,300 ..... C 1

Fairfield, 39,729 ..... C 1
Findlay, 35,703 ..... B 1
Fostoria, 14,983 ..... B 2
Fremont, 17,648 ..... B 2
Garfield Heights, 31,739 ..... h 9
Greenville, 12,863 ..... B 1
Hamilton, 61,368 ..... C 1
Ironton, 12,751 ..... D 3
Kent, 28,835 ..... A 4
Kettering, 60,569 ..... C 1
Lakewood, 59,718 ..... A 4

Lancaster, 34,507 ..... C 3
Lima, 45,549 ..... B 1
Lorain, 71,245 ..... A 4
Mansfield, 50,627 ..... B 3
Maple Heights, 27,089 ..... h 9
Marietta, 15,026 ..... C 4
Marion, 34,075 ..... B 2
Massillon, 31,007 ..... B 4
Medina, 19,231 ..... A 4
Mentor, 47,358 ..... A 4
Middletown, 46,022 ..... C 1

Mount Vernon, 14,550 ..... B 3
Newark, 44,389 ..... B 3
New Philadelphia,
    15,698 ..... B 4
Niles, 21,128 ..... A 5
Norwalk, 14,731 ..... A 3
North Olmsted, 34,204 ..... h 9
Norwalk, 14,731 ..... A 3
Norwood, 23,674 ..... o13
Oxford, 18,937 ..... C 1
Parma, 87,876 ..... A 4
Parma Heights, 21,448 ..... h 9

Piqua, 20,612 ..... B 1
Portsmouth, 22,676 ..... D 3
Reynoldsburg, 25,748 ..... C 3
Salem, 12,233 ..... B 5
Sandusky, 29,764 ..... A 3
Shaker Heights, 30,831 ..... h 9
South Euclid, 23,866 ..... g 9
Springfield, 70,487 ..... C 2
Steubenville, 22,125 ..... B 5
Stow, 27,702 ..... A 4
Strongsville, 35,308 ..... A 4

Tiffin, 18,604 ..... A 2
Toledo, 332,943 ..... A 2
Upper Arlington, 34,128 ..... B 2
Urbana, 11,353 ..... C 2
Warren, 50,793 ..... A 5
Westerville, 30,269 ..... B 3
Whitehall, 20,572 ..... m11
Wooster, 22,191 ..... B 4
Xenia, 24,664 ..... C 2
Youngstown, 95,732 ..... A 5
Zanesville, 26,778 ..... C 4

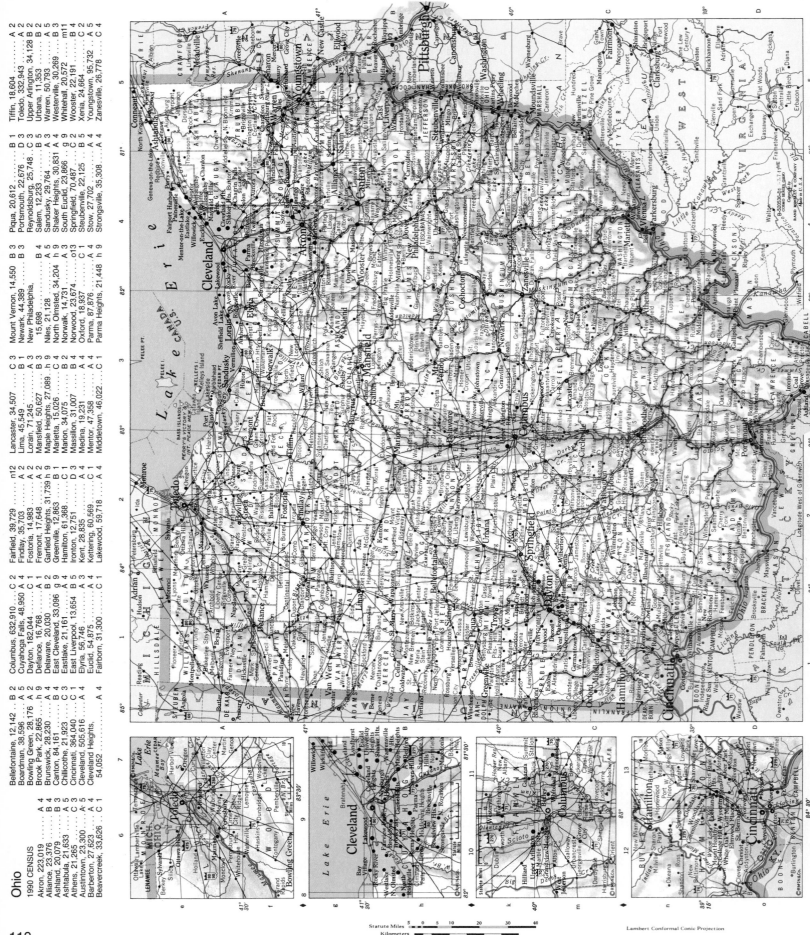

Lambert Conformal Conic Projection

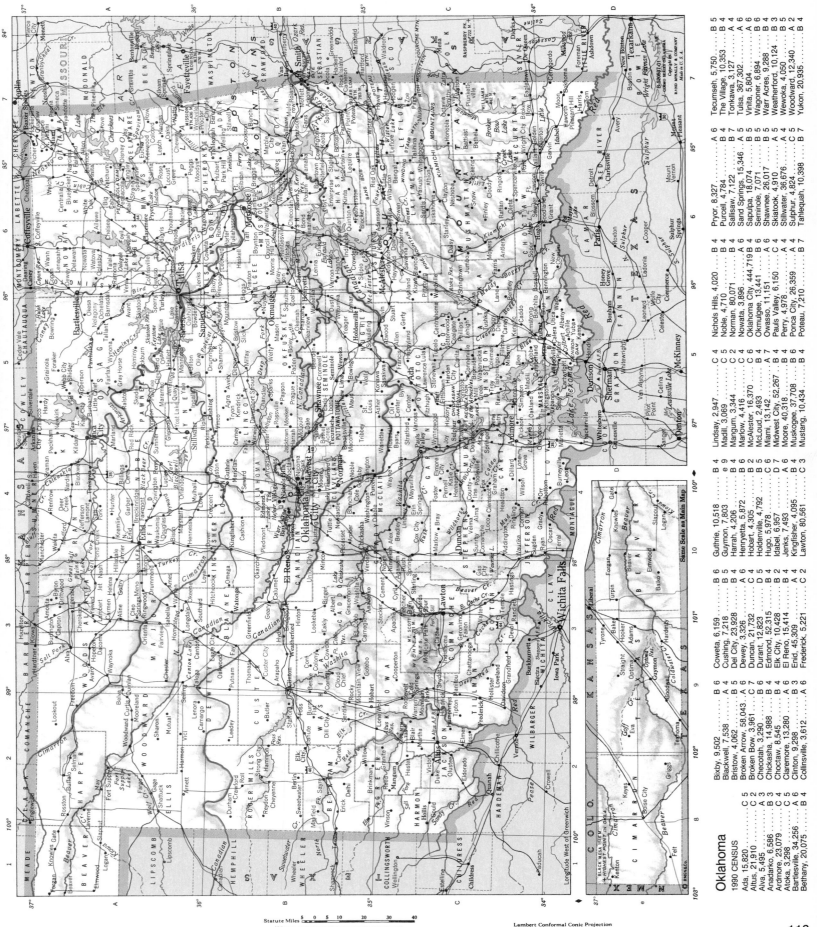

Oklahoma

1990 CENSUS

Ada, 15,820	C 5	
Altus, 21,910	C 2	
Alva, 5,495	A 3	
Anadarko, 6,586	C 4	
Atoka, 3,298	C 5	
Bartlesville, 34,256	A 6	
Bethany, 20,075	B 4	

Bixby, 9,502	B 6	
Blackwell, 7,538	A 4	
Bristow, 4,062	B 5	
Broken Arrow, 58,043	A 6	
Broken Bow, 3,961	C 7	
Checotah, 3,290	B 6	
Chickasha, 14,988	B 4	
Choctaw, 8,545	B 4	
Claremore, 13,280	A 6	
Clinton, 9,298	B 3	
Collinsville, 3,612	A 6	

Coweta, 6,159	B 6	
Cushing, 7,218	B 5	
Del City, 23,928	B 4	
Dewey, 3,326	A 6	
Duncan, 21,732	C 4	
Durant, 12,823	D 5	
Edmond, 52,315	B 4	
Elk City, 10,428	B 2	
El Reno, 15,414	B 4	
Enid, 45,309	A 4	
Frederick, 5,221	C 2	

Guthrie, 10,518	B 4	
Guymon, 7,803	e 9	
Harrah, 4,206	B 4	
Henryetta, 5,872	B 6	
Hobart, 4,305	B 2	
Holdenville, 4,792	B 5	
Hugo, 5,978	C 6	
Idabel, 6,957	D 7	
Jenks, 7,493	B 6	
Kingfisher, 4,095	B 4	
Lawton, 80,561	C 3	

Lindsay, 2,947	B 4	
Madill, 3,069	C 5	
Mangum, 3,344	C 2	
Marlow, 4,416	C 4	
McAlester, 16,370	B 6	
McLoud, 2,493	B 4	
Miami, 13,142	A 7	
Midwest City, 52,267	B 4	
Moore, 40,318	B 4	
Muskogee, 37,708	B 6	
Mustang, 10,434	B 4	

Nichols Hills, 4,020	C 4	
Noble, 4,710	C 5	
Norman, 80,071	C 4	
Nowata, 3,896	A 6	
Oklahoma City, 444,719	B 4	
Okmulgee, 13,441	A 6	
Owasso, 11,151	A 6	
Pauls Valley, 6,150	C 4	
Perry, 4,978	A 4	
Ponca City, 26,359	A 4	
Poteau, 7,210	B 7	

Pryor, 8,327	A 6	
Purcell, 4,784	B 4	
Sallisaw, 7,122	B 7	
Sand Springs, 15,346	A 5	
Sapulpa, 18,074	B 5	
Seminole, 7,071	B 5	
Shawnee, 26,017	B 5	
Skiatook, 4,910	A 5	
Stillwater, 36,676	A 4	
Sulphur, 4,824	C 5	
Tahlequah, 10,398	B 7	

Tecumseh, 5,750	B 5	
The Village, 10,353	B 4	
Tonkawa, 3,127	A 4	
Tulsa, 367,302	A 6	
Vinita, 5,804	A 6	
Wagoner, 6,894	B 6	
Warr Acres, 9,288	B 4	
Weatherford, 10,124	B 3	
Wewoka, 4,050	B 5	
Woodward, 12,340	A 2	
Yukon, 20,935	B 4	

Statute Miles

Kilometers

Lambert Conformal Conic Projection

Same Scale as Main Map

Oregon

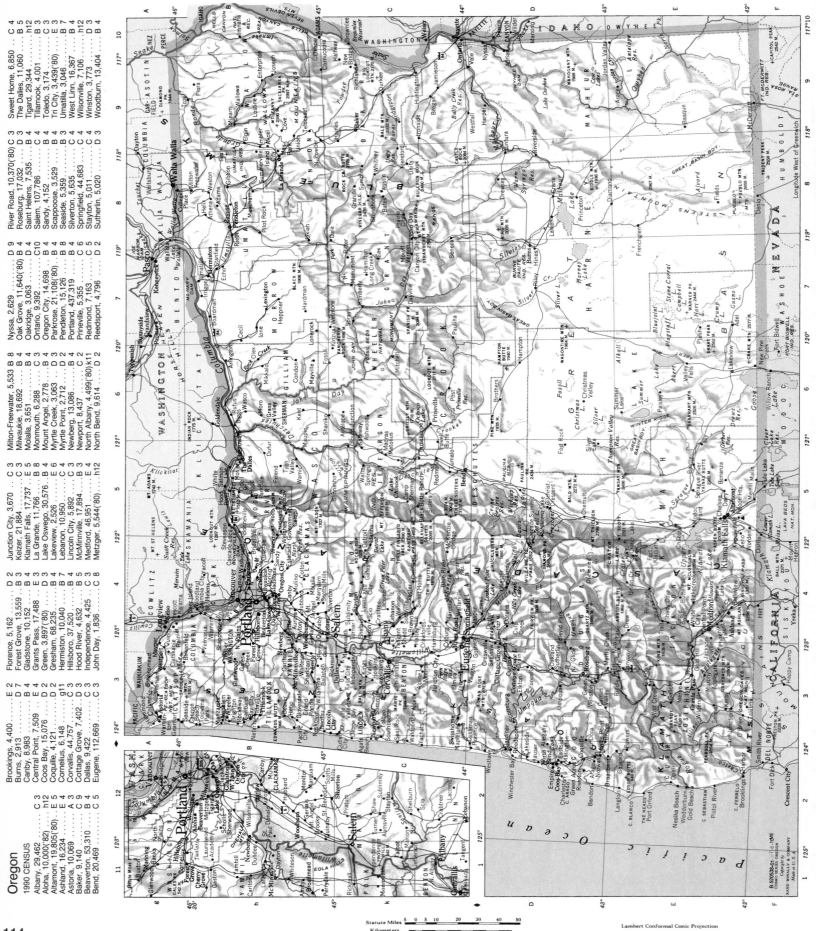

1990 CENSUS

Albany, 29,462	C 3
Aloha, 10,000('82)	h12
Altamont, 19,805('80)	E 5
Ashland, 16,234	E 4
Astoria, 10,069	A 3
Baker, 9,140	C 9
Beaverton, 53,310	B 4
Bend, 20,469	C 5

Brookings, 4,400	E 2
Burns, 2,913	D 7
Canby, 8,983	B 4
Central Point, 7,509	E 4
Coos Bay, 15,076	D 2
Coquille, 4,121	D 2
Cornelius, 6,148	g11
Corvallis, 44,757	C 3
Cottage Grove, 7,402	D 3
Dallas, 9,422	C 3
Eugene, 112,669	D 3

Florence, 5,162	D 2
Forest Grove, 13,559	B 3
Gladstone, 10,152	B 4
Grants Pass, 17,488	E 3
Green, 3,897('80)	D 3
Gresham, 68,235	B 4
Hermiston, 10,040	B 7
Hillsboro, 37,520	B 4
Hood River, 4,632	B 5
Independence, 4,425	C 3
John Day, 1,836	C 8

Junction City, 3,670	C 3
Keizer, 21,884	C 3
Klamath Falls, 17,737	E 5
La Grande, 11,766	B 8
Lake Oswego, 30,576	B 4
Lakeview, 2,526	E 6
Lebanon, 10,950	C 3
Lincoln City, 5,892	C 2
McMinnville, 17,894	B 3
Medford, 46,951	E 4
Metzger, 5,544('80)	h12

Milton-Freewater, 5,533	B 8
Milwaukie, 18,692	B 4
Molalla, 3,651	C 3
Monmouth, 6,288	C 3
Mount Angel, 2,778	C 4
Myrtle Creek, 3,063	D 3
Myrtle Point, 2,712	D 2
Newberg, 13,086	B 4
Newport, 8,437	C 2
North Albany, 4,499('80)	k11
North Bend, 9,614	D 2

Nyssa, 2,629	D 9
Oak Grove, 11,640('80)	B 4
Oakridge, 3,063	C10
Ontario, 9,392	B 4
Oregon City, 14,698	B 4
Parkrose, 21,108('80)	B 4
Pendleton, 15,126	B 8
Portland, 437,319	B 4
Prineville, 5,355	C 6
Redmond, 7,163	C 5
Reedsport, 4,796	D 2

River Road, 10,370('80)	C 3
Roseburg, 17,032	D 3
Saint Helens, 7,535	B 4
Salem, 107,786	C 4
Sandy, 4,152	B 4
Scappoose, 3,529	B 3
Seaside, 5,359	C 4
Silverton, 5,635	C 4
Springfield, 44,683	D 3
Stayton, 5,011	C 5
Sutherlin, 5,020	D 3

Sweet Home, 6,850	C 4
The Dalles, 11,060	B 5
Tigard, 29,344	h12
Tillamook, 4,001	B 3
Toledo, 3,174	C 3
Tri City, 3,439('80)	E 3
Umatilla, 3,046	B 7
West Linn, 16,367	B 4
Wilsonville, 7,106	h12
Winston, 3,773	D 3
Woodburn, 13,404	B 4

Statute Miles

Kilometers

Lambert Conformal Conic Projection

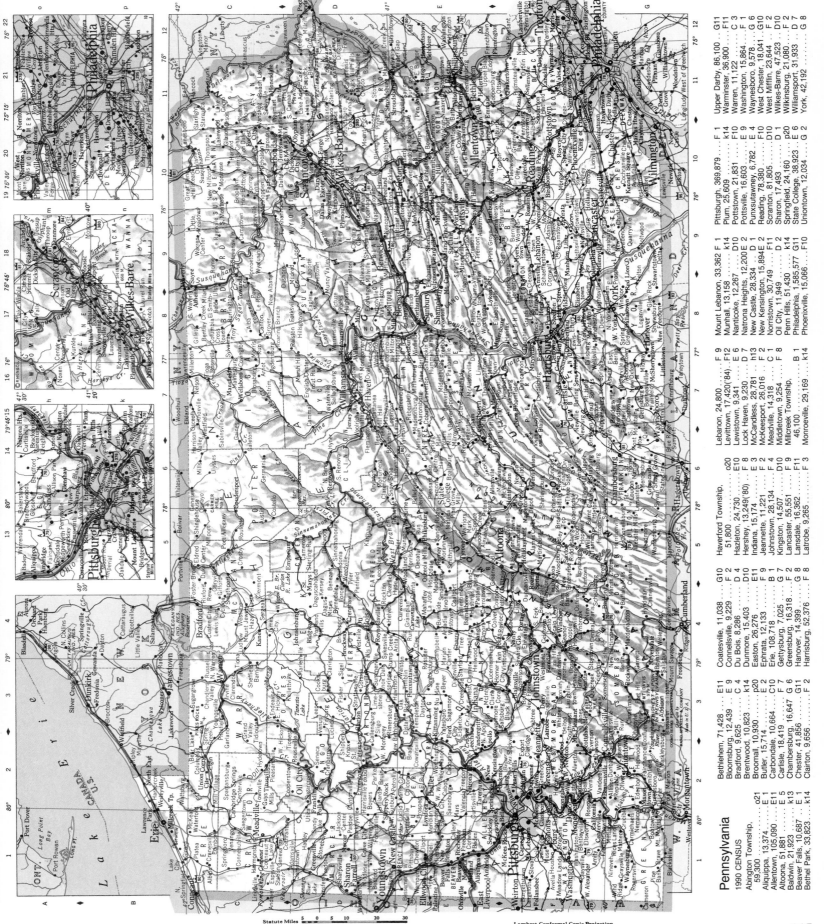

Pennsylvania

1990 CENSUS

Abington Township, 59,300	o21	Coatesville, 11,038	E11
Aliquippa, 13,374	E1	Connellsville, 9,229	F2
Allentown, 105,090	E11	Bradford, 9,625	C4
Altoona, 51,881	E5	Du Bois, 8,286	D10
Baldwin, 21,923	k13	Dunmore, 15,403	D10
Beaver Falls, 10,687	E1	Easton, 26,276	E11
Bethel Park, 33,823	k14	Ephrata, 12,133	F2
Bethlehem, 71,428	E11	Erie, 108,718	B1
Bloomsburg, 12,439	E9	Gettysburg, 7,025	G7
Bradford, 9,625	C4	Greensburg, 16,318	F2
Brentwood, 10,823	k14	Hanover, 14,399	G11
Broomall, 10,930	p20	Harrisburg, 52,376	F8
Butler, 15,714	E2		
Carbondale, 10,664	C10	Haverford Township, 51,800	o20
Carlisle, 18,419	F7	Hazleton, 24,730	E10
Chambersburg, 16,647	G6	Hershey, 13,249('80)	F8
Chester, 41,856	G11	Indiana, 15,174	E3
Clairton, 9,656	F2	Jeannette, 11,221	F2
		Johnstown, 28,134	F4
		Kingston, 14,507	D10
		Lancaster, 55,551	F9
		Latrobe, 9,265	F3
		Lebanon, 24,800	F9
		Levittown, 17,240('84)	F12
		Lock Haven, 9,230	D7
		McCandless, 28,781	h13
		McKeesport, 26,016	F2
		Meadville, 14,318	C1
		Middletown, 9,254	F8
		Millcreek Township, 46,100	B1
		Monroeville, 29,169	k14
		Mount Lebanon, 33,362	F1
		Munhall, 13,158	k14
		Nanticoke, 12,267	D10
		Natrona Heights, 12,200	E2
		New Castle, 28,334	E1
		New Kensington, 15,894	E2
		Norristown, 30,749	F11
		Oil City, 11,949	D2
		Penn Hills, 51,430	k14
		Philadelphia, 1,585,577	G11
		Phoenixville, 15,066	F10
		Pittsburgh, 369,879	F1
		Plum, 25,609	k14
		Pottstown, 21,831	F10
		Pottsville, 16,603	E9
		Punxsutawney, 6,782	E4
		Reading, 78,380	F10
		Scranton, 81,805	D10
		Sharon, 17,493	D1
		Springfield, 24,160	p20
		State College, 38,923	E6
		Uniontown, 12,034	G2
		Upper Darby, 86,100	G11
		Warminster, 36,900	F11
		Warren, 11,122	C3
		Washington, 15,864	F1
		Waynesboro, 9,578	G6
		West Chester, 18,041	G10
		West Mifflin, 23,644	F2
		Wilkes-Barre, 47,523	D10
		Wilkinsburg, 21,080	p20
		Williamsport, 31,933	D7
		York, 42,192	G8

Statute Miles 5 0 10 20 30
Kilometers 5 0 5 10 25 35 45

Lambert Conformal Conic Projection

Rhode Island

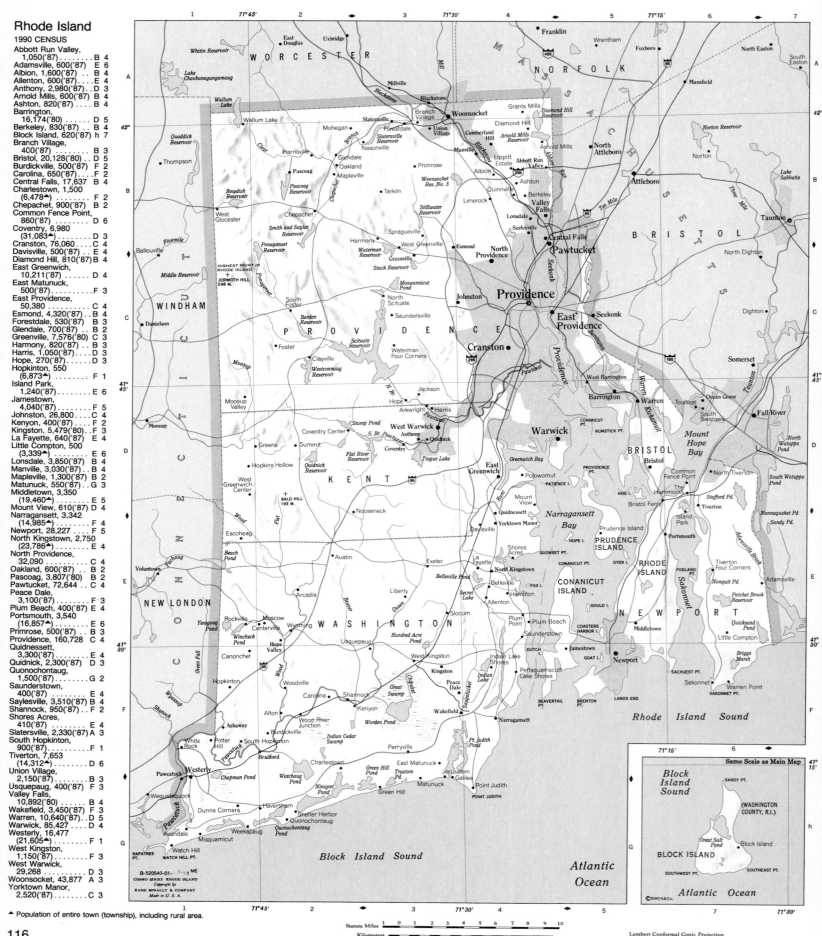

Rhode Island

1990 CENSUS

Abbott Run Valley,
  1,050('87) . . . . . B 4
Adamsville, 600('87) . E 6
Albion, 1,600('87) . . B 4
Allenton, 600('87) . . . . E 4
Anthony, 2,980('87) . . D 3
Arnold Mills, 600('87) B 4
Ashton, 820('87) . . . . B 4
Barrington,
  16,174('80) . . . . D 5
Berkeley, 830('87) . . B 4
Block Island, 620('87) h 7
Branch Village,
  400('87) . . . . B 3
Bristol, 20,128('80) . . B 4
Burdickville, 500('87) . F 2
Carolina, 650('87) . . . F 2
Central Falls, 17,637 . B 4
Charlestown, 1,500
  (6,478▲) . . . . F 2
Chepachet, 900('87) . B 2
Common Fence Point,
  860('87) . . . . D 6
Coventry, 6,980
  (31,083▲) . . . . . . D 3
Cranston, 76,060 . . . C 4
Davisville, 500('87) . . E 4
Diamond Hill, 810('87) B 4
East Greenwich,
  10,211('87) . . . . . D 4
East Matunuck,
  500('87) . . . . F 3
East Providence,
  50,380 . . . . C 4
Esmond, 4,320('87) . . B 4
Forestdale, 530('87) . B 3
Glendale, 700('87) . . B 2
Greenville, 7,576('80) C 3
Harmony, 820('87) . . B 3
Harris, 1,050('87) . . . D 3
Hope, 270('87) . . . . . D 3
Hopkinton, 550
  (6,873▲) . . . . F 1
Island Park,
  1,240('87) . . . . E 6
Jamestown,
  4,040('87) . . . . . . F 5
Johnston, 26,800 . . . C 4
Kenyon, 400('87) . . . F 2
Kingston, 5,479('80) . E 4
La Fayette, 640('87) . E 4
Little Compton, 500
  (3,339▲) . . . . E 6
Lonsdale, 3,850('87) . B 4
Manville, 3,030('87) . B 4
Mapleville, 1,300('87) B 2
Matunuck, 550('87) . . G 3
Middletown, 3,350
  (19,460▲) . . . . . . E 5
Mount View, 610('87) D 4
Narragansett, 3,342
  (14,985▲) . . . . . . F 4
Newport, 28,227 . . . . F 5
North Kingstown, 2,750
  (23,786▲) . . . . . . E 4
North Providence,
  32,090 . . . . C 4
Oakland, 600('87) . . B 2
Pascoag, 3,807('80) . B 2
Pawtucket, 72,644 . . C 4
Peace Dale,
  3,100('87) . . . . . . F 3
Plum Beach, 400('87) E 4
Portsmouth, 3,540
  (16,857▲) . . . . . . E 6
Primrose, 500('87) . . B 4
Providence, 160,728 . C 4
Quidnessett,
  3,300('87) . . . . . . E 4
Quidnick, 2,300('87) . D 3
Quonochontaug,
  1,500('87) . . . . . . G 2
Saunderstown,
  400('87) . . . . E 4
Saylesville, 3,510('87) B 4
Shannock, 950('87) . . F 2
Shores Acres,
  410('87) . . . . E 4
Slatersville, 2,330('87) A 3
South Hopkinton,
  900('87) . . . . F 1
Tiverton, 7,653
  (14,312▲) . . . . . . D 6
Union Village,
  2,150('87) . . . . . . B 3
Usquepaug, 400('87) F 3
Valley Falls,
  10,892('80) . . . . . B 4
Wakefield, 3,450('87) F 3
Warren, 10,640('87) . D 5
Warwick, 85,427 . . . D 4
Westerly, 16,477
  (21,605▲) . . . . . . F 1
West Kingston,
  1,150('87) . . . . . . F 3
West Warwick,
  29,268 . . . . D 3
Woonsocket, 43,877 . A 3
Yorktown Manor,
  2,520('87) . . . . . . C 3

▲ Population of entire town (township), including rural area.

116

B-520540-01-
COSMO SERIES RHODE ISLAND
Copyright by
RAND M℠NALLY & COMPANY
Made in U.S.A.

Same Scale as Main Map

Block
Island
Sound

(WASHINGTON
COUNTY, R.I.)

BLOCK ISLAND

©RM℠N&Co.

Atlantic
Ocean

Statute Miles
Kilometers

Lambert Conformal Conic Projection

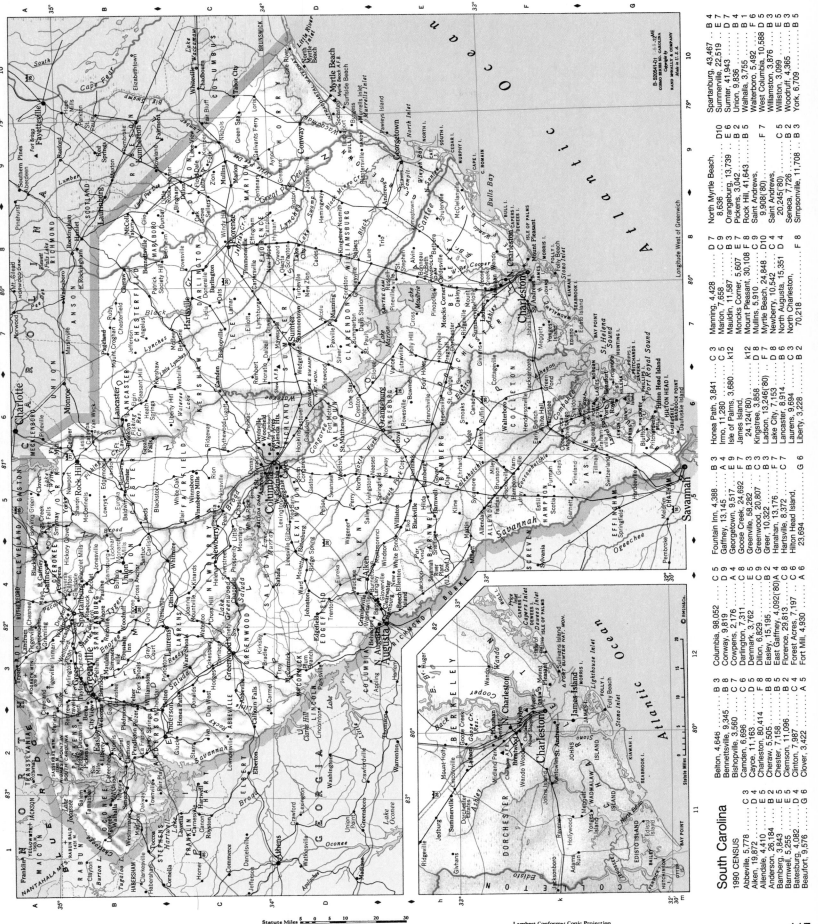

South Carolina

Statute Miles

Kilometers

Lambert Conformal Conic Projection

South Carolina

1990 CENSUS

South Dakota

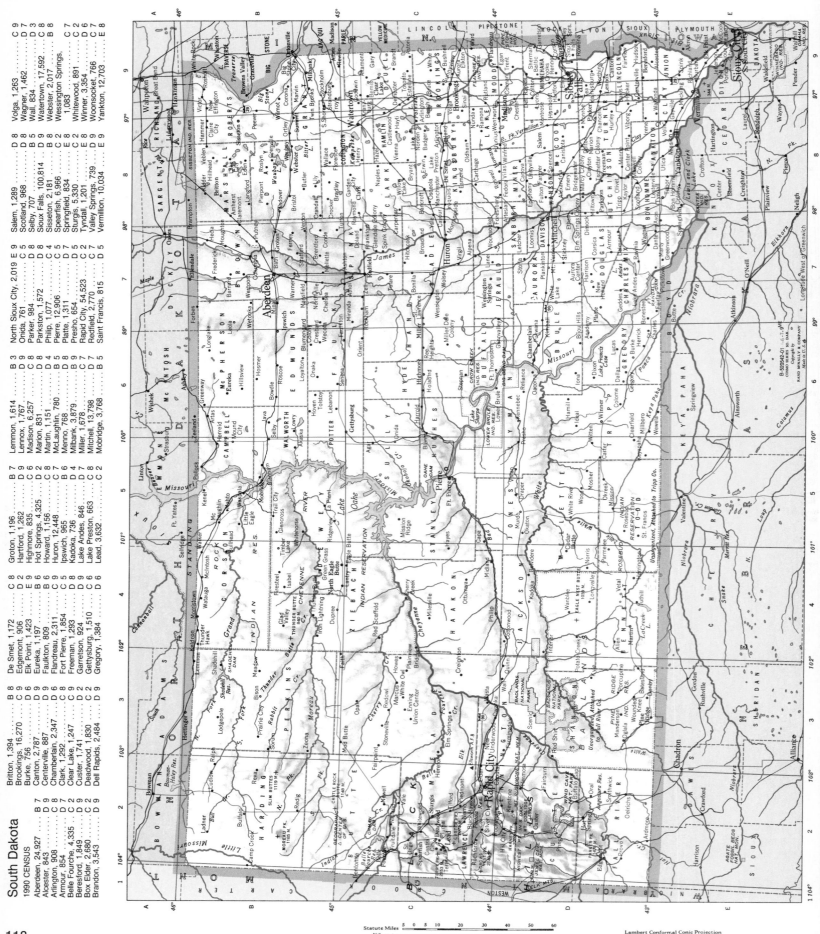

South Dakota

1990 CENSUS

Aberdeen, 24,927	C	8
Alcester, 843	D	9
Arlington, 908	C	8
Armour, 854	D	7
Belle Fourche, 4,335	C	2
Beresford, 1,849	D	9
Box Elder, 2,680	C	2
Brandon, 3,543	D	9

Britton, 1,394	B	8
Brookings, 16,270	C	9
Burke, 756	D	6
Canton, 2,787	D	9
Centerville, 887	D	9
Chamberlain, 2,347	C	6
Clark, 1,292	C	8
Clear Lake, 1,247	C	9
Custer, 1,741	D	2
Deadwood, 1,830	C	2
Dell Rapids, 2,484	D	9

De Smet, 1,172	C	8
Edgemont, 906	D	2
Elk Point, 1,423	E	9
Eureka, 1,197	B	6
Faulkton, 809	C	6
Flandreau, 2,311	C	9
Fort Pierre, 1,854	C	5
Freeman, 1,293	D	8
Garretson, 924	D	9
Gettysburg, 1,510	C	6
Gregory, 1,384	D	6

Groton, 1,196	B	7
Hartford, 1,262	D	9
Highmore, 835	C	6
Hot Springs, 4,325	D	2
Howard, 809	C	8
Huron, 12,448	C	7
Ipswich, 965	C	6
Kadoka, 736	D	4
Lake Andes, 846	D	7
Lake Preston, 663	C	8
Lead, 3,632	C	2

Lemmon, 1,614	B	3
Lennox, 1,767	D	9
Madison, 6,257	C	8
Marion, 831	D	8
Martin, 1,151	D	4
McLaughlin, 780	B	5
Menno, 768	D	8
Milbank, 3,879	C	9
Miller, 1,678	C	7
Mitchell, 13,798	D	8
Mobridge, 3,768	C	5

North Sioux City, 2,019	E	5
Onida, 761	C	5
Parker, 984	D	8
Parkston, 1,572	D	8
Philip, 1,077	C	4
Pierre, 12,906	C	5
Platte, 1,311	D	7
Presho, 654	D	5
Rapid City, 54,523	C	2
Redfield, 2,770	C	7
Saint Francis, 815	D	5

Salem, 1,289	D	8
Scotland, 968	D	8
Selby, 707	B	5
Sioux Falls, 100,814	D	9
Sisseton, 2,181	B	8
Spearfish, 6,966	C	2
Springfield, 834	E	8
Sturgis, 5,330	C	2
Tyndall, 1,201	E	8
Valley Springs, 739	D	9
Vermillion, 10,034	E	9

Volga, 1,263	C	9
Wagner, 1,462	D	7
Wall, 834	C	8
Watertown, 17,592	B	8
Webster, 2,017	B	8
Wessington Springs, 1,083	C	7
Whitewood, 891	C	2
Winner, 3,354	D	6
Woonsocket, 766	C	7
Yankton, 12,703	E	8

Statute Miles 5 0 5 10   20   30   40   50   60

Kilometers 5 0 5 15 25 35 45 55 65 75

Lambert Conformal Conic Projection

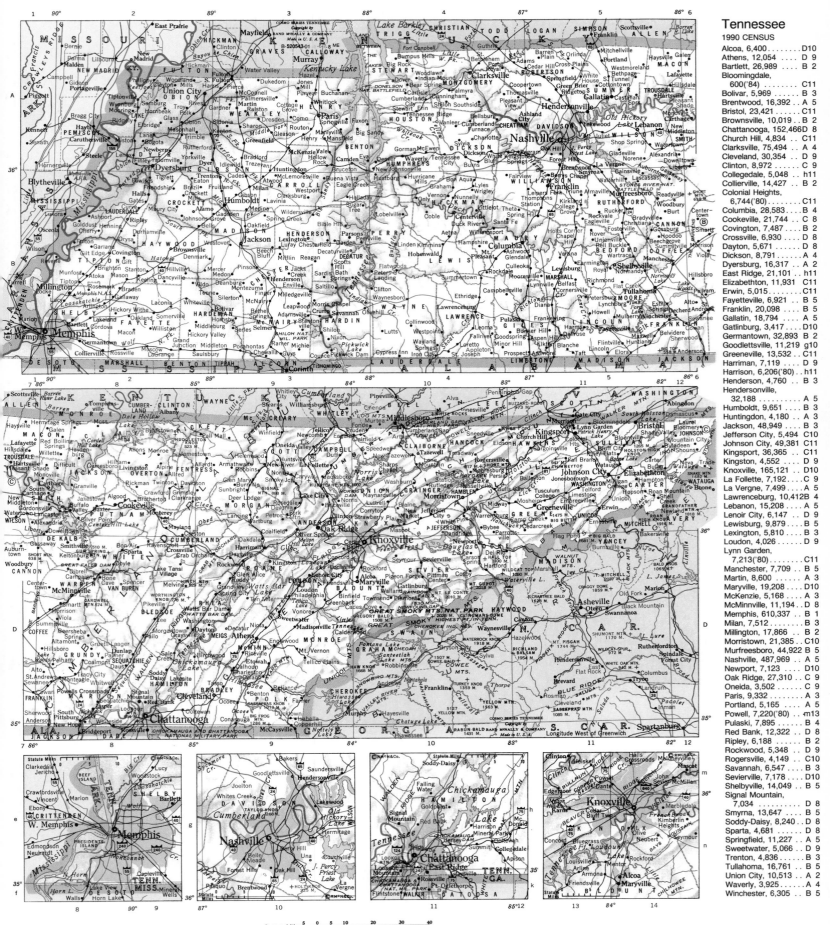

Tennessee
1990 CENSUS

Alcoa, 6,400 . . . . D10
Athens, 12,054 . . . . . D 9
Bartlett, 26,989 . . . . B 2
Bloomingdale,
600('84) C11
Bolivar, 5,969 . . . . . . B 3
Brentwood, 16,392 . . A 5
Bristol, 23,421 . . . . C11
Brownsville, 10,019 . . B 2
Chattanooga, 152,466 D 8
Church Hill, 4,834 . . C11
Clarksville, 75,494 . . A 4
Cleveland, 30,354 . . D 9
Clinton, 8,972 . . . . . C 9
Collegedale, 5,048 . . h11
Collierville, 14,427 . . B 2
Colonial Heights,
6,744('80) C11
Columbia, 28,583 . . . B 4
Cookeville, 21,744 . . C 8
Covington, 7,487 . . . B 3
Crossville, 6,930 . . . D 8
Dayton, 5,671 . . . . . D 8
Dickson, 8,791 . . . . A 4
Dyersburg, 16,317 . . A 2
East Ridge, 21,101 . . h11
Elizabethton, 11,931 C11
Erwin, 5,015 . . . . . . C11
Fayetteville, 6,921 . . B 5
Franklin, 20,098 . . . B 5
Gallatin, 18,794 . . . . A 5
Gatlinburg, 3,417 . . D10
Germantown, 32,893 B 2
Goodlettsville, 11,219 g10
Greeneville, 13,532 . . C11
Harriman, 7,119 . . . . D 9
Harrison, 6,206('80) . . h11
Henderson, 4,760 . . B 3
Hendersonville,
32,188 . . . . A 5
Humboldt, 9,651 . . . B 3
Huntingdon, 4,180 . . A 3
Jackson, 48,949 . . . B 3
Jefferson City, 5,494 C10
Johnson City, 49,381 C11
Kingsport, 36,365 . . C11
Kingston, 4,552 . . . . D 9
Knoxville, 165,121 . . D10
La Follette, 7,192 . . C 9
La Vergne, 7,499 . . . A 5
Lawrenceburg, 10,412 B 4
Lebanon, 15,208 . . . A 5
Lenoir City, 6,147 . . D 9
Lewisburg, 9,879 . . B 5
Lexington, 5,810 . . . B 3
Loudon, 4,026 . . . . . D 9
Lynn Garden,
7,213('80) C11
Manchester, 7,709 . . B 5
Martin, 8,600 . . . . . A 3
Maryville, 19,208 . . D10
McKenzie, 5,168 . . . A 3
McMinnville, 11,194 . D 8
Memphis, 610,337 . . D 2
Milan, 7,512 . . . . . B 3
Millington, 17,866 . . B 2
Morristown, 21,385 . . C10
Murfreesboro, 44,922 B 5
Nashville, 487,969 . . A 5
Newport, 7,123 . . . . D10
Oak Ridge, 27,310 . . C 9
Oneida, 3,502 . . . . . C 9
Paris, 9,332 . . . . . . A 3
Portland, 5,165 . . . . A 5
Powell, 7,220('80) . . m13
Pulaski, 7,895 . . . . . B 4
Red Bank, 12,322 . . D 8
Ripley, 6,188 . . . . . B 3
Rockwood, 5,348 . . . D 9
Rogersville, 4,149 . . C10
Savannah, 6,547 . . . B 3
Sevierville, 7,178 . . . D10
Shelbyville, 14,049 . . B 5
Signal Mountain,
7,034 . . . . D 8
Smyrna, 13,647 . . . . A 5
Soddy-Daisy, 8,240 . . D 8
Sparta, 4,681 . . . . . C 8
Springfield, 11,227 . . A 5
Sweetwater, 5,066 . . D 9
Trenton, 4,836 . . . . B 3
Tullahoma, 16,761 . . B 5
Union City, 10,513 . . A 2
Waverly, 3,925 . . . . . A 4
Winchester, 6,305 . . B 5

Texas

Texas

1990 CENSUS

Abilene, 106,654 .... C 3
Alice, 19,788 ...... F 3
Alvin, 19,220 ...... E 5
Amarillo, 157,615 .... B 2
Arlington, 261,721 .. n 9
Austin, 465,622 .... D 4
Bay City, 18,170 .... E 5
Baytown, 63,850 .... E 5
Beaumont, 114,323 .. E 6
Beeville, 13,547 .... E 4
Big Spring, 23,093 .. C 2
Borger, 15,675 ..... B 2
Brownsville, 98,962 .. G 4
Brownwood, 18,387 .. D 3
Bryan, 55,002 ..... D 4
Cleburne, 22,205 .... C 4
College Station,
    52,456 .... D 4
Conroe, 27,610 .... D 5
Copperas Cove,
    24,079 .... D 4
Corpus Christi,
    257,453 .... F 4
Corsicana, 22,911 .. C 4
Dallas, 1,006,877 ... C 4
Del Rio, 30,705 .... E 2
Denison, 21,505 .... C 4
Denton, 66,270 .... C 4
Duncanville, 35,748 .. n10
Eagle Pass, 20,651 .. E 2
Edinburg, 29,885 .... F 3
El Paso, 515,342 ... o11
Farmers Branch,
    24,250 .... n10
Fort Worth, 447,619 . C 4
Galveston, 59,070 .. E 5
Garland, 180,650 ... n10
Grand Prairie, 99,616 n10
Greenville, 23,071 .. C 4
Harlingen, 48,735 ... F 4
Hereford, 14,745 ... B 1
Houston, 1,630,553 .. E 5
Huntsville, 27,925 .. D 5
Irving, 155,037 .... n10
Kerrville, 17,384 ... D 3
Killeen, 63,535 .... D 4
Kingsville, 25,276 .. F 4
Lake Jackson, 22,776 E 5
La Porte, 27,910 ... r14
Laredo, 122,899 .... F 3
Lewisville, 46,521 .. C 4
Longview, 70,311 ... C 5
Lubbock, 186,206 ... C 2
Lufkin, 30,206 ..... D 5
Marshall, 23,682 ... C 5
McAllen, 84,021 .... F 3
Mesquite, 101,484 .. n10
Midland, 89,443 .... D 2
Mineral Wells, 14,870 C 3
Mission, 28,653 .... F 3
Missouri City, 36,176 r14
Nacogdoches, 30,872 D 5
New Braunfels,
    27,334 .... E 3
North Richland Hills,
    45,895 .... n 9
Odessa, 89,699 .... D 1
Orange, 19,381 .... D 6
Palestine, 18,042 ... C 5
Pampa, 19,959 .... B 2
Paris, 24,699 ..... C 5
Pasadena, 119,363 .. r14
Pecos, 12,069 ..... D 1
Pharr, 32,921 ..... F 3
Plainview, 21,700 .. B 2
Plano, 128,713 .... C 4
Port Arthur, 58,724 . E 6
Richardson, 74,840 . n10
Rosenberg, 20,183 .. E 4
San Angelo, 84,474 . D 2
San Antonio, 935,933 E 3
San Benito, 20,125 .. F 4
San Marcos, 28,743 . E 4
Seguin, 18,853 .... E 4
Sherman, 31,601 ... C 4
Temple, 46,109 .... D 4
Texarkana, 31,656 .. C 5
Texas City, 40,822 .. E 5
Tyler, 75,450 ..... C 5
University Park,
    22,259 .... n10
Uvalde, 14,729 .... E 3
Victoria, 55,076 ... E 4
Waco, 103,590 .... D 4
Waxahachie, 18,168 . C 4
Weslaco, 21,877 ... F 4
Wichita Falls, 96,259 . C 3

120

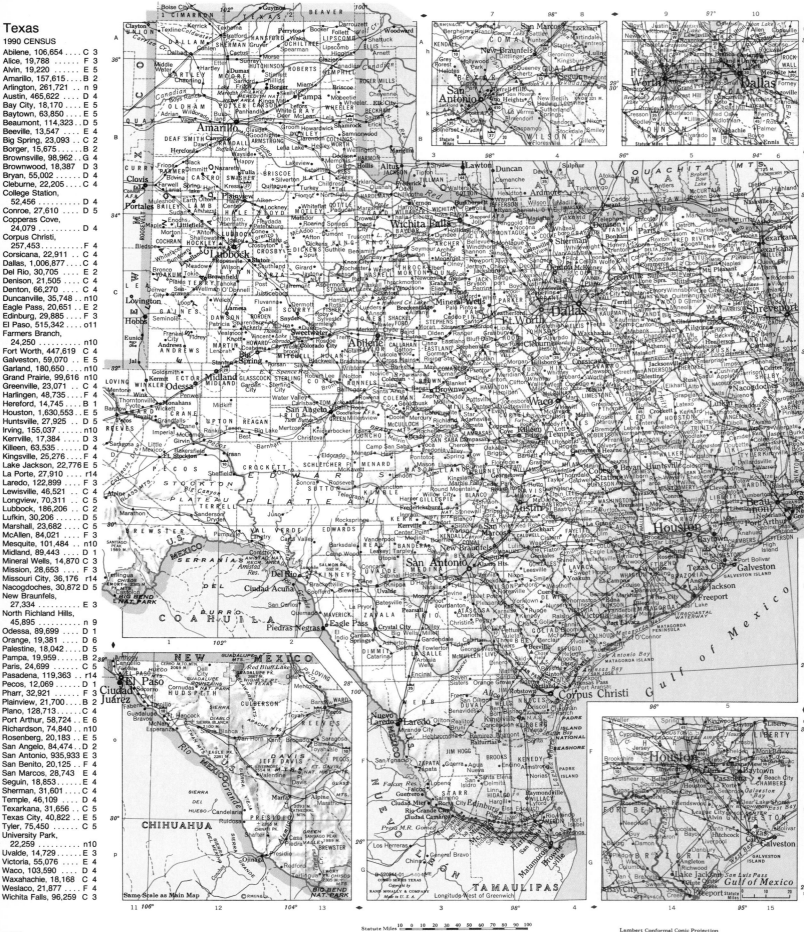

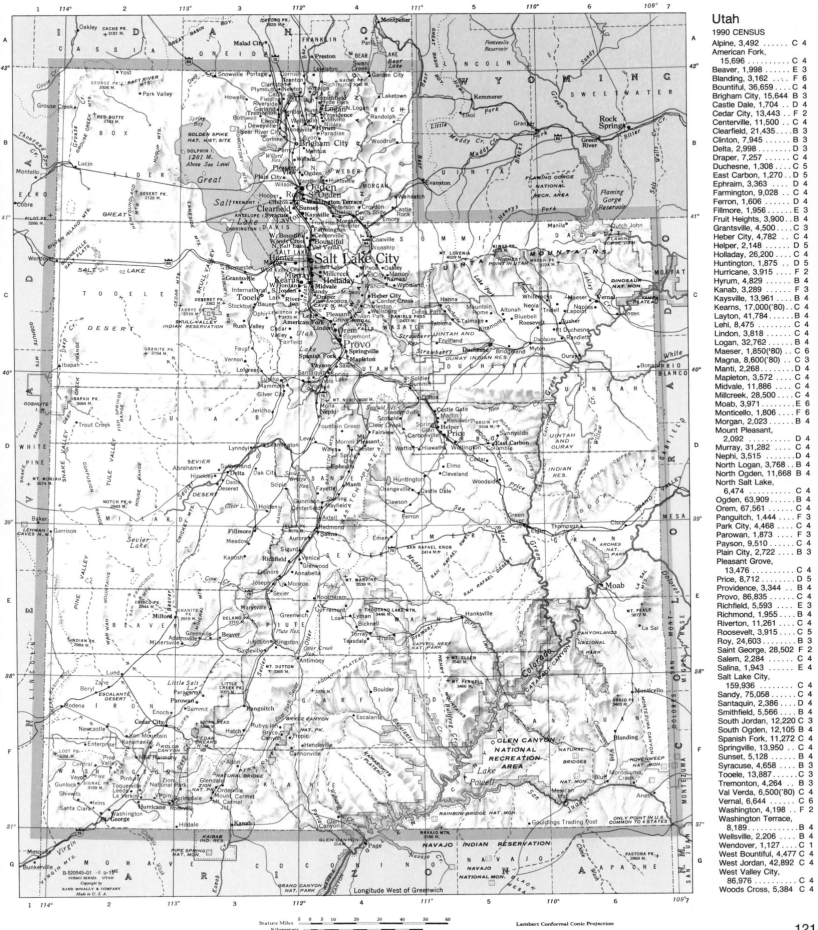

Utah

1990 CENSUS

Alpine, 3,492 ...... C 4
American Fork,
15,696 .... C 4
Beaver, 1,998 ...... E 3
Blanding, 3,162 .... F 6
Bountiful, 36,659 ... C 4
Brigham City, 15,644 B 3
Castle Dale, 1,704 .. D 4
Cedar City, 13,443 . F 2
Centerville, 11,500 . C 4
Clearfield, 21,435 ... B 3
Clinton, 7,945 ..... B 3
Delta, 2,998 ...... D 3
Draper, 7,257 ..... C 4
Duchesne, 1,308 ... C 5
East Carbon, 1,270 . D 5
Ephraim, 3,363 .... D 4
Farmington, 9,028 .. C 4
Ferron, 1,606 ..... D 4
Fillmore, 1,956 .... E 3
Fruit Heights, 3,900 . B 4
Grantsville, 4,500 ... C 3
Heber City, 4,782 .. C 4
Helper, 2,148 ..... D 5
Holladay, 26,200 ... C 4
Huntington, 1,875 .. D 5
Hurricane, 3,915 ... F 2
Hyrum, 4,829 ..... B 4
Kanab, 3,289 ..... F 3
Kaysville, 13,961 .. B 4
Kearns, 17,000('80) . C 4
Layton, 41,784 .... C 4
Lehi, 8,475 ...... C 4
Lindon, 3,818 ..... C 4
Logan, 32,762 ..... B 4
Maeser, 1,850('80) . C 6
Magna, 8,600('80) . C 4
Manti, 2,268 ...... D 4
Mapleton, 3,572 ... C 4
Midvale, 11,886 ... C 4
Millcreek, 28,500 .. C 4
Moab, 3,971 ...... E 6
Monticello, 1,806 ... F 6
Morgan, 2,023 .... B 4
Mount Pleasant,
2,092 .... D 4
Murray, 31,282 .... C 4
Nephi, 3,515 ..... D 4
North Logan, 3,768 . B 4
North Ogden, 11,668 B 4
North Salt Lake,
6,474 .... C 4
Ogden, 63,909 ..... B 4
Orem, 67,561 ..... C 4
Panguitch, 1,444 ... F 3
Park City, 4,468 ... C 4
Parowan, 1,873 ... F 3
Payson, 9,510 ..... C 4
Plain City, 2,722 ... B 3
Pleasant Grove,
13,476 .... C 4
Price, 8,712 ...... D 5
Providence, 3,344 .. B 4
Provo, 86,835 ..... C 4
Richfield, 5,593 ... E 3
Richmond, 1,955 .. B 4
Riverton, 11,261 ... C 4
Roosevelt, 3,915 ... C 5
Roy, 24,603 ...... B 3
Saint George, 28,502 F 2
Salem, 2,284 ..... C 4
Salina, 1,943 ..... E 4
Salt Lake City,
159,936 .... C 4
Sandy, 75,058 ..... C 4
Santaquin, 2,386 ... D 4
Smithfield, 5,566 .. B 4
South Jordan, 12,220 C 3
South Ogden, 12,105 B 4
Spanish Fork, 11,272 C 4
Springville, 13,950 . C 4
Sunset, 5,128 ..... B 4
Syracuse, 4,658 ... B 3
Tooele, 13,887 .... C 3
Tremonton, 4,264 .. B 3
Val Verda, 6,500('80) C 4
Vernal, 6,644 ..... C 6
Washington, 4,198 . F 2
Washington Terrace,
8,189 .... C 4
Wellsville, 2,206 ... B 4
Wendover, 1,127 ... C 1
West Bountiful, 4,477 C 4
West Jordan, 42,892 C 4
West Valley City,
86,976 .... C 4
Woods Cross, 5,384 C 4

Statute Miles
Kilometers

Lambert Conformal Conic Projection

Vermont

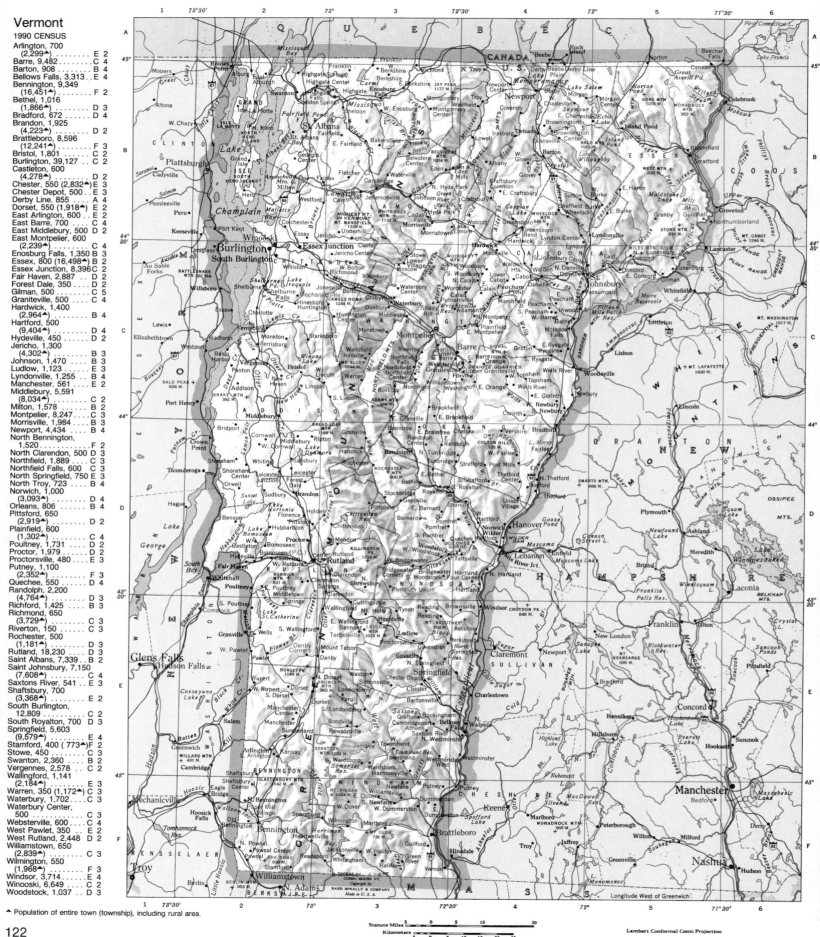

Vermont
1990 CENSUS

Arlington, 700
  (2,299▲) .... E 2
Barre, 9,482 ...... C 4
Barton, 908 .... B 4
Bellows Falls, 3,313 . E 4
Bennington, 9,349
  (16,451▲) .... F 2
Bethel, 1,016
  (1,866▲) .... D 3
Bradford, 672 ..... D 4
Brandon, 1,925
  (4,223▲) .... D 2
Brattleboro, 8,596
  (12,241▲) ...... F 3
Bristol, 1,801 ..... C 2
Burlington, 39,127 .. C 2
Castleton, 600
  (4,278▲) .... D 2
Chester, 550 (2,832▲) E 3
Chester Depot, 500 . E 3
Derby Line, 855 ... A 4
Dorset, 550 (1,918▲) . E 2
East Arlington, 600 . C 2
East Barre, 700 ... C 4
East Middlebury, 500 D 2
East Montpelier, 600
  (2,239▲) .... C 4
Enosburg Falls, 1,350 B 3
Essex, 800 (16,498▲) B 2
Essex Junction, 8,396 C 2
Fair Haven, 2,887 .. D 2
Forest Dale, 350 ... D 2
Gilman, 500 ...... C 5
Graniteville, 500 ... C 4
Hardwick, 1,400
  (2,964▲) .... B 4
Hartford, 500 ..... D 4
Hyde Park, 450
  (9,404▲) .... D 4
Hydeville, 450 .... D 2
Jericho, 1,300
  (4,302▲) .... B 3
Johnson, 1,470 .... B 3
Ludlow, 1,123 .... E 3
Lyndonville, 1,255 .. B 4
Manchester, 561 ... E 2
Middlebury, 5,591
  (8,034▲) .... C 2
Milton, 1,578 ..... B 2
Montpelier, 8,247 ... C 3
Morrisville, 1,984 .. B 3
Newport, 4,434 .... B 4
North Bennington,
  1,520 .... F 2
North Clarendon, 500 D 3
Northfield, 1,889 ... C 3
Northfield Falls, 600 . C 3
North Springfield, 750 E 3
North Troy, 723 ... B 4
Norwich, 1,000
  (3,093▲) .... D 4
Orleans, 806 ..... B 4
Pittsford, 650
  (2,919▲) .... D 2
Plainfield, 600
  (1,302▲) .... C 4
Poultney, 1,731 ... D 2
Proctor, 1,979 .... D 2
Proctorsville, 480 .. E 3
Putney, 1,100
  (2,352▲) .... F 3
Quechee, 550 ..... D 4
Randolph, 2,200
  (4,764▲) .... D 3
Richford, 1,425 ... B 3
Richmond, 650
  (3,729▲) .... C 3
Riverton, 150 ..... C 3
Rochester, 500
  (1,181▲) .... D 3
Rutland, 18,230 ... D 3
Saint Albans, 7,339 . B 2
Saint Johnsbury, 7,150
  (7,608▲) .... C 4
Saxtons River, 541 . E 3
Shaftsbury, 700
  (3,368▲) .... E 2
South Burlington,
  12,809 .... C 2
South Royalton, 700 D 3
Springfield, 5,603
  (9,579▲) .... E 4
Stamford, 400 (773▲) F 2
Stowe, 450 .... C 3
Swanton, 2,360 ... B 2
Vergennes, 2,578 .. C 2
Wallingford, 1,141
  (2,184▲) .... E 3
Warren, 350 (1,172▲) C 3
Waterbury, 1,702 .. C 3
Waterbury Center,
  500 .... C 3
Websterville, 600 ... C 4
West Pawlet, 350 .. E 2
West Rutland, 2,448 . D 2
Williamstown, 650
  (2,839▲) .... C 3
Wilmington, 550
  (1,968▲) .... F 3
Windsor, 3,714 .... E 4
Winooski, 6,649 ... C 2
Woodstock, 1,037 .. D 3

▲ Population of entire town (township), including rural area.

Statute Miles

Kilometers

Lambert Conformal Conic Projection

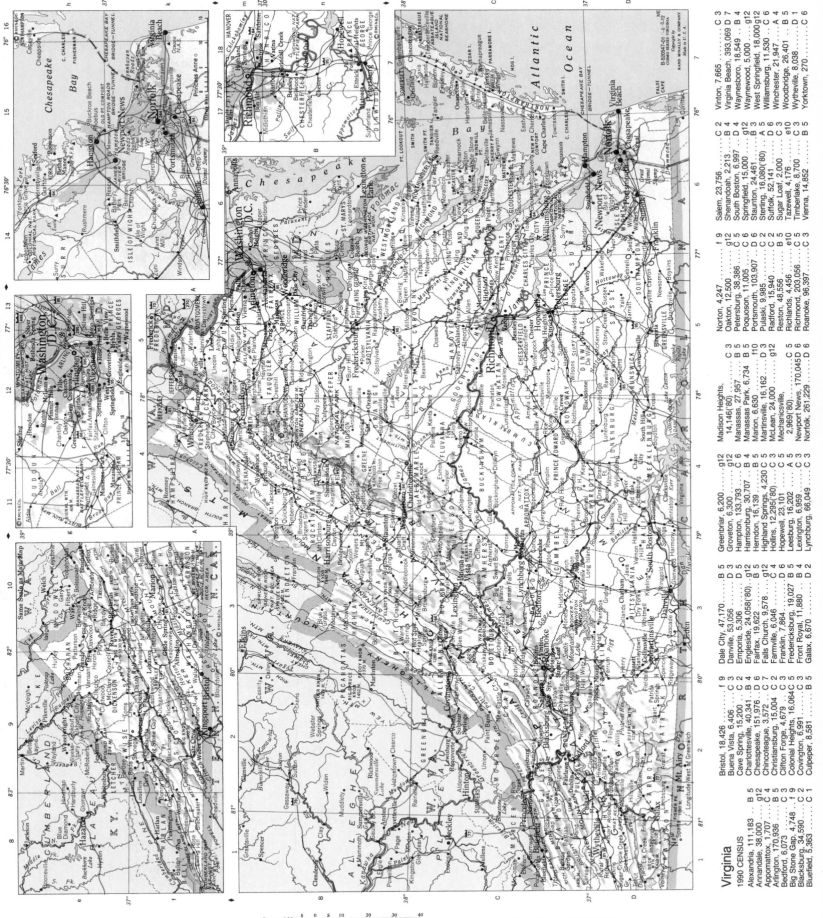

Virginia

1990 CENSUS

Statute Miles
Kilometers

Lambert Conformal Conic Projection

Washington

Sunnyside, 11,238	C 5
Tacoma, 176,664	B 3
Toppenish, 7,419	C 5
Tukwila, 11,874	f11
Tumwater, 9,976	B 3
Vancouver, 46,380	D 3
Walla Walla, 26,478	C 7
Wenatchee, 21,756	B 5
White Center,	
18,000('91)	e11
Yakima, 54,827	C 5

Richmond Highlands,	
27,900	B 3
Riverton Heights, 14,182	f11
Seattle, 516,259	B 3
Sedro Woolley, 6,031	A 3
Selah, 5,113	C 5
Shelton, 7,241	B 2
Snohomish, 6,499	B 3
Spokane, 177,196	B 8
Steilacoom, 5,728	f10
Sumner, 6,281	B 3

Port Orchard, 4,984	C 2
Port Townsend, 7,001	A 2
Prosser, 4,476	C 6
Pullman, 17,647	B 8
Puyallup, 23,875	B 3
Quincy, 3,738	B 6
Redmond, 35,800	e11
Renton, 41,688	B 3
Richland, 32,315	C 6
Richmond Beach,	
6,700('91)	B 3

Montesano, 3,064	C 2
Moses Lake, 11,235	B 6
Mount Vernon, 17,647	A 3
Oak Harbor, 17,176	A 3
Olympia, 33,840	B 3
Omak, 4,117	A 6
Othello, 4,638	C 6
Parkland, 27,300	f11
Parkwater, 4,300('91)	g14
Pasco, 20,337	C 6
Port Angeles, 17,710	A 2

Kent, 37,960	B 3
Kirkland, 40,052	B 3
Lacey, 19,279	B 3
Lakewood Center,	
62,000	B 3
Longview, 31,499	C 3
Lynden, 5,709	A 3
Lynnwood, 28,695	B 3
Marysville, 10,328	A 3
Medical Lake, 3,664	B 8
Mercer Island, 20,816	C 6

Washington
1990 CENSUS

Aberdeen, 16,565	C 2
Anacortes, 11,451	A 3
Auburn, 33,102	B 3
Bellevue, 86,874	e11
Bellingham, 52,179	A 3
Bonney Lake, 7,494	B 3
Bothell, 12,345	B 3
Bremerton, 38,142	B 3

Camas, 6,442	D 3
Centralia, 12,101	C 3
Cheney, 7,723	B 8
Chehalis, 6,527	C 3
Clarkston, 6,753	C 8
College Place, 6,308	C 7
Colville, 4,360	A 8
Coulee Dam, 1,087	B 7
Des Moines, 17,283	f11
Edmonds, 30,744	B 3
Ellensburg, 12,361	B 5

Enumclaw, 7,227	B 4
Ephrata, 5,349	B 6
Everett, 69,961	B 3
Ferndale, 5,398	f10
Fircrest, 5,258	D 5
Goldendale, 3,319	C 5
Grandview, 7,169	C 6
Hoquiam, 8,972	C 2
Issaquah, 7,786	B 3
Kelso, 11,820	C 3
Kennewick, 42,155	C 6

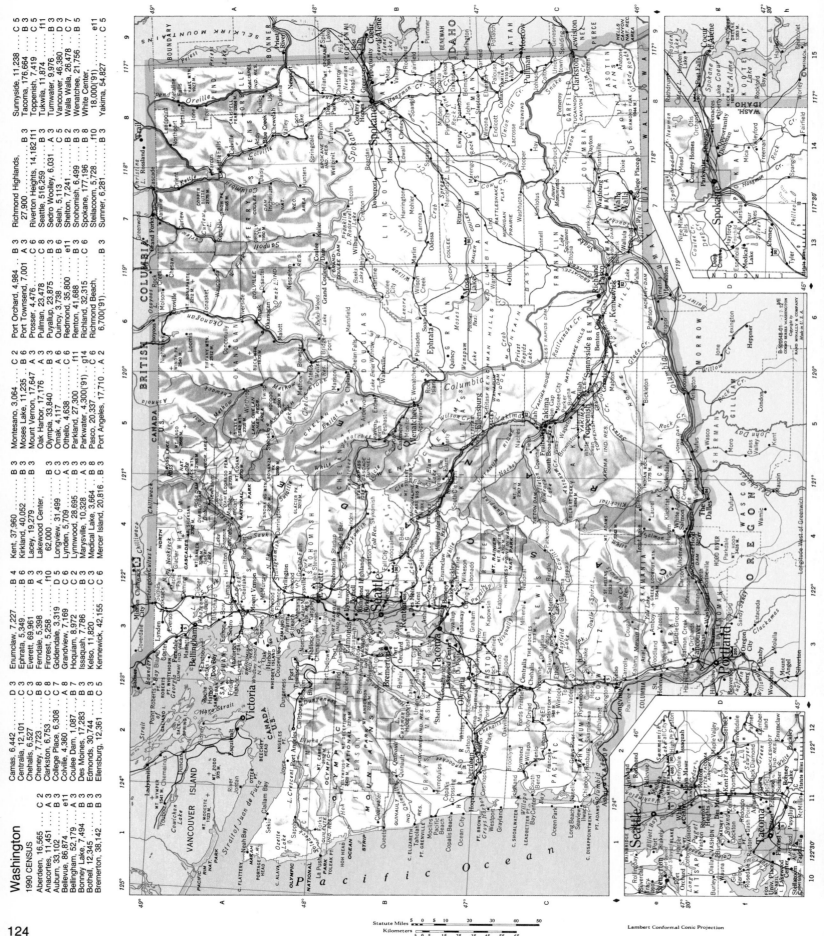

Statute Miles

Kilometers

Lambert Conformal Conic Projection

124

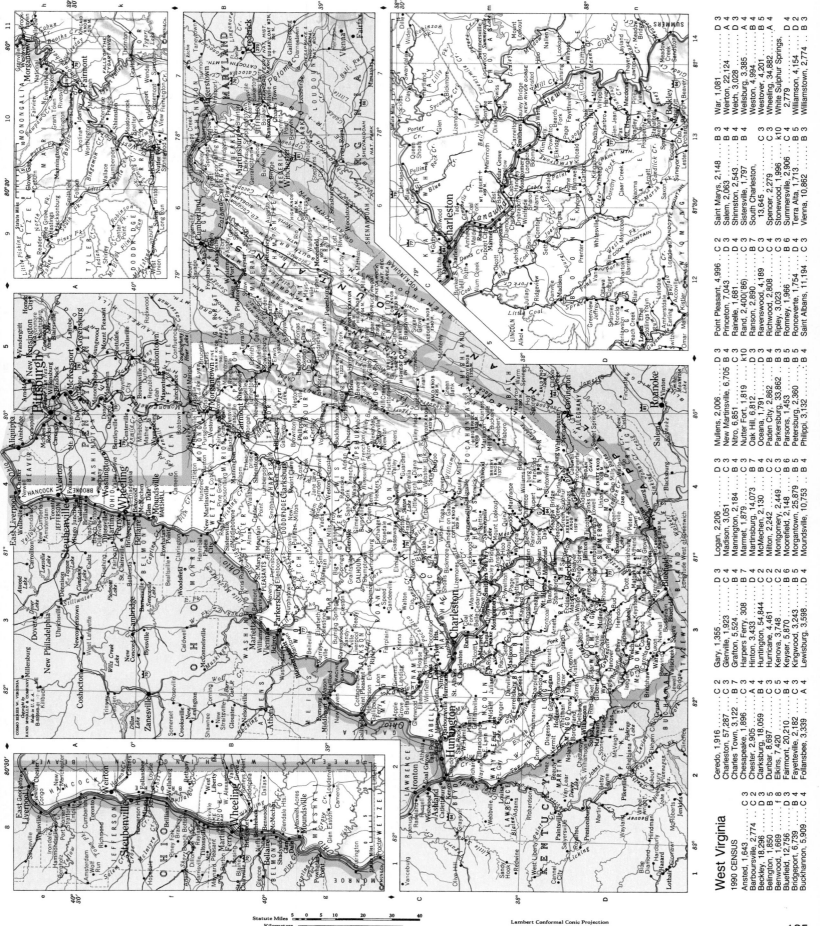

West Virginia

1990 CENSUS

Ansted, 1,643	C 3	
Barboursville, 2,774	B 4	
Beckley, 18,296	D 3	
Belington, 1,850	B 5	
Benwood, 1,669	f 8	
Bluefield, 12,756	D 3	
Bridgeport, 6,739	B 4	
Buckhannon, 5,909	C 4	

Ceredo, 1,916	C 2	
Charleston, 57,287	C 3	
Charles Town, 3,122	B 7	
Chesapeake, 1,896	C 3	
Chester, 2,905	A 4	
Clarksburg, 18,059	B 4	
Dunbar, 8,697	C 3	
Elkins, 7,420	C 5	
Fairmont, 20,210	B 4	
Fayetteville, 2,182	D 3	
Follansbee, 3,339	C 4	

Gary, 1,355	D 3	
Glenville, 1,923	C 4	
Grafton, 5,524	B 4	
Harpers Ferry, 308	B 7	
Huntington, 54,844	C 2	
Hurricane, 4,461	C 3	
Kenova, 3,748	C 2	
Keyser, 5,870	B 6	
Kingwood, 3,243	B 5	
Lewisburg, 3,598	D 4	

Logan, 2,206	D 3	
Madison, 3,051	C 3	
Mannington, 2,184	B 4	
Marmet, 1,879	C 3	
Martinsburg, 14,073	B 7	
McMechen, 2,130	f 8	
Milton, 2,242	C 3	
Montgomery, 2,449	C 3	
Moorefield, 2,148	B 6	
Morgantown, 25,879	B 5	
Moundsville, 10,753	B 4	

Mullens, 2,006	D 3	
New Martinsville, 6,705	B 4	
Nitro, 6,851	C 3	
Nutter Fort, 1,819	k10	
Oak Hill, 6,812	D 3	
Oceana, 1,791	D 3	
Paden City, 2,862	B 4	
Parkersburg, 33,862	B 5	
Parsons, 1,453	B 5	
Petersburg, 2,360	B 6	
Philippi, 3,132	B 4	

Point Pleasant, 4,996	C 2	
Princeton, 7,043	D 3	
Rainelle, 1,681	D 4	
Rand, 2,400 ('86)	C 3	
Ranson, 2,890	B 7	
Ravenswood, 4,189	C 3	
Richwood, 2,808	C 4	
Ripley, 3,023	C 3	
Romney, 1,966	B 6	
Ronceverte, 1,754	D 4	
Saint Albans, 11,194	C 3	

Saint Marys, 2,148	C 2	
Salem, 2,063	D 3	
Shinnston, 2,543	D 4	
Sistersville, 1,797	B 7	
South Charleston, 13,645	B 4	
Spencer, 2,279	C 3	
Stonewood, 1,996	k10	
Summersville, 2,906	C 4	
Terra Alta, 1,713	B 5	
Vienna, 10,862	C 3	

War, 1,081	D 3	
Weirton, 22,124	A 4	
Welch, 3,028	A 4	
Wellsburg, 3,385	B 4	
Weston, 4,994	B 4	
Westover, 4,201	B 5	
Wheeling, 34,882	A 4	
White Sulphur Springs, 2,779	D 4	
Williamson, 4,154	D 2	
Williamstown, 2,774	B 3	

Wisconsin

Wisconsin
1990 CENSUS

Allouez, 14,431 . . . . h 9
Antigo, 8,276 . . . . . . C 4
Appleton, 65,695 . . . . D 5
Ashland, 8,695 . . . . . B 3
Ashwaubenon, 16,376 D 5
Baraboo, 9,203 . . . . . E 4
Beaver Dam, 14,196 . . E 5
Beloit, 35,573 . . . . . F 4
Brookfield, 35,184 . . m11
Brown Deer, 12,236 m12
Burlington, 8,855 . . . F 5
Cedarburg, 9,895 . . . . E 6
Chippewa Falls,
  12,727 . . . . D 2
Cudahy, 18,659 . . . . . F 6
De Pere, 16,569 . . . . D 5
Eau Claire, 56,856 . . . D 2
Fond du Lac, 37,757 . . E 5
Fort Atkinson, 10,227 F 5
Franklin, 21,855 . . . . n11
Germantown, 13,658 E 5
Glendale, 14,088 . . . m12
Grafton, 9,340 . . . . . E 6
Green Bay, 96,466 . . . D 6
Greendale, 15,128 . . . F 6
Greenfield, 33,403 . . n11
Hayward, 1,897 . . . . . B 2
Howard, 9,874 . . . . . D 5
Hudson, 6,378 . . . . . D 1
Janesville, 52,133 . . . F 4
Kaukauna, 11,982 . . . D 5
Kenosha, 80,352 . . . . F 6
La Crosse, 51,003 . . . E 2
Lake Geneva, 5,979 . . F 5
Little Chute, 9,207 . . . D 5
Madison, 191,262 . . . E 4
Manitowoc, 32,520 . . D 6
Marinette, 11,843 . . . C 6
Marshfield, 19,291 . . . D 3
Menasha, 14,711 . . . . D 5
Menomonee Falls,
  26,840 . . . . E 5
Menomonie, 13,547 . . D 2
Mequon, 18,885 . . . . E 6
Merrill, 9,860 . . . . . . C 4
Middleton, 13,289 . . . E 4
Milwaukee, 628,088 . . E 6
Monona, 8,637 . . . . . E 4
Monroe, 10,241 . . . . F 4
Muskego, 16,813 . . . . F 5
Neenah, 23,219 . . . . D 5
New Berlin, 33,592 . . n11
New London, 6,658 . . D 5
Oak Creek, 19,513 . . n12
Oconomowoc, 10,993 E 5
Oconto, 4,474 . . . . . D 6
Onalaska, 11,284 . . . E 2
Oshkosh, 55,006 . . . . D 5
Park Falls, 3,104 . . . . C 3
Platteville, 9,708 . . . . F 3
Portage, 8,640 . . . . . E 4
Port Washington,
  9,338 . . . . E 6
Prairie du Chien,
  5,659 . . . . E 2
Racine, 84,298 . . . . . F 6
Reedsburg, 5,834 . . . E 3
Rhinelander, 7,427 . . C 4
Rice Lake, 7,998 . . . . C 2
River Falls, 10,610 . . D 1
Saint Francis, 9,245 . n12
Shawano, 7,598 . . . . D 5
Sheboygan, 49,676 . . E 6
Shorewood, 14,116 . . E 6
South Milwaukee,
  20,958 . . . . F 6
Stevens Point, 23,006 D 4
Stoughton, 8,786 . . . F 4
Sturgeon Bay, 9,176 . D 6
Sun Prairie, 15,333 . . E 4
Superior, 27,134 . . . . B 1
Tomah, 7,570 . . . . . . E 3
Two Rivers, 13,030 . . D 6
Watertown, 19,142 . . E 5
Waukesha, 56,958 . . . F 5
Waupun, 8,207 . . . . . E 5
Wausau, 37,060 . . . . D 4
Wauwatosa, 49,366 . . m11
West Allis, 63,221 . . m11
West Bend, 23,916 . . E 5
Weston, 8,775('80) . . D 4
Whitefish Bay, 14,272 m12
Whitewater, 12,636 . . F 5
Wisconsin Dells,
  2,393 . . . . E 4
Wisconsin Rapids,
  18,245 . . . . D 4

126

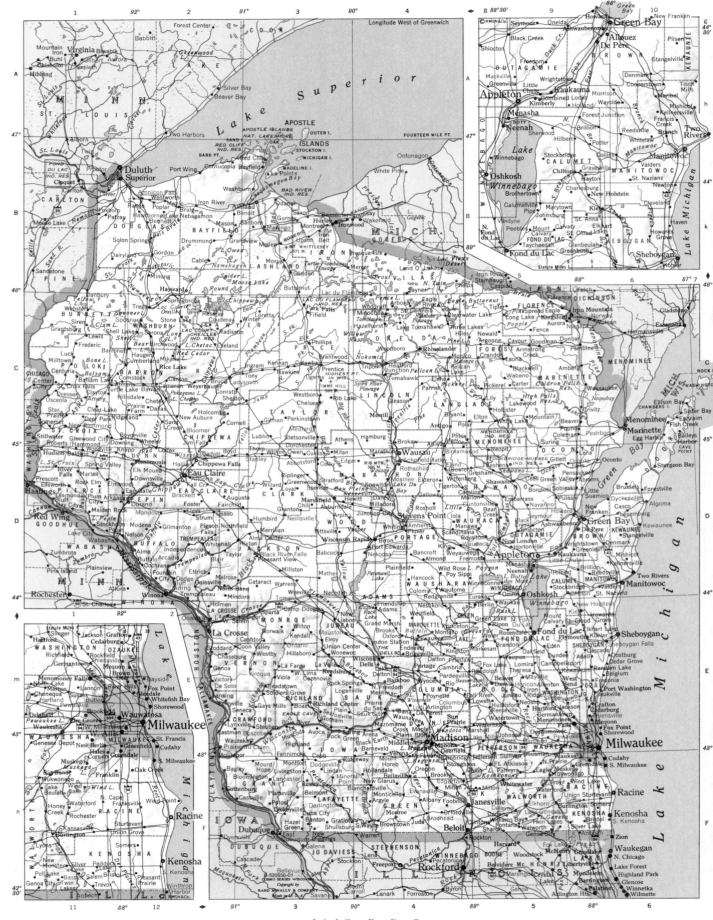

Wyoming

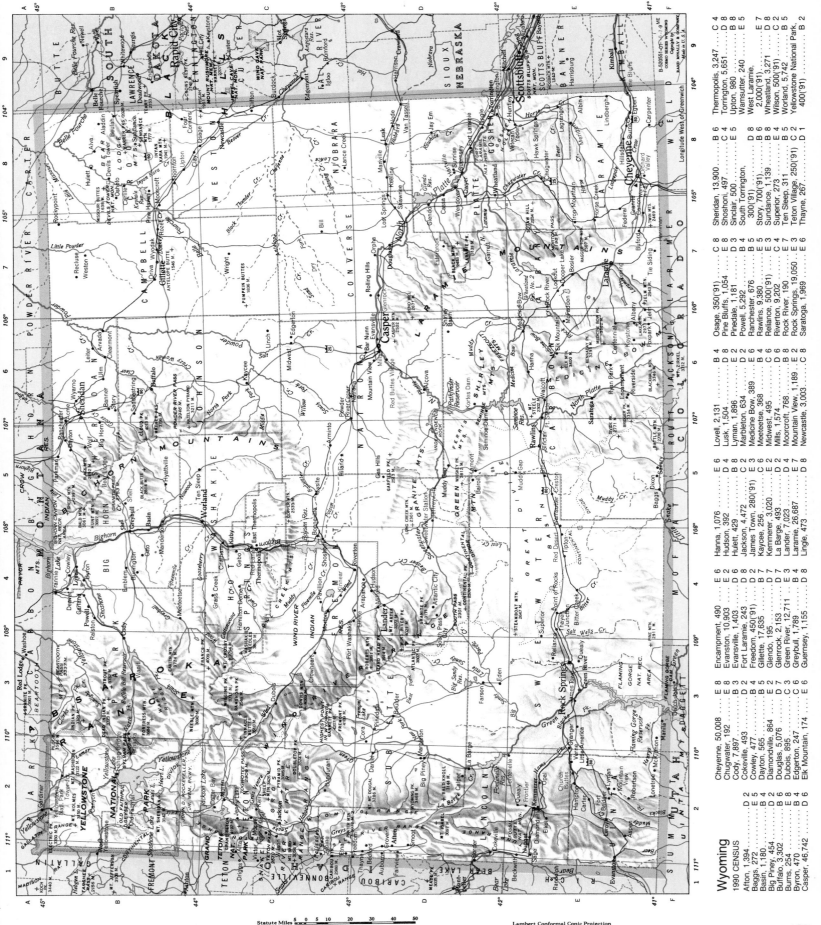

Wyoming
1990 CENSUS

Afton, 1,394	D 2	Encampment, 490	E 8
Baggs, 272	E 5	Evanston, 10,903	E 8
Basin, 1,180	B 4	Fort Laramie, 243	D 2
Big Piney, 454	D 3	Freedom, 450('91)	B 4
Buffalo, 3,302	B 6	Gillette, 17,635	B 5
Burns, 254	E 8	Glenrock, 2,153	D 7
Byron, 470	D 6	Glendo, 195	D 7
Casper, 46,742	D 6	Douglas, 5,076	D 7
		Greybull, 1,789	C 6
		Guernsey, 1,155	E 6
Cheyenne, 50,008	D 2	Hanna, 1,076	E 6
Chugwater, 192	E 7	Hudson, 392	D 3
Cody, 7,897	B 3	Hulett, 429	D 6
Cokeville, 493	D 2	Jackson, 4,472	B 2
Cowley, 477	B 4	James Town, 280('91)	D 2
Dayton, 565	B 5	Kaycee, 256	C 6
Diamondville, 864	E 2	Kemmerer, 3,020	D 7
Dubois, 895	C 3	La Barge, 493	D 2
Edgerton, 247	D 6	Lander, 7,023	D 4
Elk Mountain, 174	D 6	Laramie, 26,687	D 8
		Lingle, 473	D 8
		Lovell, 2,131	B 4
		Lusk, 1,504	D 8
		Lyman, 1,896	E 2
		Marbleton, 634	D 2
		Medicine Bow, 389	E 6
		Meeteetse, 368	B 4
		Midwest, 495	D 6
		Mills, 1,574	D 2
		Moorcroft, 768	D 4
		Mountain View, 1,189	E 7
		Newcastle, 3,003	D 8
		Osage, 350('91)	C 8
		Pine Bluffs, 1,054	E 8
		Pinedale, 1,181	D 3
		Powell, 5,292	B 5
		Ranchester, 676	B 5
		Rawlins, 9,380	E 5
		Reliance, 500('91)	E 5
		Riverton, 9,202	C 4
		Rock River, 190	E 7
		Rock Springs, 19,050	E 5
		Saratoga, 1,969	E 6
		Sheridan, 13,900	B 6
		Shoshoni, 497	C 4
		Sinclair, 500	E 5
		South Torrington,	
		300('91)	D 8
		Story, 700('91)	B 6
		Sundance, 1,139	E 4
		Superior, 273	E 5
		Ten Sleep, 311	E 7
		Teton Village, 250('91)	C 2
		Thayne, 267	D 1
		Thermopolis, 3,247	C 4
		Torrington, 5,651	C 4
		Upton, 980	E 5
		Wamsutter, 240	
		West Laramie,	
		2,000('91)	E 7
		Wheatland, 3,271	C 2
		Wilson, 500('91)	C 2
		Worland, 5,742	B 5
		Yellowstone National Park,	
		400('91)	D 1

Statute Miles 5 0 5 10 20 30 40 50

Kilometers 5 0 5 15 25 35 45 55 65 75

Lambert Conformal Conic Projection

North Polar Regions

Anchorage, 226,338
('90)............................C27
Archangel'sk, 416,000
('89)............................C 8
BELGIUM.....................D12
Berlin, 3,352,848 ('89)
(3,825,000★).........D11
CANADA.......................D22
Chicago, 2,783,726
('90)............................E21
CHINA............................F 2
Churchill, 1,186 ('81)..D22
CZECHOSLOVAKIA....E11
DENMARK....................D11
Dublin, 502,749 ('86)
(1,140,000★).........D13
Dutch Harbor, 20 ('81)..D29
Edmonton, 573,982 ('86)
(785,465★)..........D24
ESTONIA......................C10
FAEROE ISLANDS.....C13
Fairbanks, 30,843
('90)............................C27
FINLAND.....................C10
FRANCE.......................E12
Gander, 10,207 ('86)
(10,899★)...............E18
GERMANY...................D11
Godthåb, 12,217 ('90).C18
GREENLAND..............B17
Hammerfest, 7,208
('83)............................B10
Happy Valley-Goose Bay,
7,248 ('86).............D19
Helsinki, 490,034 ('88)
(1,040,000★).........C10
ICELAND.....................C14
Igarka, 16,918 ('79)...C 4
IRELAND......................D13
JAPAN..........................F35
Jekaterinburg, 1,367,000
('89) (1,620,000★)..D 6
Juneau, 26,751 ('90)..D26
Kijev (Kiev), 2,587,000
('89) (2,900,000★)..D 9
KOREA, NORTH.........E36
KOREA, SOUTH.........F36
LATVIA..........................C10
LITHUANIA..................C10
Leningrad, 4,456,000 ('89)
(5,825,000★).........D 9
LUXEMBOURG...........E12
Magadan, 152,000
('89)............................D33
MONGOLIA...................E 2
Moskva (Moscow),
8,769,000 ('89)
(13,100,000★).......D 9
Murmansk, 468,000
('89)............................C 9
NETHERLANDS..........D12
New York, 7,322,564
('90)............................E20
Nižnij Novgorod (Gorky),
1,438,000 ('89)
(2,025,000★)..........D 8
Nome, 3,500 ('90)......C29
Noril'sk, 174,000 ('89).C 4
NORWAY......................C12
Novosibirsk, 1,436,000
('89) (1,600,000★)..D 4
Ōsaka, 2,636,249 ('85)
(16,450,000★)........F35
Oslo, 452,415 ('87)
(720,000★)............D11
Ottawa, 300,763 ('86)
(819,263★)...........E20
Paris, 2,078,900 ('87)
(9,775,000★)..........E12
POLAND.......................D11
Québec, 164,580 ('86)
(603,267★).............E20
Reykjavík, 93,425 ('87)
(137,941★)............C15
RUSSIA..........................C 4
Saint John's, 96,216 ('86)
(161,901★)............E18
Sankt-Peterburg,
4,456,000 ('89)
(5,825,000★)..........D 9
Seattle, 516,259 ('90)..E25
Shenyang (Mukden),
3,910,000 ('88)
(4,370,000★).........E36
Sŏul (Seoul), 10,522,000
('89) (15,850,000★).F36
Stockholm, 672,187 ('90)
(1,449,972★).........D11
SWEDEN......................C11
Thule, 551 ('90)...........B19
Tōkyō, 8,354,615 ('85)
(27,700,000★).........F35
Ulaanbaatar (Ulan Bator),
548,400 ('89)..........E 2
UNITED KINGDOM.....D13
UNITED STATES.........F22
Vancouver, 431,147 ('86)
(1,380,729★)..........E25
Vladivostok, 648,000
('89)............................E35
Vorkuta, 116,000 ('89).C 6
Warszawa, 1,651,200
('89) (2,323,000★)..D10
Winnipeg, 594,551 ('86)
(625,304★)............E22

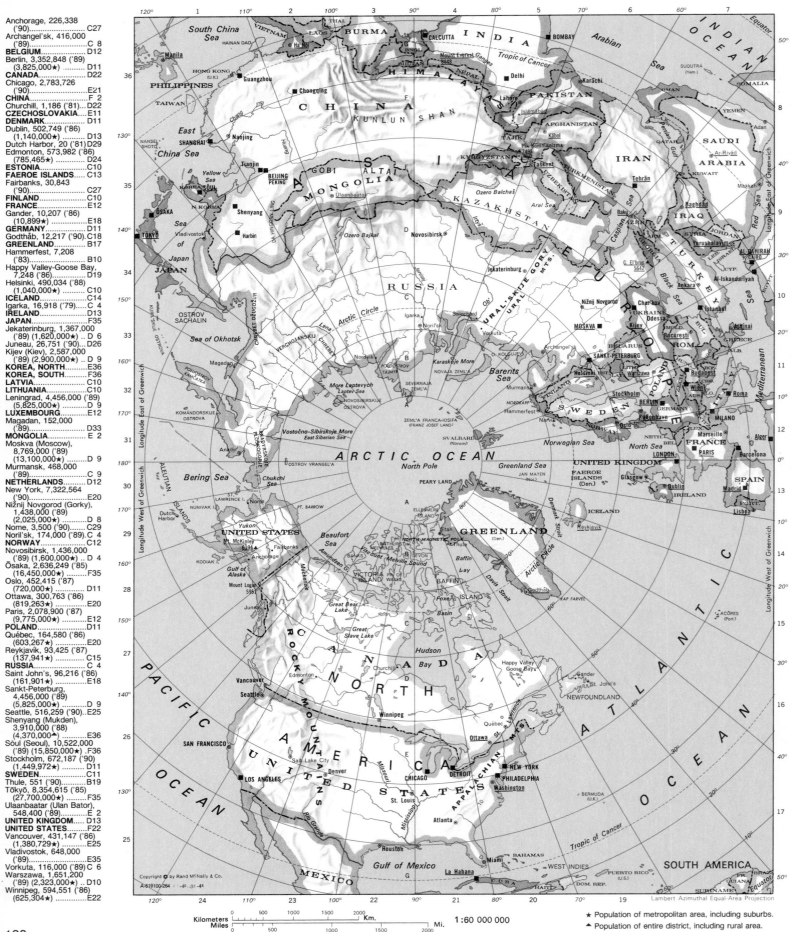

Copyright © by Rand McNally & Co.

A-519100-264   -4E- -3E- -4E

Kilometers
Miles

1:60 000 000

★ Population of metropolitan area, including suburbs.

▲ Population of entire district, including rural area.

Lambert Azimuthal Equal-Area Projection

Index to World Reference Maps

Introduction to the Index

This universal index includes in a single alphabetical list approximately 38,000 names of features that appear on the reference maps. Each name is followed by the name of the country or continent in which it is located, a map-reference key and a page reference.

Names The names of cities appear in the index in regular type. The names of all other features appear in *italics*, followed by descriptive terms (hill, mtn., state) to indicate their nature.

Names that appear in shortened versions on the maps due to space limitations are spelled out in full in the index. The portions of these names omitted from the maps are enclosed in brackets — for example, Acapulco [de Juárez].

Abbreviations of names on the maps have been standardized as much as possible. Names that are abbreviated on the maps are generally spelled out in full in the index.

Country names and names of features that extend beyond the boundaries of one country are followed by the name of the continent in which each is located. Country designations follow the names of all other places in the index. The locations of places in the United States, Canada, and the United Kingdom are further defined by abbreviations that indicate the state, province, or political division in which each is located.

All abbreviations used in the index are defined in the List of Abbreviations below.

Alphabetization Names are alphabetized in the order of the letters of the English alphabet. Spanish *ll* and *ch*, for example, are not treated as distinct letters. Furthermore, diacritical marks are disregarded in alphabetization — German or Scandinavian ä or ö are treated as a or o.

The names of physical features may appear inverted, since they are always alphabetized under the proper, not the generic, part of the name, thus: 'Gibraltar, Strait of'. Otherwise every entry, whether consisting of one word or more, is alphabetized as a single continuous entity. 'Lakeland', for example, appears after 'La Crosse' and before 'La Salle'. Names beginning with articles (Le Havre, Den Helder, Al Manşūrah) are not inverted. Names beginning 'St.', 'Ste.' and 'Sainte' are alphabetized as though spelled 'Saint'.

In the case of identical names, towns are listed first, then political divisions, then physical features. Entries that are completely identical are listed alphabetically by country name.

Map-Reference Keys and Page References The map-reference keys and page references are found in the last two columns of each entry.

Each map-reference key consists of a letter and number. The letters appear along the sides of the maps. Lowercase letters indicate reference to inset maps. Numbers appear across the tops and bottoms of the maps.

Map reference keys for point features, such as cities and mountain peaks, indicate the locations of the symbols. For extensive areal features, such as countries or mountain ranges, locations are given for the approximate centers of the features. Those for linear features, such as canals and rivers, are given for the locations of the names.

Names of some important places or features that are omitted from the maps due to space limitations are included in the index. Each of these places is identified by an asterisk (*) preceding the map-reference key.

The page number generally refers to the main map for the country in which the feature is located. Page references to two-page maps always refer to the left-hand page.

List of Abbreviations

Afg.	Afghanistan	*ctry.*	country	Isr.	Israel	N.H., U.S.	New Hampshire, U.S.	Som.	Somalia
Afr.	Africa	C.V.	Cape Verde	Isr. Occ.	Israeli Occupied	Nic.	Nicaragua	Sp. N. Afr.	Spanish North Africa
Ak., U.S.	Alaska, U.S.	Cyp.	Cyprus		Territories	Nig.	Nigeria	Sri L.	Sri Lanka
Al., U.S.	Alabama, U.S.	Czech.	Czechoslovakia	Jam.	Jamaica	N. Ire., U.K.	Northern Ireland, U.K.	*state*	state, republic, canton
Alb.	Albania	D.C., U.S.	District of Columbia,	Jord.	Jordan	N.J., U.S.	New Jersey, U.S.	St. Hel.	St. Helena
Alg.	Algeria		U.S.	Kaz.	Kazakhstan	N. Kor.	North Korea	St. K./N	St. Kitts and Nevis
Alta., Can.	Alberta, Can.	De., U.S.	Delaware, U.S.	Kir.	Kiribati	N.M., U.S.	New Mexico, U.S.	St. Luc.	St. Lucia
Am. Sam.	American Samoa	Den.	Denmark	Ks., U.S.	Kansas, U.S.	N. Mar. Is.	Northern Mariana	*stm.*	stream (river, creek)
anch.	anchorage	*dep.*	dependency, colony	Kuw.	Kuwait		Islands	S. Tom./P.	Sao Tome and
And.	Andorra	*depr.*	depression	Ky., U.S.	Kentucky, U.S.	Nmb.	Namibia		Principe
Ang.	Angola	*dept.*	department, district	Kyrg.	Kyrgyzstan	Nor.	Norway	St. P./M.	St. Pierre and
Ant.	Antarctica	*des.*	desert	*l.*	lake, pond	Norf. I.	Norfolk Island		Miquelon
Antig.	Antigua and Barbuda	Dji.	Djibouti	La., U.S.	Louisiana, U.S.	N.S., Can.	Nova Scotia, Can.	*strt.*	strait, channel, sound
Ar., U.S.	Arkansas, U.S.	Dom.	Dominica	Lat.	Latvia	Nv., U.S.	Nevada, U.S.	St. Vin.	St. Vincent and the
Arg.	Argentina	Dom. Rep.	Dominican Republic	Leb.	Lebanon	N.W. Ter.,	Northwest Territories,		Grenadines
Arm.	Armenia	Ec.	Ecuador	Leso.	Lesotho	Can.	Can.	Sud.	Sudan
Aus.	Austria	El Sal.	El Salvador	Lib.	Liberia	N.Y., U.S.	New York, U.S.	Sur.	Suriname
Austl.	Australia	Eng., U.K.	England, U.K.	Liech.	Liechtenstein	N.Z.	New Zealand	*sw.*	swamp, marsh
Az., U.S.	Arizona, U.S.	Eq. Gui.	Equatorial Guinea	Lith.	Lithuania	Oc.	Oceania	Swaz.	Swaziland
Azer.	Azerbaijan	*est.*	estuary	Lux.	Luxembourg	Oh., U.S.	Ohio, U.S.	Swe.	Sweden
b.	bay, gulf, inlet, lagoon	Est.	Estonia	Ma., U.S.	Massachusetts, U.S.	Ok., U.S.	Oklahoma, U.S.	Switz.	Switzerland
Bah.	Bahamas	Eth.	Ethiopia	Mac.	Macedonia	Ont., Can.	Ontario, Can.	Tai.	Taiwan
Bahr.	Bahrain	Eur.	Europe	Madag.	Madagascar	Or., U.S.	Oregon, U.S.	Taj.	Tajikistan
Barb.	Barbados	Faer. Is.	Faeroe Islands	Malay.	Malaysia	Pa., U.S.	Pennsylvania, U.S.	Tan.	Tanzania
B.A.T.	British Antarctic	Falk. Is.	Falkland Islands	Mald.	Maldives	Pak.	Pakistan	T./C. Is.	Turks and Caicos
	Territory	Fin.	Finland	Man., Can.	Manitoba, Can.	Pan.	Panama		Islands
B.C., Can.	British Columbia, Can.	Fl., U.S.	Florida, U.S.	Marsh. Is.	Marshall Islands	Pap. N. Gui.	Papua New Guinea	*ter.*	territory
Bdi.	Burundi	*for.*	forest, moor	Mart.	Martinique	Para.	Paraguay	Thai.	Thailand
Bel.	Belgium	Fr.	France	Maur.	Mauritania	P.E.I., Can.	Prince Edward Island,	Tn., U.S.	Tennessee, U.S.
Bela.	Belarus	Fr. Gu.	French Guiana	May.	Mayotte		Can.	Tok.	Tokelau
Ber.	Bermuda	Fr. Poly.	French Polynesia	Md., U.S.	Maryland, U.S.	*pen.*	peninsula	Trin.	Trinidad and Tobago
Bhu.	Bhutan	F.S.A.T.	French Southern and	Me., U.S.	Maine, U.S.	Phil.	Philippines	Tun.	Tunisia
B.I.O.T.	British Indian Ocean		Antarctic Territory	Mex.	Mexico	Pit.	Pitcairn	Tur.	Turkey
	Territory	Ga., U.S.	Georgia, U.S.	Mi., U.S.	Michigan, U.S.	*pl.*	plain, flat	Turk.	Turkmenistan
Bngl.	Bangladesh	Gam.	Gambia	Micron.	Federated States of	*plat.*	plateau, highland	Tx., U.S.	Texas, U.S.
Bol.	Bolivia	Geor.	Georgia		Micronesia	Pol.	Poland	U.A.E.	United Arab Emirates
Boph.	Bophuthatswana	Ger.	Germany	Mid. Is.	Midway Islands	Port.	Portugal	Ug.	Uganda
Bos.	Bosnia and	Gib.	Gibraltar	*mil.*	military installation	P.R.	Puerto Rico	U.K.	United Kingdom
	Hercegovina	Grc.	Greece	Mn., U.S.	Minnesota, U.S.	*prov.*	province, region	Ukr.	Ukraine
Bots.	Botswana	Gren.	Grenada	Mo., U.S.	Missouri, U.S.	Que., Can.	Quebec, Can.	Ur.	Uruguay
Braz.	Brazil	Grnld.	Greenland	Mol.	Moldova	*reg.*	physical region	U.S.	United States
Bru.	Brunei	Guad.	Guadeloupe	Mon.	Monaco	*res.*	reservoir	Ut., U.S.	Utah, U.S.
Br. Vir. Is.	British Virgin Islands	Guat.	Guatemala	Mong.	Mongolia	Reu.	Reunion	Uzb.	Uzbekistan
Bul.	Bulgaria	Gui.	Guinea	Monts.	Montserrat	*rf.*	reef, shoal	Va., U.S.	Virginia, U.S.
Burkina	Burkina Faso	Gui.-B.	Guinea-Bissau	Mor.	Morocco	R.I., U.S.	Rhode Island, U.S.	*val.*	valley, watercourse
c.	cape, point	Guy.	Guyana	Moz.	Mozambique	Rom.	Romania	Vat.	Vatican City
Ca., U.S.	California, U.S.	Hi., U.S.	Hawaii, U.S.	Mrts.	Mauritius	Rw.	Rwanda	Ven.	Venezuela
Cam.	Cameroon	*hist.*	historic site, ruins	Ms., U.S.	Mississippi, U.S.	S.A.	South America	Viet.	Vietnam
Camb.	Cambodia	*hist. reg.*	historic region	Mt., U.S.	Montana, U.S.	S. Afr.	South Africa	V.I.U.S.	Virgin Islands (U.S.)
Can.	Canada	H.K.	Hong Kong	*mth.*	river mouth or channel	Sask., Can.	Saskatchewan, Can.	*vol.*	volcano
Cay. Is.	Cayman Islands	Hond.	Honduras	*mtn.*	mountain	Sau. Ar.	Saudi Arabia	Vt., U.S.	Vermont, U.S.
Cen. Afr.	Central African	Hung.	Hungary	*mts.*	mountains	S.C., U.S.	South Carolina, U.S.	Wa., U.S.	Washington, U.S.
Rep.	Republic	*i.*	island	Mwi.	Malawi	*sci.*	scientific station	Wal./F.	Wallis and Futuna
Christ. I.	Christmas Island	Ia., U.S.	Iowa, U.S.	N.A.	North America	Scot., U.K.	Scotland, U.K.	Wi., U.S.	Wisconsin, U.S.
clf.	cliff, escarpment	I.C.	Ivory Coast	N.B., Can.	New Brunswick, Can.	S.D., U.S.	South Dakota, U.S.	W. Sah.	Western Sahara
co.	county, parish	Ice.	Iceland	N.C., U.S.	North Carolina, U.S.	Sen.	Senegal	W. Sam.	Western Samoa
Co., U.S.	Colorado, U.S.	*ice*	ice feature, glacier	N. Cal.	New Caledonia	Sey.	Seychelles	*wtfl.*	waterfall
Col.	Colombia	Id., U.S.	Idaho, U.S.	N. Cyp.	North Cyprus	Sing.	Singapore	W.V., U.S.	West Virginia, U.S.
Com.	Comoros	Il., U.S.	Illinois, U.S.	N.D., U.S.	North Dakota, U.S.	S. Kor.	South Korea	Wy., U.S.	Wyoming, U.S.
cont.	continent	In., U.S.	Indiana, U.S.	Ne., U.S.	Nebraska, U.S.	S.L.	Sierra Leone	Yugo.	Yugoslavia
C.R.	Costa Rica	Indon.	Indonesia	Neth.	Netherlands	Slo.	Slovenia	Yukon, Can.	Yukon Territory, Can.
crat.	crater	I. of Man	Isle of Man	Neth. Ant.	Netherlands Antilles	S. Mar.	San Marino	Zam.	Zambia
Cro.	Croatia	Ire.	Ireland	Newf., Can.	Newfoundland, Can.	Sol. Is.	Solomon Islands	Zimb.	Zimbabwe
Ct., U.S.	Connecticut, U.S.	*is.*	islands						

Index

A

Name	Map Ref	Page
Aachen, Ger.	E6	8
Aalen, Ger.	G10	8
Aalst, Bel.	E4	8
Äänekoski, Fin.	E15	6
Aarau, Switz.	E15	10
Aarschot, Bel.	E4	8
Aba, China	E7	26
Aba, Nig.	G7	42
Ābādān, Iran	B4	46
Abaeté, Braz.	E6	57
Abajo Peak, mtn., Ut., U.S.	F6	121
Abakan, Russia	G12	24
Abancay, Peru	F4	54
Abashiri, Japan	o22	30a
Abasolo, Mex.	E7	62
Abaya, Lake, l., Eth.	G2	46
Abaza, Russia	G12	24
Abbadia San Salvatore, Italy	G6	14
Abbaye, Point, c., Mi., U.S.	B2	99
Abbeville, Fr.	B8	10
Abbeville, Al., U.S.	D4	78
Abbeville, Ga., U.S.	E3	87
Abbeville, La., U.S.	E3	95
Abbeville, S.C., U.S.	C3	117
Abbeville, co., S.C., U.S.	C2	117
Abbotsford, Wi., U.S.	D3	126
Abbottābād, Pak.	C5	38
Abbott Butte, mtn., Or., U.S.	E4	114
Abbott Run, stm., U.S.	B4	116
Abbott Run Valley, R.I., U.S.	B4	116
'Abd al-Kūrī, i., Yemen	F5	46
Abe, Lake, l., Afr.	F3	46
Abéché, Chad	F10	42
Abéjar, Spain	D9	12
Abengourou, I.C.	G5	42
Abeokuta, Nig.	G6	42
Aberayron, Wales, U.K.	I8	7
Aberdeen, Scot., U.K.	D10	7
Aberdeen, Id., U.S.	G6	89
Aberdeen, Md., U.S.	A5	97
Aberdeen, Ms., U.S.	B5	101
Aberdeen, N.C., U.S.	B3	110
Aberdeen, Oh., U.S.	D2	112
Aberdeen, S.D., U.S.	B7	118
Aberdeen, Wa., U.S.	C2	124
Aberdeen Lake, l., N.W. Ter., Can.	D13	66
Aberdeen Proving Ground, mil., Md., U.S.	A5	97
Abernathy, Tx., U.S.	C2	120
Abert, Lake, l., Or., U.S.	E6	114
Abert Rim, clf, Or., U.S.	E6	114
Aberystwyth, Wales, U.K.	I8	7
Abhā, Sau. Ar.	E3	46
Abidjan, I.C.	G4	42
Abilene, Ks., U.S.	D6	93
Abilene, Tx., U.S.	C3	120
Abingdon, Il., U.S.	C3	90
Abingdon, Md., U.S.	B5	97
Abingdon, Va., U.S.	f10	123
Abington, Ma., U.S.	B6	98
Abington [Township], Pa., U.S.	o21	115
Abisko, Swe.	B12	6
Abita Springs, La., U.S.	D5	95
Abitibi, stm., Ont., Can.	o19	73
Abitibi, Lake, l., Can.	G17	66
Abohar, India	E6	38
Abomey, Benin	G6	42
Aborigen, Pik, mtn., Russia	E23	24
Abraham Lake, res., Alta., Can.	C2	68
Abraham Lincoln Birthplace National Historic Site, hist., Ky., U.S.	C4	94
Abrantes, Port.	F3	12
Absaroka Range, mts., U.S.	F7	127
Absarokee, Mt., U.S.	E7	103
Absecon, N.J., U.S.	E4	107
Absecon Inlet, b., N.J., U.S.	E4	107
Abū 'Alī, i., Sau. Ar.	C4	46
Abu Dhabi see Abū Zaby, U.A.E.	D5	46
Abū Hamad, Sudan	E12	42
Abū Kamāl, Syria	B7	40
Abukuma-sanchi, mts., Japan	E13	30
Abū Madd, Ra's, c., Sau. Ar.	D2	46
Abunā, Braz.	E5	54
Abū Shajarah, Ra's, c., Sudan	D13	42
Abū Zaby, U.A.E.	D5	46
Academia, co., La., U.S.	B3	112
Acadia, co., La., U.S.	D3	95
Acadia National Park, Me., U.S.	D4	96
Acajutla, El Sal.	H3	64
Acámbaro, Mex.	G9	62
Acaponeta, Mex.	F7	62
Acapulco [de Juárez], Mex.	I10	62
Acarai Mountains, mts., S.A.	C7	54
Acaraú, Braz.	D10	54
Acarigua, Ven.	C8	58
Acatlán [de Osorio], Mex.	H10	62
Acayucan, Mex.	I12	62
Accomack, co., Va., U.S.	C7	123
Accoville, W.V., U.S.	D3	125
Accra, Ghana	G5	42
Acerra, Italy	I9	14
Achaguas, Ven.	D8	58
Achalpur, India	B4	37
Acheng, China	B12	26
Achí, Col.	C5	58
Achill Island, i., Ire.	H2	7
Achtubinsk, Russia	H7	22
Ačinsk, Russia	F12	24
Acireale, Italy	L10	14
Ackerman, Ms., U.S.	B4	101
Ackley, Ia., U.S.	B4	92
Acklins Island, i., Bah.	C10	64
Acoma Indian Reservation, N.M., U.S.	C2	108
Aconcagua, Cerro, mtn., Arg.	C2	56
Açores (Azores), is., Port.	D11	2
Acquapendente, Italy	G6	14
Acqui Terme, Italy	E3	14
Acre, stm., S.A.	E5	54
Acri, Italy	J11	14
Acton, Ma., U.S.	B5	98
Acton Vale, Que., Can.	D5	74
Acushnet, Ma., U.S.	C6	98
Acworth, Ga., U.S.	B2	87
Ada, Mn., U.S.	C2	100
Ada, Oh., U.S.	B2	112
Ada, Ok., U.S.	C5	113
Ada, co., Id., U.S.	F2	89
Ada, Mount, mtn., Ak., U.S.	m22	79
Adair, Ia., U.S.	C3	92
Adair, Ok., U.S.	A6	113
Adair, co., Ia., U.S.	C3	92
Adair, co., Ky., U.S.	C4	94
Adair, co., Mo., U.S.	A5	102
Adair, co., Ok., U.S.	B7	113
Adair, Cape, c., N.W. Ter., Can.	B18	66
Adairsville, Ga., U.S.	B2	87
Adairville, Ky., U.S.	D3	94
Adak Island, i., Ak., U.S.	E4	79
Adak Naval Station, mil., Ak., U.S.	E4	79
Ādam, Oman	D6	46
Adamantina, Braz.	F3	57
Adamawa, mts., Afr.	G8	42
Adam Island, i., Md., U.S.	D5	97
Adams, Ma., U.S.	A1	98
Adams, Mn., U.S.	G6	100
Adams, N.Y., U.S.	B4	109
Adams, Wi., U.S.	E4	126
Adams, co., Co., U.S.	B6	83
Adams, co., Id., U.S.	E2	89
Adams, co., Il., U.S.	D2	90
Adams, co., In., U.S.	C8	91
Adams, co., Ia., U.S.	C3	92
Adams, co., Ms., U.S.	D2	101
Adams, co., Ne., U.S.	D7	104
Adams, co., N.D., U.S.	C3	111
Adams, co., Oh., U.S.	D2	112
Adams, co., Pa., U.S.	G7	115
Adams, co., Wa., U.S.	B7	124
Adams, co., Wi., U.S.	D4	126
Adams, Mount, mtn., N.H., U.S.	B4	106
Adams, Mount, mtn., Wa., U.S.	C4	124
Adams Bridge, rf., Asia	H5	37
Adams Point, c., Mi., U.S.	C7	99
Adams Run, S.C., U.S.	k11	117
Adamstown, Pa., U.S.	F9	115
Adamsville, Al., U.S.	f7	78
Adamsville, R.I., U.S.	E6	116
Adamsville, Tn., U.S.	B3	119
Adamsville Brook, stm., R.I., U.S.	E6	116
'Adan (Aden), Yemen	F4	46
Adana, Tur.	H15	4
Adapazan, Tur.	G14	4
Adarama, Sudan	E12	42
Ad-Dabbah, Sudan	E12	42
Ad-Dahnā, des., Sau. Ar.	D4	46
Ad-Dammām, Sau. Ar.	C5	46
Ad-Dawādimī, Sau. Ar.	D3	46
Ad-Dawhah (Doha), Qatar	C5	46
Addis, La., U.S.	D4	95
Addis Ababa see Adis Abeba, Eth.	G2	46
Addison, Al., U.S.	A2	78
Addison, Ct., U.S.	C5	84
Addison, Il., U.S.	k8	90
Addison, N.Y., U.S.	C3	109
Addison, co., Vt., U.S.	C2	122
Ad-Dīwānīyah, Iraq	B3	46
Ad-Duwaym, Sudan	F12	42
Addyston, Oh., U.S.	o12	112
Adel, Ga., U.S.	E3	87
Adel, Ia., U.S.	C3	92
Adelaide, Austl.	F7	50
Adelaide Peninsula, pen., N.W. Ter., Can.	C13	66
Adelanto, Ca., U.S.	E5	82
Aden, Gulf of, b.	F4	46
Aden see 'Adan, Yemen	F4	46
Adieu, Cape, c., Austl.	F6	50
Adige, stm., Italy	D7	14
Adigrat, Eth.	F2	46
Ādilābād, India	C5	37
Adimi, Russia	H21	24
Adirondack Mountains, mts., N.Y., U.S.	A6	109
Adis Abeba, Eth.	G2	46
Admiralty Bay, b., Ak., U.S.	A9	79
Admiralty Inlet, b., N.W. Ter., Can.	B15	66
Admiralty Island, i., Ak., U.S.	m22	79
Admiralty Islands, is., Pap. N. Gui.	k16	50a
Adobe Acres, N.M., U.S.	*B3	108
Adobe Creek Reservoir, res., Co., U.S.	C7	83
Adolfo López Mateos, Presa, res., Mex.	E6	62
Ādoni, India	E4	37
Adour, stm., Fr.	I7	10
Adra, Spain	I8	12
Adrano, Italy	L9	14
Adrar, Alg.	C5	42
Adria, Italy	D7	14
Adrian, Ga., U.S.	D4	87
Adrian, Mi., U.S.	G6	99
Adrian, Mn., U.S.	G3	100
Adrian, Mo., U.S.	C3	102
Adriatic Sea, Eur.	G11	4
Advance, Mo., U.S.	D8	102
Adyča, stm., Russia	D21	24
Aegean Sea	J8	16
Afars and Issas see Djibouti, ctry., Afr.	F3	46
Afghanistan, ctry., Asia	C1	36
Afikpo, Nig.	G7	42
Åfjord, Nor.	E8	6
Afmadu, Som.	A8	44
Afognak Island, i., Ak., U.S.	D9	79
Africa	D6	41
Afton, Ia., U.S.	C3	92
Afton, Mn., U.S.	F6	100
Afton, Ok., U.S.	A7	113
Afton, Wy., U.S.	D2	127
'Afula, Isr.	C4	40
Afyon, Tur.	H14	4
Agadez, Niger	E7	42
Agadir, Mor.	B4	42
Agalega Islands, is., Mrts.	D11	44
Agalta, Cordillera de, mts., Hond.	G5	64
Agapa, Russia	C11	24
Agartala, India	I14	38
Agate Fossil Beds National Monument, Ne., U.S.	B2	104
Agattu Island, i., Ak., U.S.	E2	79
Agawam, Ma., U.S.	B2	98
Agen, Fr.	H7	10
Agency, Ia., U.S.	D5	92
Agency, Mo., U.S.	B3	102
Āghā Jārī, Iran	B4	46
Agira, Italy	L9	14
Agnone, Italy	H9	14
Agoura Hills, Ca., U.S.	m11	82
Āgra, India	G8	38
Ágreda, Spain	D10	12
Ağrı Dağı (Mount Ararat), mtn., Tur.	H16	4
Agrigento, Italy	L8	14
Agrínion, Grc.	K5	16
Agropoli, Italy	I9	14
Agua Caliente, Mex.	F7	62
Agua Caliente Grande, Mex.	D5	62
Aguachica, Col.	C6	58
Água Clara, Braz.	F2	57
Agua Fria, N.M., U.S.	B3	108
Agua Fria, stm., Az., U.S.	D3	80
Agua Prieta, Mex.	B5	62
Aguascalientes, Mex.	G8	62
Águas Formosas, Braz.	D8	57
Águeda, Port.	E3	12
Águila, Az., U.S.	D2	80
Aguilar, Spain	H7	12
Águilas, Spain	H10	12
Agulhas, Cape, c., S. Afr.	H3	44
Agustín Codazzi, Col.	B6	58
Agustín Codazzi, Col.	I11	64
Ahaggar, mts., Alg.	D7	42
Ahipara Bay, b., N.Z.	A4	52
Ahklun Mountains, mts., Ak., U.S.	D7	79
Ahlen, Ger.	D7	8
Ahmadābād, India	I5	38
Ahmadnagar, India	C3	37
Ahmadpur East, Pak.	F4	38
Ahmar Mountains, mts., Eth.	G3	46
Ahtanum Creek, stm., Wa., U.S.	C5	124
Ahu, China	A7	28
Ahuacatlán, Mex.	G7	62
Ahvāz, Iran	B4	46
Ahvenanmaa (Åland), is., Fin.	F12	6
Aialik, Cape, c., Ak., U.S.	D10	79
Aichach, Ger.	G11	8
Aiea, Hi., U.S.	B4	88
Aihun, China	A12	26
Aijal, India	I15	38
Aiken, S.C., U.S.	D4	117
Aiken, co., S.C., U.S.	D4	117
Ailsa Craig, Ont., Can.	D3	73
Aim, Russia	F20	24
Aimorés, Braz.	E8	57
Ainslie Lake, l., N.S., Can.	C8	71
Ainsworth, Ne., U.S.	B6	104
Aipe, Col.	F5	58
Air, mts., Niger	E7	42
Airdrie, Alta., Can.	D3	68
Aire-sur-l'Adour, Fr.	I6	10
Air Force Island, i., N.W. Ter., Can.	C18	66
Air Park West, Ne., U.S.	*D9	104
Aisne, stm., Fr.	C10	10
Aïssa, Djebel, mtn., Alg.	B5	42
Aitape, Pap. N. Gui.	k15	50a
Aitkin, Mn., U.S.	D5	100
Aitkin, co., Mn., U.S.	D5	100
Aix, Mount, mtn., Wa., U.S.	C4	124
Aix-en-Provence, Fr.	I12	10
Aix-la-Chapelle see Aachen, Ger.	E6	8
Aix-les-Bains, Fr.	G12	10
Aizu-wakamatsu, Japan	E12	30
Ajaguz, Kaz.	H10	24
Ajan, Russia	F21	24
Ajan, stm., Russia	C13	24
Ajax, Ont., Can.	D6	73
Ajdābīyah, Libya	B10	42
Ajjer, Tassili n', plat., Alg.	C7	42
'Ajlūn, Jord.	C4	40
Ajmer, India	G6	38
Ajo, Az., U.S.	E3	80
Ajo, Cabo de, c., Spain	B8	12
Ajtos, Bul.	G11	16
Akademii, Zaliv, b., Russia	G21	24
Akaltara, India	A7	37
Akan, Japan	p22	30a
'Akasha East, Sudan	D12	42
Akashi, Japan	H7	30
Akçakale, Tur.	A6	40
Ak-Chin Indian Reservation, Az., U.S.	E3	80
Akesu, China	C3	26
Akharnaí, Grc.	K7	16
Akhisar, Tur.	H13	4
Akiachak, Ak., U.S.	C7	79
Akimiski Island, i., N.W. Ter., Can.	F16	66
Akita, Japan	C13	30
Akjoujt, Maur.	E3	42
'Akko (Acre), Isr.	C4	40
Aklavik, N.W. Ter., Can.	C6	66
Akō, Japan	H7	30
Akobo, stm., Afr.	G12	42
Akola, India	B4	37
Akordat, Eth.	E2	46
Akot, India	B4	37
Akpatok Island, i., N.W. Ter., Can.	D19	66
Akron, Co., U.S.	A7	83
Akron, In., U.S.	B5	91
Akron, Ia., U.S.	B1	92
Akron, N.Y., U.S.	B2	109
Akron, Oh., U.S.	A4	112
Akron, Pa., U.S.	F9	115
Aksaray, Tur.	H14	4
Akşehir, Tur.	H14	4
Aksum, Eth.	F2	46
Akt'ubinsk, Kaz.	G9	22
Akureyri, Ice.	B4	6a
Al, Nor.	F7	6
Alabama, state, U.S.	C3	78
Alabama, stm., Al., U.S.	D2	78
Alabaster, Al., U.S.	B3	78
Alachua, Fl., U.S.	C4	86
Alachua, co., Fl., U.S.	C4	86
Alagoinhas, Braz.	B9	57
Alagón, Spain	D10	12
Alajuela, C.R.	I5	64
Alakanuk, Ak., U.S.	C7	79
Alalakeiki Channel, strt., Hi., U.S.	C5	88
Al-'Alamayn, Egypt	B11	42
Alamance, co., N.C., U.S.	B3	110
Al-'Amārah, Iraq	B4	46
Alameda, Ca., U.S.	h8	82
Alameda, N.M., U.S.	B3	108
Alameda, co., Ca., U.S.	D3	82
Alameda Naval Air Station, mil., Ca., U.S.	h8	82
Alamito Creek, stm., Tx., U.S.	p12	120
Alamo, Ga., U.S.	D4	87
Alamo, Nv., U.S.	F6	105
Alamo, Tn., U.S.	B2	119
Alamo, Tx., U.S.	F3	120
Alamogordo, N.M., U.S.	E4	108
Alamo Heights, Tx., U.S.	E3	120
Alamo Hueco Mountains, mts., N.M., U.S.	F1	108
Alamosa, Co., U.S.	D5	83
Alamosa, co., Co., U.S.	D5	83
Alamosa, stm., Co., U.S.	D4	83
Alamosa Creek, stm., N.M., U.S.	D2	108
Alamosa East, Co., U.S.	D5	83
Alanäs, Swe.	D10	6
Alanya, Tur.	A3	40
Alapaha, Ga., U.S.	E3	87
Alapaha, stm., U.S.	E3	87
Al-'Aqabah, Jord.	E4	40
Alaşehir, Tur.	K12	16
Alashanyouqi, China	C7	26
Alaska, state, U.S.	C9	79
Alaska, Gulf of, b., Ak., U.S.	D10	79
Alaska Peninsula, pen., Ak., U.S.	D8	79
Alaska Range, mts., Ak., U.S.	C9	79
Alassio, Italy	E3	14
Alatna, stm., Ak., U.S.	B9	79
Al-'Atrūn, Sudan	E11	42
Alava, Cape, c., Wa., U.S.	A1	124
Alazeja, stm., Russia	C24	24
Alba, Italy	E3	14
Albacete, Spain	G10	12
Alba de Tormes, Spain	E6	12
Albaida, Spain	G11	12
Albanel, Lac, l., Que., Can.	F18	66
Albania, ctry., Eur.	G11	4
Albano Laziale, Italy	H7	14
Albany, Austl.	G3	50
Albany, Ga., U.S.	E2	87
Albany, Il., U.S.	B3	90
Albany, In., U.S.	D7	91
Albany, Ky., U.S.	D4	94
Albany, La., U.S.	g10	95
Albany, Mn., U.S.	E4	100
Albany, Mo., U.S.	A3	102
Albany, N.Y., U.S.	C7	109
Albany, Or., U.S.	C3	114
Albany, Tx., U.S.	C3	120
Albany, Wi., U.S.	F4	126
Albany, co., N.Y., U.S.	C6	109
Albany, co., Wy., U.S.	E7	127
Albany, stm., Ont., Can.	o18	73
Albatross Bay, b., Austl.	B8	50
Al-Batrūn, Leb.	B4	40
Al-Bawītī, Egypt	C11	42
Albemarle, N.C., U.S.	B2	110
Albemarle, co., Va., U.S.	C4	123
Albemarle Lake, l., Ms., U.S.	C2	101
Albemarle Sound, strt., N.C., U.S.	A6	110
Albenga, Italy	E3	14
Albergaria-a-Velha, Port.	E3	12
Albert, Fr.	B9	10
Albert, Lake, l., Afr.	A6	44
Alberta, prov., Can.	C4	68
Alberta, Mount, mtn., Alta., Can.	C2	68
Albert City, Ia., U.S.	B3	92
Albert Lea, Mn., U.S.	G5	100
Albert Nile, stm., Ug.	H12	42
Alberton, P.E.I., Can.	C5	71
Albertson, N.Y., U.S.	k13	109
Albertville, Fr.	G13	10
Albertville, Al., U.S.	A3	78
Albertville, Mn., U.S.	E5	100
Albertville see Kalemie, Zaire	C5	44
Albi, Fr.	I9	10
Albia, Ia., U.S.	C5	92
Albion, Il., U.S.	E5	90
Albion, In., U.S.	B7	91
Albion, Mi., U.S.	F6	99
Albion, Ne., U.S.	C7	104
Albion, N.Y., U.S.	B2	109
Albion, Pa., U.S.	C1	115
Albion, R.I., U.S.	B4	116
Albion, Wa., U.S.	C8	124
Alborán, Isla de, i., Spain	J8	12
Ålborg, Den.	H7	6
Alborz, Reshteh-ye Kūhhā-ye, mts., Iran	J8	22
Albufeira, Port.	H3	12
Albuñol, Spain	I8	12
Albuquerque, N.M., U.S.	B3	108
Alburquerque, Spain	F4	12
Alburtis, Pa., U.S.	F10	115
Albury, Austl.	G9	50
Alcácer do Sal, Port.	G3	12
Alcalá de Guadaira, Spain	H6	12
Alcalá de Henares, Spain	E8	12
Alcalá la Real, Spain	H8	12
Alcalde, N.M., U.S.	A3	108
Alcamo, Italy	L7	14
Alcañices, Spain	D5	12
Alcañiz, Spain	D11	12
Alcántara, Braz.	D10	54
Alcántara, Spain	F5	12
Alcantarilla, Spain	H10	12
Alcaraz, Spain	G9	12
Alcázar de San Juan, Spain	F8	12
Alcester, S.D., U.S.	D9	118
Alcira, Spain	F11	12
Alcoa, Tn., U.S.	D10	119
Alcobaça, Braz.	D9	57
Alcobaça, Port.	F3	12
Alcolu, S.C., U.S.	D7	117
Alcona, co., Mi., U.S.	D7	99
Alconchel, Spain	G4	12
Alcorn, co., Ms., U.S.	A5	101
Alcoy, Spain	G11	12
Aldabra Islands, atoll, Sey.	C9	44
Aldan, Russia	F19	24
Aldan, stm., Russia	E20	24
Aldanskoje Nagorje, plat., Russia	F19	24
Alden, Ia., U.S.	B4	92
Alden, Mn., U.S.	G5	100
Alden, N.Y., U.S.	C2	109
Alder Brook, stm., Vt., U.S.	B4	122
Aldershot, Eng., U.K.	J12	7
Alderson, W.V., U.S.	D4	125
Aldrich, Al., U.S.	B3	78
Aledo, Il., U.S.	B3	90
Aleg, Maur.	E3	42
Alegres Mountain, mtn., N.M., U.S.	C2	108
Alegrete, Braz.	B5	56
Alejsk, Russia	G10	24
Aleksandrov, Russia	E21	18
Aleksandrovsk-Sachalinskij, Russia	G22	24
Aleksejevsk, Russia	F15	24
Aleksin, Russia	G20	18
Além Paraíba, Braz.	F7	57
Alençon, Fr.	D7	10
Alenuihaha Channel, strt., Hi., U.S.	C5	88
Aleppo see Halab, Syria	A5	40
Alert Bay, B.C., Can.	D4	69
Alès, Fr.	H11	10
Alessandria, Italy	E3	14
Alessano, Italy	J13	14
Ålesund, Nor.	E6	6
Aleutian Islands, is., Ak., U.S.	E3	79
Aleutian Range, mts., Ak., U.S.	D9	79
Aleutka, Russia	H24	24
Alevina, Mys, c., Russia	F24	24
Alex, Ok., U.S.	C4	113
Alexander, co., Il., U.S.	F4	90
Alexander, co., N.C., U.S.	B1	110
Alexander, Lake, l., Mn., U.S.	D4	100
Alexander Archipelago, is., Ak., U.S.	D12	79
Alexander Bay, S. Afr.	G3	44
Alexander City, Al., U.S.	C4	78
Alexander Island, i., Ant.	B6	47
Alexandra, N.Z.	F2	52
Alexandretta see Iskenderun Körfezi, b., Tur.	A4	40
Alexandria, Ont., Can.	B10	73
Alexandria, In., U.S.	D6	91
Alexandria, Ky., U.S.	B5	94
Alexandria, La., U.S.	C3	95
Alexandria, Mn., U.S.	E3	100
Alexandria, Tn., U.S.	A5	119
Alexandria, Va., U.S.	B5	123
Alexandria see Al-Iskandarīyah, Egypt	B11	42
Alexandroúpolis, Grc.	I9	16
Alexis, Il., U.S.	B3	90
Alfalfa, co., Ok., U.S.	A3	113
Alfaro, Ec.	I3	58
Alfaro, Spain	C10	12
Alfarrás, Spain	D12	12
Al-Fāshir, Sudan	F11	42
Al-Fayyūm, Egypt	C12	42
Alfeld, Ger.	D9	8
Alfenas, Braz.	F6	57
Alfred, Ont., Can.	B10	73
Alfred, N.Y., U.S.	C3	109
Algarve, hist. reg., Port.	H3	12
Algeciras, Spain	I6	12
Algemesí, Spain	F11	12
Alger, Alg.	A6	42
Alger, Oh., U.S.	B2	112
Alger, co., Mi., U.S.	B4	99
Algeria, ctry., Afr.	C6	42
Al-Ghaydah, Yemen	E5	46
Alghero, Italy	I3	14
Al-Ghurdaqah, Egypt	C12	42
Algiers see Alger, Alg.	A6	42
Algoma, Wi., U.S.	D6	126
Algona, Ia., U.S.	A3	92
Algona, Wa., U.S.	B3	124
Algonac, Mi., U.S.	F8	99
Algonquin, Il., U.S.	A5	90
Algonquin Provincial Park, Ont., Can.	B6	73
Algood, Tn., U.S.	C8	119
Algorta, Ur.	C5	56
Al-Hadīthah, Iraq	B3	46
Al-Haffah, Syria	B5	40
Al-Hamād, pl., Sau. Ar.	B2	46
Alhama de Granada, Spain	H8	12
Alhambra, Ca., U.S.	m12	82
Al-Hariq, Sau. Ar.	D4	46
Al-Harūj al-Aswad, hills, Libya	C9	42
Al-Hasakah, Syria	A7	40
Alhaurín el Grande, Spain	I7	12
Al-Hawrah, Yemen	F4	46
Al-Hijāz (Hejaz), reg., Sau. Ar.	C2	46
Al-Hillah, Iraq	B3	46
Al-Hirmil, Leb.	B5	40
Al-Hudaydah, Yemen	F3	46
Al-Hufūf, Sau. Ar.	C4	46
Aliaga, Spain	E11	12
Alicante, Spain	G11	12
Alice, Tx., U.S.	F3	120
Alice Lake, l., Ms., U.S.	C7	100
Aliceville, Al., U.S.	B1	78
Alice Springs, Austl.	D6	50
Alīgarh, India	G8	38
Alijos, Escollos, Mex.	E2	62
Alingsås, Swe.	H9	6
Alīpur Duār, India	G13	38
Aliquippa, Pa., U.S.	E1	115
Al-Iskandarīyah (Alexandria), Egypt	B11	42
Al-Ismā'īlīyah, Egypt	B12	42
Aliwal North, S. Afr.	H5	44
Alix, Alta., Can.	C4	68
Al-Jabal al-Akhdar, mts., Oman	D6	46
Al-Jafr, Jord.	D5	40
Al-Jaghbūb, Libya	C10	42
Al-Jawf, Libya	D10	42
Al-Jawf, Sau. Ar.	C2	46
Al-Jazīrah, reg., Sudan	F12	42

Name	Map Ref	Page
Aljezur, Port.	H3	12
Al-Jīzah, Egypt	B12	42
Al-Junaynah, Sudan	F10	42
Aljustrel, Port.	H3	12
Alkali Lake, l., Nv., U.S.	B2	105
Alkali Lake, l., Or., U.S.	E6	114
Alkaline Lake, l., N.D., U.S.	C6	111
Al-Karak, Jord.	D4	40
Al-Kawm, Syria	B6	40
Al-Khābūr, stm., Syria	A7	40
Al-Khalīl, Isr. Occ.	D4	40
Al-Khandaq, Sudan	E12	42
Al-Khārijah, Egypt	C12	42
Al-Khartūm (Khartoum), Sudan	E12	42
Al-Khasab, Oman	C6	46
Al-Khubar, Sau. Ar.	C5	46
Al-Khums, Libya	B8	42
Alkmaar, Neth.	C4	8
Al-Kuwayt, Kuw.	C5	46
Allach-Jun', Russia	E21	24
Al-Lādhiqīyah (Latakia), Syria	B4	40
Allagash, stm., Me., U.S.	B3	96
Allagash Lake, l., Me., U.S.	B3	96
Allāhābād, India	H9	38
Allamakee, co., Ia., U.S.	A6	92
Allan, Sask., Can.	F2	75
Allanche, Fr.	G9	10
Allanmyo, Burma	E3	34
Allardt, Tn., U.S.	C9	119
Allatoona Lake, res., Ga., U.S.	B2	87
Allegan, Mi., U.S.	F5	99
Allegan, co., Mi., U.S.	F5	99
Allegany, N.Y., U.S.	C2	109
Allegany, co., Md., U.S.	k13	97
Allegany, co., N.Y., U.S.	C2	109
Allegany Indian Reservation, N.Y., U.S.	C2	109
Alleghany, co., N.C., U.S.	A1	110
Alleghany, co., Va., U.S.	C2	123
Allegheny, co., Pa., U.S.	E2	115
Allegheny, stm., U.S.	E2	115
Allegheny Reservoir, res., U.S.	B4	115
Allemands, Lac Des, l., La., U.S.	E5	95
Allen, Ok., U.S.	C5	113
Allen, co., In., U.S.	B7	91
Allen, co., Ks., U.S.	E8	93
Allen, co., Ky., U.S.	D3	94
Allen, co., La., U.S.	D3	95
Allen, co., Oh., U.S.	B1	112
Allen, Mount, mtn., Ak., U.S.	C11	79
Allendale, N.J., U.S.	A4	107
Allendale, S.C., U.S.	E5	117
Allendale, co., S.C., U.S.	F5	117
Allen Park, Mi., U.S.	p15	99
Allenton, R.I., U.S.	E4	116
Allenton, Wi., U.S.	E5	126
Allentown, Pa., U.S.	E11	115
Allentsteig, Aus.	G15	8
Alleppey, India	H4	37
Aller, stm., Ger.	C9	8
Allerton, Point, c., Ma., U.S.	B6	98
Allgäuer Alpen, mts., Eur.	H10	8
Alliance, Ne., U.S.	B3	104
Alliance, Oh., U.S.	B4	112
Alligator, stm., N.C., U.S.	B6	110
Alligator Lake, l., Me., U.S.	D4	96
Allison, Ia., U.S.	B5	92
Allison, Pa., U.S.	G2	115
Allison Park, Pa., U.S.	h14	115
Alliston, Ont., Can.	C5	73
Al-Līth, Sau. Ar.	D3	46
Allouez, Wi., U.S.	h9	126
Alloway Creek, stm., N.J., U.S.	D2	107
Al-Luhayyah, Yemen	E3	46
Allumette Lake, l., Can.	B7	73
Allyn, Wa., U.S.	B3	124
Alma, Que., Can.	A6	74
Alma, Ar., U.S.	B1	81
Alma, Ga., U.S.	E4	87
Alma, Ks., U.S.	C7	93
Alma, Mi., U.S.	E6	99
Alma, Ne., U.S.	D6	104
Alma, Wi., U.S.	D2	126
Alma-Ata, Kaz.	I9	24
Almada, Port.	G2	12
Al-Madīnah (Medina), Sau. Ar.	D2	46
Al-Mafraq, Jord.	C5	40
Almagro, Spain	G8	12
Al-Manāmah, Bahr.	C5	46
Almanor, Lake, l., Ca., U.S.	B3	82
Almansa, Spain	G10	12
Al-Mansūrah, Egypt	B12	42
Al-Marj, Libya	B10	42
Almas, Pico das, mtn., Braz.	F10	54
Al-Maṣīrah, i., Oman	D6	46
Al-Mawsil, Iraq	A3	46
Al-Mayādīn, Syria	B7	40
Almazán, Spain	D9	12
Almelo, Neth.	C6	8
Almenara, Braz.	D8	57
Almendralejo, Spain	G5	12
Almería, Spain	I9	12
Al'metjevsk, Russia	G8	22
Al-Minyā, Egypt	C12	42
Almirante, Pan.	J6	64
Al-Mismīyah, Syria	C5	40
Almodôvar, Port.	H3	12
Almodóvar del Campo, Spain	G7	12
Almont, Mi., U.S.	F7	99
Almonte, Ont., Can.	B8	73
Almonte, Spain	H5	12
Almora, India	F8	38
Al-Mubarraz, Sau. Ar.	C4	46
Al-Mubarraz, Sau. Ar.	D4	46
Al-Muglad, Sudan	F11	42
Al-Muharraq, Bahr.	C5	46
Al-Mukallā, Yemen	F4	46
Al-Mukhā, Yemen	F3	46
Al-Muwaylih, Sau. Ar.	C2	46
Alnwick, Eng., U.K.	D4	7
Aloândia, Braz.	C4	57
Aloha, Or., U.S.	h12	114
Alor, Pulau, i., Indon.	G7	32
Álora, Spain	I7	12
Alor Setar, Malay.	K6	34
Aloysius, Mount, mtn., Austl.	E5	50
Alpena, Mi., U.S.	C7	99
Alpena, co., Mi., U.S.	D7	99
Alpharetta, Ga., U.S.	B2	87
Alpiarça, Port.	F3	12
Alpine, Az., U.S.	D6	80
Alpine, Tx., U.S.	D1	120
Alpine, Ut., U.S.	C4	121
Alpine, co., Ca., U.S.	C4	82
Alps, mts., Eur.	F9	4
Al-Qadārif, Sudan	F13	42
Al-Qāhirah (Cairo), Egypt	B12	42
Al-Qāmishlī, Syria	A7	40
Al-Qaryah ash-Sharqīyah, Libya	B8	42
Al-Qaryatayn, Syria	B5	40
Al-Qasr, Egypt	C4	46
Al-Qatīf, Sau. Ar.	C5	46
Al-Qatrūn, Libya	D8	42
Al-Qaysūmah, Sau. Ar.	C4	40
Al-Qunaytirah, Syria	C4	40
Al-Qunfudhah, Sau. Ar.	E3	46
Al-Qusayr, Egypt	C12	42
Al-Qutayfah, Syria	C5	40
Alsace, hist. reg., Fr.	E14	10
Alsasua, Spain	C9	12
Alsfeld, Ger.	E9	8
Alta, Nor.	B14	6
Alta, Ia., U.S.	B2	92
Altadena, Ca., U.S.	m12	82
Altagracia, Ven.	B7	58
Altagracia de Orituco, Ven.	C9	58
Altai, mts., Asia	B4	26
Altaj (Jesönbulag), Mong.	B6	26
Altamaha, stm., Ga., U.S.	E4	87
Altamira, Braz.	D8	54
Altamont, Il., U.S.	D5	90
Altamont, Ks., U.S.	E8	93
Altamont, Or., U.S.	E5	114
Altamont, Tn., U.S.	D8	119
Altamonte Springs, Fl., U.S.	D5	86
Altamura, Italy	I11	14
Altar, Mex.	B4	62
Altar, Desierto de, des., Mex.	B3	62
Altata, Mex.	E6	62
Altavista, Va., U.S.	C3	123
Altdorf, Switz.	F15	10
Altenburg, Ger.	E12	8
Altheimer, Ar., U.S.	C4	81
Altiplano, plat., S.A.	G5	54
Alto, Ga., U.S.	B3	87
Alto, N.M., U.S.	D4	108
Alton, Il., U.S.	E3	90
Alton, Ia., U.S.	B2	92
Alton, Mo., U.S.	E6	102
Alton, N.H., U.S.	D4	106
Altona, Man., Can.	E3	70
Alton Bay, N.H., U.S.	D4	106
Altoona, Al., U.S.	A3	78
Altoona, Fl., U.S.	D5	86
Altoona, Ia., U.S.	C4	92
Altoona, Pa., U.S.	E5	115
Altoona, Wi., U.S.	D2	126
Alto Parnaíba, Braz.	E9	54
Altötting, Ger.	G12	8
Altun Shan, mts., China	D4	26
Alturas, Ca., U.S.	B3	82
Altus, Ok., U.S.	C2	113
Altus Air Force Base, mil., Ok., U.S.	C2	113
Altus Reservoir, res., Ok., U.S.	C2	113
Al-'Ubaylah, Sau. Ar.	D5	46
Al-Ubayyid, Sudan	F12	42
Al-Uqsur (Luxor), Egypt	C12	42
Alva, Fl., U.S.	F5	86
Alva, Ok., U.S.	A3	113
Alvarado, Mex.	H12	62
Alvarado, Tx., U.S.	C4	120
Álvaro Obregón, Presa, res., Mex.	D5	62
Älvdalen, Swe.	F10	6
Alvin, Tx., U.S.	E5	120
Alvinston, Ont., Can.	E3	73
Älvkarleby, Swe.	F11	6
Alvord, Lake, l., Or., U.S.	E8	114
Älvsbyn, Swe.	D13	6
Alwar, India	G7	38
Alzamaj, Russia	F13	24
Ama, La., U.S.	k11	95
Amadeus, Lake, l., Austl.	D6	50
Amadjuak Lake, l., N.W. Ter., Can.	C18	66
Amador, co., Ca., U.S.	C3	82
Amagansett, N.Y., U.S.	n16	109
Amagasaki, Japan	H8	30
Amakusa-nada, Japan	J2	30
Amakusa-shotō, is., Japan	J3	30
Amål, Swe.	G9	6
Amalapuram, India	D7	37
Amalfi, Italy	I9	14
Amalner, India	J6	38
Amambaí, stm., Braz.	G1	57
Amambaí, Serra de, mts., S.A.	H7	54
Amami-Ō-shima, i., Japan	w29	31b
Amami-shotō, is., Japan	x29	31b
Amana, U.S.	C6	92
Amantea, Italy	J11	14
Amares, Port.	D3	12
Amargosa, stm., U.S.	G5	82
Amargosa Desert, des., U.S.	G5	105
Amargosa Range, mts., U.S.	G5	105
Amarillo, Tx., U.S.	B2	120
Amatignak Island, i., Ak., U.S.	E4	79
Amazon (Solimões) (Amazonas), stm., S.A.	D7	54
Ambāla, India	E7	38
Ambarčik, Russia	D26	24
Ambāsamudram, India	H4	37
Ambato, Ec.	H3	58
Ambatolampy, Madag.	E9	44
Ambatondrazaka, Madag.	E9	44
Amberg, Ger.	F11	8
Ambérieu-en-Bugey, Fr.	G1	10
Ambert, Fr.	G10	10
Ambikāpur, India	I10	38
Ambilobe, Madag.	D9	44
Amble, Eng., U.K.	F11	7
Ambler, Pa., U.S.	F11	115
Amboise, Fr.	E7	10
Ambon, Indon.	F8	32
Ambositra, Madag.	F9	44
Ambovombe, Madag.	G9	44
Amboy, Il., U.S.	B4	90
Ambre, Cap d', c., Madag.	D9	44
Ambridge, Pa., U.S.	E1	115
Ambrières, Fr.	D6	10
Ambriz, Ang.	C2	44
Āmbūr, India	F5	37
Amchitka Island, i., Ak., U.S.	E3	79
Amchitka Pass, strt., Ak., U.S.	E4	79
Ameca, Mex.	G7	62
Amecameca [de Juárez], Mex.	H10	62
Amelia, La., U.S.	E4	95
Amelia, Oh., U.S.	C1	112
Amelia, co., Va., U.S.	C4	123
Amelia Court House, Va., U.S.	C5	123
Amelia Island, i., Fl., U.S.	k9	86
American, stm., Ca., U.S.	C3	82
Americana, Braz.	G5	57
American Falls, Id., U.S.	G6	89
American Falls Dam, Id., U.S.	G6	89
American Falls Reservoir, res., Id., U.S.	F5	89
American Fork, Ut., U.S.	C4	121
American Highland, plat., Ant.	B20	47
American Samoa, dep., Oc.	G1	2
Americus, Ga., U.S.	D2	87
Americus, Ks., U.S.	D7	93
Amersfoort, Neth.	C5	8
Amery, Wi., U.S.	C1	126
Ames, Ia., U.S.	B4	92
Amesbury, Ma., U.S.	A6	98
Amfilokhía, Grc.	K5	16
Ámfissa, Grc.	K6	16
Amga, Russia	E20	24
Amga, stm., Russia	E20	24
Amgun', stm., Russia	G21	24
Amherst, Ma., U.S.	B2	98
Amherst, N.H., U.S.	E3	106
Amherst, N.Y., U.S.	C2	109
Amherst, Oh., U.S.	A3	112
Amherst, Va., U.S.	C3	123
Amherst, Wi., U.S.	D4	126
Amherst, co., Va., U.S.	C3	123
Amherstburg, Ont., Can.	E1	73
Amherstdale, W.V., U.S.	n12	125
Amiens, Fr.	C9	10
Amīndīvi Islands, is., India	G2	37
Amirante Islands, is., Sey.	C10	44
Amisk Lake, l., Sask., Can.	C4	75
Amistad National Recreation Area, Tx., U.S.	E2	120
Amistad Reservoir, res., N.A.	C9	62
Amite, La., U.S.	D5	95
Amite, co., Ms., U.S.	D3	101
Amite, stm., La., U.S.	D5	95
Amity, Or., U.S.	B3	114
Amityville, N.Y., U.S.	n15	109
Amlia Island, i., Ak., U.S.	E5	79
'Ammān, Jord.	D4	40
Ammänsaari, Fin.	D17	6
Ammon, Id., U.S.	F7	89
Ammonoosuc, stm., N.H., U.S.	B3	106
Amo, stm., Asia	G13	38
Amory, Ms., U.S.	B5	101
Åmot, Nor.	K7	6
Amoy see Xiamen, China	E12	12
Amposta, Spain	B4	37
Amrāvati, India	J4	38
Amreli, India	I6	38
Amritsar, India	E6	38
Amroha, India	F8	38
Amsterdam, Neth.	C4	8
Amsterdam, N.Y., U.S.	C6	109
Amstetten, Aus.	G14	8
Am Timan, Chad	F10	42
Amu Darya (Amudarja), stm., Asia	I10	22
Amukta Pass, strt., Ak., U.S.	E5	79
Amundsen Gulf, b., N.W. Ter., Can.	B8	66
Amundsen Sea, Ant.	B1	47
Amuntai, Indon.	F6	32
Amur (Heilongjiang), stm., Asia	G21	24
An, Burma	D2	34
Anabar, stm., Russia	C16	24
Anaco, Ven.	C10	58
Anacoco, La., U.S.	C2	95
Anaconda, Mt., U.S.	D4	103
Anaconda Range, mts., Mt., U.S.	E3	103
Anacortes, Wa., U.S.	A3	124
Anacostia, stm., U.S.	C4	97
Anacostia, Northwest Branch, stm., Md., U.S.	B3	97
Anadarko, Ok., U.S.	B3	113
Anadyr', Russia	E29	24
Anadyr', stm., Russia	E29	24
Anadyrskij Zaliv, b., Russia	E30	24
Anagni, Italy	H8	14
Anaheim, Ca., U.S.	F5	82
Anahola, Hi., U.S.	A2	88
Anahuac, Tx., U.S.	E5	120
Ānai Mudi, mtn., India	G4	37
Anakāpalle, India	D7	37
Analalava, Madag.	D9	44
Ana María, Golfo de, b., Cuba	D8	64
Anamosa, Ia., U.S.	B6	92
Anamur, Tur.	H14	4
Anamur Burnu, c., Tur.	A3	40
Anan, Japan	I7	30
Anand, India	I5	38
Anantapur, India	E4	37
Anantnāg (Islāmābād), India	D6	38
Anápolis, Braz.	D4	57
Anastasia Island, i., Fl., U.S.	C5	86
Añatuya, Arg.	B4	56
'Anazah, Jabal, mtn., Asia	C6	40
Ancaster, Ont., Can.	D4	73
Ancha, Sierra, mts., Az., U.S.	D4	80
Anchang, China	E9	28
Anchorage, Ak., U.S.	C10	79
Anchorage, Ky., U.S.	g11	94
Anchor Point, Ak., U.S.	D9	79
Anchor Point, c., Ak., U.S.	h15	79
Ancienne-Lorette, Que., Can.	C6	74
Anclote Keys, is., Fl., U.S.	D4	86
Ancona, Italy	F8	14
Ancud, Chile	E2	56
Ancud, Golfo de, b., Chile	E2	56
Andalucía, hist. reg., Spain	H7	12
Andalusia, Al., U.S.	D3	78
Andalusia, Il., U.S.	B3	90
Andaman Islands, is., India	H2	34
Andaman Sea, Asia	I3	34
Andermatt, Switz.	F15	10
Andernach, Ger.	E7	8
Anderson, Ak., U.S.	C10	79
Anderson, Ca., U.S.	B2	82
Anderson, In., U.S.	D6	91
Anderson, Mo., U.S.	E3	102
Anderson, S.C., U.S.	B2	117
Anderson, co., Ks., U.S.	D8	93
Anderson, co., Ky., U.S.	C4	94
Anderson, co., S.C., U.S.	B2	117
Anderson, co., Tn., U.S.	C9	119
Anderson, co., Tx., U.S.	D5	120
Anderson, stm., N.W. Ter., Can.	C7	66
Anderson, stm., U.S.	H4	91
Anderson, stm., Wa., U.S.	B8	124
Anderson Ranch Reservoir, res., Id., U.S.	F3	89
Andes, mts., S.A.	F4	53
Andes, Lake, l., S.D., U.S.	D7	118
Andhra Pradesh, state, India	I12	22
Andižan, Uzb.	I12	22
Andkhvoy, Afg.	B1	38
Andong, China	C11	26
Andong, S. Kor.	D12	26
Andorra, And.	C13	12
Andorra, ctry., Eur.	G8	4
Andover, Ks., U.S.	g12	93
Andover, Ma., U.S.	A5	98
Andover, Mn., U.S.	m12	100
Andover, Oh., U.S.	A5	112
Andover Lake, res., Ct., U.S.	C6	84
Andradina, Braz.	F3	57
Andreanof Islands, is., Ak., U.S.	E4	79
Andrew, co., Mo., U.S.	B3	102
Andrew Island, i., N.S., Can.	D9	71
Andrews, In., U.S.	C6	91
Andrews, N.C., U.S.	f9	110
Andrews, S.C., U.S.	E8	117
Andrews, Tx., U.S.	C1	120
Andrews, co., Tx., U.S.	C1	120
Andrews Air Force Base, mil., Md., U.S.	C4	97
Andria, Italy	H11	14
Ándros, i., Grc.	L8	16
Androscoggin, co., Me., U.S.	D2	96
Androscoggin, stm., Me., U.S.	D2	96
Androscoggin Lake, l., Me., U.S.	D2	96
Andros Island, i., Bah.	B8	64
Andros Town, Bah.	B9	64
Andújar, Spain	G7	12
Anduo, China	D14	38
Anegada Passage, strt., N.A.	E16	64
Anfeng, China	C9	28
Anfu, China	H3	28
Ang'angxi, China	B11	26
Angara, stm., Russia	F13	24
Angarsk, Russia	G14	24
Ånge, Swe.	E10	6
Ángel, Salto (Angel Falls), wtfl, Ven.	E11	58
Ángel de la Guarda, Isla, i., Mex.	B2	62
Angeles, Phil.	q19	32
Angeles Forest, c., Wa., U.S.	A2	124
Angel Falls see Ángel, Salto, wtfl, Ven.	E11	58
Angelholm, Swe.	H9	6
Angelina, co., Tx., U.S.	D5	120
Angels Camp, Ca., U.S.	C3	82
Angermünde, Ger.	B13	8
Angers, Fr.	D8	10
Angerville, Fr.	D8	10
Angicos, Braz.	E11	54
Angier, N.C., U.S.	B4	110
Ângk Tasaôm, Camb.	I8	34
Angleton, Tx., U.S.	E5	120
Angmagssalik, Grnld.	C25	66
Angol, Chile	D2	56
Angola, In., U.S.	A8	91
Angola, N.Y., U.S.	C1	109
Angola, ctry., Afr.	D3	44
Angola Swamp, sw., N.C., U.S.	C5	110
Angoon, Ak., U.S.	D13	79
Angostura Reservoir, res., S.D., U.S.	D2	118
Angoulême, Fr.	G7	10
Angra dos Reis, Braz.	G6	57
Anguilla, Ms., U.S.	C3	101
Anguilla, dep., N.A.	E16	64
Anguille, Cape, c., Newf., Can.	E2	72
Angul, India	J11	38
Anhai, China	K7	28
Anhui, prov., China	E10	26
Aniak, Ak., U.S.	C8	79
Animas, stm., U.S.	D3	83
Animas Mountains, mts., N.M., U.S.	F1	108
Animas Peak, mtn., N.M., U.S.	F2	108
Animas Valley, val., N.M., U.S.	F1	108
Anita, Ia., U.S.	C3	92
Anjār, India	I4	38
Anji, China	E8	28
Anjiang, China	H2	28
Anjou, Que., Can.	p19	74
Anjouan, i., Com.	D8	44
Ankang, China	E8	28
Ankara, Tur.	H14	4
Ankavandra, Madag.	E9	44
Ankazoabo, Madag.	F8	44
Ankazobe, Madag.	E9	44
Ankeny, Ia., U.S.	C4	92
Anklesvar, India	B2	37
Anlong, China	B8	34
Anlu, China	D2	28
Ann, Cape, c., Ma., U.S.	A6	98
Anna, Il., U.S.	F4	90
Anna, Oh., U.S.	B1	112
Anna, Lake, res., Va., U.S.	B5	123
Annaba (Bône), Alg.	A7	42
Annaberg-Buchholz, Ger.	E12	8
An-Nabk, Syria	B5	40
An-Nafūd, des., Sau. Ar.	C3	46
An-Najaf, Iraq	B3	46
Anna Maria, Fl., U.S.	p10	86
Anna Maria Island, i., Fl., U.S.	q10	86
Annandale, Mn., U.S.	E4	100
Annandale, Va., U.S.	g12	123
Annapolis, Md., U.S.	C5	97
Annapolis, stm., N.S., Can.	E4	71
Annapolis Junction, Md., U.S.	B4	97
Annapolis Royal, N.S., Can.	E4	71
Annapurna, mtn., Nepal	G10	38
Ann Arbor, Mi., U.S.	F7	99
Anna Regina, Guy.	D13	58
An-Nāsirīyah, Iraq	B4	46
Annawan, Il., U.S.	B4	90
Anne Arundel, co., Md., U.S.	B4	97
Annecy, Fr.	G13	10
Annemasse, Fr.	F13	10
Annette, Ak., U.S.	n24	79
Anniston, Al., U.S.	B4	78
Annobón, i., Eq. Gui.	I7	42
Annonay, Fr.	G11	10
An-Nuhūd, Sudan	F11	42
Annville, Pa., U.S.	F8	115
Anoka, Mn., U.S.	E5	100
Anoka, co., Mn., U.S.	E5	100
Anqing, China	I2	28
Anren, China	H2	28
Ansbach, Ger.	F10	8
Anshan, China	C11	26
Anshun, China	A8	34
Anson, Me., U.S.	D3	96
Anson, Tx., U.S.	C3	120
Anson, co., N.C., U.S.	B2	110
Ansonia, Ct., U.S.	D3	84
Ansonia, Oh., U.S.	B1	112
Ansted, W.V., U.S.	C3	125
Antakya, Tur.	H15	4
Antalaha, Madag.	D10	44
Antalya, Tur.	H14	4
Antalya, Gulf of see Antalya Körfezi, b., Tur.	A2	40
Antalya Körfezi, b., Tur.	A2	40
Antananarivo, Madag.	E9	44
Antarctica	A18	47
Antarctic Peninsula, pen., Ant.	C6	47
Antelope, co., Ne., U.S.	B7	104
Antelope Creek, stm., Wy., U.S.	C7	127
Antelope Island, i., Ut., U.S.	B3	121
Antelope Peak, mtn., Nv., U.S.	B7	105
Antelope Range, mts., Nv., U.S.	D7	105
Antelope Reservoir, res., Or., U.S.	E9	114
Antelope Wash, val., Nv., U.S.	D5	105
Antequera, Spain	H7	12
Antero, Mount, mtn., Co., U.S.	C4	83
Antero Reservoir, res., Co., U.S.	C5	83
Anthon, Ia., U.S.	B2	92
Anthony, Fl., U.S.	C4	86
Anthony, Ks., U.S.	E5	93
Anthony, N.M., U.S.	F3	108
Anthony, R.I., U.S.	D3	116
Anthony, Tx., U.S.	o11	120
Anthony Creek, stm., W.V., U.S.	D4	125
Anti Atlas, mts., Mor.	C4	42
Antibes, Fr.	I14	10
Anticosti, Île d', i., Que., Can.	k14	74
Antietam National Battlefield, hist., Md., U.S.	B2	97
Antigo, Wi., U.S.	C4	126
Antigua and Barbuda, ctry., N.A.	F17	64
Antioch, Ca., U.S.	h9	82
Antioch, Il., U.S.	A5	90
Antioch see Antakya, Tur.	H15	4
Antisana, vol., Ec.	H3	58
Antlers, Ok., U.S.	C6	113
Antofagasta, Chile	A2	56
Antofalla, Salar de, pl., Arg.	B3	56
Anton, Tx., U.S.	C1	120
Antongila, Helodrano, b., Madag.	E9	44
António Enes, Moz.	E7	44
Antônio João, Braz.	G1	57
Antonito, Co., U.S.	D5	83
Antora Peak, mtn., Co., U.S.	C4	83
Antrim, N.H., U.S.	D3	106
Antrim, co., Mi., U.S.	C5	99
Antrodoco, Italy	G8	14
Antsirabe, Madag.	E9	44
Antsiranana, Madag.	D9	44
Antwerp, Oh., U.S.	A1	112
Antwerp see Antwerpen, Bel.	D4	8
Antwerpen (Antwerp), Bel.	D4	8
Anuradhapura, Sri L.	H6	37
Anxi, China	C6	26
Anxi, China	J7	28
Anyang, China	D9	26
Anyi, China	G4	28
Anyuan, China	H2	28
Anyuan, China	J4	28
Anžero-Sudžensk, Russia	F11	24
Anzio, Italy	H7	14
Anžu, Ostrova, is., Russia	B23	24
Aoiz, Spain	C10	12
Aöós (Vijosë), stm., Eur.	J4	16
Aôral, Phnum, mtn., Camb.	H8	34
Aosta, Italy	D2	14
Aoukâr, reg., Maur.	E4	42
Aozou, Chad	D9	42
Apache, Ok., U.S.	C3	113
Apache, co., Az., U.S.	B6	80
Apache Junction, Az., U.S.	m9	80
Apache Peak, mtn., Az., U.S.	F5	80
Apalachee Bay, b., Fl., U.S.	B2	86
Apalachicola, Fl., U.S.	C2	86
Apalachicola, stm., Fl., U.S.	B1	86
Apalachicola Bay, b., Fl., U.S.	C2	86
Apaporis, stm., S.A.	H7	58
Aparri, Phil.	B7	32
Apatzingán [de la Constitución], Mex.	H8	62
Apeldoorn, Neth.	C5	8
Apennines see Appennino, mts., Italy	F7	14
Apex, N.C., U.S.	B4	110
Apishapa, stm., Co., U.S.	D6	83
Apizaco, Mex.	H10	62
Aplington, Ia., U.S.	B5	92

Name	Map Ref	Page
Apo, Mount, mtn., Phil.	D8	32
Apolda, Ger.	D11	8
Apollo, Pa., U.S.	E2	115
Apopka, Fl., U.S.	D5	86
Apopka, Lake, l., Fl., U.S.	D5	86
Aporé, Braz.	E2	57
Apostle Islands, is., Wi., U.S.	A3	126
Apostle Islands National Lakeshore, Wi., U.S.	A3	126
Appalachia, Va., U.S.	f9	123
Appalachian Mountains, mts., N.A.	D10	76
Appanoose, co., Ia., U.S.	D5	92
Appiano, It.	C6	14
Apple, stm., Wi., U.S.	C1	126
Apple Creek, Oh., U.S.	B4	112
Applegate, Or., U.S.	E3	114
Applegate, stm., Or., U.S.	E3	114
Appleton, Mn., U.S.	E2	100
Appleton, Wi., U.S.	D5	126
Appleton City, Mo., U.S.	C3	102
Apple Valley, Ca., U.S.	E5	82
Apple Valley, Mn., U.S.	n12	100
Applewood, Co., U.S.	*B5	83
Appleyard, Wa., U.S.	B5	124
Appling, Ga., U.S.	E4	87
Appling, co., Ga., U.S.	E4	87
Appomattox, Va., U.S.	C4	123
Appomattox, co., Va., U.S.	C4	123
Appomattox, stm., Va., U.S.	C4	123
Appomattox Court House National Historical Park, Va., U.S.	C4	123
Apua Point, c., Hi., U.S.	D6	88
Apucarana, Braz.	G3	57
Apure, stm., Ven.	D9	58
Apurímac, stm., Peru	F4	54
Aqaba, Gulf of, b.	E4	40
Āqcheh, Afg.	B2	38
Āq Koprūk, Afg.	B2	38
Aquarius Mountains, mts., Az., U.S.	C2	80
Aquidauana, Braz.	H7	54
Arab, Al., U.S.	A3	78
'Arab, Bahr al-, stm., Sudan	G11	42
Arabelo, Ven.	E10	58
Arabi, La., U.S.	k11	95
Arabian Desert see Sharqīyah, Aṣ-Ṣaḥrā' al-, des., Egypt	C12	42
Arabian Sea	E17	2
Aracaju, Braz.	F11	54
Aracati, Braz.	D11	54
Araçatuba, Braz.	F3	57
Aracena, Spain	H5	12
Araçuaí, Braz.	D7	57
Arad, Rom.	C5	16
Arafura Sea	G9	32
Arago, Cape, c., Or., U.S.	D2	114
Aragon, Ga., U.S.	B1	87
Aragón, hist. reg., Spain	D11	12
Araguacema, Braz.	E9	54
Aragua de Barcelona, Ven.	C10	58
Araguari, Braz.	E4	57
Arak, Alg.	C6	42
Arāk, Iran	B4	46
Arakan Yoma, mts., Burma	E3	34
Aral Sea, Asia	H10	22
Arambaza, Col.	I6	58
Aranda de Duero, Spain	D8	12
Arandas, Mex.	G8	62
Ārani, India	F5	37
Aran Island, i., Ire.	G4	7
Aran Islands, is., Ire.	H3	7
Aranjuez, Spain	E8	12
Aransas, co., Tx., U.S.	E4	120
Aransas Bay, b., Tx., U.S.	E4	120
Aransas Pass, Tx., U.S.	F4	120
Aranyaprathet, Thai.	H7	34
Arao, Japan	I3	30
Arapaho, Ok., U.S.	B3	113
Arapahoe, Ne., U.S.	D6	104
Arapahoe, co., Co., U.S.	B6	83
Arapiraca, Braz.	E11	54
Arapongas, Braz.	G3	57
Araraquara, Braz.	F4	57
Ararat, Austl.	G8	50
Ararat, Mount see Ağrı Dağı, mtn., Tur.	H16	4
Arauca, Col.	D7	58
Araure, Ven.	C8	58
Arāvalli Range, mts., India	H5	38
Araxá, Braz.	E5	57
Araya, Punta de, c., Ven.	B10	58
Arba Minch, Eth.	G2	46
Arbois, Fr.	F12	10
Arbon, Switz.	E16	10
Arborg, Man., Can.	D3	70
Arbroath, Scot., U.K.	E10	7
Arbuckle, Lake, l., Fl., U.S.	E5	86
Arbuckle Mountains, mts., Ok., U.S.	C4	113
Arbuckles, Lake of the, res., Ok., U.S.	C5	113
Arcachon, Fr.	H5	10
Arcade, Ca., U.S.	*C3	82
Arcade, Ga., U.S.	B3	87
Arcade, N.Y., U.S.	C2	109
Arcadia, Ca., U.S.	m12	82
Arcadia, Fl., U.S.	E5	86
Arcadia, In., U.S.	D5	91
Arcadia, La., U.S.	B3	95
Arcadia, Mo., U.S.	D7	102
Arcadia, S.C., U.S.	B4	117
Arcadia, Wi., U.S.	D2	126
Arcanum, Oh., U.S.	C1	112
Arcata, Ca., U.S.	B1	82
Arc Dome, mtn., Nv., U.S.	E4	105
Archangel'sk, Russia	E6	22
Archbald, Pa., U.S.	m18	115
Archbold, Oh., U.S.	A1	112
Archdale, N.C., U.S.	B3	110
Archer, Fl., U.S.	C4	86
Archer, co., Tx., U.S.	C3	120
Archer City, Tx., U.S.	C3	120
Arches National Park, Ut., U.S.	E6	121
Archidona, Spain	H7	12
Archie, Mo., U.S.	C3	102
Archuleta, co., Co., U.S.	D3	83
Arcis-sur-Aube, Fr.	D11	10
Arco, Id., U.S.	F5	89
Arco de Baúlhe, Port.	D4	12
Arcola, Il., U.S.	D5	90
Arcos de la Frontera, Spain	I6	12
Arctic Bay, N.W. Ter., Can.	B15	66
Arctic Ocean	A32	128
Arda, stm., Eur.	H9	16
Ardabīl, Iran	J7	22
Ardalstangen, Nor.	F6	6
Ardennes, reg., Eur.	E5	8
Ardlussa, Scot., U.K.	E7	7
Ardmore, Al., U.S.	A3	78
Ardmore, In., U.S.	A5	91
Ardmore, Ok., U.S.	C4	113
Ardmore, Tn., U.S.	B5	119
Ardsley, N.Y., U.S.	g13	109
Åre, Swe.	E9	6
Arecibo, P.R.	E14	64
Arena, Point, c., Ca., U.S.	C2	82
Arena, Punta, c., Mex.	F5	62
Arenac, co., Mi., U.S.	D7	99
Arenas de San Pedro, Spain	E6	12
Arendal, Nor.	G7	6
Arequipa, Peru	G4	54
Arès, Fr.	H5	10
Arévalo, Spain	D7	12
Arezzo, Italy	F6	14
Arganda, Spain	E8	12
Arga-Sala, stm., Russia	D15	24
Argelès-Gazost, Fr.	I7	10
Argenta, Italy	E6	14
Argenta, Il., U.S.	D5	90
Argentan, Fr.	D6	10
Argentat, Fr.	G8	10
Argentera, mtn., Italy	E2	14
Argentina, ctry., S.A.	C4	56
Argentino, Lago, l., Arg.	G2	56
Argenton-sur-Creuse, Fr.	F8	10
Argonne, reg., Fr.	C12	10
Árgos, Grc.	L6	16
Argos, In., U.S.	B5	91
Argostólion, Grc.	K4	16
Argun' (Ergun), stm., Asia	A11	26
Argyle, Mn., U.S.	B2	100
Argyle, Wi., U.S.	F4	126
Århus, Den.	H8	6
Ariano Irpino, Italy	H10	14
Arica, Chile	G4	54
Arica, Col.	I7	58
Arichat, N.S., Can.	D8	71
Arid, Cape, c., Austl.	F4	50
Arikaree, stm., U.S.	B8	83
Arima, Trin.	I17	64
Arinos, stm., Braz.	F7	54
Aripuanã, Braz.	E6	54
Aripuanã, stm., Braz.	E7	54
Ariquemes, Braz.	E6	54
Arismendi, Ven.	C8	58
Aristazabal Island, i., B.C., Can.	C3	69
Ariton, Al., U.S.	D4	78
Arizona, state, U.S.	C4	80
Arizona Sunsites, Az., U.S.	F6	80
Arizpe, Mex.	B4	62
Arjay, Ky., U.S.	D6	94
Arjeplog, Swe.	C11	6
Arjona, Col.	B5	58
Arkabutla Lake, res., Ms., U.S.	A4	101
Arkadelphia, Ar., U.S.	C2	81
Arkansas, co., Ar., U.S.	C4	81
Arkansas, state, U.S.	C3	81
Arkansas, stm., U.S.	D8	76
Arkansas City, Ks., U.S.	E6	93
Arklow, Ire.	I6	7
Arkoma, Ok., U.S.	B7	113
Arkonam, India	F5	37
Arktičeskogo Instituta, Ostrova, is., Russia	B10	24
Arles, Fr.	I11	10
Arlington, Ga., U.S.	E2	87
Arlington, Ma., U.S.	B5	98
Arlington, Mn., U.S.	F4	100
Arlington, Ne., U.S.	C9	104
Arlington, N.Y., U.S.	D7	109
Arlington, N.C., U.S.	A2	110
Arlington, Oh., U.S.	B2	112
Arlington, S.C., U.S.	B3	117
Arlington, S.D., U.S.	C8	118
Arlington, Tn., U.S.	B2	119
Arlington, Tx., U.S.	n9	120
Arlington, Vt., U.S.	E2	122
Arlington, Va., U.S.	B5	123
Arlington, Wa., U.S.	A3	124
Arlington, co., Va., U.S.	g12	123
Arlington, Lake, res., Tx., U.S.	n9	120
Arlington Heights, Il., U.S.	A5	90
Arma, Ks., U.S.	E9	93
Armada, Mi., U.S.	F8	99
Armagh, Que., Can.	C7	74
Armavir, Russia	H6	22
Armenia, Col.	E5	58
Armenia, ctry., Asia	I6	22
Armentières, Fr.	B9	10
Armidale, Austl.	F10	50
Armijo, N.M., U.S.	k7	108
Armour, S.D., U.S.	D7	118
Armstrong, B.C., Can.	D8	69
Armstrong, Ia., U.S.	A3	92
Armstrong, co., Pa., U.S.	E2	115
Armstrong, co., Tx., U.S.	B2	120
Armstrong, Mount, mtn., Yukon, Can.	D6	66
Armstrong Creek, stm., W.V., U.S.	m13	125
Arnaudville, La., U.S.	D4	95
Arnedo, Spain	C9	12
Arnett, W.V., U.S.	D3	125
Arnhem, Neth.	D5	8
Arnhem, Cape, c., Austl.	B7	50
Arnhem Land, reg., Austl.	B6	50
Árnissa, Grc.	I5	16
Arno, stm., Italy	F5	14
Arnold, Mn., U.S.	D6	100
Arnold, Mo., U.S.	C7	102
Arnold, Ne., U.S.	C5	104
Arnold Mills, R.I., U.S.	B4	116
Arnold Mills Reservoir, res., R.I., U.S.	B4	116
Arnold's Cove, Newf., Can.	E4	72
Arnolds Park, Ia., U.S.	A2	92
Arnprior, Ont., Can.	B8	73
Arnsberg, Ger.	D8	8
Arnstadt, Ger.	E10	8
Arona, Italy	D3	14
Aroostook, co., Me., U.S.	B4	96
Ar-Rabʿ al-Khālī, des., Asia	C6	46
Arrah, India	H11	38
Ar-Rahad, Sudan	F12	42
Ar-Ramādī, Iraq	B3	46
Ar-Ramthā, Jord.	C4	40
Ar-Raqqah, Syria	B7	40
Arras, Fr.	B9	10
Arrecife, Spain	C3	42
Arriaga, Mex.	I13	62
Arronches, Port.	F4	12
Arrowhead Mountain Lake, res., Vt., U.S.	B2	122
Arrowrock Reservoir, res., Id., U.S.	F3	89
Arrowwood Lake, res., N.D., U.S.	B7	111
Arroyo de la Luz, Spain	F5	12
Arroyo Grande, Ca., U.S.	E3	82
Ar-Rusayriṣ, Sudan	F12	42
Ar-Rutbah, Iraq	C7	46
Arsenjev, Russia	I20	24
Árta, Grc.	J4	16
Artá, Spain	F15	12
Artemisa, Cuba	C6	64
Artemus, Ky., U.S.	D6	94
Artenay, Fr.	D8	10
Arter, Mount, mtn., Wy., U.S.	D4	127
Artesia, N.M., U.S.	E5	108
Arthabaska, Que., Can.	C6	74
Arthur, Ont., Can.	D4	73
Arthur, Il., U.S.	D5	90
Arthur, co., Ne., U.S.	C4	104
Arthur, Lake, l., La., U.S.	D3	95
Arthur, Lake, res., Pa., U.S.	E1	115
Arthur Kill, stm., N.J., U.S.	k8	107
Arthurs Town, Bah.	B10	64
Artigas, Ur.	C5	56
Art'om, Russia	I20	24
Art'omovsk, Russia	G12	24
Artvin, Tur.	G16	4
Arua, Ug.	H12	42
Aruanã, Braz.	C3	57
Aruba, dep., N.A.	H13	64
Arunachal Pradesh, ter., India	F16	38
Aruppukkottai, India	H5	37
Arusha, Tan.	B7	44
Aruwimi, stm., Zaire	A5	44
Arvada, Co., U.S.	B5	83
Arvi, India	B5	37
Arvidsjaur, Swe.	D12	6
Arvika, Swe.	G9	6
Arvin, Ca., U.S.	E4	82
Arvon, Mount, mtn., Mi., U.S.	B2	99
Arvonia, Va., U.S.	C4	123
Arzachena, Italy	H4	14
Arzignano, Italy	D6	14
Arzúa, Spain	C3	12
Asadābād, Afg.	C4	38
Asahi-dake, mtn., Japan	p20	30a
Asahikawa, Japan	p20	30a
Asansol, India	I12	38
Asbestos, Que., Can.	D6	74
Asbury Park, N.J., U.S.	C4	107
Ascensión, Mex.	E10	62
Ascension, co., La., U.S.	D5	95
Ascensión, Bahía de la, b., Mex.	H16	62
Aschabad, Turk.	J9	22
Aschaffenburg, Ger.	F9	8
Aschersleben, Ger.	D11	8
Asciano, Italy	F6	14
Ascoli Piceno, Italy	G8	14
Ascoli Satriano, Italy	H10	14
Aseb, Eth.	F3	46
Āsela, Eth.	G2	46
Åsele, Swe.	D11	6
Åsen, Nor.	E8	6
Asenovgrad, Bul.	G8	16
Ashaway, R.I., U.S.	F1	116
Ashburn, Ga., U.S.	E3	87
Ashburn, Va., U.S.	B5	123
Ashburton, N.Z.	E3	52
Ashcroft, B.C., Can.	D7	69
Ashdown, Ar., U.S.	D1	81
Ashe, co., N.C., U.S.	A1	110
Asheboro, N.C., U.S.	B3	110
Ashepoo, stm., S.C., U.S.	F6	117
Asherton, Tx., U.S.	E3	120
Asheville, N.C., U.S.	f10	110
Ash Flat, Ar., U.S.	A4	81
Ashford, Eng., U.K.	J13	7
Ashford, Al., U.S.	D4	78
Ashford, W.V., U.S.	m12	125
Ash Grove, Mo., U.S.	D4	102
Ashibetsu, Japan	p20	30a
Ashikaga, Japan	F12	30
Ashizuri-zaki, c., Japan	J6	30
Ashkhabad see Aschabad, Turk.	J9	22
Ashland, Al., U.S.	B4	78
Ashland, Il., U.S.	D3	90
Ashland, Ks., U.S.	E4	93
Ashland, Ky., U.S.	B7	94
Ashland, Me., U.S.	B4	96
Ashland, Ma., U.S.	g10	98
Ashland, Mo., U.S.	C5	102
Ashland, Ne., U.S.	C9	104
Ashland, N.H., U.S.	C3	106
Ashland, Oh., U.S.	B3	112
Ashland, Or., U.S.	E4	114
Ashland, Pa., U.S.	E9	115
Ashland, Va., U.S.	C5	123
Ashland, Wi., U.S.	B3	126
Ashland, co., Oh., U.S.	B3	112
Ashland, co., Wi., U.S.	B3	126
Ashland, Mount, mtn., Or., U.S.	E4	114
Ashland City, Tn., U.S.	A4	119
Ashley, In., U.S.	A7	91
Ashley, N.D., U.S.	C6	111
Ashley, Oh., U.S.	B3	112
Ashley, Pa., U.S.	n17	115
Ashley, co., Ar., U.S.	D4	81
Ashley, stm., S.C., U.S.	F7	117
Ashley Creek, stm., Ut., U.S.	C6	121
Ashmore, Il., U.S.	D5	90
Ashokan Reservoir, res., N.Y., U.S.	D6	109
Ashqelon, Isr.	D4	40
Ash-Shaqrā', Sau. Ar.	C4	46
Ash-Shāriqah, U.A.E.	C6	46
Ash-Shawbak, Jord.	D4	40
Ashtabula, Oh., U.S.	A5	112
Ashtabula, co., Oh., U.S.	A5	112
Ashtabula, Lake, res., N.D., U.S.	B8	111
Ashton, Id., U.S.	E7	89
Ashton, Il., U.S.	B4	90
Ashton, Md., U.S.	B3	97
Ashton, R.I., U.S.	B4	116
Ashuanipi Lake, l., Newf., Can.	h8	72
Ashuelot, stm., N.H., U.S.	E2	106
Ashville, Al., U.S.	B3	78
Ashville, Oh., U.S.	C3	112
Ashwaubenon, Wi., U.S.	D5	126
Asia	D12	84
Asia, Kepulauan, is., Indon.	E9	32
Asia Minor, reg., Tur.	H14	4
Asino, Russia	F11	24
'Asīr, reg., Sau. Ar.	E3	46
'Asīr, Ras c., Som.	F5	46
Askham, S. Afr.	G4	44
Askvoll, Nor.	F5	6
Asmara see Asmera, Eth.	E2	46
Asmera, Eth.	E2	46
Asotin, Wa., U.S.	C8	124
Asotin, co., Wa., U.S.	C8	124
Asotin Creek, stm., Wa., U.S.	C8	124
Aspang Markt, Aus.	H16	8
Aspen, Co., U.S.	B4	83
Aspen Butte, mtn., Or., U.S.	E4	114
Aspermont, Tx., U.S.	C2	120
Aspinwall, Pa., U.S.	k14	115
Aspiring, Mount, mtn., N.Z.	F2	52
Aspres-sur-Buëch, Fr.	H12	10
Aspy Bay, b., N.S., Can.	C9	71
Assabet, stm., Ma., U.S.	g9	98
As-Ṣabyā, Sau. Ar.	E3	46
As-Sallūm, Egypt	B11	42
As-Salt, Jord.	C4	40
Assam, state, India	G15	38
As-Samāwah, Iraq	B4	46
Assateague Island, i., Md., U.S.	D7	97
Assateague Island National Seashore	D7	97
Assawoman Bay, b., Md., U.S.	D7	97
Assen, Neth.	C6	8
Assiniboine, stm., Can.	E2	70
Assiniboine, Mount, mtn., Can.	D3	68
Assis, Braz.	G3	57
Assisi, Italy	F7	14
As-Sulaymānīyah, Iraq	A4	46
As-Sulaymānīyah, Sau. Ar.	D4	46
As-Sulayyil, Sau. Ar.	D4	46
Assumption, Il., U.S.	D4	90
Assumption, co., La., U.S.	E4	95
Assumption Island, i., Sey.	C9	44
As-Suwār, Syria	B7	40
As-Suwaydā', Syria	C5	40
As-Suways (Suez), Egypt	C12	42
Asti, Italy	E3	14
Astorga, Spain	C5	12
Astoria, Il., U.S.	C3	90
Astoria, Or., U.S.	A3	114
Astove Island, i., Sey.	D9	44
Astrachan', Russia	H7	22
Astrakhan see Astrachan', Russia	H7	22
Astudillo, Spain	C7	12
Asunción, Para.	B5	56
Aswān, Egypt	D12	42
Aswān High Dam, Egypt	D12	42
Asyūṭ, Egypt	C12	42
Atacama, Desierto de, des., Chile	A3	56
Atacama, Puna de, plat., S.A.	A3	56
Atacama, Salar de, pl., Chile	A3	56
Ataco, Col.	F5	58
Atakpamé, Togo	G6	42
Atami, Japan	G12	30
Atar, Maur.	D3	42
Atascadero, Ca., U.S.	E3	82
Atascosa, co., Tx., U.S.	E3	120
'Atbarah, Sudan	E12	42
'Atbarah (Atbara), stm., Afr.	E12	42
Atchafalaya, stm., La., U.S.	D4	95
Atchafalaya Bay, b., La., U.S.	E4	95
Atchison, Ks., U.S.	C8	93
Atchison, co., Ks., U.S.	C8	93
Atchison, co., Mo., U.S.	A2	102
Ateca, Spain	D10	12
Athabasca, Alta., Can.	B4	68
Athabasca, stm., Alta., Can.	f8	68
Athabasca, Lake, l., Can.	m7	75
Athena, Or., U.S.	B8	114
Athenry, Ire.	H4	7
Athens, Ont., Can.	C9	73
Athens, Al., U.S.	A3	78
Athens, Ga., U.S.	C3	87
Athens, Il., U.S.	D4	90
Athens, N.Y., U.S.	C7	109
Athens, Oh., U.S.	C3	112
Athens, Pa., U.S.	C8	115
Athens, Tn., U.S.	D9	119
Athens, Tx., U.S.	C5	120
Athens, W.V., U.S.	D3	125
Athens, Wi., U.S.	C3	126
Athens, co., Oh., U.S.	C3	112
Athens see Athínai, Grc.	L7	16
Athínai (Athens), Grc.	L7	16
Athlone, Ire.	H5	7
Athol, Ma., U.S.	A3	98
Ati, Chad	F9	42
Atienza, Spain	D9	12
Atik Lake, l., Man., Can.	B4	70
Atikonak Lake, l., Newf., Can.	h8	72
Atka Island, i., Ak., U.S.	E5	79
Atkins, Ar., U.S.	B3	81
Atkins, Va., U.S.	D1	123
Atkinson, Il., U.S.	B3	90
Atkinson, Ne., U.S.	B7	104
Atkinson, N.H., U.S.	E4	106
Atkinson, co., Ga., U.S.	E4	87
Atlanta, Ga., U.S.	C2	87
Atlanta, Il., U.S.	C4	90
Atlanta, In., U.S.	D5	91
Atlanta, Mi., U.S.	C6	99
Atlanta, Tx., U.S.	C5	120
Atlantic, Ia., U.S.	C2	92
Atlantic, N.C., U.S.	C6	110
Atlantic, co., N.J., U.S.	E3	107
Atlantic Beach, Fl., U.S.	m9	86
Atlantic City, N.J., U.S.	E4	107
Atlantic Highlands, N.J., U.S.	C4	107
Atlantic Ocean	F10	2
Atlantic Peak, mtn., Wy., U.S.	D3	127
Atlas Mountains, mts., Afr.	B5	42
Atlas Saharien, mts., Alg.	B6	42
Atmore, Al., U.S.	D2	78
Atna Peak, mtn., B.C., Can.	C3	69
Atoka, Ok., U.S.	C5	113
Atoka, Tn., U.S.	B2	119
Atoka, co., Ok., U.S.	C5	113
Atoka Reservoir, res., Ok., U.S.	C5	113
Atotonilco el Alto, Mex.	G8	62
Atrato, stm., Col.	D4	58
Aṭ-Ṭafīlah, Jord.	D4	40
Aṭ-Ṭā'if, Sau. Ar.	D3	46
Attala, co., Ms., U.S.	B4	101
Attalla, Al., U.S.	A3	78
Attawapiskat, stm., Ont., Can.	n18	73
Attica, In., U.S.	D3	91
Attica, Ks., U.S.	E5	93
Attica, N.Y., U.S.	C2	109
Attica, Oh., U.S.	A3	112
Attleboro, Ma., U.S.	C5	98
Attopeu, Laos	G9	34
Attow, Ben, mtn., Scot., U.K.	D7	7
Attu Island, i., Ak., U.S.	E2	79
Ättūr, India	G5	37
Atwater, Ca., U.S.	D3	82
Atwater, Mn., U.S.	E4	100
Atwater, Ont., Can.	D3	73
Atwood, Ont., Can.	D3	73
Atwood, Il., U.S.	D5	90
Atwood, Ks., U.S.	C2	93
Atwood, Tn., U.S.	B3	119
Atwood Lake, res., Oh., U.S.	B4	112
Auau Channel, strt., Hi., U.S.	C5	88
Aubagne, Fr.	I12	10
Aube, stm., Fr.	D11	10
Auberry, Ca., U.S.	D4	82
Aubigny-sur-Nère, Fr.	E9	10
Aubin, Fr.	H9	10
Auburn, Al., U.S.	C4	78
Auburn, Ca., U.S.	C3	82
Auburn, Ga., U.S.	B3	87
Auburn, Il., U.S.	D4	90
Auburn, In., U.S.	B7	91
Auburn, Ks., U.S.	D8	93
Auburn, Ky., U.S.	D3	94
Auburn, Me., U.S.	D2	96
Auburn, Ma., U.S.	B4	98
Auburn, Mi., U.S.	E6	99
Auburn, Ne., U.S.	D10	104
Auburn, N.Y., U.S.	C4	109
Auburn, Wa., U.S.	B3	124
Auburndale, Fl., U.S.	D5	86
Auburn Heights, Mi., U.S.	F7	99
Aubusson, Fr.	G9	10
Auch, Fr.	I7	10
Aucilla, stm., Fl., U.S.	B3	86
Auckland, N.Z.	B5	52
Audincourt, Fr.	E13	10
Audrain, co., Mo., U.S.	B6	102
Audubon, Ia., U.S.	C3	92
Audubon, N.J., U.S.	D2	107
Audubon, co., Ia., U.S.	C2	92
Aue, Ger.	E12	8
Auglaize, co., Oh., U.S.	B1	112
Auglaize, stm., Oh., U.S.	A1	112
Au Gres, Mi., U.S.	D7	99
Augsburg, Ger.	G10	8
Augusta, Italy	L10	14
Augusta, Ar., U.S.	B4	81
Augusta, Ga., U.S.	C5	87
Augusta, Ks., U.S.	E7	93
Augusta, Ky., U.S.	B6	94
Augusta, Me., U.S.	D3	96
Augusta, Mi., U.S.	F5	99
Augusta, Wi., U.S.	D2	126
Augusta, co., Va., U.S.	B3	123
Augustus, Mount, mtn., Austl.	D3	50
Aulander, N.C., U.S.	A5	110
Auld, Lake, l., Austl.	D4	50
Aulneau Peninsula, pen., Ont., Can.	E4	70
Ault, Co., U.S.	A6	83
Aumont-Aubrac, Fr.	H10	10
Aumsville, Or., U.S.	k12	114
Aurangābād, India	C3	37
Auray, Fr.	E4	10
Aurelia, Ia., U.S.	B2	92
Aurich, Ger.	B7	8
Aurillac, Fr.	H9	10
Auriflama, Braz.	F3	57
Aurora, Ont., Can.	C5	73
Aurora, Co., U.S.	B6	83
Aurora, Il., U.S.	B5	90
Aurora, In., U.S.	F8	91
Aurora, Mn., U.S.	C6	100
Aurora, Mo., U.S.	E4	102
Aurora, Ne., U.S.	D7	104
Aurora, Oh., U.S.	A4	112
Aurora, S.D., U.S.	C9	118
Aurora, Ut., U.S.	E4	121
Aurora, co., S.D., U.S.	D7	118
Aus, Nmb.	G3	44
Au Sable, Mi., U.S.	D7	99
Au Sable, stm., Mi., U.S.	D6	99
Ausable, stm., N.Y., U.S.	f11	109
Au Sable Forks, N.Y., U.S.	f11	109
Au Sable Point, c., Mi., U.S.	B4	99
Au Sable Point, c., Mi., U.S.	D7	99
Auschwitz see Oświęcim, Pol.		
Austell, Ga., U.S.	h7	87
Austin, In., U.S.	G6	91
Austin, Mn., U.S.	G6	100
Austin, Nv., U.S.	D4	105
Austin, Tx., U.S.	D4	120
Austin, co., Tx., U.S.	E4	120
Austin, Lake, l., Austl.	E3	50

Name	Map Ref	Page
Austin Channel, strt., N.W. Ter., Can.	A12	66
Austintown, Oh., U.S.	A5	112
Austinville, Va., U.S.	D2	123
Australia, ctry., Oc.	D6	50
Australian Capital Territory, ter., Austl.	G9	50
Austria, ctry., Eur.	F10	8
Autauga, co., Al., U.S.	C3	78
Autaugaville, Al., U.S.	C3	78
Autlán de Navarro, Mex.	H7	62
Autun, Fr.	F11	10
Auxerre, Fr.	E10	10
Auxier, Ky., U.S.	C7	94
Auxi-le-Château, Fr.	B9	10
Auxonne, Fr.	E12	10
Auxvasse, Mo., U.S.	B6	102
Auyán Tepuy, mtn., Ven.	E11	58
Auzances, Fr.	F9	10
Ava, Mo., U.S.	E5	102
Avallon, Fr.	E10	10
Avalon, Ca., U.S.	F4	82
Avalon, Pa., U.S.	h13	115
Avalon, Lake, res., N.M., U.S.	E5	108
Avalon Peninsula, pen., Newf., Can.	E5	72
Avaré, Braz.	G4	57
Aveiro, Port.	E3	12
Avella, Pa., U.S.	F1	115
Avellaneda, Arg.	C5	56
Avellino, Italy	I9	14
Avenal, Ca., U.S.	E3	82
Avery, co., N.C., U.S.	e11	110
Aves, Islas de, is., Ven.	A9	58
Avesnes, Fr.	B10	10
Avesta, Swe.	F11	6
Avezzano, Italy	G8	14
Aviemore, Scot., U.K.	D9	7
Avignon, Fr.	I11	10
Ávila, Spain	E7	12
Avilés, Spain	B6	12
Avilla, In., U.S.	B7	91
Avis, Pa., U.S.	D7	115
Avispa, Cerro, mtn., Ven.	G10	58
Aviston, Il., U.S.	E4	90
Aviz, Port.	F4	12
Avoca, Ia., U.S.	C2	92
Avoca, Pa., U.S.	m18	115
Avola, Italy	M10	14
Avon, Ct., U.S.	B4	84
Avon, Il., U.S.	C3	90
Avon, Ma., U.S.	B5	98
Avon, Mn., U.S.	E4	100
Avon, N.Y., U.S.	C3	109
Avon, Oh., U.S.	A3	112
Avondale, Az., U.S.	D3	80
Avondale, Co., U.S.	C6	83
Avondale, Ga., U.S.	G10	115
Avondale Estates, Ga., U.S.	h8	87
Avon Lake, Ia., U.S.	e8	92
Avon Lake, Oh., U.S.	A3	112
Avonmore, Pa., U.S.	E3	115
Avon Park, Fl., U.S.	E5	86
Avoyelles, co., La., U.S.	C3	95
Avranches, Fr.	D5	10
Awaji-shima, i., Japan	H7	30
Awash, stm., Eth.	F3	46
Awbārī, Libya	C8	42
Awe, Loch, l., Scot., U.K.	E7	7
Awjilah, Libya	C10	42
Axiós (Vardar), stm., Eur.	I6	16
Axis, Al., U.S.	E1	78
Axtell, Ne., U.S.	D6	104
Ayabe, Japan	G8	30
Ayacucho, Peru	F4	54
Ayamonte, Spain	H4	12
Ayapel, Col.	C5	58
Ayaviri, Peru	F4	54
Aybak, Afg.	B3	38
Ayden, N.C., U.S.	B5	110
Aydın, Tur.	H13	4
Ayer, Ma., U.S.	A4	98
Ayers Cliff, Que., Can.	D5	74
Ayeyarwady (Irrawaddy), stm., Burma	G3	34
Áyion Óros, pen., Grc.	I8	16
Áyios Nikólaos, Grc.	N9	16
Aylesbury, Eng., U.K.	J12	7
Aylesford, N.S., Can.	D5	71
Aylmer, Mount, mtn., Alta., Can.	D3	68
Aylmer East, Que., Can.	D2	74
Aylmer Lake, l., N.W. Ter., Can.	D11	66
Aylmer West, Ont., Can.	E4	73
Ayora, Spain	F10	12
'Ayoûn el 'Atroûs, Maur.	E4	42
Ayr, Scot., U.K.	F8	7
Ayre, Point of, c., I. of Man	G8	7
Ayu, Kepulauan, is., Indon.	E9	32
Ayvalık, Tur.	J10	16
Azambuja, Port.	F3	12
Azamgarh, India	G10	38
Azare, Nig.	F8	42
Azerbaijan, ctry., Asia	I7	22
Aziscohos Lake, l., Me., U.S.	C1	96
Azle, Tx., U.S.	n9	120
Azogues, Ec.	I3	58
Azores see Açores, is., Port.	D11	2
Azov, Sea of see Azovskoje more, Eur.	H5	22
Azovskoje more (Sea of Azov), Eur.	H5	22
Aztec, N.M., U.S.	A2	108
Aztec Peak, mtn., Az., U.S.	D5	80
Aztec Ruins National Monument, N.M., U.S.	A1	108
Azua, Dom. Rep.	E12	64
Azuaga, Spain	G6	12
Azuero, Península de, pen., Pan.	K7	64
Azul, Arg.	D5	56
Azur, Côte d', Fr.	I14	10
Azusa, Ca., U.S.	m13	82
Az-Zaqāzīq, Egypt	D2	40
Az-Zarqā', Jord.	C5	40
Az-Zāwiyah, Libya	B8	42
Azzel Matti, Sebkha, pl., Alg.	C6	42

B

Name	Map Ref	Page
Ba, stm., Viet.	H10	34
Babaeski, Tur.	H11	16
Babahoyo, Ec.	H3	58
Babar, Kepulauan, is., Indon.	G8	32
Babb Creek, stm., Pa., U.S.	C7	115
Babbitt, Mn., U.S.	C7	100
Babbitt, Nv., U.S.	E3	105
B'abdā, Leb.	C4	40
Bāb el-Mandeb see Mandeb, Bāb el-, strt.	F3	46
Babine, stm., B.C., Can.	B4	69
Babine Lake, l., B.C., Can.	B5	69
Babine Range, mts., B.C., Can.	B4	69
Bábol, Iran	J8	22
Baboquivari Mountains, mts., Az., U.S.	F4	80
Baboquivari Peak, mtn., Az., U.S.	F4	80
Babuyan Islands, is., Phil.	B7	32
Babylon, N.Y., U.S.	n15	109
Baca, co., Co., U.S.	D8	83
Bacabal, Braz.	D10	54
Bacan, Pulau, i., Indon.	F8	32
Bacău, Rom.	C10	16
Bac Can, Viet.	C8	34
Bacerac, Mex.	B5	62
Bachaquero, Ven.	C7	58
Bachta, Russia	E11	24
Bachu, China	D2	26
Back, stm., N.W. Ter., Can.	C13	66
Back, stm., S.C., U.S.	h12	117
Backbone Mountain, mtn., U.S.	m12	97
Backnang, Ger.	G9	8
Bac Lieu, Viet.	J8	34
Bac Ninh, Viet.	D9	34
Bacolod, Phil.	C7	32
Bacon, co., Ga., U.S.	E4	87
Baconton, Ga., U.S.	E2	87
Bacoor, Phil.	q19	33b
Bad, stm., S.D., U.S.	C5	118
Bad, stm., Wi., U.S.	B3	126
Badagara, India	G3	37
Badajia, China	B9	28
Badajoz, Spain	G5	12
Badalona, Spain	D14	12
Badanah, Sau. Ar.	B3	46
Bad Aussee, Aus.	H13	8
Bad Axe, Mi., U.S.	E8	99
Baddeck, N.S., Can.	C9	71
Bad Doberan, Ger.	A11	8
Bad Ems, Ger.	E7	8
Baden, Aus.	G16	8
Baden, Ont., Can.	D4	73
Baden, Pa., U.S.	E1	115
Baden, Switz.	E15	10
Baden-Baden, Ger.	G8	8
Badgastein, Aus.	H13	8
Badger, Newf., Can.	D3	72
Bad Hersfeld, Ger.	E9	8
Bad Homburg [vor der Höhe], Ger.	E8	8
Bad Honnef, Ger.	E7	8
Badin, N.C., U.S.	B2	110
Badin Lake, res., N.C., U.S.	B2	110
Bad Ischl, Aus.	H13	8
Bad Kissingen, Ger.	E10	8
Bad Kreuznach, Ger.	F7	8
Bad Lauterberg, Ger.	D10	8
Bad Nauheim, Ger.	E8	8
Bad Neustadt an der Saale, Ger.	E10	8
Bad Oldesloe, Ger.	B10	8
Bad Reichenhall, Ger.	H12	8
Bad River Indian Reservation, Wi., U.S.	B3	126
Bad Salzungen, Ger.	E10	8
Bad Schwartau, Ger.	B10	8
Bad Segeberg, Ger.	B10	8
Bad Tölz, Ger.	H11	8
Badulla, Sri L.	I6	37
Badwater Creek, stm., Wy., U.S.	C5	127
Bad Wildungen, Ger.	D9	8
Bad Wörishofen, Ger.	G10	8
Baena, Spain	H7	12
Baeza, Spain	H8	12
Bafatá, Gui.-B.	F3	42
Baffin Bay, b., N.A.	B14	61
Baffin Bay, b., Tx., U.S.	E4	120
Baffin Island, i., N.W. Ter., Can.	C18	66
Bafwasende, Zaire	A5	44
Bagaha, India	G11	38
Bāgalkot, India	D3	37
Bagansiapiapi, Indon.	M6	34
Bağarası, Tur.	L11	16
Bagdad, Az., U.S.	C2	80
Bagdad, Fl., U.S.	u14	86
Bagdad see Baghdād, Iraq	B3	46
Bagdarin, Russia	G16	24
Bagé, Braz.	C6	56
Baggs, Wy., U.S.	E5	127
Baghdād, Iraq	B3	46
Bagheria, Italy	K8	14
Baghlān, Afg.	B3	38
Baghrān Khowleh, Afg.	D1	38
Bagley, Mn., U.S.	C3	100
Bagnères-de-Bigorre, Fr.	I7	10
Bagnères-de-Luchon, Fr.	J7	10
Bagnols-sur-Cèze, Fr.	H11	10
Bago, Burma	F3	34
Baguio, Phil.	p19	32
Bahamas, ctry., N.A.	B9	64
Bahāwalnagar, Pak.	F5	38
Bahāwalpur, Pak.	F4	38
Bahía, Islas de la, is., Hond.	F4	64
Bahía Blanca, Arg.	D4	56
Bahía de Caráquez, Ec.	H2	58
Bahia Kino, Mex.	C4	62
Bahir Dar, Eth.	F2	46
Bahraich, India	G9	38
Bahrain, ctry., Asia	C5	46
Baia-Mare, Rom.	B7	16
Bai Bung, Muy, c., Viet.	J8	34
Baicheng, China	B11	26
Baicheng, China	C3	26
Baidoa, Som.	H3	46
Baie-Comeau, Que., Can.	k13	74
Baie-d'Urfé, Que., Can.	q19	74
Baie-Saint-Paul, Que., Can.	B7	74
Baie Verte, Newf., Can.	D3	72
Baigneux-les-Juifs, Fr.	E11	10
Baiju, China	B9	28
Bailén, Spain	G8	12
Bailey, co., Tx., U.S.	B1	120
Bailey Island, Me., U.S.	g8	96
Bailey Island, i., S.C., U.S.	k11	117
Baileys Crossroads, Va., U.S.	g12	123
Bainbridge, Ga., U.S.	F2	87
Bainbridge, In., U.S.	E4	91
Bainbridge, Oh., U.S.	C2	112
Bainbridge Island, i., Wa., U.S.	e10	124
Bain-de-Bretagne, Fr.	E5	10
Baing, Indon.	H7	32
Baird, Tx., U.S.	C3	120
Bairdford, Pa., U.S.	h14	115
Baird Inlet, b., Ak., U.S.	C7	79
Baird Mountains, mts., Ak., U.S.	B7	79
Bais, Fr.	D6	10
Baise, China	C9	34
Baishuijiang, China	E8	26
Baiyin, China	D7	26
Baiyunebo, China	C9	26
Baja, Hung.	I18	8
Baja, Punta, c., Mex.	C4	62
Baja California, pen., Mex.	D3	62
Bajanchongor, Mong.	B7	26
Bajkal, Ozero (Lake Baykal), l., Russia	G15	24
Bajkal'skoje, Russia	F15	24
Bajkit, Russia	E13	24
Bajkonyr, Kaz.	E4	22
Bajo Baudó, Col.	D4	58
Baker, La., U.S.	D4	95
Baker, Mt., U.S.	D12	103
Baker, Or., U.S.	C9	114
Baker, co., Fl., U.S.	B4	86
Baker, co., Ga., U.S.	E2	87
Baker, co., Or., U.S.	C9	114
Baker, stm., N.H., U.S.	C3	106
Baker, Mount, mtn., Wa., U.S.	A4	124
Baker Air Force Base, mil., Ar., U.S.	B6	81
Baker Butte, mtn., Az., U.S.	C4	80
Baker Island, i., U.S.	n22	79
Baker Lake, N.W. Ter., Can.	D13	66
Baker Lake, l., Me., U.S.	B3	96
Baker Lake, res., Wa., U.S.	A4	124
Bakersfield, Ca., U.S.	E4	82
Bakers Island, i., Ma., U.S.	f12	98
Bakerstown, Pa., U.S.	h14	115
Bakhtarān, Iran	B4	46
Bakhtegān, Daryācheh-ye, l., Iran	C5	46
Bakır, stm., Tur.	J11	16
Bakoye, stm., Afr.	F4	42
Baku, Azer.	I7	22
Balabac Island, i., Phil.	D6	32
Balabac Strait, strt., Asia	D6	32
Ba'labakk (Baalbek), Leb.	B5	40
Balachna, Russia	E26	18
Bālāghāt, India	C4	37
Bālāghāt Range, mts., India	D12	37
Balaguer, Spain	C12	12
Balakovo, Russia	G7	22
Balallan, Scot., U.K.	C6	7
Balāngīr, India	B7	37
Balašicha, Russia	F20	18
Balasore, India	J12	38
Balašov, Russia	G6	22
Balaton, Mn., U.S.	F3	100
Balaton, l., Hung.	I17	8
Balbriggan, Ire.	H6	7
Balcarres, Sask., Can.	G4	75
Balchaš, Ozero, l., Kaz.	H9	24
Bald Eagle Lake, l., Mn., U.S.	m12	100
Bald Eagle Lake, l., Mn., U.S.	D10	100
Baldhill Dam, N.D., U.S.	B7	111
Bald Knob, Ar., U.S.	B4	81
Bald Knoll, mtn., Wy., U.S.	D2	127
Bald Mountain, mtn., Or., U.S.	D5	114
Bald Mountain, mtn., Or., U.S.	C9	114
Bald Mountain, mtn., Wy., U.S.	B5	127
Bald Mountains, mts., N.C., U.S.	f10	110
Baldwin, Fl., U.S.	B5	86
Baldwin, Ga., U.S.	B3	87
Baldwin, La., U.S.	E4	95
Baldwin, Mi., U.S.	E5	99
Baldwin, Pa., U.S.	k14	115
Baldwin, S.C., U.S.	B5	117
Baldwin, Wi., U.S.	D1	126
Baldwin, co., Al., U.S.	E2	78
Baldwin, co., Ga., U.S.	C3	87
Baldwin City, Ks., U.S.	D8	93
Baldwinsville, N.Y., U.S.	B4	109
Baldwinville, Ma., U.S.	A3	98
Baldwyn, Ms., U.S.	A5	101
Baldy Mountain, mtn., B.C., Can.	D7	69
Baldy Mountain, mtn., Man., Can.	D1	70
Baldy Mountain, mtn., Mt., U.S.	B7	103
Baldy Mountain, mtn., N.M., U.S.	A4	108
Baldy Peak, mtn., Az., U.S.	D6	80
Baleares, Islas (Balearic Islands), is., Spain	F14	12
Balearic Islands see Baleares, Islas, is., Spain	E15	12
Baleine, Rivière à la, stm., Que., Can.	g13	74
Balej, Russia	G17	24
Balfate, Hond.	G4	64
Balfour, N.C., U.S.	f10	110
Bali, i., Indon.	G5	32
Bali, Laut (Bali Sea), Indon.	G6	32
Balıkesir, Tur.	H13	4
Balikpapan, Indon.	F6	32
Balimo, Pap. N. Gui.	G11	32
Balingen, Ger.	G8	8
Balintang Channel, strt., Phil.	B7	32
Baliza, Braz.	D2	57
Balkan Mountains see Stara Planina, mts., Eur.	G8	16
Balkh, Afg.	B2	38
Balkhash, Lake see Balchaš, Ozero, l., Kaz.	H9	24
Ball, La., U.S.	C3	95
Ballachulish, Scot., U.K.	E7	7
Ballālpur, India	C5	37
Ballarat, Austl.	G8	50
Ballard, co., Ky., U.S.	e8	94
Ball Club Lake, l., Mn., U.S.	C5	100
Ballenas, Canal de, strt., Mex.	C3	62
Ball Ground, Ga., U.S.	B2	87
Ballia, India	H11	38
Ballina, Ire.	G3	7
Ballinger, Tx., U.S.	D3	120
Ballinrobe, Ire.	H3	7
Ball Mountain Lake, res., Vt., U.S.	E3	122
Ballston Spa, N.Y., U.S.	C7	109
Ballwin, Mo., U.S.	f12	102
Bally, Pa., U.S.	F10	115
Ballycastle, N. Ire., U.K.	F6	7
Ballymena, N. Ire., U.K.	G6	7
Ballyshannon, Ire.	G4	7
Balmaceda, Chile	A3	56
Balmoral, N.B., Can.	B3	71
Balmoral, Scot., U.K.	D9	7
Balmville, N.Y., U.S.	D6	109
Balovale, Zam.	D4	44
Balrāmpur, India	G10	38
Balsam Lake, Wi., U.S.	C1	126
Balsam Lake, l., Wi., U.S.	C1	126
Balsas, Braz.	E9	54
Baltasar Brum, Ur.	C5	56
Baltic, Ct., U.S.	C7	84
Baltic, S.D., U.S.	D9	118
Baltic Sea, Eur.	H12	6
Baltijsk, Russia	G2	18
Baltijskaja Kosa, spit, Eur.	A19	8
Baltimore, Ire.	J3	7
Baltimore, Md., U.S.	B4	97
Baltimore, Oh., U.S.	C3	112
Baltimore, co., Md., U.S.	B4	97
Baltimore Highlands, Md., U.S.	h11	97
Baluchistan, hist. reg., Asia	D1	36
Bālurghāt, India	H13	38
Balygyčan, Russia	E24	24
Balzar, Ec.	H3	58
Bamako, Mali	F4	42
Bambana, stm., Nic.	H6	64
Bambari, Cen. Afr. Rep.	G10	42
Bamberg, Ger.	F10	8
Bamberg, S.C., U.S.	E5	117
Bamberg, co., S.C., U.S.	E5	117
Bamenda, Cam.	G8	42
Bāmīān, Afg.	C2	38
Bamialia, Zaire	A5	44
Banana, Zaire	C2	44
Bananal, Ilha do, i., Braz.	F8	54
Banana River, b., Fl., U.S.	D6	86
Banās, Ra's, c., Egypt	D13	42
Banbridge, N. Ire., U.K.	G6	7
Banbury, Eng., U.K.	I11	7
Bancroft, Ont., Can.	B7	73
Bancroft, Ia., U.S.	A3	92
Bānda, India	H9	38
Banda, Kepulauan, is., Indon.	F8	32
Banda, Laut (Banda Sea), Indon.	G8	32
Banda Aceh, Indon.	D2	32
Bandama, stm., I.C.	G4	42
Bandar Beheshtī, Iran	C7	46
Bandar-e 'Abbās, Iran	C6	46
Bandar-e Būshehr, Iran	C5	46
Bandar-e Lengeh, Iran	C5	46
Bandar Seri Begawan, Bru.	E5	32
Banded Peak, mtn., Co., U.S.	D4	83
Bandeira, Pico da, mtn., Braz.	F8	57
Bandelier National Monument, N.M., U.S.	B3	108
Bandera, co., Tx., U.S.	E3	120
Banderas, Bahía de, b., Mex.	G7	62
Bandırma, Tur.	G13	4
Bandon, Ire.	J4	7
Bandon, Or., U.S.	D2	114
Bandundu, Zaire	B3	44
Bandung, Indon.	m13	32
Banes, Cuba	D10	64
Banff, Scot., U.K.	D10	7
Banff National Park, Alta., Can.	D2	68
Bangalore, India	F4	37
Bangassou, Cen. Afr. Rep.	H10	42
Banggai, Kepulauan, is., Indon.	F7	32
Banggi, Pulau, i., Malay.	D6	32
Banghāzī, Libya	B10	42
Bangil, Indon.	m16	33a
Bangka, i., Indon.	F4	32
Bangkalan, Indon.	m16	33a
Bangkinang, Indon.	N6	34
Bangkok see Krung Thep, Thai.	H6	34
Bangladesh, ctry., Asia	E6	36
Bangor, N. Ire., U.K.	G7	7
Bangor, Wales, U.K.	H8	7
Bangor, Me., U.S.	D4	96
Bangor, Mi., U.S.	F4	99
Bangor, Pa., U.S.	E11	115
Bangor Township, Mi., U.S.	E7	99
Bangs, Tx., U.S.	D3	120
Bangs, Mount, mtn., Az., U.S.	A2	80
Bangui, Cen. Afr. Rep.	H9	42
Bangweulu, Lake, l., Zam.	D5	44
Bani, Dom. Rep.	E12	64
Banī Mazār, Egypt	C12	42
Banister, stm., Va., U.S.	D4	123
Banī Suwayf, Egypt	C12	42
Bāniyās, Syria	B4	40
Banja Luka, Bos.	E12	14
Banjarmasin, Indon.	F5	32
Banjul, Gam.	F2	42
Bankhead Lake, res., Al., U.S.	B2	78
Banks, co., Ga., U.S.	B3	87
Banks Island, i., B.C., Can.	C2	69
Banks Island, i., N.W. Ter., Can.	B8	66
Banks Lake, res., Wa., U.S.	B6	124
Banks Strait, strt., Austl.	H9	50
Bānkura, India	I12	38
Bann, stm., N. Ire., U.K.	G6	7
Banner, co., Ne., U.S.	C2	104
Banner Elk, N.C., U.S.	A1	110
Banning, Ca., U.S.	F5	82
Bannock, co., Id., U.S.	G6	89
Bannock Peak, mtn., Id., U.S.	F6	89
Bannock Range, mts., Id., U.S.	G6	89
Bannu, Pak.	D4	38
Baños de Cerrato, Spain	D7	12
Ban Pak Phraek, Thai.	J6	34
Ban Phak Phang, Thai.	F6	34
Ban Pong, Thai.	H5	34
Banská Bystrica, Czech.	G19	8
Bānswāra, India	I6	38
Bantam, stm., Ct., U.S.	B3	84
Bantam Lake, l., Ct., U.S.	C3	84
Bantry, Ire.	J3	7
Banyak, Kepulauan, is., Indon.	M4	34
Banyuwangi, Indon.	n17	33a
Baoding, China	D10	26
Baofeng, China	B2	28
Bao Ha, Viet.	C8	34
Baoji, China	E8	26
Baoshan, China	B5	34
Baotou, China	C8	26
Baoying, China	B8	28
Ba'qūbah, Iraq	B3	46
Baquedano, Chile	A3	56
Baraboo, Wi., U.S.	E4	126
Baraboo, stm., Wi., U.S.	E3	126
Baracoa, Cuba	D10	64
Baraga, Mi., U.S.	B2	99
Baraga, co., Mi., U.S.	B2	99
Barakī Barak, Afg.	D3	38
Baram, stm., Malay.	E5	32
Bārāmati, India	C3	37
Bārāmūla, India	C6	38
Bārān, India	H7	38
Baranagar, India	I13	38
Baranoa, Col.	B5	58
Baranof Island, i., Ak., U.S.	m22	79
Baranoviči, Bela.	E5	18
Barataria, La., U.S.	E6	95
Barataria Bay, b., La., U.S.	E6	95
Barat Daya, Kepulauan, is., Indon.	G8	32
Barbacena, Braz.	F7	57
Barbados, ctry., N.A.	H18	64
Barbar, Sudan	E12	42
Barbas, Cabo, c., W. Sah.	D2	42
Barbastro, Spain	C12	12
Barbate de Franco, Spain	I6	12
Barberena, Guat.	G2	64
Barbers Point, c., Hi., U.S.	B3	88
Barbers Point Naval Air Station, mil., Hi., U.S.	g9	88
Barberton, Oh., U.S.	A4	112
Barbezieux, Fr.	G6	10
Barbosa, Col.	E6	58
Barbour, co., Al., U.S.	D4	78
Barbour, co., W.V., U.S.	B4	125
Barboursville, W.V., U.S.	C2	125
Barbourville, Ky., U.S.	D6	94
Barbuda, i., Antig.	F17	64
Barcaldine, Austl.	D9	50
Barcellona Pozzo di Gotto, Italy	K10	14
Barcelona, Spain	D14	12
Barcelona, Ven.	B10	58
Barcelos, Braz.	D6	54
Barcelos, Port.	D3	12
Barcroft, Lake, res., Va., U.S.	g12	123
Barden Reservoir, res., R.I., U.S.	C2	116
Bardera, Som.	H3	46
Bardīyah, Libya	B11	42
Bardstown, Ky., U.S.	C4	94
Bardufoss, Nor.	B12	6
Bardwell, Ky., U.S.	f9	94
Bardwell Lake, res., Tx., U.S.	C4	120
Bareilly, India	F8	38
Barents Sea, Eur.	B8	128
Barfleur, Fr.	C5	10
Bargersville, In., U.S.	E5	91
Bar Harbor, Me., U.S.	D4	96
Bari, Italy	H11	14
Barīkowt, Afg.	C4	38
Barillas, Guat.	G2	64
Barinas, Ven.	C7	58
Barinitas, Ven.	C7	58
Baripāda, India	J12	38
Barisāl, Bngl.	I14	38
Barisan, Pegunungan, mts., Indon.	F3	32
Barito, stm., Indon.	F5	32
Barker Heights, N.C., U.S.	f10	110
Barkhamsted Reservoir, res., Ct., U.S.	B3	84
Barkley, Ky., U.S.	f10	94
Barkley Sound, strt., B.C., Can.	E5	69
Barkly Tableland, plat., Austl.	C7	50
Bark Point, c., Wi., U.S.	B2	126
Barksdale Air Force Base, mil., La., U.S.	B2	95
Bar-le-Duc, Fr.	D12	10
Barlee, Lake, l., Austl.	E3	50
Barletta, Italy	H11	14
Barling, Ar., U.S.	B1	81
Barlow, Ky., U.S.	e8	94
Barmer, India	H4	38
Barmouth, Wales, U.K.	I8	7
Barnaul, Russia	G10	24
Barnegat, N.J., U.S.	D4	107
Barnegat Inlet, b., N.J., U.S.	D4	107
Barnes, co., N.D., U.S.	B7	111
Barnesboro, Pa., U.S.	E4	115
Barnes Sound, strt., Fl., U.S.	G6	86
Barnesville, Ga., U.S.	C2	87
Barnesville, Mn., U.S.	D2	100
Barnesville, Oh., U.S.	C4	112
Barneville-Carteret, Fr.	C5	10
Barnhart, Ok., U.S.	C7	102
Barnsdall, Ok., U.S.	A5	113
Barnsley, Eng., U.K.	H11	7
Barnstable, Ma., U.S.	C7	98
Barnstable, co., Ma., U.S.	C7	98
Barnstaple, Eng., U.K.	J8	7
Barnwell, S.C., U.S.	E5	117
Barnwell, co., S.C., U.S.	E5	117
Baroda, India	I5	38
Barpeta, India	G14	38
Barqah (Cyrenaica), reg., Libya	B10	42
Barques, Pointe aux, c., Mi., U.S.	D8	99
Barquisimeto, Ven.	B8	58
Barra, Braz.	F10	57
Barra, Braz.	F7	54
Barra, Ponta da, c., Moz.	F7	44
Barrackville, W.V., U.S.	B4	125
Barra do Corda, Braz.	E9	54
Barra Falsa, Ponta da, c., Moz.	F7	44
Barra Mansa, Braz.	G6	57

Name	Map Ref	Page
Barrancabermeja, Col.	D6	58
Barranca del Cobre, Parque Nacional, Mex.	D6	62
Barrancas, Ven.	C11	58
Barrancos, Port.	G5	12
Barranquilla, Col.	B5	58
Barras, Braz.	D10	54
Barrax, Spain	F9	12
Barre, Vt., U.S.	C4	122
Barre, Lake, l., La., U.S.	E5	95
Barre Falls Reservoir, res., Ma., U.S.	B4	98
Barreiras, Braz.	B6	57
Barreiro, Port.	G2	12
Barreiros, Braz.	E11	54
Barrême, Fr.	I13	10
Barren, co., Ky., U.S.	D4	94
Barren, stm., Ky., U.S.	C3	94
Barren Island, i., Md., U.S.	D5	97
Barren Islands, is., Ak., U.S.	h15	79
Barren River Lake, res., Ky., U.S.	D3	94
Barretos, Braz.	F4	57
Barrett, W.V., U.S.	D3	125
Barrhead, Alta., Can.	B3	68
Barrie, Ont., Can.	C5	73
Barrie Island, i., Ont., Can.	B2	73
Barrière, B.C., Can.	D7	69
Barrington, Il., U.S.	A5	90
Barrington, N.J., U.S.	D2	107
Barrington, R.I., U.S.	D5	116
Barrington, stm., R.I., U.S.	C5	116
Barron, Wi., U.S.	C2	126
Barron, co., Wi., U.S.	C2	126
Barron Lake, Mi., U.S.	G4	99
Barrow, Ak., U.S.	A8	79
Barrow, co., Ga., U.S.	B3	87
Barrow, Point, c., Ak., U.S.	A8	79
Barrow Creek, Austl.	D6	50
Barrow-in-Furness, Eng., U.K.	G9	7
Barrow Island, i., Austl.	D3	50
Barrow Strait, strt., N.W. Ter., Can.	B14	66
Barry, Il., U.S.	D2	90
Barry, co., Mi., U.S.	F5	99
Barry, co., Mo., U.S.	E4	102
Barrys Bay, Ont., Can.	B7	73
Bārsi, India	C3	37
Barstow, Ca., U.S.	E5	82
Bar-sur-Aube, Fr.	D11	10
Barth, Ger.	A12	8
Bartholomew, co., In., U.S.	F6	91
Bartholomew, Bayou, stm., U.S.	D4	81
Bartica, Guy.	D13	58
Bartlesville, Ok., U.S.	A6	113
Bartlett, N.H., U.S.	B4	106
Bartlett, Tn., U.S.	B2	119
Bartlett, Tx., U.S.	D4	120
Bartlett Reservoir, res., Az., U.S.	D4	80
Bartletts Ferry Dam, U.S.	C4	78
Barton, Oh., U.S.	B5	112
Barton, Vt., U.S.	B4	122
Barton, co., Ks., U.S.	D5	93
Barton, co., Mo., U.S.	D3	102
Barton, stm., Vt., U.S.	B4	122
Bartonville, Il., U.S.	C4	90
Bartow, Fl., U.S.	E5	86
Bartow, co., Ga., U.S.	B2	87
Barú, Volcán, vol., Pan.	J6	64
Bāruni, India	H11	38
Baruun Urt, Mong.	B9	26
Barvas, Scot., U.K.	C6	7
Basalt, Co., U.S.	B3	83
Basankusu, Zaire	A3	44
Basatongwula Shan, mtn., China	D14	38
Bascuñán, Cabo, c., Chile	B2	56
Basehor, Ks., U.S.	k16	93
Basel (Bâle), Switz.	E14	10
Bashan Lake, l., Ct., U.S.	D6	84
Bashaw, Alta., Can.	C4	68
Bashi Channel, strt., Asia	G11	26
Basilan Island, i., Phil.	D7	32
Basildon, Eng., U.K.	J13	7
Basile, La., U.S.	D3	95
Basin, Wy., U.S.	B4	127
Basingstoke, Eng., U.K.	J11	7
Basīrhāt, India	I13	38
Basīt, Ra's al-, c., Syria	B4	40
Baskahegan Lake, l., Me., U.S.	C5	96
Baskatong, Réservoir, res., Que., Can.	G17	66
Basking Ridge, N.J., U.S.	B3	107
Basoko, Zaire	A4	44
Basra see Al-Basrah, Iraq	B4	46
Bassano, Alta., Can.	D4	68
Bassano del Grappa, Italy	D6	14
Bassari, Togo	G6	42
Bassas da India, rf., Reu.	F7	44
Basse-Terre, Guad.	F17	64
Basseterre, St. K./N.	F16	64
Basse-Terre, i., Guad.	F17	64
Bassett, Ne., U.S.	B6	104
Bassett, Va., U.S.	D3	123
Bassett Peak, mtn., Az., U.S.	E5	80
Bass Islands, is., Oh., U.S.	A3	112
Bass Lake, In., U.S.	B4	91
Bass Strait, strt., Austl.	G9	50
Basswood Lake, l., Mn., U.S.	B7	100
Basti, India	G10	38
Bastogne, Bel.	E5	8
Bastrop, La., U.S.	B4	95
Bastrop, Tx., U.S.	D4	120
Bastrop, co., Tx., U.S.	D4	120
Bastuträsk, Swe.	D13	6
Bata, Eq. Gui.	H7	42
Bataan Peninsula, pen., Phil.	q19	33b
Batabanó, Golfo de, b., Cuba	C6	64
Batagaj, Russia	D20	24
Bataguaçu, Braz.	F2	57
Bataiporã, Braz.	G2	57
Batāla, India	E6	38
Batalha, Port.	F3	12
Batamaj, Russia	E6	24
Batang, China	E6	26
Batangas, Phil.	r19	33b
Batan Islands, is., Phil.	A7	32
Batanta, Pulau, i., Indon.	F9	32
Batatais, Braz.	F5	57
Batavia, Il., U.S.	B5	90
Batavia, N.Y., U.S.	C2	109
Batavia, Oh., U.S.	C1	112
Batchelor Bay, b., N.C., U.S.	B6	110
Bătdâmbâng, Camb.	H7	34
Batepito, Mex.	B5	62
Bates, co., Mo., U.S.	C3	102
Batesburg, S.C., U.S.	D4	117
Batesville, Ar., U.S.	B4	81
Batesville, In., U.S.	F7	91
Batesville, Ms., U.S.	A4	101
Bath, N.B., Can.	C2	71
Bath, Ont., Can.	C8	73
Bath, Eng., U.K.	J10	7
Bath, Me., U.S.	E3	96
Bath, N.Y., U.S.	C3	109
Bath, Pa., U.S.	E11	115
Bath, S.C., U.S.	D4	117
Bath, co., Ky., U.S.	B6	94
Bath, co., Va., U.S.	B3	123
Bathurst, N.B., Can.	B4	71
Bathurst, Cape, c., N.W. Ter., Can.	B7	66
Bathurst Inlet, N.W. Ter., Can.	C11	66
Bathurst Inlet, b., N.W. Ter., Can.	C11	66
Bathurst Island, i., Austl.	B6	50
Bathurst Island, i., N.W. Ter., Can.	A12	66
Batiscan, stm., Que., Can.	B5	74
Batna, Alg.	A7	42
Batouri, Cam.	H8	42
Batsto, stm., N.J., U.S.	D3	107
Batten Kill, stm., U.S.	E2	122
Batticaloa, Sri L.	I6	37
Battle, stm., Can.	F10	66
Battle Creek, Ia., U.S.	B2	92
Battle Creek, Mi., U.S.	F5	99
Battle Creek, Ne., U.S.	C8	104
Battle Ground, In., U.S.	C4	91
Battle Ground, Wa., U.S.	D3	124
Battle Lake, Mn., U.S.	D3	100
Battle Mountain, Nv., U.S.	C5	105
Battle Mountain, mtn., Wy., U.S.	E5	127
Batu, mtn., Eth.	G2	46
Batu, Kepulauan, is., Indon.	O5	34
Batu Pahat, Malay.	N7	34
Baturité, Braz.	D11	54
Baubau, Indon.	G7	32
Bauchi, Nig.	F7	42
Baud, Fr.	E3	10
Baudette, Mn., U.S.	B4	100
Bauld, Cape, c., Newf., Can.	C4	72
Baume-les-Dames, Fr.	E13	10
Baunei, Italy	I4	14
Bauru, Braz.	F4	57
Baús, Braz.	E2	57
Bautzen, Ger.	D14	8
Bawean, Pulau, i., Indon.	G5	32
Baxley, Ga., U.S.	E4	87
Baxter, Ia., U.S.	C4	92
Baxter, Mn., U.S.	D4	100
Baxter, Tn., U.S.	C8	119
Baxter, co., Ar., U.S.	A3	81
Baxter Springs, Ks., U.S.	E9	93
Bay, Ar., U.S.	B5	81
Bay, co., Fl., U.S.	u16	86
Bay, co., Mi., U.S.	E6	99
Bay, Laguna de, l., Phil.	q19	33b
Bayamo, Cuba	D9	64
Bayan Har Shan, mts., China	D6	26
Bayard, Ne., U.S.	C2	104
Bayard, N.M., U.S.	E1	108
Bayboro, N.C., U.S.	B6	110
Bay Bulls, Newf., Can.	E5	72
Bay City, Mi., U.S.	E7	99
Bay City, Or., U.S.	B3	114
Bay City, Tx., U.S.	E5	120
Bay de Verde, Newf., Can.	D5	72
Bayerische Alpen, mts., Eur.	H11	8
Bayeux, Fr.	C6	10
Bayfield, Ont., Can.	D3	73
Bayfield, Co., U.S.	D3	83
Bayfield, Wi., U.S.	B3	126
Bayfield, co., Wi., U.S.	B2	126
Bayındır, Tur.	K11	16
Baykonur see Bajkonyr, Kaz.	H11	22
Baylor, co., Tx., U.S.	C3	120
Bay Mills Indian Reservation, Mi., U.S.	B6	99
Bay Minette, Al., U.S.	E2	78
Bayo, Spain	B3	12
Bayona, Spain	C3	12
Bayonne, Fr.	I5	10
Bayonne, N.J., U.S.	B4	107
Bayou Bodcau Reservoir, res., La., U.S.	B2	95
Bayou D'Arbonne Lake, res., La., U.S.	B3	95
Bayou George, Fl., U.S.	u16	86
Bayou Goula, La., U.S.	D4	95
Bayou La Batre, Al., U.S.	E1	78
Bay Point, c., S.C., U.S.	G7	117
Bayport, Mn., U.S.	E6	100
Bayport, N.Y., U.S.	n15	109
Bayramiç, Tur.	J10	16
Bayreuth, Ger.	F11	8
Bay Ridge, Md., U.S.	C5	97
Bay Roberts, Newf., Can.	E5	72
Bayrūt (Beirut), Leb.	C4	40
Bays, Lake of, l., Ont., Can.	B5	73
Bay Saint Louis, Ms., U.S.	E4	101
Bay Shore, N.Y., U.S.	E7	109
Bayshore Gardens, Fl., U.S.	q10	86
Bay Springs, Ms., U.S.	D4	101
Baytown, Tx., U.S.	E5	120
Bayview, Al., U.S.	f7	78
Bay Village, Oh., U.S.	h9	112
Baza, Spain	H9	12
Bazaruto, Ilha do, i., Moz.	F7	44
Bazas, Fr.	H6	10
Beach, N.D., U.S.	C1	111
Beachburg, Ont., Can.	B8	73
Beach City, Oh., U.S.	B4	112
Beach Haven Inlet, b., N.J., U.S.	D4	107
Beach Pond, res., U.S.	C8	84
Beachville, Ont., Can.	D4	73
Beachwood, N.J., U.S.	D4	107
Beachy Head, c., Eng., U.K.	K13	7
Beacon, N.Y., U.S.	D7	109
Beacon Falls, Ct., U.S.	D3	84
Beaconsfield, Que., Can.	q19	74
Beadle, co., S.D., U.S.	C7	118
Beagle Gulf, b., Austl.	B6	50
Bealanana, Madag.	D9	44
Beale, Cape, c., B.C., Can.	E5	69
Beale Air Force Base, mil., Ca., U.S.	C3	82
Bear, De., U.S.	B3	85
Bear, stm., U.S.	B3	121
Bear Creek, Al., U.S.	A2	78
Bear Creek, stm., U.S.	E2	93
Bear Creek, stm., Or., U.S.	E4	114
Bear Creek, stm., Wy., U.S.	E8	127
Bearden, Ar., U.S.	D3	81
Beardstown, Il., U.S.	C3	90
Bear Inlet, b., N.C., U.S.	C5	110
Bear Lake, co., Id., U.S.	G7	89
Bear Lake, l., U.S.	A4	121
Bear Lake, l., Wi., U.S.	C2	126
Bear Lodge Mountains, mts., Wy., U.S.	B8	127
Bear Mountain, mtn., Or., U.S.	D4	114
Bearpaw Mountains, mts., Mt., U.S.	B7	103
Bear River, N.S., Can.	E4	71
Bear River City, Ut., U.S.	B3	121
Beartooth Pass, Wy., U.S.	B3	127
Beartooth Range, mts., U.S.	E7	103
Bear Town, Ms., U.S.	D3	101
Beasain, Spain	B9	12
Beas de Segura, Spain	G9	12
Beata, Isla, i., Dom. Rep.	F12	64
Beatrice, Ne., U.S.	D9	104
Beatton, stm., B.C., Can.	E8	66
Beatty, Nv., U.S.	G5	105
Beattyville, Ky., U.S.	C6	94
Beaucaire, Fr.	I11	10
Beaufort, N.C., U.S.	C6	110
Beaufort, S.C., U.S.	G6	117
Beaufort, co., N.C., U.S.	B5	110
Beaufort, co., S.C., U.S.	G6	117
Beaufort Marine Corps Air Station, mil., S.C., U.S.	F6	117
Beaufort Sea, N.A.	B7	61
Beaufort West, S. Afr.	H4	44
Beaugency, Fr.	E8	10
Beauharnois, Que., Can.	D4	74
Beau Lake, l., Me., U.S.	A3	96
Beauly, Scot., U.K.	D8	7
Beaumont, Alta., Can.	C4	68
Beaumont, Ms., U.S.	D5	101
Beaumont, Tx., U.S.	D5	120
Beaumont-sur-Sarthe, Fr.	D7	10
Beaune, Fr.	E11	10
Beauport, Que., Can.	n17	74
Beaupré, Que., Can.	B7	74
Beaupréau, Fr.	E5	10
Beauregard, co., La., U.S.	D2	95
Beausejour, Man., Can.	D3	70
Beauvais, Fr.	C9	10
Beauvoir-sur-Niort, Fr.	F6	10
Beaver, Ok., U.S.	A1	113
Beaver, Pa., U.S.	E1	115
Beaver, Ut., U.S.	E3	121
Beaver, W.V., U.S.	D3	125
Beaver, co., Ok., U.S.	e10	113
Beaver, co., Pa., U.S.	E1	115
Beaver, co., Ut., U.S.	E2	121
Beaver, stm., Can.	D7	66
Beaver, stm., Can.	B2	75
Beaver, stm., U.S.	A2	113
Beaver, stm., N.Y., U.S.	B6	109
Beaver, stm., R.I., U.S.	E2	116
Beaver, stm., Ut., U.S.	E2	121
Beaverbank, N.S., Can.	E6	71
Beaver Brook, stm., U.S.	E4	106
Beaver City, Ne., U.S.	D6	104
Beavercreek, Oh., U.S.	C1	112
Beaver Creek, stm., U.S.	E4	104
Beaver Creek, stm., U.S.	C8	127
Beaver Creek, stm., N.D., U.S.	C1	111
Beaver Creek, stm., N.D., U.S.	C5	111
Beaver Creek, stm., Ok., U.S.	C3	113
Beaver Creek, stm., Tn., U.S.	m13	119
Beaver Creek, stm., Wy., U.S.	D4	127
Beaverdale, Pa., U.S.	F4	115
Beaver Dam, Ky., U.S.	C3	94
Beaver Dam, Wi., U.S.	E5	126
Beaverdam Branch, stm., De., U.S.	F3	85
Beaverdam, res., Wi., U.S.	E5	126
Beaver Falls, Pa., U.S.	E1	115
Beaverhead, co., Mt., U.S.	E3	103
Beaverhead, stm., Mt., U.S.	E4	103
Beaverhead Mountains, mts., U.S.	D5	89
Beaverhill Lake, l., Alta., Can.	C4	68
Beaver Island, i., Mi., U.S.	C5	99
Beaver Lake, res., Ar., U.S.	A2	81
Beaverlodge, Alta., Can.	B1	68
Beaver Meadows, Pa., U.S.	E10	115
Beaver Run Reservoir, res., Pa., U.S.	F2	115
Beavertail Point, c., R.I., U.S.	F4	116
Beaverton, Or., U.S.	B4	114
Beāwar, India	G6	38
Bebedouro, Braz.	F4	57
Bécancour, Que., Can.	C5	74
Bečej, Yugo.	D4	16
Becerreá, Spain	C4	12
Béchar, Alg.	B5	42
Becharof Lake, l., Ak., U.S.	D8	79
Beckemeyer, Il., U.S.	E4	90
Becker, Mn., U.S.	E5	100
Becker, co., Mn., U.S.	D3	100
Beckham, co., Ok., U.S.	B2	113
Beckley, W.V., U.S.	D3	125
Beckum, Ger.	D8	8
Becky Peak, mtn., Nv., U.S.	D7	105
Bédarieux, Fr.	I10	10
Bedford, Que., Can.	D5	74
Bedford, Eng., U.K.	I12	7
Bedford, In., U.S.	G5	91
Bedford, Ia., U.S.	D3	92
Bedford, Ky., U.S.	B4	94
Bedford, Ma., U.S.	B5	98
Bedford, N.H., U.S.	E3	106
Bedford, Oh., U.S.	A4	112
Bedford, Pa., U.S.	F4	115
Bedford, Va., U.S.	C3	123
Bedford Hills, N.Y., U.S.	D7	109
Bedford, co., Pa., U.S.	G4	115
Bedford, co., Tn., U.S.	B5	119
Bedford, co., Va., U.S.	C3	123
Bee, co., Tx., U.S.	E4	120
Beebe, Que., Can.	D5	74
Beebe, Ar., U.S.	B4	81
Beecher, Il., U.S.	B6	90
Beecher, Mi., U.S.	*E7	99
Beech Fork, stm., Ky., U.S.	C4	94
Beech Grove, In., U.S.	E5	91
Beech Island, S.C., U.S.	E4	117
Beemer, Ne., U.S.	C9	104
Bee Ridge, Fl., U.S.	q11	86
Beersheba see Be'er Sheva', Isr.	D4	40
Be'er Sheva', Isr.	D4	40
Beeton, Ont., Can.	C5	73
Beeville, Tx., U.S.	E4	120
Befale, Zaire	A4	44
Befandriana, Madag.	E9	44
Beggs, Ok., U.S.	B5	113
Begi, Eth.	G1	46
Behbehān, Iran	B5	46
Behm Canal, strt., Ak., U.S.	n24	79
Bei, stm., China	G9	26
Bei'an, China	B12	26
Beihai, China	D10	34
Beijing (Peking), China	D10	26
Beijing Shih, China	C10	26
Beipiao, China	C11	26
Beira, Moz.	E6	44
Beirut see Bayrūt, Leb.	C4	40
Beja, Port.	G4	12
Béja, Tun.	M4	14
Bejaïa, Alg.	A7	42
Béjar, Spain	E6	12
Békéscsaba, Hung.	I21	8
Bekily, Madag.	F9	44
Bela, India	H9	38
Bel Air, Md., U.S.	A5	97
Belaja Cerkov', Ukr.	H4	22
Belalcázar, Spain	G6	12
Bel Alton, Md., U.S.	D4	97
Belampalli, India	C5	37
Belarus, ctry., Eur.	H10	18
Bela Vista, Braz.	A5	56
Belaya Tserkov' see Belaja Cerkov', Ukr.	H4	22
Belcamp, Md., U.S.	B5	97
Belcherāgh, Afg.	C1	38
Belcher Islands, is., N.W. Ter., Can.	E17	66
Belchertown, Ma., U.S.	B3	98
Belchite, Spain	D11	12
Belcourt, N.D., U.S.	A6	111
Belden, Ms., U.S.	A5	101
Belding, Mi., U.S.	E5	99
Beled Weyne, Som.	H4	46
Belém, Braz.	D9	54
Belen, N.M., U.S.	C3	108
Belfair, Wa., U.S.	B3	124
Belfast, N. Ire., U.K.	G7	7
Belfast, Me., U.S.	D3	96
Belfield, N.D., U.S.	C2	111
Belford, N.J., U.S.	C4	107
Belfort, Fr.	E13	10
Belfry, Ky., U.S.	C7	94
Belgaum, India	E3	37
Belgium, Wi., U.S.	E6	126
Belgium, ctry., Eur.	E8	4
Belgorod, Russia	G5	22
Belgrade, Mn., U.S.	E3	100
Belgrade, Mt., U.S.	E5	103
Belgrade see Beograd, Yugo.	E4	16
Belhaven, N.C., U.S.	B6	110
Belin, Fr.	H6	10
Belington, W.V., U.S.	B5	125
Belitung, i., Indon.	F4	32
Belize, ctry., N.A.	F3	64
Belize City, Belize	F3	64
Belknap, co., N.H., U.S.	C3	106
Belknap Crater, crat., Or., U.S.	C5	114
Bell, co., Ky., U.S.	D6	94
Bell, co., Tx., U.S.	D4	120
Bellac, Fr.	F8	10
Bella Coola, stm., B.C., Can.	C4	69
Bellaire, Mi., U.S.	D5	99
Bellaire, Oh., U.S.	B5	112
Bellaire, Tx., U.S.	r14	120
Bellamy, Al., U.S.	C1	78
Bellary, India	E4	37
Bellavista, Peru	E3	54
Bella Vista, Ar., U.S.	A1	81
Bellbrook, Oh., U.S.	C1	112
Belle, Mo., U.S.	C6	102
Belle, W.V., U.S.	m13	125
Belle, stm., La., U.S.	k9	95
Belleair, Fl., U.S.	p10	86
Belle Bay, b., Newf., Can.	E4	72
Belle Chasse, La., U.S.	E5	95
Bellefontaine, Oh., U.S.	B2	112
Bellefonte, Pa., U.S.	E6	115
Belle Fourche, S.D., U.S.	C2	118
Belle Fourche, stm., U.S.	C3	118
Belle Fourche Reservoir, res., S.D., U.S.	C2	118
Bellegarde, Fr.	F12	10
Belle Glade, Fl., U.S.	F6	86
Belle Isle, Fl., U.S.	D5	86
Belle Isle, i., Newf., Can.	C4	72
Belle Isle, Strait of, strt., Newf., Can.	C3	72
Belle Meade, Tn., U.S.	g10	119
Belle Plaine, Ia., U.S.	C5	92
Belle Plaine, Ks., U.S.	E6	93
Belle Plaine, Mn., U.S.	F5	100
Belle River, Ont., Can.	E2	73
Belle Rose, La., U.S.	D4	95
Belle Vernon, Pa., U.S.	F2	115
Belleview, Fl., U.S.	C4	86
Belle View, Va., U.S.	g12	123
Belleville, Ont., Can.	C7	73
Belleville, Il., U.S.	E4	90
Belleville, Ks., U.S.	C6	93
Belleville, Mi., U.S.	p15	99
Belleville, N.J., U.S.	B4	107
Belleville, Pa., U.S.	E6	115
Belleville, Wi., U.S.	F4	126
Belleville Pond, l., R.I., U.S.	E4	116
Bellevue, Ia., U.S.	B7	92
Bellevue, Ky., U.S.	h13	94
Bellevue, Mi., U.S.	F5	99
Bellevue, Ne., U.S.	C10	104
Bellevue, Oh., U.S.	A3	112
Bellevue, Pa., U.S.	F1	115
Bellevue, Wa., U.S.	e11	124
Belley, Fr.	G12	10
Bellflower, Ca., U.S.	n12	82
Bellingham, Ma., U.S.	B5	98
Bellingham, Wa., U.S.	A3	124
Bellingshausen Sea, Ant.	B4	47
Bellinzona, Switz.	F16	10
Bell Island, i., Newf., Can.	C4	72
Bellmawr, N.J., U.S.	D2	107
Bello, Col.	D5	58
Bellows Falls, Vt., U.S.	E4	122
Bell Peninsula, pen., N.W. Ter., Can.	D16	66
Bellport, N.Y., U.S.	n16	109
Bells, Tn., U.S.	B2	119
Bells, stm., W.V., U.S.	m13	125
Belluno, Italy	C7	14
Bell Ville, Arg.	C4	56
Bellville, Oh., U.S.	B3	112
Bellville, Tx., U.S.	E4	120
Bellwood, Il., U.S.	k9	90
Bellwood, Pa., U.S.	E5	115
Bellwood, Va., U.S.	n18	123
Belmar, N.J., U.S.	C4	107
Belmond, Ia., U.S.	B4	92
Belmont, Ont., Can.	E3	73
Belmont, Ca., U.S.	h8	82
Belmont, Ma., U.S.	g11	98
Belmont, Ms., U.S.	A5	101
Belmont, N.H., U.S.	D4	106
Belmont, N.C., U.S.	B1	110
Belmont, W.V., U.S.	B3	125
Belmont, Wi., U.S.	F3	126
Belmont, co., Oh., U.S.	C4	112
Belmonte, Braz.	C9	57
Belmonte, Port.	E4	12
Belmonte, Spain	F9	12
Belmopan, Belize	F3	64
Belmullet, Ire.	G2	7
Bel-Nor, Mo., U.S.	f13	102
Belo, Madag.	E8	44
Beloeil, Que., Can.	D4	74
Belogorsk, Russia	G19	24
Belo Horizonte, Braz.	E7	57
Beloit, Ks., U.S.	C5	93
Beloit, Oh., U.S.	B5	112
Beloit, Wi., U.S.	F4	126
Beloit North, Wi., U.S.	*F4	126
Beloje, Ozero, l., Russia	A20	18
Belorado, Spain	C8	12
Beloje more (White Sea), Russia	D5	22
Beloreck, Russia	G9	22
Belorussia see Belarus, ctry., Eur.	H10	18
Belovo, Russia	G11	24
Belpre, Oh., U.S.	C4	112
Belt, Mt., U.S.	C5	103
Belted Range, mts., Nv., U.S.	F5	105
Belton, Mo., U.S.	C3	102
Belton, S.C., U.S.	B3	117
Belton, Tx., U.S.	D4	120
Belton Lake, res., Tx., U.S.	D4	120
Beltrami, co., Mn., U.S.	B3	100
Beltsville, Md., U.S.	B4	97
Belucha, Gora, mtn., Asia	H11	24
Belvedere, S.C., U.S.	D4	117
Belvedere Marittimo, Italy	J10	14
Belvidere, Il., U.S.	A5	90
Belvidere, N.J., U.S.	B2	107
Belyj, Ostrov, i., Russia	C8	24
Belyj Jar, Russia	F11	24
Belzoni, Ms., U.S.	B3	101
Bement, Il., U.S.	D5	90
Bemidji, Mn., U.S.	C4	100
Bemidji, Lake, l., Mn., U.S.	C4	100
Benabarre, Spain	C12	12
Bena-Dibele, Zaire	B4	44
Benavente, Port.	G3	12
Benavente, Spain	C6	12
Benavides, Tx., U.S.	F3	120
Benbrook Lake, res., Tx., U.S.	n9	120
Bend, Or., U.S.	C5	114
Ben Davis Point, c., N.J., U.S.	E2	107
Bendeleben, Mount, mtn., Ak., U.S.	B7	79
Bendigo, Austl.	G8	50
Benedict, Md., U.S.	C4	97
Benedito Leite, Braz.	E10	54
Benevento, Italy	H9	14
Benewah, co., Id., U.S.	B2	89
Bengal, Bay of, b., Asia	F6	36
Bengbu, China	C6	28
Benghazi see Banghāzī, Libya	B10	42
Bengkalis, Indon.	N7	34
Bengkulu, Indon.	F3	32
Benguela, Ang.	D2	44
Benham, Ky., U.S.	D7	94
Ben Hill, co., Ga., U.S.	E3	87
Beni, stm., Bol.	F5	54
Béni Abbès, Alg.	B5	42
Benicarló, Spain	E12	12
Benicia, Ca., U.S.	C2	82
Beni-Mellal, Mor.	B4	42
Benin, ctry., Afr.	G6	42
Benin, Bight of, b., Afr.	G6	42
Benin City, Nig.	G7	42
Benisa, Spain	G12	12
Benito Juárez, Presa, res., Mex.	I12	62
Benjamin Constant, Braz.	D4	54

Name	Map Ref	Page
Benjamín Hill, Mex.	B4	62
Benkelman, Ne., U.S.	D4	104
Benld, Il., U.S.	D6	90
Bennett, Co., U.S.	B6	83
Bennett, co., S.D., U.S.	D4	118
Bennettsville, S.C., U.S.	B8	117
Bennington, Ne., U.S.	g12	104
Bennington, N.H., U.S.	D3	106
Bennington, Vt., U.S.	F2	122
Bennington, co., Vt., U.S.	E2	122
Benoit, Ms., U.S.	B2	101
Bénoué (Benue), stm., Afr.	G8	42
Bensenville, Il., U.S.	B6	90
Bensheim, Ger.	F8	8
Bensley, Va., U.S.	C5	123
Benson, Az., U.S.	F5	80
Benson, Mn., U.S.	E3	100
Benson, N.C., U.S.	B4	110
Benson, co., N.D., U.S.	A6	111
Bent, co., Co., U.S.	D7	83
Bentley, Alta., Can.	C3	68
Bentleyville, Pa., U.S.	F1	115
Benton, Ar., U.S.	C3	81
Benton, Il., U.S.	E5	90
Benton, Ks., U.S.	E6	93
Benton, Ky., U.S.	f9	94
Benton, La., U.S.	B2	95
Benton, Pa., U.S.	D9	115
Benton, Tn., U.S.	B7	119
Benton, Wi., U.S.	F3	126
Benton, co., Ar., U.S.	A1	81
Benton, co., In., U.S.	C3	91
Benton, co., Ia., U.S.	B5	92
Benton, co., Mn., U.S.	E4	100
Benton, co., Ms., U.S.	A4	101
Benton, co., Mo., U.S.	C4	102
Benton, co., Or., U.S.	C3	114
Benton, co., Tn., U.S.	A3	119
Benton, co., Wa., U.S.	C6	124
Benton City, Wa., U.S.	C6	124
Benton Harbor, Mi., U.S.	F4	99
Benton Heights, Mi., U.S.	F4	99
Bentonville, Ar., U.S.	A1	81
Ben Treang, Viet.	I9	34
Bent's Old Fort National Historic Site, hist., Co., U.S.	C7	83
Benue (Bénoué), stm., Afr.	G7	42
Benwood, W.V., U.S.	f8	125
Benxi, China	C11	26
Benzie, co., Mi., U.S.	D4	99
Beograd (Belgrade), Yugo.	E4	16
Beowawe, Nv., U.S.	C5	105
Beppu, Japan	I4	30
Berau, Teluk, b., Indon.	F9	32
Berbera, Som.	F4	46
Berbérati, Cen. Afr. Rep.	H9	42
Berchtesgaden, Ger.	H13	8
Berck, Fr.	B8	10
Berdigest'ach, Russia	E19	24
Berdsk, Russia	G10	24
Berea, Ky., U.S.	C5	94
Berea, Oh., U.S.	A4	112
Berea, S.C., U.S.	B3	117
Berens, stm., Can.	F13	66
Berens, stm., Can.	C3	70
Beresford, S.D., U.S.	D9	118
Berg, Nor.	B11	6
Berga, Spain	C13	12
Bergama, Tur.	J11	16
Bergamo, Italy	D4	14
Bergen, Nor.	F5	6
Bergen, co., N.J., U.S.	A4	107
Bergen [auf Rügen], Ger.	A13	8
Bergenfield, N.J., U.S.	B4	107
Bergen op Zoom, Neth.	D4	8
Bergerac, Fr.	H7	10
Bergland, Mi., U.S.	m12	99
Bergstrom Air Force Base, mil., Tx., U.S.	D4	120
Berhampore, India	H13	38
Berhampur, India	C8	37
Beringovskij, Russia	D30	128
Bering Sea	m18	76a
Bering Strait, strt.	m18	76a
Berja, Spain	I9	12
Berkåk, Nor.	E7	6
Berkeley, Ca., U.S.	D2	82
Berkeley, Mo., U.S.	f13	102
Berkeley, R.I., U.S.	B4	116
Berkeley, co., S.C., U.S.	E8	117
Berkeley, co., W.V., U.S.	B6	125
Berkeley Heights, N.J., U.S.	B4	107
Berkeley Springs, W.V., U.S.	B6	125
Berkley, Mi., U.S.	F7	99
Berkner Island, i., Ant.	B8	47
Berks, co., Pa., U.S.	F9	115
Berkshire, co., Ma., U.S.	B1	98
Berkshire Hills, hills, Ma., U.S.	B1	98
Berlin, Ger.	C13	8
Berlin, Ct., U.S.	C5	84
Berlin, Md., U.S.	D7	97
Berlin, N.H., U.S.	B4	106
Berlin, N.J., U.S.	D3	107
Berlin, Pa., U.S.	G4	115
Berlin, Wi., U.S.	E5	126
Berlin Lake, res., Oh., U.S.	A4	112
Bermeo, Spain	B9	12
Bermuda, dep., N.A.	F14	10
Bern (Berne), Switz.	F14	10
Bernalillo, N.M., U.S.	B3	108
Bernalillo, co., N.M., U.S.	B3	108
Bernardsville, N.J., U.S.	B4	107
Bernasconi, Arg.	C13	56
Bernau bei Berlin, Ger.	C7	8
Bernay, Fr.	C7	10
Bernburg, Ger.	D11	8
Berne, In., U.S.	C8	91
Bernice, La., U.S.	B3	95
Bernier Island, i., Austl.	D2	50
Bernina, Piz, mtn., Eur.	F16	10
Beroroha, Madag.	F9	44
Berre, Étang de b., Fr.	I12	10
Berrien, co., Ga., U.S.	E3	87
Berrien, co., Mi., U.S.	G4	99
Berrien Springs, Mi., U.S.	G4	99
Berry, Al., U.S.	B2	78
Berryessa, Lake, res., Ca., U.S.	C2	82
Berry Hill, Tn., U.S.	g10	119
Berry Islands, is., Bah.	B9	64
Berryville, Ar., U.S.	A2	81
Berryville, Va., U.S.	A5	123
Berthierville, Que., Can.	C4	74
Berthoud, Co., U.S.	A5	83
Berthoud Pass, Co., U.S.	B5	83
Bertie, co., N.C., U.S.	A5	110
Bertoua, Cam.	H8	42
Bertrand, Mo., U.S.	E8	102
Bertrand, Ne., U.S.	D6	104
Berwick, Ia., U.S.	e8	92
Berwick, La., U.S.	E4	95
Berwick, Me., U.S.	E2	96
Berwick, Pa., U.S.	E9	115
Berwick-upon-Tweed, Eng., U.K.	F10	7
Berwyn, Alta., Can.	A2	68
Berwyn, Il., U.S.	k9	90
Berwyn, Pa., U.S.	o20	115
Besalampy, Madag.	E8	44
Besançon, Fr.	E13	10
Beskid Mountains, mts., Eur.	F19	8
Bessemer, Al., U.S.	B3	78
Bessemer, Mi., U.S.	n11	99
Bessemer City, N.C., U.S.	B1	110
Best'ach, Russia	E19	24
Betanzos, Spain	B3	12
Bétaré Oya, Cam.	G8	42
Betatakin Ruin, hist., Az., U.S.	A5	80
Bethalto, Il., U.S.	E3	90
Bethany, Ct., U.S.	D4	84
Bethany, Il., U.S.	D5	90
Bethany, Mo., U.S.	A3	102
Bethany, Ok., U.S.	B4	113
Bethany, W.V., U.S.	A4	125
Bethany Beach, De., U.S.	F5	85
Bethel, Ak., U.S.	C7	79
Bethel, Ct., U.S.	D2	84
Bethel, Me., U.S.	D2	96
Bethel, N.C., U.S.	B5	110
Bethel, Oh., U.S.	D1	112
Bethel, Vt., U.S.	D3	122
Bethel Park, Pa., U.S.	k14	115
Bethel Springs, Tn., U.S.	B3	119
Bethesda, Md., U.S.	B4	97
Bethesda, Oh., U.S.	C3	112
Bethlehem, S. Afr.	G5	44
Bethlehem, Ct., U.S.	C3	84
Bethlehem, N.H., U.S.	B3	106
Bethlehem, Pa., U.S.	E11	115
Bethlehem see Bayt Lahm, Jord.	D4	40
Béthune, Fr.	B9	10
Beticos, Sistemas, mts., Spain	H8	12
Betioky, Madag.	F8	44
Betong, Malay.	M6	34
Betroka, Madag.	F9	44
Betsiboka, stm., Madag.	E9	44
Betsie, Point, c., Mi., U.S.	D4	99
Betsy Layne, Ky., U.S.	C7	94
Bette, mtn., Libya	D9	42
Bettendorf, Ia., U.S.	C7	92
Bettiah, India	G11	38
Betül, India	B4	37
Betzdorf, Ger.	E7	8
Beulah, Co., U.S.	C6	83
Beulah, N.D., U.S.	B4	111
Beulah, Lake, l., Ms., U.S.	B3	101
Beulaville, N.C., U.S.	C5	110
B. Everett Jordan Lake, res., N.C., U.S.	B3	110
Beverley, Austl.	F3	50
Beverley, Eng., U.K.	H12	7
Beverley Head, c., Newf., Can.	D2	72
Beverly, Ma., U.S.	A6	98
Beverly, N.J., U.S.	C3	107
Beverly, Oh., U.S.	C4	112
Beverly, W.V., U.S.	C5	125
Beverly Hills, Ca., U.S.	m12	82
Beverly Shores, In., U.S.	A4	91
Bexar, co., Tx., U.S.	E3	120
Bexley, Oh., U.S.	m11	112
Beypore, India	G3	37
Bežeck, Russia	D19	18
Béziers, Fr.	I10	10
Bhadrakh, India	J12	38
Bhadrāvati, India	F3	37
Bhāgalpur, India	H12	38
Bhakkar, Pak.	E4	38
Bhaktapur, Nepal	G11	38
Bhandāra, India	B5	37
Bharatpur, India	G7	38
Bhatinda, India	E6	38
Bhātpāra, India	I13	38
Bhāvnagar, India	J5	38
Bhilai, India	B6	37
Bhilwāra, India	H6	38
Bhīma, stm., India	D4	37
Bhīmavaram, India	D6	37
Bhind, India	G8	38
Bhiwandi, India	C2	37
Bhiwāni, India	F7	38
Bhopāl, India	I7	38
Bhubaneswar, India	J11	38
Bhuj, India	I3	38
Bhusāwal, India	B3	37
Bhutan, ctry., Asia	D7	36
Bia, Phou, mtn., Laos	E7	34
Biafra, Bight of, b., Afr.	H7	42
Biak, i., Indon.	F10	32
Biała Podlaska, Pol.	C23	8
Białystok, Pol.	B23	8
Biarritz, Fr.	I5	10
Biasca, Switz.	F15	10
Bibai, Japan	p19	30a
Bibb, co., Al., U.S.	C2	78
Bibb, co., Ga., U.S.	D3	87
Biberach an der Riss, Ger.	G9	8
Bic, Que., Can.	A9	74
Bic, Île du, i., Que., Can.	A9	74
Biche, Lac la, l., Alta., Can.	B4	68
Bicknell, In., U.S.	G3	91
Bida, Nig.	G7	42
Bīdar, India	D4	37
Biddeford, Me., U.S.	E2	96
Bideford, Eng., U.K.	J8	7
Bidwell, Mount, mtn., Ca., U.S.	B3	82
Biel [Bienne], Switz.	E14	10
Bielefeld, Ger.	C8	8
Bieler Lake, l., N.W. Ter., Can.	B18	66
Bielersee, l., Switz.	E14	10
Biella, Italy	D3	14
Bielsko-Biała, Pol.	F19	8
Bien Hoa, Viet.	I9	34
Bienville, co., La., U.S.	B2	95
Bienville, Lac, l., Que., Can.	g12	74
Big, stm., Mo., U.S.	c7	102
Biga, Tur.	I11	16
Bigadiç, Tur.	J12	16
Big Bald, mtn., Ga., U.S.	B2	87
Big Bald Mountain, mtn., N.B., Can.	B3	71
Big Baldy, mtn., Id., U.S.	E3	89
Big Baldy Mountain, mtn., Mt., U.S.	D6	103
Big Bay De Noc, b., Mi., U.S.	C4	99
Big Bear City, Ca., U.S.	E5	82
Big Belt Mountains, mts., Mt., U.S.	D5	103
Big Bend, Wi., U.S.	n11	126
Big Bend Dam, S.D., U.S.	C6	118
Big Bend National Park, Tx., U.S.	E1	120
Big Birch Lake, l., Mn., U.S.	E4	100
Big Black, stm., Me., U.S.	B3	96
Big Black, stm., Ms., U.S.	C3	101
Big Blue, stm., In., U.S.	E6	91
Big Burro Mountains, mts., N.M., U.S.	E1	108
Big Cabin Creek, stm., Ok., U.S.	A6	113
Big Coal, stm., W.V., U.S.	C3	125
Big Costilla Peak, mtn., N.M., U.S.	A4	108
Big Creek, stm., Tn., U.S.	e8	119
Big Creek Lake, res., Al., U.S.	E1	78
Big Creek Peak, mtn., Id., U.S.	E5	89
Big Cypress Indian Reservation, Fl., U.S.	F5	86
Big Cypress Swamp, sw., Fl., U.S.	F5	86
Big Darby Creek, stm., Oh., U.S.	C2	112
Big Delta, Ak., U.S.	C10	79
Big Duke Dam, N.C., U.S.	B2	110
Big Eau Pleine, stm., Wi., U.S.	D3	126
Big Eau Pleine Reservoir, res., Wi., U.S.	D4	126
Big Escambia Creek, stm., Al., U.S.	D2	78
Big Flats, N.Y., U.S.	C4	109
Bigfork, Mt., U.S.	B2	103
Big Fork, stm., Mn., U.S.	B5	100
Biggs, Ca., U.S.	C3	82
Big Hatchet Peak, mtn., N.M., U.S.	F1	108
Big Hole, stm., Mt., U.S.	E4	103
Big Hole National Battlefield, hist., Mt., U.S.	E3	103
Big Horn, co., Mt., U.S.	E9	103
Big Horn, co., Wy., U.S.	B4	127
Bighorn Canyon National Recreation Area, U.S.	F8	103
Bighorn Lake, res., U.S.	A8	103
Bighorn Mountains, mts., U.S.	B5	127
Big Horn Mountains, mts., Az., U.S.	D2	80
Big Kandiyohi Lake, l., Mn., U.S.	F4	100
Big Lake, Mn., U.S.	E5	100
Big Lake, Tx., U.S.	D2	120
Big Lake, l., Me., U.S.	C5	96
Biglerville, Pa., U.S.	G7	115
Big Lookout Mountain, mtn., Or., U.S.	C9	114
Big Lost, stm., Id., U.S.	F5	89
Big Mossy Point, c., Man., Can.	C2	70
Big Mountain, mtn., Nv., U.S.	B2	105
Big Muddy, stm., Il., U.S.	F4	90
Big Nemaha, stm., Ne., U.S.	D10	104
Big Otter, stm., Va., U.S.	C3	123
Big Pine, Ca., U.S.	D5	82
Big Pine Creek, stm., In., U.S.	D3	91
Big Pine Mountain, mtn., Ca., U.S.	E4	82
Big Piney, Wy., U.S.	D2	127
Big Piney, stm., Mo., U.S.	D5	102
Bigpoint, Ms., U.S.	E5	101
Big Rapids, Mi., U.S.	E5	99
Big Rib, stm., Wi., U.S.	C3	126
Big River, Sask., Can.	D2	75
Big Sable Point, c., Mi., U.S.	D4	99
Big Sandy, stm., U.S.	B6	103
Big Sandy, Tx., U.S.	C5	120
Big Sandy, stm., Az., U.S.	C2	80
Big Sandy, stm., Tn., U.S.	A3	119
Big Sandy, stm., Wy., U.S.	D3	127
Big Sandy Creek, stm., W.V., U.S.	C3	125
Big Sandy Lake, l., Mn., U.S.	D5	100
Big Sandy Reservoir, res., Wy., U.S.	D3	127
Big Sheep Mountain, mtn., Mt., U.S.	C11	103
Big Sioux, stm., U.S.	E9	118
Big Smoky Valley, val., Nv., U.S.	E4	105
Big Snowy Mountains, mts., Mt., U.S.	D7	103
Big Southern Butte, mtn., Id., U.S.	F5	89
Big South Fork, stm., Ky., U.S.	k13	94
Big Spring, Tx., U.S.	C2	120
Big Stone, co., Mn., U.S.	E2	100
Big Stone City, S.D., U.S.	B9	118
Big Stone Gap, Va., U.S.	f9	123
Big Stone Lake, l., U.S.	E2	100
Big Sunflower, stm., Ms., U.S.	B3	101
Big Thompson, stm., Co., U.S.	A5	83
Big Timber, Mt., U.S.	E7	103
Big Trout Lake, l., Ont., Can.	n17	73
Big Walnut Creek, stm., Oh., U.S.	m11	112
Big Wood, stm., Id., U.S.	F4	89
Bihać, Bos.	D10	14
Bihār, India	H11	38
Bihār, state, India	H11	38
Biharamulo, Tan.	B6	44
Bihoro, Japan	p22	30a
Bija, stm., Russia	G11	24
Bijāpur, India	C6	37
Bijāpur, India	D3	37
Bijsk, Russia	G11	24
Bīkaner, India	F5	38
Bikin, Russia	H20	24
Bikoro, Zaire	B3	44
Bilāspur, India	I10	38
Bilauktaung Range, mts., Asia	G5	34
Bilbao, Spain	B9	12
Bilimora, India	B2	37
Bilk Creek Mountains, mts., Nv., U.S.	B3	105
Billerica, Ma., U.S.	A5	98
Billings, Mo., U.S.	D4	102
Billings, Mt., U.S.	E8	103
Billings, co., N.D., U.S.	B2	111
Billings Heights, Mt., U.S.	E8	103
Bill Williams, stm., Az., U.S.	C1	80
Bill Williams Mountain, mtn., Az., U.S.	B3	80
Bilma, Niger	E8	42
Biloxi, Ms., U.S.	E5	101
Biloxi, stm., Ms., U.S.	E4	101
Biloxi Bay, b., Ms., U.S.	f8	101
Biltmore Forest, N.C., U.S.	f10	110
Bimini Islands, is., Bah.	B8	64
Bīna-Etāwa, India	H8	38
Bindura, Zimb.	E6	44
Binéfar, Spain	D12	12
Binga, Monte, mtn., Afr.	E6	44
Bingamon Creek, stm., W.V., U.S.	k10	125
Bingen, Ger.	F7	8
Bingen, Wa., U.S.	D4	124
Binger, Ok., U.S.	B3	113
Bingham, Me., U.S.	C3	96
Bingham, co., Id., U.S.	F6	89
Binghamton, N.Y., U.S.	C5	109
Binhai (Dongkan), China	A8	28
Binjai, Indon.	M5	34
Bintimani, mtn., S.L.	G3	42
Biograd, Cro.	F10	14
Bioko, i., Eq. Gui.	H7	42
Bīr, India	C3	37
Birao, Cen. Afr. Rep.	F10	42
Bīrātnagar, Nepal	G12	38
Birch, stm., W.V., U.S.	C4	125
Birch Island, i., Man., Can.	C2	70
Birch Lake, l., Mn., U.S.	C7	100
Birch River, Man., Can.	C1	70
Birch Run, Mi., U.S.	E7	99
Birchwood City, Md., U.S.	*f9	97
Birchy Bay, Newf., Can.	D4	72
Bird Creek, stm., Ok., U.S.	A6	113
Bird Island, Mn., U.S.	F4	100
Bird Island, i., N.C., U.S.	D4	110
Birdsboro, Pa., U.S.	F10	115
Birdum, Austl.	C6	50
Birecik, Tur.	A5	40
Bīrganj, Nepal	G11	38
Birigui, Braz.	F3	57
Biril'ussy, Russia	F12	24
Bīrjand, Iran	K9	22
Birkenfeld, Ger.	F7	8
Birkenhead, Eng., U.K.	H9	7
Bîrlad, Rom.	C11	16
Birmingham, Eng., U.K.	I11	7
Birmingham, Al., U.S.	B3	78
Birmingham, Mi., U.S.	F7	99
Birmitrapur, India	I11	38
Bir Mogrein, Maur.	C3	42
Birobidžan, Russia	H20	24
Biron, Wi., U.S.	D4	126
Birr, Ire.	H5	7
Bi'r Safājah, Egypt	C12	42
Birtle, Man.	D1	70
Bisbee, Az., U.S.	F6	80
Biscarrosse, Fr.	G7	10
Biscay, Bay of, b., Eur.	G7	4
Biscayne, Key, i., Fl., U.S.	s13	86
Biscayne Bay, b., Fl., U.S.	G6	86
Biscayne National Monument, Fl., U.S.	G6	86
Biscayne Park, Fl., U.S.	s13	86
Bisceglie, Italy	H11	14
Bischofshofen, Aus.	H13	8
Biscoe, N.C., U.S.	B3	110
Bishnupur, India	I12	38
Bishop, Ca., U.S.	D4	82
Bishop, Tx., U.S.	F4	120
Bishop Auckland, Eng., U.K.	G11	7
Bishop's Falls, Newf., Can.	D4	72
Bishopville, S.C., U.S.	C7	117
Biškek, Kyrg.	I12	22
Biskra, Alg.	B7	42
Bismarck, Il., U.S.	C6	90
Bismarck, Mo., U.S.	D7	102
Bismarck, N.D., U.S.	C5	111
Bismarck Archipelago, is., Pap. N. Gui.	m16	50a
Bismarck Range, mts., Pap. N. Gui.	m15	50a
Bison Peak, mtn., Co., U.S.	B5	83
Bissau, Gui.-B.	F2	42
Bistineau, Lake, l., La., U.S.	B2	95
Bistrița, Rom.	B8	16
Bitola, Mac.	H5	16
Bitonto, Italy	H11	14
Bitter Creek, stm., Wy., U.S.	E4	127
Bitterfeld, Ger.	D12	8
Bitterfontein, S. Afr.	H3	44
Bitter Lake, l., S.D., U.S.	B8	118
Bitterroot, stm., Mt., U.S.	D2	103
Bitterroot Range, mts., U.S.	B3	89
Bitti, Italy	I4	14
Biwabik, Mn., U.S.	C6	100
Biwa-ko, l., Japan	G9	30
Bixby, Ok., U.S.	B6	113
Biyang, China	A2	28
Bizen, Japan	H7	30
Bizerte, Tun.	L4	14
Bjelovar, Cro.	D11	14
Black (Lixian) (Da), stm., Asia	D8	34
Black, stm., Az., U.S.	D5	80
Black, stm., Ar., U.S.	B4	81
Black, stm., La., U.S.	C4	95
Black, stm., Mi., U.S.	C8	99
Black, stm., N.Y., U.S.	B4	109
Black, stm., S.C., U.S.	D8	117
Black, stm., Vt., U.S.	E3	122
Black, stm., Vt., U.S.	B4	122
Black, stm., Wi., U.S.	D2	126
Blackall, Austl.	D9	50
Black Bear Creek, stm., Ok., U.S.	A4	113
Blackbeard Island, i., Ga., U.S.	E5	87
Blackburn, Eng., U.K.	H10	7
Blackburn, Mount, mtn., Ak., U.S.	C11	79
Black Butte, mtn., Mt., U.S.	F5	103
Black Butte Lake, res., Ca., U.S.	C2	82
Black Canyon, val., Co., U.S.	C3	83
Black Canyon City, Az., U.S.	C3	80
Black Canyon of the Gunnison National Monument, Co., U.S.	C3	83
Black Creek, B.C., Can.	E5	69
Black Creek, Wi., U.S.	D5	126
Black Creek, stm., N.M., U.S.	B1	108
Black Creek, stm., S.C., U.S.	B7	117
Black Diamond, Alta., Can.	D3	68
Black Diamond, Wa., U.S.	B4	124
Blackduck, Mn., U.S.	C4	100
Black Eagle, Mt., U.S.	C5	103
Black Earth, Wi., U.S.	E4	126
Blackfalds, Alta., Can.	C4	68
Blackfeet Indian Reservation, Mt., U.S.	B4	103
Blackfoot, Id., U.S.	F6	89
Blackfoot, stm., Mt., U.S.	C3	103
Blackfoot Mountains, mts., Id., U.S.	F7	89
Blackfoot Reservoir, res., Id., U.S.	G7	89
Blackford, co., In., U.S.	D7	91
Black Forest see Schwarzwald, mts., Ger.	G8	8
Blackhall Mountain, mtn., Wy., U.S.	E6	127
Black Hawk, S.D., U.S.	C2	118
Black Hawk, co., Ia., U.S.	B5	92
Black Hills, mts., U.S.	C2	118
Blackjack Mountain, mtn., Ga., U.S.	h8	87
Black Lake, Que., Can.	C6	74
Black Lake, l., Mi., U.S.	C6	99
Black Lake, l., N.Y., U.S.	f9	109
Black Lick, Pa., U.S.	F3	115
Blacklick Estates, Oh., U.S.	*m11	112
Black Mesa, mtn., Ok., U.S.	e8	113
Black Mingo Creek, stm., S.C., U.S.	D9	117
Blackmore, Mount, mtn., Mt., U.S.	E6	103
Black Mountain, N.C., U.S.	f10	110
Black Mountain, mtn., U.S.	D7	94
Black Mountain, mtn., Az., U.S.	E4	80
Black Mountain, mtn., Co., U.S.	A5	83
Black Mountain, mtn., Id., U.S.	C3	89
Black Mountain, mtn., Mt., U.S.	D4	103
Black Mountain, mtn., Or., U.S.	B7	114
Black Mountain, mtn., Wy., U.S.	B5	127
Black Mountains, mts., Az., U.S.	B1	80
Black Peak, mtn., Az., U.S.	C1	80
Black Pine Peak, mtn., Id., U.S.	G5	89
Blackpool, Eng., U.K.	H9	7
Black Range, mts., N.M., U.S.	D2	108
Black River Falls, Wi., U.S.	D3	126
Black Rock, Ar., U.S.	A4	81
Black Rock, N.M., U.S.	B1	108
Black Rock Desert, des., Nv., U.S.	B3	105
Black Rock Range, mts., Nv., U.S.	B3	105
Blacksburg, S.C., U.S.	A4	117
Blacksburg, Va., U.S.	C2	123
Black Sea	G14	4
Blacks Fork, stm., U.S.	E3	127
Blackshear, Ga., U.S.	E4	87
Blackstone, Ma., U.S.	B4	98
Blackstone, Va., U.S.	C5	123
Blackstone, stm., R.I., U.S.	B4	116
Black Thunder Creek, stm., Wy., U.S.	C8	127
Blackville, N.B., Can.	C4	71
Blackville, S.C., U.S.	E5	117
Black Volta (Volta Noire), stm., Afr.	G5	42
Blackwalnut Point, c., Md., U.S.	C5	97
Black Warrior, stm., Al., U.S.	C2	78
Blackwater, stm., Fl., U.S.	u15	86
Blackwater, stm., Md., U.S.	D5	97
Blackwater, stm., N.H., U.S.	D3	106
Blackwater, stm., Va., U.S.	D6	123
Blackwater Reservoir, res., N.H., U.S.	D3	106
Blackwell, Ok., U.S.	A4	113
Blackwood, N.J., U.S.	D2	107
Bladen, co., N.C., U.S.	C4	110
Bladenboro, N.C., U.S.	C4	110
Bladensburg, Md., U.S.	f9	97
Blades, De., U.S.	F3	85
Blagoevgrad, Bul.	G7	16
Blagoveščensk, Russia	G19	24
Blaine, Mn., U.S.	m12	100
Blaine, Tn., U.S.	C10	119
Blaine, Wa., U.S.	A3	124
Blaine, co., Id., U.S.	F4	89
Blaine, co., Mt., U.S.	B7	103
Blaine, co., Ne., U.S.	C6	104
Blaine, co., Ok., U.S.	B3	113
Blaine Lake, Sask., Can.	E2	75
Blair, Ne., U.S.	C9	104
Blair, Ok., U.S.	C2	113
Blair, W.V., U.S.	n12	125
Blair, Wi., U.S.	D2	126
Blair, co., Pa., U.S.	E5	115
Blair Athol, Austl.	D9	50
Blairstown, Ia., U.S.	C5	92
Blairsville, Pa., U.S.	F3	115
Blake Island, i., Wa., U.S.	e11	124
Blakely, Ga., U.S.	E2	87
Blakely, Pa., U.S.	m18	115
Blake Point, c., Mi., U.S.	h10	99
Blanc, Cap, c., Afr.	D2	42
Blanc, Mont (Monte Bianco), mtn., Eur.	G13	10
Blanca Peak, mtn., Co., U.S.	D5	83
Blanchard, Ok., U.S.	B4	113
Blanchard, stm., Oh., U.S.	A1	112
Blanchardville, Wi., U.S.	F4	126
Blanchester, Oh., U.S.	C2	112
Blanco, Tx., U.S.	D3	120

Name	Map Ref	Page
Blanco, co., Tx., U.S.	D3	120
Blanco, Cape, c., Or., U.S.	E2	114
Bland, Mo., U.S.	C6	102
Bland, co., Va., U.S.	C1	123
Blanding, Ut., U.S.	F6	121
Blandinsville, Il., U.S.	C3	90
Blanes, Spain	D14	12
Blangkedjeren, Indon.	M4	34
Blangy-sur-Bresle, Fr.	C8	10
Blanquilla, Isla, i., Ven.	B10	58
Blantyre, Mwi.	E7	44
Blasdell, N.Y., U.S.	C2	109
Blawnox, Pa., U.S.	k14	115
Blaye-et-Sainte-Luce, Fr.	G6	10
Bleckley, co., Ga., U.S.	D3	87
Bled, Slo.	C9	14
Bledsoe, co., Tn., U.S.	D8	119
Blende, Co., U.S.	C6	83
Blenheim, Ont., Can.	E3	73
Blenheim, N.Z.	D4	52
Blennerhassett, W.V., U.S.	B3	125
Bléré, Fr.	E7	10
Blida, Alg.	A6	42
Blind, stm., La., U.S.	h10	95
Blind River, Ont., Can.	A2	73
Blissfield, Mi., U.S.	G7	99
Blitar, Indon.	n16	32
Block Island, R.I., U.S.	h7	116
Block Island, i., R.I., U.S.	h7	116
Block Island Sound, strt., U.S.	G2	116
Bloemfontein, S. Afr.	G5	44
Bloemhof, S. Afr.	G5	44
Blois, Fr.	E8	10
Blood Mountain, mtn., Ga., U.S.	B3	87
Bloodsworth Island, i., Md., U.S.	D5	97
Bloodvein, stm., Can.	D3	70
Bloody Foreland, c., Ire.	F4	7
Bloomer, Wi., U.S.	C2	126
Bloomfield, Ont., Can.	D7	73
Bloomfield, Ct., U.S.	B5	84
Bloomfield, In., U.S.	F4	91
Bloomfield, Ia., U.S.	D5	92
Bloomfield, Ky., U.S.	C4	94
Bloomfield, Mo., U.S.	E8	102
Bloomfield, Ne., U.S.	B8	104
Bloomfield, N.J., U.S.	h8	107
Bloomfield, N.M., U.S.	A2	108
Bloomfield Hills, Mi., U.S.	o15	99
Bloomingdale, Ga., U.S.	D5	87
Bloomingdale, Il., U.S.	k8	90
Bloomingdale, N.J., U.S.	A4	107
Bloomingdale, Tn., U.S.	C11	119
Blooming Prairie, Mn., U.S.	G5	100
Bloomington, Il., U.S.	C4	90
Bloomington, In., U.S.	F4	91
Bloomington, Mn., U.S.	F5	100
Bloomington, Tx., U.S.	E4	120
Bloomington, Wi., U.S.	F3	126
Bloomington, Lake, res., Il., U.S.	C5	90
Bloomsburg, Pa., U.S.	E9	115
Bloomville, Oh., U.S.	B2	112
Blora, Indon.	m15	33a
Blossburg, Pa., U.S.	C7	115
Blossom, Tx., U.S.	C5	120
Blount, co., Al., U.S.	B3	78
Blount, co., Tn., U.S.	D10	119
Blountstown, Fl., U.S.	B1	86
Blountsville, Al., U.S.	A3	78
Blountville, Tn., U.S.	C11	119
Blowing Rock, N.C., U.S.	A1	110
Bludenz, Aus.	H9	8
Blue, stm., Co., U.S.	B4	83
Blue, stm., in., U.S.	H5	91
Blue, stm., Mo., U.S.	k10	102
Blue, stm., Ok., U.S.	C5	113
Blue Ash, Oh., U.S.	o13	112
Blue Buck Point, c., La., U.S.	E2	95
Blue Creek, W.V., U.S.	m13	125
Blue Creek, stm., W.V., U.S.	m13	125
Blue Cypress Lake, l., Fl., U.S.	E6	86
Blue Diamond, Nv., U.S.	G6	105
Blue Earth, Mn., U.S.	G4	100
Blue Earth, co., Mn., U.S.	G4	100
Blue Earth, stm., Mn., U.S.	G4	100
Bluefield, Va., U.S.	C1	123
Bluefield, W.V., U.S.	D3	125
Bluefields, Nic.	H6	64
Blue Grass, Ia., U.S.	C7	92
Blue Hill, Me., U.S.	D4	96
Blue Hill, Ne., U.S.	D7	104
Blue Hill Range, hills, Ma., U.S.	h11	98
Blue Hills, Ct., U.S.	B5	84
Blue Island, Il., U.S.	B6	90
Bluejoint Lake, l., Or., U.S.	E7	114
Blue Lake, Ca., U.S.	B2	82
Blue Mesa Reservoir, res., Co., U.S.	C3	83
Blue Mound, Il., U.S.	D4	90
Blue Mountain, Ms., U.S.	A4	101
Blue Mountain, mtn., Mt., U.S.	C12	103
Blue Mountain, mtn., N.M., U.S.	D2	108
Blue Mountain, mtn., Pa., U.S.	F6	115
Blue Mountain Lake, res., Ar., U.S.	B2	81
Blue Mountain Peak, mtn., Jam.	E9	64
Blue Nile (Al-Bahr al-Azraq), stm., Afr.	F12	42
Blue Point, Me., U.S.	g7	96
Blue Rapids, Ks., U.S.	C7	93
Blue Ridge, Ga., U.S.	B2	87
Blue Ridge, Va., U.S.	C3	123
Blue Ridge, mtn., U.S.	E10	76
Blue Ridge Summit, Pa., U.S.	G2	115
Blue Springs, Mo., U.S.	h11	102
Bluestone, stm., W.V., U.S.	D3	125
Bluestone Lake, res., U.S.	D4	125
Bluewell, W.V., U.S.	D3	125
Bluff City, Tn., U.S.	C11	119
Bluff Creek, stm., Ok., U.S.	A4	113
Bluff Lake, res., Ms., U.S.	B5	101
Bluff Park, Al., U.S.	g7	78
Bluffs, Il., U.S.	D3	90
Bluffton, In., U.S.	C7	91
Bluffton, Oh., U.S.	B2	112
Bluffton, S.C., U.S.	G6	117
Blumenau, Braz.	B7	56
Bly, Or., U.S.	E5	114
Blying Sound, strt., Ak., U.S.	h17	79
Blyth, Ont., Can.	D3	73
Blyth, Eng., U.K.	F11	7
Blythe, Ca., U.S.	F6	82
Blytheville, Ar., U.S.	B6	81
Bø, Nor.	B10	6
Bø, Nor.	G7	6
Bo, S.L.	G3	42
Boaco, Nic.	H5	64
Boalsburg, Pa., U.S.	E6	115
Boa Nova, Braz.	C8	57
Boardman, Oh., U.S.	A5	112
Boardman, Or., U.S.	B7	114
Boa Vista, Braz.	C6	54
Boavita, Col.	D6	58
Boaz, Al., U.S.	A3	78
Bobbili, India	C7	37
Bobbio, Italy	E4	14
Bobcaygeon, Ont., Can.	C6	73
Böblingen, Ger.	G9	8
Bobo Dioulasso, Burkina	F5	42
Bobrujsk, Bela.	H12	18
Bobtown, Pa., U.S.	G2	115
Bobures, Ven.	C7	58
Boby, Pic, mtn., Madag.	F9	44
Boca Chica Key, i., Fl., U.S.	H5	86
Boca Ciega Bay, b., Fl., U.S.	p10	86
Bôca do Acre, Braz.	E5	54
Boca Grande, Fl., U.S.	F4	86
Boca Raton, Fl., U.S.	F6	86
Bocas del Toro, Pan.	J6	64
Bocholt, Ger.	D6	8
Bochum, Ger.	D7	8
Bodajbo, Russia	F16	24
Bodega Head, c., Ca., U.S.	C2	82
Bodele, reg., Chad	E9	42
Boden, Swe.	D13	6
Bodensee, l., Eur.	H9	8
Bodhan, India	C4	37
Bodie Island, i., N.C., U.S.	B7	110
Bodinäyakkanūr, India	G4	37
Bodkin Point, c., Md., U.S.	B5	97
Bodø, Nor.	C10	6
Boende, Zaire	B4	44
Boën-sur-Lignon, Fr.	G10	10
Boerne, Tx., U.S.	E3	120
Boeuf, stm., La., U.S.	C4	95
Boeuf, Lake, l., La., U.S.	k10	95
Bogale, Burma	F3	34
Bogalusa, La., U.S.	D6	95
Bogart, Ga., U.S.	C3	87
Bogata, Tx., U.S.	C5	120
Bogenfels, Nmb.	G3	44
Boger City, N.C., U.S.	B1	110
Bognes, Nor.	B10	6
Bogor, Indon.	m13	32
Bogorodick, Russia	H21	18
Bogorodsk, Russia	E26	18
Bogotá see Santa Fe de Bogotá, Col.	E5	58
Bogotol, Russia	F11	24
Bogra, Bngl.	H13	38
Bogučany, Russia	F13	24
Bogue Chitto, Ms., U.S.	D3	101
Bogue Chitto, stm., U.S.	D5	95
Bogue Inlet, b., N.C., U.S.	C5	110
Bogue Phalia, stm., Ms., U.S.	B3	101
Bo Hai, b., China	D10	26
Bohain-en-Vermandois, Fr.	C10	10
Bohemia see Čechy, hist. reg., Czech.	F14	8
Bohemian Forest, mts., Eur.	F12	8
Bohol, i., Phil.	D7	32
Boiano, Italy	H9	14
Boigu, i., Austl.	A8	50
Boiling Springs, N.C., U.S.	B1	110
Boiling Springs, Pa., U.S.	F7	115
Bois Blanc Island, i., Mi., U.S.	C6	99
Bois Brule, stm., Wi., U.S.	B2	126
Boischâtel, Que., Can.	C6	74
Bois-des-Filion, Que., Can.	p19	74
Bois de Sioux, stm., Mn., U.S.	E2	100
Boise, Id., U.S.	F2	89
Boise, co., Id., U.S.	F3	89
Boise City, Ok., U.S.	e8	113
Boissevain, Man., Can.	E1	70
Boissevain, Va., U.S.	e10	123
Boistfort Peak, mtn., Wa., U.S.	C2	124
Boizenburg, Ger.	B10	8
Bojador, Cabo, c., W. Sah.	C3	42
Bojeador, Cape, c., Phil.	B7	32
Bojnūrd, Iran	J9	22
Bojonegoro, Indon.	m15	33a
Boké, Gui.	F3	42
Boketu, China	B11	26
Boknafjorden, Nor.	G5	6
Boksitogorsk, Russia	B16	18
Bokungu, Zaire	B4	44
Bolama, Gui.-B.	F2	42
Bolbec, Fr.	C7	10
Bolesławiec, Pol.	D15	8
Boley, Ok., U.S.	B5	113
Bolgatanga, Ghana	F5	42
Boli, China	B13	26
Bolingbrook, Il., U.S.	k8	90
Bolívar, Arg.	D4	56
Bolivar, Mo., U.S.	D4	102
Bolivar, Oh., U.S.	B4	112
Bolivar, Tn., U.S.	B3	119
Bolivar, W.V., U.S.	B7	125
Bolívar, co., Ms., U.S.	B3	101
Bolívar, Cerro, mtn., Ven.	D11	58
Bolívar, Lake, l., Ms., U.S.	B3	101
Bolívar, Pico, mtn., Ven.	C7	58
Bolivia, ctry., S.A.	G5	54
Bollène, Fr.	H11	10
Bollinger, co., Mo., U.S.	D7	102
Bollnäs, Swe.	F11	6
Bollullos par del Condado, Spain	H5	12
Bolobo, Zaire	B3	44
Bologna, Italy	E6	14
Bologoje, Russia	D17	18
Bolotnoje, Russia	F10	24
Bolsena, Italy	G6	14
Bol'šereck, Russia	F23	24
Bol'ševik, Russia	E23	24
Bol'ševik, Ostrov, i., Russia	B14	24
Bol'šoj An'uj, stm., Russia	D26	24
Bol'šoj Begičev, Ostrov, i., Russia	C16	24
Bol'šoj L'achovskij, Ostrov, i., Russia	C22	24
Bolton, Eng., U.K.	H10	7
Bolton, Ms., U.S.	C3	101
Bolton Lakes, l., Ct., U.S.	B6	84
Bolton Landing, N.Y., U.S.	B7	109
Bolzano (Bozen), Italy	C6	14
Boma, Zaire	C2	44
Bombala, Austl.	G9	50
Bombarral, Port.	F2	12
Bombay, India	C2	37
Bombay Hook Island, i., De., U.S.	C4	85
Bom Despacho, Braz.	E6	57
Bomoseen, Lake, l., Vt., U.S.	D2	122
Bomu (Mbomou), stm., Afr.	H10	42
Bon, Cap, c., Tun.	A8	42
Bon Accord, Alta., Can.	C4	68
Bon Air, Va., U.S.	C5	123
Bonaire, Ga., U.S.	D3	87
Bonaire, i., Neth. Ant.	H13	64
Bonanza Peak, mtn., Wa., U.S.	A5	124
Bonao, Dom. Rep.	E12	64
Bonaparte, Mount, mtn., Wa., U.S.	A6	124
Bonaparte Archipelago, is., Austl.	B5	50
Bonarbridge, Scot., U.K.	D8	7
Bonasila Dome, mtn., Ak., U.S.	C7	79
Bonaventure, Que., Can.	A4	71
Bonavista, Newf., Can.	D5	72
Bonavista, Cape, c., Newf., Can.	D5	72
Bonavista Bay, b., Newf., Can.	G22	66
Bonavista Bay, b., Newf., Can.	D5	72
Bond, co., Il., U.S.	E4	90
Bondeno, Italy	E6	14
Bondo, Zaire	H10	42
Bondoukou, I.C.	G5	42
Bondowoso, Indon.	m16	33a
Bondsville, Ma., U.S.	B3	98
Bonduel, Wi., U.S.	D5	126
Bondurant, Ia., U.S.	C4	92
Bone, Teluk, b., Indon.	F7	32
Bone Lake, l., Wi., U.S.	C1	126
Bongandanga, Zaire	A4	44
Bongor, Chad	F9	42
Bonham, Tx., U.S.	C4	120
Bon Homme, co., S.D., U.S.	D8	118
Bonifay, Fl., U.S.	u16	86
Bonifati, Capo, c., Italy	J10	14
Bonita Springs, Fl., U.S.	F5	86
Bonn, Ger.	E7	8
Bonneauville, Pa., U.S.	G7	115
Bonne Bay, b., Newf., Can.	D3	72
Bonner, co., Id., U.S.	A2	89
Bonners Ferry, Id., U.S.	A2	89
Bonner Springs, Ks., U.S.	C9	93
Bonnet Carre Floodway, La., U.S.	h11	95
Bonne Terre, Mo., U.S.	D7	102
Bonneval, Fr.	D8	10
Bonneville, Fr.	F13	10
Bonneville, co., Id., U.S.	F7	89
Bonneville Dam, U.S.	B4	114
Bonneville Peak, mtn., Id., U.S.	F6	89
Bonneville Salt Flats, pl., Ut., U.S.	C2	121
Bonney Lake, Wa., U.S.	B3	124
Bonnie Doone, N.C., U.S.	B4	110
Bonny Reservoir, res., Co., U.S.	B8	83
Bonnyville, Alta., Can.	B5	68
Bono, Ar., U.S.	B5	81
Bonorva, Italy	I3	14
Bon Secour, Al., U.S.	E2	78
Bonthe, S.L.	G3	42
Booker, Tx., U.S.	A2	120
Booker T. Washington National Monument, Va., U.S.	C3	123
Boomer, W.V., U.S.	C3	125
Boone, Ia., U.S.	B4	92
Boone, N.C., U.S.	A1	110
Boone, co., Ar., U.S.	A2	81
Boone, co., Il., U.S.	A5	90
Boone, co., In., U.S.	D4	91
Boone, co., Ia., U.S.	B3	92
Boone, co., Ky., U.S.	B5	94
Boone, co., Mo., U.S.	B5	102
Boone, co., Ne., U.S.	C7	104
Boone, co., W.V., U.S.	C3	125
Boone, stm., Ia., U.S.	B4	92
Boone Lake, res., Tn., U.S.	C11	119
Booneville, Ar., U.S.	B2	81
Booneville, Ms., U.S.	A5	101
Boonsboro, Md., U.S.	A2	97
Boonton, N.J., U.S.	B4	107
Boonville, In., U.S.	H3	91
Boonville, Mo., U.S.	C5	102
Boonville, N.Y., U.S.	B5	109
Boonville, N.C., U.S.	A2	110
Boothbay Harbor, Me., U.S.	E3	96
Boothia, Gulf of, b., N.W. Ter., Can.	B14	66
Boothia Peninsula, pen., N.W. Ter., Can.	B14	66
Booths Creek, stm., W.V., U.S.	h11	125
Boothville, La., U.S.	E6	95
Booué, Gabon	B2	44
Boquete, Pan.	J6	64
Boquillas del Carmen, Mex.	C8	62
Bor, Russia	E27	18
Bor, Sudan	G12	42
Boraha, Nosy, i., Madag.	E9	44
Borah Peak, mtn., Id., U.S.	E5	89
Borås, Swe.	H9	6
Bordeaux, Fr.	H6	10
Borden, co., Tx., U.S.	C2	120
Borden Peninsula, pen., N.W. Ter., Can.	B16	66
Bordentown, N.J., U.S.	C3	107
Bordertown, Austl.	G8	50
Borgå (Porvoo), Fin.	F15	6
Borgarnes, Ice.	C3	4
Borger, Tx., U.S.	B2	120
Borgne, Lake, b., La., U.S.	D6	95
Borgo, Italy	C6	14
Borgo San Dalmazzo, Italy	E2	14
Borgosesia, Italy	D3	14
Borgo Val di Taro, Italy	E4	14
Borisov, Bela.	G11	18
Borja, Spain	D10	12
Borjas Blancas, Spain	D12	12
Borken, Ger.	D6	8
Borlänge, Swe.	F10	6
Borlu, Tur.	K12	16
Borneo (Kalimantan), i., Asia	E5	32
Bornholm, i., Den.	I10	6
Bornova, Tur.	K11	16
Borogoncy, Russia	E20	24
Boron, Ca., U.S.	E5	82
Boronga Islands, is., Burma	E2	34
Borovici, Russia	C16	18
Borrego Springs, Ca., U.S.	F5	82
Bort-les-Orgues, Fr.	G9	10
Borūjerd, Iran	B4	46
Borz'a, Russia	G17	24
Bosa, Italy	I3	14
Bosanska Gradiška, Bos.	D12	14
Bosanska Krupa, Bos.	E11	14
Bosanski Novi, Bos.	D11	14
Bosanski Petrovac, Bos.	E11	14
Bosaso, Som.	F4	46
Boscobel, Wi., U.S.	E3	126
Boshan, China	D10	26
Bosnia and Hercegovina, ctry., Eur.	E12	14
Bosporus see İstanbul Boğazı, strt., Tur.	H13	16
Bosque, co., Tx., U.S.	D4	120
Bossangoa, Cen. Afr. Rep.	G9	42
Bossembélé, Cen. Afr. Rep.	G9	42
Bossier, co., La., U.S.	B2	95
Bossier City, La., U.S.	B2	95
Bosten Hu, l., China	C4	26
Boston, Eng., U.K.	I12	7
Boston, Ga., U.S.	F3	87
Boston, Ma., U.S.	B5	98
Boston Bay, b., Ma., U.S.	B6	98
Boston Mountains, mts., Ar., U.S.	B2	81
Boswell, Ok., U.S.	C6	113
Boswell, Pa., U.S.	F3	115
Botād, India	I4	38
Boteti, stm., Bots.	F4	44
Botetourt, co., Va., U.S.	C3	123
Bothell, Wa., U.S.	B3	124
Bothnia, Gulf of, b., Eur.	E12	6
Bothwell, Ont., Can.	E3	73
Botkins, Oh., U.S.	B1	112
Botoşani, Rom.	B10	16
Botswana, ctry., Afr.	F4	44
Bottenhavet (Selkämeri), b., Eur.	F12	6
Bottenviken (Perämeri), b., Eur.	D14	6
Bottineau, N.D., U.S.	A5	111
Bottineau, co., N.D., U.S.	A4	111
Botucatu, Braz.	G4	57
Botwood, Newf., Can.	D4	72
Bouaflé, I.C.	G4	42
Bouaké, I.C.	G4	42
Bouar, Cen. Afr. Rep.	G9	42
Bou Arada, Tun.	M4	14
Boucherville, Que., Can.	D4	74
Bouctouche, N.B., Can.	C5	71
Boudreaux, Lake, l., La., U.S.	E5	95
Bou Ficha, Tun.	M5	14
Bougainville Reef, rf., Austl.	C9	50
Bougouni, Mali	F4	42
Bouillon, Bel.	F5	8
Boulder, Co., U.S.	A5	83
Boulder, Mt., U.S.	D4	103
Boulder, co., Co., U.S.	A5	83
Boulder City, Nv., U.S.	H7	105
Boulevard Heights, Md., U.S.	f9	97
Boulogne-Billancourt, Fr.	D9	10
Boulogne-sur-Gesse, Fr.	I7	10
Boulogne-sur-Mer, Fr.	B8	10
Bouna, I.C.	G5	42
Boundary, co., Id., U.S.	A2	89
Boundary Bay, b., Wa., U.S.	A3	124
Boundary Peak, mtn., Nv., U.S.	F3	105
Bound Brook, N.J., U.S.	B3	107
Bountiful, Ut., U.S.	C4	121
Bourbeuse, stm., Mo., U.S.	C6	102
Bourbon, In., U.S.	B5	91
Bourbon, Mo., U.S.	C6	102
Bourbon, co., Ks., U.S.	E9	93
Bourbon, co., Ky., U.S.	B5	94
Bourbonnais, Il., U.S.	B6	90
Bourbonnais, hist. reg., Fr.	F9	10
Bourbonne-les-Bains, Fr.	E12	10
Bourem, Mali	E5	42
Bourg, La., U.S.	E5	95
Bourganeuf, Fr.	G8	10
Bourg-en-Bresse, Fr.	F12	10
Bourges, Fr.	E9	10
Bourg-Lastic, Fr.	G9	10
Bourgogne, hist. reg., Fr.	E11	10
Bourgoin, Fr.	G12	10
Bourg-Saint-Andéol, Fr.	H11	10
Bourg-Saint-Maurice, Fr.	G13	10
Bourke, Austl.	F9	50
Bournemouth, Eng., U.K.	K11	7
Bou Saâda, Alg.	A6	42
Bouse, Az., U.S.	D2	80
Boussac, Fr.	F9	10
Bousso, Chad	F9	42
Boutte, La., U.S.	k11	95
Bøvågen, Nor.	F6	6
Bovalino Marina, Italy	K11	14
Bovec, Slo.	C8	14
Bøverdal, Nor.	F7	6
Bovey, Mn., U.S.	C5	100
Bovina, Tx., U.S.	B1	120
Bow, N.H., U.S.	D3	106
Bow, stm., Alta., Can.	D4	68
Bowbells, N.D., U.S.	A2	111
Bowden, Alta., Can.	D4	68
Bowdish Reservoir, res., R.I., U.S.	B1	116
Bowdon, Ga., U.S.	C1	87
Bowen, Austl.	C9	50
Bowie, Az., U.S.	E6	80
Bowie, Md., U.S.	C4	97
Bowie, Tx., U.S.	C4	120
Bowie, co., Tx., U.S.	C5	120
Bow Island, Alta., Can.	E5	68
Bow Lake, l., N.H., U.S.	D4	106
Bowling Green, Fl., U.S.	E5	86
Bowling Green, Ky., U.S.	C3	94
Bowling Green, Mo., U.S.	B6	102
Bowling Green, Oh., U.S.	A2	112
Bowling Green, S.C., U.S.	A5	117
Bowling Green, Va., U.S.	B5	123
Bowman, Ga., U.S.	B3	87
Bowman, N.D., U.S.	C2	111
Bowman, S.C., U.S.	E6	117
Bowman, co., N.D., U.S.	C2	111
Bowman Creek, stm., Pa., U.S.	m16	115
Bowman-Haley Lake, res., N.D., U.S.	C2	111
Bowron, stm., B.C., Can.	C7	69
Bowstring Lake, l., Mn., U.S.	C5	100
Box Butte, co., Ne., U.S.	B2	104
Box Butte Reservoir, res., Ne., U.S.	B2	104
Box Elder, S.D., U.S.	C2	118
Box Elder, co., Ut., U.S.	B2	121
Boxford, Ma., U.S.	A6	98
Boxian, China	B4	28
Boyce, La., U.S.	C3	95
Boyceville, Wi., U.S.	C1	126
Boyd, Tx., U.S.	C4	120
Boyd, co., Ky., U.S.	B7	94
Boyd, co., Ne., U.S.	B7	104
Boyden, Ia., U.S.	A2	92
Boyd Lake, l., Me., U.S.	C4	96
Boyer, stm., Ia., U.S.	C2	92
Boyertown, Pa., U.S.	F10	115
Boykins, Va., U.S.	D5	123
Boyle, Alta., Can.	B4	68
Boyle, Ire.	H4	7
Boyle, Ms., U.S.	B3	101
Boyle, co., Ky., U.S.	C5	94
Boyne City, Mi., U.S.	C6	99
Boynton Beach, Fl., U.S.	F6	86
Boysen Reservoir, res., Wy., U.S.	C4	127
Boys Town, Ne., U.S.	g12	104
Bozburun, Tur.	M12	16
Boz Dağ, mtn., Tur.	L13	16
Bozeman, Mt., U.S.	E6	103
Bozeman Pass, Mt., U.S.	E6	103
Bozoum, Cen. Afr. Rep.	G9	42
Bra, Italy	E2	14
Bracciano, Italy	G7	14
Bracebridge, Ont., Can.	B5	73
Bräcke, Swe.	E10	6
Bracken, co., Ky., U.S.	B5	94
Brackenridge, Pa., U.S.	h15	115
Brackettville, Tx., U.S.	E2	120
Braddock, Pa., U.S.	k14	115
Braddock Heights, Md., U.S.	B2	97
Braddock Point, c., S.C., U.S.	G6	117
Bradenton, Fl., U.S.	E4	86
Bradenville, Pa., U.S.	F3	115
Bradford, Ont., Can.	C5	73
Bradford, Eng., U.K.	H11	7
Bradford, Ar., U.S.	B4	81
Bradford, Oh., U.S.	B1	112
Bradford, Pa., U.S.	C4	115
Bradford, R.I., U.S.	F2	116
Bradford, Tn., U.S.	A3	119
Bradford, Vt., U.S.	D4	122
Bradford, co., Fl., U.S.	C4	86
Bradford, co., Pa., U.S.	C8	115
Bradfordwoods, Pa., U.S.	h13	115
Bradley, Il., U.S.	B6	90
Bradley, Me., U.S.	D4	96
Bradley, W.V., U.S.	D3	125
Bradley, co., Ar., U.S.	D3	81
Bradley, co., Tn., U.S.	D9	119
Bradley Beach, N.J., U.S.	C4	107
Bradner, Oh., U.S.	A2	112
Bradshaw, Md., U.S.	B5	97
Bradshaw Mountains, mts., Az., U.S.	C3	80
Brady, Tx., U.S.	D3	120
Braga, Port.	D3	12
Bragado, Arg.	D4	56
Bragança, Braz.	D9	54
Bragança, Port.	D5	12
Braham, Mn., U.S.	E5	100
Brāhmanbāria, Bngl.	I14	38
Brāhmani, stm., India	J11	38
Brahmaputra (Yarlung), stm., Asia	G15	38
Braich y Pwll, c., Wales, U.K.	I8	7
Braidwood, Il., U.S.	B5	90
Brăila, Rom.	D11	16
Brainerd, Mn., U.S.	D4	100
Braintree, Ma., U.S.	B5	98
Brake, Ger.	B8	8
Brampton, Ont., Can.	D5	73
Bramsche, Ger.	C7	8
Bramwell, W.V., U.S.	D3	125
Branch, co., Mi., U.S.	G5	99
Branch, stm., R.I., U.S.	B3	116
Branch, stm., Wi., U.S.	h10	126
Branch Lake, l., Me., U.S.	D4	96
Branch Village, R.I., U.S.	B3	116
Branchville, S.C., U.S.	E6	117
Branco, stm., Braz.	C6	54
Brandberg, mtn., Nmb.	F2	44
Brandbu, Nor.	F8	6
Brandenburg, Ger.	C12	8
Brandenburg, Ky., U.S.	C3	94
Brandon, Man., Can.	E2	70
Brandon, Fl., U.S.	E4	86
Brandon, Ms., U.S.	C4	101
Brandon, S.C., U.S.	B3	117
Brandon, S.D., U.S.	D9	118
Brandon, Vt., U.S.	D2	122
Brandon, Wi., U.S.	E5	126
Brandvlei, S. Afr.	H4	44
Brandy Peak, mtn., Or., U.S.	E3	114
Brandywine, Md., U.S.	C4	97
Brandywine Creek, stm., U.S.	A3	85
Branford, Ct., U.S.	D4	84
Branford Hills, Ct., U.S.	D4	84
Br'ansk, Russia	H17	18
Branson, Mo., U.S.	E4	102
Brantford, Ont., Can.	D4	73
Brantley, Al., U.S.	D3	78
Brantley, co., Ga., U.S.	E4	87
Brantôme, Fr.	G7	10
Brant Rock, Ma., U.S.	B6	98
Brantville, N.B., Can.	B5	71
Bras d'Or Lake, l., N.S., Can.	D9	71
Brasília, Braz.	C5	57
Braşov, Rom.	D9	16
Brasstown Bald, mtn., U.S.	B3	87
Brassua Lake, res., Me., U.S.	C3	96
Bratenahl, Oh., U.S.	g9	112
Bratislava, Czech.	G17	8

Name	Map Ref	Page
Bratsk, Russia	F14	24
Bratskoje Vodochranilišče, res., Russia	F14	24
Brattleboro, Vt., U.S.	F3	122
Braunau [am Inn], Aus.	G13	8
Braunschweig, Ger.	C10	8
Brava, Som.	H3	46
Brava, Costa, Spain	D15	12
Bravo del Norte (Rio Grande), stm., N.A.	F6	76
Brawley, Ca., U.S.	F6	82
Brawley Peaks, mts., Nv., U.S.	E3	105
Braxton, co., W.V., U.S.	C4	125
Bray, Ire.	H6	7
Bray, Ok., U.S.	C4	113
Bray Island, i., N.W. Ter., Can.	C17	66
Braymer, Mo., U.S.	B4	102
Brazeau, stm., Alta., Can.	C2	68
Brazil, In., U.S.	E3	91
Brazil, ctry., S.A.	E7	54
Brazoria, In., U.S.	r14	120
Brazoria, Tx., U.S.	E5	120
Brazoria, co., Tx., U.S.	D4	120
Brazos, co., Tx., U.S.	D4	120
Brazos, stm., Tx., U.S.	D4	120
Brazzaville, Congo	B3	44
Brčko, Bos.	E2	16
Brea, Ca., U.S.	n13	82
Breakenridge, Mount, mtn., B.C., Can.	E7	69
Breathitt, co., Ky., U.S.	C6	94
Breaux Bridge, La., U.S.	D4	95
Brebes, Indon.	m14	33a
Breckenridge, Co., U.S.	B4	83
Breckenridge, Mi., U.S.	E6	99
Breckenridge, Mn., U.S.	D2	100
Breckenridge, Tx., U.S.	C3	120
Breckinridge, co., Ky., U.S.	C3	94
Brecksville, Oh., U.S.	A4	112
Brecon Beacons National Park, Wales, U.K.	J9	7
Breda, Neth.	D4	8
Bredstedt, Ger.	A8	8
Breese, Il., U.S.	E4	90
Bréhal, Fr.	D5	10
Brekstad, Nor.	E7	6
Bremen, Ger.	B8	8
Bremen, Ga., U.S.	C1	87
Bremen, In., U.S.	B5	91
Bremen, Oh., U.S.	C3	112
Bremer, co., Ia., U.S.	B5	92
Bremerhaven, Ger.	B8	8
Bremerton, Wa., U.S.	B3	124
Bremond, Tx., U.S.	D4	120
Brenham, Tx., U.S.	D4	120
Brenner Pass, Eur.	B6	14
Breno, Italy	D5	14
Brent, Al., U.S.	C2	78
Brent, Fl., U.S.	u14	86
Brenton Point, c., R.I., U.S.	F5	116
Brentwood, Ca., U.S.	h9	82
Brentwood, Md., U.S.	f9	97
Brentwood, Mo., U.S.	f13	102
Brentwood, N.Y., U.S.	E7	109
Brentwood, Pa., U.S.	k14	115
Brentwood, S.C., U.S.	k11	117
Brentwood, Tn., U.S.	A5	119
Brescia, Italy	D5	14
Breslau see Wrocław, Pol.		
Bressanone, Italy	C6	14
Bressuire, Fr.	F6	10
Brest, Bela.	I6	18
Brest, Fr.	D2	10
Bretagne, hist. reg., Fr.	D3	10
Breton Islands, is., La., U.S.	E6	95
Breton Sound, strt., La., U.S.	E6	95
Brevard, N.C., U.S.	f10	110
Brevard, co., Fl., U.S.	E6	86
Brevoort Lake, l., Mi., U.S.	B6	99
Brewer, Me., U.S.	D4	96
Brewster, Ma., U.S.	C7	98
Brewster, N.Y., U.S.	D7	109
Brewster, Oh., U.S.	B4	112
Brewster, Wa., U.S.	A6	124
Brewster, co., Tx., U.S.	E1	120
Brewster Islands, is., Ma., U.S.	g12	98
Brewton, Al., U.S.	D2	78
Brežice, Slo.	D10	14
Bria, Cen. Afr. Rep.	G10	42
Brian Boru Peak, mtn., B.C., Can.	B4	69
Briançon, Fr.	H13	10
Brian Head, mtn., Ut., U.S.	F3	121
Briare, Fr.	E9	10
Briceville, Tn., U.S.	C9	119
Brick [Township], N.J., U.S.	C4	107
Bricquebec, Fr.	C5	10
Bridal Veil Falls, wtfl, Ut., U.S.	C4	121
Bridgehampton, N.Y., U.S.	n16	109
Bridgeport, Al., U.S.	A4	78
Bridgeport, Ct., U.S.	E3	84
Bridgeport, Il., U.S.	E6	90
Bridgeport, Mi., U.S.	E7	99
Bridgeport, Ne., U.S.	C2	104
Bridgeport, Oh., U.S.	B5	112
Bridgeport, Pa., U.S.	o20	115
Bridgeport, Tx., U.S.	C4	120
Bridgeport, Wa., U.S.	B6	124
Bridgeport, W.V., U.S.	B4	125
Bridger, Mt., U.S.	E8	103
Bridger Peak, mtn., Wy., U.S.	E5	127
Bridger Range, mts., Mt., U.S.	E6	103
Bridgeton, Mo., U.S.	C7	102
Bridgeton, N.J., U.S.	E2	107
Bridgetown, Barb.	H18	64
Bridgetown, N.S., Can.	E4	71
Bridgeville, De., U.S.	F3	85
Bridgeville, Pa., U.S.	k13	115
Bridgewater, Ma., U.S.	C6	98
Bridgewater, N.J., U.S.	B3	107
Bridgewater, Va., U.S.	B4	123
Bridgman, Mi., U.S.	G4	99
Bridgton, Me., U.S.	D2	96
Bridgwater, Eng., U.K.	J9	7
Bridlington, Eng., U.K.	G12	7
Briec, Fr.	D2	10
Brielle, N.J., U.S.	C4	107
Brienne-le-Château, Fr.	D11	10
Brienz, Switz.	F15	10
Brig, Switz.	F14	10
Brigantine, N.J., U.S.	E4	107
Brigantine Beach, N.J., U.S.	E4	107
Brigden, Ont., Can.	E2	73
Briggs Marsh, sw., R.I., U.S.	F6	116
Brigham City, Ut., U.S.	B3	121
Brighton, Ont., Can.	C7	73
Brighton, Eng., U.K.	K12	7
Brighton, Al., U.S.	B3	78
Brighton, Co., U.S.	B6	83
Brighton, Il., U.S.	D3	90
Brighton, Ia., U.S.	C6	92
Brighton, Mi., U.S.	F7	99
Brighton, N.Y., U.S.	B3	109
Brighton, Tn., U.S.	B2	119
Brighton Indian Reservation, Fl., U.S.	E5	86
Brihuega, Spain	E9	12
Brilliant, Al., U.S.	A2	78
Brilliant, Oh., U.S.	B5	112
Brillion, Wi., U.S.	D5	126
Brilon, Ger.	D8	8
Brimfield, Il., U.S.	C4	90
Brindisi, Italy	I12	14
Brinkley, Ar., U.S.	C4	81
Brinnon, Wa., U.S.	B3	124
Brioude, Fr.	G10	10
Brisbane, Austl.	E10	50
Briscoe, co., Tx., U.S.	B2	120
Bristol, N.B., Can.	C2	71
Bristol, Eng., U.K.	J10	7
Bristol, Ct., U.S.	C4	84
Bristol, In., U.S.	A6	91
Bristol, N.H., U.S.	C3	106
Bristol, R.I., U.S.	D5	116
Bristol, Tn., U.S.	C11	119
Bristol, Vt., U.S.	C2	122
Bristol, Va., U.S.	f9	123
Bristol, co., Ma., U.S.	C5	98
Bristol, co., R.I., U.S.	D5	116
Bristol Bay, b., Ak., U.S.	D7	79
Bristol Channel, strt., U.K.	J8	7
Bristow [Township], Pa., U.S.	F12	115
Bristow, Ok., U.S.	B5	113
British Columbia, prov., Can.	C6	69
British Honduras see Belize, ctry., N.A.	F3	64
British Indian Ocean Territory, dep., I.O.	G17	2
British Mountains, mts., N.A.	C5	66
British Solomon Islands see Solomon Islands, ctry., Oc.	G23	2
Britstown, S. Afr.	H4	44
Britt, Ia., U.S.	A4	92
Brittany see Bretagne, hist. reg., Fr.	D3	10
Britton, S.D., U.S.	B8	118
Brive-la-Gaillarde, Fr.	G8	10
Briviesca, Spain	C8	12
Brno, Czech.	F16	8
Broach, India	B2	37
Broad, stm., S.C., U.S.	C5	117
Broad Brook, Ct., U.S.	B5	84
Broadford, Scot., U.K.	D7	7
Broadkill, stm., De., U.S.	E4	85
Broadkill Beach, De., U.S.	E5	85
Broad Law, mtn., Scot., U.K.	F9	7
Broad Run, stm., Va., U.S.	g11	123
Broadus, Mt., U.S.	E11	103
Broadview Heights, Oh., U.S.	h9	112
Broadwater, co., Mt., U.S.	D5	103
Broadway, N.C., U.S.	B3	110
Broadway, Va., U.S.	B4	123
Brockport, N.Y., U.S.	B3	109
Brockton, Ma., U.S.	B5	98
Brockton Reservoir, res., Ma., U.S.	h11	98
Brockville, Ont., Can.	C9	73
Brockway, Pa., U.S.	D4	115
Brodeur Peninsula, pen., N.W. Ter., Can.	B15	66
Brodhead, Ky., U.S.	C5	94
Brodhead, Wi., U.S.	F4	126
Brodheadsville, Pa., U.S.	E11	115
Broken Arrow, Ok., U.S.	A6	113
Broken Bow, Ne., U.S.	C6	104
Broken Bow, Ok., U.S.	C7	113
Broken Bow Lake, res., Ok., U.S.	C7	113
Broken Hill, Austl.	F8	50
Brokopondo, Sur.	B8	54
Brome, Lac, l., Que., Can.	D5	74
Bromptonville, Que., Can.	D6	74
Bromsgrove, Eng., U.K.	I10	7
Bronlund Peak, mtn., B.C., Can.	E7	66
Brønnøysund, Nor.	D9	6
Bronson, Fl., U.S.	C4	86
Bronte, Italy	L9	14
Bronx, N.Y., U.S.	E7	109
Bronxville, N.Y., U.S.	h13	109
Brook, In., U.S.	C3	91
Brooke, co., W.V., U.S.	A4	125
Brookfield, N.S., Can.	D6	71
Brookfield, Ct., U.S.	D2	84
Brookfield, Il., U.S.	k9	90
Brookfield, Mo., U.S.	B4	102
Brookfield, Oh., U.S.	*B5	123
Brookfield, Wi., U.S.	m11	126
Brookfield Center, Ct., U.S.	D2	84
Brookhaven, Ms., U.S.	D3	101
Brookhaven, W.V., U.S.	h11	125
Brookings, Or., U.S.	E2	114
Brookings, S.D., U.S.	C9	118
Brookings, co., S.D., U.S.	C9	118
Brookland, Ar., U.S.	B5	81
Brooklandville, Md., U.S.	g10	97
Brooklet, Ga., U.S.	D5	87
Brookline, Ma., U.S.	B5	98
Brooklyn, N.S., Can.	E5	71
Brooklyn, Ct., U.S.	B8	84
Brooklyn, In., U.S.	E5	91
Brooklyn, Ia., U.S.	C5	92
Brooklyn, Mi., U.S.	F6	99
Brooklyn, Ms., U.S.	D4	101
Brooklyn, Oh., U.S.	h9	112
Brooklyn, Wi., U.S.	F4	126
Brooklyn Center, Mn., U.S.	E5	100
Brooklyn Park, Md., U.S.	h11	97
Brooklyn Park, Mn., U.S.	m12	100
Brookneal, Va., U.S.	C4	123
Brook Park, Oh., U.S.	h9	112
Brookport, Il., U.S.	F5	90
Brooks, Alta., Can.	D5	68
Brooks, Ky., U.S.	g11	94
Brooks, co., Ga., U.S.	F3	87
Brooks, co., Tx., U.S.	F3	120
Brooks Air Force Base, mil., Tx., U.S.	k7	120
Brookshire, Tx., U.S.	E5	120
Brookside, Al., U.S.	f7	78
Brookside, De., U.S.	B3	85
Brooks Range, mts., Ak., U.S.	B9	79
Brookston, In., U.S.	C4	91
Brooksville, Fl., U.S.	D4	86
Brooksville, Ky., U.S.	B5	94
Brooksville, Ms., U.S.	B5	101
Brookville, In., U.S.	F8	91
Brookville, Oh., U.S.	C1	112
Brookville, Pa., U.S.	D3	115
Brookville Lake, res., In., U.S.	E7	91
Brookwood, Al., U.S.	B2	78
Brookwood, N.J., U.S.	C4	107
Broomall, Pa., U.S.	p20	115
Broome, Austl.	C4	50
Broome, co., N.Y., U.S.	C5	109
Broomfield, Co., U.S.	B5	83
Broons, Fr.	D4	10
Brossard, Que., Can.	q20	74
Brou, Fr.	D8	10
Broussard, La., U.S.	D4	95
Broward, co., Fl., U.S.	F6	86
Browerville, Mn., U.S.	D4	100
Brown, co., Il., U.S.	D3	90
Brown, co., In., U.S.	F5	91
Brown, co., Ks., U.S.	C8	93
Brown, co., Mn., U.S.	F4	100
Brown, co., Ne., U.S.	B6	104
Brown, co., Oh., U.S.	D2	112
Brown, co., S.D., U.S.	B7	118
Brown, co., Tx., U.S.	D3	120
Brown, co., Wi., U.S.	D6	126
Brown, Point, c., Wa., U.S.	C1	124
Brown City, Mi., U.S.	E8	99
Brown Deer, Wi., U.S.	m12	126
Brownfield, Tx., U.S.	C1	120
Browning, Mt., U.S.	B3	103
Brownlee Dam, U.S.	E2	89
Brownlee Reservoir, res., U.S.	C10	114
Browns, stm., Vt., U.S.	B2	122
Browns Branch, stm., De., U.S.	E3	85
Brownsburg, In., U.S.	E5	91
Brownsburg, Que., Can.	D3	74
Brownsdale, Mn., U.S.	G6	100
Browns Inlet, b., N.C., U.S.	C5	110
Browns Mills, N.J., U.S.	D3	107
Brownstown, In., U.S.	G5	91
Browns Valley, Mn., U.S.	E2	100
Brownsville, Fl., U.S.	s13	86
Brownsville, Ky., U.S.	C3	94
Brownsville, Or., U.S.	C4	114
Brownsville, Pa., U.S.	F2	115
Brownsville, Tn., U.S.	B2	119
Brownsville, Tx., U.S.	G4	120
Brownton, Mn., U.S.	F4	100
Brownville Junction, Me., U.S.	C3	96
Brownwood, Tx., U.S.	D3	120
Brownwood, Lake, res., Tx., U.S.	D3	120
Broxton, Ga., U.S.	E4	87
Bruay-en-Artois, Fr.	B9	10
Bruce, Ms., U.S.	B4	101
Bruce, Wi., U.S.	C2	126
Bruce, Mount, mtn., Austl.	D3	50
Bruce National Park, Ont., Can.	B3	73
Bruce Peninsula, pen., Ont., Can.	B3	73
Bruceton, Tn., U.S.	A3	119
Bruchsal, Ger.	F8	8
Bruck an der Leitha, Aus.	H16	8
Bruck an der Mur, Aus.	H15	8
Bruderheim, Alta., Can.	C4	68
Brugge, Bel.	D3	8
Bruin Point, mtn., Ut., U.S.	D6	121
Brule, co., S.D., U.S.	D6	118
Brule, stm., U.S.	C5	126
Brule Lake, l., Mn., U.S.	k9	100
Brundidge, Al., U.S.	D4	78
Bruneau, stm., U.S.	G3	89
Brunei, ctry., Asia	E5	32
Brunico, Italy	C6	14
Brunkeberg, Nor.	G7	6
Bruno, Sask., Can.	E3	75
Brunsbüttel, Ger.	B9	8
Brunswick, Ga., U.S.	E5	87
Brunswick, Me., U.S.	E3	96
Brunswick, Md., U.S.	B2	97
Brunswick, Mo., U.S.	B4	102
Brunswick, Oh., U.S.	A4	112
Brunswick, co., N.C., U.S.	C4	110
Brunswick, co., Va., U.S.	D5	123
Brunswick Naval Air Station, mil., Me., U.S.	E3	96
Brush, Co., U.S.	A7	83
Brushy Mountains, mts., N.C., U.S.	B1	110
Brusly, La., U.S.	D4	95
Brussels, Ont., Can.	D3	73
Brussels see Bruxelles, Bel.	E4	8
Bruxelles (Brussel), Bel.	E4	8
Bryan, Oh., U.S.	A1	112
Bryan, Tx., U.S.	D4	120
Bryan, co., Ga., U.S.	D5	87
Bryan, co., Ok., U.S.	D5	113
Bryans Road, Md., U.S.	C3	97
Bryant, Ar., U.S.	C3	81
Bryantville, Ma., U.S.	B6	98
Bryce Canyon National Park, Ut., U.S.	F3	121
Bryn Mawr, Wa., U.S.	e11	124
Bryson City, N.C., U.S.	f9	110
Brzeg, Pol.	E17	8
Bsharrī, Leb.	B5	40
Būbiyān, i., Kuw.	C4	46
Bucaramanga, Col.	B5	58
Buccaneer Archipelago, is., Austl.	C4	50
Buchanan, Lib.	G3	42
Buchanan, Ga., U.S.	C1	87
Buchanan, Mi., U.S.	G4	99
Buchanan, Va., U.S.	C3	123
Buchanan, co., Ia., U.S.	B6	92
Buchanan, co., Mo., U.S.	B3	102
Buchanan, co., Va., U.S.	e9	123
Buchan Gulf, b., N.W. Ter., Can.	B18	66
Buchans, Newf., Can.	D3	72
Buchara, Uzb.	J10	22
Bucharest see București, Rom.	E10	16
Buchholz, Ger.	B9	8
Buckatunna, Ms., U.S.	D5	101
Buckeye, Az., U.S.	D3	80
Buckeye Lake, Oh., U.S.	C3	112
Buckhannon, W.V., U.S.	C4	125
Buckhorn Lake, res., Ky., U.S.	C6	94
Buckingham, Que., Can.	D2	74
Buckingham, co., Va., U.S.	C4	123
Buckley, Wa., U.S.	B3	124
Bucklin, Ks., U.S.	E4	93
Bucklin, Mo., U.S.	B5	102
Buckner, Mo., U.S.	h11	102
Bucks, co., Pa., U.S.	F11	115
Buckskin Mountains, mts., Az., U.S.	C2	80
Bucksport, Me., U.S.	D4	96
Bucksport, S.C., U.S.	D9	117
București (Bucharest), Rom.	E10	16
Bucyrus, Oh., U.S.	B3	112
Buda, Tx., U.S.	D4	120
Budapest, Hung.	H19	8
Budaun, India	F8	38
Budd Lake, l., N.J., U.S.	B3	107
Buddusò, Italy	I4	14
Bude, Eng., U.K.	K8	7
Bude, Ms., U.S.	D3	101
Buea, Cam.	H7	42
Buechel, Ky., U.S.	B4	94
Buena, N.J., U.S.	D3	107
Buena, Wa., U.S.	C5	124
Buena Park, Ca., U.S.	n12	82
Buena Vista, Bol.	G6	54
Buena Vista, Co., U.S.	C4	83
Buena Vista, Ga., U.S.	D2	87
Buena Vista, Va., U.S.	C3	123
Buena Vista, co., Ia., U.S.	B2	92
Buenópolis, Braz.	D6	57
Buenos Aires, Arg.	C5	56
Buffalo, Ia., U.S.	C7	92
Buffalo, Mn., U.S.	E5	100
Buffalo, Mo., U.S.	D4	102
Buffalo, N.Y., U.S.	C2	109
Buffalo, Ok., U.S.	A2	113
Buffalo, S.C., U.S.	B4	117
Buffalo, Tx., U.S.	D5	120
Buffalo, W.V., U.S.	C3	125
Buffalo, Wi., U.S.	D2	126
Buffalo, Wy., U.S.	B6	127
Buffalo, co., Ne., U.S.	D6	104
Buffalo, co., S.D., U.S.	C6	118
Buffalo, co., Wi., U.S.	D2	126
Buffalo, stm., Ar., U.S.	B3	81
Buffalo, stm., Mn., U.S.	D2	100
Buffalo, stm., Tn., U.S.	B4	119
Buffalo, stm., Wi., U.S.	D2	126
Buffalo Bill Reservoir, res., Wy., U.S.	B3	127
Buffalo Center, Ia., U.S.	A4	92
Buffalo Creek, stm., W.V., U.S.	f8	125
Buffalo Creek, stm., W.V., U.S.	h10	125
Buffalo Creek, stm., W.V., U.S.	n12	125
Buffalo Grove, Il., U.S.	h9	90
Buffalo Lake, Mn., U.S.	F4	100
Buffalo Lake, l., Alta., Can.	C4	68
Buffalo Lake, l., N.W. Ter., Can.	D9	66
Buffalo Lake, res., Wi., U.S.	E4	126
Buffumville Lake, res., Ma., U.S.	B4	98
Buford, Ga., U.S.	B2	87
Bug, stm., Eur.	E12	4
Buga, Col.	F4	58
Bugøynes, Nor.	B17	6
Bugsuk Island, i., Phil.	D6	32
Bugul'ma, Russia	G8	22
Buhl, Id., U.S.	G4	89
Buhl, Mn., U.S.	C6	100
Buhler, Ks., U.S.	D6	93
Buies Creek, N.C., U.S.	B4	110
Buj, Russia	C24	18
Bujalance, Spain	D11	12
Bujaraloz, Spain	D11	12
Bujumbura, Bdi.	B5	44
Bukačača, Russia	G17	24
Bukama, Zaire	C5	44
Bukavu, Zaire	B5	44
Bukittinggi, Indon.	F3	32
Bukoba, Tan.	B6	44
Bukovina, hist. reg., Eur.	B9	16
Bula, Indon.	F9	32
Bulan, Ky., U.S.	C6	94
Bulandshahr, India	F7	38
Bulawayo, Zimb.	F5	44
Buldan, Tur.	K12	16
Buldāna, India	B4	37
Bulgan, Mong.	B5	26
Bulgaria, ctry., Eur.	G12	4
Bulkley, stm., B.C., Can.	B4	69
Bull Creek, stm., S.D., U.S.	D6	118
Bulle, Switz.	F14	10
Bullfinch, Austl.	F3	50
Bullfrog Creek, stm., Ut., U.S.	F5	121
Bullhead City, Az., U.S.	B1	80
Bull Island, i., S.C., U.S.	G6	117
Bull Island, i., S.C., U.S.	F8	117
Bull Island, i., S.C., U.S.	D9	117
Bullitt, co., Ky., U.S.	C4	94
Bulloch, co., Ga., U.S.	D5	87
Bullock, co., Al., U.S.	C4	78
Bullock Creek, Mi., U.S.	E6	99
Bull Run, stm., Va., U.S.	g11	123
Bullrun Rock, mtn., Or., U.S.	C8	114
Bulls Bay, b., S.C., U.S.	F8	117
Bulls Gap, Tn., U.S.	C10	119
Bull Shoals, Ar., U.S.	A3	81
Bull Shoals Lake, res., U.S.	A3	81
Bully Creek Reservoir, res., Or., U.S.	C9	114
Bulsār, India	B2	37
Bulukumba, Indon.	G7	32
Bumba, Zaire	A4	44
Bumping, stm., Wa., U.S.	C4	124
Buna, Tx., U.S.	D6	120
Bunbury, Austl.	F3	50
Buncombe, co., N.C., U.S.	f10	110
Buncrana, Ire.	F5	7
Bundaberg, Austl.	D10	50
Būndi, India	H6	38
Bundoran, Ire.	G4	7
Bungo-suidō, strt., Japan	I5	30
Bunia, Zaire	A6	44
Bunker Hill, Il., U.S.	D4	90
Bunker Hill, In., U.S.	C5	91
Bunker Hill, W.V., U.S.	B6	125
Bunker Hill, W.V., U.S.	m12	125
Bunker Hill, mtn., Nv., U.S.	D4	105
Bunkerville, Nv., U.S.	G7	105
Bunkie, La., U.S.	D3	95
Bunnell, Fl., U.S.	C5	86
Buñol, Spain	F11	12
Buntok, Indon.	F5	32
Buolkalach, Russia	C17	24
Buon Me Thuot, Viet.	H10	34
Buor-Chaja, Guba, b., Russia	C20	24
Buor-Chaja, Mys, c., Russia	C20	24
Bura, Kenya	B7	44
Burao, Som.	G4	46
Buras, La., U.S.	E6	95
Buraydah, Sau. Ar.	C3	46
Burbank, Ca., U.S.	E4	82
Burbank, Il., U.S.	k9	90
Burbank, Wa., U.S.	C7	124
Burdickville, R.I., U.S.	F2	116
Burdur, Tur.	H14	4
Burdwān, India	I12	38
Bureau, co., Il., U.S.	B4	90
Bureinskij Chrebet, mts., Russia	G20	24
Bureja, stm., Russia	G20	24
Burfjord, Nor.	B13	6
Burgas, Bul.	G11	16
Bur Gavo, Som.	B8	44
Burgaw, N.C., U.S.	C5	110
Burg [bei Magdeburg], Ger.	C11	8
Burgdorf, Switz.	E14	10
Burgeo, Newf., Can.	E3	72
Burgettstown, Pa., U.S.	F1	115
Burghausen, Ger.	G12	8
Burghūth, Sabkhat al-, l., Syria	B7	40
Burgin, China	B4	26
Burgin, Ky., U.S.	C5	94
Burglengenfeld, Ger.	F12	8
Burgos, Spain	C8	12
Burgsteinfurt, Ger.	C7	8
Burgundy see Bourgogne, hist. reg., Fr.	E11	10
Burhaniye, Tur.	J10	16
Burhānpur, India	B4	37
Burica, Punta, c., N.A.	E4	64
Burin, Newf., Can.	E4	72
Burin Peninsula, pen., Newf., Can.	E4	72
Buriram, Thai.	G7	34
Burjasot, Spain	F11	12
Burkburnett, Tx., U.S.	B3	120
Burke, S.D., U.S.	D6	118
Burke, co., Ga., U.S.	C4	87
Burke, co., N.C., U.S.	B1	110
Burke, co., N.D., U.S.	A3	111
Burke Channel, strt., B.C., Can.	C4	69
Burkesville, Ky., U.S.	D4	94
Burketown, Austl.	C7	50
Burkina Faso, ctry., Afr.	F5	42
Burk's Falls, Ont., Can.	B5	73
Burleigh, co., N.D., U.S.	C5	111
Burleson, Tx., U.S.	n9	120
Burleson, co., Tx., U.S.	D4	120
Burley, Id., U.S.	G5	89
Burlingame, Ca., U.S.	h8	82
Burlingame, Ks., U.S.	D8	93
Burlington, Ont., Can.	D5	73
Burlington, Co., U.S.	B8	83
Burlington, Ia., U.S.	D6	92
Burlington, Ks., U.S.	D8	93
Burlington, Ky., U.S.	A5	94
Burlington, Ma., U.S.	f11	98
Burlington, N.C., U.S.	A3	110
Burlington, N.D., U.S.	A4	111
Burlington, Vt., U.S.	C2	122
Burlington, Wa., U.S.	A3	124
Burlington, Wi., U.S.	F5	126
Burlington, co., N.J., U.S.	D3	107
Burlington Beach, In., U.S.	B3	91
Burlington Junction, Mo., U.S.	A2	102
Burma, ctry., Asia	A2	32
Burnaby, B.C., Can.	E6	69
Burnet, Tx., U.S.	D3	120
Burnet, co., Tx., U.S.	D3	120
Burnett, co., Wi., U.S.	C1	126
Burney, Ca., U.S.	B3	82
Burnham, Pa., U.S.	E6	115
Burnie, Austl.	H9	50
Burns, Or., U.S.	D7	114
Burns, Tn., U.S.	A4	119
Burns, Wy., U.S.	E8	127
Burns Flat, Ok., U.S.	B2	113
Burnside, Ky., U.S.	D5	94
Burns Paiute Indian Reservation, Or., U.S.	D7	114
Burnsville, Mn., U.S.	F5	100
Burnsville, Ms., U.S.	A5	101
Burnsville, N.C., U.S.	f10	110
Burnsville Lake, res., W.V., U.S.	C4	125
Burnt Islands, Newf., Can.	E2	72
Burnt Mills, Lake, l., Va., U.S.	k14	123
Burntside Lake, l., Mn., U.S.	C6	100
Burntwood, stm., Man., Can.	B2	70
Burravoe, Scot., U.K.	A11	7
Burr Oak, Mi., U.S.	G5	99
Burr Oak Reservoir, res., Oh., U.S.	C3	112
Burrton, Ks., U.S.	D6	93
Bursa, Tur.	G13	4
Būr Sa'īd (Port Said), Egypt	B12	42
Būr Sūdān (Port Sudan), Sudan	E13	42

Name	Map Ref	Page
Burt, co., Ne., U.S.	C9	104
Burt Lake, l., Mi., U.S.	C6	99
Burton, Mi., U.S.	F7	99
Burton, Oh., U.S.	A4	112
Burton upon Trent, Eng., U.K.	I11	7
Burtts Corner, N.B., Can.	C3	71
Buru, i., Indon.	F8	32
Burundi, ctry., Afr.	B5	44
Burwell, Ne., U.S.	C6	104
Burwick, Scot., U.K.	C10	7
Bury Saint Edmunds, Eng., U.K.	I13	7
Busalla, Italy	E3	14
Buşayrah, Syria	B7	40
Bushnell, Fl., U.S.	D4	86
Bushnell, Il., U.S.	C3	90
Bush River, b., Md., U.S.	B5	97
Buşrá ash-Shām, Syria	C5	40
Busselton, Austl.	F3	50
Busto Arsizio, Italy	D3	14
Busuanga Island, i., Phil.	C7	32
Buta, Zaire	H10	42
Butare, Rw.	B5	44
Butehaqi, China	B11	26
Bute Inlet, b., B.C., Can.	D5	69
Butler, Al., U.S.	C1	78
Butler, Ga., U.S.	D2	87
Butler, In., U.S.	B8	91
Butler, Ky., U.S.	B5	94
Butler, Mo., U.S.	C3	102
Butler, N.J., U.S.	B4	107
Butler, Oh., U.S.	B3	112
Butler, Pa., U.S.	E2	115
Butler, Wi., U.S.	m11	126
Butler, co., Al., U.S.	D3	78
Butler, co., Ia., U.S.	B5	92
Butler, co., Ks., U.S.	E7	93
Butler, co., Ky., U.S.	C3	94
Butler, co., Mo., U.S.	E7	102
Butler, co., Ne., U.S.	C8	104
Butler, co., Oh., U.S.	C1	112
Butler, co., Pa., U.S.	E2	115
Butner, N.C., U.S.	A4	110
Buttahatchee, stm., U.S.	B5	101
Butte, Mt., U.S.	E4	103
Butte, co., Ca., U.S.	C3	82
Butte, co., Id., U.S.	F5	89
Butte, co., S.D., U.S.	C2	118
Butte des Morts, Lake, l., Wi., U.S.	D5	126
Butte Mountains, mts., Nv., U.S.	D6	105
Butternut Lake, l., Wi., U.S.	C5	126
Butterworth, Malay.	L6	34
Butt of Lewis, c., Scot., U.K.	C6	7
Buttonwillow, Ca., U.S.	E4	82
Butts, co., Ga., U.S.	C3	87
Butuan, Phil.	D8	32
Butung, Pulau, i., Indon.	F7	32
Bützow, Ger.	B11	8
Buxtehude, Ger.	B9	8
Buxton, N.C., U.S.	B7	110
Büyükmenderes, stm., Tur.	L11	16
Buzançais, Fr.	F8	10
Buzău, Rom.	D10	16
Búzi, stm., Moz.	F6	44
Buzuluk, Russia	G8	22
Buzzards Bay, Ma., U.S.	C6	98
Buzzards Bay, b., Ma., U.S.	C6	98
Byam Channel, strt., N.W. Ter., Can.	A11	66
Byam Martin Island, i., N.W. Ter., Can.	A12	66
Bydgoszcz, Pol.	B18	8
Byers, Co., U.S.	B6	83
Byesville, Oh., U.S.	C4	112
Byhalia, Ms., U.S.	A4	101
Bylas, Az., U.S.	D5	80
Bylot Island, i., N.W. Ter., Can.	B17	66
Byng, Ok., U.S.	C5	113
Byrdstown, Tn., U.S.	C8	119
Byron, Ga., U.S.	D3	87
Byron, Il., U.S.	A4	90
Byron, Mn., U.S.	F6	100
Byron, Wy., U.S.	B4	127
Byrranga, Gory, mts., Russia	B14	24
Bytantaj, stm., Russia	D20	24
Bytom (Beuthen), Pol.	E18	8
Byxelkrok, Swe.	H11	6

C

Name	Map Ref	Page
Caacupé, Para.	B5	56
Cabaiguán, Cuba	C8	64
Caballo Mountains, mts., N.M., U.S.	E2	108
Caballo Reservoir, res., N.M., U.S.	E2	108
Cabanatuan, Phil.	q19	32
Cabano, Que., Can.	B9	74
Cabarrus, co., N.C., U.S.	B2	110
Cabbage Swamp, sw., Fl., U.S.	m9	86
Cabell, co., W.V., U.S.	C2	125
Cabeza del Buey, Spain	G6	12
Cabimas, Ven.	B7	58
Cabin Creek, W.V., U.S.	m13	125
Cabin Creek, stm., W.V., U.S.	m13	125
Cabinda, Ang.	C2	44
Cabinda, dept., Ang.	C2	44
Cabinet Gorge Reservoir, res., U.S.	B1	103
Cabinet Mountains, mts., Mt., U.S.	B1	103
Cabin John, Md., U.S.	C3	97
Cabo Frio, Braz.	G7	57
Cabonga, Réservoir, res., Que., Can.	k11	74
Cabool, Mo., U.S.	D5	102
Caborca, Mex.	B3	62
Cabot, Ar., U.S.	C3	81
Cabot, Mount, mtn., N.H., U.S.	A4	106
Cabot Head, c., Ont., Can.	B3	73
Cabot Strait, strt., Can.	G21	66
Cabra, Spain	H7	12
Cabri, Sask., Can.	G1	75
Cabrillo National Monument, Ca., U.S.	o15	82
Cabrobó, Braz.	E11	54
Cabruta, Ven.	D9	58
Caçador, Braz.	B6	56
Čačak, Yugo.	F4	16
Cacapon, stm., W.V., U.S.	B6	125
Cáceres, Braz.	G7	54
Cáceres, Col.	D5	58
Cáceres, Spain	F5	12
Cache, Ok., U.S.	C3	113
Cache, co., Ut., U.S.	B4	121
Cache, stm., Ar., U.S.	C4	81
Cache, stm., Il., U.S.	F4	90
Cache Bay, Ont., Can.	A5	73
Cache Creek, B.C., Can.	D7	69
Cache la Poudre, stm., Co., U.S.	A5	83
Cache Mountain, mtn., Ak., U.S.	B10	79
Cache Peak, mtn., Id., U.S.	G5	89
Cachimbo, Serra do, mts., Braz.	E7	54
Cachoeira, Braz.	B9	57
Cachoeira do Sul, Braz.	C6	56
Cachoeiro de Itapemirim, Braz.	F8	57
Cacólo, Ang.	D3	44
Caconda, Ang.	D3	44
Cactus Flat, pl., Nv., U.S.	F5	105
Cactus Peak, mtn., Nv., U.S.	F5	105
Caddo, Ok., U.S.	C5	113
Caddo, co., La., U.S.	B2	95
Caddo, co., Ok., U.S.	B3	113
Caddo, stm., Ar., U.S.	C2	81
Caddo Creek, stm., Ok., U.S.	C4	113
Caddo Lake, l., U.S.	B2	95
Cader Idris, mtn., Wales, U.K.	I9	7
Cadillac, Fr.	H6	10
Cadillac, Mi., U.S.	D5	99
Cadillac Mountain, mtn., Me., U.S.	D4	96
Cádiz, Spain	I5	12
Cadiz, Ky., U.S.	D2	94
Cadiz, Oh., U.S.	B4	112
Cádiz, Golfo de, b., Eur.	I4	12
Cadott, Wi., U.S.	D2	126
Caen, Fr.	C6	10
Caernarvon, Wales, U.K.	H8	7
Caesar Creek Lake, res., Oh., U.S.	C2	112
Caeté, Braz.	E7	57
Cagayan de Oro, Phil.	D7	32
Cagayan Islands, is., Phil.	D7	32
Çagda, Russia	F20	24
Cagli, Italy	F7	14
Cagliari, Italy	J4	14
Caguas, P.R.	E14	64
Cahaba, stm., Al., U.S.	C2	78
Caha Mountains, mts., Ire.	J3	7
Cahirciveen, Ire.	J2	7
Cahokia, Il., U.S.	E3	90
Cahore Point, c., Ire.	I6	7
Cahors, Fr.	H8	10
Caiapó, Serra, mts., Braz.	D2	57
Caibarién, Cuba	C8	64
Caicara, Ven.	D9	58
Caicos Islands, is., T./C. Is.	D12	64
Caicos Passage, strt., N.A.	C11	64
Caillou Bay, b., La., U.S.	E5	95
Caillou Lake, l., La., U.S.	E5	95
Cairnbrook, Pa., U.S.	F4	115
Cairngorm Mountains, mts., Scot., U.K.	D9	7
Cairns, Austl.	C9	50
Cairo, Ga., U.S.	F2	87
Cairo, Il., U.S.	F4	90
Cairo, N.Y., U.S.	D7	104
Cairo see Al-Qāhirah, Egypt	B12	42
Caiundo, Ang.	E3	44
Cajamarca, Peru	E3	54
Cajàzeiras, Braz.	E11	54
Calabar, Nig.	H7	42
Calabozo, Ven.	C9	58
Calahorra, Spain	C10	12
Calais, Fr.	B8	10
Calais, Me., U.S.	C5	96
Calais, Pas de (Strait of Dover), strt., Eur.	K14	7
Calamar, Col.	B5	58
Calamian Group, is., Phil.	C6	32
Calamocha, Spain	E10	12
Calamus, stm., Ne., U.S.	B6	104
Calanda, Spain	E11	12
Calapan, Phil.	r19	33b
Călăraşi, Rom.	E11	16
Calatayud, Spain	D10	12
Calaveras, co., Ca., U.S.	C3	82
Calcasieu, co., La., U.S.	D2	95
Calcasieu, stm., La., U.S.	D2	95
Calcasieu Lake, l., La., U.S.	E2	95
Calcasieu Pass, strt., La., U.S.	E2	95
Calcoene, Braz.	C8	54
Calcutta, India	I13	38
Calcutta, Oh., U.S.	B5	112
Calcutta Lake, l., Nv., U.S.	B2	105
Caldas da Rainha, Port.	F2	12
Calderwood, Tn., U.S.	D10	119
Caldron Falls Reservoir, res., Wi., U.S.	C5	126
Caldwell, Id., U.S.	F2	89
Caldwell, Ks., U.S.	E6	93
Caldwell, N.J., U.S.	B4	107
Caldwell, Oh., U.S.	C4	112
Caldwell, Tx., U.S.	D4	120
Caldwell, co., Ky., U.S.	C2	94
Caldwell, co., La., U.S.	B3	95
Caldwell, co., Mo., U.S.	B3	102
Caldwell, co., N.C., U.S.	B1	110
Caldwell, co., Tx., U.S.	E4	120
Caledon, Ont., Can.	D5	73
Caledonia, Mi., U.S.	F5	99
Caledonia, Mn., U.S.	G7	100
Caledonia, N.Y., U.S.	C3	109
Caledonia, co., Vt., U.S.	B4	122
Calera, Al., U.S.	B3	78
Calexico, Ca., U.S.	F6	82
Calgary, Alta., Can.	D3	68
Calhoun, Ga., U.S.	B2	87
Calhoun, Ky., U.S.	C2	94
Calhoun, co., Al., U.S.	B4	78
Calhoun, co., Ar., U.S.	D3	81
Calhoun, co., Fl., U.S.	B1	86
Calhoun, co., Ga., U.S.	E2	87
Calhoun, co., Il., U.S.	D3	90
Calhoun, co., Ia., U.S.	B3	92
Calhoun, co., Mi., U.S.	F5	99
Calhoun, co., Ms., U.S.	B4	101
Calhoun, co., S.C., U.S.	D6	117
Calhoun, co., Tx., U.S.	E4	120
Calhoun, co., W.V., U.S.	C3	125
Calhoun City, Ms., U.S.	B4	101
Calhoun Falls, S.C., U.S.	C2	117
Cali, Col.	F4	58
Calico Rock, Ar., U.S.	A3	81
Caliente, Nv., U.S.	F7	105
Calicut, India	G3	37
California, Mo., U.S.	C5	102
California, Pa., U.S.	F2	115
California, state, U.S.	D4	82
California, Golfo de, b., Mex.	D4	62
California Aqueduct, Ca., U.S.	E4	82
Calimere, Point, c., India	G5	37
Calipatria, Ca., U.S.	F6	82
Calispell Peak, mtn., Wa., U.S.	A8	124
Calistoga, Ca., U.S.	C2	82
Calitri, Italy	I10	14
Callac, Fr.	D3	10
Callaghan, Mount, mtn., Nv., U.S.	D5	105
Callahan, co., Tx., U.S.	C3	120
Callao, Peru	F3	54
Callaway, co., Mo., U.S.	C6	102
Calling Lake, l., Alta., Can.	B4	68
Calloway, co., Ky., U.S.	f9	94
Callosa de Ensarriá, Spain	G11	12
Calmar, Alta., Can.	C4	68
Calmar, Ia., U.S.	A6	92
Caloosahatchee, stm., Fl., U.S.	F5	86
Caltagirone, Italy	L9	14
Caltanissetta, Italy	L9	14
Calumet, Mi., U.S.	A2	99
Calumet, co., Wi., U.S.	D5	126
Calumet, Lake, l., Il., U.S.	k9	90
Calumet City, Il., U.S.	B6	90
Calunda, Ang.	D4	44
Calvert, Tx., U.S.	D4	120
Calvert, co., Md., U.S.	C4	97
Calvert City, Ky., U.S.	e9	94
Calverton, Md., U.S.	*B4	97
Calverton Park, Mo., U.S.	f13	102
Calvinia, S. Afr.	H3	44
Camacho, Mex.	E8	62
Camacupa, Ang.	D3	44
Camaguán, Ven.	C9	58
Camagüey, Cuba	D9	64
Camaná, Peru	G4	54
Camanche, Ia., U.S.	C7	92
Camano Island, i., Wa., U.S.	A3	124
Cam Ranh, Viet.	I10	34
Camaquã, Braz.	C6	56
Camas, Wa., U.S.	D3	124
Camas, co., Id., U.S.	F4	89
Cambados, Spain	C3	12
Cambay, India	I5	38
Cambodia (Kampuchea), ctry., Asia	C3	32
Cambrai, Fr.	B10	10
Cambria, Ca., U.S.	E3	82
Cambria, Wi., U.S.	E4	126
Cambria, co., Pa., U.S.	E4	115
Cambrian Mountains, mts., Wales, U.K.	I9	7
Cambridge, Ont., Can.	D4	73
Cambridge, Eng., U.K.	I13	7
Cambridge, Il., U.S.	B3	90
Cambridge, Ia., U.S.	C4	92
Cambridge, Md., U.S.	C5	97
Cambridge, Ma., U.S.	B5	98
Cambridge, Mn., U.S.	E5	100
Cambridge, Ne., U.S.	D5	104
Cambridge, N.Y., U.S.	B7	109
Cambridge, Oh., U.S.	B4	112
Cambridge, Wi., U.S.	F4	126
Cambridge Bay, N.W. Ter., Can.	C11	66
Cambridge City, In., U.S.	E7	91
Cambridge Reservoir, res., Ma., U.S.	g10	98
Cambridge Springs, Pa., U.S.	C1	115
Cambuci, Braz.	F8	57
Camden, Al., U.S.	D2	78
Camden, Ar., U.S.	D3	81
Camden, De., U.S.	D3	85
Camden, In., U.S.	C4	91
Camden, Me., U.S.	D3	96
Camden, N.J., U.S.	D2	107
Camden, N.Y., U.S.	B5	109
Camden, Oh., U.S.	C1	112
Camden, S.C., U.S.	C6	117
Camden, Tn., U.S.	A3	119
Camden, co., Ga., U.S.	F5	87
Camden, co., Mo., U.S.	C5	102
Camden, co., N.J., U.S.	D3	107
Camden, co., N.C., U.S.	A6	110
Camdenton, Mo., U.S.	D5	102
Camelback Mountain, mtn., Az., U.S.	k9	80
Cameron, Az., U.S.	B4	80
Cameron, La., U.S.	E2	95
Cameron, Mo., U.S.	B3	102
Cameron, Tx., U.S.	D4	120
Cameron, W.V., U.S.	B4	125
Cameron, Wi., U.S.	C2	126
Cameron, co., La., U.S.	E2	95
Cameron, co., Pa., U.S.	D5	115
Cameron, co., Tx., U.S.	F4	120
Cameron Highlands, Malay.	L6	34
Cameron Hills, hills, Can.	E9	66
Cameroon, ctry., Afr.	G8	42
Cameroon Mountain, mtn., Cam.	H7	42
Cametá, Braz.	D9	54
Camilla, Ga., U.S.	E2	87
Camino, Ca., U.S.	C3	82
Camiranga, Braz.	D9	54
Camissombo, Ang.	C4	44
Cam Lo, Viet.	F9	34
Cammack Village, Ar., U.S.	C3	81
Camooweal, Austl.	C7	50
Camorta Island, i., India	J2	34
Camp, co., Tx., U.S.	C5	120
Campana, Isla, i., Chile	F1	56
Campanero, Cerro, mtn., Ven.	E10	58
Campbell, Ca., U.S.	k8	82
Campbell, Fl., U.S.	D5	86
Campbell, Mo., U.S.	E7	102
Campbell, Oh., U.S.	A5	112
Campbell, co., Ky., U.S.	B5	94
Campbell, co., S.D., U.S.	B5	118
Campbell, co., Tn., U.S.	C9	119
Campbell, co., Va., U.S.	C3	123
Campbell, co., Wy., U.S.	B7	127
Campbellford, Ont., Can.	C7	73
Campbell Hill, hill, Oh., U.S.	B2	112
Campbell Lake, l., Or., U.S.	E7	114
Campbellsburg, In., U.S.	G5	91
Campbellsburg, Ky., U.S.	B4	94
Campbellsport, Wi., U.S.	E5	126
Campbellsville, Ky., U.S.	C4	94
Campbellton, N.B., Can.	A3	71
Campbellton, Newf., Can.	D4	72
Campbeltown, Scot., U.K.	F7	7
Campeche, Mex.	H14	62
Campeche, Bahía de, b., Mex.	H13	62
Camperville, Man., Can.	D1	70
Camp Hill, Al., U.S.	C4	78
Camp Hill, Pa., U.S.	F8	115
Camp H. M. Smith Marine Corps Base, mil., Hi., U.S.	g10	88
Camp Howard Ridge, mtn., Id., U.S.	D2	89
Campina Grande, Braz.	E11	54
Campinas, Braz.	G5	57
Camp Lejeune Marine Corps Base, mil., N.C., U.S.	C5	110
Campoalegre, Col.	F5	58
Campo Alegre de Goiás, Braz.	D5	57
Campobasso, Italy	H9	14
Campobello Island, i., N.B., Can.	E3	71
Campo Belo, Braz.	F6	57
Campo de Criptana, Spain	F8	12
Campo de la Cruz, Col.	B5	58
Campo Grande, Braz.	F1	57
Campo Maior, Braz.	D10	54
Campos, Braz.	F8	57
Campos do Jordão, Braz.	G6	57
Camp Pendleton Marine Corps Base, mil., Ca., U.S.	F5	82
Camp Point, Il., U.S.	C2	90
Camp Springs, Md., U.S.	f9	97
Campti, La., U.S.	C2	95
Campton, N.H., U.S.	C3	106
Camp Verde, Az., U.S.	C4	80
Camp Verde Indian Reservation, Az., U.S.	C4	80
Cam Ranh, Viet.	I10	34
Camrose, Alta., Can.	C4	68
Canaan, Ct., U.S.	A2	84
Canaan, N.H., U.S.	C2	106
Canaan, stm., N.B., Can.	C4	71
Canada, ctry., N.A.	D14	66
Canada Bay, b., Newf., Can.	C3	72
Canada Falls Lake, res., Me., U.S.	C2	96
Canadensis, Pa., U.S.	D11	115
Canadian, Tx., U.S.	B2	120
Canadian, co., Ok., U.S.	B3	113
Canadian, stm., U.S.	D6	76
Canajoharie, N.Y., U.S.	C6	109
Çanakkale, Tur.	G13	4
Çanakkale Boğazı (Dardanelles), strt., Tur.	I10	16
Canal Flats, B.C., Can.	D10	69
Canal Fulton, Oh., U.S.	B4	112
Canal Winchester, Oh., U.S.	C3	112
Canandaigua, N.Y., U.S.	C3	109
Canandaigua Lake, l., N.Y., U.S.	C3	109
Cananea, Mex.	B4	62
Cañar, Ec.	I3	58
Canarias, Islas (Canary Islands), is., Spain	C2	42
Canary Islands see Canarias, Islas, is., Spain	C2	42
Cañas, C.R.	I5	64
Canastota, N.Y., U.S.	B5	109
Canaveral, Cape, c., Fl., U.S.	D6	86
Canaveral National Seashore, Fl., U.S.	D6	86
Canavieiras, Braz.	C9	57
Canberra, Austl.	G9	50
Canby, Mn., U.S.	F2	100
Canby, Or., U.S.	B4	114
Cancale, Fr.	D5	10
Cancon, Fr.	H7	10
Cancún, Mex.	G16	62
Candeleda, Spain	E6	12
Candiac, Que., Can.	q19	74
Candle Lake, l., Sask., Can.	D3	75
Candler, co., Ga., U.S.	D4	87
Candlewood, Lake, l., Ct., U.S.	D1	84
Candlewood Isle, Ct., U.S.	D2	84
Candlewood Shores, Ct., U.S.	D2	84
Cando, N.D., U.S.	A6	111
Candor, N.C., U.S.	B3	110
Cane, stm., La., U.S.	C2	95
Cañete, Spain	E10	12
Caney, Ks., U.S.	E8	93
Caney, stm., Ok., U.S.	A5	113
Caney Creek, stm., Tx., U.S.	r14	120
Caney Fork, stm., Tn., U.S.	C8	119
Canfield, Oh., U.S.	A5	112
Canfranc, Spain	C11	12
Cangas de Onís, Spain	B6	12
Cangombe, Ang.	D3	44
Canguçu, Braz.	C6	56
Cangzhou, China	D10	26
Caniapiscau, stm., Que., Can.	g13	74
Caniapiscau, Lac, l., Que., Can.	F19	66
Canicattì, Italy	L8	14
Canistear Reservoir, res., N.J., U.S.	A4	107
Canisteo, N.Y., U.S.	C3	109
Canisteo, stm., N.Y., U.S.	C3	109
Canistota, S.D., U.S.	D8	118
Cañitas, Mex.	F8	62
Çankırı, Tur.	G14	4
Canmore, Alta., Can.	D3	68
Cannanore, India	G3	37
Cannelton, In., U.S.	I4	91
Cannes, Fr.	I14	10
Canning, N.S., Can.	D5	71
Cannon, co., Tn., U.S.	B5	119
Cannon, stm., Mn., U.S.	F5	100
Cannon Air Force Base, mil., N.M., U.S.	C6	108
Cannonball, stm., N.D., U.S.	C5	111
Cannon Beach, Or., U.S.	B3	114
Cannondale, Ct., U.S.	E2	84
Cannon Falls, Mn., U.S.	F6	100
Cannonsburg, Ky., U.S.	B7	94
Canon, Ga., U.S.	B3	87
Canon City, Co., U.S.	C5	83
Canonsburg, Pa., U.S.	F1	115
Canosa [di Puglia], Italy	H11	14
Cantábrica, Cordillera, mts., Spain	B7	12
Cantalejo, Spain	D8	12
Cantanhede, Port.	E3	12
Cantaura, Ven.	C10	58
Canterbury, Eng., U.K.	J14	7
Canterbury, De., U.S.	D3	85
Canterbury Bight, N.Z.	F3	52
Can Tho, Viet.	I8	34
Canton, Ct., U.S.	B4	84
Canton, Ga., U.S.	B2	87
Canton, Il., U.S.	C3	90
Canton, Ks., U.S.	D6	93
Canton, Ma., U.S.	B5	98
Canton, Ms., U.S.	C3	101
Canton, Mo., U.S.	A6	102
Canton, N.Y., U.S.	f9	109
Canton, N.C., U.S.	f10	110
Canton, Oh., U.S.	B4	112
Canton, Ok., U.S.	A3	113
Canton, Pa., U.S.	C8	115
Canton, S.D., U.S.	D9	118
Canton, Tx., U.S.	C5	120
Canton see Guangzhou, China	L2	28
Canton Lake, res., Ok., U.S.	A3	113
Cantonment, Fl., U.S.	u14	86
Cantù, Italy	D4	14
Canutillo, Tx., U.S.	o11	120
Canyon, Tx., U.S.	B2	120
Canyon, co., Id., U.S.	F2	89
Canyon City, Or., U.S.	C8	114
Canyon de Chelly National Monument, Az., U.S.	A6	80
Canyon Ferry Lake, res., Mt., U.S.	D5	103
Canyon Lake, Tx., U.S.	E3	120
Canyon Lake, res., Tx., U.S.	E3	120
Canyonlands National Park, Ut., U.S.	E6	121
Canyonville, Or., U.S.	E3	114
Cao Bang, Viet.	C9	34
Capac, Mi., U.S.	F8	99
Cap-à-l'Aigle, Que., Can.	B7	74
Cap-aux-Meules, Que., Can.	B8	71
Cap-de-la-Madeleine, Que., Can.	C5	74
Cape Breton Highlands National Park, N.S., Can.	C9	71
Cape Breton Island, i., N.S., Can.	C9	71
Cape Broyle, Newf., Can.	E5	72
Cape Canaveral, Fl., U.S.	D6	86
Cape Charles, Va., U.S.	C6	123
Cape Coast, Ghana	G5	42
Cape Cod Bay, b., Ma., U.S.	C7	98
Cape Cod National Seashore, Ma., U.S.	C6	98
Cape Coral, Fl., U.S.	F5	86
Cape Dorset, N.W. Ter., Can.	D17	66
Cape Elizabeth, Me., U.S.	E2	96
Cape Fear, stm., N.C., U.S.	C4	110
Cape Girardeau, Mo., U.S.	D8	102
Cape Girardeau, co., Mo., U.S.	D8	102
Cape Hatteras National Seashore, N.C., U.S.	B7	110
Cape Horn Mountain, mtn., Id., U.S.	E3	89
Cape Island, i., S.C., U.S.	E9	117
Cape Lookout National Seashore, N.C., U.S.	C6	110
Cape May, N.J., U.S.	F3	107
Cape May, co., N.J., U.S.	E3	107
Cape May Court House, N.J., U.S.	E3	107
Capers Inlet, b., S.C., U.S.	k12	117
Capers Island, i., S.C., U.S.	G6	117
Capers Island, i., S.C., U.S.	F8	117
Cape Sable Island, i., N.S., Can.	F4	71
Cape Town (Kaapstad), S. Afr.	H3	44
Cape Verde, ctry., Afr.	E11	2
Cape York Peninsula, pen., Austl.	B8	50
Cap-Haïtien, Haiti	E11	64
Capim, stm., Braz.	D9	54
Capitan, N.M., U.S.	D4	108
Capitan Mountains, mts., N.M., U.S.	D4	108
Capitan Peak, mtn., N.M., U.S.	D4	108
Capitol Heights, Ia., U.S.	e8	92
Capitol Heights, Md., U.S.	C4	97
Capitol Peak, mtn., Nv., U.S.	B4	105
Capitol Reef National Park, Ut., U.S.	E4	121
Čapljina, Bos.	F12	14
Cap-Pelé, N.B., Can.	C5	71
Capreol, Ont., Can.	p19	73
Capri, Italy	I9	14
Caprivi Strip, hist. reg., Nmb.	E4	44
Cap-Rouge, Que., Can.	n17	74
Capron, Va., U.S.	D5	123
Captain Cook, Hi., U.S.	D6	88
Captieux, Fr.	H6	10
Captiva, Fl., U.S.	F4	86
Captiva Island, i., Fl., U.S.	F4	86
Capua, Italy	H9	14
Capulin Volcano National Monument, N.M., U.S.	A6	108
Caquetá (Japurá), stm., S.A.	D5	54
Çara, Russia	F17	24
Çara, stm., Russia	F17	24
Caracaraí, Braz.	C6	54
Caracas, Ven.	B9	58
Carajás, Serra dos, mts., Braz.	E8	54
Carangola, Braz.	F7	57
Caraquet, N.B., Can.	B5	71

Name	Map Ref	Page
Caratasca, Laguna de, b., Hond.	G6	64
Caratinga, Braz.	E7	57
Carauari, Braz.	D5	54
Caravaca, Spain	G10	12
Caravelas, Braz.	D9	57
Caraway, Ar., U.S.	B5	81
Carballo, Spain	B3	12
Carberry, Man., Can.	E2	70
Carbon, co., Mt., U.S.	E7	103
Carbon, co., Pa., U.S.	D10	115
Carbon, co., Ut., U.S.	D5	121
Carbon, co., Wy., U.S.	E5	127
Carbondale, Co., U.S.	B3	83
Carbondale, Il., U.S.	F4	90
Carbondale, Ks., U.S.	D8	93
Carbondale, Pa., U.S.	C10	115
Carbonear, Newf., Can.	E5	72
Carboneras de Guadazaon, Spain	F10	12
Carbon Hill, Al., U.S.	B2	78
Carbonia, Italy	J3	14
Carcagente, Spain	F11	12
Carcassonne, Fr.	I9	10
Carcross, Yukon, Can.	D6	66
Cárdenas, Cuba	C7	64
Cárdenas, Mex.	F10	62
Cardiff, Wales, U.K.	J9	7
Cardigan, Wales, U.K.	I8	7
Cardigan Bay, b., P.E.I., Can.	C7	71
Cardigan Bay, b., Wales, U.K.	I8	7
Cardinal, Ont., Can.	C9	73
Cardington, Oh., U.S.	B3	112
Cardston, Alta., Can.	E4	68
Cardwell, Mo., U.S.	E7	102
Cardžou, Turk.	J10	22
Carencro, La., U.S.	D3	95
Carentan, Fr.	C5	10
Caretta, W.V., U.S.	D3	125
Carey, Id., U.S.	F5	89
Carey, Oh., U.S.	B2	112
Carey, Lake, l., Austl.	E4	50
Caribbean Sea	G10	64
Cariboo Mountains, mts., B.C., Can.	C7	69
Caribou, Me., U.S.	B5	96
Caribou, co., Id., U.S.	G7	89
Caribou Island, i., N.S., Can.	D7	71
Caribou Lake, l., Me., U.S.	C3	96
Caribou Mountain, mtn., Id., U.S.	F7	89
Caribou Mountains, mts., Alta., Can.	f7	68
Caribou Range, mts., Id., U.S.	F7	89
Carignan, Fr.	C12	10
Cariñena, Spain	D10	12
Carinhanha, Braz.	C7	57
Carini, Italy	K8	14
Caripito, Ven.	B11	58
Carl Blackwell, Lake, res., Ok., U.S.	A4	113
Carleton, Mi., U.S.	F7	99
Carleton, Mount, mtn., N.B., Can.	B3	71
Carleton Place, Ont., Can.	B8	73
Carlin, Nv., U.S.	C5	105
Carlinville, Il., U.S.	D4	90
Carlisle, Eng., U.K.	G10	7
Carlisle, Ar., U.S.	C4	81
Carlisle, In., U.S.	G3	91
Carlisle, Ia., U.S.	C4	92
Carlisle, Ky., U.S.	B5	94
Carlisle, Oh., U.S.	C1	112
Carlisle, Pa., U.S.	F7	115
Carlisle, co., Ky., U.S.	f8	94
Carl Junction, Mo., U.S.	D3	102
Carlow, Ire.	I6	7
Carlsbad, Ca., U.S.	F5	82
Carlsbad, N.M., U.S.	E5	108
Carlsbad Caverns National Park, N.M., U.S.	E5	108
Carlstadt, N.J., U.S.	h8	107
Carlton, Mn., U.S.	D6	100
Carlton, Or., U.S.	B3	114
Carlton, co., Mn., U.S.	D6	100
Carlyle, Il., U.S.	E4	90
Carlyle Lake, res., Il., U.S.	E4	90
Carmacks, Yukon, Can.	D5	66
Carmagnola, Italy	E2	14
Carman, Man., Can.	E2	70
Carmanville, Newf., Can.	D4	72
Carmarthen, Wales, U.K.	J8	7
Carmaux, Fr.	H9	10
Carmel, Ca., U.S.	D3	82
Carmel, In., U.S.	E5	91
Carmel, N.Y., U.S.	D7	109
Carmel Head, c., Wales, U.K.	H8	7
Carmen, Isla, i., Mex.	E4	62
Carmen, Isla del, i., Mex.	H14	62
Carmen de Patagones, Arg.	E4	56
Carmi, Il., U.S.	E5	90
Carmi, Lake, l., Vt., U.S.	B3	122
Carmona, Spain	H6	12
Carnarvon, Austl.	D2	50
Carnarvon, S. Afr.	H4	44
Carnation, Wa., U.S.	B4	124
Carndonagh, Ire.	F5	7
Carnegie, Ok., U.S.	B3	113
Carnegie, Pa., U.S.	F1	115
Carnegie, Lake, l., Austl.	E4	50
Carneys Point, N.J., U.S.	D2	107
Carniche, Alpi, mts., Eur.	C8	14
Car Nicobar Island, i., India	J2	34
Carnsore Point, c., Ire.	I6	7
Caro, Mi., U.S.	E7	99
Carol City, Fl., U.S.	s13	86
Caroleen, N.C., U.S.	B1	110
Carolina, Braz.	E9	54
Carolina, Col.	D5	58
Carolina, R.I., U.S.	F2	116
Carolina, W.V., U.S.	k10	125
Carolina Beach, N.C., U.S.	C5	110
Caroline, co., Md., U.S.	C6	97
Caroline, co., Va., U.S.	C5	123
Caroní, stm., Ven.	D11	58
Carora, Ven.	B7	58
Carpathian Mountains, mts., Eur.	F12	4
Carpații Meridionali, mts., Rom.	D8	16
Carpentaria, Gulf of, b., Austl.	B7	50
Carpenter Dam, Ar., U.S.	g7	81
Carpentersville, Il., U.S.	A5	90
Carpentras, Fr.	H12	10
Carpi, Italy	E5	14
Carpinteria, Ca., U.S.	E4	82
Carquefou, Fr.	E5	10
Carrabelle, Fl., U.S.	C2	86
Carrara, Italy	E5	14
Carrauntoohill, mtn., Ire.	I3	7
Carrboro, N.C., U.S.	B3	110
Carreta, Punta, c., Peru	F3	54
Carrickfergus, N. Ire., U.K.	G7	7
Carrickmacross, Ire.	H6	7
Carrie, Mount, mtn., Wa., U.S.	B2	124
Carriere, Ms., U.S.	E4	101
Carrier Mills, Il., U.S.	F5	90
Carrillo, Mex.	D8	62
Carrington, N.D., U.S.	B6	111
Carrington Island, i., Ut., U.S.	C3	121
Carrión de los Condes, Spain	C7	12
Carrizo Creek, stm., U.S.	A1	120
Carrizo Mountain, mtn., N.M., U.S.	D4	108
Carrizo Mountains, mts., U.S.	A6	80
Carrizo Springs, Tx., U.S.	*E3	120
Carrizozo, N.M., U.S.	D4	108
Carroll, Ia., U.S.	B3	92
Carroll, co., Ar., U.S.	A2	81
Carroll, co., Ga., U.S.	C1	87
Carroll, co., Il., U.S.	A4	90
Carroll, co., In., U.S.	C4	91
Carroll, co., Ia., U.S.	B3	92
Carroll, co., Ky., U.S.	B4	94
Carroll, co., Md., U.S.	A3	97
Carroll, co., Ms., U.S.	B4	101
Carroll, co., Mo., U.S.	B4	102
Carroll, co., N.H., U.S.	C4	106
Carroll, co., Oh., U.S.	B4	112
Carroll, co., Tn., U.S.	B3	119
Carroll, co., Va., U.S.	D2	123
Carrollton, Al., U.S.	B1	78
Carrollton, Ga., U.S.	C1	87
Carrollton, Il., U.S.	D3	90
Carrollton, Ky., U.S.	B4	94
Carrollton, Mi., U.S.	E7	99
Carrollton, Mo., U.S.	B4	102
Carrollton, Oh., U.S.	B4	112
Carrolltown, Pa., U.S.	E4	115
Carrot, stm., Can.	B8	75
Carry Falls Reservoir, res., N.Y., U.S.	f10	109
Čarsk, Kaz.	H10	24
Carson, Ca., U.S.	n12	82
Carson, Wa., U.S.	D4	124
Carson, co., Tx., U.S.	B2	120
Carson, stm., Nv., U.S.	D2	105
Carson City, Mi., U.S.	E6	99
Carson City, Nv., U.S.	D2	105
Carson Lake, l., Nv., U.S.	D3	105
Carson Sink, l., Nv., U.S.	D3	105
Carson Spring, Tn., U.S.	D10	119
Carstairs, Alta., Can.	D3	68
Carswell Air Force Base, mil., Tx., U.S.	n9	120
Cartagena, Col.	B5	58
Cartagena, Spain	H11	12
Cartago, Col.	E5	58
Cartago, C.R.	J6	64
Carter, co., Ky., U.S.	B6	94
Carter, co., Mo., U.S.	E7	102
Carter, co., Mt., U.S.	E12	103
Carter, co., Ok., U.S.	C4	113
Carter, co., Tn., U.S.	C11	119
Carteret, N.J., U.S.	B4	107
Carteret, co., N.C., U.S.	C6	110
Carter Lake, Ia., U.S.	C2	92
Carter Mountain, mtn., Wy., U.S.	B3	127
Carters Lake, res., Ga., U.S.	B2	87
Cartersville, Ga., U.S.	B2	87
Carterville, Il., U.S.	F4	90
Carterville, Mo., U.S.	D3	102
Carthage, Il., U.S.	C2	90
Carthage, In., U.S.	E6	91
Carthage, Ms., U.S.	C4	101
Carthage, Mo., U.S.	D3	102
Carthage, N.Y., U.S.	B5	109
Carthage, N.C., U.S.	B3	110
Carthage, Tn., U.S.	C8	119
Carthage, Tx., U.S.	C5	120
Cartier Island, i., Austl.	B4	50
Cartwright, Newf., Can.	B3	72
Cartwright, Ok., U.S.	D5	113
Caruaru, Braz.	E11	54
Carúpano, Ven.	B11	58
Caruthersville, Mo., U.S.	E8	102
Carver, Ma., U.S.	C6	98
Carver, Mn., U.S.	F5	100
Carver, co., Mn., U.S.	F5	100
Carville, La., U.S.	h9	95
Cary, Il., U.S.	A5	90
Cary, N.C., U.S.	B4	110
Caryville, Tn., U.S.	C9	119
Casablanca (Dar-el-Beida), Mor.	B4	42
Casacalenda, Italy	H9	14
Casa Grande, Az., U.S.	E4	80
Casa Grande National Monument, Az., U.S.	E4	80
Casale Monferrato, Italy	D3	14
Casarano, Italy	I13	14
Casas Adobes, Az., U.S.	E5	80
Casas Ibáñez, Spain	F10	12
Cascade, Co., U.S.	C6	83
Cascade, Id., U.S.	E2	89
Cascade, Ia., U.S.	B6	92
Cascade, Mt., U.S.	C5	103
Cascade, co., Mt., U.S.	C5	103
Cascade Locks, Or., U.S.	B5	114
Cascade Range, mts., N.A.	C2	76
Cascade Reservoir, res., Id., U.S.	E3	89
Cascade Tunnel, Wa., U.S.	B4	124
Cascais, Port.	G2	12
Cascina, Italy	F5	14
Casco Bay, b., Me., U.S.	E3	96
Caserta, Italy	H9	14
Caseville, Mi., U.S.	E7	99
Casey, Il., U.S.	D6	90
Casey, co., Ky., U.S.	C5	94
Casey, Mount, mtn., Id., U.S.	A2	89
Casey Key, i., Fl., U.S.	E4	86
Cashion, Az., U.S.	m8	80
Cashmere, Wa., U.S.	B5	124
Cashton, Wi., U.S.	E3	126
Casigua, Ven.	C6	58
Caspe, Spain	D11	12
Casper, Wy., U.S.	D6	127
Casper Mountain, mtn., Wy., U.S.	D6	127
Caspian, Mi., U.S.	B2	99
Caspian Lake, l., Vt., U.S.	B4	122
Caspian Sea	G17	4
Cass, co., Il., U.S.	D3	90
Cass, co., In., U.S.	C5	91
Cass, co., Ia., U.S.	C3	92
Cass, co., Mi., U.S.	G4	99
Cass, co., Mn., U.S.	D4	100
Cass, co., Mo., U.S.	C3	102
Cass, co., Ne., U.S.	D9	104
Cass, co., N.D., U.S.	C8	111
Cass, co., Tx., U.S.	C5	120
Cass, stm., Mi., U.S.	E7	99
Cassano allo Ionio, Italy	J11	14
Cass City, Mi., U.S.	E7	99
Casselberry, Fl., U.S.	D5	86
Casselman, Ont., Can.	B9	73
Casselman, stm., U.S.	k12	97
Casselton, N.D., U.S.	C8	111
Cassia, co., Id., U.S.	G5	89
Cassiar, B.C., Can.	m17	69
Cassinga, Ang.	E3	44
Cassino, Italy	H8	14
Cass Lake, Mn., U.S.	C4	100
Cass Lake, l., Mn., U.S.	C4	100
Cassopolis, Mi., U.S.	G4	99
Cassville, Ga., U.S.	B2	87
Cassville, Mo., U.S.	E4	102
Cassville, Wi., U.S.	F3	126
Castalia, Oh., U.S.	A3	112
Castanea, Pa., U.S.	D7	115
Castanheira de Pêra, Port.	E3	12
Castel del Piano, Italy	G6	14
Castelfranco Veneto, Italy	D6	14
Castellammare del Golfo, Italy	K7	14
Castellammare [di Stabia], Italy	I9	14
Castellane, Fr.	I13	10
Castellón de la Plana, Spain	F11	12
Castelnaudary, Fr.	I8	10
Castelo Branco, Port.	F4	12
Castelsarrasin, Fr.	H8	10
Castelvetrano, Italy	L7	14
Castets, Fr.	I5	10
Castiglione del Lago, Italy	F7	14
Castilla, Peru	E2	54
Castilla la Nueva, hist. reg., Spain	F8	12
Castillo de San Marcos National Monument, Fl., U.S.	n9	86
Castine, Me., U.S.	D4	96
Castle Air Force Base, mil., Ca., U.S.	D3	82
Castlebar, Ire.	H3	7
Castleberry, Al., U.S.	D2	78
Castle Dale, Ut., U.S.	D4	121
Castle Dome Mountains, mts., Az., U.S.	D1	80
Castle Dome Peak, mtn., Az., U.S.	D1	80
Castlegar, B.C., Can.	E9	69
Castle Hayne, N.C., U.S.	C5	110
Castle Hills, De., U.S.	i7	85
Castle Mountain, mtn., Yukon, Can.	D5	66
Castle Mountains, mts., Mt., U.S.	D6	103
Castle Peak, mtn., Co., U.S.	B4	83
Castle Peak, mtn., Id., U.S.	E4	89
Castle Point, Mo., U.S.	f13	102
Castle Rock, Co., U.S.	B6	83
Castle Rock, Wa., U.S.	C3	124
Castle Rock, mtn., Or., U.S.	C8	114
Castle Rock Lake, res., Wi., U.S.	E4	126
Castleton, Vt., U.S.	D2	122
Castletown, I. of Man	G8	7
Castletown Berehaven, Ire.	J3	7
Castlewood, Va., U.S.	f9	123
Castor, Alta., Can.	D5	68
Castor, stm., Mo., U.S.	D7	102
Castres, Fr.	I9	10
Castries, St. Luc.	G17	64
Castro, Braz.	B6	56
Castro, co., Tx., U.S.	B1	120
Castro Daire, Port.	E4	12
Castro del Río, Spain	H7	12
Castropol, Spain	B4	12
Castro Valley, Ca., U.S.	h8	82
Castrovillari, Italy	J11	14
Castroville, Tx., U.S.	E3	120
Castuera, Spain	G6	12
Caswell, co., N.C., U.S.	A3	110
Catacamas, Hond.	G5	64
Cataguases, Braz.	F7	57
Catahoula, co., La., U.S.	C4	95
Catahoula Lake, l., La., U.S.	C3	95
Catalão, Braz.	E5	57
Catalina, Newf., Can.	D5	72
Catalina, Chile	B3	56
Catamarca, Arg.	B3	56
Catamayo, Ec.	I3	58
Catanduanes Island, i., Phil.	C7	32
Catanduva, Braz.	F4	57
Catania, Italy	L10	14
Catanzaro, Italy	K11	14
Cataouatche, Lake, l., La., U.S.	k11	95
Catarman, Phil.	C7	32
Catasauqua, Pa., U.S.	E11	115
Catastrophe, Cape, c., Austl.	F7	50
Catawba, co., N.C., U.S.	B1	110
Catawba, stm., S.C., U.S.	B6	117
Catawba, South Fork, stm., N.C., U.S.	B1	110
Catawissa, Pa., U.S.	E9	115
Catawissa Creek, stm., Pa., U.S.	E9	115
Catete, Ang.	C2	44
Cathance Lake, l., Me., U.S.	D5	96
Cathcart, S. Afr.	H5	44
Cathedral City, Ca., U.S.	F5	82
Cathedral of the Pines, N.H., U.S.	E3	106
Catherine, Lake, res., Ar., U.S.	C3	81
Cat Island, i., Bah.	B10	64
Cat Island, i., Fl., U.S.	f12	86
Cat Island, i., Ms., U.S.	E4	101
Cat Island, i., S.C., U.S.	E9	117
Catlettsburg, Ky., U.S.	B7	94
Catlin, Il., U.S.	C6	90
Catnip Mountain, mtn., Nv., U.S.	B2	105
Catoche, Cabo, c., Mex.	G16	62
Cato Island, i., Austl.	D11	50
Catonsville, Md., U.S.	B4	97
Catoosa, Ok., U.S.	A6	113
Catoosa, co., Ga., U.S.	B1	87
Catorce, Mex.	F9	62
Catron, co., N.M., U.S.	D1	108
Catskill, N.Y., U.S.	C7	109
Catskill Mountains, mts., N.Y., U.S.	C6	109
Catt, Mount, mtn., B.C., Can.	B3	69
Cattaraugus, co., N.Y., U.S.	C2	109
Cattaraugus Creek, stm., N.Y., U.S.	C2	109
Cattaraugus Indian Reservation, N.Y., U.S.	C2	109
Cattolica, Italy	F7	14
Catus, Fr.	H8	10
Caubvick, Mount (Mont d'Iberville), mtn., Can.	f9	72
Cauca, stm., Col.	D5	58
Caucasia, Col.	C5	58
Caucasus, mts., Eur.	I6	22
Caucomgomoc Lake, l., Me., U.S.	B3	96
Caudry, Fr.	B10	10
Caulonia, Italy	K11	14
Çaúngula, Ang.	C3	44
Čaunskaja Guba, b., Russia	D27	24
Cauquenes, Chile	D2	56
Caura, stm., Ven.	D10	58
Caussade, Fr.	H8	10
Cauvery, stm., India	G5	37
Cavalaire-sur-Mer, Fr.	I13	10
Cavalier, N.D., U.S.	A8	111
Cavalier, co., N.D., U.S.	A7	111
Cavan, Ire.	G5	7
Cave City, Ar., U.S.	B4	81
Cave City, Ky., U.S.	C4	94
Cave Creek, Az., U.S.	D4	80
Cave Junction, Or., U.S.	E3	114
Cave Point, c., Wi., U.S.	D6	126
Cave Run Lake, res., Ky., U.S.	B6	94
Cave Spring, Ga., U.S.	B1	87
Cave Spring, Va., U.S.	C2	123
Cavetown, Md., U.S.	A2	97
Caviana, Ilha, i., Braz.	C8	54
Cavite, Phil.	q19	33b
Cawood, Ky., U.S.	D6	94
Cawston, B.C., Can.	E8	69
Caxambu, Braz.	F6	57
Caxias, Braz.	D10	54
Caxias do Sul, Braz.	B6	56
Caxito, Ang.	C2	44
Cayambe, Ec.	G3	58
Cayambe, vol., Ec.	H4	58
Cayce, S.C., U.S.	D5	117
Cayenne, Fr. Gu.	C8	54
Cayman Brac, i., Cay. Is.	E8	64
Cayman Islands, dep., N.A.	E7	64
Cayuga, In., U.S.	E3	91
Cayuga, co., N.Y., U.S.	C4	109
Cayuga Heights, N.Y., U.S.	C4	109
Cayuga Lake, l., N.Y., U.S.	C4	109
Cazenovia, N.Y., U.S.	C5	109
Cazères, Fr.	I8	10
Cazin, Bos.	E10	14
Cazorla, Spain	H8	12
Čeboksary, Russia	F7	22
Cebollar, Arg.	B3	56
Cebreros, Spain	E7	12
Cebu, Phil.	C7	32
Cebu, i., Phil.	C7	32
Čečerleg, Mong.	B7	26
Čechov, Russia	F20	18
Čechy, hist. reg., Czech.	F14	8
Cecil, co., Md., U.S.	A6	97
Cecil Field Naval Air Station, mil., Fl., U.S.	B5	86
Cecilia, Ky., U.S.	C4	94
Cecina, Italy	F5	14
Cedar, co., Ia., U.S.	C6	92
Cedar, co., Mo., U.S.	D4	102
Cedar, co., Ne., U.S.	B8	104
Cedar, stm., U.S.	C6	92
Cedar, stm., Ne., U.S.	B7	104
Cedar, stm., Wa., U.S.	B4	124
Cedar Bluff, Al., U.S.	A4	78
Cedar Bluff Reservoir, res., Ks., U.S.	D4	93
Cedar Bluff Two, Tn., U.S.	D9	119
Cedar Breaks National Monument, Ut., U.S.	F3	121
Cedarburg, Wi., U.S.	E6	126
Cedar City, Ut., U.S.	F2	121
Cedar Creek, stm., N.J., U.S.	D4	107
Cedar Creek, stm., N.D., U.S.	C3	111
Cedar Creek, stm., Oh., U.S.	e7	112
Cedar Creek Lake, res., Tx., U.S.	C4	120
Cedar Crest, N.M., U.S.	k8	108
Cedaredge, Co., U.S.	C3	83
Cedar Falls, Ia., U.S.	B5	92
Cedar Grove, N.J., U.S.	B4	107
Cedar Grove, W.V., U.S.	C3	125
Cedar Grove, Wi., U.S.	E6	126
Cedar Hill, Mo., U.S.	g12	102
Cedar Hill, Tx., U.S.	n10	120
Cedarhurst, N.Y., U.S.	k13	109
Cedar Island, i., N.C., U.S.	C6	110
Cedar Island, i., S.C., U.S.	E9	117
Cedar Island, i., Va., U.S.	C7	123
Cedar Key, Fl., U.S.	C3	86
Cedar Keys, is., Fl., U.S.	C3	86
Cedar Lake, In., U.S.	B3	91
Cedar Lake, l., Man., Can.	C1	70
Cedar Lake, res., Il., U.S.	F4	90
Cedar Mountain, mtn., Ca., U.S.	B3	82
Cedar Point, c., Md., U.S.	D5	97
Cedar Point, c., Oh., U.S.	A3	112
Cedar Point, c., Oh., U.S.	e7	112
Cedar Rapids, Ia., U.S.	C6	92
Cedar Springs, Mi., U.S.	E5	99
Cedartown, Ga., U.S.	B1	87
Cedar Vale, Ks., U.S.	E7	93
Cedarville, Oh., U.S.	C2	112
Cedros, Isla, i., Mex.	C2	62
Ceduna, Austl.	F6	50
Cefalù, Italy	K9	14
Čegdomyn, Russia	G20	24
Cegléd, Hung.	H19	8
Cehegín, Spain	G10	12
Čela, Ang.	D3	44
Čel'abinsk, Russia	F10	22
Celano, Italy	G8	14
Celanova, Spain	C4	12
Celaya, Mex.	G9	62
Cele, China	B9	38
Celebes Sea, Asia	E7	32
Celebes see Sulawesi, i., Indon.	F7	32
Celina, Oh., U.S.	B1	112
Celina, Tn., U.S.	C8	119
Celina, Tx., U.S.	C4	120
Celinograd, Kaz.	G8	24
Celje, Slo.	C10	14
Celle, Ger.	C10	8
Cement, Ok., U.S.	C3	113
Cementon, Pa., U.S.	E10	115
Centennial Mountains, mts., Id., U.S.	E7	89
Center, Co., U.S.	D4	83
Center, N.D., U.S.	B4	111
Center, Tx., U.S.	D5	120
Centerbrook, Ct., U.S.	D6	84
Centereach, N.Y., U.S.	n15	109
Centerburg, Oh., U.S.	B3	112
Center Hill Lake, res., Tn., U.S.	C8	119
Center Moriches, N.Y., U.S.	n16	109
Center Mountain, mtn., Id., U.S.	D3	89
Center Point, Al., U.S.	f7	78
Center Point, Ia., U.S.	B6	92
Centerville, In., U.S.	E8	91
Centerville, Ia., U.S.	D5	92
Centerville, La., U.S.	E4	95
Centerville, Ma., U.S.	C7	98
Centerville, Oh., U.S.	C1	112
Centerville, Pa., U.S.	F2	115
Centerville, S.D., U.S.	D9	118
Centerville, Tn., U.S.	B4	119
Centerville, Ut., U.S.	C4	121
Cento, Italy	E6	14
Central, N.M., U.S.	E1	108
Central, S.C., U.S.	B2	117
Central, Cordillera, mts., Bol.	G6	54
Central, Cordillera, mts., Col.	E5	58
Central, Cordillera, mts., Peru	E3	54
Central, Massif, mts., Fr.	G10	10
Central, Planalto, plat., Braz.	G9	54
Central, Sistema, mts., Spain	E6	12
Central African Republic, ctry., Afr.	G10	42
Central City, Co., U.S.	B5	83
Central City, Il., U.S.	E4	90
Central City, Ia., U.S.	B6	92
Central City, Ky., U.S.	C2	94
Central City, Ne., U.S.	C7	104
Central City, Pa., U.S.	F4	115
Central Falls, R.I., U.S.	B5	116
Central Heights, Az., U.S.	D5	80
Centralia, Il., U.S.	E4	90
Centralia, Mo., U.S.	B5	102
Centralia, Wa., U.S.	C3	124
Central Islip, N.Y., U.S.	n15	109
Central Lake, Mi., U.S.	C5	99
Central Makrān Range, mts., Pak.	D1	36
Central Point, Wa., U.S.	C2	124
Central Point, Or., U.S.	E4	114
Central Square, N.Y., U.S.	B4	109
Central Valley, Ca., U.S.	B2	82
Central Valley, N.Y., U.S.	D6	109
Central Village, Ct., U.S.	C8	84
Centre, Al., U.S.	A4	78
Centre, co., Pa., U.S.	E6	115
Centre Hall, Pa., U.S.	E6	115
Centreville, Al., U.S.	C2	78
Centreville, Il., U.S.	E3	90
Centreville, Md., U.S.	B5	97
Centreville, Mi., U.S.	G5	99
Centreville, Ms., U.S.	D2	101
Centuria, Wi., U.S.	C1	126
Century, Fl., U.S.	u14	86
Cepu, Indon.	m15	33a
Ceram Sea see Seram, Laut, Indon.	F8	32
Cerbat Mountains, mts., Az., U.S.	B1	80
Ceredo, W.V., U.S.	C2	125
Čeremchovo, Russia	G14	24
Čerepovec, Russia	B20	18
Ceres, Ca., U.S.	D3	82
Ceresco, Ne., U.S.	C9	104
Céret, Fr.	J9	10
Cereté, Col.	C5	58
Cerf Island, i., Sey.	C10	44
Cerignola, Italy	H10	14
Cérilly, Fr.	F9	10
Čerkassy, Ukr.	H4	22
Çerkeş, Tur.	I6	22
Čerkessk, Russia	G4	18
Černigov, Ukr.	G4	22
Černobyl' (Chernobyl), Ukr.	G4	22
Černogorsk, Russia	G12	24
Černovcy, Ukr.	H3	22
Černyševskij, Russia	E16	24
Cerralvo, Isla, i., Mex.	E5	62
Cerritos, Mex.	F9	62
Cerro de Pasco, Peru	F3	54
Cerro Gordo, Il., U.S.	D5	90
Cerro Gordo, co., Ia., U.S.	A4	92
Čerskij, Russia	D26	24
Čerskogo, Chrebet, mts., Russia	E23	24
Cervera del Río Alhama, Spain	C10	12
Cervera de Pisuerga, Spain	C7	12
Cervia, Italy	E7	14
Cesena, Italy	E7	14
Ceśenatico, Italy	E7	14
České Budějovice, Czech.	G14	8
Cessnock, Austl.	F10	50
Ceuta, Sp. N. Afr.	A4	42
Ceyhan, Tur.	A4	40
Ceyhan, Tur.	A7	40
Ceylânpınar, Tur.	A7	40
Ceylon see Sri Lanka, ctry., Asia	H5	36
Chabanais, Fr.	G7	10
Chabarovsk, Russia	H21	24
Chachoengsao, Thai.	H6	34
Chaco, stm., N.M., U.S.	A1	108
Chaco Culture National Historic Park, N.M., U.S.	A2	108

Name	Map Ref	Page
Chacon, Cape, c., Ak., U.S.	n24	79
Chad, ctry., Afr.	E9	42
Chad, Lake (Lac Tchad), l., Afr.	F8	42
Chadbourn, N.C., U.S.	C4	110
Chadds Ford, Pa., U.S.	G10	115
Chadileuvú, stm., Arg.	D3	56
Chadron, Ne., U.S.	B3	104
Chadwicks, N.Y., U.S.	B5	109
Chaffee, Mo., U.S.	D8	102
Chaffee, co., Co., U.S.	C4	83
Chaffin, Ma., U.S.	B4	98
Chaghcharān, Afg.	C1	38
Chagny, Fr.	F11	10
Chagos Archipelago, is., B.I.O.T.	G17	2
Chagrin Falls, Oh., U.S.	A4	112
Chaibāsā, India	I11	38
Chaîne Annamitique, mts., Asia	F9	34
Chakachamna Lake, l., Ak., U.S.	g15	79
Chalais, Fr.	G7	10
Chalbi Desert, des., Kenya	H2	46
Chalcuapa, El Sal.	H3	64
Chaleur Bay, b., Can.	B4	71
Chalfonte, De., U.S.	h7	85
Chālisgaon, India	B3	37
Chalk River, Ont., Can.	A7	73
Challans, Fr.	F5	10
Challis, Id., U.S.	E4	89
Chalmette, La., U.S.	E6	95
Chalonnes-sur-Loire, Fr.	E6	10
Châlons-sur-Marne, Fr.	D11	10
Chalon-sur-Saône, Fr.	F11	10
Châlus, Fr.	G7	10
Cham, Ger.	F12	8
Chama, N.M., U.S.	A3	108
Chama, Rio, stm., N.M., U.S.	A3	108
Chaman, Pak.	E2	38
Chambal, stm., India	G7	38
Chamberlain, S.D., U.S.	D6	118
Chamberlain Lake, l., Me., U.S.	B3	96
Chamberlin, Mount, mtn., Ak., U.S.	B10	79
Chambers, co., Al., U.S.	C4	78
Chambers, co., Tx., U.S.	E5	120
Chambersburg, Pa., U.S.	G6	115
Chambers Island, i., Wi., U.S.	C6	126
Chambéry, Fr.	G12	10
Chambi, Jebel, mtn., Tun.	A7	42
Chamblee, Ga., U.S.	h8	87
Chambly, Que., Can.	D4	74
Chambon-sur-Voueize, Fr.	F9	10
Chamisal, N.M., U.S.	A4	108
Chamonix-Mont-Blanc, Fr.	G13	10
Champagne, hist. reg., Fr.	D11	10
Champagnole, Fr.	F12	10
Champaign, Il., U.S.	C5	90
Champaign, co., Il., U.S.	C5	90
Champaign, co., Oh., U.S.	B2	112
Champassak, Laos	G8	34
Champion, Oh., U.S.	A5	112
Champlain, Lake, l., N.A.	C12	76
Champlin, Mn., U.S.	m12	100
Chāmrājnagar Rāmasamudram, India	G4	37
Chañaral, Chile	B2	56
Chance, Md., U.S.	D6	97
Chanch, Mong.	A7	26
Chanchelulla Peak, mtn., Ca., U.S.	B2	82
Chandalar, stm., Ak., U.S.	B10	79
Chandausi, India	F8	38
Chandeleur Islands, is., La., U.S.	E7	95
Chandeleur Sound, strt., La., U.S.	E6	95
Chandīgarh, India	E7	38
Chandler, Que., Can.	k14	74
Chandler, Az., U.S.	D4	80
Chandler, In., U.S.	H3	91
Chandler, Ok., U.S.	B5	113
Chandler, Tx., U.S.	C5	120
Chandler Heights, Az., U.S.	m9	80
Chāndpur, Bngl.	I14	38
Chāndpur, India	F8	38
Chandrapur, India	C5	37
Chandyga, Russia	E21	24
Chang (Yangtze), stm., China	E10	26
Changajn Nuruu, mts., Mong.	B6	26
Changchun, China	C12	26
Changde, China	F9	26
Changhua, Tai.	K9	28
Changjiang, China	J5	28
Changli, China	D10	26
Changsha, China	G1	28
Changshu, China	D9	28
Changzhi, China	D9	26
Changzhou (Changchow), China	D8	28
Chanhassen, Mn., U.S.	n11	100
Chanka, Ozero (Xingkathu), l., Asia	I20	24
Channahon, Il., U.S.	B5	90
Channapatna, India	F4	37
Channel Islands, is., Eur.	C4	10
Channel Islands National Park, Ca., U.S.	F4	82
Channel Lake, Il., U.S.	H8	90
Channel-Port-aux-Basques, Newf., Can.	E2	72
Channelview, Tx., U.S.	r14	120
Chantada, Spain	C4	12
Chantajskoje, Ozero, l., Russia	D12	24
Chanthaburi, Thai.	H7	34
Chantilly, Va., U.S.	g12	123
Chantrey Inlet, b., N.W. Ter., Can.	C13	66
Chanute, Ks., U.S.	E8	93
Chanute Air Force Base, mil., Il., U.S.	C5	90
Chaoan, China	L5	28
Chao Phraya, stm., Thai.	G6	34
Chapala, Lago de, l., Mex.	G8	62
Chaparral, Col.	F5	58
Chapčeranga, Russia	H16	24
Chapel Hill, N.C., U.S.	B3	110
Chapel Hill, Tn., U.S.	B5	119
Chaplin, stm., Ky., U.S.	C4	94
Chaplin Lake, l., Sask., Can.	G2	75
Chapman, Ks., U.S.	D6	93
Chapman Pond, l., R.I., U.S.	F1	116
Chapmanville, W.V., U.S.	D2	125
Chappaquiddick Island, i., Ma., U.S.	D7	98
Chappell, Ne., U.S.	C3	104
Chāpra, India	H11	38
Chapultepec, mtn., Mex.	F8	62
Charadai, Arg.	B5	56
Charcas, Mex.	F9	62
Chardon, Oh., U.S.	A4	112
Chardzhou see Čardžou, Turk.	J10	22
Charenton, La., U.S.	E4	95
Chari, stm., Afr.	F9	42
Chārīkār, Afg.	C3	38
Chariton, Ia., U.S.	C4	92
Chariton, co., Mo., U.S.	B4	102
Chariton, stm., U.S.	A5	102
Charity, Guy.	D13	58
Char'kov, Ukr.	G5	22
Charleroi, Bel.	E4	8
Charleroi, Pa., U.S.	F2	115
Charles, co., Md., U.S.	C3	97
Charles, stm., Ma., U.S.	B5	98
Charles, Cape, c., Va., U.S.	C6	123
Charles A. Goodwin Dam, Ct., U.S.	B3	84
Charlesbourg, Que., Can.	n17	74
Charles City, Ia., U.S.	A5	92
Charles City, co., Va., U.S.	C5	123
Charles Island, i., N.W. Ter., Can.	D18	66
Charles Mill Lake, res., Oh., U.S.	B3	112
Charles Mix, co., S.D., U.S.	D7	118
Charles Mound, hill, Il., U.S.	A3	90
Charleston, Ar., U.S.	B1	81
Charleston, Il., U.S.	D5	90
Charleston, Ms., U.S.	A3	101
Charleston, Mo., U.S.	E8	102
Charleston, Or., U.S.	D2	114
Charleston, S.C., U.S.	F8	117
Charleston, Tn., U.S.	D9	119
Charleston, W.V., U.S.	C3	125
Charleston, co., S.C., U.S.	F8	117
Charleston Air Force Base, mil., S.C., U.S.	k11	117
Charleston Naval Shipyard, mil., S.C., U.S.	k12	117
Charleston Peak, mtn., Nv., U.S.	G6	105
Charlestown, In., U.S.	H6	91
Charlestown, N.H., U.S.	D2	106
Charlestown, R.I., U.S.	F2	116
Charles Town, W.V., U.S.	B7	125
Charleville, Austl.	E9	50
Charleville-Mézières, Fr.	C11	10
Charlevoix, Mi., U.S.	C5	99
Charlevoix, co., Mi., U.S.	C5	99
Charlevoix, Lake, l., Mi., U.S.	C5	99
Charlo, N.B., Can.	B3	71
Charlotte, Mi., U.S.	F6	99
Charlotte, N.C., U.S.	B2	110
Charlotte, Tx., U.S.	E3	120
Charlotte, co., Fl., U.S.	F5	86
Charlotte, co., Va., U.S.	C4	123
Charlotte Amalie, V.I.U.S.	E15	64
Charlotte Hall, Md., U.S.	D4	97
Charlotte Harbor, Fl., U.S.	F4	86
Charlotte Harbor, b., Fl., U.S.	F4	86
Charlottenberg, Swe.	G9	6
Charlottesville, Va., U.S.	B4	123
Charlottetown, P.E.I., Can.	C6	71
Charlton, co., Ga., U.S.	F4	87
Charmco, W.V., U.S.	C4	125
Charmes, Fr.	D13	10
Charny, Que., Can.	C6	74
Charolles, Fr.	F11	10
Chārsadda, Pak.	C4	38
Charters Towers, Austl.	D9	50
Chartres, Fr.	D8	10
Char Us Nuur, l., Mong.	B5	26
Chascomús, Arg.	D5	56
Chase, B.C., Can.	D8	69
Chase, Md., U.S.	B5	97
Chase, co., Ks., U.S.	D7	93
Chase, co., Ne., U.S.	D4	104
Chase City, Va., U.S.	D4	123
Chase Field Naval Air Station, mil., Tx., U.S.	E4	120
Chaska, Mn., U.S.	F5	100
Chassahowitzka Bay, b., Fl., U.S.	D4	86
Chassell, Mi., U.S.	B2	99
Chatanbulag, Mong.	C8	26
Chatanga, Russia	C14	24
Chatanga, stm., Russia	C14	24
Chatangskij Zaliv, b., Russia	C15	24
Châteaubriant, Fr.	E5	10
Château-du-Loir, Fr.	E7	10
Châteaudun, Fr.	D8	10
Château-Gontier, Fr.	E6	10
Châteauguay, Que., Can.	D4	74
Château-Landon, Fr.	D9	10
Châteaulin, Fr.	D2	10
Châteaumeillant, Fr.	F9	10
Châteauneuf-sur-Charente, Fr.	G6	10
Châteauneuf-sur-Loire, Fr.	E9	10
Château-Renault, Fr.	E7	10
Château-Richer, Que., Can.	C6	74
Châteauroux, Fr.	F8	10
Château-Thierry, Fr.	C10	10
Châtellerault, Fr.	F7	10
Chatfield, Mn., U.S.	G6	100
Chatgal, Mong.	A7	26
Chatham, N.B., Can.	B4	71
Chatham, Ont., Can.	E2	73
Chatham, Eng., U.K.	J13	7
Chatham, Il., U.S.	D4	90
Chatham, La., U.S.	B3	95
Chatham, Ma., U.S.	C8	98
Chatham, N.J., U.S.	B4	107
Chatham, N.Y., U.S.	C7	109
Chatham, Va., U.S.	D3	123
Chatham, co., Ga., U.S.	E5	87
Chatham, co., N.C., U.S.	B3	110
Chatham Strait, strt., Ak., U.S.	m22	79
Châtillon, Italy	D2	14
Châtillon-Coligny, Fr.	E9	10
Châtillon-sur-Indre, Fr.	F8	10
Châtillon-sur-Seine, Fr.	E11	10
Chatom, Al., U.S.	D1	78
Chatsworth, Ga., U.S.	B2	87
Chatsworth, Il., U.S.	C5	90
Chatsworth Reservoir, res., Ca., U.S.	m11	82
Chattahoochee, Fl., U.S.	B2	86
Chattahoochee, co., Ga., U.S.	D2	87
Chattahoochee, stm., U.S.	E1	87
Chattanooga, Tn., U.S.	D8	119
Chattaroy, W.V., U.S.	D2	125
Chattooga, co., Ga., U.S.	B1	87
Chatuge Lake, res., U.S.	g9	110
Chatyrka, Russia	E29	24
Chaudière, stm., Que., Can.	C7	74
Chau Doc, Viet.	I8	34
Chauk, Burma	D3	34
Chaumont, Fr.	D12	10
Chauncey, Oh., U.S.	C3	112
Chauny, Fr.	C10	10
Chautauqua, co., Ks., U.S.	E7	93
Chautauqua, co., N.Y., U.S.	C1	109
Chautauqua Lake, l., N.Y., U.S.	C1	109
Chauvigny, Fr.	F7	10
Chauvin, La., U.S.	E5	95
Chavakkad, India	G4	37
Chaves, Port.	D4	12
Chaves, co., N.M., U.S.	D5	108
Cháviva, Col.	E6	58
Chbukha Dzong, Bhu.	G13	38
Cheaha Mountain, mtn., Al., U.S.	B4	78
Cheat, Shavers Fork, stm., W.V., U.S.	B5	125
Cheatham, co., Tn., U.S.	A4	119
Chebanse, Il., U.S.	C6	90
Cheboygan, Mi., U.S.	C6	99
Cheboygan, co., Mi., U.S.	C6	99
Chech, Erg, des., Afr.	C5	42
Checotah, Ok., U.S.	B6	113
Chedabucto Bay, b., N.S., Can.	D8	71
Cheduba Island, i., Burma	E2	34
Cheektowaga, N.Y., U.S.	C2	109
Cheeseman Lake, res., Co., U.S.	B5	83
Chehalem Mountains, mts., Or., U.S.	h12	114
Chehalis, Wa., U.S.	C3	124
Chehalis, stm., Wa., U.S.	C2	124
Cheju-do, i., S. Kor.	E12	26
Chelan, Wa., U.S.	B5	124
Chelan, co., Wa., U.S.	B4	124
Chelan, Lake, l., Wa., U.S.	A5	124
Chelan Mountains, mts., Wa., U.S.	A5	124
Chełm, Pol.	D23	8
Chełmno, Pol.	B18	8
Chelmsford, Eng., U.K.	J13	7
Chelmsford, Ma., U.S.	A5	98
Chelsea, Que., Can.	D2	74
Chelsea, Al., U.S.	g7	78
Chelsea, Ma., U.S.	B5	98
Chelsea, Mi., U.S.	F6	99
Chelsea, Ok., U.S.	A6	113
Cheltenham, Eng., U.K.	J10	7
Cheltenham, Md., U.S.	C4	97
Chelva, Spain	F11	12
Chelyabinsk see Čel'abinsk, Russia	F10	22
Chelyan, W.V., U.S.	C3	125
Chemehuevi Indian Reservation, Ca., U.S.	E6	82
Chemnitz, Ger.	E12	8
Chemquasabamticook Lake (Ross Lake), l., Me., U.S.	B3	96
Chemung, co., N.Y., U.S.	C4	109
Chemung, stm., Pa., U.S.	C8	115
Chemung Lake, l., Ont., Can.	C6	73
Chenāb, stm., Asia	E5	38
Chenachane, Alg.	C6	42
Chenango, co., N.Y., U.S.	C5	109
Chenango, stm., N.Y., U.S.	C5	109
Chenango Bridge, N.Y., U.S.	C5	109
Chenes, River Aux, b., La., U.S.	k12	95
Chénéville, Que., Can.	D2	74
Cheney, Ks., U.S.	E6	93
Cheney, Wa., U.S.	B8	124
Cheney Reservoir, res., Ks., U.S.	E6	93
Cheneyville, La., U.S.	C3	95
Chengde, China	C10	26
Chengdu, China	E7	26
Chengutu, Zimb.	E6	44
Chenoa, Il., U.S.	C5	90
Chenoweth, Or., U.S.	B5	114
Chepachet, R.I., U.S.	B2	116
Chepachet, stm., R.I., U.S.	B2	116
Chepo, Pan.	J8	64
Chequamegon Bay, b., Wi., U.S.	B3	126
Cheraw, S.C., U.S.	B8	117
Cherbourg, Fr.	C5	10
Chergui, Chott ech, l., Alg.	B6	42
Cherkassy see Čerkassy, Ukr.	H4	22
Chernigov see Černigov, Ukr.	G4	22
Chernobyl see Černobyl', Ukr.	G4	22
Cherokee, Al., U.S.	A2	78
Cherokee, Ia., U.S.	B2	92
Cherokee, Ks., U.S.	E9	93
Cherokee, Ok., U.S.	A3	113
Cherokee, co., Al., U.S.	A4	78
Cherokee, co., Ga., U.S.	B2	87
Cherokee, co., Ia., U.S.	B2	92
Cherokee, co., Ks., U.S.	E9	93
Cherokee, co., N.C., U.S.	f8	110
Cherokee, co., Ok., U.S.	B6	113
Cherokee, co., S.C., U.S.	A4	117
Cherokee, co., Tx., U.S.	D5	120
Cherokee Indian Reservation, N.C., U.S.	f9	110
Cherokee Lake, l., Tn., U.S.	C10	119
Cherokees, Lake O' The, res., Ok., U.S.	A7	113
Cherokee Village, Ar., U.S.	A4	81
Cherry, co., Ne., U.S.	B4	104
Cherry Creek, stm., S.D., U.S.	C3	118
Cherry Hill, N.J., U.S.	D2	107
Cherry Point, c., Va., U.S.	C6	123
Cherry Point Marine Corps Air Station, mil., N.C., U.S.	C6	110
Cherryvale, Ks., U.S.	E8	93
Cherry Valley, Ar., U.S.	B5	81
Cherry Valley, Il., U.S.	A5	90
Cherryville, N.C., U.S.	B1	110
Cherson, Ukr.	H4	22
Chesaning, Mi., U.S.	E6	99
Chesapeake, Oh., U.S.	D3	112
Chesapeake, Va., U.S.	D6	123
Chesapeake, W.V., U.S.	C3	125
Chesapeake and Delaware Canal, U.S.	B3	85
Chesapeake Bay, b., U.S.	D11	76
Chesapeake Bay Bridge-Tunnel, Va., U.S.	D7	123
Chesapeake Beach, Md., U.S.	C4	97
Chesapeake City, Md., U.S.	A6	97
Chesdin, Lake, res., Va., U.S.	C5	123
Cheshire, Ct., U.S.	D4	84
Cheshire, co., N.H., U.S.	E2	106
Cheshire Reservoir, res., Ma., U.S.	A1	98
Chesley, Ont., Can.	C3	73
Chesnee, S.C., U.S.	A4	117
Chester, Eng., U.K.	H10	7
Chester, Ca., U.S.	B3	82
Chester, Ct., U.S.	D6	84
Chester, Il., U.S.	F4	90
Chester, Md., U.S.	C5	97
Chester, Mt., U.S.	B6	103
Chester, N.H., U.S.	E4	106
Chester, N.Y., U.S.	D6	109
Chester, Pa., U.S.	G11	115
Chester, S.C., U.S.	B5	117
Chester, Vt., U.S.	E3	122
Chester, Va., U.S.	C5	123
Chester, W.V., U.S.	A4	125
Chester, co., Pa., U.S.	G10	115
Chester, co., S.C., U.S.	B5	117
Chester, co., Tn., U.S.	B3	119
Chester, stm., Md., U.S.	B5	97
Chester Basin, N.S., Can.	E5	71
Chester Depot, Vt., U.S.	E3	122
Chesterfield, In., U.S.	D6	91
Chesterfield, S.C., U.S.	B7	117
Chesterfield, co., S.C., U.S.	B7	117
Chesterfield, co., Va., U.S.	C5	123
Chesterfield, Îles, is., N. Cal.	C11	50
Chesterfield Inlet, N.W. Ter., Can.	D14	66
Chesterfield Inlet, b., N.W. Ter., Can.	D14	66
Chesterton, In., U.S.	A3	91
Chestertown, Md., U.S.	B5	97
Chesterville, Ont., Can.	B9	73
Chesuncook Lake, l., Me., U.S.	C3	96
Cheswick, Pa., U.S.	h14	115
Cheswold, De., U.S.	D3	85
Cheta, stm., Russia	C13	24
Chetco, stm., Or., U.S.	E2	114
Chetek, Wi., U.S.	C2	126
Chetek, Lake, l., Wi., U.S.	C2	126
Chetopa, Ks., U.S.	E8	93
Chetumal Bay, b., N.A.	H15	62
Chetwynd, B.C., Can.	B7	69
Cheval Blanc, Pointe du, c., Haiti	E11	64
Cheviot, Oh., U.S.	C1	112
Chevreuil, Point, c., La., U.S.	E4	95
Chevy Chase, Md., U.S.	C3	97
Chewack, stm., Wa., U.S.	A5	124
Chew Bahir (Lake Stefanie), l., Afr.	H2	46
Chewelah, Wa., U.S.	A8	124
Cheyenne, Ok., U.S.	B2	113
Cheyenne, Wy., U.S.	E8	127
Cheyenne, co., Co., U.S.	C8	83
Cheyenne, co., Ks., U.S.	C2	93
Cheyenne, co., Ne., U.S.	C2	104
Cheyenne, stm., U.S.	C4	118
Cheyenne, Dry Fork, stm., Wy., U.S.	C7	127
Cheyenne River Indian Reservation, S.D., U.S.	B4	118
Cheyenne Wells, Co., U.S.	C8	83
Chezhou, China	J1	28
Chhatarpur, India	H8	38
Chhindwāra, India	I8	38
Chi, stm., Thai.	G8	34
Chiai, Tai.	L9	28
Chiali, Tai.	L9	28
Chiang Khan, Thai.	F6	34
Chiang Mai, Thai.	E5	34
Chiang Rai, Thai.	E5	34
Chiari, Italy	D4	14
Chiavari, Italy	E4	14
Chiavenna, Italy	C4	14
Chiba, Japan	G13	30
Chiblow Lake, l., Ont., Can.	A1	73
Chibougamau, Que., Can.	k12	74
Chibuto, Moz.	F6	44
Chicago, Il., U.S.	B6	90
Chicago Heights, Il., U.S.	B6	90
Chicago Sanitary and Ship Canal, Il., U.S.	k8	90
Chicamacomico, stm., Md., U.S.	D6	97
Chicapa, stm., Afr.	C4	44
Chichagof Island, i., Ak., U.S.	m22	79
Chichāwatni, Pak.	E5	38
Chichén Itzá, Mex.	G15	62
Chichibu, Japan	G12	30
Chickahominy, stm., Va., U.S.	C5	123
Chickamauga, Al., U.S.	B1	87
Chickamauga and Chattanooga National Military Park, U.S.	k11	119
Chickamauga Dam, Tn., U.S.	h11	119
Chickamauga Lake, res., Tn., U.S.	D8	119
Chickasaw, Al., U.S.	E1	78
Chickasaw, co., Ia., U.S.	A5	92
Chickasaw, co., Ms., U.S.	B4	101
Chickasawhay, stm., Ms., U.S.	D5	101
Chickasaw National Recreation Area, Ok., U.S.	C5	113
Chickasha, Ok., U.S.	B4	113
Chickasha, Lake, res., Ok., U.S.	B3	113
Chickwolnepy Stream, stm., N.H., U.S.	A4	106
Chiclana de la Frontera, Spain	I5	12
Chiclayo, Peru	E3	54
Chico, Ca., U.S.	C3	82
Chicoa, Moz.	E6	44
Chicopee, Ma., U.S.	B2	98
Chicora, Pa., U.S.	E2	115
Chicot Island, i., La., U.S.	E6	95
Chicoutimi, Que., Can.	A6	74
Chicoutimi, stm., Que., Can.	A6	74
Chidambaram, India	G5	37
Chidley, Cape, c., Can.	D20	66
Chiefland, Fl., U.S.	C4	86
Chieri, Italy	D2	14
Chieti, Italy	G9	14
Chifeng, China	C10	26
Chigasaki, Japan	G12	30
Chignecto, Cape, c., N.S., Can.	D5	71
Chignecto Bay, b., Can.	D5	71
Ch'ihu, Tai.	L9	28
Chihuahua, Mex.	C6	62
Chikaskia, stm., U.S.	A4	113
Chik Ballāpur, India	F4	37
Chikmagalūr, India	F3	37
Chilakalūrupet, India	D6	37
Chilapa de Alvarez, Mex.	I10	62
Chīlās, Pak.	C6	38
Childersburg, Al., U.S.	B3	78
Childress, Tx., U.S.	B2	120
Childress, co., Tx., U.S.	B2	120
Chile, ctry., S.A.	C2	56
Chilete, Peru	E3	54
Chilhowie, Va., U.S.	f10	123
Chililabombwe (Bancroft), Zam.	D5	44
Chilka Lake, l., India	C8	37
Chilko, stm., B.C., Can.	D6	69
Chilko Lake, l., B.C., Can.	D5	69
Chillán, Chile	D2	56
Chillicothe, Il., U.S.	C4	90
Chillicothe, Mo., U.S.	B4	102
Chillicothe, Oh., U.S.	C3	112
Chilliwack, B.C., Can.	E7	69
Chillum, Md., U.S.	f9	97
Chiloé, Isla de, i., Chile	E2	56
Chilok, Russia	G16	24
Chiloquin, Or., U.S.	E5	114
Chilpancingo [de los Bravos], Mex.	I10	62
Chilton, Wi., U.S.	D5	126
Chilton, co., Al., U.S.	C3	78
Chilung, Tai.	J10	28
Chilwa, Lake, l., Afr.	E7	44
Chimacum, Wa., U.S.	A3	124
Chimayo, N.M., U.S.	A4	108
Chimborazo, vol., Ec.	H3	54
Chimbote, Peru	E3	54
Chimkent see Čimkent, Kaz.	I11	22
Chimki, Russia	F20	18
Chimney Rock, mtn., Ne., U.S.	C2	104
China, ctry., Asia	D7	26
China Grove, N.C., U.S.	B2	110
China Lake, l., Me., U.S.	D3	96
Chinandega, Nic.	H4	64
Chincha Alta, Peru	F3	54
Chinchilla de Monte Aragón, Spain	G10	12
Chincoteague, Va., U.S.	C7	123
Chincoteague Bay, b., U.S.	D7	97
Chinde, Moz.	E7	44
Chindwin, stm., Burma	C3	34
Chingleput, India	F5	37
Chingola, Zam.	D5	44
Ch'ingshui, Tai.	K9	28
Chin Hills, hills, Burma	D2	34
Chinhoyi, Zimb.	E6	44
Chiniot, Pak.	E5	38
Chinitna Point, c., Ak., U.S.	h15	79
Chinju, S. Kor.	D12	26
Chinko, stm., Cen. Afr. Rep.	G10	42
Chinkuashih, Tai.	J10	28
Chinle, Az., U.S.	A6	80
Chinmen Tao, i., Tai.	K7	28
Chino, Ca., U.S.	F5	82
Chinon, Fr.	E7	10
Chinook, Mt., U.S.	B7	103
Chinook, Wa., U.S.	C2	124
Chinook, Lake, res., Or., U.S.	C5	114
Chino Valley, Az., U.S.	C3	80
Chinshan, Tai.	J10	28
Chioggia, Italy	D7	14
Chipata, Zam.	D6	44
Chipita Park, Co., U.S.	C6	83
Chipley, Fl., U.S.	u16	86
Chipman, N.B., Can.	C4	71
Chipola, stm., Fl., U.S.	B1	86
Chippewa, co., Mi., U.S.	B6	99
Chippewa, co., Mn., U.S.	E3	100
Chippewa, co., Wi., U.S.	C2	126
Chippewa, stm., Mn., U.S.	E3	100
Chippewa, stm., Wi., U.S.	D2	126
Chippewa, Lake, l., Wi., U.S.	C2	126
Chippewa Falls, Wi., U.S.	D2	126
Chipuxet, stm., R.I., U.S.	F3	116
Chiquimula, Guat.	G3	64
Chiquinquirá, Col.	E6	58
Chīrāla, India	D6	37
Chirfa, Niger	D8	42
Chirgis Nuur, l., Mong.	B5	26
Chiricahua Mountains, mts., Az., U.S.	E6	80
Chiricahua National Monument, Az., U.S.	F6	80
Chiricahua Peak, mtn., Az., U.S.	F6	80
Chiriguaná, Col.	C6	58
Chirikof Island, i., Ak., U.S.	D8	79
Chiriquí, Golfo, b., Pan.	K6	64
Chiriquí, Laguna de, b., Pan.	J7	64
Chiripó, Cerro, mtn., C.R.	J6	64
Chisago, co., Mn., U.S.	E6	100
Chisago City, Mn., U.S.	E6	100
Chisholm, Mn., U.S.	C6	100
Chishtiān Mandi, Pak.	F5	38
Chisos Mountains, mts., Tx., U.S.	E1	120
Chitato, Ang.	C4	44
Chitembo, Ang.	D3	44
Chitina, Ak., U.S.	g19	79
Chitipa, Mwi.	C6	44
Chitorgarh, India	H6	38
Chitose, Japan	q19	30a
Chitradurga, India	E4	37
Chitrāl, Pak.	C4	38
Chitré, Pan.	K7	64
Chittagong, Bngl.	I14	38
Chittenango, N.Y., U.S.	B5	109
Chittenden, co., Vt., U.S.	C2	122

Name	Map Ref	Page

Chittenden Reservoir, res., Vt., U.S. D3 122
Chittoor, India F5 37
Chiusi, Italy F6 14
Chivasso, Italy D2 14
Choapan, Mex. I12 62
Chocolate Mountains, mts., U.S. F6 82
Chocontá, Col. E6 58
Choctaw, Ok., U.S. B4 113
Choctaw, co., Al., U.S. C1 78
Choctaw, co., Ms., U.S. B4 101
Choctaw, co., Ok., U.S. C6 113
Choctawhatchee Bay, b., Fl., U.S. u15 86
Choctaw Indian Reservation, Ms., U.S. C4 101
Choele-Choel, Arg. D3 56
Cholet, Fr. E6 10
Cholmsk, Russia H22 24
Choluteca, Hond. H4 64
Choma, Zam. E5 44
Chomutov, Czech. E13 8
Chon Buri, Thai. H6 34
Chone, Ec. H2 58
Ch'ŏngjin, N. Kor. C12 26
Ch'ŏngju, S. Kor. D12 26
Chongmingdao, i., China D10 28
Chongqing, China F8 26
Chŏnju, S. Kor. D12 26
Chonos, Archipiélago de los, is., Chile F2 56
Chonuu, Russia D22 24
Choptank, stm., Md., U.S. C6 97
Chōshi, Japan G13 28
Chos Malal, Arg. D2 56
Choteau, Mt., U.S. C4 103
Chouteau, Ok., U.S. A6 113
Chouteau, co., Mt., U.S. C6 103
Chovd, Mong. B5 26
Chövsgöl Nuur, l., Mong. A7 26
Chowan, co., N.C., U.S. A6 110
Chowan, stm., N.C., U.S. A6 110
Chowchilla, Ca., U.S. D3 82
Chrisman, Il., U.S. D6 90
Christanshåb, Grnld. C22 66
Christchurch, N.Z. E4 52
Christian, co., Il., U.S. D4 90
Christian, co., Ky., U.S. D2 94
Christian, co., Mo., U.S. E4 102
Christian, Cape, c., N.W. Ter., Can. B19 66
Christiana, De., U.S. B3 85
Christiana, Pa., U.S. G9 115
Christiansburg, Va., U.S. C2 123
Christian Sound, strt., Ak., U.S. n22 79
Christiansted, V.I.U.S. F15 64
Christina, stm., De., U.S. A5 68
Christina, Lake, l., Alta., Can. B3 85
Christina, Lake, l., Mn., U.S. D3 100
Christina Peak, mtn., Nv., U.S. D6 105
Christmas, Fl., U.S. D5 86
Christmas Island, dep., Oc. H4 32
Christmas Lake, l., Or., U.S. D6 114
Christopher, Il., U.S. F4 90
Chroma, stm., Russia C22 24
Chrzanów, Pol. E19 8
Chubbuck, Id., U.S. G6 89
Chugach Islands, is., Ak., U.S. h16 79
Chugach Mountains, mts., Ak., U.S. g18 79
Chūgoku-sanchi, mts., Japan H5 30
Chugwater, Wy., U.S. E8 127
Chugwater Creek, stm., Wy., U.S. E8 127
Chukai, Malay. L7 34
Chukchi Sea C30 128
Chula Vista, Ca., U.S. F5 82
Chulucanas, Peru E2 54
Chumphon, Thai. I5 34
Chum Saeng, Thai. G6 34
Chunchi, Ec. I3 58
Ch'unch'ŏn, S. Kor. D12 26
Chunchula, Al., U.S. E1 78
Ch'ungju, S. Kor. D12 26
Chungking see Chongqing, China F8 26
Chungli, Tai. K10 28
Chungyang Shanmo, mts., Tai. L10 28
Chuŏr Phnum Krâvanh, mts., Asia H7 34
Chupadera Mesa, mtn., N.M., U.S. D3 108
Chupaderos, Mex. F8 62
Chuquicamata, Chile A3 56
Chur, Switz. F16 10
Church Hill, Tn., U.S. C11 119
Churchill, Man., Can. f9 70
Churchill, co., Nv., U.S. D3 105
Churchill, stm., Can. E13 66
Churchill, stm., Newf., Can. h9 72
Churchill, Cape, c., Man., Can. f9 70
Churchill, Mount, mtn., B.C., Can. E6 69
Churchill Falls, wtfl, Newf., Can. h8 72
Churchill Lake, l., Sask., Can. m7 75
Churchill Lake, l., Me., U.S. B3 96
Church Point, La., U.S. D3 95
Church Rock, N.M., U.S. B1 108
Churchton, Md., U.S. C4 97
Churchville, N.Y., U.S. B3 109
Churu, India F6 38
Churubusco, In., U.S. B7 91
Churuguara, Ven. B8 58
Chuska Mountains, mts., U.S. A6 80
Chutag, Mong. B7 26
Chuxian, China C7 28
Chuxiong, China B6 34
Chužir, Russia G15 24
Cianjur, Indon. G4 32
Cibecue, Az., U.S. C5 80
Cibinong, Indon. m13 33a
Cibola, co., N.M., U.S. C1 108
Cibolo Creek, stm., Tx., U.S. h7 120
Cicero, Il., U.S. B6 90
Cicero, In., U.S. D5 91
Ciechanów, Pol. C20 8
Ciego de Avila, Cuba D8 64
Ciempozuelos, Spain E8 12
Ciénaga, Col. B5 58
Cienfuegos, Cuba C7 64

Cieszyn, Pol. F18 8
Cieza, Spain G10 12
Cifuentes, Spain E9 12
Cikampek, Indon. m13 33a
Cilacap, Indon. m14 33a
Cilleruelo de Bezana, Spain C8 12
Cimarron, Ks., U.S. E3 93
Cimarron, N.M., U.S. A5 108
Cimarron, co., Ok., U.S. e8 113
Çimkent, Kaz. I11 22
Çınarcık, Tur. I13 16
Cincinnati, Oh., U.S. C1 112
Çine, Tur. L12 16
Çiney, Bel. E5 8
Cinnaminson, N.J., U.S. D3 107
Cipa, stm., Russia F17 24
Cipolletti, Arg. D3 56
Circle, Ak., U.S. B11 79
Circle, Mt., U.S. C11 103
Circle Pines, Mn., U.S. m12 100
Circleville, Oh., U.S. C3 112
Cirebon, Indon. m14 32
Cirencester, Eng., U.K. J11 7
Cirié, Italy D2 14
Cirò Marina, Italy J12 14
Cisco, Tx., U.S. C3 120
Cispus, stm., Wa., U.S. C4 124
Cissna Park, Il., U.S. C6 90
Cistierna, Spain C6 12
Cita, Russia G16 24
Citra, Fl., U.S. C4 86
Citronelle, Al., U.S. D1 78
Citrus, co., Fl., U.S. D4 86
Città di Castello, Italy F7 14
City of Refuge National Historical Park, Hi., U.S. D5 88
City View, S.C., U.S. B3 117
Ciudad, Mex. F7 62
Ciudad Acuña, Mex. C9 62
Ciudad Altamirano, Mex. H9 62
Ciudad Bolívar, Ven. C11 58
Ciudad Bolivia, Ven. C7 58
Ciudad Camargo, Mex. D7 62
Ciudad Chetumal, Mex. H15 62
Ciudad del Carmen, Mex. H14 62
Ciudad del Maíz, Mex. F10 62
Ciudad de México (Mexico City), Mex. H10 62
Ciudad de Nutrias, Ven. C8 58
Ciudad de Valles, Mex. G10 62
Ciudadela, Spain E15 12
Ciudad Guayana, Ven. C11 58
Ciudad Guzmán, Mex. H8 62
Ciudad Hidalgo, Mex. H9 62
Ciudad Ixtepec, Mex. I12 62
Ciudad Jiménez, Mex. D7 62
Ciudad Juárez, Mex. B6 62
Ciudad Madero, Mex. F11 62
Ciudad Mante, Mex. F10 62
Ciudad Melchor Múzquiz, Mex. D9 62
Ciudad Obregón, Mex. D5 62
Ciudad Ojeda (Lagunillas), Ven. B7 58
Ciudad Piar, Ven. D11 58
Ciudad Real, Spain G8 12
Ciudad Rodrigo, Spain E5 12
Ciudad Victoria, Mex. F10 62
Civita Castellana, Italy G7 14
Civitanova Marche, Italy F8 14
Civitavecchia, Italy G6 14
Civray, Fr. F7 10
C.J. Strike Reservoir, res., Id., U.S. G3 89
Clackamas, Or., U.S. h12 114
Clackamas, co., Or., U.S. B4 114
Clacton-on-Sea, Eng., U.K. J14 7
Claflin, Ks., U.S. D5 93
Claiborne, co., Ms., U.S. D3 101
Claiborne, co., Tn., U.S. C10 119
Claiborne, Lake, res., La., U.S. B3 95
Clair, N.B., Can. B1 71
Claire, Lake, l., Alta., Can. f8 68
Clair Engle Lake, res., Ca., U.S. B2 82
Clairton, Pa., U.S. F2 115
Clallam, co., Wa., U.S. B1 124
Clallam Bay, Wa., U.S. A1 124
Clamecy, Fr. E10 10
Clam Lake, l., Wi., U.S. C1 126
Clan Alpine Mountains, mts., Nv., U.S. D4 105
Clanton, Al., U.S. C3 78
Clanwilliam, S. Afr. H3 44
Clara City, Mn., U.S. F3 100
Clara Peak, mtn., Az., U.S. C2 80
Clare, Mi., U.S. E6 99
Clare, co., Mi., U.S. E6 99
Claremont, Ca., U.S. m13 82
Claremont, N.H., U.S. D2 106
Claremont, N.C., U.S. B1 110
Claremont, mtn., Ca., U.S. C3 82
Claremore, Ok., U.S. A6 113
Claremorris, Ire. H3 7
Clarence, Mo., U.S. B5 102
Clarence Strait, strt., Ak., U.S. n23 79
Clarendon, Ar., U.S. C4 81
Clarendon, Tx., U.S. B2 120
Clarendon, co., S.C., U.S. D7 117
Clarendon, stm., Vt., U.S. E2 122
Clarendon Hills, Il., U.S. k9 90
Clarenville, Newf., Can. D4 72
Claresholm, Alta., Can. D4 68
Claridge, Pa., U.S. F2 115
Clarinda, Ia., U.S. D2 92
Clarines, Ven. C10 58
Clarion, Ia., U.S. B4 92
Clarion, Pa., U.S. D3 115
Clarion, co., Pa., U.S. D3 115
Clarion, stm., Pa., U.S. D3 115
Clarión, Isla, i., Mex. H2 62
Clarissa, Mn., U.S. D4 100
Clark, N.J., U.S. B4 107
Clark, S.D., U.S. C8 118
Clark, co., Ar., U.S. C2 81
Clark, co., Id., U.S. E6 89
Clark, co., In., U.S. H6 91
Clark, co., Ks., U.S. E4 93
Clark, co., Ky., U.S. C5 94

Clark, co., Mo., U.S. A6 102
Clark, co., Nv., U.S. G6 105
Clark, co., Oh., U.S. C2 112
Clark, co., S.D., U.S. C8 118
Clark, co., Wa., U.S. D3 124
Clark, co., Wi., U.S. D3 126
Clark, Lake, l., Ak., U.S. C9 79
Clark, Point, c., Ont., Can. C3 73
Clarkdale, Az., U.S. C3 80
Clarkdale, Ga., U.S. h7 87
Clarke, co., Al., U.S. D2 78
Clarke, co., Ga., U.S. C3 87
Clarke, co., Ia., U.S. C4 92
Clarke, co., Ms., U.S. C5 101
Clarke, co., Va., U.S. A4 123
Clarkesville, Ga., U.S. B3 87
Clarkfield, Mn., U.S. F3 100
Clark Fork, stm., U.S. C1 103
Clarks, La., U.S. B3 95
Clarks, stm., Ky., U.S. f9 94
Clarksburg, Md., U.S. B3 97
Clarksburg, W.V., U.S. B4 125
Clarksdale, Ms., U.S. A3 101
Clarks Grove, Mn., U.S. G5 100
Clark's Harbour, N.S., Can. F4 71
Clarks Hill, In., U.S. D4 91
Clarkson, Ky., U.S. C3 94
Clarkson, Ne., U.S. C8 104
Clarks Summit, Pa., U.S. m18 115
Clarkston, Ga., U.S. h8 87
Clarkston, Mi., U.S. F7 99
Clarkston, Ut., U.S. B3 121
Clarkston, Wa., U.S. C8 124
Clarksville, Ar., U.S. B2 81
Clarksville, De., U.S. F5 85
Clarksville, In., U.S. H6 91
Clarksville, Ia., U.S. B5 92
Clarksville, Tn., U.S. A4 119
Clarksville, Tx., U.S. C5 120
Clarksville, Va., U.S. D4 123
Clarkton, Mo., U.S. E8 102
Clarkton, N.C., U.S. C4 110
Clatskanie, Or., U.S. A3 114
Clatsop, co., Or., U.S. A3 114
Claude, Tx., U.S. B2 120
Clausthal-Zellerfeld, Ger. D10 8
Clawson, Mi., U.S. o15 99
Claxton, Ga., U.S. D5 87
Clay, Ky., U.S. C2 94
Clay, co., Al., U.S. B4 78
Clay, co., Ar., U.S. A5 81
Clay, co., Fl., U.S. B5 86
Clay, co., Ga., U.S. E2 87
Clay, co., Il., U.S. E5 90
Clay, co., In., U.S. F3 91
Clay, co., Ia., U.S. A2 92
Clay, co., Ks., U.S. C6 93
Clay, co., Ky., U.S. C6 94
Clay, co., Mn., U.S. D2 100
Clay, co., Ms., U.S. B5 101
Clay, co., Mo., U.S. B3 102
Clay, co., Ne., U.S. D7 104
Clay, co., N.C., U.S. f9 110
Clay, co., S.D., U.S. E8 118
Clay, co., Tn., U.S. C8 119
Clay, co., Tx., U.S. C3 120
Clay, co., W.V., U.S. C3 125
Clay Center, Ks., U.S. C6 93
Clay Center, Ne., U.S. D7 104
Clay City, Il., U.S. E5 90
Clay City, In., U.S. F3 91
Clay City, Ky., U.S. C6 94
Clay Creek, stm., S.D., U.S. D8 118
Claymont, De., U.S. A4 85
Claypool, Az., U.S. D5 80
Claysburg, Pa., U.S. F5 115
Claysville, Pa., U.S. F1 115
Clayton, Al., U.S. D4 78
Clayton, Ga., U.S. B3 87
Clayton, In., U.S. E4 91
Clayton, La., U.S. C4 95
Clayton, Mo., U.S. f13 102
Clayton, N.J., U.S. D2 107
Clayton, N.M., U.S. A6 108
Clayton, N.Y., U.S. A4 109
Clayton, N.C., U.S. B4 110
Clayton, Ok., U.S. C6 113
Clayton, co., Ga., U.S. C2 87
Clayton, co., Ia., U.S. B6 92
Claytor Lake, res., Va., U.S. C2 123
Clear, stm., R.I., U.S. B2 116
Clear Boggy Creek, stm., Ok., U.S. C5 113
Clear Creek, co., Co., U.S. B5 83
Clear Creek, stm., Tn., U.S. C9 119
Clear Creek, stm., Wy., U.S. B6 127
Cleare, Cape, c., Ak., U.S. D10 79
Clearfield, Ky., U.S. B6 94
Clearfield, Pa., U.S. D5 115
Clearfield, Ut., U.S. B3 121
Clearfield, co., Pa., U.S. D5 115
Clear Fork, stm., W.V., U.S. D3 125
Clear Fork, stm., W.V., U.S. n13 125
Clearlake, Ia., U.S. A4 92
Clear Lake, Ia., U.S. A4 92
Clear Lake, S.C., U.S. C9 118
Clearlake, Wa., U.S. A3 124
Clear Lake, Wi., U.S. C1 126
Clear Lake, l., Ia., U.S. A4 92
Clear Lake, l., Ca., U.S. C2 82
Clear Lake, res., Ca., U.S. B3 82
Clear Lake Reservoir, res., Ca., U.S. B3 82
Clear Lake Shores, Tx., U.S. r15 120
Clear Stream, stm., N.H., U.S. g7 106
Clearwater, Fl., U.S. E4 86
Clearwater, S.C., U.S. E4 117
Clearwater, co., Id., U.S. C3 89
Clearwater, co., Mn., U.S. C3 100
Clearwater, stm., Can. A5 68
Clearwater, stm., Id., U.S. C2 89
Clearwater, stm., Mn., U.S. C3 100
Clearwater Lake, res., Mo., U.S. D7 102
Clearwater Mountains, mts., Id., U.S. C2 89

Cleburne, Tx., U.S. C4 120
Cleburne, co., Al., U.S. B4 78
Cleburne, co., Ar., U.S. B3 81
Cle Elum, Wa., U.S. B5 124
Cle Elum, stm., Wa., U.S. B4 124
Cle Elum Lake, res., Wa., U.S. B4 124
Clementon, N.J., U.S. D3 107
Clemmons, N.C., U.S. A2 110
Clemson, S.C., U.S. B2 117
Clendenin, W.V., U.S. C3 125
Clendening Lake, res., Oh., U.S. B4 112
Cleona, Pa., U.S. F9 115
Clermont, Que., Can. B7 74
Clermont, Fr. C9 10
Clermont, Fl., U.S. D5 86
Clermont, co., Oh., U.S. C1 112
Clermont-Ferrand, Fr. G10 10
Cles, Italy C6 14
Cleveland, Al., U.S. A3 78
Cleveland, Ga., U.S. B3 87
Cleveland, Mn., U.S. F5 100
Cleveland, Ms., U.S. B3 101
Cleveland, N.C., U.S. B2 110
Cleveland, Oh., U.S. A4 112
Cleveland, Ok., U.S. A5 113
Cleveland, Tn., U.S. D9 119
Cleveland, Tx., U.S. D5 120
Cleveland, Wi., U.S. k10 126
Cleveland, co., Ar., U.S. D3 81
Cleveland, co., N.C., U.S. B1 110
Cleveland, co., Ok., U.S. B4 113
Cleveland, Mount, mtn., Mt., U.S. B3 103
Cleveland Heights, Oh., U.S. A4 112
Cleves, Oh., U.S. o12 112
Clewiston, Fl., U.S. F6 86
Cliff Island, i., Me., U.S. g7 96
Clifford, Ont., Can. D4 73
Cliffside, N.C., U.S. B1 110
Cliffside Park, N.J., U.S. h9 107
Clifton, Az., U.S. D6 80
Clifton, Co., U.S. B2 83
Clifton, Il., U.S. C6 90
Clifton, N.J., U.S. B4 107
Clifton, S.C., U.S. B4 117
Clifton, Tn., U.S. B4 119
Clifton, Tx., U.S. D4 120
Clifton Forge, Va., U.S. C3 123
Clifton Knolls, N.Y., U.S. C7 109
Clifton Springs, N.Y., U.S. C3 109
Clinch, co., Ga., U.S. F4 87
Clinch, stm., U.S. D9 119
Clinchco, Va., U.S. e9 123
Clinch Mountain, mtn., U.S. C10 119
Clingmans Dome, mtn., U.S. D10 119
Clinton, B.C., Can. D7 69
Clinton, Ont., Can. D3 73
Clinton, Ar., U.S. B3 81
Clinton, Ct., U.S. D5 84
Clinton, Il., U.S. C5 90
Clinton, In., U.S. E3 91
Clinton, Ia., U.S. C7 92
Clinton, Ky., U.S. f9 94
Clinton, La., U.S. D4 95
Clinton, Me., U.S. D3 96
Clinton, Md., U.S. C4 97
Clinton, Ma., U.S. B4 98
Clinton, Mi., U.S. F7 99
Clinton, Ms., U.S. C3 101
Clinton, Mo., U.S. C4 102
Clinton, N.Y., U.S. B5 109
Clinton, N.C., U.S. C4 110
Clinton, Ok., U.S. B3 113
Clinton, S.C., U.S. C4 117
Clinton, Tn., U.S. C9 119
Clinton, Ut., U.S. B3 121
Clinton, Wa., U.S. B3 124
Clinton, Wi., U.S. F5 126
Clinton, co., Il., U.S. E4 90
Clinton, co., In., U.S. D4 91
Clinton, co., Ia., U.S. C7 92
Clinton, co., Ky., U.S. D4 94
Clinton, co., Mi., U.S. F6 99
Clinton, co., Mo., U.S. B3 102
Clinton, co., N.Y., U.S. f11 109
Clinton, co., Oh., U.S. C2 112
Clinton, co., Pa., U.S. D6 115
Clinton, Lake, res., Il., U.S. C5 90
Clinton-Colden Lake, l., N.W. Ter., Can. D11 66
Clinton Lake, res., Ks., U.S. m15 93
Clinton Reservoir, res., N.J., U.S. A4 107
Clintonville, Wi., U.S. D5 126
Clintwood, Va., U.S. e9 123
Clio, Al., U.S. D4 78
Clio, Mi., U.S. E7 99
Clio, S.C., U.S. B8 117
Clive, Ia., U.S. e8 92
Clogher Head, c., Ire. H6 7
Cloncurry, Austl. D8 50
Clonmel, Ire. I5 7
Cloppenburg, Ger. C8 8
Cloquet, Mn., U.S. D6 100
Cloquet, stm., Mn., U.S. C6 100
Closter, N.J., U.S. B5 107
Clothier, W.V., U.S. n12 125
Cloud, co., Ks., U.S. C6 93
Cloudcroft, N.M., U.S. E4 108
Cloud Peak, mtn., Wy., U.S. B5 127
Clover, S.C., U.S. A5 117
Cloverdale, Al., U.S. A2 78
Cloverdale, Ca., U.S. C2 82
Cloverdale, In., U.S. E4 91
Cloverport, Ky., U.S. C3 94
Clovis, Ca., U.S. D4 82
Clovis, N.M., U.S. C6 108
Cluj-Napoca, Rom. C7 16
Cluny, Fr. F11 10
Cluses, Fr. F13 10
Clusone, Italy D4 14
Clute, Tx., U.S. r14 120
Clutha, stm., N.Z. G2 52
Clyde, N.W. Ter., Can. B19 66
Clyde, Ks., U.S. C6 93
Clyde, N.Y., U.S. B4 109
Clyde, N.C., U.S. f10 110
Clyde, Oh., U.S. A3 112
Clyde, Tx., U.S. C3 120
Clyde, stm., Scot., U.K. F9 7

Clyde, Firth of, est., Scot., U.K. . . . F7 7
Clymer, Pa., U.S. E3 115
Coachella, Ca., U.S. F5 82
Coachella Canal, Ca., U.S. F6 82
Coacoyole, Mex. E6 62
Coahoma, Tx., U.S. C2 120
Coahoma, co., Ms., U.S. A3 101
Coal, co., Ok., U.S. C5 113
Coal, stm., W.V., U.S. C3 125
Coal Branch, N.B., Can. C4 71
Coal City, Il., U.S. B5 90
Coalcomán de Matamoros, Mex. H8 62
Coal Creek, stm., Ok., U.S. B6 113
Coaldale, Alta., Can. E4 68
Coal Fork, W.V., U.S. C3 125
Coal Fork, stm., W.V., U.S. m13 125
Coalgate, Ok., U.S. C5 113
Coal Grove, Oh., U.S. D3 112
Coal Hill, Ar., U.S. B2 81
Coalhurst, Alta., Can. E4 68
Coalinga, Ca., U.S. D3 82
Coalmont, Tn., U.S. D8 119
Coalville, Ut., U.S. C4 121
Coalwood, W.V., U.S. D3 125
Coari, Braz. D6 54
Coasters Harbor Island, i., R.I., U.S. E5 116
Coast Mountains, mts., N.A. E6 66
Coast Ranges, mts., U.S. C2 76
Coatepeque, Guat. G2 64
Coatesville, Pa., U.S. G10 115
Coaticook, Que., Can. D6 74
Coats, N.C., U.S. B4 110
Coats Island, i., N.W. Ter., Can. D16 66
Coats Land, reg., Ant. B10 47
Coatzacoalcos, Mex. H12 62
Cobalt, Ont., Can. p19 73
Cobb, co., Ga., U.S. C2 87
Cobb, stm., Mn., U.S. G5 100
Cobble Mountain Reservoir, res., Ma., U.S. B2 98
Cobbosseecontee Lake, l., Me., U.S. D3 96
Cobden, Ont., Can. B8 73
Cobden, Il., U.S. F4 90
Cobequid Mountains, mts., N.S., Can. D5 71
Cobham, stm., Can. C4 70
Cobija, Bol. F5 54
Cobleskill, N.Y., U.S. C6 109
Cobourg, Ont., Can. D6 73
Cóbuè, Moz. D6 44
Cobun Creek, stm., W.V., U.S. h11 125
Coburg, Ger. E10 8
Coburg, Or., U.S. C3 114
Coburg Island, i., N.W. Ter., Can. A17 66
Cochabamba, Bol. G5 54
Cocheco, stm., N.H., U.S. D5 106
Cochin, India H4 37
Cochise, co., Az., U.S. F5 80
Cochise Head, mtn., Az., U.S. E6 80
Cochiti Indian Reservation, N.M., U.S. h8 108
Cochiti Reservoir, res., N.M., U.S. B3 108
Cochituate, Ma., U.S. g10 98
Cochituate, Lake, l., Ma., U.S. g10 98
Cochran, Ga., U.S. D3 87
Cochran, co., Tx., U.S. C1 120
Cochrane, Alta., Can. D3 68
Cochrane, Ont., Can. o19 73
Cochranton, Pa., U.S. C1 115
Cocke, co., Tn., U.S. D10 119
Cockeysville, Md., U.S. B4 97
Cockrell Hill, Tx., U.S. n10 120
Coco, stm., N.A. G6 64
Coco, Isla del, i., C.R. B1 54
Cocoa, Fl., U.S. D6 86
Cocoa Beach, Fl., U.S. D6 86
Coco Channel, strt., Asia H2 34
Coco Islands, is., Burma G2 34
Coconino, co., Az., U.S. B3 80
Cocopah Indian Reservation, Az., U.S. E1 80
Côcos, Braz. C6 57
Cocula, Mex. G8 62
Cod, Cape, c., Ma., U.S. C7 98
Codajás, Braz. D6 54
Coden, Al., U.S. E1 78
Codigoro, Italy E7 14
Codington, co., S.D., U.S. C8 118
Codogno, Italy D4 14
Codroipo, Italy D7 14
Cody, Wy., U.S. B3 127
Coeburn, Va., U.S. f9 123
Coen, Austl. B8 50
Coetivy Island, i., Sey. C11 44
Coeur d'Alene, Id., U.S. B2 89
Coeur d'Alene, stm., Id., U.S. B2 89
Coeur d'Alene Indian Reservation, Id., U.S. B2 89
Coeur d'Alene Lake, res., Id., U.S. B2 89
Coeur d'Alene Mountains, mts., Id., U.S. B2 89
Coffee, co., Al., U.S. D3 78
Coffee, co., Ga., U.S. E4 87
Coffee, co., Tn., U.S. B5 119
Coffeeville, Ms., U.S. B4 101
Coffey, co., Ks., U.S. D8 93
Coffeyville, Ks., U.S. E8 93
Coffs Harbour, Austl. F10 50
Coggon, Ia., U.S. B6 92
Cognac, Fr. G6 10
Cohansey, stm., N.J., U.S. E2 107
Cohasset, Ma., U.S. B6 98
Cohasset, Mn., U.S. C5 100
Cohocton, stm., N.Y., U.S. C3 109
Cohoes, N.Y., U.S. C7 109
Cohoon, Lake, res., Va., U.S. k14 123
Cohutta Mountain, mtn., Ga., U.S. B2 87
Coiba, Isla de, i., Pan. K7 64
Coimbatore, India G4 37
Coimbra, Braz. F7 57
Coimbra, Port. E3 12
Çoin, Spain I7 12
Cojbalsan, Mong. B9 26
Cokato, Mn., U.S. E4 100
Coke, co., Tx., U.S. D2 120
Çokeville, Wy., U.S. D2 127
Çokurdach, Russia C23 24

Name	Map Ref	Page
Colatina, Braz.	E8	57
Colbert, Ok., U.S.	D5	113
Colbert, co., Al., U.S.	A2	78
Colborne, Ont., Can.	C7	73
Colby, Ks., U.S.	C2	93
Colby, Wi., U.S.	D3	126
Colchester, Eng., U.K.	J13	7
Colchester, Ct., U.S.	C6	84
Colchester, Il., U.S.	C3	90
Colcord, Ok., U.S.	A7	113
Cold, stm., N.H., U.S.	C4	106
Cold, stm., N.H., U.S.	D2	106
Cold Bay, Ak., U.S.	E7	79
Cold Lake, Alta., Can.	B5	68
Cold Spring, Ky., U.S.	A5	94
Cold Spring, Mn., U.S.	E4	100
Coldwater, Ont., Can.	C5	73
Coldwater, Ks., U.S.	E4	93
Coldwater, Mi., U.S.	G5	99
Coldwater, Ms., U.S.	A4	101
Coldwater, Oh., U.S.	A3	101
Coldwater, stm., Ms., U.S.	B1	112
Coldwater Creek, stm., U.S.	A3	101
Colebrook, N.H., U.S.	e9	113
Colebrook River Lake, res., Ct., U.S.	g7	106
Cole, co., Mo., U.S.	C5	102
Colebrook River Lake, res., Ct., U.S.	A3	84
Cole Camp, Mo., U.S.	C4	102
Coleen, stm., Ak., U.S.	B11	79
Coleman, Mi., U.S.	E6	99
Coleman, Tx., U.S.	D3	120
Coleman, Wi., U.S.	C5	126
Coleman, co., Tx., U.S.	D3	120
Coleraine, N. Ire., U.K.	F6	7
Coleraine, Mn., U.S.	C5	100
Coles, co., Il., U.S.	D5	90
Colesberg, S. Afr.	H5	44
Colfax, Ca., U.S.	C3	82
Colfax, In., U.S.	D4	91
Colfax, Ia., U.S.	C4	92
Colfax, La., U.S.	C3	95
Colfax, Wa., U.S.	C8	124
Colfax, Wi., U.S.	D2	126
Colfax, co., Ne., U.S.	C8	104
Colfax, co., N.M., U.S.	A5	108
Colhué Huapi, Lago, l., Arg.	F3	56
Colima, Mex.	H8	62
Colima, Nevado de, mtn., Mex.	H8	62
Colinas, Braz.	E10	54
Coll, i., Scot., U.K.	E6	7
College, Ak., U.S.	B10	79
Collegedale, Tn., U.S.	h11	119
College Park, Ga., U.S.	h2	87
College Park, Md., U.S.	C4	97
College Place, Wa., U.S.	C7	124
College Station, Ar., U.S.	C3	81
College Station, Tx., U.S.	D4	120
Collegeville, In., U.S.	C3	91
Collegeville, Pa., U.S.	F11	115
Colleton, co., S.C., U.S.	F6	117
Collier, co., Fl., U.S.	F5	86
Collier Bay, b., Austl.	C4	50
Colliers, W.V., U.S.	f8	125
Collierville, Tn., U.S.	B2	119
Collin, co., Tx., U.S.	C4	120
Collingdale, Pa., U.S.	p20	115
Collingswood, N.J., U.S.	D2	107
Collingsworth, co., Tx., U.S.	B2	120
Collingwood, Ont., Can.	C4	73
Collins, Ms., U.S.	D4	101
Collins Park, De., U.S.	B3	85
Collinsville, Al., U.S.	A4	78
Collinsville, Ct., U.S.	B4	84
Collinsville, Il., U.S.	E4	90
Collinsville, Ms., U.S.	C5	101
Collinsville, Ok., U.S.	A6	113
Collinsville, Va., U.S.	D3	123
Collinwood, Tn., U.S.	B4	119
Collooney, Ire.	G4	7
Colmar, Fr.	D14	10
Colmar Manor, Md., U.S.	f9	97
Colmenar, Spain	I7	12
Colmenar de Oreja, Spain	E8	12
Colmenar Viejo, Spain	E8	12
Colo, Ia., U.S.	B4	92
Cologne see Köln, Ger.	E6	8
Coloma, Mi., U.S.	F4	99
Colomb-Béchar see Béchar, Alg.	B5	42
Colombia, ctry., S.A.	C4	54
Colombo, Sri L.	I5	37
Colón, Cuba	C7	64
Colón, Pan.	J8	64
Colon, Mi., U.S.	G5	99
Colon, Archipiélago de (Galapagos Islands), is., Ec.	m15	58a
Colonia Dora, Arg.	B4	56
Colonia Las Heras, Arg.	F3	56
Colonial Beach, Va., U.S.	B6	123
Colonial Heights, Tn., U.S.	C11	119
Colonial Heights, Va., U.S.	C5	123
Colonial National Historical Park, Va., U.S.	C6	123
Colonia Vicente Guerrero, Mex.	B1	62
Colonie, N.Y., U.S.	C7	109
Coloradas, Lomas, hills, Arg.	E4	56
Colorado, co., Tx., U.S.	E4	120
Colorado, state, U.S.	B5	83
Colorado, stm., Arg.	D4	56
Colorado, stm., N.A.	E4	76
Colorado, stm., N.A.	E4	76
Colorado City, Az., U.S.	A3	80
Colorado City, Co., U.S.	D6	83
Colorado City, Tx., U.S.	C2	120
Colorado City, Lake, res., Tx., U.S.	C2	120
Colorado National Monument, Co., U.S.	B2	83
Colorado River Aqueduct, Ca., U.S.	F6	82
Colorado River Indian Reservation, U.S.	D1	80
Colorado Springs, Co., U.S.	C6	83
Colotlán, Mex.	F8	62
Colquitt, Ga., U.S.	E2	87
Colquitt, co., Ga., U.S.	E3	87
Colstrip, Mt., U.S.	E10	103
Colton, S.D., U.S.	D9	118
Coltons Point, Md., U.S.	D4	97
Columbia, Al., U.S.	D4	78
Columbia, Il., U.S.	E3	90
Columbia, Ky., U.S.	C4	94
Columbia, Md., U.S.	B4	97
Columbia, Ms., U.S.	D4	101
Columbia, Mo., U.S.	C5	102
Columbia, N.C., U.S.	B6	110
Columbia, Pa., U.S.	F9	115
Columbia, S.C., U.S.	C5	117
Columbia, Tn., U.S.	B4	119
Columbia, co., Ar., U.S.	D2	81
Columbia, co., Fl., U.S.	B4	86
Columbia, co., Ga., U.S.	C4	87
Columbia, co., N.Y., U.S.	C7	109
Columbia, co., Or., U.S.	B3	114
Columbia, co., Pa., U.S.	D9	115
Columbia, co., Wa., U.S.	C7	124
Columbia, co., Wi., U.S.	E4	126
Columbia, stm., N.A.	G8	66
Columbia, Mount, mtn., Can.	C2	68
Columbia City, In., U.S.	B7	91
Columbia City, Or., U.S.	B4	114
Columbia Falls, Mt., U.S.	B2	103
Columbia Heights, Mn., U.S.	m12	100
Columbia Lake, res., Ct., U.S.	C6	84
Columbia Mountains, mts., B.C., Can.	C7	69
Columbiana, Al., U.S.	B3	78
Columbiana, Oh., U.S.	B5	112
Columbiana, co., Oh., U.S.	B5	112
Columbiaville, Mi., U.S.	E7	99
Columbus, Ga., U.S.	D2	87
Columbus, In., U.S.	F6	91
Columbus, Ks., U.S.	E9	93
Columbus, Ms., U.S.	B5	101
Columbus, Mt., U.S.	E7	103
Columbus, Ne., U.S.	C8	104
Columbus, N.M., U.S.	F2	108
Columbus, N.C., U.S.	f10	110
Columbus, Oh., U.S.	C2	112
Columbus, Tx., U.S.	E4	120
Columbus, Wi., U.S.	E4	126
Columbus, co., N.C., U.S.	C4	110
Columbus Air Force Base, mil., Ms., U.S.	B5	101
Columbus Grove, Oh., U.S.	B1	112
Columbus Junction, Ia., U.S.	C6	92
Columbus Lake, res., Ms., U.S.	B5	101
Colusa, Ca., U.S.	C2	82
Colusa, co., Ca., U.S.	C2	82
Colver, Pa., U.S.	E4	115
Colville, Wa., U.S.	A8	124
Colville, stm., Ak., U.S.	B9	79
Colville, stm., Wa., U.S.	A8	124
Colville Indian Reservation, Wa., U.S.	A6	124
Colvos Passage, strt., Wa., U.S.	f10	124
Colwich, Ks., U.S.	E6	93
Colwood, B.C., Can.	h12	69
Comacchio, Italy	E7	14
Comal, co., Tx., U.S.	E3	120
Comanche, Ok., U.S.	C4	113
Comanche, Tx., U.S.	D3	120
Comanche, co., Ks., U.S.	E4	93
Comanche, co., Ok., U.S.	C3	113
Comanche, co., Tx., U.S.	D3	120
Comandante Fontana, Arg.	B5	56
Comayagua, Hond.	G4	64
Combahee, stm., S.C., U.S.	F6	117
Combarbalá, Chile	C2	56
Combeaufontaine, Fr.	E12	10
Combined Locks, Wi., U.S.	h9	126
Combourg, Fr.	D5	10
Combs, Ky., U.S.	C6	94
Comer, Ga., U.S.	B3	87
Comfort, Tx., U.S.	E3	120
Comilla, Bngl.	I14	38
Comitán [de Domínguez], Mex.	I13	62
Comite, stm., La., U.S.	D4	95
Commentry, Fr.	F9	10
Commerce, Ga., U.S.	B3	87
Commerce, Ok., U.S.	A7	113
Commerce, Tx., U.S.	C5	120
Commerce City, Co., U.S.	B6	83
Committee Bay, b., N.W. Ter., Can.	C15	66
Common Fence Point, R.I., U.S.	D6	116
Como, Italy	D4	14
Como, Ms., U.S.	A4	101
Como, Lago di, l., Italy	C4	14
Comodoro Rivadavia, Arg.	F3	56
Comorin, Cape, c., India	H4	37
Comoros, ctry., Afr.	D8	44
Compiègne, Fr.	C9	10
Compton, Que., Can.	D6	74
Compton, Ca., U.S.	n12	82
Comstock, Mi., U.S.	F5	99
Con, stm., Viet.	E8	34
Cona, stm., Russia	E16	24
Conakry, Gui.	G3	42
Conanicut Island, i., R.I., U.S.	E5	116
Conanicut Point, c., R.I., U.S.	E5	116
Concarneau, Fr.	E3	10
Conceição do Araguaia, Braz.	E9	54
Concepción, Arg.	B3	56
Concepción, Bol.	G6	54
Concepción, Chile	D2	56
Concepción, Para.	A5	56
Concepción, Laguna, l., Bol.	G6	54
Concepción, Volcán, vol., Nic.	I5	64
Concepción del Oro, Mex.	E9	62
Concepción del Uruguay, Arg.	C5	56
Conception, Point, c., Ca., U.S.	E3	82
Conception Bay, b., Newf., Can.	E5	72
Conception Bay South, Newf., Can.	E5	72
Conchas Lake, res., N.M., U.S.	B5	108
Conches, Fr.	D7	10
Concho, co., Tx., U.S.	D3	120
Concho, stm., Tx., U.S.	D2	120
Conchos, stm., Mex.	C7	62
Concord, Ca., U.S.	h8	82
Concord, Ma., U.S.	B5	98
Concord, Mi., U.S.	F6	99
Concord, Mo., U.S.	g13	102
Concord, N.H., U.S.	D3	106
Concord, N.C., U.S.	B2	110
Concord, stm., Ma., U.S.	A5	98
Concordia, Arg.	C5	56
Concordia, Mex.	F6	62
Concordia, Ks., U.S.	C6	93
Concordia, Mo., U.S.	C4	102
Concordia, co., La., U.S.	C4	95
Concrete, Wa., U.S.	A4	124
Condé, Fr.	D6	10
Condom, Fr.	I7	10
Condon, Or., U.S.	B6	114
Condoto, Col.	E4	58
Conecuh, co., Al., U.S.	D2	78
Conecuh, stm., Al., U.S.	D3	78
Conegliano, Italy	D7	14
Conejos, co., Co., U.S.	D4	83
Conejos, stm., Co., U.S.	D4	83
Conejos Peak, mtn., Co., U.S.	D4	83
Conemaugh, Pa., U.S.	F4	115
Conemaugh River Lake, res., Pa., U.S.	F3	115
Confolens, Fr.	F7	10
Congamond Lakes, l., U.S.	A4	84
Congaree, stm., S.C., U.S.	D6	117
Congaree Swamp National Monument, S.C., U.S.	D6	117
Congo, ctry., Afr.	B2	44
Congo (Zaïre), stm., Afr.	C2	44
Congress, Az., U.S.	C3	80
Conimicut Point, c., R.I., U.S.	D5	116
Conitaca, Mex.	E6	62
Conklin, N.Y., U.S.	C5	109
Conn, Lough, l., Ire.	G3	7
Connaught, hist. reg., Ire.	H3	7
Conneaut, Oh., U.S.	A5	112
Conneaut Creek, stm., Oh., U.S.	A5	112
Conneaut Lake, l., Pa., U.S.	C1	115
Connecticut, stm., U.S.	C12	76
Connecticut, state, U.S.	C5	84
Connell, Wa., U.S.	C7	124
Connellsville, Pa., U.S.	F2	115
Connemara, reg., Ire.	H3	7
Connersville, In., U.S.	E7	91
Conover, N.C., U.S.	B1	110
Conowingo, Md., U.S.	A5	97
Conrad, Ia., U.S.	B5	92
Conrad, Mt., U.S.	B5	103
Conroe, Tx., U.S.	D5	120
Conselheiro Lafaiete, Braz.	F7	57
Conshohocken, Pa., U.S.	F11	115
Con Son, i., Viet.	J9	34
Consort, Alta., Can.	C5	68
Constance, Lake see Bodensee, l., Eur.	H9	8
Constanța, Rom.	E12	16
Constantina, Spain	H6	12
Constantine (Qacentina), Alg.	A7	42
Constantine, Mi., U.S.	G5	99
Constantine, Cape, c., Ak., U.S.	D8	79
Consuegra, Spain	F8	12
Contai, India	J12	38
Contas, Rio de, stm., Braz.	C9	57
Content Keys, is., Fl., U.S.	H5	86
Continental, Oh., U.S.	A1	112
Continental Peak, mtn., Wy., U.S.	D4	127
Continental Reservoir, res., Co., U.S.	D3	83
Contoocook, N.H., U.S.	D3	106
Contoocook, stm., N.H., U.S.	D3	106
Contra Costa, co., Ca., U.S.	D3	82
Contrecoeur, Que., Can.	D4	74
Contres, Fr.	E8	10
Contwoyto Lake, l., N.W. Ter., Can.	C10	66
Convención, Col.	C6	58
Conversano, Italy	I12	14
Converse, In., U.S.	C6	91
Converse, S.C., U.S.	B4	117
Converse, co., Wy., U.S.	C7	127
Convoy, Oh., U.S.	B1	112
Conway, Ar., U.S.	B3	81
Conway, Fl., U.S.	D5	86
Conway, Mo., U.S.	D5	102
Conway, N.H., U.S.	C4	106
Conway, N.C., U.S.	A5	110
Conway, Pa., U.S.	E1	115
Conway, S.C., U.S.	D9	117
Conway, co., Ar., U.S.	B3	81
Conway, Lake, res., Ar., U.S.	B3	81
Conway Lake, l., N.H., U.S.	C4	106
Conway Springs, Ks., U.S.	E6	93
Conyers, Ga., U.S.	C2	87
Cooch Behar, India	G13	38
Cook, Mn., U.S.	C6	100
Cook, co., Ga., U.S.	E3	87
Cook, co., Il., U.S.	B6	90
Cook, co., Mn., U.S.	k9	100
Cook, Cape, c., B.C., Can.	D4	69
Cook, Mount, mtn., N.Z.	E3	52
Cooke, co., Tx., U.S.	C4	120
Cookes Peak, mtn., N.M., U.S.	E2	108
Cookeville, Tn., U.S.	C8	119
Cook Inlet, b., Ak., U.S.	D9	79
Cook Islands, dep., Oc.	H2	2
Cook Point, c., Md., U.S.	C5	97
Cookshire, Que., Can.	D6	74
Cookson, Ok., U.S.	B7	113
Cookstown, N. Ire., U.K.	G6	7
Cook Strait, strt., N.Z.	D5	52
Cooktown, Austl.	C9	50
Cooleemee, N.C., U.S.	B2	110
Coolgardie, Austl.	F4	50
Coolidge, Az., U.S.	E4	80
Coolidge, Ga., U.S.	E3	87
Cooma, Austl.	G9	50
Coonoor, India	G4	37
Coon Rapids, Ia., U.S.	C3	92
Coon Rapids, Mn., U.S.	E5	100
Coon Valley, Wi., U.S.	E2	126
Cooper, Tx., U.S.	C5	120
Cooper, co., Mo., U.S.	C5	102
Cooper, stm., S.C., U.S.	F8	117
Cooper Mountain, mtn., Ak., U.S.	g17	79
Coopersburg, Pa., U.S.	F11	115
Cooperstown, N.Y., U.S.	C6	109
Cooperstown, N.D., U.S.	B7	111
Coopersville, Mi., U.S.	E5	99
Coos, co., N.H., U.S.	A4	106
Coos, co., Or., U.S.	D2	114
Coos, stm., Or., U.S.	D2	114
Coosa, co., Al., U.S.	C3	78
Coosa, stm., U.S.	C3	78
Coosada, Al., U.S.	C3	78
Coosawhatchie, stm., S.C., U.S.	F5	117
Coos Bay, Or., U.S.	D2	114
Copalis Beach, Wa., U.S.	B1	124
Copan, Ok., U.S.	A6	113
Copan Reservoir, res., Ok., U.S.	A6	113
Copenhagen see København, Den.	I9	6
Copiah, co., Ms., U.S.	D3	101
Copiapó, Chile	B2	56
Coplay, Pa., U.S.	E10	115
Copparo, Italy	E6	14
Copper, stm., Ak., U.S.	C11	79
Copperas Cove, Tx., U.S.	D4	120
Copper Butte, mtn., Wa., U.S.	A7	124
Coppermine, N.W. Ter., Can.	C9	66
Coppermine, stm., N.W. Ter., Can.	C10	66
Copper Mountain, mtn., Wy., U.S.	C5	127
Copper Mountains, mts., Az., U.S.	E2	80
Coquille, Or., U.S.	D2	114
Coquimbo, Chile	B2	56
Coral Gables, Fl., U.S.	G6	86
Coral Harbour, N.W. Ter., Can.	D16	66
Coral Sea, Oc.	B10	50
Coralville, Ia., U.S.	C6	92
Coralville Lake, res., Ia., U.S.	C5	92
Corantijn (Corentyne), stm., S.A.	E14	58
Coraopolis, Pa., U.S.	E1	115
Corato, Italy	H11	14
Corbeil-Essonnes, Fr.	D9	10
Corbigny, Fr.	E10	10
Corbin, Ky., U.S.	D5	94
Corcoran, Ca., U.S.	D4	82
Corcoran, Mn., U.S.	m11	100
Corcovado, Golfo, b., Chile	E2	56
Corcovado, Volcán, vol., Chile	E2	56
Corcubión, Spain	C2	12
Cordele, Ga., U.S.	E3	87
Cordell, Ok., U.S.	B3	113
Cordell Hull Lake, res., Tn., U.S.	C8	119
Cordes, Fr.	H8	10
Córdoba, Arg.	C4	56
Córdoba, Mex.	H11	62
Córdoba, Spain	H7	12
Cordova, Al., U.S.	B2	78
Cordova, Ak., U.S.	C10	79
Cordova, N.M., U.S.	A4	108
Cordova, N.C., U.S.	C3	110
Cordova Peak, mtn., Ak., U.S.	C10	79
Corentyne (Corantijn), stm., S.A.	E14	58
Corfu see Kérkira, Grc.	J3	16
Coria, Spain	F5	12
Coria del Río, Spain	H5	12
Corigliano Calabro, Italy	J11	14
Coringa Islets, is., Austl.	C9	50
Corinna, Me., U.S.	D3	96
Corinne, Ut., U.S.	B3	121
Corinth, Ms., U.S.	A5	101
Corinth, N.Y., U.S.	B7	109
Corinth see Kórinthos, Grc.	L6	16
Corinto, Braz.	E6	57
Cork, Ire.	J4	7
Corlay, Fr.	D3	10
Corleone, Italy	L8	14
Corleto Perticara, Italy	I11	14
Çorlu, Tur.	H11	16
Cormorant Lake, l., Man., U.S.	B1	70
Cornelia, Ga., U.S.	B3	87
Cornélio Procópio, Braz.	G3	57
Cornelius, N.C., U.S.	B2	110
Cornelius, Or., U.S.	g11	114
Cornell, Wi., U.S.	C2	126
Corner Brook, Newf., Can.	D3	72
Cornersville, Tn., U.S.	B5	119
Cornfield Point, c., Ct., U.S.	D6	84
Cornie Bayou, stm., U.S.	D3	81
Corning, Ar., U.S.	A5	81
Corning, Ca., U.S.	C2	82
Corning, Ia., U.S.	D3	92
Corning, N.Y., U.S.	C3	109
Cornish, Me., U.S.	E2	96
Corn Islands, is., Nic.	H6	64
Corno Grande, mtn., Italy	G8	14
Cornville, Az., U.S.	C4	80
Cornwall, Ont., Can.	B10	73
Cornwall, Pa., U.S.	F9	115
Cornwallis Island, i., N.W. Ter., Can.	A14	66
Cornwall on Hudson, N.Y., U.S.	D6	109
Coro, Ven.	B8	58
Corocoro, Bol.	G5	54
Coroico, Bol.	G5	54
Coromandel Coast, India	F6	37
Coromandel Peninsula, pen., N.Z.	B5	52
Corona, Ca., U.S.	F5	82
Coronado, Ca., U.S.	F5	82
Coronado National Memorial, Az., U.S.	F5	80
Coronation, Alta., Can.	C5	68
Coronation Gulf, b., N.W. Ter., Can.	C10	66
Coronation Island, i., Ak., U.S.	n22	79
Coronel Dorrego, Arg.	D4	56
Coronel Fabriciano, Braz.	E7	57
Coronel Pringles, Arg.	D4	56
Coronel Suárez, Arg.	D4	56
Coropuna, Nevado, mtn., Peru	G4	54
Corpus Christi, Tx., U.S.	F4	120
Corpus Christi Naval Air Station, mil., Tx., U.S.	F4	120
Corral de Almaguer, Spain	F8	12
Correctionville, Ia., U.S.	B2	92
Correggio, Italy	E5	14
Corrente, stm., Braz.	B7	57
Corrib, Lough, l., Ire.	H3	7
Corrientes, Arg.	B5	56
Corrientes, Cabo, c., Col.	E4	58
Corrientes, Cabo, c., Cuba	D4	64
Corrientes, Cabo, c., Mex.	G7	62
Corrigan, Tx., U.S.	D5	120
Corriganville, Md., U.S.	k13	97
Corry, Pa., U.S.	C2	115
Corse (Corsica), i., Fr.	m19	11a
Corsica, S.D., U.S.	D7	118
Corsica see Corse, i., Fr.	m19	11a
Corsicana, Tx., U.S.	C4	120
Corson, co., S.D., U.S.	B4	118
Corson Inlet, b., N.J., U.S.	E3	14
Cortemilia, Italy	D2	14
Cortez, Co., U.S.	q10	86
Cortez, Fl., U.S.	C5	105
Cortez Mountains, mts., Nv., U.S.	C7	14
Cortina d'Ampezzo, Italy	B5	90
Cortland, Il., U.S.	B5	90
Cortland, N.Y., U.S.	C4	109
Cortland, Oh., U.S.	A5	112
Cortland, co., N.Y., U.S.	C4	109
Çorum, Tur.	G14	4
Corumbá, Braz.	G7	54
Corumbá, stm., Braz.	E4	57
Corunna, Mi., U.S.	F6	99
Corvallis, Or., U.S.	C3	114
Corydon, In., U.S.	H5	91
Corydon, Ia., U.S.	D4	92
Corydon, Ky., U.S.	C2	94
Coryell, co., Tx., U.S.	D4	120
Cosalá, Mex.	E6	62
Cosamaloapan [de Carpio], Mex.	H12	62
Cosenza, Italy	J11	14
Coshocton, Oh., U.S.	B4	112
Coshocton, co., Oh., U.S.	B4	112
Cosmoledo Group, is., Sey.	C9	44
Cosmopolis, Wa., U.S.	C2	124
Cosmos, Mn., U.S.	F4	100
Cosne-sur-Loire, Fr.	E9	10
Cossatot, stm., Ar., U.S.	C1	81
Costa Mesa, Ca., U.S.	n13	82
Costa Rica, Mex.	C4	62
Costa Rica, ctry., N.A.	I5	64
Costilla, co., Co., U.S.	D5	83
Cotabato, Phil.	D7	32
Coteau-Landing, Que., Can.	D3	74
Cotentin, pen., Fr.	C5	10
Cotonou, Benin	G6	42
Cotopaxi, vol., Ec.	H3	58
Cottage Grove, Mn., U.S.	n13	100
Cottage Grove, Or., U.S.	D3	114
Cottage Grove Reservoir, res., Or., U.S.	D3	114
Cottam, Ont., Can.	E2	73
Cottbus, Ger.	D14	8
Cotter, Ar., U.S.	A3	81
Cottiennes, Alpes (Alpi Cozie), mts., Eur.	H13	10
Cottle, co., Tx., U.S.	B2	120
Cottleville, Mo., U.S.	f12	102
Cotton, co., Ok., U.S.	C3	113
Cottondale, Al., U.S.	B2	78
Cotton Plant, Ar., U.S.	B4	81
Cottonport, La., U.S.	C3	95
Cotton Valley, La., U.S.	B2	95
Cottonwood, Al., U.S.	D4	78
Cottonwood, Az., U.S.	C3	80
Cottonwood, Ca., U.S.	B2	82
Cottonwood, Id., U.S.	C2	89
Cottonwood, Mn., U.S.	F3	100
Cottonwood, co., Mn., U.S.	F3	100
Cottonwood, stm., U.S.	D7	93
Cottonwood, stm., Mn., U.S.	F3	100
Cottonwood Creek, stm., Wy., U.S.	C4	127
Cottonwood Falls, Ks., U.S.	D7	93
Cotuit, Ma., U.S.	C7	98
Cotulla, Tx., U.S.	E3	120
Coudersport, Pa., U.S.	C5	115
Cougar Reservoir, res., Or., U.S.	C4	114
Couhé, Fr.	F7	10
Coulee Creek, stm., Wa., U.S.	g13	124
Coulee Dam, Wa., U.S.	B7	124
Coulee Dam National Recreation Area, Wa., U.S.	A7	124
Coulommiers, Fr.	D10	10
Coulterville, Il., U.S.	E4	90
Counce, Tn., U.S.	B3	119
Council, Id., U.S.	E2	89
Council Bluffs, Ia., U.S.	C2	92
Council Grove, Ks., U.S.	D7	93
Council Grove Lake, res., Ks., U.S.	D7	93
Council Mountain, mtn., Id., U.S.	E2	89
Country Homes, Wa., U.S.	B8	124
Coupeville, Wa., U.S.	A3	124
Courtenay, B.C., Can.	E5	69
Courte Oreilles, Lac, l., Wi., U.S.	C2	126
Courtland, Ont., Can.	E4	73
Courtland, Al., U.S.	A2	78
Courtland, Va., U.S.	D5	123
Coushatta, La., U.S.	B2	95
Coutances, Fr.	C5	10
Coutras, Fr.	G6	10
Cove Creek, stm., Ut., U.S.	E3	121
Covedale, Oh., U.S.	o12	112
Coventry, Eng., U.K.	I11	7
Coventry, Ct., U.S.	B6	84
Coventry, R.I., U.S.	D3	116
Cove Point, c., Md., U.S.	D5	97
Covilhã, Port.	E4	12
Covina, Ca., U.S.	m13	82
Covington, Ga., U.S.	C3	87
Covington, In., U.S.	D3	91
Covington, Ky., U.S.	A5	94
Covington, La., U.S.	D5	95
Covington, Oh., U.S.	B1	112
Covington, Tn., U.S.	B2	119
Covington, Va., U.S.	C3	123
Covington, co., Al., U.S.	D3	78
Covington, co., Ms., U.S.	D4	101
Cowan, Tn., U.S.	B5	119
Cowan, Lake, l., Austl.	F4	50
Cowansville, Que., Can.	D5	74
Cowarts, Al., U.S.	D4	78
Cow Creek, stm., Wa., U.S.	C7	124
Cowee Mountains, mts., N.C., U.S.	f9	110
Cowen, Mount, mtn., Mt., U.S.	E6	103
Coweta, Ok., U.S.	B6	113
Coweta, co., Ga., U.S.	C2	87
Cow Head, Newf., Can.	D3	72
Cowichan Bay, B.C., Can.	g12	69
Cow Lakes, l., Or., U.S.	D9	114
Cowley, Wy., U.S.	B4	127

Name	Map Ref	Page

Cowley, co., Ks., U.S. ... E7 93
Cowlington, Ok., U.S. ... B7 113
Cowlitz, co., Wa., U.S. ... C2 124
Cowlitz, stm., Wa., U.S. ... C3 124
Cowpasture, stm., Va., U.S. ... B3 123
Cowpen Mountain, mtn., Ga., U.S. ... B2 87
Cowpens, S.C., U.S. ... A4 117
Coxim, Braz. ... E1 57
Coxsackie, N.Y., U.S. ... C7 109
Cox's Bāzār, Bngl. ... J14 38
Cox's Cove, Newf., Can. ... D2 72
Coyhaique, Chile ... F2 56
Cozad, Ne., U.S. ... D6 104
Cozumel, Isla de, i., Mex. ... G16 62
Crab Creek, stm., Wa., U.S. ... C6 124
Crab Creek, stm., Wa., U.S. ... B7 124
Crab Orchard, Ky., U.S. ... C5 94
Crab Orchard, Tn., U.S. ... D9 119
Crab Orchard, W.V., U.S. ... n13 125
Crab Orchard Lake, res., Il., U.S. ... F4 90
Crabtree, Pa., U.S. ... F3 115
Crabtree Mills, Que., Can. ... A5 74
Cradock, S. Afr. ... H5 44
Crafton, Pa., U.S. ... k13 115
Craig, Ak., U.S. ... D13 79
Craig, Co., U.S. ... A3 83
Craig, co., Ok., U.S. ... A6 113
Craig, co., Va., U.S. ... C2 123
Craig Air Force Base, mil., Al., U.S. ... C3 78
Craig Creek, stm., Va., U.S. ... C2 123
Craighead, co., Ar., U.S. ... B5 81
Craigsville, Va., U.S. ... B3 123
Craigsville, W.V., U.S. ... C4 125
Crailsheim, Ger. ... F10 8
Craiova, Rom. ... E7 16
Cramerton, N.C., U.S. ... B1 110
Cranberry Lake, l., N.Y., U.S. ... A6 109
Cranberry Portage, Man., Can. ... B1 70
Cranbrook, B.C., Can. ... E10 69
Crandall, Tx., U.S. ... n10 120
Crandon, Wi., U.S. ... C5 126
Crane, Az., U.S. ... *E1 80
Crane, Mo., U.S. ... E4 102
Crane, Tx., U.S. ... D1 120
Crane, co., Tx., U.S. ... D1 120
Crane Creek, stm., Oh., U.S. ... e7 112
Crane Creek Reservoir, res., Id., U.S. ... E2 89
Crane Lake, l., Il., U.S. ... C3 90
Crane Lake, l., Mn., U.S. ... B6 100
Crane Mountain, mtn., Or., U.S. ... E6 114
Crane Prairie Reservoir, res., Or., U.S. ... D5 114
Cranford, N.J., U.S. ... B4 107
Cranston, R.I., U.S. ... C4 116
Craon, Fr. ... E6 10
Craponne, Fr. ... G10 10
Crater Lake, l., Or., U.S. ... E4 114
Crater Lake National Park, Or., U.S. ... E4 114
Craters of the Moon National Monument, Id., U.S. ... F5 89
Cratéus, Braz. ... E10 54
Crato, Braz. ... E11 54
Craufurd, Cape, c., N.W. Ter., Can. ... B16 66
Craven, co., N.C., U.S. ... B5 110
Crawford, Ga., U.S. ... C3 87
Crawford, Ms., U.S. ... B5 101
Crawford, Ne., U.S. ... B2 104
Crawford, co., Ar., U.S. ... B1 81
Crawford, co., Ga., U.S. ... D3 87
Crawford, co., Il., U.S. ... D6 90
Crawford, co., In., U.S. ... H4 91
Crawford, co., Ia., U.S. ... B2 92
Crawford, co., Ks., U.S. ... E9 93
Crawford, co., Mi., U.S. ... D6 99
Crawford, co., Mo., U.S. ... D6 102
Crawford, co., Oh., U.S. ... B3 112
Crawford, co., Pa., U.S. ... C1 115
Crawford, co., Wi., U.S. ... E3 126
Crawford Lake, l., Me., U.S. ... C5 96
Crawford Notch State Park, N.H., U.S. ... B4 106
Crawfordsville, Ar., U.S. ... B5 81
Crawfordsville, In., U.S. ... D4 91
Crawfordville, Fl., U.S. ... B2 86
Crazy Mountains, mts., Mt., U.S. ... D6 103
Crazy Peak, mtn., Mt., U.S. ... D6 103
Crazy Woman Creek, stm., Wy., U.S. ... B6 127
Creal Springs, Il., U.S. ... F5 90
Cree, stm., Sask., Can. ... E11 54
Creedmoor, N.C., U.S. ... A4 110
Creek, co., Ok., U.S. ... B5 113
Cree Lake, l., Sask., Can. ... m7 75
Creemore, Ont., Can. ... C4 73
Creighton, Ne., U.S. ... B8 104
Creighton, Pa., U.S. ... h14 115
Creil, Fr. ... C9 10
Crema, Italy ... D4 14
Cremona, Italy ... D5 14
Crenshaw, Ms., U.S. ... A3 101
Crenshaw, co., Al., U.S. ... D3 78
Creola, Al., U.S. ... E1 78
Cres, Cro. ... E9 14
Cresaptown, Md., U.S. ... k13 97
Crescent, Ok., U.S. ... B4 113
Crescent, Or., U.S. ... D5 114
Crescent, Lake, l., Wa., U.S. ... A2 124
Crescent City, Ca., U.S. ... B1 82
Crescent City, Fl., U.S. ... C5 86
Crescent Lake, l., Fl., U.S. ... C5 86
Crescent Lake, l., Or., U.S. ... D5 114
Crescent Springs, Ky., U.S. ... h13 94
Cresco, Ia., U.S. ... A5 92
Cresskill, N.J., U.S. ... h9 107
Cresson, Pa., U.S. ... F4 115
Cressona, Pa., U.S. ... E9 115
Crest, Fr. ... H12 10
Crested Butte, Co., U.S. ... C4 83
Crest Hill, Il., U.S. ... k8 90
Crestline, Oh., U.S. ... B3 112
Creston, B.C., Can. ... E9 69
Creston, Ia., U.S. ... C3 92

Creston, Oh., U.S. ... B4 112
Crestone Peak, mtn., Co., U.S. ... D5 83
Crestview, Fl., U.S. ... u15 86
Crestview, Hi., U.S. ... g10 88
Crestwood, Ky., U.S. ... B4 94
Crestwood Village, N.J., U.S. ... D4 107
Creswell, Or., U.S. ... D3 114
Crete, Il., U.S. ... B6 90
Crete, Ne., U.S. ... D9 104
Crete see Kríti, i., Grc. ... N8 16
Creve Coeur, Il., U.S. ... C4 90
Crevillente, Spain ... G11 12
Crewe, Eng., U.K. ... H10 7
Crewe, Va., U.S. ... C4 123
Criciúma, Braz. ... B7 56
Cricket, N.C., U.S. ... A1 110
Cridersville, Oh., U.S. ... B1 112
Crikvenica, Cro. ... D9 14
Crimea see Krymskij poluostrov, pen., Ukr. ... H4 22
Crimmitschau, Ger. ... E12 8
Crisfield, Md., U.S. ... E6 97
Crisp, co., Ga., U.S. ... E3 87
Cristalândia, Braz. ... F9 54
Cristalina, Braz. ... D5 57
Cristianópolis, Braz. ... D4 57
Cristóbal Colón, Pico, mtn., Col. ... B6 58
Crittenden, Ky., U.S. ... B5 94
Crittenden, co., Ar., U.S. ... B5 81
Crittenden, co., Ky., U.S. ... e9 94
Crivitz, Wi., U.S. ... C6 126
Crnomelj, Slo. ... D10 14
Croatia, ctry., Eur. ... D10 14
Crocker, Mo., U.S. ... D5 102
Crockett, Ca., U.S. ... g8 82
Crockett, Tx., U.S. ... D5 120
Crockett, co., Tn., U.S. ... B2 119
Crockett, co., Tx., U.S. ... D2 120
Crofton, Ky., U.S. ... C2 94
Crofton, Md., U.S. ... B4 97
Crofton, Ne., U.S. ... B8 104
Croix, Lac la, l., Mn., U.S. ... B6 100
Croker, Cape, c., Ont., Can. ... C4 73
Croker Island, i., Austl. ... B6 50
Cromarty, Scot., U.K. ... D8 7
Cromona, Ky., U.S. ... C7 94
Cromwell, Ct., U.S. ... C5 84
Crook, co., Or., U.S. ... C6 114
Crook, co., Wy., U.S. ... B8 127
Crooked, stm., Or., U.S. ... C6 114
Crooked Creek, stm., Ak., U.S. ... E3 93
Crooked Creek, stm., Pa., U.S. ... C7 115
Crooked Creek Lake, res., Pa., U.S. ... E3 115
Crooked Island, i., Bah. ... C10 64
Crooked Island Passage, strt., Bah. ... C10 64
Crooked Lake, l., Fl., U.S. ... E5 86
Crooked Lake, l., Mn., U.S. ... B7 100
Crooks, S.D., U.S. ... D9 118
Crooks Lake, l., Nv., U.S. ... B2 105
Crookston, Mn., U.S. ... C2 100
Crooksville, Oh., U.S. ... C3 112
Crosby, Mn., U.S. ... D5 100
Crosby, N.D., U.S. ... A2 111
Crosby, Tx., U.S. ... r14 120
Crosby, co., Tx., U.S. ... C2 120
Crosby, Mount, mtn., Wy., U.S. ... C3 127
Crosbyton, Tx., U.S. ... C2 120
Cross, co., Ar., U.S. ... B5 81
Cross Bay, b., Man., Can. ... C2 70
Cross City, Fl., U.S. ... C3 86
Cross Creek, stm., W.V., U.S. ... f8 125
Crossett, Ar., U.S. ... D4 81
Crossfield, Alta., Can. ... D3 68
Cross Island, i., Me., U.S. ... D5 96
Cross Lake, Man., Can. ... B3 70
Crosslake, Mn., U.S. ... D4 100
Cross Lake, l., Me., U.S. ... A4 96
Cross Lake, res., La., U.S. ... B2 95
Cross Lanes, W.V., U.S. ... C3 125
Crossman Peak, mtn., Az., U.S. ... C1 80
Cross Plains, Tn., U.S. ... A5 119
Cross Plains, Tx., U.S. ... C3 120
Cross Plains, Wi., U.S. ... E4 126
Cross Sound, strt., Ak., U.S. ... k21 79
Crossville, Al., U.S. ... A4 78
Crossville, Il., U.S. ... E5 90
Crossville, Tn., U.S. ... D8 119
Croswell, Mi., U.S. ... E8 99
Crothersville, In., U.S. ... G6 91
Crotone, Italy ... J12 14
Croton-on-Hudson, N.Y., U.S. ... D7 109
Crouse, N.C., U.S. ... B1 110
Crow, stm., Mn., U.S. ... F4 100
Crow Agency, Mt., U.S. ... E9 103
Crow Creek, stm., U.S. ... A6 83
Crow Creek Indian Reservation, S.D., U.S. ... C6 118
Crowder, Ms., U.S. ... A3 101
Crowell, Tx., U.S. ... C3 120
Crow Indian Reservation, Mt., U.S. ... E9 103
Crowley, La., U.S. ... D3 95
Crowley, Tx., U.S. ... n9 120
Crowley, co., Co., U.S. ... C7 83
Crowley, Lake, res., Ca., U.S. ... D4 82
Crowleys Ridge, mtn., U.S. ... B5 81
Crown Point, In., U.S. ... B3 91
Crown Point, La., U.S. ... k11 95
Crownpoint, N.M., U.S. ... B1 108
Crown Prince Frederick Island, i., N.W. Ter., Can. ... B15 66
Crow Peak, mtn., Mt., U.S. ... D5 103
Crowsnest Pass, Alta., Can. ... E3 68
Crowsnest Pass, Can. ... E3 68
Crow Wing, co., Mn., U.S. ... D4 100
Crow Wing, stm., Mn., U.S. ... D4 100
Croydon, Austl. ... C8 50
Crozet, Va., U.S. ... B4 123
Crozon, Fr. ... D2 10
Crucea, Cuba ... C7 64
Cruces, Cuba ... C7 64
Crump Lake, l., Or., U.S. ... E7 114
Cruz del Eje, Arg. ... C4 56
Cruzeiro do Sul, Braz. ... E4 54
Crystal, Mn., U.S. ... m12 100
Crystal, stm., Co., U.S. ... B3 83
Crystal Bay, Nv., U.S. ... D1 105

Crystal Bay, b., Fl., U.S. ... D4 86
Crystal Beach, Fl., U.S. ... D4 86
Crystal City, Man., Can. ... E2 70
Crystal City, Mo., U.S. ... C7 102
Crystal City, Tx., U.S. ... E3 120
Crystal Falls, Mi., U.S. ... B2 99
Crystal Lake, Fl., U.S. ... u16 86
Crystal Lake, Il., U.S. ... A5 90
Crystal Lake, l., Ct., U.S. ... B6 84
Crystal Lake, l., Mi., U.S. ... D4 99
Crystal Lake, l., N.H., U.S. ... D4 106
Crystal Lake, l., Vt., U.S. ... B4 122
Crystal Lawns, Il., U.S. ... k8 90
Crystal Pond, res., Ct., U.S. ... B7 84
Crystal River, Fl., U.S. ... D4 86
Crystal Springs, Ms., U.S. ... D3 101
Cuando (Kwando), stm., Afr. ... E4 44
Cuangar, Ang. ... E3 44
Cuango, Ang. ... C3 44
Cuango (Kwango), stm., Afr. ... C3 44
Cuanza, stm., Ang. ... C3 44
Cuauhtémoc, Mex. ... C6 62
Cuautla, Mex. ... H10 62
Cuba, Port. ... G4 12
Cuba, Il., U.S. ... C3 90
Cuba, Mo., U.S. ... C6 102
Cuba, N.M., U.S. ... A3 108
Cuba, N.Y., U.S. ... C2 109
Cuba, ctry., N.A. ... D8 64
Cuba City, Wi., U.S. ... F3 126
Cubango (Okavango), stm., Afr. ... E3 44
Cubero, N.M., U.S. ... B2 108
Cucharas, Mex. ... F7 62
Cucharas, stm., Co., U.S. ... D6 83
Cudahy, Wi., U.S. ... F6 126
Cuddalore, India ... G5 37
Cuddapah, India ... E5 37
Cuddy Mountain, mtn., Id., U.S. ... E2 89
Čudskoje Ozero (Peipsi Järv), l., Eur. ... C10 18
Cuéllar, Spain ... D7 12
Cuenca, Ec. ... I3 58
Cuenca, Spain ... E9 12
Cuencamé [de Ceniceros], Mex. ... E8 62
Cuernavaca, Mex. ... H10 62
Cuero, Tx., U.S. ... E4 120
Cuers, Fr. ... I13 10
Cuervos, Mex. ... A2 62
Cuevas del Almanzora, Spain ... H10 12
Cuglieri, Italy ... I3 14
Cuiabá, Braz. ... G7 54
Cuiseaux, Fr. ... F12 10
Cuito, stm., Ang. ... E3 44
Cuito-Cuanavale, Ang. ... E3 44
Cuivre, West Fork, stm., Mo., U.S. ... B6 102
Čukotskij, Mys, c., Russia ... E31 24
Čukotskij Poluostrov, pen., Russia ... D30 24
Culberson, co., Tx., U.S. ... o12 120
Culbertson, Mt., U.S. ... B12 103
Culbertson, Ne., U.S. ... D5 104
Culebra Peak, mtn., Co., U.S. ... D5 83
Culiacán, Mex. ... E6 62
Cullen, La., U.S. ... B2 95
Cullman, Al., U.S. ... A3 78
Cullman, co., Al., U.S. ... A3 78
Culloden, W.V., U.S. ... C2 125
Cullowhee, N.C., U.S. ... f9 110
Čul'man, Russia ... F18 24
Culpeper, Va., U.S. ... B4 123
Culpeper, co., Va., U.S. ... B5 123
Culver, In., U.S. ... B5 91
Culver City, Ca., U.S. ... m12 82
Culvers Lake, l., N.J., U.S. ... A3 107
Čulym, Russia ... F10 24
Cumali, Tur. ... M11 16
Cumaná, Ven. ... B10 58
Cumanacoa, Ven. ... B11 58
Cumbal, Nevado de, mtn., Col. ... G4 58
Cumberland, B.C., Can. ... E5 69
Cumberland, Ky., U.S. ... D7 94
Cumberland, Md., U.S. ... k13 97
Cumberland, Wi., U.S. ... C2 126
Cumberland, co., U.S. ... D5 90
Cumberland, co., Il., U.S. ... D5 90
Cumberland, co., Ky., U.S. ... D4 94
Cumberland, co., Me., U.S. ... E2 96
Cumberland, co., N.J., U.S. ... E2 107
Cumberland, co., N.C., U.S. ... C4 110
Cumberland, co., Pa., U.S. ... F7 115
Cumberland, co., Tn., U.S. ... D8 119
Cumberland, co., Va., U.S. ... C4 123
Cumberland, stm., U.S. ... D4 94
Cumberland, Lake, res., Ky., U.S. ... D5 94
Cumberland Center, Me., U.S. ... g7 96
Cumberland Foreside, Me., U.S. ... E2 96
Cumberland Gap, U.S. ... D6 94
Cumberland Gap National Historical Park, U.S. ... D6 94
Cumberland Hill, R.I., U.S. ... B4 116
Cumberland Island National Seashore, Ga., U.S. ... F5 87
Cumberland Islands, is., Austl. ... D9 50
Cumberland Lake, l., Sask., Can. ... C4 75
Cumberland Peninsula, pen., N.W. Ter., Can. ... C19 66
Cumberland Sound, strt., N.W. Ter., Can. ... C19 66
Cumbres Pass, Co., U.S. ... D4 83
Cumikan, Russia ... G21 24
Cuming, co., Ne., U.S. ... C9 104
Cumming, Ga., U.S. ... B2 87
Cumnock, Scot., U.K. ... F8 7
Čuna, stm., Russia ... F13 24
Cuna, stm., Russia ... E13 24
Cunani, Braz. ... C8 54
Cunene, stm., Afr. ... E2 44
Cuneo, Italy ... E2 14
Cunnamulla, Austl. ... E9 50
Cunningham, Ky., U.S. ... f9 94
Cupar, Sask., Can. ... G3 75
Curaçao, i., Neth. Ant. ... H13 64
Curecanti National Recreation Area, Co., U.S. ... C3 83
Curepipe, Mrts. ... F11 44
Curiapo, Ven. ... C12 58
Curicó, Chile ... C2 56
Curitiba, Braz. ... B7 56
Curlew Creek, stm., Wa., U.S. ... A7 124

Curlew Lake, l., Wa., U.S. ... A7 124
Curralinho, Braz. ... D9 54
Currant Mountain, mtn., Nv., U.S. ... E6 105
Current, stm., U.S. ... A5 81
Currituck, co., N.C., U.S. ... A6 110
Curry, co., N.M., U.S. ... C6 108
Curry, co., Or., U.S. ... E2 114
Curtis, Ne., U.S. ... D5 104
Curtisville, Pa., U.S. ... E2 115
Curvelo, Braz. ... E6 57
Curwensville, Pa., U.S. ... E4 115
Curwensville Lake, res., Pa., U.S. ... E4 115
Curwood, Mount, mtn., Mi., U.S. ... B2 99
Cushing, Ok., U.S. ... B5 113
Cushman, Lake, res., Wa., U.S. ... B2 124
Cusseta, Ga., U.S. ... D2 87
Custer, S.D., U.S. ... D2 118
Custer, Co., U.S. ... C5 83
Custer, co., Id., U.S. ... E5 89
Custer, co., Mt., U.S. ... C6 103
Custer, co., Ne., U.S. ... C6 104
Custer, co., Ok., U.S. ... B2 113
Custer, co., S.D., U.S. ... D2 118
Custer Battlefield National Monument, Mt., U.S. ... E9 103
Cut Bank, Mt., U.S. ... B4 103
Cut Bank Creek, stm., N.D., U.S. ... A4 111
Cutchogue, N.Y., U.S. ... m16 109
Cuthbert, Ga., U.S. ... E2 87
Cutler Ridge, Fl., U.S. ... s13 86
Cut Off, La., U.S. ... E5 95
Cutro, Italy ... J11 14
Cuttack, India ... J11 38
Cuttyhunk Island, i., Ma., U.S. ... D6 98
Cuxhaven, Ger. ... B8 8
Cuyahoga, co., Oh., U.S. ... A4 112
Cuyahoga, stm., Oh., U.S. ... A4 112
Cuyahoga Falls, Oh., U.S. ... A4 112
Cuyama, stm., Ca., U.S. ... E4 82
Cuyamaca Peak, mtn., Ca., U.S. ... F5 82
Cuyo Islands, is., Phil. ... C7 32
Cuyuni, stm., S.A. ... D13 58
Cuzco, Peru ... F4 54
C.W. McConaughy, Lake, res., Ne., U.S. ... C4 104
Cyclades see Kikládhes, is., Grc. ... L8 16
Cynthiana, In., U.S. ... H2 91
Cynthiana, Ky., U.S. ... B5 94
Cypress Creek, stm., Tx., U.S. ... r14 120
Cypress Hills Provincial Park, Sask., Can. ... H1 75
Cypress Lake, l., Fl., U.S. ... D5 86
Cypress Quarters, Fl., U.S. ... E6 86
Cypress Swamp, sw., U.S. ... F4 85
Cyprus, ctry., Asia ... B3 40
Cyril, Ok., U.S. ... C3 113
Czechoslovakia, ctry., Eur. ... F11 4
Częstochowa, Pol. ... E19 8

D

Dabeiba, Col. ... D4 58
Dabhoi, India ... I5 38
Dabie Shan, mts., China ... D4 28
Dabola, Gui. ... F3 42
Dacca see Dhaka, Bngl. ... I14 38
Dachaidan, China ... B16 38
Dachau, Ger. ... G11 8
Dacono, Co., U.S. ... A6 83
Dacula, Ga., U.S. ... C3 87
Dadanawa, Guy. ... F13 58
Dade, co., Fl., U.S. ... G6 86
Dade, co., Ga., U.S. ... B1 87
Dade, co., Mo., U.S. ... D4 102
Dade City, Fl., U.S. ... D4 86
Dadeville, Al., U.S. ... C4 78
Dadeville, In., U.S. ... D6 91
Dahart, Tx., U.S. ... A1 120
Dahlonega, Ga., U.S. ... B3 87
Dahomey see Benin, ctry., Afr. ... G6 42
Dahra, Libya ... C9 42
Dahy, Nafūd ad-, des., Sau. Ar. ... D4 46
Daimiel, Spain ... F8 12
Daingerfield, Tx., U.S. ... C5 120
Dairen see Dalian, China ... D11 26
Dakar, Sen. ... F2 42
Dakhla, W. Sah. ... D2 42
Dakota, co., Mn., U.S. ... F5 100
Dakota, co., Ne., U.S. ... B9 104
Dakota City, Ia., U.S. ... B3 92
Dakota City, Ne., U.S. ... B9 104
Dalandzadgad, Mong. ... C7 26
Da Lat, Viet. ... I10 34
Dälbandin, Pak. ... D1 36
Dalby, Austl. ... E10 50
Dale, In., U.S. ... H4 91
Dale, co., Al., U.S. ... D4 78
Dale City, Va., U.S. ... B5 123
Dale Hollow Lake, res., U.S. ... C8 119
Daleville, Al., U.S. ... D4 78
Daleville, In., U.S. ... D6 91
Dalhart, Tx., U.S. ... A1 120
Dalhousie, N.B., Can. ... A3 71
Dalhousie, Cape, c., N.W. Ter., Can. ... B7 66
Dali, China ... B6 34
Dalian, China ... D11 26
Dall, Mount, mtn., Ak., U.S. ... f15 79
Dallam, co., Tx., U.S. ... A1 120
Dallas, Ga., U.S. ... C2 87
Dallas (part of Melcher), Ia., U.S. ... C4 92
Dallas, N.C., U.S. ... B1 110
Dallas, Or., U.S. ... C3 114
Dallas, Pa., U.S. ... D10 115
Dallas, Tx., U.S. ... C4 120
Dallas, co., Al., U.S. ... C2 78
Dallas, co., Ar., U.S. ... D3 81
Dallas, co., Ia., U.S. ... C3 92

Dallas, co., Mo., U.S. ... D4 102
Dallas, co., Tx., U.S. ... C4 120
Dallas Center, Ia., U.S. ... C4 92
Dallas City, Il., U.S. ... C2 90
Dallas Naval Air Station, mil., Tx., U.S. ... n9 120
Dallastown, Pa., U.S. ... G8 115
Dall Island, i., Ak., U.S. ... n23 79
Dalmacija, hist. reg., Eur. ... F11 14
Dalmatia see Dalmacija, hist. reg., Eur. ... F11 14
Daloa, I.C. ... G4 42
Dalqū, Sudan ... D12 42
Dalton, Ga., U.S. ... B2 87
Dalton, Ma., U.S. ... B1 98
Dalton, Oh., U.S. ... B4 112
Dalton, Pa., U.S. ... C10 115
Daltonganj, India ... H11 38
Dalton Gardens, Id., U.S. ... B2 89
Dalwallinu, Austl. ... F3 50
Daly City, Ca., U.S. ... h8 82
Damān, India ... B2 37
Damān, ter., India ... B2 37
Damar, Pulau, i., Indon. ... G8 32
Damariscotta, Me., U.S. ... D3 96
Damariscotta Lake, l., Me., U.S. ... D3 96
Damascus, Md., U.S. ... B3 97
Damascus, Va., U.S. ... f10 123
Damascus see Dimashq, Syria ... C5 40
Dāmāvand, Qolleh-ye, mtn., Iran ... J8 22
Damba, Ang. ... C3 44
Damoh, India ... I8 38
Dampar, Tasek, l., Malay. ... M7 34
Dampier, Austl. ... D3 50
Dampier, Selat, strt., Indon. ... F9 32
Dampier Archipelago, is., Austl. ... D3 50
Dan, stm., U.S. ... D3 123
Dana, In., U.S. ... E3 91
Danakil Plain, pl., Eth. ... F3 46
Da Nang, Viet. ... F10 34
Danbury, Ct., U.S. ... D2 84
Danbury, Tx., U.S. ... r14 120
Dand, Afg. ... E1 38
Dandridge, Tn., U.S. ... C10 119
Dane, co., Wi., U.S. ... E4 126
Dangla, Eth. ... F2 46
Dania, Fl., U.S. ... F6 86
Daniels, co., Mt., U.S. ... B11 103
Danielson, Ct., U.S. ... B8 84
Daniels Pass, Ut., U.S. ... C4 121
Danilov, Russia ... C23 18
Danlí, Hond. ... G4 64
Dannemora, N.Y., U.S. ... f11 109
Dansville, N.Y., U.S. ... C3 109
Dante, Va., U.S. ... f9 123
Danube, stm., Eur. ... G13 4
Danube, Mouths of the, mth., Eur. ... D13 16
Danvers, Il., U.S. ... C4 90
Danvers, Ma., U.S. ... A6 98
Danville, Que., Can. ... D5 74
Danville, Ar., U.S. ... B2 81
Danville, Ca., U.S. ... h9 82
Danville, Il., U.S. ... C6 90
Danville, In., U.S. ... E4 91
Danville, Ia., U.S. ... D6 92
Danville, Ky., U.S. ... C5 94
Danville, Oh., U.S. ... B3 112
Danville, Pa., U.S. ... E8 115
Danville, Va., U.S. ... D3 123
Danyang, China ... C8 28
Danzig, Gulf of, b., Eur. ... A19 8
Danzig see Gdańsk, Pol. ... A18 8
Daocheng, China ... F7 26
Dapango, Togo ... F6 42
Daphne, Al., U.S. ... E2 78
Dar'ā, Syria ... C5 40
Darakht-e Yaḥyá, Afg. ... E3 38
Dārayyā, Syria ... A7 40
Darbāsīyah, Syria ... A7 40
Darbhanga, India ... G11 38
Darby, Mt., U.S. ... D2 103
Darby, Pa., U.S. ... G11 115
Darchan, Mong. ... B8 26
Dardanelle, Ar., U.S. ... B2 81
Dardanelle Lake, res., Ar., U.S. ... B2 81
Dardanelles see Çanakkale Boğazı, strt., Tur. ... I10 16
Dare, co., N.C., U.S. ... B7 110
Dar es Salaam, Tan. ... C7 44
Dargaville, N.Z. ... A4 52
Dari, China ... E6 26
Darien, Ct., U.S. ... E2 84
Darien, Ga., U.S. ... E5 87
Darien, Wi., U.S. ... F5 126
Dariganga, Mong. ... B9 26
Darjeeling, India ... G13 38
Darke, co., Oh., U.S. ... B1 112
Darley Woods, De., U.S. ... h8 85
Darling, stm., Austl. ... F9 50
Darling, Lake, res., N.D., U.S. ... A4 111
Darling Range, mts., Austl. ... F3 50
Darlington, Eng., U.K. ... G11 7
Darlington, In., U.S. ... D4 91
Darlington, Md., U.S. ... A5 97
Darlington, S.C., U.S. ... C8 117
Darlington, Wi., U.S. ... F3 126
Darlington, co., S.C., U.S. ... C8 117
Darnah, Libya ... B10 42
Daroca, Spain ... D10 12
Darrah, Mount, mtn., Can. ... E3 68
Darrington, Wa., U.S. ... A4 124
Dartmoor National Park, Eng., U.K. ... K9 7
Dartmouth, Eng., U.K. ... K9 7
Dartmouth, Pap. N. Gui. ... G11 32
Darwin, Austl. ... B6 50
Dašinčilen, Mong. ... B7 26
Dassel, Mn., U.S. ... E4 100
Datia, India ... H8 38
Datil Mountains, mts., N.M., U.S. ... C2 108
D'at'kovo, Russia ... H17 18
Datong, China ... C9 26
Datu, Tanjung, c., Asia ... M10 34
Dāūd Khel, Pak. ... D4 38
Daufuskie Island, i., S.C., U.S. ... G6 117
Daugavpils, Lat. ... F9 18
Daulatābād (Shirin Tagāo), Afg. ... B1 38
Daule, Ec. ... G2 58

143

Name	Map Ref	Page
Dauphin, Man., Can.	D1	70
Dauphin, co., Pa., U.S.	F8	115
Dauphin, stm., Man., Can.	D2	70
Dauphin Island, Al., U.S.	E1	78
Dauphin Island, i., Al., U.S.	E1	78
Dauphin Lake, l., Man., Can.	D2	70
Dāvangere, India	E3	37
Davao, Phil.	D8	32
Davao Gulf, b., Phil.	D8	32
Daveluyville, Que., Can.	C5	74
Davenport, Fl., U.S.	D5	86
Davenport, Ia., U.S.	C7	92
Davenport, Ok., U.S.	B5	113
Davenport, Wa., U.S.	B7	124
David, Pan.	J6	64
David City, Ne., U.S.	C8	104
Davidson, N.C., U.S.	B2	110
Davidson, co., N.C., U.S.	B2	110
Davidson, co., Tn., U.S.	A5	119
Davidsville, Pa., U.S.	F4	115
Davie, Fl., U.S.	F6	86
Davie, co., N.C., U.S.	B2	110
Daviess, co., In., U.S.	G3	91
Daviess, co., Ky., U.S.	C2	94
Daviess, co., Mo., U.S.	B3	102
Davis, Ca., U.S.	C3	82
Davis, Ok., U.S.	C4	113
Davis, W.V., U.S.	B5	125
Davis, co., Ia., U.S.	D5	92
Davis, co., Ut., U.S.	C3	121
Davis, Mount, mtn., Pa., U.S.	G3	115
Davis Creek, stm., W.V., U.S.	m12	125
Davis Dam, U.S.	H7	105
Davis Islands, is., Fl., U.S.	p11	86
Davis Lake, l., Or., U.S.	E5	114
Davis-Monthan Air Force Base, mil., Az., U.S.	E5	80
Davison, Mi., U.S.	E7	99
Davison, co., S.D., U.S.	D7	118
Davisville, R.I., U.S.	E4	116
Davos, Switz.	F16	10
Dawa (Daua), stm., Afr.	H3	46
Dawei, Burma	G5	34
Dawes, co., Ne., U.S.	B2	104
Daws Island, i., S.C., U.S.	G6	117
Dawson, Ga., U.S.	E2	87
Dawson, Mn., U.S.	F2	100
Dawson, co., Ga., U.S.	B2	87
Dawson, co., Mt., U.S.	C11	103
Dawson, co., Ne., U.S.	D6	104
Dawson, co., Tx., U.S.	C1	120
Dawson, Mount, mtn., B.C., Can.	D9	69
Dawson Creek, B.C., Can.	B7	69
Dawson Springs, Ky., U.S.	C2	94
Dax, Fr.	I5	10
Day, co., S.D., U.S.	B8	118
Dayr az-Zawr, Syria	B7	40
Daysland, Alta., Can.	C4	68
Dayton, In., U.S.	D4	91
Dayton, Ia., U.S.	B3	92
Dayton, Ky., U.S.	h14	94
Dayton, Md., U.S.	B4	97
Dayton, Mn., U.S.	m12	100
Dayton, Nv., U.S.	D2	105
Dayton, Oh., U.S.	C1	112
Dayton, Or., U.S.	B3	114
Dayton, Tn., U.S.	D8	119
Dayton, Tx., U.S.	D5	120
Dayton, Va., U.S.	B4	123
Dayton, Wa., U.S.	C8	124
Dayton, Wy., U.S.	B5	127
Daytona Beach, Fl., U.S.	C5	86
Da Yunhe, China	B8	34
Dayville, Ct., U.S.	B8	84
De Aar, S. Afr.	H4	44
Dead, North Branch, stm., Me., U.S.	C2	96
Dead, South Branch, stm., Me., U.S.	C2	96
Dead Creek, stm., Vt., U.S.	C2	122
Dead Diamond, stm., N.H., U.S.	g7	106
Dead Indian Peak, mtn., Wy., U.S.	B3	127
Dead Lake, l., Mn., U.S.	D3	100
Dead Lakes, l., Fl., U.S.	B1	86
Deadman Bay, b., Fl., U.S.	C3	86
Deadman Creek, stm., Wa., U.S.	g14	124
Deadmans Cay, Bah.	C10	64
Dead Sea, l., Asia	D4	40
Deadwood, S.D., U.S.	C2	118
Deadwood Reservoir, res., Id., U.S.	E3	89
Deaf Smith, co., Tx., U.S.	B1	120
Deale, Md., U.S.	C4	97
Deal Island, Md., U.S.	D6	97
Deal Island, i., Md., U.S.	D6	97
Dean, stm., B.C., Can.	C4	69
Dean Channel, strt., B.C., Can.	C4	69
Deán Funes, Arg.	C4	56
Dearborn, Mi., U.S.	F7	99
Dearborn, co., In., U.S.	F7	91
Dearborn Heights, Mi., U.S.	p15	99
Dearg, Beinn, mtn., Scot., U.K.	D8	7
Dease Strait, strt., N.W. Ter., Can.	C11	66
Death Valley, val., Ca., U.S.	D5	82
Death Valley National Monument, U.S.	D5	82
Deauville, Fr.	C7	10
De Baca, co., N.M., U.S.	C5	108
De Bary, Fl., U.S.	D5	86
Debauch Mountain, mtn., Ak., U.S.	C8	79
Dębica, Pol.	E21	8
Debrecen, Hung.	H21	8
Debre Markos, Eth.	F2	46
Debre Tabor, Eth.	F2	46
De Cade, Lake, l., La., U.S.	E5	95
Decatur, Al., U.S.	A3	78
Decatur, Ar., U.S.	A1	81
Decatur, Ga., U.S.	C2	87
Decatur, Il., U.S.	D5	90
Decatur, In., U.S.	C8	91
Decatur, Mi., U.S.	F5	99
Decatur, Ms., U.S.	C4	101
Decatur, Ne., U.S.	B9	104
Decatur, Tn., U.S.	D9	119
Decatur, Tx., U.S.	C4	120
Decatur, co., Ga., U.S.	F2	87
Decatur, co., In., U.S.	F6	91
Decatur, co., Ia., U.S.	D4	92
Decatur, co., Ks., U.S.	C3	93
Decatur, co., Tn., U.S.	B3	119
Decaturville, Tn., U.S.	B3	119
Decazeville, Fr.	H9	10
Deccan, plat., India	E4	37
Deception, Mount, mtn., Wa., U.S.	B2	124
Decherd, Tn., U.S.	B5	119
Děčín, Czech.	E14	8
Decize, Fr.	F10	10
Deckerville, Mi., U.S.	E8	99
Decorah, Ia., U.S.	A6	92
Dedham, Ma., U.S.	B5	98
Dédougou, Burkina	F5	42
Dedovsk, Russia	F20	18
Deep, stm., N.C., U.S.	B3	110
Deep Creek, stm., Ut., U.S.	C2	121
Deep Creek, stm., Ut., U.S.	B3	121
Deep Creek, stm., Ut., U.S.	F3	121
Deep Creek, stm., Wa., U.S.	g13	124
Deep Creek Lake, res., Md., U.S.	k12	97
Deep Creek Mountains, mts., Id., U.S.	G6	89
Deep Fork, stm., Ok., U.S.	B5	113
Deep Inlet, b., Newf., Can.	g10	72
Deep Red Creek, stm., Ok., U.S.	C3	113
Deep River, Ont., Can.	A7	73
Deep River, Ct., U.S.	D6	84
Deer Creek, stm., Oh., U.S.	C2	112
Deer Creek Indian Reservation, Mn., U.S.	C5	100
Deerfield, Il., U.S.	h9	90
Deerfield, Ks., U.S.	E2	93
Deerfield, Ma., U.S.	A2	98
Deerfield, Mi., U.S.	G7	99
Deerfield, Wi., U.S.	E4	126
Deerfield, stm., Ma., U.S.	A2	98
Deerfield Beach, Fl., U.S.	F6	86
Deer Island, pen., Ma., U.S.	g12	98
Deer Island, i., Ms., U.S.	f8	101
Deer Isle, i., Me., U.S.	D4	96
Deer Lake, Newf., Can.	D3	72
Deer Lake, l., Newf., Can.	D3	72
Deer Lake, l., Mn., U.S.	C5	100
Deer Lodge, Mt., U.S.	D4	103
Deer Lodge, co., Mt., U.S.	E3	103
Deer Park, N.Y., U.S.	n15	109
Deer Park, Oh., U.S.	o13	112
Deer Park, Wa., U.S.	B8	124
Deer Peak, mtn., Co., U.S.	C5	83
Deer River, Mn., U.S.	C5	100
Deesa, India	H5	38
Defiance, Oh., U.S.	A1	112
Defiance, co., Oh., U.S.	A1	112
Defiance, Mount, mtn., Or., U.S.	B5	114
De Forest, Wi., U.S.	E4	126
De Funiak Springs, Fl., U.S.	u15	86
Degeh-Bur, Eth.	G3	46
Dégelis, Que., Can.	B9	74
Deggendorf, Ger.	G12	8
De Graff, Oh., U.S.	B2	112
De Gray Lake, res., Ar., U.S.	C2	81
Dehiwala-Mount Lavinia, Sri L.	I5	37
Dehra Dūn, India	E8	38
Dehri, India	H11	38
Dehu, India	C2	37
Dehui, China	C12	26
Dej, Rom.	B7	16
Deje, Swe.	G9	6
De Kalb, Il., U.S.	B5	90
De Kalb, Ms., U.S.	C5	101
De Kalb, Tx., U.S.	C5	120
De Kalb, co., Al., U.S.	A4	78
De Kalb, co., Ga., U.S.	C2	87
De Kalb, co., Il., U.S.	B5	90
De Kalb, co., In., U.S.	B7	91
De Kalb, co., Mo., U.S.	B3	102
De Kalb, co., Tn., U.S.	D8	119
Dekese, Zaire	B4	44
Delafield, Wi., U.S.	m11	126
Delanco, N.J., U.S.	C3	107
De Land, Fl., U.S.	C5	86
Delano, Ca., U.S.	E4	82
Delano, Mn., U.S.	E5	100
Delano Peak, mtn., Ut., U.S.	E3	121
Delaronde Lake, l., Sask., Can.	C2	75
Delavan, Il., U.S.	C4	90
Delavan, Wi., U.S.	F5	126
Delaware, Oh., U.S.	B2	112
Delaware, co., In., U.S.	D7	91
Delaware, co., Ia., U.S.	B6	92
Delaware, co., N.Y., U.S.	C5	109
Delaware, co., Oh., U.S.	B2	112
Delaware, co., Ok., U.S.	A7	113
Delaware, co., Pa., U.S.	G11	115
Delaware, state, U.S.	D3	85
Delaware, East Branch, stm., N.Y., U.S.	C5	109
Delaware Bay, b., U.S.	D11	76
Delaware City, De., U.S.	B3	85
Delaware Lake, res., Oh., U.S.	B3	112
Delaware Water Gap, N.J., U.S.	B2	107
Delaware Water Gap National Recreation Area, U.S.	B2	107
Delbarton, W.V., U.S.	D2	125
Delcambre, La., U.S.	E4	95
Del City, Ok., U.S.	B4	113
Delémont, Switz.	E14	10
De Leon, Tx., U.S.	C3	120
De Leon Springs, Fl., U.S.	C5	86
Delft, Neth.	C4	8
Delfzijl, Neth.	B6	8
Delgado, Cabo, c., Moz.	D8	44
Delhi, India	F7	38
Delhi, La., U.S.	B4	95
Delhi, N.Y., U.S.	C6	109
Delicias, Mex.	C7	62
De Lisle, Ms., U.S.	E4	101
Delitzsch, Ger.	D12	8
Dellenbaugh, Mount, mtn., Az., U.S.	A2	80
Dell Rapids, S.D., U.S.	D9	118
Del Mar, Ca., U.S.	o15	82
Delmar, De., U.S.	G3	85
Delmar, Md., U.S.	D6	97
Delmar, N.Y., U.S.	C7	109
Delmenhorst, Ger.	B8	8
Delnice, Cro.	D9	14
Del Norte, Co., U.S.	D4	83
Del Norte, co., Ca., U.S.	B2	82
De-Longa, Ostrova, is., Russia	B23	24
Deloraine, Man., Can.	E1	70
Del Park Manor, De., U.S.	i7	85
Delphi, In., U.S.	C4	91
Delphos, Oh., U.S.	B1	112
Delran, N.J., U.S.	C3	107
Delray Beach, Fl., U.S.	F6	86
Del Rio, Tx., U.S.	E2	120
Delson, Que., Can.	q19	74
Delta, Co., U.S.	C2	83
Delta, Oh., U.S.	A2	112
Delta, co., Co., U.S.	C3	83
Delta, co., Mi., U.S.	C3	99
Delta, co., Tx., U.S.	C5	120
Delta, reg., Ms., U.S.	B3	101
Delta Junction, Ak., U.S.	C10	79
Delta Peak, mtn., B.C., Can.	A3	69
Delta Reservoir, res., N.Y., U.S.	B5	109
Deltaville, Va., U.S.	C6	123
Deltona, Fl., U.S.	D5	86
Demarest, N.J., U.S.	h9	107
Deming, N.M., U.S.	E2	108
Demirci, Tur.	J12	16
Demirköy, Tur.	H11	16
Demmin, Ger.	B13	8
Demopolis, Al., U.S.	C2	78
Demorest, Ga., U.S.	B3	87
Demotte, In., U.S.	B3	91
Denain, Fr.	B10	10
Denali National Park, Ak., U.S.	C9	79
Denare Beach, Sask., Can.	C4	75
Denham Springs, La., U.S.	D5	95
Den Helder, Neth.	C4	8
Denia, Spain	G12	12
Denison, Ia., U.S.	B2	92
Denison, Tx., U.S.	C4	120
Denison Dam, U.S.	D5	113
Denizli, Tur.	H13	14
Denmark, S.C., U.S.	E5	117
Denmark, Wi., U.S.	D6	126
Denmark, ctry., Eur.	D9	4
Denmark Strait, strt.	C15	128
Dennehotso, Az., U.S.	A6	80
Dennis, Ma., U.S.	C7	98
Dennison, Oh., U.S.	B4	112
Dennis Port, Ma., U.S.	C7	98
Denny Terrace, S.C., U.S.	C5	117
Denpasar, Indon.	G6	32
Dent, co., Mo., U.S.	D6	102
Denton, Md., U.S.	C6	97
Denton, N.C., U.S.	B2	110
Denton, Tx., U.S.	C4	120
Denton, co., Tx., U.S.	C4	120
Denver, Co., U.S.	B6	83
Denver, Ia., U.S.	B5	92
Denver, Pa., U.S.	F9	115
Denver, co., Co., U.S.	B6	83
Denver City, Tx., U.S.	C1	120
Denville, N.J., U.S.	B4	107
Deogarh, India	H12	38
Deolāli, India	C2	37
Deoria, India	G10	38
De Pere, Wi., U.S.	D5	126
Depew, N.Y., U.S.	C2	109
Depoe Bay, Or., U.S.	C2	114
Depok, Indon.	m13	33a
Deposit, N.Y., U.S.	C5	109
Depue, Il., U.S.	B4	90
Deqin, China	F6	26
De Queen, Ar., U.S.	C1	81
De Queen Reservoir, res., Ar., U.S.	C1	81
De Quincy, La., U.S.	D2	95
Dera Ghāzi Khān, Pak.	E4	38
Dera Ismāil Khān, Pak.	E4	38
Derby, Austl.	C4	50
Derby, Eng., U.K.	I11	7
Derby, Ct., U.S.	D3	84
Derby, Ks., U.S.	E6	93
Derby, Vt., U.S.	B4	122
Derby Line, Vt., U.S.	A4	122
Derg, Lough, l., Ire.	I4	7
De Ridder, La., U.S.	D2	95
Derma, Ms., U.S.	B4	101
Dermott, Ar., U.S.	D4	81
Dernieres, Isles, is., La., U.S.	E5	95
Derry, N.H., U.S.	E4	106
Derry, Pa., U.S.	F3	115
Derval, Fr.	E5	10
Derventa, Bos.	E12	14
Derwood, Md., U.S.	B3	97
Desaguadero, stm., Arg.	C3	56
Des Allemands, La., U.S.	E5	95
Des Arc, Ar., U.S.	C4	81
Desbiens, Que., Can.	A6	74
Descartes, Fr.	F7	10
Deschaillons [-sur-Saint-Laurent], Que., Can.	C5	74
Deschambault, Que., Can.	C6	74
Deschambault Lake, l., Sask., Can.	C4	75
Deschutes, co., Or., U.S.	D5	114
Deschutes, stm., Or., U.S.	B6	114
Dese, Eth.	F2	46
Deseado, stm., Arg.	F3	56
Deseret Peak, mtn., Ut., U.S.	C3	121
Deseronto, Ont., Can.	C7	73
Desert Creek Peak, mtn., Nv., U.S.	E2	105
Desert Hot Springs, Ca., U.S.	F5	82
Desert Peak, mtn., Ut., U.S.	B2	121
Desert Valley, val., Nv., U.S.	B3	105
Desha, Ar., U.S.	B4	81
Desha, co., Ar., U.S.	D4	81
Deshler, Ne., U.S.	D8	104
Deshler, Oh., U.S.	A2	112
Des Lacs, stm., N.D., U.S.	A4	111
Desloge, Mo., U.S.	D7	102
De Smet, S.D., U.S.	C8	118
Des Moines, Ia., U.S.	C4	92
Des Moines, co., Ia., U.S.	D6	92
Des Moines, stm., U.S.	D5	92
Des Moines, Wa., U.S.	B3	124
De Soto, Il., U.S.	F4	90
De Soto, Ia., U.S.	C3	92
De Soto, Ks., U.S.	D9	93
De Soto, Mo., U.S.	C7	102
De Soto, co., Fl., U.S.	E5	86
De Soto, co., La., U.S.	B2	95
De Soto, co., Ms., U.S.	A3	101
Despard, W.V., U.S.	k10	125
Des Peres, Mo., U.S.	f13	102
Des Plaines, Il., U.S.	A6	90
Des Plaines, stm., U.S.	k8	90
Desroches, Île, i., Sey.	C10	44
Dessau, Ger.	D12	8
Destin, Fl., U.S.	u15	86
Destrehan, La., U.S.	E5	95
Desvres, Fr.	B8	10
Detmold, Ger.	D8	8
Detour, Point, c., Mi., U.S.	C4	99
Detroit, Mi., U.S.	F7	99
Detroit Lake, res., Or., U.S.	C4	114
Detroit Lakes, Mn., U.S.	D3	100
Deuel, co., Ne., U.S.	C3	104
Deuel, co., S.D., U.S.	C9	118
Deutsche Bucht, b., Ger.	A7	8
Deutschlandsberg, Aus.	I15	8
Deux-Montagnes, Que., Can.	p19	74
Deux Montagnes, Lac des, l., Que., Can.	q19	74
Deva, Rom.	D6	16
Devakottai, India	H5	37
De Valls Bluff, Ar., U.S.	C4	81
DeView, Bayou, stm., Ar., U.S.	B4	81
Devils Lake, N.D., U.S.	A7	111
Devils Lake, l., N.D., U.S.	A6	111
Devils Paw, mtn., Ak., U.S.	k23	79
Devils Postpile National Monument, Ca., U.S.	D4	82
Devils Tower National Monument, Wy., U.S.	B8	127
Devil Track Lake, l., Mn., U.S.	k9	100
Devine, Tx., U.S.	E3	120
DeVola, Oh., U.S.	C4	112
Devon, Alta., Can.	C4	68
Devon Island, i., N.W. Ter., Can.	A15	66
Devonport, Austl.	H9	50
Devonport, N.Z.	B5	52
Devonshire, De., U.S.	h7	85
Dewa-kyūryō, hills, Japan	C13	30
Dewar, Ok., U.S.	B6	113
Dewās, India	I7	38
Dewees Inlet, b., S.C., U.S.	k12	117
Dewees Island, i., S.C., U.S.	F8	117
Dewey, Az., U.S.	C3	80
Dewey, co., Ok., U.S.	B2	113
Dewey, co., S.D., U.S.	B4	118
Dewey Beach, De., U.S.	F5	85
Dewey Lake, res., Ky., U.S.	C7	94
Deweyville, Tx., U.S.	D6	120
De Witt, Ar., U.S.	C4	81
De Witt, Ia., U.S.	C7	92
De Witt, Mi., U.S.	F6	99
De Witt, N.Y., U.S.	B4	109
De Witt, co., Il., U.S.	C5	90
De Witt, co., Tx., U.S.	E4	120
Dexter, Ia., U.S.	C3	92
Dexter, Me., U.S.	C3	96
Dexter, Mi., U.S.	F7	99
Dexter, Mo., U.S.	E8	102
Dexter, N.M., U.S.	D5	108
Dexter, Lake, l., Fl., U.S.	C5	86
Dezfūl, Iran	B4	46
Dezhou, China	D10	26
Dhaka, Bngl.	I14	38
Dhamār, Yemen	F3	46
Dhamtari, India	B6	37
Dhānbād, India	I12	38
Dhār, India	I6	38
Dharmapuri, India	F5	37
Dharmavaram, India	E4	37
Dhārwār, India	E3	37
Dhaulāgiri, mtn., Nepal	F10	38
Dholpur, India	G8	38
Dhorāji, India	J4	38
Dhrol, India	I4	38
Dhubri, India	G13	38
Dhule, India	B3	37
Diable, Île du, i., Fr. Gu.	B8	54
Diablo, Canyon, val., Az., U.S.	C4	80
Diablo, Mount, mtn., Ca., U.S.	h9	82
Diablo Dam, Wa., U.S.	A4	124
Diablo Lake, res., Wa., U.S.	A4	124
Diablo Range, mts., Ca., U.S.	D3	82
Diamante, Arg.	C4	56
Diamantina, Braz.	E7	57
Diamantino, Braz.	F7	54
Diamond Head, crat., Hi., U.S.	g11	88
Diamond Hill, R.I., U.S.	B4	116
Diamond Hill Reservoir, res., R.I., U.S.	A4	116
Diamond Lake, Il., U.S.	h9	90
Diamond Lake, l., Or., U.S.	D4	114
Diamond Mountains, mts., Nv., U.S.	D6	105
Diamond Peak, mtn., Co., U.S.	A2	83
Diamond Peak, mtn., Id., U.S.	E5	89
Diamond Peak, mtn., Or., U.S.	D4	114
Diamond Peak, mtn., Wa., U.S.	C8	124
Diamondville, Wy., U.S.	E2	127
Diaz, Ar., U.S.	B4	81
Dibaya, Zaire	C4	44
D'Iberville, Ms., U.S.	E5	101
Diboll, Tx., U.S.	D5	120
Dibrugarh, India	G16	38
Dickens, co., Tx., U.S.	C2	120
Dickenson, co., Va., U.S.	e9	123
Dickerson, Md., U.S.	B3	97
Dickey, co., N.D., U.S.	C7	111
Dickeyville, Wi., U.S.	F3	126
Dickinson, N.D., U.S.	C3	111
Dickinson, co., Ia., U.S.	A2	92
Dickinson, co., Ks., U.S.	D6	93
Dickinson, co., Mi., U.S.	B3	99
Dickinson Dam, N.D., U.S.	C3	111
Dickson, Ok., U.S.	C5	113
Dickson, Tn., U.S.	A4	119
Dickson, co., Tn., U.S.	A4	119
Dickson City, Pa., U.S.	D10	115
Didsbury, Alta., Can.	D3	68
Die, Fr.	H12	10
Dieburg, Ger.	F8	8
Dieciocho de Marzo, Mex.	E11	62
Diefenbaker, Lake, res., Sask., Can.	F2	75
Diégo-Suarez see Antsiranana, Madag.	D9	44
Dien Bien Phu, Viet.	D7	34
Diepholz, Ger.	C8	8
Dieppe, N.B., Can.	C5	71
Dieppe, Fr.	C8	10
Dierks, Ar., U.S.	C1	81
Dieuze, Fr.	D13	10
Digboi, India	G16	38
Dighton, Ks., U.S.	D3	93
Digne, Fr.	H13	10
Digoin, Fr.	F10	10
Dijon, Fr.	E12	10
Dike, Ia., U.S.	B5	92
Dikson, Russia	C10	24
Dili, Indon.	G8	32
Dillard, Or., U.S.	D3	114
Dill City, Ok., U.S.	B2	113
Dilley, Tx., U.S.	E3	120
Dillingen [an der Donau], Ger.	G10	8
Dillingham, Ak., U.S.	D8	79
Dillon, Mt., U.S.	E4	103
Dillon, S.C., U.S.	C9	117
Dillon, co., S.C., U.S.	C9	117
Dillon Lake, res., Oh., U.S.	B3	112
Dillon Reservoir, res., Co., U.S.	B4	83
Dillonvale, Oh., U.S.	B5	112
Dillsboro, In., U.S.	F7	91
Dillsburg, Pa., U.S.	F7	115
Dilolo, Zaire	D4	44
Dilworth, Mn., U.S.	D2	100
Dimāpur, India	H15	38
Dimashq (Damascus), Syria	C5	40
Dimitrovgrad, Bul.	G9	16
Dimitrovgrad, Russia	G7	18
Dimmit, co., Tx., U.S.	E3	120
Dimmitt, Tx., U.S.	B1	120
Dimona, Isr.	D4	40
Dimondale, Mi., U.S.	F6	99
Dinagat Island, i., Phil.	C8	32
Dinājpur, Bngl.	H13	38
Dinan, Fr.	D4	10
Dinant, Bel.	E4	8
Dinar, Tur.	F11	14
Dinara, mts., Eur.	F11	14
Dinaric Alps see Dinara, mts., Eur.	F11	14
Dindigul, India	G4	37
Dinghai, China	E11	28
Dingle, Ire.	I2	7
Dingmans Ferry, Pa., U.S.	D12	115
Dingolfing, Ger.	G12	8
Dingqing, China	E16	38
Dingri, China	F12	38
Dingshan, China	D8	28
Dingwall, Scot., U.K.	D8	7
Dinh Lap, Viet.	D9	34
Dinner Point, c., Fl., U.S.	D4	86
Dinosaur National Monument, U.S.	C6	121
Dinuba, Ca., U.S.	D4	82
Dinwiddie, co., Va., U.S.	C5	123
Diourbel, Sen.	F2	42
Dipkarpaz, N. Cyp.	B4	40
Dipolog, Phil.	D7	32
Dire Dawa, Eth.	G3	46
Diriamba, Nic.	I4	64
Dirico, Ang.	E4	44
Dirk Hartog Island, i., Austl.	E2	50
Dirty Devil, stm., Ut., U.S.	E5	121
Disappointment, Cape, c., Falk. Is.	G9	56
Disappointment, Cape, c., Wa., U.S.	C1	124
Disappointment, Lake, l., Austl.	D4	50
Disentis, Switz.	F15	10
Dishman, Wa., U.S.	g14	124
Disko, i., Grnld.	C22	66
Disko Bugt, b., Grnld.	C22	66
Dismal, stm., Ne., U.S.	C5	104
Disraëli, Que., Can.	D6	74
District of Columbia, dept., U.S.	f8	97
Diu, India	J4	38
Diu, ter., India	J4	38
Divernon, Il., U.S.	D4	90
Divide, co., N.D., U.S.	A2	111
Divide Peak, mtn., Wy., U.S.	E5	127
Divinópolis, Braz.	F6	57
Divisor, Serra do, plat., S.A.	E4	54
Dix, stm., Ky., U.S.	C5	94
Dixfield, Me., U.S.	D2	96
Dixie, co., Fl., U.S.	C3	86
Dixie Valley, val., Nv., U.S.	D4	105
Dixon, Ca., U.S.	C3	82
Dixon, Il., U.S.	B4	90
Dixon, Mo., U.S.	D5	102
Dixon, N.M., U.S.	A4	108
Dixon, co., Ne., U.S.	B9	104
Dixon Entrance, strt., N.A.	F6	69
Dixonville, Pa., U.S.	E3	115
Diyarbakır, Tur.	H16	4
Dja, stm., Afr.	H8	42
Djakarta see Jakarta, Indon.	m13	33a
Djambala, Congo	B2	44
Djanet, Alg.	D7	42
Djebel Abiod, Tun.	M4	14
Djebibina, Tun.	M5	14
Djemmal, Tun.	N5	14
Djerba, Île de, i., Tun.	B8	42
Djerid, Chott, sw., Tun.	B7	42
Djibouti, Dji.	F3	46
Djibouti, ctry., Afr.	F3	46
Dmitrija Lapteva, Proliv, strt., Russia	C22	24

Name	Map Ref	Page
Dmitrov, Russia	E20	18
Dnepr, stm., Eur.	H4	22
Dneprodzeržinsk, Ukr.	H4	22
Dnepropetrovsk, Ukr.	H4	22
Dnestr, stm., Eur.	H3	22
Dnieper see Dnepr, stm., Eur.	H4	22
Dniester see Dnestr, stm., Eur.	H3	22
Dno, Russia	D12	18
Do Āb-e Mīkh-e Zarrīn, Afg.	C2	38
Doaktown, N.B., Can.	C3	71
Doany, Madag.	D9	44
Doba, Chad	E9	42
Dobbiaco, Italy	C7	14
Dobbs Ferry, N.Y., U.S.	g13	109
Döbeln, Ger.	D13	8
Doberai, Jazirah, pen., Indon.	F9	32
Dobo, Indon.	G9	32
Doboj, Bos.	E2	16
Dobrič, Bul.	F11	16
Dobruš, Bela.	I14	18
Dobson, N.C., U.S.	A2	110
Doce, stm., Braz.	E8	57
Docena, Al., U.S.	f7	78
Dock Junction, Ga., U.S.	*E5	87
Doctors Lake, l., Fl., U.S.	m8	86
Doddridge, co., W.V., U.S.	B4	125
Dodecanese see Dhodhekánisos, is., Grc.	M10	16
Dodge, Ne., U.S.	C9	104
Dodge, co., Ga., U.S.	D3	87
Dodge, co., Mn., U.S.	G6	100
Dodge, co., Ne., U.S.	C9	104
Dodge, co., Wi., U.S.	E5	126
Dodge Center, Mn., U.S.	F6	100
Dodge City, Ks., U.S.	E3	93
Dodgeville, Wi., U.S.	F3	126
Dodoma, Tan.	C7	44
Doerun, Ga., U.S.	E3	87
Doe Run, Mo., U.S.	D7	102
Doetinchem, Neth.	D6	8
Dog, stm., Vt., U.S.	C3	122
Dogai Coring, l., China	C13	38
Dog Island, i., Fl., U.S.	C2	86
Dog Keys Pass, strt., Ms., U.S.	g8	101
Dog Lake, l., Man., Can.	D2	70
Dogondoutchi, Niger	F6	42
Doha see Ad-Dawḥah, Qatar	C5	46
Dohad, India	I6	38
Doiran, Lake, l., Eur.	H6	16
Dokka, Nor.	F8	6
Dokkum, Neth.	B5	8
Dolak, Pulau, i., Indon.	G10	32
Dolbeau, Que., Can.	k12	74
Dol-de-Bretagne, Fr.	D5	10
Dolgeville, N.Y., U.S.	B6	109
Dolianova, Italy	J4	14
Dolisie, Congo	B2	44
Dollar Bay, Mi., U.S.	A2	99
Dolo, Som.	H3	46
Dolomite, Al., U.S.	B3	78
Dolomites see Dolomiti, mts., Italy	C6	14
Dolomiti, mts., Italy	C6	14
Dolores, Arg.	D5	56
Dolores, Col.	F5	58
Dolores, Co., U.S.	D2	83
Dolores, co., Co., U.S.	D2	83
Dolores, stm., U.S.	E7	121
Dolores Hidalgo, Mex.	G9	62
Dolphin and Union Strait, strt., N.W. Ter., Can.	C9	66
Dolphin Island, i., Ut., U.S.	B3	121
Dolton, Il., U.S.	k9	90
Dombås, Nor.	E7	6
Dome Mountain, mtn., Az., U.S.	k9	80
Dome Peak, mtn., Co., U.S.	B3	83
Domeyko, Chile	B2	56
Domeyko, Cordillera, mts., Chile	A3	56
Domfront, Fr.	D6	10
Dominica, ctry., N.A.	G17	64
Dominica Channel, strt., N.A.	G17	64
Dominican Republic, ctry., N.A.	E12	64
Dominion, Cape, c., N.W. Ter., Can.	C18	66
Domodedovo, Russia	F20	18
Domodossola, Italy	C3	14
Domžale, Slo.	C9	14
Don, stm., Russia	H6	22
Dona Ana, N.M., U.S.	E3	108
Dona Ana, co., N.M., U.S.	E2	108
Donaldsonville, La., U.S.	D4	95
Donalsonville, Ga., U.S.	E2	87
Donaueschingen, Ger.	H8	8
Donauwörth, Ger.	G10	8
Don Benito, Spain	G6	12
Doncaster, Eng., U.K.	H11	7
Dondo, Ang.	C2	44
Dondra Head, c., Sri L.	J6	37
Doneck, Ukr.	H5	22
Doneraile, S.C., U.S.	C8	117
Donetsk see Doneck, Ukr.	H5	22
Donga, stm., Nig.	G8	42
Dongara, Austl.	E2	50
Dongchuan, China	A7	34
Dongfang, China	H8	26
Dongfang (Basuo), China	E10	34
Dongguan, China	L2	28
Donghai Dao, i., China	D11	34
Dong Hoi, Viet.	F9	32
Dongsheng, China	L6	28
Dongtai, China	C9	28
Dongting Hu, l., China	F1	28
Doniphan, Mo., U.S.	E7	102
Doniphan, Ne., U.S.	D7	104
Doniphan, co., Ks., U.S.	C8	93
Donkey Creek, stm., Wy., U.S.	B7	127
Donkin, N.S., Can.	C10	71
Donley, co., Tx., U.S.	B2	120
Donna, Tx., U.S.	F3	120
Donnacona, Que., Can.	C6	74
Donnellson, Ia., U.S.	D6	92
Donner Pass, Ca., U.S.	C3	82
Donora, Pa., U.S.	F2	115
Donskoj, Russia	H21	18
Dooly, co., Ga., U.S.	D3	87
Doonerak, Mount, mtn., Ak., U.S.	B9	79

Door, co., Wi., U.S.	D6	126
Dora, Al., U.S.	B2	78
Doraville, Ga., U.S.	h8	87
Dorcheat, Bayou, stm., U.S.	B2	95
Dorchester, N.B., Can.	D5	71
Dorchester, Eng., U.K.	K10	7
Dorchester, Ne., U.S.	D8	104
Dorchester, co., Md., U.S.	D5	97
Dorchester, co., S.C., U.S.	E7	117
Dorchester, Cape, c., N.W. Ter., Can.	C17	66
Dordogne, stm., Fr.	H8	10
Dordrecht, Neth.	D4	8
Doré Lake, l., Sask., Can.	C2	75
Dorena Lake, res., Or., U.S.	D3	114
Dores do Indaiá, Braz.	E6	57
Dorgali, Italy	I4	14
Dori, Burkina	F5	42
Dorion-Vaudreuil, Que., Can.	q18	74
Dormont, Pa., U.S.	k13	115
Dornbirn, Aus.	H9	8
Dorothy Pond, Ma., U.S.	B4	98
Dorr, Mi., U.S.	F5	99
Dorset, Vt., U.S.	E2	122
Dorsey, Md., U.S.	B4	97
Dortmund, Ger.	D7	8
Dorton, Ky., U.S.	C7	94
Dorval, Que., Can.	q19	74
Dos Bahías, Cabo, c., Arg.	E3	56
Dothan, Al., U.S.	D4	78
Douai, Fr.	B10	10
Douala, Cam.	H7	42
Douarnenez, Fr.	D2	10
Double Beach, Ct., U.S.	D4	84
Doublespring Pass, Id., U.S.	E5	89
Double Springs, Al., U.S.	A2	78
Doubletop Peak, mtn., Wy., U.S.	C2	127
Doubs, stm., Eur.	E12	10
Dougherty, co., Ga., U.S.	E2	87
Douglas, I. of Man	G8	7
Douglas, Az., U.S.	F6	80
Douglas, Ga., U.S.	E4	87
Douglas, Mi., U.S.	F4	99
Douglas, Wy., U.S.	D7	127
Douglas, co., Co., U.S.	B6	83
Douglas, co., Ga., U.S.	C2	87
Douglas, co., Il., U.S.	D5	90
Douglas, co., Ks., U.S.	D8	93
Douglas, co., Mn., U.S.	E3	100
Douglas, co., Mo., U.S.	E5	102
Douglas, co., Ne., U.S.	C9	104
Douglas, co., Nv., U.S.	E2	105
Douglas, co., Or., U.S.	D3	114
Douglas, co., S.D., U.S.	D7	118
Douglas, co., Wa., U.S.	B6	124
Douglas, co., Wi., U.S.	B2	126
Douglas, Mount, mtn., Ak., U.S.	D9	79
Douglas Channel, strt., B.C., Can.	C3	69
Douglas Lake, l., Mi., U.S.	C6	99
Douglas Lake, res., Tn., U.S.	D10	119
Douglass, Ks., U.S.	E7	93
Douglastown, N.B., Can.	B4	71
Douglasville, Ga., U.S.	C2	87
Dourada, Serra, plat., Braz.	B4	57
Dourados, Braz.	G1	57
Douro (Duero), stm., Eur.	D4	12
Dousman, Wi., U.S.	E5	126
Dove Creek, Co., U.S.	D2	83
Dover, Eng., U.K.	J14	7
Dover, Ar., U.S.	B2	81
Dover, De., U.S.	D3	85
Dover, Fl., U.S.	D4	86
Dover, Ma., U.S.	h10	98
Dover, N.H., U.S.	D5	106
Dover, N.J., U.S.	B3	107
Dover, Oh., U.S.	B4	112
Dover, Pa., U.S.	F8	115
Dover, Tn., U.S.	A4	119
Dover, Strait of (Pas de Calais), strt., Eur.	J14	7
Dover Air Force Base, mil., De., U.S.	D4	85
Dover-Foxcroft, Me., U.S.	C3	96
Dover Plains, N.Y., U.S.	D7	109
Dowagiac, Mi., U.S.	G4	99
Dowlat Yār, Afg.	C1	38
Downers Grove, Il., U.S.	B5	90
Downey, Ca., U.S.	n12	82
Downey, Id., U.S.	G6	89
Downingtown, Pa., U.S.	F10	115
Downpatrick, N. Ire., U.K.	G7	7
Downpatrick Head, c., Ire.	G3	7
Downs, Ks., U.S.	C5	93
Downs Mountain, mtn., Wy., U.S.	C3	127
Downton, Mount, mtn., B.C., Can.	C5	69
Downs, Ia., U.S.	B4	92
Dowshī, Afg.	C3	38
Doylestown, Oh., U.S.	B4	112
Doylestown, Pa., U.S.	F11	115
Doyline, La., U.S.	B2	95
Dráa, Oued, val., Afr.	C4	42
Dracena, Braz.	F3	57
Drachten, Neth.	B6	8
Dracut, Ma., U.S.	A5	98
Draguignan, Fr.	I13	10
Drain, Or., U.S.	D3	114
Drake, Co., U.S.	D6	47
Drake Passage, strt., S.A.	D6	47
Drake Peak, mtn., Or., U.S.	E6	114
Dráma, Grc.	H8	16
Drammen, Nor.	G8	6
Draper, Ut., U.S.	C4	121
Drau (Drava), stm., Eur.	C8	14
Drava (Drau), stm., Eur.	D13	14
Drayton, Ont., Can.	D4	73
Drayton, N.D., U.S.	A8	111
Drayton, S.C., U.S.	B4	117
Drayton Plains, Mi., U.S.	F7	99
Drayton Valley, Alta., Can.	C3	68
Dresden, Ont., Can.	E2	73
Dresden, Ger.	D13	8
Dresden, Oh., U.S.	B3	112
Dresden, Tn., U.S.	A3	119
Dresslerville, Nv., U.S.	E2	105
Dreux, Fr.	D8	10
Drew, Ms., U.S.	B3	101
Drew, co., Ar., U.S.	D4	81
Drews Reservoir, res., Or., U.S.	E6	114
Drexel, Mo., U.S.	C3	102
Drexel, N.C., U.S.	B1	110

Drexel, Oh., U.S.	C1	112
Drift, Ky., U.S.	C7	94
Driggs, Id., U.S.	F7	89
Driskill Mountain, hill, La., U.S.	B3	95
Drogheda, Ire.	H6	7
Drumheller, Alta., Can.	D4	68
Drummond, Ok., U.S.	A4	113
Drummond, Lake, l., Va., U.S.	D6	123
Drummond Island, i., Mi., U.S.	C7	99
Drummondville, Que., Can.	D5	74
Drumright, Ok., U.S.	B5	113
Družina, Russia	D23	24
Drybranch, W.V., U.S.	m13	125
Dry Cimarron, stm., U.S.	A6	108
Dry Creek Mountain, mtn., Nv., U.S.	B5	105
Dryden, Ont., Can.	o16	73
Dryden, N.Y., U.S.	C4	109
Dry Fork, stm., Mo., U.S.	D6	102
Dry Fork, stm., W.V., U.S.	D3	125
Dry Fork, stm., W.V., U.S.	B5	125
Dry Ridge, Ky., U.S.	B5	94
Dry Tortugas, is., Fl., U.S.	H5	86
Duarte, Pico, mtn., Dom. Rep.	E12	64
Dubach, La., U.S.	B3	95
Dubai see Dubayy, U.A.E.	C6	46
Dubawnt, stm., N.W. Ter., Can.	D12	66
Dubawnt Lake, l., N.W. Ter., Can.	D12	66
Du Bay, Lake, res., Wi., U.S.	D4	126
Dubayy (Dubai), U.A.E.	C6	46
Dubbo, Austl.	F9	50
Dublin (Baile Átha Cliath), Ire.	H6	7
Dublin, Ga., U.S.	D4	87
Dublin, In., U.S.	E7	91
Dublin, N.H., U.S.	E2	106
Dublin, Oh., U.S.	k10	112
Dublin, Pa., U.S.	F11	115
Dublin, Tx., U.S.	C3	120
Dublin, Va., U.S.	C2	123
Dubna, Russia	E20	18
Dubois, In., U.S.	H4	91
Du Bois, Pa., U.S.	D4	115
Dubois, Wy., U.S.	C3	127
Dubois, co., In., U.S.	H4	91
Duboistown, Pa., U.S.	D7	115
Dubrovnik, Cro.	G13	14
Dubuque, Ia., U.S.	B7	92
Dubuque, co., Ia., U.S.	B7	92
Duchesne, Ut., U.S.	C5	121
Duchesne, co., Ut., U.S.	C5	121
Duchesne, stm., Ut., U.S.	C5	121
Duchess, Austl.	D7	50
Duck, stm., Tn., U.S.	B4	119
Duck Bay, Man., Can.	C1	70
Duck Creek, stm., Oh., U.S.	C4	112
Duck Creek, stm., Wi., U.S.	h9	126
Duck Lake, Sask., Can.	E2	75
Duck Lake, l., Me., U.S.	C4	96
Duck Mountain Provincial Park, Sask., Can.	F5	75
Duck Valley Indian Reservation, U.S.	B5	105
Duckwater Indian Reservation, Nv., U.S.	E6	105
Duckwater Peak, mtn., Nv., U.S.	F6	105
Dudelange, Lux.	F6	8
Dudinka, Russia	D11	24
Dudley, Ma., U.S.	B4	98
Duenweg, Mo., U.S.	D3	102
Duero (Douro), stm., Eur.	D5	12
Due West, S.C., U.S.	C3	117
Duffer Peak, mtn., Nv., U.S.	B3	105
Dufour Spitze, mtn., Eur.	G14	10
Duga Resa, Cro.	D10	14
Dugdemona, stm., La., U.S.	B3	95
Dugger, In., U.S.	F3	91
Duida, Cerro, mtn., Ven.	F10	58
Duifken Point, c., Austl.	B8	50
Duisburg, Ger.	D6	8
Duk Fadiat, Sudan	G12	42
Dulce, N.M., U.S.	A2	108
Dulgalach, stm., Russia	D20	24
Duluth, Ga., U.S.	B2	87
Duluth, Mn., U.S.	D6	100
Dūmā, Syria	C5	40
Dumaguete, Phil.	D7	32
Dumaran Island, i., Phil.	C6	32
Dumaring, Indon.	E6	32
Dumas, Ar., U.S.	D4	81
Dumas, Tx., U.S.	B2	120
Dumbarton, Scot., U.K.	F8	7
Dumfries, Scot., U.K.	F9	7
Dumfries, Va., U.S.	B5	123
Dumont, Ia., U.S.	B5	92
Dumont, N.J., U.S.	B5	107
Dumyāṭ, Egypt	B12	42
Dunaújváros, Hung.	I18	8
Dunbar, Pa., U.S.	G2	115
Dunbar, W.V., U.S.	C3	125
Duncan, B.C., Can.	E6	69
Duncan, Az., U.S.	E6	80
Duncan, Ok., U.S.	C4	113
Duncan, co., S.C., U.S.	B3	117
Duncan Falls, Oh., U.S.	C4	112
Duncan Lake, res., B.C., Can.	D9	69
Duncannon, Pa., U.S.	F7	115
Duncansville, Pa., U.S.	F5	115
Duncanville, Tx., U.S.	n10	120
Dundalk, Ont., Can.	C4	73
Dundalk, Ire.	G6	7
Dundalk, Md., U.S.	B4	97
Dundas, Ont., Can.	D5	73
Dundas Peninsula, pen., N.W. Ter., Can.	B10	66
Dundee, S. Afr.	G6	44
Dundee, Scot., U.K.	E9	7
Dundee, Fl., U.S.	D5	86
Dundee, Il., U.S.	A5	90
Dundee, Mi., U.S.	G7	99
Dundee, N.Y., U.S.	C4	109
Dundee, Or., U.S.	h11	114
Dundy, co., Ne., U.S.	D4	104
Dunedin, N.Z.	F3	52
Dunedin, Fl., U.S.	D4	86
Dunfermline, Scot., U.K.	E9	7
Dungarvan, Ire.	I5	7
Dungun, Malay.	L7	34

Dungeness, stm., Wa., U.S.	A2	124
Dungun, Malay.	L7	34
Dunham, Que., Can.	D5	74
Dunhua, China	C12	26
Dunhuang, China	C5	26
Dunkard Creek, stm., U.S.	B4	125
Dunkerque, Fr.	A9	10
Dunkerton, Ia., U.S.	B5	92
Dunkirk, In., U.S.	D7	91
Dunkirk, N.Y., U.S.	C1	109
Dunkirk, Oh., U.S.	B2	112
Dunklin, co., Mo., U.S.	E7	102
Dunkwa, Ghana	G5	42
Dún Laoghaire, Ire.	H6	7
Dunlap, Il., U.S.	C4	90
Dunlap, In., U.S.	A6	91
Dunlap, Ia., U.S.	C2	92
Dunlap, Tn., U.S.	D8	119
Dunleith, De., U.S.	i7	85
Dunloup Creek, stm., W.V., U.S.	n13	125
Dunmore, Pa., U.S.	D10	115
Dunmore, Lake, l., Vt., U.S.	D2	122
Dunn, N.C., U.S.	B4	110
Dunn, co., N.D., U.S.	B3	111
Dunn, co., Wi., U.S.	D2	126
Dunnellon, Fl., U.S.	C4	86
Dunnville, Ont., Can.	E5	73
Dunqulah, Sudan	E12	42
Duns, Scot., U.K.	F10	7
Dunseith, N.D., U.S.	A5	111
Dunsmuir, Ca., U.S.	B2	82
Duntou, China	F8	28
Dunville, Newf., Can.	E5	72
Dunwoody, Ga., U.S.	h8	87
Duomaer, China	E2	26
Du Page, co., Il., U.S.	B5	90
Du Page, stm., Il., U.S.	k8	90
Duplin, co., N.C., U.S.	C5	110
Dupont, Co., U.S.	B6	83
Dupont, Pa., U.S.	n18	115
Dupont City, W.V., U.S.	m12	125
Dupont Manor, De., U.S.	B1	41
Dupont Manor, De., U.S.	D3	85
Duque de Caxias, Braz.	G7	57
Duque de York, Isla, i., Chile	G1	56
Duquesne, Pa., U.S.	F2	115
Du Quoin, Il., U.S.	E4	90
Durand, Il., U.S.	A4	90
Durand, Mi., U.S.	F6	99
Durand, Wi., U.S.	D2	126
Durango, Mex.	E7	62
Durango, Spain	B9	12
Durango, Co., U.S.	D3	83
Durant, Ia., U.S.	C7	92
Durant, Ms., U.S.	B4	101
Durant, Ok., U.S.	D5	113
Durazno, Ur.	C5	56
Durban, S. Afr.	G6	44
Đurđevac, Cro.	C12	14
Düren, Ger.	E6	8
Durg, India	B6	37
Durgāpur, India	I12	38
Durham, Ont., Can.	C4	73
Durham, Eng., U.K.	G11	7
Durham, Ca., U.S.	C3	82
Durham, Ct., U.S.	D5	84
Durham, N.H., U.S.	D5	106
Durham, N.C., U.S.	B4	110
Durham, co., N.C., U.S.	A4	110
Durness, Scot., U.K.	C8	7
Durrell, Newf., Can.	D4	72
Durrës, Alb.	H3	16
Dursunbey, Tur.	J12	16
D'Urville, Tanjung, c., Indon.	F10	32
Duryea, Pa., U.S.	D10	115
Dušanbe, Taj.	J11	22
Dušekan, Russia	E15	24
Dushan, China	B9	34
Dushanbe see Dušanbe, Taj.	J11	22
Duson, La., U.S.	D3	95
Düsseldorf, Ger.	D6	8
Dutchess, co., N.Y., U.S.	D7	109
Dutch Island, i., R.I., U.S.	F4	116
Dutton, Ont., Can.	E3	73
Dutton, Mount, mtn., Ut., U.S.	E3	121
Duval, co., Fl., U.S.	B5	86
Duval, co., Tx., U.S.	F3	120
Duxbury, Ma., U.S.	B6	98
Duyun, China	A9	34
Dwight, Il., U.S.	B5	90
Dwight D. Eisenhower Lock, N.Y., U.S.	f9	109
Dworshak Reservoir, res., Id., U.S.	C3	89
Dyer, In., U.S.	A2	91
Dyer, Tn., U.S.	A3	119
Dyer, co., Tn., U.S.	A2	119
Dyer, Cape, c., N.W. Ter., Can.	C20	66
Dyer Island, i., R.I., U.S.	E5	116
Dyersburg, Tn., U.S.	A2	119
Dyersville, Ia., U.S.	B6	92
Dyess Air Force Base, mil., Tx., U.S.	C3	120
Dysart, Ia., U.S.	B5	92
Džalinda, Russia	G18	24
Džambul, Kaz.	I12	22
Dzaoudzi, May.	D9	44
Džardžan, Russia	D18	24
Dzavchan, stm., Mong.	B5	26
Dzeržinsk, Russia	E26	18
Dzeržinskoje, Kaz.	H10	24
Džezkazgan, Kaz.	H11	22
Dzhambul see Džambul, Kaz.	I12	22
Dzierżoniów (Reichenbach), Pol.	E16	8
Džugdžur, Chrebet, mts., Russia	F21	24

E

Eads, Co., U.S.	C8	83
Eagan, Mn., U.S.	n12	100
Eagar, Az., U.S.	C6	80
Eagle, Co., U.S.	B4	83
Eagle, Id., U.S.	F2	89
Eagle, Ne., U.S.	h12	104
Eagle, Wi., U.S.	F5	126
Eagle, co., Co., U.S.	B4	83
Eagle, stm., Newf., Can.	B2	72

Eagle Creek Reservoir, res., In., U.S.	E5	91
Eagle Grove, Ia., U.S.	B4	92
Eagle Key, i., Fl., U.S.	G6	86
Eagle Lake, Me., U.S.	A4	96
Eagle Lake, Mn., U.S.	F5	100
Eagle Lake, Tx., U.S.	E4	120
Eagle Lake, l., Ca., U.S.	B3	82
Eagle Lake, l., Me., U.S.	B3	96
Eagle Lake, l., Me., U.S.	A4	96
Eagle Lake, l., Ms., U.S.	C3	101
Eagle Lake, l., Wi., U.S.	C5	126
Eagle Mountain, mtn., Mn., U.S.	k9	100
Eagle Mountain Lake, res., Tx., U.S.	m9	120
Eagle Nest Lake, l., N.M., U.S.	A4	108
Eagle Pass, Tx., U.S.	E2	120
Eagle Peak, mtn., Ca., U.S.	B3	82
Eagle Point, Or., U.S.	E4	114
Eagle River, Wi., U.S.	C4	126
Eagletail Mountains, mts., Az., U.S.	D2	80
Eagletail Peak, mtn., Az., U.S.	D2	80
Eagletown, Ok., U.S.	C7	113
Earle, Ar., U.S.	B5	81
Earlham, Ia., U.S.	C3	92
Earlimart, Ca., U.S.	E4	82
Earlington, Ky., U.S.	C2	94
Earlville, Il., U.S.	B5	90
Earlville, Ia., U.S.	B6	92
Early, Ia., U.S.	B2	92
Early, co., Ga., U.S.	E2	87
Earth, Tx., U.S.	B1	120
Easley, S.C., U.S.	B2	117
East, stm., Ct., U.S.	D5	84
East, stm., N.Y., U.S.	k13	109
East, stm., Wi., U.S.	h9	126
East Alton, Il., U.S.	E3	90
East Angus, Que., Can.	D6	74
East Arlington, Vt., U.S.	E2	122
East Aurora, N.Y., U.S.	C2	109
East Bangor, Pa., U.S.	E11	115
East Bank, W.V., U.S.	m13	125
East Barre, Vt., U.S.	C4	122
East Baton Rouge, co., La., U.S.	D4	95
East Bay, b., Fl., U.S.	u16	86
East Bay, b., Tx., U.S.	R15	120
East Beckwith Mountain, mtn., Co., U.S.	C3	83
East Berlin, Ct., U.S.	C5	84
East Berlin, Pa., U.S.	G8	115
East Bernard, Tx., U.S.	E4	120
East Bernstadt, Ky., U.S.	C5	94
East Bethel, Mn., U.S.	E5	100
East Billerica, Ma., U.S.	f11	98
Eastborough, Ks., U.S.	g12	93
Eastbourne, Eng., U.K.	K13	7
East Brady, Pa., U.S.	E2	115
East Branch Clarion River Lake, res., Pa., U.S.	C4	115
East Brewton, Al., U.S.	D2	78
East Bridgewater, Ma., U.S.	B6	98
East Brimfield Lake, res., Ma., U.S.	B3	98
East Brooklyn, Ct., U.S.	B8	84
East Broughton, Que., Can.	C6	74
East Brunswick, N.J., U.S.	C4	107
East Butte, mtn., Mt., U.S.	B5	103
East Cache Creek, stm., Ok., U.S.	C3	113
East Cape, c., Fl., U.S.	G5	86
East Carbon, Ut., U.S.	D5	121
East Carroll, co., La., U.S.	B4	95
East Chicago, In., U.S.	A3	91
East China Sea, Asia	E12	26
East Chop, c., Ma., U.S.	D6	98
East Cleveland, Oh., U.S.	g9	112
East Cote Blanche Bay, b., La., U.S.	E4	95
East Dennis, Ma., U.S.	C7	98
East Derry, N.H., U.S.	E4	106
East Detroit, Mi., U.S.	p16	99
East Douglas, Ma., U.S.	B4	98
East Dubuque, Il., U.S.	A3	90
Eastend, Sask., Can.	H1	75
Easter Island see Pascua, Isla de, i., Chile	H5	2
Eastern Bay, b., Md., U.S.	C5	97
Eastern Channel see Tsushima-kaikyō, strt., Japan	I2	30
Eastern Ghāts, mts., India	F5	37
Eastern Neck Island, i., Md., U.S.	B5	97
Eastern Point, c., Ma., U.S.	f13	98
Easterville, Man., Can.	C2	70
East Falkland, i., Falk. Is.	G5	56
East Falmouth, Ma., U.S.	C6	98
East Feliciana, co., La., U.S.	D4	95
East Flat Rock, N.C., U.S.	f10	110
East Fork, stm., Wy., U.S.	D3	127
East Fork Lake, res., Oh., U.S.	C1	112
East Gaffney, S.C., U.S.	A4	117
East Galesburg, Il., U.S.	C3	90
East Granby, Ct., U.S.	B5	84
East Grand Forks, Mn., U.S.	C2	100
East Grand Rapids, Mi., U.S.	F5	99
East Greenville, Pa., U.S.	F10	115
East Greenwich, R.I., U.S.	D4	116
East Gwillimbury, Ont., Can.	C5	73
East Hampstead, N.H., U.S.	E4	106
East Hampton, Ct., U.S.	C5	84
Easthampton, Ma., U.S.	B2	98
East Hanover, N.J., U.S.	*B4	107
East Hartford, Ct., U.S.	B5	84
East Hartland, Ct., U.S.	B4	84
East Haven, Ct., U.S.	D5	84
East Helena, Mt., U.S.	D5	103
East Jordan, Mi., U.S.	C5	99
Eastlake, Oh., U.S.	A4	112
East Lake Tohopekaliga, l., Fl., U.S.	D5	86
Eastland, Tx., U.S.	C3	120
Eastland, co., Tx., U.S.	C3	120
East Lansing, Mi., U.S.	F6	99
East Las Vegas, Nv., U.S.	G6	105
East Liverpool, Oh., U.S.	B5	112
East London (Oos-Londen), S. Afr.	H5	44
East Longmeadow, Ma., U.S.	B3	98
East Los Angeles, Ca., U.S.	m12	82
East Lyme, Ct., U.S.	D7	84

Index

Name	Map Ref	Page
East Lynn Lake, res., W.V., U.S.	C2	125
Eastmain, stm., Que., Can.	F17	66
Eastmain-Opinaca, Réservoir, res., Que., Can.	h11	74
Eastman, Que., Can.	D5	74
Eastman, Ga., U.S.	D3	87
East Matunuck, R.I., U.S.	F3	116
East Middlebury, Vt., U.S.	D2	122
East Millinocket, Me., U.S.	C4	96
East Moline, Il., U.S.	B3	90
East Montpelier, Vt., U.S.	C4	122
East Naples, Fl., U.S.	F5	86
East Newnan, Ga., U.S.	C2	87
East Nishnabotna, stm., Ia., U.S.	C2	92
East Norriton, Pa., U.S.	o20	115
East Olympia, Wa., U.S.	C3	124
Easton, Md., U.S.	C5	97
Easton, Pa., U.S.	E11	115
Easton Reservoir, res., Ct., U.S.	E2	84
East Orange, N.J., U.S.	B4	107
East Orleans, Ma., U.S.	C8	98
Eastover, S.C., U.S.	D6	117
East Palatka, Fl., U.S.	C5	86
East Palestine, Oh., U.S.	B5	112
East Pass, strt., Fl., U.S.	C2	86
East Pea Ridge, W.V., U.S.	C2	125
East Peoria, Il., U.S.	C4	90
East Pepperell, Ma., U.S.	A4	98
East Petersburg, Pa., U.S.	F9	115
East Pittsburgh, Pa., U.S.	k14	115
Eastpoint, Fl., U.S.	C2	86
East Point, Ga., U.S.	C2	87
East Point, c., P.E.I., Can.	C8	71
East Point, c., Ma., U.S.	B6	98
East Point, c., N.J., U.S.	E2	107
Eastport, Newf., Can.	D5	72
Eastport, Me., U.S.	D6	96
East Prairie, Mo., U.S.	E8	102
East Providence, R.I., U.S.	C4	116
East Pryor Mountain, mtn., Mt., U.S.	E8	103
East Quogue, N.Y., U.S.	n16	109
East Range, mts., Nv., U.S.	C4	105
East Ridge, Tn., U.S.	h11	119
East River, Ct., U.S.	D5	84
East Rochester, N.Y., U.S.	B3	109
East Rockingham, N.C., U.S.	C3	110
East Rutherford, N.J., U.S.	h8	107
East Saint Louis, Il., U.S.	E3	90
East Selkirk, Man., Can.	D3	70
Eastsound, Wa., U.S.	A3	124
East Spencer, N.C., U.S.	B2	110
East Stroudsburg, Pa., U.S.	D11	115
East Tawas, Mi., U.S.	D7	99
East Troy, Wi., U.S.	F5	126
East Vestal, N.Y., U.S.	C4	109
East View, W.V., U.S.	k10	125
East Walker, stm., U.S.	E2	105
East Walpole, Ma., U.S.	h11	98
East Wareham, Ma., U.S.	C6	98
East Washington, Pa., U.S.	F1	115
East Wenatchee, Wa., U.S.	B5	124
East Windsor, N.J., U.S.	C3	107
East York, Ont., Can.	D5	73
Eaton, Co., U.S.	A6	83
Eaton, In., U.S.	D7	91
Eaton, Oh., U.S.	C1	112
Eaton, co., Mi., U.S.	F6	99
Eaton Rapids, Mi., U.S.	F6	99
Eatonton, Ga., U.S.	C3	87
Eatontown, N.J., U.S.	C4	107
Eatonville, Wa., U.S.	C3	124
Eau Claire, Wi., U.S.	D2	126
Eau Claire, co., Wi., U.S.	D2	126
Eau Claire, stm., Wi., U.S.	D2	126
Eau Claire, Lac à l', l., Que., Can.	g11	74
Eauze, Fr.	I7	10
Ebano, Mex.	F10	62
Ebba Ksour, Tun.	N3	14
Ebbw Vale, Wales, U.K.	J9	7
Ebensburg, Pa., U.S.	F4	115
Eberndorf, Aus.	I14	8
Eberswalde, Ger.	C13	8
Ebetsu, Japan	p19	30a
Ebingen, Ger.	G9	8
Ebinur Hu, l., China	B3	26
Eboli, Italy	I10	14
Ebolowa, Cam.	H8	42
Ebro, stm., Spain	E12	12
Ebro, Delta del, Spain	E12	12
Eccles, W.V., U.S.	n13	125
Echo Bay, Nv., U.S.	G7	105
Echo Lake, l., Me., U.S.	D3	96
Echo Lake, l., Vt., U.S.	B5	122
Echols, co., Ga., U.S.	F4	87
Écija, Spain	H6	12
Eckernförde, Ger.	A9	8
Eckhart Mines, Md., U.S.	k13	97
Eckville, Alta., Can.	C3	68
Eclectic, Al., U.S.	C3	78
Eclipse Sound, strt., N.W. Ter., Can.	B17	66
Écommoy, Fr.	E7	10
Econfina, stm., Fl., U.S.	B3	86
Economy, Pa., U.S.	*h13	115
Écorces, Rivière aux, stm., Que., Can.	A6	74
Ecorse, Mi., U.S.	p15	99
Ecru, Ms., U.S.	A4	101
Ector, co., Tx., U.S.	D1	120
Ecuador, ctry., S.A.	D3	54
Ed, Swe.	G8	6
Edcouch, Tx., U.S.	F4	120
Eddy, co., N.M., U.S.	E5	108
Eddy, co., N.D., U.S.	B7	111
Eddystone, Pa., U.S.	p20	115
Eddyville, Ia., U.S.	C5	92
Eddyville, Ky., U.S.	e9	94
Ede, Neth.	C5	8
Edéa, Cam.	H8	42
Eden, Ga., U.S.	D5	87
Eden, Md., U.S.	D6	97
Eden, N.Y., U.S.	C2	109
Eden, N.C., U.S.	A3	110
Eden, Tx., U.S.	D3	120
Edenderry, Ire.	H5	7
Eden Prairie, Mn., U.S.	n12	100
Edenton, N.C., U.S.	A6	110
Eden Valley, Mn., U.S.	E4	100
Edgar, Ne., U.S.	D8	104
Edgar, Wi., U.S.	D4	126
Edgar, co., Il., U.S.	D6	90
Edgard, La., U.S.	D5	95
Edgartown, Ma., U.S.	D6	98
Edgecombe, co., N.C., U.S.	B5	110
Edgecombe, Cape, c., Ak., U.S.	m21	79
Edgefield, S.C., U.S.	D4	117
Edgefield, co., S.C., U.S.	D4	117
Edgeley, N.D., U.S.	C7	111
Edgemere, Md., U.S.	B5	97
Edgemont, S.D., U.S.	D2	118
Edgemoor, De., U.S.	A3	85
Edgerton, Ks., U.S.	D8	93
Edgerton, Mn., U.S.	G2	100
Edgerton, Oh., U.S.	A1	112
Edgerton, Wi., U.S.	F4	126
Edgerton, Wy., U.S.	C6	127
Edgewater, Al., U.S.	f7	78
Edgewater, Fl., U.S.	D6	86
Edgewater, Md., U.S.	C4	97
Edgewater, N.J., U.S.	h9	107
Edgewater Park, N.J., U.S.	C3	107
Edgewood, In., U.S.	D6	91
Edgewood, Ia., U.S.	B6	92
Edgewood, Ky., U.S.	h13	94
Edgewood, Md., U.S.	B5	97
Edgewood, N.M., U.S.	B3	108
Edgewood, Oh., U.S.	A5	112
Edgewood, Pa., U.S.	k14	115
Edgewood, Wa., U.S.	f11	124
Edgeworth, Pa., U.S.	h13	115
Edina, Mn., U.S.	F5	100
Edina, Mo., U.S.	A5	102
Edinboro, Pa., U.S.	C1	115
Edinburg, Il., U.S.	D4	90
Edinburg, Tx., U.S.	F3	120
Edinburg, Va., U.S.	B4	123
Edinburgh, Scot., U.K.	F9	7
Edinburgh, In., U.S.	F6	91
Edirne, Tur.	G13	4
Edison, Ga., U.S.	E2	87
Edison, N.J., U.S.	B4	107
Edisto, stm., S.C., U.S.	E6	117
Edisto Island, i., S.C., U.S.	F7	117
Edith, Mount, mtn., Mt., U.S.	D5	103
Edjeleh, Alg.	C7	42
Edmond, Ok., U.S.	B4	113
Edmonds, Wa., U.S.	B3	124
Edmondson Heights, Md., U.S.	*g10	97
Edmonson, co., Ky., U.S.	C3	94
Edmonton, Alta., Can.	C4	68
Edmonton, Ky., U.S.	D4	94
Edmore, Mi., U.S.	E5	99
Edmunds, co., S.D., U.S.	B6	118
Edmundston, N.B., Can.	B1	71
Edna, Tx., U.S.	E4	120
Edon, Oh., U.S.	A1	112
Édouard, Lac, l., Que., Can.	B5	74
Edremit, Tur.	J11	16
Edrengiyn Nuruu, mts., Mong.	C6	26
Edsbyn, Swe.	F10	6
Edson, Alta., Can.	C2	68
Edson Butte, mtn., Or., U.S.	E2	114
Eduardo Castex, Arg.	D4	56
Edward, Lake, l., Afr.	B5	44
Edwards, Ms., U.S.	C3	101
Edwards, co., Il., U.S.	E5	90
Edwards, co., Ks., U.S.	E4	93
Edwards, co., Tx., U.S.	E2	120
Edwards Air Force Base, mil., Ca., U.S.	E5	82
Edwardsburg, Mi., U.S.	G4	99
Edwards Butte, mtn., Or., U.S.	B3	114
Edwardsville, Il., U.S.	E4	90
Edwardsville, Ks., U.S.	k16	93
Edwardsville, Pa., U.S.	n17	115
Eel, stm., Ca., U.S.	B2	82
Eel, stm., In., U.S.	F3	91
Eel, stm., In., U.S.	C6	91
Effigy Mounds National Monument, Ia., U.S.	A6	92
Effingham, Il., U.S.	D5	90
Effingham, co., Ga., U.S.	D5	87
Effingham, co., Il., U.S.	D5	90
Efland, N.C., U.S.	A3	110
Egan Range, mts., Nv., U.S.	E7	105
Eganville, Ont., Can.	B7	73
Egede og Rothes Fjord, Grnld.	C25	66
Egedesminde, Grnld.	C22	66
Eger, Hung.	H20	8
Egersund, Nor.	G5	6
Eggenfelden, Ger.	G12	8
Egg Harbor City, N.J., U.S.	D3	107
Egg Island Point, c., N.J., U.S.	E2	107
Égletons, Fr.	G9	10
Eglin Air Force Base, mil., Fl., U.S.	u15	86
Egmont, Mount, mtn., N.Z.	C5	52
Egmont Bay, b., P.E.I., Can.	C5	71
Egmont Channel, strt., Fl., U.S.	p10	86
Egmont Key, i., Fl., U.S.	p10	86
Egvekinot, Russia	D29	24
Egypt, ctry., Afr.	C11	42
Egypt, Lake of, res., Il., U.S.	F5	90
Ehingen, Ger.	G9	8
Ehrenberg, Az., U.S.	D1	80
Éibar, Spain	B9	12
Eichstätt, Ger.	G11	8
Eidsvoll, Nor.	F8	6
Eielson Air Force Base, mil., Ak., U.S.	C10	79
Eifel, mts., Ger.	E6	8
Eighty Mile Beach, Austl.	C4	50
Eil, Som.	G4	46
Eilenburg, Ger.	D12	8
Eindhoven, Neth.	D5	8
Einsiedeln, Switz.	E15	10
Eirunepé, Braz.	E5	54
Eisenach, Ger.	E10	8
Eisenberg, Ger.	E11	8
Eisenerz, Aus.	H14	8
Eisenhower, Mount, mtn., N.H., U.S.	B4	106
Eisenhüttenstadt, Ger.	C14	8
Eisenstadt, Aus.	H16	8
Eisleben, Ger.	D11	8
Ejea de los Caballeros, Spain	C10	12
Ekiatapskij Chrebet, mts., Russia	D29	24
Ekimčan, Russia	G20	24
Ekwan, stm., Ont., Can.	F16	66
Elaine, Ar., U.S.	C5	81
El Asnam, Alg.	A6	42
Elat, Isr.	E4	40
Elâziğ, Tur.	H15	4
Elba, Al., U.S.	D3	78
Elba, Isola d', i., Italy	G5	14
El Banco, Col.	C6	58
El Barco de Valdeorras, Spain	C5	12
Elbasan, Alb.	H4	16
El Baúl, Ven.	C8	58
Elbe (Labe), stm., Eur.	B9	8
Elberfeld, In., U.S.	H3	91
Elbert, co., Co., U.S.	B6	83
Elbert, co., Ga., U.S.	B4	87
Elbert, Mount, mtn., Co., U.S.	B4	83
Elberta, Ga., U.S.	D3	87
Elberton, Ga., U.S.	B4	87
Elbeuf, Fr.	C8	10
Elblag (Elbing), Pol.	A19	8
El Bonillo, Spain	G9	12
El Bordo, Col.	F4	58
Elbow, stm., Alta., Can.	D3	68
Elbow Lake, Mn., U.S.	E3	100
El'brus, Gora (Mount Elbrus), mtn., Russia	I6	22
El Burgo de Osma, Spain	D8	12
Elburn, Il., U.S.	B5	90
Elburz Mountains see Alborz, Reshteh-ye Kūhhā-ye, Iran	J8	22
El Cajon, Ca., U.S.	F5	82
El Callao, Ven.	D12	58
El Campo, Tx., U.S.	E4	120
El Capitan, mtn., Mt., U.S.	D2	103
El Capitan Reservoir, res., Ca., U.S.	o16	82
El Carmen, Ca., U.S.	A3	56
El Carmen de Bolívar, Col.	C5	58
El Centro, Ca., U.S.	F6	82
El Cerrito, Col.	F4	58
El Cerrito, Ca., U.S.	h8	82
Elche, Spain	G11	12
Elche de la Sierra, Spain	G9	12
El Cozón, Mex.	B3	62
El Cuervo Butte, mtn., N.M., U.S.	k9	108
Elda, Spain	G11	12
El Desemboque, Mex.	C3	62
El Diviso, Col.	G3	58
El Djouf, des., Afr.	D4	42
Eldon, Ia., U.S.	D5	92
Eldon, Mo., U.S.	C5	102
Eldora, Ia., U.S.	B4	92
Eldorado, Mex.	E6	62
El Dorado, Ar., U.S.	D3	81
El Dorado, Il., U.S.	F5	90
El Dorado, Ks., U.S.	E7	93
El Dorado, Tx., U.S.	D2	120
El Dorado, co., Ca., U.S.	C3	82
Eldorado Peak, mtn., Wa., U.S.	A4	124
Eldorado Springs, Co., U.S.	B5	83
El Dorado Springs, Mo., U.S.	D3	102
Eldoret, Kenya	A7	44
Eldridge, Ia., U.S.	C7	92
Eleanor, W.V., U.S.	C3	125
Electra, Tx., U.S.	C3	120
Electra Lake, res., Co., U.S.	D3	83
Electric Peak, mtn., Co., U.S.	C5	83
Electric Peak, mtn., Mt., U.S.	E6	103
Elektrostal', Russia	F21	22
El Encanto, Col.	H6	58
Elephant Butte Reservoir, res., N.M., U.S.	D2	108
El Estor, Guat.	G3	64
Eleuthera, i., Bah.	B9	64
Eleven Mile Canyon Reservoir, res., Co., U.S.	C5	83
Eleven Point, stm., U.S.	A4	81
Elevsís, Grc.	K7	16
El Fahs, Tun.	M4	14
El Ferrol del Caudillo, Spain	B3	12
El Galpón, Arg.	B4	56
Elgin, Scot., U.K.	D9	7
Elgin, Il., U.S.	A5	90
Elgin, Ia., U.S.	B6	92
Elgin, Mn., U.S.	F6	100
Elgin, Ne., U.S.	C7	104
Elgin, N.D., U.S.	C4	111
Elgin, Ok., U.S.	C3	113
Elgin, Or., U.S.	B9	114
Elgin, S.C., U.S.	B6	117
Elgin, Tx., U.S.	D4	120
El Goléa, Alg.	B6	42
El Golfo de Santa Clara, Mex.	B2	62
Elgon, Mount, mtn., Afr.	A6	44
El Hadjira, Tun.	N6	14
El Hank, clf, Afr.	D4	42
El Haouaria, Tun.	L6	14
Elida, Oh., U.S.	B1	112
Elisabethville see Lubumbashi, Zaire	D5	44
Elizabeth, Austl.	F7	50
Elizabeth, Co., U.S.	B6	83
Elizabeth, N.J., U.S.	B4	107
Elizabeth, W.V., U.S.	B3	125
Elizabeth, Cape, c., Wa., U.S.	B1	124
Elizabeth City, N.C., U.S.	A6	110
Elizabeth Islands, is., Ma., U.S.	D6	98
Elizabeth Reef, atoll, Austl.	E11	50
Elizabethton, Tn., U.S.	C11	119
Elizabethtown, Ky., U.S.	C4	94
Elizabethtown, N.C., U.S.	C4	110
Elizabethtown, Pa., U.S.	F8	115
Elizabethville, Pa., U.S.	E8	115
El-Jadida, Mor.	B4	42
El Jebel, Co., U.S.	B3	83
El Morro National Monument, N.M., U.S.	B1	108
Elk, Pol.	B21	8
Elk, co., Ks., U.S.	E7	93
Elk, co., Pa., U.S.	D5	115
Elk, stm., U.S.	A2	78
Elk, stm., Co., U.S.	A4	83
Elk, stm., Ks., U.S.	E7	93
Elk, stm., Tn., U.S.	B5	119
Elk, stm., Wi., U.S.	C3	126
Elkader, Ia., U.S.	B6	92
El Kairouan, Tun.	N5	14
Elk City, Id., U.S.	D3	89
Elk City, Ok., U.S.	B2	113
Elk City Lake, res., Ks., U.S.	E7	93
Elk Creek, stm., Ok., U.S.	B2	113
Elk Creek, stm., S.D., U.S.	C3	118
El Kef, Tun.	M3	14
Elkford, B.C., Can.	D10	69
Elk Grove, Ca., U.S.	C3	82
Elk Grove Village, Il., U.S.	h9	90
Elkhart, In., U.S.	A6	91
Elkhart, Ks., U.S.	E2	93
Elkhart, Tx., U.S.	D5	120
Elkhart, co., In., U.S.	A6	91
Elkhart, stm., In., U.S.	B6	91
Elkhead Mountains, mts., Co., U.S.	A3	83
Elkhorn, Man., Can.	E1	70
Elk Horn, Ia., U.S.	C2	92
Elkhorn, Ne., U.S.	g12	104
Elkhorn, Wi., U.S.	F5	126
Elkhorn, stm., Ne., U.S.	B7	104
Elkhorn Peaks, mts., Id., U.S.	F7	89
Elkin, N.C., U.S.	A2	110
Elkins, Ar., U.S.	A1	81
Elkins, W.V., U.S.	C5	125
Elkland, Pa., U.S.	C7	115
Elk Mills, Md., U.S.	A6	97
Elk Mound, Wi., U.S.	D2	126
Elk Mountain, Wy., U.S.	E6	127
Elk Mountain, mtn., N.M., U.S.	D1	108
Elk Mountain, mtn., Wy., U.S.	E6	127
Elk Mountains, mts., U.S.	D1	118
Elk Mountains, mts., Co., U.S.	B3	83
Elko, Nv., U.S.	C6	105
Elko, co., Nv., U.S.	B6	105
Elk Peak, mtn., Mt., U.S.	D6	103
Elk Point, Alta., Can.	C5	68
Elk Point, S.D., U.S.	E9	118
Elk Rapids, Mi., U.S.	D5	99
El Krib, Tun.	M4	14
Elkridge, Md., U.S.	B4	97
Elk River, Mn., U.S.	E5	100
Elkton, Ky., U.S.	D2	94
Elkton, Md., U.S.	A6	97
Elkton, Mi., U.S.	E7	99
Elkton, S.D., U.S.	C9	118
Elkton, Va., U.S.	B4	123
Elkview, W.V., U.S.	m13	125
Elkville, Il., U.S.	F4	90
Ellaville, Ga., U.S.	D2	87
Ellen, Mount, mtn., Ut., U.S.	E5	121
Ellendale, De., U.S.	E4	85
Ellendale, N.D., U.S.	C7	111
Ellensburg, Wa., U.S.	C5	124
Ellenton, Fl., U.S.	E4	86
Ellenville, N.Y., U.S.	D6	109
Ellerbe, N.C., U.S.	B3	110
Ellerslie, Md., U.S.	k13	97
Ellesmere Island, i., N.W. Ter., Can.	A21	128
Ellice Islands see Tuvalu, ctry., Oc.	G24	2
Ellicott City, Md., U.S.	B4	97
Ellijay, Ga., U.S.	B2	87
Ellington, Ct., U.S.	B6	84
Ellington, Mo., U.S.	D7	102
Ellinwood, Ks., U.S.	D5	93
Elliot Lake, Ont., Can.	A2	73
Elliott, Ms., U.S.	B4	101
Elliott, co., Ky., U.S.	B6	94
Elliott Bay, b., Wa., U.S.	e11	124
Elliott Key, i., Fl., U.S.	G6	86
Ellis, Ks., U.S.	D4	93
Ellis, co., Ks., U.S.	D4	93
Ellis, co., Ok., U.S.	A2	113
Ellis, co., Tx., U.S.	C4	120
Ellis, stm., N.H., U.S.	B4	106
Elliston, Va., U.S.	C2	123
Ellisville, Ms., U.S.	D4	101
Ellisville, Mo., U.S.	f12	102
Ellon, Scot., U.K.	D10	7
Elloree, S.C., U.S.	D6	117
Ellport, Pa., U.S.	E1	115
Ellsworth, Ks., U.S.	D5	93
Ellsworth, Me., U.S.	D4	96
Ellsworth, Wi., U.S.	D1	126
Ellsworth, co., Ks., U.S.	D5	93
Ellsworth Air Force Base, mil., S.D., U.S.	C2	118
Ellwangen, Ger.	G10	8
Ellwood City, Pa., U.S.	E1	115
Elm, stm., N.D., U.S.	B8	111
Elma, Ia., U.S.	A5	92
Elma, Wa., U.S.	C2	124
El Mahdia, Tun.	N6	14
El Manteco, Ven.	D11	58
Elm City, N.C., U.S.	B5	110
Elm Creek, Ne., U.S.	D6	104
El Médano, Mex.	E4	62
Elmendorf Air Force Base, mil., Ak., U.S.	C10	79
Elm Grove, Wi., U.S.	m11	126
Elmhurst, Il., U.S.	B5	90
Elmhurst, Pa., U.S.	D10	115
Elmira, N.Y., U.S.	C4	109
El Mirage, Az., U.S.	k8	80
Elmira Heights, N.Y., U.S.	C4	109
El Moknine, Tun.	N5	14
Elmont, N.Y., U.S.	k13	109
Elmora, Pa., U.S.	E4	115
Elmore, Mn., U.S.	G4	100
Elmore, Oh., U.S.	A2	112
Elmore, co., Al., U.S.	C3	78
Elmore, co., Id., U.S.	F3	89
Elmsdale, N.S., Can.	E6	71
Elmshorn, Ger.	B9	8
Elm Springs, Ar., U.S.	A1	81
Elmvale, Ont., Can.	C5	73
Elmwood, Il., U.S.	C3	90
Elmwood, Ne., U.S.	D9	104
Elmwood, Wi., U.S.	D1	126
Elmwood Park, Il., U.S.	k9	90
Elmwood Park, N.J., U.S.	h8	107
Elmwood Place, Oh., U.S.	o13	112
Elne, Fr.	J9	10
Elnora, In., U.S.	G3	91
Eloise, Fl., U.S.	E5	86
Elon College, N.C., U.S.	A3	110
Elora, Ont., Can.	D4	73
Elorza, Ven.	D8	58
El Oued, Alg.	B7	42
Eloy, Az., U.S.	E4	80
El Palmar, Ven.	D12	58
El Paso, Il., U.S.	C4	90
El Paso, Tx., U.S.	o11	120
El Paso, co., Co., U.S.	C6	83
El Paso, co., Tx., U.S.	o11	120
El Pilar, Ven.	B11	58
El Pital, Cerro, mtn., N.A.	G3	64
El Portal, Fl., U.S.	s13	86
El Prado, N.M., U.S.	A4	108
El Progreso, Hond.	G4	64
El Puente del Arzobispo, Spain	F6	12
El Puerto de Santa María, Spain	I5	12
El Quelite, Mex.	F6	62
El Reno, Ok., U.S.	B4	113
Elrose, Sask., Can.	F1	75
Elroy, Wi., U.S.	E3	126
Elsa, Tx., U.S.	F3	120
Elsah, Il., U.S.	E3	90
El Salto, Mex.	F7	62
El Salvador, ctry., N.A.	H3	64
El Sauce, Nic.	H4	64
El Sauzal, Mex.	B1	62
Elsberry, Mo., U.S.	B7	102
Elsie, Mi., U.S.	E6	99
Elsinore, Ut., U.S.	E3	121
Elsmere, De., U.S.	B3	85
Elsmere, Ky., U.S.	B5	94
El Socorro, Ven.	C10	58
El Sombrero, Ven.	C9	58
Elspe, Ger.	D8	8
Elsterwerda, Ger.	D13	8
El Tigre, Col.	F8	58
El Tigre, Ven.	C10	58
El Tocuyo, Ven.	C8	58
Elton, La., U.S.	D3	95
El Toro Marine Corps Air Station, mil., Ca., U.S.	n13	82
El Trapiche, Col.	F4	58
El Triunfo, Mex.	F4	62
El Turbio, Arg.	G2	56
Elūru, India	D6	37
El Vado Reservoir, res., N.M., U.S.	A3	108
Elvas, Port.	G4	12
Elverum, Nor.	F8	6
El Vigía, Ven.	C7	58
Elvins, Mo., U.S.	D7	102
Elwell, Lake, res., Mt., U.S.	B5	103
Elwha, stm., Wa., U.S.	A2	124
Elwood, In., U.S.	D6	91
Elwood, Ks., U.S.	C9	93
Elwood, Ne., U.S.	D6	104
Ely, Eng., U.K.	I13	7
Ely, Mn., U.S.	C7	100
Ely, Nv., U.S.	D7	105
Elyria, Oh., U.S.	A3	112
Elysburg, Pa., U.S.	E8	115
Emanuel, co., Ga., U.S.	D4	87
Embarcación, Arg.	A4	56
Embarras, stm., Il., U.S.	E6	90
Embarrass, stm., Wi., U.S.	D5	126
Embro, Ont., Can.	D4	73
Embrun, Fr.	H13	10
Emden, Ger.	B7	8
Emerald, Austl.	D9	50
Emerson, Man., Can.	E3	70
Emerson, Ga., U.S.	B2	87
Emerson, Ne., U.S.	B9	104
Emerson, N.J., U.S.	h8	107
Emery, co., Ut., U.S.	E5	121
Emet, Tur.	J13	16
Emily, Mn., U.S.	D5	100
Emily, Lake, l., Mn., U.S.	E3	100
Eminence, Ky., U.S.	B4	94
Emmaus, Pa., U.S.	E11	115
Emmen, Neth.	C6	8
Emmendingen, Ger.	G7	8
Emmet, co., Ia., U.S.	A3	92
Emmet, co., Mi., U.S.	C6	99
Emmetsburg, Ia., U.S.	A3	92
Emmett, Id., U.S.	F2	89
Emmiganūru, India	E4	37
Emmitsburg, Md., U.S.	A3	97
Emmonak, Ak., U.S.	C7	79
Emmons, co., N.D., U.S.	C5	111
Emory Peak, mtn., Tx., U.S.	E1	120
Empalme, Mex.	D4	62
Empangeni, S. Afr.	G6	44
Empedrado, Arg.	B5	56
Empire, La., U.S.	E6	95
Empire, Nv., U.S.	C2	105
Empoli, Italy	F5	14
Emporia, Ks., U.S.	D7	93
Emporia, Va., U.S.	D5	123
Emporium, Pa., U.S.	D5	115
Empty Quarter see Ar-Rab' al-Khālī, des., Asia	D5	46
Emsdetten, Ger.	C7	8
Emsworth, Pa., U.S.	h13	115
Encampment, Wy., U.S.	E6	127
Encarnación, Para.	B5	56
Encinitas, Ca., U.S.	F5	82
Encontrados, Ven.	C6	58
Ende, Indon.	G7	32
Enderby, B.C., Can.	D8	69
Enderby Land, reg., Ant.	C18	47
Enderlin, N.D., U.S.	C8	111
Enders Reservoir, res., Ne., U.S.	D4	104
Endicott, N.Y., U.S.	C4	109
Endicott Mountains, mts., Ak., U.S.	B9	79
Endless Lake, l., Me., U.S.	C4	96
Endwell, N.Y., U.S.	C4	109
Enfida, Tun.	M5	14
Enfield (Thompsonville), Ct., U.S.	B5	84
Enfield, N.H., U.S.	C2	106
Enfield, N.C., U.S.	A5	110
Engel's, Russia	G7	22
Enggano, Pulau, i., Indon.	G3	32

Name	Map Ref	Page
England, Ar., U.S.	C4	81
England, ter., U.K.	I11	7
England Air Force Base, mil., La., U.S.	C3	95
Englee, Newf., Can.	C3	72
Engleside, Va., U.S.	g12	123
Englewood, Co., U.S.	B6	83
Englewood, Fl., U.S.	F4	86
Englewood, N.J., U.S.	B5	107
Englewood, Oh., U.S.	C1	112
Englewood, Tn., U.S.	D9	119
Englewood Cliffs, N.J., U.S.	h9	107
English, In., U.S.	H5	91
English Bāzār, India	H13	38
English Channel (La Manche), strt., Eur.	B5	10
Enguera, Spain	G11	12
Enid, Ok., U.S.	A4	113
Enid Lake, res., Ms., U.S.	A4	101
Enigma, Ga., U.S.	E3	87
Enka, N.C., U.S.	f10	110
Enkhuizen, Neth.	C5	8
Enköping, Swe.	G11	6
Enmelen, Russia	D30	24
Enna, Italy	L9	14
Ennadai Lake, l., N.W. Ter., Can.	D12	66
Ennedi, plat., Chad	E10	42
Ennis, Ire.	I4	7
Ennis, Mt., U.S.	E5	103
Ennis, Tx., U.S.	C4	120
Enniskillen, N. Ire., U.K.	G5	7
Enoch, Ut., U.S.	F2	121
Enola, Pa., U.S.	F8	115
Enon, Oh., U.S.	*C2	112
Enoree, S.C., U.S.	B4	117
Enoree, stm., S.C., U.S.	B3	117
Enosburg Falls, Vt., U.S.	B3	122
Enriquillo, Dom. Rep.	F12	64
Enschede, Neth.	C6	8
Ensenada, Mex.	B1	62
Enshi, China	E8	26
Enshū-nada, Japan	H10	30
Ensley, Fl., U.S.	u14	86
Entebbe, Ug.	A6	44
Enterprise, Al., U.S.	D4	78
Enterprise, Ks., U.S.	D6	93
Enterprise, Or., U.S.	B9	114
Enterprise, Ut., U.S.	F2	121
Enterprise, W.V., U.S.	B4	125
Entiat, stm., Wa., U.S.	B5	124
Entiat, Lake, l., Wa., U.S.	B5	124
Entiat Mountains, mts., Wa., U.S.	B5	124
Entrayques, Fr.	H9	10
Entre-Rios, Moz.	D7	44
Enugu, Nig.	G7	42
Enumclaw, Wa., U.S.	B4	124
Envigado, Col.	D5	58
Eola Hills, hills, Or., U.S.	h11	114
Épernay, Fr.	C10	10
Ephraim, Ut., U.S.	D4	121
Ephrata, Pa., U.S.	F9	115
Ephrata, Wa., U.S.	B6	124
Épila, Spain	D10	12
Épinal, Fr.	D13	10
Epping, Eng., U.K.	D4	106
Epworth, Ia., U.S.	B7	92
Equatorial Guinea, ctry., Afr.	H7	42
Eraclea, Italy	D7	14
Erath, La., U.S.	E3	95
Erath, co., Tx., U.S.	C3	120
Erdek, Tur.	I11	16
Erdemli, Tur.	A4	40
Erebus, Mount, mtn., Ant.	B29	47
Erechim, Braz.	B6	56
Erfurt, Ger.	E11	8
Erichsen Lake, l., N.W. Ter., Can.	B16	66
Erick, Ok., U.S.	B2	113
Erickson, Man., Can.	D2	70
Erie, Co., U.S.	A5	83
Erie, Il., U.S.	B3	90
Erie, Ks., U.S.	E8	93
Erie, Mi., U.S.	G7	99
Erie, Pa., U.S.	B1	115
Erie, co., N.Y., U.S.	C2	109
Erie, co., Oh., U.S.	A3	112
Erie, co., Pa., U.S.	C1	115
Erie, Lake, l., N.A.	C10	76
Erie Canal, N.Y., U.S.	B5	109
Erimo-misaki, c., Japan	r21	30a
Erin, Ont., Can.	D4	73
Erin, Tn., U.S.	A4	119
Eritrea, hist. reg., Eth.	E2	46
Erlangen, Ger.	F11	8
Erlanger, Ky., U.S.	A5	94
Erlian, China	C9	26
Erling, Lake, l., Ar., U.S.	D2	81
Ermelo, S. Afr.	G5	44
Ermenak, Tur.	A3	40
Ernākulam, India	H4	37
Erne, Lower Lough, l., N. Ire., U.K.	G5	7
Ernée, Fr.	D6	10
Erode, India	G4	37
Errigal, mtn., Ire.	F4	7
Ertai, China	B5	26
Erwin, N.C., U.S.	B4	110
Erwin, Tn., U.S.	C11	119
Erzgebirge (Krušné hory), mts., Eur.	E12	8
Erzincan, Tur.	H15	4
Erzurum, Tur.	H16	4
Esashi, Japan	A13	30
Esbjerg, Den.	I7	6
Escalante, Ut., U.S.	F4	121
Escalante, stm., Ut., U.S.	F4	121
Escalón, Mex.	D7	62
Escalon, Ca., U.S.	D3	82
Escambia, co., Al., U.S.	D2	78
Escambia, co., Fl., U.S.	u14	86
Escambia, stm., Fl., U.S.	u14	86
Escanaba, Mi., U.S.	C3	99
Escanaba, stm., Mi., U.S.	B3	99
Escarpada Point, c., Phil.	B7	32
Escatawpa, Ms., U.S.	E5	101
Escatawpa, stm., U.S.	D5	101
Esch-sur-Alzette, Lux.	F5	8
Eschwege, Ger.	D10	8
Escondido, Ca., U.S.	F5	82
Escoumins, Rivière des, stm., Que., Can.	A8	74
Escuinapa [de Hidalgo], Mex.	F7	62
Escuintla, Guat.	G2	64
Escuintla, Mex.	J13	62
Escuminac, Point, c., N.B., Can.	B5	71
Esfahān, Iran	B5	46
Eshkāshem, Afg.	B4	38
Eskilstuna, Swe.	G11	6
Eskimo Lakes, l., N.W. Ter., Can.	C6	66
Eskimo Point, N.W. Ter., Can.	D14	66
Eskişehir, Tur.	H14	4
Eşme, Tur.	K12	16
Esmeralda, co., Nv., U.S.	F4	105
Esmeraldas, Ec.	G3	58
Esmond, R.I., U.S.	B4	116
Espalion, Fr.	H9	10
Espanola, Ont., Can.	A3	73
Espanola, N.M., U.S.	B3	108
Esparto, Ca., U.S.	C2	82
Espelkamp, Ger.	C8	8
Esperance, Austl.	F4	50
Espinal, Col.	E5	58
Espinhaço, Serra do, mts., Braz.	C7	57
Espinho, Port.	D3	12
Espíritu Santo, Bahía del, b., Mex.	H16	62
Espíritu Santo, Isla del, i., Mex.	E4	62
Espoo (Esbo), Fin.	F15	6
Espy, Pa., U.S.	D9	115
Esquel, Arg.	E2	56
Esquimalt, B.C., Can.	E6	69
Esquina, Arg.	B5	56
Essaouira, Mor.	B4	42
Essen, Ger.	D7	8
Essendon, Mount, mtn., Austl.	D4	50
Essequibo, stm., Guy.	E13	58
Es Sers, Tun.	M4	14
Essex, Ont., Can.	E2	73
Essex, Ct., U.S.	D6	84
Essex, Ia., U.S.	D2	92
Essex, Md., U.S.	B5	97
Essex, Ma., U.S.	A6	98
Essex, Vt., U.S.	B2	122
Essex, co., Ma., U.S.	A5	98
Essex, co., N.J., U.S.	B4	107
Essex, co., N.Y., U.S.	B7	109
Essex, co., Vt., U.S.	B5	122
Essex, co., Va., U.S.	C6	123
Essex Junction, Vt., U.S.	C2	122
Essexville, Mi., U.S.	E7	99
Esslingen, Ger.	G9	8
Es Smala es Souassi, Tun.	N5	14
Est, Cap, c., Madag.	E10	44
Est, Pointe de l', c., Que., Can.	G20	66
Estacada, Or., U.S.	B4	114
Estaca de Bares, Punta de la, c., Spain	B4	12
Estacado, Llano, pl., U.S.	C1	120
Estados, Isla de los, i., Arg.	G4	56
Estancia, N.M., U.S.	C3	108
Estcourt, S. Afr.	G5	44
Este, Italy	D6	14
Estelí, Nic.	H4	64
Estella, Spain	C9	12
Estelline, S.D., U.S.	C9	118
Estepona, Spain	I6	12
Esternay, Fr.	D10	10
Estero Bay, b., Ca., U.S.	E3	82
Estero Bay, b., Fl., U.S.	F5	86
Estero Island, i., Fl., U.S.	F5	86
Estes Park, Co., U.S.	A5	83
Estherville, Ia., U.S.	A3	92
Estherwood, La., U.S.	D3	95
Estill, S.C., U.S.	F5	117
Estill, co., Ky., U.S.	C6	94
Estill Springs, Tn., U.S.	B5	119
Estonia, ctry., Eur.	C9	18
Estremoz, Port.	G4	12
Esztergom, Hung.	H18	8
Etah, Grnld.	B20	128
Etah, India	G8	38
Étampes, Fr.	D9	10
Étang-du-Nord, Que., Can.	B8	71
Étaples, Fr.	B8	10
Etāwah, India	G8	38
Ethel, W.V., U.S.	n12	125
Ethiopia, ctry., Afr.	G2	46
Etna, Pa., U.S.	k14	115
Etna, Monte, vol., Italy	L9	14
Etobicoke, Ont., Can.	D5	73
Etolin Island, i., Ak., U.S.	m23	79
Etolin Strait, strt., Ak., U.S.	C6	79
Etoshapan, pl., Nmb.	E3	44
Etowah, Tn., U.S.	D9	119
Etowah, co., Al., U.S.	A3	78
Etowah, stm., Ga., U.S.	B2	87
Ettelbruck, Lux.	F6	8
Ettlingen, Ger.	G8	8
Ettrick, Va., U.S.	C5	123
Eu, Fr.	B8	10
Eucla, Austl.	F5	50
Euclid, Oh., U.S.	A4	112
Eudora, Ar., U.S.	D4	81
Eudora, Ks., U.S.	D8	93
Eufaula, Al., U.S.	D4	78
Eufaula, Ok., U.S.	B6	113
Eufaula Lake, res., Ok., U.S.	B6	113
Eugene, Or., U.S.	C3	114
Eugenia, Punta, c., Mex.	D2	62
Eunice, La., U.S.	D3	95
Eunice, N.M., U.S.	E3	108
Eupora, Ms., U.S.	B4	101
Euphrates (Al-Furāt), stm., Asia	A2	46
Eureka, Ca., U.S.	B1	82
Eureka, Il., U.S.	C4	90
Eureka, Ks., U.S.	E7	93
Eureka, Mo., U.S.	f12	102
Eureka, Mt., U.S.	B1	103
Eureka, Nv., U.S.	D6	105
Eureka, S.C., U.S.	B5	117
Eureka, S.D., U.S.	B6	118
Eureka, co., Nv., U.S.	D5	105
Eureka Springs, Ar., U.S.	A2	81
Europa, Île, i., Reu.	F8	44
Europa Point, c., Gib.	I6	12
Europe	E11	4
Euskirchen, Ger.	E6	8
Eustis, Fl., U.S.	D5	86
Eutaw, Al., U.S.	C2	78
Eutin, Ger.	A10	8
Eutsuk Lake, l., B.C., Can.	C4	69
Evangeline, co., La., U.S.	D3	95
Evans, Co., U.S.	A6	83
Evans, Ga., U.S.	C4	87
Evans, W.V., U.S.	C3	125
Evans, co., Ga., U.S.	D5	87
Evans, Lac, l., Que., Can.	F17	66
Evans, Mount, mtn., Co., U.S.	B5	83
Evansburg, Alta., Can.	C3	68
Evans City, Pa., U.S.	E1	115
Evansdale, Ia., U.S.	B5	92
Evans Strait, strt., N.W. Ter., Can.	D16	66
Evanston, Il., U.S.	A6	90
Evanston, Wy., U.S.	E2	127
Evansville, Il., U.S.	E4	90
Evansville, In., U.S.	I2	91
Evansville, Wi., U.S.	F4	126
Evansville, Wy., U.S.	D6	127
Evart, Mi., U.S.	E5	99
Evarts, Ky., U.S.	D6	94
Eveleth, Mn., U.S.	C6	100
Everard, Lake, l., Austl.	F7	50
Everest, Mount, mtn., Asia	G12	38
Everett, Ma., U.S.	g11	98
Everett, Pa., U.S.	F5	115
Everett, Wa., U.S.	B3	124
Everett Lake, res., N.H., U.S.	D3	106
Everglades National Park, Fl., U.S.	G5	86
Evergreen, Al., U.S.	D3	78
Evergreen, Co., U.S.	B5	83
Evergreen Park, Il., U.S.	k9	90
Everly, Ia., U.S.	A2	92
Everson, Wa., U.S.	A3	124
Evesham, Eng., U.K.	I11	7
Evje, Nor.	G6	6
Évora, Port.	G4	12
Évreux, Fr.	C8	10
Évros (Marica) (Meriç), stm., Eur.	H10	16
E.V. Spence Reservoir, res., Tx., U.S.	D2	120
Évvoia, i., Grc.	K7	16
Ewa, Hi., U.S.	B3	88
Ewa Beach, Hi., U.S.	B3	88
Ewa Beach, Hi., U.S.	g9	88
Ewing Township, N.J., U.S.	C3	107
Ewo, Congo	B2	44
Excelsior Mountain, mtn., Ca., U.S.	C4	82
Excelsior Mountains, mts., Nv., U.S.	E3	105
Excelsior Springs, Mo., U.S.	B3	102
Executive Committee Range, mts., Ant.	B36	47
Exeter, Ont., Can.	D3	73
Exeter, Eng., U.K.	K9	7
Exeter, Ca., U.S.	D4	82
Exeter, Ne., U.S.	D8	104
Exeter, N.H., U.S.	E5	106
Exeter, Pa., U.S.	D10	115
Exeter, co., N.H., U.S.	E5	106
Exeter Sound, strt., N.W. Ter., Can.	C20	66
Exira, Ia., U.S.	C3	92
Exmore, Va., U.S.	C7	123
Exmouth, Eng., U.K.	K9	7
Exmouth Gulf, b., Austl.	D2	50
Experiment, Ga., U.S.	C2	87
Exploits, stm., Newf., Can.	D3	72
Exploits, Bay of, b., Newf., Can.	D4	72
Export, Pa., U.S.	F2	115
Exuma Sound, strt., Bah.	B9	64
Eyasi, Lake, l., Tan.	B6	44
Eylar Mountain, mtn., Ca., U.S.	D3	82
Eymoutiers, Fr.	G8	10
Eyota, Mn., U.S.	G6	100
Eyre (North), Lake, l., Austl.	E7	50
Eyre (South), Lake, l., Austl.	E7	50
Eyre Peninsula, pen., Austl.	F7	50

F

Name	Map Ref	Page
Fabens, Tx., U.S.	o11	120
Fabius, stm., Mo., U.S.	A6	102
Fabriano, Italy	F7	14
Facatativá, Col.	E5	58
Factoryville, Pa., U.S.	C10	115
Fada, Chad	E10	42
Fada Ngourma, Burkina	F6	42
Faddejevskij, Ostrov, i., Russia	B22	24
Faenza, Italy	E6	14
Faeroe Islands, dep., Eur.	C6	4
Fagernes, Nor.	F7	6
Fagersta, Swe.	F10	6
Fairacres, N.M., U.S.	E3	108
Fairbank, Ia., U.S.	B5	92
Fairbanks, Ak., U.S.	C10	79
Fair Bluff, N.C., U.S.	C3	110
Fairborn, Oh., U.S.	C1	112
Fairburn, Ga., U.S.	C2	87
Fairbury, Il., U.S.	C5	90
Fairbury, Ne., U.S.	D8	104
Fairchance, Pa., U.S.	G2	115
Fairchild Air Force Base, mil., Wa., U.S.	g13	124
Fairdale, Ky., U.S.	B4	94
Fairfax, Ca., U.S.	C2	82
Fairfax, De., U.S.	A3	85
Fairfax, Ia., U.S.	C6	92
Fairfax, Mn., U.S.	F4	100
Fairfax, Mo., U.S.	A2	102
Fairfax, Ok., U.S.	A5	113
Fairfax, S.C., U.S.	F5	117
Fairfax, Va., U.S.	B5	123
Fairfax, co., Va., U.S.	B5	123
Fairfield, Al., U.S.	B3	78
Fairfield, Ca., U.S.	C2	82
Fairfield, Ct., U.S.	E2	84
Fairfield, Il., U.S.	E5	90
Fairfield, Ia., U.S.	C6	92
Fairfield, Me., U.S.	D3	96
Fairfield, Mt., U.S.	C5	103
Fairfield, Oh., U.S.	n12	112
Fairfield, Tx., U.S.	D4	120
Fairfield, co., Ct., U.S.	D2	84
Fairfield, co., Oh., U.S.	C3	112
Fairfield, co., S.C., U.S.	C5	117
Fairfield Bay, Ar., U.S.	B3	81
Fairfield Pond, l., Vt., U.S.	B3	122
Fair Grove, Mo., U.S.	D4	102
Fair Grove, N.C., U.S.	B2	110
Fairhaven, Ma., U.S.	C6	98
Fair Haven, Mi., U.S.	F8	99
Fair Haven, N.J., U.S.	C4	107
Fair Haven, Vt., U.S.	D2	122
Fairhope, Al., U.S.	E2	78
Fair Isle, i., Scot., U.K.	B11	7
Fairland, In., U.S.	E6	91
Fairland, Ok., U.S.	A7	113
Fair Lawn, N.J., U.S.	h8	107
Fairlawn, Va., U.S.	C2	123
Fairlea, W.V., U.S.	D4	125
Fairmont, Il., U.S.	C6	90
Fairmont, Mn., U.S.	G4	100
Fairmont, Ne., U.S.	D8	104
Fairmont, N.C., U.S.	C3	110
Fairmont, W.V., U.S.	B4	125
Fairmount, Ga., U.S.	B2	87
Fairmount, In., U.S.	D6	91
Fairmount Heights, Md., U.S.	f9	97
Fairoaks, Pa., U.S.	h13	115
Fair Plain, Mi., U.S.	F4	99
Fairport, N.Y., U.S.	B3	109
Fairport Harbor, Oh., U.S.	A4	112
Fairvale, N.B., Can.	D4	71
Fairview, Alta., Can.	A1	68
Fairview, Mt., U.S.	C12	103
Fairview, N.J., U.S.	h8	107
Fairview, Ok., U.S.	A3	113
Fairview, Pa., U.S.	B1	115
Fairview, Tn., U.S.	B4	119
Fairview, Ut., U.S.	D4	121
Fairview Heights, Il., U.S.	E3	90
Fairview Park, In., U.S.	E3	91
Fairview Park, Oh., U.S.	g9	112
Fairview Peak, mtn., Nv., U.S.	D3	105
Fairview Peak, mtn., Or., U.S.	D4	114
Fairway, Ks., U.S.	k16	93
Fairweather, Mount, mtn., N.A.	E5	66
Faisalabad, Pak.	E5	38
Faison, N.C., U.S.	B4	110
Faizābād, India	G10	38
Fakenham, Eng., U.K.	I13	7
Fakfak, Indon.	F9	32
Falaise, Fr.	D6	10
Falam, Burma	C2	34
Falconer, N.Y., U.S.	C1	109
Falcon Heights, Mn., U.S.	n12	100
Falcon Heights, Or., U.S.	E5	114
Falcon Reservoir, res., N.A.	D10	62
Falfurrias, Tx., U.S.	F3	120
Falher, Alta., Can.	B2	68
Falkenberg, Swe.	H9	6
Falkensee, Ger.	C13	8
Falkenstein, Ger.	E12	8
Falkland Islands (Islas Malvinas), dep., S.A.	G5	56
Falköping, Swe.	G9	6
Falkville, Al., U.S.	A3	78
Fall, stm., Ks., U.S.	E7	93
Fall Branch, Tn., U.S.	C11	119
Fallbrook, Ca., U.S.	F5	82
Fall City, Wa., U.S.	B4	124
Fall Creek, Wi., U.S.	D2	126
Falling Creek, stm., Va., U.S.	n17	123
Falling Rock Creek, stm., W.V., U.S.	m13	125
Fall Mountain Lake, Ct., U.S.	C4	84
Fallon, Nv., U.S.	D3	105
Fallon, co., Mt., U.S.	D12	103
Fallon Indian Reservation, Nv., U.S.	D3	105
Fallon Naval Air Station, mil., Nv., U.S.	D3	105
Fall River, Ma., U.S.	C5	98
Fall River, Wi., U.S.	E4	126
Fall River, co., S.D., U.S.	D2	118
Fall River Lake, res., Ks., U.S.	E7	93
Falls, co., Tx., U.S.	D4	120
Falls Church, Va., U.S.	g12	123
Falls City, Ne., U.S.	D10	104
Falls City, Or., U.S.	C3	114
Falls Creek, Pa., U.S.	D4	115
Fallston, Md., U.S.	A5	97
Falmouth, N.S., Can.	E5	71
Falmouth, Eng., U.K.	K7	7
Falmouth, Ky., U.S.	B5	94
Falmouth, Me., U.S.	E2	96
Falmouth, Ma., U.S.	C6	98
Falmouth, Va., U.S.	B5	123
False Cape, c., Fl., U.S.	D6	86
False Cape, c., Va., U.S.	D7	123
False Divi Point, c., India	E6	37
Falset, Spain	D12	12
Falun, Swe.	F10	6
Famagusta see Gazimağusa, N. Cyp.	B3	40
Famatina, Nevado de, mts., Arg.	B3	56
Fancy Farm, Ky., U.S.	f9	94
Fangcheng, China	B1	28
Fannin, co., Ga., U.S.	B2	87
Fannin, co., Tx., U.S.	C4	120
Fanny, Mount, mtn., Or., U.S.	B9	114
Fano, Italy	F8	14
Faradje, Zaire	H11	42
Faradofay, Madag.	G9	44
Farafangana, Madag.	F9	44
Farāh, Afg.	C1	36
Faranah, Gui.	F3	42
Farasān, Jazā'ir, is., Sau. Ar.	E3	46
Farewell, Cape, c., N.Z.	D4	52
Fargo, Ga., U.S.	F4	87
Fargo, N.D., U.S.	C9	111
Faribault, Mn., U.S.	F5	100
Faribault, co., Mn., U.S.	G4	100
Farīdpur, Bngl.	I13	38
Färjestaden, Swe.	H11	6
Farley, Ia., U.S.	B6	92
Farmer City, Il., U.S.	C5	90
Farmers Branch, Tx., U.S.	n10	120
Farmersburg, In., U.S.	F3	91
Farmerville, La., U.S.	B3	95
Farmingdale, Me., U.S.	D3	96
Farmington, Ar., U.S.	A1	81
Farmington, Ct., U.S.	C4	84
Farmington, Il., U.S.	C3	90
Farmington, Ia., U.S.	D6	92
Farmington, Me., U.S.	D2	96
Farmington, Mi., U.S.	p15	99
Farmington, Mn., U.S.	F5	100
Farmington, Mo., U.S.	D7	102
Farmington, N.H., U.S.	D4	106
Farmington, N.M., U.S.	A1	108
Farmington, Ut., U.S.	C4	121
Farmington, stm., Ct., U.S.	B4	84
Farmington Hills, Mi., U.S.	o15	99
Farmland, In., U.S.	D7	91
Farmville, N.C., U.S.	B5	110
Farmville, Va., U.S.	C4	123
Farnham, Que., Can.	D5	74
Faro, Braz.	D7	54
Faro, Port.	H4	12
Faro, Punta del, c., Italy	K10	14
Fårösund, Swe.	H12	6
Farquhar Group, is., Sey.	D10	44
Farrell, Pa., U.S.	D1	115
Farrukhābād, India	G8	38
Fartak, Ra's, c., Yemen	E5	46
Farvel, Kap, c., Grnld.	E24	66
Farwell, Mi., U.S.	E6	99
Farwell, Tx., U.S.	B1	120
Fasano, Italy	I12	14
Fatehpur, India	H9	38
Fatehpur, India	G6	38
Faulk, co., S.D., U.S.	B6	118
Faulkland Heights, De., U.S.	i7	85
Faulkner, co., Ar., U.S.	B3	81
Faulkton, S.D., U.S.	B6	118
Fauquier, co., Va., U.S.	B5	123
Fauske, Nor.	C10	6
Favara, Italy	L8	14
Faverges, Fr.	G13	10
Fawnie Nose, mtn., B.C., Can.	C5	69
Fayette, Al., U.S.	B2	78
Fayette, Ia., U.S.	B6	92
Fayette, Ms., U.S.	D2	101
Fayette, Mo., U.S.	B5	102
Fayette, Oh., U.S.	A1	112
Fayette, co., Al., U.S.	B2	78
Fayette, co., Ga., U.S.	C2	87
Fayette, co., Il., U.S.	D5	90
Fayette, co., In., U.S.	E7	91
Fayette, co., Ia., U.S.	B6	92
Fayette, co., Ky., U.S.	B5	94
Fayette, co., Oh., U.S.	C2	112
Fayette, co., Pa., U.S.	G2	115
Fayette, co., Tn., U.S.	B2	119
Fayette, co., Tx., U.S.	E4	120
Fayette, co., W.V., U.S.	C3	125
Fayetteville, Ar., U.S.	A1	81
Fayetteville, Ga., U.S.	C2	87
Fayetteville, N.C., U.S.	B4	110
Fayetteville, Pa., U.S.	G6	115
Fayetteville, Tn., U.S.	B5	119
Fayetteville, W.V., U.S.	C3	125
Fāzilka, India	E6	38
Fazzān (Fezzan), reg., Libya	C8	42
Fdérik, Maur.	D3	42
Fear, Cape, c., N.C., U.S.	D5	110
Feather, stm., Ca., U.S.	C3	82
Fécamp, Fr.	C7	10
Federalsburg, Md., U.S.	C6	97
Feeding Hills, Ma., U.S.	B2	98
Fehmarn Belt, strt., Eur.	A11	8
Feijó, Braz.	E4	54
Feira de Santana, Braz.	B9	57
Felanitx, Spain	F15	12
Feldbach, Aus.	I15	8
Feldkirch, Aus.	H9	8
Feldkirchen in Kärnten, Aus.	I14	8
Félix Gómez, Mex.	C4	62
Felletin, Fr.	G9	10
Fellsmere, Fl., U.S.	E6	86
Felton, Ca., U.S.	D2	82
Felton, De., U.S.	D3	85
Feltre, Italy	C6	14
Femundsenden, Nor.	F8	6
Fence, stm., Mi., U.S.	B2	99
Fence Lake, l., Wi., U.S.	C4	126
Fenelon Falls, Ont., Can.	C6	73
Fengcheng, China	G4	28
Fengzhen, China	C9	26
Fenimore Pass, strt., Ak., U.S.	E4	79
Fennimore, Wi., U.S.	F3	126
Fennville, Mi., U.S.	F4	99
Fenton, Mi., U.S.	F7	99
Fentress, co., Tn., U.S.	C9	119
Fenwick Island, i., S.C., U.S.	k11	117
Fenyang, China	D9	26
Feodosija, Ukr.	H5	22
Fer, Point au, c., La., U.S.	E4	95
Ferdinand, In., U.S.	H4	91
Fergana, Uzb.	I12	22
Fergus, Ont., Can.	D4	73
Fergus, co., Mt., U.S.	C7	103
Fergus Falls, Mn., U.S.	D2	100
Ferguson, Ky., U.S.	C5	94
Ferguson, Mo., U.S.	C7	102
Ferme-Neuve, Que., Can.	C2	74
Fermo, Italy	F8	14
Fermont, Que., Can.	h13	74
Fermoy, Ire.	I4	7
Fernandina Beach, Fl., U.S.	B5	86
Fernando de Noronha, Ilha, i., Braz.	D12	54
Fernandópolis, Braz.	F3	57
Fernando Póo see Bioko, i., Eq. Gui.	H7	42
Fernán-Núñez, Spain	H7	12
Fern Creek, Ky., U.S.	g11	94
Ferndale, Ca., U.S.	B1	82
Ferndale, Md., U.S.	B4	97
Ferndale, Mi., U.S.	p15	99
Ferndale, Pa., U.S.	F4	115
Ferndale, Wa., U.S.	A3	124
Fernie, B.C., Can.	E10	69
Fern Ridge Lake, res., Or., U.S.	C3	114
Fernwood, Id., U.S.	B2	89
Fernwood, Ms., U.S.	D3	101
Ferrara, Italy	E6	14

Name	Map Ref	Page
Ferreira do Alentejo, Port.	G3	12
Ferrelo, Cape, c., Or., U.S.	E2	114
Ferriday, La., U.S.	C4	95
Ferris, Tx., U.S.	C4	120
Ferris Mountains, mts., Wy., U.S.	D5	127
Ferron, Ut., U.S.	D4	121
Ferrum, Va., U.S.	D2	123
Ferry, co., Wa., U.S.	A7	124
Ferry Farms, Va., U.S.	B5	123
Ferryland, Newf., Can.	E5	72
Ferry Point, c., N.J., U.S.	k7	107
Fertile, Mn., U.S.	C2	100
Fès, Mor.	B5	42
Feshi, Zaire	C3	44
Fessenden, N.D., U.S.	B6	111
Festus, Mo., U.S.	C7	102
Fès see Fès, Mor.		
Fethiye, Tur.	M13	16
Feuilles, Rivière aux, stm., Que., Can.	g12	74
Feurs, Fr.	G11	10
Feyzābād, Afg.	B4	38
Fez see Fès, Mor.		
Fez, Mor.	B5	42
Fianarantsoa, Madag.	F9	44
Ficksburg, S. Afr.	G5	44
Fidalgo Island, i., Wa., U.S.	A3	124
Fidenza, Italy	E5	14
Fieldale, Va., U.S.	D3	123
Fields, Lake, l., La., U.S.	B3	86
Fields, Lake, l., La., U.S.	k10	95
Fier, Alb.	I3	16
Fifteenmile Creek, stm., Wy., U.S.	B4	127
Fifteen Mile Falls Reservoir, res., U.S.	C5	122
Figeac, Fr.	H9	10
Figueira da Foz, Port.	E3	12
Figueras, Spain	C14	12
Figuig, Mor.	B5	42
Fiji, ctry., Oc.	H1	2
Filchner Ice Shelf, Ant.	B9	47
Filer, Id., U.S.	G4	89
Fillmore, Ca., U.S.	E4	82
Fillmore, Ut., U.S.	E3	121
Fillmore, co., Mn., U.S.	G6	100
Fillmore, co., Ne., U.S.	D8	104
Finale Ligure, Italy	E3	14
Findlay, Il., U.S.	D5	90
Findlay, Oh., U.S.	A2	112
Finisterre, Cabo de, c., Spain	C2	12
Finland, ctry., Eur.	C13	4
Finland, Gulf of, b., Eur.	G16	6
Finlay, stm., B.C., Can.	E7	66
Finley, Tn., U.S.	A2	119
Finn Mountain, mtn., Ak., U.S.	C8	79
Finney, co., Ks., U.S.	D3	93
Finse, Nor.	F6	6
Finspång, Swe.	G10	6
Finsterwalde, Ger.	D13	8
Fiorenzuola d'Arda, Italy	E4	14
Fircrest, Wa., U.S.	f10	124
Firebaugh, Ca., U.S.	D3	82
Firenze (Florence), Italy	F6	14
Firenzuola, Italy	E6	14
Firestone, Co., U.S.	A6	83
Firminy, Fr.	G11	10
Firozābād, India	G8	38
Firozpur, India	E6	38
First Connecticut Lake, l., N.H., U.S.	f7	106
Fish, stm., Al., U.S.	E2	78
Fish, stm., Me., U.S.	A4	96
Fish Creek, stm., W.V., U.S.	g8	125
Fisher, Il., U.S.	C5	90
Fisher, co., Tx., U.S.	C2	120
Fisher Bay, b., Man., Can.	D3	70
Fishermans Island, i., Va., U.S.	h15	123
Fishers, In., U.S.	E5	91
Fishers Island, i., N.Y., U.S.	m16	109
Fishers Peak, mtn., Co., U.S.	D6	83
Fisher Strait, strt., N.W. Ter., Can.	D16	66
Fishersville, Va., U.S.	B4	123
Fishing Bay, b., Md., U.S.	D5	97
Fishing Creek, Md., U.S.	D5	97
Fishing Creek, stm., N.C., U.S.	A5	110
Fishing Creek, stm., S.C., U.S.	B5	117
Fishing Creek, stm., W.V., U.S.	B4	125
Fishing Creek Reservoir, res., S.C., U.S.	B6	117
Fishkill, N.Y., U.S.	D7	109
Fish Lake, l., Ut., U.S.	E4	121
Fish River Lake, l., Me., U.S.	B4	96
Fishtrap Lake, res., Ky., U.S.	C7	94
Fiskdale, Ma., U.S.	B3	98
Fitchburg, Ma., U.S.	A4	98
Fitzgerald, Ga., U.S.	E3	87
Fitz Roy, Arg.	F3	56
Fitzroy, stm., Austl.	C4	50
Fitzroy, Monte (Cerro Chaltel), mtn., S.A.	F2	56
Fitzroy Crossing, Austl.	C5	50
Fitzwilliam, N.H., U.S.	E2	106
Fitzwilliam Island, i., Ont., Can.	B3	73
Five Island Lake, l., Ia., U.S.	A3	92
Fivemile Creek, stm., Wy., U.S.	C4	127
Five Points, N.M., U.S.	B3	108
Flagler, co., Fl., U.S.	C5	86
Flagler Beach, Fl., U.S.	C5	86
Flagstaff, Az., U.S.	B4	80
Flagstaff Lake, l., Or., U.S.	E7	114
Flambeau, stm., Wi., U.S.	C3	126
Flamborough Head, c., Eng., U.K.	G12	7
Flaming Gorge Dam, Ut., U.S.	C6	121
Flaming Gorge National Recreation Area, U.S.	E3	127
Flaming Gorge Reservoir, res., U.S.	E3	127
Flanagan, Il., U.S.	C5	90
Flandreau, S.D., U.S.	C9	118
Flandreau Indian Reservation, S.D., U.S.	C9	118
Flat, stm., Mi., U.S.	E5	99
Flat, stm., N.C., U.S.	A4	110
Flat, stm., R.I., U.S.	E2	116
Flat Brook, stm., N.J., U.S.	A3	107
Flathead, co., Mt., U.S.	B2	103
Flathead, South Fork, stm., Mt., U.S.	C3	103
Flathead Indian Reservation, Mt., U.S.	C2	103
Flathead Lake, l., Mt., U.S.	C2	103
Flathead Valley, val., Mt., U.S.	C2	103
Flat Lake, l., La., U.S.	k9	95
Flat Lick, Ky., U.S.	D6	94
Flatonia, Tx., U.S.	E4	120
Flat River, Mo., U.S.	D7	102
Flat River Reservoir, res., R.I., U.S.	D3	116
Flat Rock, Mi., U.S.	F7	99
Flat Rock, N.C., U.S.	f10	110
Flatrock, stm., In., U.S.	F6	91
Flattery, Cape, c., Wa., U.S.	A1	124
Flatwoods, Ky., U.S.	B7	94
Fleetwood, Eng., U.K.	H9	7
Fleetwood, Pa., U.S.	F10	115
Flekkefjord, Nor.	G6	6
Fleming, co., Ky., U.S.	B6	94
Fleming-Neon, Ky., U.S.	C7	94
Flemingsburg, Ky., U.S.	B6	94
Flemington, N.J., U.S.	B3	107
Flemington, Pa., U.S.	D7	115
Flensburg, Ger.	A9	8
Flers, Fr.	D6	10
Fletcher, N.C., U.S.	f10	110
Fletcher, Oh., U.S.	C3	113
Fleurance, Fr.	I7	10
Flinders, stm., Austl.	C8	50
Flinders Island, i., Austl.	G9	50
Flin Flon, Man., Can.	E1	70
Flint, Wales, U.K.	H9	7
Flint, Mi., U.S.	E7	99
Flint, stm., Ga., U.S.	E2	87
Flint City, Al., U.S.	A3	78
Flint Creek Range, mts., Mt., U.S.	D3	103
Flint Run, stm., W.V., U.S.	k9	125
Flippin, Ar., U.S.	A3	81
Flomaton, Al., U.S.	D2	78
Flora, Il., U.S.	E5	90
Flora, In., U.S.	C4	91
Flora, Ms., U.S.	C3	101
Florac, Fr.	H10	10
Florala, Al., U.S.	D3	78
Floral City, Fl., U.S.	D4	86
Florence, Al., U.S.	A2	78
Florence, Az., U.S.	D4	80
Florence, Co., U.S.	C5	83
Florence, Ks., U.S.	D7	93
Florence, Ky., U.S.	A5	94
Florence, Ms., U.S.	C3	101
Florence, N.J., U.S.	C3	107
Florence, Or., U.S.	D2	114
Florence, S.C., U.S.	C8	117
Florence, co., S.C., U.S.	C8	117
Florence, co., Wi., U.S.	C5	126
Florence see Firenze, Italy	F6	14
Florenceville, N.B., Can.	C2	71
Florencia, Col.	G5	58
Flores, i., Indon.	G7	32
Flores, Laut (Flores Sea), Indon.	G6	32
Floresville, Tx., U.S.	E3	120
Florham Park, N.J., U.S.	B4	107
Floriano, Braz.	E10	54
Florianópolis, Braz.	B7	56
Florida, Col.	F4	58
Florida, Cuba	D8	64
Florida, N.Y., U.S.	D6	109
Florida, state, U.S.	E5	86
Florida, Cape, c., Fl., U.S.	G6	86
Florida, Straits of, strt., N.A.	B7	64
Florida Bay, b., Fl., U.S.	H6	86
Floridablanca, Col.	D6	58
Florida City, Fl., U.S.	G6	86
Florida Keys, is., Fl., U.S.	H6	86
Florida Mountains, mts., N.M., U.S.	E2	108
Florida State Indian Reservation, Fl., U.S.	F5	86
Florien, La., U.S.	C2	95
Florissant, Mo., U.S.	f13	102
Florissant Fossil Beds National Monument, Co., U.S.	C5	83
Florø, Nor.	F5	6
Flossmoor, Il., U.S.	k9	90
Flovilla, Ga., U.S.	C3	87
Flower Brook, stm., Vt., U.S.	E2	122
Flowery Branch, Ga., U.S.	B3	87
Flowood, Ms., U.S.	C3	101
Floyd, co., Ga., U.S.	B1	87
Floyd, co., In., U.S.	H6	91
Floyd, co., Ia., U.S.	A5	92
Floyd, co., Ky., U.S.	C7	94
Floyd, co., Tx., U.S.	B2	120
Floyd, co., Va., U.S.	D2	123
Floyd, stm., Ia., U.S.	B1	92
Floydada, Tx., U.S.	C2	120
Floyds Fork, stm., Ky., U.S.	B4	94
Floyds Knobs, In., U.S.	H6	91
Flushing, Mi., U.S.	E7	99
Flushing, Oh., U.S.	B4	112
Flushing see Vlissingen, Neth.	D3	8
Fluvanna, co., Va., U.S.	C4	123
Fly, stm.	m15	50a
Foard, co., Tx., U.S.	B3	120
Foça, Tur.	K10	16
Focşani, Rom.	D11	16
Fogang (Shijiao), China	L2	28
Foggia, Italy	H10	14
Fogland Point, c., R.I., U.S.	E6	116
Fogo, Newf., Can.	D4	72
Fogo, Cape, c., Newf., Can.	D5	72
Fogo Island, i., Newf., Can.	D4	72
Fohnsdorf, Aus.	H14	8
Foix, Fr.	J8	10
Foley, Al., U.S.	E2	78
Foley, Mn., U.S.	E5	100
Foley Island, i., N.W. Ter., Can.	C17	66
Foligno, Italy	G7	14
Folkestone, Eng., U.K.	J14	7
Folkston, Ga., U.S.	F4	87
Follansbee, W.V., U.S.	A4	125
Follonica, Italy	G5	14
Folly Beach, S.C., U.S.	F8	117
Folly Island, i., S.C., U.S.	F8	117
Folsom, Ca., U.S.	C3	82
Fonda, Ia., U.S.	B3	92
Fond du Lac, Wi., U.S.	E5	126
Fond du Lac, co., Wi., U.S.	E5	126
Fond du Lac Indian Reservation, Mn., U.S.	D6	100
Fondi, Italy	H8	14
Fondouk el Aouareb, Tun.	N4	14
Fonni, Italy	I4	14
Fonseca, Col.	B6	58
Fonseca, Golfo de, b., N.A.	H4	64
Fontainebleau, Fr.	D9	10
Fontana, Ca., U.S.	m14	82
Fontana, Wi., U.S.	F5	126
Fontana Lake, res., N.C., U.S.	f9	110
Fontanelle, Ia., U.S.	C3	92
Fonte Boa, Braz.	D5	54
Fontenelle Reservoir, res., Wy., U.S.	D2	127
Fontur, c., Ice.	B5	4
Foochow see Fuzhou, China	I8	28
Footville, Wi., U.S.	F4	126
Foraker, Mount, mtn., Ak., U.S.	f16	79
Forbach, Fr.	C13	10
Forbach, Ger.	G8	8
Forbes, Mount, mtn., Alta., Can.	D2	68
Forcalquier, Fr.	I12	10
Forchheim, Ger.	F11	8
Ford, co., Il., U.S.	C5	90
Ford, co., Ks., U.S.	E4	93
Ford, stm., Mi., U.S.	C3	99
Ford City, Ca., U.S.	E4	82
Ford City, Pa., U.S.	E2	115
Førde, Nor.	F5	6
Fordoche, La., U.S.	D4	95
Fords Prairie, Wa., U.S.	C2	124
Fordyce, Ar., U.S.	D3	81
Forel, Mont, mtn., Grnld.	C25	66
Foreman, Ar., U.S.	D1	81
Forest, Ont., Can.	D2	73
Forest, Ms., U.S.	C4	101
Forest, Oh., U.S.	B2	112
Forest, co., Pa., U.S.	C3	115
Forest, co., Wi., U.S.	C5	126
Forest, stm., N.D., U.S.	A8	111
Forest Acres, S.C., U.S.	C6	117
Forestburg, Alta., Can.	C4	68
Forest City, Ia., U.S.	A4	92
Forest City, N.C., U.S.	B1	110
Forest City, Pa., U.S.	C11	115
Forestdale, R.I., U.S.	B3	116
Forest Dale, Vt., U.S.	D2	122
Forest Glen, La., U.S.	h12	95
Forest Grove, Or., U.S.	B3	114
Forest Hill, Md., U.S.	A5	97
Forest Hills, Pa., U.S.	k14	115
Forest Knolls, Ca., U.S.	g7	82
Forest Lake, Mn., U.S.	E6	100
Forest Park, Ga., U.S.	h8	87
Forest Park, Il., U.S.	k9	90
Forest Park, La., U.S.	*B3	95
Forest Park, Oh., U.S.	*n12	112
Forfar, Scot., U.K.	E10	7
Forillon, Parc National de, Que., Can.	k14	74
Fork Creek, stm., W.V., U.S.	m12	125
Forked Deer, stm., Tn., U.S.	B2	119
Forkland, Al., U.S.	C2	78
Forks, Wa., U.S.	B1	124
Forlì, Italy	E7	14
Formia, Italy	H8	14
Formiga, Braz.	F6	57
Formosa, Arg.	B5	56
Formosa, Braz.	C5	57
Formosa, Serra, plat., Braz.	F8	54
Formosa see Taiwan, i., Asia	L9	28
Forney, Tx., U.S.	C4	120
Fornovo di Taro, Italy	E5	14
Forrest, Austl.	F5	50
Forrest, Il., U.S.	C5	90
Forrest, co., Ms., U.S.	D4	101
Forrest City, Ar., U.S.	B5	81
Forreston, Il., U.S.	A4	90
Forrester Island, i., Ak., U.S.	n23	79
Forsayth, Austl.	C8	50
Forst, Ger.	D14	8
Forsyth, Ga., U.S.	C3	87
Forsyth, Il., U.S.	D5	90
Forsyth, Mo., U.S.	E4	102
Forsyth, Mt., U.S.	D10	103
Forsyth, co., Ga., U.S.	B2	87
Forsyth, co., N.C., U.S.	A2	110
Fortaleza, Braz.	D11	54
Fort Apache Indian Reservation, Az., U.S.	D5	80
Fort-Archambault see Sarh, Chad	G9	42
Fort Ashby, W.V., U.S.	B6	125
Fort Atkinson, Wi., U.S.	F5	126
Fort Augustus, Scot., U.K.	D8	7
Fort Beaufort, S. Afr.	H5	44
Fort Belknap Indian Reservation, Mt., U.S.	B8	103
Fort Belvoir, mil., Va., U.S.	g12	123
Fort Bend, co., Tx., U.S.	E5	120
Fort Benjamin Harrison, mil., In., U.S.	k10	91
Fort Benning, mil., Ga., U.S.	D2	87
Fort Benton, Mt., U.S.	C6	103
Fort Berthold Indian Reservation, N.D., U.S.	B3	111
Fort Bidwell Indian Reservation, Ca., U.S.	B3	82
Fort Bliss, mil., Tx., U.S.	o11	120
Fort Bragg, Ca., U.S.	C2	82
Fort Bragg, mil., N.C., U.S.	B3	110
Fort Branch, In., U.S.	H2	91
Fort Calhoun, Ne., U.S.	C9	104
Fort Campbell, mil., U.S.	A4	119
Fort Carson, mil., Co., U.S.	C6	83
Fort Chipewyan, Alta., Can.	f8	68
Fort Clatsop National Memorial, hist., Or., U.S.	A3	114
Fort Cobb, Ok., U.S.	B3	113
Fort Cobb Reservoir, res., Ok., U.S.	B3	113
Fort Collins, Co., U.S.	A5	83
Fort Coulonge, Que., Can.	B8	73
Fort Davis National Historic Site, hist., Tx., U.S.	o13	120
Fort Defiance, Az., U.S.	B6	80
Fort-de-France, Mart.	G17	64
Fort Deposit, Al., U.S.	D3	78
Fort Detrick, mil., Md., U.S.	B3	97
Fort Devens, mil., Ma., U.S.	f9	98
Fort Dix, mil., N.J., U.S.	C3	107
Fort Dodge, Ia., U.S.	B3	92
Fort Donelson National Battlefield, Tn., U.S.	A4	119
Fort Edward, N.Y., U.S.	B7	109
Fort Erie, Ont., Can.	E6	73
Fortescue, stm., Austl.	D3	50
Fort Eustis, mil., Va., U.S.	h14	123
Fort Fairfield, Me., U.S.	B5	96
Fort Frances, Ont., Can.	o16	73
Fort Franklin, N.W. Ter., Can.	C8	66
Fort Gaines, Ga., U.S.	E1	87
Fort Gay, W.V., U.S.	C2	125
Fort Gibson, Ok., U.S.	B6	113
Fort Gibson Lake, res., Ok., U.S.	A6	113
Fort Good Hope, N.W. Ter., Can.	C7	66
Fort Gordon, mil., Ga., U.S.	C4	87
Fort Greely, mil., Ak., U.S.	C10	79
Fort Hall, Id., U.S.	F6	89
Fort Hall Indian Reservation, Id., U.S.	F6	89
Fort Hood, mil., Tx., U.S.	D4	120
Fort Howard, Md., U.S.	B5	97
Fort Huachuca, mil., Az., U.S.	F5	80
Fortín Coronel Eugenio Garay, Para.	H6	54
Fort Jackson, mil., S.C., U.S.	C6	117
Fort Jefferson National Monument, Fl., U.S.	H4	86
Fort Kent, Me., U.S.	A4	96
Fort Knox, mil., Ky., U.S.	B4	94
Fort-Lamy see N'Djamena, Chad	F9	42
Fort Laramie, Wy., U.S.	D8	127
Fort Laramie National Historic Site, hist., Wy., U.S.	D8	127
Fort Lauderdale, Fl., U.S.	F6	86
Fort Lawn, S.C., U.S.	B6	117
Fort Leavenworth, mil., Ks., U.S.	C9	93
Fort Lee, N.J., U.S.	B5	107
Fort Lee, mil., Va., U.S.	C5	123
Fort Leonard Wood, mil., Mo., U.S.	D5	102
Fort Lewis, mil., Wa., U.S.	B3	124
Fort Liard, N.W. Ter., Can.	D8	66
Fort Loramie, Oh., U.S.	B1	112
Fort Loudon, Pa., U.S.	G6	115
Fort Loudoun Lake, res., Tn., U.S.	D9	119
Fort Lupton, Co., U.S.	A6	83
Fort MacArthur, mil., Ca., U.S.	n12	82
Fort Macleod, Alta., Can.	E4	68
Fort Madison, Ia., U.S.	D6	92
Fort Matanzas National Monument, Fl., U.S.	C5	86
Fort McClellan, mil., Al., U.S.	B4	78
Fort McDermitt Indian Reservation, U.S.	B4	105
Fort McDowell Indian Reservation, Az., U.S.	D4	80
Fort McHenry National Monument And Historic Shrine, Md., U.S.	g11	97
Fort McMurray, Alta., Can.	A5	68
Fort Meade, Fl., U.S.	E5	86
Fort Meade, mil., Md., U.S.	B4	97
Fort Meadow Reservoir, res., Ma., U.S.	g9	98
Fort Mill, S.C., U.S.	A6	117
Fort Mitchell, Al., U.S.	C4	78
Fort Mitchell, Ky., U.S.	h13	94
Fort Mojave Indian Reservation, U.S.	C1	80
Fort Monmouth, mil., N.J., U.S.	C4	107
Fort Monroe, mil., Va., U.S.	h15	123
Fort Morgan, Co., U.S.	A7	83
Fort Myer, mil., Va., U.S.	g12	123
Fort Myers, Fl., U.S.	F5	86
Fort Myers Beach, Fl., U.S.	F5	86
Fort Nelson, B.C., Can.	m18	69
Fort Norman, N.W. Ter., Can.	D7	66
Fort Oglethorpe, Ga., U.S.	B1	87
Fort Ord, mil., Ca., U.S.	D3	82
Fort Payne, Al., U.S.	A4	78
Fort Peck Indian Reservation, Mt., U.S.	B11	103
Fort Peck Lake, res., Mt., U.S.	C9	103
Fort Pierce, Fl., U.S.	E6	86
Fort Pierce Inlet, b., Fl., U.S.	E6	86
Fort Pierre, S.D., U.S.	C5	118
Fort Plain, N.Y., U.S.	C6	109
Fort Polk, mil., La., U.S.	C2	95
Fort Portal, Ug.	A6	44
Fort Providence, N.W. Ter., Can.	D9	66
Fort Randall Dam, S.D., U.S.	D7	118
Fort Recovery, Oh., U.S.	B1	112
Fort Reliance, N.W. Ter., Can.	D11	66
Fort Resolution, N.W. Ter., Can.	D10	66
Fort Richardson, mil., Ak., U.S.	C10	79
Fort Riley, mil., Ks., U.S.	C7	93
Fort Ritchie, mil., Md., U.S.	A3	97
Fort Rucker, mil., Al., U.S.	D4	78
Fort Saint James, B.C., Can.	B5	69
Fort Saint John, B.C., Can.	A7	69
Fort Saskatchewan, Alta., Can.	C4	68
Fort Scott, Ks., U.S.	E9	93
Fort Shafter, mil., Hi., U.S.	g10	88
Fort Shawnee, Oh., U.S.	B1	112
Fort Sheridan, mil., Il., U.S.	h9	90
Fort Sill, mil., Ok., U.S.	C3	113
Fort Simpson, N.W. Ter., Can.	D8	66
Fort Smith, N.W. Ter., Can.	D10	66
Fort Smith, Ar., U.S.	B1	81
Fort Stewart, mil., Ga., U.S.	D5	87
Fort Stockton, Tx., U.S.	D1	120
Fort Sumner, N.M., U.S.	C5	108
Fort Sumter National Monument, S.C., U.S.	k12	117
Fort Supply Lake, res., Ok., U.S.	A2	113
Fort Thomas, Ky., U.S.	h14	94
Fort Totten, N.D., U.S.	B7	111
Fort Totten Indian Reservation, N.D., U.S.	B7	111
Fortuna, Ca., U.S.	B1	82
Fortune, Newf., Can.	E4	72
Fortune Bay, b., Newf., Can.	E4	72
Fort Union National Monument, N.M., U.S.	B5	108
Fort Valley, Ga., U.S.	D3	87
Fort Vermilion, Alta., Can.	f7	68
Fortville, In., U.S.	E6	91
Fort Wainwright, mil., Ak., U.S.	C10	79
Fort Walton Beach, Fl., U.S.	u15	86
Fort Washington Forest, Md., U.S.	C4	97
Fort Wayne, In., U.S.	B7	91
Fort William, Scot., U.K.	E7	7
Fort Wingate, N.M., U.S.	B1	108
Fort Worth, Tx., U.S.	C4	120
Fort Wright, Ky., U.S.	h13	94
Forty Fort, Pa., U.S.	D10	115
Fort Yukon, Ak., U.S.	B10	79
Fort Yuma Indian Reservation, Ca., U.S.	F6	82
Foshan, China	L2	28
Fossano, Italy	E2	14
Fossil Butte National Monument, Wy., U.S.	E2	127
Fossil Lake, l., Or., U.S.	D6	114
Fossombrone, Italy	F7	14
Foss Reservoir, res., Ok., U.S.	B2	113
Fosston, Mn., U.S.	C3	100
Foster, Or., U.S.	C4	114
Foster, co., N.D., U.S.	B6	111
Foster Village, Hi., U.S.	g10	88
Fostoria, Oh., U.S.	A2	112
Fougamou, Gabon	B2	44
Fougères, Fr.	D5	10
Fouke, Ar., U.S.	D2	81
Foula, i., Scot., U.K.	A10	7
Foumban, Cam.	G8	42
Fountain, Co., U.S.	C6	83
Fountain, co., In., U.S.	D3	91
Fountain City, In., U.S.	E8	91
Fountain City, Wi., U.S.	D2	126
Fountain Hill, Pa., U.S.	E11	115
Fountain Inn, S.C., U.S.	B3	117
Fountain Peak, mtn., Ca., U.S.	E6	82
Fountain Place, La., U.S.	*D4	95
Fourche LaFave, stm., Ar., U.S.	C2	81
Fourche Maline, stm., Ok., U.S.	C6	113
Fourmies, Fr.	B11	10
Four Mountains, Islands of, is., Ak., U.S.	E6	79
Four Oaks, N.C., U.S.	B4	110
Fowler, Ca., U.S.	D4	82
Fowler, Co., U.S.	C6	83
Fowler, In., U.S.	C3	91
Fowler, Mi., U.S.	E6	99
Fowlerville, Mi., U.S.	F6	99
Fox, stm., Man., Can.	B4	70
Fox, stm., U.S.	B5	90
Fox, stm., U.S.	A6	102
Fox, stm., Mi., U.S.	B4	99
Fox, stm., Wi., U.S.	D5	126
Foxboro, Ont., Can.	C7	73
Foxboro, Ma., U.S.	B5	98
Fox Creek, Alta., Can.	B2	68
Foxe Basin, b., N.W. Ter., Can.	C17	66
Foxe Channel, strt., N.W. Ter., Can.	D16	66
Foxe Peninsula, pen., N.W. Ter., Can.	D17	66
Fox Island, i., R.I., U.S.	E4	116
Fox Island, i., Wa., U.S.	f10	124
Fox Islands, is., Ak., U.S.	E6	79
Fox Lake, Il., U.S.	A5	90
Fox Lake, Wi., U.S.	E5	126
Fox Lake, l., Il., U.S.	h8	90
Fox Mountain, mtn., Nv., U.S.	B2	105
Fox Point, Wi., U.S.	E6	126
Fox River Grove, Il., U.S.	h8	90
Foxworth, Ms., U.S.	D4	101
Foz do Cunene, Ang.	E2	44
Foz do Iguaçu, Braz.	B6	56
Frackville, Pa., U.S.	E9	115
Fraga, Spain	D12	12
Framingham, Ma., U.S.	B5	98
Franca, Braz.	F5	57
Francavilla Fontana, Italy	I12	14
France, ctry., Eur.	F8	4
Francesville, In., U.S.	C4	91
Franceville, Gabon	B2	44
Francis, Lake, l., N.H., U.S.	f7	106
Francis Case, Lake, res., S.D., U.S.	D6	118
Francistown, Bots.	F5	44
Francofonte, Italy	L9	14
Franconia, N.H., U.S.	B3	106
Franconia Notch, N.H., U.S.	B3	106
Francs Peak, mtn., Wy., U.S.	C3	127
Frankenberg, Ger.	E13	8
Frankenberg-Eder, Ger.	D8	8
Frankenmuth, Mi., U.S.	E7	99
Frankford, Ont., Can.	C7	73
Frankford, De., U.S.	F5	85
Frankfort, Il., U.S.	m9	90
Frankfort, In., U.S.	D4	91
Frankfort, Ks., U.S.	C7	93
Frankfort, Ky., U.S.	B5	94
Frankfort, Mi., U.S.	D4	99
Frankfort, N.Y., U.S.	B5	109
Frankfort, Oh., U.S.	C2	112
Frankfurt am Main, Ger.	E8	8
Frankfurt an der Oder, Ger.	C14	8
Franklin, Ga., U.S.	C1	87
Franklin, In., U.S.	F5	91
Franklin, Ky., U.S.	D3	94
Franklin, La., U.S.	E4	95
Franklin, Ma., U.S.	B5	98
Franklin, Ne., U.S.	D7	104
Franklin, N.H., U.S.	D3	106
Franklin, N.J., U.S.	A3	107
Franklin, N.C., U.S.	f9	110
Franklin, Oh., U.S.	C1	112
Franklin, Pa., U.S.	D2	115
Franklin, Tn., U.S.	B5	119
Franklin, Tx., U.S.	D4	120
Franklin, Va., U.S.	D6	123
Franklin, W.V., U.S.	C5	125
Franklin, Wi., U.S.	n11	126
Franklin, co., Al., U.S.	A2	78
Franklin, co., Ar., U.S.	B2	81
Franklin, co., Fl., U.S.	C2	86

Name	Map Ref	Page
Franklin, co., Ga., U.S.	B3	87
Franklin, co., Id., U.S.	G7	89
Franklin, co., Il., U.S.	E4	90
Franklin, co., In., U.S.	F7	91
Franklin, co., Ia., U.S.	B4	92
Franklin, co., Ks., U.S.	D8	93
Franklin, co., Ky., U.S.	B5	94
Franklin, co., La., U.S.	B4	95
Franklin, co., Me., U.S.	C2	96
Franklin, co., Ma., U.S.	A2	98
Franklin, co., Ms., U.S.	D3	101
Franklin, co., Mo., U.S.	C6	102
Franklin, co., Ne., U.S.	D7	104
Franklin, co., N.Y., U.S.	f10	109
Franklin, co., N.C., U.S.	A4	110
Franklin, co., Oh., U.S.	B2	112
Franklin, co., Pa., U.S.	G6	115
Franklin, co., Tn., U.S.	B5	119
Franklin, co., Tx., U.S.	C5	120
Franklin, co., Vt., U.S.	B2	122
Franklin, co., Va., U.S.	D3	123
Franklin, co., Wa., U.S.	C6	124
Franklin, Point, c., Ak., U.S.	A8	79
Franklin Bay, b., N.W. Ter., Can.	C7	66
Franklin D. Roosevelt Lake, res., Wa., U.S.	B7	124
Franklin Falls Reservoir, res., N.H., U.S.	C3	106
Franklin Grove, Il., U.S.	B4	90
Franklin Lake, l., N.W. Ter., Can.	C13	66
Franklin Lake, l., Nv., U.S.	C6	105
Franklin Mountains, mts., N.W. Ter., Can.	D8	66
Franklin Park, Il., U.S.	k9	90
Franklin Park, Pa., U.S.	*h13	115
Franklin Strait, strt., N.W. Ter., Can.	B13	66
Franklinton, La., U.S.	D5	95
Franklinton, N.C., U.S.	A4	110
Franklinville, N.Y., U.S.	C2	109
Frankston, Tx., U.S.	C5	120
Frankton, In., U.S.	D6	91
Frascati, Italy	H7	14
Fraser, stm., B.C., Can.	E7	69
Fraser, stm., Newf., Can.	g9	72
Fraser, Mount, mtn., Can.	C8	69
Fraserburgh, Scot., U.K.	D10	7
Fraser Lake, B.C., Can.	B5	69
Fraser Plateau, plat., B.C., Can.	D6	69
Frauenfeld, Switz.	E15	10
Frazee, Mn., U.S.	D3	100
Frazeysburg, Oh., U.S.	B3	112
Frazier Park, Ca., U.S.	E4	82
Fr'azino, Russia	F21	18
Frederic, Wi., U.S.	C1	126
Frederica, De., U.S.	D4	85
Fredericia, Den.	I7	6
Frederick, Co., U.S.	A6	83
Frederick, Md., U.S.	B3	97
Frederick, Ok., U.S.	C2	113
Frederick, co., Md., U.S.	B3	97
Frederick, co., Va., U.S.	A4	123
Fredericksburg, Ia., U.S.	B5	92
Fredericksburg, Tx., U.S.	D3	120
Fredericksburg, Va., U.S.	B5	123
Frederick Sound, strt., Ak., U.S.	m23	79
Fredericktown, Mo., U.S.	D7	102
Fredericktown, Oh., U.S.	B3	112
Fredericktown, Pa., U.S.	F1	115
Fredericton, N.B., Can.	D3	71
Fredericton Junction, N.B., Can.	D3	71
Frederikshåb, Grnld.	D23	66
Frederikshavn, Den.	H8	6
Fredonia, Az., U.S.	A3	80
Fredonia, Ks., U.S.	E8	93
Fredonia, N.Y., U.S.	C1	109
Fredonia, Wi., U.S.	E6	126
Fredrikstad, Nor.	G8	6
Freeborn, co., Mn., U.S.	G5	100
Freeburg, Il., U.S.	E4	90
Freedom, Pa., U.S.	E1	115
Freedom, Wy., U.S.	D2	127
Freehold, N.J., U.S.	C4	107
Freeland, Mi., U.S.	E6	99
Freeland, Pa., U.S.	D10	115
Freelandville, In., U.S.	G3	91
Freel Peak, mtn., Ca., U.S.	C4	82
Freels, Cape, c., Newf., Can.	D5	72
Freels, Cape, c., Newf., Can.	E5	72
Freeman, S.D., U.S.	D8	118
Freeman, Lake, l., In., U.S.	C4	91
Freemansburg, Pa., U.S.	E11	115
Freemason Island, i., La., U.S.	E7	95
Freeport, Bah.	A8	64
Freeport, Il., U.S.	A4	90
Freeport, Me., U.S.	E2	96
Freeport, N.Y., U.S.	n15	109
Freeport, Pa., U.S.	E2	115
Freeport, Tx., U.S.	E5	120
Freer, Tx., U.S.	F3	120
Freestone, co., Tx., U.S.	D4	120
Freetown, S.L.	G3	42
Freetown, In., U.S.	G5	91
Freezeout Mountains, mts., Wy., U.S.	D6	127
Fregenal de la Sierra, Spain	G5	12
Freiberg, Ger.	E13	8
Freiburg [im Breisgau], Ger.	H7	8
Freising, Ger.	G14	8
Freistadt, Aus.	D13	8
Freital, Ger.	I13	10
Fréjus, Fr.	D2	72
Fremont, Ca., U.S.	A8	91
Fremont, In., U.S.	C5	99
Fremont, Ia., U.S.	E5	99
Fremont, Mi., U.S.	C9	104
Fremont, Ne., U.S.	B5	110
Fremont, N.C., U.S.	A2	112
Fremont, Oh., U.S.		
Fremont, co., Co., U.S.	C5	83
Fremont, co., Id., U.S.	E7	89
Fremont, co., Ia., U.S.	D2	92
Fremont, co., Wy., U.S.	C4	127
Fremont Island, i., Ut., U.S.	B3	121
Fremont Lake, l., Wy., U.S.	D3	127
Fremont Peak, mtn., Wy., U.S.	C3	127
French Broad, stm., U.S.	D10	119
Frenchburg, Ky., U.S.	C6	94
French Creek, stm., Pa., U.S.	C2	115
French Frigate Shoals, rf., Hi., U.S.	C8	54
French Guiana, dep., S.A.	G4	91
French Lick, In., U.S.	G4	91
Frenchman Bay, b., Me., U.S.	D4	96
Frenchman Creek, stm., U.S.	D4	104
French Hills, hills, Wa., U.S.	C6	124
Frenchman Lake, l., Nv., U.S.	G6	105
French Polynesia, dep., Oc.	G3	2
French Settlement, La., U.S.	D5	95
Freshfield, Mount, mtn., Can.	D2	68
Fresnillo, Mex.	F8	62
Fresno, Ca., U.S.	D4	82
Fresno, co., Ca., U.S.	D4	82
Fresno Reservoir, res., Mt., U.S.	B6	103
Freudenstadt, Ger.	G8	8
Frewsbury, N.Y., U.S.	C1	109
Fria, Cape, c., Nmb.	E2	44
Friars Point, Ms., U.S.	A3	101
Frías, Arg.	B3	56
Fribourg (Freiburg), Switz.	F14	10
Friday Harbor, Wa., U.S.	A2	124
Fridley, Mn., U.S.	m12	100
Friedberg, Ger.	H16	8
Friedrichshafen, Ger.	H9	8
Friend, Ne., U.S.	D8	104
Friendsville, Tn., U.S.	D9	119
Fries, Va., U.S.	D2	123
Friesland, hist. reg., Neth.	B5	8
Frio, co., Tx., U.S.	E3	120
Frio, stm., Tx., U.S.	E3	120
Frio, Cabo, c., Braz.	G7	57
Friona, Tx., U.S.	B1	120
Fripps Island, i., S.C., U.S.	G7	117
Frisco, Co., U.S.	B4	83
Frisco City, Al., U.S.	D2	78
Frisco Peak, mtn., Ut., U.S.	E2	121
Frissell, Mount, mtn., U.S.	A2	84
Fritch, Tx., U.S.	B2	120
Fritzlar, Ger.	D9	8
Friza, Proliv, strt., Russia	H23	24
Frobisher Bay, b., N.W. Ter., Can.	D19	66
Frobisher Lake, l., Sask., Can.	m7	75
Frohnleiten, Aus.	H15	8
Frontenac, Ks., U.S.	E9	93
Frontier, co., Ne., U.S.	D5	104
Front Range, mts., Co., U.S.	A5	83
Front Royal, Va., U.S.	B4	123
Frosinone, Italy	H8	14
Frostburg, Md., U.S.	k13	97
Frostproof, Fl., U.S.	E5	86
Fruita, Co., U.S.	B2	83
Fruit Heights, Ut., U.S.	B4	121
Fruitland, Id., U.S.	F2	89
Fruitland, Md., U.S.	D6	97
Fruitland, N.M., U.S.	A1	108
Fruitland Park, Fl., U.S.	D5	86
Fruitport, Mi., U.S.	E4	99
Fruitvale, B.C., Can.	E9	69
Fruitvale, Co., U.S.	B2	83
Fruitvale, Wa., U.S.	C5	124
Fruitville, Fl., U.S.	E4	86
Frunze see Bishkek, Kyrg.	I12	22
Frutigen, Switz.	F14	10
Fryeburg, Me., U.S.	D2	96
Fuchū, Japan	H6	30
Fuencaliente, Spain	G7	12
Fuente de Cantos, Spain	G5	12
Fuente-obejuna, Spain	G6	12
Fuerteventura, i., Spain	C3	42
Fuji, Japan	G11	30
Fuji, Mount see Fuji-san, vol., Japan	G11	30
Fujian, prov., China	F10	26
Fujin, China	B13	26
Fujinomiya, Japan	G11	30
Fuji-san (Fujiyama), vol., Japan	G11	30
Fujisawa, Japan	G12	30
Fujiyama see Fuji-san, vol., Japan	G11	30
Fuji-yoshida, Japan	G11	30
Fukagawa, Japan	p20	30a
Fukaya, Japan	F12	30
Fukuchiyama, Japan	G8	30
Fukue, Japan	J1	30
Fukui, Japan	F9	30
Fukuoka, Japan	I3	30
Fukushima, Japan	E13	30
Fukushima, Japan	r18	30a
Fukuyama, Japan	H6	30
Fūlādī, Kūh-e, mtn., Afg.	C2	38
Fulda, Ger.	E9	8
Fulda, Mn., U.S.	G3	100
Fullerton, Ca., U.S.	n13	82
Fullerton, Ne., U.S.	C8	104
Fulton, Il., U.S.	B3	90
Fulton, Ky., U.S.	f9	94
Fulton, Md., U.S.	B4	97
Fulton, Ms., U.S.	A5	101
Fulton, Mo., U.S.	C6	102
Fulton, N.Y., U.S.	B4	109
Fulton, co., Ar., U.S.	A4	81
Fulton, co., Ga., U.S.	C2	87
Fulton, co., Il., U.S.	C3	90
Fulton, co., In., U.S.	B5	91
Fulton, co., Ky., U.S.	f8	94
Fulton, co., N.Y., U.S.	B6	109
Fulton, co., Oh., U.S.	A1	112
Fulton, co., Pa., U.S.	G5	115
Fultondale, Al., U.S.	f7	78
Funabashi, Japan	G13	30
Funchal, Port.	B2	42
Fundación, Col.	B5	58
Fundy, Bay of, b., Can.	D4	71
Fundy National Park, N.B., Can.	D4	71
Funkstown, Md., U.S.	A2	97
Fuquay-Varina, N.C., U.S.	B4	110
Furano, Japan	p20	30a
Furmanov, Russia	D24	18
Furnace Brook, stm., Vt., U.S.	D3	122
Furnas, co., Ne., U.S.	D6	104
Furnas, Reprêsa de, res., Braz.	F5	57
Furneaux Group, is., Austl.	H9	50
Furqlus, Syria	B5	40
Fürstenfeld, Aus.	H16	8
Fürstenfeldbruck, Ger.	G11	8
Fürstenwalde, Ger.	C14	8
Fürth, Ger.	F10	8
Furth im Wald, Ger.	F12	8
Furudal, Swe.	F10	6
Fushun, China	C11	26
Füssen, Ger.	H10	8
Fuxian, China	D11	26
Fuxian, China	D8	26
Fuxinshi, China	C11	26
Fuyang, China	C4	28
Fuyang, China	G5	28
Fuzhou, China	I8	28
Fuzhou (Foochow), China	I8	28
Fyffe, Al., U.S.	A4	78

G

Name	Map Ref	Page
Gabbs, Nv., U.S.	E4	105
Gabès, Tun.	B8	42
Gabès, Golfe de, b., Tun.	B8	42
Gabon, ctry., Afr.	B2	44
Gaborone, Bots.	F5	44
Gabriel Strait, strt., N.W. Ter., Can.	D19	66
Gabriola, B.C., Can.	f12	69
Gabrovo, Bul.	G9	16
Gadag, India	E3	37
Gäddede, Swe.	D10	6
Gadsden, Al., U.S.	A3	78
Gadsden, co., Fl., U.S.	B2	86
Gaeta, Italy	H8	14
Gaffney, S.C., U.S.	A4	117
Gafsa, Tun.	B7	42
Gage, co., Ne., U.S.	D9	104
Gagetown, N.B., Can.	D3	71
Gagliano del Capo, Italy	J13	14
Gagnoa, I.C.	G4	42
Gahanna, Oh., U.S.	k11	112
Gaillac, Fr.	I8	10
Gaillard, Lake, l., Ct., U.S.	D5	84
Gaines, co., Tx., U.S.	C1	120
Gainesboro, Tn., U.S.	C8	119
Gaines Creek, stm., Ok., U.S.	C6	113
Gainesville, Fl., U.S.	C4	86
Gainesville, Ga., U.S.	B3	87
Gainesville, Mo., U.S.	E5	102
Gainesville, Tx., U.S.	C4	120
Gainesville, Va., U.S.	g11	123
Gairdner, Lake, l., Austl.	F7	50
Gaithersburg, Md., U.S.	B3	97
Galán, Cerro, mtn., Arg.	B3	56
Galapagos Islands see Colón, Archipiélago de, is., Ec.	m15	58a
Galashiels, Scot., U.K.	F10	7
Galati, Rom.	D12	16
Galatia, Il., U.S.	F5	90
Galatina, Italy	I13	14
Galax, Va., U.S.	D2	123
Galena, Ak., U.S.	C8	79
Galena, Il., U.S.	A3	90
Galena, Ks., U.S.	E9	93
Galeota Point, c., Trin.	I17	64
Galera, Punta, c., Chile	D2	56
Galera, Punta, c., Ec.	G2	58
Galesburg, Il., U.S.	C3	90
Galesburg, Mi., U.S.	F5	99
Gales Ferry, Ct., U.S.	D7	84
Galesville, Md., U.S.	C4	97
Galesville, Wi., U.S.	D2	126
Galeton, Pa., U.S.	C6	115
Galič, Russia	C25	18
Galicia, hist. reg., Eur.	F21	8
Galicia, hist. reg., Spain	B3	12
Galilee, Sea of see Kinneret, Yam, l., Isr.	C4	40
Galion, Oh., U.S.	B3	112
Galisteo Creek, stm., N.M., U.S.	k8	108
Galiuro Mountains, mts., Az., U.S.	E5	80
Galka'yo, Som.	G4	46
Gallant, Al., U.S.	A3	78
Gallarate, Italy	D3	14
Gallatin, Mo., U.S.	B4	102
Gallatin, Tn., U.S.	A5	119
Gallatin, co., Il., U.S.	F5	90
Gallatin, co., Ky., U.S.	B5	94
Gallatin, co., Mt., U.S.	E5	103
Gallatin, stm., Mt., U.S.	E5	103
Gallatin Range, mts., Mt., U.S.	E5	103
Gallaway, Tn., U.S.	B2	119
Galle, Sri L.	I6	37
Gallia, co., Oh., U.S.	D3	112
Galliano, La., U.S.	E5	95
Gallinas, Punta, c., Col.	A7	58
Gallinas Mountains, mts., N.M., U.S.	C2	108
Gallipoli, Italy	I12	14
Gallipoli see Gelibolu, Tur.	I10	16
Gallipolis, Oh., U.S.	D3	112
Gallitzin, Pa., U.S.	F4	115
Gällivare, Swe.	C13	6
Gallo Mountains, mts., N.M., U.S.	C1	108
Galloo Island, i., N.Y., U.S.	B4	109
Galloway, Mull of, c., Scot., U.K.	G8	7
Gallup, N.M., U.S.	B1	108
Galt, Ca., U.S.	C3	82
Galtür, Aus.	I10	8
Galty Mountains, mts., Ire.	I4	7
Galva, Il., U.S.	B3	90
Galva, Ks., U.S.	D6	93
Galveston, In., U.S.	C5	91
Galveston, Tx., U.S.	E5	120
Galveston, co., Tx., U.S.	E5	120
Galveston Bay, b., Tx., U.S.	E5	120
Galveston Island, i., Tx., U.S.	E5	120
Gálvez, Arg.	C4	56
Galway, Ire.	H3	7
Gambela, Eth.	G1	46
Gambell, Ak., U.S.	C5	79
Gambia, ctry., Afr.	F2	42
Gambia (Gambie), stm., Afr.	F2	42
Gambier, Oh., U.S.	B3	112
Gambo, Newf., Can.	D4	72
Gambrills, Md., U.S.	B4	97
Gamleby, Swe.	H11	6
Ganado, Az., U.S.	B6	80
Ganado, Tx., U.S.	E4	120
Gananoque, Ont., Can.	C8	73
Ganda, Ang.	D2	44
Gandak, stm., Asia	G11	38
Gander, Newf., Can.	D4	72
Gander, stm., Newf., Can.	D4	72
Ganderkesee, Ger.	B8	8
Gander Lake, l., Newf., Can.	D4	72
Gandesa, Spain	D12	12
Gāndhīnagar, India	I5	38
Gāndhī Sāgar, res., India	H6	38
Gandia, Spain	G11	12
Gangāpur, India	G7	38
Gangāwati, India	E4	37
Gangdisê Shan, mts., China	E10	38
Ganges, B.C., Can.	g12	69
Ganges (Ganga) (Padma), stm., Asia	I13	38
Ganges, Mouths of the, mth., Asia	J13	38
Gang Mills, N.Y., U.S.	C3	109
Gangtok, India	G13	38
Gangu, China	E8	26
Gannat, Fr.	F10	10
Gannett Peak, mtn., Wy., U.S.	C3	127
Gansu, prov., China	D7	26
Gantt, S.C., U.S.	B3	117
Gantt Lake, res., Al., U.S.	D3	78
Ganzhou, China	J3	28
Ganzi, China	E7	26
Gao, Mali	E5	42
Gaokeng, China	H2	28
Gaoyou, China	C8	28
Gaozhou, China	D11	34
Gap, Fr.	H13	10
Gap, Pa., U.S.	G9	115
Gar, China	E9	38
Garanhuns, Braz.	E11	54
Garber, Ok., U.S.	A4	113
Garberville, Ca., U.S.	B2	82
Garça, Braz.	G4	57
Garda, Lago di, l., Italy	D5	14
Gardelegen, Ger.	C11	8
Garden, co., Ne., U.S.	C3	104
Gardena, Ca., U.S.	n12	82
Garden City, Ga., U.S.	D5	87
Garden City, Id., U.S.	F2	89
Garden City, Ks., U.S.	E3	93
Garden City, Mi., U.S.	p15	99
Garden City, Mo., U.S.	C3	102
Gardendale, Al., U.S.	B3	78
Garden Grove, Ca., U.S.	n13	82
Garden Island, i., Mi., U.S.	C5	99
Garden Plain, Ks., U.S.	E6	93
Garden Reach, India	I13	38
Gardēz, Afg.	D3	38
Gardiner, Me., U.S.	D3	96
Gardiner, Mt., U.S.	E6	103
Gardiner, Or., U.S.	D2	114
Gardiners Island, i., N.Y., U.S.	m16	109
Gardner, Il., U.S.	B5	90
Gardner, Ks., U.S.	D9	93
Gardner, Ma., U.S.	A4	98
Gardner Canal, strt., B.C., Can.	C3	69
Gardner Lake, l., Ct., U.S.	C6	84
Gardner Lake, l., Me., U.S.	D5	96
Gardner Pinnacles, Hi., U.S.	k14	88
Gardnerville, Nv., U.S.	E2	105
Gardone Val Trompia, Italy	D5	14
Garfield, N.J., U.S.	h8	107
Garfield, co., Co., U.S.	B2	83
Garfield, co., Mt., U.S.	C9	103
Garfield, co., Ne., U.S.	C6	104
Garfield, co., Ok., U.S.	A4	113
Garfield, co., Ut., U.S.	F4	121
Garfield, co., Wa., U.S.	C8	124
Garfield Heights, Oh., U.S.	h9	112
Garfield Mountain, mtn., Mt., U.S.	F4	103
Garfield Peak, mtn., Wy., U.S.	D5	127
Garibaldi, Or., U.S.	B3	114
Garibaldi, Mount, mtn., B.C., Can.	E6	69
Garies, S. Afr.	H3	44
Garissa, Kenya	B7	44
Garland, N.C., U.S.	C4	110
Garland, Tx., U.S.	n10	120
Garland, Ut., U.S.	B3	121
Garland, co., Ar., U.S.	C2	81
Garlin, Fr.	I6	10
Garm ab, Afg.	D1	38
Garmisch-Partenkirchen, Ger.	H11	8
Garnavillo, Ia., U.S.	B6	92
Garner, Ia., U.S.	A4	92
Garner, N.C., U.S.	B4	110
Garnet Range, mts., Mt., U.S.	D3	103
Garnett, Ks., U.S.	D8	93
Garnish, Newf., Can.	E4	72
Garonne, stm., Eur.	H6	10
Garoua, Cam.	G8	42
Garrard, co., Ky., U.S.	C5	94
Garretson, S.D., U.S.	D9	118
Garrett, In., U.S.	B7	91
Garrett, co., Md., U.S.	k12	97
Garrett Park, Md., U.S.	B3	97
Garrettsville, Oh., U.S.	A4	112
Garrison, Ky., U.S.	B6	94
Garrison, Md., U.S.	B4	97
Garrison, N.D., U.S.	B4	111
Garrison Dam, N.D., U.S.	B4	111
Garrovillas, Spain	F5	12
Garry Lake, l., N.W. Ter., Can.	C12	66
Garsen, Kenya	B8	44
Garut, Indon.	m13	33a
Garvin, co., Ok., U.S.	C4	113
Gary, In., U.S.	A3	91
Gary, W.V., U.S.	D3	125
Garysburg, N.C., U.S.	A5	110
Garyville, La., U.S.	D5	95
Garza, co., Tx., U.S.	C2	120
Garza-Little Elm Reservoir, res., Tx., U.S.	C4	120
Garzón, Col.	F5	58
Gas City, In., U.S.	D6	91
Gasconade, co., Mo., U.S.	C6	102
Gasconade, stm., Mo., U.S.	C6	102
Gascoyne, stm., Austl.	E3	50
Gasparilla Island, i., Fl., U.S.	F4	86
Gaspé, Que., Can.	k14	74
Gaspé, Cape, c., N.S., Can.	k13	74
Gaspésie, Péninsule de la, pen., Que., Can.	k13	74
Gassaway, W.V., U.S.	C4	125
Gassville, Ar., U.S.	A3	81
Gaston, In., U.S.	D7	91
Gaston, N.C., U.S.	A5	110
Gaston, S.C., U.S.	D5	117
Gaston, co., N.C., U.S.	B1	110
Gaston, Lake, res., U.S.	A5	110
Gaston Dam, N.C., U.S.	A5	110
Gastonia, N.C., U.S.	B1	110
Gátas, Akrotírion, c., Cyp.	B3	40
Gatčina, Russia	B13	18
Gate City, Va., U.S.	f9	123
Gates, N.Y., U.S.	*B3	109
Gates, Tn., U.S.	B2	119
Gates, co., N.C., U.S.	A6	110
Gateshead, Eng., U.K.	G11	7
Gateshead Island, i., N.W. Ter., Can.	B12	66
Gates of the Arctic National Park, Ak., U.S.	B9	79
Gatesville, Tx., U.S.	D4	120
Gatineau, Que., Can.	D2	74
Gatineau, stm., Que., Can.	D2	74
Gatineau, Parc de la, Que., Can.	D2	74
Gatlinburg, Tn., U.S.	D10	119
Gaucín, Spain	I6	12
Gauhāti, India	G14	38
Gauley, stm., W.V., U.S.	C3	125
Gauley Bridge, W.V., U.S.	C3	125
Gautier, Ms., U.S.	f8	101
Gauting, Ger.	G11	8
Gavá, Spain	D14	12
Gavins Point Dam, U.S.	B8	104
Gävle, Swe.	F11	6
Gavrilov-Jam, Russia	D22	18
Gawler, Austl.	F7	50
Gawler Ranges, mts., Austl.	F7	50
Gaya, India	H11	38
Gay Head, c., Ma., U.S.	D6	98
Gaylord, Mi., U.S.	C6	99
Gaylord, Mn., U.S.	F4	100
Gayndah, Austl.	E10	50
Gaza see Ghazzah, Isr. Occ.	D4	40
Gaziantep, Tur.	H15	4
Gazimağusa, N. Cyp.	B3	40
Gazimağusa Körfezi, b., N. Cyp.	B4	40
Gbarnga, Lib.	G4	42
Gdańsk (Danzig), Pol.	A18	8
Gdynia, Pol.	A18	8
Gearhart, Or., U.S.	A3	114
Gearhart Mountain, mtn., Or., U.S.	E6	114
Geary, N.B., Can.	D3	71
Geary, Ok., U.S.	B3	113
Geary, co., Ks., U.S.	D7	93
Geauga, co., Oh., U.S.	A4	112
Gebze, Tur.	I13	16
Gediz, stm., Tur.	K11	16
Geel, Bel.	D4	8
Geelong, Austl.	G8	50
Ge'ermu, China	B16	38
Geesthacht, Ger.	B10	8
Geilo, Nor.	F7	6
Geislingen, Ger.	G9	8
Geistown, Pa., U.S.	F4	115
Geist Reservoir, res., In., U.S.	E6	91
Gejiu (Kokiu), China	C7	34
Gela, Italy	L9	14
Gelibolu, Tur.	I10	16
Gelibolu Yarımadası (Gallipoli Peninsula), pen., Tur.	I10	16
Gelsenkirchen, Ger.	D7	8
Gem, co., Id., U.S.	E2	89
Gembloux, Bel.	E4	8
Gemena, Zaire	H9	42
Gemlik, Tur.	I13	16
Gemona del Friuli, Italy	C8	14
Genale (Juba), stm., Afr.	G3	46
General Alvear, Arg.	C3	56
General Bravo, Mex.	E10	62
General Carneiro, Braz.	C2	57
General Levalle, Arg.	C4	56
General Pico, Arg.	D4	56
General Pinedo, Arg.	B4	56
General Roca, Arg.	D3	56
General Villegas, Arg.	D4	56
Genesee, Id., U.S.	C2	89
Genesee, co., Mi., U.S.	E7	99
Genesee, co., N.Y., U.S.	B2	109
Genesee, stm., N.Y., U.S.	C2	109
Geneseo, Il., U.S.	B3	90
Geneseo, N.Y., U.S.	C3	109
Geneva, Al., U.S.	D4	78
Geneva, Il., U.S.	B5	90
Geneva, In., U.S.	C8	91
Geneva, Ne., U.S.	D8	104
Geneva, N.Y., U.S.	C4	109
Geneva, Oh., U.S.	A5	112
Geneva, co., Al., U.S.	D4	78
Geneva, Lake, l., Eur.	F13	10
Geneva, Lake, l., Wi., U.S.	F5	126
Geneva see Genève, Switz.	F13	10
Geneva-on-the-Lake, Oh., U.S.	A5	112
Genève, Switz.	F13	10
Genk, Bel.	E5	8
Genkai-nada, Japan	I3	30
Genoa, Il., U.S.	A5	90
Genoa, Ne., U.S.	C8	104
Genoa, Nv., U.S.	D2	105
Genoa, Oh., U.S.	A2	112
Genoa City, Wi., U.S.	F5	126
Genoa see Genova, Italy	E3	14
Genola, Ut., U.S.	D4	121
Genova (Genoa), Italy	E3	14
Genova, Golfo di, b., Italy	E3	14
Gent (Gand), Bel.	D3	8
Genteng, Indon.	n17	33a
Genthin, Ger.	C12	8
Gentry, Ar., U.S.	A1	81
Gentry, co., Mo., U.S.	A3	102
Geographe Bay, b., Austl.	F3	50
George, S. Afr.	H4	44
George, Ia., U.S.	A2	92
George, co., Ms., U.S.	E5	101
George, stm., Que., Can.	g13	74
George, Cape, c., N.S., Can.	D8	71
George, Lake, l., Ug.	B6	44
George, Lake, l., N.Y., U.S.	B7	109
George Air Force Base, mil., Ca., U.S.	E5	82

Name	Map Ref	Page
George B. Stevenson Reservoir, res., Pa., U.S.	D6	115
George Peak, mtn., Ut., U.S.	B2	121
Georgetown, P.E.I., Can.	C7	71
Georgetown, Cay. Is.	E7	64
Georgetown, Gam.	F3	42
Georgetown, Guy.	D13	58
George Town (Pinang), Malay.	L6	34
Georgetown, Ca., U.S.	C3	82
Georgetown, Co., U.S.	B5	83
Georgetown, Ct., U.S.	D2	84
Georgetown, De., U.S.	F4	85
Georgetown, Il., U.S.	E1	87
Georgetown, In., U.S.	D6	90
Georgetown, Ky., U.S.	H6	91
Georgetown, Ma., U.S.	B5	94
Georgetown, Oh., U.S.	A6	98
Georgetown, S.C., U.S.	D2	112
Georgetown, Tx., U.S.	E9	117
Georgetown, co., S.C., U.S.	D4	120
George Washington Birthplace National Monument, Va., U.S.	E9 / B6	117 / 123
George Washington Carver National Monument, Mo., U.S.	E3	102
George West, Tx., U.S.	E3	120
Georgia, ctry., Asia	I6	22
Georgia, state, U.S.	D3	87
Georgia, Strait of, strt., N.A.	B2	76
Georgiana, Al., U.S.	D3	78
Georgian Bay, b., Ont., Can.	B3	73
Georgina, stm., Austl.	D7	50
Gera, Ger.	E12	8
Gerald, Mo., U.S.	C6	102
Geraldine, Al., U.S.	A4	78
Geral do Paraná, Serra, hills, Braz.	C5	57
Geraldton, Austl.	E2	50
Geraldton, Ont., Can.	o18	73
Gérardmer, Fr.	D13	10
Gerber Reservoir, res., Or., U.S.	E5	114
Gerdine, Mount, mtn., Ak., U.S.	C9	79
Gereshk, Afg.	E1	38
Gérgal, Spain	H9	12
Gering, Ne., U.S.	C2	104
Gerlach, Nv., U.S.	C2	105
Germantown, Il., U.S.	E4	90
Germantown, Md., U.S.	B3	97
Germantown, Oh., U.S.	C1	112
Germantown, Tn., U.S.	B2	119
Germantown, Wi., U.S.	E5	126
Germany, ctry., Eur.	E10	4
Germiston, S. Afr.	G5	44
Gerona, Spain	D14	12
Geronimo, Ok., U.S.	C3	113
Gervais, Or., U.S.	B4	114
Geseke, Ger.	D8	8
Getafe, Spain	E8	12
Gettysburg, Pa., U.S.	G7	115
Gettysburg, S.D., U.S.	C6	118
Ghāghra, stm., Asia	G10	38
Ghana, ctry., Afr.	G5	42
Ghanzi, Bots.	F4	44
Gharbīyah, Aş-Şahrā' al- (Western Desert), des., Egypt	C11	42
Ghardaïa, Alg.	B6	42
Gharyān, Libya	B8	42
Ghāt, Libya	D8	42
Ghawdex, i., Malta	M9	14
Ghazāl, Bahr al-, stm., Sudan	G12	42
Ghāziābād, India	F7	38
Ghāzīpur, India	H10	38
Ghaznī, Afg.	D3	38
Ghazzah (Gaza), Isr. Occ.	D4	40
Ghedi, Italy	D5	14
Gheen, Mn., U.S.	C6	100
Ghent see Gent, Bel.	D3	8
Gheorghe Gheorghiu-Dej, Rom.	C10	16
Ghīn, Tall, mtn., Syria	C5	40
Ghudāmis, Libya	B7	42
Giants Neck, Ct., U.S.	D7	84
Gibbon, Mn., U.S.	F4	100
Gibbon, Ne., U.S.	D7	104
Gibbons, Alta., Can.	C4	68
Gibbstown, N.J., U.S.	D2	107
Gibeon, Nmb.	G3	44
Gibraltar, Gib.	I6	4
Gibraltar, dep., Eur.	H6	4
Gibraltar, Strait of (Estrecho de Gibraltar), strt.	J6	12
Gibraltar Point, c., Eng., U.K.	H13	7
Gibsland, La., U.S.	B2	95
Gibson, Ga., U.S.	C4	87
Gibson, co., In., U.S.	H2	91
Gibson, co., Tn., U.S.	A3	119
Gibson, Oh., U.S.	A2	112
Gibson City, Il., U.S.	C5	90
Gibson Desert, des., Austl.	D4	50
Gibsonia, Pa., U.S.	h14	115
Gibson Island, i., Md., U.S.	B5	97
Gibsons, B.C., Can.	E6	69
Gibsonton, Fl., U.S.	p11	86
Gibsonville, N.C., U.S.	A3	110
Giddings, Tx., U.S.	D4	120
Gideon, Mo., U.S.	E8	102
Gien, Fr.	E9	10
Giessen, Ger.	E8	8
Gifford, Fl., U.S.	E6	86
Gifford, Il., U.S.	C5	90
Gifu, Japan	G9	30
Gig Harbor, Wa., U.S.	B3	124
Gihon, stm., Vt., U.S.	B3	122
Gijón, Spain	B6	12
Gila, co., Az., U.S.	D5	80
Gila, stm., U.S.	E3	80
Gila Bend, Az., U.S.	E3	80
Gila Bend Indian Reservation, Az., U.S.	D3	80
Gila Bend Mountains, mts., Az., U.S.	D2	80
Gila Cliff Dwellings National Monument, N.M., U.S.	D1	108
Gila Mountains, mts., Az., U.S.	D6	80
Gila Peak, mtn., Az., U.S.	D6	80
Gila River Indian Reservation, Az., U.S.	D4	80
Gilbert, Az., U.S.	D4	80
Gilbert, Ia., U.S.	B4	92
Gilbert, La., U.S.	B4	95
Gilbert, Mn., U.S.	C6	100
Gilbert Islands see Kiribati, ctry., Oc.	G24	2
Gilbert Peak, mtn., Wa., U.S.	C4	124
Gilbert Plains, Man., Can.	D1	70
Gilbertsville, Ky., U.S.	f9	94
Gilbertsville, Pa., U.S.	F10	115
Gilbertville, Ia., U.S.	B5	92
Gilchrist, Or., U.S.	D5	114
Gilchrist, co., Fl., U.S.	C4	86
Gilcrest, Co., U.S.	A6	83
Giles, co., Tn., U.S.	B4	119
Giles, co., Va., U.S.	C2	123
Gilford Island, i., B.C., Can.	D4	69
Gilgit, Pak.	C6	38
Gillam, Man., Can.	A4	70
Gillespie, Il., U.S.	D4	90
Gillespie, co., Tx., U.S.	D3	120
Gillespie Dam, Az., U.S.	D3	80
Gillett, Ar., U.S.	C4	81
Gillett, Wi., U.S.	D5	126
Gillette, Wy., U.S.	B7	127
Gilliam, co., Or., U.S.	B6	114
Gilman, Il., U.S.	C5	90
Gilman, Vt., U.S.	C5	122
Gilmanton, N.H., U.S.	D4	106
Gilmer, Tx., U.S.	C5	120
Gilmer, co., Ga., U.S.	B2	87
Gilmer, co., W.V., U.S.	C4	125
Gilo, stm., Eth.	G1	46
Gilpin, co., Co., U.S.	B5	83
Gilroy, Ca., U.S.	D3	82
Gil'uj, stm., Russia	G19	24
Giluwe, Mount, mtn., Pap. N. Gui.	m15	50a
Gimli, Man., Can.	D3	70
Ginosa, Italy	I11	14
Ginowan, Japan	y27	31b
Gioia del Colle, Italy	I11	14
Gioia Tauro, Italy	K10	14
Girard, Il., U.S.	D4	90
Girard, Ks., U.S.	E9	93
Girard, Oh., U.S.	A5	112
Girard, Pa., U.S.	B1	115
Girardot, Col.	E5	58
Girardville, Pa., U.S.	E9	115
Giresun, Tur.	G15	4
Giridih, India	H12	38
Girifalco, Italy	K11	14
Girne, N. Cyp.	B3	40
Girwa, stm., Asia	F9	38
Gisborne, N.Z.	C7	52
Gisenyi, Rw.	B5	44
Gisors, Fr.	C8	10
Giugliano [in Campania], Italy	I9	14
Giulianova, Italy	G8	14
Giurgiu, Rom.	F9	16
Givet, Fr.	B11	10
Givors, Fr.	G11	10
Giyon, Eth.	G2	46
Giza see Al-Jīzah, Egypt	B12	42
Gižiga, Russia	E26	24
Gižiginskaja Guba, b., Russia	E25	24
Gjandža, Azer.	I7	22
Gjoa Haven, N.W. Ter., Can.	C13	66
Gjirokastër, Alb.	I4	16
Glacier, co., Mt., U.S.	B3	103
Glacier Bay, b., Ak., U.S.	k21	79
Glacier Bay National Park, Ak., U.S.	D12	79
Glacier National Park, B.C., Can.	D9	69
Glacier National Park, Mt., U.S.	B2	103
Glacier Peak, mtn., Wa., U.S.	A4	124
Gladbrook, Ia., U.S.	B5	92
Glade Creek, stm., Wa., U.S.	C6	124
Glade Creek, stm., W.V., U.S.	n14	125
Glade Creek, stm., W.V., U.S.	n13	125
Glades, co., Fl., U.S.	F5	86
Glade Spring, Va., U.S.	f10	123
Gladewater, Tx., U.S.	C5	120
Gladstone, Austl.	D10	50
Gladstone, Man., Can.	D2	70
Gladstone, Mi., U.S.	C4	99
Gladstone, Mo., U.S.	h10	102
Gladstone, Or., U.S.	B4	114
Gladwin, Mi., U.S.	E6	99
Gladwin, co., Mi., U.S.	D6	99
Gláma, stm., Nor.	F8	6
Glarner Alpen, mts., Switz.	F15	10
Glarus, Switz.	E16	10
Glascock, co., Ga., U.S.	C4	87
Glasford, Il., U.S.	C4	90
Glasgow, Scot., U.K.	F8	7
Glasgow, Ky., U.S.	C4	94
Glasgow, Mo., U.S.	B5	102
Glasgow, Mt., U.S.	B10	103
Glasgow, Va., U.S.	C3	123
Glasgow, W.V., U.S.	m13	125
Glassboro, N.J., U.S.	D2	107
Glasscock, co., Tx., U.S.	D2	120
Glassport, Pa., U.S.	F2	115
Glastonbury, Ct., U.S.	C5	84
Glauchau, Ger.	E12	8
Glazier Lake, l., Me., U.S.	A3	96
Glazov, Russia	F8	22
Gleason, Tn., U.S.	A3	119
Gleisdorf, Aus.	H15	8
Glen Allan, Ms., U.S.	B2	101
Glen Allen, Va., U.S.	C5	123
Glenboro, Man., Can.	E2	70
Glenbrook, Nv., U.S.	D2	105
Glen Burnie, Md., U.S.	B4	97
Glen Canyon Dam, Az., U.S.	A4	80
Glen Canyon National Recreation Area, U.S.	F5	121
Glencoe, Ont., Can.	E3	73
Glencoe, Al., U.S.	B4	78
Glencoe, Il., U.S.	A6	90
Glencoe, Mn., U.S.	F4	100
Glen Cove, N.Y., U.S.	h13	109
Glendale, Az., U.S.	D3	80
Glendale, Ca., U.S.	m12	82
Glendale, Ms., U.S.	D4	101
Glendale, Oh., U.S.	C1	112
Glendale, Or., U.S.	E3	114
Glendale, R.I., U.S.	B2	116
Glendale, S.C., U.S.	B4	117
Glen Dale, W.V., U.S.	B4	125
Glendale, Wi., U.S.	m12	126
Glendale Heights, W.V., U.S.	g8	125
Glendive, Mt., U.S.	C12	103
Glendo, Wy., U.S.	D7	127
Glendo Reservoir, res., Wy., U.S.	D8	127
Glenelg, Md., U.S.	B4	97
Glen Ellis Falls, wtfl, N.H., U.S.	B4	106
Glen Ellyn, Il., U.S.	k8	90
Glenham, W.V., U.S.	D7	109
Glen Innes, Austl.	E10	50
Glen Jean, W.V., U.S.	D3	125
Glen Lake, l., Mi., U.S.	D5	99
Glen Lyon, Pa., U.S.	D9	115
Glenmora, La., U.S.	D3	95
Glenn, co., Ca., U.S.	C2	82
Glennallen, Ak., U.S.	f19	79
Glenns Ferry, Id., U.S.	G3	89
Glennville, Ga., U.S.	E5	87
Glenolden, Pa., U.S.	p20	115
Glenpool, Ok., U.S.	B5	113
Glen Raven, N.C., U.S.	A3	110
Glen Ridge, N.J., U.S.	h8	107
Glen Rock, N.J., U.S.	h8	107
Glen Rock, Pa., U.S.	G8	115
Glenrock, Wy., U.S.	D7	127
Glen Rose, Tx., U.S.	C4	120
Glens Falls, N.Y., U.S.	B7	109
Glen Ullin, N.D., U.S.	C4	111
Glenview, Il., U.S.	h9	90
Glenview Naval Air Station, mil., Il., U.S.	h9	90
Glenville, Mn., U.S.	G5	100
Glenville, W.V., U.S.	C4	125
Glenwood, Newf., Can.	D4	72
Glenwood, Ar., U.S.	C2	81
Glenwood, Ga., U.S.	D4	87
Glenwood, Ia., U.S.	C2	92
Glenwood, Mn., U.S.	E3	100
Glenwood, Va., U.S.	D3	123
Glenwood City, Wi., U.S.	C1	126
Glenwood Springs, Co., U.S.	B3	83
Glidden, Ia., U.S.	B3	92
Glide, Or., U.S.	D3	114
Glina, Cro.	D11	14
Glittertinden, mtn., Nor.	F7	6
Gliwice (Gleiwitz), Pol.	E18	8
Globe, Az., U.S.	D5	80
Gloggnitz, Aus.	H15	8
Gloster, Ms., U.S.	D2	101
Gloucester, Ont., Can.	h12	73
Gloucester, Eng., U.K.	J10	7
Gloucester, Ma., U.S.	A6	98
Gloucester, Va., U.S.	C6	123
Gloucester, co., N.J., U.S.	D2	107
Gloucester, co., Va., U.S.	C6	123
Gloucester City, N.J., U.S.	D2	107
Gloucester Point, Va., U.S.	C6	123
Glouster, Oh., U.S.	C3	112
Glover Island, i., Newf., Can.	D3	72
Gloversville, N.Y., U.S.	B6	109
Glovertown, Newf., Can.	D4	72
Gloverville, S.C., U.S.	E4	117
Gluck, S.C., U.S.	C2	117
Glücksburg, Ger.	A9	8
Glückstadt, Ger.	B9	8
Glyndon, Md., U.S.	B4	97
Glyndon, Mn., U.S.	D2	100
Glynn, co., Ga., U.S.	E5	87
Gmünd, Aus.	G14	8
Gmunden, Aus.	H13	8
Gnadenhutten, Oh., U.S.	B4	112
Gnarp, Swe.	E11	6
Gniezno, Pol.	C17	8
Gnjilane, Yugo.	G5	16
Gō, stm., Japan	H5	30
Goa, ter., India	E2	37
Goat Island, i., R.I., U.S.	F5	116
Goat Mountain, mtn., Mt., U.S.	C3	103
Goat Rock Dam, U.S.	C4	78
Goba, Eth.	G3	46
Gobabis, Nmb.	F3	44
Gobi, des., Asia	C7	26
Gobles, Mi., U.S.	F5	99
Godāvari, stm., India	D6	37
Goddard, Ks., U.S.	E6	93
Goderich, Ont., Can.	D3	73
Godfrey, Il., U.S.	E3	90
Godhavn, Grnld.	C22	66
Godhra, India	I5	38
Godoy Cruz, Arg.	C3	56
Gods, stm., Man., Can.	A5	70
Gods Lake, l., Man., Can.	B4	70
Godthåb, Grnld.	D22	66
Godwin Austen see K2, mtn., Asia	C7	38
Goéland, Lac au, l., Que., Can.	G17	66
Goélands, Lac aux, l., Que., Can.	E20	66
Goff Creek, stm., Ok., U.S.	e9	113
Goffstown, N.H., U.S.	D3	106
Gogebic, co., Mi., U.S.	n12	99
Gogebic, Lake, l., Mi., U.S.	m12	99
Goiana, Braz.	D4	57
Goiânia, Braz.	C3	57
Goiás, Braz.	C3	57
Gojra, Pak.	E5	38
Gokāk, India	D3	37
Gökçeada, i., Tur.	I9	16
Gol'čicha, Russia	C10	24
Golconda, Il., U.S.	F5	90
Golconda, Nv., U.S.	C4	105
Gold Bar, Wa., U.S.	B4	124
Gold Beach, Or., U.S.	E2	114
Golden, B.C., Can.	D9	69
Golden, Co., U.S.	B5	83
Golden City, Mo., U.S.	D3	102
Goldendale, Wa., U.S.	D5	124
Golden Gate Bridge, Ca., U.S.	h7	82
Golden Gate National Recreation Area, U.S.	h7	82
Golden Hinde, mtn., B.C., Can.	E5	69
Golden Meadow, La., U.S.	E5	95
Golden Spike National Historic Site, hist., Ut., U.S.	B3	121
Golden Valley, Mn., U.S.	n12	100
Golden Valley, co., Mt., U.S.	D7	103
Golden Valley, co., N.D., U.S.	B2	111
Goldfield, Ia., U.S.	B4	92
Goldfield, Nv., U.S.	F4	105
Gold Hill, Or., U.S.	E3	114
Goldsboro, N.C., U.S.	B5	110
Goldsby, Ok., U.S.	B4	113
Goldthwaite, Tx., U.S.	D3	120
Golf Manor, Oh., U.S.	o13	112
Goliad, Tx., U.S.	E4	120
Goliad, co., Tx., U.S.	E4	120
Golspie, Scot., U.K.	D9	7
Gomati, stm., India	G9	38
Gombe, stm., Tan.	B6	44
Gomel', Bela.	I14	18
Gomera, i., Spain	C2	42
Gómez Palacio, Mex.	E8	62
Gonābād, Iran	K9	22
Gonaïves, Haiti	E11	64
Gonam, Russia	F20	24
Gonam, stm., Russia	F28	24
Gonâve, Golfe de la, b., Haiti	E11	64
Gonâve, Île de la, i., Haiti	E11	64
Gonda, India	G9	38
Gondal, India	J4	38
Gonder, Eth.	F2	46
Gondia, India	B6	37
Gondomar, Port.	D3	12
Gönen, Tur.	I11	16
Gônoura, Japan	I2	30
Gonzales, Ca., U.S.	D3	82
Gonzales, La., U.S.	D5	95
Gonzales, Tx., U.S.	E4	120
Gonzales, co., Tx., U.S.	E4	120
Gonzalez, Fl., U.S.	u14	86
Goochland, co., Va., U.S.	C5	123
Goode, Mount, mtn., Ak., U.S.	g18	79
Goodfellow Air Force Base, mil., Tx., U.S.	D2	120
Good Hope, Cape of, c., S. Afr.	H3	44
Good Hope Mountain, mtn., B.C., Can.	D5	69
Goodhue, co., Mn., U.S.	F6	100
Gooding, Id., U.S.	G4	89
Gooding, co., Id., U.S.	F4	89
Goodland, In., U.S.	C3	91
Goodland, Ks., U.S.	C2	93
Goodlettsville, Tn., U.S.	g10	119
Goodman, Ms., U.S.	C4	101
Goodman, Mo., U.S.	E3	102
Good Pine, La., U.S.	C3	95
Goodsprings, Nv., U.S.	H6	105
Goodview, Mn., U.S.	F7	100
Goodwater, Al., U.S.	B3	78
Goodwell, Ok., U.S.	e9	113
Goodyear, Az., U.S.	D3	80
Goole, Eng., U.K.	H12	7
Goondiwindi, Austl.	E10	50
Goose, stm., N.D., U.S.	B8	111
Goose Bay, b., Newf., Can.	B1	72
Gooseberry Creek, stm., Wy., U.S.	B4	127
Goose Creek, S.C., U.S.	F7	117
Goose Creek, stm., U.S.	G5	89
Goose Creek, stm., U.S.	C3	123
Goose Creek Reservoir, res., S.C., U.S.	k11	117
Goose Lake, l., U.S.	B3	82
Goose Pond, l., N.H., U.S.	C2	106
Göppingen, Ger.	G9	8
Gorakhpur, India	G10	38
Gorda, Punta, c., Cuba	C6	64
Gordil, Cen. Afr. Rep.	G10	42
Gordo, Al., U.S.	B2	78
Gordon, Ga., U.S.	D3	87
Gordon, Ne., U.S.	B3	104
Gordon, co., Ga., U.S.	B2	87
Gordonsville, Tn., U.S.	C8	119
Gordonsville, Va., U.S.	B4	123
Gore, Eth.	G2	46
Gore, N.Z.	G2	52
Gore, Ok., U.S.	B6	113
Gore Bay, Ont., Can.	B2	73
Gore Point, c., Ak., U.S.	h16	79
Gore Range, mts., Co., U.S.	B4	83
Goreville, Il., U.S.	F5	90
Gorey, Ire.	I6	7
Gorgān, Iran	J8	22
Gorham, Me., U.S.	E2	96
Gorham, N.H., U.S.	B4	106
Gorinchem, Neth.	D4	8
Gorizia, Italy	D8	14
Gorki, Bela.	G13	18
Gorki see Nižnij Novgorod, Russia	E27	18
Görlitz, Ger.	B13	8
Gorlovka, Ukr.	H5	22
Gorman, Tx., U.S.	C3	120
Gornja Radgona, Slo.	C10	14
Gorno-Altajsk, Russia	G11	24
Gorodec, Russia	E26	18
Gorontalo, Indon.	E7	32
Gort, Ire.	H4	7
Gorzów Wielkopolski (Landsberg an der Warthe), Pol.	C15	8
Goshen, In., U.S.	A6	91
Goshen, N.Y., U.S.	D6	109
Goshen, Oh., U.S.	C1	112
Goshen, co., Wy., U.S.	D8	127
Goshute Indian Reservation, U.S.	D7	105
Goshute Lake, l., Nv., U.S.	C7	105
Goshute Mountains, mts., Nv., U.S.	C7	105
Goslar, Ger.	D10	8
Gosper, co., Ne., U.S.	D6	104
Gosport, In., U.S.	F4	91
Göteborg (Gothenburg), Swe.	H8	6
Gotemba, Japan	G11	30
Gotha, Ger.	E10	8
Gothenburg see Göteborg, Swe.	H8	6
Gothenburg, Ne., U.S.	D5	104
Gotland, i., Swe.	H12	6
Gotō-rettō, is., Japan	J1	30
Göttingen, Ger.	D9	8
Gouda, Neth.	C4	8
Gouin, Réservoir, res., Que., Can.	k12	74
Goulburn, Austl.	F9	50
Goulburn Islands, is., Austl.	B6	50
Gould, Ar., U.S.	D4	81
Goulding, Fl., U.S.	u14	86
Gould Island, i., R.I., U.S.	E5	116
Goulds, Fl., U.S.	s13	86
Gourdon, Fr.	H8	10
Gouré, Niger	F8	42
Gourin, Fr.	D3	10
Gournay-en-Bray, Fr.	C8	10
Gouverneur, N.Y., U.S.	f9	109
Gove, co., Ks., U.S.	D3	93
Governador Valadares, Braz.	E8	57
Governors Harbour, Bah.	B9	64
Govind Balabh Pant Sāgar, res., India	H10	38
Govind Sāgar, res., India	E7	38
Gowanda, N.Y., U.S.	C2	109
Gower, Mo., U.S.	B3	102
Gowmal (Gumal), stm., Asia	D3	38
Gowmal Kalay, Afg.	D3	38
Gowrie, Ia., U.S.	B3	92
Goya, Arg.	B5	56
Gozo see Ghawdex, i., Malta	M9	14
Graaff-Reinet, S. Afr.	H4	44
Grabill, In., U.S.	B8	91
Grace, Id., U.S.	G7	89
Graceville, Fl., U.S.	u16	86
Graceville, Mn., U.S.	E2	100
Gracewood, Ga., U.S.	C4	87
Gracias a Dios, Cabo, c., N.A.	G6	64
Gradaús, Braz.	E8	54
Gradaús, Serra dos, plat., Braz.	E8	54
Grado, Italy	D8	14
Grady, co., Ga., U.S.	F2	87
Grady, co., Ok., U.S.	C4	113
Graettinger, Ia., U.S.	A3	92
Grafton, Austl.	E10	50
Grafton, Il., U.S.	E3	90
Grafton, Ma., U.S.	B4	98
Grafton, N.D., U.S.	A8	111
Grafton, Oh., U.S.	A3	112
Grafton, Va., U.S.	h15	123
Grafton, W.V., U.S.	B4	125
Grafton, Wi., U.S.	E6	126
Grafton, co., N.H., U.S.	C3	106
Grafton, Cape, c., Austl.	C9	50
Graham, N.C., U.S.	A3	110
Graham, Tx., U.S.	C3	120
Graham, co., Az., U.S.	E5	80
Graham, co., Ks., U.S.	C4	93
Graham, co., N.C., U.S.	f9	110
Graham, Lake, res., Tx., U.S.	C3	120
Graham, Mount, mtn., Az., U.S.	E6	80
Graham Island, i., B.C., Can.	C1	69
Graham Lake, l., Me., U.S.	D4	96
Graham Moore, Cape, c., N.W. Ter., Can.	B17	66
Grahamstown, S. Afr.	H5	44
Grahn, Ky., U.S.	B6	94
Grainger, co., Tn., U.S.	C10	119
Grain Valley, Mo., U.S.	B3	102
Grajaú, Braz.	E9	54
Grajaú, stm., Braz.	E9	54
Gramat, Fr.	H8	10
Grambling, La., U.S.	B3	95
Gramercy, La., U.S.	h10	95
Grammichele, Italy	L9	14
Grampian Mountains, mts., Scot., U.K.	E8	7
Granada, Col.	F6	58
Granada, Nic.	I5	64
Granada, Spain	H8	12
Granard, Ire.	H5	7
Granby, Que., Can.	D5	74
Granby, Co., U.S.	A5	83
Granby, Ct., U.S.	B4	84
Granby, Mo., U.S.	E3	102
Granby, Lake, res., Co., U.S.	A5	83
Gran Canaria, i., Spain	C2	42
Gran Chaco, pl., S.A.	A4	56
Grand, co., Co., U.S.	A4	83
Grand, co., Ut., U.S.	E6	121
Grand, stm., Ont., Can.	D4	73
Grand, stm., U.S.	E5	99
Grand, stm., Mo., U.S.	A4	102
Grand, stm., Oh., U.S.	A4	112
Grand, stm., S.D., U.S.	B4	118
Grandas, Spain	B5	12
Grand Bahama, i., Bah.	A8	64
Grand Bank, Newf., Can.	E4	72
Grand-Bassam, I.C.	G5	42
Grand Bay, N.B., Can.	D3	71
Grand Bay, Al., U.S.	E1	78
Grand Bend, Ont., Can.	D3	73
Grand Blanc, Mi., U.S.	F7	99
Grand Caillou, La., U.S.	E5	95
Grand Canal, Ire.	H5	7
Grand Canal see Da Yunhe, China	E10	26
Grand Canyon, Az., U.S.	A3	80
Grand Canyon, val., Az., U.S.	A3	80
Grand Canyon National Park, Az., U.S.	B3	80
Grand Cayman, i., Cay. Is.	E7	64
Grand Centre, Alta., Can.	B5	68
Grand Coteau, La., U.S.	D3	95
Grand Coulee, Wa., U.S.	B6	124
Grand Coulee Dam, Wa., U.S.	B6	124
Grande, stm., Bol.	G6	54
Grande, stm., Braz.	E3	57
Grande, Bahía, b., Arg.	G3	56
Grande, Boca, mth., Ven.	C12	58
Grande, Ilha, i., Braz.	G1	57
Grande, Rio (Bravo del Norte), stm., U.S.	F7	76
Grande-Anse, N.B., Can.	B4	71
Grande Cache, Alta., Can.	C1	68
Grande Comore, i., Com.	D8	44
Grande de Matagalpa, stm., Nic.	H5	64
Grande de Santiago, Río, stm., Mex.	G7	62
Grande do Gurupá, Ilha, i., Braz.	D8	54
Grande-Entrée, Que., Can.	B8	71
Grande Prairie, Alta., Can.	B1	68
Grand Erg de Bilma, des., Niger	E8	42
Grand Erg Occidental, des., Alg.	B6	42
Grand Erg Oriental, des., Alg.	B7	42
Grande rivière de la Baleine, stm., Que., Can.	g11	74

Index

Name	Map Ref	Page
Grande Ronde, stm., U.S.	C8	124
Grandes, Salinas, pl., Arg.	B4	56
Grandes-Bergeronnes, Que., Can.	A8	74
Grande-Terre, i., Guad.	F17	64
Grand Falls (Grand-Sault), N.B., Can.	B2	71
Grand Falls, Newf., Can.	D4	72
Grand Falls, wtfl, Me., U.S.	C5	96
Grandfather Mountain, mtn., N.C., U.S.	A1	110
Grandfield, Ok., U.S.	C3	113
Grand Forks, B.C., Can.	E8	69
Grand Forks, N.D., U.S.	B8	111
Grand Forks, co., N.D., U.S.	B8	111
Grand Forks Air Force Base, mil., N.D., U.S.	B8	111
Grand-Fougeray, Fr.	E5	10
Grand Harbour, N.B., Can.	E3	71
Grand Haven, Mi., U.S.	E4	99
Grand Island, Ne., U.S.	D7	104
Grand Island, i., La., U.S.	D6	95
Grand Island, i., Mi., U.S.	B4	99
Grand Isle, La., U.S.	E6	95
Grand Isle, co., Vt., U.S.	B2	122
Grand Isle, i., La., U.S.	E6	95
Grand Junction, Co., U.S.	B2	83
Grand Junction, Ia., U.S.	B3	92
Grand Lake, l., N.B., Can.	D3	71
Grand Lake, l., Newf., Can.	D3	72
Grand Lake, l., La., U.S.	E3	95
Grand Lake, l., La., U.S.	E6	95
Grand Lake, l., Mi., U.S.	C7	99
Grand Lake, l., Oh., U.S.	B1	112
Grand Lake Matagamon, l., Me., U.S.	B4	96
Grand Lake Seboeis, l., Me., U.S.	B4	96
Grand Ledge, Mi., U.S.	F6	99
Grand Manan Island, i., N.B., Can.	E3	71
Grand Marais, Mn., U.S.	k9	100
Grand Meadow, Mn., U.S.	G6	100
Grand-Mère, Que., Can.	C5	74
Grand Mound, Ia., U.S.	C7	92
Grand Portage Indian Reservation, Mn., U.S.	k10	100
Grand Portage National Monument, Mn., U.S.	h10	100
Grand Prairie, Tx., U.S.	n10	120
Grand Rapids, Mi., U.S.	F5	99
Grand Rapids, Mn., U.S.	C5	100
Grand Rapids, Oh., U.S.	f6	112
Grand Rivière de la Baleine, stm., Que., Can.	E17	66
Grand-Saint-Bernard, Tunnel du, Eur.	G14	10
Grand Saline, Tx., U.S.	C5	120
Grand Terre Islands, is., La., U.S.	E6	95
Grand Teton, mtn., Wy., U.S.	C2	127
Grand Teton National Park, Wy., U.S.	C2	127
Grand Tower, Il., U.S.	F4	90
Grand Traverse, co., Mi., U.S.	D5	99
Grand Traverse Bay, b., Mi., U.S.	C5	99
Grand Turk, T./C. Is.	D12	64
Grand Valley, Ont., Can.	D4	73
Grandview, Man., Can.	D1	70
Grandview, In., U.S.	I4	91
Grandview, Mo., U.S.	C3	102
Grandview, Wa., U.S.	C6	124
Grandview Heights, Oh., U.S.	m10	112
Grandville, Mi., U.S.	F5	99
Grandy, N.C., U.S.	A7	110
Granger, In., U.S.	A5	91
Granger, Ia., U.S.	C4	92
Granger, Tx., U.S.	D4	120
Granger, Wa., U.S.	C5	124
Grangeville, Id., U.S.	D2	89
Granisle, B.C., Can.	B4	69
Granite, Ok., U.S.	C2	113
Granite, co., Mt., U.S.	D3	103
Granite City, Il., U.S.	E3	90
Granite Falls, Mn., U.S.	F3	100
Granite Falls, N.C., U.S.	B1	110
Granite Falls, Wa., U.S.	A4	124
Granite Lake, res., Newf., Can.	D3	72
Granite Mountain, mtn., Ak., U.S.	B7	79
Granite Mountains, mts., Az., U.S.	E2	80
Granite Mountains, mts., Wy., U.S.	D5	127
Granite Pass, Wy., U.S.	B5	127
Granite Peak, mtn., Mt., U.S.	E7	103
Granite Peak, mtn., Nv., U.S.	B4	105
Granite Peak, mtn., Nv., U.S.	C2	105
Granite Peak, mtn., Ut., U.S.	C2	121
Granite Peak, mtn., Ut., U.S.	E3	121
Granite Peak, mtn., Wy., U.S.	C2	127
Granite Quarry, N.C., U.S.	B2	110
Granite Range, mts., Nv., U.S.	C2	105
Graniteville, S.C., U.S.	D4	117
Graniteville, Vt., U.S.	C4	122
Granollers, Spain	D14	12
Grant, Al., U.S.	A3	78
Grant, Mi., U.S.	E5	99
Grant, Ne., U.S.	D4	104
Grant, co., Ar., U.S.	C3	81
Grant, co., In., U.S.	D6	91
Grant, co., Ks., U.S.	E2	93
Grant, co., Ky., U.S.	B5	94
Grant, co., La., U.S.	C3	95
Grant, co., Mn., U.S.	E2	100
Grant, co., Ne., U.S.	C4	104
Grant, co., N.M., U.S.	E1	108
Grant, co., N.D., U.S.	C4	111
Grant, co., Ok., U.S.	A4	113
Grant, co., Or., U.S.	C7	114
Grant, co., S.D., U.S.	B9	118
Grant, co., Wa., U.S.	B6	124
Grant, co., W.V., U.S.	B5	125
Grant, co., Wi., U.S.	F3	126
Grant, Mount, mtn., Nv., U.S.	E3	105
Grant City, Mo., U.S.	A3	102
Grantham, Eng., U.K.	I12	7
Grant Park, Il., U.S.	B6	90
Grant Range, mts., Nv., U.S.	E6	105
Grants, N.M., U.S.	B2	108
Grantsburg, Wi., U.S.	C1	126
Grants Pass, Or., U.S.	E3	114
Grantsville, Ut., U.S.	C3	121
Grantsville, W.V., U.S.	C3	125
Grant Town, W.V., U.S.	B4	125
Grantville, Ga., U.S.	C2	87
Granville, Fr.	D5	10
Granville, Il., U.S.	B4	90
Granville, N.Y., U.S.	B7	109
Granville, Oh., U.S.	B3	112
Granville, W.V., U.S.	h11	125
Granville, co., N.C., U.S.	A4	110
Granville Lake, l., Man., Can.	C1	70
Granvin, Nor.	F6	6
Grapeland, Tx., U.S.	D5	120
Grapeview, Wa., U.S.	B3	124
Grapevine, Tx., U.S.	C4	120
Grapevine Lake, res., Tx., U.S.	n9	120
Grapevine Peak, mtn., Nv., U.S.	G4	105
Gras, Lac de l., N.W. Ter., Can.	D10	66
Grasonville, Md., U.S.	C5	97
Grass, stm., Man., Can.	B2	70
Grass, stm., N.Y., U.S.	f9	109
Grasse, Fr.	I13	10
Grass Lake, Il., U.S.	h8	90
Grass Lake, Mi., U.S.	F6	99
Grass Lake, l., Il., U.S.	h8	90
Grass Valley, Ca., U.S.	C3	82
Grassy Brook, stm., Vt., U.S.	E3	122
Grassy Lake, l., La., U.S.	k9	95
Grates Point, c., Newf., Can.	D5	72
Gratiot, co., Mi., U.S.	E6	99
Gratis, Oh., U.S.	C1	112
Grave Creek, stm., W.V., U.S.	g8	125
Gravelly Branch, stm., De., U.S.	F4	85
Gravelly Range, mts., Mt., U.S.	E4	103
Gravenhurst, Ont., Can.	C5	73
Grave Peak, mtn., Id., U.S.	C4	89
Graves, co., Ky., U.S.	f9	94
Gravette, Ar., U.S.	A1	81
Gravina in Puglia, Italy	I11	14
Gray, Fr.	E12	10
Gray, Ga., U.S.	C3	87
Gray, Ky., U.S.	D5	94
Gray, La., U.S.	k10	95
Gray, Me., U.S.	g7	96
Gray, co., Ks., U.S.	E3	93
Gray, co., Tx., U.S.	B2	120
Grayback Mountain, mtn., Or., U.S.	E3	114
Gray Court, S.C., U.S.	B3	117
Grayland, Wa., U.S.	C1	124
Grayling, Mi., U.S.	D6	99
Graylyn Crest, De., U.S.	A3	85
Grays Harbor, co., Wa., U.S.	B2	124
Grays Harbor, b., Wa., U.S.	C1	124
Grayslake, Il., U.S.	A5	90
Grays Lake, sw., Id., U.S.	F7	89
Grayson, Ky., U.S.	B7	94
Grayson, co., Ky., U.S.	C3	94
Grayson, co., Tx., U.S.	C4	120
Grayson, co., Va., U.S.	D1	123
Grayson Lake, res., Ky., U.S.	B7	94
Grays Peak, mtn., Co., U.S.	B5	83
Gray Summit, Mo., U.S.	g12	102
Graysville, Al., U.S.	f7	78
Graysville, Tn., U.S.	D8	119
Grayville, Il., U.S.	E5	90
Graz, Aus.	H15	8
Gr'azi, Russia	I22	18
Great Abaco, i., Bah.	A9	64
Great Artesian Basin, Austl.	D8	50
Great Australian Bight, Austl.	F5	50
Great Averill Pond, l., Vt., U.S.	B5	122
Great Barrier Reef, rf., Austl.	C9	50
Great Barrington, Ma., U.S.	B1	98
Great Basin National Park, Nv., U.S.	E7	105
Great Bay, b., N.H., U.S.	D5	106
Great Bay, b., N.J., U.S.	D4	107
Great Bear Lake, l., N.W. Ter., Can.	C9	66
Great Bend, Ks., U.S.	D5	93
Great Captain Island, i., Ct., U.S.	F1	84
Great Channel, strt., Asia	K3	34
Great Dismal Swamp, sw., U.S.	D6	123
Great Divide Basin, Wy., U.S.	E4	127
Great Dividing Range, mts., Austl.	D9	50
Great East Lake, l., U.S.	C5	106
Great Egg Harbor, stm., N.J., U.S.	D3	107
Greater Antilles, is., N.A.	D10	64
Greater Sunda Islands, is., Asia	F4	32
Great Exuma, i., Bah.	C10	64
Great Falls, Mt., U.S.	C5	103
Great Falls, S.C., U.S.	B6	117
Great Falls, wtfl, Md., U.S.	B3	97
Great Falls Dam, Tn., U.S.	B5	119
Great Guana Cay, i., Bah.	B9	64
Great Himalaya Range, mts., Asia	F10	38
Greathouse Peak, mtn., Mt., U.S.	D7	103
Great Inagua, i., Bah.	D11	64
Great Indian Desert (Thar Desert), des., Asia	G4	38
Great Island, spit, Ma., U.S.	C7	98
Great Island, i., N.C., U.S.	B6	110
Great Karroo, plat., S. Afr.	H4	44
Great Lakes Naval Training Center, mil., Il., U.S.	h9	90
Great Miami, stm., U.S.	C1	112
Great Misery Island, i., Ma., U.S.	f12	98
Great Moose Lake, l., Me., U.S.	D3	96
Great Neck, N.Y., U.S.	h13	109
Great Nicobar, i., India	K2	34
Great Pee Dee, stm., U.S.	D9	117
Great Plain of the Koukdjuak, pl., N.W. Ter., Can.	C18	66
Great Plains, c., N.A.	E10	61
Great Point, c., Ma., U.S.	D7	98
Great Ruaha, stm., Tan.	C7	44
Great Sacandaga Lake, l., N.Y., U.S.	C6	109
Great Salt Lake, l., Ut., U.S.	B3	121
Great Salt Lake Desert, des., Ut., U.S.	C2	121
Great Salt Plains Lake, res., Ok., U.S.	A3	113
Great Salt Pond, b., R.I., U.S.	h7	116
Great Sand Dunes National Monument, Co., U.S.	D5	83
Great Sandy Desert, des., Austl.	D4	50
Great Slave Lake, l., N.W. Ter., Can.	D10	66
Great Smoky Mountains, mts., U.S.	B8	119
Great Smoky Mountains National Park, U.S.	B8	119
Great Swamp, sw., R.I., U.S.	F3	116
Great Victoria Desert, des., Austl.	E5	50
Great Village, N.S., Can.	D6	71
Great Wass Island, i., Me., U.S.	D5	96
Great Yarmouth, Eng., U.K.	I14	7
Greece, N.Y., U.S.	B3	109
Greece, ctry., Eur.	H12	4
Greeley, Co., U.S.	A6	83
Greeley, co., Ks., U.S.	D2	93
Greeley, co., Ne., U.S.	C7	104
Greeley Junction, Me., U.S.	C3	96
Green, Or., U.S.	D3	114
Green, co., Ky., U.S.	C4	94
Green, co., Wi., U.S.	F4	126
Green, stm., U.S.	D5	76
Green, stm., U.S.	A1	83
Green, stm., U.S.	F3	122
Green, stm., U.S.	B4	90
Green, stm., Ky., U.S.	C2	94
Green, stm., Wa., U.S.	B3	124
Green Acres, De., U.S.	i8	85
Greenacres, Wa., U.S.	B8	124
Greenacres City, Fl., U.S.	F6	86
Greenback, Tn., U.S.	D9	119
Green Bay, Wi., U.S.	D6	126
Green Bay, b., U.S.	D3	99
Greenbelt, Md., U.S.	C4	97
Greenbriar, Va., U.S.	g12	123
Greenbrier, Ar., U.S.	B3	81
Green Brier, Tn., U.S.	A5	119
Greenbrier, co., W.V., U.S.	D4	125
Greenbrier, stm., W.V., U.S.	D4	125
Greenbush, Mn., U.S.	B2	100
Greencastle, In., U.S.	E4	91
Greencastle, Pa., U.S.	G6	115
Green City, Mo., U.S.	A5	102
Green Cove Springs, Fl., U.S.	C5	86
Greendale, In., U.S.	F8	91
Greendale, Wi., U.S.	F6	126
Greene, Ia., U.S.	B5	92
Greene, N.Y., U.S.	C5	109
Greene, co., Al., U.S.	C1	78
Greene, co., Ar., U.S.	A5	81
Greene, co., Ga., U.S.	C3	87
Greene, co., Il., U.S.	D3	90
Greene, co., In., U.S.	F4	91
Greene, co., Ia., U.S.	B3	92
Greene, co., Ms., U.S.	D5	101
Greene, co., Mo., U.S.	D4	102
Greene, co., N.Y., U.S.	C6	109
Greene, co., N.C., U.S.	B5	110
Greene, co., Oh., U.S.	C2	112
Greene, co., Pa., U.S.	G1	115
Greene, co., Tn., U.S.	C11	119
Greene, co., Va., U.S.	B4	123
Greeneville, Tn., U.S.	C11	119
Green Fall, stm., U.S.	F1	116
Greenfield, Ca., U.S.	D3	82
Greenfield, Il., U.S.	D3	90
Greenfield, In., U.S.	E6	91
Greenfield, Ia., U.S.	C3	92
Greenfield, Ma., U.S.	A2	98
Greenfield, Mo., U.S.	D4	102
Greenfield, N.H., U.S.	E3	106
Greenfield, Oh., U.S.	C2	112
Greenfield, Tn., U.S.	A3	119
Greenfield, Wi., U.S.	n12	126
Greenfield Plaza, Ia., U.S.	e8	92
Green Forest, Ar., U.S.	A2	81
Green Harbor, Ma., U.S.	B6	98
Green Hill Pond, l., R.I., U.S.	G3	116
Greenhills, Oh., U.S.	n12	112
Green Lake, Wi., U.S.	E4	126
Green Lake, co., Wi., U.S.	E4	126
Green Lake, l., Me., U.S.	D4	96
Green Lake, l., Wi., U.S.	E4	126
Greenland, Ar., U.S.	B1	81
Greenland, N.H., U.S.	D5	106
Greenland, dep., N.A.	B16	61
Greenland Sea	B13	128
Greenlee, co., Az., U.S.	D6	80
Green Lookout Mountain, mtn., Wa., U.S.	D3	124
Green Mountain, mtn., Wy., U.S.	D5	127
Green Mountain Reservoir, res., Co., U.S.	B4	83
Green Mountains, mts., Vt., U.S.	F2	122
Greenock, Scot., U.K.	F8	7
Greenock, Pa., U.S.	F2	115
Green Peter Lake, res., Or., U.S.	C4	114
Green Pond, Al., U.S.	B2	78
Green Pond, l., N.J., U.S.	A4	107
Greenport, N.Y., U.S.	m16	109
Green River, Ut., U.S.	E5	121
Green River, Wy., U.S.	E3	127
Green River Lake, res., Ky., U.S.	C4	94
Green River Lock and Dam, U.S.	I2	91
Green River Reservoir, res., Vt., U.S.	B3	122
Green Rock, Il., U.S.	B3	90
Greensboro, Al., U.S.	C2	78
Greensboro, Ga., U.S.	C3	87
Greensboro, Md., U.S.	C6	97
Greensboro, N.C., U.S.	A3	110
Greensburg, In., U.S.	F7	91
Greensburg, Ks., U.S.	E4	93
Greensburg, Ky., U.S.	C4	94
Greensburg, Pa., U.S.	F2	115
Greens Peak, mtn., Az., U.S.	C6	80
Green Springs, Oh., U.S.	A2	112
Greensville, co., Va., U.S.	D5	123
Green Swamp, sw., N.C., U.S.	C4	110
Greentown, In., U.S.	D6	91
Greenup, Il., U.S.	D5	90
Greenup, Ky., U.S.	B7	94
Greenup, co., Ky., U.S.	B7	94
Green Valley, Az., U.S.	F5	80
Greenview, Il., U.S.	C4	90
Greenville, Lib.	G4	42
Greenville, Al., U.S.	D3	78
Greenville, Ca., U.S.	B3	82
Greenville, De., U.S.	A3	85
Greenville, Ga., U.S.	C2	87
Greenville, Il., U.S.	E4	90
Greenville, Ky., U.S.	C2	94
Greenville, Me., U.S.	C3	96
Greenville, Mi., U.S.	E5	99
Greenville, Ms., U.S.	B2	101
Greenville, N.H., U.S.	E3	106
Greenville, N.C., U.S.	B5	110
Greenville, Oh., U.S.	B1	112
Greenville, Pa., U.S.	D1	115
Greenville, R.I., U.S.	C3	116
Greenville, S.C., U.S.	B3	117
Greenville, Tx., U.S.	C4	120
Greenville, co., S.C., U.S.	B3	117
Greenville Creek, stm., Oh., U.S.	B1	112
Greenville Junction, Me., U.S.	C3	96
Greenwich, Ct., U.S.	E1	84
Greenwich, N.Y., U.S.	B7	109
Greenwich, Oh., U.S.	A3	112
Greenwich Bay, b., R.I., U.S.	D4	116
Greenwich Point, c., Ct., U.S.	E1	84
Greenwood, Ar., U.S.	B1	81
Greenwood, B.C., Can.	E8	69
Greenwood, De., U.S.	E3	85
Greenwood, In., U.S.	E5	91
Greenwood, La., U.S.	B2	95
Greenwood, Ms., U.S.	B3	101
Greenwood, Mo., U.S.	k11	102
Greenwood, Pa., U.S.	E5	115
Greenwood, S.C., U.S.	C3	117
Greenwood, Wi., U.S.	D3	126
Greenwood, co., Ks., U.S.	E7	93
Greenwood, co., S.C., U.S.	C3	117
Greenwood, Lake, res., In., U.S.	G4	91
Greenwood, Lake, res., S.C., U.S.	C4	117
Greenwood Lake, N.Y., U.S.	A4	107
Greenwood Lake, l., U.S.	A4	107
Greenwood Lake, l., Mn., U.S.	C7	100
Greer, S.C., U.S.	B3	117
Greer, co., Ok., U.S.	C2	113
Greers Ferry Lake, res., Ar., U.S.	B3	81
Greeson, Lake, res., Ar., U.S.	C2	81
Gregg, co., Tx., U.S.	C5	120
Gregory, S.D., U.S.	D6	118
Gregory, co., S.D., U.S.	D6	118
Greifswald, Ger.	A13	8
Greilickville, Mi., U.S.	D5	99
Greiz, Ger.	E12	8
Grenada, Ms., U.S.	B4	101
Grenada, co., Ms., U.S.	B4	101
Grenada, ctry., N.A.	H17	64
Grenada Lake, res., Ms., U.S.	B4	101
Grenadine Islands, is., N.A.	H17	64
Grenchen, Switz.	E14	10
Grenoble, Fr.	G12	10
Grenville, Que., Can.	D3	74
Grenville, Cape, c., Austl.	B8	50
Grenville, Point, c., Wa., U.S.	B1	124
Gresham, Or., U.S.	B4	114
Gresik, Indon.	m16	33a
Gretna, Man., Can.	E3	70
Gretna, Fl., U.S.	B2	86
Gretna, La., U.S.	E5	95
Gretna, Ne., U.S.	C9	104
Gretna, Va., U.S.	D3	123
Greven, Ger.	C7	8
Grevená, Grc.	I5	16
Grevesmühlen, Ger.	B11	8
Grey, stm., Newf., Can.	E3	72
Greybull, Wy., U.S.	B4	127
Greybull, stm., Wy., U.S.	B4	127
Greylock, Mount, mtn., Ma., U.S.	A1	98
Greymouth, N.Z.	E3	52
Greys, stm., Wy., U.S.	C2	127
Gridley, Ca., U.S.	C3	82
Gridley, Il., U.S.	C5	90
Griffin, Ga., U.S.	C2	87
Griffiss Air Force Base, mil., N.Y., U.S.	B5	109
Griffith, Austl.	F9	50
Griffith, In., U.S.	A3	91
Grifton, N.C., U.S.	B5	110
Griggs, co., N.D., U.S.	B7	111
Griggsville, Il., U.S.	D3	90
Grik, Malay.	L6	34
Grimes, Ia., U.S.	C4	92
Grimes, co., Tx., U.S.	D4	120
Grimmen, Ger.	A13	8
Grimsby, Ont., Can.	D5	73
Grimsby, Eng., U.K.	H12	7
Grimselpass, Switz.	F15	10
Grimshaw, Alta., Can.	A2	68
Grimsley, Tn., U.S.	C9	119
Grimstad, Nor.	G7	6
Grindall Creek, Va., U.S.	n18	123
Grinnell, Ia., U.S.	C5	92
Grinnell Peninsula, pen., N.W. Ter., Can.	A14	66
Gris-Nez, Cap, c., Fr.	B8	10
Grissom Air Force Base, mil., In., U.S.	C5	91
Griswold, Ia., U.S.	C2	92
Grizzly Mountain, mtn., Id., U.S.	B2	89
Grizzly Mountain, mtn., Or., U.S.	C6	114
Grizzly Mountain, mtn., Wa., U.S.	A7	124
Groais Island, i., Newf., Can.	C3	72
Grodno, Bela.	H6	18
Groesbeck, Tx., U.S.	D4	120
Grombalia, Tun.	M5	14
Gronau, Ger.	C6	8
Grong, Nor.	D9	6
Groningen, Neth.	B6	8
Groom Lake, l., Nv., U.S.	F6	105
Groom Range, mts., Nv., U.S.	F6	105
Groote Eylandt, i., Austl.	B7	50
Grootfontein, Nmb.	E3	44
Gros Morne National Park, Newf., Can.	D3	72
Grosse Isle Naval Air Station, mil., Mi., U.S.	p15	99
Grossenhain, Ger.	D13	8
Grosse Pointe, Mi., U.S.	*p16	99
Grosse Pointe Park, Mi., U.S.	p16	99
Grosse Pointe Woods, Mi., U.S.	p16	99
Grosseto, Italy	G6	14
Grossglockner, mtn., Aus.	H12	8
Grossmont, Ca., U.S.	o16	82
Gros Ventre, stm., Wy., U.S.	C2	127
Gros Ventre Range, mts., Wy., U.S.	C2	127
Groswater Bay, b., Newf., Can.	F21	66
Groton, Ct., U.S.	D7	84
Groton, N.Y., U.S.	C4	109
Groton, S.D., U.S.	B7	118
Groton Long Point, Ct., U.S.	I12	84
Grottaglie, Italy	H10	14
Grottaminarda, Italy	H10	14
Grottoes, Va., U.S.	B4	123
Grouse Creek, Ut., U.S.	B2	121
Grouse Creek Mountain, mtn., Id., U.S.	E5	89
Grove, Ok., U.S.	A7	113
Grove City, Fl., U.S.	F4	86
Grove City, Oh., U.S.	C2	112
Grove City, Pa., U.S.	D1	115
Grove Hill, Al., U.S.	D2	78
Groveland, Fl., U.S.	D5	86
Groveland, Ma., U.S.	A5	98
Grove Point, c., Md., U.S.	B5	97
Groveport, Oh., U.S.	C3	112
Grover City, Ca., U.S.	E3	82
Groves, Tx., U.S.	E6	120
Groveton, N.H., U.S.	A3	106
Groveton, Tx., U.S.	D5	120
Groveton, Va., U.S.	g12	123
Groveton Gardens, Va., U.S.	*B5	123
Grovetown, Ga., U.S.	C4	87
Groveville, N.J., U.S.	C3	107
Growler Peak, mtn., Az., U.S.	E2	80
Groznyj, Russia	I7	22
Grudziądz, Pol.	B18	8
Gruetli-Laager, Tn., U.S.	D8	119
Grulla, Tx., U.S.	F3	120
Grundy, Va., U.S.	e9	123
Grundy, co., Il., U.S.	B5	90
Grundy, co., Ia., U.S.	B5	92
Grundy, co., Mo., U.S.	A4	102
Grundy, co., Tn., U.S.	D8	119
Grundy Center, Ia., U.S.	B5	92
Grunthal, Man., Can.	E3	70
Gruver, Tx., U.S.	A2	120
Guacanayabo, Golfo de, b., Cuba	D9	64
Guachochic, Mex.	D6	62
Guadalajara, Mex.	G8	62
Guadalajara, Spain	E8	12
Guadalcanal, i., Sol.Is.	A11	50
Guadalquivir, stm., Spain	H6	12
Guadalupe, Mex.	E9	62
Guadalupe, Az., U.S.	m9	80
Guadalupe, Ca., U.S.	E3	82
Guadalupe, co., N.M., U.S.	C5	108
Guadalupe, co., Tx., U.S.	E4	120
Guadalupe Garzarón, Mex.	E9	62
Guadalupe Mountains, mts., U.S.	E5	108
Guadalupe Mountains National Park, Tx., U.S.	o12	120
Guadalupe Peak, mtn., Tx., U.S.	o12	120
Guadeloupe, dep., N.A.	F17	64
Guadeloupe Passage, strt., N.A.	F17	64
Guadiana, stm., Eur.	H4	12
Guadix, Spain	H8	12
Guafo, Isla i., Chile	E2	56
Guajará Mirim, Braz.	F5	54
Gualeguaychú, Arg.	C5	56
Guam, dep., Oc.	F22	2
Guamini, Arg.	D4	56
Guamo, Col.	E5	58
Guampí, Sierra de, mts., Ven.	B5	54
Guanaja, Isla de, i., Hond.	F5	64
Guanajuato, Mex.	G9	62
Guanambi, Braz.	C7	57
Guanare, Ven.	C8	58
Guanarito, Ven.	C8	58
Guanay, Cerro, mtn., Ven.	E9	58
Guane, Cuba	C5	64
Guang'an, China	E8	26
Guangdong, prov., China	G9	26
Guanghua, China	E9	26
Guangxi Zhuang Zizhiqu, prov., China	G8	26
Guangyuan, China	E8	26
Guangzhou (Canton), China	L2	28
Guano Lake, l., Or., U.S.	E7	114
Guantánamo, Cuba	D10	64
Guanxian, China	E7	26
Guápiles, C.R.	I6	64
Guaporé (Iténez), stm., S.A.	G5	54
Guaqui, Bol.	G5	54
Guarabira, Braz.	E11	54
Guaranda, Ec.	H3	58
Guarapuava, Braz.	B6	56
Guaratinguetá, Braz.	G6	57
Guarda, Port.	E4	12
Guardo, Spain	C7	12
Guárico, Embalse del, res., Ven.	C9	58
Guarulhos, Braz.	G5	57
Guarus, Braz.	F8	57
Guasave, Mex.	E5	62
Guasdualito, Ven.	D7	58
Guatemala, Guat.	G2	64
Guatemala, ctry., N.A.	G2	64
Guaviare, stm., Col.	F8	58
Guaxupé, Braz.	F5	57
Guayama, P.R.	F14	64
Guayaquil, Ec.	I3	58
Guayaquil, Golfo de, b., S.A.	I2	58
Guaymallén, Arg.	C3	56
Guaymas, Mex.	D4	62
Gubbio, Italy	F7	14
Guben, Ger.	D14	8
Guchengzi, China	D7	26
Gūdalūr, India	G4	37
Gudiyāttam, India	F5	37
Gūdūr, India	E5	37
Guebwiller, Fr.	E14	10
Guelma, Alg.	A7	42
Guelph, Ont., Can.	D4	73
Guérande, Fr.	E4	10
Guéret, Fr.	F8	10
Guernsey, Wy., U.S.	D8	127
Guernsey, co., Oh., U.S.	B4	112
Guernsey, dep., Eur.	C4	10
Gueydan, La., U.S.	D3	95
Guga, Russia	G21	24
Guibes, Nmb.	G3	44
Güicán, Col.	D6	58
Guichen, Fr.	E5	10
Guiding, China	A9	34

Name	Map Ref	Page
Guijuelo, Spain	E6	12
Guilford, Ct., U.S.	D5	84
Guilford, Me., U.S.	C3	96
Guilford, co., N.C., U.S.	A3	110
Guilin (Kweilin), China	B11	34
Guillaumes, Fr.	H13	10
Guimarães, Port.	D3	12
Guin, Al., U.S.	B2	78
Guinea, ctry., Afr.	F3	42
Guinea, Gulf of, b., Afr.	H6	42
Guinea-Bissau, ctry., Afr.	F2	42
Güines, Cuba	C6	64
Guingamp, Fr.	D3	10
Güira de Melena, Cuba	C6	64
Guiratinga, Braz.	G8	54
Güiria, Ven.	B11	58
Guixian, China	C10	34
Guiyang (Kweiyang), China	A9	34
Guizhou, prov., China	F8	26
Gujarat, state, India	I4	38
Gūjar Khān, Pak.	D5	38
Gujrānwāla, Pak.	D6	38
Gujrāt, Pak.	D6	38
Gulbarga, India	D4	37
Guledagudda, India	D3	37
Gulf, co., Fl., U.S.	C1	86
Gulf Gate Estates, Fl., U.S.	E4	86
Gulf Islands National Seashore, U.S.	E5	101
Gulfport, Fl., U.S.	E4	86
Gulfport, Ms., U.S.	E4	101
Gulf Shores, Al., U.S.	E2	78
Gull Island, i., N.C., U.S.	B7	110
Gullivan Bay, b., Fl., U.S.	G5	86
Gull Lake, l., Alta., Can.	C4	68
Gull Lake, l., Mn., U.S.	D4	100
Güllük, Tur.	L11	16
Gülpınar, Tur.	J10	16
Gulu, Ug.	H12	42
Gumal (Gowmal), stm., Asia	D3	38
Gumboro, De., U.S.	G4	85
Gummersbach, Ger.	D7	8
Guna, India	H7	38
Gunisao, stm., Man., Can.	C3	70
Gunnarn, Swe.	D11	6
Gunnison, Co., U.S.	C4	83
Gunnison, Ms., U.S.	B3	101
Gunnison, Ut., U.S.	D4	121
Gunnison, co., Co., U.S.	C3	83
Gunnison, stm., Co., U.S.	C2	83
Gunnison, Mount, mtn., Co., U.S.	C3	83
Gunpowder Neck, c., Md., U.S.	B5	97
Gunpowder River, b., Md., U.S.	B5	97
Guntakal, India	E4	37
Gunter Air Force Base, mil., Al., U.S.	C3	78
Guntersville, Al., U.S.	A3	78
Guntersville Lake, res., Al., U.S.	A3	78
Guntown, Ms., U.S.	A5	101
Guntūr, India	D6	37
Gunungsitoli, Indon.	N4	34
Günzburg, Ger.	G10	8
Gunzenhausen, Ger.	F10	8
Gurdāspur, India	D6	38
Gurdon, Ar., U.S.	D2	81
Guri, Embalse, res., Ven.	D11	58
Gurjev, Kaz.	H8	22
Gurley, Al., U.S.	A3	78
Gurnee, Il., U.S.	h9	90
Gurnet Point, c., Ma., U.S.	B6	98
Gurupi, Braz.	F9	54
Gurupi, stm., Braz.	D9	54
Gusau, Nig.	F7	42
Gus'-Chrustal'nyj, Russia	F23	18
Gusev, Russia	G5	18
Gushi, China	C4	28
Gushikawa, Japan	y27	31b
Gusinoozersk, Russia	G15	24
Guspini, Italy	J3	14
Gustav Holm, Kap, c., Grnld.	C26	66
Gustine, Ca., U.S.	D3	82
Güstrow, Ger.	B12	8
Gütersloh, Ger.	D8	8
Guthrie, Ky., U.S.	D2	94
Guthrie, Ok., U.S.	B4	113
Guthrie, W.V., U.S.	m12	125
Guthrie, co., Ia., U.S.	C3	92
Guthrie Center, Ia., U.S.	C3	92
Guttenberg, Ia., U.S.	B6	92
Guttenberg, N.J., U.S.	h8	107
Guyana, ctry., S.A.	B7	54
Guyandotte, stm., W.V., U.S.	C2	125
Guymon, Ok., U.S.	e9	113
Guysborough, N.S., Can.	D8	71
Guyton, Ga., U.S.	D5	87
Güzelyurt Körfezi, b., N. Cyp.	B3	40
Gwādar, Pak.	D1	36
Gwai, Zimb.	E5	44
Gwalior, India	G8	38
Gwanda, Zimb.	F5	44
Gweru, Zimb.	E5	44
Gwinhurst, De., U.S.	h8	85
Gwinn, Mi., U.S.	B3	99
Gwinner, N.D., U.S.	C8	111
Gwinnett, co., Ga., U.S.	C2	87
Gwydyr Bay, b., Ak., U.S.	A10	79
Gwynns Falls, stm., Md., U.S.	g10	97
Gympie, Austl.	E10	50
Gyöngyös, Hung.	H19	8
Győr, Hung.	H17	8
Gypsum, Co., U.S.	B4	83

H

Name	Map Ref	Page
Haakon, co., S.D., U.S.	C4	118
Haapajärvi, Fin.	E15	6
Haapamäki, Fin.	E15	6
Haar, Ger.	G11	8
Haarlem, Neth.	C4	8
Haast, N.Z.	E2	52
Habersham, co., Ga., U.S.	B3	87
Habiganj, Bngl.	H14	38
Hachijō-jima, i., Japan	E14	26
Hachinohe, Japan	B14	30
Hachiōji, Japan	G12	30
Hackberry, La., U.S.	E2	95
Hackensack, N.J., U.S.	B4	107
Hackensack, stm., N.J., U.S.	h8	107
Hackettstown, N.J., U.S.	B3	107
Hackleburg, Al., U.S.	A2	78
Hadd, Ra's al-, c., Oman	D6	46
Haddam, Ct., U.S.	D5	84
Haddock, Ga., U.S.	C3	87
Haddonfield, N.J., U.S.	D2	107
Haddon Heights, N.J., U.S.	D2	107
Hadejia, stm., Nig.	F8	42
Hadera, Isr.	C4	40
Haderslev, Den.	I7	6
Hadīyah, Sau. Ar.	C2	46
Hadjeb el Aïoun, Tun.	N4	14
Hadley Bay, b., N.W. Ter., Can.	B11	66
Hadley Lake, l., Me., U.S.	D5	96
Hadlock, Wa., U.S.	A3	124
Ha Dong, Viet.	D8	34
Hadramawt, reg., Yemen	E4	46
Haeju, N. Kor.	D12	26
Häfizābād, Pak.	D5	38
Hafun, Ras, c., Som.	F5	46
Hagan, La., U.S.	D5	87
Hagemeister Island, i., Ak., U.S.	D7	79
Hagen, Ger.	D7	8
Hagerman, Id., U.S.	G4	89
Hagerman, N.M., U.S.	D5	108
Hagerstown, In., U.S.	E7	91
Hagerstown, Md., U.S.	A2	97
Hagfors, Swe.	F9	6
Haggin, Mount, mtn., Mt., U.S.	D3	103
Hagi, Japan	H4	30
Ha Giang, Viet.	C8	34
Hague, Sask., Can.	E2	75
Hague, Cap de la, c., Fr.	C5	10
Haguenau, Fr.	D14	10
Hagues Peak, mtn., Co., U.S.	A5	83
Ha! Ha!, Baie des, b., Que., Can.	C2	72
Hahira, Ga., U.S.	F3	87
Hahnville, La., U.S.	E5	95
Haicheng, China	C11	26
Hai Duong, Viet.	D9	34
Haifa see Hefa, Isr.	C4	40
Haikou, China	D11	34
Haiku, Hi., U.S.	C5	88
Hā'il, Sau. Ar.	C3	46
Hailaer, China	B10	26
Hailey, Id., U.S.	F4	89
Haileybury, Ont., Can.	p20	73
Haileyville, Ok., U.S.	C6	113
Haimen, China	C9	28
Haimen, China	L5	28
Haimen, China	H8	26
Hainan Dao, i., China	E10	34
Haines, Ak., U.S.	D12	79
Haines City, Fl., U.S.	D5	86
Haines Junction, Yukon, Can.	D5	66
Hainfeld, Aus.	G15	8
Haining, China	E9	28
Hai Phong, Viet.	D9	34
Haizhou, China	A8	28
Hakodate, Japan	r18	30a
Hāla, Pak.	H3	38
Halab (Aleppo), Syria	A5	40
Halawa, Cape, c., Hi., U.S.	B5	88
Halawa Heights, Hi., U.S.	g10	88
Halbā, Leb.	B5	40
Halberstadt, Ger.	D11	8
Halden, Nor.	G8	6
Haldensleben, Ger.	C11	8
Haldimand, Ont., Can.	E5	73
Haldwāni, India	F8	38
Hale, co., Tx., U.S.	B2	120
Hale, co., Al., U.S.	C2	78
Haleakala Crater, crat., Hi., U.S.	C5	88
Haleakala National Park, Hi., U.S.	C6	88
Hale Center, Tx., U.S.	B2	120
Haleiwa, Hi., U.S.	B3	88
Hales Corners, Wi., U.S.	n11	126
Halethorpe, Md., U.S.	B4	97
Haleyville, Al., U.S.	A2	78
Half Moon Bay, Ca., U.S.	k8	82
Halfway, Md., U.S.	A2	97
Halibut Point, c., Ma., U.S.	A6	98
Haliburton, Ont., Can.	B6	73
Halifax, N.S., Can.	E6	71
Halifax, Va., U.S.	D4	123
Halifax, co., N.C., U.S.	A5	110
Halifax, co., Va., U.S.	D4	123
Halifax Bay, b., Austl.	C9	50
Haliimaile, Hi., U.S.	C5	88
Halkirk, Scot., U.K.	C9	7
Hall, co., Ga., U.S.	B3	87
Hall, co., Ne., U.S.	D7	104
Hall, co., Tx., U.S.	B2	120
Hallam Peak, mtn., B.C., Can.	C8	69
Hallandale, Fl., U.S.	G6	86
Halla-san, mtn., S. Kor.	E12	26
Halle, Ger.	D11	8
Hällefors, Swe.	G10	6
Hallein, Aus.	H13	8
Hallettsville, Tx., U.S.	E4	120
Hallie, Wi., U.S.	D2	126
Hall Island, i., Ak., U.S.	C5	79
Hall Meadow Brook Reservoir, res., Ct., U.S.	B3	84
Hall Mountain, mtn., Wa., U.S.	A8	124
Hällnäs, Swe.	D12	6
Hallock, Mn., U.S.	B2	100
Hallowell, Me., U.S.	D3	96
Hall Peninsula, pen., N.W. Ter., Can.	D19	66
Halls, Tn., U.S.	B2	119
Hallsberg, Swe.	G10	6
Halls Creek, Austl.	C5	50
Halls Creek, stm., Ut., U.S.	F5	121
Halls Crossroads, Tn., U.S.	m14	119
Halls Stream, stm., N.H., U.S.	f7	106
Hallstavik, Swe.	F12	6
Hallstead, Pa., U.S.	C10	115
Hallsville, Mo., U.S.	B5	102
Hallsville, Tx., U.S.	C5	120
Halmahera, i., Indon.	E8	32
Halmahera, Laut, Indon.	F8	32
Halmstad, Swe.	H9	6
Halsey, Or., U.S.	C3	114
Hälsingborg see Helsingborg, Swe.	H9	6
Halstad, Ks., U.S.	E6	93
Halstead, Ks., U.S.	E6	93
Haltern, Ger.	D7	8
Haltiatunturi, mtn., Eur.	B13	6
Halton Hills, Ont., Can.	D5	73
Hamada, Japan	H5	30
Hamadān, Iran	B4	46
Hamāh, Syria	B5	40
Hamamatsu, Japan	H10	30
Hamar, Nor.	F8	6
Hamblen, co., Tn., U.S.	C10	119
Hamburg, Ger.	B9	8
Hamburg, Ar., U.S.	D4	81
Hamburg, Ia., U.S.	D2	92
Hamburg, N.Y., U.S.	C2	109
Hamburg, Pa., U.S.	E10	115
Hamden, Ct., U.S.	D4	84
Hamden, Oh., U.S.	C3	112
Hameenlinna, Fin.	F15	6
Hamel, Mn., U.S.	m11	100
Hameln, Ger.	C9	8
Hamersley Range, mts., Austl.	D3	50
Hamhŭng, N. Kor.	D12	26
Hami, China	C5	26
Hamilton, Ber.	E14	76
Hamilton, Ont., Can.	D5	73
Hamilton, N.Z.	B5	52
Hamilton, Scot., U.K.	F8	7
Hamilton, Al., U.S.	A2	78
Hamilton, Il., U.S.	C2	90
Hamilton, In., U.S.	A8	91
Hamilton, Ms., U.S.	B5	101
Hamilton, Mo., U.S.	B3	102
Hamilton, Mt., U.S.	D2	103
Hamilton, N.Y., U.S.	C5	109
Hamilton, Oh., U.S.	C1	112
Hamilton, Tx., U.S.	D3	120
Hamilton, Va., U.S.	A5	123
Hamilton, co., Fl., U.S.	B3	86
Hamilton, co., Il., U.S.	E5	90
Hamilton, co., In., U.S.	D5	91
Hamilton, co., Ia., U.S.	B4	92
Hamilton, co., Ks., U.S.	E2	93
Hamilton, co., Ne., U.S.	D7	104
Hamilton, co., N.Y., U.S.	B6	109
Hamilton, co., Oh., U.S.	C1	112
Hamilton, co., Tn., U.S.	D8	119
Hamilton, co., Tx., U.S.	D3	120
Hamilton, Lake, res., Ar., U.S.	C2	81
Hamilton, Mount, mtn., Ak., U.S.	C8	79
Hamilton, Mount, mtn., Ca., U.S.	k9	82
Hamilton, Mount, mtn., Nv., U.S.	D6	105
Hamilton Inlet, b., Newf., Can.	A2	72
Hamilton Reservoir, res., Ma., U.S.	B3	98
Hamilton Sound, strt., Newf., Can.	D4	72
Hamilton Square, N.J., U.S.	C3	107
Hamiota, Man., Can.	D1	70
Haiti (Haïti), ctry., N.A.	E11	64
Hamlet, In., U.S.	B4	91
Hamlet, N.C., U.S.	C3	110
Hamlet, Mount, mtn., Ak., U.S.	D6	79
Hamlin, Pa., U.S.	D11	115
Hamlin, Tx., U.S.	C2	120
Hamlin, W.V., U.S.	C2	125
Hamlin, co., S.D., U.S.	C8	118
Hamlin, co., Oh., U.S.	B2	112
Hamlin Lake, l., Mi., U.S.	D4	99
Hamm, Ger.	D7	8
Hammamet, Tun.	M5	14
Hammam Lif, Tun.	M5	14
Hammerdal, Swe.	E10	6
Hammonasset, stm., Ct., U.S.	D5	84
Hammonasset Point, c., Ct., U.S.	E5	84
Hammond, In., U.S.	A2	91
Hammond, La., U.S.	D5	95
Hammond, Wi., U.S.	D1	126
Hammond Bay, b., Mi., U.S.	C6	99
Hammonton, N.J., U.S.	D3	107
Hampden, Newf., Can.	D3	72
Hampden, Me., U.S.	D4	96
Hampden, co., Ma., U.S.	B2	98
Hampden Highlands, Me., U.S.	D4	96
Hampshire, co., Ma., U.S.	A5	90
Hampshire, co., W.V., U.S.	B6	125
Hampstead, Md., U.S.	A4	97
Hampstead, N.C., U.S.	C5	110
Hampton, N.B., Can.	D4	71
Hampton, Ar., U.S.	D3	81
Hampton, Ia., U.S.	B4	92
Hampton, N.H., U.S.	E5	106
Hampton, S.C., U.S.	F5	117
Hampton, Tn., U.S.	C11	119
Hampton, Va., U.S.	C6	123
Hampton, co., S.C., U.S.	F5	117
Hampton Bays, N.Y., U.S.	n16	109
Hampton Beach, N.H., U.S.	E5	106
Hampton Butte, mtn., Or., U.S.	D6	114
Hampton Roads, b., Va., U.S.	k15	123
Hampton Roads Bridge-Tunnel, Va., U.S.	k15	123
Hams Fork, stm., Wy., U.S.	E2	127
Hamtramck, Mi., U.S.	p15	99
Hana, Hi., U.S.	C6	88
Hanahan, S.C., U.S.	F7	117
Hanalei Bay, b., Hi., U.S.	A2	88
Hanamaki, Japan	C14	30
Hanamaulu, Hi., U.S.	B2	88
Hanapepe, Hi., U.S.	B2	88
Hanau, Ger.	E8	8
Hanceville, Al., U.S.	A3	78
Hancock, Md., U.S.	A1	97
Hancock, Mi., U.S.	A2	99
Hancock, Mn., U.S.	E3	100
Hancock, co., Ga., U.S.	C3	87
Hancock, co., Il., U.S.	C2	90
Hancock, co., In., U.S.	E6	91
Hancock, co., Ia., U.S.	A4	92
Hancock, co., Ky., U.S.	C3	94
Hancock, co., Me., U.S.	D4	96
Hancock, co., Ms., U.S.	E4	101
Hancock, co., Oh., U.S.	A2	112
Hancock, co., Tn., U.S.	C10	119
Hancock, co., W.V., U.S.	A4	125
Hand, co., S.D., U.S.	C6	118
Handa, Japan	H9	30
Handan, China	D9	26
Hando, Som.	F5	46
HaNegev, reg., Isr.	D4	40
Hanford, Ca., U.S.	D4	82
Hangchow see Hangzhou, China	E9	28
Hangzhou (Hangchow), China	E9	28
Hangzhou Wan, b., China	E9	28
Hanish, Jazā'ir, is., Yemen	F3	46
Hanjiang, China	J8	28
Hankinson, N.D., U.S.	C9	111
Hanna, Alta., Can.	D5	68
Hanna, Wy., U.S.	E6	127
Hanna City, Il., U.S.	C4	90
Hannahville Indian Reservation, Mi., U.S.	C3	99
Hannibal, Mo., U.S.	B6	102
Hannover, Ger.	C9	8
Ha Noi, Viet.	D8	34
Hanover, Ont., Can.	C3	73
Hanover, In., U.S.	G7	91
Hanover, Ks., U.S.	C7	93
Hanover, Ma., U.S.	B6	98
Hanover, Mn., U.S.	m11	100
Hanover, N.H., U.S.	C2	106
Hanover, Pa., U.S.	G8	115
Hanover, co., Va., U.S.	C5	123
Hanover Park, Il., U.S.	k8	90
Hansen, Id., U.S.	G4	89
Hansford, co., Tx., U.S.	A2	120
Hanson, Ma., U.S.	B6	98
Hanson, co., S.D., U.S.	D8	118
Hantsport, N.S., Can.	D5	71
Hanzhong, China	E8	26
Haparanda, Swe.	D15	6
Hapeville, Ga., U.S.	C2	87
Happy Valley, N.H., U.S.	E5	108
Happy Valley-Goose Bay, Newf., Can.	B1	72
Harahan, La., U.S.	k11	95
Haralson, co., Ga., U.S.	C1	87
Harare, Zimb.	E6	44
Harash, Bi'r al-, well, Libya	C10	42
Harbeson, De., U.S.	F4	85
Harbin, China	B12	26
Harbor, Or., U.S.	E2	114
Harbor Beach, Mi., U.S.	E8	99
Harborcreek, Pa., U.S.	B2	115
Harbor Springs, Mi., U.S.	C6	99
Harbour Breton, Newf., Can.	E4	72
Harbour Grace, Newf., Can.	E5	72
Harcuvar Mountains, mts., Az., U.S.	D2	80
Harda, India	I7	38
Hardangerfjorden, Nor.	F5	6
Hardee, co., Fl., U.S.	E5	86
Hardeeville, S.C., U.S.	G5	117
Hardeman, co., Tn., U.S.	B2	119
Hardeman, co., Tx., U.S.	B3	120
Hardin, Il., U.S.	D3	90
Hardin, Mt., U.S.	E9	103
Hardin, co., Il., U.S.	F5	90
Hardin, co., Ia., U.S.	B4	92
Hardin, co., Ky., U.S.	C4	94
Hardin, co., Oh., U.S.	B2	112
Hardin, co., Tn., U.S.	B3	119
Hardin, co., Tx., U.S.	D5	120
Harding, co., N.M., U.S.	B5	108
Harding, co., S.D., U.S.	B2	118
Harding, Lake, res., U.S.	C4	78
Hardinsburg, Ky., U.S.	C3	94
Hardisty, Alta., Can.	C5	68
Hardwār, India	F8	38
Hardwick, Ga., U.S.	C3	87
Hardwick, Vt., U.S.	B4	122
Hardwood Ridge, mtn., Pa., U.S.	D11	115
Hardy, co., W.V., U.S.	B6	125
Hardy Lake, res., In., U.S.	G6	91
Hare Bay, Newf., Can.	D4	72
Hare Bay, b., Newf., Can.	C4	72
Harer, Eth.	G3	46
Harford, co., Md., U.S.	A5	97
Hargeysa, Som.	G3	46
Harihar, India	E3	37
Harīrūd (Tedžen), stm., Asia	J10	22
Harkers Island, N.C., U.S.	C6	110
Harlan, In., U.S.	B8	91
Harlan, Ia., U.S.	C2	92
Harlan, Ky., U.S.	D6	94
Harlan, co., Ky., U.S.	D6	94
Harlan, co., Ne., U.S.	D6	104
Harlan County Lake, res., Ne., U.S.	E6	104
Harlem, Fl., U.S.	F6	86
Harlem, Ga., U.S.	C4	87
Harlem, Mt., U.S.	B8	103
Harleyville, S.C., U.S.	E7	117
Harlingen, Neth.	B5	8
Harlingen, Tx., U.S.	F4	120
Harlow, Eng., U.K.	J13	7
Harlowton, Mt., U.S.	D7	103
Harmon, co., Ok., U.S.	C2	113
Harmon Creek, stm., W.V., U.S.	f8	125
Harmony, In., U.S.	E3	91
Harmony, Mn., U.S.	G6	100
Harmony, Pa., U.S.	E1	115
Harmony, R.I., U.S.	B3	116
Harnett, co., N.C., U.S.	B4	110
Harney, co., Or., U.S.	D7	114
Harney, Lake, l., Fl., U.S.	D5	86
Harney Lake, l., Or., U.S.	D7	114
Harney Peak, mtn., S.D., U.S.	D2	118
Härnösand, Swe.	E11	6
Haro, Spain	C9	12
Haro Strait, strt., Wa., U.S.	A2	124
Harper, Lib.	H4	42
Harper, Ks., U.S.	E5	93
Harper, co., Ks., U.S.	E5	93
Harper, co., Ok., U.S.	A2	113
Harper, Mount, mtn., Ak., U.S.	C11	79
Harpers Ferry, Ia., U.S.	A6	92
Harpers Ferry National Historical Park, W.V., U.S.	B7	125
Harpersville, Al., U.S.	B3	78
Harpeth, stm., Tn., U.S.	A5	119
Harquahala Mountain, mtn., Az., U.S.	D2	80
Harquahala Mountains, mts., Az., U.S.	D2	80
Harrah, Ok., U.S.	B4	113
Harricana, stm., Can.	F17	66
Harriman, Tn., U.S.	D9	119
Harriman Reservoir, res., Vt., U.S.	F3	122
Harrington, De., U.S.	E3	85
Harrington Park, N.J., U.S.	h9	107
Harris, Mn., U.S.	E6	100
Harris, R.I., U.S.	D3	116
Harris, co., Ga., U.S.	D2	87
Harris, co., Tx., U.S.	E5	120
Harris, Lake, l., Fl., U.S.	D5	86
Harrisburg, Ar., U.S.	B5	81
Harrisburg, Il., U.S.	F5	90
Harrisburg, Or., U.S.	C3	114
Harrisburg, Pa., U.S.	F8	115
Harrisburg, S.D., U.S.	D9	118
Harrison, Ar., U.S.	A2	81
Harrison, Mi., U.S.	D6	99
Harrison, N.J., U.S.	k8	107
Harrison, N.Y., U.S.	h13	109
Harrison, Oh., U.S.	C1	112
Harrison, Tn., U.S.	h11	119
Harrison, co., In., U.S.	H5	91
Harrison, co., Ia., U.S.	C2	92
Harrison, co., Ky., U.S.	B5	94
Harrison, co., Ms., U.S.	E4	101
Harrison, co., Mo., U.S.	A3	102
Harrison, co., Oh., U.S.	B4	112
Harrison, co., Tx., U.S.	C5	120
Harrison, co., W.V., U.S.	B4	125
Harrison, Cape, c., Newf., Can.	g10	72
Harrison Bay, b., Ak., U.S.	A9	79
Harrisonburg, Va., U.S.	B4	123
Harrison Hot Springs, B.C., Can.	f14	69
Harrison Lake, l., B.C., Can.	E7	69
Harrisonville, Mo., U.S.	C3	102
Harriston, Ont., Can.	D4	73
Harristown, Il., U.S.	D4	90
Harrisville, R.I., U.S.	B2	116
Harrisville, Ut., U.S.	B4	121
Harrisville, W.V., U.S.	B3	125
Harrodsburg, Ky., U.S.	C5	94
Harrogate, Eng., U.K.	G11	7
Harrow, Ont., Can.	E2	73
Harry S. Truman Reservoir, res., Mo., U.S.	C4	102
Harry Strunk Lake, res., Ne., U.S.	D5	104
Harstad, Nor.	B11	6
Hart, Mi., U.S.	E4	99
Hart, Tx., U.S.	B1	120
Hart, co., Ga., U.S.	B4	87
Hart, co., Ky., U.S.	C4	94
Hart, Lake, l., Fl., U.S.	D5	86
Hartford, Al., U.S.	D4	78
Hartford, Ar., U.S.	B1	81
Hartford, Ct., U.S.	B5	84
Hartford, Il., U.S.	E3	90
Hartford, Ia., U.S.	C4	92
Hartford, Ky., U.S.	C3	94
Hartford, Mi., U.S.	F4	99
Hartford, S.D., U.S.	D9	118
Hartford, Vt., U.S.	D4	122
Hartford, Wi., U.S.	E5	126
Hartford, co., Ct., U.S.	B4	84
Hartford City, In., U.S.	D7	91
Hartington, Ne., U.S.	B8	104
Hart Lake, l., Or., U.S.	E7	114
Hartland, N.B., Can.	C2	71
Hartland, Me., U.S.	D3	96
Hartland, Wi., U.S.	E5	126
Hartland Point, c., Eng., U.K.	J8	7
Hartlepool, Eng., U.K.	G11	7
Hartley, Ia., U.S.	A2	92
Hartley, co., Tx., U.S.	B1	120
Hartney, Man., Can.	E1	70
Hartselle, Al., U.S.	A3	78
Hartshorne, Ok., U.S.	C6	113
Hartsville, S.C., U.S.	C7	117
Hartsville, Tn., U.S.	A5	119
Hartville, Oh., U.S.	B4	112
Hartwell, Ga., U.S.	B4	87
Hartwell Lake, res., U.S.	B1	117
Härnösand, Swe.	E11	6
Harvard, Il., U.S.	A5	90
Harvard, Ne., U.S.	D7	104
Harvard, Mount, mtn., Co., U.S.	C4	83
Harvey, La., U.S.	B6	90
Harvey, La., U.S.	E5	95
Harvey, Mi., U.S.	B3	99
Harvey, N.D., U.S.	B6	111
Harvey, co., Ks., U.S.	D6	93
Harvey Lake, res., Pa., U.S.	m16	115
Harveys Creek, stm., Pa., U.S.	n16	115
Harwich, Eng., U.K.	J14	7
Harwich Port, Ma., U.S.	C7	98
Harwinton, Ct., U.S.	B3	84
Haryana, state, India	F7	38
Harz, mts., Ger.	D10	8
Hasbrouck Heights, N.J., U.S.	h8	107
Haskell, Ar., U.S.	C3	81
Haskell, Ok., U.S.	B6	113
Haskell, Tx., U.S.	C3	120
Haskell, co., Ks., U.S.	E3	93
Haskell, co., Ok., U.S.	B6	113
Haskell, co., Tx., U.S.	C3	120
Haskovo, Bul.	H9	16
Hassan, India	F4	37
Hassayampa, stm., Az., U.S.	D3	80
Hasselt, Bel.	E5	8
Hassfurt, Ger.	E10	8
Hässleholm, Swe.	H9	6
Hastings, Ont., Can.	C7	73
Hastings, N.Z.	C6	52
Hastings, Eng., U.K.	K13	7
Hastings, Mi., U.S.	F5	99
Hastings, Mn., U.S.	F6	100
Hastings, Ne., U.S.	D7	104
Hastings, co., Ont., Can.	C7	73
Hastings-on-Hudson, N.Y., U.S.	h13	109
Hatch, N.M., U.S.	E2	108
Hatchet Lake, l., N.S., Can.	E6	71
Hatchie, stm., Tn., U.S.	B2	119
Hatcheneha, Lake, l., Fl., U.S.	D5	86

Name	Map Ref	Page
Hat Creek, stm., S.D., U.S.	E2	118
Hatfield, In., U.S.	I3	91
Hatfield, Pa., U.S.	F11	115
Hāthras, India	E8	34
Ha Tinh, Viet.	G8	38
Hat Mountain, mtn., Az., U.S.	E3	80
Hatteras, N.C., U.S.	B7	110
Hatteras, Cape, c., N.C., U.S.	B7	110
Hatteras Inlet, b., N.C., U.S.	B7	110
Hattiesburg, Ms., U.S.	D4	101
Hatton, N.D., U.S.	B8	111
Hat Yai, Thai.	K6	34
Haubstadt, In., U.S.	H2	91
Haugesund, Nor.	G5	6
Haughton, La., U.S.	B2	95
Haukivuori, Fin.	E16	6
Hauser, Or., U.S.	D2	114
Haut, Isle au, i., Me., U.S.	D4	96
Haut Atlas, mts., Mor.	B4	42
Hauula, Hi., U.S.	B4	88
Havana, Fl., U.S.	B2	86
Havana, Il., U.S.	C3	90
Havana see La Habana, Cuba	C6	64
Havant, Eng., U.K.	K12	7
Havasu, Lake, res., U.S.	C1	80
Havasupai Indian Reservation, Az., U.S.	A3	80
Havelberg, Ger.	C12	8
Havelock, Ont., Can.	C7	73
Havelock, N.C., U.S.	C6	110
Haven, Ks., U.S.	E6	93
Haverford [Township], Pa., U.S.	o20	115
Haverhill, Ma., U.S.	A5	98
Hāveri, India	E3	37
Haverstraw, N.Y., U.S.	D7	109
Haviland, Ks., U.S.	E4	93
Havířov, Czech.	F18	8
Havre, Mt., U.S.	B7	103
Havre de Grace, Md., U.S.	A5	97
Havre North, Mt., U.S.	B7	103
Haw, stm., N.C., U.S.	B3	110
Hawaii, co., Hi., U.S.	D6	88
Hawaii, state, U.S.	C5	88
Hawaii, i., Hi., U.S.	D6	88
Hawaiian Islands, is., Hi., U.S.	m14	88
Hawaii Volcanoes National Park, Hi., U.S.	D6	88
Hawarden, Ia., U.S.	A1	92
Hawesville, Ky., U.S.	C3	94
Hawi, Hi., U.S.	C6	88
Hawick, Scot., U.K.	F10	7
Hawke Bay, b., N.Z.	C6	52
Hawkesbury, Ont., Can.	B10	73
Hawkesbury Island, i., B.C., Can.	C3	69
Hawkins, co., Tn., U.S.	C11	119
Hawkinsville, Ga., U.S.	D3	87
Hawley, Mn., U.S.	D2	100
Hawley, Pa., U.S.	D11	115
Haworth, N.J., U.S.	h9	107
Haw River, N.C., U.S.	A3	110
Hawthorne, Ca., U.S.	n12	82
Hawthorne, Fl., U.S.	C4	86
Hawthorne, Nv., U.S.	E3	105
Hawthorne, N.J., U.S.	B4	107
Hawthorne, N.Y., U.S.	g13	109
Haxtun, Co., U.S.	A8	83
Hay, Austl.	F8	50
Hay, stm., Austl.	D7	50
Hay, stm., Can.	E9	66
Hay, Cape, c., N.W. Ter., Can.	B10	66
Hayange, Fr.	C13	10
Hayden, Az., U.S.	E5	80
Hayden, Co., U.S.	A3	83
Hayden Lake, l., Id., U.S.	B2	89
Hayes, La., U.S.	D3	95
Hayes, co., Ne., U.S.	D4	104
Hayes, stm., Man., Can.	B5	70
Hayes, Mount, mtn., Ak., U.S.	C10	79
Hayfield, Mn., U.S.	G6	100
Hayford Peak, mtn., Nv., U.S.	G6	105
Haymock Lake, l., Me., U.S.	B3	96
Haynesville, La., U.S.	B2	95
Hayneville, Al., U.S.	C3	78
Hayrabolu, Tur.	H11	16
Hay River, N.W. Ter., Can.	D9	66
Hays, Ks., U.S.	D4	93
Hays, N.C., U.S.	A1	110
Hays, co., Tx., U.S.	D3	120
Hays Canyon Peak, mtn., Nv., U.S.	B2	105
Hay Springs, Ne., U.S.	B3	104
Haystack Mountain, mtn., Nv., U.S.	B6	105
Haysville, Ks., U.S.	g12	93
Hayti, Mo., U.S.	E8	102
Hayti Heights, Mo., U.S.	E8	102
Hayward, Ca., U.S.	h8	82
Hayward, Wi., U.S.	B2	126
Haywood, co., N.C., U.S.	f9	110
Haywood, co., Tn., U.S.	B2	119
Hazard, Ky., U.S.	C6	94
Hazardville, Ct., U.S.	B5	84
Hazārībāgh, India	I11	38
Hazel Crest, Il., U.S.	k9	90
Hazel Dell, Wa., U.S.	D3	124
Hazel Green, Al., U.S.	A3	78
Hazel Green, Wi., U.S.	F3	126
Hazel Park, Mi., U.S.	p15	99
Hazelton Pyramid, mtn., Wy., U.S.	B5	127
Hazelwood, N.C., U.S.	f10	110
Hazen, Ar., U.S.	C4	81
Hazen, N.D., U.S.	B4	111
Hazen Bay, b., Ak., U.S.	C6	79
Hazlehurst, Ga., U.S.	E4	87
Hazlehurst, Ms., U.S.	D3	101
Hazleton, Ia., U.S.	B6	92
Hazleton, Pa., U.S.	E10	115
Head Harbor Island, i., Me., U.S.	D5	96
Headland, Al., U.S.	D4	78
Headley, Mount, mtn., Mt., U.S.	C1	103
Healdsburg, Ca., U.S.	C2	82
Healdton, Ok., U.S.	C4	113
Healy, Ak., U.S.	C10	79
Heard, co., Ga., U.S.	C1	87
Hearne, Tx., U.S.	D4	120
Hearst, Ont., Can.	o19	73
Heart, stm., N.D., U.S.	C3	111
Heart Butte Dam, N.D., U.S.	C4	111
Heart Lake, l., Wy., U.S.	B2	127
Heart's Content, Newf., Can.	E5	72
Heath, Oh., U.S.	B3	112
Heath Springs, S.C., U.S.	B6	117
Heavener, Ok., U.S.	C7	113
Hebbronville, Tx., U.S.	F3	120
Hebei, prov., China	D10	26
Heber, Az., U.S.	C5	80
Heber City, Ut., U.S.	C4	121
Heber Springs, Ar., U.S.	B3	81
Hébertville, Que., Can.	A6	74
Hebgen Lake, res., Mt., U.S.	F5	103
Hebrides, is., Scot., U.K.	D6	4
Hebron, N.S., Can.	F3	71
Hebron, Il., U.S.	A5	90
Hebron, In., U.S.	B3	91
Hebron, Ky., U.S.	h13	94
Hebron, Md., U.S.	D6	97
Hebron, Ne., U.S.	D8	104
Hebron, N.D., U.S.	C3	111
Hebron, Oh., U.S.	C3	112
Hebron see Al-Khalīl, Jord.	D4	40
Hecate Strait, strt., B.C., Can.	C2	69
Heceta Island, i., Ak., U.S.	n23	79
Hechi, China	B9	34
Hechingen, Ger.	G8	8
Hechuan, China	E8	26
Hecla Island, i., Man., Can.	D3	70
Hector, Mn., U.S.	F4	100
Hedemora, Swe.	F10	6
He Devil, mtn., Id., U.S.	D2	89
Hedrick, Ia., U.S.	C5	92
Heerenveen, Neth.	C5	8
Heerlen, Neth.	E5	8
Hefa (Haifa), Isr.	C4	40
Hefei, China	D6	28
Heflin, Al., U.S.	B4	78
Hefner, Lake, res., Ok., U.S.	B4	113
Hegang, China	B13	26
Hegins, Pa., U.S.	E9	115
Heide, Ger.	A9	8
Heidelberg, Ger.	F8	8
Heidelberg, Ms., U.S.	D5	101
Heidenheim, Ger.	F10	8
Heidenreichstein, Aus.	G15	8
Heidrick, Ky., U.S.	D6	94
Heihe (Naqula), China	A13	26
Heilbron, S. Afr.	G5	44
Heilbronn, Ger.	F9	8
Heilongjiang, prov., China	B12	26
Heilongjiang (Amur), stm., Asia	G19	24
Heinola, Fin.	F16	6
Hejaz see Al-Ḥijāz, reg., Sau. Ar.	C2	46
Hekla, vol., Ice.	C4	6
Hekou, China	C7	34
Helena, Al., U.S.	B3	78
Helena, Ar., U.S.	C5	81
Helena, Ga., U.S.	D4	87
Helena, Mt., U.S.	D4	103
Helena, Ok., U.S.	A3	113
Helensburgh, Scot., U.K.	E8	7
Helgoland, i., Ger.	A7	8
Helgoländer Bucht, b., Ger.	A8	8
Hellam, Pa., U.S.	G8	115
Hellertown, Pa., U.S.	E11	115
Hellesylt, Nor.	E6	6
Hellín, Spain	G10	12
Hells Canyon, val., U.S.	B10	114
Hells Canyon National Recreation Area, U.S.	B10	114
Hell-Ville, Madag.	D9	44
Helmand, stm., Asia	C2	36
Helmond, Neth.	D5	8
Helmsdale, Scot., U.K.	C9	7
Helmstedt, Ger.	C10	8
Helotes, Tx., U.S.	h7	120
Helper, Ut., U.S.	D5	121
Helsingborg, Swe.	H9	6
Helsingfors see Helsinki, Fin.	F15	6
Helsingør (Elsinore), Den.	H9	6
Helsinki (Helsingfors), Fin.	F15	6
Hematite, Mo., U.S.	C7	102
Hemet, Ca., U.S.	F5	82
Hemingford, Ne., U.S.	B2	104
Hemingway, S.C., U.S.	D9	117
Hemlock, Mi., U.S.	E6	99
Hemlock Reservoir, res., Ct., U.S.	E2	84
Hemmingford, Que., Can.	D4	74
Hemphill, Tx., U.S.	D6	120
Hemphill, co., Tx., U.S.	B2	120
Hempstead, N.Y., U.S.	n15	109
Hempstead, Tx., U.S.	D4	120
Hempstead, co., Ar., U.S.	D2	81
Hemse, Swe.	H12	6
Henagar, Al., U.S.	A4	78
Henan, prov., China	E9	26
Henderson, Ky., U.S.	C2	94
Henderson, La., U.S.	D4	95
Henderson, Mn., U.S.	F5	100
Henderson, Ne., U.S.	D8	104
Henderson, Nv., U.S.	G7	105
Henderson, N.C., U.S.	A4	110
Henderson, Tn., U.S.	B3	119
Henderson, Tx., U.S.	C5	120
Henderson, co., Il., U.S.	C3	90
Henderson, co., Ky., U.S.	C2	94
Henderson, co., N.C., U.S.	f10	110
Henderson, co., Tn., U.S.	B3	119
Henderson, co., Tx., U.S.	C5	120
Henderson's Point, Ms., U.S.	g7	101
Hendersonville, N.C., U.S.	f10	110
Hendersonville, Tn., U.S.	A5	119
Hendricks, Mn., U.S.	F2	100
Hendricks, co., In., U.S.	E4	91
Hendry, co., Fl., U.S.	F5	86
Hengelo, Neth.	C6	8
Hengshan, China	H1	28
Hengyang, China	F9	26
Henlawson, W.V., U.S.	n12	125
Henlopen, Cape, c., De., U.S.	E5	85
Hennef, Ger.	E7	8
Hennepin, co., Mn., U.S.	E5	100
Hennessey, Ok., U.S.	A4	113
Henniker, N.H., U.S.	D3	106
Henning, Mn., U.S.	D3	100
Henning, Tn., U.S.	B2	119
Henrico, co., Va., U.S.	C5	123
Henrietta, N.C., U.S.	B1	110
Henrietta, Tx., U.S.	C3	120
Henrietta Maria, Cape, c., Ont., Can.	n19	73
Henry, Il., U.S.	B4	90
Henry, co., Al., U.S.	D4	78
Henry, co., Ga., U.S.	C2	87
Henry, co., Il., U.S.	B3	90
Henry, co., In., U.S.	E7	91
Henry, co., Ia., U.S.	C6	92
Henry, co., Ky., U.S.	B4	94
Henry, co., Mo., U.S.	C4	102
Henry, co., Oh., U.S.	A1	112
Henry, co., Tn., U.S.	A3	119
Henry, co., Va., U.S.	D3	123
Henry, Mount, mtn., Mt., U.S.	B1	103
Henryetta, Ok., U.S.	B6	113
Henry Kater, Cape, c., N.W. Ter., Can.	C19	66
Henrys Fork, stm., U.S.	E2	127
Henryville, Que., Can.	D4	74
Henryville, In., U.S.	G6	91
Hensall, Ont., Can.	D3	73
Henzada, Burma	F3	34
Hephzibah, Ga., U.S.	C4	87
Heppner, Or., U.S.	B7	114
Hepu (Lianzhou), China	D10	34
Herāt, Afg.	C1	36
Herbes, Isle aux, i., Al., U.S.	E1	78
Herbignac, Fr.	E4	10
Herculaneum, Mo., U.S.	C7	102
Hereford, Eng., U.K.	I10	7
Hereford, Md., U.S.	A4	97
Hereford, Tx., U.S.	B1	120
Hereford Inlet, b., N.J., U.S.	E3	107
Herford, Ger.	C8	8
Herington, Ks., U.S.	D7	93
Herkimer, N.Y., U.S.	B6	109
Herkimer, co., N.Y., U.S.	B5	109
Hermann, Mo., U.S.	C6	102
Hermano Peak, mtn., Co., U.S.	D2	83
Hermantown, Mn., U.S.	D6	100
Hermanus, S. Afr.	H3	44
Herminie, Pa., U.S.	F2	115
Hermiston, Or., U.S.	B7	114
Hermitage, Newf., Can.	E4	72
Hermitage, Ar., U.S.	D3	81
Hermitage Bay, b., Newf., Can.	E3	72
Hermosillo, Mex.	C4	62
Hernando, Fl., U.S.	D4	86
Hernando, Ms., U.S.	A4	101
Hernando, co., Fl., U.S.	D4	86
Herndon, Va., U.S.	B5	123
Herning, Den.	H7	6
Heron Lake, Mn., U.S.	G3	100
Herrera del Duque, Spain	F6	12
Herrera de Pisuerga, Spain	C7	12
Herrin, Il., U.S.	F4	90
Herring Bay, b., Md., U.S.	C4	97
Herring Cove, N.S., Can.	E6	71
Herrington Lake, res., Ky., U.S.	C5	94
Herscher, Il., U.S.	B5	90
Hershey, Pa., U.S.	F8	115
Hertford, N.C., U.S.	A6	110
Hertford, co., N.C., U.S.	A5	110
Hervás, Spain	E6	12
Hervey Bay, b., Austl.	E10	50
Hesdin, Fr.	B9	10
Hesperia, Ca., U.S.	E5	82
Hesperia, Mi., U.S.	E4	99
Hesperus Mountain, mtn., Co., U.S.	D2	83
Hesston, Ks., U.S.	D6	93
Hetian, China	B8	38
Hettinger, N.D., U.S.	D3	111
Hettinger, co., N.D., U.S.	C3	111
Heyburn, Id., U.S.	G5	89
Heyworth, Il., U.S.	C5	90
Hialeah, Fl., U.S.	G6	86
Hiawatha, Ia., U.S.	B6	92
Hiawatha, Ks., U.S.	C8	93
Hibbing, Mn., U.S.	C6	100
Hickam Air Force Base, mil., Hi., U.S.	g10	88
Hickman, Ky., U.S.	f8	94
Hickman, Ne., U.S.	D9	104
Hickman, co., Ky., U.S.	f8	94
Hickman, co., Tn., U.S.	B4	119
Hickory, N.C., U.S.	B1	110
Hickory, co., Mo., U.S.	D4	102
Hicksville, N.Y., U.S.	E7	109
Hicksville, Oh., U.S.	A1	112
Hico, Tx., U.S.	D3	120
Hidaka-sammyaku, mts., Japan	q20	30a
Hidalgo, Mex.	E10	62
Hidalgo, Tx., U.S.	F3	120
Hidalgo, co., N.M., U.S.	F1	108
Hidalgo, co., Tx., U.S.	F3	120
Hidalgo del Parral, Mex.	D7	62
Hiddenite, N.C., U.S.	B1	110
Hieroglyphic Mountains, mts., Az., U.S.	k8	80
Hierro, i., Spain	C2	42
Higashiōsaka, Japan	H8	30
Higbee, Mo., U.S.	B5	102
Higganum, Ct., U.S.	D5	84
Higgins Lake, l., Mi., U.S.	D6	99
Higgins Millpond, res., Md., U.S.	C5	97
Higginsville, Mo., U.S.	B4	102
High Bridge, N.J., U.S.	B3	107
High Falls Reservoir, res., Wi., U.S.	C5	126
High Island, i., Mi., U.S.	C5	99
Highland, Il., U.S.	E4	90
Highland, In., U.S.	A3	91
Highland, Ks., U.S.	C8	93
Highland, Mi., U.S.	o14	99
Highland, N.Y., U.S.	D7	109
Highland, Wi., U.S.	E3	126
Highland, co., Oh., U.S.	C2	112
Highland, co., Va., U.S.	B3	123
Highland Lake, l., Me., U.S.	g7	96
Highland Lakes, N.J., U.S.	A4	107
Highland Park, Il., U.S.	A6	90
Highland Park, Mi., U.S.	p15	99
Highland Park, Tx., U.S.	n10	120
Highland Peak, mtn., Ca., U.S.	C4	82
Highland Point, c., Fl., U.S.	G5	86
Highlands, N.J., U.S.	C5	107
Highlands, N.C., U.S.	f9	110
Highlands, Tx., U.S.	r14	120
Highlands, co., Fl., U.S.	E5	86
Highland Springs, Va., U.S.	C5	123
High Level, Alta., Can.	F7	68
Highmore, S.D., U.S.	C6	118
High Point, N.C., U.S.	B2	110
High Prairie, Alta., Can.	B2	68
High Ridge, Mo., U.S.	g12	102
High River, Alta., Can.	D4	68
Highrock Lake, l., Man., Can.	B1	70
High Spire, Pa., U.S.	F8	115
High Springs, Fl., U.S.	C4	86
Hightstown, N.J., U.S.	C3	107
Highwood, Il., U.S.	A6	90
Highwood Baldy, mtn., Mt., U.S.	C6	103
Highwood Mountains, mts., Mt., U.S.	C6	103
Higüerote, Ven.	B9	58
Higüey, Dom. Rep.	E13	64
Híjar, Spain	D11	12
Hikari, Japan	I4	30
Hikone, Japan	G9	30
Hiko Range, mts., Nv., U.S.	F6	105
Hilbert, Wi., U.S.	D5	126
Hildale, Ut., U.S.	F3	121
Hilden, N.S., Can.	D6	71
Hildesheim, Ger.	C9	8
Hill, co., Mt., U.S.	B6	103
Hill, co., Tx., U.S.	D4	120
Hill City, Ks., U.S.	C4	93
Hill City, S.D., U.S.	D2	118
Hillcrest, Il., U.S.	B4	90
Hillcrest Heights, Md., U.S.	C4	97
Hilliard, Fl., U.S.	B5	86
Hilliard, Oh., U.S.	k10	112
Hill Island Lake, l., N.W. Ter., Can.	D11	66
Hill Lake, l., Ar., U.S.	h10	81
Hills, Ia., U.S.	C6	92
Hills, Mn., U.S.	G2	100
Hillsboro, Il., U.S.	D4	90
Hillsboro, Ks., U.S.	D6	93
Hillsboro, Mo., U.S.	C7	102
Hillsboro, N.H., U.S.	D3	106
Hillsboro, N.D., U.S.	B8	111
Hillsboro, Oh., U.S.	C2	112
Hillsboro, Or., U.S.	B4	114
Hillsboro, Tx., U.S.	C4	120
Hillsboro, Wi., U.S.	E3	126
Hillsboro Canal, Fl., U.S.	F6	86
Hillsborough, N.B., Can.	D5	71
Hillsborough, N.C., U.S.	A3	110
Hillsborough, co., Fl., U.S.	E4	86
Hillsborough, co., N.H., U.S.	E3	106
Hillsborough Bay, b., P.E.I., Can.	C6	71
Hillsburgh, Ont., Can.	D4	73
Hills Creek Lake, res., Or., U.S.	D4	114
Hillsdale, Mi., U.S.	G6	99
Hillsdale, N.J., U.S.	g8	107
Hillsdale, co., Mi., U.S.	G6	99
Hillside, N.J., U.S.	k8	107
Hillsville, Pa., U.S.	D1	115
Hillsville, Va., U.S.	D2	123
Hilo, Hi., U.S.	D6	88
Hilo Bay, b., Hi., U.S.	D6	88
Hilton, N.Y., U.S.	B3	109
Hilton Head Island, S.C., U.S.	G6	117
Hilton Head Island, i., S.C., U.S.	G6	117
Hilversum, Neth.	C5	8
Himachal Pradesh, ter., India	E7	38
Himalayas, mts., Asia	F10	38
Himeji, Japan	F9	30
Himi, Japan	F10	30
Hims (Homs), Syria	B5	40
Hinchinbrook Island, i., Austl.	C9	50
Hinchinbrook Island, i., Ak., U.S.	g18	79
Hinckley, Il., U.S.	B5	90
Hinckley, Mn., U.S.	D6	100
Hinckley, Ut., U.S.	D3	121
Hinckley Reservoir, res., N.Y., U.S.	B5	109
Hindaun, India	G7	38
Hindman, Ky., U.S.	C7	94
Hinds, co., Ms., U.S.	C3	101
Hindu Kush, mts., Asia	B4	38
Hindupur, India	F4	37
Hines, Or., U.S.	D7	114
Hinesville, Ga., U.S.	E5	87
Hinganghāt, India	B5	37
Hingham, Ma., U.S.	B6	98
Hingham Bay, b., Ma., U.S.	g12	98
Hingoli, India	C4	37
Hinojosa del Duque, Spain	G6	12
Hinsdale, Il., U.S.	k9	90
Hinsdale, N.H., U.S.	E2	106
Hinsdale, co., Co., U.S.	D3	83
Hinton, Alta., Can.	C2	68
Hinton, Ia., U.S.	B1	92
Hinton, Ok., U.S.	B3	113
Hinton, W.V., U.S.	D4	125
Hirado, Japan	I2	30
Hīrākud, res., India	J10	38
Hiram, Ga., U.S.	C2	87
Hiram, Oh., U.S.	A4	112
Hirara, Japan	G12	26
Hiratsuka, Japan	G12	30
Hirosaki, Japan	B14	30
Hiroshima, Japan	H5	30
Hirson, Fr.	C11	10
Hisār, India	F6	38
Hispaniola, i., N.A.	E12	64
Hita, Japan	I3	30
Hitachi, Japan	F13	30
Hitchcock, Tx., U.S.	r14	120
Hitchcock, co., Ne., U.S.	D4	104
Hitchcock Lake, Ct., U.S.	C4	84
Hitoyoshi, Japan	J3	30
Hitra, i., Nor.	E7	6
Hiwassee, stm., Tn., U.S.	D9	119
Hiwassee Lake, res., N.C., U.S.	f8	110
Hjørring, Den.	H7	6
Ho, Ghana	G5	42
Hoa Binh, Viet.	D8	34
Hoagland, In., U.S.	C8	91
Hoback, stm., Wy., U.S.	C2	127
Hobart, Austl.	H9	50
Hobart, In., U.S.	A3	91
Hobart, Ok., U.S.	B2	113
Hobbs, N.M., U.S.	E6	108
Hobe Sound, Fl., U.S.	E6	86
Hobo, Col.	F5	58
Hoboken, N.J., U.S.	k8	107
Höchstadt an der Aisch, Ger.	F10	8
Hockessin, De., U.S.	A3	85
Hocking, co., Oh., U.S.	C3	112
Hocking, stm., Oh., U.S.	C3	112
Hockley, co., Tx., U.S.	C1	120
Hodgeman, co., Ks., U.S.	D4	93
Hodgenville, Ky., U.S.	C4	94
Hodges Village Reservoir, res., Ma., U.S.	B4	98
Hódmezővásárhely, Hung.	I20	8
Hodna, Chott el, l., Alg.	J16	12
Hodonín, Czech.	G17	8
Hof, Ger.	E11	8
Hoffman Estates, Il., U.S.	h8	90
Hofgeismar, Ger.	D9	8
Hofheim in Unterfranken, Ger.	E10	8
Hofors, Swe.	F11	6
Hōfu, Japan	H4	30
Hogansville, Ga., U.S.	C2	87
Hogback Mountain, mtn., Mt., U.S.	F4	103
Hog Island, i., Fl., U.S.	C3	86
Hog Island, i., Mi., U.S.	C5	99
Hog Island, i., N.C., U.S.	B6	110
Hog Island, i., R.I., U.S.	D5	116
Hog Island, i., Va., U.S.	C7	123
Hoh, stm., Wa., U.S.	B1	124
Hohenau an der March, Aus.	G16	8
Hohenwald, Tn., U.S.	B4	119
Hohe Tauern, mts., Aus.	H12	8
Hoh Head, c., Wa., U.S.	B1	124
Hohhot, China	C9	26
Hohoe, Ghana	H3	42
Hōhoku, Japan	H3	30
Hoh Xil Shan, mts., China	G10	34
Hoi An, Viet.	G10	34
Hoisington, Ks., U.S.	D5	93
Hokah, Mn., U.S.	G7	100
Hoke, co., N.C., U.S.	B3	110
Hokes Bluff, Al., U.S.	B4	78
Hokitika, N.Z.	E3	52
Hokkaidō, i., Japan	p20	30a
Holbrook, Az., U.S.	C5	80
Holbrook, Ma., U.S.	B5	98
Holcomb, Ks., U.S.	E3	93
Holden, Ma., U.S.	B4	98
Holden, Mo., U.S.	C4	102
Holden, W.V., U.S.	D2	125
Holdenville, Ok., U.S.	B5	113
Holdrege, Ne., U.S.	D6	104
Hole in the Mountain Peak, mtn., Nv., U.S.	C6	105
Holgate, Oh., U.S.	A1	112
Holguín, Cuba	D9	64
Höljes, Swe.	F9	6
Hollabrunn, Aus.	G16	8
Holladay, Ut., U.S.	C4	121
Holland, In., U.S.	H3	91
Holland, Mi., U.S.	F4	99
Holland, Oh., U.S.	A2	112
Holland, Tx., U.S.	D4	120
Hollandale, Ms., U.S.	B3	101
Holland Island, i., Md., U.S.	D5	97
Holland see Netherlands, ctry., Eur.	E9	4
Holland Point, c., Md., U.S.	C4	97
Holland Straits, strt., Md., U.S.	D5	97
Holley, N.Y., U.S.	B2	109
Holliday, Tx., U.S.	C3	120
Hollidaysburg, Pa., U.S.	F5	115
Hollins, Va., U.S.	C3	123
Hollis, Ok., U.S.	C2	113
Hollister, Ca., U.S.	D3	82
Hollister, Mo., U.S.	E4	102
Holliston, Ma., U.S.	B5	98
Holloman Air Force Base, mil., N.M., U.S.	E3	108
Hollow Rock, Tn., U.S.	A3	119
Hollowtop Mountain, mtn., Mt., U.S.	E4	103
Holly, Co., U.S.	C8	83
Holly, Mi., U.S.	F7	99
Holly Grove, Ar., U.S.	C5	81
Holly Hill, Fl., U.S.	C5	86
Holly Hill, S.C., U.S.	E7	117
Holly Pond, Al., U.S.	A3	78
Holly Ridge, Mi., U.S.	C5	99
Holly Shelter Swamp, sw., N.C., U.S.	C5	110
Holly Springs, Ga., U.S.	B2	87
Holly Springs, Ms., U.S.	A4	101
Holly Springs, N.C., U.S.	B4	110
Hollywood, Al., U.S.	A4	78
Hollywood, Fl., U.S.	F6	86
Hollywood, Md., U.S.	D5	97
Hollywood, S.C., U.S.	k11	117
Hollywood Indian Reservation, Fl., U.S.	r3	86
Holman Island, N.W. Ter., Can.	B9	66
Holmen, Wi., U.S.	E2	126
Holmes, co., Fl., U.S.	u16	86
Holmes, co., Ms., U.S.	B3	101
Holmes, co., Oh., U.S.	B4	112
Holmes, Mount, mtn., Wy., U.S.	B2	127
Holmes Reefs, rf., Austl.	C9	50
Holstebro, Den.	H7	6
Holstein, Ia., U.S.	B2	92
Holsteinsborg, Grnld.	C22	66
Holston, stm., Tn., U.S.	C11	119
Holston, Middle Fork, stm., Va., U.S.	f10	123
Holsworthy, Eng., U.K.	K8	7
Holt, Al., U.S.	B2	78
Holt, Mi., U.S.	F6	99
Holt, co., Mo., U.S.	A2	102
Holt, co., Ne., U.S.	B7	104
Holt Lake, res., Al., U.S.	B2	78
Holton, Ks., U.S.	C8	93
Holtville, Ca., U.S.	F6	82

Name	Map Ref	Page

Holualoa, Hi., U.S. ... D6 88
Holy Cross, Mountain of the, mtn., Co., U.S. ... B4 83
Holyhead, Wales, U.K. ... H8 7
Holyoke, Co., U.S. ... A8 83
Holyoke, Ma., U.S. ... B2 98
Holyoke Range, hills, Ma., U.S. ... B2 98
Holzminden, Ger. ... D9 8
Hombori Tondo, mtn., Mali ... E5 42
Homburg, Ger. ... F7 8
Home Bay, b., N.W. Ter., Can. ... C19 66
Homecroft, In., U.S. ... m10 91
Homedale, Id., U.S. ... F2 89
Home Hill, Austl. ... C9 50
Homeland, Ga., U.S. ... F4 87
Home Place, In., U.S. ... E5 91
Homer, Ak., U.S. ... D9 79
Homer, Ga., U.S. ... B3 87
Homer, Il., U.S. ... C6 90
Homer, La., U.S. ... B2 95
Homer, Mi., U.S. ... F6 99
Homer, N.Y., U.S. ... C4 109
Homer City, Pa., U.S. ... E3 115
Homerville, Ga., U.S. ... E4 87
Homer Youngs Peak, mtn., Mt., U.S. ... E3 103
Homestead, Fl., U.S. ... G6 86
Homestead, Pa., U.S. ... k14 115
Homestead Air Force Base, mil., Fl., U.S. ... G6 86
Homestead National Monument of America, Ne., U.S. ... D9 104
Homewood, Al., U.S. ... g7 78
Homewood, Il., U.S. ... B6 90
Homewood, Oh., U.S. ... C1 112
Hominy, Ok., U.S. ... A5 113
Hominy Creek, stm., Ok., U.S. ... A5 113
Homme Dam, N.D., U.S. ... A8 111
Homochitto, stm., Ms., U.S. ... D2 101
Homosassa, Fl., U.S. ... D4 86
Homs see Ḩimş, Syria ... B5 40
Honaker, Va., U.S. ... e10 123
Honaunau, Hi., U.S. ... D6 88
Honda, Col. ... E5 58
Hondo, Japan ... J3 30
Hondo, Tx., U.S. ... E3 120
Hondo, stm., N.A. ... H15 62
Hondo, Rio, stm., N.M., U.S. ... D4 108
Honduras, ctry., N.A. ... G4 64
Honduras, Gulf of, b., N.A. ... F4 64
Honea Path, S.C., U.S. ... C3 117
Hønefoss, Nor. ... F8 6
Honeoye Falls, N.Y., U.S. ... C3 109
Honesdale, Pa., U.S. ... C11 115
Honey Brook, Pa., U.S. ... F10 115
Honey Grove, Tx., U.S. ... C5 120
Honey Lake, l., Ca., U.S. ... B3 82
Honeypot Glen, Ct., U.S. ... C4 84
Honeyville, Ut., U.S. ... B3 121
Hon Gai, Viet. ... D9 34
Honga River, b., Md., U.S. ... D5 97
Hongdong, China ... D9 26
Honghu, China ... F2 28
Hong Kong, dep., Asia ... M3 28
Hongliuyuan, China ... C6 26
Honguedo, Détroit d', strt., Que., Can. ... G20 66
Hongze Hu, l., China ... B7 28
Honiara, Sol.Is. ... A11 50
Honjō, Japan ... F12 30
Honningsvåg, Nor. ... A15 6
Honokaa, Hi., U.S. ... C6 88
Honolulu, Hi., U.S. ... B4 88
Honolulu, co., Hi., U.S. ... B3 88
Honolulu International Airport, Hi., U.S. ... g10 88
Honomu, Hi., U.S. ... D6 88
Honouliuli, Hi., U.S. ... g9 88
Honshū, i., Japan ... F10 30
Honuapo Bay, b., Hi., U.S. ... D6 88
Hood, co., Tx., U.S. ... C4 120
Hood, Mount, mtn., Or., U.S. ... B5 114
Hood Canal, b., Wa., U.S. ... B2 124
Hoodoo Peak, mtn., Wa., U.S. ... A5 124
Hood River, Or., U.S. ... B5 114
Hood River, co., Or., U.S. ... B5 114
Hoodsport, Wa., U.S. ... B2 124
Hoogeveen, Neth. ... C6 8
Hooker, Ok., U.S. ... e9 113
Hooker, co., Ne., U.S. ... C4 104
Hook Head, c., Ire. ... I6 7
Hooksett, N.H., U.S. ... D4 106
Hoonah, Ak., U.S. ... D12 79
Hoopa Valley Indian Reservation, Ca., U.S. ... B2 82
Hooper, Ne., U.S. ... C9 104
Hooper Bay, Ak., U.S. ... C6 79
Hooper Islands, is., Md., U.S. ... D5 97
Hooper Strait, strt., Md., U.S. ... D5 97
Hoopes Reservoir, res., De., U.S. ... A3 85
Hoopeston, Il., U.S. ... C6 90
Hoorn, Neth. ... C5 8
Hoosac Range, mts., U.S. ... A1 98
Hoosic, stm., U.S. ... C7 109
Hoosick Falls, N.Y., U.S. ... C7 109
Hoover Dam, U.S. ... G7 105
Hoover Reservoir, res., Oh., U.S. ... B3 112
Hooverson Heights, W.V., U.S. ... f8 125
Hopatcong, N.J., U.S. ... B3 107
Hopatcong, Lake, l., N.J., U.S. ... A3 107
Hope, B.C., Can. ... E7 69
Hope, Ar., U.S. ... D2 81
Hope, In., U.S. ... F6 91
Hope, R.I., U.S. ... D3 116
Hope, Ben, mtn., Scot., U.K. ... C8 7
Hope, Point, c., Ak., U.S. ... B6 79
Hopedale, Il., U.S. ... C4 90
Hopedale, Ma., U.S. ... B4 98
Hope Island, i., R.I., U.S. ... E4 116
Hope Mills, N.C., U.S. ... C4 110
Hopes Advance, Cap, c., Que., Can. ... f13 74
Hopetown, S. Afr. ... G4 44
Hope Valley, R.I., U.S. ... E2 116
Hopewell, Va., U.S. ... C5 123
Hopewell Junction, N.Y., U.S. ... D7 109

Hopi Indian Reservation, Az., U.S. ... A5 80
Hopkins, Mn., U.S. ... n12 100
Hopkins, S.C., U.S. ... D6 117
Hopkins, co., Ky., U.S. ... C2 94
Hopkins, co., Tx., U.S. ... C5 120
Hopkinsville, Ky., U.S. ... D2 94
Hopkinton, Ia., U.S. ... B6 92
Hopkinton, Ma., U.S. ... B4 98
Hopkinton, R.I., U.S. ... F1 116
Hopkinton Lake, res., N.H., U.S. ... D3 106
Hopwood, Pa., U.S. ... G2 115
Hoquiam, Wa., U.S. ... C2 124
Horace, N.D., U.S. ... C9 111
Horace Mountain, mtn., Ak., U.S. ... B10 79
Horatio, Ar., U.S. ... D1 81
Horgen, Switz. ... E15 10
Horicon, Wi., U.S. ... E5 126
Horine, Mo., U.S. ... C7 102
Hormuz, Strait of, strt., Asia ... C6 46
Horn, Aus. ... G15 8
Horn, Cape see Hornos, Cabo de, c., Chile ... H3 56
Hornell, N.Y., U.S. ... C3 109
Hornersville, Mo., U.S. ... E7 102
Horn Island, i., Ms., U.S. ... E5 101
Horn Island Pass, strt., Ms., U.S. ... g8 101
Horn Lake, Ms., U.S. ... A3 101
Hornos, Cabo de (Cape Horn), c., Chile ... H3 56
Horn Plateau, plat., N.W. Ter., Can. ... D9 66
Horqin Youyi Qianqi, China ... B11 26
Horry, co., S.C., U.S. ... D10 117
Horse, stm., Ct., U.S. ... C6 84
Horse Cave, Ky., U.S. ... C4 94
Horse Creek, stm., U.S. ... E8 127
Horse Creek Reservoir, res., Co., U.S. ... C7 83
Horsehead Lake, l., N.D., U.S. ... B6 111
Horseheads, N.Y., U.S. ... C4 109
Horse Heaven Hills, hills, Wa., U.S. ... C6 124
Horsens, Den. ... I7 6
Horse Peak, mtn., N.M., U.S. ... D1 108
Horseshoe Bend, Id., U.S. ... F2 89
Horseshoe Bend National Military Park, Al., U.S. ... C4 78
Horseshoe Cove, b., Fl., U.S. ... C3 86
Horseshoe Point, c., Fl., U.S. ... C3 86
Horseshoe Reservoir, res., Az., U.S. ... C4 80
Horsham, Austl. ... G8 50
Horten, Nor. ... G8 6
Horton, Ks., U.S. ... C8 93
Hortonia, Lake, l., Vt., U.S. ... D2 122
Hortonville, Wi., U.S. ... D5 126
Hoschton, Ga., U.S. ... B3 87
Hoshangābād, India ... I7 38
Hoshiārpur, India ... E6 38
Hospers, Ia., U.S. ... A2 92
Hospet, India ... E4 37
Hospitalet, Spain ... D14 12
Hosta Butte, mtn., N.M., U.S. ... B1 108
Hoste, Isla, i., Chile ... H3 56
Hotchkiss, Co., U.S. ... C3 83
Hot Creek Range, mts., Nv., U.S. ... E5 105
Hot Creek Valley, val., Nv., U.S. ... E5 105
Hoting, Swe. ... D11 6
Hot Spring, co., Ar., U.S. ... C2 81
Hot Springs, S.D., U.S. ... D2 118
Hot Springs, co., Wy., U.S. ... C4 127
Hot Springs National Park, Ar., U.S. ... C2 81
Hot Springs National Park, Ar., U.S. ... C2 81
Hot Springs Peak, mtn., Ca., U.S. ... B3 82
Hot Springs Peak, mtn., Nv., U.S. ... B4 105
Hottah Lake, l., N.W. Ter., Can. ... C9 66
Houghton, Mi., U.S. ... A2 99
Houghton, N.Y., U.S. ... C2 109
Houghton, co., Mi., U.S. ... A2 99
Houghton Lake, Mi., U.S. ... D6 99
Houghton Lake, l., Mi., U.S. ... D6 99
Houghton Lake Heights, Mi., U.S. ... D6 99
Houlton, Me., U.S. ... B5 96
Houma, China ... D9 26
Houma, La., U.S. ... E5 95
House Springs, Mo., U.S. ... g12 102
Houston, De., U.S. ... E3 85
Houston, Mn., U.S. ... G7 100
Houston, Ms., U.S. ... B4 101
Houston, Mo., U.S. ... D6 102
Houston, Pa., U.S. ... F1 115
Houston, Tx., U.S. ... E5 120
Houston, co., Al., U.S. ... D4 78
Houston, co., Ga., U.S. ... D3 87
Houston, co., Mn., U.S. ... G7 100
Houston, co., Tn., U.S. ... A4 119
Houston, co., Tx., U.S. ... D5 120
Houston, stm., La., U.S. ... D2 95
Houston, Lake, res., Tx., U.S. ... r14 120
Houston Intercontinental Airport, Tx., U.S. ... r14 120
Houtman Rocks, Austl. ... E2 50
Houtzdale, Pa., U.S. ... E5 115
Hovenweep National Monument, Ut., U.S. ... F6 121
Hovmantorp, Swe. ... H10 6
Howard, Ks., U.S. ... E7 93
Howard, S.D., U.S. ... C8 118
Howard, Wi., U.S. ... D5 126
Howard, co., Ar., U.S. ... C2 81
Howard, co., In., U.S. ... C5 91
Howard, co., Ia., U.S. ... A5 92
Howard, co., Md., U.S. ... B4 97
Howard, co., Mo., U.S. ... B5 102
Howard, co., Ne., U.S. ... C7 104
Howard, co., Tx., U.S. ... C2 120
Howard City, Mi., U.S. ... E5 99
Howard Hanson Reservoir, res., Wa., U.S. ... B4 124
Howard Lake, Mn., U.S. ... E4 100
Howard Prairie Lake, res., Or., U.S. ... E4 114
Howards Grove-Millersville, Wi., U.S. ... E6 126
Howell, Mi., U.S. ... F7 99
Howell, co., Mo., U.S. ... E6 102

Howells, Ne., U.S. ... C8 104
Howe Sound, strt., B.C., Can. ... E6 69
Howick, Que., Can. ... D4 74
Howland, Me., U.S. ... C4 96
Howrah, India ... I13 38
Hoxie, Ar., U.S. ... A5 81
Hoxie, Ks., U.S. ... C3 93
Höxter, Ger. ... D9 8
Hoy, i., Scot., U.K. ... C9 7
Høyanger, Nor. ... F6 6
Hoyerswerda, Ger. ... D14 8
Hoyos, Spain ... E5 12
Hoyt Lakes, Mn., U.S. ... C6 100
Hradec Králové, Czech. ... E15 8
Hsilo, Tai. ... L9 28
Hsinchu, Tai. ... K9 28
Hsüehchia, Tai. ... L9 28
Huacho, Peru ... F3 54
Huachuca City, Az., U.S. ... F5 80
Hua Hin, Thai. ... H5 34
Huahua, stm., Nic. ... G6 64
Huaian, China ... B8 28
Huainan, China ... C6 28
Huaiyang, China ... B3 28
Huaiyin, China ... B8 28
Huaiyuan, China ... C6 28
Hualalai, vol., Hi., U.S. ... D6 88
Hualapai Indian Reservation, Az., U.S. ... B2 80
Hualapai Peak, mtn., Az., U.S. ... C2 80
Hualien, Tai. ... L10 28
Huallaga, stm., Peru ... E3 54
Huallanca, Peru ... E3 54
Huamachuco, Peru ... E3 54
Huambo, Ang. ... D3 44
Huancayo, Peru ... F3 54
Huang (Yellow), stm., China ... D10 26
Huangchuan, China ... C4 28
Huangling, China ... D8 26
Huangshi, China ... E4 28
Huangyan, China ... G10 28
Huánuco, Peru ... E3 54
Huaraz, Peru ... E3 54
Huascarán, Nevado, mtn., Peru ... E3 54
Huasco, Chile ... B2 56
Huatabampo, Mex. ... D5 62
Huauchinango, Mex. ... G10 62
Hubbard, Ia., U.S. ... B4 92
Hubbard, Oh., U.S. ... A5 112
Hubbard, Or., U.S. ... B4 114
Hubbard, Tx., U.S. ... D4 120
Hubbard, co., Mn., U.S. ... C4 100
Hubbard Creek Lake, res., Tx., U.S. ... C3 120
Hubbard Lake, l., Mi., U.S. ... D7 99
Hubbardton, stm., Vt., U.S. ... D2 122
Hubbell, Mi., U.S. ... A2 99
Hubei, prov., China ... E9 26
Hubli, India ... E3 37
Huckleberry Mountain, mtn., Or., U.S. ... D4 114
Huddersfield, Eng., U.K. ... H11 7
Huddinge, Swe. ... G11 6
Hudiksvall, Swe. ... F11 6
Hudson, Que., Can. ... D3 74
Hudson, Co., U.S. ... A6 83
Hudson, Fl., U.S. ... D4 86
Hudson, Il., U.S. ... C5 90
Hudson, Ia., U.S. ... B5 92
Hudson, Ma., U.S. ... B4 98
Hudson, Mi., U.S. ... G6 99
Hudson, N.H., U.S. ... E4 106
Hudson, N.Y., U.S. ... C7 109
Hudson, N.C., U.S. ... B1 110
Hudson, Oh., U.S. ... A4 112
Hudson, Wi., U.S. ... D1 126
Hudson, Wy., U.S. ... D4 127
Hudson, co., N.J., U.S. ... B4 107
Hudson, co., Oh., U.S. ... E7 109
Hudson, Lake, res., Ok., U.S. ... A6 113
Hudson Bay, b., Can. ... D15 66
Hudson Falls, N.Y., U.S. ... B7 109
Hudson Hope, B.C., Can. ... A6 69
Hudson Lake, In., U.S. ... A4 91
Hudson Strait, strt., Can. ... D18 66
Hudsonville, Mi., U.S. ... F5 99
Hudspeth, co., Tx., U.S. ... o12 120
Hue, Viet. ... F9 34
Huehuetenango, Guat. ... G2 64
Huelma, Spain ... H8 12
Huelva, Spain ... H5 12
Huércal-Overa, Spain ... H10 12
Huerfano, co., Co., U.S. ... D5 83
Huerfano, stm., Co., U.S. ... D6 83
Huerfano Mountain, mtn., N.M., U.S. ... A2 108
Huesca, Spain ... C11 12
Hueytown, Al., U.S. ... g6 78
Huffakers, Nv., U.S. ... D2 105
Hugh Butler Lake, res., Ne., U.S. ... D5 104
Hughenden, Austl. ... D8 50
Hughes, Ar., U.S. ... C5 81
Hughes, co., Ok., U.S. ... B5 113
Hughes, co., S.D., U.S. ... C5 118
Hughes, North Fork, stm., W.V., U.S. ... B3 125
Hughes, South Fork, stm., W.V., U.S. ... B3 125
Hughesville, Md., U.S. ... C4 97
Hughesville, Pa., U.S. ... D8 115
Hugo, Co., U.S. ... B7 83
Hugo, Mn., U.S. ... m13 100
Hugo, Ok., U.S. ... C6 113
Hugo, Lake, res., Ok., U.S. ... C6 113
Hugoton, Ks., U.S. ... E2 93
Huidong, China ... A7 34
Huila, Nevado del, mtn., Col. ... F4 58
Huili, China ... A7 34
Huinan, China ... C12 26
Huittinen (Lauttakylä), Fin. ... F14 6
Huitzuco [de los Figueroa], Mex. ... H10 62
Huixtla, Mex. ... J13 62
Huiyang (Huizhou), China ... L3 28
Hulah Lake, res., Ok., U.S. ... A5 113
Hulan, China ... B12 26
Hulett, Wy., U.S. ... B8 127
Hull, Que., Can. ... D2 74

Hull, Ia., U.S. ... A1 92
Hull, Ma., U.S. ... B6 98
Hultsfred, Swe. ... H10 6
Hulun Nur, l., China ... B10 26
Humaitá, Braz. ... E6 54
Humansville, Mo., U.S. ... D4 102
Humble, Tx., U.S. ... E5 120
Humboldt, Az., U.S. ... C3 80
Humboldt, Ia., U.S. ... B3 92
Humboldt, Ks., U.S. ... E8 93
Humboldt, Ne., U.S. ... D10 104
Humboldt, Tn., U.S. ... B3 119
Humboldt, co., Ca., U.S. ... B2 82
Humboldt, co., Ia., U.S. ... B3 92
Humboldt, co., Nv., U.S. ... B3 105
Humboldt, stm., Nv., U.S. ... C3 105
Humboldt Range, mts., Nv., U.S. ... C3 105
Hummels Wharf, Pa., U.S. ... E8 115
Humphrey, Ar., U.S. ... C4 81
Humphrey, Ne., U.S. ... C8 104
Humphreys, co., Ms., U.S. ... B3 101
Humphreys, co., Tn., U.S. ... A4 119
Humphreys, Mount, mtn., Ca., U.S. ... D4 82
Humphreys Peak, mtn., Az., U.S. ... B4 80
Hunan, prov., China ... F9 26
Hundred Acre Pond, l., R.I., U.S. ... E3 116
Hunedoara, Rom. ... D6 16
Hünfeld, Ger. ... E9 8
Hungary, ctry., Eur. ... F11 4
Hungŏ'ou Hsū, i., Tai. ... M10 28
Hüngnam, N. Kor. ... D12 26
Hungry Horse, Mt., U.S. ... B2 103
Hungry Horse Reservoir, res., Mt., U.S. ... B3 103
Hunsrück, mts., Ger. ... F6 8
Hunt, co., Tx., U.S. ... C4 120
Hunt, stm., R.I., U.S. ... D4 116
Hunterdon, co., N.J., U.S. ... B3 107
Hunter Island, i., Austl. ... H8 50
Hunter Island, i., B.C., Can. ... D3 69
Huntertown, In., U.S. ... B7 91
Huntingburg, In., U.S. ... H4 91
Huntingdon, Que., Can. ... D3 74
Huntingdon, Pa., U.S. ... F6 115
Huntingdon, Tn., U.S. ... A3 119
Huntingdon, co., Pa., U.S. ... F5 115
Hunting Island, i., S.C., U.S. ... G7 117
Huntington, Ar., U.S. ... B1 81
Huntington, In., U.S. ... C7 91
Huntington, N.Y., U.S. ... E7 109
Huntington, Tx., U.S. ... D5 120
Huntington, Ut., U.S. ... D5 121
Huntington, W.V., U.S. ... C2 125
Huntington, co., In., U.S. ... C6 91
Huntington Beach, Ca., U.S. ... F4 82
Huntington Lake, res., In., U.S. ... C7 91
Huntington Woods, Mi., U.S. ... p15 99
Huntingtown, Md., U.S. ... C4 97
Huntland, Tn., U.S. ... B5 119
Huntley, Il., U.S. ... A5 90
Hunt Mountain, mtn., Wy., U.S. ... B5 127
Huntsville, Ont., Can. ... B5 73
Huntsville, Al., U.S. ... A3 78
Huntsville, Ar., U.S. ... A2 81
Huntsville, Mo., U.S. ... B5 102
Huntsville, Tn., U.S. ... C9 119
Huntsville, Tx., U.S. ... D5 120
Huon Gulf, b., Pap. N. Gui. ... m16 50a
Hurao, China ... B13 26
Hurd, Cape, c., Ont., Can. ... B3 73
Hurley, Ms., U.S. ... E5 101
Hurley, N.M., U.S. ... E1 108
Hurley, N.Y., U.S. ... D6 109
Hurley, Wi., U.S. ... B3 126
Hurlock, Md., U.S. ... C6 97
Huron, Ca., U.S. ... A3 112
Huron, S.D., U.S. ... C7 118
Huron, co., Mi., U.S. ... E7 99
Huron, co., Oh., U.S. ... A3 112
Huron, stm., Mi., U.S. ... p14 99
Huron, Lake, l., N.A. ... C10 76
Huron Mountains, hills, Mi., U.S. ... B3 99
Hurricane, Ut., U.S. ... F2 121
Hurricane, W.V., U.S. ... C2 125
Hurst, Il., U.S. ... F4 90
Hurt, Va., U.S. ... C3 123
Hurtsboro, Al., U.S. ... C4 78
Húsavík, Ice. ... B4 4
Huskvarna, Swe. ... H10 6
Hustisford, Wi., U.S. ... E5 126
Husum, Ger. ... A9 8
Hutchins, Tx., U.S. ... n10 120
Hutchinson, Ks., U.S. ... D6 93
Hutchinson, Mn., U.S. ... F4 100
Hutchinson, co., S.D., U.S. ... D8 118
Hutchinson, co., Tx., U.S. ... B2 120
Hutchinson Island, i., Fl., U.S. ... E6 86
Hutchinson Island, i., S.C., U.S. ... k11 117
Hutch Mountain, mtn., Az., U.S. ... C4 80
Hüttental, Ger. ... E8 8
Huttig, Ar., U.S. ... D3 81
Huwei, Tai. ... L9 28
Huxley, Ia., U.S. ... C4 92
Huy, Bel. ... E4 8
Huzhou, China ... E9 28
Hvar, Cro. ... F11 14
Hwange, Zimb. ... E5 44
Hwang Ho see Huang, stm., China ... D10 26
Hyannis, Ma., U.S. ... C7 98
Hyannis Port, Ma., U.S. ... C7 98
Hyattsville, Md., U.S. ... C4 97
Hybla Valley, Va., U.S. ... g12 123
Hyco, stm., Va., U.S. ... D3 123
Hyco Lake, res., N.C., U.S. ... A3 110
Hydaburg, Ak., U.S. ... D13 79
Hyde, Pa., U.S. ... D5 115
Hyde, co., N.C., U.S. ... B6 110
Hyde, co., S.D., U.S. ... C6 118
Hyde Park, Guy. ... D13 58
Hyde Park, N.Y., U.S. ... D7 109
Hyde Park, Ut., U.S. ... B4 121
Hydeville, Vt., U.S. ... D2 122

Hydro, Ok., U.S. ... B3 113
Hyères, Fr. ... I13 10
Hyesan, N. Kor. ... C12 26
Hymera, In., U.S. ... F3 91
Hyndman, Pa., U.S. ... G4 115
Hyndman Peak, mtn., Id., U.S. ... F4 89
Hyrum, Ut., U.S. ... B4 121
Hythe, Alta., Can. ... B1 68
Hyūga, Japan ... J4 30
Hyūga-nada, Japan ... J4 30
Hyvinkää, Fin. ... F15 6

I

Iamonia, Lake, l., Fl., U.S. ... B2 86
Iaşi, Rom. ... B11 16
Iatt, Lake, res., La., U.S. ... C3 95
Ibadan, Nig. ... G6 42
Ibagué, Col. ... E5 58
Ibapah Peak, mtn., Ut., U.S. ... D2 121
Ibarra, Ec. ... G3 58
Ibb, Yemen ... F3 46
Iberia, Mo., U.S. ... C5 102
Iberia, co., La., U.S. ... E4 95
Iberville, Que., Can. ... D4 74
Iberville, co., La., U.S. ... D4 95
Iberville, Mont d' (Mount Caubvick), mtn., Can. ... g14 74
Ibiá, Braz. ... E5 57
Ibicaraí, Braz. ... C9 57
Ibiza, Spain ... G13 12
Ibiza, i., Spain ... G13 12
Ibo, Moz. ... D8 44
Içá (Putumayo), stm., S.A. ... I8 58
Içana, Braz. ... C5 54
Içana, stm., S.A. ... C5 54
Ice Harbor Dam, Wa., U.S. ... C7 124
İçel, Tur. ... H14 4
Iceland, ctry., Eur. ... B4 4
Ichalkaranji, India ... D3 37
Ich Bogd Uul, mtn., Mong. ... C7 26
Ichinomiya, Japan ... G9 30
Ichinoseki, Japan ... D14 30
Icicle Creek, stm., Wa., U.S. ... B5 124
Icó, Braz. ... E11 54
Icy Cape, c., Ak., U.S. ... A7 79
Icy Strait, strt., Ak., U.S. ... k22 79
Ida, Mi., U.S. ... G7 99
Ida, co., Ia., U.S. ... B2 92
Ida, Lake, l., Mn., U.S. ... D3 100
Idabel, Ok., U.S. ... D7 113
Ida Grove, Ia., U.S. ... B2 92
Idaho, co., Id., U.S. ... D3 89
Idaho, state, U.S. ... E3 89
Idaho Falls, Id., U.S. ... F6 89
Idaho Springs, Co., U.S. ... B5 83
Idalou, Tx., U.S. ... C2 120
Idamay, W.V., U.S. ... k10 125
Idanha-a-Nova, Port. ... F4 12
Idäppädi, India ... G4 37
Idar-Oberstein, Ger. ... F7 8
Idaville, In., U.S. ... C4 91
Ider, Al., U.S. ... A4 78
Idfū, Egypt ... D12 42
Idlib, Syria ... B5 40
Idolo, Isla del, i., Mex. ... G11 62
Ieper, Bel. ... E2 8
Ierápetra, Grc. ... N9 16
Iesi, Italy ... F8 14
Ife, Nig. ... G6 42
Iferouâne, Niger ... E7 42
Iforas, Adrar des, mts., Afr. ... D6 42
Iglesias, Italy ... J3 14
Igloolik, N.W. Ter., Can. ... C16 66
Ignacio, Co., U.S. ... D3 83
Iguaçu, Saltos do (Iguassu Falls), wtfl, S.A. ... B6 56
Iguala, Mex. ... H10 62
Igualada, Spain ... D13 12
Iguape, Braz. ... A7 56
Iguatu, Braz. ... E11 54
Iguéla, Gabon ... B1 44
Iguidi, Erg, dunes, Afr. ... C4 42
Ihosy, Madag. ... F9 44
Iida, Japan ... G10 30
Iisalmi, Fin. ... E16 6
Iizuka, Japan ... I3 30
IJmuiden, Neth. ... C4 8
IJsselmeer (Zuiderzee), Neth. ... C5 8
Ika, Russia ... F15 24
Ikela, Zaire ... B4 44
Ikerre, Nig. ... G7 42
Ila, Nig. ... G6 42
Ilagan, Phil. ... B7 32
Ilan, Tai. ... K10 28
Ilbenge, Russia ... E18 24
Île-à-la-Crosse, Lac, l., Sask., Can. ... B2 75
Ilebo, Zaire ... B4 44
Île-de-France, hist. reg., Fr. ... C9 10
Île-Perrot, Que., Can. ... q19 74
Ilhéus, Braz. ... C9 57
Ili, stm., Asia ... I13 22
Iliamna Lake, l., Ak., U.S. ... D8 79
Iliamna Volcano, vol., Ak., U.S. ... C9 79
Ilion, N.Y., U.S. ... B5 109
Ilio Point, c., Hi., U.S. ... B4 88
Ilirska Bistrica, Slo. ... D9 14
Ilkal, India ... E4 37
Illampu, Nevado, mtn., Bol. ... G5 54
Illapel, Chile ... C2 56
Illescas, Mex. ... F8 62
Illiers, Fr. ... D8 10
Illimani, Nevado, mtn., Bol. ... G5 54
Illinois, state, U.S. ... C4 90
Illinois, stm., U.S. ... A7 113
Illinois, stm., Il., U.S. ... B5 90
Illinois, stm., Or., U.S. ... E3 114
Illinois Peak, mtn., U.S. ... B3 89
Illiopolis, Il., U.S. ... D4 90
Illizi, Alg. ... C7 42
Ill'mo, Mo., U.S. ... D8 102
Il'men', Ozero, l., Russia ... C14 18
Ilo, Peru ... G4 54
Iloilo, Phil. ... C7 32

Name	Map Ref	Page
Ilomantsi, Fin.	E18	6
Ilorin, Nig.	G6	42
Il'pyrskij, Russia	F26	24
Ilwaco, Wa., U.S.	C1	124
Imabari, Japan	H6	30
Iman, Russia	H20	24
Imari, Japan	I2	30
Imatra, Fin.	F17	6
Imboden, Ar., U.S.	A4	81
Imlay, Nv., U.S.	C3	105
Imlay City, Mi., U.S.	E7	99
Immenstadt, Ger.	H10	8
Immokalee, Fl., U.S.	F5	86
Imnaha, stm., Or., U.S.	B10	114
Imola, Italy	E6	14
Imperatriz, Braz.	E9	54
Imperia, Italy	F3	14
Imperial, Ca., U.S.	F6	82
Imperial, Mo., U.S.	C7	102
Imperial, Ne., U.S.	D4	104
Imperial, Pa., U.S.	k13	115
Imperial, co., Ca., U.S.	F6	82
Imperial Beach, Ca., U.S.	o15	82
Imperial Dam, U.S.	E1	80
Imperial Reservoir, res., U.S.	E1	80
Imperial Valley, val., Ca., U.S.	F6	82
Impfondo, Congo	A3	44
Imphāl, India	H15	38
Imst, Aus.	H10	8
Imuris, Mex.	B4	62
Ina, Japan	G10	30
Inari, Fin.	B16	6
Inca, Spain	F14	12
Incekum Burnu, c., Tur.	A3	40
Inch'ŏn, S. Kor.	D12	26
Incline Village, Nv., U.S.	D2	105
Independence, Ia., U.S.	B6	92
Independence, Ks., U.S.	E8	93
Independence, Ky., U.S.	B5	94
Independence, La., U.S.	D5	95
Independence, Mo., U.S.	B3	102
Independence, Or., U.S.	C3	114
Independence, Va., U.S.	D1	123
Independence, Wi., U.S.	D2	126
Independence, co., Ar., U.S.	B4	81
Independence, stm., N.Y., U.S.	B5	109
Independence Mountains, mts., Nv., U.S.	C5	105
Independence National Historical Park, Pa., U.S.	p21	115
Independence Rock, mtn., Wy., U.S.	D5	127
India, ctry., Asia	E4	36
Indian, stm., Ont., Can.	B7	73
Indian, stm., De., U.S.	F4	85
Indian, stm., Mi., U.S.	B4	99
Indian, stm., N.Y., U.S.	A5	109
Indiana, Pa., U.S.	E3	115
Indiana, co., Pa., U.S.	E3	115
Indiana, state, U.S.	E5	91
Indiana Dunes National Lakeshore, In., U.S.	A3	91
Indianapolis, In., U.S.	E5	91
Indian Bay, b., Fl., U.S.	D4	86
Indian Cedar Swamp, sw., R.I., U.S.	F2	116
Indian Creek, stm., Oh., U.S.	C1	112
Indian Creek, stm., S.D., U.S.	B2	118
Indian Creek, stm., Tn., U.S.	B3	119
Indian Creek, stm., W.V., U.S.	D4	125
Indian Creek, stm., W.V., U.S.	k9	125
Indian Head, Md., U.S.	C3	97
Indian Island, i., N.C., U.S.	B6	110
Indian Lake, i., Mi., U.S.	C4	99
Indian Lake, l., N.Y., U.S.	B6	109
Indian Lake, l., Oh., U.S.	B2	112
Indian Lake, l., R.I., U.S.	F4	116
Indian Neck, Ct., U.S.	D4	84
Indian Ocean	G17	2
Indianola, Ia., U.S.	C4	92
Indianola, Ms., U.S.	B3	101
Indianola, Ne., U.S.	D5	104
Indian Peak, mtn., Ut., U.S.	E2	121
Indian Peak, mtn., Wy., U.S.	B3	127
Indian Prairie Canal, Fl., U.S.	E5	86
Indian River, co., Fl., U.S.	E6	86
Indian River, Mi., U.S.	D6	86
Indian River Bay, b., De., U.S.	F5	85
Indian Rock, mtn., Wa., U.S.	D5	124
Indian Rocks Beach, Fl., U.S.	p10	86
Indian Springs, Nv., U.S.	G6	105
Indian Stream, stm., N.H., U.S.	f7	106
Indiantown, Fl., U.S.	E6	86
Indian Trail, N.C., U.S.	B2	110
Indigirka, stm., Russia	C23	24
Indio, Ca., U.S.	F5	82
Indispensable Reefs, rf., Sol.Is.	B12	50
Indonesia, ctry., Asia	F6	32
Indore, India	I6	38
Indoukâl-n-Taghès, mtn., Niger	E7	42
Indramayu, Indon.	m14	33a
Indrāvati, stm., India	C6	37
Indus, stm., Asia	H2	38
Inegöl, Tur.	I13	16
Infiernillo, Presa del, res., Mex.	H9	62
I-n-Gall, Niger	E7	42
Ingalls, In., U.S.	E6	91
Ingalls Park, Il., U.S.	B5	90
Ingersoll, Ont., Can.	D4	73
Ingham, Austl.	C9	50
Ingham, co., Mi., U.S.	F6	99
Ingleside, Tx., U.S.	F4	120
Inglewood, Ca., U.S.	n12	82
Ingolstadt, Ger.	G11	8
Ingraham, Lake, l., Fl., U.S.	G5	86
Ingram, Pa., U.S.	k13	115
In Guezzam, Alg.	E7	42
Inhambane, Moz.	F7	44
Inhambupe, Braz.	F11	54
Inhaminga, Moz.	E6	44
Inharrime, Moz.	F7	44
Inírida, stm., Col.	F8	58
Inkerman, N.B., Can.	B5	71
Inkom, Id., U.S.	G6	89
Inkster, Mi., U.S.	p15	99
Inland Sea see Seto-naikai, Japan	H6	30

Inle Lake, l., Burma	D4	34
Inman, Ks., U.S.	D6	93
Inman, S.C., U.S.	A3	117
Inn (En), stm., Eur.	G13	8
Innamincka, Austl.	E8	50
Inner Hebrides, is., Scot., U.K.	E6	7
Innisfail, Alta., Can.	C4	68
Innsbruck, Aus.	H11	8
Inola, Ok., U.S.	A6	113
Inongo, Zaire	B3	44
Inowrocław, Pol.	C18	8
In Salah, Alg.	C6	42
Inscription House Ruin, hist., Az., U.S.	A5	80
Insein, Burma	F4	34
Institute, W.V., U.S.	m12	125
Interlachen, Fl., U.S.	C5	86
Interlaken, Switz.	F14	10
International Falls, Mn., U.S.	B5	100
Inthanon, Doi, mtn., Thai.	E5	34
Intiyaco, Arg.	B4	56
Intracoastal Waterway, U.S.	E4	95
Inukjuak, Que., Can.	g11	74
Inveraray, Scot., U.K.	E7	7
Invercargill, N.Z.	G2	52
Inverell, Austl.	E10	50
Inver Grove Heights, Mn., U.S.	n12	100
Invermere, B.C., Can.	D9	69
Inverness, Scot., U.K.	D8	7
Inverness, Ca., U.S.	C2	82
Inverness, Fl., U.S.	D4	86
Inverness, Ms., U.S.	B3	101
Inverurie, Scot., U.K.	D10	7
Investigator Group, is., Austl.	F6	50
Investigator Strait, strt., Austl.	G7	50
Invisible Mountain, mtn., Id., U.S.	F5	89
Inwood, Ia., U.S.	A1	92
Inwood, N.Y., U.S.	k13	109
Inwood, W.V., U.S.	B6	125
Inyangani, mtn., Zimb.	E6	44
Inyan Kara Creek, stm., Wy., U.S.	B8	127
Inyan Kara Mountain, mtn., Wy., U.S.	B8	127
Inyo, co., Ca., U.S.	D5	82
Inyo, Mount, mtn., Ca., U.S.	D5	82
Inyo Mountains, mts., Ca., U.S.	D4	82
Ioánnina, Grc.	J4	16
Iola, Ks., U.S.	E8	93
Iola, Wi., U.S.	D4	126
Iona, Id., U.S.	F7	89
Ione, Ca., U.S.	C3	82
Ionia, Mi., U.S.	F5	99
Ionia, co., Mi., U.S.	F5	99
Ionian Islands see Iónioi Nísoi, is., Grc.	K4	16
Ionian Sea, Eur.	H11	4
Iónioi Nísoi, is., Grc.	K4	16
Iosco, co., Mi., U.S.	D7	99
Iota, La., U.S.	D3	95
Iowa, La., U.S.	D2	95
Iowa, co., Ia., U.S.	C5	92
Iowa, co., Wi., U.S.	E3	126
Iowa, state, U.S.	C4	92
Iowa, stm., Ia., U.S.	C6	92
Iowa, West Branch, stm., Ia., U.S.	B4	92
Iowa City, Ia., U.S.	C6	92
Iowa Falls, Ia., U.S.	B4	92
Iowa Indian Reservation, U.S.	C8	93
Iowa Lake, l., U.S.	A3	92
Iowa Park, Tx., U.S.	C3	120
Ipameri, Braz.	D4	57
Iphigenia Bay, b., Ak., U.S.	n22	79
Ipiales, Col.	G4	58
Ipiaú, Braz.	C9	57
Ipoh, Malay.	L6	34
Ipswich, Austl.	E10	50
Ipswich, Eng., U.K.	I14	7
Ipswich, Ma., U.S.	A6	98
Ipswich, S.D., U.S.	B6	118
Ipswich, stm., Ma., U.S.	A5	98
Ipu, Braz.	D10	54
Iqaluit, N.W. Ter., Can.	D19	66
Iquique, Chile	H4	54
Iquitos, Peru	D4	54
Iraan, Tx., U.S.	D2	120
Iráklion, Grc.	N9	16
Iran, ctry., Asia	B5	46
Iran Mountains, mts., Asia	E5	32
Trānshahr, Iran	C7	46
Irapa, Ven.	B11	58
Irapuato, Mex.	G9	62
Iraq, ctry., Asia	B3	46
Irazú, Volcán, vol., C.R.	J6	64
Irbid, Jord.	A3	46
Irbil, Iraq	B2	46
Iredell, co., N.C., U.S.	B2	110
Ireland, ctry., Eur.	E6	4
Iriga, Phil.	r20	32
Irion, co., Tx., U.S.	D2	120
Iringa, Tan.	C7	44
Iriri, stm., Braz.	D8	54
Irish, Mount, mtn., Nv., U.S.	F6	105
Irish Sea, Eur.	H8	7
Irkutsk, Russia	G14	24
Irmo, S.C., U.S.	C5	117
Iron, co., Mi., U.S.	B2	99
Iron, co., Mo., U.S.	D7	102
Iron, co., Ut., U.S.	F2	121
Iron, co., Wi., U.S.	B3	126
Irondale, Al., U.S.	f7	78
Irondequoit, N.Y., U.S.	B3	109
Iron Gate, val., Eur.	E6	16
Iron Gate Reservoir, res., Eur.	E5	16
Iron Gate Reservoir, res., Ca., U.S.	B2	82
Iron Mountain, Mi., U.S.	C2	99
Iron Mountain, mtn., Az., U.S.	D4	80
Iron Mountains, mts., U.S.	D1	123
Iron Ridge, Wi., U.S.	E5	126
Iron River, Mi., U.S.	B2	99
Iron River, Wi., U.S.	B2	126
Ironton, Mo., U.S.	D7	102
Ironton, Oh., U.S.	D3	112
Ironwood, Mi., U.S.	n11	99
Iroquois, Ont., Can.	C9	73
Iroquois, co., Il., U.S.	C6	90
Iroquois, stm., U.S.	C6	90
Iroquois, Lake, l., Vt., U.S.	B2	122
Iroquois Falls, Ont., Can.	o19	73

Irrawaddy see Ayeyarwady, stm., Burma	G3	34
Irricana, Alta., Can.	D4	68
Irrigon, Or., U.S.	B7	114
Irtyš (Ertix), stm., Asia	F11	22
Irumu, Zaire	A5	44
Irún, Spain	B10	12
Irurzun, Spain	C10	12
Irú Tepuy, mtn., Ven.	E12	58
Irvine, Scot., U.K.	F8	7
Irvine, Ca., U.S.	n13	82
Irvine, Ky., U.S.	C6	94
Irving, Tx., U.S.	n10	120
Irvington, Al., U.S.	E1	78
Irvington, Il., U.S.	E4	90
Irvington, Ky., U.S.	C3	94
Irvington, N.J., U.S.	k8	107
Irvington, N.Y., U.S.	g13	109
Irwin, Pa., U.S.	F2	115
Irwin, co., Ga., U.S.	E3	87
Irwinton, Ga., U.S.	D3	87
Isabel, Mount, mtn., Wy., U.S.	D2	127
Isabela, co., Mi., U.S.	E6	99
Isabella, Cordillera, mts., Nic.	G5	64
Isabella Indian Reservation, Mi., U.S.	E6	99
Isabella Lake, l., Mn., U.S.	C7	100
Ísafjördur, Ice.	B3	4
Isahaya, Japan	J3	30
Isanti, Mn., U.S.	E5	100
Isanti, co., Mn., U.S.	E5	100
Isar, stm., Eur.	G11	8
Ischia, Italy	I8	14
Ise, Japan	H9	30
Isernia, Italy	H9	14
Isesaki, Japan	F12	30
Ise-wan, b., Japan	H9	30
Isherton, Guy.	F13	58
Ishikari-wan, b., Japan	p18	30a
Ishinomaki, Japan	D14	30
Ishpeming, Mi., U.S.	B3	99
Isinglass, stm., N.H., U.S.	D4	106
Isiolo, Kenya	A7	44
Isiro, Zaire	H11	42
Iskele, N. Cyp.	B3	40
İskenderun, Tur.	H15	4
İskenderun Körfezi, b., Tur.	A4	40
Iskitim, Russia	G10	24
Islâhiye, Tur.	A5	40
Islāmābād, Pak.	D5	38
Islamorada, Fl., U.S.	H6	86
Isla Mujeres, Mex.	G16	62
Island, co., Wa., U.S.	A3	124
Island Beach, N.J., U.S.	D4	107
Island City, Or., U.S.	B8	114
Island Falls, Me., U.S.	B4	96
Island Lake, l., Man., Can.	C4	70
Island Park, R.I., U.S.	E6	116
Island Park Reservoir, res., Id., U.S.	E7	89
Island Pond, Vt., U.S.	B5	122
Island Pond, l., N.H., U.S.	E4	106
Islands, Bay of, b., Newf., Can.	D2	72
Isla Vista, Ca., U.S.	E4	82
Islay, i., Scot., U.K.	F6	7
Isle-aux-Morts, Newf., Can.	E2	72
Isle of Man, dep., Eur.	E7	4
Isle of Palms, S.C., U.S.	k12	117
Isle of Wight, co., Va., U.S.	D6	123
Isle of Wight Bay, b., Md., U.S.	D7	97
Isle Royale National Park, Mi., U.S.	h9	99
Islesboro Island, i., Me., U.S.	D4	96
Isleta, N.M., U.S.	C3	108
Isleta Indian Reservation, N.M., U.S.	C3	108
Islington, Ma., U.S.	h11	98
Isola, Ms., U.S.	B3	101
Isola della Scala, Italy	D5	14
Ispica, Italy	M9	14
Israel (Yisra'el), ctry., Asia	D4	40
Israel, stm., N.H., U.S.	B3	106
Issano, Guy.	E13	58
Issaquah, Wa., U.S.	B3	124
Issaquena, co., Ms., U.S.	C2	101
Issoire, Fr.	G10	10
Issoudun, Fr.	F8	10
Is-sur-Tille, Fr.	E12	10
İstanbul, Tur.	G13	4
İstanbul Boğazı (Bosporus), strt., Tur.	H13	16
Isto, Mount, mtn., Ak., U.S.	B11	79
Istokpoga, Lake, l., Fl., U.S.	E5	86
Itabaiana, Braz.	F11	54
Itaberaí, Braz.	G9	54
Itaberaí, Braz.	E7	57
Itabira, Braz.	C9	57
Itabuna, Braz.	D5	58
Itacoatiara, Braz.	D7	54
Itagüí, Col.	D7	54
Itaituba, Braz.	B7	56
Itajaí, Braz.	G6	57
Itajubá, Braz.	C4	120
Italy, Tx., U.S.	G10	4
Italy, ctry., Eur.	F8	57
Itaperuna, Braz.	C8	57
Itapetinga, Braz.	C8	57
Itapetininga, Braz.	G4	57
Itapeva, Braz.	G4	57
Itapicuru, stm., Braz.	D10	54
Itapira, Braz.	G5	57
Itaquari, Braz.	E8	57
Itararé, Braz.	H4	57
Itārsi, India	I7	38
Itasca, Il., U.S.	k8	90
Itasca, Tx., U.S.	C4	120
Itasca, co., Mn., U.S.	C5	100
Itasca, Lake, l., Mn., U.S.	C3	100
Itawamba, co., Ms., U.S.	A5	101
Ithaca, Mi., U.S.	E6	99
Ithaca, N.Y., U.S.	C4	109
Itō, Japan	H12	30
Itta Bena, Ms., U.S.	B3	101
Ittiri, Italy	I3	14
Ituberá, Braz.	B9	57
Ituiutaba, Braz.	E4	57
Itumbiara, Braz.	E4	57
Ituni, Guy.	E13	58
Ituri, stm., Zaire	A5	44

Iturup, Ostrov (Etorofu-tō), i., Russia	I23	24
Ituverava, Braz.	F5	57
Ituxi, stm., Braz.	E5	54
Itzehoe, Ger.	B9	8
Iuka, Ms., U.S.	A5	101
Iva, S.C., U.S.	C2	117
Ivanhoe, Mn., U.S.	F2	100
Ivanić Grad, Cro.	D11	14
Ivano-Frankivsk, Ukr.	H2	22
Ivanovo, Russia	D23	18
Ivigtut, Grnld.	D23	66
Ivinheima, stm., Braz.	G2	57
Ivins, Ut., U.S.	F2	121
Ivory Coast, ctry., Afr.	G4	42
Ivoryton, Ct., U.S.	D6	84
Ivrea, Italy	D2	14
Iwaki (Taira), Japan	E13	30
Iwakuni, Japan	H5	30
Iwanai, Japan	q18	30a
Iwanuma, Japan	D13	30
Iwo, Nig.	G6	42
Ixtacihuatl, vol., Mex.	H10	62
Iyo-nada, Japan	I5	30
Izabal, Lago de, l., Guat.	G3	64
Izard, co., Ar., U.S.	A4	81
Izegem, Bel.	E3	8
Iževsk, Russia	F8	22
İzmir, Tur.	H13	4
İzmit, Tur.	G13	4
Iznalloz, Spain	H8	12
İznik Gölü, l., Tur.	I13	16
Izozog, Bañados de, sw., Bol.	G6	54
Izúcar de Matamoros, Mex.	H10	62
Izuhara, Japan	H2	30
Izumo, Japan	G5	30
Izu-shotō, is., Japan	H12	30
Izvestij CIK, Ostrova, is., Russia	B10	24

J

Jabalpur, India	I8	38
Jabbūl, Sabkhat al-, l., Syria	A5	40
Jablah, Syria	B4	40
Jablonec nad Nisou, Czech.	E15	8
Jaboatão, Braz.	E11	54
Jabrïn, well, Sau. Ar.	D4	46
Jaca, Spain	C11	12
Jacarèzinho, Braz.	G4	57
Jáchal, Arg.	C3	56
Jacinto City, Tx., U.S.	r14	120
Jack, co., Tx., U.S.	C3	120
Jackfish Lake, l., Sask., Can.	D1	75
Jackman, Me., U.S.	C2	96
Jackman Station, Me., U.S.	C2	96
Jack Mountain, mtn., Mt., U.S.	D4	103
Jack Mountain, mtn., Wa., U.S.	A5	124
Jackpot, Nv., U.S.	B7	105
Jacksboro, Tn., U.S.	C9	119
Jacksboro, Tx., U.S.	C3	120
Jacks Mountain, mtn., Pa., U.S.	E6	115
Jackson, Al., U.S.	D2	78
Jackson, Ca., U.S.	C3	82
Jackson, Ga., U.S.	C3	87
Jackson, Ky., U.S.	C6	94
Jackson, La., U.S.	D4	95
Jackson, Mi., U.S.	F6	99
Jackson, Mn., U.S.	G4	100
Jackson, Ms., U.S.	C3	101
Jackson, Mo., U.S.	D8	102
Jackson, Oh., U.S.	C3	112
Jackson, S.C., U.S.	E4	117
Jackson, Tn., U.S.	B3	119
Jackson, Wi., U.S.	E5	126
Jackson, Wy., U.S.	C2	127
Jackson, co., Al., U.S.	A3	78
Jackson, co., Ar., U.S.	B4	81
Jackson, co., Co., U.S.	A4	83
Jackson, co., Fl., U.S.	B1	86
Jackson, co., Ga., U.S.	B3	87
Jackson, co., Il., U.S.	F4	90
Jackson, co., In., U.S.	G5	91
Jackson, co., Ia., U.S.	B7	92
Jackson, co., Ks., U.S.	C8	93
Jackson, co., Ky., U.S.	C5	94
Jackson, co., La., U.S.	B3	95
Jackson, co., Mi., U.S.	F6	99
Jackson, co., Mn., U.S.	G3	100
Jackson, co., Ms., U.S.	E5	101
Jackson, co., Mo., U.S.	B3	102
Jackson, co., N.C., U.S.	f9	110
Jackson, co., Oh., U.S.	C3	112
Jackson, co., Ok., U.S.	C2	113
Jackson, co., Or., U.S.	E4	114
Jackson, co., S.D., U.S.	C4	118
Jackson, co., Tn., U.S.	C8	119
Jackson, co., Tx., U.S.	E4	120
Jackson, co., W.V., U.S.	C3	125
Jackson, co., Wi., U.S.	D3	126
Jackson, stm., Va., U.S.	C3	123
Jackson, Lake, l., Fl., U.S.	E5	86
Jackson, Lake, l., Fl., U.S.	B2	86
Jackson, Mount, mtn., N.H., U.S.	B4	106
Jackson Center, Oh., U.S.	B1	112
Jackson Lake, res., Wy., U.S.	C2	127
Jackson Mountains, mts., Nv., U.S.	B3	105
Jackson's Arm, Newf., Can.	D3	72
Jacksons Gap, Al., U.S.	C4	78
Jacksonville, Al., U.S.	B4	78
Jacksonville, Ar., U.S.	C3	81
Jacksonville, Fl., U.S.	B5	86
Jacksonville, Il., U.S.	D3	90
Jacksonville, N.C., U.S.	C5	110
Jacksonville, Or., U.S.	E4	114
Jacksonville, Tx., U.S.	D5	120
Jacksonville Beach, Fl., U.S.	B5	86
Jacksonville Naval Air Station, mil., Fl., U.S.	B5	86
Jacmel, Haiti	E11	64
Jacobābād, Pak.	F3	38
Jacques-Cartier, stm., Que., Can.	B6	74
Jacques-Cartier, Détroit de, strt., Que., Can.	h8	72

Jacquet River, N.B., Can.	B4	71
Jadraque, Spain	E9	12
Jaén, Peru	E3	54
Jaén, Spain	H8	12
Jaffna, Sri L.	H6	37
Jaffrey, N.H., U.S.	E2	106
Jaffr, Qâ' al-, depr., Jord.	D5	40
Jagādhri, India	E7	38
Jagdalpur, India	C7	37
Jagersfontein, S. Afr.	G5	44
Jagodnoje, Russia	E23	24
Jagtiāl, India	C5	37
Jaguarão, Braz.	C6	56
Jahrom, Iran	C5	46
Jaidak, Afg.	G6	38
Jaipur, India	E12	14
Jajce, Bos.	m13	32
Jakarta, Indon.	m13	32
Jakobshavn, Grnld.	C22	66
Jakobstad (Pietarsaari), Fin.	E14	6
Jakutsk, Russia	E19	24
Jal, N.M., U.S.	E6	108
Jalālābād, Afg.	C4	38
Jalapa, Guat.	G3	64
Jalapa Enríquez, Mex.	H11	62
Jālgaon, India	B3	37
Jālna, India	C3	37
Jalostotitlán, Mex.	G8	62
Jalpaiguri, India	G13	38
Jalta, Ukr.	I4	22
Jaltepec, stm., Mex.	I12	62
Jamaica, ctry., N.A.	E9	64
Jamaica Bay, b., N.Y., U.S.	k13	109
Jamaica Channel, strt., N.A.	E10	64
Jamālpur, Bngl.	H13	38
Jamālpur, India	H12	38
Jamame, Som.	A8	44
Jambi, Indon.	F3	32
Jambol, Bul.	G10	16
James, stm., U.S.	C7	76
James, stm., Mo., U.S.	E4	102
James, stm., Va., U.S.	C5	123
James, Lake, l., In., U.S.	A7	91
James, Lake, res., N.C., U.S.	B1	110
James Bay, b., Can.	F16	66
James Branch, stm., De., U.S.	F3	85
Jamesburg, N.J., U.S.	C4	107
James City, N.C., U.S.	B5	110
James City, co., Va., U.S.	C6	123
James Island, S.C., U.S.	k12	117
James Island, i., Md., U.S.	C5	97
James Island, i., S.C., U.S.	F8	117
James River Bridge, Va., U.S.	k15	123
Jamestown, In., U.S.	E4	91
Jamestown, Ky., U.S.	D4	94
Jamestown, N.Y., U.S.	C1	109
Jamestown, N.C., U.S.	B3	110
Jamestown, N.D., U.S.	C7	111
Jamestown, Oh., U.S.	C2	112
Jamestown, R.I., U.S.	F5	116
Jamestown, Tn., U.S.	C9	119
James Town, Wy., U.S.	E3	127
Jamestown Dam, N.D., U.S.	C7	111
Jamestown Reservoir, res., N.D., U.S.	C7	111
Jamiltepec, Mex.	I11	62
Jamkhandi, India	D3	37
Jammu, India	D6	38
Jammu and Kashmir, dep., Asia	C6	38
Jāmnagar, India	I4	38
Jāmpur, Pak.	F4	38
Jämsä, Fin.	F15	6
Jamshedpur, India	I12	38
Jamsk, Russia	F24	24
Jamūi, India	H12	38
Jamuna, stm., Bngl.	H13	38
Jana, stm., Russia	C21	24
Janaucu, Ilha, i., Braz.	C8	54
Janesville, Ca., U.S.	B3	82
Janesville, Ia., U.S.	B5	92
Janesville, Mn., U.S.	F5	100
Janesville, Wi., U.S.	F4	126
Jangipur, India	H13	38
Janīn, Jord.	C4	40
Janskij, Russia	D20	24
Janskij Zaliv, b., Russia	C21	24
Januária, Braz.	C6	57
Jaora, India	I6	38
Japan, ctry., Asia	D14	26
Japan, Sea of, Asia	D13	26
Japurá (Caquetá), stm., S.A.	D5	54
Jaqué, Pan.	K8	64
Jarābulus, Syria	A6	40
Jaraiz de la Vera, Spain	E6	12
Jarash, Jord.	C4	40
Jarcevo, Russia	F15	18
Jardines de la Reina, is., Cuba	D8	64
Jari, stm., Braz.	D8	54
Jaridih, India	I12	38
Jaroslavl', Russia	D22	18
Jarosław, Pol.	E22	8
Jarrettsville, Md., U.S.	A5	97
Järvenpää, Fin.	F15	6
Järvsö, Swe.	F11	6
Jask, Iran	C6	46
Jasmine Estates, Fl., U.S.	D4	86
Jasnyj, Russia	G19	24
Jasonville, In., U.S.	F3	91
Jasper, Al., U.S.	B2	78
Jasper, Fl., U.S.	B4	86
Jasper, Ga., U.S.	B2	87
Jasper, In., U.S.	H4	91
Jasper, Mo., U.S.	D3	102
Jasper, Tn., U.S.	D8	119
Jasper, Tx., U.S.	D6	120
Jasper, co., Ga., U.S.	C3	87
Jasper, co., Il., U.S.	D5	90
Jasper, co., In., U.S.	B3	91
Jasper, co., Ia., U.S.	C4	92
Jasper, co., Ms., U.S.	C4	101
Jasper, co., Mo., U.S.	D3	102
Jasper, co., S.C., U.S.	G5	117
Jasper, co., Tx., U.S.	D6	120
Jasper National Park, Alta., Can.	C1	68
Jataí, Braz.	D3	57
Játiva, Spain	G11	12

Name	Map Ref	Page
Jatni, India	J11	38
Jaú, Braz.	G4	57
Jauaperi, stm., Braz.	C6	54
Jauja, Peru	F3	54
Jaunpur, India	H10	38
Java see Jawa, i., Indon.	G4	32
Javari (Yavarí), stm., S.A.	D4	54
Java Sea see Jawa, Laut, Indon.	G4	32
Jävre, Swe.	D13	6
Jawa, i., Indon.	G4	32
Jawa, Laut (Java Sea), Indon.	G4	32
Jaworzno, Pol.	E19	8
Jay, Ok., U.S.	A7	113
Jay, co., In., U.S.	D7	91
Jaya, Puncak, mtn., Indon.	F10	32
Jayapura, Indon.	F11	32
Jayb, Wādī al-, val., Asia	D4	40
J. B. Thomas, Lake, res., Tx., U.S.	C2	120
Jean, Nv., U.S.	H6	105
Jeanerette, La., U.S.	E4	95
Jean Lafitte National Historical Park, La., U.S.	k12	95
Jeannette, Pa., U.S.	F2	115
Jebba, Nig.	G6	42
Jeddore Lake, res., Newf., Can.	D3	72
Jeff Davis, co., Ga., U.S.	E4	87
Jeff Davis, co., Tx., U.S.	o12	120
Jefferson, Ga., U.S.	B3	87
Jefferson, Ia., U.S.	B3	92
Jefferson, La., U.S.	k11	95
Jefferson, N.C., U.S.	A1	110
Jefferson, Oh., U.S.	A5	112
Jefferson, Or., U.S.	C3	114
Jefferson, S.C., U.S.	B7	117
Jefferson, Tx., U.S.	C5	120
Jefferson, Wi., U.S.	E5	126
Jefferson, co., Al., U.S.	B3	78
Jefferson, co., Ar., U.S.	C3	81
Jefferson, co., Co., U.S.	B5	83
Jefferson, co., Fl., U.S.	B3	86
Jefferson, co., Ga., U.S.	C4	87
Jefferson, co., Id., U.S.	F6	89
Jefferson, co., Il., U.S.	E5	90
Jefferson, co., In., U.S.	G6	91
Jefferson, co., Ia., U.S.	C5	92
Jefferson, co., Ks., U.S.	C8	93
Jefferson, co., Ky., U.S.	B4	94
Jefferson, co., La., U.S.	E5	95
Jefferson, co., Ms., U.S.	D2	101
Jefferson, co., Mo., U.S.	C7	102
Jefferson, co., Mt., U.S.	D4	103
Jefferson, co., Ne., U.S.	D8	104
Jefferson, co., N.Y., U.S.	A5	109
Jefferson, co., Oh., U.S.	B5	112
Jefferson, co., Ok., U.S.	C4	113
Jefferson, co., Or., U.S.	C5	114
Jefferson, co., Pa., U.S.	D3	115
Jefferson, co., Tn., U.S.	C10	119
Jefferson, co., Tx., U.S.	E5	120
Jefferson, co., Wa., U.S.	B1	124
Jefferson, co., W.V., U.S.	B7	125
Jefferson, co., Wi., U.S.	E5	126
Jefferson, stm., U.S.	E5	103
Jefferson, Mount, mtn., Id., U.S.	E7	89
Jefferson, Mount, mtn., Nv., U.S.	E5	105
Jefferson, Mount, mtn., Or., U.S.	C5	114
Jefferson City, Mo., U.S.	C5	102
Jefferson City, Tn., U.S.	C10	119
Jefferson Davis, co., La., U.S.	D3	95
Jefferson Davis, co., Ms., U.S.	D4	101
Jefferson Farms, co., U.S.	i7	89
Jefferson Proving Ground, mil., In., U.S.	G7	91
Jeffersontown, Ky., U.S.	B4	94
Jeffersonville, Ga., U.S.	D3	87
Jeffersonville, In., U.S.	H6	91
Jeffersonville, Ky., U.S.	C6	94
Jeffersonville, Oh., U.S.	C2	112
Jeffrey, W.V., U.S.	D3	125
Jeffrey City, Wy., U.S.	D5	127
Jeffries Creek, stm., S.C., U.S.	C8	117
Jefremov, Russia	H21	18
Jegorjevsk, Russia	F22	18
Jehossee Island, i., S.C., U.S.	k11	117
Jejsk, Russia	H5	22
Jekaterinburg, Russia	F10	22
Jekyll Island, i., Ga., U.S.	E5	87
Jelec, Russia	I21	18
Jelenia Góra (Hirschberg), Pol.	E15	8
Jelgava, Lat.	E6	18
Jellico, Tn., U.S.	C9	119
Jelm Mountain, mtn., Wy., U.S.	E7	127
Jeloguj, stm., Russia	E11	24
Jember, Indon.	n16	32
Jemez, stm., N.M., U.S.	k7	108
Jemez Canyon Dam, N.M., U.S.	k7	108
Jemez Indian Reservation, N.M., U.S.	h7	108
Jemez Pueblo, N.M., U.S.	B3	108
Jemison, Al., U.S.	C3	78
Jena, Ger.	E11	8
Jena, La., U.S.	C3	95
Jenašimskij Polkan, Gora, mtn., Russia	F12	24
Jendouba (Souk el Arba), Tun.	M3	14
Jenisej, stm., Russia	D11	24
Jenisejsk, Russia	F12	24
Jenisejskij Zaliv, b., Russia	C10	24
Jenkins, Ky., U.S.	C7	94
Jenkins, co., Ga., U.S.	D5	87
Jenkintown, Pa., U.S.	o21	115
Jenks, Ok., U.S.	A6	113
Jennings, La., U.S.	D3	95
Jennings, Mo., U.S.	f13	102
Jennings, co., In., U.S.	G6	91
Jensen Beach, Fl., U.S.	E6	86
Jepara, Indon.	m15	33a
Jequié, Braz.	B8	57
Jequitinhonha, stm., Braz.	D9	57
Jerada, Mor.	B5	42
Jerauld, co., S.D., U.S.	C7	118
Jérémie, Haiti	E10	64
Jeremoabo, Braz.	F11	54
Jerevan, Arm.	I6	22
Jerez de García Salinas, Mex.	F8	62
Jerez de la Frontera, Spain	I5	12
Jerez de los Caballeros, Spain	G5	12
Jericho, Vt., U.S.	B3	122
Jericho see Arīḥā, Jord.	D4	40
Jerimoth Hill, hill, R.I., U.S.	C1	116
Jermyn, Pa., U.S.	C10	115
Jerofej Pavlovič, Russia	G18	24
Jerome, Az., U.S.	C3	80
Jerome, Id., U.S.	G4	89
Jerome, Pa., U.S.	F4	115
Jerome, co., Id., U.S.	G4	89
Jeropol, Russia	D27	24
Jersey, co., Il., U.S.	D3	90
Jersey, dep., Eur.	C4	10
Jersey City, N.J., U.S.	B4	107
Jersey Mountain, mtn., Id., U.S.	E3	89
Jersey Shore, Pa., U.S.	D7	115
Jerseyville, Il., U.S.	D3	90
Jerusalem see Yerushalayim, Isr.	D4	40
Jervis Inlet, b., B.C., Can.	D6	69
Jesenice, Slo.	C9	14
Jessamine, co., Ky., U.S.	C5	94
Jessore, Bngl.	I13	38
Jessup, Md., U.S.	B4	97
Jessup, Pa., U.S.	m18	115
Jesup, Ga., U.S.	E5	87
Jesup, Ia., U.S.	B5	92
Jesup, Lake, l., Fl., U.S.	D5	86
Jésus, Île, i., Que., Can.	p19	74
Jesús Carranza, Mex.	I12	62
Jetmore, Ks., U.S.	D4	93
Jeumont, Fr.	B11	10
Jever, Ger.	B7	8
Jevpatorija, Ukr.	H4	22
Jewel Cave National Monument, S.D., U.S.	D2	118
Jewell, Ia., U.S.	B4	92
Jewell, co., Ks., U.S.	C5	93
Jewett City, Ct., U.S.	C8	84
Jeypore, India	C7	37
Jhang Maghiāna, Pak.	E5	38
Jhānsi, India	H8	38
Jharia, India	I12	38
Jhelum, Pak.	D5	38
Jhelum, stm., Asia	E5	38
Jiading, China	D10	28
Jiaganj, India	H13	38
Jiamusi, China	B13	26
Jian, China	H3	28
Jianchuan, China	A5	34
Jiangmen, China	M2	28
Jiangsu, prov., China	E10	26
Jiangxi, prov., China	F10	26
Jiangyin, China	D9	28
Jiangzi, China	F13	38
Jianou, China	H7	28
Jianshui, China	C7	34
Jiaoxian, China	D10	26
Jiaozuo, China	D9	26
Jiashan, China	C6	28
Jiawang, China	A6	28
Jiaxian, China	A2	28
Jiaxing, China	E9	28
Jiazi, China	M5	28
Jicarilla Apache Indian Reservation, N.M., U.S.	A2	108
Jiddah, Sau. Ar.	D2	46
Jieshou, China	B4	28
Jieyang, China	L5	28
Jihlava, Czech.	F15	8
Jijiga, Eth.	G3	46
Jijona, Spain	G11	12
Jilemutu, China	A11	26
Jilin, China	C12	26
Jilin, prov., China	C12	26
Jima, Eth.	G2	46
Jimena de la Frontera, Spain	I6	12
Jim Hogg, co., Tx., U.S.	F3	120
Jim Lake, res., N.D., U.S.	B7	111
Jim Thorpe, Pa., U.S.	E10	115
Jim Wells, co., Tx., U.S.	F3	120
Jinan (Tsinan), China	D10	26
Jīnd, India	F7	38
Jingdezhen (Kingtechen), China	F6	28
Jingjiang, China	C9	28
Jingxi, China	C9	34
Jinhua, China	F8	28
Jining, China	D10	26
Jining, China	C9	26
Jinja, Ug.	A6	44
Jinning (Jiukunyang), China	B7	34
Jinotega, Nic.	H4	64
Jinshi, China	F9	26
Jinxian, China	D11	26
Jinzhou, China	C11	26
Jiparaná, stm., Braz.	E6	54
Jipijapa, Ec.	H2	58
Jirjā, Egypt	C12	42
Jisr ash-Shughūr, Syria	B5	40
Jiujiang, China	F4	28
Jiuling Shan, mts., China	G3	28
Jiumangya, China	B14	38
Jiuquan, China	D6	26
Jixi, China	B13	26
Joaçaba, Braz.	B6	56
Joanna, S.C., U.S.	C4	117
João Pessoa, Braz.	E12	54
Joaquín V. González, Arg.	B4	56
Job Peak, mtn., Nv., U.S.	D3	105
Jobson (Vera), Arg.	B4	56
Jocassee, Lake, res., U.S.	B1	117
Jódar, Spain	H8	12
Jo Daviess, co., Il., U.S.	A3	90
Jodhpur, India	G5	38
Joe Batt's Arm [-Barr'd Islands-Shoal Bay], Newf., Can.	D4	72
Joensuu, Fin.	E17	6
Joes Brook, stm., Vt., U.S.	C4	122
Joes Creek, stm., W.V., U.S.	m12	125
Joffre, Arg.	D3	56
Jogjakarta see Yogyakarta, Indon.	G5	32
Johannesburg, S. Afr.	G5	44
John, Cape, c., N.S., Can.	D6	71
John Day, Or., U.S.	C8	114
John Day, stm., Or., U.S.	B6	114
John Day Dam, U.S.	D5	124
John Day Fossil Beds National Monument, Or., U.S.	C6	114
John F. Kennedy Space Center, sci., Fl., U.S.	D6	86
John H. Kerr Dam, Va., U.S.	D4	123
John H. Kerr Reservoir, res., U.S.	D4	123
John Martin Reservoir, res., Co., U.S.	C7	83
John Muir National Historical Site, hist., Ca., U.S.	h8	82
John o' Groats, Scot., U.K.	C9	7
John Redmond Reservoir, res., Ks., U.S.	D8	93
John Sevier, Tn., U.S.	m14	119
Johns Island, i., S.C., U.S.	F7	117
Johnson, Ks., U.S.	E2	93
Johnson, Vt., U.S.	B3	122
Johnson, co., Ar., U.S.	B2	81
Johnson, co., Ga., U.S.	D4	87
Johnson, co., Il., U.S.	F5	90
Johnson, co., In., U.S.	F5	91
Johnson, co., Ia., U.S.	C6	92
Johnson, co., Ks., U.S.	D9	93
Johnson, co., Ky., U.S.	C7	94
Johnson, co., Mo., U.S.	C4	102
Johnson, co., Ne., U.S.	D9	104
Johnson, co., Tn., U.S.	C12	119
Johnson, co., Tx., U.S.	C4	120
Johnson, co., Wy., U.S.	B6	127
Johnsonburg, Pa., U.S.	D4	115
Johnson City, N.Y., U.S.	C5	109
Johnson City, Tn., U.S.	C11	119
Johnson City, Tx., U.S.	D3	120
Johnson Creek, Wi., U.S.	E5	126
Johnsonville, S.C., U.S.	D9	117
Johns Pass, strt., Fl., U.S.	p10	86
Johnston, Ia., U.S.	e8	92
Johnston, R.I., U.S.	C4	116
Johnston, S.C., U.S.	D4	117
Johnston, co., N.C., U.S.	B4	110
Johnston, co., Ok., U.S.	C5	113
Johnston City, Il., U.S.	F5	90
Johnston Key, i., Fl., U.S.	H5	86
Johnstown, Co., U.S.	A6	83
Johnstown, N.Y., U.S.	B6	109
Johnstown, Oh., U.S.	B3	112
Johnstown, Pa., U.S.	F4	115
John W. Flannagan Reservoir, res., Va., U.S.	e9	123
Johor Baharu, Malay.	N7	34
Joigny, Fr.	E10	10
Joiner, Ar., U.S.	B5	81
Joinvile, Braz.	B7	56
Joinville, Fr.	D12	10
Jokkmokk, Swe.	C12	6
Joliet, Il., U.S.	B5	90
Joliette, Que., Can.	C4	74
Jolo Island, i., Phil.	D7	32
Jombang, Indon.	m16	33a
Jones, Ok., U.S.	B4	113
Jones, co., Ga., U.S.	C3	87
Jones, co., Ia., U.S.	B6	92
Jones, co., Ms., U.S.	D4	101
Jones, co., N.C., U.S.	B5	110
Jones, co., S.D., U.S.	D5	118
Jones, co., Tx., U.S.	C3	120
Jonesboro, Ar., U.S.	B5	81
Jonesboro, Ga., U.S.	C2	87
Jonesboro, Il., U.S.	F4	90
Jonesboro, In., U.S.	D6	91
Jonesboro, La., U.S.	B3	95
Jonesborough, Tn., U.S.	C11	119
Jonesburg, Mo., U.S.	C6	102
Jones Creek, Tx., U.S.	s14	120
Jones Mill, Ar., U.S.	C3	81
Jonesport, Me., U.S.	D5	96
Jones Sound, strt., N.W. Ter., Can.	A15	66
Jonestown, Ms., U.S.	A3	101
Jonesville, La., U.S.	C4	95
Jonesville, Mi., U.S.	G6	99
Jonesville, N.C., U.S.	A2	110
Jonesville, S.C., U.S.	B4	117
Jonesville, Va., U.S.	f8	123
Jongkha, China	F11	38
Jönköping, Swe.	H10	6
Jonquière, Que., Can.	A6	74
Jonzac, Fr.	F6	10
Joplin, Mo., U.S.	D3	102
Joppatowne, Md., U.S.	B5	97
Jordan, Mn., U.S.	F5	100
Jordan, ctry., Asia	D5	40
Jordan, stm., Asia	C4	40
Jordan, stm., Ut., U.S.	C4	121
Jordan Creek, stm., U.S.	E9	114
Jordan Lake, res., Al., U.S.	C3	78
Jorhāt, India	G16	38
Jörn, Swe.	D13	6
Jornado del Muerto, des., N.M., U.S.	D3	108
Jos, Nig.	G7	42
José Battle y Ordóñez, Ur.	C5	56
Joseph, Or., U.S.	B9	114
Joseph, Lac, l., Newf., Can.	h8	72
Joseph Bonaparte Gulf, b., Austl.	B5	50
Joseph City, Az., U.S.	C5	80
Josephine, co., Or., U.S.	E3	114
Joshua, Tx., U.S.	n9	120
Joshua Tree, Ca., U.S.	E5	82
Joshua Tree National Monument, Ca., U.S.	F6	82
Joškar-Ola, Russia	F7	22
Jourdanton, Tx., U.S.	E3	120
Joutsijärvi, Fin.	C16	6
Jovellanos, Cuba	C7	64
J. Percy Priest Lake, res., Tn., U.S.	A5	119
Juab, co., Ut., U.S.	D3	121
Juan Aldama, Mex.	E8	62
Juan de Fuca, Strait of, strt., N.A.	G8	66
Juan de Nova, Île, i., Reu.	E8	44
Juárez, Arg.	D5	56
Juàzeiro, Braz.	E10	54
Juàzeiro do Norte, Braz.	E11	54
Jūbā, Sudan	H12	42
Juba (Genale), stm., Afr.	H3	46
Juchitán [de Zaragoza], Mex.	I12	62
Judenburg, Aus.	H14	8
Judith, stm., Mt., U.S.	C7	103
Judith, Point, c., R.I., U.S.	G4	85
Judith Basin, co., Mt., U.S.	C6	103
Judith Island, i., N.C., U.S.	B6	110
Judith Mountains, mts., Mt., U.S.	C7	103
Judith Peak, mtn., Mt., U.S.	C7	103
Judoma, stm., Russia	F21	24
Judsonia, Ar., U.S.	B4	81
Juigalpa, Nic.	H5	64
Juiz de Fora, Braz.	F7	57
Jukagirskoje Ploskogorje, plat., Russia	D24	24
Jukte, Russia	E15	24
Julesburg, Co., U.S.	A8	83
Juliaca, Peru	G4	54
Julian, Ca., U.S.	F5	82
Julian, W.V., U.S.	C3	125
Julian Alps, mts., Eur.	C8	14
Juliana Top, mtn., Sur.	C7	54
Julianehåb, Grnld.	D23	66
Jülich, Ger.	E6	8
Jullundur, India	E6	38
Jumbo Peak, mtn., Nv., U.S.	G7	105
Jumentos Cays, is., Bah.	C10	64
Jumet, Bel.	E4	8
Jumilla, Spain	G10	12
Jump, stm., Wi., U.S.	C3	126
Jumla, Bots.	F4	44
Junāgadh, India	J4	38
Junction, Tx., U.S.	D3	120
Junction City, Ar., U.S.	D3	81
Junction City, Ks., U.S.	C7	93
Junction City, Ky., U.S.	C5	94
Junction City, La., U.S.	A3	95
Junction City, Or., U.S.	C3	114
Jundiaí, Braz.	G5	57
Juneau, Ak., U.S.	D13	79
Juneau, Wi., U.S.	E5	126
Juneau, co., Wi., U.S.	E3	126
June in Winter, Lake, l., Fl., U.S.	E5	86
Jungfrau, mtn., Switz.	F14	10
Junggar Pendi, China	B4	26
Juniata, Ne., U.S.	D7	104
Juniata, co., Pa., U.S.	F7	115
Juniata, stm., Pa., U.S.	F7	115
Junín, Arg.	C4	56
Junín, Lago de, l., Peru	F3	54
Junín de los Andes, Arg.	D2	56
Junior Lake, l., Me., U.S.	C4	96
Juniper Mountains, mts., Az., U.S.	B2	80
Junipero Serra Peak, mtn., Ca., U.S.	D3	82
Junsele, Swe.	E11	6
Jupiter, Fl., U.S.	F6	86
Jupiter Inlet, b., Fl., U.S.	F6	86
Jupiter Island, i., Fl., U.S.	E6	86
Jura, mts., Eur.	F13	10
Jura, i., Scot., U.K.	F7	7
Jurga, Russia	F10	24
Jūrmala, Lat.	E6	18
Juruá, stm., S.A.	D5	54
Juruena, stm., Braz.	E7	54
Justin, Tx., U.S.	C4	120
Justo Daract, Arg.	C3	56
Jutaí, stm., Braz.	D5	54
Jüterbog, Ger.	D13	8
Jutiapa, Guat.	G3	64
Juticalpa, Hond.	G4	64
Jutland see Jylland, pen., Den.	H7	6
Juventud, Isla de la (Isle of Pines), i., Cuba	D6	64
Juwara, Oman	E6	46
Juža, Russia	E25	18
Južno-Sachalinsk, Russia	H22	24
Južnyj, Mys, c., Russia	F25	24
Južnyj Bug, stm., Ukr.	H3	22
Jwayyā, Leb.	C4	40
Jylland, pen., Den.	H7	6
Jyväskylä, Fin.	E15	6

K

Name	Map Ref	Page
K2 (Qogir Feng), mtn., Asia	C7	38
Kaaawa, Hi., U.S.	f10	88
Kaala, mtn., Hi., U.S.	f9	88
Kaala Djerda, Tun.	N3	14
Kaalualu Bay, b., Hi., U.S.	E6	88
Kaaumakua, Puu, mtn., Hi., U.S.	f10	88
Kabale, Ug.	B5	44
Kabalo, Zaire	C5	44
Kabambare, Zaire	B5	44
Kâbdalis, Swe.	C12	6
Kabetogama Lake, l., Mn., U.S.	B5	100
Kabīr Kūh, mts., Iran	B4	46
Kābol, Afg.	C3	38
Kabompo, stm., Zam.	D4	44
Kabongo, Zaire	C5	44
Kābul, stm., Asia	C4	38
Kabwe (Broken Hill), Zam.	D5	44
Kachess Lake, res., Wa., U.S.	B4	124
K'achta, Russia	G15	24
Kačug, Russia	G15	24
Kadan Kyun, i., Burma	H5	34
Kadiri, India	E5	37
Kadoka, S.D., U.S.	D4	118
Kaduna, Nig.	F7	42
Kāduqlī, Sudan	F11	42
Kadykčan, Russia	E23	24
Kaédi, Maur.	E3	42
Kaena Point, c., Hi., U.S.	B3	88
Kaesŏng, N. Kor.	D12	26
Kafia Kingi, Sudan	G10	42
Kafue, stm., Zam.	D5	44
Kaga, Japan	F9	30
Kagamigahara, Japan	G9	30
Kagaznagar, India	C5	37
Kagoshima, Japan	K3	30
Kahaluu, Hi., U.S.	D6	88
Kahaluu, Hi., U.S.	g10	88
Kahana Bay, b., Hi., U.S.	f10	88
Kahemba, Zaire	C3	44
Kahoka, Mo., U.S.	A6	102
Kahoolawe, i., Hi., U.S.	C5	88
Kahramanmaraş, Tur.	H15	4
Kahuku, Hi., U.S.	B4	88
Kahuku Point, c., Hi., U.S.	B4	88
Kahului, Hi., U.S.	C5	88
Kahului Bay, b., Hi., U.S.	C5	88
Kai, Kepulauan, is., Indon.	G9	32
Kaibab Indian Reservation, Az., U.S.	A3	80
Kaieteur Fall, wtfl, Guy.	E13	58
Kaifeng, China	E9	26
Kaikoura, N.Z.	E4	52
Kaili, China	A10	34
Kailua, Hi., U.S.	B4	88
Kailua Bay, b., Hi., U.S.	g11	88
Kailua Kona, Hi., U.S.	D6	88
Kaimana, Indon.	F9	32
Kaimanawa Mountains, mts., N.Z.	C5	52
Kainan, Japan	H8	30
Kaiserslautern, Ger.	F7	8
Kaitangata, N.Z.	G2	52
Kaiwi Channel, strt., Hi., U.S.	B4	88
Kajaani, Fin.	D16	6
Kajakī, Band-e, res., Afg.	D1	38
Kajan, stm., Indon.	E6	32
Kajang, Malay.	M6	34
Kakamas, S. Afr.	G4	44
Kaka Point, c., Hi., U.S.	C5	88
Kake, Ak., U.S.	D13	79
Kakegawa, Japan	H11	30
Kakie, Bots.	F4	44
Kākināda, India	D7	37
Kakogawa, Japan	H7	30
Kaladan, stm., Asia	D2	34
Ka Lae, c., Hi., U.S.	E6	88
Kalahari Desert, des., Afr.	F4	44
Kālahasti, India	F5	37
Kalaheo, Hi., U.S.	B2	88
Kalajoki, Fin.	D14	6
Kalakan, Russia	F17	24
Kalām, Pak.	C5	38
Kalama, Wa., U.S.	C3	124
Kalámai, Grc.	L6	16
Kalamazoo, Mi., U.S.	F5	99
Kalamazoo, co., Mi., U.S.	F5	99
Kalamazoo, stm., Mi., U.S.	F5	99
Kalasin, Thai.	F7	34
Kalāt, Pak.	F2	38
Kalaupapa Peninsula, pen., Hi., U.S.	B5	88
Kalawao, co., Hi., U.S.	B5	88
Kalb, Ra's al-, c., Yemen	F4	46
Kale, Tur.	L12	16
Kaleden, B.C., Can.	E8	69
Kalemie (Albertville), Zaire	C5	44
Kalena, Puu, mtn., Hi., U.S.	g9	88
Kalgin Island, i., Ak., U.S.	g16	79
Kalgoorlie, Austl.	F4	50
Kalima, Zaire	B5	44
Kálimnos, Grc.	M10	16
Kaliningrad (Königsberg), Russia	G3	18
Kalinkoviči, Bela.	I12	18
Kalispel Indian Reservation, Wa., U.S.	A8	124
Kalispell, Mt., U.S.	B2	103
Kalisz, Pol.	D18	8
Kalkaska, Mi., U.S.	D5	99
Kalkaska, co., Mi., U.S.	D5	99
Kalmar, Swe.	H11	6
Kalohi Channel, strt., Hi., U.S.	C4	88
Kālol, India	I5	38
Kaloli Point, c., Hi., U.S.	D7	88
Kalona, Ia., U.S.	C6	92
Kalone Peak, mtn., B.C., Can.	C4	69
Kaluga, Russia	G19	18
Kalutara, Sri L.	I5	37
Kamaishi, Japan	C14	30
Kamakou, mtn., Hi., U.S.	B5	88
Kamakura, Japan	G12	30
Kamālia, Pak.	E5	38
Kamarān, i., Yemen	E3	46
Kamas, Ut., U.S.	C4	121
Kamba, China	F13	38
Kambam, India	H4	37
Kambar, Pak.	G2	38
Kamčatka, stm., Russia	F25	24
Kamčatka, Poluostrov, pen., Russia	F25	24
Kamčatskij Zaliv, b., Russia	F26	24
Kamen', stm., Russia	D12	24
Kamen'-na-Obi, Russia	G10	24
Kamenz, Ger.	D14	8
Kamiah, Id., U.S.	C2	89
Kamiak Butte, mtn., Wa., U.S.	C8	124
Kamienna Góra, Pol.	E16	8
Kamilukuak Lake, l., N.W. Ter., Can.	D12	66
Kamina, Zaire	C5	44
Kaminak Lake, l., N.W. Ter., Can.	D13	66
Kaminuriak Lake, l., N.W. Ter., Can.	D13	66
Kamitsushima, Japan	H2	30
Kamloops, B.C., Can.	D7	69
Kamo, Japan	E12	30
Kāmoke, Pak.	E6	38
Kampala, Ug.	A6	44
Kampar, Malay.	L6	34
Kampen, Neth.	C5	8
Kampeska, Lake, l., S.D., U.S.	C8	118
Kâmpóng Cham, Camb.	H8	34
Kâmpóng Chhnǎng, Camb.	H8	34
Kâmpóng Saôm, Camb.	I7	34
Kâmpóng Saôm, Chhâk, b., Camb.	I7	34
Kâmpóng Thum, Camb.	H8	34
Kâmpôt, Camb.	I8	34
Kāmthi, India	B5	37
Kamuela (Waimea), Hi., U.S.	C6	88
Kamui-misaki, c., Japan	p18	30a
Kan, stm., Asia	H9	34
Kanab, Ut., U.S.	F3	121
Kanab Creek, stm., U.S.	A3	80
Kanabec, co., Mn., U.S.	E5	100
Kanaga Island, i., Ak., U.S.	E4	79

Name	Map Ref	Page
Kanairiktok, stm., Newf., Can.	g9	72
Kananga (Luluabourg), Zaire	C4	44
Kanapou Bay, b., Hi., U.S.	C5	88
Kanata, Ont., Can.	B9	73
Kanawha, Ia., U.S.	B4	92
Kanawha, co., W.V., U.S.	C3	125
Kanawha, stm., W.V., U.S.	C3	125
Kanazawa, Japan	F9	30
Kanchanaburi, Thai.	G5	34
Kānchenjunga, mtn., Asia	G13	38
Kānchipuram, India	F5	37
Kandhkot, Pak.	F3	38
Kāndi, India	I13	38
Kandiyohi, co., Mn., U.S.	E3	100
Kandy, Sri L.	I6	37
Kane, Pa., U.S.	C4	115
Kane, co., Il., U.S.	B5	90
Kane, co., Ut., U.S.	F3	121
Kaneohe, Hi., U.S.	B4	88
Kaneohe Bay, b., Hi., U.S.	g10	88
Kaneohe Bay Marine Corps Air Station, mil., Hi., U.S.	g10	88
Kangar, Malay.	K6	34
Kangaroo Island, i., Austl.	G7	50
Kangean, Kepulauan, is., Indon.	G6	32
Kangnŭng, S. Kor.	D12	26
Kango, Gabon	A2	44
Kangto, mtn., Asia	G15	38
Kaniama, Zaire	C4	44
Kankakee, Il., U.S.	B6	90
Kankakee, co., Il., U.S.	B6	90
Kankakee, stm., U.S.	B5	90
Kankan, Gui.	F4	42
Kanmaw Kyun, i., Burma	I5	34
Kannapolis, N.C., U.S.	B2	110
Kannauj, India	G8	38
Kannonkoski, Fin.	E15	6
Kannus, Fin.	E14	6
Kano, Nig.	F7	42
Kanonji, Japan	H6	30
Kanopolis, Ks., U.S.	D5	93
Kanopolis Lake, res., Ks., U.S.	D5	93
Kanoya, Japan	K3	30
Kānpur, India	G9	38
Kansas, Il., U.S.	D6	90
Kansas, state, U.S.	D5	93
Kansas, stm., Ks., U.S.	C7	93
Kansas City, Ks., U.S.	C9	93
Kansas City, Mo., U.S.	B3	102
Kansk, Russia	F13	24
Kantō-sammyaku, mts., Japan	F11	30
Kanuma, Japan	F12	30
Kanye, Bots.	F5	44
Kaohsiung, Tai.	M9	28
Kaohsiunghsien, Tai.	M9	28
Kaokoveld, plat., Nmb.	E2	44
Kaolack, Sen.	F2	42
Kapaa, Hi., U.S.	A2	88
Kapaau, Hi., U.S.	C6	88
Kapadvanj, India	I5	38
Kapanga, Zaire	C4	44
Kapapa Island, i., Hi., U.S.	g10	88
Kapfenberg, Aus.	H15	8
Kaplan, La., U.S.	D3	95
Kaposvár, Hung.	I17	8
Kaptai, Bngl.	I15	38
Kapuas, stm., Indon.	F4	32
Kapūrthala, India	E6	38
Kapuskasing, Ont., Can.	o19	73
Karabük, Tur.	G14	4
Karacabey, Tur.	I12	16
Karaçaköy, Tur.	H12	16
Karāchi, Pak.	H2	38
Karād, India	D3	37
Karaganda, Kaz.	H8	24
Karaginskij, Ostrov, i., Russia	F26	24
Karaginskij Zaliv, b., Russia	F26	24
Karagoš, Gora, mtn., Russia	G11	24
Kāraikkudi, India	G5	37
Karakelong, Pulau, i., Indon.	E8	32
Karakoram Range, mts., Asia	C7	38
Karakumskij kanal, Turk.	J10	22
Karaman, Tur.	H14	4
Karaman, Tur.	L13	16
Karamay, China	B3	26
Karamürsel, Tur.	I13	16
Kāranja, India	B4	37
Karasburg, Nmb.	G3	44
Karasjok, Nor.	B15	6
Karatsu, Japan	I2	30
Karaul, Russia	C10	24
Karauli, India	G7	38
Karawang, Indon.	m13	33a
Karawanken, mts., Eur.	C9	14
Karbalā', Iraq	B3	46
Kårböle, Swe.	F10	6
Karcag, Hung.	H20	8
Kardhitsa, Grc.	J5	16
Kârdžali, Bul.	H9	16
Kargasok, Russia	F10	24
Karhula, Fin.	F16	6
Kariba, Zimb.	E5	44
Kariba, Lake, res., Afr.	E5	44
Karibib, Nmb.	F3	44
Karigasniemi, Fin.	B15	6
Karimata, Kepulauan, is., Indon.	F4	32
Karimata, Selat (Karimata Strait), strt., Indon.	F4	32
Karīmganj, India	H15	38
Karīmnagar, India	C5	37
Karin, Som.	F4	46
Karis (Karjaa), Fin.	F14	6
Kariya, Japan	H9	30
Karkabet, Eth.	E2	46
Karlovac, Cro.	D10	14
Karlovo, Bul.	G8	16
Karlovy Vary, Czech.	E12	8
Karlshamn, Swe.	H10	6
Karlskoga, Swe.	G10	6
Karlskrona, Swe.	H10	6
Karlsruhe, Ger.	F8	8
Karlstad, Swe.	G9	6
Karlstad, Mn., U.S.	B2	100

Name	Map Ref	Page
Karnāl, India	F7	38
Karnaphuli Reservoir, res., Bngl.	I15	38
Karnataka, state, India	E3	37
Karnes, co., Tx., U.S.	E4	120
Karnes City, Tx., U.S.	E4	120
Karns, Tn., U.S.	n13	119
Karonga, Mwi.	C6	44
Kárpathos, i., Grc.	N11	16
Karpeníson, Grc.	K5	16
Kars, Tur.	G16	4
Kärsämäki, Fin.	E15	6
Karši, Uzb.	J11	22
Kartal, Tur.	I13	16
Karufa, Indon.	F9	32
Karungi, Swe.	C14	6
Karūr, India	G5	37
Karvinā, Czech.	F18	8
Kārwār, India	E3	37
Kasai (Cassai), stm., Afr.	B3	44
Kasaji, Zaire	D4	44
Kasama, Zam.	C6	44
Kasanga, Tan.	C6	44
Kasaoka, Japan	H6	30
Kāsaragod, India	F3	37
Kasba Lake, l., N.W. Ter., Can.	D12	66
Kaseda, Japan	K3	30
Kasempa, Zam.	D5	44
Kasenga, Zaire	D5	44
Kasese, Zaire	B5	44
Kāsganj, India	G8	38
Kāshān, Iran	B5	46
Kashi, China	D2	26
Kashima-nada, Japan	F13	30
Kashīpur, India	F8	38
Kashiwa, Japan	G12	30
Kashiwazaki, Japan	E11	30
Kashmir see Jammu and Kashmir, dep., Asia	C6	38
Kasimov, Russia	G24	18
Kašin, Russia	D20	18
Kašira, Russia	G21	18
Kaskaskia, stm., Il., U.S.	D5	90
Kaskö (Kaskinen), Fin.	E13	6
Kaslo, B.C., Can.	E9	69
Kasongo, Zaire	B5	44
Kasota, Mn., U.S.	F5	100
Kasr, Ra's, c., Sudan	E13	42
Kassalā, Sudan	E13	42
Kassel, Ger.	D9	8
Kasson, Mn., U.S.	F6	100
Kastoria, Grc.	I5	16
Kasugai, Japan	G9	30
Kasūr, Pak.	E6	38
Katahdin, Mount, mtn., Me., U.S.	C4	96
Katanga Plateau, plat., Zaire	D5	44
Katchall Island, i., India	K2	34
Katerini, Grc.	I6	16
Kates Needle, mtn., Ak., U.S.	m24	79
Katherine, Austl.	B6	50
Kāthiāwār, pen., India	I4	38
Kathleen, Fl., U.S.	D4	86
Kāthmāndau, Nepal	G11	38
Katihār, India	H12	38
Katiola, I.C.	G4	42
Katmai, Mount, mtn., Ak., U.S.	D9	79
Katmai National Park, Ak., U.S.	D9	79
Katmandu see Kāthmāndau, Nepal	G11	38
Katowice, Pol.	E19	8
Kātrīnā, Jabal, mtn., Egypt	C12	42
Katrineholm, Swe.	G11	6
Katsina, Nig.	F7	42
Katsuta, Japan	F13	30
Kattegat, strt., Eur.	H8	6
Katy, Tx., U.S.	r14	120
Kauai, i., Hi., U.S.	B1	88
Kauai, i., Hi., U.S.	A2	88
Kauai Channel, strt., Hi., U.S.	B3	88
Kau Desert, des., Hi., U.S.	D6	88
Kaufbeuren, Ger.	H10	8
Kaufman, Tx., U.S.	C4	120
Kaufman, co., Tx., U.S.	C4	120
Kauiki Head, c., Hi., U.S.	C6	88
Kaukauna, Wi., U.S.	D5	126
Kaukauveld, mts., Afr.	F3	44
Kaula Island, i., Hi., U.S.	m15	88
Kaulakahi Channel, strt., Hi., U.S.	A2	88
Kaumakani, Hi., U.S.	B2	88
Kaunakakai, Hi., U.S.	B4	88
Kauna Point, c., Hi., U.S.	D6	88
Kaunas, Lith.	G6	18
Kaura Namoda, Nig.	F7	42
Kaustinen, Fin.	E14	6
Kavača, Russia	E27	24
Kavacik, Tur.	J12	16
Kavalerovo, Russia	I21	24
Kaválla, Grc.	I8	16
Kavaratti, India	G2	37
Kavieng, Pap. N. Gui.	k17	50a
Kawagoe, Japan	G12	30
Kawaguchi, Japan	G12	30
Kawaihoa Point, c., Hi., U.S.	B1	88
Kawaikini, mtn., Hi., U.S.	A2	88
Kawambwa, Zam.	C5	44
Kawanoe, Japan	H6	30
Kawasaki, Japan	G12	30
Kawich Peak, mtn., Nv., U.S.	F5	105
Kawich Range, mts., Nv., U.S.	F5	105
Kaw Lake, res., Ok., U.S.	A5	113
Kawm Umbū, Egypt	D12	42
Kay, co., Ok., U.S.	A4	113
Kayankulam, India	H4	37
Kaycee, Wy., U.S.	C6	127
Kayenta, Az., U.S.	A5	80
Kayes, Mali	F3	42
Kayseri, Tur.	H15	4
Kaysville, Ut., U.S.	B4	121
Kažačinskoje, Russia	F12	24
Kazačje, Russia	C21	24
Kazakhstan, ctry., Asia	H11	22
Kazan', Russia	F7	22
Kazanlâk, Bul.	G9	16
Kāzerūn, Iran	C5	46
Keaau, Hi., U.S.	D6	88
Keahiakahoe, Puu, mtn., Hi., U.S.	g10	88
Keahole Point, c., Hi., U.S.	D5	88

Name	Map Ref	Page
Kealaikahiki Channel, strt., Hi., U.S.	C5	88
Kealaikahiki Point, c., Hi., U.S.	C5	88
Kealakekua, Hi., U.S.	D6	88
Kealia, Hi., U.S.	A2	88
Keams Canyon, Az., U.S.	B5	80
Keanapapa Point, c., Hi., U.S.	C4	88
Keansburg, N.J., U.S.	C4	107
Kearney, Mo., U.S.	B3	102
Kearney, Ne., U.S.	D6	104
Kearney, co., Ne., U.S.	D7	104
Kearns, Ut., U.S.	C4	121
Kearny, Az., U.S.	D5	80
Kearny, N.J., U.S.	h8	107
Kearny, co., Ks., U.S.	D2	93
Kebri Dehar, Eth.	G3	46
Kechika, stm., B.C., Can.	E7	66
Kecskemét, Hung.	I19	8
Kedgwick, N.B., Can.	B2	71
Kediri, Indon.	m16	32
Kedon, Russia	E25	24
Kédougou, Sen.	F3	42
Kędzierzyn, Pol.	E18	8
Keego Harbor, Mi., U.S.	o15	99
Keele Peak, mtn., Yukon, Can.	D6	66
Keelung see Chilung, Tai.	J10	28
Keene, N.H., U.S.	E2	106
Keene, Tx., U.S.	n9	120
Keeper Hill, hill, Ire.	I4	7
Keeseville, N.Y., U.S.	f11	109
Keesler Air Force Base, mil., Ms., U.S.	E5	101
Keetmanshoop, Nmb.	G3	44
Keet Seel Ruin, hist., Az., U.S.	A5	80
Keewatin, Ont., Can.	E4	70
Keewatin, Mn., U.S.	C5	100
Kefallinía, i., Grc.	K4	16
Keffi, Nig.	G7	42
Keflavík, Ice.	C3	4
Ke Ga, Mui, c., Viet.	H10	34
Kegonsa, Lake, l., Wi., U.S.	F4	126
Keiser, Ar., U.S.	B5	81
Keith, Scot., U.K.	D10	7
Keith, co., Ne., U.S.	C4	104
Keizer, Or., U.S.	C3	114
Kejimkujik National Park, N.S., Can.	E4	71
Kekaha, Hi., U.S.	B2	88
Kelafo, Eth.	G3	46
Kelang, Malay.	M6	34
Kelheim, Ger.	G11	8
Kelibia, Tun.	M6	14
Keller, Tx., U.S.	n9	120
Kellett, Cape, c., N.W. Ter., Can.	B7	66
Kelleys Island, i., Oh., U.S.	A3	112
Kellogg, Id., U.S.	B2	89
Kellogg, Ia., U.S.	C5	92
Kelloselkä, Fin.	C17	6
Kelly Air Force Base, mil., Tx., U.S.	k7	120
Kelly Island, i., De., U.S.	D4	85
Kellyville, Ok., U.S.	B5	113
Kélo, Chad	G9	42
Kelotijärvi, Fin.	B14	6
Kelowna, B.C., Can.	E8	69
Kelso, Wa., U.S.	C3	124
Keluang, Malay.	M7	34
Kemerovo, Russia	F11	24
Kemi, Fin.	D15	6
Kemijärvi, Fin.	C16	6
Kemijoki, stm., Fin.	C15	6
Kemmerer, Wy., U.S.	E2	127
Kemp, Tx., U.S.	C4	120
Kemp, Lake, res., Tx., U.S.	C3	120
Kemper, co., Ms., U.S.	C5	101
Kemps Bay, Bah.	B9	64
Kempt, Lac, l., Que., Can.	G18	66
Kempten [Allgäu], Ger.	H10	8
Kemptville, Ont., Can.	B9	73
Kemul, Kong, mtn., Indon.	E6	32
Kenai, Ak., U.S.	C9	79
Kenai Fjords National Park, Ak., U.S.	D10	79
Kenai Mountains, mts., Ak., U.S.	h16	79
Kenai Peninsula, pen., Ak., U.S.	h16	79
Kenansville, N.C., U.S.	C5	110
Kenbridge, Va., U.S.	D4	123
Kendall, Fl., U.S.	s13	86
Kendall, co., Il., U.S.	B5	90
Kendall, co., Tx., U.S.	E3	120
Kendall, Cape, c., N.W. Ter., Can.	D15	66
Kendall Park, N.J., U.S.	C3	107
Kendallville, In., U.S.	B7	91
Kendari, Indon.	F7	32
Kenedy, Tx., U.S.	E4	120
Kenedy, co., Tx., U.S.	F4	120
Kenema, S.L.	G3	42
Kenesaw, Ne., U.S.	D7	104
Kēng Tung, Burma	D5	34
Kenhardt, S. Afr.	G4	44
Kenilworth, Il., U.S.	h9	90
Kenitra, Mor.	B4	42
Kenly, N.C., U.S.	A3	111
Kenmare, N.D., U.S.	A3	111
Kenmore, N.Y., U.S.	C2	109
Kennaday Peak, mtn., Wy., U.S.	E6	127
Kennebago Lake, l., Me., U.S.	C2	96
Kennebec, co., Me., U.S.	D3	96
Kennebec, stm., Me., U.S.	D3	96
Kennebunk, Me., U.S.	E2	96
Kennebunkport, Me., U.S.	E2	96
Kennedy Entrance, strt., Ak., U.S.	D9	79
Kennedy Peak, mtn., Burma	C2	34
Kenner, La., U.S.	E5	95
Kennett, Mo., U.S.	E7	102
Kennett Square, Pa., U.S.	G10	115
Kennewick, Wa., U.S.	C6	124
Kenn Reefs, rf., Austl.	D11	50
Kennydale, Wa., U.S.	e11	124
Keno, Or., U.S.	E5	114
Kénogami, Lac, l., Que., Can.	A6	74
Kenora, Ont., Can.	o16	73

Name	Map Ref	Page
Kenosha, Wi., U.S.	F6	126
Kenosha, co., Wi., U.S.	F5	126
Kenova, W.V., U.S.	C2	125
Kensett, Ar., U.S.	B4	81
Kensico Reservoir, res., N.Y., U.S.	g13	109
Kensington, P.E.I., Can.	C6	71
Kensington, Ct., U.S.	C4	84
Kensington, Md., U.S.	B3	97
Kent, Oh., U.S.	A4	112
Kent, Wa., U.S.	B3	124
Kent, co., Ne., U.S.	D3	85
Kent, co., Md., U.S.	B5	97
Kent, co., Mi., U.S.	E5	99
Kent, co., R.I., U.S.	D2	116
Kent, co., Tx., U.S.	C2	120
Kent City, Mi., U.S.	E5	99
Kent Island, i., De., U.S.	D4	85
Kent Island, i., Md., U.S.	C5	97
Kentland, In., U.S.	C3	91
Kenton, De., U.S.	D3	85
Kenton, Oh., U.S.	B2	112
Kenton, Tn., U.S.	A2	119
Kenton, co., Ky., U.S.	B5	94
Kent Peninsula, pen., N.W. Ter., Can.	C11	66
Kent Point, c., Md., U.S.	C5	97
Kentucky, state, U.S.	C4	94
Kentucky, stm., Ky., U.S.	B5	94
Kentwood, La., U.S.	D5	95
Kentwood, Mi., U.S.	F5	99
Kenvil, N.J., U.S.	B3	107
Kenvir, Ky., U.S.	D6	94
Kenya, ctry., Afr.	B7	44
Kenya, Mount see Kirinyaga, mtn., Kenya	B7	44
Kenyon, Mn., U.S.	F6	100
Kenyon, R.I., U.S.	F2	116
Keokea, Hi., U.S.	C5	88
Keokuk, Ia., U.S.	D6	92
Keokuk, co., Ia., U.S.	C5	92
Keokuk Lock and Dam, U.S.	D6	92
Keosauqua, Ia., U.S.	D6	92
Keota, Ia., U.S.	C6	92
Keota, Ok., U.S.	B7	113
Keowee, Lake, res., S.C., U.S.	B2	117
Kepi, Indon.	G10	32
Kerala, state, India	G4	37
Kerč, Ukr.	H5	22
Keremeos, B.C., Can.	E8	69
Keren, Eth.	E2	46
Kerens, Tx., U.S.	C4	120
Kerguélen, Îles, is., F.S.A.T.	J17	2
Kerhonkson, N.Y., U.S.	D6	109
Kericho, Kenya	B7	44
Kerinci, Gunung, mtn., Indon.	F3	32
Kerkhoven, Mn., U.S.	E3	100
Kérkira (Corfu), Grc.	J3	16
Kérkira, i., Grc.	J3	16
Kermān, Iran	C7	46
Kerme Körfezi, b., Tur.	M11	16
Kermit, Tx., U.S.	D1	120
Kermode, Mount, mtn., B.C., Can.	C2	69
Kern, co., Ca., U.S.	E4	82
Kern, stm., Ca., U.S.	E4	82
Kernersville, N.C., U.S.	A2	110
Kernville, Ca., U.S.	E4	82
Kerr, co., Tx., U.S.	D3	120
Kerr, Lake, l., Fl., U.S.	C5	86
Kerrville, Tx., U.S.	D3	120
Kerry Head, c., Ire.	I3	7
Kersey, Co., U.S.	A6	83
Kershaw, S.C., U.S.	B6	117
Kershaw, co., S.C., U.S.	C6	117
Kerulen (Cherlen), stm., Asia	B9	26
Kesagami Lake, l., Ont., Can.	F16	66
Keşan, Tur.	I10	16
Kesennuma, Japan	D14	30
Keshena, Wi., U.S.	D5	126
Kesteven, co., Eng., U.K.	I12	7
Keta, Ozero, l., Russia	D11	24
Ketchikan, Ak., U.S.	D13	79
Ketchum, Id., U.S.	F4	89
Kettering, Eng., U.K.	I12	7
Kettering, Oh., U.S.	C1	112
Kettle, stm., Mn., U.S.	D6	100
Kettle Creek, stm., Pa., U.S.	D6	115
Kettle Creek Lake, res., Pa., U.S.	D6	115
Kettle Falls, Wa., U.S.	A7	124
Keuka Lake, l., N.Y., U.S.	C3	109
Kew, T./C. Is.	D11	64
Kewanee, Il., U.S.	B4	90
Kewaskum, Wi., U.S.	E5	126
Kewaunee, Wi., U.S.	D6	126
Kewaunee, co., Wi., U.S.	D6	126
Keweenaw, co., Mi., U.S.	A2	99
Keweenaw Bay, b., Mi., U.S.	B2	99
Keweenaw Peninsula, pen., Mi., U.S.	A3	99
Keweenaw Point, c., Mi., U.S.	A3	99
Keya Paha, co., Ne., U.S.	B6	104
Keya Paha, stm., U.S.	B6	104
Keyhole Reservoir, res., Wy., U.S.	B8	127
Key Largo, Fl., U.S.	G6	86
Keyport, N.J., U.S.	C4	107
Keyser, W.V., U.S.	B6	125
Keystone, W.V., U.S.	D3	125
Keystone Heights, Fl., U.S.	C4	86
Keystone Lake, res., Ok., U.S.	A5	113
Keystone Peak, mtn., Az., U.S.	F4	80
Keysville, Va., U.S.	C4	123
Key West, Fl., U.S.	H5	86
Key West Naval Air Station, mil., Fl., U.S.	H5	86
Kezar Falls, Me., U.S.	E2	96
Kezar Lake, l., Me., U.S.	D2	96
Kežma, Russia	F14	24
Khadki (Kirkee), India	C2	37
Khairpur, Pak.	G3	38
Khalkís, Grc.	K7	16
Khambhāliya, India	I3	38
Khambhāt, Gulf of, b., India	B2	37
Khамgaon, India	B4	37
Khammam, India	D6	37
Khānābād, Afg.	B3	38
Khānaqīn, Iraq	B4	46
Khandwa, India	B4	37

Name	Map Ref	Page
Khānewāl, Pak.	E4	38
Khaniá, Grc.	N8	16
Khanna, India	E7	38
Khānpur, Pak.	F4	38
Khān Yūnus, Isr. Occ.	D4	40
Kharagpur, India	I12	38
Khargon, India	J6	38
Kharkov see Char'kov, Ukr.	E5	22
Khartoum see Al-Khartūm, Sudan	E12	42
Kherson see Cherson, Ukr.	H4	22
Khíos, Grc.	K10	16
Kholm, Afg.	B2	38
Khong, Laos	G8	34
Khong Sédone, Laos	G8	34
Khon Kaen, Thai.	F7	34
Khóra Sfakíon, Grc.	N8	16
Khorramābād, Iran	B4	46
Khorramshahr, Iran	B4	46
Khouribga, Mor.	B4	42
Khowst, Afg.	D3	38
Khulna, Bngl.	I13	38
Khunjerab Pass, Asia	B6	38
Khurja, India	F7	38
Khūryān Mūryān (Kuria Muria Isla, is., Oman	E6	46
Khushāb, Pak.	D5	38
Khvājeh Mohammad, Kūh-e, mts., Afg.	B4	38
Khvoy, Iran	J6	22
Khyber Pass, Asia	C4	38
Kiamichi, stm., Ok., U.S.	C6	113
Kiamika, stm., Que., Can.	C2	74
Kiana, Ak., U.S.	B7	79
Kiawah Island, i., S.C., U.S.	F7	117
Kibangou, Congo	B2	44
Kibombo, Zaire	B5	44
Kibre Mengist, Eth.	G2	46
Kičevo, Mac.	H4	16
Kichčik, Russia	G25	24
Kickamuit, stm., R.I., U.S.	D5	116
Kickapoo, stm., Wi., U.S.	E3	126
Kickapoo, Lake, res., Tx., U.S.	C3	120
Kickapoo Indian Reservation, Ks., U.S.	C8	93
Kicking Horse Pass, Can.	D2	68
Kidal, Mali	E6	42
Kidder, co., N.D., U.S.	C6	111
Kidira, Sen.	F3	42
Kiefer, Ok., U.S.	B5	113
Kiel, Ger.	A10	8
Kiel, Wi., U.S.	E5	126
Kielce, Pol.	E20	8
Kieler Bucht, b., Ger.	A10	8
Kiester, Mn., U.S.	G5	100
Kiev see Kijev, Ukr.	G4	22
Kiffa, Maur.	E3	42
Kigali, Rw.	B5	44
Kigoma, Tan.	B5	44
Kihei, Hi., U.S.	C5	88
Kihniö, Fin.	E14	6
Kiholo Bay, b., Hi., U.S.	D5	88
Kii-suidō, strt., Japan	I7	30
Kijev (Kiev), Ukr.	G4	22
Kikinda, Yugo.	D4	16
Kikládhes, is., Grc.	L8	16
Kikwit, Zaire	C3	44
Kilauea, Hi., U.S.	A2	88
Kilauea Crater, crat., Hi., U.S.	D6	88
Kilauea Point, c., Hi., U.S.	A2	88
Kilgore, Tx., U.S.	C5	120
Kilimanjaro, mtn., Tan.	B7	44
Kilis, Tur.	A5	40
Kilkee, Ire.	I3	7
Kilkenny, Ire.	I5	7
Kilkís, Grc.	H6	16
Killala, Ire.	H3	7
Killaloe Station, Ont., Can.	B7	73
Killam, Alta., Can.	C5	68
Killarney, Man., Can.	E2	70
Killarney, Ire.	I3	7
Killarney Provincial Park, Ont., Can.	A3	73
Killdeer, N.D., U.S.	B3	111
Killen, Al., U.S.	A2	78
Killian, La., U.S.	h10	95
Killik, stm., Ak., U.S.	B9	79
Killona, La., U.S.	h11	95
Killorglin, Ire.	I3	7
Kilmarnock, Scot., U.K.	F8	7
Kilmarnock, Va., U.S.	C6	123
Kilmichael, Ms., U.S.	B4	101
Kiln, Ms., U.S.	E4	101
Kilombero, stm., Tan.	C7	44
Kilosa, Tan.	C7	44
Kilpisjärvi, Fin.	B13	6
Kilwa, Zaire	C5	44
Kilwa Kivinje, Tan.	C7	44
Kimball, Mn., U.S.	E4	100
Kimball, Ne., U.S.	C2	104
Kimball, S.D., U.S.	D7	118
Kimball, co., Ne., U.S.	C2	104
Kimball, Mount, mtn., Ak., U.S.	C11	79
Kimberley, B.C., Can.	E9	69
Kimberley, S. Afr.	G4	44
Kimberley Plateau, plat., Austl.	C5	50
Kimberlin Heights, Tn., U.S.	n14	119
Kimberly, Al., U.S.	B3	78
Kimberly, Id., U.S.	G5	89
Kimberly, W.V., U.S.	m13	125
Kimberly, Wi., U.S.	h9	126
Kimble, co., Tx., U.S.	D3	120
Kimch'aek, N. Kor.	C12	26
Kimovsk, Russia	H21	18
Kimry, Russia	E20	18
Kinabalu, Gunong, mtn., Malay.	D6	32
Kinbasket Lake, res., B.C., Can.	D8	69
Kincaid, Il., U.S.	D4	90
Kincaid, W.V., U.S.	m13	125
Kincaid, Lake, res., Il., U.S.	D4	90
Kincardine, Ont., Can.	C3	73
Kincheloe Air Force Base, mil., Mi., U.S.	B6	99
Kinder, La., U.S.	D3	95
Kindia, Gui.	F3	42
Kindu, Zaire	B5	44

Name	Map Ref	Page
Kinešma, Russia	D25	18
King, N.C., U.S.	A2	110
King, Wi., U.S.	D4	126
King, co., Tx., U.S.	C2	120
King, co., Wa., U.S.	D4	124
King and Queen, co., Va., U.S.	C6	123
Kingaroy, Austl.	E10	50
King City, Ca., U.S.	D3	82
King City, Mo., U.S.	A3	102
King Cove, Ak., U.S.	E7	79
Kingfield, Me., U.S.	D2	96
Kingfisher, Ok., U.S.	B4	113
Kingfisher, co., Ok., U.S.	B3	113
King George, co., Va., U.S.	B5	123
King Island, i., Austl.	G8	50
King Island, i., B.C., Can.	C4	69
King Lear Peak, mtn., Nv., U.S.	B3	105
King Leopold Ranges, mts., Austl.	C5	50
Kingman, Az., U.S.	B1	80
Kingman, Ks., U.S.	E5	93
Kingman, co., Ks., U.S.	E5	93
King Mountain, mtn., Or., U.S.	E3	114
King Mountain, mtn., Or., U.S.	D8	114
King Peak, mtn., Ca., U.S.	B1	82
Kings, Ms., U.S.	C3	101
Kings, co., Ca., U.S.	D4	82
Kings, co., N.Y., U.S.	E7	109
Kings, stm., Ar., U.S.	A2	81
Kings, stm., Ca., U.S.	D4	82
Kings, stm., Nv., U.S.	B3	105
King Salmon, Ak., U.S.	D8	79
Kingsburg, Ca., U.S.	D4	82
Kingsbury, co., S.D., U.S.	C8	118
Kings Canyon National Park, Ca., U.S.	D4	82
Kingsey-Falls, Que., Can.	D5	74
Kingsford, Mi., U.S.	C2	99
Kingsland, Ga., U.S.	F5	87
Kingsland, Tx., U.S.	D3	120
Kingsley, Ia., U.S.	B2	92
Kingsley, Mi., U.S.	D5	99
King's Lynn, Eng., U.K.	I13	7
Kings Mountain, N.C., U.S.	B1	110
King Sound, strt., Austl.	C4	50
Kings Park West, Va., U.S.	*B5	123
Kings Peak, mtn., Ut., U.S.	C5	121
King's Point, Newf., Can.	D3	72
Kingsport, Tn., U.S.	C11	119
Kingston, Ont., Can.	C8	73
Kingston, Jam.	E9	64
Kingston, Ga., U.S.	B2	87
Kingston, Id., U.S.	B2	89
Kingston, Ma., U.S.	C6	98
Kingston, N.H., U.S.	E4	106
Kingston, N.Y., U.S.	D6	109
Kingston, Oh., U.S.	C3	112
Kingston, Ok., U.S.	D5	113
Kingston, Pa., U.S.	D10	115
Kingston, R.I., U.S.	F3	116
Kingston, Tn., U.S.	D9	119
Kingston Springs, Tn., U.S.	A4	119
Kingston upon Hull, Eng., U.K.	H12	7
Kingstown, St. Vin.	H17	64
Kingstree, S.C., U.S.	D8	117
Kingsville, Ont., Can.	E2	73
Kingsville, Md., U.S.	B5	97
Kingsville (North Kingsville), Oh., U.S.	A5	112
Kingsville, Tx., U.S.	F4	120
Kingsville Naval Air Station, mil., Tx., U.S.	F4	120
King William, co., Va., U.S.	C5	123
King William Island, i., N.W. Ter., Can.	C13	66
King William's Town, S. Afr.	H5	44
Kingwood, W.V., U.S.	B5	125
Kinistino, Sask., Can.	E3	75
Kinkaid Lake, res., Il., U.S.	F4	90
Kinloch, Mo., U.S.	f13	102
Kinmundy, Il., U.S.	E5	90
Kinna, Swe.	H9	6
Kinnairds Head, c., Scot., U.K.	D10	7
Kinnelon, N.J., U.S.	B4	107
Kinneret, Yam, l., Isr.	C4	40
Kinney, co., Tx., U.S.	E2	120
Kinross, Scot., U.K.	E9	7
Kinsale, Ire.	J4	7
Kinsarvik, Nor.	F6	6
Kinsey, Al., U.S.	D4	78
Kinshasa (Léopoldville), Zaire	B3	44
Kinsley, Ks., U.S.	E4	93
Kinston, N.C., U.S.	B5	110
Kintyre, pen., Scot., U.K.	F7	7
Kintyre, Mull of, c., Scot., U.K.	F7	7
Kinyeti, mtn., Sudan	H12	42
Kiowa, Ks., U.S.	E5	93
Kiowa, Ok., U.S.	C6	113
Kiowa, co., Co., U.S.	C8	83
Kiowa, co., Ks., U.S.	E4	93
Kiowa, co., Ok., U.S.	C2	113
Kiowa Creek, stm., Ok., U.S.	A1	113
Kipembawe, Tan.	C6	44
Kipili, Tan.	C6	44
Kipnuk, Ak., U.S.	C7	79
Kipushi, Zaire	D5	44
Kirbyville, Tx., U.S.	D6	120
Kirchdorf an der Krems, Aus.	H14	8
Kirenga, stm., Russia	F15	24
Kirensk, Russia	F15	24
Kirghizia see Kyrgyzstan, ctry., Asia	I12	22
Kiribati, ctry., Oc.	G24	2
Kırıkhan, Tur.	A5	40
Kırıkkale, Tur.	H14	4
Kirin see Jilin, China	C12	26
Kirinyaga (Mount Kenya), mtn., Kenya	B7	44
Kırkağaç, Tur.	J11	16
Kirkcaldy, Scot., U.K.	E9	7
Kirkcudbright, Scot., U.K.	G9	7
Kirkenes, Nor.	B18	6
Kirkland, Il., U.S.	A5	90
Kirkland, Wa., U.S.	B3	124
Kirkland Lake, Ont., Can.	o19	73
Kırklareli, Tur.	H11	16
Kirklin, In., U.S.	D5	91
Kirkūk, Iraq	A3	46
Kirkwall, Scot., U.K.	C10	7
Kirkwood, De., U.S.	B3	85
Kirkwood, Il., U.S.	C3	90
Kirkwood, Mo., U.S.	f13	102
Kirov, Russia	F7	22
Kirov, Russia	G17	18
Kirovograd, Ukr.	H4	22
Kirovskij, Russia	G25	24
Kırşehir, Tur.	H14	4
Kirthar Range, mts., Pak.	G2	38
Kirtland, N.M., U.S.	A1	108
Kirtland Air Force Base, mil., N.M., U.S.	k7	108
Kiruna, Swe.	C13	6
Kirwin Reservoir, res., Ks., U.S.	C4	93
Kiryū, Japan	F12	30
Kisa, Swe.	H10	6
Kisangani (Stanleyville), Zaire	A5	44
Kisarazu, Japan	G12	30
K.I. Sawyer Air Force Base, mil., Mi., U.S.	B3	99
Kisel'ovsk, Russia	G11	24
Kishanganj, India	G12	38
Kishangarh, India	G6	38
Kishinev see Kišin'ov, Mol.	H3	22
Kishiwada, Japan	H8	30
Kishorganj, Bngl.	H14	38
Kishwaukee, stm., Il., U.S.	A5	90
Kišin'ov, Mol.	H3	22
Kiska Island, i., Ak., U.S.	E3	79
Kiskunfélegyháza, Hung.	I19	8
Kiskunhalas, Hung.	I19	8
Kislovodsk, Russia	I6	22
Kismayu, Som.	B8	44
Kissidougou, Gui.	G3	42
Kissimmee, Fl., U.S.	D5	86
Kissimmee, stm., Fl., U.S.	E5	86
Kissimmee, Lake, l., Fl., U.S.	E5	86
Kississing Lake, l., Man., Can.	B1	70
Kistanje, Cro.	F10	14
Kistler, W.V., U.S.	D3	125
Kisumu, Kenya	B6	44
Kitaibaraki, Japan	F13	30
Kitakami, stm., Japan	C14	30
Kitakami-sanchi, mts., Japan	C14	30
Kitakyūshū, Japan	I3	30
Kitale, Kenya	A6	44
Kitami, Japan	p21	30a
Kitami-sanchi, mts., Japan	o20	30a
Kit Carson, co., Co., U.S.	C8	83
Kitchener, Ont., Can.	D4	73
Kíthira, i., Grc.	M6	16
Kitimat, B.C., Can.	B3	69
Kitsap, co., Wa., U.S.	B3	124
Kitscoty, Alta., Can.	C5	68
Kittanning, Pa., U.S.	E2	115
Kittatinny Mountain, mtn., U.S.	B2	107
Kittery, Me., U.S.	E2	96
Kittery Point, Me., U.S.	E2	96
Kittilä, Fin.	C15	6
Kittitas, Wa., U.S.	C5	124
Kittitas, co., Wa., U.S.	B4	124
Kitts, Ky., U.S.	D6	94
Kittson, co., Mn., U.S.	B2	100
Kitty Hawk, N.C., U.S.	A7	110
Kitty Hawk Bay, b., N.C., U.S.	A7	110
Kitwe, Zam.	D5	44
Kitzbühel, Aus.	H12	8
Kitzingen, Ger.	F10	8
Kivu, Lac, l., Afr.	B5	44
Kızıl, stm., Tur.	G14	4
Kjustendil, Bul.	G6	16
Kladno, Czech.	E14	8
Klagenfurt, Aus.	I14	8
Klaipėda (Memel), Lith.	F4	18
Klamath, co., Or., U.S.	E5	114
Klamath, stm., U.S.	B2	82
Klamath Falls, Or., U.S.	E5	114
Klamath Mountains, mts., U.S.	E2	114
Klangenan, Indon.	m14	33a
Klarälven, stm., Eur.	F9	6
Klawock, Ak., U.S.	D13	79
Kleberg, co., Tx., U.S.	F4	120
Klerksdorp, S. Afr.	G5	44
Kleve, Ger.	D6	8
Klickitat, Wa., U.S.	D4	124
Klickitat, co., Wa., U.S.	D4	124
Klickitat, stm., Wa., U.S.	C4	124
Klimovsk, Russia	F20	18
Klin, Russia	E19	18
Klincy, Russia	I15	18
Kłodzko, Pol.	E16	8
Klondike, hist. reg., Yukon, Can.	D5	66
Klondike Gold Rush National Historical Park, Ak., U.S.	k22	79
Klosterneuburg, Aus.	G16	8
Kluane Lake, l., Yukon, Can.	D5	66
Klutina Lake, l., Ak., U.S.	g19	79
Knapp Creek, stm., W.V., U.S.	C5	125
Knee Lake, l., Man., Can.	B4	70
Kneža, Bul.	F8	16
Knife, stm., N.D., U.S.	B3	111
Knightdale, N.C., U.S.	B4	110
Knight Inlet, b., B.C., Can.	D5	69
Knight Island, i., Ak., U.S.	g18	79
Knightstown, In., U.S.	E6	91
Knightsville, In., U.S.	E3	91
Knightville Reservoir, res., Ma., U.S.	B2	98
Knin, Cro.	E11	14
Knittelfeld, Aus.	H14	8
Knob Noster, Mo., U.S.	C4	102
Knokke, Bel.	D3	8
Knollwood, W.V., U.S.	m12	125
Knott, co., Ky., U.S.	C6	94
Knox, In., U.S.	B4	91
Knox, Pa., U.S.	D2	115
Knox, co., Il., U.S.	B3	90
Knox, co., In., U.S.	G3	91
Knox, co., Ky., U.S.	D6	94
Knox, co., Me., U.S.	D4	96
Knox, co., Mo., U.S.	A5	102
Knox, co., Ne., U.S.	B8	104
Knox, co., Oh., U.S.	B3	112
Knox, co., Tn., U.S.	C10	119
Knox, co., Tx., U.S.	C3	120
Knox, Cape, c., B.C., Can.	B1	69
Knox City, Tx., U.S.	C3	120
Knoxville, Il., U.S.	C3	90
Knoxville, Ia., U.S.	C4	92
Knoxville, Tn., U.S.	D10	119
Knysna, S. Afr.	H4	44
Kōbe, Japan	H8	30
København (Copenhagen), Den.	I9	6
Koblenz, Ger.	E7	8
Kobrin, Bela.	I7	18
Kobuk, stm., Ak., U.S.	B8	79
Kobuk Valley National Park, Ak., U.S.	B8	79
Kočani, Mac.	H6	16
Kočevje, Slo.	D9	14
Koch Peak, mtn., Mt., U.S.	E5	103
Kodiak, Ak., U.S.	D9	79
Kodiak Island, i., Ak., U.S.	D9	79
Koes, Nmb.	G3	44
Kofa Mountains, mts., Az., U.S.	D2	80
Köflach, Aus.	H15	8
Kōfu, Japan	G11	30
Koga, Japan	F12	30
Kogaluc, Baie, b., Que., Can.	E17	66
Kogaluk, stm., Newf., Can.	g9	72
Kohala Mountains, mts., Hi., U.S.	C6	88
Kohāt, Pak.	D4	38
Kohima, India	H16	38
Kohler, Wi., U.S.	E6	126
Kohtla-Järve, Est.	B10	18
Kokand, Uzb.	I12	22
Kokanee Glacier Provincial Park, B.C., Can.	E9	69
Kokemäki, Fin.	F14	6
Kokkola (Gamlakarleby), Fin.	E14	6
Koko Head, c., Hi., U.S.	B4	88
Kokolik, stm., Ak., U.S.	B7	79
Kokomo, In., U.S.	D5	91
Kokonau, Indon.	F10	32
Kokopo, Pap. N. Gui.	k17	50a
Kokosing, stm., Oh., U.S.	B3	112
Koksoak, stm., Que., Can.	E19	66
Kokstad, S. Afr.	H5	44
Kolaka, Indon.	F7	32
Kola Peninsula see Kol'skij poluostrov, pen., Russia	D5	22
Kolār, India	F5	37
Kolār Gold Fields, India	F5	37
Kol'čugino, Russia	E22	18
Kolda, Sen.	F3	42
Kolhāpur, India	D3	37
Kolín, Czech.	E15	8
Kollegāl, India	F4	37
Köln (Cologne), Ger.	E6	8
Koloa, Hi., U.S.	B2	88
Kołobrzeg, Pol.	A15	8
Kolomna, Russia	F21	18
Kolpaševo, Russia	F10	24
Kolpino, Russia	B13	18
Kol'skij poluostrov (Kola Peninsula), pen., Russia	D5	22
Kolwezi, Zaire	D5	44
Kolyma, stm., Russia	D25	24
Kolymskaja Nizmennost', pl., Russia	D24	24
Komárno, Czech.	H18	8
Komatsu, Japan	F9	30
Komló, Hung.	I18	8
Kommunizma, pik, mtn., Taj.	J12	22
Komoé, stm., Afr.	G5	42
Komotiní, Grc.	H9	16
Komsomolec, Ostrov, i., Russia	A12	24
Komsomol'sk-na-Amure, Russia	G21	24
Komsomol'skoj Pravdy, Ostrova, is., Russia	B15	24
Konahuanui, Puu, mtn., Hi., U.S.	g10	88
Konakovo, Russia	E19	18
Konawa, Ok., U.S.	C5	113
Konch, India	H8	38
Kondrovo, Russia	G18	18
Köng, Kaôh, i., Camb.	I7	34
Kongolo, Zaire	C5	44
Kongsberg, Nor.	G7	6
Kongsvinger, Nor.	F8	6
Kongsvoll, Nor.	E7	6
Kongur Shan, mtn., China	A6	38
Königs Wusterhausen, Ger.	C13	8
Konin, Pol.	C18	8
Konjic, Bos.	F12	14
Konomoc, Lake, res., Ct., U.S.	D7	84
Konqi, stm., China	C4	26
Konstanz, Ger.	H9	8
Kontagora, Nig.	F7	42
Kontiomäki, Fin.	D17	6
Kon Tum, Viet.	G10	34
Konya, Tur.	H14	4
Konza, Kenya	B7	44
Koochiching, co., Mn., U.S.	B4	100
Koolau Range, mts., Hi., U.S.	f10	88
Koontz Lake, In., U.S.	B5	91
Kooskia, Id., U.S.	C3	89
Kootenai, co., Id., U.S.	B2	89
Kootenay Lake, l., B.C., Can.	E9	69
Kootenay National Park, B.C., Can.	D9	69
Kopargaon, India	C3	37
Koper, Slo.	D8	14
Kopetdag, chrebet, mts., Asia	J9	22
Köping, Swe.	G10	6
Koppal, India	E4	37
Koppang, Nor.	F8	6
Koppel, Pa., U.S.	E1	115
Koprivnica, Cro.	C11	14
Kor'akskoje Nagorje, mts., Russia	E27	24
Korba, India	I10	38
Korbach, Ger.	D8	8
Korçë, Alb.	I4	16
Korčula, Cro.	G12	14
Korea, North, ctry., Asia	C12	26
Korea, South, ctry., Asia	D12	26
Korea Bay, b., Asia	D11	26
Korea Strait, strt., Asia	E12	26
Korf, Russia	E27	24
Korhogo, I.C.	G4	42
Korinthiakós Kólpos, b., Grc.	K6	16
Kórinthos (Corinth), Grc.	L6	16
Kōriyama, Japan	E13	30
Korliki, Russia	E10	24
Korogwe, Tan.	C7	44
Koronis, Lake, l., Mn., U.S.	E4	100
Koro Toro, Chad	E9	42
Korovin Volcano, vol., Ak., U.S.	E5	79
Korsakov, Russia	H22	24
Korsnäs, Fin.	E13	6
Korso, Fin.	F15	6
Kortrijk (Courtrai), Bel.	E3	8
Koruçam Burnu, c., N. Cyp.	B3	40
Koš-Ağač, Russia	D15	6
Kosciusko, Ms., U.S.	B4	101
Kosciusko, co., In., U.S.	B5	91
Kosciusko, Mount, mtn., Austl.	G9	50
Koshkonong, Lake, l., Wi., U.S.	F5	126
Košice, Czech.	G21	8
Kosovska Mitrovica, Yugo.	G4	16
Kossuth, co., Ia., U.S.	A3	92
Kostroma, Russia	D23	18
Koszalin (Köslin), Pol.	A16	8
Kota, India	H6	38
Kota Baharu, Malay.	K7	34
Kotabumi, Indon.	F3	32
Kot Addu, Pak.	E4	38
Kota Kinabalu (Jesselton), Malay.	D6	32
Kotel'nyj, Ostrov, i., Russia	B21	24
Köthen, Ger.	D11	8
Kotka, Fin.	F16	6
Kot Kapūra, India	E6	38
Kotlas, Russia	E7	22
Kotlik, Ak., U.S.	C7	79
Kotor Varoš, Bos.	E12	14
Kotovsk, Russia	I24	18
Kotri, Pak.	H3	38
Kötschach [-Mauthen], Aus.	I12	8
Kottagüdem, India	D6	37
Kottayam, India	H4	37
Kotte, Sri L.	I5	37
Kotto, stm., Cen. Afr. Rep.	G10	42
Kotuj, stm., Russia	C14	24
Kotzebue, Ak., U.S.	B7	79
Kotzebue Sound, strt., Ak., U.S.	B7	79
Kouchibouguac National Park, N.B., Can.	C5	71
Koudougou, Burkina	F5	42
Koula-Moutou, Gabon	B2	44
Koumra, Chad	G9	42
Kountze, Tx., U.S.	D5	120
Koussi, Emi, mtn., Chad	E9	42
Koutiala, Mali	F4	42
Kouts, In., U.S.	B3	91
Kouvola, Fin.	F16	6
Kovrov, Russia	E24	18
Kowkcheh, stm., Afg.	B4	38
Kowloon (Jiulong), H.K.	M3	28
Kowt-e 'Ashrow, Afg.	C3	38
Koyukuk, stm., Ak., U.S.	B8	79
Koza, Japan	y27	31b
Kozáni, Grc.	I5	16
Kra, Isthmus of, Asia	I5	34
Krâchéh, Camb.	H9	34
Kragerø, Nor.	G7	6
Kragujevac, Yugo.	E4	16
Kraków, Pol.	E19	8
Kraljevica, Cro.	D9	14
Kraljevo, Yugo.	F4	16
Kramfors, Swe.	E11	6
Krångede, Swe.	E11	6
Kranj, Slo.	C9	14
Krasneno, Russia	E27	24
Krasnodar, Russia	H5	22
Krasnogorsk, Russia	F20	18
Krasnojarsk, Russia	F12	24
Krasnoje, Ozero, l., Russia	E28	24
Krasnosel'kup, Russia	D10	24
Krasnozavodsk, Russia	E21	18
Krebs, Ok., U.S.	C6	113
Kremenčug, Ukr.	H4	22
Kremmling, Co., U.S.	A4	83
Krems an der Donau, Aus.	G15	8
Kresta, Zaliv, b., Russia	D30	24
Kribi, Cam.	H7	42
Kričov, Bela.	H14	18
Krishna, stm., India	D5	37
Krishnanagar, India	I13	38
Kristiansand, Nor.	G7	6
Kristianstad, Swe.	H10	6
Kristiansund, Nor.	E6	6
Kristinehamn, Swe.	G10	6
Kríti, i., Grc.	N8	16
Kritikón Pélagos, Grc.	N8	16
Krivoj Rog, Ukr.	H4	22
Krivoy Rog see Krivoj Rog, Ukr.	H4	22
Krnov, Czech.	E17	8
Kroken, Nor.	D10	6
Kroměříž, Czech.	F17	8
Kronach, Ger.	E11	8
Kröng Khémôreăh Phumint, Camb.	I7	34
Kronockij Zaliv, b., Russia	G26	24
Kronoki, Russia	G26	24
Kronštadt, Russia	B12	18
Kroonstad, S. Afr.	G5	44
Kropotkin, Russia	F17	24
Krosno, Pol.	F21	8
Krotz Springs, La., U.S.	D4	95
Krško, Slo.	D10	14
Kr'ukovo, Russia	D25	24
Krung Thep (Bangkok), Thai.	H6	34
Kruševac, Yugo.	F5	16
Krušné hory (Erzgebirge), mts., Eur.	E12	8
Kruzenšterna, Proliv, strt., Russia	H24	24
Kruzof Island, i., Ak., U.S.	m21	79
Krymskij poluostrov (Crimea), pen., Ukr.	H4	22
Ksar-es-Souk, Mor.	B5	42
Ksenjevka, Russia	G17	24
Ksour Essaf, Tun.	N5	14
Kuala Kangsar, Malay.	L6	34
Kualakapuas, Indon.	F5	32
Kuala Krai, Malay.	L7	34
Kuala Kubu Baharu, Malay.	M6	34
Kuala Lumpur, Malay.	M6	34
Kuala Nerang, Malay.	K6	34
Kuala Pilah, Malay.	M7	34
Kuala Terengganu, Malay.	L7	34
Kuantan, Malay.	M7	34
Kubokawa, Japan	I6	30
Kuche, China	C3	26
Kuching, Malay.	E5	32
Kudat, Malay.	D6	32
Kudus, Indon.	m15	32
Kuee Ruins, hist., Hi., U.S.	D6	88
Kufstein, Aus.	H12	8
Kuhmo, Fin.	D17	6
Kuito, Ang.	D3	44
Kuiu Island, i., Ak., U.S.	m23	79
Kuivaniemi, Fin.	D15	6
Kukawa, Nig.	F8	42
Kula, Tur.	K12	16
Kula, Hi., U.S.	C5	88
Kula Kangri, mtn., Bhu.	F14	38
Kulebaki, Russia	F25	18
Kulen Vakuf, Bos.	E11	14
Kulim, Malay.	L6	34
Kulmbach, Ger.	E11	8
Kulpmont, Pa., U.S.	E9	115
Kulunqi, China	C11	26
Kumagaya, Japan	F12	30
Kumajri, Arm.	I6	22
Kumamoto, Japan	J3	30
Kumano, Japan	I9	30
Kumano-nada, Japan	I9	30
Kumanovo, Mac.	G5	16
Kumasi, Ghana	G5	42
Kumbakonam, India	G5	37
Kume-shima, i., Japan	y26	31b
Kumo, Nig.	F8	42
Kumon Range, mts., Burma	B4	34
Kumukahi, Cape, c., Hi., U.S.	D7	88
Kuna, Id., U.S.	F2	89
Kunašir, Ostrov (Kunashiri-tō), i., Russia	I23	24
Kundiān, Pak.	D4	38
Kundla, India	J4	38
Kunes, Nor.	A16	6
Kunghit Island, i., B.C., Can.	C2	69
Kuningan, Indon.	m14	33a
Kunlun Shan, mts., China	B12	38
Kunming, China	B7	34
Kunsan, S. Kor.	D12	26
Kunshan, China	D9	28
Kuopio, Fin.	E16	6
Kupang, Indon.	H7	32
Kupreanof Island, i., Ak., U.S.	m23	79
Kupres, Bos.	E12	14
Kura, stm., Asia	I7	22
Kurashiki, Japan	H6	30
Kurayoshi, Japan	G6	30
Kure, Japan	H5	30
Kure Island, i., Hi., U.S.	k12	88
Kurejka, stm., Russia	D11	24
Kurenalus, Fin.	D16	6
Kurgan, Russia	F10	24
Kurgan-T'ube, Taj.	B3	38
Kurikka, Fin.	E14	6
Kuril'sk, Russia	H23	24
Kuril'skije Ostrova (Kuril Islands), is., Russia	H23	24
Kurmuk, Sudan	F12	42
Kurnool, India	E5	37
Kurow, N.Z.	F3	52
Kursk, Russia	G5	22
Kurtistown, Hi., U.S.	D6	88
Kuruman, S. Afr.	G4	44
Kurume, Japan	I3	30
Kurumkan, Russia	G16	24
Kurunegala, Sri L.	I6	37
Kuşadası Körfezi, b., Tur.	L11	16
Kuş Gölü, l., Tur.	I11	16
Kushima, Japan	K4	30
Kushiro, Japan	q22	30a
Kushtia, Bngl.	I13	38
Kushui, China	C5	26
Kuskokwim, stm., Ak., U.S.	C8	79
Kuskokwim Bay, b., Ak., U.S.	D7	79
Kuskokwim Mountains, mts., Ak., U.S.	C8	79
Küstī, Sudan	F12	42
K'us'ur, Russia	C19	24
Kut, Ko, i., Thai.	I7	34
Kutaisi, Geor.	I6	22
Kūt al-Imāra, Iraq	B4	46
Kutch, Gulf of, b., India	I3	38
Kutina, Cro.	D11	14
Kutno, Pol.	C19	8
Kutu, Zaire	B3	44
Kutztown, Pa., U.S.	E10	115
Kuujjuaq, Que., Can.	g13	74
Kuusamo, Fin.	D17	6
Kuusankoski, Fin.	F16	6
Kuvango, Ang.	D3	44
Kuwait, ctry., Asia	C4	46
Kuwait see Al-Kuwayt, Kuw.	C4	46
Kuwana, Japan	G9	30
Kuybyshev see Samara, Russia	G8	22
Kuzneck, Russia	G7	22
Kvikkjokk, Swe.	C11	6
Kwando (Cuando), stm., Afr.	E4	44
Kwangchow see Guangzhou, China	L2	28
Kwangju, S. Kor.	D12	26
Kwango (Cuango), stm., Afr.	B3	44
Kwekwe, Zimb.	E5	44
Kwethluk, Ak., U.S.	C7	79
Kwidzyn, Pol.	B18	8
Kwigillingok, Ak., U.S.	D7	79
Kwilu (Cuilo), stm., Afr.	B3	44
Kyaiklat, Burma	F3	34
Kyaikto, Burma	F4	34
Kyle, Tx., U.S.	E4	120

Name	Map Ref	Page
Kyle of Lochalsh, Scot., U.K.	D7	7
Kyoga, Lake, l., Ug.	A6	44
Kyōto, Japan	G8	30
Kyuquot Sound, strt., B.C., Can.	E4	69
Kyūshū, i., Japan	I3	30
Kyūshū-sanchi, mts., Japan	J4	30
Kyyjärvi, Fin.	E15	6
Kyrgyzstan, ctry., Asia	I12	22
Kyzyl, Russia	G12	24
Kzyl-Orda, Kaz.	I11	22

L

Name	Map Ref	Page
Laa an der Thaya, Aus.	G16	8
La Almunia de Doña Godina, Spain	D10	12
La Asunción, Ven.	B11	58
Laau Point, c., Hi., U.S.	B4	88
L'Abacou, Pointe, c., Haiti	E11	64
Labadieville, La., U.S.	E5	95
La Bañeza, Spain	C6	12
La Barca, Mex.	G8	62
La Barge, Wy., U.S.	D2	127
La Barge Creek, stm., Wy., U.S.	D2	127
La Baule, Fr.	E4	10
Labé, Gui.	F3	42
Labe (Elbe), stm., Eur.	E14	8
La Belle, Fl., U.S.	F5	86
La Belle, Mo., U.S.	A6	102
Labette, co., Ks., U.S.	E8	93
Labin, Cro.	D9	14
La Bisbal, Spain	D15	12
Labouheyre, Fr.	H6	10
Labrador, reg., Newf., Can.	g9	72
Labrador City, Newf., Can.	h8	72
Labrador Sea, N.A.	E22	66
Lábrea, Braz.	E6	54
Labutta, Burma	F3	34
La Canada Flintridge, Ca., U.S.	m12	82
La Cañiza, Spain	C3	12
La Canourgue, Fr.	H10	10
La Carolina, Spain	G8	12
Lacaune, Fr.	I9	10
Lac-Bouchette, Que., Can.	A5	74
Lac-Brome, Que., Can.	D5	74
Laccadive Sea, Asia	H3	3
Lac-Carré, Que., Can.	C3	74
Lac Courte Oreilles Indian Reservation, Wi., U.S.	C2	126
Lac du Bonnet, Man., Can.	D3	70
Lac du Flambeau, Wi., U.S.	B4	126
Lac du Flambeau Indian Reservation, Wi., U.S.	C3	126
La Ceiba, Hond.	G4	64
La Ceiba, Ven.	C7	58
La Center, Ky., U.S.	e9	94
Lac-Etchemin, Que., Can.	C7	74
Lacey, Wa., U.S.	B3	124
La Charité [-sur-Loire], Fr.	E10	10
La Châtre, Fr.	F8	10
La Chaux-de-Fonds, Switz.	E13	10
Lachine, Que., Can.	D4	74
La Chorrera, Col.	H6	58
La Chorrera, Pan.	J8	64
Lachute, Que., Can.	D3	74
La Ciotat, Fr.	I12	10
Lackawanna, N.Y., U.S.	C2	109
Lackawanna, co., Pa., U.S.	D10	115
Lackland Air Force Base, mil., Tx., U.S.	k7	120
Lac La Biche, Alta., Can.	B5	68
Lac la Hache, B.C., Can.	D7	69
Laclede, co., Mo., U.S.	D5	102
Lac-Mégantic, Que., Can.	D7	74
Lacolle, Que., Can.	D4	74
Lacombe, Alta., Can.	C4	68
Lacombe, La., U.S.	D6	95
Lacon, Il., U.S.	B4	90
Laconia, N.H., U.S.	C4	106
La Conner, Wa., U.S.	A3	124
Lacoochee, Fl., U.S.	D4	86
La Coruña, Spain	B3	12
Lac qui Parle, co., Mn., U.S.	F2	100
Lac qui Parle, stm., Mn., U.S.	F2	100
La Creek Lake, l., S.D., U.S.	D4	118
La Crescent, Mn., U.S.	G7	100
La Crete, Alta., Can.	f7	68
La Crosse, In., U.S.	B4	91
La Crosse, Ks., U.S.	D4	93
La Crosse, Wi., U.S.	E2	126
La Crosse, co., Wi., U.S.	E2	126
La Crosse, stm., Wi., U.S.	E3	126
La Cruz, Nic.	H5	64
La Cygne, Ks., U.S.	D9	93
Ladd, Il., U.S.	B4	90
Ladies Island, i., S.C., U.S.	G6	117
Lādīz, Iran	C7	46
Lādnun, India	G6	38
Ladoga, In., U.S.	E4	91
Ladoga, Lake see Ladožskoje Ozero, l., Russia	F18	6
La Dorada, Col.	E5	58
Ladožskoje Ozero (Lake Ladoga), l., Russia	F18	6
Ladson, S.C., U.S.	F7	117
Lady Lake, Fl., U.S.	D5	86
Lady Laurier, Mount, mtn., B.C., Can.	A6	69
Ladysmith, B.C., Can.	E6	69
Ladysmith, S. Afr.	G5	44
Ladysmith, Wi., U.S.	C2	126
Lae, Pap. N. Gui.	m16	50a
La Encantada, Cerro de, mtn., Mex.	B2	62
La Esmeralda, Ven.	F10	58
La Esperanza, Hond.	G3	64
La Estrada, Spain	C3	12
La Farge, Wi., U.S.	E3	126
Lafayette, Al., U.S.	C4	78
Lafayette, Co., U.S.	B5	83
Lafayette, Ga., U.S.	B1	87
Lafayette, In., U.S.	D4	91
Lafayette, La., U.S.	D3	95
Lafayette, N.C., U.S.	B3	110
Lafayette, Or., U.S.	B3	114
Lafayette, R.I., U.S.	E4	116
Lafayette, Tn., U.S.	A5	119
Lafayette, co., Ar., U.S.	D2	81
Lafayette, co., Fl., U.S.	C3	86
Lafayette, co., La., U.S.	D3	95
Lafayette, co., Ms., U.S.	A4	101
Lafayette, co., Mo., U.S.	B4	102
Lafayette, co., Wi., U.S.	F3	126
Lafayette, Mount, mtn., N.H., U.S.	B3	106
La Feria, Tx., U.S.	F4	120
La Ferté-Bernard, Fr.	D7	10
La Ferté-Macé, Fr.	D6	10
La Ferté-Saint-Aubin, Fr.	E8	10
Lafia, Nig.	G7	42
Lafitte, La., U.S.	k11	95
La Flèche, Fr.	E6	10
La Follette, Tn., U.S.	C9	119
La Fontaine, In., U.S.	C6	91
La Fortuna, C.R.	I5	64
Lafourche, La., U.S.	E5	95
Lafourche, co., La., U.S.	E5	95
La France, S.C., U.S.	B2	117
La Fregeneda, Spain	E5	12
La Fría, Ven.	C6	58
La Fuente de San Esteban, Spain	E5	12
Lågen, stm., Nor.	F8	6
Laghouat, Alg.	B6	42
Lago, Mount, mtn., Wa., U.S.	A5	124
Lagonegro, Italy	I10	14
Lagos, Nig.	G6	42
Lagos de Moreno, Mex.	G9	62
La Goulette, Tun.	M5	14
La Grand'Combe, Fr.	H11	10
La Grande, Or., U.S.	B8	114
La Grande, stm., Que., Can.	h11	74
La Grande Deux, Réservoir, res., Que., Can.	h11	74
La Grange, Austl.	C4	50
La Grange, Ga., U.S.	C1	87
La Grange, Il., U.S.	B6	90
Lagrange, In., U.S.	A7	91
La Grange, Ky., U.S.	B4	94
La Grange, Mo., U.S.	A6	102
La Grange, N.C., U.S.	B5	110
Lagrange, Oh., U.S.	A3	112
La Grange, Tx., U.S.	E4	120
Lagrange, co., In., U.S.	A7	91
La Grange Park, Il., U.S.	k9	90
La Gran Sabana, pl., Ven.	E12	58
La Grita, Ven.	C7	58
La Guadeloupe (Saint-Evariste), Que., Can.	D7	74
La Guaira, Ven.	B9	58
La Guajira, Península de, pen., S.A.	A7	58
Laguardia, Spain	C9	12
La Guardia, Spain	D3	12
La Guerche-de-Bretagne, Fr.	E5	10
La Guerche-sur-l'aubois, Fr.	F9	10
Laguiole, Fr.	H9	10
Laguna, N.M., U.S.	B2	108
Laguna Beach, Ca., U.S.	F5	82
Laguna Dam, U.S.	E1	80
Laguna Indian Reservation, N.M., U.S.	C2	108
Lagunillas, Bol.	G6	54
La Habana (Havana), Cuba	C6	64
La Habra, Ca., U.S.	n13	82
Lahaina, Hi., U.S.	C5	88
La Harpe, Il., U.S.	C3	90
La Harpe, Ks., U.S.	E8	93
Lahat, Indon.	F3	32
La Have, stm., N.S., Can.	E5	71
La Haye-du-Puits, Fr.	C5	10
Lahij, Yemen	F3	46
Laholm, Swe.	H9	6
Lahoma, Ok., U.S.	A3	113
Lahontan Reservoir, res., Nv., U.S.	D2	105
Lahore, Pak.	E6	38
Lahr, Ger.	G7	8
Lahti, Fin.	F15	6
Laie, Hi., U.S.	B4	88
L'Aigle, Fr.	D7	10
Laignes, Fr.	E11	10
Laihia, Fin.	E14	6
Laingsburg, S. Afr.	H4	44
Laingsburg, Mi., U.S.	F6	99
Lairg, Scot., U.K.	C8	7
Laissac, Fr.	H9	10
Laiyang, China	D11	26
La Jara, Co., U.S.	D5	83
La Joya, Mex.	A2	62
La Junta, Mex.	C6	62
La Junta, Co., U.S.	D7	83
Lake, co., Ca., U.S.	C2	82
Lake, co., Co., U.S.	B4	83
Lake, co., Fl., U.S.	D5	86
Lake, co., Il., U.S.	A6	90
Lake, co., In., U.S.	B3	91
Lake, co., Mi., U.S.	E5	99
Lake, co., Mn., U.S.	C7	100
Lake, co., Mt., U.S.	C2	103
Lake, co., Oh., U.S.	A4	112
Lake, co., Or., U.S.	E6	114
Lake, co., S.D., U.S.	C8	118
Lake, co., Tn., U.S.	A2	119
Lake Alfred, Fl., U.S.	D5	86
Lake Andes, S.D., U.S.	D7	118
Lake Ariel, Pa., U.S.	D11	115
Lake Arrowhead, Ca., U.S.	E5	82
Lake Arthur, La., U.S.	D3	95
Lake Barcroft, Va., U.S.	*B5	123
Lake Benton, Mn., U.S.	F2	100
Lake Bluff, Il., U.S.	A6	90
Lake Butler, Fl., U.S.	B4	86
Lake Charles, La., U.S.	D2	95
Lake Chelan National Recreation Area, Wa., U.S.	A5	124
Lake City, Ar., U.S.	B5	81
Lake City, Fl., U.S.	B4	86
Lake City, Ia., U.S.	B3	92
Lake City, Mi., U.S.	D5	99
Lake City, Mn., U.S.	F6	100
Lake City, Pa., U.S.	B1	115
Lake City, S.C., U.S.	D8	117
Lake City, Tn., U.S.	C9	119
Lake Clark National Park, Ak., U.S.	C9	79
Lake Cowichan, B.C., Can.	g11	69
Lake Creek, stm., Wa., U.S.	B7	124
Lake Crystal, Mn., U.S.	F4	100
Lake Delta, N.Y., U.S.	B5	109
Lake Delton, Wi., U.S.	E4	126
Lake District National Park, Eng., U.K.	G9	7
Lake Elsinore, Ca., U.S.	F5	82
Lake Erie Beach, N.Y., U.S.	C1	109
Lakefield, Ont., Can.	C6	73
Lakefield, Mn., U.S.	G3	100
Lake Forest, Il., U.S.	A6	90
Lake Fork, stm., Ut., U.S.	C5	121
Lake Geneva, Wi., U.S.	F5	126
Lake Hamilton, Ar., U.S.	g7	81
Lake Harbour, N.W. Ter., Can.	D19	66
Lake Havasu City, Az., U.S.	C1	80
Lake Helen, Fl., U.S.	D5	86
Lakehurst, N.J., U.S.	C4	107
Lakehurst Naval Air Station, mil., N.J., U.S.	C4	107
Lake in the Hills, Il., U.S.	h8	90
Lake Jackson, Tx., U.S.	r14	120
Lake Katrine, N.Y., U.S.	D7	109
Lakeland, Fl., U.S.	D5	86
Lakeland, Ga., U.S.	E3	87
Lake Linden, Mi., U.S.	A2	99
Lake Louise, Alta., Can.	D2	68
Lake Magdalene, Fl., U.S.	o11	86
Lake Mary, Fl., U.S.	D5	86
Lake Mead National Recreation Area, U.S.	H7	105
Lake Meredith National Recreation Area, Tx., U.S.	B2	120
Lake Mills, Ia., U.S.	A4	92
Lake Mills, Wi., U.S.	E5	126
Lakemore, Oh., U.S.	A4	112
Lake Mountain, mtn., Wy., U.S.	E6	127
Lake Nebagamon, Wi., U.S.	B2	126
Lake Odessa, Mi., U.S.	F5	99
Lake of the Woods, co., Mn., U.S.	B4	100
Lake Orion, Mi., U.S.	F7	99
Lake Oswego, Or., U.S.	B4	114
Lake Ozark, Mo., U.S.	C5	102
Lake Park, Fl., U.S.	F6	86
Lake Park, Ia., U.S.	A2	92
Lake Park, Mn., U.S.	D2	100
Lake Placid, Fl., U.S.	E5	86
Lake Placid, N.Y., U.S.	A7	109
Lake Pontchartrain Causeway, La., U.S.	h11	95
Lakeport, Ca., U.S.	C2	82
Lake Preston, S.D., U.S.	C8	118
Lake Providence, La., U.S.	B4	95
Lake Range, mts., Nv., U.S.	C2	105
Lake Ridge, Va., U.S.	*B5	123
Lake Shore, Md., U.S.	B5	97
Lakeshore, Ms., U.S.	E4	101
Lakeside, Az., U.S.	C6	80
Lakeside, Ca., U.S.	F5	82
Lakeside, Ct., U.S.	D3	84
Lakeside, Mt., U.S.	B2	103
Lakeside, Oh., U.S.	A3	112
Lakeside, Or., U.S.	D2	114
Lakeside Park, Ky., U.S.	h13	94
Lake Station, In., U.S.	A3	91
Lake Station, Ok., U.S.	A5	113
Lake Stevens, Wa., U.S.	A3	124
Lake Superior Provincial Park, Ont., Can.	p18	73
Lake Swamp, stm., S.C., U.S.	D8	117
Lake Tansi Village, Tn., U.S.	D8	119
Lake Valley, val., Nv., U.S.	E7	105
Lake View, Ia., U.S.	B2	92
Lakeview, Mi., U.S.	E5	99
Lakeview, Oh., U.S.	B2	112
Lakeview, Or., U.S.	E6	114
Lake View, S.C., U.S.	C9	117
Lake Villa, Il., U.S.	h8	90
Lake Village, Ar., U.S.	D4	81
Lake Village, In., U.S.	B3	91
Lakeville, Ct., U.S.	B2	84
Lakeville, In., U.S.	A5	91
Lakeville, Ma., U.S.	C6	98
Lakeville, Mn., U.S.	F5	100
Lake Waccamaw, N.C., U.S.	C4	110
Lake Wales, Fl., U.S.	E5	86
Lakewood, Ca., U.S.	n12	82
Lakewood, Co., U.S.	B5	83
Lakewood, Il., U.S.	D5	90
Lakewood, Ia., U.S.	f8	92
Lakewood, N.J., U.S.	C4	107
Lakewood, N.Y., U.S.	C1	109
Lakewood, Oh., U.S.	A4	112
Lakewood Center, Wa., U.S.	B3	124
Lake Worth, Fl., U.S.	F6	86
Lake Worth Inlet, b., Fl., U.S.	F7	86
Lake Zurich, Il., U.S.	h8	90
Lakhīmpur, India	G9	38
Lakin, Ks., U.S.	E2	93
Lakota, N.D., U.S.	A7	111
Lakselv, Nor.	A15	6
Lakshadweep, state, India	H3	37
Lakshadweep, is., India	H2	37
Lalbenque, Fr.	H8	10
La Libertad, Guat.	F2	64
La Libertad, Mex.	C3	62
Lalinde, Fr.	H7	10
La Línea, Spain	I6	12
Lalitpur, India	H8	38
Lalitpur, Nepal	G11	38
La Loupe, Fr.	D8	10
La Luz, N.M., U.S.	E4	108
Lama, Ozero, l., Russia	D12	24
La Maddalena, Italy	H4	14
La Madrid, Arg.	B3	56
La Malbaie, Que., Can.	B7	74
La Mancha, Mex.	E8	62
La Mancha, reg., Spain	G8	12
Lamar, Ar., U.S.	B2	81
Lamar, Co., U.S.	D8	83
Lamar, Mo., U.S.	D3	102
Lamar, Pa., U.S.	D7	115
Lamar, S.C., U.S.	C7	117
Lamar, co., Al., U.S.	B1	78
Lamar, co., Ga., U.S.	C2	87
Lamar, co., Ms., U.S.	D4	101
Lamar, co., Tx., U.S.	C5	120
Lamar, stm., Wy., U.S.	B2	127
Lamarche, Fr.	D12	10
La Mauricie, Parc National de, Que., Can.	C5	74
Lamb, co., Tx., U.S.	B1	120
Lambaréné, Gabon	B2	44
Lambert, Ms., U.S.	A3	101
Lambert Glacier, Ant.	B19	47
Lamberton, Mn., U.S.	F3	100
Lambert's Bay, S. Afr.	H3	44
Lambertville, Mi., U.S.	G7	99
Lambertville, N.J., U.S.	C3	107
Lambton, Cape, c., N.W. Ter., Can.	B8	66
Lame Deer, Mt., U.S.	E10	103
Lamego, Port.	D4	12
Lamèque, N.B., Can.	B5	71
Lamèque, Île, i., N.B., Can.	B5	71
La Mesa, Ca., U.S.	F5	82
La Mesa, N.M., U.S.	E3	108
Lamesa, Tx., U.S.	C2	120
Lamia, Grc.	K6	16
Lamoille, Nv., U.S.	C6	105
Lamoille, co., Vt., U.S.	B3	122
Lamoille, stm., Vt., U.S.	B3	122
La Moine, stm., Il., U.S.	C3	90
Lamoni, Ia., U.S.	D4	92
Lamont, Alta., Can.	C4	68
Lamont, Ca., U.S.	E4	82
La Monte, Mo., U.S.	C4	102
La Motte, Isle, i., Vt., U.S.	B2	122
Lamotte-Beuvron, Fr.	E9	10
La Moure, co., N.D., U.S.	C7	111
Lampang, Thai.	E5	34
Lampasas, Tx., U.S.	D3	120
Lampasas, co., Tx., U.S.	D3	120
Lampedusa, Isola di, i., Italy	N7	14
Lampertheim, Ger.	F8	8
Lampman, Sask., Can.	H4	75
Lamprey, stm., N.H., U.S.	D4	106
Lamu, Kenya	B8	44
La Mure, Fr.	H12	10
Lanai, i., Hi., U.S.	C5	88
Lanai City, Hi., U.S.	C5	88
Lanaihale, mtn., Hi., U.S.	C5	88
Lanark, Ont., Can.	C8	73
Lanark, Il., U.S.	A4	90
Lanbi Kyun, i., Burma	I5	34
Lancaster, Ont., Can.	B10	73
Lancaster, Eng., U.K.	G10	7
Lancaster, Ca., U.S.	E4	82
Lancaster, Ky., U.S.	C5	94
Lancaster, Mo., U.S.	A5	102
Lancaster, N.H., U.S.	B3	106
Lancaster, N.Y., U.S.	C2	109
Lancaster, Oh., U.S.	C3	112
Lancaster, Pa., U.S.	F9	115
Lancaster, S.C., U.S.	B6	117
Lancaster, Tx., U.S.	n10	120
Lancaster, Wi., U.S.	F3	126
Lancaster, co., Ne., U.S.	D9	104
Lancaster, co., Pa., U.S.	G9	115
Lancaster, co., S.C., U.S.	B6	117
Lancaster, co., Va., U.S.	C6	123
Lancaster Sound, strt., N.W. Ter., Can.	B16	66
Lance Creek, stm., Wy., U.S.	C8	127
Lanciano, Italy	G9	14
Landau, Ger.	F8	8
Landau an der Isar, Ger.	G12	8
Land Between the Lakes, park, U.S.	f9	94
Lander, Wy., U.S.	D4	127
Lander, co., Nv., U.S.	C4	105
Landerneau, Fr.	D2	10
Landess, In., U.S.	C6	91
Landete, Spain	F10	12
Landis, N.C., U.S.	B2	110
Lando, S.C., U.S.	B5	117
Landquart, Switz.	F16	10
Land's End, c., Eng., U.K.	K7	7
Lands End, c., R.I., U.S.	F5	116
Landshut, Ger.	G12	8
Landskrona, Swe.	I9	6
Lane, co., Ks., U.S.	D3	93
Lane, co., Or., U.S.	C4	114
Lanesboro, Mn., U.S.	G7	100
Lanett, Al., U.S.	C4	78
Langar, Afg.	B5	38
Långban, Swe.	G10	6
Langdon, N.D., U.S.	A7	111
Langeac, Fr.	G10	10
Langeais, Fr.	E7	10
Langeloth, Pa., U.S.	F1	115
Langenhagen, Ger.	C9	8
Langenthal, Switz.	E14	10
Langholm, Scot., U.K.	F9	7
Langhorne, Pa., U.S.	F12	115
Langlade, co., Wi., U.S.	C4	126
Langley, B.C., Can.	f13	69
Langley, S.C., U.S.	E4	117
Langley, Wa., U.S.	A3	124
Langley Air Force Base, mil., Va., U.S.	h15	123
Langley Park, Md., U.S.	f9	97
Langnau, Switz.	F14	10
Langogne, Fr.	H10	10
Langon, Fr.	H6	10
Langres, Fr.	E12	10
Langsa, Indon.	E2	32
Lang Son, Viet.	D9	34
Langston, Ok., U.S.	B4	113
Languedoc, hist. reg., Fr.	I9	10
L'Anguille, stm., Ar., U.S.	B5	81
Langzhong, China	E8	26
Lanham, Md., U.S.	C4	97
Lanier, co., Ga., U.S.	E3	87
Lannilis, Fr.	D2	10
Lannion, Fr.	D3	10
L'Annonciation, Que., Can.	C3	74
Lansdale, Pa., U.S.	F11	115
Lansdowne, Md., U.S.	B4	97
L'Anse, Mi., U.S.	B2	99
L'Anse-au-Loup, Newf., Can.	C3	72
L'Anse Indian Reservation, Mi., U.S.	B2	99
Lansford, Pa., U.S.	E10	115
Lansing, Il., U.S.	B6	90
Lansing, Ia., U.S.	A6	92
Lansing, Ks., U.S.	C9	93
Lansing, Mi., U.S.	F6	99
Lantana, Fl., U.S.	F6	86
Lantau Island, i., H.K.	M2	28
Lanusei, Italy	J4	14
Lanxi, China	F8	28
Lanzarote, i., Spain	C3	42
Lanzhou, China	D7	26
Laoag, Phil.	B7	32
Lao Cai, Viet.	C7	34
Laon, Fr.	C10	10
La Oroya, Peru	F3	54
Laos, ctry., Asia	B3	32
Lapalisse, Fr.	F10	10
La Palma, Col.	E5	58
La Palma, Pan.	J8	64
La Palma, i., Spain	C2	42
La Paragua, Ven.	D11	58
La Paz, Arg.	C5	56
La Paz, Arg.	C3	56
La Paz, Bol.	G5	54
La Paz, Mex.	E4	62
La Paz, Az., U.S.	D2	80
La Paz, co., Az., U.S.	D2	80
La Paz, Bahía de, b., Mex.	E4	62
Lapeer, Mi., U.S.	E7	99
Lapeer, co., Mi., U.S.	E7	99
Lapel, In., U.S.	D6	91
La Perouse Strait, strt., Asia	B15	26
La Piedad [Cavadas], Mex.	G8	62
La Pine, Or., U.S.	D5	114
Lapinlahti, Fin.	E16	6
La Place, La., U.S.	h11	95
Lapland, reg., Eur.	C14	6
La Plata, Arg.	C5	56
La Plata, Md., U.S.	C3	97
La Plata, Mo., U.S.	A5	102
La Plata, co., Co., U.S.	D3	83
La Plata Mountains, mts., Co., U.S.	D3	83
La Plata Peak, mtn., Co., U.S.	B4	83
La Platte, stm., Vt., U.S.	C2	122
La Pocatière, Que., Can.	B7	74
Laporte, Co., U.S.	A5	83
La Porte, In., U.S.	A4	91
La Porte, Tx., U.S.	r14	120
La Porte, co., In., U.S.	A4	91
La Porte City, Ia., U.S.	B5	92
Lappeenranta, Fin.	F17	6
La Prairie, Que., Can.	D4	74
La Pryor, Tx., U.S.	E3	120
Laptevych, More (Laptev Sea), Russia	B19	24
Lapua, Fin.	E14	6
La Puebla, Spain	F15	12
La Puebla de Montalbán, Spain	F7	12
La Push, Wa., U.S.	B1	124
Lapwai, Id., U.S.	C2	89
La Quiaca, Arg.	A3	56
L'Aquila, Italy	G8	14
Lār, Iran	C5	46
Larache, Mor.	A4	42
Laramie, Wy., U.S.	E7	127
Laramie, co., Wy., U.S.	E8	127
Laramie, stm., Wy., U.S.	E7	127
Laramie Mountains, mts., Wy., U.S.	D7	127
Laramie Peak, mtn., Wy., U.S.	D7	127
Larantuka, Indon.	G7	32
L'Arbresle, Fr.	G11	10
Lärbro, Swe.	H12	6
Larche, Col de, Eur.	H13	10
Larchmont, N.Y., U.S.	h13	109
Larchwood, Ia., U.S.	A1	92
Laredo, Tx., U.S.	F3	120
La Réole, Fr.	H6	10
Largeau, Chad	E9	42
L'argentière-la-Bessée, Fr.	H13	10
Lar Gerd, Afg.	C2	38
Largo, Fl., U.S.	E4	86
Largo, Cañón, val., N.M., U.S.	A2	108
Largo, Key, i., Fl., U.S.	G6	86
Largs, Scot., U.K.	F8	7
Larimer, co., Co., U.S.	A5	83
Larimore, N.D., U.S.	B8	111
La Rioja, Arg.	B3	56
Lárisa, Grc.	J6	16
Larjak, Russia	E10	24
Lārkāna, Pak.	G3	38
Lark Harbour, Newf., Can.	D2	72
Larkspur, Ca., U.S.	h7	82
Lárnax (Larnaca), Cyp.	B3	40
Larne, N. Ire., U.K.	G7	7
Larned, Ks., U.S.	D4	93
La Robla, Spain	C6	12
La Roca de la Sierra, Spain	F5	12
La Rochefoucauld, Fr.	G7	10
La Rochelle, Fr.	F5	10
La Roche-sur-Yon, Fr.	F5	10
La Roda, Spain	F9	12
La Romana, Dom. Rep.	E13	64
Larose, La., U.S.	E5	95
La Rubia, Arg.	C4	56
Larue, co., Ky., U.S.	C4	94
Laruns, Fr.	J6	10

Index

Name	Map Ref	Page
Larvik, Nor.	G7	6
LaSalle, Que., Can.	q19	74
La Salle, Co., U.S.	A6	83
La Salle, Il., U.S.	B4	90
La Salle, co., Il., U.S.	B4	90
La Salle, co., La., U.S.	C3	95
La Salle, co., Tx., U.S.	E3	120
Las Animas, Co., U.S.	C7	83
Las Animas, co., Co., U.S.	D6	83
Las Anod, Som.	G4	46
La Sarre, Que., Can.	k11	74
Las Casitas, Cerro, mtn., Mex.	F5	62
Las Choapas, Mex.	I12	62
La Scie, Newf., Can.	D4	72
Las Colimas, Mex.	E10	62
Las Cruces, N.M., U.S.	E3	108
Las Delicias, Mex.	J14	62
La Selle, Pic, mtn., Haiti	E11	64
La Serena, Chile	B2	56
Las Escobas, Mex.	B2	62
La Seyne, Fr.	I12	10
Las Flores, Arg.	D5	56
Lashio, Burma	C4	34
Laško, Slo.	A4	56
Las Lomitas, Arg.	A4	56
Las Minas, Cerro, mtn., Hond.	G3	64
La Solana, Spain	G8	12
Las Palmas de Gran Canaria, Spain	C2	42
La Spezia, Italy	E4	14
Las Piedras, Ur.	C5	56
Las Plumas, Arg.	E3	56
Lassen, co., Ca., U.S.	B3	82
Lassen Peak, vol., Ca., U.S.	B3	82
Lassen Volcanic National Park, Ca., U.S.	B3	82
L'Assomption, Que., Can.	D4	74
Las Termas, Arg.	B4	56
Last Mountain Lake, l., Sask., Can.	F3	75
Las Tórtolas, Cerro, mtn., S.A.	C5	56
Las Varas, Mex.	C5	62
Las Vegas, Nv., U.S.	G6	105
Las Vegas, N.M., U.S.	B4	108
Latacunga, Ec.	H3	58
Latah, co., Id., U.S.	C2	89
Latakia see Al-Lādhiqīyah, Syria	B4	40
La Teste-de-Buch, Fr.	H5	10
Lathrop, Mo., U.S.	B3	102
Lathrop Wells, Nv., U.S.	G5	105
Latimer, co., Ok., U.S.	C6	113
Latina, Italy	H7	14
Laton, Ca., U.S.	D4	82
La Tortuga, Isla, i., Ven.	B10	58
Latour Peak, mtn., Id., U.S.	B2	89
Latrobe, Pa., U.S.	F3	115
Latta, S.C., U.S.	C9	117
La Tuque, Que., Can.	B5	74
Lātūr, India	C4	37
Latvia, ctry., Eur.	D7	18
Lauchhammer, Ger.	D5	8
Lauderdale, Ms., U.S.	C5	101
Lauderdale, co., Al., U.S.	A2	78
Lauderdale, co., Ms., U.S.	C5	101
Lauderdale, co., Tn., U.S.	B2	119
Lauderdale Lakes, Fl., U.S.	r13	86
Lauenburg, Ger.	B10	8
Laughlin, Nv., U.S.	H7	105
Laughlin Air Force Base, mil., Tx., U.S.	E2	120
Laughlin Peak, mtn., N.M., U.S.	A5	108
Laughlintown, Pa., U.S.	F3	115
Launceston, Austl.	H9	50
Launceston, Eng., U.K.	K8	7
Launching Point, c., P.E.I., Can.	C7	71
La Union, El Sal.	H4	64
La Unión, Spain	H11	12
La Unión, Ven.	C9	58
La Urbana, Ven.	C9	58
Laurel, De., U.S.	F3	85
Laurel, Fl., U.S.	E4	86
Laurel, Md., U.S.	B4	97
Laurel, Ms., U.S.	D4	101
Laurel, Mt., U.S.	E8	103
Laurel, Ne., U.S.	B8	104
Laurel, Va., U.S.	C5	123
Laurel, co., Ky., U.S.	C5	94
Laurel, co., Ky., U.S.	C5	94
Laurel Bay, S.C., U.S.	G6	117
Laurel Creek, stm., W.V., U.S.	n14	125
Laurel Creek, stm., W.V., U.S.	m12	125
Laureldale, Pa., U.S.	F10	115
Laurel Fork, stm., W.V., U.S.	C5	125
Laurel Hill, N.C., U.S.	C3	110
Laurel River Lake, res., Ky., U.S.	D5	94
Laurence G. Hanscom Air Force Base, mil., Ma., U.S.	g10	98
Laurence Harbor, N.J., U.S.	C4	107
Laurens, Ia., U.S.	B3	92
Laurens, S.C., U.S.	C3	117
Laurens, co., Ga., U.S.	D4	87
Laurens, co., S.C., U.S.	C3	117
Laurentides, Que., Can.	D4	74
Laurentides, Parc Provincial des, Que., Can.	B6	74
Laurier, Que., Can.	C6	74
Laurière, Fr.	F8	10
Laurierville, Que., Can.	C6	74
Laurinburg, N.C., U.S.	C3	110
Laurium, Mi., U.S.	A2	99
Lausanne, Switz.	F13	10
Laut, Pulau, i., Indon.	F6	32
Laut, Pulau, i., Indon.	L9	34
Lautaro, Chile	D2	56
Lauterbach, Ger.	E9	8
Laut Kecil, Kepulauan, is., Indon.	F6	32
Lauzon, Que., Can.	C6	74
Lava Beds National Monument, Ca., U.S.	B3	82
Lavaca, Ar., U.S.	B1	81
Lavaca, co., Tx., U.S.	E4	120
Lavagh More, mtn., Ire.	G4	7
Laval, Que., Can.	D4	74
Laval, Fr.	D6	10
La Vale, Md., U.S.	k13	97
Lavaltrie, Que., Can.	D4	74
Lavapié, Punta, c., Chile	D2	56
Laveen, Az., U.S.	m8	80
La Vega, Dom. Rep.	E12	64
La Vela, Cabo de c., Col.	A6	58
Lavello, Italy	H10	14
L'Avenir, Que., Can.	D5	74
La Vergne, Tn., U.S.	A5	119
La Verkin, Ut., U.S.	F2	121
La Verne, Ca., U.S.	m13	82
Laverne, Ok., U.S.	A2	113
La Veta, Co., U.S.	D5	83
Lavia, Fin.	F14	6
La Vista, Ca., U.S.	*h8	87
La Vista, Ne., U.S.	g12	104
Lavonia, Ga., U.S.	B3	87
Lavon Lake, res., Tx., U.S.	m10	120
La Voulte-sur-Rhône, Fr.	H11	10
Lavras, Braz.	F6	57
Lawai, Hi., U.S.	B2	88
Lawang, Indon.	m16	33a
Lawers, Ben, mtn., Scot., U.K.	E8	7
Lawn, Newf., Can.	E4	72
Lawrence, In., U.S.	E5	91
Lawrence, Ks., U.S.	D8	93
Lawrence, Ma., U.S.	A5	98
Lawrence, Mi., U.S.	F4	99
Lawrence, N.Y., U.S.	k13	109
Lawrence, co., Al., U.S.	A2	78
Lawrence, co., Ar., U.S.	A4	81
Lawrence, co., Il., U.S.	E6	90
Lawrence, co., In., U.S.	G4	91
Lawrence, co., Ky., U.S.	B7	94
Lawrence, co., Ms., U.S.	D3	101
Lawrence, co., Mo., U.S.	D4	102
Lawrence, co., Oh., U.S.	D3	112
Lawrence, co., Pa., U.S.	E1	115
Lawrence, co., Tn., U.S.	B4	119
Lawrenceburg, In., U.S.	F8	91
Lawrenceburg, Ky., U.S.	B5	94
Lawrenceburg, Tn., U.S.	B4	119
Lawrence Park, Pa., U.S.	B1	115
Lawrenceville, Ga., U.S.	C3	87
Lawrenceville, Il., U.S.	E6	90
Lawrenceville, Va., U.S.	D5	123
Lawson, Mo., U.S.	B3	102
Lawsonia, Md., U.S.	E6	97
Lawtell, La., U.S.	D3	95
Lawton, Mi., U.S.	F5	99
Lawton, Ok., U.S.	C3	113
Lawz, Jabal al-, mtn., Sau. Ar.	C2	46
Lay Lake, res., Al., U.S.	B3	78
Laysan Island, i., Hi., U.S.	k13	88
Layton, Ut., U.S.	B4	121
La Zarca, Mex.	E7	62
Lazarev, Russia	G22	24
Lazi, China	F12	38
Lea, co., N.M., U.S.	D6	108
Leachville, Ar., U.S.	B5	81
Lead, S.D., U.S.	C2	118
Leadbetter Point, c., Wa., U.S.	C1	124
Leadville, Co., U.S.	B4	83
Leadwood, Mo., U.S.	D7	102
Leaf, stm., Ms., U.S.	D5	101
Leaf Rapids, Man., Can.	A1	70
Leake, co., Ms., U.S.	C4	101
Leakesville, Ms., U.S.	D5	101
Lealman, Fl., U.S.	p10	86
Leamington, Ont., Can.	E2	73
Leary, Ga., U.S.	E2	87
Leatherman Peak, mtn., Id., U.S.	E5	89
Leavenworth, Ks., U.S.	C9	93
Leavenworth, Wa., U.S.	B5	124
Leavenworth, co., Ks., U.S.	C8	93
Leavittsburg, Oh., U.S.	A5	112
Leawood, Ks., U.S.	D9	93
Lebanon, De., U.S.	D4	85
Lebanon, Il., U.S.	E4	90
Lebanon, In., U.S.	D5	91
Lebanon, Ky., U.S.	C4	94
Lebanon, Mo., U.S.	D5	102
Lebanon, N.H., U.S.	C2	106
Lebanon, Oh., U.S.	C1	112
Lebanon, Or., U.S.	C4	114
Lebanon, Pa., U.S.	F9	115
Lebanon, Tn., U.S.	A5	119
Lebanon, Va., U.S.	f9	123
Lebanon, co., Pa., U.S.	F8	115
Lebanon, ctry., Asia	C4	40
Lebanon Junction, Ky., U.S.	C4	94
Le Blanc, Fr.	F8	10
Lebo, Ks., U.S.	D8	93
Lebork, Pol.	A17	8
Lebrija, Spain	I5	12
Lecce, Italy	I13	14
Lecco, Italy	D4	14
Le Center, Mn., U.S.	F5	100
Le Cheylard, Fr.	H11	10
La Claire, Ia., U.S.	C7	92
Lecompte, La., U.S.	C3	95
Lecompton, Ks., U.S.	C8	93
Le Creusot, Fr.	F11	10
Leduc, Alta., Can.	C4	68
Lee, Ma., U.S.	B1	98
Lee, co., Al., U.S.	C4	78
Lee, co., Ar., U.S.	C5	81
Lee, co., Fl., U.S.	F5	86
Lee, co., Ga., U.S.	E2	87
Lee, co., Il., U.S.	B4	90
Lee, co., Ia., U.S.	D6	92
Lee, co., Ky., U.S.	C6	94
Lee, co., Ms., U.S.	A5	101
Lee, co., N.C., U.S.	B3	110
Lee, co., S.C., U.S.	C7	117
Lee, co., Tx., U.S.	D4	120
Lee, co., Va., U.S.	f8	123
Lee, Lake, l., Ms., U.S.	B3	101
Leechburg, Pa., U.S.	E2	115
Leech Lake, l., Mn., U.S.	C4	100
Leech Lake Indian Reservation, Mn., U.S.	C4	100
Lee Creek, stm., U.S.	B1	81
Leeds, Eng., U.K.	H11	7
Leeds, Al., U.S.	B3	78
Leelanau, co., Mi., U.S.	D5	99
Leelanau, Lake, l., Mi., U.S.	C5	99
Lee Park, Pa., U.S.	n17	115
Leer, Ger.	B7	8
Leesburg, Fl., U.S.	D5	86
Leesburg, Ga., U.S.	E2	87
Leesburg, Oh., U.S.	C2	112
Leesburg, Va., U.S.	A5	123
Lees Summit, Mo., U.S.	C3	102
Leesville, La., U.S.	C2	95
Leesville, S.C., U.S.	D4	117
Leesville Lake, res., Va., U.S.	C3	123
Leeton, Mo., U.S.	C4	102
Leetonia, Oh., U.S.	B5	112
Leetsdale, Pa., U.S.	h13	115
Leeuwarden, Neth.	B5	8
Leeuwin, Cape, c., Austl.	F3	50
Leeward Islands, is., N.A.	F17	64
Leflore, co., Ms., U.S.	B3	101
Le Flore, co., Ok., U.S.	C7	113
Legal, Alta., Can.	C4	68
Legazpi, Phil.	r20	33b
Leghorn see Livorno, Italy	F5	14
Legnago, Italy	D6	14
Legnano, Italy	D3	14
Legnica (Liegnitz), Pol.	D16	8
Le Grand, Ca., U.S.	D3	82
Le Grand, Ia., U.S.	B5	92
Le Havre, Fr.	C7	10
Lehi, Ut., U.S.	C4	121
Lehigh, co., Pa., U.S.	E10	115
Lehigh, stm., Pa., U.S.	E10	115
Lehigh Acres, Fl., U.S.	F5	86
Lehighton, Pa., U.S.	E10	115
Lehua Island, i., Hi., U.S.	A1	88
Lehutu, Bots.	F4	44
Leiah, Pak.	E4	38
Leibnitz, Aus.	I15	8
Leicester, Eng., U.K.	I11	7
Leicester, Ma., U.S.	B4	98
Leichhardt, stm., Austl.	C7	50
Leiden, Neth.	C4	8
Leighton, Al., U.S.	A2	78
Leikanger, Nor.	F6	6
Leinster, hist. reg., Ire.	H5	7
Leinster, Mount, mtn., Ire.	I6	7
Leipsic, De., U.S.	D3	85
Leipsic, Oh., U.S.	A2	112
Leipsic, stm., De., U.S.	C3	85
Leipzig, Ger.	D12	8
Leiria, Port.	F3	12
Leisler, Mount, mtn., Austl.	D5	50
Leisure City, Fl., U.S.	s13	86
Leitchfield, Ky., U.S.	C3	94
Leitrim, Ire.	G4	7
Leiyang, China	I1	29
Leizhou Bandao, pen., China	D11	34
Leland, Il., U.S.	B5	90
Leland, Ms., U.S.	B3	101
Leleiwi Point, c., Hi., U.S.	D7	88
Leleque, Arg.	E2	56
Leli Shan, mtn., China	D9	38
Le Locle, Switz.	E13	10
Le Lude, Fr.	E7	10
Le Maire, Estrecho de, strt., Arg.	G4	56
Le Mans, Fr.	D7	10
Le Mars, Ia., U.S.	B1	92
Leme, Braz.	G5	57
Lemesós (Limassol), Cyp.	B3	40
Lemgo, Ger.	C8	8
Lemhi, co., Id., U.S.	E4	89
Lemhi, stm., Id., U.S.	E5	89
Lemhi Pass, Id., U.S.	E5	89
Lemhi Range, mts., Id., U.S.	E5	89
Lemmon, S.D., U.S.	B3	118
Lemmon, Mount, mtn., Az., U.S.	E5	80
Lemmon Valley, Nv., U.S.	D2	105
Lemon, Lake, l., In., U.S.	F5	91
Lemon Grove, Ca., U.S.	o15	82
Lemon Fair, stm., Vt., U.S.	C2	122
Lemon Island, i., S.C., U.S.	G6	117
Lemont, Il., U.S.	B5	90
Lemont, Pa., U.S.	E6	115
Lemonweir, stm., Wi., U.S.	D3	126
Lemoore, Ca., U.S.	D4	82
Lemoore Naval Air Station, mil., Ca., U.S.	D4	82
Lempa, stm., N.A.	H3	64
Lem Peak, mtn., Id., U.S.	E5	89
Lena, Il., U.S.	A4	90
Lena, stm., Russia	C19	24
Lenawee, co., Mi., U.S.	G6	99
Lencloître, Fr.	F7	10
Lenexa, Ks., U.S.	D9	93
Lenghu, China	D5	26
Leninabad, Taj.	I11	22
Leningrad see Sankt-Peterburg, Russia	B13	18
Leninogorsk, Kaz.	G10	24
Leninsk-Kuzneckij, Russia	G11	24
Leninskoje, Russia	H20	24
Lennox, S.D., U.S.	D9	118
Lennox, Ca., U.S.	n12	82
Lennoxville, Que., Can.	D6	74
Lenoir, N.C., U.S.	B1	110
Lenoir, co., N.C., U.S.	B5	110
Lenoir City, Tn., U.S.	D9	119
Lenore Lake, l., Sask., Can.	E3	75
Lenore Lake, l., Wa., U.S.	B6	124
Lenox, Ga., U.S.	E3	87
Lenox, Ia., U.S.	D3	92
Lenox, Ma., U.S.	B1	98
Lens, Fr.	B9	10
Lensk, Russia	E16	24
Lentini, Italy	L10	14
Leo, In., U.S.	B7	91
Leoben, Aus.	H15	8
Leominster, Eng., U.K.	I10	7
Leominster, Ma., U.S.	A4	98
León, Nic.	H4	64
Leon, Ia., U.S.	D4	92
León, Spain	C6	12
Leon, Ks., U.S.	E7	93
Leon, co., Fl., U.S.	B2	86
Leon, co., Tx., U.S.	D4	120
Leonard, Tx., U.S.	C4	120
Leonardo, N.J., U.S.	C4	107
Leonardtown, Md., U.S.	D4	97
Leonberg, Ger.	G9	8
León [de los Aldamas], Mex.	G9	62
Leonia, N.J., U.S.	h9	107
Leonora, Austl.	E4	50
Leonville, La., U.S.	D4	95
Léopold II, Lac see Mai-Ndombe, Lac, l., Zaire	B3	44
Leopoldina, Braz.	F7	57
Léopoldville see Kinshasa, Zaire	B3	44
Leoti, Ks., U.S.	D2	93
Le Palais, Fr.	E3	10
Lepanto, Ar., U.S.	B5	81
Lepe, Spain	H4	12
Leping, China	G6	28
Lepontine, Alpi, mts., Eur.	F15	10
Le Puy, Fr.	G10	10
Lercara Friddi, Italy	L8	14
Lerici, Italy	E4	14
Lérida, Col.	E3	58
Lérida, Spain	D12	12
Lerma, Spain	C8	12
Le Roy, Il., U.S.	C5	90
Le Roy, Ia., U.S.	G6	92
Le Roy, N.Y., U.S.	C3	109
Lerwick, Scot., U.K.	A11	7
Léry, Que., Can.	q19	74
Lery, Lake, l., La., U.S.	k12	95
Les Andelys, Fr.	C8	10
Lesbos see Lésvos, i., Grc.	J10	16
Les Cayes, Haiti	E11	64
Les Échelles, Fr.	G12	10
Les Herbiers, Fr.	F5	10
Leskovac, Yugo.	G5	16
Leslie, Mi., U.S.	F6	99
Leslie, S.C., U.S.	B6	117
Leslie, co., Ky., U.S.	C6	94
Lesosavodsk, Russia	H20	24
Lesotho, ctry., Afr.	G5	44
Les Sables-d'Olonne, Fr.	F5	10
Lesser Antilles, is.	G17	64
Lesser Slave Lake, l., Alta., Can.	B3	68
Lesser Sunda Islands, is., Indon.	G6	32
Lester Prairie, Mn., U.S.	F4	100
Le Sueur, Mn., U.S.	F5	100
Le Sueur, co., Mn., U.S.	F5	100
Lésvos (Lesbos), i., Grc.	J10	16
Leszno, Pol.	D16	8
Letcher, co., Ky., U.S.	C7	94
Lethbridge, Alta., Can.	E4	68
Lethbridge, Newf., Can.	D5	72
Lethem, Guy.	F13	58
Le Thillot, Fr.	E13	10
Leti, Kepulauan, is., Indon.	G8	32
Leticia, Col.	J8	58
Le Tréport, Fr.	B8	10
Letsók-Aw Kyun, i., Burma	I5	34
Letterkenny, Ire.	G5	7
Leutkirch, Ger.	H10	8
Leuven, Bel.	E5	8
Levádhia, Grc.	K6	16
Levante, Riviera di, Italy	E4	14
Leveland, Tx., U.S.	C1	120
Leveque, Cape, c., Austl.	C4	50
Leverkusen, Ger.	D6	8
Le Vigan, Fr.	I10	10
Lévis, Que., Can.	C6	74
Levisa Fork, stm., U.S.	C7	94
Levittown, N.Y., U.S.	E7	109
Levittown, Pa., U.S.	F12	115
Levy, co., Fl., U.S.	C4	86
Levy Lake, l., Fl., U.S.	C4	86
Lewes, Eng., U.K.	K13	7
Lewes, De., U.S.	E5	85
Lewes and Rehoboth Canal, De., U.S.	F5	85
Lewis, co., Id., U.S.	C2	89
Lewis, co., Ky., U.S.	B6	94
Lewis, co., Mo., U.S.	A6	102
Lewis, co., N.Y., U.S.	B5	109
Lewis, co., Tn., U.S.	B4	119
Lewis, co., Wa., U.S.	C3	124
Lewis, co., W.V., U.S.	C4	125
Lewis, stm., Wa., U.S.	C4	124
Lewis, Isle of, i., Scot., U.K.	C6	7
Lewis, Mount, mtn., Nv., U.S.	C5	105
Lewis and Clark, co., Mt., U.S.	C4	103
Lewis and Clark Cavern, Mt., U.S.	D5	103
Lewis and Clark Lake, res., U.S.	E8	118
Lewisburg, Oh., U.S.	C1	112
Lewisburg, Pa., U.S.	E8	115
Lewisburg, Tn., U.S.	B5	119
Lewisburg, W.V., U.S.	D4	125
Lewis Creek, stm., Vt., U.S.	C2	122
Lewis Lake, l., Wy., U.S.	B2	127
Lewisport, Ky., U.S.	C3	94
Lewisporte, Newf., Can.	D4	72
Lewis Smith Lake, res., Al., U.S.	B1	78
Lewiston, Id., U.S.	C1	89
Lewiston, Me., U.S.	D2	96
Lewiston, Mn., U.S.	G7	100
Lewiston, N.Y., U.S.	B1	109
Lewiston, Ut., U.S.	B4	121
Lewiston Peak, mtn., Ut., U.S.	C3	121
Lewiston Woodville, N.C., U.S.	A5	110
Lewistown, Il., U.S.	C3	90
Lewistown, Mt., U.S.	C7	103
Lewistown, Pa., U.S.	E6	115
Lewisville, Ar., U.S.	D2	81
Lewisville, Tx., U.S.	C4	120
Lewisville Lake, res., Tx., U.S.	C4	120
Lexington, Al., U.S.	A2	78
Lexington, Il., U.S.	C5	90
Lexington, Ky., U.S.	B5	94
Lexington, Ma., U.S.	B5	98
Lexington, Mi., U.S.	E8	99
Lexington, Ms., U.S.	B3	101
Lexington, Mo., U.S.	B4	102
Lexington, Ne., U.S.	D6	104
Lexington, N.C., U.S.	B2	110
Lexington, Oh., U.S.	B3	112
Lexington, Ok., U.S.	B4	113
Lexington, S.C., U.S.	D5	117
Lexington, Tn., U.S.	B3	119
Lexington, Va., U.S.	C3	123
Lexington, co., S.C., U.S.	D5	117
Lexington Park, Md., U.S.	D5	97
Leyte, i., Phil.	C7	32
Leyte Gulf, b., Phil.	C8	32
Lhasa, China	F14	38
Lhokseumawe, Indon.	D2	32
Lianhua Shan, mts., China	L4	28
Lianxian, China	G9	26
Lianyungang, China	E10	26
Liao, stm., China	C11	26
Liaocheng, China	D10	26
Liaodong Wan, b., China	C11	26
Liaoning, prov., China	C11	26
Liaotung, Gulf of see Liaodong Wan, b., China	C11	26
Liaoyang, China	C11	26
Liaoyuan, China	C12	26
Liard, stm., Can.	E8	66
Libby, Mt., U.S.	B1	103
Libenge, Zaire	H9	42
Liberal, Ks., U.S.	E3	93
Liberal, Mo., U.S.	D3	102
Liberec, Czech.	E15	8
Liberia, C.R.	I5	64
Liberia, ctry., Afr.	G4	42
Libertad, Ven.	C8	58
Liberty, In., U.S.	E8	91
Liberty, Ky., U.S.	C5	94
Liberty, Ms., U.S.	D3	101
Liberty, Mo., U.S.	B3	102
Liberty, N.Y., U.S.	D6	109
Liberty, N.C., U.S.	B3	110
Liberty, S.C., U.S.	B2	117
Liberty, Tx., U.S.	D5	120
Liberty, co., Fl., U.S.	B2	86
Liberty, co., Ga., U.S.	E5	87
Liberty, co., Mt., U.S.	B5	103
Liberty, co., Tx., U.S.	D5	120
Liberty Center, Oh., U.S.	A1	112
Liberty Lake, Wa., U.S.	g14	124
Liberty Lake, res., Md., U.S.	B4	97
Libertyville, Il., U.S.	A6	90
Lībīyah, Aş-Şaḥrā' al- (Libyan Desert), des., Afr.	D11	42
Libourne, Fr.	H6	10
Libreville, Gabon	A1	44
Libuse, La., U.S.	C3	95
Libya, ctry., Afr.	C9	42
Libyan Desert see Lībīyah, Aş-Şaḥrā' al-, des., Afr.	D11	42
Licata, Italy	L8	14
Lichinga, Moz.	D7	44
Lichtenfels, Ger.	E11	8
Lick Creek, stm., Tn., U.S.	C11	119
Licking, Mo., U.S.	D6	102
Licking, co., Oh., U.S.	B3	112
Licking, stm., Ky., U.S.	B6	94
Lida, Bela.	H8	18
Lida, Lake, l., Mn., U.S.	D3	100
Lidgerwood, N.D., U.S.	C8	111
Lidköping, Swe.	G9	6
Lido di Ostia, Italy	H7	14
Liechtenstein, ctry., Eur.	F9	4
Liège, Bel.	E5	8
Lieksa, Fin.	E18	6
Lienz, Aus.	I12	8
Liepāja, Lat.	E4	18
Lier, Bel.	D4	8
Liestal, Switz.	E14	10
Liévin, Fr.	B9	10
Lièvre, Rivière du, stm., Que., Can.	D2	74
Liezen, Aus.	H14	8
Lifford, Ire.	G5	7
Ligao, Phil.	r20	33b
Lighthouse Inlet, b., S.C., U.S.	k12	117
Lighthouse Point, c., Fl., U.S.	C2	86
Lighthouse Point, c., Fl., U.S.	F6	86
Lighthouse Point, c., La., U.S.	E3	95
Lighthouse Point, c., Mi., U.S.	C5	99
Lightning Creek, stm., Wy., U.S.	C8	127
Ligny-en-Barrois, Fr.	D12	10
Ligonier, In., U.S.	B6	91
Ligonier, Pa., U.S.	F3	115
Ligurian Sea, Eur.	F3	14
Lihou Reefs, rf., Austl.	C10	50
Lihue, Hi., U.S.	B2	88
Lijiang, China	F7	26
Likasi (Jadotville), Zaire	D5	44
Likino-Dulevo, Russia	F22	18
Liknes, Nor.	G6	6
Likouala, stm., Congo	B3	44
Lilbourn, Mo., U.S.	E8	102
Lilburn, Ga., U.S.	h8	87
Liling, China	H2	28
Lille, Fr.	B10	10
Lillehammer, Nor.	F8	6
Lillestrøm, Nor.	G8	6
Lillian, Al., U.S.	E2	78
Lillington, N.C., U.S.	B4	110
Lillinonah, Lake, l., Ct., U.S.	C2	84
Lillo, Spain	F8	12
Lillooet, B.C., Can.	D7	69
Lillooet, stm., B.C., Can.	D6	69
Lilly, Pa., U.S.	F4	115
Lilly Fork, stm., W.V., U.S.	m13	125
Lilly Grove, W.V., U.S.	D3	125
Lilongwe, Mwi.	D6	44
Lily, Ky., U.S.	C5	94
Lima, Peru	F3	54
Lima, N.Y., U.S.	C3	109
Lima, Oh., U.S.	B1	112
Lima Reservoir, res., Mt., U.S.	F4	103
Limassol see Lemesós, Cyp.	B3	40
Limbdi, India	I4	38
Limburg an der Lahn, Ger.	E8	8
Limeira, Braz.	G5	57
Limerick, Ire.	I4	7
Limestone, Me., U.S.	B5	96
Limestone, co., Al., U.S.	A2	78
Limestone, co., Tx., U.S.	D4	120
Limestone Point, pen., Man., Can.	C2	70
Liminka, Fin.	D15	6

Name	Map Ref	Page
Limmen Bight, Austl.	B7	50
Límnos, i., Grc.	J9	16
Limoges, Ont., Can.	B9	73
Limoges, Fr.	G8	10
Limón, C.R.	I6	64
Limón, Hond.	G5	64
Limon, Co., U.S.	B7	83
Limousins, Plateau du, plat., Fr.	G8	10
Limoux, Fr.	I9	10
Limpopo, stm., Afr.	F6	44
Linares, Chile	D2	56
Linares, Col.	G4	58
Linares, Mex.	E10	62
Linares, Spain	G8	12
Lincoln, Arg.	C4	56
Lincoln, Ont., Can.	D5	73
Lincoln, Eng., U.K.	H12	7
Lincoln, Al., U.S.	B3	78
Lincoln, Ar., U.S.	B1	81
Lincoln, Ca., U.S.	C3	82
Lincoln, De., U.S.	E4	85
Lincoln, Id., U.S.	F6	89
Lincoln, Il., U.S.	C4	90
Lincoln, Ks., U.S.	C5	93
Lincoln, Me., U.S.	C4	96
Lincoln, Ma., U.S.	g10	98
Lincoln, Mo., U.S.	C4	102
Lincoln, Ne., U.S.	D9	104
Lincoln, N.H., U.S.	B3	106
Lincoln, co., Ar., U.S.	D4	81
Lincoln, co., Co., U.S.	C7	83
Lincoln, co., Ga., U.S.	C4	87
Lincoln, co., Id., U.S.	G4	89
Lincoln, co., Ks., U.S.	C5	93
Lincoln, co., Ky., U.S.	C5	94
Lincoln, co., La., U.S.	B3	95
Lincoln, co., Me., U.S.	D3	96
Lincoln, co., Mn., U.S.	F2	100
Lincoln, co., Ms., U.S.	D3	101
Lincoln, co., Mo., U.S.	B7	102
Lincoln, co., Mt., U.S.	B1	103
Lincoln, co., Ne., U.S.	D5	104
Lincoln, co., Nv., U.S.	F6	105
Lincoln, co., N.M., U.S.	D4	108
Lincoln, co., N.C., U.S.	B1	110
Lincoln, co., Ok., U.S.	B5	113
Lincoln, co., Or., U.S.	C3	114
Lincoln, co., S.D., U.S.	D9	118
Lincoln, co., Tn., U.S.	B5	119
Lincoln, co., Wa., U.S.	B7	124
Lincoln, co., W.V., U.S.	C2	125
Lincoln, co., Wi., U.S.	C4	126
Lincoln, co., Wy., U.S.	D2	127
Lincoln, Mount, mtn., Co., U.S.	B4	83
Lincoln Acres, Ca., U.S.	o15	82
Lincoln City, Or., U.S.	C3	114
Lincoln Heights, Oh., U.S.	o13	112
Lincoln Park, Co., U.S.	C5	83
Lincoln Park, Ga., U.S.	D2	87
Lincoln Park, Mi., U.S.	p15	99
Lincoln Park, N.J., U.S.	B4	107
Lincolnshire, Il., U.S.	h9	90
Lincoln Tomb State Memorial, hist., Il., U.S.	D4	90
Lincolnton, Ga., U.S.	C4	87
Lincolnton, N.C., U.S.	B1	110
Lincolnville, S.C., U.S.	h11	117
Lincolnwood, Il., U.S.	h9	90
Lincroft, N.J., U.S.	C4	107
Lindale, Ga., U.S.	B1	87
Lindale, Tx., U.S.	C5	120
Lindau, Ger.	H9	8
Linden, Al., U.S.	C2	78
Linden, In., U.S.	D4	91
Linden, Mi., U.S.	F7	99
Linden, N.J., U.S.	k8	107
Linden, Tn., U.S.	B4	119
Linden, Tx., U.S.	C5	120
Lindenhurst, Il., U.S.	h8	90
Lindenhurst, N.Y., U.S.	n15	109
Lindenwold, N.J., U.S.	D3	107
Lindesnes, c., Nor.	G6	6
Lindi, Tan.	C7	44
Lindon, Ut., U.S.	C4	121
Lindsay, Ont., Can.	C6	73
Lindsay, Ca., U.S.	D4	82
Lindsay, Ok., U.S.	C4	113
Lindsborg, Ks., U.S.	D6	93
Lindstrom, Mn., U.S.	E6	100
Linesville, Pa., U.S.	C1	115
Lineville, Al., U.S.	B4	78
Lingao, China	D10	34
Lingayen, Phil.	B7	32
Lingen, Ger.	C7	8
Lingga, Kepulauan, is., Indon.	F3	32
Lingle, Wy., U.S.	D8	127
Linglestown, Pa., U.S.	F8	115
Lingling, China	A11	34
Linh, Ngoc, mtn., Viet.	G9	34
Linhai, China	G10	34
Linière, Que., Can.	C7	74
Linjiang, China	C12	26
Linköping, Swe.	G6	6
Linkou, China	B13	26
Linn, Mo., U.S.	C6	102
Linn, co., Ia., U.S.	B6	92
Linn, co., Ks., U.S.	D9	93
Linn, co., Mo., U.S.	B4	102
Linn, co., Or., U.S.	C4	114
Lino Lakes, Mn., U.S.	m12	100
Linqing, China	D10	26
Linru, China	A1	28
Lins, Braz.	F4	57
Lintao, China	D7	26
Linthicum Heights, Md., U.S.	B4	97
Linton, In., U.S.	F3	91
Linton, N.D., U.S.	C5	111
Linwood, N.J., U.S.	E3	107
Linxi, China	C10	26
Linxia, China	D7	26
Linyi, China	D10	26
Linz, Aus.	G14	8
Lion, Golfe du, b., Fr.	I11	10
Lipa, Phil.	r19	33b
Lipeck, Russia	I22	18
Lippstadt, Ger.	D8	8
Lipscomb, Al., U.S.	B3	78
Lipscomb, co., Tx., U.S.	A2	120
Lira, Ug.	H12	42
Liria, Spain	F11	12
Lisala, Zaire	A4	44
Lisboa (Lisbon), Port.	G2	12
Lisbon, Ia., U.S.	C6	92
Lisbon, Me., U.S.	D2	96
Lisbon, Md., U.S.	B3	97
Lisbon, N.H., U.S.	B3	106
Lisbon, N.D., U.S.	C8	111
Lisbon, Oh., U.S.	B5	112
Lisbon Center, Me., U.S.	f7	96
Lisbon Falls, Me., U.S.	E2	96
Lisbon see Lisboa, Port.	G2	12
Lisburne, Cape, c., Ak., U.S.	B6	79
Lishui, China	G8	28
Lisianski Island, i., Hi., U.S.	k13	88
Lisičansk, Ukr.	H5	22
Lisieux, Fr.	C7	10
Lisle, Il., U.S.	k8	90
L'Isle Jourdain, Fr.	F7	10
L'Isle-Jourdain, Fr.	I8	10
L'Islet-sur-Mer, Que., Can.	B7	74
L'Isle-Verte, Que., Can.	A8	74
Lismore, Austl.	E10	50
Listowel, Ont., Can.	D4	73
Listowel, Ire.	I3	7
Lit, Swe.	E10	6
Litang, China	G8	26
Litchfield, Ct., U.S.	C3	84
Litchfield, Il., U.S.	D4	90
Litchfield, Mi., U.S.	F6	99
Litchfield, Mn., U.S.	E4	100
Litchfield, co., Ct., U.S.	B2	84
Litchfield Park, Az., U.S.	m8	80
Lithia Springs, Ga., U.S.	h7	87
Lithonia, Ga., U.S.	C2	87
Lithuania, ctry., Eur.	F6	18
Litija, Slo.	C9	14
Lititz, Pa., U.S.	F9	115
Litovko, Russia	H21	24
Little, stm., U.S.	B5	81
Little, stm., U.S.	D7	113
Little, stm., Ct., U.S.	C7	84
Little, stm., Ky., U.S.	D2	94
Little, stm., La., U.S.	C3	95
Little, stm., N.C., U.S.	B3	110
Little, stm., Ok., U.S.	B5	113
Little, stm., S.C., U.S.	C2	117
Little, stm., Tn., U.S.	n14	119
Little, stm., Vt., U.S.	C3	122
Little, stm., Va., U.S.	D2	123
Little Abaco Island, i., Bah.	A9	64
Little Acres, Az., U.S.	D5	80
Little Andaman, i., India	I2	34
Little Arkansas, stm., Ks., U.S.	D6	93
Little Belt Mountains, mts., Mt., U.S.	D6	103
Little Bighorn, stm., U.S.	E9	103
Little Black, stm., Me., U.S.	A3	96
Little Blue, stm., U.S.	C6	93
Little Blue, stm., In., U.S.	H5	91
Little Bow, stm., Alta., Can.	D4	68
Little Cacapon, stm., W.V., U.S.	B6	125
Little Catalina, Newf., Can.	D5	72
Little Cayman, i., Cay. Is.	E7	64
Little Cedar, stm., Ia., U.S.	A5	92
Little Churchill, stm., Man., Can.	A4	70
Little Chute, Wi., U.S.	D5	126
Little Coal, stm., W.V., U.S.	C3	125
Little Colorado, stm., Az., U.S.	B4	80
Little Compton, R.I., U.S.	E6	116
Little Creek, De., U.S.	D4	85
Little Creek Naval Amphibious Base, mil., Va., U.S.	k15	123
Little Creek Peak, mtn., Ut., U.S.	F3	121
Little Current, Ont., Can.	B3	73
Little Diomede Island, i., Ak., U.S.	B6	79
Little Egg Harbor, b., N.J., U.S.	D4	107
Little Egg Inlet, b., N.J., U.S.	E4	107
Little Falls, Mn., U.S.	E4	100
Little Falls, N.J., U.S.	B4	107
Little Falls, N.Y., U.S.	B6	109
Little Ferry, N.J., U.S.	h8	107
Littlefield, Tx., U.S.	C1	120
Little Fishing Creek, stm., W.V., U.S.	h9	125
Littlefork, Mn., U.S.	B5	100
Little Fork, stm., Mn., U.S.	B5	100
Little Goose Creek, stm., Wy., U.S.	B6	127
Little Gunpowder Falls, stm., Md., U.S.	A4	97
Little Humboldt, stm., Nv., U.S.	B4	105
Little Inagua, i., Bah.	D11	64
Little Kanawha, stm., W.V., U.S.	C4	125
Little Lake, Mi., U.S.	B3	99
Little Lake, i., La., U.S.	E5	95
Little Lynches, stm., S.C., U.S.	C7	117
Little Manatee, stm., Fl., U.S.	p11	86
Little Mecatina, stm., Can.	h9	72
Little Miami, stm., Oh., U.S.	C1	112
Little Minch, strt., Scot., U.K.	D6	7
Little Missouri, stm., U.S.	B6	76
Little Missouri, stm., Ar., U.S.	D2	81
Little Muddy, stm., Il., U.S.	E4	90
Little Muddy, stm., N.D., U.S.	A2	111
Little Nicobar, i., India	K2	34
Little Osage, stm., U.S.	E9	93
Little Otter Creek, stm., Vt., U.S.	C2	122
Little Owyhee, stm., U.S.	B5	105
Little Pee Dee, stm., S.C., U.S.	C9	117
Little Powder, stm., U.S.	F11	103
Little Red, stm., Ar., U.S.	B4	81
Little River, co., Ar., U.S.	D1	81
Little River Inlet, b., S.C., U.S.	D10	117
Little Rock, Ar., U.S.	C3	81
Little Rock, stm., U.S.	A1	92
Little Rock Air Force Base, mil., Ar., U.S.	C3	81
Little Sable Point, c., Mi., U.S.	E4	99
Little Salt Lake, l., Ut., U.S.	F3	121
Little Sandy, stm., Ky., U.S.	B6	94
Little Sandy Creek, stm., Wy., U.S.	D3	127
Little Sebago Lake, l., Me., U.S.	g7	96
Little Silver, N.J., U.S.	C4	107
Little Sioux, stm., U.S.	B2	92
Little Sioux, West Fork, stm., Ia., U.S.	B2	92
Little Smoky, stm., Alta., Can.	B2	68
Little Snake, stm., U.S.	A2	83
Little Spokane, stm., Wa., U.S.	B8	124
Littlestown, Pa., U.S.	G7	115
Little Tallapoosa, stm., U.S.	B4	78
Little Tenmile Creek, stm., W.V., U.S.	k10	125
Little Tennessee, stm., U.S.	D9	119
Littleton, Co., U.S.	B6	83
Littleton, Me., U.S.	B5	96
Littleton, Ma., U.S.	f10	98
Littleton, N.H., U.S.	B3	106
Littleton, N.C., U.S.	A5	110
Littleville, Al., U.S.	A2	78
Little Wabash, stm., Il., U.S.	E5	90
Little Walnut, stm., Ks., U.S.	g13	93
Little White, stm., S.D., U.S.	D5	118
Little Wolf, stm., Wi., U.S.	D4	126
Little Wood, stm., Id., U.S.	F4	89
Liuan, China	D5	28
Liuhe, China	C7	28
Liuzhou, China	B10	34
Live Oak, Ca., U.S.	C3	82
Live Oak, Fl., U.S.	B4	86
Live Oak, co., Tx., U.S.	E3	120
Livermore, Ca., U.S.	h9	82
Livermore, Ky., U.S.	C2	94
Livermore, Mount, mtn., Tx., U.S.	o12	120
Livermore Falls, Me., U.S.	D2	96
Liverpool, Eng., U.K.	H10	7
Liverpool, Cape, c., N.W. Ter., Can.	B17	66
Livingston, Al., U.S.	C1	78
Livingston, Ca., U.S.	D3	82
Livingston, Il., U.S.	E4	90
Livingston, La., U.S.	D5	95
Livingston, Mt., U.S.	E6	103
Livingston, N.J., U.S.	B4	107
Livingston, Tn., U.S.	C8	119
Livingston, Tx., U.S.	D5	120
Livingston, co., Il., U.S.	C5	90
Livingston, co., Ky., U.S.	e9	94
Livingston, co., La., U.S.	D5	95
Livingston, co., Mi., U.S.	F7	99
Livingston, co., Mo., U.S.	B4	102
Livingston, co., N.Y., U.S.	C3	109
Livingston Lake, res., Tx., U.S.	D5	120
Livingstone, Zam.	E5	44
Livingstonia, Mwi.	D6	44
Livno, Bos.	F12	14
Livny, Russia	I20	18
Livonia, La., U.S.	D4	95
Livonia, Mi., U.S.	F7	99
Livorno (Leghorn), Italy	F5	14
Liyang, China	D8	28
Lizard Head Pass, Co., U.S.	D3	83
Lizard Head Peak, mtn., Wy., U.S.	D3	127
Lizard Point, c., Eng., U.K.	L7	7
Lizella, Ga., U.S.	D3	87
Ljubljana, Slo.	C9	14
Ljungby, Swe.	H9	6
Ljusdal, Swe.	F11	6
Llandudno, Wales, U.K.	H9	7
Llanelli, Wales, U.K.	J8	7
Llanes, Spain	B7	12
Llanidloes, Wales, U.K.	I9	7
Llano, Tx., U.S.	D3	120
Llano, co., Tx., U.S.	D3	120
Llano, stm., Tx., U.S.	D3	120
Llanos, pl., S.A.	E7	58
Llanwrtyd Wells, Wales, U.K.	I9	7
Llera, Mex.	F10	62
Llerena, Spain	G5	12
Lloyd, Ky., U.S.	B7	94
Lloydminster, Alta., Can.	C5	68
Lloyds, stm., Newf., Can.	D3	72
Lluchmayor, Spain	F14	12
Llullaillaco, Volcán, vol., S.A.	A3	56
Lo, stm., Viet.	C8	34
Loami, Il., U.S.	D4	90
Loange, stm., Afr.	C3	44
Lobaye, stm., Cen. Afr. Rep.	G9	42
Lobelville, Tn., U.S.	B4	119
Lobito, Ang.	D2	44
Lobos de Afuera, Islas, is., Peru	E2	54
Lobos de Tierra, Isla, i., Peru	E2	54
Lobster Lake, l., Me., U.S.	C3	96
Locarno, Switz.	F15	10
Lochaline, Scot., U.K.	E7	7
Lochboisdale, Scot., U.K.	D5	7
Loches, Fr.	E7	10
Lochgilphead, Scot., U.K.	E7	7
Loch Lomond, Va., U.S.	*B5	123
Loch Raven Reservoir, res., Md., U.S.	B4	97
Lochsa, stm., Id., U.S.	C3	89
Lockeport, N.S., Can.	F4	71
Lockesburg, Ar., U.S.	D1	81
Lockhart, Tx., U.S.	E4	120
Lock Haven, Pa., U.S.	D7	115
Lockland, Oh., U.S.	o13	112
Lockney, Tx., U.S.	B2	120
Lockport, Il., U.S.	B5	90
Lockport, La., U.S.	E5	95
Lockport, N.Y., U.S.	B2	109
Lockwood, Mo., U.S.	D4	102
Lockwood, Mt., U.S.	E8	103
Loc Ninh, Viet.	I9	34
Locust, stm., U.S.	B2	110
Locust Fork, stm., Al., U.S.	B3	78
Locust Grove, Ga., U.S.	C2	87
Locust Grove, Ok., U.S.	A6	113
Lod, Isr.	D4	40
Lodejnoje Polje, Russia	A16	18
Lodève, Fr.	I10	10
Lodgepole Creek, stm., U.S.	C3	104
Lodi, Italy	D4	14
Lodi, Ca., U.S.	C3	82
Lodi, N.J., U.S.	h8	107
Lodi, Oh., U.S.	A3	112
Lodi, Wi., U.S.	E4	126
Lodja, Zaire	B4	44
Lodore, Canyon of, val., Co., U.S.	A2	83
Lodwar, Kenya	H2	46
Łódź, Pol.	D19	8
Loffa, stm., Afr.	G3	42
Logan, Ia., U.S.	C2	92
Logan, Ks., U.S.	C4	93
Logan, N.M., U.S.	B6	108
Logan, Oh., U.S.	C3	112
Logan, Ut., U.S.	B4	121
Logan, W.V., U.S.	D3	125
Logan, co., Ar., U.S.	B2	81
Logan, co., Co., U.S.	A7	83
Logan, co., Il., U.S.	C4	90
Logan, co., Ks., U.S.	D2	93
Logan, co., Ky., U.S.	D3	94
Logan, co., Ne., U.S.	C5	104
Logan, co., N.D., U.S.	C6	111
Logan, co., Oh., U.S.	B2	112
Logan, co., Ok., U.S.	B4	113
Logan, co., W.V., U.S.	D3	125
Logan, Mount, mtn., Yukon, Can.	D4	66
Logan, Mount, mtn., Wa., U.S.	A5	124
Logan Lake, B.C., Can.	D7	69
Logan Martin Lake, res., Al., U.S.	B3	78
Logan Pass, Mt., U.S.	B2	103
Logansport, In., U.S.	C5	91
Logansport, La., U.S.	C2	95
Loganville, Ga., U.S.	C3	87
Loganville, Pa., U.S.	G8	115
Loggieville, N.B., Can.	B4	71
Log Lane Village, Co., U.S.	A7	83
Logone, stm., Afr.	F9	42
Logroño, Spain	C9	12
Logrosán, Spain	F6	12
Lohr, Ger.	E9	8
Loi-Kaw, Burma	E4	34
Loimaa, Fin.	F14	6
Loire, stm., Fr.	E5	10
Loja, Ec.	J3	58
Loja, Spain	H7	12
Lokolama, Zaire	B3	44
Lol, stm., Sudan	G11	42
Lola, Mount, mtn., Ca., U.S.	C3	82
Lolo, Mt., U.S.	D2	103
Lolo Pass, U.S.	C4	89
Lomami, stm., Zaire	B4	44
Lombard, Il., U.S.	k8	90
Lomblen, Pulau, i., Indon.	G7	32
Lombok, i., Indon.	G6	32
Lomé, Togo	G6	42
Lomela, Zaire	B4	44
Lomela, stm., Zaire	B4	44
Lomira, Wi., U.S.	E5	126
Lomond, Loch, l., Scot., U.K.	E8	7
Lomonosov, Russia	B12	18
Lompoc, Ca., U.S.	E3	82
Łomża, Pol.	B22	8
Lonaconing, Md., U.S.	k13	97
Lonavale, India	C2	37
Loncoche, Chile	D2	56
London, Ont., Can.	E3	73
London, Eng., U.K.	J12	7
London, Ar., U.S.	B2	81
London, Ky., U.S.	C5	94
London, Oh., U.S.	C2	112
Londonderry, N. Ire., U.K.	G5	7
Londonderry, N.H., U.S.	E4	106
Londonderry, Cape, c., Austl.	B5	50
Londonderry, Isla, i., Chile	H2	56
Londontown, Md., U.S.	C4	97
Londrina, Braz.	G3	57
Lone Grove, Ok., U.S.	C4	113
Lone Mountain, mtn., Nv., U.S.	E4	105
Lone Pine, Ca., U.S.	D4	82
Lone Tree, Ia., U.S.	C6	92
Long, co., Ga., U.S.	E5	87
Longa, Proliv, strt., Russia	C29	24
Longarone, Italy	C7	14
Long Bar Harbor, Md., U.S.	B5	97
Long Beach, Ca., U.S.	F4	82
Long Beach, In., U.S.	A4	91
Long Beach, Md., U.S.	D5	97
Long Beach, Ms., U.S.	g7	101
Long Beach, N.Y., U.S.	E7	109
Long Beach, Wa., U.S.	C1	124
Long Beach Naval Shipyard, mil., Ca., U.S.	n12	82
Longboat Key, Fl., U.S.	q10	86
Longboat Key, i., Fl., U.S.	E4	86
Longboat Pass, strt., Fl., U.S.	q10	86
Long Branch, N.J., U.S.	C5	107
Long Creek Mountain, mtn., Wy., U.S.	D5	127
Longeau, Fr.	E12	10
Long Grove, Ia., U.S.	C7	92
Long Harbour [-Mount Arlington Heights], Newf., Can.	E5	72
Long Island, i., Bah.	C10	64
Long Island, i., N.S., Can.	E3	71
Long Island, i., Me., U.S.	g7	96
Long Island, i., Ma., U.S.	g12	98
Long Island, i., N.Y., U.S.	E7	109
Long Island Sound, strt., U.S.	C8	84
Longjiang, China	B11	26
Long Key, i., Fl., U.S.	H6	86
Long Lake, Il., U.S.	h8	90
Long Lake, l., Me., U.S.	D2	96
Long Lake, l., Me., U.S.	A4	96
Long Lake, l., Mi., U.S.	C7	99
Long Lake, l., Mi., U.S.	D5	99
Long Lake, l., N.Y., U.S.	B6	109
Long Lake, l., Wa., U.S.	f10	124
Long Lake, l., Wi., U.S.	C2	126
Longli, China	A9	34
Longmeadow, Ma., U.S.	B2	98
Longmont, Co., U.S.	A5	83
Long Point, c., Man., Can.	C2	70
Long Point, pen., Ont., Can.	E4	73
Long Pond, res., Fl., U.S.	C4	86
Long Prairie, Mn., U.S.	E4	100
Long Range Mountains, mts., Newf., Can.	D3	72
Longreach, Austl.	D8	50
Longs Peak, mtn., Co., U.S.	A5	83
Longué, Fr.	E6	10
Longueuil, Que., Can.	D4	74
Longuyon, Fr.	C12	10
Long View, N.C., U.S.	B1	110
Longview, Tx., U.S.	C5	120
Longview, Wa., U.S.	C3	124
Longwy, Fr.	C12	10
Long Xuyen, Viet.	I8	34
Lonigo, Italy	D6	14
Löningen, Ger.	C7	8
Lonoke, Ar., U.S.	C4	81
Lonoke, co., Ar., U.S.	C4	81
Lønsdal, Nor.	C10	6
Lonsdale, Mn., U.S.	F5	100
Lonsdale, R.I., U.S.	B4	116
Lons-le-Saunier, Fr.	F12	10
Loogootee, In., U.S.	G4	91
Lookout, Ky., U.S.	C7	94
Lookout, Cape, c., N.C., U.S.	C6	110
Lookout, Point, c., Mi., U.S.	d7	99
Lookout Mountain, Tn., U.S.	h11	119
Lookout Mountain, mtn., U.S.	D8	119
Lookout Mountain, mtn., Or., U.S.	C6	114
Lookout Pass, U.S.	B3	89
Lookout Point Lake, res., Or., U.S.	D4	114
Loon Lake, Wa., U.S.	A8	124
Loon Lake, l., Me., U.S.	B3	96
Loop Creek, stm., W.V., U.S.	m13	125
Loop Head, c., Ire.	I3	7
Loosahatchie, stm., Tn., U.S.	B2	119
Lopatina, Gora, mtn., Russia	G22	24
Lopatka, Mys, c., Russia	G25	24
Lop Buri, Thai.	G6	34
Lopez, Cap, c., Gabon	B1	44
López Collada, Mex.	B3	62
Lopez Island, i., Wa., U.S.	A3	124
Lop Nur, l., China	C5	26
Lora del Río, Spain	H6	12
Lorain, Oh., U.S.	A3	112
Lorain, co., Oh., U.S.	A3	112
Loramie, Lake, res., Oh., U.S.	B1	112
Lorca, Spain	H10	12
Lord Howe Island, i., Austl.	F11	50
Lordsburg, N.M., U.S.	E1	108
Loreauville, La., U.S.	D4	95
Lorena, Braz.	G6	57
Lorenzo, Tx., U.S.	C2	120
Loreto, Braz.	E9	54
Loreto, Col.	I7	58
Loreto, Mex.	F9	62
Lorette, Man., Can.	E3	70
Loretteville, Que., Can.	C6	74
Loretto, Ky., U.S.	C4	94
Loretto, Pa., U.S.	F4	115
Loretto, Tn., U.S.	B4	119
Lorica, Col.	C5	58
Lorient, Fr.	E3	10
L'Orignal, Ont., Can.	B10	73
Loring Air Force Base, mil., Me., U.S.	B5	96
Loriol [-du-Comtat], Fr.	H11	10
Loris, S.C., U.S.	C10	117
Lorne, N.B., Can.	B3	71
Lörrach, Ger.	H7	8
Lorraine, hist. reg., Fr.	D13	10
Los Alamos, N.M., U.S.	B3	108
Los Alamos, co., N.M., U.S.	B3	108
Los Aldamas, Mex.	D10	62
Los Altos, Ca., U.S.	k8	82
Los Ángeles, Chile	D2	56
Los Angeles, Ca., U.S.	E4	82
Los Angeles, co., Ca., U.S.	E4	82
Los Angeles Aqueduct, Ca., U.S.	E4	82
Los Banos, Ca., U.S.	D3	82
Los Blancos, Arg.	A4	56
Los Fresnos, Tx., U.S.	F4	120
Los Gatos, Ca., U.S.	D2	82
Los Lagos, Chile	D2	56
Los Lunas, N.M., U.S.	C3	108
Los Mochis, Mex.	E5	62
Los Palacios y Villafranca, Spain	H6	12
Los Pinos, stm., U.S.	D3	83
Los Ranchos de Albuquerque, N.M., U.S.	n12	108
Los Roques, Islas, is., Ven.	B9	58
Lost, stm., U.S.	G4	91
Lost, stm., Wa., U.S.	A5	124
Lost, stm., W.V., U.S.	B6	125
Lost Creek, stm., Wy., U.S.	D4	127
Los Teques, Ven.	B9	58
Los Testigos, Islas, is., Ven.	B11	58
Lost Peak, mtn., Ut., U.S.	F2	121
Lost Ranger Peak, mtn., Co., U.S.	A4	83
Lost River Glacial Caverns, N.H., U.S.	B3	106
Lost River, mts., Id., U.S.	E5	89
Lost Trail Pass, U.S.	D5	89
Los Vilos, Chile	C2	56
Los Yébenes, Spain	F8	12
Lota, Chile	D2	56
Lotawana, Lake, res., Mo., U.S.	k11	102
Lotbinière, Que., Can.	C6	74
Louang Namtha, Laos	C4	34
Louangphrabang, Laos	E7	34
Loudéac, Fr.	D4	10
Loudon, Tn., U.S.	D9	119
Loudon, co., Tn., U.S.	D9	119
Loudonville, Oh., U.S.	B3	112
Loudoun, co., Va., U.S.	A5	123
Loudun, Fr.	E7	10
Louga, Sen.	E2	42
Loughrea, Ire.	H4	7
Louhans, Fr.	F12	10
Louisa, Ky., U.S.	B7	94
Louisa, co., Ia., U.S.	C6	92
Louisa, co., Va., U.S.	C5	123

Name	Map Ref	Page
Louisa, Lake, l., Fl., U.S.	D5	86
Louisbourg, N.S., Can.	D10	71
Louisburg, Ks., U.S.	D9	93
Louisburg, N.C., U.S.	A4	110
Louisdale, N.S., Can.	D8	71
Louise, Lake, l., Ak., U.S.	f18	79
Louise Island, i., B.C., Can.	C2	69
Louiseville, Que., Can.	C5	74
Louisiade Archipelago, is., Pap. N. Gui.	B10	50
Louisiana, Mo., U.S.	B6	102
Louisiana, state, U.S.	C3	95
Louisiana Point, c., La., U.S.	E2	95
Louis Trichardt, S. Afr.	F5	44
Louisville, Al., U.S.	D4	78
Louisville, Co., U.S.	B5	83
Louisville, Ga., U.S.	C4	87
Louisville, Il., U.S.	E5	90
Louisville, Ky., U.S.	B4	94
Louisville, Ms., U.S.	B4	101
Louisville, Ne., U.S.	D9	104
Louisville, Oh., U.S.	B4	112
Louis-XIV, Pointe, c., Que., Can.	h11	74
Loulé, Port.	H3	12
Loup, co., Ne., U.S.	C6	104
Loup, stm., Ne., U.S.	C8	104
Loup City, Ne., U.S.	C7	104
Lourdes, Newf., Can.	D2	72
Lourdes, Fr.	I6	10
Lourenço Marques see Maputo, Moz.	G6	44
Louth, Eng., U.K.	H12	7
Louviers, Fr.	C8	10
Louviers, Co., U.S.	B6	83
Love, co., Ok., U.S.	D4	113
Loveč, Bul.	F8	16
Loveland, Co., U.S.	A5	83
Loveland, Oh., U.S.	n13	112
Loveland Park, Oh., U.S.	C1	112
Loveland Pass, Co., U.S.	B5	83
Lovell, Wy., U.S.	B4	127
Lovelock, Nv., U.S.	C3	105
Lovely, Ky., U.S.	C7	94
Lovenia, Mount, mtn., Ut., U.S.	C5	121
Love Point, c., Md., U.S.	B5	97
Lovere, Italy	D5	14
Loves Park, Il., U.S.	A4	90
Lovettsville, Va., U.S.	A5	123
Loving, N.M., U.S.	E5	108
Loving, co., Tx., U.S.	D1	120
Lovington, Il., U.S.	D5	90
Lovington, Ia., U.S.	e8	92
Lovington, N.M., U.S.	E6	108
Lövstabruk, Swe.	F11	6
Low, Cape, c., N.W. Ter., Can.	D15	66
Lowden, Ia., U.S.	C7	92
Lowell, Ar., U.S.	A1	81
Lowell, In., U.S.	B3	91
Lowell, Ma., U.S.	A5	98
Lowell, Mi., U.S.	F5	99
Lowell, N.C., U.S.	B1	110
Lowell, Or., U.S.	D4	114
Lowell, Lake, res., Id., U.S.	F2	89
Lowellville, Oh., U.S.	A5	112
Lower Arrow Lake, res., B.C., Can.	E8	69
Lower Brule Indian Reservation, S.D., U.S.	C6	118
Lower California see Baja California, pen., Mex.	D3	62
Lower Hutt, N.Z.	D5	52
Lower Klamath Lake, l., Ca., U.S.	B3	82
Lower Matecumbe Key, i., Fl., U.S.	H6	86
Lower Monumental Lake, res., Wa., U.S.	C7	124
Lower New York Bay, b., N.J., U.S.	B4	107
Lower Otay Lake, res., Ca., U.S.	o16	82
Lower Paia, Hi., U.S.	C5	88
Lower Red Lake, l., Mn., U.S.	C3	100
Lower Rice Lake, l., Mn., U.S.	C3	100
Lower Salmon Dam, Id., U.S.	G4	89
Lower West Pubnico, N.S., Can.	F4	71
Lowestoft, Eng., U.K.	I14	7
Lowndes, co., Al., U.S.	C3	78
Lowndes, co., Ga., U.S.	F3	87
Lowndes, co., Ms., U.S.	B5	101
Lowry Air Force Base, mil., Co., U.S.	B6	83
Lowry City, Mo., U.S.	C4	102
Lowville, N.Y., U.S.	B5	109
Loxley, Al., U.S.	E2	78
Loyal, Wi., U.S.	D3	126
Loyall, Ky., U.S.	D6	94
Loyalsock Creek, stm., Pa., U.S.	D8	115
Loznica, Yugo.	E3	16
Lozoyuela, Spain	E8	12
Lua, stm., Zaire	H9	42
Lualaba, stm., Zaire	B5	44
Lua Makika, crat., Hi., U.S.	C5	88
Luanda, Ang.	C2	44
Luang Praban Range, mts., Asia	E6	34
Luanguinga, stm., Afr.	D4	44
Luangwa, stm., Afr.	D6	44
Luanshya, Zam.	D5	44
Luarca, Spain	B5	12
Luau, Ang.	E5	44
Lubang Island, i., Phil.	C7	32
Lubango, Ang.	D2	44
Lübben, Ger.	D13	8
Lübbenau, Ger.	D13	8
Lubbock, Tx., U.S.	C2	120
Lubbock, co., Tx., U.S.	C2	120
Lubec, Me., U.S.	D6	96
Lübeck, Ger.	B10	8
Lübecker Bucht, b., Ger.	A11	8
L'ubercy, Russia	F20	18
Lubilash, stm., Zaire	C4	44
Lubin, Pol.	D16	8
Lublin, Pol.	D22	8
Lubudi, Zaire	C4	44
Lubuksikaping, Indon.	N6	34
Lubumbashi (Élisabethville), Zaire	D5	44
Lubutu, Zaire	B5	44
Lucama, N.C., U.S.	B4	110
Lucan, Ont., Can.	D3	73
Lucania, Mount, mtn., Yukon, Can.	D4	66
Lucas, co., Ia., U.S.	C4	92
Lucas, co., Oh., U.S.	A2	112
Lucasville, Oh., U.S.	D3	112
Lucca, Italy	F5	14
Luce, co., Mi., U.S.	B5	99
Luce Bay, b., Scot., U.K.	G8	7
Lucedale, Ms., U.S.	E5	101
Lucena, Phil.	r19	33b
Lucena, Spain	H7	12
Lucena del Cid, Spain	E11	12
Luc-en-Diois, Fr.	H12	10
Lucera, Italy	H10	14
Lucerne, Ca., U.S.	C2	82
Lucerne see Luzern, Switz.	E15	10
Lucernemines, Pa., U.S.	E3	115
Lucerne Valley, Ca., U.S.	E5	82
Luceville, Que., Can.	A9	74
Luchiang, Tai.	K9	28
Lüchow, Ger.	C11	8
Lucira, Ang.	D2	44
Luck, Ukr.	G3	22
Luck, Wi., U.S.	C1	126
Luckeesarai, India	H12	38
Luckenwalde, Ger.	C13	8
Lucknow, Ont., Can.	D3	73
Lucknow, India	G9	38
Lucky Peak Lake, res., Id., U.S.	F3	89
Luçon, Fr.	F5	10
Lüderitz, Nmb.	G3	44
Ludhiäna, India	E6	38
Ludington, Mi., U.S.	E4	99
Ludlow, Ky., U.S.	h13	94
Ludlow, Ma., U.S.	B3	98
Ludlow, Vt., U.S.	E3	122
Ludowici, Ga., U.S.	E5	87
Ludvika, Swe.	F10	6
Ludwigsburg, Ger.	G9	8
Ludwigsfelde, Ger.	C13	8
Ludwigshafen, Ger.	F8	8
Luena, stm., Ang.	D4	44
Luene, Ang.	D3	44
Lufeng, China	M4	28
Lufkin, Tx., U.S.	D5	120
Luga, Russia	C12	18
Lugano, Switz.	F15	10
Lugansk, Ukr.	H5	22
Lugenda, stm., Moz.	D7	44
Lugh Ganane, Som.	H3	46
Lugnaquillia Mountain, mtn., Ire.	I6	7
Lugo, Italy	E6	14
Lugo, Spain	B4	12
Lugoff, S.C., U.S.	C6	117
Lugoj, Rom.	D5	16
Luhit, stm., Asia	G16	38
Luilaka, stm., Zaire	B4	44
Luino, Italy	C3	14
Lukachukai, Az., U.S.	A6	80
Luke Air Force Base, mil., Az., U.S.	D3	80
Lukulu, Zam.	D4	44
Lula, La., U.S.	B3	87
Luleå, Swe.	D14	6
Lüleburgaz, Tur.	H11	16
Luling, La., U.S.	k11	95
Luling, Tx., U.S.	E4	120
Lulonga, stm., Zaire	A3	44
Lumajang, Indon.	n16	33a
Lumber, stm., U.S.	C9	117
Lumber City, Ga., U.S.	E4	87
Lumberport, W.V., U.S.	B4	125
Lumberton, Ms., U.S.	D4	101
Lumberton, N.C., U.S.	C3	110
Lumbrales, Spain	E5	12
Lumby, B.C., Can.	D8	69
Lumding, India	H15	38
Lummi Indian Reservation, Wa., U.S.	A3	124
Lumpkin, Ga., U.S.	D2	87
Lumpkin, co., Ga., U.S.	B2	87
Lumsden, Newf., Can.	D5	72
Luna, co., N.M., U.S.	E2	108
Luna Pier, Mi., U.S.	G7	99
Lund, Swe.	I9	6
Lund, Nv., U.S.	E6	105
Lundar, Man., Can.	D2	70
Lundazi, Zam.	D6	44
Lüneburg, Ger.	B10	8
Lüneburger Heide, reg., Ger.	B10	8
Lunel, Fr.	I11	10
Lunenburg, Ma., U.S.	A4	98
Lunenburg, co., Va., U.S.	D4	123
Lunéville, Fr.	D13	10
Lunga, stm., Zam.	D5	44
Luohe, China	B3	28
Luolong, China	E17	38
Luopu, China	B9	38
Luoyang, China	E9	28
Lürah, stm., Afg.	D2	38
Luray, Va., U.S.	B4	123
Lure, Fr.	E13	10
Lure, Lake, res., N.C., U.S.	f10	110
Lurgan, N. Ire., U.K.	G6	7
Lúrio, stm., Moz.	D7	44
Lusaka, Zam.	D5	44
Lusambo, Zaire	B4	44
Lusby, Md., U.S.	D5	97
Luseland, Sask., Can.	E1	75
Lushan, China	B1	28
Lushnje, Alb.	I3	16
Lushoto, Tan.	B7	44
Lüshun (Port Arthur), China	D11	26
Lusk, Wy., U.S.	D8	127
Lussac-les-Châteaux, Fr.	F7	10
Lutcher, La., U.S.	D5	95
Luther, Ok., U.S.	B4	113
Luthersville, Ga., U.S.	C2	87
Lutherville-Timonium, Md., U.S.	B4	97
Luton, Eng., U.K.	J12	7
Lutsk see Luck, Ukr.	G3	22
Luttrell, Tn., U.S.	C10	119
Lutz, Fl., U.S.	D4	86
Luverne, Al., U.S.	D3	78
Luverne, Mn., U.S.	G2	100
Luwegu, stm., Tan.	C7	44
Luxapallila Creek, stm., U.S.	B5	101
Luxembourg, Lux.	F6	8
Luxembourg, ctry., Eur.	F9	4
Luxemburg, Wi., U.S.	D6	126
Luxomni, Ga., U.S.	h8	87
Luxora, Ar., U.S.	B6	81
Luzern, Switz.	E15	10
Luzerne, Pa., U.S.	n17	115
Luzerne, co., Pa., U.S.	D9	115
Luzhou, China	F8	26
Luzon, i., Phil.	B7	32
Luzon Strait, strt., Asia	G11	26
Luzy, Fr.	F10	10
L'vov, Ukr.	H2	22
Lyckasele, Swe.	D12	6
Lycoming, co., Pa., U.S.	D7	115
Lycoming Creek, stm., Pa., U.S.	D7	115
Lydenburg, S. Afr.	G6	44
Lyell, Mount, mtn., Can.	D2	68
Lyford, Tx., U.S.	F4	120
Lykens, Pa., U.S.	E8	115
Lyle, Wa., U.S.	D4	124
Lyman, S.C., U.S.	B3	117
Lyman, Wy., U.S.	E2	127
Lyman, co., S.D., U.S.	D6	118
Lyman Lake, res., Az., U.S.	C6	80
Lynch, Ky., U.S.	D7	94
Lynchburg, Oh., U.S.	C2	112
Lynchburg, Tn., U.S.	B5	119
Lynchburg, Va., U.S.	C3	123
Lynches, stm., S.C., U.S.	D8	117
Lynden, Wa., U.S.	A3	124
Lynde Point, c., Ct., U.S.	D6	84
Lyndhurst, N.J., U.S.	h8	107
Lyndhurst, Oh., U.S.	g9	112
Lyndon, Ks., U.S.	D8	93
Lyndon, Ky., U.S.	g11	94
Lyndon B. Johnson National Historical Site, hist., Tx., U.S.	D3	120
Lyndon B. Johnson Space Center, sci., Tx., U.S.	r14	120
Lyndonville, Vt., U.S.	B4	122
Lyndora, Pa., U.S.	E2	115
Lynher Reef, rf., Austl.	C4	50
Lynn, Al., U.S.	A2	78
Lynn, In., U.S.	D8	91
Lynn, Ma., U.S.	B6	98
Lynn, co., Tx., U.S.	C2	120
Lynn, Lake, res., W.V., U.S.	B5	125
Lynn Canal, b., Ak., U.S.	k22	79
Lynne Acres, Md., U.S.	*B4	97
Lynnfield, Ma., U.S.	f11	98
Lynn Garden, Tn., U.S.	C11	119
Lynn Garden, Tn., U.S.	A9	119
Lynn Haven, Fl., U.S.	u16	86
Lynnhaven Roads, b., Va., U.S.	k15	123
Lynnville, In., U.S.	H3	91
Lynnwood, Wa., U.S.	B3	124
Lynton, Eng., U.K.	J9	7
Lynwood, Ca., U.S.	n12	82
Lyon, co., Ia., U.S.	A1	92
Lyon, co., Ks., U.S.	D7	93
Lyon, co., Ky., U.S.	C1	94
Lyon, co., Mn., U.S.	F3	100
Lyon, co., Nv., U.S.	D2	105
Lyons, Co., U.S.	A5	83
Lyons, Ga., U.S.	D4	87
Lyons, Il., U.S.	k9	90
Lyons, In., U.S.	G3	91
Lyons, Ks., U.S.	D5	93
Lyons, Mi., U.S.	F6	99
Lyons, Ne., U.S.	C9	104
Lyons, N.Y., U.S.	B3	109
Lyons, Or., U.S.	C4	114
Lyster Station, Que., Can.	C6	74
Lytle, Tx., U.S.	E3	120

M

Name	Map Ref	Page
Ma, stm., Asia	D8	34
Maalaea Bay, b., Hi., U.S.	C5	88
Ma'ān, Jord.	D4	40
Maanshan, China	D7	28
Ma'arrat an-Nu'mān, Syria	B5	40
Maas (Meuse), stm., Eur.	D5	8
Maastricht, Neth.	E5	8
Mabank, Tx., U.S.	C4	120
Mabaruma, Guy.	C13	58
Mabel, Mn., U.S.	G7	100
Maben, Ms., U.S.	B4	101
Mableton, Ga., U.S.	h7	87
Mabscott, W.V., U.S.	D3	125
Mabton, Wa., U.S.	C5	124
Mača, Russia	F17	24
Macaé, Braz.	G8	57
Macão, Port.	F3	12
Macao see Macau, dep., Asia	M2	28
Macapá, Braz.	C8	54
Macará, Ec.	J3	58
Macarani, Braz.	C8	57
Macas, Ec.	I3	58
Macau, Braz.	E11	54
Macau (Aomen), Macao	M2	28
Macau (Aomen), dep., Asia	M2	28
MacClenny, Fl., U.S.	B4	86
MacDill Air Force Base, mil., Fl., U.S.	E4	86
Macdonnell Ranges, mts., Austl.	D6	50
MacDowell Reservoir, res., N.H., U.S.	E2	106
Macduff, Scot., U.K.	D10	7
Macedo de Cavaleiros, Port.	D5	12
Macedonia, Oh., U.S.	A4	112
Macedonia, ctry., Eur.	H5	16
Macedonia, hist. reg., Eur.	H6	16
Maceió, Braz.	E11	54
Macerata, Italy	F8	14
Maces Bay, b., N.B., Can.	D3	71
MacGregor, Man., Can.	E2	70
Machačkala, Russia	I7	22
Machagai, Arg.	B4	56
Machala, Ec.	I3	58
Machecoul, Fr.	E5	10
Machias, Me., U.S.	D5	96
Machias, stm., Me., U.S.	B4	96
Machias, stm., Me., U.S.	D5	96
Machias, stm., Me., U.S.	D5	96
Machias Lakes, l., Me., U.S.	C5	96
Machilīpatnam (Bandar), India	D6	37
Machiques, Ven.	B6	58
Macho, Arroyo del, val., N.M., U.S.	C4	108
Machupicchu, Peru	F4	54
Macina, reg., Mali	F4	42
Mackay, Austl.	D9	50
Mackay, Lake, l., Austl.	D5	50
MacKenzie, B.C., Can.	B6	69
Mackenzie, stm., N.W. Ter., Can.	C6	66
Mackenzie Bay, b., Can.	C5	66
Mackenzie Mountains, mts., Can.	D7	66
Mackinac, co., Mi., U.S.	B5	99
Mackinac, Straits of, strt., Mi., U.S.	C6	99
Mackinac Bridge, Mi., U.S.	C6	99
Mackinac Island, i., Mi., U.S.	C6	99
Mackinaw, Il., U.S.	C4	90
Mackinaw, stm., Il., U.S.	C4	90
Mackinaw City, Mi., U.S.	C6	99
Maclear, S. Afr.	H5	44
Macmillan, stm., Yukon, Can.	D6	66
Macomb, Il., U.S.	C3	90
Macomb, co., Mi., U.S.	F8	99
Macomer, Italy	I3	14
Mâcon, Fr.	F11	10
Macon, Ga., U.S.	D3	87
Macon, Il., U.S.	D5	90
Macon, Ms., U.S.	B5	101
Macon, Mo., U.S.	B5	102
Macon, co., Al., U.S.	C4	78
Macon, co., Ga., U.S.	D2	87
Macon, co., Il., U.S.	D5	90
Macon, co., Mo., U.S.	B5	102
Macon, co., N.C., U.S.	f9	110
Macon, co., Tn., U.S.	A5	119
Macon, Bayou, stm., U.S.	B4	95
Macoupin, co., Il., U.S.	D4	90
MacTier, Ont., Can.	B5	73
Macungie, Pa., U.S.	E10	115
Mad, stm., Ca., U.S.	B2	82
Mad, stm., Ct., U.S.	B3	84
Mad, stm., N.H., U.S.	C3	106
Mad, stm., Oh., U.S.	C2	112
Mad, stm., Vt., U.S.	C3	122
Ma'dabā, Jord.	D4	40
Madagascar, ctry., Afr.	E9	44
Madame, Isle, i., N.S., Can.	D9	71
Madanapalle, India	F5	37
Madang, Pap. N. Gui.	m16	50a
Mädäripur, Bngl.	I14	38
Madawaska, Me., U.S.	A4	96
Madawaska, stm., Can.	B9	74
Madawaska, co., Ont., Can.	B7	73
Madawaska Lake, l., Me., U.S.	A4	96
Maddaloni, Italy	H9	14
Madeira, Oh., U.S.	o13	112
Madeira, i., Port.	B2	42
Madeira, stm., S.A.	E6	54
Madeira, Arquipélago da (Madeira Islands), is., Port.	B2	42
Mädelegabel, mtn., Eur.	E17	10
Madeleine, Îles de la, is., Que., Can.	B8	71
Madelia, Mn., U.S.	F4	100
Madeline Island, i., Wi., U.S.	B3	126
Madera, Ca., U.S.	D3	82
Madera, co., Ca., U.S.	D4	82
Madhubani, India	G12	38
Madhya Pradesh, state, India	I8	38
Madill, Ok., U.S.	C5	113
Madingou, Congo	B2	44
Madison, Al., U.S.	A3	78
Madison, Ct., U.S.	D5	84
Madison, Fl., U.S.	B3	86
Madison, Ga., U.S.	C3	87
Madison, In., U.S.	G7	91
Madison, Ks., U.S.	D7	93
Madison, Me., U.S.	D3	96
Madison, Mn., U.S.	E2	100
Madison, Ms., U.S.	C3	101
Madison, Ne., U.S.	C8	104
Madison, N.J., U.S.	B4	107
Madison, N.C., U.S.	A3	110
Madison, Oh., U.S.	A4	112
Madison, S.D., U.S.	D8	118
Madison, W.V., U.S.	C3	125
Madison, Wi., U.S.	E4	126
Madison, co., Al., U.S.	A3	78
Madison, co., Ar., U.S.	B2	81
Madison, co., Fl., U.S.	B3	86
Madison, co., Ga., U.S.	B3	87
Madison, co., Id., U.S.	F7	89
Madison, co., Il., U.S.	E4	90
Madison, co., In., U.S.	D6	91
Madison, co., Ia., U.S.	C3	92
Madison, co., Ky., U.S.	C5	94
Madison, co., La., U.S.	B4	95
Madison, co., Ms., U.S.	C3	101
Madison, co., Mo., U.S.	D7	102
Madison, co., Mt., U.S.	E5	103
Madison, co., Ne., U.S.	C8	104
Madison, co., N.Y., U.S.	C5	109
Madison, co., N.C., U.S.	f10	110
Madison, co., Oh., U.S.	C2	112
Madison, co., Tn., U.S.	B3	119
Madison, co., Tx., U.S.	D5	120
Madison, co., Va., U.S.	B4	123
Madison, stm., Mt., U.S.	E5	103
Madison Heights, Mi., U.S.	o15	99
Madison Heights, Va., U.S.	C3	123
Madison Lake, Mn., U.S.	F5	100
Madison Range, mts., Mt., U.S.	E5	103
Madisonville, Ky., U.S.	C2	94
Madisonville, La., U.S.	D5	95
Madisonville, Tn., U.S.	D9	119
Madisonville, Tx., U.S.	D5	120
Madiun, Indon.	m15	32
Madoc, Ont., Can.	C7	73
Mado Gashi, Kenya	B7	44
Madras, India	F6	37
Madras, Or., U.S.	C5	114
Madre, Laguna, b., Mex.	E11	62
Madre, Laguna, b., Tx., U.S.	F4	120
Madre, Sierra, mts., N.A.	J14	62
Madre, Sierra, mts., Phil.	B7	32
Madre de Dios, stm., S.A.	F5	54
Madre de Dios, Isla, i., Chile	G1	56
Madre del Sur, Sierra, mts., Mex.	I10	62
Madre Occidental, Sierra, mts., Mex.	E6	62
Madre Oriental, Sierra, mts., Mex.	F9	62
Madrid, Spain	E8	12
Madrid, Ia., U.S.	C4	92
Madridejos, Spain	F8	12
Maduo, China	E6	26
Madura, i., Indon.	G5	32
Madurai, India	H5	37
Maebashi, Japan	F12	30
Mae Hong Son, Thai.	E4	34
Maeser, Ut., U.S.	C6	121
Mae Sot, Thai.	F5	34
Maestra, Sierra, mts., Cuba	D9	64
Maevatanana, Madag.	E9	44
Mafia Island, i., Tan.	C7	44
Mafikeng, S. Afr.	G5	44
Mafra, Braz.	B7	56
Magadan, Russia	F24	24
Magadi, Kenya	B7	44
Magallanes, Estrecho de (Strait of Magellan), strt., S.A.	G2	56
Magangué, Col.	C5	58
Magazine, Ar., U.S.	B2	81
Magazine Mountain, mtn., Ar., U.S.	B2	81
Magdagači, Russia	G19	24
Magdalena, Bol.	F6	54
Magdalena, Mex.	B4	62
Magdalena, N.M., U.S.	C2	108
Magdalena, stm., Col.	B5	58
Magdalena, Bahía, b., Mex.	E3	62
Magdalena, Isla, i., Chile	E2	56
Magdalena Mountains, mts., N.M., U.S.	D2	108
Magdeburg, Ger.	C11	8
Magee, Ms., U.S.	D4	101
Magelang, Indon.	m15	33a
Magellan, Strait of see Magallanes, Estrecho de, strt., S.A.	G2	56
Magenta, Italy	D3	14
Maggie Creek, stm., Nv., U.S.	C5	105
Maggiore, Lago, l., Eur.	C3	14
Magic Reservoir, res., Id., U.S.	F4	89
Magione, Italy	F7	14
Magna, Ut., U.S.	C3	121
Magnetawan, stm., Ont., Can.	B4	73
Magnitogorsk, Russia	G9	22
Magnolia, Ar., U.S.	D2	81
Magnolia, Ky., U.S.	C4	94
Magnolia, Ms., U.S.	D3	101
Magnolia, N.C., U.S.	C4	110
Magnolia, Oh., U.S.	B4	112
Magoffin, co., Ky., U.S.	C6	94
Magog, Que., Can.	D5	74
Magothy River, b., Md., U.S.	B4	97
Magpie, Lac, l., Que., Can.	F20	66
Magrath, Alta., Can.	E4	68
Magruder Mountain, mtn., Nv., U.S.	F4	105
Maguarinho, Cabo, c., Braz.	D9	54
Magway, Burma	D3	34
Mahābād, Iran	J7	22
Mahābhārat Range, mts., Nepal	F10	38
Mahaicony Village, Guy.	D14	58
Mahajamba, Baie de la, b., Madag.	E9	44
Mahajanga, Madag.	E9	44
Mahakam, stm., Indon.	E6	32
Mahānadi, stm., India	J11	38
Mahanoro, Madag.	E9	44
Mahanoy City, Pa., U.S.	E9	115
Mahārāshtra, state, India	C3	37
Maha Sarakham, Thai.	F7	34
Mahaska, co., Ia., U.S.	C5	92
Mahattat al-Qaṭrānah, Jord.	D5	40
Mahattat Harad, Sau. Ar.	D4	46
Mahbūbnagar, India	D4	37
Mahé Island, i., Sey.	B11	44
Mahenge, Tan.	C7	44
Mahi, stm., India	I5	38
Mahmūd-e 'Erāqī, Afg.	C3	38
Mahnomen, Mn., U.S.	C3	100
Mahnomen, co., Mn., U.S.	C3	100
Mahoba, India	H8	38
Mahogany Mountain, mtn., Or., U.S.	D9	114
Mahomet, Il., U.S.	C5	90
Mahón, Spain	F16	12
Mahone Bay, N.S., Can.	E5	71
Mahoning, co., Oh., U.S.	B5	112
Mahoning, stm., U.S.	A5	112
Mahopac, N.Y., U.S.	D7	109
Mahuva, India	J4	38
Mahwah, N.J., U.S.	A4	107
Maiden, N.C., U.S.	B1	110
Maidenhead, Eng., U.K.	J13	7
Maidstone, Eng., U.K.	J13	7
Maidstone Lake, l., Vt., U.S.	B5	122
Maiduguri, Nig.	F8	42
Maili, Hi., U.S.	g9	88
Maili Point, c., Hi., U.S.	g9	88
Maillezais, Fr.	F6	10
Main, stm., Ger.	F9	8
Mainburg, Ger.	G11	8
Main Channel, strt., Ont., Can.	B3	73
Mai-Ndombe, Lac, l., Zaire	B3	44
Maine, state, U.S.	C3	96
Mainland, i., Scot., U.K.	B9	7

Name	Map Ref	Page
Mainland, i., Scot., U.K.	A11	7
Main Pass, strt., La., U.S.	E6	95
Mainz, Ger.	E8	8
Maipo, Volcán, vol., S.A.	C3	56
Maipú, Arg.	D5	56
Maiquetía, Ven.	B9	58
Maisonnette, N.B., Can.	B4	71
Maitland, Austl.	F10	50
Maitland, Ont., Can.	C9	73
Maize, Ks., U.S.	g12	93
Maizuru, Japan	G8	30
Maja, stm., Russia	F20	24
Majene, Indon.	F6	32
Maji, Eth.	G2	46
Majkop, Russia	I6	22
Majno-Pyl'gino, Russia	E29	24
Major, co., Ok., U.S.	A3	113
Majorca see Mallorca, i., Spain	F15	12
Makaha, Hi., U.S.	g9	88
Makaha Point, c., Hi., U.S.	A2	88
Makah Indian Reservation, Wa., U.S.	A1	124
Makahuena Point, c., Hi., U.S.	B2	88
Makakilo City, Hi., U.S.	g9	88
Makale, Indon.	F6	32
Makapuu Head, c., Hi., U.S.	B4	88
Makarska, Cro.	F12	14
Makasar, Selat (Makassar Strait), strt., Indon.	F6	32
Makasar see Ujungpandang, Indon.	G6	32
Makawao, Hi., U.S.	C5	88
Makaweli, Hi., U.S.	B2	88
Makeni, S.L.	G3	42
Makgadikgadi Pans, pl., Bots.	F5	44
Makhachkala see Machačkala, Russia	I7	22
Makindu, Kenya	B7	44
M'akit, Russia	E24	24
Makkah (Mecca), Sau. Ar.	D2	46
Maklakovo, Russia	F12	24
Makó, Hung.	I20	8
Makokou, Gabon	A2	44
Makthar, Tun.	N4	14
Makumbi, Zaire	C4	44
Makurazaki, Japan	K3	30
Makurdi, Nig.	G7	42
Makushin Volcano, vol., Ak., U.S.	E6	79
Malabar, Fl., U.S.	D6	86
Malabar Coast, India	G4	37
Malabo, Eq. Gui.	H7	42
Malacca, Strait of, strt., Asia	M6	34
Malad City, Id., U.S.	G6	89
Málaga, Col.	D6	58
Málaga, Spain	I7	12
Malagón, Spain	F8	12
Malaimbandy, Madag.	F9	44
Malaja Kuril'skaja Gr'ada (Habomai-shotō), is., Russia	p24	30a
Malakāl, Sudan	G12	42
Malakoff, Tx., U.S.	C4	120
Malang, Indon.	m16	32
Malanje, Ang.	C3	44
Malanville, Benin	F6	42
Mälaren, l., Swe.	G11	6
Malargüe, Arg.	D3	56
Malartic, Que., Can.	k11	74
Malaspina Glacier, Ak., U.S.	D11	79
Malatya, Tur.	H15	4
Malawi, ctry., Afr.	D6	44
Malaya, reg., Malay.	M7	34
Malay Peninsula, pen., Asia	K6	34
Malaysia, ctry., Asia	E3	32
Malbaie, stm., Que., Can.	B7	74
Malbork, Pol.	A19	8
Malcolm, Austl.	E4	50
Malden, Ma., U.S.	B5	98
Malden, Mo., U.S.	E8	102
Malden, W.V., U.S.	m12	125
Maldives, ctry., Asia	I2	37
Maldonado, Ur.	C6	56
Mālegaon, India	B3	37
Malek Dīn, Afg.	D3	38
Malha Wells, Sudan	E11	42
Malheur, co., Or., U.S.	D9	114
Malheur, stm., Or., U.S.	D9	114
Malheur Lake, l., Or., U.S.	D8	114
Mali, ctry., Afr.	E5	42
Malibu, Ca., U.S.	m11	82
Malik, Wādī al-, val., Sudan	E11	42
Malin, Or., U.S.	E5	114
Malindi, Kenya	B8	44
Malino, Bukit, mtn., Indon.	E6	32
Malka, Russia	G25	24
Malkāpur, India	B4	37
Malkara, Tur.	I10	16
Mallaig, Scot., U.K.	D7	7
Mallawī, Egypt	C12	42
Malletts Bay, b., Vt., U.S.	B2	122
Mallnitz, Aus.	I13	8
Mallorca, i., Spain	F14	12
Mallow, Ire.	I4	7
Malmberget, Swe.	C13	6
Malmédy, Bel.	E6	8
Malmesbury, S. Afr.	H3	44
Malmö, Swe.	I9	6
Malmstrom Air Force Base, mil., Mt., U.S.	C5	103
Malolos, Phil.	q19	33b
Malone, N.Y., U.S.	f10	109
Maloney Reservoir, res., Ne., U.S.	C5	104
Måløy, Nor.	F5	6
Malpaso, Presa de, res., Mex.	I13	62
Malpelo, Isla de, i., Col.	C2	54
Malpeque Bay, b., P.E.I., Can.	C6	71
Malta, Il., U.S.	B5	90
Malta, Mt., U.S.	B9	103
Malta Channel, strt., Eur.	M9	14
Maltahöhe, Nmb.	F3	44
Maluku (Moluccas), is., Indon.	F8	32
Maluku, Laut (Molucca Sea), Indon.	F7	32
Malung, Swe.	F9	6
Malvern, Ar., U.S.	C3	81
Malvern, Ia., U.S.	D2	92
Malvern, Oh., U.S.	B4	112
Malvern, Pa., U.S.	o19	115
Malverne, N.Y., U.S.	k13	109
Malyj An'uj, stm., Russia	D26	24
Malyj Tajmyr, Ostrov, i., Russia	B15	24
Mama, Russia	F16	24
Mamala Bay, b., Hi., U.S.	g10	88
Mamaroneck, N.Y., U.S.	h13	109
Mamberamo, stm., Indon.	F10	32
Mamers, Fr.	D7	10
Mamfe, Cam.	G7	42
Mammoth, Az., U.S.	E5	80
Mammoth Cave National Park, Ky., U.S.	C4	94
Mammoth Lakes, Ca., U.S.	D4	82
Mammoth Spring, Ar., U.S.	A4	81
Mamoré, stm., S.A.	F5	54
Mamou, Gui.	F3	42
Mamou, La., U.S.	D3	95
Man, I.C.	G4	42
Man, W.V., U.S.	D3	125
Manacapuru, Braz.	D6	54
Manacor, Spain	F15	12
Manado, Indon.	E7	32
Managua, Nic.	H4	64
Managua, Lago de, l., Nic.	H4	64
Manakara, Madag.	F9	44
Manama see Al-Manāmah, Bahr.	C5	46
Manana Island, i., Hi., U.S.	g11	88
Mananara, Madag.	E9	44
Mananjary, Madag.	F9	44
Manantico Creek, stm., N.J., U.S.	E3	107
Mana Point, c., Hi., U.S.	A2	88
Manas, China	C4	26
Manasquan, N.J., U.S.	C4	107
Manasquan, stm., N.J., U.S.	C4	107
Manassa, Co., U.S.	D5	83
Manassas, Va., U.S.	B5	123
Manassas National Battlefield Park, Va., U.S.	g11	123
Manassas Park, Va., U.S.	B5	123
Manatee, co., Fl., U.S.	E4	86
Manatee, stm., Fl., U.S.	E4	86
Manaus, Braz.	D6	54
Manawa, Wi., U.S.	D5	126
Manbij, Syria	A5	40
Mancelona, Mi., U.S.	D5	99
Mancha Real, Spain	H8	12
Manchester, Eng., U.K.	H10	7
Manchester, Ct., U.S.	B5	84
Manchester, Ga., U.S.	D2	87
Manchester, Ia., U.S.	B6	92
Manchester, Ky., U.S.	C6	94
Manchester, Me., U.S.	D3	96
Manchester, Md., U.S.	A4	97
Manchester, Ma., U.S.	A6	98
Manchester, Mo., U.S.	f12	102
Manchester, N.H., U.S.	E4	106
Manchester, N.Y., U.S.	C3	109
Manchester, Oh., U.S.	D2	112
Manchester, Pa., U.S.	F8	115
Manchester, Tn., U.S.	B5	119
Manchester, Vt., U.S.	E2	122
Manchester Center, Vt., U.S.	E2	122
Manchuria, reg., China	B12	26
Manciano, Italy	G6	14
Mancos, Co., U.S.	D2	83
Mancos, stm., U.S.	D2	83
Mand, stm., Iran	C5	46
Manda, Tan.	D6	44
Mandal, Nor.	G6	6
Mandalay, Burma	C4	34
Mandalgov', Mong.	B8	26
Mandan, N.D., U.S.	C5	111
Mandas, Italy	J4	14
Mandasor, India	H6	38
Mandeb, Bāb el-, strt.	E3	46
Mandeville, Jam.	E6	64
Mandeville, La., U.S.	D5	95
Mandi Bahāuddīn, Pak.	D5	38
Mandimba, Moz.	D7	44
Mandla, India	I9	38
Manduria, Italy	I12	14
Māndvi, India	I3	38
Mandya, India	F4	37
Manerbio, Italy	D5	14
Manfredonia, Italy	H10	14
Mangabeiras, Chapada das, hills, Braz.	F9	54
Mangalore, India	F3	37
Mangkalihat, Tanjung, c., Indon.	E6	32
Manglares, Cabo, c., Col.	G3	58
Mangoche, Mwi.	D7	44
Mangoky, stm., Madag.	F8	44
Mangole, Pulau, i., Indon.	F8	32
Mängrol, India	J4	38
Mangrove Cay, i., Bah.	B9	64
Mangualde, Port.	E4	12
Mangum, Ok., U.S.	C2	113
Mangya, China	D5	26
Manhattan, Ks., U.S.	C7	93
Manhattan, Mt., U.S.	E5	103
Manhattan Beach, Ca., U.S.	n12	82
Manhattan Island, i., N.Y., U.S.	h13	109
Manheim, Pa., U.S.	F9	115
Manhuaçu, Braz.	F7	57
Manicoré, Braz.	E6	54
Manicouagan, stm., Que., Can.	F19	66
Manicouagan, Réservoir, res., Que., Can.	h13	74
Manila, Phil.	q19	32
Manila, Ar., U.S.	B5	81
Manila, Ut., U.S.	C7	121
Manila Bay, b., Phil.	C7	32
Manilla, Ia., U.S.	C2	92
Manipur, ter., India	H15	38
Manisa, Tur.	K11	16
Manistee, Mi., U.S.	D4	99
Manistee, co., Mi., U.S.	D4	99
Manistee, stm., Mi., U.S.	D5	99
Manistique, Mi., U.S.	C4	99
Manistique, stm., Mi., U.S.	B4	99
Manistique Lake, l., Mi., U.S.	B5	99
Manito, Il., U.S.	C4	90
Manitoba, prov., Can.	C3	70
Manitoba, Lake, l., Man., Can.	D2	70
Manitou, Man., Can.	E2	70
Manitou, Lake, l., Ont., Can.	B3	73
Manitou Island, i., Mi., U.S.	A3	99
Manitou Lake, l., Sask., Can.	E1	75
Manitoulin Island, i., Ont., Can.	B3	73
Manitou Springs, Co., U.S.	C6	83
Manitowoc, Wi., U.S.	D6	126
Manitowoc, co., Wi., U.S.	D6	126
Manitowoc, stm., Wi., U.S.	h10	126
Maniwaki, Que., Can.	C2	74
Manizales, Col.	E5	58
Mānjra, stm., India	C4	37
Mankato, Ks., U.S.	C5	93
Mankato, Mn., U.S.	F5	100
Mankoya, Zam.	D4	44
Manlius, N.Y., U.S.	C5	109
Manlléu, Spain	C14	12
Manly, Ia., U.S.	A4	92
Manmād, India	B3	37
Mannar, Gulf of, b., Asia	H5	37
Mannārgudi, India	G5	37
Mannar Island, i., Sri L.	H5	37
Mannford, Ok., U.S.	A5	113
Mannheim, Ger.	F8	8
Manning, Alta., Can.	A2	68
Manning, Ia., U.S.	C2	92
Manning, S.C., U.S.	D7	117
Mannington, W.V., U.S.	B4	125
Manns Creek, stm., W.V., U.S.	n14	125
Mannville, Alta., Can.	C5	68
Manokin, stm., Md., U.S.	D6	97
Manokotak, Ak., U.S.	D7	79
Manokwari, Indon.	F9	32
Manomet, Ma., U.S.	C6	98
Manomet Point, c., Ma., U.S.	C6	98
Manono, Zaire	C5	44
Manor, Tx., U.S.	D4	120
Manosque, Fr.	I12	10
Manouane, Lac, l., Que., Can.	h12	74
Manresa, Spain	D13	12
Mānsa, India	F6	38
Mansa, Zam.	D5	44
Manseau, Que., Can.	C5	74
Mansel Island, i., N.W. Ter., Can.	D17	66
Mansfield, Eng., U.K.	H11	7
Mansfield, Ar., U.S.	B1	81
Mansfield, Il., U.S.	C5	90
Mansfield, La., U.S.	B2	95
Mansfield, Ma., U.S.	B5	98
Mansfield, Mo., U.S.	D5	102
Mansfield, Oh., U.S.	B3	112
Mansfield, Pa., U.S.	C7	115
Mansfield, Tx., U.S.	n9	120
Mansfield, Mount, mtn., Vt., U.S.	B3	122
Mansfield Center, Ct., U.S.	B7	84
Mansfield Hollow Lake, res., Ct., U.S.	B7	84
Manson, Ia., U.S.	B3	92
Manson, Wa., U.S.	B5	124
Mansonville, Que., Can.	D5	74
Mansura, La., U.S.	C3	95
Manta, Ec.	H2	58
Mantachie, Ms., U.S.	A5	101
Manteca, Ca., U.S.	D3	82
Manteno, Il., U.S.	B6	90
Manteo, N.C., U.S.	B7	110
Mantes-la-Jolie, Fr.	D8	10
Manti, Ut., U.S.	D4	121
Mantiqueira, Serra da, mts., Braz.	F6	57
Manton, Mi., U.S.	D5	99
Mantorville, Mn., U.S.	F6	100
Mantova, Italy	D5	14
Mantua, Oh., U.S.	A4	112
Mantua, Ut., U.S.	B4	121
Manturovo, Russia	C27	18
Manukau Harbour, b., N.Z.	B5	52
Manumuskin, stm., N.J., U.S.	E3	107
Manus Island, i., Pap. N. Gui.	k16	50a
Manvel, Tx., U.S.	r14	120
Manville, N.J., U.S.	B3	107
Manville, R.I., U.S.	B4	116
Many, La., U.S.	C2	95
Many Farms, Az., U.S.	A6	80
Manzanares, Spain	F8	12
Manzanillo, Cuba	D9	64
Manzanillo, Mex.	H7	62
Manzano Mountains, mts., N.M., U.S.	C3	108
Manzano Peak, mtn., N.M., U.S.	C3	108
Manzhouli, China	B10	26
Mao, Chad	F9	42
Maoke, Pegunungan, mts., Indon.	F10	32
Mapastepec, Mex.	J13	62
Mapi, Indon.	G10	32
Mapia, Kepulauan, is., Indon.	E9	32
Mapimí, Mex.	E8	62
Mapimí, Bolsón de, des., Mex.	D8	62
Mapire, Ven.	D10	58
Maple, stm., U.S.	A7	118
Maple, stm., Ia., U.S.	B2	92
Maple, stm., N.D., U.S.	C8	111
Maple Bluff, Wi., U.S.	E4	126
Maple Grove, Mn., U.S.	m12	100
Maple Heights, Oh., U.S.	h9	112
Maple Lake, Mn., U.S.	E5	100
Maple Plain, Mn., U.S.	m11	100
Maple Shade, N.J., U.S.	D2	107
Maplesville, Al., U.S.	C3	78
Mapleton, Ia., U.S.	B2	92
Mapleton, Mn., U.S.	G5	100
Mapleton, N.D., U.S.	C8	111
Mapleton, Or., U.S.	C3	114
Mapleton, Ut., U.S.	C4	121
Maple Valley, Wa., U.S.	f11	124
Mapleville, R.I., U.S.	B2	116
Maplewood, Mn., U.S.	n12	100
Maplewood, Mo., U.S.	f13	102
Maplewood, N.J., U.S.	B4	107
Maputo (Lourenço Marques), Moz.	G6	44
Maqueda, Spain	E7	12
Maquela do Zombo, Ang.	C3	44
Maquinchao, Arg.	E3	56
Maquoketa, Ia., U.S.	B7	92
Maquoketa, stm., Ia., U.S.	B6	92
Maquoketa, North Fork, stm., Ia., U.S.	B7	92
Mar, Serra do, clf, Braz.	A7	56
Marabá, Braz.	E9	54
Maracá, Ilha de, i., Braz.	C8	54
Maracaibo, Ven.	B7	58
Maracaibo, Lago de, l., Ven.	C7	58
Maracay, Ven.	B9	58
Marādah, Libya	C9	42
Maradi, Niger	F7	42
Marāgheh, Iran	J7	22
Maragogipe, Braz.	B9	57
Marahuaca, Cerro, mtn., Ven.	F10	58
Marais des Cygnes, stm., U.S.	D8	93
Marajó, Baía de, b., Braz.	D9	54
Marajó, Ilha de, i., Braz.	D9	54
Maralal, Kenya	A7	44
Marambaia, Ilha da, i., Braz.	G7	57
Marana, Az., U.S.	E4	80
Marang, Malay.	L7	34
Marañón, stm., Peru	D3	54
Marans, Fr.	F5	10
Marapanim, Braz.	D9	54
Marathon, Fl., U.S.	H5	86
Marathon, Wi., U.S.	D4	126
Marathon, co., Wi., U.S.	D4	126
Marawī, Sudan	E1	46
Marble, Mn., U.S.	C5	100
Marble, N.C., U.S.	f9	110
Marble Bar, Austl.	D3	50
Marble Canyon, val., Az., U.S.	A4	80
Marble Falls, Tx., U.S.	D3	120
Marblehead, Ma., U.S.	B6	98
Marble Hill, Mo., U.S.	D8	102
Marbleton, Wy., U.S.	D2	127
Marburg an der Lahn, Ger.	E8	8
Marbury, Md., U.S.	C3	97
Marcaria, Italy	D5	14
Marceline, Mo., U.S.	B5	102
Marcellus, Mi., U.S.	F5	99
March (Morava), stm., Eur.	G16	8
Marcha, Russia	E18	24
March Air Force Base, mil., Ca., U.S.	F5	82
Marche-en-Famenne, Bel.	E5	8
Marchena, Spain	H6	12
Mar Chiquita, Laguna, l., Arg.	C4	56
Marco, Fl., U.S.	G5	86
Marcus, Ia., U.S.	B2	92
Marcus Baker, Mount, mtn., Ak., U.S.	g18	79
Marcus Hook, Pa., U.S.	G11	115
Marcy, Mount, mtn., N.Y., U.S.	A7	109
Mardān, Pak.	C5	38
Mar del Plata, Arg.	D5	56
Mardin, Tur.	H16	4
Mareeba, Austl.	C9	50
Mareg, Som.	H4	46
Marengo, Il., U.S.	A5	90
Marengo, In., U.S.	H5	91
Marengo, Ia., U.S.	C5	92
Marengo, co., Al., U.S.	C2	78
Marennes, Fr.	G5	10
Marfa, Tx., U.S.	o12	120
Margaret, Al., U.S.	B3	78
Margarita, Isla de, i., Ven.	B10	58
Margate, Fl., U.S.	F6	86
Margate City, N.J., U.S.	E3	107
Margherita Peak, mtn., Afr.	A5	44
Marghī, Afg.	C2	38
Margrethe, Lake, l., Mi., U.S.	D6	99
Maria Cleofas, Isla, i., Mex.	G6	62
Maria Madre, Isla, i., Mex.	G6	62
Maria Magdalena, Isla, i., Mex.	G6	62
Marian, Lake, l., Fl., U.S.	E5	86
Marianao, Cuba	C6	64
Marianna, Ar., U.S.	C5	81
Marianna, Fl., U.S.	B1	86
Marias, stm., Mt., U.S.	B4	103
Marias, Islas, is., Mex.	G6	62
Marias Pass, Mt., U.S.	B3	103
Mariato, Punta, c., Pan.	K7	64
Maribor, Slo.	C10	14
Marica (Évros) (Meriç), stm., Eur.	G9	16
Maricopa, Az., U.S.	E3	80
Maricopa, co., Az., U.S.	D3	80
Maricopa Mountains, mts., Az., U.S.	m7	80
Marie-Galante, i., Guad.	G17	64
Mariehamn, Fin.	F12	6
Mariemont, Oh., U.S.	o13	112
Mariental, Nmb.	F3	44
Marienville, Pa., U.S.	D3	115
Maries, co., Mo., U.S.	C6	102
Mariestad, Swe.	G9	6
Marietta, Ga., U.S.	C2	87
Marietta, Oh., U.S.	C4	112
Marietta, Ok., U.S.	D4	113
Marietta, S.C., U.S.	A2	117
Marieville, Que., Can.	D4	74
Marília, Braz.	G4	57
Marimba, Ang.	C3	44
Marín, Spain	C3	12
Marin, co., Ca., U.S.	C2	82
Marinduque Island, i., Phil.	C7	32
Marine City, Mi., U.S.	F8	99
Marine On St. Croix, Mn., U.S.	E6	100
Marinette, Wi., U.S.	C6	126
Marinette, co., Wi., U.S.	C5	126
Maringá, Braz.	G3	57
Marinha Grande, Port.	F3	12
Marion, Al., U.S.	C2	78
Marion, Ar., U.S.	B5	81
Marion, Il., U.S.	F5	90
Marion, In., U.S.	C6	91
Marion, Ia., U.S.	B6	92
Marion, Ks., U.S.	D6	93
Marion, Ky., U.S.	e9	94
Marion, La., U.S.	B3	95
Marion, Mi., U.S.	D5	99
Marion, Ms., U.S.	C5	101
Marion, N.C., U.S.	B1	110
Marion, Oh., U.S.	B2	112
Marion, Pa., U.S.	G6	115
Marion, S.C., U.S.	C9	117
Marion, S.D., U.S.	D8	118
Marion, Va., U.S.	f10	123
Marion, Wi., U.S.	D5	126
Marion, co., Al., U.S.	A2	78
Marion, co., Ar., U.S.	A3	81
Marion, co., Fl., U.S.	C4	86
Marion, co., Ga., U.S.	D2	87
Marion, co., Il., U.S.	E4	90
Marion, co., In., U.S.	E5	91
Marion, co., Ia., U.S.	C4	92
Marion, co., Ks., U.S.	D6	93
Marion, co., Ky., U.S.	C4	94
Marion, co., Ms., U.S.	D4	101
Marion, co., Mo., U.S.	B6	102
Marion, co., Oh., U.S.	B2	112
Marion, co., Or., U.S.	C4	114
Marion, co., S.C., U.S.	C9	117
Marion, co., Tn., U.S.	D8	119
Marion, co., Tx., U.S.	C5	120
Marion, co., W.V., U.S.	B4	125
Marion, Lake, res., S.C., U.S.	E7	117
Marion Station, Md., U.S.	D6	97
Marionville, Mo., U.S.	D4	102
Maripa, Ven.	D10	58
Mariposa, Ca., U.S.	D3	82
Mariposa, co., Ca., U.S.	D3	82
Mariscal Estigarribia, Para.	A4	56
Marissa, Il., U.S.	E4	90
Maritime Alps, mts., Eur.	H14	10
Mariupol' (Ždanov), Ukr.	H5	22
Marka, Som.	H3	46
Markaryd, Swe.	H9	6
Markdale, Ont., Can.	C4	73
Marked Tree, Ar., U.S.	B5	81
Markesan, Wi., U.S.	E5	126
Markham, Ont., Can.	D5	73
Markham, Il., U.S.	k9	90
Markham, Tx., U.S.	E4	120
Markham, Mount, mtn., Ant.	A29	47
Markland Lock and Dam, U.S.	B5	94
Markle, In., U.S.	C7	91
Markovo, Russia	E28	24
Marks, Ms., U.S.	A3	101
Marksville, La., U.S.	C3	95
Marktredwitz, Ger.	E12	8
Mark Twain Lake, res., Mo., U.S.	B6	102
Marlboro, N.Y., U.S.	D7	109
Marlboro, Va., U.S.	n17	123
Marlboro, co., S.C., U.S.	B8	117
Marlborough, Ct., U.S.	C6	84
Marlborough, Ma., U.S.	B4	98
Marlborough, N.H., U.S.	E2	106
Marle, Fr.	C10	10
Marlette, Mi., U.S.	E7	99
Marley, Md., U.S.	B4	97
Marlin, Tx., U.S.	D4	120
Marlinton, W.V., U.S.	C4	125
Marlow, Ok., U.S.	C4	113
Marlowe, W.V., U.S.	B7	125
Marlton, N.J., U.S.	D3	107
Marmaduke, Ar., U.S.	A5	81
Marmande, Fr.	H7	10
Marmara Adası, i., Tur.	I11	16
Marmara Denizi (Sea of Marmara), Tur.	I12	16
Marmaris, Tur.	M12	16
Marmet, W.V., U.S.	C3	125
Marmora, Ont., Can.	C7	73
Marne, stm., Fr.	C10	10
Maroa, Il., U.S.	C5	90
Maroa, Ven.	F9	58
Maroantsetra, Madag.	E9	44
Maromokotro, mtn., Madag.	D9	44
Marondera, Zimb.	E6	44
Maros (Mureş), stm., Eur.	C4	16
Maroua, Cam.	F8	42
Marovoay, Madag.	E9	44
Marquesas Keys, is., Fl., U.S.	H4	86
Marquette, Mi., U.S.	B3	99
Marquette, co., Mi., U.S.	B3	99
Marquette, co., Wi., U.S.	E4	126
Marquette Heights, Il., U.S.	C4	90
Marquise, Fr.	B8	10
Marrah, Jabal, mtn., Sudan	F10	42
Marrakech, Mor.	B4	42
Marrero, La., U.S.	E5	95
Mars, Pa., U.S.	E1	115
Marsabit, Kenya	H2	46
Marsala, Italy	L7	14
Marsá Matrūh, Egypt	B11	42
Marseille, Fr.	J12	10
Marseille, Il., U.S.	B5	90
Marseille-en-Beauvaisis, Fr.	C8	10
Marseilles, Il., U.S.	B5	90
Marshall, Sask., Can.	D1	75
Marshall, Ar., U.S.	B3	81
Marshall, Il., U.S.	D6	90
Marshall, Mi., U.S.	F6	99
Marshall, Mn., U.S.	F3	100
Marshall, Mo., U.S.	B4	102
Marshall, N.C., U.S.	f10	110
Marshall, Tx., U.S.	C5	120
Marshall, Wi., U.S.	E4	126
Marshall, co., Al., U.S.	A3	78
Marshall, co., Il., U.S.	B4	90
Marshall, co., In., U.S.	B5	91
Marshall, co., Ia., U.S.	C4	92
Marshall, co., Ks., U.S.	C7	93
Marshall, co., Ky., U.S.	f9	94
Marshall, co., Mn., U.S.	B2	100
Marshall, co., Ms., U.S.	A4	101
Marshall, co., Ok., U.S.	C5	113
Marshall, co., S.D., U.S.	B8	118
Marshall, co., Tn., U.S.	B5	119
Marshall, co., W.V., U.S.	B4	125
Marshall, De., U.S.	B3	85
Marshalltown, Ia., U.S.	B5	92
Marshallville, Ga., U.S.	D3	87
Marshes Siding, Ky., U.S.	D5	94
Marshfield, Ma., U.S.	B6	98

Marshfield, Mo., U.S. — D5 102
Marshfield, Wi., U.S. — D3 126
Marshfield Hills, Ma., U.S. — B6 98
Marsh Fork, stm., W.V., U.S. — n13 125
Marsh Harbour, Bah. — A9 64
Mars Hill, Me., U.S. — B5 96
Mars Hill, N.C., U.S. — f10 110
Marsh Island, i., La., U.S. — E4 95
Marsh Lake, res., Mn., U.S. — E2 100
Marsh Peak, mtn., Ut., U.S. — C6 121
Marshville, N.C., U.S. — C2 110
Marsing, Id., U.S. — F2 89
Märsta, Swe. — G11 6
Marston, Mo., U.S. — E8 102
Mart, Tx., U.S. — D4 120
Martaban, Gulf of, b., Burma — F4 34
Marthasville, Mo., U.S. — C6 102
Martha's Vineyard, i., Ma., U.S. — D6 98
Martigny, Switz. — F14 10
Martigues, Fr. — I12 10
Martin, Czech. — F18 8
Martin, Ky., U.S. — C7 94
Martin, S.D., U.S. — D4 118
Martin, Tn., U.S. — A3 119
Martin, co., Fl., U.S. — E6 86
Martin, co., In., U.S. — G4 91
Martin, co., Ky., U.S. — C7 94
Martin, co., Mn., U.S. — G4 100
Martin, co., N.C., U.S. — B5 110
Martin, co., Tx., U.S. — C2 120
Martina Franca, Italy — I12 14
Martinez, Ca., U.S. — C2 82
Martinez, Ga., U.S. — C4 87
Martínez de la Torre, Mex. — G11 62
Martinique, dep., N.A. — G17 64
Martin Lake, res., Al., U.S. — C4 78
Martin Point, c., Ak., U.S. — A11 79
Martinsberg, Aus. — G15 8
Martinsburg, Pa., U.S. — F5 115
Martinsburg, W.V., U.S. — B7 125
Martins Ferry, Oh., U.S. — B5 112
Martinsville, Il., U.S. — D6 90
Martinsville, In., U.S. — F5 91
Martinsville, Va., U.S. — D3 123
Martos, Spain — H8 12
Martre, Lac la, l., N.W. Ter., Can. — D9 66
Martti, Fin. — C17 6
Marugame, Japan — H6 30
Ma'rūt, Afg. — E2 38
Marvejols, Fr. — H10 10
Marvell, Ar., U.S. — C5 81
Marvine, Mount, mtn., Ut., U.S. — E4 121
Mary, Turk. — J10 22
Mary, stm., Nv., U.S. — E3 100
Mary, Lake, l., Ms., U.S. — D2 101
Maryborough, Austl. — E10 50
Maryland, state, U.S. — B4 97
Maryland City, Md., U.S. — B4 97
Maryland Heights, Mo., U.S. — f13 102
Maryland Point, c., Md., U.S. — D3 97
Maryport, Eng., U.K. — G9 7
Marys, stm., Nv., U.S. — B6 105
Marys Peak, mtn., Or., U.S. — C3 114
Marystown, Newf., Can. — E4 72
Marysville, Ca., U.S. — C3 82
Marysville, Ks., U.S. — C7 93
Marysville, Mi., U.S. — F8 99
Marysville, Oh., U.S. — B2 112
Marysville, Pa., U.S. — F8 115
Marysville, Wa., U.S. — A3 124
Maryville, Mo., U.S. — A3 102
Maryville, Tn., U.S. — D10 119
Marzūq, Libya — C8 42
Marzūq, Idehan, reg., Libya — C8 42
Masai Steppe, plat., Tan. — B7 44
Masaka, Ug. — B6 44
Masan, S. Kor. — D12 26
Masasi, Tan. — D7 44
Masaya, Nic. — I4 64
Masbate Island, i., Phil. — C7 32
Mascarene Islands, is., Afr. — F11 44
Mascoma, stm., N.H., U.S. — C2 106
Mascoma, Lake, l., N.H., U.S. — C2 106
Mascot, Tn., U.S. — C10 119
Mascota, Mex. — G7 62
Mascouche, Que., Can. — D4 74
Mascoutah, Il., U.S. — E4 90
Maseru, Leso. — G5 44
Mashābīh, i., Sau. Ar. — C2 46
Mashapaug Pond, l., Ct., U.S. — A7 84
Masherbrum, mtn., Pak. — C7 38
Mashhad, Iran — J9 22
Masi Manimba, Zaire — B3 44
Masindi, Ug. — H12 42
Masjed Soleymān, Iran — B4 46
Mask, Lough, l., Ire. — H3 7
Maskanah, Syria — A6 40
Maskinongé, Que., Can. — C4 74
Mason, Mi., U.S. — F6 99
Mason, Nv., U.S. — E2 105
Mason, Oh., U.S. — C1 112
Mason, Tx., U.S. — D3 120
Mason, W.V., U.S. — B2 125
Mason, co., Il., U.S. — C4 90
Mason, co., Ky., U.S. — B6 94
Mason, co., Mi., U.S. — D4 99
Mason, co., Tx., U.S. — D3 120
Mason, co., Wa., U.S. — B2 124
Mason, co., W.V., U.S. — C3 125
Mason City, Il., U.S. — C4 90
Mason City, Ia., U.S. — A4 92
Masontown, Pa., U.S. — G2 115
Masontown, W.V., U.S. — B5 125
Masqat (Muscat), Oman — D6 46
Massa, Italy — E5 14
Massabesic Lake, l., N.H., U.S. — E4 106
Massac, co., Il., U.S. — F5 90
Massachusetts, state, U.S. — B4 98
Massachusetts Bay, b., Ma., U.S. — B6 98
Massacre Lake, l., Nv., U.S. — B2 105
Massafra, Italy — I12 14
Massa Marittima, Italy — F5 14
Massangena, Moz. — F6 44

Massapoag Lake, l., Ma., U.S. — h11 98
Massarosa, Italy — F5 14
Massasecum, Lake, l., N.H., U.S. — D3 106
Massena, N.Y., U.S. — f10 109
Massenya, Chad — F9 42
Masset, B.C., Can. — C1 69
Massey, Ont., Can. — A2 73
Massif Central see Central, Massif, mts., Fr. — G10 10
Massillon, Oh., U.S. — B4 112
Massive, Mount, mtn., Co., U.S. — B4 83
Masterton, N.Z. — D5 52
Mastic Beach, N.Y., U.S. — n16 109
Mastung, Pak. — F2 38
Masuda, Japan — H4 30
Masury, Oh., U.S. — A5 112
Matadi, Zaire — C2 44
Matagalpa, Nic. — H5 64
Matagorda, co., Tx., U.S. — E5 120
Matagorda Bay, b., Tx., U.S. — E4 120
Matagorda Island, i., Tx., U.S. — E4 120
Matagorda Peninsula, pen., Tx., U.S. — E5 120
Matale, Sri L. — I6 37
Matamoras, Pa., U.S. — D12 115
Matamoros, Mex. — E11 62
Matamoros de la Laguna, Mex. — E8 62
Matandu, stm., Tan. — C7 44
Matane, Que., Can. — k13 74
Matanuska, stm., Ak., U.S. — g18 79
Matanzas, Cuba — C7 64
Matanzas Inlet, b., Fl., U.S. — C5 86
Matara, Sri L. — J6 37
Mataró, Spain — D14 12
Matatiele, S. Afr. — H5 44
Matawan, N.J., U.S. — C4 107
Matehuala, Mex. — F9 62
Mateira, Braz. — D4 57
Matelica, Italy — F7 14
Matera, Italy — I11 14
Mateur, Tun. — L4 14
Matewan, W.V., U.S. — D2 125
Mather, Pa., U.S. — G1 115
Mather Air Force Base, mil., Ca., U.S. — C3 82
Mather Peaks, mts., Wy., U.S. — B5 127
Mathews, La., U.S. — E5 95
Mathews, Va., U.S. — C6 123
Mathews, co., Va., U.S. — C6 123
Mathews, Lake, l., Ca., U.S. — n14 82
Mathis, Tx., U.S. — E4 120
Mathiston, Ms., U.S. — B4 101
Mathura, India — G7 38
Matías Romero, Mex. — I12 62
Matinicus Island, i., Me., U.S. — E3 96
Mätli, Pak. — H3 38
Mato, Cerro, mtn., Ven. — D10 58
Matoaca, Va., U.S. — n18 123
Mato Grosso, Braz. — F7 54
Mato Grosso, Planalto do, plat., Braz. — G7 54
Matosinhos, Port. — D3 12
Matou, Tai. — L9 28
Matrah, Oman — D6 46
Matsqui, B.C., Can. — f13 69
Matsudo, Japan — G12 30
Matsue, Japan — G6 30
Matsumae, Japan — r18 30a
Matsumoto, Japan — F10 30
Matsusaka, Japan — H9 30
Matsu Tao, i., Tai. — I8 28
Matsuyama, Japan — I5 30
Mattagami, stm., Ont., Can. — F16 66
Mattamiscontis Lake, l., Me., U.S. — C4 96
Mattamuskeet, Lake, l., N.C., U.S. — B6 110
Mattancheri, India — H4 37
Mattapoisett, Ma., U.S. — C6 98
Mattaponi, stm., Va., U.S. — C5 123
Mattawa, Ont., Can. — A6 73
Mattawamkeag, Me., U.S. — C4 96
Mattawamkeag, stm., Me., U.S. — C4 96
Mattawamkeag Lake, l., Me., U.S. — C4 96
Matterhorn, mtn., Eur. — G14 10
Matterhorn, mtn., Nv., U.S. — B6 105
Matteson, Il., U.S. — k9 90
Matthews, Mo., U.S. — E8 102
Matthews, N.C., U.S. — B2 110
Matthews Ridge, Guy. — D12 58
Matthew Town, Bah. — D11 64
Mattighofen, Aus. — G13 8
Mattituck, N.Y., U.S. — n16 109
Mattoon, Il., U.S. — D5 90
Mattoon, Lake, res., Il., U.S. — D5 90
Mattydale, N.Y., U.S. — B4 109
Matunuck, R.I., U.S. — G3 116
Maturín, Ven. — C11 58
Maúa, Moz. — D7 44
Maubeuge, Fr. — B10 10
Maud, Ok., U.S. — B5 113
Maugansville, Md., U.S. — A2 97
Maui, co., Hi., U.S. — B5 88
Maui, i., Hi., U.S. — C6 88
Mauldin, S.C., U.S. — B3 117
Mauléon-Licharre, Fr. — I6 10
Maulvi Bāzār, Bngl. — H14 38
Maumee, Oh., U.S. — A2 112
Maumee, stm., U.S. — A1 112
Maumee Bay, b., U.S. — G7 99
Maumelle, Lake, res., Ar., U.S. — C3 81
Maun, Bots. — E4 44
Mauna Kea, vol., Hi., U.S. — D6 88
Maunaloa, Hi., U.S. — B4 88
Mauna Loa, vol., Hi., U.S. — D6 88
Maunalua Bay, b., Hi., U.S. — g10 88
Maunath Bhanjan, India — H10 38
Maunawili, Hi., U.S. — g10 88
Mau Rānīpur, India — H8 38
Maurepas, Lake, l., La., U.S. — D5 95
Mauriac, Fr. — G9 10
Maurice, Ia., U.S. — B1 92
Maurice, stm., N.J., U.S. — E2 107
Mauritania, ctry., Afr. — D3 42
Mauritius, ctry., Afr. — F11 44
Maurs, Fr. — H9 10
Maury, co., Tn., U.S. — B4 119
Maury City, Tn., U.S. — B2 119

Maury Island, i., Wa., U.S. — f11 124
Mauston, Wi., U.S. — E3 126
Mauterndorf, Aus. — H13 8
Mauthausen, Aus. — G14 8
Maverick, co., Tx., U.S. — E2 120
Maw-Daung Pass, Asia — I5 34
Mawlaik, Burma — C3 34
Mawlamyine (Moulmein), Burma — F4 34
Maw Taung, mtn., Asia — I5 34
Maxinkuckee, Lake, l., In., U.S. — B5 91
Max Meadows, Va., U.S. — D2 123
Maxton, N.C., U.S. — C3 110
Maxville, Ont., Can. — B10 73
Maxwell, Ia., U.S. — C4 92
Maxwell Acres, W.V., U.S. — g8 125
Maxwell Air Force Base, mil., Al., U.S. — C3 78
Mayaguana, i., Bah. — C11 64
Mayaguana Passage, strt., Bah. — C11 64
Mayagüez, P.R. — E14 64
Maya Mountains, mts., N.A. — F3 64
Maybole, Scot., U.K. — F8 7
Mayen, Ger. — E7 8
Mayenne, Fr. — D6 10
Mayer, Az., U.S. — C3 80
Mayerthorpe, Alta., Can. — C3 68
Mayes, co., Ok., U.S. — A6 113
Mayesville, S.C., U.S. — D7 117
Mayfield, Ky., U.S. — f9 94
Mayfield, Pa., U.S. — C10 115
Mayfield Heights, Oh., U.S. — A4 112
Mayfield Lake, res., Wa., U.S. — C3 124
Mayflower, Ar., U.S. — C3 81
Mayking, Ky., U.S. — C7 94
Maymyo, Burma — C4 34
Maynard, Ma., U.S. — B5 98
Maynardville, Tn., U.S. — C10 119
Mayne, B.C., Can. — g12 69
Mayo, Yukon, Can. — D5 66
Mayo, Md., U.S. — C4 97
Mayo, S.C., U.S. — A4 117
Mayodan, N.C., U.S. — A3 110
Mayotte, ter., Afr. — D9 44
Mayotte, i., May. — D9 44
May Park, Or., U.S. — B8 114
Mayport Naval Station, mil., Fl., U.S. — B5 86
Maysville, Ga., U.S. — B3 87
Maysville, Ky., U.S. — B6 94
Maysville, Mo., U.S. — B3 102
Maysville, N.C., U.S. — C5 110
Maysville, Ok., U.S. — C4 113
Mayumba, Gabon — B2 44
Māyūram, India — G5 37
Mayville, Mi., U.S. — E7 99
Mayville, N.Y., U.S. — C1 109
Mayville, N.D., U.S. — B8 111
Mayville, Wi., U.S. — E5 126
Maywood, Il., U.S. — k9 90
Maywood, N.J., U.S. — h8 107
Maywood Park, Or., U.S. — *B4 114
Mazabuka, Zam. — E5 44
Mazamet, Fr. — I9 10
Mazara del Vallo, Italy — L7 14
Mazār-e Sharīf, Afg. — B2 38
Mazaruni, stm., Guy. — E13 58
Mazatenango, Guat. — G2 64
Mazatlán, Mex. — F6 62
Mazatzal Mountains, mts., Az., U.S. — C4 80
Mazatzal Peak, mtn., Az., U.S. — C4 80
Mazeppa, Mn., U.S. — F6 100
Mazoe, stm., Afr. — E6 44
Mazomanie, Wi., U.S. — E4 126
Mazon, Il., U.S. — B5 90
Mbabane, Swaz. — G6 44
Mbaïki, Cen. Afr. Rep. — H9 42
Mbala, Zam. — C6 44
Mbale, Ug. — B6 44
Mbandaka (Coquilhatville), Zaire — A3 44
Mbanza-Ngungu, Zaire — C2 44
M'banz Congo, Ang. — C2 44
Mbeya, Tan. — C6 44
Mbomou (Bomu), stm., Afr. — H10 42
Mbout, Maur. — E3 42
Mbuji-Mayi (Bakwanga), Zaire — C4 44
McAdam, N.B., Can. — D2 71
McAdoo, Pa., U.S. — E9 115
McAfee Peak, mtn., Nv., U.S. — B6 105
McAlester, Ok., U.S. — C6 113
McAlester, Lake, res., Ok., U.S. — B6 113
McAllen, Tx., U.S. — F3 120
McAlmont, Ar., U.S. — h10 81
McAlpine, Md., U.S. — B4 97
McAlpine Lock and Dam, U.S. — H6 91
McArthur, Oh., U.S. — C3 112
McBee, S.C., U.S. — C7 117
McCall, Id., U.S. — E2 89
McCalla, Al., U.S. — g6 78
McCamey, Tx., U.S. — D1 120
McCammon, Id., U.S. — G6 89
McCandless, Pa., U.S. — h13 115
McCartney Mountain, mtn., Mt., U.S. — E4 103
McCaysville, Ga., U.S. — B2 87
McChord Air Force Base, mil., Wa., U.S. — f11 124
McClain, co., Ok., U.S. — C4 113
McCleary, Wa., U.S. — B2 124
McClellan Air Force Base, mil., Ca., U.S. — C3 82
McClintock, Mount, mtn., Ant. — A28 47
McCloud, Ca., U.S. — B2 82
McClure, Pa., U.S. — E7 115
McClusky, N.D., U.S. — B5 111
McColl, S.C., U.S. — B8 117
McComas, W.V., U.S. — D3 125
McComb, Ms., U.S. — D3 101
McComb, Oh., U.S. — A2 112
McCone, co., Mt., U.S. — C11 103
McConnell Air Force Base, mil., Ks., U.S. — g12 93
McConnellsburg, Pa., U.S. — G6 115
McConnelsville, Oh., U.S. — C4 112
McCook, Ne., U.S. — D5 104
McCook, co., S.D., U.S. — D8 118

McCordsville, In., U.S. — E6 91
McCormick, S.C., U.S. — D3 117
McCormick, co., S.C., U.S. — D3 117
McCracken, co., Ky., U.S. — e9 94
McCreary, Man., Can. — D2 70
McCreary, co., Ky., U.S. — D5 94
McCrory, Ar., U.S. — B4 81
McCulloch, co., Tx., U.S. — D3 120
McCullough Mountain, mtn., Nv., U.S. — H6 105
McCurtain, co., Ok., U.S. — C7 113
McDermitt, Nv., U.S. — B4 105
McDonald, co., Mo., U.S. — E3 102
McDonough, Ga., U.S. — C2 87
McDonough, co., Il., U.S. — C3 90
McDougall, Mount, mtn., Wy., U.S. — D2 127
McDowell, Ky., U.S. — C7 94
McDowell, co., N.C., U.S. — f10 110
McDowell, co., W.V., U.S. — D3 125
McDowell Mountains, mts., Az., U.S. — k9 80
McDowell Peak, mtn., Az., U.S. — k9 80
McDuffie, co., Ga., U.S. — C4 87
McElroy Creek, stm., W.V., U.S. — k9 125
McEwen, Tn., U.S. — A4 119
McFarland, Ca., U.S. — E4 82
McFarland, Wi., U.S. — E4 126
McGehee, Ar., U.S. — D4 81
McGill, Nv., U.S. — D7 105
McGrath, Ak., U.S. — C8 79
McGregor, Ia., U.S. — A6 92
McGregor, Tx., U.S. — D4 120
McGregor, stm., B.C., Can. — B7 69
McGregor Lake, l., Alta., Can. — D4 68
McGuire, Mount, mtn., Id., U.S. — D4 89
McGuire Air Force Base, mil., N.J., U.S. — C3 107
McHenry, Il., U.S. — A5 90
McHenry, Md., U.S. — k12 97
McHenry, co., Il., U.S. — A5 90
McHenry, co., N.D., U.S. — A5 111
McIntosh, Mn., U.S. — C3 100
McIntosh, co., Ga., U.S. — E5 87
McIntosh, co., N.D., U.S. — C6 111
McIntosh, co., Ok., U.S. — B6 113
McKean, co., Pa., U.S. — C4 115
McKee, Ky., U.S. — C6 94
McKeesport, Pa., U.S. — F2 115
McKees Rocks, Pa., U.S. — F1 115
McKenzie, Tn., U.S. — A3 119
McKenzie, co., N.D., U.S. — B2 111
McKenzie, stm., Or., U.S. — C4 114
McKinley, co., N.M., U.S. — B1 108
McKinley, Mount, mtn., Ak., U.S. — C9 79
McKinleyville, Ca., U.S. — B1 82
McKinney, Tx., U.S. — C4 120
McKinney, Lake, l., Ks., U.S. — E2 93
McKittrick Summit, mtn., Ca., U.S. — E4 82
McLaughlin, S.D., U.S. — B5 118
McLean, Il., U.S. — C4 90
McLean, Va., U.S. — g12 123
McLean, co., Il., U.S. — C4 90
McLean, co., Ky., U.S. — C2 94
McLean, co., N.D., U.S. — B4 111
McLeansboro, Il., U.S. — E5 90
McLennan, Alta., Can. — B2 68
McLennan, co., Tx., U.S. — D4 120
McLeod, co., Mn., U.S. — F4 100
McLeod, Lake, l., Austl. — D2 50
M'Clintock Channel, strt., N.W. Ter., Can. — B12 66
McLoud, Ok., U.S. — B4 113
McLoughlin, Mount, mtn., Or., U.S. — D4 114
McLouth, Ks., U.S. — C8 93
McMechen, W.V., U.S. — B4 125
McMillan, Lake, res., N.M., U.S. — E5 108
McMinn, co., Tn., U.S. — D9 119
McMinnville, Or., U.S. — B3 114
McMinnville, Tn., U.S. — D8 119
McMullen, co., Tx., U.S. — E3 120
McNairy, co., Tn., U.S. — B3 119
McNary, Az., U.S. — C6 80
McNary Dam, U.S. — B7 114
McNeil, Ar., U.S. — D2 81
McNeil, Mount, mtn., B.C., Can. — B2 69
McNeil Island, i., Wa., U.S. — f10 124
McNeill, Ms., U.S. — E4 101
McPherson, Ks., U.S. — D6 93
McPherson, co., Ks., U.S. — D6 93
McPherson, co., Ne., U.S. — C4 104
McPherson, co., S.D., U.S. — B6 118
McQueeney, Tx., U.S. — h7 120
McRae, Ar., U.S. — B4 81
McRae, Ga., U.S. — D4 87
McRoberts, Ky., U.S. — C7 94
McSherrystown, Pa., U.S. — G7 115
Mead, Ne., U.S. — B8 124
Mead, Lake, res., U.S. — A1 80
Meade, Ks., U.S. — E3 93
Meade, co., Ks., U.S. — E3 93
Meade, co., Ky., U.S. — C3 94
Meade, co., S.D., U.S. — C3 118
Meade, stm., Ak., U.S. — B8 79
Meaden Peak, mtn., Co., U.S. — A3 83
Meade Peak, mtn., Id., U.S. — G7 89
Meadow, W.V., U.S. — C4 125
Meadow Creek, stm., W.V., U.S. — n14 125
Meadow Lands, Pa., U.S. — F1 115
Meadow Valley Wash, val., Nv., U.S. — F7 105
Meadowview, Va., U.S. — f10 123
Meadville, Pa., U.S. — C1 115
Meaford, Ont., Can. — C4 73
Meagher, co., Mt., U.S. — D6 103
Mealhada, Port. — E3 12
Meander Creek Reservoir, res., Oh., U.S. — A5 112
Meath, hist. reg., Ire. — H5 7
Meaux, Fr. — D9 10
Mebane, N.C., U.S. — A3 110
Mecca, Ca., U.S. — F5 82
Mecca see Makkah, Sau. Ar. — D2 46
Mechanic Falls, Me., U.S. — D2 96

Mechanicsburg, Oh., U.S. — B2 112
Mechanicsburg, Pa., U.S. — F7 115
Mechanicsville, Ia., U.S. — C6 92
Mechanicsville, Md., U.S. — D4 97
Mechanicville, N.Y., U.S. — C7 109
Mechant, Lake, l., La., U.S. — E4 95
Mechelen, Bel. — D4 8
Mecklenburg, co., N.C., U.S. — B2 110
Mecklenburg, co., Va., U.S. — D4 123
Mecklenburg, hist. reg., Ger. — B12 8
Mecklenburger Bucht, b., Ger. — A11 8
Mecosta, co., Mi., U.S. — E5 99
Medan, Indon. — E2 32
Medanosa, Punta, c., Arg. — F3 56
Medaryville, In., U.S. — B4 91
Meddybemps Lake, l., Me., U.S. — C5 96
Medeiros Neto, Braz. — D8 57
Medellín, Col. — D5 58
Médenine, Tun. — B8 42
Medfield, Ma., U.S. — h10 98
Medford, Ma., U.S. — B5 98
Medford, Mn., U.S. — F5 100
Medford, Ok., U.S. — A4 113
Medford, Or., U.S. — E4 114
Medford, Wi., U.S. — C3 126
Medford Lakes, N.J., U.S. — D3 107
Medgidia, Rom. — E12 16
Media, Pa., U.S. — G11 115
Mediapolis, Ia., U.S. — C6 92
Mediaş, Rom. — C8 16
Medical Lake, Wa., U.S. — B8 124
Medicine Bow, Wy., U.S. — E6 127
Medicine Bow, stm., Wy., U.S. — E6 127
Medicine Bow Mountains, mts., U.S. — E6 127
Medicine Bow Peak, mtn., Wy., U.S. — E6 127
Medicine Hat, Alta., Can. — D5 68
Medicine Lodge, Ks., U.S. — E5 93
Medicine Lodge, stm., U.S. — E4 93
Medina, N.Y., U.S. — B2 109
Medina, Oh., U.S. — A4 112
Medina, Tn., U.S. — B3 119
Medina, Wa., U.S. — e11 124
Medina, co., Oh., U.S. — A4 112
Medina, co., Tx., U.S. — E3 120
Medina, stm., Tx., U.S. — k7 120
Medina see Al-Madīnah, Sau. Ar. — D2 46
Medinaceli, Spain — D9 12
Medina del Campo, Spain — D7 12
Medina de Ríoseco, Spain — D6 12
Mediterranean Sea — D14 2
Medjez el Bab, Tun. — M4 14
Médoc, reg., Fr. — G5 10
Medora, In., U.S. — G5 91
Médouneu, Gabon — A2 44
Medway, Me., U.S. — C4 96
Medway, Ma., U.S. — B5 98
Medway, stm., N.S., Can. — E5 71
Meekatharra, Austl. — E3 50
Meeker, Co., U.S. — A3 83
Meeker, Ok., U.S. — B5 113
Meeker, co., Mn., U.S. — E4 100
Meelpaeg Lake, res., Newf., Can. — D3 72
Meerut, India — F7 38
Meeteetse, Wy., U.S. — B4 127
Mega, Eth. — H2 46
Mégantic, Lac, l., Que., Can. — D7 74
Mégantic, Mont, mtn., Que., Can. — D6 74
Mégara, Grc. — K7 16
Meggett, S.C., U.S. — F7 117
Meghalaya, state, India — H14 38
Meherrin, stm., U.S. — f11 123
Mehlville, Mo., U.S. — f13 102
Mehsāna, India — I5 38
Mehtar Lām, Afg. — C4 38
Mehun-sur-Yèvre, Fr. — E9 10
Meigs, Ga., U.S. — E2 87
Meigs, co., Oh., U.S. — C3 112
Meigs, co., Tn., U.S. — D9 119
Meiktila, Burma — D3 34
Meiningen, Ger. — E10 8
Meissen, Ger. — D13 8
Meixian, China — K5 28
Mekambo, Gabon — A2 44
Mekele, Eth. — F2 46
Meknès, Mor. — B4 42
Mekong, stm., Asia — H8 34
Melaka, Malay. — M7 34
Melanesia, is., Oc. — G23 2
Melbourne, Austl. — G8 50
Melbourne, Ar., U.S. — A4 81
Melbourne, Fl., U.S. — D6 86
Melbourne, Ia., U.S. — C4 92
Melbourne, Ky., U.S. — h14 94
Melbourne Beach, Fl., U.S. — D6 86
Melcher, Ia., U.S. — C4 92
Meldorf, Ger. — A9 8
Mélèzes, Rivière aux, stm., Que., Can. — g12 74
Melfi, Chad — F9 42
Melfi, Italy — I10 14
Melgaço, Port. — C3 12
Melhus, Nor. — E8 6
Melilla, Sp. N. Afr. — A5 42
Melita, Man., Can. — E1 70
Melito di Porto Salvo, Italy — L10 14
Melitopol', Ukr. — H5 22
Melk, Aus. — G15 8
Mellansel, Swe. — E12 6
Melle, Fr. — F6 10
Mellen, Wi., U.S. — B3 126
Mellerud, Swe. — G9 6
Mellette, co., S.D., U.S. — D5 118
Mellish Reef, atoll, Austl. — C11 50
Melo, Ur. — C6 56
Melocheville, Que., Can. — q19 74
Melrhir, Chott, l., Alg. — B7 42
Melrose, Fl., U.S. — C4 86
Melrose, Ma., U.S. — B5 98
Melrose, Mn., U.S. — E4 100
Melrose, N.M., U.S. — C6 108
Melton Hill Lake, res., Tn., U.S. — D9 119
Melton Mowbray, Eng., U.K. — I12 7

Name	Map Ref	Page
Melun, Fr.	D9	10
Melvern Lake, res., Ks., U.S.	D8	93
Melville, La., U.S.	D4	95
Melville, Lake, l., Newf., Can.	A4	72
Melville Hills, hills, N.W. Ter., Can.	C8	66
Melville Island, i., Austl.	B6	50
Melville Island, i., N.W. Ter., Can.	A10	66
Melville Peninsula, pen., N.W. Ter., Can.	C16	66
Melvin, Ky., U.S.	C7	94
Memmingen, Ger.	H10	8
Memphis, Fl., U.S.	p10	86
Memphis, Mi., U.S.	F8	99
Memphis, Mo., U.S.	A5	102
Memphis, Tn., U.S.	B1	119
Memphis, Tx., U.S.	B2	120
Memphis Naval Air Station, mil., Tn., U.S.	B2	119
Mena, Ar., U.S.	C1	81
Menahga, Mn., U.S.	D3	100
Ménaka, Mali	E6	42
Menan, Id., U.S.	F7	89
Menands, N.Y., U.S.	C7	109
Menard, Tx., U.S.	D3	120
Menard, co., Il., U.S.	C4	90
Menard, co., Tx., U.S.	D3	120
Menasha, Wi., U.S.	D5	126
Mendawai, stm., Indon.	F5	32
Mende, Fr.	H10	10
Mendenhall, Ms., U.S.	D4	101
Méndez, Ec.	I3	58
Mendham, N.J., U.S.	B3	107
Mendi, Eth.	G2	46
Mendip Hills, hills, Eng., U.K.	J10	7
Mendocino, co., Ca., U.S.	C2	82
Mendon, Il., U.S.	C2	90
Mendon, Mi., U.S.	F5	99
Mendon, Ut., U.S.	B4	121
Mendota, Ca., U.S.	D3	82
Mendota, Il., U.S.	B4	90
Mendota, Lake, l., Wi., U.S.	E4	126
Mendoza, Arg.	C3	56
Mene de Mauroa, Ven.	B7	58
Mene Grande, Ven.	C7	58
Menemen, Tur.	K11	16
Menfi, Italy	L7	14
Mengzhi, China	C7	34
Mengzi, China	B5	34
Menifee, co., Ky., U.S.	C6	94
Menlo Park, Ca., U.S.	k8	82
Menno, S.D., U.S.	D8	118
Menominee, Mi., U.S.	C3	99
Menominee, co., Mi., U.S.	C3	99
Menominee, co., Wi., U.S.	C5	126
Menominee, stm., U.S.	C6	126
Menominee Indian Reservation, Wi., U.S.	C5	126
Menomonee, stm., Wi., U.S.	m11	126
Menomonee Falls, Wi., U.S.	E5	126
Menomonie, Wi., U.S.	D2	126
Menongue, Ang.	D3	44
Menorca, i., Spain	F16	12
Mentawai, Kepulauan, is., Indon.	F2	32
Menton, Fr.	I14	10
Mentone, In., U.S.	B5	91
Mentor, Oh., U.S.	A4	112
Mentor-on-the-Lake, Oh., U.S.	A4	112
Menzel Bourguiba, Tun.	L4	14
Meoqui, Mex.	C7	62
Meppel, Neth.	C6	8
Meppen, Ger.	C7	8
Mequon, Wi., U.S.	E6	126
Mer, Fr.	E8	10
Meramec, stm., Mo., U.S.	C7	102
Merano (Meran), Italy	C6	14
Merasheen Island, i., Newf., Can.	E4	72
Merauke, Indon.	G11	32
Meraux, La., U.S.	k12	95
Mercaderes, Col.	G4	58
Merced, Ca., U.S.	D3	82
Merced, co., Ca., U.S.	D3	82
Merced, stm., Ca., U.S.	D3	82
Mercedes, Arg.	B5	56
Mercedes, Arg.	C3	56
Mercedes, Tx., U.S.	F4	120
Mercedes, Ur.	C5	56
Mercer, Pa., U.S.	D1	115
Mercer, Wi., U.S.	B3	126
Mercer, co., Il., U.S.	B3	90
Mercer, co., Ky., U.S.	C5	94
Mercer, co., Mo., U.S.	A4	102
Mercer, co., N.J., U.S.	C3	107
Mercer, co., N.D., U.S.	B4	111
Mercer, co., Oh., U.S.	B1	112
Mercer, co., Pa., U.S.	D1	115
Mercer, co., W.V., U.S.	D3	125
Mercer Island, Wa., U.S.	e11	124
Mercer Island, i., Wa., U.S.	e11	124
Mercersburg, Pa., U.S.	G6	115
Mercerville, N.J., U.S.	C3	107
Mercier, Que., Can.	D4	74
Meredith, N.H., U.S.	C3	106
Meredith, Lake, l., Co., U.S.	C7	83
Meredith, Lake, res., Tx., U.S.	B2	120
Meredosia, Il., U.S.	D3	90
Meredosia, Lake, l., Il., U.S.	D3	90
Mergui (Myeik), Burma	H5	34
Mergui Archipelago, is., Burma	H4	34
Meriç (Marica) (évros), stm., Eur.	H10	16
Mérida, Mex.	G15	62
Mérida, Spain	G5	12
Mérida, Ven.	C7	58
Meriden, Ct., U.S.	C4	84
Meriden, Ks., U.S.	C8	93
Meridian, Id., U.S.	F2	89
Meridian, Ms., U.S.	C5	101
Meridian, Pa., U.S.	E2	115
Meridian, Tx., U.S.	D4	120
Meridian Hills, In., U.S.	k10	91
Meridian Naval Air Station, mil., Ms., U.S.	C5	101
Meridianville, Al., U.S.	A3	78
Mérignac, Fr.	H6	10
Merikarvia, Fin.	F13	6
Meriwether, co., Ga., U.S.	C2	87
Merkel, Tx., U.S.	C2	120
Merlin, Ont., Can.	E2	73
Mermentau, La., U.S.	D3	95
Mermentau, stm., La., U.S.	E3	95
Meron, Hare, mtn., Isr.	C4	40
Merriam, Ks., U.S.	k16	93
Merrick, co., Ne., U.S.	C7	104
Merrickville, Ont., Can.	C9	73
Merrill, Ia., U.S.	B1	92
Merrill, Mi., U.S.	E6	99
Merrill, Or., U.S.	E5	114
Merrill, Wi., U.S.	C4	126
Merrillville, In., U.S.	B3	91
Merrimac, Ma., U.S.	A5	98
Merrimack, N.H., U.S.	E4	106
Merrimack, co., N.H., U.S.	D3	106
Merrimack, stm., U.S.	A5	98
Merritt, B.C., Can.	D7	69
Merritt Island, Fl., U.S.	D6	86
Merritt Reservoir, res., Ne., U.S.	B5	104
Merrymeeting Lake, l., N.H., U.S.	D4	106
Merryville, La., U.S.	D2	95
Merseburg, Ger.	D11	8
Merthyr Tydfil, Wales, U.K.	J9	7
Mértola, Port.	H4	12
Merton, Wi., U.S.	m11	126
Méru, Fr.	C9	10
Merwin Lake, res., Wa., U.S.	C3	124
Merzig, Ger.	F6	8
Mesa, Az., U.S.	D4	80
Mesa, co., Co., U.S.	C2	83
Mesabi Range, hills, Mn., U.S.	C6	100
Mesagne, Italy	I12	14
Mesa Mountain, mtn., Co., U.S.	D4	83
Mesa Verde National Park, Co., U.S.	D2	83
Mescalero, N.M., U.S.	D4	108
Mescalero Indian Reservation, N.M., U.S.	D4	108
Mesilla, N.M., U.S.	E3	108
Mesolóngion, Grc.	K5	16
Mesopotamia, reg., Asia	G7	105
Mesquite, Nv., U.S.	G7	105
Mesquite, N.M., U.S.	E3	108
Mesquite, Tx., U.S.	n10	120
Messalo, stm., Moz.	D7	44
Messalonskee Lake, l., Me., U.S.	D3	96
Messina, Italy	K10	14
Messina, S. Afr.	F5	44
Messina, Stretto di, strt., Italy	K10	14
Mesta (Néstos), stm., Eur.	H7	16
Mestre, Italy	D7	14
Meta, stm., S.A.	D9	58
Métabetchouan, Que., Can.	A6	74
Métabetchouane, stm., Que., Can.	A5	74
Metairie, La., U.S.	k11	95
Metamora, Il., U.S.	C4	90
Metán, Arg.	B3	56
Metcalfe, Ont., Can.	B9	73
Metcalfe, Ms., U.S.	B2	101
Metcalfe, co., Ky., U.S.	C4	94
Metedeconk, North Branch, stm., N.J., U.S.	C4	107
Metedeconk, South Branch, stm., N.J., U.S.	C3	107
Meteghan, N.S., Can.	E3	71
Meteghan River, N.S., Can.	E3	71
Meteor Crater, crat., Az., U.S.	C4	80
Methow, stm., Wa., U.S.	A5	124
Methuen, Ma., U.S.	A5	98
Metković, Cro.	F12	14
Metlakatla, Ak., U.S.	D13	79
Metlatonoc, Mex.	I10	62
Metlika, Slo.	D10	14
Metonga, Lake, l., Wi., U.S.	C5	126
Metro, Indon.	k12	33a
Metropolis, Il., U.S.	F5	90
Mettawee, stm., U.S.	E2	122
Metter, Ga., U.S.	D4	87
Mettür, India	G4	37
Metuchen, N.J., U.S.	B4	107
Metz, Fr.	C13	10
Metzger, Or., U.S.	h12	114
Meuse (Maas), stm., Eur.	E5	8
Mexia, Tx., U.S.	D4	120
Mexia, Lake, res., Tx., U.S.	D4	120
Mexiana, Ilha, i., Braz.	D9	54
Mexicali, Mex.	A2	62
Mexico, In., U.S.	C5	91
Mexico, Mo., U.S.	B6	102
Mexico (México), ctry., N.A.	F8	62
Mexico, Gulf of, b., N.A.	F9	76
Mexico City see Ciudad de México, Mex.	H10	62
Meximieux, Fr.	G12	10
Meycauayan, Phil.	q19	33b
Meyersdale, Pa., U.S.	G3	115
Meymaneh, Afg.	C1	38
Meyrueis, Fr.	H10	10
Meždurečensk, Russia	G11	24
Mèze, Fr.	I10	10
Mezőtúr, Hung.	H20	8
Mezquital, Mex.	F7	62
Mezzolombardo, Italy	C6	14
Mhow, India	I6	38
Miami, Az., U.S.	D5	80
Miami, Fl., U.S.	G6	86
Miami, Ok., U.S.	A7	113
Miami, co., In., U.S.	C5	91
Miami, co., Ks., U.S.	D9	93
Miami, co., Oh., U.S.	B1	112
Miami Beach, Fl., U.S.	G6	86
Miami Canal, Fl., U.S.	F6	86
Miami International Airport, Fl., U.S.	G6	86
Miamisburg, Oh., U.S.	C1	112
Miami Shores, Fl., U.S.	G6	86
Miami Springs, Fl., U.S.	G6	86
Miandrivazo, Madag.	E9	44
Mīāneh, Iran	J7	22
Mianus Reservoir, res., U.S.	E1	84
Miānwāli, Pak.	D4	38
Mica Mountain, mtn., Az., U.S.	E5	80
Micco, Fl., U.S.	E6	86
Miccosukee, Lake, res., Fl., U.S.	B2	86
Michelson, Mount, mtn., Ak., U.S.	B11	79
Michie, Tn., U.S.	B3	119
Michigamme, Lake, l., Mi., U.S.	B2	99
Michigamme Reservoir, res., Mi., U.S.	B2	99
Michigan, state, U.S.	E6	99
Michigan, stm., Co., U.S.	A4	83
Michigan, Lake, l., U.S.	C9	76
Michigan Center, Mi., U.S.	F6	99
Michigan City, In., U.S.	A4	91
Michigan Island, i., Wi., U.S.	A3	126
Michikamau Lake, l., Newf., Can.	F20	66
Michipicoten Island, i., Ont., Can.	G15	66
Micronesia, is., Oc.	F23	2
Mičurinsk, Russia	I23	18
Middelburg, Neth.	D3	8
Middelburg, S. Afr.	H4	44
Middelharnis, Neth.	D4	8
Middle, stm., Ia., U.S.	C3	92
Middle Andaman, i., India	H2	34
Middleboro (Middleborough Center), Ma.	C6	98
Middlebourne, W.V., U.S.	B4	125
Middleburg, Fl., U.S.	B5	86
Middleburg, Pa., U.S.	E7	115
Middleburg Heights, Oh., U.S.	h9	112
Middlebury, Ct., U.S.	C3	84
Middlebury, In., U.S.	A6	91
Middlebury, Vt., U.S.	C2	122
Middlefield, Ct., U.S.	C5	84
Middlefield, Oh., U.S.	A4	112
Middle Island Creek, stm., W.V., U.S.	B3	125
Middle Nodaway, stm., Ia., U.S.	C3	92
Middle Park, val., Co., U.S.	A4	83
Middle Patuxent, stm., Md., U.S.	B4	97
Middleport, N.Y., U.S.	B2	109
Middleport, Oh., U.S.	C3	112
Middle Raccoon, stm., Ia., U.S.	C3	92
Middle River, Md., U.S.	B5	97
Middlesboro, Ky., U.S.	D6	94
Middlesex, N.J., U.S.	B4	107
Middlesex, N.C., U.S.	B4	110
Middlesex, co., Ct., U.S.	D5	84
Middlesex, co., Ma., U.S.	A5	98
Middlesex, co., N.J., U.S.	C4	107
Middlesex, co., Va., U.S.	C6	123
Middlesex Fells Reservation, Ma., U.S.	g11	98
Middleton, N.S., Can.	E4	71
Middleton, Id., U.S.	F2	89
Middleton, Ma., U.S.	A5	98
Middleton Reef, atoll, Austl.	E11	50
Middletown, Ct., U.S.	C5	84
Middletown, De., U.S.	C3	85
Middletown, In., U.S.	D6	91
Middletown, Ky., U.S.	g11	94
Middletown, Md., U.S.	B2	97
Middletown, N.J., U.S.	C4	107
Middletown, N.Y., U.S.	D6	109
Middletown, Oh., U.S.	C1	112
Middletown, Pa., U.S.	F8	115
Middletown, R.I., U.S.	E5	116
Middletown, Va., U.S.	A4	123
Middleville, Mi., U.S.	F5	99
Midfield, Al., U.S.	g7	78
Midland, Ont., Can.	C5	73
Midland, Mi., U.S.	E6	99
Midland, N.C., U.S.	B2	110
Midland, Pa., U.S.	E1	115
Midland, Tx., U.S.	D1	120
Midland, co., Mi., U.S.	E6	99
Midland, co., Tx., U.S.	D1	120
Midland City, Al., U.S.	D4	78
Midland Park, Ks., U.S.	g12	93
Midland Park, N.J., U.S.	A4	107
Midland Park, S.C., U.S.	k11	117
Midleton, Ire.	J4	7
Midlothian, Il., U.S.	k9	90
Midlothian, Tx., U.S.	C4	120
Midnapore, India	I12	38
Midongy Sud, Madag.	F9	44
Midvale, Ut., U.S.	C4	121
Midville, Ga., U.S.	D4	87
Midway, B.C., Can.	E8	69
Midway, De., U.S.	F5	85
Midway, Ky., U.S.	B5	94
Midway, Pa., U.S.	G7	115
Midway, Ut., U.S.	C4	121
Midway Islands, dep., Oc.	E1	2
Midwest, Wy., U.S.	C6	127
Midwest City, Ok., U.S.	B4	113
Mielec, Pol.	E21	8
Mieres, Spain	B6	12
Miesbach, Ger.	H11	8
Mifflin, co., Pa., U.S.	E6	115
Mifflinburg, Pa., U.S.	E7	115
Mifflinville, Pa., U.S.	D9	115
Miguel Alemán, Presa, res., Mex.	H11	62
Miguel Auza, Mex.	E8	62
Mihajlovgrad, Bul.	F7	16
Mihara, Japan	H6	30
Mikasa, Japan	p19	30a
Mikkeli, Fin.	F16	6
Mikumi, Tan.	C7	44
Milaca, Mn., U.S.	E5	100
Milagro, Arg.	C3	56
Milagro, Ec.	I3	58
Milam, co., Tx., U.S.	D4	120
Milan, Ga., U.S.	D3	87
Milan, Il., U.S.	B3	90
Milan, In., U.S.	F7	91
Milan, Mi., U.S.	F7	99
Milan, Mo., U.S.	A4	102
Milan, N.M., U.S.	B2	108
Milan, Oh., U.S.	A3	112
Milan, Tn., U.S.	B3	119
Milan see Milano, Italy	D4	14
Milano (Milan), Italy	D4	14
Milâs, Tur.	L11	16
Milazzo, Italy	K10	14
Milbank, S.D., U.S.	B9	118
Mildmay, Ont., Can.	C3	73
Mildura, Austl.	F8	50
Milesburg, Pa., U.S.	E6	115
Miles City, Mt., U.S.	D11	103
Milestone, Sask., Can.	G3	75
Milford, Ct., U.S.	E3	84
Milford, De., U.S.	E4	85
Milford, Il., U.S.	C6	90
Milford, In., U.S.	B6	91
Milford, Ia., U.S.	A2	92
Milford, Me., U.S.	D4	96
Milford, Ma., U.S.	B4	98
Milford, Mi., U.S.	F7	99
Milford, Ne., U.S.	D8	104
Milford, N.H., U.S.	E3	106
Milford, Oh., U.S.	C1	112
Milford, Pa., U.S.	D12	115
Milford, Ut., U.S.	E2	121
Milford Haven, Wales, U.K.	J7	7
Milford Lake, res., Ks., U.S.	C6	93
Milford Station, N.S., Can.	D6	71
Mililani Town, Hi., U.S.	g9	88
Milk River, Alta., Can.	E4	68
Mill, stm., Ma., U.S.	h9	98
Millard, co., Ut., U.S.	D2	121
Millau, Fr.	H10	10
Millbrae, Ca., U.S.	h8	82
Millbrook, Ont., Can.	C6	73
Millbrook, Al., U.S.	C3	78
Mill Brook, stm., Vt., U.S.	B5	122
Millburn, N.J., U.S.	B4	107
Millbury, Ma., U.S.	B4	98
Millbury, Oh., U.S.	e7	112
Mill City, Or., U.S.	C4	114
Millcreek, Ut., U.S.	C4	121
Mill Creek, W.V., U.S.	C5	125
Mill Creek, stm., N.J., U.S.	D4	107
Mill Creek, stm., Oh., U.S.	B2	112
Mill Creek, stm., Tn., U.S.	g10	119
Mill Creek, stm., W.V., U.S.	C3	125
Mill Creek, stm., W.V., U.S.	m13	125
Millcreek Township, Pa., U.S.	B1	115
Milledgeville, Ga., U.S.	C3	87
Milledgeville, Il., U.S.	B4	90
Mille Îles, Rivière des, stm., Que., Can.	p19	74
Mille Lacs, co., Mn., U.S.	E5	100
Mille Lacs, Lac des, l., Ont., Can.	G14	66
Mille Lacs Indian Reservation, Mn., U.S.	D5	100
Mille Lacs Lake, l., Mn., U.S.	D5	100
Millen, Ga., U.S.	D5	87
Miller, S.D., U.S.	C7	118
Miller, co., Ar., U.S.	D2	81
Miller, co., Ga., U.S.	E2	87
Miller, co., Mo., U.S.	C5	102
Miller, Mount, mtn., Ak., U.S.	C11	79
Miller Peak, mtn., Az., U.S.	F5	80
Miller Run, stm., Vt., U.S.	B4	122
Millers, stm., Ma., U.S.	A3	98
Millersburg, In., U.S.	A6	91
Millersburg, Ky., U.S.	B5	94
Millersburg, Oh., U.S.	B4	112
Millersburg, Pa., U.S.	E8	115
Millersport, Oh., U.S.	C3	112
Millersville, Pa., U.S.	F9	115
Millet, Alta., Can.	C4	68
Mill Hall, Pa., U.S.	D7	115
Milliken, Co., U.S.	A6	83
Millington, Mi., U.S.	E7	99
Millington, Tn., U.S.	B2	119
Millinocket, Me., U.S.	C4	96
Millinocket Lake, l., Me., U.S.	B4	96
Millinocket Lake, l., Me., U.S.	C3	96
Millis, Ma., U.S.	B5	98
Millport, Al., U.S.	B1	78
Millry, Al., U.S.	D1	78
Mills, Wy., U.S.	D6	127
Mills, co., Ia., U.S.	C2	92
Mills, co., Tx., U.S.	D3	120
Millsboro, De., U.S.	F4	85
Millsboro, Pa., U.S.	G1	115
Millstadt, Il., U.S.	E3	90
Millstone, stm., N.J., U.S.	C4	107
Milltown, In., U.S.	H5	91
Milltown, N.J., U.S.	C4	107
Milltown [-Head of Bay d'Espoir], Newf., Can.	E4	72
Milltown Malbay, Ire.	I3	7
Millvale, Pa., U.S.	k14	115
Mill Valley, Ca., U.S.	D2	82
Millville, Ma., U.S.	B4	98
Millville, N.J., U.S.	E2	107
Millville, Ut., U.S.	B4	121
Millville Lake, N.H., U.S.	E4	106
Millwood, Wa., U.S.	g14	124
Millwood Lake, res., Ar., U.S.	D1	81
Milner Dam, Id., U.S.	G5	89
Milnor, N.D., U.S.	C8	111
Milo, Ia., U.S.	C4	92
Milo, Me., U.S.	C4	96
Milparinka, Austl.	F7	50
Milroy, In., U.S.	F7	91
Milroy, Pa., U.S.	E6	115
Milstead, Ga., U.S.	C3	87
Milton, Ont., Can.	D5	73
Milton, Fl., U.S.	u14	86
Milton, In., U.S.	E7	91
Milton, Ky., U.S.	B5	94
Milton, Ma., U.S.	B5	98
Milton, N.H., U.S.	D5	106
Milton, Pa., U.S.	D8	115
Milton, Vt., U.S.	B2	122
Milton, Wa., U.S.	f11	124
Milton, W.V., U.S.	C2	125
Milton, Wi., U.S.	F5	126
Milton, Lake, l., Oh., U.S.	A4	112
Miltona, Lake, l., Mn., U.S.	D3	100
Milton Reservoir, res., Co., U.S.	A6	83
Milverton, Ont., Can.	D4	73
Milwaukee, Wi., U.S.	E6	126
Milwaukee, co., Wi., U.S.	E6	126
Milwaukee, stm., Wi., U.S.	m12	126
Milwaukie, Or., U.S.	B4	114
Mimizan, Fr.	H5	10
Mims, Fl., U.S.	D6	86
Min, stm., China	I7	28
Mina, Nv., U.S.	E3	105
Minahasa, pen., Indon.	E7	32
Minamata, Japan	J3	30
Minas, Ur.	C5	56
Minas, Sierra de las, mts., Guat.	G3	64
Minas Basin, b., N.S., Can.	D5	71
Minas Channel, strt., N.S., Can.	D5	71
Minas de Barroterán, Mex.	D9	62
Minas Novas, Braz.	D7	57
Minatare, Ne., U.S.	C2	104
Minatitlán, Mex.	I12	62
Minco, Ok., U.S.	B4	113
Mindanao, i., Phil.	D7	32
Mindanao, stm., Phil.	D7	32
Mindanao Sea, Phil.	D7	32
Mindelheim, Ger.	G10	8
Minden, Ger.	C8	8
Minden, La., U.S.	B2	95
Minden, Ne., U.S.	D7	104
Minden, Nv., U.S.	E2	105
Minden, W.V., U.S.	D3	125
Mindoro, i., Phil.	C7	32
Mindoro Strait, strt., Phil.	C7	32
Mine Hill, N.J., U.S.	B3	107
Mineiros, Braz.	D2	57
Mineola, N.Y., U.S.	E7	109
Mineola, Tx., U.S.	C5	120
Miner, Mo., U.S.	E8	102
Miner, co., S.D., U.S.	D8	118
Mineral, co., Co., U.S.	D4	83
Mineral, co., Mt., U.S.	C1	103
Mineral, co., Nv., U.S.	E3	105
Mineral, co., W.V., U.S.	B6	125
Mineral Point, Wi., U.S.	F3	126
Mineral Springs, Ar., U.S.	D2	81
Mineral Wells, Tx., U.S.	C3	120
Minersville, Pa., U.S.	E9	115
Minersville, Ut., U.S.	E3	121
Minerva, Oh., U.S.	B4	112
Minervino Murge, Italy	H11	14
Minetto, N.Y., U.S.	B4	109
Mingo, co., W.V., U.S.	D2	125
Mingo Junction, Oh., U.S.	B5	112
Minho (Miño), stm., Eur.	D3	12
Minidoka, co., Id., U.S.	G5	89
Minidoka Dam, Id., U.S.	G5	89
Minier, Il., U.S.	C4	90
Minisink Island, i., N.J., U.S.	A3	107
Minitonas, Man., Can.	C1	70
Minna, Nig.	G7	42
Minneapolis, Ks., U.S.	C6	93
Minneapolis, Mn., U.S.	F5	100
Minnedosa, Man., Can.	D2	70
Minnedosa, stm., Man., Can.	D1	70
Minnehaha, co., S.D., U.S.	D9	118
Minneola, Ks., U.S.	E3	93
Minneota, Mn., U.S.	F3	100
Minnesota, state, U.S.	E4	100
Minnesota, stm., Mn., U.S.	G5	100
Minnesota Lake, Mn., U.S.	G5	100
Minnetonka, Mn., U.S.	n12	100
Minnetonka, Lake, l., Mn., U.S.	n11	100
Minnewaska, Lake, l., Mn., U.S.	E3	100
Miño (Minho), stm., Eur.	D3	12
Minocqua, Wi., U.S.	C4	126
Minonk, Il., U.S.	C4	90
Minooka, Il., U.S.	B5	90
Minot, N.D., U.S.	A4	111
Minot Air Force Base, mil., N.D., U.S.	A4	111
Minquadale, De., U.S.	i7	85
Minsk, Bela.	H10	18
Mińsk Mazowiecki, Pol.	C21	8
Minster, Oh., U.S.	B1	112
Mint Hill, N.C., U.S.	B2	110
Minto, N.B., Can.	C3	71
Minto Inlet, b., N.W. Ter., Can.	B9	66
Minturn, Co., U.S.	B4	83
Minturno, Italy	H8	14
Minusinsk, Russia	G12	24
Minute Man National Historical Park, Ma., U.S.	g10	98
Minxian, China	E7	26
Mio, Mi., U.S.	D6	99
Mira, stm., Eur.	D7	14
Mirabel, Que., Can.	D3	74
Miraflores, Col.	G6	58
Miraflores, Col.	G6	58
Miraj, India	D3	37
Miramar, Fl., U.S.	s13	86
Miramar Naval Air Station, mil., Ca., U.S.	F5	82
Miramas, Fr.	I11	10
Mirambeau, Fr.	G6	10
Miramichi Bay, b., N.B., Can.	B5	71
Miranda de Ebro, Spain	C9	12
Miranda do Douro, Port.	D5	12
Mirande, Fr.	I7	10
Mirandela, Port.	D4	12
Mirandola, Italy	E6	14
Mirbāt, Oman	E5	46
Mirebeau-sur-Bèze, Fr.	E12	10
Miri, Malay.	E5	32
Mirnyj, Russia	E16	24
Mirpur Khās, Pak.	H3	38
Mirror Lake, l., N.H., U.S.	C4	106
Mirzāpur, India	H10	38
Misawa, Japan	B14	30
Miscouche, P.E.I., Can.	C6	71
Miscou Island, i., N.B., Can.	B5	71
Miscou Point, c., N.B., Can.	A5	71
Misenheimer, N.C., U.S.	B2	110
Mishawaka, In., U.S.	A5	91
Misheguk Mountain, mtn., Ak., U.S.	B7	79
Mishicot, Wi., U.S.	D6	126
Mishmi Hills, hills, Asia	F16	38
Misima Island, i., Pap. N. Gui.	B10	50
Miskitos, Cayos, is., Nic.	G6	64
Miskolc, Hung.	G20	8

Name	Map Ref	Page
Misool, Pulau, i., Indon.	F9	32
Mispillion, stm., De., U.S.	E4	85
Misrātah, Libya	B9	42
Missaukee, co., Mi., U.S.	D5	99
Missaukee, Lake, l., Mi., U.S.	D5	99
Mission, Ks., U.S.	m16	93
Mission, S.D., U.S.	D5	118
Mission, Tx., U.S.	F3	120
Mission Range, mts., Mt., U.S.	C3	103
Mission Viejo, Ca., U.S.	n13	82
Missisquoi, stm., Vt., U.S.	B3	122
Missisquoi Bay, b., Vt., U.S.	A2	122
Mississauga, Ont., Can.	D5	73
Mississinewa, stm., U.S.	D7	91
Mississinewa Lake, res., In., U.S.	C6	91
Mississippi, co., Ar., U.S.	B5	81
Mississippi, co., Mo., U.S.	E8	102
Mississippi, state, U.S.	C4	101
Mississippi, stm., U.S.	E8	76
Mississippi Delta, La., U.S.	E6	95
Mississippi Sound, strt., U.S.	E5	101
Mississippi State, Ms., U.S.	B5	101
Missoula, Mt., U.S.	D2	103
Missoula, co., Mt., U.S.	D2	103
Missouri, state, U.S.	C5	102
Missouri, stm., U.S.	C7	76
Missouri City, Tx., U.S.	r14	120
Missouri Valley, Ia., U.S.	C2	92
Mistassini, Que., Can.	h12	74
Mistassini, Lac, l., Que., Can.	h12	74
Misti, Volcán, vol., Peru	G4	54
Mistretta, Italy	L9	14
Mita, Punta de, c., Mex.	G7	62
Mitchell, Austl.	E9	50
Mitchell, Ont., Can.	D3	73
Mitchell, Il., U.S.	E3	90
Mitchell, In., U.S.	G5	91
Mitchell, Ne., U.S.	C2	104
Mitchell, S.D., U.S.	D7	118
Mitchell, co., Ga., U.S.	E2	87
Mitchell, co., Ia., U.S.	A5	92
Mitchell, co., Ks., U.S.	C5	93
Mitchell, co., N.C., U.S.	e10	110
Mitchell, co., Tx., U.S.	C2	120
Mitchell, stm., Austl.	C8	50
Mitchell, Lake, res., Al., U.S.	C3	78
Mitchell, Mount, mtn., N.C., U.S.	f10	110
Mitchell Island, i., La., U.S.	E6	95
Mitchellville, Ia., U.S.	C4	92
Mitilíni, Grc.	J10	16
Mitkof Island, i., Ak., U.S.	m23	79
Mito, Japan	F13	30
Mitsiwa, Eth.	E2	46
Mitsuke, Japan	E11	30
Mittenwald, Ger.	H11	8
Mittweida, Ger.	E12	8
Mitú, Col.	G7	58
Mitumba, Monts, mts., Zaire	C5	44
Mitwaba, Zaire	C5	44
Mitzic, Gabon	A2	44
Miura, Japan	G12	30
Mixian, China	A2	28
Miyako, Japan	C14	30
Miyako-jima, i., Japan	C14	30
Miyakonojō, Japan	K4	30
Miyazaki, Japan	K4	30
Miyoshi, Japan	H5	30
Miyun, China	C10	26
Mizdah, Libya	B8	42
Mizen Head, c., Ire.	J3	7
Mizoram, ter., India	I15	38
Mizpe Ramon, Isr.	D4	40
Mizque, Bol.	G5	54
Mjölby, Swe.	G10	6
Mjøsa, l., Nor.	F8	6
Mkalama, Tan.	B6	44
Mladá Boleslav, Czech.	E14	8
Mława, Pol.	B20	8
Mo, Nor.	C10	6
Moab, Ut., U.S.	E6	121
Moanda, Gabon	B2	44
Moapa River Indian Reservation, Nv., U.S.	G7	105
Moate, Ire.	H5	7
Mobara, Japan	G13	30
Mobaye, Cen. Afr. Rep.	H10	42
Moberly, Mo., U.S.	B5	102
Mobile, Al., U.S.	E1	78
Mobile, co., Al., U.S.	E1	78
Mobile, stm., Al., U.S.	E1	78
Mobile Bay, b., Al., U.S.	E1	83
Mobridge, S.D., U.S.	B5	118
Moçambique, Moz.	E7	44
Mocanaqua, Pa., U.S.	D9	115
Mocha, Isla, i., Chile	D2	56
Mochudi, Bots.	F5	44
Mocksville, N.C., U.S.	B2	110
Moclips, Wa., U.S.	B1	124
Môco, Serra do, mtn., Ang.	D3	44
Mocoa, Col.	G4	58
Mococa, Braz.	F5	57
Moctezuma, Mex.	C5	62
Mocuba, Moz.	E7	44
Modane, Fr.	G13	10
Model Reservoir, res., Co., U.S.	D6	83
Modena, Italy	E5	14
Modesto, Ca., U.S.	D3	82
Modica, Italy	M9	14
Mödling, Aus.	G16	8
Modoc, co., Ca., U.S.	B3	82
Modowi, Indon.	F9	32
Moengo, Sur.	B8	54
Moenkopi, Az., U.S.	A4	80
Moffat, Scot., U.K.	F9	7
Moffat, co., Co., U.S.	A2	83
Moffat Tunnel, Co., U.S.	B5	83
Moffett Field Naval Air Station, mil., Ca., U.S.	k8	82
Moga, India	E6	38
Mogadishu see Muqdisho, Som.	H4	46
Mogadore, Oh., U.S.	A4	112
Mogadouro, Port.	D5	12
Mogaung, Burma	B4	34
Mogi das Cruzes, Braz.	G5	57
Mogil'ov, Bela.	H13	18
Mogi-Mirim, Braz.	G5	57
Mogincual, Moz.	E8	44
Mogoča, Russia	G17	24
Mogočin, Russia	F10	24
Mogok, Burma	C4	34
Mogollon Mountains, mts., N.M., U.S.	D1	108
Mogollon Rim, clf, Az., U.S.	C5	80
Mogotón, Pico, mtn., N.A.	H4	64
Mohall, N.D., U.S.	A4	111
Mohave, co., Az., U.S.	B1	80
Mohave, Lake, res., U.S.	H7	105
Mohave Mountains, mts., Az., U.S.	C1	80
Mohave Valley, Az., U.S.	C1	80
Mohawk, N.Y., U.S.	C5	109
Mohawk, stm., N.H., U.S.	g7	106
Mohawk, stm., N.Y., U.S.	C6	109
Mohawk Lake, l., N.J., U.S.	A3	107
Mohawk Mountains, mts., Az., U.S.	E2	80
Moheli, i., Com.	D8	44
Mohican, stm., Oh., U.S.	B3	112
Mohinora, Cerro, mtn., Mex.	D6	62
Mohnton, Pa., U.S.	F10	115
Moi, Nor.	G6	6
Moisie, Que., Can.	h8	72
Moisie, stm., Que., Can.	F19	66
Moissac, Fr.	H8	10
Mojave, Ca., U.S.	E4	82
Mojave, stm., Ca., U.S.	E5	82
Mojave Desert, des., Ca., U.S.	E5	82
Mojjero, stm., Russia	D14	24
Mojo, Eth.	G2	46
Mokapu Peninsula, pen., Hi., U.S.	g10	88
Mokapu Point, c., Hi., U.S.	g11	88
Mokelumne, stm., Ca., U.S.	C3	82
Mokena, Il., U.S.	k9	90
Mokp'o, S. Kor.	E12	26
Moku Manu, i., Hi., U.S.	g11	88
Mol, Bel.	D5	8
Molalla, Or., U.S.	B4	114
Moldau see Vltava, stm., Czech.	F14	8
Molde, Nor.	E6	6
Moldova, ctry., Eur.	H3	22
Molepolole, Bots.	F5	44
Molfetta, Italy	H11	14
Molina de Aragón, Spain	E10	12
Molina de Segura, Spain	G10	12
Moline, Il., U.S.	B3	90
Moline, Mi., U.S.	F5	99
Molins de Rey, Spain	D14	12
Mollendo, Peru	G4	54
Mölln, Ger.	B10	8
Mölndal, Swe.	H9	6
Molodečno, Bela.	G9	18
Molokai, i., Hi., U.S.	B5	88
Molokini, i., Hi., U.S.	C5	88
Molson Lake, l., Man., Can.	B3	70
Molucca Sea see Maluku, Laut, Indon.	F7	32
Moluccas see Maluku, is., Indon.	F8	32
Moma, Moz.	E7	44
Moma, stm., Russia	D22	24
Mombasa, Kenya	B7	44
Mombetsu, Japan	o21	30a
Momence, Il., U.S.	B6	90
Momotombo, Volcán, vol., Nic.	H4	64
Mon, stm., Burma	D3	34
Mona, Canal de la, strt., N.A.	E14	64
Mona, Isla, i., P.R.	E14	64
Monaca, Pa., U.S.	E1	115
Monaco, ctry., Eur.	G9	4
Monadhliath Mountains, mts., Scot., U.K.	D8	7
Monadnock, Mount, mtn., N.H., U.S.	E2	106
Monadnock Mountain, mtn., Vt., U.S.	B5	122
Monahans, Tx., U.S.	D1	120
Monarch Mills, S.C., U.S.	B4	117
Monarch Pass, Co., U.S.	C4	83
Monashee Mountains, mts., B.C., Can.	D8	69
Monastir, Tun.	N5	14
Moncalieri, Italy	D2	14
Monção, Braz.	D9	54
Mönchengladbach, Ger.	D6	8
Monchique, Port.	H3	12
Moncks Corner, S.C., U.S.	E7	117
Monclova, Mex.	D9	62
Moncton, N.B., Can.	C5	71
Mondoñedo, Spain	B4	12
Mondovì, Italy	E2	14
Mondovi, Wi., U.S.	D2	126
Mondragone, Italy	H8	14
Monee, Il., U.S.	B6	90
Monessen, Pa., U.S.	F2	115
Monett, Mo., U.S.	E4	102
Monette, Ar., U.S.	B5	81
Monfalcone, Italy	D8	14
Monforte de Lemos, Spain	C4	12
Monfort Heights, Oh., U.S.	*o12	112
Mong Cai, Viet.	D9	34
Möng Hsat, Burma	D5	34
Monghyr, India	H12	38
Mongo, Chad	F9	42
Mongol Altajn Nuruu, mts., Asia	B5	26
Mongolia, ctry., Asia	B7	26
Mongu, Zam.	E4	44
Monhegan Island, i., Me., U.S.	E3	96
Monida Pass, U.S.	E6	89
Moniteau, co., Mo., U.S.	C5	102
Monitor Range, mts., Nv., U.S.	E5	105
Monitor Valley, val., Nv., U.S.	D5	105
Monmouth, Il., U.S.	C3	90
Monmouth, Or., U.S.	C3	114
Monmouth, co., N.J., U.S.	C4	107
Monmouth Beach, N.J., U.S.	C5	107
Monmouth Mountain, mtn., B.C., Can.	D6	69
Mono, co., Ca., U.S.	D4	82
Monocacy, stm., Md., U.S.	B3	97
Mono Lake, l., Ca., U.S.	D4	82
Monomonac, Lake, l., U.S.	E3	106
Monomoy Island, i., Ma., U.S.	C7	98
Monomoy Point, c., Ma., U.S.	C7	98
Monon, In., U.S.	C4	91
Monona, Ia., U.S.	A6	92
Monona, Wi., U.S.	E4	126
Monona, co., Ia., U.S.	B1	92
Monona, Lake, l., Wi., U.S.	E4	126
Monongah, W.V., U.S.	B4	125
Monongahela, Pa., U.S.	F2	115
Monongahela, stm., U.S.	G2	115
Monongalia, co., W.V., U.S.	B4	125
Monopoli, Italy	I12	14
Monóvar, Spain	G11	12
Monreal del Campo, Spain	E10	12
Monroe, Ga., U.S.	C3	87
Monroe, In., U.S.	C8	91
Monroe, Ia., U.S.	C4	92
Monroe, La., U.S.	B3	95
Monroe, Mi., U.S.	G7	99
Monroe, N.C., U.S.	C2	110
Monroe, N.Y., U.S.	D6	109
Monroe, Oh., U.S.	C1	112
Monroe, Ut., U.S.	E3	121
Monroe, Wa., U.S.	B4	124
Monroe, Wi., U.S.	F4	126
Monroe, co., Al., U.S.	D2	78
Monroe, co., Ar., U.S.	C4	81
Monroe, co., Fl., U.S.	G5	86
Monroe, co., Ga., U.S.	D3	87
Monroe, co., Il., U.S.	E3	90
Monroe, co., In., U.S.	F4	91
Monroe, co., Ia., U.S.	D5	92
Monroe, co., Ky., U.S.	D4	94
Monroe, co., Mi., U.S.	G7	99
Monroe, co., Ms., U.S.	B5	101
Monroe, co., Mo., U.S.	B5	102
Monroe, co., N.Y., U.S.	B3	109
Monroe, co., Oh., U.S.	C4	112
Monroe, co., Pa., U.S.	D11	115
Monroe, co., Tn., U.S.	D9	119
Monroe, co., W.V., U.S.	D4	125
Monroe, co., Wi., U.S.	E3	126
Monroe Center, Ct., U.S.	D3	84
Monroe City, Mo., U.S.	B6	102
Monroe Lake, res., In., U.S.	F5	91
Monroe Park, De., U.S.	h7	85
Monroeville, Al., U.S.	D2	78
Monroeville, In., U.S.	C8	91
Monroeville, Oh., U.S.	A3	112
Monroeville, Pa., U.S.	k14	115
Monrovia, Lib.	G3	42
Monrovia, Ca., U.S.	m13	82
Monrovia, In., U.S.	E5	91
Mons, Bel.	E3	8
Monson, Ma., U.S.	B3	98
Mont-Joli, Que., Can.	A9	74
Montague, P.E.I., Can.	C7	71
Montague, Ca., U.S.	B2	82
Montague, Mi., U.S.	E4	99
Montague, co., Tx., U.S.	C4	120
Montague, Isla, i., Mex.	B2	62
Montague Island, i., Ak., U.S.	D10	79
Montague Peak, mtn., Ak., U.S.	g18	79
Montague Strait, strt., Ak., U.S.	h18	79
Montaigu, Fr.	F5	10
Montalbán, Spain	E11	12
Montalcino, Italy	F6	14
Montalegre, Port.	D4	12
Mont Alto, Pa., U.S.	G6	115
Montana, state, U.S.	D7	103
Montánchez, Spain	F5	12
Montargis, Fr.	D9	10
Montauban, Fr.	H8	10
Montauk, N.Y., U.S.	m17	109
Montbard, Fr.	E11	10
Montbéliard, Fr.	E13	10
Mont Belvieu, Tx., U.S.	E5	120
Montblanch, Spain	D13	12
Montbrison, Fr.	G11	10
Montcalm, co., Mi., U.S.	E5	99
Montchanin, De., U.S.	h7	85
Montclair, Ca., U.S.	m13	82
Montclair, N.J., U.S.	B4	107
Mont Clare, Pa., U.S.	o19	115
Mont-de-Marsan, Fr.	I6	10
Montdidier, Fr.	C9	10
Monteagle, Tn., U.S.	D8	119
Monteagudo, Bol.	G6	54
Monte Azul, Braz.	C7	57
Montebello, Que., Can.	D3	74
Montebello, Ca., U.S.	m12	82
Monte Caseros, Arg.	C5	56
Montecatini Terme, Italy	F5	14
Monte Comán, Arg.	C3	56
Montecristi, Dom. Rep.	E12	64
Montecristi, Ec.	H2	58
Montefiascone, Italy	G7	14
Montego Bay, Jam.	E9	64
Montegut, La., U.S.	E5	95
Montélimar, Fr.	H11	10
Montello, Nv., U.S.	B7	105
Montello, Wi., U.S.	E4	126
Montemorelos, Mex.	E10	62
Montemor-o-Novo, Port.	G3	12
Montendre, Fr.	G6	10
Montenegro, state, Yugo.	G3	16
Montenero di Bisaccia, Italy	H9	14
Montepuez, Moz.	D7	44
Montepulciano, Italy	F6	14
Monte Quemado, Arg.	B4	56
Montereau-faut-Yonne, Fr.	D9	10
Monterey, Ca., U.S.	D3	82
Monterey, Tn., U.S.	C8	119
Monterey, co., Ca., U.S.	D3	82
Monterey Bay, b., Ca., U.S.	D2	82
Monterey Park, Ca., U.S.	m12	82
Montería, Col.	C5	58
Monterotondo, Italy	G7	14
Monterrey, Mex.	E9	62
Montesano, Wa., U.S.	C2	124
Monte Sant'Angelo, Italy	H10	14
Montes Claros, Braz.	D7	57
Montevallo, Al., U.S.	B3	78
Montevarchi, Italy	F6	14
Montevideo, Mn., U.S.	F3	100
Montevideo, Ur.	C5	56
Monte Vista, Co., U.S.	D4	83
Montezuma, Ga., U.S.	D2	87
Montezuma, In., U.S.	E3	91
Montezuma, Ia., U.S.	C5	92
Montezuma, Ks., U.S.	E3	93
Montezuma, co., Co., U.S.	D2	83
Montezuma Castle National Monument, Az., U.S.	C4	80
Montezuma Peak, mtn., Az., U.S.	D3	80
Montgomery, Al., U.S.	C3	78
Montgomery, Il., U.S.	B5	90
Montgomery, La., U.S.	C3	95
Montgomery, Mn., U.S.	F5	100
Montgomery, N.Y., U.S.	D6	109
Montgomery, Pa., U.S.	D8	115
Montgomery, W.V., U.S.	C3	125
Montgomery, co., Al., U.S.	C3	78
Montgomery, co., Ar., U.S.	C2	81
Montgomery, co., Ga., U.S.	D4	87
Montgomery, co., Il., U.S.	D4	90
Montgomery, co., In., U.S.	D4	91
Montgomery, co., Ia., U.S.	C2	92
Montgomery, co., Ks., U.S.	E8	93
Montgomery, co., Ky., U.S.	B6	94
Montgomery, co., Md., U.S.	B3	97
Montgomery, co., Ms., U.S.	B4	101
Montgomery, co., Mo., U.S.	C6	102
Montgomery, co., N.Y., U.S.	C6	109
Montgomery, co., N.C., U.S.	B3	110
Montgomery, co., Oh., U.S.	C1	112
Montgomery, co., Pa., U.S.	F11	115
Montgomery, co., Tn., U.S.	A4	119
Montgomery, co., Tx., U.S.	D5	120
Montgomery, co., Va., U.S.	C2	123
Montgomery City, Mo., U.S.	C6	102
Monthey, Switz.	F13	10
Monticello, Ar., U.S.	D4	81
Monticello, Fl., U.S.	B3	86
Monticello, Ga., U.S.	C3	87
Monticello, Il., U.S.	C5	90
Monticello, In., U.S.	C4	91
Monticello, Ia., U.S.	B6	92
Monticello, Ky., U.S.	D5	94
Monticello, Mn., U.S.	E5	100
Monticello, Ms., U.S.	D3	101
Monticello, N.Y., U.S.	D6	109
Monticello, Ut., U.S.	F6	121
Monticello, Wi., U.S.	F4	126
Montichiari, Italy	D5	14
Montignac, Fr.	G8	10
Montijo, Port.	G3	12
Montijo, Spain	G5	12
Montilla, Spain	H7	12
Montivilliers, Fr.	C7	10
Mont-Joli, Que., Can.	A9	74
Mont-Laurier, Que., Can.	C2	74
Mont-Louis, Que., Can.	J9	10
Montluçon, Fr.	F9	10
Montmagny, Que., Can.	C7	74
Montmorenci, S.C., U.S.	D4	117
Montmorency, co., Mi., U.S.	C6	99
Montmorillon, Fr.	F7	10
Montmort, Fr.	D10	10
Montoro, Spain	G7	12
Montour, co., Pa., U.S.	D8	115
Montour Falls, N.Y., U.S.	C4	109
Montoursville, Pa., U.S.	D8	115
Montpelier, Id., U.S.	G7	89
Montpelier, In., U.S.	C7	91
Montpelier, Oh., U.S.	A1	112
Montpelier, Vt., U.S.	C3	122
Montpellier, Fr.	I10	10
Montréal, Que., Can.	D4	74
Montreal, Wi., U.S.	B3	126
Montréal, Île de, i., Que., Can.	q19	74
Montreal, Lake, l., Sask., Can.	C3	75
Montréal-Nord, Que., Can.	p19	74
Montreat, N.C., U.S.	f10	110
Montreuil-Bellay, Fr.	E6	10
Montreux, Switz.	F13	10
Mont-Rolland, Que., Can.	D3	74
Montrose, B.C., Can.	E9	69
Montrose, Scot., U.K.	E10	7
Montrose, Al., U.S.	E2	78
Montrose, Co., U.S.	C3	83
Montrose, Ia., U.S.	D6	92
Montrose, Mi., U.S.	E7	99
Montrose, Pa., U.S.	C10	115
Montrose, Va., U.S.	m18	123
Montrose, co., Co., U.S.	C2	83
Mont-Royal, Que., Can.	p19	74
Montserrat, dep., N.A.	F16	64
Mont-Tremblant, Parc Provincial du, Que., Can.	C3	74
Montvale, N.J., U.S.	A4	107
Montville, Ct., U.S.	D7	84
Montville, co., U.S.	B6	83
Monument Beach, Ma., U.S.	C6	98
Monument Peak, mtn., Co., U.S.	B3	83
Monument Peak, mtn., Id., U.S.	G4	89
Monument Valley, val., Az., U.S.	A5	80
Monywa, Burma	C3	34
Monza, Italy	D4	14
Monzón, Spain	D12	12
Moodus, Ct., U.S.	D6	84
Moody, Tx., U.S.	D4	120
Moody, co., S.D., U.S.	C9	118
Moon Lake, l., Ms., U.S.	A3	101
Moora, Austl.	F3	50
Moorcroft, Wy., U.S.	B8	127
Moore, Ok., U.S.	B4	113
Moore, co., N.C., U.S.	B3	110
Moore, co., Tn., U.S.	B5	119
Moore, co., Tx., U.S.	B2	120
Moore Dam, U.S.	B3	106
Moorefield, W.V., U.S.	B6	125
Mooreland, Ok., U.S.	A2	113
Moores Creek National Military Park, N.C., U.S.	C4	110
Moores Hill, In., U.S.	F7	91
Moorestown, N.J., U.S.	D3	107
Mooresville, In., U.S.	E5	91
Mooresville, N.C., U.S.	B2	110
Moorhead, Mn., U.S.	D2	100
Moorhead, Ms., U.S.	B3	101
Mooringsport, La., U.S.	B2	95
Moose, stm., N.H., U.S.	B4	106
Moose, stm., N.Y., U.S.	B5	109
Moose, stm., Vt., U.S.	B5	122
Moosehead Lake, l., Me., U.S.	C3	96
Moose Jaw, stm., Sask., Can.	G3	75
Moose Lake, Man., Can.	C1	70
Moose Lake, Mn., U.S.	D6	100
Moose Lake, l., Wi., U.S.	B2	126
Mooseleuk Stream, stm., Me., U.S.	B4	96
Mooselookmeguntic Lake, l., Me., U.S.	D2	96
Moose Mountain Creek, stm., Sask., Can.	H4	75
Moose Mountain Provincial Park, Sask., Can.	H4	75
Moosic, Pa., U.S.	m18	115
Moosup, Ct., U.S.	C8	84
Moosup, stm., U.S.	C1	116
Mopang Lake, l., Me., U.S.	D5	96
Mopti, Mali	F5	42
Moquegua, Peru	G4	54
Mora, Port.	G3	12
Mora, Spain	F8	12
Mora, Swe.	F10	6
Mora, Mn., U.S.	E5	100
Mora, N.M., U.S.	B4	108
Mora, co., N.M., U.S.	A5	108
Mora, stm., N.M., U.S.	A4	119
Morādābād, India	F8	38
Morada Nova de Minas, Braz.	E6	57
Morafenobe, Madag.	E8	44
Moraleda, Canal, strt., Chile	E2	56
Morant Cays, is., Jam.	F9	64
Mor'arovskij Zaton, Russia	F10	24
Moratuwa, Sri L.	I5	37
Morava, hist. reg., Czech.	F17	8
Morava (March), stm., Eur.	G16	8
Moravia, Ia., U.S.	D5	92
Moravia see Morava, hist. reg., Czech.	F17	8
Morawhanna, Guy.	C13	58
Moray Firth, est., Scot., U.K.	D9	7
Morden, Man., Can.	E2	70
More, Ben, mtn., Scot., U.K.	E8	7
More Assynt, Ben, mtn., Scot., U.K.	C8	7
Moreau, stm., S.D., U.S.	B3	118
Moreauville, La., U.S.	C4	95
Morecambe, Eng., U.K.	G10	7
Moree, Austl.	E9	50
Morehead, Ky., U.S.	B6	94
Morehead City, N.C., U.S.	C6	110
Morehouse, Mo., U.S.	E8	102
Morehouse, co., La., U.S.	B4	95
Morelia, Mex.	H9	62
Morella, Spain	E11	12
Morena, India	G8	38
Morenci, Az., U.S.	D6	80
Morenci, Mi., U.S.	G6	99
Moresby Island, i., B.C., Can.	C2	69
Moreuil, Fr.	C9	10
Morey, Lake, l., Vt., U.S.	D4	122
Morey Peak, mtn., Nv., U.S.	E5	105
Morgan, Mn., U.S.	F4	100
Morgan, Ut., U.S.	B4	121
Morgan, co., Al., U.S.	A3	78
Morgan, co., Co., U.S.	A7	83
Morgan, co., Ga., U.S.	C3	87
Morgan, co., Il., U.S.	D3	90
Morgan, co., In., U.S.	F5	91
Morgan, co., Ky., U.S.	C6	94
Morgan, co., Mo., U.S.	C5	102
Morgan, co., Oh., U.S.	C4	112
Morgan, co., Tn., U.S.	C9	119
Morgan, co., Ut., U.S.	B4	121
Morgan, co., W.V., U.S.	B6	125
Morgan City, La., U.S.	E4	95
Morganfield, Ky., U.S.	C2	94
Morgan Hill, Ca., U.S.	D3	82
Morgan Island, i., S.C., U.S.	G6	117
Morgan Point, c., Ct., U.S.	E4	84
Morganton, N.C., U.S.	B1	110
Morgantown, In., U.S.	F5	91
Morgantown, Ky., U.S.	C3	94
Morgantown, Ms., U.S.	D2	101
Morgantown, Tn., U.S.	D8	119
Morgantown, W.V., U.S.	B5	125
Morganza, La., U.S.	D4	95
Mori, Japan	q18	30a
Moriah, Mount, mtn., Nv., U.S.	D7	105
Moriarty, N.M., U.S.	C3	108
Morinville, Alta., Can.	C4	68
Morioka, Japan	C14	30
Morkoka, stm., Russia	D16	24
Morlaix, Fr.	D3	10
Morley, Mo., U.S.	D8	102
Mormon Peak, mtn., Nv., U.S.	G7	105
Morning Sun, Ia., U.S.	C6	92
Mornington Island, i., Austl.	C7	50
Morobe, Pap. N. Gui.	m16	50a
Morocco, In., U.S.	C3	91
Morocco, ctry., Afr.	B4	42
Morogoro, Tan.	C7	44
Morombe, Madag.	F8	44
Morón, Cuba	C8	64
Morondava, Madag.	F8	44
Morón de la Frontera, Spain	H6	12
Moroni, Com.	D8	44
Moroni, Ut., U.S.	D4	121
Morošečnoje, Russia	F25	24
Morotai, i., Indon.	E8	32
Morrill, Ne., U.S.	C2	104
Morrill, co., Ne., U.S.	C2	104
Morrilton, Ar., U.S.	B3	81
Morrinhos, Braz.	D4	57
Morris, Man., Can.	E3	70
Morris, Al., U.S.	B3	78
Morris, Il., U.S.	B5	90

Name	Map Ref	Page
Morris, Mn., U.S.	E3	100
Morris, Ok., U.S.	B6	113
Morris, co., Ks., U.S.	D7	93
Morris, co., N.J., U.S.	B3	107
Morris, co., Tx., U.S.	C5	120
Morrisburg, Ont., Can.	C9	73
Morris Island, i., S.C., U.S.	F8	117
Morrison, Il., U.S.	B4	90
Morrison, co., Mn., U.S.	D4	100
Morrison City, Tn., U.S.	C11	119
Morrisonville, Il., U.S.	D4	90
Morrisonville, N.Y., U.S.	f11	109
Morris Plains, N.J., U.S.	B4	107
Morristown, In., U.S.	E6	91
Morristown, Mn., U.S.	F5	100
Morristown, N.J., U.S.	B4	107
Morristown, Tn., U.S.	C10	119
Morristown National Historical Park, N.J., U.S.	B3	107
Morrisville, N.Y., U.S.	C5	109
Morrisville, Pa., U.S.	F12	115
Morrisville, Vt., U.S.	B3	122
Morro, Ec.	I2	58
Morro, Punta el, c., Chile	B2	56
Morro Bay, Ca., U.S.	E3	82
Morro do Chapéu, Braz.	F10	54
Morrow, Ga., U.S.	C2	87
Morrow, Oh., U.S.	C1	112
Morrow, co., Oh., U.S.	B3	112
Morrow, co., Or., U.S.	B7	114
Moršansk, Russia	H24	18
Morse, La., U.S.	D3	95
Morse Reservoir, res., In., U.S.	D5	91
Morses Creek, stm., N.J., U.S.	k8	107
Mortagne, Fr.	D7	10
Mortagne-sur-Sèvre, Fr.	E6	10
Mortara, Italy	D3	14
Mortes, Rio das, stm., Braz.	G8	54
Morton, Il., U.S.	C4	90
Morton, Ms., U.S.	C4	101
Morton, Tx., U.S.	C1	120
Morton, Wa., U.S.	C3	124
Morton, co., Ks., U.S.	E2	93
Morton, co., N.D., U.S.	C4	111
Morton Grove, Il., U.S.	h9	90
Morton Pass, Wy., U.S.	E7	127
Mortons Gap, Ky., U.S.	C2	94
Morven, mtn., Scot., U.K.	C9	7
Morvi, India	I4	38
Morwell, Austl.	G9	50
Mosbach, Ger.	F9	8
Moscos Islands, is., Burma	G4	34
Moscow, Id., U.S.	C2	89
Moscow, Pa., U.S.	m18	115
Moscow Mills, Mo., U.S.	C7	102
Moscow see Moskva, Russia	F20	18
Mosel (Moselle), stm., Eur.	F6	8
Moselle, Ms., U.S.	D4	101
Moselle (Mosel), stm., Eur.	F6	8
Moses Coulee, val., Wa., U.S.	B6	124
Moses Lake, Wa., U.S.	B6	124
Moses Lake, l., Wa., U.S.	C11	119
Mosheim, Tn., U.S.	B7	44
Moshi, Tan.	D4	126
Mosinee, Wi., U.S.	D9	18
Mosjøen, Nor.	F20	18
Moskva (Moscow), Russia	F3	58
Mosquera, Col.	A5	112
Mosquito Creek Lake, res., Oh., U.S.	D6	86
Mosquito Lagoon, b., Fl., U.S.	J7	64
Mosquitos, Golfo de los, b., Pan.	G8	6
Moss, Nor.	B3	44
Mossaka, Congo	D2	95
Moss Bluff, La., U.S.	B2	44
Mosselbaai, S. Afr.	H4	44
Mossendjo, Congo	E11	54
Mossoró, Braz.	E5	101
Moss Point, Ms., U.S.	E13	8
Most, Czech.	A6	42
Mostaganem, Alg.	F12	14
Mostar, Bos.	C6	56
Mostardas, Braz.	D24	66
Møsting, Kap, c., Grnld.	D6	12
Moswansicut Pond, l., R.I., U.S.	C3	116
Mota del Marquès, Spain	G10	6
Motala, Swe.	F8	7
Motherwell, Scot., U.K.	G11	38
Motīhāri, India	F10	12
Motilla del Palancar, Spain	B2	120
Motley, co., Tx., U.S.	I8	12
Motril, Spain	C3	111
Mott, N.D., U.S.	H4	41
Motueka, N.Z.	G15	62
Motul de Felipe Carrillo Puerto, Mex.	F12	24
Motygino, Russia	D12	64
Mouchoir Passage, strt., N.A.	E3	42
Moudjéria, Maur.	E3	42
Mouila, Gabon	G8	50
Moulamein Creek, stm., Austl.	F10	10
Moulins, Fr.	F3	34
Moulmeingyun, Burma	A2	78
Moulouya, Oued, stm., Mor.	D5	92
Moulton, Al., U.S.	D5	92
Moulton, Ia., U.S.	E7	117
Moultrie, Ga., U.S.	n11	100
Moultrie, co., Il., U.S.	B3	101
Moultrie, Lake, res., S.C., U.S.	F4	90
Mound, Mn., U.S.	D9	93
Mound Bayou, Ms., U.S.	A2	102
Mound City, Il., U.S.	C2	112
Mound City, Ks., U.S.	C9	100
Mound City, Mo., U.S.	B4	125
Mound City Group National Monument, Oh., U.S.		
Moundou, Chad		
Moundridge, Ks., U.S.		
Mounds, Il., U.S.		
Mounds, Ok., U.S.		
Mounds View, Mn., U.S.		
Moundsville, W.V., U.S.		
Moundville, Al., U.S.	C2	78
Mountainair, N.M., U.S.	C3	108
Mountainaire, Az., U.S.	B4	80
Mountain Brook, Al., U.S.	g7	78
Mountain City, Ga., U.S.	B3	87
Mountain City, Nv., U.S.	B6	105
Mountain City, Tn., U.S.	C12	119
Mountain Fork, stm., U.S.	C7	113
Mountain Grove, Mo., U.S.	D5	102
Mountain Home, Ar., U.S.	A3	81
Mountain Home, Id., U.S.	F3	89
Mountain Home Air Force Base, mil., Id., U.S.	F3	89
Mountain Iron, Mn., U.S.	C6	100
Mountain Lake, Mn., U.S.	G4	100
Mountain Lake Park, Md., U.S.	m12	97
Mountain Nile (Bahr al-Jabal), stm., Sudan	G12	42
Mountain Pine, Ar., U.S.	C2	81
Mountainside, N.J., U.S.	B4	107
Mountain View, Ar., U.S.	B3	81
Mountain View, Ca., U.S.	k8	82
Mountain View, Mo., U.S.	D6	102
Mountain View, N.M., U.S.	C3	108
Mountain View, Ok., U.S.	B3	113
Mountain View, Wy., U.S.	E2	127
Mountain Village, Ak., U.S.	C7	79
Mount Airy, Md., U.S.	B3	97
Mount Airy, N.C., U.S.	A2	110
Mount Albert, Ont., Can.	C5	73
Mount Angel, Or., U.S.	B4	114
Mount Arlington, N.J., U.S.	B3	107
Mount Ayr, Ia., U.S.	D3	92
Mount Carmel, Il., U.S.	E6	90
Mount Carmel, Il., U.S.	o13	112
Mount Carmel, Oh., U.S.	C1	112
Mount Carmel, Pa., U.S.	E9	115
Mount Carmel [-Mitchell's Brook-Saint Catherine's], Newf., Can.	E5	72
Mount Carroll, Il., U.S.	A4	90
Mount Clare, W.V., U.S.	B4	125
Mount Clemens, Mi., U.S.	F8	99
Mount Desert Island, i., Me., U.S.	D4	96
Mount Dora, Fl., U.S.	D5	86
Mount Forest, Ont., Can.	D4	73
Mount Gambier, Austl.	H7	50
Mount Gay, W.V., U.S.	D2	125
Mount Gilead, N.C., U.S.	B3	110
Mount Gilead, Oh., U.S.	B3	112
Mount Healthy, Oh., U.S.	o12	112
Mount Holly, N.J., U.S.	D3	107
Mount Holly, N.C., U.S.	B1	110
Mount Holly Springs, Pa., U.S.	F7	115
Mount Hope, Austl.	F7	50
Mount Hope, Ks., U.S.	E6	93
Mount Hope, W.V., U.S.	D3	125
Mount Hope, stm., Ct., U.S.	B7	84
Mount Hope Bay, b., U.S.	D6	116
Mount Horeb, Wi., U.S.	E4	126
Mount Ida, Ar., U.S.	C2	81
Mount Isa, Austl.	D7	50
Mount Jackson, Va., U.S.	B4	123
Mount Jewett, Pa., U.S.	C4	115
Mount Joy, Pa., U.S.	F9	115
Mount Juliet, Tn., U.S.	A5	119
Mount Kisco, N.Y., U.S.	D7	109
Mount Lebanon, Pa., U.S.	F1	115
Mount Magnet, Austl.	E3	50
Mount Morris, Il., U.S.	A4	90
Mount Morris, Mi., U.S.	E7	99
Mount Morris, N.Y., U.S.	C3	109
Mount Olive, Al., U.S.	B3	78
Mount Olive, Il., U.S.	D4	90
Mount Olive, Ms., U.S.	D4	101
Mount Olive, N.C., U.S.	B4	110
Mount Olive, Tn., U.S.	n14	119
Mount Orab, Oh., U.S.	C2	112
Mount Pearl, Newf., Can.	E5	72
Mount Penn, Pa., U.S.	F10	115
Mount Pleasant, Ia., U.S.	D6	92
Mount Pleasant, Mi., U.S.	E6	99
Mount Pleasant, N.C., U.S.	B2	110
Mount Pleasant, Pa., U.S.	F2	115
Mount Pleasant, S.C., U.S.	F8	117
Mount Pleasant, Tn., U.S.	B4	119
Mount Pleasant, Tx., U.S.	C5	120
Mount Pleasant, Ut., U.S.	D4	121
Mount Pocono, Pa., U.S.	D11	115
Mount Prospect, Il., U.S.	A6	90
Mount Pulaski, Il., U.S.	C4	90
Mountrail, co., N.D., U.S.	A3	111
Mount Rainier, Md., U.S.	f9	97
Mount Rainier National Park, Wa., U.S.	C4	124
Mount Revelstoke National Park, B.C., Can.	D8	69
Mount Rogers National Recreation Area, Va., U.S.	D1	123
Mount Rushmore National Memorial, hist., S.D., U.S.	D2	118
Mount Savage, Md., U.S.	k13	97
Mount Shasta, Ca., U.S.	B2	82
Mount Sterling, Il., U.S.	D3	90
Mount Sterling, Ky., U.S.	B6	94
Mount Sterling, Oh., U.S.	C2	112
Mount Uniacke, N.S., Can.	E6	71
Mount Union, Pa., U.S.	F6	115
Mount Vernon, Al., U.S.	D1	78
Mount Vernon, Ga., U.S.	D4	87
Mount Vernon, Il., U.S.	E5	90
Mount Vernon, In., U.S.	I2	91
Mount Vernon, Ia., U.S.	C6	92
Mount Vernon, Ky., U.S.	C5	94
Mount Vernon, Mo., U.S.	D4	102
Mount Vernon, N.Y., U.S.	h13	109
Mount Vernon, Oh., U.S.	B3	112
Mount Vernon, Tx., U.S.	C5	120
Mount Vernon, Wa., U.S.	A3	124
Mount View, R.I., U.S.	D4	116
Mount Washington, Ky., U.S.	B4	94
Mount Wolf, Pa., U.S.	F8	115
Mount Zion, Il., U.S.	D5	90
Moura, Braz.	D6	54
Mourne Mountains, mts., N. Ire., U.K.	G6	7
Moussoro, Chad	F9	42
Moutong, Indon.	E7	32
Moville, Ia., U.S.	B1	92
Mowequa, Il., U.S.	D4	90
Mower, co., Mn., U.S.	G6	100
Moxee City, Wa., U.S.	C5	124
Moxos, Llanos de, pl., Bol.	G6	54
Moyahua, Mex.	G8	62
Moyale, Kenya	H2	46
Moyen Atlas, mts., Mor.	B5	42
Moyeuvre-Grande, Fr.	C13	10
Moyock, N.C., U.S.	A6	110
Moyu, China	B8	38
Možajsk, Russia	F19	18
Mozambique, ctry., Afr.	E6	44
Mozambique Channel, strt., Afr.	E8	44
Mozyr' (Mozyr), Bela.	G3	22
Mpanda, Tan.	C6	44
Mpika, Zam.	D6	44
Mporokoso, Tan.	D8	44
Muang Khammouan, Laos	F8	34
Muang Pakxan, Laos	E7	34
Muar, Malay.	M7	34
Muaratewe, Indon.	F5	32
Mūārī, Rās, c., Pak.	H2	38
Mücheln, Ger.	D11	8
Muchinga Mountains, mts., Zam.	D6	44
Muckleshoot Indian Reservation, Wa., U.S.	f11	124
Mud, stm., Ky., U.S.	C3	94
Mud, stm., Mn., U.S.	B3	100
Mud, stm., W.V., U.S.	C2	125
Mudanjiang, China	C12	26
Mud Creek, stm., Ok., U.S.	C4	113
Muddy Boggy Creek, stm., Ok., U.S.	C6	113
Muddy Creek, stm., Ut., U.S.	E4	121
Muddy Creek, stm., Wy., U.S.	D6	127
Muddy Creek, stm., Wy., U.S.	E5	127
Muddy Creek, stm., Wy., U.S.	C4	127
Muddy Creek, stm., Wy., U.S.	E2	127
Muddy Mountains, mts., Nv., U.S.	G7	105
Muddy Peak, mtn., Nv., U.S.	G7	105
Mud Lake, l., Me., U.S.	A4	96
Mud Lake, l., Nv., U.S.	F4	105
Mudon, Burma	F4	34
Muenster, Tx., U.S.	C4	120
Mufulira, Zam.	D5	44
Mu Gia, Deo (Mu Gia Pass), Asia	F8	34
Muğla, Tur.	H13	4
Mühldorf, Ger.	G12	8
Muhlenberg, co., Ky., U.S.	C2	94
Mühlhausen, Ger.	D10	8
Mühlviertel, reg., Aus.	G14	8
Muhola, Fin.	E15	6
Muirkirk, Md., U.S.	E4	97
Muiron Islands, is., Austl.	D2	50
Muir Woods National Monument, Ca., U.S.	h7	82
Mukden see Shenyang, China	C11	26
Mukilteo, Wa., U.S.	B3	124
Mukwonago, Wi., U.S.	F5	126
Mula, Spain	G10	12
Mulanje, Mwi.	E7	44
Mulberry, Ar., U.S.	B1	81
Mulberry, Fl., U.S.	E4	86
Mulberry, In., U.S.	D4	91
Mulberry, N.C., U.S.	A1	110
Mulberry, stm., Ar., U.S.	B1	81
Mulberry Fork, stm., Al., U.S.	B3	78
Muldraugh, Ky., U.S.	C4	94
Muldrow, Ok., U.S.	B7	113
Muleshoe, Tx., U.S.	B1	120
Mulgrave, N.S., Can.	D8	71
Mulhacén, mtn., Spain	H8	12
Mulhall, Ok., U.S.	A4	113
Mulhouse, Fr.	E14	10
Mull, Island of, i., Scot., U.K.	E6	7
Mullan, Id., U.S.	B3	89
Mullan Pass, Mt., U.S.	D4	103
Mullens, W.V., U.S.	D3	125
Muller, Pegunungan, mts., Indon.	E5	32
Mullet Key, i., Fl., U.S.	p10	86
Mullett Lake, l., Mi., U.S.	C6	99
Mullewa, Austl.	E3	50
Mullica, stm., N.J., U.S.	D3	107
Mullins, S.C., U.S.	C9	117
Multān, Pak.	E4	38
Multnomah, co., Or., U.S.	B4	114
Mulvane, Ks., U.S.	E6	93
Mumbwa, Zam.	D5	44
Mummy Range, mts., Co., U.S.	A5	83
Muna, Pulau, i., Indon.	F7	32
Muncar, Indon.	n17	33a
München (Munich), Ger.	G11	8
Muncie, In., U.S.	D7	91
Muncy, Pa., U.S.	D8	115
Munday, Tx., U.S.	C3	120
Mundelein, Il., U.S.	A5	90
Münden, Ger.	D9	8
Munford, Al., U.S.	B4	78
Munford, Tn., U.S.	B2	119
Munfordville, Ky., U.S.	C4	94
Mungbere, Zaire	H11	42
Munhango, Ang.	D3	44
Munhall, Pa., U.S.	k14	115
Munich see München, Ger.	G11	8
Munising, Mi., U.S.	B4	99
Munster, Ger.	C10	8
Münster, Ger.	D7	8
Munster, In., U.S.	A2	91
Munster, hist. reg., Ire.	I4	7
Munsungan Lake, l., Me., U.S.	B3	96
Munuscong Lake, l., Mi., U.S.	B6	99
Muong Sing, Laos	D6	34
Muqayshit, i., U.A.E.	D5	46
Muqdisho, Som.	H4	46
Mur (Mura), stm., Eur.	I15	8
Mura (Mur), stm., Eur.	I16	8
Murat, Fr.	G9	10
Murat, stm., Tur.	H16	4
Muravera, Italy	J4	14
Murça, Port.	D4	12
Murchison, stm., Austl.	E3	50
Murcia, Spain	H10	12
Murderkill, stm., De., U.S.	D4	85
Murdo, S.D., U.S.	D5	118
Mureș (Maros), stm., Eur.	C5	16
Muret, Fr.	I8	10
Murfreesboro, Ar., U.S.	C2	81
Murfreesboro, N.C., U.S.	A5	110
Murfreesboro, Tn., U.S.	B5	119
Mūrīān, Hāmūn-e, l., Iran	C6	46
Murmansk, Russia	B22	18
Murom, Russia	F25	18
Muroran, Japan	q18	30a
Muros, Spain	C2	12
Muroto, Japan	I7	30
Muroto-zaki, c., Japan	I7	30
Murphy, Mo., U.S.	g13	102
Murphy, N.C., U.S.	f8	110
Murphy Island, i., S.C., U.S.	E9	117
Murphysboro, Il., U.S.	F4	90
Murray, Ia., U.S.	C4	92
Murray, Ky., U.S.	f9	94
Murray, Ut., U.S.	C4	121
Murray, co., Ga., U.S.	B2	87
Murray, co., Mn., U.S.	F3	100
Murray, co., Ok., U.S.	C4	113
Murray, stm., Austl.	F7	50
Murray, Lake, res., Ok., U.S.	C4	113
Murray, Lake, res., S.C., U.S.	C5	117
Murray Head, c., P.E.I., Can.	C7	71
Murraysburg, S. Afr.	H4	44
Murrayville, Il., U.S.	B3	87
Murrells Inlet, S.C., U.S.	D9	117
Murrells Inlet, b., S.C., U.S.	D10	117
Murten, Switz.	F14	10
Murukta, Russia	D14	24
Murwāra, India	I9	38
Murwillumbah, Austl.	E10	50
Mürzzuschlag, Aus.	H15	8
Muş, Tur.	H16	4
Musay'īd, Qatar	D5	46
Muscat and Oman see Oman, ctry., Asia	D6	46
Muscatatuck, stm., In., U.S.	G5	91
Muscatine, Ia., U.S.	C6	92
Muscatine, co., Ia., U.S.	C6	92
Muscat see Masqaṭ, Oman	D6	46
Musclow, Mount, mtn., B.C., Can.	C4	69
Muscoda, Wi., U.S.	E3	126
Muscogee, co., Ga., U.S.	D2	87
Musconetcong, stm., N.J., U.S.	B4	107
Muscooten Bay, l., Il., U.S.	C3	90
Muse, Pa., U.S.	F1	115
Musgrave, Austl.	B8	50
Musgrave Harbour, Newf., Can.	D5	72
Musgrave Ranges, mts., Austl.	E6	50
Musgravetown, Newf., Can.	D5	72
Mushin, Nig.	G6	42
Muskeg Bay, b., Mn., U.S.	B3	100
Muskeget Island, i., Ma., U.S.	D7	98
Muskego, Wi., U.S.	F5	126
Muskego Lake, l., Wi., U.S.	n11	126
Muskegon, Mi., U.S.	E4	99
Muskegon, co., Mi., U.S.	E4	99
Muskegon, stm., Mi., U.S.	E4	99
Muskegon Heights, Mi., U.S.	E4	99
Muskegon Lake, l., Mi., U.S.	E4	99
Muskingum, co., Oh., U.S.	B4	112
Muskingum, stm., Oh., U.S.	C4	112
Muskogee, Ok., U.S.	B6	113
Muskogee, co., Ok., U.S.	B6	113
Musoma, Tan.	B6	44
Musquacook Lakes, l., Me., U.S.	B3	96
Musquodoboit Harbour, N.S., Can.	E6	71
Musselshell, co., Mt., U.S.	D8	103
Musselshell, stm., Mt., U.S.	D9	103
Mussidan, Fr.	G7	10
Mussuma, Ang.	D4	44
Mustafakemalpaşa, Tur.	I12	16
Mustang, Ok., U.S.	B4	113
Mustinka, stm., Mn., U.S.	E2	100
Mut, Tur.	A3	40
Mutare, Zimb.	E6	44
Mutoraj, Russia	E14	24
Mutsu, Japan	A14	30
Mutsu-wan, b., Japan	A13	30
Mutton Mountains, mts., Or., U.S.	C5	114
Muzaffarābād, Pak.	C5	38
Muzaffarnagar, India	F7	38
Muzaffarpur, India	G11	38
Muzon, Cape, c., Ak., U.S.	n23	79
Muztag, mtn., China	B9	38
Muztag, mtn., China	B12	38
Mvuma, Zimb.	E6	44
Mwanza, Tan.	B6	44
Mweelrea, mtn., Ire.	H3	7
Mweka, Zaire	B4	44
Mwenezi, Zimb.	F6	44
Mweru, Lake, l., Afr.	C5	44
Mwinilunga, Zam.	D4	44
Myakka, stm., Fl., U.S.	E4	86
Myanaung, Burma	F3	34
Myaungmya, Burma	F2	34
Myerstown, Pa., U.S.	F9	115
Myingyan, Burma	D3	34
Myitkyinā, Burma	B4	34
Myllymäki, Fin.	E15	6
Mymensingh, Bngl.	H14	38
Mynämäki, Fin.	F13	6
Myrskylä (Mörskom), Fin.	F15	6
Myrtle Beach, S.C., U.S.	D10	117
Myrtle Beach Air Force Base, mil., S.C., U.S.	D10	117
Myrtle Grove, Fl., U.S.	u14	86
Myrtle Point, Or., U.S.	D2	114
Mysen, Nor.	G8	6
Mysore, India	F4	37
Mys Šmidta, Russia	D30	24
Mystic, Ct., U.S.	i9	84
Mystic Lakes, l., Ma., U.S.	g11	98
My Tho, Viet.	I9	34
Mytišči, Russia	F20	18
Mzimba, Mwi.	D6	44
Mzuzu, Mwi.	D6	44

N

Naalehu, Hi., U.S.	D6	88
Naas, Ire.	H6	7
Nabadwīp, India	I13	38
Naberežnyje Čelny, Russia	F8	22
Nabeul, Tun.	M5	14
Nabī Shu'ayb, Jabal an-, mtn., Yemen	E3	46
Nabnasset, Ma., U.S.	A5	98
Nābulus, Isr. Occ.	C4	40
Nacala-Velha, Moz.	D8	44
Naches, stm., Wa., U.S.	C5	124
Nachingwea, Tan.	D7	44
Nachodka, Russia	I20	24
Nacimiento, Lake, res., Ca., U.S.	E3	82
Naco, Mex.	B5	62
Naco, Az., U.S.	F6	80
Nacogdoches, Tx., U.S.	D5	120
Nacogdoches, co., Tx., U.S.	D5	120
Nadiād, India	I5	39
Nadym, stm., Russia	E8	24
Næstved, Den.	I8	6
Naga, Phil.	r20	32
Nagahama, Japan	G9	30
Nagaland, state, India	H16	38
Nagano, Japan	F11	30
Nagaoka, Japan	E11	30
Nāgappattinam, India	G5	37
Nagasaki, Japan	J2	30
Nāgaur, India	G5	38
Nāgda, India	I6	38
Nāgercoil, India	H4	37
Nago, Japan	y27	31b
Nagornyj, Russia	F18	24
Nagoya, Japan	G9	30
Nāgpur, India	B5	37
Nags Head, N.C., U.S.	B7	110
Nagykanizsa, Hung.	H19	8
Nagykőrös, Hung.	H19	8
Naha, Japan	y27	31b
Nahant, Ma., U.S.	g12	98
Nahariyya, Isr.	C4	40
Nahmakanta Lake, l., Me., U.S.	C3	96
Nahunta, Ga., U.S.	E5	87
Naidong, China	F14	38
Nain, Newf., Can.	g9	72
Nāʾīn, Iran	B5	46
Nairn, Scot., U.K.	D9	7
Nairobi, Kenya	B7	44
Najafābād, Iran	B5	46
Nájera, Spain	C9	12
Najin, N. Kor.	C13	26
Nakaminato, Japan	F13	30
Nakatsu, Japan	I4	30
Nakatsugawa, Japan	G10	30
Nakhon Pathom, Thai.	H6	34
Nakhon Phanom, Thai.	F8	34
Nakhon Ratchasima, Thai.	G7	34
Nakhon Sawan, Thai.	G6	34
Nakhon Si Thammarat, Thai.	J5	34
Nakina, Ont., Can.	o18	73
Naknek, Ak., U.S.	D8	79
Naknek Lake, l., Ak., U.S.	D8	79
Nakskov, Den.	I8	6
Nakuru, Kenya	B7	44
Nakusp, B.C., Can.	D9	69
Nal'čik see Nal'čik, Russia	I6	22
Nal'čik, Russia	I6	22
Nalgonda, India	D5	37
Nālūt, Libya	B8	42
Namak, Daryācheh-ye, l., Iran	K8	22
Namangan, Uzb.	I12	22
Namanock Island, i., N.J., U.S.	A3	107
Namapa, Moz.	D7	44
Namatanai, Pap. N. Gui.	k17	50a
Nambour, Austl.	E10	50
Namcha Barwa see Namjagbarwa Feng, mtn., China	F16	38
Nam Co, l., China	E14	38
Nam Dinh, Viet.	D9	34
Namekagon, stm., Wi., U.S.	B2	126
Namekagon Lake, l., Wi., U.S.	B2	126
Namhkam, Burma	C4	34
Namib Desert, des., Nmb.	F2	44
Namibe, Ang.	E2	44
Namibia, ctry., Afr.	F3	44
Namjagbarwa Feng, mtn., China	F16	38
Namlea, Indon.	F8	32
Namna, Id., U.S.	F2	89
Nampa, Id., U.S.	F2	89
Namp'o, N. Kor.	D12	26
Nampula, Moz.	E7	44
Namsos, Nor.	D8	6
Namur, Bel.	E4	8
Nanaimo, B.C., Can.	E5	69
Nanakuli, Hi., U.S.	B3	88
Nanao, Japan	E9	30
Nance, co., Ne., U.S.	C7	104
Nanchang, China	G4	28
Nanchong, China	E8	26
Nancy, Fr.	D13	10
Nanda Devi, mtn., India	E8	38
Nānded, India	C4	37
Nandurbār, India	B3	37
Nandyāl, India	E5	37
Nānga Parbat, mtn., Pak.	C6	38
Nangqian (Xiangda), China	D17	38
Nanjing (Nanking), China	C7	28
Nanking see Nanjing, China	I6	30
Nankoku, Japan	C10	26
Nankou, China	F9	28
Nan Ling, mts., China	C10	34
Nanning, China	I7	28
Nanping, China		
Nansei-shotō (Ryukyu Islands), is., Japan	F12	26
Nansemond, stm., Va., U.S.	k14	123
Nantes, Fr.	E5	10
Nanticoke, Ont., Can.	E4	73
Nanticoke, Pa., U.S.	D10	115
Nanticoke, stm., U.S.	D6	97
Nanton, Alta., Can.	D4	68
Nantong, China	C9	28

Name	Map Ref	Page
Nant'ou, Tai.	L9	28
Nantua, Fr.	F12	10
Nantucket, Ma., U.S.	D7	98
Nantucket, co., Ma., U.S.	D7	98
Nantucket Island, i., Ma., U.S.	D7	98
Nantucket Sound, strt., Ma., U.S.	C7	98
Nantuxent Point, c., N.J., U.S.	E2	107
Nanty Glo, Pa., U.S.	F4	115
Nanuet, N.Y., U.S.	g12	109
Nanuque, Braz.	D8	57
Nanxiang, China	D10	28
Nanxiong, China	J3	28
Nanyang, China	B1	28
Naoetsu, Japan	E11	30
Naoma, W.V., U.S.	n13	125
Naomi Peak, mtn., Ut., U.S.	B4	121
Náousa, Grc.	I6	16
Napa, Ca., U.S.	C2	82
Napa, co., Ca., U.S.	C2	82
Napanee, Ont., Can.	C8	73
Napatree Point, c., R.I., U.S.	G1	116
Napavine, Wa., U.S.	C3	124
Naperville, Il., U.S.	B5	90
Napier, N.Z.	C6	52
Napierville, Que., Can.	D4	74
Naples, Fl., U.S.	F5	86
Naples, Tx., U.S.	C5	120
Naples, Ut., U.S.	C6	121
Naples see Napoli, Italy	I9	14
Napo, stm., S.A.	I6	58
Napoleon, N.D., U.S.	C6	111
Napoleon, Oh., U.S.	A1	112
Napoleonville, La., U.S.	E4	95
Napoli (Naples), Italy	I9	14
Nappanee, In., U.S.	B5	91
Nara, Japan	H8	30
Nara, Mali	E4	42
Naracoorte, Austl.	G8	50
Naramata, B.C., Can.	E8	69
Naranja, Fl., U.S.	G6	86
Narasapur, India	D6	37
Narasaraopet, India	D6	37
Narathiwat, Thai.	K6	34
Nārāyanganj, Bngl.	I14	38
Narberth, Pa., U.S.	p20	115
Narbonne, Fr.	I9	10
Nardò, Italy	I13	14
Narew, stm., Eur.	C21	8
Nārīn Ghar, Afg.	B3	38
Narita, Japan	G13	30
Narmada, stm., India	J5	38
Nārnaul, India	F7	38
Narni, Italy	G7	14
Naro-Fominsk, Russia	F19	18
Narragansett, R.I., U.S.	F4	116
Narragansett Bay, b., R.I., U.S.	E5	116
Narraguagus, stm., Me., U.S.	D5	96
Narrows, Va., U.S.	C2	123
Narsimhapur, India	I8	38
Narssaq, Grnld.	D23	66
Naruto, Japan	H7	30
Narva, Est.	B11	18
Narvik, Nor.	B11	6
Naselle, Wa., U.S.	C2	124
Nash, Tx., U.S.	C5	120
Nash, co., N.C., U.S.	A4	110
Nashawena Island, i., Ma., U.S.	D6	98
Nash Stream, stm., N.H., U.S.	A4	106
Nashua, Ia., U.S.	B5	92
Nashua, N.H., U.S.	E4	106
Nashua, stm., U.S.	E3	106
Nashville, Ar., U.S.	D2	81
Nashville, Ga., U.S.	E3	87
Nashville, Il., U.S.	E4	90
Nashville, In., U.S.	F5	91
Nashville, Mi., U.S.	F5	99
Nashville, N.C., U.S.	B5	110
Nashville, Tn., U.S.	A5	119
Nashwauk, Mn., U.S.	C5	100
Nāsik, India	C2	37
Nāsir, Sudan	G12	42
Naskaupi, stm., Newf., Can.	g9	72
Nassau, Bah.	B9	64
Nassau, co., Fl., U.S.	B5	86
Nassau, co., N.Y., U.S.	E7	109
Nassau, stm., Fl., U.S.	k8	86
Nassau Sound, b., Fl., U.S.	B5	86
Nasser, Lake, res., Afr.	D12	42
Nässjö, Swe.	H10	6
Nasukoin Mountain, mtn., Mt., U.S.	B2	103
Natal, Braz.	E11	54
Natalbany, La., U.S.	D5	95
Natalia, Tx., U.S.	E3	120
Natashquan, stm., Can.	h9	72
Natchaug, stm., Ct., U.S.	B7	84
Natchez, Ms., U.S.	D2	101
Natchitoches, La., U.S.	C2	95
Natchitoches, co., La., U.S.	C2	95
Nāthdwāra, India	H5	38
Natick, Ma., U.S.	B5	98
National City, Ca., U.S.	F5	82
Natron, Lake, l., Afr.	B7	44
Natrona, co., Wy., U.S.	D5	127
Natrona Heights, Pa., U.S.	E2	115
Nattaung, mtn., Burma	E4	34
Natuna Besar, i., Indon.	M10	34
Natuna Besar, Kepulauan, is., Indon.	M10	34
Natuna Selatan, Kepulauan, is., Indon.	M10	34
Natural Bridge, Ut., U.S.	F3	121
Natural Bridge, Va., U.S.	C3	123
Natural Bridges National Monument, Ut., U.S.	F6	121
Naturaliste, Cape, c., Austl.	F3	50
Nauen, Ger.	C12	8
Naugatuck, Ct., U.S.	D3	84
Naugatuck, stm., Ct., U.S.	D3	84
Naumburg, Ger.	D11	8
Naushon Island, i., Ma., U.S.	D6	98
Nautilus Park, Ct., U.S.	D7	84
Nauvoo, Il., U.S.	C2	90
Nava del Rey, Spain	D6	12
Navahermosa, Spain	F7	12
Navajo, co., Az., U.S.	B5	80
Navajo Dam, N.M., U.S.	A2	108
Navajo Indian Reservation, U.S.	A4	80
Navajo Mountain, mtn., Ut., U.S.	F5	121
Navajo National Monument, Az., U.S.	A5	80
Navajo Reservoir, res., U.S.	A2	108
Navalcarnero, Spain	E7	12
Navalmoral de la Mata, Spain	F6	12
Navalvillar de Pela, Spain	F6	12
Navan, Ont., Can.	B9	73
Navan, Ire.	H6	7
Navarin, Mys, c., Russia	E29	24
Navarino, Isla, i., Chile	H3	56
Navarre, Oh., U.S.	B4	112
Navarro, co., Tx., U.S.	D4	120
Navasota, Tx., U.S.	D4	120
Navassa Island, i., N.A.	E10	64
Navoi, Uzb.	I11	22
Navojoa, Mex.	D5	62
Navolato, Mex.	E6	62
Navsāri, India	B2	37
Nawābganj, Bngl.	H13	38
Nawābganj, India	G9	38
Nawābshāh, Pak.	G3	38
Nāwah, Afg.	D2	38
Nawalgarh, India	G6	38
Nawiliwili Bay, b., Hi., U.S.	B2	88
Náxos, i., Grc.	L9	16
Nayak, Afg.	C2	38
Naylor, Mo., U.S.	E7	102
Nayoro, Japan	o20	30a
Nazaré, Braz.	B9	57
Nazaré, Port.	F2	12
Nazareth, Pa., U.S.	E11	115
Nazca, Peru	F4	54
Naze, Japan	w29	31b
Nazilli, Tur.	L12	16
Nazko, stm., B.C., Can.	C6	69
Ndélé, Cen. Afr. Rep.	G10	42
N'Djamena (Fort-Lamy), Chad	F9	42
Ndola, Zam.	D5	44
Neagh, Lough, l., N. Ire., U.K.	G6	7
Neah Bay, Wa., U.S.	A1	124
Néa Páfos (Paphos), Cyp.	B3	40
Neápolis, Grc.	M7	16
Near Islands, is., Ak., U.S.	E2	79
Nebo, Mount, mtn., Ut., U.S.	D4	121
Nebraska, state, U.S.	C6	104
Nebraska City, Ne., U.S.	D10	104
Nechako, stm., B.C., Can.	C5	69
Neches, stm., Tx., U.S.	D5	120
Nechí, Col.	C5	58
Neckar, stm., Ger.	F9	8
Necker Island, i., Hi., U.S.	m15	88
Necochea, Arg.	D5	56
Nederland, Co., U.S.	B5	83
Nederland, Tx., U.S.	E6	120
Nedrow, N.Y., U.S.	C4	109
Needham, Ma., U.S.	g11	98
Needle Mountain, mtn., Wy., U.S.	B3	127
Needles, Ca., U.S.	E6	82
Needville, Tx., U.S.	r14	120
Neenah, Wi., U.S.	D5	126
Neepawa, Man., Can.	D2	70
Neffs, Oh., U.S.	B5	112
Neffsville, Pa., U.S.	F9	115
Negage, Ang.	C3	44
Negaunee, Mi., U.S.	B3	99
Negele, Eth.	G2	46
Negev Desert see Hanegev, reg., Isr.	D4	40
Negley, Oh., U.S.	B5	112
Negombo, Sri L.	I5	37
Negra, Punta, c., Peru	E2	54
Negro, stm., Arg.	E4	56
Negro, stm., S.A.	H12	58
Negros, i., Phil.	C7	32
Neguac, N.B., Can.	B4	71
Nehalem, stm., Or., U.S.	A3	114
Nehbandān, Iran	B7	46
Neheim-Hüsten, Ger.	D7	8
Neiba, Bahía de, b., Dom. Rep.	E12	64
Neijiang, China	F8	26
Neill Point, c., Wa., U.S.	f11	124
Neillsville, Wi., U.S.	D3	126
Nei Monggol Zizhiqu (Inner Mongolia), prov., China	C10	26
Neisse (Nysa Łużycka), stm., Eur.	D14	8
Neiva, Col.	F5	58
Neja, Russia	C26	18
Nekemte, Eth.	G2	46
Nekoosa, Wi., U.S.	D4	126
Nelidovo, Russia	E15	18
Neligh, Ne., U.S.	B7	104
Nel'kan, Russia	F21	24
Nellikuppam, India	G5	37
Nellis Air Force Base, mil., Nv., U.S.	G6	105
Nellore, India	E5	37
Nelson, B.C., Can.	E9	69
Nelson, N.Z.	D4	52
Nelson, Ne., U.S.	D7	104
Nelson, co., Ky., U.S.	C4	94
Nelson, co., N.D., U.S.	B7	111
Nelson, co., Va., U.S.	C4	123
Nelson, stm., Man., Can.	A4	70
Nelsonville, Oh., U.S.	C3	112
Néma, Maur.	E4	42
Nemacolin, Pa., U.S.	G2	115
Nemadji, stm., U.S.	B1	126
Nemaha, co., Ks., U.S.	C7	93
Nemaha, co., Ne., U.S.	D10	104
Nemours, Fr.	D9	10
Nemuro, Japan	p23	30a
Nemuro Strait, strt., Asia	o23	30a
Nenagh, Ire.	I4	7
Nenana, Ak., U.S.	C10	79
Neodesha, Ks., U.S.	E8	93
Neoga, Il., U.S.	D5	90
Neola, Ia., U.S.	C2	92
Neola, Ut., U.S.	C5	121
Neopit, Wi., U.S.	D5	126
Neosho, Mo., U.S.	E3	102
Neosho, co., Ks., U.S.	E8	93
Neosho, stm., Ok., U.S.	A6	113
Nepal (Nepāl), ctry., Asia	D5	36
Nepālganj, Nepal	F9	38
Nepaug Reservoir, res., Ct., U.S.	B3	84
Nepean, Ont., Can.	h12	73
Nepewassi Lake, l., Ont., Can.	A4	73
Nephi, Ut., U.S.	D4	121
Nepisiguit, stm., N.B., Can.	B3	71
Nepisiguit Bay, b., N.B., Can.	B4	71
Neponset, stm., Ma., U.S.	h11	98
Neptune, N.J., U.S.	C4	107
Neptune Beach, Fl., U.S.	B5	86
Neptune City, N.J., U.S.	C4	107
Nerastro, Sarīr, des., Libya	D10	42
Nerčinskij Zavod, Russia	G17	24
Nerechta, Russia	D23	18
Neriquinha, Ang.	E4	44
Nerva, Spain	H5	12
Nesbyen, Nor.	F7	6
Nescopeck, Pa., U.S.	D9	115
Neshanic, stm., N.J., U.S.	C3	107
Neshoba, co., Ms., U.S.	C4	101
Neskaupstadur, Ice.	B5	4
Nesna, Nor.	C9	6
Nesowadnehunk, l., Me., U.S.	B3	96
Nesquehoning, Pa., U.S.	E10	115
Ness, co., Ks., U.S.	D4	93
Ness, Loch, l., Scot., U.K.	D8	7
Ness City, Ks., U.S.	D4	93
Néstos (Mesta), stm., Eur.	H8	16
Netanya, Isr.	C4	40
Netcong, N.J., U.S.	B3	107
Netherlands, ctry., Eur.	E9	4
Netherlands Antilles (Nederlandse Antillen), dep., N.A.	H13	64
Netrakona, Bngl.	H14	38
Nettie, W.V., U.S.	C4	125
Nettilling Lake, l., N.W. Ter., Can.	C18	66
Nett Lake, l., Mn., U.S.	B5	100
Nett Lake Indian Reservation, Mn., U.S.	B6	100
Nettleton, Ms., U.S.	A5	101
Nettuno, Italy	H7	14
Neubrandenburg, Ger.	B13	8
Neuburg an der Donau, Ger.	G11	8
Neuchâtel, Switz.	F13	10
Neuchâtel, Lac de, l., Switz.	F13	10
Neufchâteau, Bel.	F5	8
Neufchâteau, Fr.	D12	10
Neufchâtel-en-Bray, Fr.	C8	10
Neuillé-Pont-Pierre, Fr.	E7	10
Neumünster, Ger.	A9	8
Neunkirchen, Aus.	H16	8
Neunkirchen/Saar, Ger.	F7	8
Neuquén, Arg.	D3	56
Neuruppin, Ger.	C12	8
Neuse, stm., N.C., U.S.	B6	110
Neusiedler See, l., Eur.	H16	8
Neuss, Ger.	D6	8
Neustadt Jan der Aisch—, Ger.	F10	8
Neustadt in Holstein, Ger.	A10	8
Neustrelitz, Ger.	B13	8
Neu-Ulm, Ger.	G10	8
Neustadt an der Weinstrasse, Ger.	F8	8
Nevada, Ia., U.S.	B4	92
Nevada, Mo., U.S.	D3	102
Nevada, co., Ar., U.S.	D2	81
Nevada, co., Ca., U.S.	C3	82
Nevada, state, U.S.	D5	105
Nevada, Sierra, mts., Spain	H8	12
Nevada, Sierra, mts., Ca., U.S.	D4	82
Nevada City, Ca., U.S.	C3	82
Nevado, Cerro, mtn., Arg.	D3	56
Nevado, Cerro, mtn., Col.	F5	58
Nevers, Fr.	E10	10
Neversink, stm., N.Y., U.S.	D6	109
Nevis, i., St. K./N.	F16	64
Nevis, Ben, mtn., Scot., U.K.	E7	7
New, stm., U.S.	C3	125
New, stm., Az., U.S.	k8	80
New, stm., N.C., U.S.	C5	110
New Albany, In., U.S.	H6	91
New Albany, Ms., U.S.	A4	101
New Albany, Oh., U.S.	k11	112
New Amsterdam, Guy.	D14	58
Newark, Ar., U.S.	B4	81
Newark, Ca., U.S.	h8	82
Newark, De., U.S.	B3	85
Newark, Il., U.S.	B5	90
Newark, N.J., U.S.	B4	107
Newark, N.Y., U.S.	B3	109
Newark, Oh., U.S.	B3	112
Newark Bay, b., N.J., U.S.	k8	107
Newark Lake, l., Nv., U.S.	D6	105
New Athens, Il., U.S.	E4	90
New Augusta, Ms., U.S.	D4	101
Newaygo, Mi., U.S.	E5	99
Newaygo, co., Mi., U.S.	E5	99
New Baden, Il., U.S.	E4	90
New Baltimore, Mi., U.S.	F8	99
New Bedford, Ma., U.S.	C6	98
New Bedford, Pa., U.S.	D1	115
Newberg, Or., U.S.	B4	114
New Berlin, Wi., U.S.	n11	126
New Bern, N.C., U.S.	B5	110
Newbern, Tn., U.S.	A2	119
Newberry, Fl., U.S.	C4	86
Newberry, Mi., U.S.	B5	99
Newberry, S.C., U.S.	C4	117
Newberry, co., S.C., U.S.	C4	117
New Bethlehem, Pa., U.S.	D3	115
New Bloomfield, Pa., U.S.	F7	115
New Boston, Mi., U.S.	p15	99
New Boston, Oh., U.S.	D3	112
New Boston, Tx., U.S.	C5	120
New Braunfels, Tx., U.S.	E3	120
New Bremen, Oh., U.S.	B1	112
New Brighton, Mn., U.S.	m12	100
New Brighton, Pa., U.S.	E1	115
New Britain, Ct., U.S.	C4	84
New Britain, i., Pap. N. Gui.	m16	50a
New Brockton, Al., U.S.	D4	78
New Brunswick, N.J., U.S.	C4	107
New Brunswick, prov., Can.	C3	71
New Buffalo, Mi., U.S.	G4	99
Newburg, Wi., U.S.	E5	126
Newburgh, Ont., Can.	C8	73
Newburgh, In., U.S.	I3	91
Newburgh, N.Y., U.S.	D6	109
Newburgh Heights, Oh., U.S.	h9	112
Newburyport, Ma., U.S.	A6	98
New Caledonia, dep., Oc.	H24	2
New Canaan, Ct., U.S.	E2	84
New Carlisle, In., U.S.	A4	91
New Carlisle, Oh., U.S.	C1	112
Newcastle, Austl.	F10	50
Newcastle, N.B., Can.	C4	71
Newcastle, S. Afr.	G5	44
Newcastle, S. Ire., U.K.	G7	7
New Castle, Al., U.S.	B3	78
New Castle, Co., U.S.	B3	83
New Castle, De., U.S.	B3	85
New Castle, In., U.S.	E7	91
New Castle, Ky., U.S.	B4	94
New Castle, Pa., U.S.	D1	115
Newcastle, Ok., U.S.	B4	113
New Castle, co., De., U.S.	B3	85
New Castle, Wy., U.S.	C8	127
Newcastle upon Tyne, Eng., U.K.	G11	7
Newcastle Waters, Austl.	C6	50
New City, N.Y., U.S.	D6	109
Newcomerstown, Oh., U.S.	B4	112
New Concord, Oh., U.S.	C4	112
New Cumberland, Pa., U.S.	F8	115
New Cumberland, W.V., U.S.	A4	125
Newdegate, Austl.	F3	50
New Delhi, India	F7	38
Newell, Ia., U.S.	B2	92
Newell, S.D., U.S.	C2	118
Newell, W.V., U.S.	A4	125
New Ellenton, S.C., U.S.	E4	117
New England, N.D., U.S.	C3	111
Newenham, Cape, c., Ak., U.S.	D7	79
Newfane, N.Y., U.S.	B2	109
Newfields, N.H., U.S.	D5	106
New Florence, Mo., U.S.	C6	102
Newfound Gap, U.S.	f9	110
Newfound Lake, l., N.H., U.S.	C3	106
Newfoundland, prov., Can.	D4	72
Newfoundland, i., Newf., Can.	D3	72
New Franklin, Mo., U.S.	B5	102
New Freedom, Pa., U.S.	G8	115
New Georgia, i., Sol.Is.	A11	50
New Germany, N.S., Can.	E5	71
New Glarus, Wi., U.S.	F4	126
New Guinea, i.	m14	50a
Newhall, Ia., U.S.	C6	92
New Hampshire, state, U.S.	C3	106
New Hampton, Ia., U.S.	A5	92
New Hanover, co., N.C., U.S.	C5	110
New Hanover, i., Pap. N. Gui.	k17	50a
New Harbour, Newf., Can.	E5	72
New Harmony, In., U.S.	H2	91
New Hartford, Ct., U.S.	B4	84
New Hartford, Ia., U.S.	B5	92
New Haven, Ct., U.S.	D4	84
New Haven, In., U.S.	B7	91
New Haven, Ky., U.S.	C4	94
New Haven, Mi., U.S.	F8	99
New Haven, Mo., U.S.	C6	102
New Haven, W.V., U.S.	C3	125
New Haven, co., Ct., U.S.	D4	84
New Haven, stm., Vt., U.S.	C2	122
New Haven Harbor, b., Ct., U.S.	E4	84
New Hazelton, B.C., Can.	B4	69
New Hebrides see Vanuatu, ctry., Oc.	H24	2
New Holland, Ga., U.S.	B3	87
New Holland, Pa., U.S.	F9	115
New Holstein, Wi., U.S.	E5	126
New Hope, Al., U.S.	A3	78
New Hope, Ky., U.S.	C4	94
New Hope, Mn., U.S.	m12	100
New Hope, Pa., U.S.	F12	115
New Hudson, Mi., U.S.	o14	99
New Iberia, La., U.S.	D4	95
Newington, Ct., U.S.	C5	84
New Inlet, b., N.C., U.S.	D5	110
New Ireland, i., Pap. N. Gui.	k17	50a
New Jersey, state, U.S.	C4	107
New Johnsonville, Tn., U.S.	A4	119
New Kensington, Pa., U.S.	E2	115
New Kent, co., Va., U.S.	C5	123
Newkirk, Ok., U.S.	A4	113
New Laguna, N.M., U.S.	B2	108
New Lake, l., N.C., U.S.	B6	110
New Lenox, Il., U.S.	B6	90
New Lexington, Oh., U.S.	C3	112
New Lisbon, Wi., U.S.	E3	126
New Liskeard, Ont., Can.	p20	73
Newllano, La., U.S.	C2	95
New London, Ct., U.S.	D7	84
New London, Ia., U.S.	D6	92
New London, Mn., U.S.	E4	100
New London, Mo., U.S.	B6	102
New London, Oh., U.S.	A3	112
New London, Wi., U.S.	D5	126
New London, co., Ct., U.S.	C7	84
New London Submarine Base, mil., Ct., U.S.	D7	84
New Madison, Oh., U.S.	C1	112
New Madrid, Mo., U.S.	E8	102
New Madrid, co., Mo., U.S.	E8	102
Newman, Ca., U.S.	D3	82
Newman, Il., U.S.	D6	90
New Manchester, W.V., U.S.	e8	125
Newman Grove, Ne., U.S.	C8	104
Newman Lake, l., Wa., U.S.	B8	124
Newmanstown, Pa., U.S.	F9	115
New Market, Ont., Can.	C5	73
New Market, Al., U.S.	A3	78
New Market, In., U.S.	E4	91
Newmarket, N.H., U.S.	D5	106
New Market, Tn., U.S.	C10	119
New Market, Va., U.S.	B4	123
New Martinsville, W.V., U.S.	B4	125
New Matamoras, Oh., U.S.	C4	112
New Mexico, state, U.S.	C3	108
New Miami, Oh., U.S.	C1	112
New Milford, Ct., U.S.	C2	84
New Milford, N.J., U.S.	h8	107
New Milford, Pa., U.S.	C10	115
Newnan, Ga., U.S.	C2	87
Newnans Lake, l., Fl., U.S.	C4	86
New Norfolk, Austl.	H9	50
New Orleans, La., U.S.	E5	95
New Orleans Naval Air Station, mil., La., U.S.	k11	95
New Oxford, Pa., U.S.	G7	115
New Palestine, In., U.S.	E6	91
New Paltz, N.Y., U.S.	D6	109
New Paris, In., U.S.	B6	91
New Paris, Oh., U.S.	C1	112
New Philadelphia, Oh., U.S.	B4	112
New Philadelphia, Pa., U.S.	E9	115
New Plymouth, N.Z.	C5	52
New Plymouth, Id., U.S.	F2	89
New Point Comfort, c., Va., U.S.	C6	123
Newport, Eng., U.K.	K11	7
Newport, Wales, U.K.	J9	7
Newport, Ar., U.S.	B4	81
Newport, De., U.S.	B3	85
Newport, In., U.S.	E3	91
Newport, Ky., U.S.	A5	94
Newport, Me., U.S.	D3	96
Newport, Mi., U.S.	G7	99
Newport, N.H., U.S.	D2	106
Newport, N.C., U.S.	C6	110
Newport, Oh., U.S.	C4	112
Newport, Or., U.S.	C2	114
Newport, Pa., U.S.	F7	115
Newport, R.I., U.S.	F5	116
Newport, Tn., U.S.	D10	119
Newport, Vt., U.S.	B4	122
Newport, Wa., U.S.	A8	124
Newport, co., R.I., U.S.	E5	116
Newport Beach, Ca., U.S.	n13	82
Newport News, Va., U.S.	D6	123
New Port Richey, Fl., U.S.	D4	86
New Prague, Mn., U.S.	F5	100
New Preston, Ct., U.S.	C2	84
New Providence, N.J., U.S.	B4	107
New Providence, i., Bah.	B9	64
Newquay, Eng., U.K.	K7	7
New Richland, Mn., U.S.	G5	100
New Richmond, Que., Can.	A4	71
New Richmond, Oh., U.S.	D1	112
New Richmond, Wi., U.S.	C1	126
New River Inlet, b., N.C., U.S.	C5	110
New Roads, La., U.S.	D4	95
New Rochelle, N.Y., U.S.	E7	109
New Rockford, N.D., U.S.	B7	111
New Ross, Ire.	I6	7
Newry, N. Ire., U.K.	G6	7
New Salem, N.D., U.S.	C4	111
New Sarpy, La., U.S.	k11	95
New Sharon, Ia., U.S.	C5	92
New Site, Al., U.S.	B4	78
New Smyrna Beach, Fl., U.S.	C6	86
New South Wales, state, Austl.	F9	50
New Straitsville, Oh., U.S.	C3	112
New Tazewell, Tn., U.S.	C10	119
Newton, Al., U.S.	D4	78
Newton, Ga., U.S.	E2	87
Newton, Il., U.S.	E5	90
Newton, Ia., U.S.	C4	92
Newton, Ks., U.S.	D6	93
Newton, Ma., U.S.	B5	98
Newton, Ms., U.S.	C4	101
Newton, N.J., U.S.	A3	107
Newton, N.C., U.S.	B1	110
Newton, Tx., U.S.	D6	120
Newton, Ut., U.S.	B4	121
Newton, co., Ar., U.S.	B2	81
Newton, co., Ga., U.S.	C3	87
Newton, co., In., U.S.	B3	91
Newton, co., Ms., U.S.	C4	101
Newton, co., Mo., U.S.	E3	102
Newton, co., Tx., U.S.	D6	120
Newton Falls, Oh., U.S.	A5	112
Newton Lake, res., Il., U.S.	E5	90
Newtown, Ct., U.S.	D2	84
New Town, N.D., U.S.	B3	111
Newtown, Oh., U.S.	C1	112
Newtownabbey, N. Ire., U.K.	G7	7
Newtownards, N. Ire., U.K.	G7	7
Newtown Square, Pa., U.S.	p20	115
New Ulm, Mn., U.S.	F4	100
New Vienna, Oh., U.S.	C2	112
Newville, Pa., U.S.	F7	115
New Washington, In., U.S.	G6	91
New Washington, Oh., U.S.	B3	112
New Waterford, Oh., U.S.	B5	112
New Westminster, B.C., Can.	E6	69
New Whiteland, In., U.S.	E5	91
New Wilmington, Pa., U.S.	D1	115
New Windsor, Il., U.S.	B3	90
New Windsor, Md., U.S.	A3	97
New Windsor, N.Y., U.S.	D6	109
New World Island, i., Newf., Can.	D4	72
New York, co., N.Y., U.S.	k13	109
New York, state, U.S.	C6	109
New York Mills, Mn., U.S.	D3	100
New Zealand, ctry., Oc.		
Nežin, Ukr.	G4	22
Nez Perce, co., Id., U.S.	C2	89
Nez Perce Indian Reservation, Id., U.S.	C2	89
Ngami, Lake, l., Bots.	F4	44
Nganglong Kangri, mts., China	D10	38
Nganjuk, Indon.	m15	33a
Ngaoundéré, Cam.	G8	42

Name	Map Ref	Page

Nguigmi, Niger ... F8 42
Nguru, Nig. ... F8 42
Nha Trang, Viet. ... H10 34
Niafounké, Mali ... E5 42
Niagara, Wi., U.S. ... C6 126
Niagara, co., N.Y., U.S. ... B2 109
Niagara Falls, Ont., Can. ... D5 73
Niagara Falls, N.Y., U.S. ... B1 109
Niagara-on-the-Lake, Ont., Can. ... D5 73
Niamey, Niger ... F6 42
Niangara, Zaire ... H11 42
Niangua, stm., Mo., U.S. ... D5 102
Niantic, Ct., U.S. ... D7 84
Nias, Pulau, i., Indon. ... N4 34
Nibley, Ut., U.S. ... B4 121
Nicaragua, ctry., N.A. ... H5 64
Nicaragua, Lago de, l., Nic. ... I5 64
Nicastro (Lamezia Terme), Italy ... K11 14
Nicatous Lake, l., Me., U.S. ... C4 96
Nice, Fr. ... I14 10
Niceville, Fl., U.S. ... u15 86
Nichinan, Japan ... K4 30
Nicholas, co., Ky., U.S. ... B6 94
Nicholas, co., W.V., U.S. ... C4 125
Nicholas Channel, strt., N.A. ... C7 64
Nicholasville, Ky., U.S. ... C5 94
Nicholls, Ga., U.S. ... E4 87
Nichols Hills, Ok., U.S. ... B4 113
Nicholson, Ms., U.S. ... E4 101
Nickajack Res., res., Tn., U.S. ... D8 119
Nickel Centre, Ont., Can. ... p19 73
Nickerson, Ks., U.S. ... D5 93
Nicobar Islands, is., India ... J2 34
Nicolet, Que., Can. ... C5 74
Nicolet, stm., Que., Can. ... C5 74
Nicolet, Lake, l., Mi., U.S. ... B6 99
Nicollet, Mn., U.S. ... F4 100
Nicollet, co., Mn., U.S. ... F4 100
Nicolls Town, Bah. ... B8 64
Nicoma Park, Ok., U.S. ... B4 113
Nicosia, Cyp. ... B3 40
Nicosia, N. Cyp. ... B3 40
Nicosia, Italy ... L9 14
Nicoya, Golfo de, b., C.R. ... J5 64
Nicoya, Península de, pen., C.R. ... I5 64
Niebüll, Ger. ... A8 8
Nienburg, Ger. ... C9 8
Nieuw Nickerie, Sur. ... B7 54
Nieves, Mex. ... E8 62
Nigadoo, N.B., Can. ... B4 71
Niger, ctry., Afr. ... E7 42
Niger, stm., Afr. ... G7 42
Nigeria, ctry., Afr. ... G7 42
Nigríta, Grc. ... I7 16
Nihoa, i., Hi., U.S. ... m15 88
Niigata, Japan ... E12 30
Niihama, Japan ... I6 30
Niihau, i., Hi., U.S. ... B1 88
Niinisalo, Fin. ... F14 6
Niitsu, Japan ... E12 30
Nijar, Spain ... I9 12
Nijmegen, Neth. ... D5 8
Nikishka, Ak., U.S. ... g16 79
Nikkō, Japan ... F12 30
Nikolajev, Ukr. ... H4 22
Nikolajevsk-na-Amure, Russia ... G22 24
Nikolayev see Nikolajev, Ukr. ... H4 22
Nikšić, Yugo. ... G2 16
Niland, Ca., U.S. ... F6 82
Nile (Nahr an-Nil), stm., Afr. ... C12 42
Niles, Il., U.S. ... h9 90
Niles, Mi., U.S. ... G4 99
Niles, Oh., U.S. ... A5 112
Nileshwar, India ... F3 37
Nīmach, India ... H6 38
Nimba, Mont, mtn., Afr. ... G4 42
Nîmes, Fr. ... I11 10
Nimrod Lake, res., Ar., U.S. ... C2 81
Nine Degree Channel, strt., India ... H2 37
Nine Mile Creek, stm., Ut., U.S. ... D5 121
Ninemile Point, c., Mi., U.S. ... C6 99
Ninety Six, S.C., U.S. ... F10 28
Ningbo, China ... C9 34
Ningming, China ... C9 34
Ningxia Huizu Zizhiqu, prov., China ... D8 26
Ninh Binh, Viet. ... D8 34
Ninigret Pond, l., R.I., U.S. ... G2 116
Ninilchik, Ak., U.S. ... C9 79
Ninnescah, stm., Ks., U.S. ... E6 93
Niobrara, co., Wy., U.S. ... C8 127
Niobrara, stm., U.S. ... B7 104
Niono, Mali ... F4 42
Nioro du Sahel, Mali ... E4 42
Niort, Fr. ... F6 10
Niota, Tn., U.S. ... D9 119
Nipāni, India ... D3 37
Nipigon, Lake, l., Ont., Can. ... o17 73
Nipissing, Lake, l., Ont., Can. ... A5 73
Nipomo, Ca., U.S. ... E3 82
Nipple Mountain, mtn., Co., U.S. ... C5 37
Nirmal, India ... F5 16
Niš, Yugo. ... F4 12
Nisa, Port. ... u30 31b
Nishinoomote, Japan ... H7 30
Nishiwaki, Japan ... C7 109
Niskayuna, N.Y., U.S. ... C3 124
Nisqually, stm., Wa., U.S. ... D4 100
Nisswa, Mn., U.S. ... G7 57
Niterói, Braz. ... G18 8
Nitra, Czech. ... C3 125
Nitro, W.V., U.S. ... H1 2
Niue, dep., Oc. ... E4 8
Nivelles, Bel. ... E3 70
Niverville, Man., Can. ... A5 83
Niwot, Co., U.S. ... D4 102
Nixa, Mo., U.S. ... D2 105
Nixon, Nv., U.S. ... E4 120
Nixon, Tx., U.S. ... C5 40
Nizāmābād, India ... A5 40
Nizip, Tur. ... F13 24
Nižn'aja Pojma, Russia ... E12 24
Nižn'aja Tunguska, stm., Russia ...

Nižneangarsk, Russia ... F15 24
Nižneilimsk, Russia ... F14 24
Nižneudinsk, Russia ... G13 24
Nižnij Novgorod (Gorki), Russia ... E27 18
Nizza Monferrato, Italy ... E3 14
Njombe, Tan. ... C6 44
Nkhota Kota, Mwi. ... D6 44
Nkongsamba, Cam. ... H7 42
Noākhāli, Bngl. ... I14 38
Noank, Ct., U.S. ... D8 84
Noatak, Ak., U.S. ... B7 79
Noatak, stm., Ak., U.S. ... B7 79
Nobel, Ont., Can. ... B4 73
Nobeoka, Japan ... J4 30
Noble, Ok., U.S. ... B4 113
Noble, co., Il., U.S. ... B7 91
Noble, co., In., U.S. ... B7 91
Noble, co., Oh., U.S. ... C4 112
Noble, co., Ok., U.S. ... A4 113
Nobles, co., Mn., U.S. ... G3 100
Noblesville, In., U.S. ... D6 91
Noboribetsu, Japan ... q19 30a
Nocatee, Fl., U.S. ... E5 86
Nochixtlán, Mex. ... I11 62
Nocona, Tx., U.S. ... C4 120
Nodaway, co., Mo., U.S. ... A3 102
Nodaway, stm., U.S. ... A2 102
Noel, Mo., U.S. ... E3 102
Nogales, Mex. ... B4 62
Nogales, Az., U.S. ... F5 80
Nōgata, Japan ... I3 30
Nogent-le-Rotrou, Fr. ... D7 10
Noginsk, Russia ... F21 18
Nogoyá, Arg. ... C5 56
Noirmoutier, Fr. ... E4 10
Nojima-zaki, c., Japan ... H12 30
Nokia, Fin. ... F14 6
Nokomis, Fl., U.S. ... E4 86
Nokomis, Il., U.S. ... D4 90
Nokomis, Lake, res., Wi., U.S. ... C4 126
Nolan, co., Tx., U.S. ... C2 120
Nolichucky, stm., Tn., U.S. ... C10 119
Nolin, stm., Ky., U.S. ... C3 94
Nolin Lake, res., Ky., U.S. ... C3 94
Nomans Land, i., Ma., U.S. ... D6 98
Nombre de Dios, Mex. ... F7 62
Nome, Ak., U.S. ... C6 79
Nomininque, Que., Can. ... C2 74
Nonacho Lake, l., N.W. Ter., Can. ... D11 66
Nonesuch, stm., Me., U.S. ... g7 96
Nong'an, China ... C12 26
Nong Khai, Thai. ... F7 34
Nonquit Pond, l., R.I., U.S. ... E6 116
Nontron, Fr. ... G7 10
Nooksack, North Fork, stm., Wa., U.S. ... A4 124
Nooksack, South Fork, stm., Wa., U.S. ... A3 124
Noordoost Polder, reg., Neth. ... C5 8
Noorvik, Ak., U.S. ... B7 79
Nootka Island, i., B.C., Can. ... G7 66
Nootka Sound, strt., B.C., Can. ... E4 69
No Point, Point, c., Md., U.S. ... D5 97
Noquebay, Lake, l., Wi., U.S. ... C6 126
Noranda, Que., Can. ... k11 74
Nora Springs, Ia., U.S. ... A5 92
Norborne, Mo., U.S. ... B4 102
Norco, La., U.S. ... E5 95
Norcross, Ga., U.S. ... C2 87
Norden, Ger. ... B7 8
Nordenham, Ger. ... B8 8
Nordenšel'da, Archipelag, is., Russia ... B13 24
Norderney, i., Ger. ... B7 8
Nordfjordeid, Nor. ... F5 6
Nordfold, Nor. ... C10 6
Nordhausen, Ger. ... D10 8
Nordhorn, Ger. ... C7 8
Nordkapp, c., Nor. ... A15 6
Nordkjosbotn, Nor. ... B12 6
Nördlingen, Ger. ... G10 8
Nordmaling, Swe. ... E12 6
Nordreisa, Nor. ... B13 6
Nordre Strømfjord, Grnld. ... C22 66
Nordvik, Russia ... C16 24
Norfolk, Ct., U.S. ... B3 84
Norfolk, Ne., U.S. ... B8 104
Norfolk, N.Y., U.S. ... f9 109
Norfolk, Va., U.S. ... D6 123
Norfolk, co., Ma., U.S. ... B5 98
Norfolk Naval Base, mil., Va., U.S. ... k15 123
Norfolk Naval Shipyard, mil., Va., U.S. ... k15 123
Norfork Dam, Ar., U.S. ... A3 81
Norfork Lake, res., Ar., U.S. ... A3 81
Noril'sk, Russia ... D11 24
Norland, Fl., U.S. ... s13 86
Norlina, N.C., U.S. ... A4 110
Normal, Il., U.S. ... C5 90
Norman, Ok., U.S. ... B4 113
Norman, co., Mn., U.S. ... C2 100
Norman, Lake, res., N.C., U.S. ... B2 110
Normandie, hist. reg., Fr. ... D6 10
Normandy see Normandie, hist. reg., Fr. ... D6 10
Norman Park, Ga., U.S. ... E3 87
Normanton, Austl. ... C8 50
Norman Wells, N.W. Ter., Can. ... C7 66
Norphlet, Ar., U.S. ... D3 81
Norquincó, Arg. ... E2 56
Norridge, Il., U.S. ... k9 90
Norridgewock, Me., U.S. ... D3 96
Norris, S.C., U.S. ... B2 117
Norris, Tn., U.S. ... C9 119
Norris Arm, Newf., Can. ... D4 72
Norris Dam, Tn., U.S. ... C9 119
Norris Lake, res., Tn., U.S. ... C10 119
Norris Point, Newf., Can. ... D3 72
Norristown, Pa., U.S. ... F11 115
Norrköping, Swe. ... G11 6
Norrtälje, Swe. ... G12 6
Norseman, Austl. ... F4 50
Norsk, Russia ... G19 24
Norte, Serra do, plat., Braz. ... F7 54

North, S.C., U.S. ... D5 117
North, stm., Al., U.S. ... B2 78
North, stm., Ia., U.S. ... f8 92
North, stm., Ma., U.S. ... h12 98
North, stm., W.V., U.S. ... B6 125
North, Cape, c., N.S., Can. ... B9 71
North Adams, Ma., U.S. ... A1 98
North Albany, Or., U.S. ... k11 114
Northam, Austl. ... F3 50
North America ... E10 61
North Amherst, Ma., U.S. ... B2 98
North Andaman, i., India ... H2 34
North Andover, Ma., U.S. ... A5 98
North Andrews Gardens, Fl., U.S. ... *r13 86
North Anna, stm., Va., U.S. ... B5 123
North Anson, Me., U.S. ... D3 96
North Apollo, Pa., U.S. ... E2 115
North Arapaho Peak, mtn., Co., U.S. ... A5 83
North Arlington, N.J., U.S. ... h8 107
North Atlanta, Ga., U.S. ... h8 87
North Attleboro, Ma., U.S. ... C5 98
North Augusta, S.C., U.S. ... D4 117
North Aurora, Il., U.S. ... k8 90
North Baltimore, Oh., U.S. ... A2 112
North Bay, Ont., Can. ... A5 73
North Beach, Md., U.S. ... C4 97
North Belmont, N.C., U.S. ... B1 110
North Bend, Ne., U.S. ... C9 104
North Bend, Or., U.S. ... D2 114
North Bend, Wa., U.S. ... B4 124
North Bennington, Vt., U.S. ... F2 122
North Bergen, N.J., U.S. ... h8 107
North Berwick, Me., U.S. ... E2 96
Northborough, Ma., U.S. ... B4 98
North Branch, Mi., U.S. ... E7 99
North Branch, Mn., U.S. ... E6 100
North Branch, N.H., U.S. ... D3 106
North Branch, N.J., U.S. ... B3 107
North Branford, Ct., U.S. ... D4 84
Northbridge, Ma., U.S. ... B4 98
Northbrook, Il., U.S. ... h9 90
North Brookfield, Ma., U.S. ... B3 98
North Brunswick, N.J., U.S. ... C4 107
North Caldwell, N.J., U.S. ... B4 107
North Canadian, stm., Ok., U.S. ... A5 113
North Canton, Ga., U.S. ... B2 87
North Canton, Oh., U.S. ... B4 112
North Cape, c., P.E.I., Can. ... B6 71
North Cape May, N.J., U.S. ... F3 107
North Cape see Nordkapp, c., Nor. ... A15 6
North Caribou Lake, l., Ont., Can. ... F14 66
North Carolina, state, U.S. ... B3 110
North Cascades National Park, Wa., U.S. ... A4 124
North Channel, strt., Ont., Can. ... A2 73
North Channel, strt., U.K. ... F7 7
North Charleston, S.C., U.S. ... F8 117
North Chicago, Il., U.S. ... A6 90
North Clarendon, Vt., U.S. ... D3 122
North College Hill, Oh., U.S. ... o12 112
North Conway, N.H., U.S. ... B4 106
North Corbin, Ky., U.S. ... D5 94
North Crossett, Ar., U.S. ... D4 81
North Cyprus, ctry., Asia ... B3 40
North Dakota, state, U.S. ... B5 111
North Dartmouth, Ma., U.S. ... C6 98
North Druid Hills, Ga., U.S. ... *h8 87
North Eagle Butte, S.D., U.S. ... B4 118
North East, Md., U.S. ... A6 97
North East, Pa., U.S. ... B2 115
Northeast, stm., Md., U.S. ... A6 97
Northeast Cape, c., Ak., U.S. ... C6 79
Northeast Cape Fear, stm., N.C., U.S. ... C5 110
Northeast Harbor, Me., U.S. ... D4 96
Northeast Henrietta, N.Y., U.S. ... *B3 109
North Easton, Ma., U.S. ... B5 98
Northeast Pond, l., N.H., U.S. ... D5 106
Northeast Providence Channel, strt., Bah. ... B9 64
North Edisto, stm., S.C., U.S. ... k11 117
Northeim, Ger. ... D9 8
North English, Ia., U.S. ... C5 92
North English, stm., Ia., U.S. ... C5 92
North Enid, Ok., U.S. ... A4 113
Northern Cheyenne Indian Reservation, Mt., U.S. ... E10 103
Northern Indian Lake, l., Man., Can. ... A3 70
Northern Ireland, ter., U.K. ... G6 7
Northern Territory, ter., Austl. ... C6 50
North Falmouth, Ma., U.S. ... C6 98
Northfield, Mn., U.S. ... F5 100
Northfield, N.H., U.S. ... D3 106
Northfield, N.J., U.S. ... E3 107
Northfield, Oh., U.S. ... h9 112
Northfield, Vt., U.S. ... C3 122
Northfield Falls, Vt., U.S. ... C3 122
North Flinders Ranges, mts., Austl. ... F7 50
North Fond du Lac, Wi., U.S. ... E5 126
Northford, Ct., U.S. ... D4 84
North Fork Reservoir, res., Or., U.S. ... B4 114
North Fort Myers, Fl., U.S. ... F5 86
North Fox Island, i., Mi., U.S. ... C5 99
North Frisian Islands, is., Eur. ... A8 8
Northglenn, Co., U.S. ... B6 83
North Gower, Ont., Can. ... B9 73
North Grafton, Ma., U.S. ... B4 98
North Grosvenordale, Ct., U.S. ... B8 84
North Gulfport, Ms., U.S. ... E4 101
North Haledon, N.J., U.S. ... B4 107
North Hampton, N.H., U.S. ... E5 106
North Hartland Reservoir, res., Vt., U.S. ... D4 122
North Hatley, Que., Can. ... D6 74

North Haven, Ct., U.S. ... D4 84
North Head, N.B., Can. ... E3 71
North Hero Island, i., Vt., U.S. ... B2 122
North Horn Lake, l., Tn., U.S. ... e8 119
North Industry, Oh., U.S. ... B4 112
North Inlet, b., S.C., U.S. ... E9 117
North Island, i., N.Z. ... C5 52
North Island, i., S.C., U.S. ... E9 117
North Island Naval Air Station, mil., Ca., U.S. ... o15 82
North Islands, is., La., U.S. ... E7 95
North Judson, In., U.S. ... B4 91
North Kansas City, Mo., U.S. ... h10 102
North Kingstown, R.I., U.S. ... E4 116
North Kingsville, Oh., U.S. ... A5 112
North La Junta, Co., U.S. ... C7 83
North Lake, l., Wy., U.S. ... D7 127
North Las Vegas, Nv., U.S. ... G6 105
North La Veta Pass, Co., U.S. ... D5 83
North Lewisburg, Oh., U.S. ... B2 112
North Liberty, Ia., U.S. ... C6 92
North Liberty, In., U.S. ... A5 91
North Lima, Oh., U.S. ... B5 112
North Little Rock, Ar., U.S. ... C3 81
North Logan, Ut., U.S. ... B4 121
North Loon Mountain, mtn., Id., U.S. ... D3 89
North Magnetic Pole ... B22 128
North Mamm Peak, mtn., Co., U.S. ... B3 83
North Manchester, In., U.S. ... C6 91
North Manitou Island, i., Mi., U.S. ... C4 99
North Mankato, Mn., U.S. ... F4 100
North Merrydale, La., U.S. ... *D4 95
North Miami, Fl., U.S. ... G6 86
North Miami Beach, Fl., U.S. ... s13 86
North Middletown, Ky., U.S. ... B5 94
North Moose Lake, l., Man., Can. ... B1 70
North Mountain, mtn., Pa., U.S. ... D9 115
North Muskegon, Mi., U.S. ... E4 99
North Myrtle Beach, S.C., U.S. ... D10 117
North Naples, Fl., U.S. ... F5 86
North New River Canal, Fl., U.S. ... F6 86
North Ogden, Ut., U.S. ... B4 121
North Olmsted, Oh., U.S. ... h9 112
North Palisade, mtn., Ca., U.S. ... D4 82
North Park, Il., U.S. ... A4 90
North Park, val., Co., U.S. ... A4 83
North Pass, strt., La., U.S. ... E7 95
North Pembroke, Ma., U.S. ... B6 98
North Plainfield, N.J., U.S. ... B4 107
North Plains, Or., U.S. ... B4 114
North Platte, Ne., U.S. ... C5 104
North Platte, stm., U.S. ... C6 76
North Point, c., Md., U.S. ... B5 97
North Point, c., Mi., U.S. ... C7 99
North Pole ... A12 128
Northport, Al., U.S. ... B2 78
North Prairie, Wi., U.S. ... F5 126
North Providence, R.I., U.S. ... C4 116
North Raccoon, stm., Ia., U.S. ... C3 92
North Reading, Ma., U.S. ... f11 98
North Richland Hills, Tx., U.S. ... n9 120
Northridge, Oh., U.S. ... C2 112
North Ridgeville, Oh., U.S. ... A3 112
North Royalton, Oh., U.S. ... h9 112
North Rustico, P.E.I., Can. ... C6 71
North Salem, Ind., U.S. ... E4 106
North Salt Lake, Ut., U.S. ... C4 121
North Santee, stm., S.C., U.S. ... E9 117
North Saskatchewan, stm., Can. ... F10 66
North Schell Peak, mtn., Nv., U.S. ... D7 105
North Scituate, Ma., U.S. ... h12 98
North Sea, Eur. ... D8 4
North Shoshone Peak, mtn., Nv., U.S. ... D4 105
North Sioux City, S.D., U.S. ... E9 118
North Skunk, stm., Ia., U.S. ... C5 92
North Springfield, Vt., U.S. ... E3 122
North Springfield Reservoir, res., Vt., U.S. ... E4 122
North Star, De., U.S. ... A3 85
North St. Paul, Mn., U.S. ... m13 100
North Stratford, N.H., U.S. ... A3 106
North Sudbury, Ma., U.S. ... g10 98
North Swanzey, N.H., U.S. ... E2 106
North Syracuse, N.Y., U.S. ... B4 109
North Tarrytown, N.Y., U.S. ... D7 109
North Terre Haute, In., U.S. ... E3 91
North Thompson, stm., B.C., Can. ... D8 69
North Tonawanda, N.Y., U.S. ... B2 109
North Troy, Vt., U.S. ... B4 122
North Tunica, Ms., U.S. ... A3 101
North Twin Lake, l., Wi., U.S. ... B4 126
Northumberland, co., Pa., U.S. ... D8 115
Northumberland, co., Va., U.S. ... C6 123
Northumberland National Park, Eng., U.K. ... F10 7
Northumberland Strait, strt., Can. ... C6 71
North Umpqua, stm., Or., U.S. ... D3 114
North Uxbridge, Ma., U.S. ... B4 98
Northvale, N.J., U.S. ... g9 107
North Vancouver, B.C., Can. ... E6 69
North Vassalboro, Me., U.S. ... D3 96
North Vernon, In., U.S. ... F6 91
Northville, Mi., U.S. ... p15 99
North Wales, Pa., U.S. ... F11 115
North Walpole, N.H., U.S. ... D2 106
North Warren, Pa., U.S. ... C3 115
North Webster, In., U.S. ... B6 91
North West Cape, c., Austl. ... D2 50
Northwest Miramichi, stm., N.B., Can. ... B3 71
Northwest Providence Channel, strt., Bah. ... A8 64
Northwest Territories, prov., Can. ... C13 66
North Wildwood, N.J., U.S. ... E3 107
North Wilkesboro, N.C., U.S. ... A1 110
North Windham, Ct., U.S. ... C7 84
North Windham, Me., U.S. ... E2 96
Northwood, Ia., U.S. ... A4 92
Northwood, N.D., U.S. ... B8 111
Northwoods, Mo., U.S. ...

North York, Ont., Can. ... D5 73
North York, Pa., U.S. ... G8 115
North York Moors National Park, Eng., U.K. ... G12 7
Norton, N.B., Can. ... D4 71
Norton, Ks., U.S. ... C4 93
Norton, Ma., U.S. ... C5 98
Norton, Oh., U.S. ... A4 112
Norton, Va., U.S. ... f9 123
Norton, co., Ks., U.S. ... C4 93
Norton Air Force Base, mil., Ca., U.S. ... E5 82
Norton Bay, b., Ak., U.S. ... C7 79
Norton Pond, l., Vt., U.S. ... B5 122
Norton Reservoir, res., Ks., U.S. ... C3 93
Norton Shores, Mi., U.S. ... E4 99
Norton Sound, strt., Ak., U.S. ... C6 79
Nortonville, Ks., U.S. ... C8 93
Nortonville, Ky., U.S. ... C2 94
Norwalk, Ct., U.S. ... n12 82
Norwalk, Ct., U.S. ... E2 84
Norwalk, Ia., U.S. ... C4 92
Norwalk, Oh., U.S. ... A3 112
Norwalk Islands, is., Ct., U.S. ... E2 84
Norway, Me., U.S. ... D2 96
Norway, Mi., U.S. ... C3 99
Norway, ctry., Eur. ... C9 4
Norway Bay, b., N.W. Ter., Can. ... B12 66
Norway House, Man., Can. ... C3 70
Norway Lake, l., Mn., U.S. ... E3 100
Norwegian Sea, Eur. ... C12 128
Norwich, Eng., U.K. ... I14 7
Norwich, Ct., U.S. ... C7 84
Norwich, N.Y., U.S. ... C5 109
Norwich, Vt., U.S. ... D4 122
Norwood, Ont., Can. ... C7 73
Norwood, Ma., U.S. ... B5 98
Norwood, Mn., U.S. ... F5 100
Norwood, N.J., U.S. ... h9 107
Norwood, N.Y., U.S. ... f10 109
Norwood, N.C., U.S. ... B2 110
Norwood, Oh., U.S. ... o13 112
Norwood, Pa., U.S. ... p20 115
Norwoodville, Ia., U.S. ... e8 92
Noshiro, Japan ... B13 30
Notasulga, Al., U.S. ... C4 78
Notch Peak, mtn., Ut., U.S. ... D2 121
Noto, Italy ... M10 14
Notodden, Nor. ... G7 6
Notre Dame, Monts, mts., Que., Can. ... k13 74
Notre Dame Bay, b., Newf., Can. ... D4 72
Notre Dame de Lourdes, Man., Can. ... E2 70
Notre-Dame-du-Lac, Que., Can. ... B9 70
Nottawasaga Bay, b., Ont., Can. ... C4 73
Nottoway, stm., Que., Can. ... h11 74
Nottingham, Eng., U.K. ... I11 7
Nottingham Island, i., N.W. Ter., Can. ... D17 66
Nottoway, co., Va., U.S. ... C4 123
Nottoway, stm., Va., U.S. ... D5 123
Nouadhibou, Maur. ... D2 42
Nouakchott, Maur. ... E2 42
Nouamrhar, Maur. ... E2 42
Noupoort, S. Afr. ... H4 44
Nouveau-Québec, Cratère du, crat., Que., Can. ... D18 66
Nova América, Braz. ... C4 57
Nova Cruz, Braz. ... E11 54
Nova Freixo, Moz. ... D7 44
Nova Friburgo, Braz. ... G7 57
Nova Gaia, Ang. ... D3 44
Nova Gradiška, Cro. ... D12 14
Nova Iguaçu, Braz. ... G7 57
Novaja Sibir', Ostrov, i., Russia ... B23 24
Novaja Zeml'a, is., Russia ... C5 24
Nova Lima, Braz. ... E7 57
Nova Lisboa see Huambo, Ang. ... D3 44
Nova Mambone, Moz. ... F7 44
Novara, Italy ... D3 14
Nova Scotia, prov., Can. ... D6 71
Nova Sofala, Moz. ... C2 87
Novato, Ca., U.S. ... G11 12
Noveldo, Spain ... H18 8
Nové Zámky, Czech. ... C14 18
Novgorod, Russia ... p15 99
Novi, Mi., U.S. ... E3 14
Novi Ligure, Italy ... F11 16
Novi Pazar, Bul. ... F4 16
Novi Pazar, Yugo. ... D3 16
Novi Sad, Yugo. ... G10 24
Novoaltajsk, Russia ... E6 54
Novo Aripuanã, Braz. ... H8 8
Novogrudok, Bela. ... G11 24
Novokuzneck, Russia ... D10 14
Novo Mesto, Slo. ... D2 44
Novo Redondo, Ang. ... I5 22
Novorossijsk, Russia ... C15 24
Novorybnoje, Russia ... D4 128
Novosibirsk, Russia ... B22 24
Novosibirskoje Ostrova, is., Russia ... G10 24
Novosibirskoje Vodochranilišče, res., Russia ... G9 22
Novotroick, Russia ... I14 18
Novozybkov, Russia ... D11 14
Novska, Cro. ... D15 8
Nowa Sól (Neusalz), Pol. ... A6 113
Nowata, Ok., U.S. ... A6 113
Nowata, co., Ok., U.S. ... G15 38
Nowgong, India ... B5 127
Nowood, stm., Wy., U.S. ... B4 38
Nowshāk, mtn., Asia ... C4 38
Nowshera, Pak. ... F20 8
Nowy Sącz, Pol. ... F20 8
Nowy Targ, Pol. ... C1 103
Noxon Reservoir, res., Mt., U.S. ... C3 85
Noxontown Lake, res., De., U.S. ... B5 101
Noxubee, co., Ms., U.S. ... B5 101
Noxubee, stm., U.S. ... C9 70
Noyes Island, i., Ak., U.S. ... E7 44
Noyon, Fr. ... G5 42
Nozay, Fr. ...
Nsanje, Mwi. ...
Nsawam, Ghana ...

Name	Map Ref	Page
Nubanusit Lake, l., N.H., U.S.	E2	106
Nubian Desert, des., Sudan	D12	42
Nuckolls, co., Ne., U.S.	D7	104
Nucla, Co., U.S.	C2	83
Nueces, co., Tx., U.S.	F4	120
Nueces, stm., Tx., U.S.	E3	120
Nueltin Lake, l., Can.	E13	66
Nueva Casas Grandes, Mex.	B6	62
Nueva Rosita, Mex.	D9	62
Nueva San Salvador, El Sal.	H3	64
Nueve de Julio, Arg.	D4	56
Nuevitas, Cuba	D9	64
Nuevo, Golfo, b., Arg.	E4	56
Nuevo Laredo, Mex.	D10	62
Nuevo Rocafuerte, Ec.	H5	58
Nuits-Saint-Georges, Fr.	E11	10
Nukus, Uzb.	I9	22
Nulato, Ak., U.S.	C8	79
Nulhegan, stm., Vt., U.S.	B5	122
Nullagine, Austl.	D4	50
Nullarbor Plain, pl., Austl.	F5	50
Numata, Japan	F12	30
Numazu, Japan	G11	30
Numfoor, Pulau, i., Indon.	F9	32
Nun, stm., China	A12	26
Nunivak Island, i., Ak., U.S.	D6	79
Nunjiang, China	B12	26
Nuoro, Italy	I4	14
N'urba, Russia	E17	24
Nuremberg, Pa., U.S.	E9	115
Nuremberg see Nürnberg, Ger.	F11	8
Nürnberg, Ger.	F11	8
Nurri, Italy	J4	14
Nutley, N.J., U.S.	B4	107
Nutter Fort, W.V., U.S.	k10	125
Nutting Lake, Ma., U.S.	f10	98
Nuuanu Pali, Hi., U.S.	g10	88
Nyack, N.Y., U.S.	D7	109
Nyainqêntanglha Shan, mts., China	E13	38
Nyala, Sudan	F10	42
Nyanda, Zimb.	F6	44
Nyasa, Lake, l., Afr.	D6	44
Nyaunglebin, Burma	F4	34
Nybro, Swe.	H10	6
Nye, co., Nv., U.S.	E5	105
Nyenyam, China	F11	38
Nyeri, Kenya	B7	44
Nyíregyháza, Hung.	H21	8
Nykøbing, Den.	I8	6
Nyköping, Swe.	G11	6
Nylstroom, S. Afr.	F5	44
Nynäshamn, Swe.	G11	6
Nyngan, Austl.	F9	50
Nyon, Switz.	F13	10
Nyons, Fr.	H12	10
Nysa, Pol.	E17	8
Nysa Łużycka (Neisse) (Nisa), stm., Eur.	D14	8
Nyssa, Or., U.S.	D9	114
Nzérékoré, Gui.	G4	42
N'zeto, Ang.	C2	44

O

Name	Map Ref	Page
Oahe, Lake, res., U.S.	B6	76
Oahe Dam, S.D., U.S.	C5	118
Oahu, i., Hi., U.S.	B4	88
Oak Bay, B.C., Can.	h12	69
Oak Bluffs, Ma., U.S.	D6	98
Oak Creek, Co., U.S.	A4	83
Oak Creek, Wi., U.S.	n12	126
Oakdale, Ca., U.S.	D3	82
Oakdale, Ga., U.S.	h8	87
Oakdale, La., U.S.	D3	95
Oakdale, Pa., U.S.	k13	115
Oakes, N.D., U.S.	C7	111
Oakfield, N.Y., U.S.	B2	109
Oakfield, Wi., U.S.	E5	126
Oak Forest, Il., U.S.	k9	90
Oak Grove, Ky., U.S.	D2	94
Oak Grove, La., U.S.	B4	95
Oak Grove, Or., U.S.	B4	114
Oak Harbor, Oh., U.S.	A2	112
Oak Harbor, Wa., U.S.	A3	124
Oak Hill, Mi., U.S.	D4	99
Oak Hill, Oh., U.S.	D3	112
Oak Hill, W.V., U.S.	D3	125
Oak Hill, mtn., Ma., U.S.	f9	98
Oakhurst, Ok., U.S.	A5	113
Oak Island, i., Wi., U.S.	B3	126
Oak Lake, l., Man., Can.	E1	70
Oakland, Ca., U.S.	D2	82
Oakland, Il., U.S.	D5	90
Oakland, Ia., U.S.	C2	92
Oakland, Me., U.S.	D3	96
Oakland, Md., U.S.	m12	97
Oakland, Ne., U.S.	C9	104
Oakland, N.J., U.S.	A4	107
Oakland, Ok., U.S.	C5	113
Oakland, Or., U.S.	D3	114
Oakland, R.I., U.S.	B2	116
Oakland, co., Mi., U.S.	F7	99
Oakland City, In., U.S.	H3	91
Oakland Park, Fl., U.S.	r13	86
Oak Lawn, Il., U.S.	B6	90
Oaklawn, Ks., U.S.	g12	93
Oakley, Id., U.S.	G5	89
Oakley, Ks., U.S.	C3	93
Oakman, Al., U.S.	B2	78
Oakmont, Pa., U.S.	E2	115
Oak Mountain, mtn., Ga., U.S.	D2	87
Oak Orchard, De., U.S.	F5	85
Oak Park, Il., U.S.	B6	90
Oak Park, Mi., U.S.	p15	99
Oak Ridge, N.C., U.S.	A3	110
Oak Ridge, Or., U.S.	D4	114
Oak Ridge, Tn., U.S.	C9	119
Oak Ridge Reservoir, res., N.J., U.S.	A3	107
Oakton, Va., U.S.	g12	123
Oaktown, In., U.S.	G3	91

Name	Map Ref	Page
Oak Valley, N.J., U.S.	D2	107
Oakville, Ont., Can.	D5	73
Oakville, Ct., U.S.	C3	84
Oakville, Mo., U.S.	g13	102
Oakwood, Ga., U.S.	B3	87
Oakwood, Il., U.S.	C6	90
Oakwood, Oh., U.S.	C1	112
Oamaru, N.Z.	F3	52
Oaxaca [de Juárez], Mex.	I11	62
Ob', stm., Russia	D7	24
Oban, Scot., U.K.	E7	7
Obbia, Som.	G4	46
Obed, stm., Tn., U.S.	C9	119
Oberlin, Ks., U.S.	C3	93
Oberlin, La., U.S.	D3	95
Oberlin, Oh., U.S.	A3	112
Oberwart, Aus.	H16	8
Obetz, Oh., U.S.	C3	112
Obi, Kepulauan, is., Indon.	F8	32
Obi, Pulau, i., Indon.	F8	32
Óbidos, Braz.	D7	54
Obihiro, Japan	q21	30a
Obion, Tn., U.S.	A2	119
Obion, co., Tn., U.S.	A2	119
Obion, stm., Tn., U.S.	A2	119
Oblong, Il., U.S.	D6	90
Obluč'e, Russia	H20	24
Obninsk, Russia	F19	18
Obock, Dji.	F3	46
O'Brien, co., Ia., U.S.	A2	92
Obrovac, Cro.	E10	14
Observation Peak, mtn., Ca., U.S.	B3	82
Observatoire, Caye de l', i., N. Cal.	D11	50
Obuasi, Ghana	G5	42
Ocala, Fl., U.S.	C4	86
Ocaña, Col.	C6	58
Ocaña, Spain	F8	12
Occidental, Cordillera, mts., Col.	E4	58
Occidental, Cordillera, mts., Peru	F4	54
Ocean, co., N.J., U.S.	D4	107
Oceana, W.V., U.S.	D3	125
Oceana, co., Mi., U.S.	E4	99
Oceana Naval Air Station, mil., Va., U.S.	k15	123
Ocean Bluff, Ma., U.S.	B6	98
Ocean City, Fl., U.S.	u15	86
Ocean City, Md., U.S.	D7	97
Ocean City, N.J., U.S.	E3	107
Ocean Grove, Ma., U.S.	C5	98
Ocean Park, Wa., U.S.	C1	124
Oceanport, N.J., U.S.	C4	107
Oceanside, Ca., U.S.	F5	82
Ocean Springs, Ms., U.S.	E5	101
Ocean [Township], N.J., U.S.	C4	107
Ocean View, De., U.S.	F5	85
Ocha, Russia	G22	24
Ocheda Lake, l., Mn., U.S.	G3	100
Ocheyedan, stm., Ia., U.S.	A2	92
Ochiltree, co., Tx., U.S.	A2	120
Ochlockonee, stm., Fl., U.S.	B2	86
Ocho Lake, res., Or., U.S.	C6	114
Ocho Rios, Jam.	E9	64
Ochota, stm., Russia	F22	24
Ochotsk, Russia	F22	24
Ochsenfurt, Ger.	F10	8
Ocilla, Ga., U.S.	E3	87
Ockelbo, Swe.	F11	6
Ocmulgee, stm., Ga., U.S.	D3	87
Ocoee, Fl., U.S.	D5	86
Ocoee, Lake, res., Tn., U.S.	D9	119
Oconee, co., Ga., U.S.	C3	87
Oconee, co., S.C., U.S.	B1	117
Oconee, stm., Ga., U.S.	C3	87
Oconee, Lake, res., Ga., U.S.	C3	87
Oconomowoc, Wi., U.S.	E5	126
Oconto, Wi., U.S.	D6	126
Oconto, co., Wi., U.S.	D5	126
Oconto, stm., Wi., U.S.	D5	126
Oconto Falls, Wi., U.S.	D5	126
Ocotal, Nic.	H4	64
Ocotlán, Mex.	G8	62
Ocracoke Inlet, b., N.C., U.S.	B6	110
Ocracoke Island, i., N.C., U.S.	B7	110
Octoraro Creek, stm., U.S.	A5	97
Ocumare del Tuy, Ven.	B9	58
Ocussi, Indon.	G7	32
Oda, Ghana	G5	42
Oda, Jabal, mtn., Sudan	D13	42
Ōdate, Japan	B13	30
Odawara, Japan	G12	30
Odda, Nor.	F6	6
Odebolt, Ia., U.S.	B2	92
Odell, Il., U.S.	B5	90
Odell, Or., U.S.	B5	114
Odell Lake, l., Or., U.S.	E5	114
Odem, Tx., U.S.	F4	120
Odemira, Port.	H3	12
Ödemiş, Tur.	K11	16
Odense, Den.	I8	6
Odenton, Md., U.S.	B4	97
Odenville, Al., U.S.	B3	78
Oder (Odra), stm., Eur.	C14	8
Oderberg, Ger.	C14	8
Odessa, Ont., Can.	C8	73
Odessa, Ukr.	H4	22
Odessa, De., U.S.	C3	85
Odessa, Mo., U.S.	C4	102
Odessa, Tx., U.S.	D1	120
Odessa, Wa., U.S.	B7	124
Odienné, I.C.	G4	42
Odin, Il., U.S.	E4	90
Odincovo, Russia	F20	18
Odon, In., U.S.	G4	91
O'Donnell, Tx., U.S.	C2	120
Odra (Oder), stm., Eur.	C14	8
Oelsnitz, Ger.	E12	8
Oelwein, Ia., U.S.	B6	92
O'Fallon, Il., U.S.	E4	90
O'Fallon, Mo., U.S.	f12	102
Offenbach, Ger.	E8	8
Offenburg, Ger.	G7	8
Offutt Air Force Base, mil., Ne., U.S.	g3	104
Ōfunato, Japan	C14	30
Ōgaki, Japan	G9	30

Name	Map Ref	Page
Ogallala, Ne., U.S.	C4	104
Ogbomosho, Nig.	G6	42
Ogden, Ia., U.S.	B3	92
Ogden, Ks., U.S.	C7	93
Ogden, Ut., U.S.	B4	121
Ogden, Mount, mtn., N.A.	k23	79
Ogdensburg, N.J., U.S.	A3	107
Ogdensburg, N.Y., U.S.	f9	109
Ogeechee, stm., Ga., U.S.	D5	87
Ogemaw, co., Mi., U.S.	D6	99
Ogilvie Mountains, mts., Yukon, Can.	D5	66
Ogle, co., Il., U.S.	B4	90
Oglesby, Il., U.S.	B4	90
Oglethorpe, Ga., U.S.	D2	87
Oglethorpe, co., Ga., U.S.	C3	87
Oglethorpe, Mount, mtn., Ga., U.S.	B2	87
Ogooué, stm., Afr.	B1	44
Ogunquit, Me., U.S.	E2	96
Oğuzeli, Tur.	A5	40
Ohanet, Alg.	C7	42
Ōhata, Japan	A14	30
Ohatchee, Al., U.S.	B3	78
O'Higgins, Lago (Lago San Martín), l., S.A.	F2	56
Ohio, co., In., U.S.	G7	91
Ohio, co., Ky., U.S.	C3	94
Ohio, co., W.V., U.S.	A4	125
Ohio, state, U.S.	B3	112
Ohio, stm., U.S.	D9	76
Ohio Brush Creek, stm., Oh., U.S.	D2	112
Ohio City, Oh., U.S.	B1	112
Ohio Peak, mtn., Co., U.S.	C3	83
Ohioville, Pa., U.S.	E1	115
Ohoopee, stm., Ga., U.S.	D4	87
Ohrid, Lake, l., Eur.	H4	16
Öhringen, Ger.	F9	8
Oiapoque, Braz.	C8	54
Oil City, La., U.S.	B2	95
Oil City, Pa., U.S.	D2	115
Oil Creek, stm., Pa., U.S.	C3	82
Oildale, Ca., U.S.	E4	82
Oil Springs, Ont., Can.	E2	73
Oilton, Ok., U.S.	A5	113
Ōita, Japan	I4	30
Ojai, Ca., U.S.	E4	82
Ojinaga, Mex.	C7	62
Ojm'akon, Russia	E22	24
Ojo de Liebre, Laguna, b., Mex.	D2	62
Ojos del Salado, Cerro, mtn., S.A.	B3	56
Oka, stm., Russia	G14	24
Oka, stm., Russia	F25	18
Okaba, Indon.	G10	32
Okahandja, Nmb.	F3	44
Okaloosa, co., Fl., U.S.	u15	86
Okamanpeedan Lake, l., U.S.	A3	92
Okanagan Falls, B.C., Can.	E8	69
Okanagan Lake, l., B.C., Can.	D8	69
Okanagan Landing, B.C., Can.	D8	69
Okanogan, Wa., U.S.	A6	124
Okanogan, co., Wa., U.S.	A5	124
Okanogan, stm., Wa., U.S.	A5	124
Okāra, Pak.	E5	38
Okarche, Ok., U.S.	B4	113
Okatibbee Reservoir, res., Ms., U.S.	C5	101
Okauchee Lake, Wi., U.S.	*E5	126
Okavango (Cubango), stm., Afr.	E3	44
Okavango Swamp, sw., Bots.	E4	44
Ōkawa, Japan	I3	30
Okawville, Il., U.S.	E4	90
Okaya, Japan	F11	30
Okayama, Japan	H6	30
Okazaki, Japan	H10	30
Okeechobee, Fl., U.S.	E6	86
Okeechobee, co., Fl., U.S.	E6	86
Okeechobee, Lake, l., Fl., U.S.	F6	86
Okeene, Ok., U.S.	A3	113
Okefenokee Swamp, sw., U.S.	F4	87
Okemah, Ok., U.S.	B5	113
Okfuskee, co., Ok., U.S.	B5	113
Okhotsk, Sea of (Ochotskoje More), Asia	G23	24
Oki-guntō, is., Japan	F6	30
Okinawa-jima, i., Japan	y27	31b
Okinoerabu-shima, i., Japan	x28	31b
Okino-Tori-shima, i., Japan	G14	26
Oklahoma, co., Ok., U.S.	B4	113
Oklahoma, state, U.S.	B4	113
Oklahoma City, Ok., U.S.	B4	113
Oklawaha, Fl., U.S.	C5	86
Oklawaha, stm., Fl., U.S.	C5	86
Oklawaha, Lake, res., Fl., U.S.	C5	86
Okmulgee, Ok., U.S.	B6	113
Okmulgee, co., Ok., U.S.	B5	113
Okoboji, Ia., U.S.	A2	92
Okobojo Creek, stm., S.D., U.S.	C5	118
Okolona, Ky., U.S.	g11	94
Okolona, Ms., U.S.	B5	101
Okotoks, Alta., Can.	D4	68
Okt'abr'skoj Revol'ucii, Ostrov, i., Russia	B13	24
Oktibbeha, co., Ms., U.S.	B5	101
Ola, Ar., U.S.	B2	81
Olancha Peak, mtn., Ca., U.S.	D4	82
Olanchito, Hond.	G4	64
Öland, i., Swe.	H11	6
Olanta, S.C., U.S.	D8	117
Olathe, Co., U.S.	C3	83
Olathe, Ks., U.S.	D9	93
Olavarría, Arg.	D4	56
Olbia, Italy	I4	14
Ol'chon, Ostrov, i., Russia	G15	24
Olcott, N.Y., U.S.	B2	109
Old Bahama Channel, strt., N.A.	C8	64
Old Bridge, N.J., U.S.	C4	107
Oldenburg, Ger.	B8	8
Oldenburg, In., U.S.	F7	91
Oldenburg [in Holstein], Ger.	A10	8
Old Faithful Geyser, Wy., U.S.	B2	127
Old Forge, Pa., U.S.	D10	115
Old Fort, N.C., U.S.	f10	110
Oldham, co., Ky., U.S.	B4	94
Oldham, co., Tx., U.S.	B1	120
Old Harbor, Ak., U.S.	D9	79

Name	Map Ref	Page
Old Head of Kinsale, c., Ire.	J4	7
Old Hickory Lake, res., Tn., U.S.	A5	119
Oldman, stm., Alta., Can.	E4	68
Old Man of the Mountain, N.H., U.S.	B3	106
Oldmans Creek, stm., N.J., U.S.	D2	107
Old Orchard Beach, Me., U.S.	E2	96
Old Perlican, Newf., Can.	D5	72
Old Point Comfort, c., Va., U.S.	h15	123
Old Rhodes Key, i., Fl., U.S.	G6	86
Old River Lake, l., Ar., U.S.	k10	81
Old Saybrook, Ct., U.S.	D6	84
Oldsmar, Fl., U.S.	o10	86
Old Tampa Bay, b., Fl., U.S.	p10	86
Old Tappan, N.J., U.S.	g9	107
Old Topsail Inlet, b., N.C., U.S.	C5	110
Old Town, Me., U.S.	D4	96
Old Wives Lake, l., Sask., Can.	G2	75
Olean, N.Y., U.S.	C2	109
O'Leary, P.E.I., Can.	C5	71
Ølen, Nor.	G5	6
Olenij, Ostrov, i., Russia	C9	24
Olen'ok, Russia	D16	24
Olen'ok, stm., Russia	C18	24
Olen'okskij Zaliv, b., Russia	C18	24
Olentangy, stm., Oh., U.S.	B3	112
Oleśnica, Pol.	D17	8
Ol'ga, Russia	I21	24
Olga, Mount, mtn., Austl.	E6	50
Olhão, Port.	H3	12
Ólimbos, mtn., Cyp.	B3	40
Ólimbos, Óros, mtn., Grc.	I6	16
Olímpia, Braz.	F4	57
Olin, Ia., U.S.	B6	92
Olinda, Braz.	E12	54
Olite, Spain	C10	12
Oliva, Arg.	C4	56
Oliva, Spain	G11	12
Oliva de la Frontera, Spain	G5	12
Olive Branch, Ms., U.S.	A4	101
Olive Hill, Ky., U.S.	B6	94
Olivehurst, Ca., U.S.	C3	82
Oliveira, Braz.	F6	57
Olivenza, Spain	G4	12
Oliver, B.C., Can.	E8	69
Oliver, Pa., U.S.	G2	115
Oliver, co., N.D., U.S.	B4	111
Oliver Dam, U.S.	C5	78
Oliver Springs, Tn., U.S.	C9	119
Olivet, Mi., U.S.	F6	99
Olivia, Mn., U.S.	F4	100
Olla, La., U.S.	C3	95
Ollagüe, Chile	A3	56
Olmedo, Spain	D7	12
Olmito, Tx., U.S.	F4	120
Olmos, Peru	E3	54
Olmos Park, Tx., U.S.	k7	120
Olmsted, co., Mn., U.S.	G6	100
Olmsted Falls, Oh., U.S.	h9	112
Olney, Il., U.S.	E5	90
Olney, Md., U.S.	B3	97
Olney, Tx., U.S.	C3	120
Oloj, stm., Russia	D26	24
Ol'okma, stm., Russia	F18	24
Ol'okminsk, Russia	E18	24
Olomouc, Czech.	F17	8
Olongapo, Phil.	q19	33b
Oloron-Sainte-Marie, Fr.	I6	10
Olot, Spain	C14	12
Olov'annaja, Russia	G17	24
Olsztyn (Allenstein), Pol.	B20	8
Olten, Switz.	E14	10
Olton, Tx., U.S.	B1	120
Oluan Pi, c., Tai.	N9	28
Olustee, Ok., U.S.	C2	113
Ol'utorskij, Mys, c., Russia	F28	24
Olympia, Wa., U.S.	B3	124
Olympic Mountains, mts., Wa., U.S.	B2	124
Olympic National Park, Wa., U.S.	B2	124
Olympus, Mount, mtn., Wa., U.S.	B2	124
Olympus, Mount see Ólimbos, Óros, mtn., Grc.	I6	16
Olyphant, Pa., U.S.	D10	115
Omae-zaki, c., Japan	H11	30
Omagh, N. Ire., U.K.	G5	7
Omaha, Ne., U.S.	C10	104
Omaha Indian Reservation, Ne., U.S.	B9	104
Omak, Wa., U.S.	A6	124
Omak Lake, l., Wa., U.S.	A6	124
Oman, ctry., Asia	D6	46
Oman, Gulf of, b., Asia	D6	46
Omar, W.V., U.S.	D3	125
Ōma-zaki, c., Japan	A13	30
Omčak, Russia	E23	24
Omega, Ga., U.S.	E3	87
Omegna, Italy	D3	14
Omemee, Ont., Can.	C6	73
Omerville, Que., Can.	D5	74
Ometepe, Isla de, i., Nic.	I5	64
Ometepec, Mex.	I10	62
Omineca, stm., B.C., Can.	B5	69
Omineca Mountains, mts., B.C., Can.	A4	69
Ōmiya, Japan	G12	30
Ommaney, Cape, c., Ak., U.S.	D12	79
Ommanney Bay, b., N.W. Ter., Can.	B12	66
Ommen, Neth.	C6	8
Omo, stm., Eth.	G2	46
Omolon, stm., Russia	D25	24
Ompompanoosuc, stm., Vt., U.S.	D4	122
Omro, Wi., U.S.	D5	126
Omsk, Russia	F8	24
Omsukčan, Russia	E25	24
Ōmura, Japan	J2	30
Ōmuta, Japan	I3	30
Onaga, Ks., U.S.	C7	93
Onalaska, Wa., U.S.	C3	124
Onalaska, Wi., U.S.	E2	126
Onamia, Mn., U.S.	D5	100
Onancock, Va., U.S.	C7	123
Onarga, Il., U.S.	C6	90
Onawa, Ia., U.S.	B1	92

Name	Map Ref	Page
Onawa, Lake, l., Me., U.S.	C3	96
Onaway, Mi., U.S.	C6	99
Onda, Spain	F11	12
Ondangua, Nmb.	E3	44
Ondjiva, Ang.	E3	44
Öndörchaan, Mong.	B9	26
Oneco, Fl., U.S.	E4	86
Onega, Lake see Onežskoje ozero, l., Russia	E5	22
One Hundred Fifty Mile House, B.C., Can.	C7	69
One Hundred Mile House, B.C., Can.	D7	69
Oneida, Ky., U.S.	C6	94
Oneida, N.Y., U.S.	B5	109
Oneida, Oh., U.S.	C1	112
Oneida, Tn., U.S.	C9	119
Oneida, co., Id., U.S.	G6	89
Oneida, co., N.Y., U.S.	B5	109
Oneida, co., Wi., U.S.	C4	126
Oneida Lake, l., N.Y., U.S.	B5	109
O'Neill, Ne., U.S.	B7	104
Onekotan, Ostrov, i., Russia	H24	24
Oneonta, Al., U.S.	B3	78
Oneonta, N.Y., U.S.	C5	109
Onežskoje ozero, l., Russia	E5	22
Ongole, India	E6	37
Onida, S.D., U.S.	C5	118
Onitsha, Nig.	G7	42
Onoda, Japan	I4	30
Onomichi, Japan	H6	30
Onondaga, co., N.Y., U.S.	C4	109
Onondaga Indian Reservation, N.Y., U.S.	C4	109
Onota Lake, l., Ma., U.S.	B1	98
Onoway, Alta., Can.	C3	68
Onset, Ma., U.S.	C6	98
Onslow, Austl.	D3	50
Onslow, co., N.C., U.S.	C5	110
Onslow Bay, b., N.C., U.S.	C5	110
Onsted, Mi., U.S.	F6	99
Ontario, Ca., U.S.	E5	82
Ontario, Oh., U.S.	B3	112
Ontario, Or., U.S.	C10	114
Ontario, co., N.Y., U.S.	C3	109
Ontario, prov., Can.	C6	73
Ontario, Lake, l., N.A.	C11	76
Onteniente, Spain	G11	12
Ontonagon, Mi., U.S.	m12	99
Ontonagon, co., Mi., U.S.	m12	99
Ontonagon Indian Reservation, Mi., U.S.	B1	99
Onverwacht, Sur.	B7	54
Oodnadatta, Austl.	E7	50
Ooldea, Austl.	F6	50
Oolitic, In., U.S.	G4	91
Oologah, Ok., U.S.	A6	113
Oologah Lake, res., Ok., U.S.	A6	113
Ooltewah, Tn., U.S.	D8	119
Oostburg, Wi., U.S.	E6	126
Oostende (Ostende), Bel.	D2	8
Oosterhout, Neth.	D4	8
Ootacamund, India	G4	37
Ootsa Lake, l., B.C., Can.	C4	69
Opala, Zaire	B4	44
Opa-Locka, Fl., U.S.	s13	86
Opatija, Cro.	D9	14
Opava, Czech.	F17	8
Opelika, Al., U.S.	C4	78
Opelousas, La., U.S.	D3	95
Opequon Creek, stm., W.V., U.S.	B6	125
Opiscotéo, Lac, l., Que., Can.	F19	66
Opole (Oppeln), Pol.	E17	8
Opotiki, N.Z.	C6	52
Opp, Al., U.S.	D3	78
Oppdal, Nor.	E7	6
Oppelo, Ar., U.S.	B3	81
Opportunity, Wa., U.S.	B8	124
Optima Reservoir, res., Ok., U.S.	e9	113
Oquawka, Il., U.S.	C3	90
Ora, Italy	C6	14
Oracle, Az., U.S.	E5	80
Oradea, Rom.	B5	16
Oradell, N.J., U.S.	h8	107
Oradell Reservoir, res., N.J., U.S.	h9	107
Orai, India	H8	38
Oraibi, Az., U.S.	B5	80
Oran (Wahran), Alg.	A5	42
Oran, Mo., U.S.	D8	102
Orange, Austl.	F9	50
Orange, Fr.	H11	10
Orange, Ca., U.S.	n13	82
Orange, Ct., U.S.	D3	84
Orange, Ma., U.S.	A3	98
Orange, Tx., U.S.	D6	120
Orange, co., Ca., U.S.	F5	82
Orange, co., Fl., U.S.	D5	86
Orange, co., In., U.S.	G4	91
Orange, co., N.Y., U.S.	D6	109
Orange, co., N.C., U.S.	A3	110
Orange, co., Tx., U.S.	D6	120
Orange, co., Vt., U.S.	D3	122
Orange, co., Va., U.S.	B4	123
Orange (Oranje), stm., Afr.	G3	44
Orange, Cabo, c., Braz.	C8	54
Orange Beach, Al., U.S.	E2	78
Orangeburg, S.C., U.S.	E6	117
Orangeburg, co., S.C., U.S.	E6	117
Orange City, Fl., U.S.	D5	86
Orange City, Ia., U.S.	B1	92
Orange Grove, Ms., U.S.	E5	101
Orange Grove, Tx., U.S.	F4	120
Orange Lake, l., Fl., U.S.	C4	86
Orange Park, Fl., U.S.	B5	86
Orangeville, Ont., Can.	D4	73
Orangeville, Ut., U.S.	D4	121
Orange Walk, Belize	E3	64
Orani, Phil.	q19	33b
Oranienburg, Ger.	C13	8
Oranjestad, Aruba	H12	64
Orbetello, Italy	G6	14
Orbost, Austl.	G9	50
Ørbyhus, Swe.	F11	6
Orcas Island, i., Wa., U.S.	A3	124

Name	Map Ref	Page
Orcera, Spain	G9	12
Orchard City, Co., U.S.	C3	83
Orchard Homes, Mt., U.S.	D2	103
Orchard Park, N.Y., U.S.	C2	109
Orchards, Wa., U.S.	D3	124
Orchard Valley, Wy., U.S.	B9	127
Orchila, Isla i., Ven.	B9	58
Orchon, stm., Mong.	B7	26
Orcutt, Ca., U.S.	E3	82
Ord, Ne., U.S.	C7	104
Ord, Mount, mtn., Austl.	C5	50
Ordenes, Spain	B3	12
Ordway, Co., U.S.	C7	83
Ordzhonikidze see Vladikavkaz, Russia	I6	22
Oreana, Il., U.S.	D5	90
Örebro, Swe.	G10	6
Orechovo-Zujevo, Russia	F21	18
Oregon, Il., U.S.	A4	90
Oregon, Mo., U.S.	B2	102
Oregon, Oh., U.S.	A2	112
Oregon, Wi., U.S.	F4	126
Oregon, co., Mo., U.S.	E6	102
Oregon, state, U.S.	C6	114
Oregon Caves National Monument, Or., U.S.	E2	114
Oregon City, Or., U.S.	B4	114
Oregon Inlet, b., N.C., U.S.	B7	110
Orem, Ut., U.S.	C4	121
Orenburg, Russia	G9	22
Orense, Spain	C4	12
Orestiás, Grc.	H10	16
Orfordville, Wi., U.S.	F4	126
Organ Mountains, mts., N.M., U.S.	E3	108
Organ Pipe Cactus National Monument, Az., U.S.	E3	80
Orgün, Afg.	D3	38
Oriental, N.C., U.S.	B6	110
Oriental, Cordillera, mts., Col.	E6	58
Oriental, Cordillera, mts., Peru	F4	54
Orihuela, Spain	G11	12
Orillia, Ont., Can.	C5	73
Orinoco, stm., S.A.	C11	58
Orinoco, Delta del, Ven.	B10	58
Orion, Il., U.S.	B3	90
Oripää, Fin.	F14	6
Orissa, state, India	J11	38
Oristano, Italy	I3	14
Orivesi, Fin.	F15	6
Orizaba, Mex.	H11	62
Orizaba, Pico de (Volcán Citlaltépetl), vol., Mex.	H11	62
Orkney Islands, is., Scot., U.K.	B9	7
Orland, Ca., U.S.	C2	82
Orlando, Fl., U.S.	D5	86
Orland Park, Il., U.S.	k9	90
Orléans, Fr.	E8	10
Orleans, Ma., U.S.	C7	98
Orleans, In., U.S.	B4	122
Orleans, co., La., U.S.	E6	95
Orleans, co., N.Y., U.S.	B2	109
Orleans, co., Vt., U.S.	B4	122
Orléans, Île d', i., Que., Can.	C6	74
Orman Dam, S.D., U.S.	C2	118
Ormond Beach, Fl., U.S.	C5	86
Ormož, Slo.	C11	14
Ormstown, Que., Can.	D3	74
Ornans, Fr.	E13	10
Örnsköldsvik, Swe.	E12	6
Orocué, Col.	E7	58
Orofino, Id., U.S.	C2	89
Or'ol, Russia	I19	18
Oromocto, N.B., Can.	D3	71
Oromocto Lake, l., N.B., Can.	D2	71
Orono, Me., U.S.	D4	96
Oronoco, Mn., U.S.	F6	100
Oroville, Ca., U.S.	C3	82
Oroville, Wa., U.S.	A6	124
Oroville, Lake, res., Ca., U.S.	C3	82
Orrick, Mo., U.S.	B3	102
Orrville, Oh., U.S.	B4	112
Orsk, Russia	G9	22
Orta Nova, Italy	H10	14
Ortegal, Cabo, c., Spain	B4	12
Orting, Wa., U.S.	B3	124
Ortiz, Ven.	C9	58
Ortona, Italy	G9	14
Ortonville, Mi., U.S.	F7	99
Ortonville, Mn., U.S.	E2	100
Orūmīyeh (Reżā'īyeh), Iran	J7	22
Orūmīyeh, Daryācheh-ye, l., Iran	J7	22
Oruro, Bol.	G5	54
Orūzgān (Qala-I-Hazār Qadam), Afg.	D2	38
Orvieto, Italy	G7	14
Orwell, Oh., U.S.	A5	112
Orwigsburg, Pa., U.S.	E9	115
Oš, Kyrg.	I12	22
Osa, Península de, pen., C.R.	J6	64
Osage, Ia., U.S.	A5	92
Osage, Wy., U.S.	C8	127
Osage, co., Ks., U.S.	D8	93
Osage, co., Mo., U.S.	C6	102
Osage, co., Ok., U.S.	A5	113
Osage, stm., Mo., U.S.	C3	102
Osage Beach, Mo., U.S.	C5	102
Osage City, Ks., U.S.	D8	93
Ōsaka, Japan	H8	30
Ōsaka-wan, b., Japan	H8	30
Osakis, Mn., U.S.	E3	100
Osakis, Lake, l., Mn., U.S.	E3	100
Osawatomie, Ks., U.S.	D9	93
Osborne, Ks., U.S.	C5	93
Osborne, co., Ks., U.S.	C5	93
Osburn, Id., U.S.	B3	89
Osceola, Ar., U.S.	B6	81
Osceola, In., U.S.	A5	91
Osceola, Ia., U.S.	C4	92
Osceola, Mo., U.S.	C4	102
Osceola, Ne., U.S.	C8	104
Osceola, Wi., U.S.	C1	126
Osceola, co., Fl., U.S.	E5	86
Osceola, co., Ia., U.S.	A2	92
Osceola, co., Mi., U.S.	E5	99
Osceola Mills, Pa., U.S.	E5	115
Oschatz, Ger.	D12	8
Oschersleben, Ger.	C11	8
Oscoda, Mi., U.S.	D7	99
Oscoda, co., Mi., U.S.	D6	99
Oscura Mountains, mts., N.M., U.S.	D3	108
Osen, Nor.	D8	6
Osgood, In., U.S.	F7	91
Oshawa, Ont., Can.	D6	73
Oshima-hantō, pen., Japan	q18	30a
Oshkosh, Ne., U.S.	C3	104
Oshkosh, Wi., U.S.	D5	126
Oshogbo, Nig.	G6	42
Osh see Oš, Kyrg.	I12	22
Oshwe, Zaire	B3	44
Osijek, Cro.	D2	16
Osimo, Italy	F8	14
Osinniki, Russia	G11	24
Osipoviči, Bela.	H11	18
Oskaloosa, Ia., U.S.	C5	92
Oskaloosa, Ks., U.S.	C8	93
Oskarshamn, Swe.	H11	6
Oslo, Nor.	G8	6
Osmānābād, India	C4	37
Osmaniye, Tur.	A5	40
Osmond, Ne., U.S.	B8	104
Osnabrück, Ger.	C8	8
Osorno, Chile	E2	56
Osorno, Spain	C7	12
Osoyoos, B.C., Can.	E8	69
Osoyoos Lake, l., Wa., U.S.	A6	124
Ospino, Ven.	C8	58
Osprey, Fl., U.S.	E4	86
Osprey Reef, rf., Austl.	B9	50
Ossa, Mount, mtn., Austl.	H9	50
Ossabaw Island, i., Ga., U.S.	E5	87
Osseo, Mn., U.S.	m12	100
Osseo, Wi., U.S.	D2	126
Ossian, In., U.S.	C7	91
Ossian, Ia., U.S.	A6	92
Ossining, N.Y., U.S.	D7	109
Ossipee, stm., U.S.	C5	106
Ossipee Lake, l., N.H., U.S.	C4	106
Ostaškov, Russia	D16	18
Osterholz-Scharmbeck, Ger.	B8	8
Osterode, Ger.	D10	8
Östersund, Swe.	E10	6
Osterville, Ma., U.S.	C7	98
Ostrava, Czech.	F18	8
Ostrołęka, Pol.	B21	8
Ostrov, Russia	D11	18
Ostrowiec Świętokrzyski, Pol.	E21	8
Ostrów Wielkopolski, Pol.	D17	8
Ostuni, Italy	I12	14
Ōsumi-kaikyō, strt., Japan	L3	30
Ōsumi-shotō, is., Japan	u30	31b
Osuna, Spain	H6	12
Osvaldo Cruz, Braz.	F3	57
Oswegatchie, stm., N.Y., U.S.	f9	109
Oswego, Il., U.S.	B5	90
Oswego, Ks., U.S.	E8	93
Oswego, N.Y., U.S.	B4	109
Oswego, co., N.Y., U.S.	B4	109
Oswego, stm., N.J., U.S.	D4	107
Oswego, stm., N.Y., U.S.	B4	109
Oswestry, Eng., U.K.	I9	7
Oświęcim, Pol.	E19	8
Ōta, Japan	F12	30
Otaki, N.Z.	D5	52
Otaru, Japan	p18	30a
Otavi, Nmb.	E3	44
Oteen, N.C., U.S.	f10	110
Otero, co., Co., U.S.	D7	83
Otero, co., N.M., U.S.	E3	108
Othello, Wa., U.S.	C6	124
Oti, stm., Afr.	G6	42
Otish, Monts, mts., Que., Can.	F18	66
Otis Orchards, Wa., U.S.	g14	124
Otis Reservoir, res., Ma., U.S.	B1	98
Otisville, Mi., U.S.	E7	99
Otjiwarongo, Nmb.	F3	44
Otočac, Cro.	E10	14
Otoe, co., Ne., U.S.	D9	104
Otranto, Italy	I13	14
Otranto, Strait of, mth., Eur.	I2	16
Otsego, Mi., U.S.	F5	99
Otsego, co., Mi., U.S.	C6	99
Otsego, co., N.Y., U.S.	C5	109
Otsego Lake, l., N.Y., U.S.	C6	109
Ōtsu, Japan	G8	30
Otta, Nor.	F7	6
Ottauquechee, stm., Vt., U.S.	D4	122
Ottawa, Ont., Can.	B9	73
Ottawa, Il., U.S.	B5	90
Ottawa, Ks., U.S.	D8	93
Ottawa, Oh., U.S.	A1	112
Ottawa, co., Ks., U.S.	C6	93
Ottawa, co., Mi., U.S.	F4	99
Ottawa, co., Oh., U.S.	A2	112
Ottawa, co., Ok., U.S.	A7	113
Ottawa, stm., Can.	G17	66
Ottawa, stm., Oh., U.S.	e6	112
Ottawa Hills, Oh., U.S.	e6	112
Ottawa Islands, is., N.W. Ter., Can.	E16	66
Ottenby, Swe.	H11	6
Otterbein, In., U.S.	D3	91
Otter Brook, stm., N.H., U.S.	E2	106
Otter Brook Lake, res., N.H., U.S.	E2	106
Otter Creek, stm., Ut., U.S.	E4	121
Otter Creek, stm., Vt., U.S.	C2	122
Otter Creek Reservoir, res., Ut., U.S.	E4	121
Otter Islands, is., S.C., U.S.	m11	117
Otter Tail, co., Mn., U.S.	D3	100
Otter Tail, stm., Mn., U.S.	D2	100
Otter Tail Lake, l., Mn., U.S.	D3	100
Otterville, Ont., Can.	E4	73
Ottumwa, Ia., U.S.	C5	92
Otwock, Pol.	C21	8
Ötztaler Alpen, mts., Eur.	C5	14
Ouachita, co., Ar., U.S.	D3	81
Ouachita, co., La., U.S.	B3	95
Ouachita, Lake, res., Ar., U.S.	C2	81
Ouachita Mountains, mts., U.S.	E8	76
Ouadda, Cen. Afr. Rep.	G10	42
Ouagadougou, Burkina	F5	42
Ouahigouya, Burkina	F5	42
Oualâta, Maur.	E4	42
Ouallene, Alg.	D6	42
Ouanda Djallé, Cen. Afr. Rep.	G10	42
Ouarane, reg., Maur.	D3	42
Ouargla, Alg.	B7	42
Ouarzazate, Mor.	B4	42
Oubangui, stm., Afr.	A3	44
Oudtshoorn, S. Afr.	H4	44
Oued Meliz, Tun.	M3	14
Oued Zarga, Tun.	M4	14
Ouémé, stm., Benin	G6	42
Ouesso, Congo	A3	44
Ouezzane, Mor.	B4	42
Oujda, Mor.	B5	42
Oulu, Fin.	D15	6
Oulujärvi, l., Fin.	D16	6
Oum Chalouba, Chad	E10	42
Ounianga Kébir, Chad	E10	42
Ouray, Co., U.S.	C3	83
Ouray, co., Co., U.S.	C3	83
Ouray, Mount, mtn., Co., U.S.	C4	83
Ourinhos, Braz.	G4	57
Ourique, Port.	H3	12
Ouro Prêto, Braz.	F7	57
Ōu-sammyaku, mts., Japan	D13	30
Outagamie, co., Wi., U.S.	D5	126
Outardes Quatre, Réservoir, res., Que., Can.	h13	74
Outer Hebrides, is., Scot., U.K.	D5	7
Outer Island, i., Wi., U.S.	A3	126
Outer Santa Barbara Passage, strt., Ca., U.S.	F4	82
Outpost Mountain, mtn., Ak., U.S.	B9	79
Outremont, Que., Can.	p19	74
Ovalle, Chile	C2	56
Ovamboland, hist. reg., Nmb.	E3	44
Ovana, Cerro, mtn., Ven.	E9	58
Ovar, Port.	E3	12
Overbrook, Ks., U.S.	D8	93
Overgaard, Az., U.S.	C5	80
Overland, Mo., U.S.	f13	102
Overland Park, Ks., U.S.	m16	93
Overlea, Md., U.S.	B4	97
Overlea, Md., U.S.	g7	105
Overton, Nv., U.S.	G7	105
Overton, Tx., U.S.	C5	120
Overton, co., Tn., U.S.	C8	119
Övertorneå, Swe.	C14	6
Ovett, Ms., U.S.	D4	101
Ovid, Mi., U.S.	E6	99
Oviedo, Spain	B6	12
Owando, Congo	B3	44
Owasco Lake, l., N.Y., U.S.	C4	109
Owase, Japan	H9	30
Owasso, Ok., U.S.	A6	113
Owatonna, Mn., U.S.	F5	100
Owego, N.Y., U.S.	C4	109
Owen, Wi., U.S.	D3	126
Owen, co., In., U.S.	F4	91
Owen, co., Ky., U.S.	B5	94
Owen, Lake, l., Wi., U.S.	B2	126
Owen, Mount, mtn., Co., U.S.	C3	83
Owens, stm., Ca., U.S.	D4	82
Owensboro, Ky., U.S.	C2	94
Owens Cross Roads, Al., U.S.	A3	78
Owens Lake, l., Ca., U.S.	D5	82
Owen Sound, Ont., Can.	C4	73
Owen Sound, b., Ont., Can.	C4	73
Owen Stanley Range, mts., Pap. N. Gui.	m16	50a
Owensville, In., U.S.	H2	91
Owensville, Mo., U.S.	C6	102
Owensville, Oh., U.S.	C1	112
Owenton, Ky., U.S.	B5	94
Owings Mills, Md., U.S.	B4	97
Owingsville, Ky., U.S.	B6	94
Owl Creek, stm., Wy., U.S.	C4	127
Owl Creek Mountains, mts., Wy., U.S.	C4	127
Owo, Nig.	G7	42
Owosso, Mi., U.S.	E6	99
Owsley, co., Ky., U.S.	C6	94
Owyhee, Nv., U.S.	B5	105
Owyhee, co., Id., U.S.	G2	89
Owyhee, stm., U.S.	E9	114
Owyhee, Lake, res., Or., U.S.	D9	114
Owyhee Dam, Or., U.S.	D9	114
Owyhee Mountains, mts., U.S.	G2	89
Oxbow Dam, U.S.	E2	89
Oxelösund, Swe.	G11	6
Oxford, N.S., Can.	D6	71
Oxford, N.Z.	E4	52
Oxford, Eng., U.K.	J11	7
Oxford, Al., U.S.	B4	78
Oxford, Ct., U.S.	D3	84
Oxford, Ga., U.S.	C3	87
Oxford, In., U.S.	C3	91
Oxford, Ia., U.S.	C6	92
Oxford, Ks., U.S.	E6	93
Oxford, Me., U.S.	D2	96
Oxford, Md., U.S.	C5	97
Oxford, Ma., U.S.	B4	98
Oxford, Mi., U.S.	F7	99
Oxford, Ms., U.S.	A4	101
Oxford, Ne., U.S.	D6	104
Oxford, N.Y., U.S.	C5	109
Oxford, N.C., U.S.	A4	110
Oxford, Oh., U.S.	C1	112
Oxford, Pa., U.S.	G10	115
Oxford, co., Me., U.S.	D2	96
Oxford Lake, l., Man., Can.	B4	70
Oxford Peak, mtn., Id., U.S.	G6	89
Oxnard, Ca., U.S.	E4	82
Oxon Hill, Md., U.S.	f9	97
Oxus see Amu Darya, stm., Asia	I10	22
Oyama, B.C., Can.	D8	69
Oyama, Japan	F12	30
Oyem, Gabon	A2	44
Oyen, Alta., Can.	D5	68
Oyonnax, Fr.	F12	10
Oyster Bay, N.Y., U.S.	E7	109
Oyster Keys, is., Fl., U.S.	G6	86
Ozamiz, Phil.	D7	32
Ozark, Al., U.S.	D4	78
Ozark, Ar., U.S.	B2	81
Ozark, Mo., U.S.	D4	102
Ozark, co., Mo., U.S.	E5	102
Ozark Plateau, plat., U.S.	D8	76
Ozark Reservoir, res., Ar., U.S.	B1	81
Ozarks, Lake of the, res., Mo., U.S.	C5	102
Ozaukee, co., Wi., U.S.	E6	126
Özd, Hung.	G20	8
Ozernovskij, Russia	G25	24
Ozette Lake, l., Wa., U.S.	A1	124
Ozieri, Italy	I3	14
Ožogino, Ozero, l., Russia	D23	24
Ozona, Fl., U.S.	o10	86
Ozona, Tx., U.S.	D2	120
Ōzu, Japan	I5	30

P

Paarl, S. Afr.	H3	44
Pauilo, Hi., U.S.	C6	88
Pabianice, Pol.	D19	8
Pābna, Bngl.	E3	34
Pacasmayo, Peru	u14	86
Pace, Fl., U.S.	C8	84
Pachaug Pond, l., Ct., U.S.	C8	84
Pachino, Italy	M10	14
Pachuca [de Soto], Mex.	G10	62
Pacific, Mo., U.S.	C7	102
Pacific, co., Wa., U.S.	C2	124
Pacifica, Ca., U.S.	h8	82
Pacific Beach, Wa., U.S.	B1	124
Pacific City, Or., U.S.	B3	114
Pacific Creek, stm., Wy., U.S.	D3	127
Pacific Grove, Ca., U.S.	D3	82
Pacific Ocean	F2	2
Pacific Palisades, Hi., U.S.	g10	88
Pacific Ranges, mts., B.C., Can.	D4	69
Pacific Rim National Park, B.C., Can.	E5	69
Pack Monadnock Mountain, mtn., N.H., U.S.	E3	106
Packwood, Wa., U.S.	C4	124
Pacolet, S.C., U.S.	B4	117
Pacolet, stm., S.C., U.S.	A4	117
Pacolet Mills, S.C., U.S.	B4	117
Pactola Reservoir, res., S.D., U.S.	C2	118
Padang, Indon.	F3	32
Padangpanjang, Indon.	O6	34
Padangsidempuan, Indon.	N5	34
Paddock Lake, Wi., U.S.	n11	126
Paden City, W.V., U.S.	B4	125
Paderborn, Ger.	D8	8
Padova, Italy	D6	14
Padre Island, i., Tx., U.S.	F4	120
Padre Island National Seashore, Tx., U.S.	F4	120
Padrón, Spain	C3	12
Padstow, Eng., U.K.	K8	7
Padua see Padova, Italy	D6	14
Paducah, Ky., U.S.	e9	94
Paducah, Tx., U.S.	B2	120
Paektu-san, mtn., Asia	C12	26
Pafúri, Moz.	F6	44
Pag, Cro.	E10	14
Pagai Selatan, Pulau, i., Indon.	F3	32
Pagai Utara, Pulau, i., Indon.	F3	32
Page, Az., U.S.	A4	80
Page, W.V., U.S.	C3	125
Page, co., Ia., U.S.	D2	92
Page, co., Va., U.S.	B4	123
Pageland, S.C., U.S.	B7	117
Pagoda Peak, mtn., Co., U.S.	A3	83
Pagoda Point, c., Burma	G3	34
Pagosa Springs, Co., U.S.	D3	83
Paguate, N.M., U.S.	B2	108
Pahala, Hi., U.S.	D6	88
Pahang, stm., Malay.	M7	34
Pahoa, Hi., U.S.	D7	88
Pahokee, Fl., U.S.	F6	86
Pahrump, Nv., U.S.	G6	105
Pahute Mesa, mtn., Nv., U.S.	F5	105
Paia, Hi., U.S.	C5	88
Päijänne, l., Fin.	F15	6
Pailolo Channel, strt., Hi., U.S.	B5	88
Paimpol, Fr.	D3	10
Paincourtville, La., U.S.	k9	95
Painesville, Oh., U.S.	A4	112
Paint, stm., Mi., U.S.	B2	99
Paint Creek, stm., W.V., U.S.	m13	125
Paint Creek, North Fork, stm., Oh., U.S.	C2	112
Paint Creek Lake, res., Oh., U.S.	C2	112
Painted Desert, des., Az., U.S.	B4	80
Painted Post, N.Y., U.S.	C3	109
Painted Rock Reservoir, res., Az., U.S.	D3	80
Paintsville, Ky., U.S.	C7	94
Paisley, Ont., Can.	C3	73
Paisley, Scot., U.K.	F8	7
Paita, Peru	E2	54
Pajala, Swe.	C14	6
Paján, Ec.	H2	58
Pakanbaru, Indon.	E3	32
Pakaraima Mountains, mts., S.A.	E12	58
Pakistan (Pākistān), ctry., Asia	D2	36
Pakistan, East see Bangladesh, ctry., Asia	E6	36
Pakokku, Burma	D3	34
Pakowki Lake, l., Alta., Can.	E5	68
P'akupur, stm., Russia	E9	24
Pakxé, Laos	G8	34
Pala, Chad	G8	42
Palacios, Tx., U.S.	E4	120
Palamós, Spain	D15	12
Palana, Russia	F25	24
Pālanpur, India	H5	38
Palaoa Point, c., Hi., U.S.	C4	88
Palapye, Bots.	F5	44
Palatine, Il., U.S.	A5	90
Palatka, Russia	E24	24
Palatka, Fl., U.S.	C5	86
Palawan, i., Phil.	D6	32
Pālayankottai, India	H4	37
Palembang, Indon.	F3	32
Palencia, Spain	C7	12
Palermo, Italy	K8	14
Palestine, Ar., U.S.	C5	81
Palestine, Il., U.S.	D6	90
Palestine, Tx., U.S.	D5	120
Palestine, ctry., Asia	C4	40
Palestine, Lake, res., Tx., U.S.	C5	120
Paletwa, Burma	D2	34
Pālghāt, India	G4	37
Pāli, India	H5	38
Palikea, mtn., Hi., U.S.	g9	88
Palisade, Co., U.S.	B2	83
Palisades Park, N.J., U.S.	h8	107
Palisades Reservoir, res., U.S.	F7	89
Pālitāna, India	J4	38
Palk Strait, strt., Asia	H5	37
Pallastunturi, mtn., Fin.	B14	6
Palma, Moz.	D8	44
Palma del Río, Spain	H6	12
Palma [de Mallorca], Spain	F14	12
Palma di Montechiaro, Italy	L8	14
Palmanova, Italy	D8	14
Palmarito, Ven.	D7	58
Palmas, Cape, c., Lib.	H4	42
Palma Soriano, Cuba	D9	64
Palm Bay, Fl., U.S.	D6	86
Palm Beach, Fl., U.S.	F6	86
Palm Beach, co., Fl., U.S.	F6	86
Palm Beach Gardens, Fl., U.S.	*F6	86
Palmdale, Ca., U.S.	E4	82
Palmeio, Braz.	D4	57
Palmer, Ak., U.S.	C10	79
Palmer, Ma., U.S.	B3	98
Palmer, Mi., U.S.	B3	99
Palmer, Mi., U.S.	D4	101
Palmer, Ne., U.S.	C7	104
Palmer, Tn., U.S.	D8	119
Palmer, Tx., U.S.	n10	120
Palmer Lake, Co., U.S.	B6	83
Palmerston, Ont., Can.	D4	73
Palmerston, Cape, c., Austl.	D9	50
Palmerston North, N.Z.	D5	52
Palmerton, Pa., U.S.	E10	115
Palmetto, Fl., U.S.	E4	86
Palmetto, Ga., U.S.	C2	87
Palm Harbor, Fl., U.S.	o10	86
Palmi, Italy	K10	14
Palmira, Col.	F4	58
Palmira, Ec.	I3	58
Palms, Isle of, i., S.C., U.S.	F8	117
Palm Springs, Ca., U.S.	F5	82
Palm Springs, Fl., U.S.	*F6	86
Palmyra, mtn., Hi., U.S.	H5	91
Palmyra, Mo., U.S.	B6	102
Palmyra, N.J., U.S.	C2	107
Palmyra, N.Y., U.S.	B3	109
Palmyra, Pa., U.S.	F8	115
Palmyra, Wi., U.S.	F5	126
Palni, India	G4	37
Palo Alto, Ca., U.S.	D2	82
Palo Alto, co., Ia., U.S.	A3	92
Paloich, Sudan	F12	42
Palomar Mountain, mtn., Ca., U.S.	F5	82
Palomas Mountains, mts., Az., U.S.	D2	80
Palo Pinto, co., Tx., U.S.	C3	120
Palos Park, Il., U.S.	k9	90
Palos Verdes Estates, Ca., U.S.	n12	82
Palourde, Lake, l., La., U.S.	k9	95
Palouse, Wa., U.S.	C8	124
Palouse, stm., Wa., U.S.	C7	124
Palu, Indon.	F6	32
Palwal, India	F7	38
Pamekasan, Indon.	m16	33a
Pamiers, Fr.	I8	10
Pamir, mts., Asia	B3	36
Pamlico, co., N.C., U.S.	B6	110
Pamlico, stm., N.C., U.S.	B6	110
Pamlico Sound, strt., N.C., U.S.	B6	110
Pampa, Tx., U.S.	B2	120
Pampa, reg., Arg.	C4	56
Pamplico, S.C., U.S.	D8	117
Pamplona, Col.	D6	58
Pamplona, Spain	C10	12
Pamunkey, stm., Va., U.S.	C5	123
Panaca, Nv., U.S.	F7	105
Panache, Lake, l., Ont., Can.	A3	73
Panaji (Panjim), India	E2	37
Panamá, Pan.	J8	64
Panama, Ok., U.S.	B7	113
Panama, ctry., N.A.	J7	64
Panama, Gulf of, b., Pan.	J8	64
Panama, Isthmus of, Pan.	J8	64
Panama Canal, Pan.	J8	64
Panama City, Fl., U.S.	u16	86
Panama City Beach, Fl., U.S.	u16	86
Panamint Range, mts., Ca., U.S.	D5	82
Panay, i., Phil.	C7	32
Pancake Range, mts., Nv., U.S.	E6	105
Pandharpur, India	D3	37
Pandora, Oh., U.S.	B2	112
P'andž (Panj), stm., Asia	B3	36
Panevėžys, Lith.	F7	18
Pangala, Congo	B2	44
Pangburn, Ar., U.S.	B4	81
Pangkalanbuun, Indon.	F5	32
Pangkalpinang, Indon.	F4	32
Pangnirtung, N.W. Ter., Can.	C19	66
Panguitch, Ut., U.S.	F3	121
Pangutaran Group, is., Phil.	D7	32
Panhandle, Tx., U.S.	B2	120
Paniau, mtn., Hi., U.S.	B1	88
Pānīpat, India	F7	38
Panj (P'andž), stm., Asia	B4	38
Panjāb, Afg.	C2	38
Panjgūr, Pak.	D1	36
Panola, co., Ms., U.S.	A3	101
Panola, co., Tx., U.S.	C5	120
Panora, Ia., U.S.	C3	92
Pantelleria, Italy	M6	14
Panvel, India	C2	37
Panxian, China	B8	34

Name	Map Ref	Page
Panyam, Nig.	G7	42
Panyu, China	M2	28
Paola, Italy	J11	14
Paola, Ks., U.S.	D9	93
Paoli, In., U.S.	G5	91
Paoli, Pa., U.S.	o20	115
Paonia, Co., U.S.	C3	83
Pápa, Hung.	H17	8
Papago Indian Reservation, Az., U.S.	E3	80
Papaikou, Hi., U.S.	D6	88
Papantla [de Olarte], Mex.	G11	62
Papawai Point, c., Hi., U.S.	C5	88
Papenburg, Ger.	B7	8
Papillion, Ne., U.S.	C9	104
Papineauville, Que., Can.	D2	74
Papua, Gulf of, b., Pap. N. Gui.	m15	50a
Papua New Guinea, ctry., Oc.	m15	50a
Pará, stm., Braz.	D9	54
Paracatu, Braz.	D5	57
Paracatu, Braz.	D6	57
Paracel Islands, is., Asia	B5	32
Parachute, Co., U.S.	B2	83
Paradis, La., U.S.	k11	95
Paradise, stm., Newf., Can.	B3	72
Paradise, Nv., U.S.	G6	105
Paradise, stm., Newf., Can.	B3	72
Paradise Hills, N.M., U.S.	B3	108
Paradise Valley, Az., U.S.	k9	80
Paradise Valley, Nv., U.S.	B4	105
Paragould, Ar., U.S.	A5	81
Paraguaçu Paulista, Braz.	G3	57
Paraguaipoa, Ven.	B7	58
Paraguaná, Península de, pen., Ven.	B7	58
Paraguarí, Para.	B5	56
Paraguay, ctry., S.A.	A5	56
Paraguay, stm., S.A.	A5	56
Paraíba do Sul, stm., Braz.	F7	57
Parakou, Benin	G6	42
Paramagudi, India	H5	37
Paramaribo, Sur.	B7	54
Paramirim, Braz.	B7	57
Paramount, Md., U.S.	A5	97
Paramus, N.J., U.S.	h8	107
Paramušir, Ostrov, i., Russia	G25	24
Paraná, Arg.	C4	56
Paraná, Braz.	B5	57
Paraná, stm., Braz.	B5	57
Paraná, stm., S.A.	C5	56
Paranaguá, Braz.	B7	56
Paranaíba, Braz.	E3	57
Paranaíba, stm., Braz.	E3	57
Paranapanema, stm., Braz.	G3	57
Paranavaí, Braz.	G2	57
Parangaba, Braz.	D11	54
Paratinga, Braz.	B7	57
Paraúna, Braz.	D3	57
Paray-le-Monial, Fr.	F11	10
Pārbati, stm., India	H7	38
Parbhani, India	C4	37
Parchim, Ger.	B11	8
Parchment, Mi., U.S.	F5	99
Pardeeville, Wi., U.S.	E4	126
Pardo, stm., Braz.	E8	57
Pardubice, Czech.	E15	8
Parece Vela see Okino-Tori-shima, i., Japan	G14	26
Parecis, Serra dos, mts., Braz.	F7	54
Paredes de Nava, Spain	C7	12
Paren', Russia	E26	24
Parepare, Indon.	F6	32
Pargas (Parainen), Fin.	F14	6
Paria, stm., U.S.	A4	80
Paria, Gulf of, b.	I16	64
Pariaguán, Ven.	C10	58
Pariaman, Indon.	O6	34
Parícutin, vol., Mex.	H8	62
Parikkala, Fin.	F17	6
Parima, Sierra, mts., S.A.	F10	58
Pariñas, Punta, c., Peru	D2	54
Parintins, Braz.	D7	54
Paris, Ont., Can.	D4	73
Paris, Fr.	D9	10
Paris, Ar., U.S.	B2	81
Paris, Il., U.S.	D6	90
Paris, Ky., U.S.	B5	94
Paris, Mo., U.S.	B5	102
Paris, Tn., U.S.	A3	119
Paris, Tx., U.S.	C5	120
Paris Peak, mtn., Id., U.S.	G7	89
Parit Buntar, Malay.	L6	34
Park, co., Co., U.S.	B5	83
Park, co., Mt., U.S.	E6	103
Park, co., Wy., U.S.	B3	127
Park, stm., N.D., U.S.	A8	111
Parkano, Fin.	E14	6
Park City, Ks., U.S.	g12	93
Park City, Ut., U.S.	C4	121
Parkdale, P.E.I., Can.	C6	71
Parke, co., In., U.S.	E3	91
Parker, Az., U.S.	C1	80
Parker, Co., U.S.	B6	83
Parker, Fl., U.S.	u16	86
Parker, S.D., U.S.	D8	118
Parker, co., Tx., U.S.	C4	120
Parker, Cape, c., N.W. Ter., Can.	A17	66
Parker City, In., U.S.	D7	91
Parker Dam, U.S.	C1	80
Parkersburg, Ia., U.S.	B5	92
Parkersburg, W.V., U.S.	B3	125
Parkers Prairie, Mn., U.S.	D3	100
Parkesburg, Pa., U.S.	G10	115
Park Falls, Wi., U.S.	C3	126
Park Forest, Il., U.S.	B6	90
Park Hall, Md., U.S.	D5	97
Parkhill, Ont., Can.	D3	73
Park Hills, Ky., U.S.	h13	94
Parkin, Ar., U.S.	B5	81
Parkland, Wa., U.S.	f11	124
Park Layne, Oh., U.S.	C1	112
Park Range, mts., Co., U.S.	A4	83
Park Rapids, Mn., U.S.	D3	100
Park Ridge, Il., U.S.	B6	90
Park Ridge, N.J., U.S.	g8	107
Park River, N.D., U.S.	A8	111
Parkrose, Or., U.S.	B4	114
Parksley, Va., U.S.	C7	123
Parkston, S.D., U.S.	D8	118
Parksville, B.C., Can.	E5	69
Parkville, Md., U.S.	B4	97
Parkville, Mo., U.S.	B3	102
Parkwater, Wa., U.S.	g14	124
Parkwood, N.C., U.S.	B4	110
Parlākimidi, India	C8	37
Parie, Lac qui, l., Mn., U.S.	E8	100
Parlier, Ca., U.S.	D4	82
Parma, Italy	E5	14
Parma, Id., U.S.	F2	89
Parma, Mi., U.S.	F6	99
Parma, Mo., U.S.	E8	102
Parma, Oh., U.S.	A4	112
Parmachenee Lake, l., Me., U.S.	C2	96
Parma Heights, Oh., U.S.	h9	112
Parmer, co., Tx., U.S.	B1	120
Parnaíba, Braz.	D10	54
Parnaíba, stm., Braz.	D10	54
Pärnu, Est.	C7	18
Paro, Bhu.	G13	38
Parowan, Ut., U.S.	F3	121
Par Pond, res., S.C., U.S.	D5	117
Parral, Chile	D2	56
Parramore Island, i., Va., U.S.	C7	123
Parras de la Fuente, Mex.	E8	62
Parrish, Al., U.S.	B2	78
Parrsboro, N.S., Can.	D5	71
Parry, Cape, c., N.W. Ter., Can.	B8	66
Parry, Mount, mtn., B.C., Can.	C3	69
Parry Bay, b., N.W. Ter., Can.	C16	66
Parry Sound, Ont., Can.	B4	73
Parshall, N.D., U.S.	B3	111
Parsons, Ks., U.S.	E8	93
Parsons, Tn., U.S.	B3	119
Parsons, W.V., U.S.	B5	125
Parsonsburg, Md., U.S.	D7	97
Parthenay, Fr.	F6	10
Partinico, Italy	K8	14
Partridge Point, c., Newf., Can.	C3	72
Paru, stm., Braz.	D8	54
Pārvatīpuram, India	C7	37
Parys, S. Afr.	G5	44
Pasadena, Newf., Can.	D3	72
Pasadena, Ca., U.S.	E4	82
Pasadena, Md., U.S.	B4	97
Pasadena, Tx., U.S.	r14	120
Pascagoula, Ms., U.S.	E5	101
Pascagoula, stm., Ms., U.S.	E5	101
Pascagoula Bay, b., Ms., U.S.	f8	101
Pasco, Wa., U.S.	C6	124
Pasco, co., Fl., U.S.	D4	86
Pascoag, R.I., U.S.	B2	116
Pascoag Reservoir, res., R.I., U.S.	B2	116
Pascua, Isla de (Easter Island), i., Chile	H5	2
Pasewalk, Ger.	B13	8
Pasig, Phil.	q19	33b
P'asina, stm., Russia	C11	24
P'asino, Ozero, l., Russia	D11	24
P'asinskij Zaliv, b., Russia	C10	24
Pasirpengarajan, Indon.	N6	34
Pasir Puteh, Malay.	L7	34
Pasni, Pak.	D1	36
Paso de Indios, Arg.	E3	56
Paso de los Libres, Arg.	B5	56
Paso Robles, Ca., U.S.	E3	82
Pasque Island, i., Ma., U.S.	D6	98
Pasquotank, co., N.C., U.S.	A6	110
Passagem, Braz.	B7	57
Passaic, N.J., U.S.	B4	107
Passaic, co., N.J., U.S.	A4	107
Passaic, stm., N.J., U.S.	h8	107
Passamaquoddy Bay, b., Me., U.S.	C6	96
Passau, Ger.	G13	8
Pass Christian, Ms., U.S.	E4	101
Passo Fundo, Braz.	B6	56
Passos, Braz.	F5	57
Passumpsic, stm., Vt., U.S.	C4	122
Pasto, Col.	G4	58
Pastora Peak, mtn., Az., U.S.	A6	80
Pastrana, Spain	E9	12
Pasuruan, Indon.	m16	33a
Patagonia, Az., U.S.	F5	80
Patagonia, reg., Arg.	E3	56
Pātan, India	I5	38
Patapsco, stm., Md., U.S.	B4	97
Pataskala, Oh., U.S.	C3	112
Patchet Brook Reservoir, res., R.I., U.S.	E6	116
Patchogue, N.Y., U.S.	n15	109
Pate Island, i., Kenya	B8	44
Paternò, Italy	L9	14
Paterson, N.J., U.S.	B4	107
Pathānkot, India	D6	38
Pathein, Burma	F3	34
Pathfinder Reservoir, res., Wy., U.S.	D6	127
Pati, Indon.	m15	33a
Patiāla, India	E7	38
Patience Island, i., R.I., U.S.	D5	116
P'atigorsk, Russia	I6	22
Pātkai Range, mts., Asia	G16	38
Patman, Lake, res., Tx., U.S.	C5	120
Patna, India	H11	38
Patoka, In., U.S.	H2	91
Patoka, stm., In., U.S.	H2	91
Patoka, Lake, res., In., U.S.	H4	91
Patos, Braz.	E11	54
Patos, Lagoa do, b., Braz.	C6	56
Patos de Minas, Braz.	E5	57
Patquía, Arg.	C3	56
Pátrai, Grc.	K5	16
Patricio Lynch, Isla, i., Chile	F1	56
Patrick, co., Va., U.S.	D2	123
Patrick Air Force Base, mil., Fl., U.S.	D6	86
Patrocínio, Braz.	E5	57
Pattani, Thai.	K6	34
Patten, Me., U.S.	C4	96
Patterson, Ga., U.S.	E4	87
Patterson, La., U.S.	E4	95
Patterson Creek, stm., W.V., U.S.	B5	125
Pattoki, Pak.	E5	38
Patton, Pa., U.S.	E4	115
Patuākhāli, Bngl.	I14	38
Patuca, stm., Hond.	G5	64
Patuxent, stm., Md., U.S.	D4	97
Patuxent Naval Air Test Center, mil., Md., U.S.	D5	97
Pátzcuaro, Mex.	H9	62
Pau, Fr.	I6	10
Paul, Id., U.S.	G5	89
Paulding, Oh., U.S.	A1	112
Paulding, co., Ga., U.S.	C2	87
Paulding, co., Oh., U.S.	A1	112
Paulina, La., U.S.	h10	95
Paulina Mountains, mts., Or., U.S.	D5	114
Paulina Peak, mtn., Or., U.S.	E5	114
Paulins Kill, stm., N.J., U.S.	A3	107
Paulistana, Braz.	E10	54
Paulistas, Braz.	E7	57
Paullina, Ia., U.S.	B2	92
Paulo Afonso, Braz.	E11	54
Paulsboro, N.J., U.S.	D2	107
Paul Stream, stm., Vt., U.S.	B5	122
Pauls Valley, Ok., U.S.	C4	113
Paungde, Burma	E3	34
Pavia, Italy	D4	14
Pavilion Key, i., Fl., U.S.	G5	86
Pavlodar, Kaz.	G9	24
Pavlof Volcano, vol., Ak., U.S.	D7	79
Pavlovo, Russia	F26	18
Pavlovsk, Russia	G7	24
Pavlovskij Posad, Russia	F21	18
Pavo, Ga., U.S.	F3	87
Pavullo nel Frignano, Italy	E5	14
Pavón, Col.	F6	58
Pawcatuck, Ct., U.S.	D8	84
Pawcatuck, stm., R.I., U.S.	G1	116
Paw Creek, N.C., U.S.	B2	110
Pawhuska, Ok., U.S.	A5	113
Pawling, N.Y., U.S.	D7	109
Pawnee, Il., U.S.	D4	90
Pawnee, Ok., U.S.	A5	113
Pawnee, co., Ks., U.S.	D4	93
Pawnee, co., Ne., U.S.	D9	104
Pawnee, co., Ok., U.S.	A5	113
Pawnee City, Ne., U.S.	D9	104
Pawpaw, Il., U.S.	B5	90
Paw Paw, Mi., U.S.	F5	99
Paw Paw, W.V., U.S.	B6	125
Pawpaw Creek, stm., W.V., U.S.	h10	125
Pawtuckaway Pond, l., N.H., U.S.	D4	106
Pawtucket, R.I., U.S.	C4	116
Pawtuxet, stm., R.I., U.S.	C4	116
Paxton, Il., U.S.	C5	90
Paxton, Ma., U.S.	B4	98
Payakumbuh, Indon.	O6	34
Payette, Id., U.S.	E2	89
Payette, co., Id., U.S.	E2	89
Payette, North Fork, stm., Id., U.S.	E2	89
Payette, South Fork, stm., Id., U.S.	E3	89
Payette Lake, res., Id., U.S.	E3	89
Payne, Oh., U.S.	A1	112
Payne, co., Ok., U.S.	A4	113
Paynesville, Mn., U.S.	E4	100
Paysandú, Ur.	C5	56
Payson, Az., U.S.	C4	80
Payson, Il., U.S.	D2	90
Payson, Ut., U.S.	C4	121
Pazardžik, Bul.	G8	16
Pazarköy, Tur.	J11	16
Paz de Río, Col.	E6	58
Pazin, Cro.	D8	14
Pea, stm., Al., U.S.	D3	78
Peabody, Ks., U.S.	D6	93
Peabody, Ma., U.S.	A6	98
Peabody, stm., N.H., U.S.	B4	106
Peace, Can.	E9	66
Peace, stm., Fl., U.S.	E5	86
Peace Dale, R.I., U.S.	F3	116
Peace River, Alta., Can.	A2	68
Peacham Pond, res., Vt., U.S.	C4	122
Peach, co., Ga., U.S.	D3	87
Peach Point, c., Ma., U.S.	f12	98
Peach Springs, Az., U.S.	B2	80
Peak District National Park, Eng., U.K.	H11	7
Peaks Island, i., Me., U.S.	g7	96
Peale, Mount, mtn., Ut., U.S.	E6	121
Pea Patch Island, i., De., U.S.	B3	85
Pea Ridge, Ar., U.S.	A1	81
Pea Ridge National Military Park, Ar., U.S.	A1	81
Pearisburg, Va., U.S.	C2	123
Pearl, Ms., U.S.	C3	101
Pearl, stm., U.S.	D3	101
Pearland, Tx., U.S.	r14	120
Pearl and Hermes Reef, rf., Hi., U.S.	k12	88
Pearl City, Hi., U.S.	B4	88
Pearl Harbor, b., Hi., U.S.	B3	88
Pearl Harbor Naval Station, mil., Hi., U.S.	g10	88
Pearlington, Ms., U.S.	E4	101
Pearl River, La., U.S.	D6	95
Pearl River, N.Y., U.S.	g12	109
Pearl River, co., Ms., U.S.	E4	101
Pearsall, Tx., U.S.	E3	120
Pearsoll Peak, mtn., Or., U.S.	E3	114
Pearson, Ga., U.S.	E4	87
Peary Land, reg., Grnld.	A16	128
Pease, stm., Tx., U.S.	B3	120
Pease Air Force Base, mil., N.H., U.S.	D5	106
Pebane, Moz.	E7	44
Peć, Yugo.	G4	16
Pecatonica, Il., U.S.	A4	90
Pecatonica, stm., U.S.	A4	90
Pecatonica, East Branch, stm., Wi., U.S.	F4	126
Peckerwood Lake, res., Ar., U.S.	C4	81
Pečora, stm., Russia	D5	24
Pecos, N.M., U.S.	B4	108
Pecos, Tx., U.S.	D1	120
Pecos, co., Tx., U.S.	D1	120
Pecos, stm., U.S.	E6	76
Pecos National Monument, N.M., U.S.	B4	108
Peculiar, Mo., U.S.	C3	102
Peddocks Island, i., Ma., U.S.	g12	98
Pedernales, Ven.	C11	58
Pedregal, Ven.	B7	58
Pedro, Point, c., Sri L.	H6	37
Pedro de Valdivia, Chile	A3	56
Pedro Juan Caballero, Para.	G1	57
Peebles, Oh., U.S.	D2	112
Peekskill, N.Y., U.S.	D7	109
Peel, I. of Man	G8	7
Peel, stm., Can.	C5	66
Peel Point, c., N.W. Ter., Can.	B10	66
Peel Sound, strt., N.W. Ter., Can.	B13	66
Pegram, Tn., U.S.	A4	119
Pehuajó, Arg.	D4	56
Peikang, Tai.	L9	28
Peine, Ger.	C10	8
Pekalongan, Indon.	m14	33a
Pekin, Il., U.S.	C4	90
Pekin, In., U.S.	G5	91
Peking see Beijing, China	D10	26
Pelagie, Isole, is., Italy	N7	14
Pelahatchie, Ms., U.S.	C4	101
Pelée, Montagne, mtn., Mart.	G17	64
Pelee Island, i., Ont., Can.	F2	73
Peleng, Pulau, i., Indon.	F7	32
Pelham, Ont., Can.	D5	73
Pelham, Al., U.S.	B3	78
Pelham, Ga., U.S.	E2	87
Pelham, N.H., U.S.	E4	106
Pelham Manor, N.Y., U.S.	h13	109
Pelican Bay, b., Man., Can.	C1	70
Pelican Lake, l., Man., Can.	C1	70
Pelican Lake, l., Mn., U.S.	D4	100
Pelican Lake, l., Mn., U.S.	D3	100
Pelican Lake, l., Mn., U.S.	B6	100
Pelican Lake, l., Mn., U.S.	E5	100
Pelican Lake, l., Wi., U.S.	C4	126
Pelican Mountain, mtn., Alta., Can.	B4	68
Pelican Rapids, Mn., U.S.	D2	100
Pella, Ia., U.S.	C5	92
Pell City, Al., U.S.	B3	78
Pell Lake, Wi., U.S.	n11	126
Pello, Fin.	C14	6
Pelly Mountains, mts., Yukon, Can.	D6	66
Pelopónnisos, reg., Grc.	L5	16
Pelotas, Braz.	C6	56
Pelton, Lake, l., La., U.S.	E5	95
Pemadumcook Lake, l., Me., U.S.	C3	96
Pemalang, Indon.	m14	33a
Pematangsiantar, Indon.	E2	32
Pemba, Moz.	D8	44
Pemba Island, i., Tan.	C7	44
Pemberton, Austl.	F3	50
Pemberton, B.C., Can.	D6	69
Pemberville, Oh., U.S.	A2	112
Pembina, N.D., U.S.	A8	111
Pembina, co., N.D., U.S.	A8	111
Pembina, stm., Alta., Can.	C3	68
Pembroke, Ont., Can.	B7	73
Pembroke, Wales, U.K.	J8	7
Pembroke, Ga., U.S.	D5	87
Pembroke, Ky., U.S.	D2	94
Pembroke, Ma., U.S.	B6	98
Pembroke, N.C., U.S.	C3	110
Pembroke, Va., U.S.	C2	123
Pembroke Pines, Fl., U.S.	r13	86
Pemigewasset, stm., N.H., U.S.	C3	106
Pemiscot, co., Mo., U.S.	E8	102
Peñafiel, Spain	D7	12
Penápolis, Braz.	F3	57
Peñaranda de Bracamonte, Spain	E6	12
Pen Argyl, Pa., U.S.	E11	115
Peñarroya-Pueblonuevo, Spain	G6	12
Penasco, N.M., U.S.	A4	108
Peñasco, Rio, stm., N.M., U.S.	E4	108
Penbrook, Pa., U.S.	F8	115
Pender, Ne., U.S.	B9	104
Pender, co., N.C., U.S.	C4	110
Pendleton, In., U.S.	E6	91
Pendleton, Or., U.S.	B8	114
Pendleton, S.C., U.S.	B2	117
Pendleton, co., Ky., U.S.	B5	94
Pendleton, co., W.V., U.S.	C5	125
Pendley Hills, Ga., U.S.	*h8	87
Pend Oreille, co., Wa., U.S.	A8	124
Pend Oreille, Lake, l., Id., U.S.	A2	89
Pend Oreille, Mount, mtn., Id., U.S.	A2	89
Penetanguishene, Ont., Can.	C5	73
P'enghu Liehtao, is., Tai.	L8	28
Penglai, China	D11	26
Penhold, Alta., Can.	C4	68
Peniche, Port.	F2	12
Penjamo, Mex.	G9	62
Pennant Point, c., N.S., Can.	E6	71
Pennask Mountain, mtn., B.C., Can.	E7	69
Penne, Italy	G8	14
Pennell, Mount, mtn., Ut., U.S.	E5	121
Penner, stm., India	F5	37
Penn Hills, Pa., U.S.	k14	115
Pennines, mts., Eng., U.K.	G10	7
Pennines, Alpes, mts., Eur.	F14	10
Pennington, co., Mn., U.S.	B2	100
Pennington, co., S.D., U.S.	D2	118
Pennington Gap, Va., U.S.	f8	123
Pennsauken, N.J., U.S.	D2	107
Pennsboro, W.V., U.S.	B4	125
Pennsburg, Pa., U.S.	F11	115
Penns Grove, N.J., U.S.	D2	107
Pennsville, N.J., U.S.	D1	107
Pennsylvania, state, U.S.	E7	115
Pennville, In., U.S.	D7	91
Penn Yan, N.Y., U.S.	C3	109
Penobscot, co., Me., U.S.	C4	96
Penobscot, stm., Me., U.S.	C4	96
Penobscot Bay, b., Me., U.S.	D3	96
Penobscot Lake, l., Me., U.S.	C2	96
Penonomé, Pan.	J7	64
Penrith, Eng., U.K.	G10	7
Pensacola, Fl., U.S.	u14	86
Pensacola Bay, b., Fl., U.S.	u14	86
Pensacola Dam, Ok., U.S.	A6	113
Pensacola Naval Air Station, mil., Fl., U.S.	u14	86
Pentagon Mountain, mtn., Mt., U.S.	C3	103
Penticton, B.C., Can.	E8	69
Pentland Firth, strt., Scot., U.K.	C9	7
Pentwater, Mi., U.S.	E4	99
Penyu, Kepulauan, is., Indon.	G8	32
Penza, Russia	G7	22
Penzance, Eng., U.K.	K7	7
Penžina, stm., Russia	E27	24
Penžinskaja Guba, b., Russia	E26	24
Penžinskij Chrebet, mts., Russia	E27	24
Peonan Point, c., Man., Can.	D2	70
Peoria, Az., U.S.	D3	80
Peoria, Il., U.S.	C4	90
Peoria, co., Il., U.S.	C4	90
Peoria Heights, Il., U.S.	C4	90
Peotone, Il., U.S.	B6	90
Pepacton Reservoir, res., N.Y., U.S.	C6	109
Pepeekeo, Hi., U.S.	D6	88
Pepin, Wi., U.S.	D1	126
Pepin, co., Wi., U.S.	D2	126
Pepin, Lake, l., U.S.	D1	126
Pepperell, Ma., U.S.	A4	98
Pequannock, N.J., U.S.	B4	107
Pequest, stm., N.J., U.S.	B2	107
Pequop Mountains, mts., Nv., U.S.	C7	105
Pequot Lakes, Mn., U.S.	D4	100
Perabumulih, Indon.	F3	32
Percy, Il., U.S.	E4	90
Perdido, Al., U.S.	D2	78
Perdido, stm., U.S.	E2	78
Perdido Bay, b., Al., U.S.	E2	78
Pereira, Col.	E5	58
Pere Marquette, stm., Mi., U.S.	E4	99
Pereslavl'-Zalesskij, Russia	E21	18
Pergamino, Arg.	C4	56
Pergine Valsugana, Italy	C6	14
Perham, Mn., U.S.	D3	100
Péribonca, stm., Que., Can.	G18	66
Peridot, Az., U.S.	D5	80
Périgueux, Fr.	G7	10
Perijá, Sierra de, mts., S.A.	B6	58
Perkasie, Pa., U.S.	F11	115
Perkins, Ok., U.S.	B4	113
Perkins, co., Ne., U.S.	D4	104
Perkins, co., S.D., U.S.	B3	118
Perkinston, Ms., U.S.	E4	101
Perlas, Archipiélago de las, is., Pan.	J8	64
Perlas, Laguna de, b., Nic.	H6	64
Perleberg, Ger.	B11	8
Perm', Russia	F9	22
Pernik, Bul.	G7	16
Péronne, Fr.	C9	10
Perpignan, Fr.	J9	10
Perquimans, co., N.C., U.S.	A6	110
Perrine, Fl., U.S.	G6	86
Perris, Ca., U.S.	F5	82
Perro, Laguna del, l., N.M., U.S.	C4	108
Perros-Guirec, Fr.	D3	10
Perrot, Île, i., Que., Can.	q19	74
Perry, Fl., U.S.	B3	86
Perry, Ga., U.S.	D3	87
Perry, Ia., U.S.	C3	92
Perry, Ks., U.S.	C8	93
Perry, Mi., U.S.	F6	99
Perry, Mo., U.S.	B6	102
Perry, N.Y., U.S.	C2	109
Perry, Oh., U.S.	A4	112
Perry, Ok., U.S.	A4	113
Perry, Ut., U.S.	B3	121
Perry, co., Al., U.S.	C2	78
Perry, co., Ar., U.S.	C3	81
Perry, co., Il., U.S.	E4	90
Perry, co., In., U.S.	H4	91
Perry, co., Ky., U.S.	C6	94
Perry, co., Ms., U.S.	D4	101
Perry, co., Mo., U.S.	D8	102
Perry, co., Oh., U.S.	C3	112
Perry, co., Pa., U.S.	F7	115
Perry, co., Tn., U.S.	B4	119
Perry Hall, Md., U.S.	B5	97
Perry Lake, res., Ks., U.S.	C8	93
Perryman, Md., U.S.	B5	97
Perrysburg, Oh., U.S.	A2	112
Perry Stream, stm., N.H., U.S.	f7	106
Perry's Victory and International Peace Memorial, hist., Oh., U.S.	A2	112
Perryton, Tx., U.S.	A2	120
Perryville, Ar., U.S.	B3	81
Perryville, Ky., U.S.	C5	94
Perryville, Md., U.S.	A5	97
Perryville, Mo., U.S.	D8	102
Pershing, co., Nv., U.S.	C3	105
Persia see Iran, ctry., Asia	B5	46
Persian Gulf, b., Asia	C5	46
Person, co., N.C., U.S.	A3	110
Perth, Austl.	F3	50
Perth, Ont., Can.	C8	73
Perth, Scot., U.K.	E9	7
Perth Amboy, N.J., U.S.	B4	107
Perth-Andover, N.B., Can.	D10	71
Pertuis, Fr.	I12	10
Peru, Il., U.S.	B4	90
Peru, In., U.S.	C5	91
Peru, N.Y., U.S.	f11	109
Peru (Perú), ctry., S.A.	E3	54
Perugia, Italy	F7	14
Perušic, Cro.	E10	14
Pesaro, Italy	F7	14
Pescadores see P'enghu Liehtao, is., Tai.	L8	28
Pescara, Italy	G9	14

Name	Map Ref	Page
Pescia, Italy	F5	14
Peshastin, Wa., U.S.	B5	124
Peshāwar, Pak.	C4	38
Peshtigo, Wi., U.S.	C6	126
Peshtigo, stm., Wi., U.S.	C5	126
Pesqueira, Braz.	E11	54
Pessac, Fr.	H6	10
Petaḥ Tiqwa, Isr.	C4	40
Petal, Ms., U.S.	D4	101
Petaluma, Ca., U.S.	C2	82
Petatlán, Mex.	I9	62
Petawawa, Ont., Can.	B7	73
Petawawa, stm., Ont., Can.	A6	73
Petenwell Lake, res., Wi., U.S.	D4	126
Peterborough, Austl.	F7	50
Peterborough, Ont., Can.	C6	73
Peterborough, Eng., U.K.	I12	7
Peterborough, N.H., U.S.	E3	106
Peterhead, Scot., U.K.	D11	7
Peter Pond Lake, l., Sask., Can.	m7	75
Petersburg, Ak., U.S.	D13	79
Petersburg, Il., U.S.	C4	90
Petersburg, In., U.S.	H3	91
Petersburg, Mi., U.S.	G7	99
Petersburg, Oh., U.S.	B5	112
Petersburg, Tx., U.S.	C2	120
Petersburg, Va., U.S.	C5	123
Petersburg, W.V., U.S.	B5	125
Peters Creek, stm., W.V., U.S.	m14	125
Peterson, Al., U.S.	C6	78
Peterson Field, mil., Co., U.S.	A2	78
Petersville, Al., U.S.	A2	78
Petit Bois Island, i., Ms., U.S.	E5	101
Petitcodiac, N.B., Can.	D4	71
Petitcodiac, stm., N.B., Can.	C5	71
Petite Amite, stm., La., U.S.	h10	95
Petit Jean, stm., Ar., U.S.	B2	81
Petit Lac Des Allemands, l., La., U.S.	k11	95
Petit Lake, l., La., U.S.	k12	95
Petitot, stm., Can.	E8	66
Petit-Rocher, N.B., Can.	B4	71
Petitsikapau Lake, l., Newf., Can.	g8	72
Petlād, India	I5	38
Petone, N.Z.	D5	52
Petoskey, Mi., U.S.	C6	99
Petrified Forest National Park, Az., U.S.	B6	80
Petrila, Rom.	D7	16
Petrinja, Cro.	D11	14
Petroleum, co., Mt., U.S.	C8	103
Petrolia, Ont., Can.	E2	73
Petrolina, Braz.	E10	54
Petropavlovsk-Kamčatskij, Russia	G25	24
Petrópolis, Braz.	G7	57
Petros, Tn., U.S.	C9	119
Petroșani, Rom.	D7	16
Petrovsk-Zabajkal'skij, Russia	G15	24
Petrozavodsk, Russia	E4	22
Pettaquamscutt Lake Shores, R.I., U.S.	F4	116
Pettingell Peak, mtn., Co., U.S.	B5	83
Pettis, co., Mo., U.S.	C4	102
Pevek, Russia	D28	24
Pevely, Mo., U.S.	g13	102
Pewaukee, Wi., U.S.	E5	126
Pewaukee Lake, l., Wi., U.S.	m11	126
Pewee Valley, Ky., U.S.	B4	94
Péxenas, Fr.	I10	10
Pézenas, Fr.	G8	8
Pforzheim, Ger.	F8	8
Pfungstadt, Ger.	F4	34
Pha-an, Burma	E6	38
Phagwāra, India	D14	10
Phalsbourg, Fr.	D3	37
Phaltan, India	J6	34
Phangan, Ko, i., Thai.	J5	34
Phangnga, Thai.		
Phanom Dongrak, Thiu Khao, mts., Asia	G7	34
Phan Rang, Viet.	I10	34
Phan Si Pan, mtn., Viet.	C7	34
Phan Thiet, Viet.	I10	34
Pharr, Tx., U.S.	F3	120
Phatthalung, Thai.	K6	34
Phayao, Thai.	E5	34
Phelps, Ky., U.S.	C7	94
Phelps, N.Y., U.S.	C3	109
Phelps, Wi., U.S.	B4	126
Phelps, co., Mo., U.S.	D6	102
Phelps, co., Ne., U.S.	D6	104
Phelps Lake, l., N.C., U.S.	B6	110
Phenix City, Al., U.S.	C4	78
Phetchaburi, Thai.	H5	34
Philadelphia, Ms., U.S.	C4	101
Philadelphia, Pa., U.S.	G11	115
Philadelphia, co., Pa., U.S.	G12	115
Philadelphia Naval Shipyard, mil., Pa., U.S.	P21	115
Phil Campbell, Al., U.S.	A2	78
Philip, S.D., U.S.	C4	118
Philippeville, Bel.		
Philippi, W.V., U.S.	B4	125
Philippines, ctry., Asia	C7	32
Philippine Sea	E21	2
Philipsburg, Mt., U.S.	D3	103
Philipsburg, Pa., U.S.	E5	115
Philleo Lake, l., Wa., U.S.	h14	124
Phillips, Me., U.S.	D2	96
Phillips, Tx., U.S.	B2	120
Phillips, Wi., U.S.	C3	126
Phillips, co., Ar., U.S.	C5	81
Phillips, co., Co., U.S.	A8	83
Phillips, co., Ks., U.S.	C4	93
Phillips, co., Mt., U.S.	B8	103
Phillips Brook, stm., N.H., U.S.	A4	106
Phillipsburg, Ks., U.S.	C4	93
Phillipsburg, N.J., U.S.	B2	107
Philmont, N.Y., U.S.	C7	109
Philo, Il., U.S.	C5	90
Philomath, Or., U.S.	C3	114
Philpots Island, i., N.W. Ter., Can.	B17	66
Philpott Reservoir, res., Va., U.S.	D2	123
Phitsanulok, Thai.	F6	34

Phnom Penh see Phnum Pénh, Camb.	I8	34
Phnum Pénh (Phnom Penh), Camb.	I8	34
Phoenix, Az., U.S.	D3	80
Phoenix, Il., U.S.	k9	90
Phoenix, N.Y., U.S.	B4	109
Phoenix, Or., U.S.	E4	114
Phoenixville, Pa., U.S.	F10	115
Phôngsali, Laos	D7	34
Phrae, Thai.	E6	34
Phra Nakhon Si Ayutthaya, Thai.	G6	34
Phuket, Thai.	K5	34
Phuket, Ko, i., Thai.	K5	34
Phu Ly, Viet.	D8	34
Phumĭ Bĕng, Camb.	H8	34
Phumĭ Kâmpóng Trâbêk, Camb.	H8	34
Phumĭ Prêk Kák, Camb.	I7	34
Phu Quoc, Dao, i., Viet.	I7	34
Phu Tho, Viet.	D8	34
Piacenza, Italy	D4	14
Piatra-Neamt, Rom.	C10	16
Piatt, co., Il., U.S.	D5	90
Piazza Armerina, Italy	L9	14
Pibor Post, Sudan	G12	42
Picacho, Az., U.S.	E4	80
Picardie, hist. reg., Fr.	C9	10
Picayune, Ms., U.S.	E4	101
Piccadilly, Newf., Can.	D2	72
Pichanal, Arg.	A4	56
Picher, Ok., U.S.	A7	113
Pickaway, co., Oh., U.S.	C2	112
Pickens, Ms., U.S.	C4	101
Pickens, S.C., U.S.	B2	117
Pickens, co., Al., U.S.	B1	78
Pickens, co., Ga., U.S.	B2	87
Pickens, co., S.C., U.S.	B2	117
Pickerel Lake, l., Wi., U.S.	C5	126
Pickering, Ont., Can.	D5	73
Pickerington, Oh., U.S.	C3	112
Pickett, co., Tn., U.S.	C8	119
Pickwick Lake, res., U.S.	A6	101
Pickworth Point, c., Ma., U.S.	f12	98
Pico Rivera, Ca., U.S.	n12	82
Picos, Braz.	E10	54
Picquigny, Fr.	C9	10
Picton, Ont., Can.	D7	73
Pictou Island, i., N.S., Can.	D7	71
Picture Butte, Alta., Can.	E4	68
Pictured Rocks National Lakeshore, Mi., U.S.	B4	99
Pidálion, Akrotírion, c., Cyp.	B4	40
Pidurutalagala, mtn., Sri L.	I6	37
Piedmont, Al., U.S.	B4	78
Piedmont, Ca., U.S.	h8	82
Piedmont, Mo., U.S.	D7	102
Piedmont, Ok., U.S.	B4	113
Piedmont, S.C., U.S.	B3	117
Piedmont, W.V., U.S.	B5	125
Piedmont Lake, res., Oh., U.S.	B4	112
Piedra, stm., Co., U.S.	D3	83
Piedrabuena, Spain	F7	12
Piedrahita, Spain	E6	12
Piedras Blancas, Point, c., Ca., U.S.	E3	82
Piedras Negras, Guat.	F2	64
Piedras Negras, Mex.	C9	62
Pieksämäki, Fin.	E16	6
Pierce, Co., U.S.	A6	83
Pierce, Id., U.S.	C3	89
Pierce, Ne., U.S.	B8	104
Pierce, co., Ga., U.S.	E4	87
Pierce, co., Ne., U.S.	B8	104
Pierce, co., N.D., U.S.	A5	111
Pierce, co., Wa., U.S.	C3	124
Pierce, co., Wi., U.S.	D1	126
Pierce, Lake, l., Fl., U.S.	E5	86
Pierce City, Mo., U.S.	E3	102
Pierceton, In., U.S.	B6	91
Pierre, S.D., U.S.	C5	118
Pierre-Buffière, Fr.	G8	10
Pierrefonds, Que., Can.	q19	74
Pierre Part, La., U.S.	k9	95
Pierreville, Que., Can.	C5	74
Pierson, Fl., U.S.	C5	86
Pierz, Wi., U.S.	E4	100
Pietermaritzburg, S. Afr.	G6	44
Pietersburg, S. Afr.	F5	44
Pietrasanta, Italy	F5	14
Piet Retief, S. Afr.	G6	44
Pigeon, Mi., U.S.	E7	99
Pigeon, stm., In., U.S.	f9	110
Pigeon, stm., In., U.S.	A6	91
Pigeon, stm., Mn., U.S.	h10	100
Pigeon, stm., Wi., U.S.	k10	126
Pigeon Cove, Ma., U.S.	A6	98
Pigeon Forge, Tn., U.S.	D10	119
Pigeon Point, c., Mn., U.S.	h10	100
Pigg, stm., Va., U.S.	D3	123
Piggott, Ar., U.S.	A5	81
Pihlajavesi, l., Fin.	F17	6
Pihtipudas, Fin.	E15	6
Pijijiapan, Mex.	J13	62
Pikal'ovo, Russia	B17	18
Pike, co., Al., U.S.	D4	78
Pike, co., Ar., U.S.	C2	81
Pike, co., Ga., U.S.	C2	87
Pike, co., Il., U.S.	D2	90
Pike, co., In., U.S.	H3	91
Pike, co., Ky., U.S.	C7	94
Pike, co., Ms., U.S.	D3	101
Pike, co., Mo., U.S.	B6	102
Pike, co., Oh., U.S.	C2	112
Pike, co., Pa., U.S.	D11	115
Pike, stm., Wi., U.S.	C6	126
Pike Island Dam, l.,	f8	125
Pike Lake, Mn., U.S.	D6	100
Pikes Peak, mtn., Co., U.S.	C5	83
Pikesville, Md., U.S.	H3	44
Piketberg, S. Afr.	C2	112
Piketon, Oh., U.S.	C7	94
Pikeville, Ky., U.S.	D8	119
Pikeville, Tn., U.S.	B16	8
Piła (Schneidemühl), Pol.	G5	57
Pilar do Sul, Braz.	A4	56
Pilcomayo, stm., S.A.	F8	38
Pīlībhīt, India		

Pillar Point, c., Ca., U.S.	k7	82
Pilot Grove, Mo., U.S.	C5	102
Pilot Knob, Mo., U.S.	D7	102
Pilot Knob, mtn., Id., U.S.	D3	89
Pilot Mound, Man., Can.	E2	70
Pilot Mountain, N.C., U.S.	A2	110
Pilot Peak, mtn., Nv., U.S.	B7	105
Pilot Peak, mtn., Nv., U.S.	E4	105
Pilot Peak, mtn., Wy., U.S.	B3	127
Pilot Point, Tx., U.S.	C4	120
Pilot Range, mts., Nv., U.S.	B7	105
Pilot Rock, Or., U.S.	B8	114
Pilot Station, Ak., U.S.	C7	79
Pima, Az., U.S.	E6	80
Pima, co., Az., U.S.	E4	80
Pimental, Peru	E3	54
Pimmit Hills, Va., U.S.	g12	123
Pina, Spain	D11	12
Pinal, co., Az., U.S.	E4	80
Pinaleno Mountains, mts., Az., U.S.	E5	80
Pinal Mountains, mts., Az., U.S.	D5	80
Pinang see George Town, Malay.	L6	34
Pinar del Río, Cuba	C6	64
Pinardville, N.H., U.S.	E3	106
Pincher Creek, Alta., Can.	E4	68
Pinckard, Al., U.S.	D4	78
Pinckney, Mi., U.S.	F7	99
Pinckney Island, i., S.C., U.S.	G6	117
Pinckneyville, Il., U.S.	E4	90
Pinconning, Mi., U.S.	E7	99
Píndhos Óros, mts., Grc.	J5	16
Pindi Gheb, Pak.	D5	38
Pindus Mountains see Píndhos Óros, mts., Grc.	J5	16
Pine, Az., U.S.	C4	80
Pine, co., Mn., U.S.	D6	100
Pine, stm., Mi., U.S.	D5	99
Pine, stm., Mi., U.S.	D7	99
Pine, stm., N.H., U.S.	C4	106
Pine, stm., Wi., U.S.	C5	126
Pine, stm., Wi., U.S.	C4	126
Pine Barrens, reg., N.J., U.S.	D3	107
Pine Bluff, Ar., U.S.	C3	81
Pinebluff, N.C., U.S.	B3	110
Pine Bluffs, Wy., U.S.	E8	127
Pine Bridge, Ct., U.S.	D3	84
Pine Castle, Fl., U.S.	D5	86
Pine City, Mn., U.S.	E6	100
Pine Creek, stm., Nv., U.S.	C5	105
Pine Creek, stm., Pa., U.S.	C6	115
Pine Creek, stm., Wa., U.S.	B8	124
Pine Creek Lake, res., Ok., U.S.	C6	113
Pinedale, Wy., U.S.	D3	127
Pine Falls, Man., Can.	D3	70
Pine Forest Range, mts., Nv., U.S.	B3	105
Pine Grove, Pa., U.S.	E9	115
Pine Grove Mills, Pa., U.S.	E6	115
Pine Hill, N.J., U.S.	D3	107
Pine Hills, Fl., U.S.	D5	86
Pinehouse Lake, Sask., Can.	B2	75
Pinehouse Lake, l., Sask., Can.	B2	75
Pinehurst, Ma., U.S.	f11	98
Pinehurst, N.C., U.S.	B3	110
Pine Island, Mn., U.S.	F6	100
Pine Island, i., Fl., U.S.	F4	86
Pine Island Sound, strt., Fl., U.S.	F4	86
Pine Key, i., Fl., U.S.	p10	86
Pine Knot, Ky., U.S.	D5	94
Pine Lake, Ga., U.S.	h8	87
Pine Lake, l., In., U.S.	A4	91
Pine Lake, l., Wi., U.S.	C5	126
Pine Lawn, Mo., U.S.	f13	102
Pine Level, N.C., U.S.	B4	110
Pinellas, co., Fl., U.S.	D4	86
Pinellas, Point, c., Fl., U.S.	p10	86
Pinellas Park, Fl., U.S.	E4	86
Pine Mountain, Ga., U.S.	D2	87
Pine Mountain, mtn., Or., U.S.	D6	114
Pine Mountain, mtn., Wy., U.S.	E3	127
Pine Point, N.W. Ter., Can.	D10	66
Pine Point, Me., U.S.	E2	96
Pine Prairie, La., U.S.	D3	95
Pine Ridge, S.D., U.S.	D3	118
Pine Ridge Indian Reservation, S.D., U.S.	D3	118
Pine River, Mn., U.S.	D4	100
Pinerolo, Italy	E2	14
Pines, Lake O' the, res., Tx., U.S.	C5	120
Pinesdale, Mt., U.S.	D2	103
Pinetops, N.C., U.S.	B5	110
Pine Valley, val., Ut., U.S.	E2	121
Pineville, Ky., U.S.	D6	94
Pineville, La., U.S.	C3	95
Pineville, N.C., U.S.	B2	110
Pineville, W.V., U.S.	D3	125
Pinewood, S.C., U.S.	D7	117
Piney Creek, stm., W.V., U.S.	n13	125
Piney Fork, stm., W.V., U.S.	h9	125
Piney Point, Md., U.S.	D4	97
Piney View, W.V., U.S.	n13	125
Ping, stm., Thai.	F5	34
Pingdingshan, China	E9	26
Pinghu, China	E10	28
Pingliang, China	D8	26
Pingtang, China	A9	28
Pingtan Dao, i., China	J8	28
P'ingtung, Tai.	M9	28
Pingxiang, China	H2	28
Pingyao, China	D9	26
Pinhel, Port.	E4	12
Pinnacles National Monument, Ca., U.S.	D3	82
Pinneberg, Ger.	B9	8
Pinole, Ca., U.S.	h8	82
Pinopolis Dam, S.C., U.S.	E8	117
Pinos, Mount, mtn., Ca., U.S.	E4	82
Pins, Pointe aux, c., Ont., Can.	E3	73
Pinsk, Bela.	I9	18
Pinson, Al., U.S.	f7	78
Pinta, Sierra, mts., Az., U.S.	E2	80
Pintwater Range, mts., Nv., U.S.	G6	105
Pioche, Nv., U.S.	F7	105
Piombino, Italy	G5	14
Pioneer, Oh., U.S.	A1	112
Pioneer Mountains, mts., Id., U.S.	F5	89

Pioneer Mountains, mts., Mt., U.S.	E3	103
Pioner, Ostrov, i., Russia	B12	24
Piotrków Trybunalski, Pol.	D19	8
Pipe Spring National Monument, Az., U.S.	A3	80
Pipestem Creek, stm., N.D., U.S.	B6	111
Pipestone, Mn., U.S.	G2	100
Pipestone, co., Mn., U.S.	F2	100
Pipestone, stm., Ont., Can.	F14	66
Pipestone National Monument, Mn., U.S.	G2	100
Pipestone Pass, Mt., U.S.	E4	103
Pipmuacan, Réservoir, res., Que., Can.	k12	74
Piqua, Oh., U.S.	B1	112
Piracicaba, Braz.	G5	57
Piraeus see Piraiévs, Grc.	L7	16
Piraí do Sul, Braz.	A7	56
Piraiévs (Piraeus), Grc.	L7	16
Piraju, Braz.	G4	57
Piran, Slo.	D8	14
Pirané, Arg.	B5	56
Pirapora, Braz.	D6	57
Pires do Rio, Braz.	D4	57
Pírgos, Grc.	L5	16
Pirmasens, Ger.	F7	8
Pirna, Ger.	E13	8
Pirtleville, Az., U.S.	F6	80
Piru, Indon.	F8	32
Pisa, Italy	F5	14
Pisagua, Chile	G4	54
Piscataqua, stm., N.H., U.S.	D5	106
Piscataquis, co., Me., U.S.	C3	96
Piscataquis, stm., Me., U.S.	C3	96
Piscataquog, stm., N.H., U.S.	D3	106
Piscataway, N.J., U.S.	B4	107
Pisco, Peru	F3	54
Piseco Lake, l., N.Y., U.S.	B6	109
Písek, Czech.	F14	8
Pishan, China		
Pisgah, Al., U.S.	A4	78
Pisgah, Oh., U.S.	n13	112
Pisgah, Mount, mtn., Wy., U.S.	B8	127
Pisgah Forest, N.C., U.S.	f10	110
Pishan, China		
Pismo Beach, Ca., U.S.	E3	82
Pisticci, Italy	I11	14
Pistoia, Italy	F5	14
Pistolet Bay, b., Newf., Can.	C4	72
Pit, stm., Ca., U.S.	B3	82
Pitalito, Col.	G4	58
Pitcairn, Pa., U.S.	k14	115
Pitcairn, dep., Oc.	H4	2
Piteå, Swe.	D13	6
Pitești, Rom.	E8	16
Pithāpuram, India	D7	37
Pithiviers, Fr.	D9	10
Pitiquito, Mex.	B3	62
Pitkin, co., Co., U.S.	B4	83
Pitlochry, Scot., U.K.	E9	7
Pitman, N.J., U.S.	D2	107
Pitt, co., N.C., U.S.	B5	110
Pitt Island, i., B.C., Can.	C3	69
Pittsboro, In., U.S.	E5	91
Pittsboro, N.C., U.S.	B3	110
Pittsburg, Ca., U.S.	g9	82
Pittsburg, Ks., U.S.	E9	93
Pittsburg, Ky., U.S.	C5	94
Pittsburg, Tx., U.S.	C5	120
Pittsburg, co., Ok., U.S.	C6	113
Pittsburgh, Pa., U.S.	F1	115
Pittsfield, Il., U.S.	D3	90
Pittsfield, Me., U.S.	D3	96
Pittsfield, Ma., U.S.	B1	98
Pittsfield, N.H., U.S.	D4	106
Pittsfield, Vt., U.S.	D2	122
Pittston, Pa., U.S.	D10	115
Pittsville, Md., U.S.	D7	97
Pittsville, Wi., U.S.	D3	126
Pittsylvania, co., Va., U.S.	D3	123
Piu, Cerro, mtn., Nic.	H5	64
Piura, Peru	E2	54
Piute, co., Ut., U.S.	E4	121
Piute Peak, mtn., Ca., U.S.	E4	82
Piute Reservoir, res., Ut., U.S.	E3	121
Pixley, Ca., U.S.	E4	82
Pizzo, Italy	K11	14
Placentia, Newf., Can.	E5	72
Placentia Bay, b., Newf., Can.	E4	72
Placer, co., Ca., U.S.	C3	82
Placer Mountain, mtn., N.M., U.S.	k8	108
Placerville, Ca., U.S.	C3	82
Placetas, Cuba	C8	64
Placid, Lake, l., Fl., U.S.	E5	86
Placid, Lake, l., N.Y., U.S.	f11	109
Placitas, N.M., U.S.	B3	108
Plain City, Oh., U.S.	B2	112
Plain City, Ut., U.S.	B3	121
Plain Dealing, La., U.S.	B2	95
Plainfield, Ct., U.S.	C8	84
Plainfield, Il., U.S.	B5	90
Plainfield, In., U.S.	E5	91
Plainfield, N.J., U.S.	B4	107
Plainfield, Vt., U.S.	C4	122
Plainfield, Wi., U.S.	D4	126
Plainfield Heights, Mi., U.S.	*E5	99
Plains, Ga., U.S.	D2	87
Plains, Ks., U.S.	E3	93
Plains, Mt., U.S.	C2	103
Plains, Pa., U.S.	n17	115
Plains, Tx., U.S.	C1	120
Plainview, Mn., U.S.	F6	100
Plainview, Ne., U.S.	B8	104
Plainview, Tx., U.S.	B2	120
Plainville, Ct., U.S.	C4	84
Plainville, Ks., U.S.	C4	93
Plainville, Ma., U.S.	B5	98
Plainwell, Mi., U.S.	F5	99
Plaistow, N.H., U.S.	E4	106
Plankinton, S.D., U.S.	D7	118
Plano, Il., U.S.	B5	90
Plano, Tx., U.S.	C4	120
Plantagenet, Ont., Can.	B9	73
Plantation, Fl., U.S.	r13	86
Plant City, Fl., U.S.	D4	86

Plantersville, Al., U.S.	C3	78
Plantersville, Ms., U.S.	A5	101
Plantsite, Az., U.S.	D6	80
Plantsville, Ct., U.S.	C4	84
Plaquemine, La., U.S.	D4	95
Plaquemines, co., La., U.S.	E6	95
Plasencia, Spain	E5	12
Plaški, Cro.	D10	14
Plaster Rock, N.B., Can.	C2	71
Plata, Río de la, est., S.A.	D5	56
Platte, S.D., U.S.	D7	118
Platte, co., Mo., U.S.	B3	102
Platte, co., Ne., U.S.	C8	104
Platte, co., Wy., U.S.	D7	127
Platte, stm., U.S.	B3	102
Platte, stm., Mn., U.S.	E4	100
Platte, stm., Ne., U.S.	D6	104
Platte City, Mo., U.S.	B3	102
Platte Island, i., Sey.	C11	44
Platteville, I., U.S.	A6	83
Platteville, Wi., U.S.	F3	126
Plattling, Ger.	G12	8
Plattsburg, Mo., U.S.	B3	102
Plattsburgh, N.Y., U.S.	f11	109
Plattsburgh Air Force Base, mil., N.Y., U.S.	f11	109
Plattsmouth, Ne., U.S.	D10	104
Plau, Ger.	B12	8
Plauen, Ger.	E12	8
Playas Lake, l., N.M., U.S.	F2	108
Play Cu, Viet.	H9	34
Playgreen Lake, l., Man., Can.	B2	70
Pleasant, stm., Me., U.S.	C3	96
Pleasant, Lake, res., Az., U.S.	D3	80
Pleasant Gap, Pa., U.S.	E6	115
Pleasant Garden, N.C., U.S.	B3	110
Pleasant Grove, Al., U.S.	g7	78
Pleasant Grove, Ut., U.S.	C4	121
Pleasant Hill, Ca., U.S.	h8	82
Pleasant Hill, Il., U.S.	D3	90
Pleasant Hill, La., U.S.	C2	95
Pleasant Hill, Mo., U.S.	C3	102
Pleasant Hill, Oh., U.S.	B1	112
Pleasant Lake, In., U.S.	A7	91
Pleasant Lake, l., Me., U.S.	C5	96
Pleasant Lake, l., N.H., U.S.	D4	106
Pleasanton, Ca., U.S.	h9	82
Pleasanton, Ks., U.S.	D9	93
Pleasanton, Tx., U.S.	E3	120
Pleasant Prairie, Wi., U.S.	n12	126
Pleasants, co., W.V., U.S.	B3	125
Pleasant Valley, Ia., U.S.	g11	92
Pleasant Valley, Mo., U.S.	h11	102
Pleasant View, Ut., U.S.	B3	121
Pleasantville, Ia., U.S.	C4	92
Pleasantville, N.J., U.S.	E3	107
Pleasantville, N.Y., U.S.	D7	109
Pleasantville, Oh., U.S.	C3	112
Pleasure Beach, Ct., U.S.	D7	84
Pleasure Ridge Park, Ky., U.S.	g11	94
Pleasureville, Ky., U.S.	B4	94
Pleiku see Play Cu, Viet.	H9	34
Pléneuf, Fr.	D4	10
Plenty, Bay of, b., N.Z.	B6	52
Plentywood, Mt., U.S.	B12	103
Plessisville, Que., Can.	C6	74
Pleternica, Cro.	D12	14
Plétipi, Lac, l., Que., Can.	F18	66
Pleven, Bul.	F8	16
Pljevlja, Yugo.	F3	16
Ploče, Cro.	F12	14
Płock, Pol.	C19	8
Ploërmel, Fr.	D4	10
Ploiești, Rom.	E10	16
Plomosa Mountains, mts., Az., U.S.	D1	80
Plonge, Lac la, l., Sask., Can.	B2	75
Plouguenast, Fr.	D4	10
Plovdiv, Bul.	G8	16
Plover, Wi., U.S.	D4	126
Plover, stm., Wi., U.S.	D4	126
Plum, Pa., U.S.	k14	115
Plumas, co., Ca., U.S.	B3	82
Plum Coulee, Man., Can.	E3	70
Plumerville, Ar., U.S.	B3	81
Plum Island, i., Ma., U.S.	A6	98
Plummer, Id., U.S.	B2	89
Plumsteadville, Pa., U.S.	F11	115
Plumtree, Zimb.	F5	44
Plymouth, Monts.	F16	64
Plymouth, Eng., U.K.	K8	7
Plymouth, Ct., U.S.	C3	84
Plymouth, Fl., U.S.	D5	86
Plymouth, In., U.S.	B5	91
Plymouth, Ma., U.S.	C6	98
Plymouth, Mi., U.S.	p15	99
Plymouth, Mn., U.S.	m12	100
Plymouth, N.H., U.S.	C3	106
Plymouth, N.C., U.S.	B6	110
Plymouth, Oh., U.S.	B3	112
Plymouth, Pa., U.S.	D10	115
Plymouth, Wi., U.S.	E6	126
Plymouth, co., Ia., U.S.	B1	92
Plymouth, co., Ma., U.S.	C6	98
Plymouth Bay, b., Ma., U.S.	C6	98
Plzeň, Czech.	F13	8
Po, stm., Italy	E7	14
Po, stm., Va., U.S.	B5	123
Pobeda, Gora, mtn., Russia	D23	24
Pocahontas, Ar., U.S.	A5	81
Pocahontas, Il., U.S.	E4	90
Pocahontas, Ia., U.S.	B3	92
Pocahontas, co., Ia., U.S.	B3	92
Pocahontas, co., W.V., U.S.	C4	125
Pocasset, Ma., U.S.	C6	98
Pocatalico, W.V., U.S.	C3	125
Pocatalico, stm., W.V., U.S.	C3	125
Pocatello, Id., U.S.	G6	89
Počep, Russia	I16	18
Pochutla, Mex.	J11	62
Poções, Braz.	C8	57
Pocola, Ok., U.S.	B7	113
Pocomoke, stm., Md., U.S.	D6	97
Pocomoke City, Md., U.S.	D6	97
Pocomoke Sound, strt., Md., U.S.	E6	97

173

Name	Map Ref	Page
Pocono Mountains, hills, Pa., U.S.	E11	115
Pocono Pines, Pa., U.S.	D11	115
Poços de Caldas, Braz.	F5	57
Pocotopaug Lake, res., Ct., U.S.	C6	84
Podensac, Fr.	H6	10
Podkamennaja Tunguska, Russia	E12	24
Podkamennaja Tunguska, stm., Russia	E13	24
Podol'sk, Russia	F20	18
Podor, Sen.	E3	42
Podravska Slatina, Cro.	D12	14
Pofadder, S. Afr.	G3	44
Poge, Cape, c., Ma., U.S.	D7	98
Poggibonsi, Italy	F6	14
P'ohang, S. Kor.	D12	26
Pohénégamook, Que., Can.	B8	74
Pohue Bay, b., Hi., U.S.	E6	88
Poinsett, co., Ar., U.S.	B5	81
Poinsett, Lake, l., Fl., U.S.	D6	86
Poinsett, Lake, l., S.D., U.S.	C8	118
Point Clear, Al., U.S.	E2	78
Pointe a la Hache, La., U.S.	E6	95
Pointe-à-Pitre, Guad.	F17	64
Pointe-au-Pic, Que., Can.	B7	74
Pointe-Calumet, Que., Can.	p19	74
Pointe-Claire, Que., Can.	D4	74
Pointe Coupee, co., La., U.S.	D4	95
Pointe-des-Cascades, Que., Can.	q19	74
Point Edward, Ont., Can.	D2	73
Pointe-Noire, Congo	B2	44
Pointe-Verte, N.B., Can.	B4	71
Point Fortin, Trin.	I17	64
Point Hope, Ak., U.S.	B6	79
Point Imperial, mtn., Az., U.S.	A4	80
Point Judith Pond, l., R.I., U.S.	F4	116
Point Lake, l., N.W. Ter., Can.	C10	66
Point Leamington, Newf., Can.	D4	72
Point Marion, Pa., U.S.	G2	115
Point Mugu Naval Air Station, mil., Ca., U.S.	E4	82
Point of Rocks, Md., U.S.	B2	97
Point Pelee National Park, Ont., Can.	F2	73
Point Pleasant, N.J., U.S.	C4	107
Point Pleasant, W.V., U.S.	C2	125
Point Pleasant Beach, N.J., U.S.	C4	107
Point Reyes National Seashore, Ca., U.S.	C2	82
Point Roberts, Wa., U.S.	A2	124
Poipu, Hi., U.S.	B2	88
Poison Creek, stm., Wy., U.S.	C5	127
Poisson Blanc, Lac du, res., Que., Can.	C2	74
Poitiers, Fr.	F7	10
Poitou, reg., Fr.	F6	10
Poix, Fr.	C8	10
Pokegama Lake, l., Mn., U.S.	C5	100
Pokegama Lake, l., Wi., U.S.	C2	126
Polacca, Az., U.S.	B5	80
Poland, ctry., Eur.	E11	4
Polar Bear Provincial Park, Ont., Can.	n18	73
Polecat Creek, stm., Ok., U.S.	B5	113
Pol-e Khomrī, Afg.	C3	38
Polesje, reg., Eur.	I10	18
Pólis, Cyp.	B3	40
Polistena, Italy	K11	14
Polk, Pa., U.S.	D2	115
Polk, co., Ar., U.S.	C1	81
Polk, co., Fl., U.S.	E5	86
Polk, co., Ga., U.S.	C1	87
Polk, co., Ia., U.S.	C4	92
Polk, co., Mn., U.S.	C2	100
Polk, co., Mo., U.S.	D4	102
Polk, co., Ne., U.S.	C8	104
Polk, co., N.C., U.S.	f10	110
Polk, co., Or., U.S.	C3	114
Polk, co., Tn., U.S.	D9	119
Polk, co., Tx., U.S.	D5	120
Polk, co., Wi., U.S.	C1	126
Polk City, Fl., U.S.	D5	86
Polk City, Ia., U.S.	C4	92
Pol'kino, Russia	C13	24
Pollāchi, India	G4	37
Polo, Il., U.S.	B4	90
Polock, Bela.	F11	18
Polson, Mt., U.S.	C2	103
Poltava, Ukr.	H4	22
Polynesia, is., Oc.	G2	2
Pomabamba, Peru	E3	54
Pomaro, Mex.	H8	62
Pombal, Port.	F3	12
Pomerania, hist. reg., Pol.	A16	8
Pomeranian Bay, b., Eur.	A14	8
Pomeroy, Ia., U.S.	B3	92
Pomeroy, Oh., U.S.	C3	112
Pomeroy, Wa., U.S.	C8	124
Pomme de Terre, stm., Mn., U.S.	E3	100
Pomme de Terre, stm., Mo., U.S.	D4	102
Pomme de Terre Lake, res., Mo., U.S.	D4	102
Pomona, Ca., U.S.	E5	82
Pomona, Ks., U.S.	D8	93
Pomona Lake, res., Ks., U.S.	D7	93
Pompano Beach, Fl., U.S.	F6	86
Pompton Lakes, N.J., U.S.	A4	107
Ponaganset, stm., R.I., U.S.	C2	116
Ponaganset Reservoir, res., R.I., U.S.	B2	116
Ponca, Ne., U.S.	B9	104
Ponca City, Ok., U.S.	A4	113
Ponca Creek, stm., U.S.	A6	104
Ponca Indian Reservation, Ne., U.S.	B7	104
Ponce, P.R.	E14	64
Ponce de Leon Bay, b., Fl., U.S.	G5	86
Ponce de Leon Inlet, b., Fl., U.S.	C6	86
Poncha Pass, Co., U.S.	C4	83
Ponchatoula, La., U.S.	D5	95
Pond, stm., Ky., U.S.	C2	94
Pond, Ok., U.S.	A3	113
Pondera, co., Mt., U.S.	B4	103
Pond Fork, stm., W.V., U.S.	D3	125

Name	Map Ref	Page
Pondicherry, India	G5	37
Pondicherry, ter., India	G5	37
Pond Inlet, N.W. Ter., Can.	B17	66
Pone Island, i., Md., U.S.	D5	97
Ponferrada, Spain	C5	12
Ponoka, Alta., Can.	C4	68
Ponorogo, Indon.	m15	33a
Pons, Fr.	G6	10
Ponta Grossa, Braz.	B6	56
Pont-à-Mousson, Fr.	D13	10
Ponta Porã, Braz.	G1	57
Pontarlier, Fr.	F13	10
Pontassieve, Italy	F6	14
Pont-Audemer, Fr.	C7	10
Pontchartrain, Lake, l., La., U.S.	D5	95
Pontchâteau, Fr.	E4	10
Pont de Suert, Spain	C12	12
Ponte Branca, Braz.	D3	12
Ponte da Barca, Port.	C3	12
Pontedera, Italy	F5	14
Ponte de Sor, Port.	F3	12
Ponteix, Sask., Can.	H2	75
Ponte Nova, Braz.	F7	57
Pontevedra, Spain	C3	12
Ponte Vedra Beach, Fl., U.S.	B5	86
Pontgibaud, Fr.	F9	10
Pontiac, Il., U.S.	C5	90
Pontiac, Mi., U.S.	F7	99
Pontianak, Indon.	F4	32
Pontivy, Fr.	D4	10
Pont-l'Abbé, Fr.	E2	10
Pontoise, Fr.	C9	10
Pontoosuc Lake, l., Ma., U.S.	B1	98
Pontorson, Fr.	D5	10
Pontotoc, Ms., U.S.	A4	101
Pontotoc, co., Ms., U.S.	A4	101
Pontotoc, co., Ok., U.S.	C5	113
Pont-Rouge, Que., Can.	C6	74
Pontypool, Ont., Can.	C6	73
Pontypool, Wales, U.K.	J9	7
Poole, Eng., U.K.	K11	7
Pooler, Ga., U.S.	D5	87
Pooles Island, i., Md., U.S.	B5	97
Poolesville, Md., U.S.	B3	97
Poopó, Lago de, l., Bol.	G5	54
Popayán, Col.	F4	58
Pope, co., Ar., U.S.	B2	81
Pope, co., Il., U.S.	F5	90
Pope, co., Mn., U.S.	E3	100
Pope Air Force Base, mil., N.C., U.S.	B3	110
Poplar, Mt., U.S.	B11	103
Poplar, stm., Can.	C3	70
Poplar, stm., Mn., U.S.	C2	100
Poplar Bluff, Mo., U.S.	E7	102
Poplar Island, i., Md., U.S.	C5	97
Poplarville, Ms., U.S.	E4	101
Popocatépetl, Volcán, vol., Mex.	H10	62
Popokabaka, Zaire	C3	44
Popomanasiu, Mount, mtn., Sol.Is.	A11	50
Popondetta, Pap. N. Gui.	m16	50a
Popple, stm., Wi., U.S.	C5	126
Poquonock, Ct., U.S.	B5	84
Poquonock Bridge, Ct., U.S.	D7	84
Poquoson, Va., U.S.	C6	123
Porangatu, Braz.	F9	54
Porbandar, India	J3	38
Porcher Island, i., B.C., Can.	C2	69
Porcupine Mountains, mts., Mi., U.S.	m12	99
Pordenone, Italy	D7	14
Poreč, Cro.	D8	14
Pori, Fin.	F13	6
Porkkala, Fin.	G15	6
Porlamar, Ven.	B11	58
Poronajsk, Russia	H22	24
Porsgrunn, Nor.	G7	6
Portadown, N. Ire., U.K.	G6	7
Portage, In., U.S.	A3	91
Portage, Mi., U.S.	F5	99
Portage, Pa., U.S.	F4	115
Portage, Wi., U.S.	E4	126
Portage, co., Oh., U.S.	A4	112
Portage, co., Wi., U.S.	D4	126
Portage, stm., Oh., U.S.	B2	112
Portage Bay, b., Man., Can.	D2	70
Portage Head, c., Wa., U.S.	A1	124
Portage Lake, l., Me., U.S.	B4	96
Portage Lakes, Oh., U.S.	B4	112
Portage la Prairie, Man., Can.	E2	70
Portageville, Mo., U.S.	E8	102
Port Alberni, B.C., Can.	E5	69
Portalegre, Port.	F4	12
Portales, N.M., U.S.	C6	108
Port Alice, B.C., Can.	D4	69
Port Allegany, Pa., U.S.	C5	115
Port Allen, La., U.S.	D4	95
Port Angeles, Wa., U.S.	A2	124
Port Antonio, Jam.	E9	64
Port Aransas, Tx., U.S.	F4	120
Port Arthur, Tx., U.S.	E6	120
Port Arthur see Lüshun, China	D11	26
Port Augusta, Austl.	F7	50
Port au Port Bay, b., Newf., Can.	D2	72
Port au Port [West-Aguathuna-Felix Cove], Newf., Can.	D2	72
Port-au-Prince, Haiti	E11	64
Port au Prince Peninsula, pen., Newf., Can.	D2	72
Port Austin, Mi., U.S.	D7	99
Port Barre, La., U.S.	D4	95
Port-Bergé, Madag.	E9	44
Port Blair, India	I2	34
Port Blandford, Newf., Can.	D4	72
Port Bolivar, Tx., U.S.	E5	120
Port Burwell, Ont., Can.	E4	73
Port Byron, Il., U.S.	B3	90
Port Carbon, Pa., U.S.	E9	115
Port Carling, Ont., Can.	B5	73
Port-Cartier-Ouest, Que., Can.	k13	74
Port Chalmers, N.Z.	F3	52
Port Charlotte, Fl., U.S.	F4	86
Port Chester, N.Y., U.S.	E7	109
Port Clinton, Oh., U.S.	A3	112
Port Colborne, Ont., Can.	E5	73
Port Coquitlam, B.C., Can.	E6	69

Name	Map Ref	Page
Port Deposit, Md., U.S.	A5	97
Port Dickinson, N.Y., U.S.	C5	109
Port Dickson, Malay.	M6	34
Port Edward, B.C., Can.	B2	69
Port Edwards, Wi., U.S.	D4	126
Portel, Braz.	D8	54
Portel, Port.	G4	12
Port Elgin, Ont., Can.	C3	73
Port Elizabeth, S. Afr.	H5	44
Port Ellen, Scot., U.K.	F6	7
Porter, In., U.S.	A3	91
Porter, Tx., U.S.	D5	120
Porter, co., In., U.S.	B3	91
Porter Creek, stm., W.V., U.S.	m13	125
Porterdale, Ga., U.S.	C3	87
Porterville, Ca., U.S.	D4	82
Port Ewen, N.Y., U.S.	D7	109
Port Gamble Indian Reservation, Wa., U.S.	B3	124
Port-Gentil, Gabon	B1	44
Port Gibson, Ms., U.S.	D3	101
Port Harcourt, Nig.	H7	42
Port Hedland, Austl.	D3	50
Port Hood, N.S., Can.	C8	71
Port Hope, Ont., Can.	D6	73
Port Hope Simpson, Newf., Can.	B3	72
Port Hueneme, Ca., U.S.	E4	82
Port Huron, Mi., U.S.	F8	99
Portimão, Port.	H3	12
Port Isabel, Tx., U.S.	F4	120
Port Jefferson, N.Y., U.S.	n15	109
Port Jervis, N.Y., U.S.	D6	109
Portland, Austl.	G8	50
Portland, Ct., U.S.	C5	84
Portland, In., U.S.	D8	91
Portland, Me., U.S.	E2	96
Portland, Mi., U.S.	F6	99
Portland, N.D., U.S.	B8	111
Portland, Or., U.S.	B4	114
Portland, Tn., U.S.	A5	119
Portland, Tx., U.S.	F4	120
Portland, Bill of, c., Eng., U.K.	K10	7
Portland Inlet, b., B.C., Can.	B2	69
Portland Point, c., Jam.	F9	64
Port Lavaca, Tx., U.S.	E4	120
Port Lincoln, Austl.	F7	50
Port Loko, S.L.	G3	42
Port Louis, Mrts.	F11	44
Port-Lyautey see Kenitra, Mor.	B4	42
Port Macquarie, Austl.	F10	50
Port Madison Indian Reservation, Wa., U.S.	B3	124
Port McNeill, B.C., Can.	D4	69
Port McNicoll, Ont., Can.	C5	73
Port Monmouth, N.J., U.S.	C4	107
Port Moresby, Pap. N. Gui.	m16	50a
Port Morien, N.S., Can.	C10	71
Port Neches, Tx., U.S.	E6	120
Portneuf, Que., Can.	C6	74
Port Nolloth, S. Afr.	G3	44
Porto, Port.	D3	12
Porto Alegre, Braz.	C6	56
Porto Amboim, Ang.	D2	44
Portobelo, Pan.	J8	64
Porto de Moz, Braz.	D8	54
Póvoa de Varzim, Port.	D3	12
Porto Esperança, Braz.	G7	54
Porto Esperidião, Braz.	G7	54
Pôrto Feliz, Braz.	G5	57
Portoferraio, Italy	G5	14
Pôrto Ferreira, Braz.	F5	57
Port of Spain, Trin.	I17	64
Portogruaro, Italy	D7	14
Portola, Ca., U.S.	C3	82
Porto Murtinho, Braz.	H7	54
Porto Nacional, Braz.	F9	54
Porto-Novo, Benin	G6	42
Port Orange, Fl., U.S.	C6	86
Port Orchard, Wa., U.S.	B3	124
Port Orford, Or., U.S.	E2	114
Porto San Giorgio, Italy	F8	14
Porto Santo Stefano, Italy	G6	14
Pôrto São José, Braz.	G2	57
Pôrto Seguro, Braz.	D9	57
Porto Torres, Italy	I3	14
Porto União, Braz.	B6	56
Porto Velho, Braz.	E6	54
Portoviejo, Ec.	H2	58
Port Penn, De., U.S.	B3	85
Port Pirie, Austl.	F7	50
Port Richey, Fl., U.S.	D4	86
Port Rowan, Ont., Can.	E4	73
Port Royal, S.C., U.S.	G6	117
Port Royal Island, i., S.C., U.S.	G6	117
Port Royal Sound, strt., S.C., U.S.	G6	117
Port Said see Būr Sa'īd, Egypt	B12	42
Port-Sainte-Marie, Fr.	H7	10
Port Saint Joe, Fl., U.S.	C1	86
Port Saint Johns, S. Afr.	H5	44
Port Saint Lucie, Fl., U.S.	E6	86
Port Salerno, Fl., U.S.	E6	86
Port Saunders, Newf., Can.	C3	72
Port Shepstone, S. Afr.	H6	44
Portsmouth, Eng., U.K.	K11	7
Portsmouth, N.H., U.S.	D5	106
Portsmouth, Oh., U.S.	D3	112
Portsmouth, R.I., U.S.	E6	116
Portsmouth, Va., U.S.	D6	123
Portsmouth Naval Shipyard, mil., Me., U.S.	D5	106
Port Stanley, Ont., Can.	E3	73
Port Sulphur, La., U.S.	E6	95
Port Talbot, Wales, U.K.	J9	7
Port Townsend, Wa., U.S.	A3	124
Portugal, ctry., Eur.	H6	4
Portugalete, Spain	B8	12
Portuguese Guinea see Guinea-Bissau, ctry., Afr.	F2	42
Portumna, Ire.	H4	7
Port Union, Newf., Can.	D5	72
Port-Vendres, Fr.	J10	10
Port Washington, N.Y., U.S.	h13	109
Port Washington, Wi., U.S.	E6	126
Port Wentworth, Ga., U.S.	D5	87
Porum, Ok., U.S.	B6	113
Porz, Ger.	E7	8

Name	Map Ref	Page
Porzuna, Spain	F7	12
Posadas, Arg.	B5	56
Poschiavo, Switz.	F17	10
Posen, Il., U.S.	k9	90
Posey, co., In., U.S.	H2	91
Poseyville, In., U.S.	H2	91
Poso, Indon.	F7	32
Posse, Braz.	C5	57
Pössneck, Ger.	E11	8
Post, Tx., U.S.	C2	120
Post Falls, Id., U.S.	B2	89
Post Maurice Cortier (Bidon Cinq), Alg.	D6	42
Postojna, Slo.	D9	14
P'ostraja Dresva, Russia	E25	24
Postville, Ia., U.S.	A6	92
Potawatomi Indian Reservation, Ks., U.S.	C8	93
Potchefstroom, S. Afr.	G5	44
Poté, Braz.	D8	57
Poteau, Ok., U.S.	B7	113
Poteau, stm., U.S.	B7	113
Poteet, Tx., U.S.	E3	120
Potenza, Italy	I10	14
Potes, Spain	B7	12
Potgietersrus, S. Afr.	F5	44
Poth, Tx., U.S.	E3	120
Potholes Reservoir, res., Wa., U.S.	B6	124
Potiraguá, Braz.	C9	57
Potiskum, Nig.	F8	42
Potlatch, Id., U.S.	C2	89
Potomac, Md., U.S.	B3	97
Potomac, stm., U.S.	D4	97
Potomac Heights, Md., U.S.	C3	97
Potomac Park, Md., U.S.	k13	97
Potosí, Bol.	G5	54
Potosi, Mo., U.S.	D7	102
Potosí, Cerro, mtn., Mex.	E9	62
Potsdam, Ger.	C13	8
Potsdam, N.Y., U.S.	f10	109
Pottawatomie, co., Ks., U.S.	C7	93
Pottawatomie, co., Ok., U.S.	B4	113
Pottawattamie, co., Ia., U.S.	C2	92
Potter, co., Pa., U.S.	C6	115
Potter, co., S.D., U.S.	B6	118
Potter, co., Tx., U.S.	B2	120
Potter Valley, Ca., U.S.	C2	82
Potts Creek, stm., U.S.	B2	123
Pottstown, Pa., U.S.	F10	115
Pottsville, Ar., U.S.	B2	81
Pottsville, Pa., U.S.	E9	115
P'otzu, Tai.	L9	28
Pouce Coupe, B.C., Can.	B7	69
Pouch Cove, Newf., Can.	E5	72
Poughkeepsie, N.Y., U.S.	D7	109
Poulan, Ga., U.S.	E3	87
Poulsbo, Wa., U.S.	B3	124
Poultney, Vt., U.S.	D2	122
Poultney, stm., Vt., U.S.	D2	122
Pound, Va., U.S.	e9	123
Pound Gap, U.S.	C7	94
Pouso Alegre, Braz.	G6	57
Pouthisăt, Camb.	H7	34
Pouzauges, Fr.	F6	10
Póvoa de Varzim, Port.	D3	12
Povungnituk, Que., Can.	f11	74
Powassan, Ont., Can.	A5	73
Poway, Ca., U.S.	F5	82
Powder, stm., Or., U.S.	C9	114
Powder, Middle Fork, stm., Wy., U.S.	C6	127
Powder, North Fork, stm., Wy., U.S.	C6	127
Powder, South Fork, stm., Wy., U.S.	C6	127
Powder River, co., Mt., U.S.	E11	103
Powder River Pass, Wy., U.S.	B5	127
Powder Springs, Ga., U.S.	h8	87
Powell, Oh., U.S.	B2	112
Powell, Tn., U.S.	m13	119
Powell, Wy., U.S.	B4	127
Powell, co., Ky., U.S.	C6	94
Powell, co., Mt., U.S.	D4	103
Powell, stm., U.S.	C10	119
Powell, Lake, res., U.S.	F5	121
Powell, Mount, mtn., Co., U.S.	B4	83
Powell, Mount, mtn., N.M., U.S.	B1	108
Powell Butte, Or., U.S.	C5	114
Powell Park, reg., Co., U.S.	A2	83
Powell River, B.C., Can.	E5	69
Powellton, W.V., U.S.	C3	125
Power, co., Id., U.S.	G5	89
Powers, Or., U.S.	E2	114
Powerview, Man., Can.	D3	70
Poweshiek, co., Ia., U.S.	C5	92
Powhatan, Va., U.S.	C5	123
Powhatan, co., Va., U.S.	C5	123
Powhatan Point, Oh., U.S.	C5	112
Poxoreu, Braz.	C1	57
Poyang, China	F5	28
Poyang Hu, l., China	F5	28
Poygan, Lake, l., Wi., U.S.	D5	126
Poynette, Wi., U.S.	E4	126
Poza Rica de Hidalgo, Mex.	G11	62
Poznań, Pol.	C16	8
Pozo Alcón, Spain	H9	12
Pozoblanco, Spain	G7	12
Pozo Redondo Mountains, mts., Az., U.S.	E3	80
Pozuelo de Alarcón, Spain	E8	12
Pozzuoli, Italy	I9	14
Prachin Buri, Thai.	G6	34
Prachuap Khiri Khan, Thai.	I5	34
Prague, Ok., U.S.	B5	113
Prague see Praha, Czech.	E14	8
Praha (Prague), Czech.	E14	8
Prainha, Braz.	D8	54
Prairie, co., Ar., U.S.	C4	81
Prairie, co., Mt., U.S.	D11	103
Prairie, stm., Mn., U.S.	C5	100
Prairie, stm., Wi., U.S.	C4	126
Prairie City, Ia., U.S.	C4	92
Prairie City, Or., U.S.	C8	114

Name	Map Ref	Page
Prairie Creek Reservoir, res., In., U.S.	D7	91
Prairie Dog Creek, stm., U.S.	C3	93
Prairie du Chien, Wi., U.S.	E2	126
Prairie du Sac, Wi., U.S.	E4	126
Prairie Grove, Ar., U.S.	B1	81
Prairies, Rivière des, stm., Que., Can.	p19	74
Prairie View, Tx., U.S.	D5	120
Prairie Village, Ks., U.S.	m16	93
Praslin Island, i., Sey.	B11	44
Pratas Islands see Tungsha Tao, is., Tai.	G10	26
Prat de Llobregat, Spain	D14	12
Prater Mountain, mtn., Wy., U.S.	C2	127
Prato, Italy	F6	14
Pratt, Ks., U.S.	E5	93
Pratt, co., Ks., U.S.	E5	93
Prattville, Al., U.S.	C3	78
Pravia, Spain	B5	12
Preble, co., Oh., U.S.	C1	112
Predazzo, Italy	C6	14
Predlitz [-Turrach], Aus.	H13	8
Pré-en-Pail, Fr.	D6	10
Preetz, Ger.	A10	8
Premont, Tx., U.S.	F3	120
Prentiss, Ms., U.S.	D4	101
Prentiss, co., Ms., U.S.	A5	101
Prenzlau, Ger.	B13	8
Preparis Island, i., Burma	G2	34
Preparis North Channel, strt., Burma	G2	34
Preparis South Channel, strt., Burma	G2	34
Přerov, Czech.	F17	8
Prescott, Ont., Can.	C9	73
Prescott, Az., U.S.	C3	80
Prescott, Ar., U.S.	D2	81
Prescott, Wi., U.S.	D1	126
Presho, S.D., U.S.	D5	118
Presidencia Roca, Arg.	B5	56
Presidente Epitácio, Braz.	F2	57
Presidente Prudente, Braz.	G3	57
Presidential Range, mts., N.H., U.S.	B4	106
Presidio, Tx., U.S.	p12	120
Presidio, co., Tx., U.S.	o12	120
Presidio of San Francisco, mil., Ca., U.S.	h8	82
Prešov, Czech.	F21	8
Prespa, Lake, l., Eur.	I4	16
Presque Isle, Me., U.S.	B5	96
Presque Isle, co., Mi., U.S.	C6	99
Preston, Eng., U.K.	H10	7
Preston, Id., U.S.	G7	89
Preston, Ia., U.S.	B7	92
Preston, Mn., U.S.	G6	100
Preston, co., W.V., U.S.	B5	125
Preston Peak, mtn., Ca., U.S.	B2	82
Prestonsburg, Ky., U.S.	C7	94
Prestea, Gr.	B7	16
Presumpscot, stm., Me., U.S.	g7	96
Pretoria, S. Afr.	G5	44
Prettyboy Reservoir, res., Md., U.S.	A4	97
Pretty Prairie, Ks., U.S.	E5	93
Préveza, Grc.	K4	16
Prewitt Reservoir, res., Co., U.S.	A7	83
Prey Vêng, Camb.	I8	34
Pribilof Islands, is., Ak., U.S.	D5	79
Příbram, Czech.	F14	8
Price, Ut., U.S.	D5	121
Price, co., Wi., U.S.	C3	126
Price, stm., Ut., U.S.	D5	121
Price Inlet, b., S.C., U.S.	k12	117
Prichard, Al., U.S.	E1	78
Priego, Spain	E9	12
Priego de Córdoba, Spain	H7	12
Prien, Ger.	H12	8
Prieska, S. Afr.	G4	44
Priest Lake, l., Id., U.S.	A2	89
Priest Rapids Dam, Wa., U.S.	C6	124
Priest Rapids Lake, res., Wa., U.S.	C6	124
Priest River, Id., U.S.	A2	89
Prievidza, Czech.	G18	8
Prijedor, Bos.	E11	14
Prilep, Mac.	H5	16
Prim, Point, c., P.E.I., Can.	C6	71
Primghar, Ia., U.S.	A2	92
Primrose, R.I., U.S.	B3	116
Primrose Lake, l., Can.	F11	66
Prince, Lake, res., Va., U.S.	k14	123
Prince Albert National Park, Sask., Can.	C2	75
Prince Albert Sound, strt., N.W. Ter., Can.	B9	66
Prince Charles Island, i., N.W. Ter., Can.	C17	66
Prince-de-Galles, Cap du, c., Que., Can.	D18	74
Prince Edward, co., Va., U.S.	C4	123
Prince Edward Island, prov., Can.	C6	71
Prince Edward Island National Park, P.E.I., Can.	C6	71
Prince Frederick, Md., U.S.	C4	97
Prince George, B.C., Can.	C6	69
Prince George, co., Va., U.S.	C5	123
Prince Georges, co., Md., U.S.	C4	97
Prince of Wales, Cape, c., Ak., U.S.	B6	79
Prince of Wales Island, i., Austl.	B8	50
Prince of Wales Island, i., N.W. Ter., Can.	B13	66
Prince of Wales Island, i., Ak., U.S.	n23	79
Prince of Wales Strait, strt., N.W. Ter., Can.	B9	66
Prince Regent Inlet, b., N.W. Ter., Can.	B14	66
Prince Rupert, B.C., Can.	B2	69
Princes Lakes, In., U.S.	F5	91
Princess Anne, Md., U.S.	D6	97
Princess Royal Channel, strt., B.C., Can.	C3	69
Princess Royal Island, i., B.C., Can.	C3	69

Name	Map Ref	Page
Princeton, B.C., Can.	E7	69
Princeton, Fl., U.S.	G6	86
Princeton, Il., U.S.	B4	90
Princeton, In., U.S.	H2	91
Princeton, Ia., U.S.	C7	92
Princeton, Ky., U.S.	C2	94
Princeton, Me., U.S.	C5	96
Princeton, Mn., U.S.	E5	100
Princeton, Mo., U.S.	A4	102
Princeton, N.J., U.S.	C3	107
Princeton, N.C., U.S.	B4	110
Princeton, W.V., U.S.	D3	125
Princeton, Wi., U.S.	E4	126
Princeton, Mount, mtn., Co., U.S.	B4	83
Princeville, Que., Can.	C6	74
Princeville, Il., U.S.	C4	90
Princeville, N.C., U.S.	B5	110
Prince William, co., Va., U.S.	B5	123
Prince William Sound, strt., Ak., U.S.	g18	79
Príncipe, i., S. Tom./P.	A1	44
Principe Channel, strt., B.C., Can.	C3	69
Príncipe da Beira, Braz.	F6	54
Prineville, Or., U.S.	C6	114
Prineville Reservoir, res., Or., U.S.	C6	114
Pringsewu, Indon.	k12	33a
Prinzapolca, Nic.	H6	64
Prior Lake, Mn., U.S.	F5	100
Priština, Yugo.	G5	16
Pritchards Island, i., S.C., U.S.	G6	117
Pritzwalk, Ger.	B12	8
Privas, Fr.	H11	10
Privolžsk, Russia	D24	18
Probolinggo, Indon.	m16	33a
Proctor, Mn., U.S.	D6	100
Proctor, Vt., U.S.	D2	122
Proctor Lake, res., Tx., U.S.	C3	120
Proctorsville, Vt., U.S.	E3	122
Proddatūr, India	E5	37
Professor Dr. Ir. W.J. van Blommestein Meer, res., Sur.	C7	54
Progreso, Mex.	G15	62
Prokopjevsk, Russia	G11	24
Prokuplje, Yugo.	F5	16
Promontory Mountains, mts., Ut., U.S.	B3	121
Prophetstown, Il., U.S.	B4	90
Propriá, Braz.	F11	54
Prospect, Ct., U.S.	C4	84
Prospect, Ky., U.S.	g11	94
Prospect, Oh., U.S.	B2	112
Prospect, Or., U.S.	E4	114
Prospect, Pa., U.S.	E1	115
Prospect Hill, mtn., Or., U.S.	k11	114
Prospect Park, N.J., U.S.	B4	107
Prospect Park, Pa., U.S.	p20	115
Prosperity, S.C., U.S.	C4	117
Prosperity, W.V., U.S.	n13	125
Prosser, Wa., U.S.	C6	124
Prostějov, Czech.	F17	8
Protection, Ks., U.S.	E4	93
Protville, Tun.	M5	14
Provence, hist. reg., Fr.	I13	10
Providence, Ky., U.S.	C2	94
Providence, R.I., U.S.	C4	116
Providence, Ut., U.S.	B4	121
Providence, co., R.I., U.S.	C2	116
Providence, stm., R.I., U.S.	C5	116
Providence Island, i., Sey.	C10	44
Providence Point, c., R.I., U.S.	D5	116
Providencia, Isla de, i., Col.	H7	64
Providenija, Russia	E31	24
Province Lake, l., N.H., U.S.	C5	106
Provincetown, Ma., U.S.	B7	98
Provins, Fr.	D10	10
Provo, Ut., U.S.	C4	121
Provo, stm., Ut., U.S.	C5	121
Provost, Alta., Can.	C5	68
Prowers, co., Co., U.S.	D8	83
Prozor, Bos.	F12	14
Prudence Island, i., R.I., U.S.	E5	116
Prudenville, Mi., U.S.	D6	99
Prudhoe, Ak., U.S.	A10	79
Prudhoe Bay, b., Ak., U.S.	A10	79
Prüm, Ger.	E6	8
Pruszków, Pol.	C20	8
Prut, stm., Eur.	D12	16
Pryor, Mt., U.S.	E8	103
Pryor, Ok., U.S.	A6	113
Pryor Mountains, mts., Mt., U.S.	E8	103
Przemyśl, Pol.	F22	8
Pskov, Russia	D11	18
Ptolemaís, Grc.	I5	16
Ptuj, Slo.	C10	14
Pucallpa, Peru	E4	54
Pucheng, China	H7	28
Puckaway Lake, l., Wi., U.S.	E4	126
Pudukkottai, India	G5	37
Puebla de Sanabria, Spain	C5	12
Puebla de Trives, Spain	C4	12
Puebla [de Zaragoza], Mex.	H10	62
Pueblo, Co., U.S.	C6	83
Pueblo, co., Co., U.S.	C6	83
Pueblo Hundido, Chile	B2	56
Pueblo Mountain, mtn., Or., U.S.	E8	114
Pueblo Mountains, mts., Or., U.S.	E8	114
Pueblo Reservoir, res., Co., U.S.	C6	83
Puentedeume, Spain	B3	12
Puente-Genil, Spain	H7	12
Pueo Point, c., Hi., U.S.	B1	88
Puerco, stm., U.S.	C6	80
Puerco, Rio, stm., N.M., U.S.	B2	108
Puerto Aisén, Chile	F2	56
Puerto Alfonso, Col.	I7	58
Puerto Ángel, Mex.	J11	62
Puerto Armuelles, Pan.	J6	64
Puerto Asís, Col.	G4	58
Puerto Ayacucho, Ven.	E9	58
Puerto Barrios, Guat.	G3	64
Puerto Berrío, Col.	D5	58
Puerto Boyacá, Col.	E6	58
Puerto Cabello, Ven.	B8	58
Puerto Cabezas, Nic.	G6	64
Puerto Carreño, Col.	D9	58
Puerto Casado, Para.	A5	56
Puerto Chicama, Peru	E3	54
Puerto Cortés, C.R.	J6	64
Puerto Cortés, Hond.	G4	64
Puerto Cumarebo, Ven.	B8	58
Puerto de Pollensa, Spain	F15	12
Puerto de San José, Guat.	H2	64
Puerto Deseado, Arg.	F3	56
Puerto Escondido, Mex.	J11	62
Puerto Francisco de Orellana, Ec.	H4	58
Puerto Inírida, Col.	F9	58
Puerto Juárez, Mex.	G16	62
Puerto la Cruz, Ven.	B10	58
Puerto Leguízamo, Col.	H5	58
Puerto Limón, Col.	F6	58
Puertollano, Spain	G7	12
Puerto Lobos, Arg.	E3	56
Puerto Madryn, Arg.	E3	56
Puerto Maldonado, Peru	F5	54
Puerto Montt, Chile	E2	56
Puerto Morelos, Mex.	G16	62
Puerto Nariño, Col.	E9	58
Puerto Natales, Chile	G2	56
Puerto Padre, Cuba	D9	64
Puerto Peñasco, Mex.	B3	62
Puerto Plata, Dom. Rep.	E12	64
Puerto Princesa, Phil.	D6	32
Puerto Real, Spain	I5	12
Puerto Rico, dep., N.A.	E14	64
Puerto Rondón, Col.	D7	58
Puerto Suárez, Bol.	G7	54
Puerto Tejada, Col.	F4	58
Puerto Vallarta, Mex.	G7	62
Puerto Wilches, Col.	D6	58
Puget Sound, strt., Wa., U.S.	B3	124
Puget Sound Naval Shipyard, mil., Wa., U.S.	e10	124
Pugwash, N.S., Can.	D6	71
Puhi, Hi., U.S.	B2	88
Puigcerdá, Spain	C13	12
Pukalani, Hi., U.S.	C5	88
Pukaskwa National Park, Ont., Can.	o18	73
Pukch'ŏng, N. Kor.	C12	26
Pukë, Alb.	G3	16
Pukeashun Mountain, mtn., B.C., Can.	D8	69
Pukekohe, N.Z.	B5	52
Pukou, China	C7	28
Pula, Cro.	E8	14
Pulacayo, Bol.	H5	54
Pulaski, N.Y., U.S.	B4	109
Pulaski, Tn., U.S.	B4	119
Pulaski, Va., U.S.	C2	123
Pulaski, Wi., U.S.	D5	126
Pulaski, co., Ar., U.S.	C3	81
Pulaski, co., Ga., U.S.	D3	87
Pulaski, co., Il., U.S.	F4	90
Pulaski, co., In., U.S.	B4	91
Pulaski, co., Ky., U.S.	C5	94
Pulaski, co., Mo., U.S.	D5	102
Pulaski, co., Va., U.S.	C2	123
Puli, Tai.	L9	28
Puliyangudi, India	H4	37
Pulkkila, Fin.	D15	6
Pullman, Wa., U.S.	C8	124
Pulog, Mount, mtn., Phil.	B7	32
Pumphrey, Md., U.S.	h11	97
Puná, Isla, i., Ec.	I2	58
Punakha, Bhu.	G13	38
Pünch, India	D6	38
Pune (Poona), India	C2	37
Pungo Lake, l., N.C., U.S.	B6	110
Punjab, state, India	E6	38
Puno, Peru	G4	54
Punta Alta, Arg.	D4	56
Punta Arenas, Chile	G2	56
Punta Delgada, Arg.	E4	56
Punta de Mata, Ven.	C11	58
Punta Gorda, Belize	F3	64
Punta Gorda, Nic.	I6	64
Punta Gorda, Fl., U.S.	F4	86
Puntarenas, C.R.	J5	64
Punto Fijo, Ven.	B7	58
Punxsutawney, Pa., U.S.	E4	115
Puolanka, Fin.	D16	6
Purcell, Ok., U.S.	B4	113
Purcellville, Va., U.S.	A5	123
Purdy, Mo., U.S.	E4	102
Purgatoire, stm., Co., U.S.	D7	83
Purgatoire Peak, mtn., Co., U.S.	D5	83
Purí, India	K11	38
Purli, India	C4	37
Purnea, India	H12	38
Purūlia, India	I12	38
Purus (Purús), stm., S.A.	D6	54
Purvis, Ms., U.S.	D4	101
Purwakarta, Indon.	m13	33a
Purwokerto, Indon.	m14	33a
Purworejo, Indon.	m15	33a
Pusan, S. Kor.	D12	26
Pushaw Lake, l., Me., U.S.	D4	96
Pushmataha, co., Ok., U.S.	C6	113
Puškin, Russia	B13	18
Puškino, Russia	E20	18
Putao, Burma	F6	26
Putian, China	J8	28
Puting, Tanjung, c., Indon.	F5	32
Putnam, Ct., U.S.	B8	84
Putnam, co., Fl., U.S.	C5	86
Putnam, co., Ga., U.S.	C3	87
Putnam, co., Il., U.S.	B4	90
Putnam, co., In., U.S.	E4	91
Putnam, co., Mo., U.S.	A4	102
Putnam, co., N.Y., U.S.	D7	109
Putnam, co., Oh., U.S.	B1	112
Putnam, co., Tn., U.S.	C8	119
Putnam, co., W.V., U.S.	C3	125
Putney, Ga., U.S.	E2	87
Putney, Vt., U.S.	F3	122
Putorana, Plato, plat., Russia	D12	24
Puttalam, Sri L.	H5	37
Puttgarden, Ger.	A11	8
Putumayo (Içá), stm., S.A.	I7	58
Putuo, China	F11	28
Puukohola Heiau National Historic Site, hist., Hi., U.S.	D6	88
Puxico, Mo., U.S.	E7	102
Puyallup, Wa., U.S.	B3	124
Puyallup, stm., Wa., U.S.	C3	124
Puy de Dôme, mtn., Fr.	G9	10
Puy de Sancy, mtn., Fr.	G9	10
Puylaurens, Fr.	I9	10
Puyo, Ec.	H4	58
Pweto, Zaire	C5	44
Pwllheli, Wales, U.K.	I8	7
Pyapon, Burma	F3	34
Pyatigorsk see P'atigorsk, Russia	I6	22
Pyĕ (Prome), Burma	E3	34
Pyhäjoki, Fin.	D15	6
Pyhäselkä, Fin.	E17	6
Pyinmana, Burma	E4	34
Pyles Fork, stm., W.V., U.S.	h10	125
Pymatuning Reservoir, res., U.S.	C1	115
P'yŏngyang, N. Kor.	D12	26
Pyramid Lake, l., Nv., U.S.	C2	105
Pyramid Lake Indian Reservation, Nv., U.S.	D2	105
Pyramid Mountains, mts., N.M., U.S.	E1	108
Pyramid Peak, mtn., N.M., U.S.	E1	108
Pyramid Peak, mtn., Wy., U.S.	C2	127
Pyrenees, mts., Eur.	C12	12
Pyskowice, Pol.	E18	8
Pyu, Burma	E4	34

Q

Qaidam Pendi, China	B16	38
Qalāt, Afg.	D2	38
Qal'at Bīshah, Sau. Ar.	E3	46
Qal'eh-ye Kānsī, Afg.	C2	36
Qal'eh-ye Sarkārī, Afg.	C2	38
Qallābāt, Sudan	F13	42
Qamar, Ghubbat al-, b., Yemen	E5	46
Qamdo, China	E6	26
Qandahār, Afg.	E1	38
Qandala, Som.	F4	46
Qarqan, stm., China	B11	38
Qarqīn, Afg.	B2	38
Qaşr al-Burayqah, Libya	B9	42
Qaşr al-Farāfirah, Egypt	C11	42
Qatanā, Syria	C5	40
Qatar, ctry., Asia	C5	46
Qazvīn, Iran	J8	22
Qeshm, i., Iran	C6	46
Qeyşār, Afg.	C1	38
Qezi'ot, Isr.	D4	40
Qiemo, China	A11	38
Qijiang, China	F8	26
Qinā, Egypt	C12	42
Qingdao (Tsingtao), China	D11	26
Qinghai, prov., China	D6	26
Qinghai Hu, l., China	D7	26
Qingjiang, China	G4	28
Qinglong, China	B8	34
Qingyang, China	D8	26
Qingyuan, China	G8	26
Qingyuan, China	L2	28
Qinhuangdao, China	D10	26
Qin Ling, mts., China	E8	26
Qinzhou, China	D10	34
Qiongzhou Haixia, strt., China	D11	34
Qiqihar, China	B11	26
Qiryat Shemona, Isr.	C4	40
Qitai, China	C4	26
Qizān, Sau. Ar.	E3	46
Qom, Iran	B5	46
Qomsheh, Iran	B5	46
Qondūz, Afg.	B3	38
Qondūz, stm., Afg.	C3	38
Quabbin Reservoir, res., Ma., U.S.	B3	98
Quaddick Reservoir, res., Ct., U.S.	B8	84
Quail Oaks, Va., U.S.	n18	123
Quaker Hill, Ct., U.S.	D7	84
Quakertown, Pa., U.S.	F11	115
Qualicum Beach, B.C., Can.	E5	69
Quanah, Tx., U.S.	B3	120
Quang Ngai, Viet.	G10	34
Quannapowitt, Lake, l., Ma., U.S.	f11	98
Quantico, Va., U.S.	B5	123
Quantico Marine Corps Air Station, mil., Va., U.S.	B5	123
Quanzhou, China	K7	28
Quapaw, Ok., U.S.	A7	113
Qu'Appelle, Sask., Can.	G4	75
Qu'Appelle, stm., Can.	G4	75
Quarryville, Pa., U.S.	G9	115
Quartu Sant'Elena, Italy	J4	14
Quartz Lake, l., N.W. Ter., Can.	B16	66
Quartz Mountain, mtn., Or., U.S.	E4	114
Quartzsite, Az., U.S.	D1	80
Quassapaug, Lake, l., Ct., U.S.	C3	84
Quatsino Sound, strt., B.C., Can.	D3	69
Quay, co., N.M., U.S.	C6	108
Québec, Que., Can.	C6	74
Québec, prov., Can.	C5	74
Quechee, Vt., U.S.	D4	122
Quedlinburg, Ger.	D11	8
Queen, stm., R.I., U.S.	E3	116
Queen Annes, co., Md., U.S.	B5	97
Queen Bess, Mount, mtn., B.C., Can.	D5	69
Queen Charlotte, B.C., Can.	C1	69
Queen Charlotte Islands, is., B.C., Can.	C1	69
Queen Charlotte Mountains, mts., B.C., Can.	C1	69
Queen Charlotte Sound, strt., B.C., Can.	n17	69
Queen Charlotte Strait, strt., B.C., Can.	D4	69
Queen City, Mo., U.S.	A5	102
Queen City, Tx., U.S.	C5	120
Queen Creek, Az., U.S.	m9	80
Queen Maud Gulf, b., N.W. Ter., Can.	C12	66
Queen Maud Land, reg., Ant.	B14	47
Queens, co., N.Y., U.S.	E7	109
Queens Channel, strt., N.W. Ter., Can.	A13	66
Queensland, state, Austl.	D8	50
Queenstown, N.Z.	F2	52
Queenstown, S. Afr.	H5	44
Quelimane, Moz.	E7	44
Quemoy see Chinmen Tao, i., Tai.	K7	28
Querétaro, Mex.	G9	62
Querobabi, Mex.	B4	62
Quesnel, B.C., Can.	C6	69
Quesnel, stm., B.C., Can.	C6	69
Quesnel Lake, l., B.C., Can.	C7	69
Questa, N.M., U.S.	A4	108
Questembert, Fr.	E4	10
Quetico Provincial Park, Ont., Can.	o17	73
Quetta, Pak.	E2	38
Quevedo, Ec.	H3	58
Quevedo, stm., Ec.	H3	58
Quezaltenango, Guat.	G2	64
Quezon City, Phil.	q19	32
Qufu, China	D10	26
Quibdó, Col.	E4	58
Quiberon, Fr.	E3	10
Quibor, Ven.	B8	58
Quicksand Pond, l., R.I., U.S.	E6	116
Quidnessett, R.I., U.S.	D4	116
Quidnick, R.I., U.S.	D3	116
Quidnick Reservoir, res., R.I., U.S.	D2	116
Quilá, Mex.	E6	62
Quilcene, Wa., U.S.	B3	124
Quileute Indian Reservation, Wa., U.S.	B1	124
Quillan, Fr.	J9	10
Quilon, India	H4	37
Quilpie, Austl.	E8	50
Quimilí, Arg.	B4	56
Quimper, Fr.	D2	10
Quimperlé, Fr.	E3	10
Quinault, stm., Wa., U.S.	B1	124
Quinault, Lake, l., Wa., U.S.	B2	124
Quinault Indian Reservation, Wa., U.S.	B1	124
Quincemil, Peru	F4	54
Quincy, Ca., U.S.	C3	82
Quincy, Fl., U.S.	B2	86
Quincy, Il., U.S.	D2	90
Quincy, Ma., U.S.	B5	98
Quincy, Mi., U.S.	G6	99
Quincy, Wa., U.S.	B6	124
Quincy Bay, b., Ma., U.S.	g12	98
Quinebaug, Ct., U.S.	A8	84
Quinebaug, stm., Ct., U.S.	C8	84
Quinhagak, Ak., U.S.	D7	79
Qui Nhon, Viet.	H10	34
Quinlan, Tx., U.S.	C4	120
Quinn, stm., Nv., U.S.	B3	105
Quinn Canyon Range, mts., Nv., U.S.	F6	105
Quinnesec, Mi., U.S.	C3	99
Quinnipiac, stm., Ct., U.S.	D4	84
Quinter, Ks., U.S.	C3	93
Quinton, Ok., U.S.	B6	113
Quiroga, Spain	C4	12
Quitman, Ar., U.S.	B3	81
Quitman, Ga., U.S.	F3	87
Quitman, Ms., U.S.	C5	101
Quitman, Tx., U.S.	C5	120
Quitman, co., Ga., U.S.	E1	87
Quitman, co., Ms., U.S.	A3	101
Quito, Ec.	H3	58
Quixadá, Braz.	D11	54
Qujing, China	B7	34
Qumalai (Sewugou), China	C16	38
Quoich, stm., N.W. Ter., Can.	D14	66
Quonnipaug Lake, l., Ct., U.S.	D5	84
Quonochontaug, R.I., U.S.	G2	116
Quonochontaug Pond, l., R.I., U.S.	G2	116
Quonset Point, c., R.I., U.S.	E4	116
Qutdligssat, Grnld.	B22	66
Quthing, Leso.	H5	44
Quxian, China	G7	28

R

Raalte, Neth.	C6	8
Rab, Cro.	E9	14
Raba, Indon.	G6	32
Rába (Raab), stm., Eur.	H17	8
Rábade, Spain	B4	12
Rabat (Victoria), Malta	M9	14
Rabat, Mor.	B4	42
Rabaul, Pap. N. Gui.	k17	50a
Rabbit Creek, stm., S.D., U.S.	B3	118
Rabbit Ears Pass, Co., U.S.	A4	83
Rābigh, Sau. Ar.	D2	46
Rabun, co., Ga., U.S.	B3	87
Rabun Bald, mtn., Ga., U.S.	B3	87
Raccoon Creek, stm., Oh., U.S.	D3	112
Raccourci Island, i., La., U.S.	D4	95
Race, Cape, c., Newf., Can.	E5	72
Race Point, c., Ma., U.S.	B7	98
Rach Gia, Viet.	I8	34
Racibórz (Ratibor), Pol.	E18	8
Racine, W.V., U.S.	C3	125
Racine, Wi., U.S.	F5	126
Racine, co., Wi., U.S.	F5	126
Racine Dam, U.S.	C3	125
Radcliff, Ky., U.S.	C4	94
Radeberg, Ger.	D13	8
Radebeul, Ger.	D13	8
Radeče, Slo.	C10	14
Radford, Va., U.S.	C2	123
Radolfzell, Ger.	H8	8
Radom, Pol.	D21	8
Radomsko, Pol.	D19	8
Rae, N.W. Ter., Can.	D9	66
Rāe Bareli, India	G9	38
Rae Isthmus, N.W. Ter., Can.	C15	66
Rae Strait, strt., N.W. Ter., Can.	C13	66
Raetihi, N.Z.	C5	52
Rafaela, Arg.	C4	56
Rafah, Isr. Occ.	D4	40
Rafhā', Sau. Ar.	C3	46
Rafsanjān, Iran	K9	22
Rafsanjān, Iran	B6	46
Raft, stm., Id., U.S.	G5	89
Raft River Mountains, mts., Ut., U.S.	B2	121
Raga, Sudan	G11	42
Ragged Island, i., Me., U.S.	E4	96
Ragged Lake, l., Me., U.S.	C3	96
Ragged Top Mountain, mtn., Wy., U.S.	E7	127
Ragland, Al., U.S.	B3	78
Ragusa, Italy	M9	14
Ragusa see Dubrovnik, Cro.	G13	14
Rahīmyār Khān, Pak.	F4	38
Rahway, N.J., U.S.	B4	107
Rahway, stm., N.J., U.S.	k7	107
Rāichūr, India	D4	37
Raigarh, India	B7	37
Railroad Valley, val., Nv., U.S.	E6	105
Rainbow Bridge National Monument, U.S.	F5	121
Rainbow Falls, wtfl, Tn., U.S.	D10	119
Rainbow Flowage, res., Wi., U.S.	C4	126
Rainbow Lake, l., Me., U.S.	C3	96
Rainelle, W.V., U.S.	D4	125
Rainier, Or., U.S.	A4	114
Rainier, Wa., U.S.	C3	124
Rainier, Mount, mtn., Wa., U.S.	C4	124
Rains, co., Tx., U.S.	C5	120
Rainsville, Al., U.S.	A4	78
Rainy Lake, l., N.A.	G14	66
Rainy Lake, l., Mn., U.S.	B5	100
Rainy River, Ont., Can.	o16	73
Raipur, India	B6	37
Rājahmundry, India	D6	37
Raja-Jooseppi, Fin.	B17	6
Rājapālaiyam, India	H4	37
Rājasthān, prov., India	G5	38
Rājasthān Canal, India	F5	38
Rajčichinsk, Russia	H19	24
Rājkot, India	I4	37
Rāj-Nāndgaon, India	B6	37
Rājpīpla, India	J5	38
Rājshāhi, Bngl.	H13	38
Rakaposhi, mtn., Pak.	B6	38
Rakata, Pulau, i., Indon.	m12	33a
Råkvåg, Nor.	E8	6
Raleigh, Ms., U.S.	C4	101
Raleigh, N.C., U.S.	B4	110
Raleigh, W.V., U.S.	n13	125
Raleigh, co., W.V., U.S.	D3	125
Raleigh Bay, b., N.C., U.S.	C6	110
Ralls, Tx., U.S.	C2	120
Ralls, co., Mo., U.S.	B6	102
Ralston, Ne., U.S.	g12	104
Ralston Valley, val., Nv., U.S.	E4	105
Rama, Nic.	H5	64
Ramah, N.M., U.S.	B1	108
Ramah Indian Reservation, N.M., U.S.	C1	108
Rām Allāh, Jord.	D4	40
Ramapo, stm., N.J., U.S.	A4	107
Ramblewood, N.J., U.S.	D3	107
Rambouillet, Fr.	D8	10
Ramea, Newf., Can.	E3	72
Ramenskoje, Russia	F21	18
Rāmeswaram, India	H5	37
Rāmgarh, Bngl.	I14	38
Ramla, Isr.	D4	40
Ramio, mtn., Eth.	F3	46
Ramona, Ca., U.S.	F5	82
Rampart Range, mts., Co., U.S.	B5	83
Rāmpur, India	F8	38
Ramree Island, i., Burma	E2	34
Ramsay, Mi., U.S.	n12	99
Ramseur, N.C., U.S.	B3	110
Ramsey, I. of Man	G8	7
Ramsey, Il., U.S.	D4	90
Ramsey, Mn., U.S.	*E5	100
Ramsey, N.J., U.S.	A4	107
Ramsey, co., Mn., U.S.	E5	100
Ramsey, co., N.D., U.S.	A7	111
Ramsgate, Eng., U.K.	J14	7
Ramshorn Peak, mtn., Mt., U.S.	E5	103
Ramshorn Peak, mtn., Wy., U.S.	C3	127
Rāmu, Bngl.	J15	38
Ramu, stm., Pap. N. Gui.	m16	50a
Rancagua, Chile	C2	56
Rancharia, Braz.	G3	57
Rancheria Rock, mtn., Or., U.S.	C6	114
Ranchester, Wy., U.S.	B5	127
Rānchī, India	I11	38
Rancho Palos Verdes, Ca., U.S.	*n12	82
Ranchos de Taos, N.M., U.S.	A4	108
Rancocas Creek, stm., N.J., U.S.	C3	107
Rand, W.V., U.S.	C3	125
Randall, co., Tx., U.S.	B2	120
Randallstown, Md., U.S.	B4	97
Randazzo, Italy	L9	14
Randers, Den.	H8	6
Randle, Wa., U.S.	C4	124
Randleman, N.C., U.S.	B3	110
Randolph, Me., U.S.	D3	96
Randolph, Ma., U.S.	B5	98
Randolph, Ne., U.S.	B8	104
Randolph, Vt., U.S.	D3	122
Randolph, Wi., U.S.	E5	126
Randolph, co., Al., U.S.	B4	78
Randolph, co., Ar., U.S.	A4	81
Randolph, co., Ga., U.S.	E2	87
Randolph, co., Il., U.S.	E4	90
Randolph, co., In., U.S.	D7	91
Randolph, co., Mo., U.S.	B5	102
Randolph, co., N.C., U.S.	B3	110
Randolph, co., W.V., U.S.	C5	125
Randolph Air Force Base, mil., Tx., U.S.	h7	120
Randolph Hills, Md., U.S.	B3	97
Random Island, i., Newf., Can.	D5	72
Random Lake, Wi., U.S.	E6	126
Rangeley, Me., U.S.	D2	96

Name	Map Ref	Page
Rangeley Lake, l., Me., U.S.	D2	96
Rangely, Co., U.S.	A2	83
Ranger, Tx., U.S.	C3	120
Ranger Lake, l., N.M., U.S.	D6	108
Rangoon see Yangon, Burma	B2	32
Rangpur, Bngl.	H13	38
Rankin, Pa., U.S.	k14	115
Rankin, co., Ms., U.S.	C4	101
Rankin Inlet, N.W. Ter., Can.	D14	66
Rann of Kutch, pl., Asia	H3	38
Ransom, co., N.D., U.S.	C8	111
Ranson, W.V., U.S.	B7	125
Rantauprapat, Indon.	E2	32
Rantaukombola, Bulu, mtn., Indon.	F7	32
Rantoul, Il., U.S.	C5	90
Raoping, China	L6	28
Raoul, Ga., U.S.	B3	87
Rapallo, Italy	E4	14
Rapid, stm., Mn., U.S.	B4	100
Rapid City, S.D., U.S.	C2	118
Rapides, co., La., U.S.	C3	95
Rapid River, Mi., U.S.	C4	99
Rapids City, Il., U.S.	B3	90
Rappahannock, co., Va., U.S.	B4	123
Rappahannock, stm., Va., U.S.	B5	123
Raquette, stm., N.Y., U.S.	f10	109
Raquette Lake, l., N.Y., U.S.	B6	109
Raritan, N.J., U.S.	B3	107
Raritan, stm., N.J., U.S.	C4	107
Raritan Bay, b., N.J., U.S.	C4	107
Ra's al-'Ayn, Syria	A7	40
Ra's an-Naqb, Jord.	D4	40
Ras Dashen, mtn., Eth.	F2	46
Ras Djebel, Tun.	L5	14
Rasht, Iran	J7	22
Rāsipuram, India	G5	37
Rasskazovo, Russia	I24	18
Rastatt, Ger.	G8	8
Ratangarh, India	F6	38
Rätansbyn, Swe.	E10	6
Rathbun Lake, res., Ia., U.S.	D5	92
Rathdrum, Id., U.S.	B2	89
Rathenow, Ger.	C12	8
Rathkeale, Ire.	I4	7
Rathlin Island, i., N. Ire., U.K.	F6	7
Rat Islands, is., Ak., U.S.	E3	79
Ratlām, India	I6	38
Ratnāgiri, India	D2	37
Ratnapura, Sri L.	I6	37
Raton, N.M., U.S.	A5	108
Raton Pass, N.M., U.S.	A5	108
Rattlesnake Creek, stm., Oh., U.S.	C2	112
Rattlesnake Creek, stm., Wa., U.S.	C6	124
Rättvik, Swe.	F10	6
Ratz, Mount, mtn., B.C., Can.	E6	66
Ratzeburg, Ger.	B10	8
Raub, Malay.	M6	34
Rauch, Arg.	D5	56
Rauma, Fin.	F13	6
Raurkela, India	I11	38
Ravalli, co., Mt., U.S.	D2	103
Raven, Va., U.S.	e10	123
Ravena, N.Y., U.S.	C7	109
Ravenel, S.C., U.S.	k11	117
Ravenna, Italy	E7	14
Ravenna, Ky., U.S.	C6	94
Ravenna, Mi., U.S.	E5	99
Ravenna, Ne., U.S.	C7	104
Ravenna, Oh., U.S.	A4	112
Raven Park, reg., Co., U.S.	A2	83
Ravensburg, Ger.	H9	8
Ravenshoe, Austl.	C9	50
Ravensthorpe, Austl.	F3	50
Ravenswood, W.V., U.S.	C3	125
Rāwalpindi, Pak.	D5	38
Rawdon, Que., Can.	C4	74
Rawhide Creek, stm., Wy., U.S.	D8	127
Rawlings, Md., U.S.	k13	97
Rawlinna, Austl.	F5	50
Rawlins, Wy., U.S.	E5	127
Rawlins, co., Ks., U.S.	C2	93
Rawson, Arg.	E3	56
Ray, N.D., U.S.	A2	111
Ray, co., Mo., U.S.	B3	102
Ray, Cape, c., Newf., Can.	E2	72
Raya, Bukit, mtn., Indon.	F5	32
Rāyadrug, India	E4	37
Ray City, Ga., U.S.	E3	87
Raymond, Alta., Can.	E4	68
Raymond, Il., U.S.	D4	90
Raymond, Mn., U.S.	E3	100
Raymond, Ms., U.S.	C3	101
Raymond, N.H., U.S.	D4	106
Raymond, Wa., U.S.	C2	124
Raymondville, Tx., U.S.	F4	120
Raymore, Sask., Can.	F3	75
Raymore, Mo., U.S.	C3	102
Rayne, La., U.S.	D3	95
Raynham, Ma., U.S.	C5	98
Raynham Center, Ma., U.S.	C5	98
Raytown, Mo., U.S.	h11	102
Rayville, La., U.S.	B4	95
R'azan', Russia	G22	18
Razgrad, Bul.	F10	16
R'ažsk, Russia	H23	18
Reader, W.V., U.S.	B4	125
Reading, Eng., U.K.	J12	7
Reading, Ma., U.S.	A5	98
Reading, Mi., U.S.	G6	99
Reading, Oh., U.S.	C1	112
Reading, Pa., U.S.	F10	115
Readlyn, Ia., U.S.	B5	92
Reagan, co., Tx., U.S.	D2	120
Real, co., Tx., U.S.	E3	120
Realicó, Arg.	D4	56
Réalmont, Fr.	I9	10
Reamstown, Pa., U.S.	F9	115
Recanati, Italy	F8	14
Recherche, Archipelago of the, is., Austl.	F4	50
Rečica, Bela.	I13	18
Recife, Braz.	E12	54
Recklinghausen, Ger.	D7	8
Recreo, Arg.	B3	56
Rector, Ar., U.S.	A5	81
Red (Hong) (Yuan), stm., Asia	C8	34
Red, stm., N.A.	B7	76
Red, stm., U.S.	E8	76
Red, stm., Ky., U.S.	C6	94
Red, stm., Tn., U.S.	A4	119
Red Bank, N.J., U.S.	C4	107
Red Bank, Tn., U.S.	D8	119
Red Bay, Al., U.S.	A1	78
Redberry Lake, l., Sask., Can.	E2	75
Redbird, Oh., U.S.	A4	112
Red Bird, stm., Ky., U.S.	C6	94
Red Bluff, Ca., U.S.	B2	82
Red Bluff Lake, res., U.S.	o12	120
Red Boiling Springs, Tn., U.S.	C8	119
Red Bud, Il., U.S.	E4	90
Red Butte, mtn., Ut., U.S.	B2	121
Red Cedar, stm., Wi., U.S.	C2	126
Red Cedar Lake, l., Wi., U.S.	C2	126
Redcliff, Alta., Can.	D5	68
Redcliffe, Mount, mtn., Austl.	E4	50
Red Cliff Indian Reservation, Wi., U.S.	B2	126
Red Cloud, Ne., U.S.	D7	104
Redcloud Peak, mtn., Co., U.S.	D3	83
Red Deer, Alta., Can.	C4	68
Red Deer, stm., Can.	D4	68
Red Deer, stm., Can.	E4	75
Redding, Ca., U.S.	B2	82
Redding, Ct., U.S.	D2	84
Redeye, stm., Mn., U.S.	D3	100
Redfield, Ar., U.S.	C3	81
Redfield, Ia., U.S.	C3	92
Redfield, S.D., U.S.	C7	118
Redford, Mi., U.S.	F7	99
Redgranite, Wi., U.S.	D4	126
Red Hook, N.Y., U.S.	C7	109
Red Indian Lake, l., Newf., Can.	D3	72
Red Jacket, W.V., U.S.	D2	125
Redkey, In., U.S.	D7	91
Redlake, Mn., U.S.	C3	100
Red Lake, co., Mn., U.S.	C2	100
Red Lake, l., Az., U.S.	B1	80
Red Lake, stm., Mn., U.S.	C2	100
Red Lake Falls, Mn., U.S.	C2	100
Red Lake Indian Reservation, Mn., U.S.	B3	100
Redlands, Ca., U.S.	E5	82
Red Lion, Pa., U.S.	G8	115
Red Lodge, Mt., U.S.	E7	103
Red Mill Pond, l., De., U.S.	E5	85
Redmond, Or., U.S.	C5	114
Redmond, Ut., U.S.	E4	121
Redmond, Wa., U.S.	e11	124
Red Mountain, mtn., Ca., U.S.	B2	82
Red Mountain, mtn., Mt., U.S.	C4	103
Red Mountain Pass, Co., U.S.	D3	83
Red Oak, Ga., U.S.	h7	87
Red Oak, Ia., U.S.	D2	92
Red Oak, Ok., U.S.	C6	113
Red Oak, Tx., U.S.	n10	120
Red Oaks, La., U.S.	h9	95
Redon, Fr.	E4	10
Redondela, Spain	C3	12
Redondo, Port.	G4	12
Redondo, Wa., U.S.	f11	124
Redondo Beach, Ca., U.S.	n12	82
Redoubt Volcano, vol., Ak., U.S.	g15	79
Red Peak, mtn., Co., U.S.	B4	83
Red River, co., La., U.S.	B2	95
Red River, co., Tx., U.S.	C5	120
Red Rock, stm., Mt., U.S.	F4	103
Red Rock Lake, res., Ia., U.S.	C4	92
Red Sea	D2	46
Red Springs, N.C., U.S.	C3	110
Red Table Mountain, mts., Co., U.S.	B4	83
Redwater, Alta., Can.	C4	68
Redwater, stm., Mt., U.S.	C11	103
Red Willow, co., Ne., U.S.	D5	104
Redwillow, stm., Can.	B7	69
Red Wing, Mn., U.S.	F6	100
Redwood, co., Mn., U.S.	F3	100
Redwood, stm., Mn., U.S.	F3	100
Redwood City, Ca., U.S.	D2	82
Redwood Falls, Mn., U.S.	F3	100
Redwood National Park, Ca., U.S.	B2	82
Redwood Valley, Ca., U.S.	C2	82
Ree, Lough, l., Ire.	H4	7
Reed City, Mi., U.S.	E5	99
Reedley, Ca., U.S.	D4	82
Reedsburg, Wi., U.S.	E3	126
Reeds Peak, mtn., N.M., U.S.	D2	108
Reedsport, Or., U.S.	D2	114
Reedsville, Pa., U.S.	E6	115
Reedsville, Wi., U.S.	D6	126
Reedy, stm., S.C., U.S.	C3	117
Reedy Lake, l., Fl., U.S.	E5	86
Reelfoot Lake, l., Tn., U.S.	A2	119
Reese, Mi., U.S.	E7	99
Reese, stm., Nv., U.S.	C4	105
Reese Air Force Base, mil., Tx., U.S.	C1	120
Reeves, co., Tx., U.S.	o13	120
Reform, Al., U.S.	B1	78
Refugio, Tx., U.S.	E4	120
Refugio, co., Tx., U.S.	E4	120
Regen, Ger.	G13	8
Regencia, Braz.	E9	57
Regensburg, Ger.	F12	8
Reggane, Alg.	C6	42
Reggio di Calabria, Italy	K10	14
Reggio nell'Emilia, Italy	E5	14
Regina, Sask., Can.	G3	75
Regina Beach, Sask., Can.	G3	75
Rehoboth, Nmb.	F3	44
Rehoboth, Nmb.	E3	44
Rehoboth Bay, b., De., U.S.	F5	85
Rehoboth Beach, De., U.S.	F5	85
Rehovot, Isr.	D4	40
Reichenbach, Ger.	E12	8
Reid, Mount, mtn., Ak., U.S.	n24	79
Reidland, Ky., U.S.	e9	94
Reidsville, Ga., U.S.	D4	87
Reidsville, N.C., U.S.	A3	110
Reims, Fr.	C11	10
Reina Adelaida, Archipiélago, is., Chile	G2	56
Reinbeck, Ia., U.S.	B5	92
Reindeer Island, i., Man., Can.	C3	70
Reindeer Lake, l., Can.	m8	75
Reinosa, Spain	B7	12
Reisterstown, Md., U.S.	B4	97
Reliance, Wy., U.S.	E3	127
Remada, Tun.	B8	42
Remanso, Braz.	E10	54
Rembang, Indon.	m15	33a
Remington, In., U.S.	C3	91
Remiremont, Fr.	D13	10
Remmel Dam, Ar., U.S.	g8	81
Remscheid, Ger.	D7	8
Remsen, Ia., U.S.	B2	92
Rend Lake, res., Il., U.S.	E5	90
Rendova, i., Sol.Is.	A11	50
Rendsburg, Ger.	A9	8
Renforth, N.B., Can.	D4	71
Renfrew, Ont., Can.	B8	73
Rengat, Indon.	O7	34
Rennell Island, i., Sol.Is.	B12	50
Rennes, Fr.	D5	10
Reno, Nv., U.S.	D2	105
Reno, co., Ks., U.S.	E5	93
Reno, Lake, l., Mn., U.S.	E3	100
Reno Hill, mtn., Wy., U.S.	D6	127
Renovo, Pa., U.S.	D6	115
Rensselaer, In., U.S.	C3	91
Rensselaer, N.Y., U.S.	C7	109
Rensselaer, co., N.Y., U.S.	C7	109
Renton, Wa., U.S.	B3	124
Renville, Mn., U.S.	F3	100
Renville, co., Mn., U.S.	F4	100
Renville, co., N.D., U.S.	A4	111
Reo, Indon.	G7	32
Repentigny, Que., Can.	D4	74
Republic, Mi., U.S.	B3	99
Republic, Mo., U.S.	D4	102
Republic, Pa., U.S.	G2	115
Republic, Wa., U.S.	A7	124
Republic, co., Ks., U.S.	C6	93
Republican, stm., U.S.	C6	93
Repulse Bay, N.W. Ter., Can.	C15	66
Repvåg, Nor.	A15	6
Réquista, Fr.	H9	10
Reschenpass, Eur.	C5	14
Reserve, La., U.S.	h10	95
Resistencia, Arg.	B5	56
Reșița, Rom.	D5	16
Resolute, N.W. Ter., Can.	B14	66
Resolution Island, i., N.W. Ter., Can.	D20	66
Reston, Man., Can.	E1	70
Reston, Va., U.S.	B5	123
Resülhınzir, c., Tur.	A4	40
Retalhuleu, Guat.	G2	64
Rethel, Fr.	C11	10
Réthimnon, Grc.	N8	16
Reunion (Réunion), dep., Afr.	F11	44
Reus, Spain	D13	12
Reutlingen, Ger.	G9	8
Revelo, Ky., U.S.	D5	94
Revelstoke, B.C., Can.	D8	69
Revelstoke, Lake, res., B.C., Can.	D8	69
Revillagigedo, Islas de, is., Mex.	H4	62
Revillagigedo Island, i., Ak., U.S.	n24	79
Revin, Fr.	C11	10
Rewa, India	H9	38
Rex, Ga., U.S.	h8	87
Rexburg, Id., U.S.	F7	89
Rexton, N.B., Can.	C5	71
Rey, Iran	J8	22
Rey, Isla del, i., Pan.	J8	64
Reyes, Bol.	F5	54
Reyes, Point, c., Ca., U.S.	C2	82
Reyhanlı, Tur.	A5	40
Reykjavík, Ice.	C3	4
Reynolds, Ga., U.S.	D2	87
Reynolds, co., Mo., U.S.	D6	102
Reynoldsburg, Oh., U.S.	C3	112
Reynoldsville, Pa., U.S.	D4	115
Reynosa, Mex.	D10	62
Rēzekne, Lat.	E10	18
Rhaetian Alps, mts., Eur.	F16	10
Rhea, co., Tn., U.S.	D9	119
Rheine, Ger.	C7	8
Rheydt, Ger.	D6	8
Rhine (Rhein) (Rhin), stm., Eur.	D6	8
Rhinebeck, N.Y., U.S.	D7	109
Rhinelander, Wi., U.S.	C4	126
Rho, Italy	D4	14
Rhode Island, state, U.S.	D3	116
Rhode Island, i., R.I., U.S.	E5	116
Rhode Island Sound, strt., U.S.	F5	116
Rhodesia see Zimbabwe, ctry., Afr.	E5	44
Rhodes Peak, mtn., Id., U.S.	C4	89
Rhodes see Ródhos, Grc.	M12	16
Rhodope Mountains, mts., Eur.	H8	16
Rhondda, Wales, U.K.	J9	7
Rhône, stm., Eur.	H11	10
Rialto, Ca., U.S.	m14	82
Riau, Kepulauan, is., Indon.	N8	34
Riaza, Spain	D8	12
Ribadeo, Spain	B4	12
Ribadesella, Spain	B6	12
Ribeirão Prêto, Braz.	F5	57
Ribera, Italy	L8	14
Riberalta, Bol.	F5	54
Rib Lake, Wi., U.S.	C3	126
Ribnitz-Damgarten, Ger.	A12	8
Riccione, Italy	F7	14
Rice, co., Ks., U.S.	D5	93
Rice, co., Mn., U.S.	F5	100
Riceboro, Ga., U.S.	E5	87
Rice Lake, Wi., U.S.	C2	126
Rice Lake, l., Ont., Can.	C6	73
Rice Lake, l., Mn., U.S.	D5	100
Reidsville, Ga., U.S.	D4	87
Riceville, Ia., U.S.	A5	92
Rich, co., Ut., U.S.	B4	121
Rich, Cape, c., Ont., Can.	C4	73
Richards-Gebaur Air Force Base, mil., Mo., U.S.	C3	102
Richards Island, i., N.W. Ter., Can.	C6	66
Richardson, Tx., U.S.	n10	120
Richardson, co., Ne., U.S.	D10	104
Richardson Lakes, l., Me., U.S.	D2	96
Richardson Mountains, mts., Can.	C5	66
Richardton, N.D., U.S.	C3	111
Rich Creek, Va., U.S.	C2	123
Riche, Pointe, c., Newf., Can.	C3	72
Richfield, Mn., U.S.	F5	100
Richfield, Ut., U.S.	E3	121
Richford, Vt., U.S.	B3	122
Rich Hill, Mo., U.S.	C3	102
Richibucto, N.B., Can.	C5	71
Richland, Ga., U.S.	D2	87
Richland, Mo., U.S.	D5	102
Richland, Wa., U.S.	C6	124
Richland, co., Il., U.S.	E5	90
Richland, co., La., U.S.	B4	95
Richland, co., Mt., U.S.	C12	103
Richland, co., N.D., U.S.	C8	111
Richland, co., Oh., U.S.	B3	112
Richland, co., S.C., U.S.	D6	117
Richland, co., Wi., U.S.	E3	126
Richland Balsam, mtn., N.C., U.S.	f10	110
Richland Center, Wi., U.S.	E3	126
Richland Creek, stm., Tn., U.S.	B5	119
Richlands, N.C., U.S.	C5	110
Richlands, Va., U.S.	e10	123
Richlandtown, Pa., U.S.	F11	115
Richmond, Austl.	D8	50
Richmond, B.C., Can.	E6	69
Richmond, Que., Can.	D5	74
Richmond, Ca., U.S.	D2	82
Richmond, Il., U.S.	A5	90
Richmond, In., U.S.	E8	91
Richmond, Ky., U.S.	C5	94
Richmond, Me., U.S.	D3	96
Richmond, Mi., U.S.	F8	99
Richmond, Mn., U.S.	E4	100
Richmond, Mo., U.S.	B4	102
Richmond, Tx., U.S.	E5	120
Richmond, Ut., U.S.	B4	121
Richmond, Vt., U.S.	C3	122
Richmond, Va., U.S.	C5	123
Richmond, co., Ga., U.S.	C4	87
Richmond, co., N.Y., U.S.	E6	109
Richmond, co., N.C., U.S.	B3	110
Richmond, co., Va., U.S.	C6	123
Richmond Beach, Wa., U.S.	B3	124
Richmond Heights, Fl., U.S.	s13	86
Richmond Heights, Mo., U.S.	f13	102
Richmond Highlands, Wa., U.S.	B3	124
Richmond Hill, Ont., Can.	D5	73
Richmond Hill, Ga., U.S.	E5	87
Richmond National Battlefield Park, Va., U.S.	n18	123
Rich Square, N.C., U.S.	A5	110
Richton, Ms., U.S.	D5	101
Richwood, Oh., U.S.	B2	112
Richwood, W.V., U.S.	C4	125
Rickenbacker Air Force Base, mil., Oh., U.S.	m11	112
Rickman, Tn., U.S.	C8	119
Riddle, Or., U.S.	E3	114
Riddle Mountain, mtn., Or., U.S.	D8	114
Rideau, stm., Ont., Can.	B9	73
Ridgecrest, Ca., U.S.	E5	82
Ridge Farm, Il., U.S.	D6	90
Ridgefield, Ct., U.S.	D2	84
Ridgefield, N.J., U.S.	h8	107
Ridgefield, Wa., U.S.	D3	124
Ridgefield Park, N.J., U.S.	h8	107
Ridgeland, Ms., U.S.	C3	101
Ridgeland, S.C., U.S.	G6	117
Ridgeley, W.V., U.S.	B6	125
Ridgely, Md., U.S.	C6	97
Ridgely, Tn., U.S.	A2	119
Ridgetop, Tn., U.S.	A5	119
Ridgetown, Ont., Can.	E3	73
Ridgeview, W.V., U.S.	C3	125
Ridgeville, In., U.S.	D7	91
Ridgeville, S.C., U.S.	E7	117
Ridgeway, Va., U.S.	D3	123
Ridgewood, N.J., U.S.	B4	107
Ridgway, Il., U.S.	F5	90
Ridgway, Pa., U.S.	D4	115
Riding Mountain National Park, Man., Can.	D1	70
Ridley Park, Pa., U.S.	p20	115
Ried im Innkreis, Aus.	G13	8
Riesa, Ger.	D13	8
Riesi, Italy	L9	14
Rieti, Italy	G7	14
Rif, mts., Mor.	A5	42
Riffe Lake, res., Wa., U.S.	C3	124
Rifle, Co., U.S.	B3	83
Rifle, stm., Mi., U.S.	D6	99
Rift Valley, val., Afr.	B5	44
Rīga, Lat.	E7	18
Riga, Gulf of, b., Eur.	D6	18
Rigaud, Que., Can.	F7	89
Rigby, Id., U.S.	F7	89
Rigestān, reg., Afg.	C1	36
Riihimäki, Fin.	F15	6
Rijeka, Cro.	D9	14
Riley, Ks., U.S.	C7	93
Riley, co., Ks., U.S.	C7	93
Riley, Mount, mtn., N.M., U.S.	F2	108
Rimbey, Alta., Can.	C3	68
Rimersburg, Pa., U.S.	D3	115
Rimini, Italy	F7	14
Rimouski, Que., Can.	A9	74
Rimouski, stm., Que., Can.	A9	74
Rimouski-Est, Que., Can.	A9	74
Rimrock Lake, res., Wa., U.S.	C4	124
Rincon, Ga., U.S.	D5	87
Rincon Mountains, mts., Az., U.S.	E5	80
Rindal, Nor.	E7	6
Ringebu, Nor.	F8	6
Ringgold, Ga., U.S.	B1	87
Ringgold, La., U.S.	B2	95
Ringgold, co., Ia., U.S.	D3	92
Ringling, Ok., U.S.	C4	113
Ringwood, N.J., U.S.	A4	107
Rio, Il., U.S.	E6	86
Rio, Wi., U.S.	E4	126
Rio Arriba, co., N.M., U.S.	A2	108
Riobamba, Ec.	H3	58
Río Benito, Eq. Gui.	H7	42
Rio Blanco, co., Co., U.S.	B2	83
Rio Branco, Braz.	E5	54
Rio Claro, Braz.	G5	57
Río Colorado, Arg.	D4	56
Río Cuarto, Arg.	C4	56
Rio de Janeiro, Braz.	G7	57
Rio Dell, Ca., U.S.	B1	82
Rio do Sul, Braz.	B7	56
Río Gallegos, Arg.	G3	56
Rio Grande, Arg.	G3	56
Rio Grande, Braz.	C6	56
Río Grande, Mex.	F8	62
Rio Grande, Nic.	H6	64
Rio Grande, Oh., U.S.	D3	112
Rio Grande, co., Co., U.S.	D4	83
Rio Grande City, Tx., U.S.	F3	120
Rio Grande Reservoir, res., Co., U.S.	D3	83
Ríohacha, Col.	B6	58
Rio Hondo, Tx., U.S.	F4	120
Rioja, Peru	E3	54
Riom, Fr.	G10	10
Río Mayo, Arg.	F2	56
Río Negro, Embalse del, res., Ur.	C5	56
Río Negro, Pantanal do, sw., Braz.	G7	54
Rionero in Vulture, Italy	I10	14
Rio Pardo, Braz.	B6	56
Rio Pardo de Minas, Braz.	G10	54
Rio Rancho, N.M., U.S.	B3	108
Río Sucio, Col.	E5	58
Rio Verde, Braz.	D3	57
Ríoverde, Mex.	G10	62
Rio Vista, Ca., U.S.	C3	82
Rioz, Fr.	E13	10
Ripley, Ms., U.S.	A5	101
Ripley, Oh., U.S.	D2	112
Ripley, Tn., U.S.	B2	119
Ripley, W.V., U.S.	C3	125
Ripley, co., In., U.S.	F7	91
Ripley, co., Mo., U.S.	E7	102
Ripoll, Spain	C14	12
Ripon, Eng., U.K.	G11	7
Ripon, Ca., U.S.	E5	126
Ripon, Wi., U.S.	E5	126
Rippowam, stm., Ct., U.S.	E1	84
Ririe Lake, res., Id., U.S.	F7	89
Rishon leZiyyon, Isr.	D4	40
Rising Sun, De., U.S.	D3	85
Rising Sun, In., U.S.	G8	91
Rising Sun, Md., U.S.	A5	97
Rison, Ar., U.S.	D3	81
Ritchie, co., W.V., U.S.	B3	125
Ritter, Mount, mtn., Ca., U.S.	D4	82
Rittman, Oh., U.S.	B4	112
Ritzville, Wa., U.S.	B7	124
Riva, Italy	D5	14
Rivanna, stm., Va., U.S.	C4	123
Rivas, Nic.	I5	64
Rivera, Ur.	C5	56
Riverbank, Ca., U.S.	D3	82
River Bourgeois, N.S., Can.	D9	71
Riverdale, Ca., U.S.	D4	82
Riverdale, Il., U.S.	k9	90
Riverdale, Md., U.S.	C4	97
River Edge, N.J., U.S.	h8	107
River Falls, Al., U.S.	D3	78
River Falls, Wi., U.S.	D1	126
River Forest, Il., U.S.	k9	90
River Grove, Il., U.S.	k9	90
Riverhead, N.Y., U.S.	n16	109
River Hebert, N.S., Can.	D5	71
River Heights, Ut., U.S.	B4	121
River Hills, Wi., U.S.	m12	126
River Pines, Wi., U.S.	f10	98
River Ridge, La., U.S.	k11	95
River Road, Or., U.S.	C3	114
River Rouge, Mi., U.S.	p15	99
Rivers, Man., Can.	D1	70
Riverside, Al., U.S.	B3	78
Riverside, Ca., U.S.	F5	82
Riverside, Il., U.S.	k9	90
Riverside, Ia., U.S.	C6	92
Riverside, N.J., U.S.	C3	107
Riverside, Pa., U.S.	E8	115
Riverside, co., Ca., U.S.	F5	82
Riverside Reservoir, res., Co., U.S.	A6	83
Riverton, Man., Can.	D3	70
Riverton, Il., U.S.	D4	90
Riverton, Ks., U.S.	E9	93
Riverton, N.J., U.S.	C3	107
Riverton, Ut., U.S.	C4	121
Riverton, Vt., U.S.	C3	122
Riverton, Wy., U.S.	C4	127
Riverton Heights, Wa., U.S.	f11	124
River Vale, N.J., U.S.	h8	107
Riverview, Fl., U.S.	p11	86
Riverview, Mi., U.S.	p15	99
Rivesaltes, Fr.	J9	10
Rivesville, W.V., U.S.	B4	125
Riviera Beach, Fl., U.S.	F6	86
Riviera Beach, Md., U.S.	B4	97
Rivière-du-Loup, Que., Can.	B8	74
Rivière-Verte, N.B., Can.	B1	71
Rivoli, Italy	D2	14
Riyadh see Ar-Riyāḍ, Sau. Ar.	D4	46
Rize, Tur.	G16	22
Roa, Spain	D8	12
Roachdale, In., U.S.	E4	91
Roane, co., Tn., U.S.	D9	119
Roane, co., W.V., U.S.	C3	125
Roan Mountain, Tn., U.S.	C11	119
Roanne, Fr.	F11	10
Roanoke, Al., U.S.	B4	78

Name	Map Ref	Page
Roanoke, Il., U.S.	C4	90
Roanoke, In., U.S.	C7	91
Roanoke, La., U.S.	D3	95
Roanoke, Tx., U.S.	m9	120
Roanoke, Va., U.S.	C3	123
Roanoke, co., Va., U.S.	C2	123
Roanoke, stm., U.S.	A5	110
Roanoke Island, i., N.C., U.S.	B7	110
Roanoke Rapids, N.C., U.S.	A5	110
Roanoke Rapids Lake, res., U.S.	A5	110
Roaring Fork, stm., Co., U.S.	C4	83
Roaring Spring, Pa., U.S.	F5	115
Roatán, Isla de, i., Hond.	F4	64
Robbins, Il., U.S.	k9	90
Robbins, N.C., U.S.	B3	110
Robbinsdale, Mn., U.S.	m12	100
Robbinsville, N.C., U.S.	f9	110
Röbel, Ger.	B12	8
Robersonville, N.C., U.S.	B5	110
Roberta, Ga., U.S.	D2	87
Robert Lee, Tx., U.S.	D2	120
Roberts, Wi., U.S.	C1	126
Roberts, co., S.D., U.S.	B8	118
Roberts, co., Tx., U.S.	B2	120
Roberts, Point, c., Wa., U.S.	A2	124
Robert's Arm, Newf., Can.	D4	72
Roberts Creek Mountain, mtn., Nv., U.S.	D5	105
Robertsdale, Al., U.S.	E2	78
Robertsfors, Swe.	D13	6
Robert S. Kerr Reservoir, res., Ok., U.S.	B6	113
Roberts Mountain, mtn., Ak., U.S.	C6	79
Roberts Mountain, mtn., Wy., U.S.	D3	127
Robertson, co., Ky., U.S.	B5	94
Robertson, co., Tn., U.S.	A5	119
Robertson, co., Tx., U.S.	D4	120
Robertsonville, Que., Can.	C6	74
Roberts Peak, mtn., B.C., Can.	F8	66
Robertsport, Lib.	G3	42
Robertville, N.B., Can.	B4	71
Roberval, Que., Can.	A5	74
Robeson, co., N.C., U.S.	C3	110
Robins, Ia., U.S.	B6	92
Robinson, Il., U.S.	D6	90
Robinson, co., W.V., U.S.	m14	125
Robinson Fork, stm., W.V., U.S.	k9	125
Roblin, Man., Can.	D1	70
Roboré, Bol.	G7	54
Robson, Mount, mtn., B.C., Can.	C8	69
Robstown, Tx., U.S.	F4	120
Roca Partida, Isla, i., Mex.	H3	62
Roca Partida, Punta, c., Mex.	H12	62
Rocas, Atol das, atoll, Braz.	D12	54
Roccastrada, Italy	F6	14
Rocha, Ur.	C6	56
Rochefort, Fr.	G6	10
Rochelle, Ga., U.S.	E3	87
Rochelle, Il., U.S.	B4	90
Rochelle Park, N.J., U.S.	h8	107
Rochester, Il., U.S.	D4	90
Rochester, In., U.S.	B5	91
Rochester, Mi., U.S.	F7	99
Rochester, Mn., U.S.	F6	100
Rochester, N.H., U.S.	D5	106
Rochester, N.Y., U.S.	B3	109
Rochester, Pa., U.S.	E1	115
Rochester, Vt., U.S.	D3	122
Rochester, Wa., U.S.	C2	124
Rochester, Wi., U.S.	n11	126
Rock, co., Mn., U.S.	G2	100
Rock, co., Ne., U.S.	B6	104
Rock, co., Wi., U.S.	F4	126
Rock, stm., U.S.	B3	90
Rock, stm., U.S.	A1	92
Rockall, i., Scot., U.K.	D5	4
Rockaway, N.J., U.S.	B3	107
Rockaway, Or., U.S.	B3	114
Rockbridge, co., Va., U.S.	C3	123
Rockcastle, co., Ky., U.S.	C5	94
Rockcastle, stm., Ky., U.S.	C5	94
Rockcliffe Park, Ont., Can.	h12	73
Rock Creek, Mn., U.S.	E6	100
Rock Creek, stm., U.S.	B3	97
Rock Creek, stm., U.S.	h14	124
Rock Creek, stm., Nv., U.S.	C5	105
Rock Creek, stm., Or., U.S.	B6	114
Rock Creek, stm., Wa., U.S.	B8	124
Rock Creek, stm., Wa., U.S.	D5	124
Rock Creek, stm., Wy., U.S.	E6	127
Rock Creek Butte, mtn., Or., U.S.	C8	114
Rockdale, Il., U.S.	B5	90
Rockdale, Md., U.S.	B4	97
Rockdale, Tx., U.S.	D4	120
Rockdale, co., Ga., U.S.	C3	87
Rockfall, Ct., U.S.	C5	84
Rock Falls, Il., U.S.	B4	90
Rockford, Ia., U.S.	A4	90
Rockford, Ia., U.S.	A5	92
Rockford, Mi., U.S.	E5	99
Rockford, Mn., U.S.	E5	100
Rockford, Oh., U.S.	B1	112
Rockford, Tn., U.S.	D10	119
Rock Hall, Md., U.S.	B5	97
Rockhampton, Austl.	D10	50
Rock Hill, S.C., U.S.	B5	117
Rockingham, N.C., U.S.	C3	110
Rockingham, co., N.H., U.S.	D4	106
Rockingham, co., Va., U.S.	A3	110
Rockingham, co., Va., U.S.	B4	123
Rock Island, Que., Can.	D5	74
Rock Island, Il., U.S.	B3	90
Rock Island, co., Il., U.S.	B3	90
Rock Island, i., Fl., U.S.	C3	86
Rock Island, i., Wi., U.S.	C7	126
Rock Lake, l., Wa., U.S.	B8	124
Rockland, Ont., Can.	B9	73
Rockland, Me., U.S.	D3	96
Rockland, Ma., U.S.	B6	98
Rockland, co., N.Y., U.S.	D6	109
Rockledge, Fl., U.S.	D6	86
Rockledge, Pa., U.S.	o20	115
Rocklin, Ca., U.S.	C3	82
Rockmart, Ga., U.S.	B1	87
Rock Mountain, mtn., Co., U.S.	D3	83
Rockport, In., U.S.	I3	91
Rockport, Me., U.S.	D3	96
Rockport, Ma., U.S.	A6	98
Rock Port, Mo., U.S.	A2	102
Rockport, Tx., U.S.	F4	120
Rock Rapids, Ia., U.S.	A1	92
Rock River, Wy., U.S.	E7	127
Rock Sound, Bah.	B9	64
Rocksprings, Tx., U.S.	D2	120
Rock Springs, Wy., U.S.	E3	127
Rockstone, Guy.	E13	58
Rockton, Il., U.S.	A4	90
Rock Valley, Ia., U.S.	A1	92
Rockville, In., U.S.	E3	91
Rockville, Md., U.S.	B3	97
Rockville Centre, N.Y., U.S.	n15	109
Rockwall, Tx., U.S.	C4	120
Rockwall, co., Tx., U.S.	C4	120
Rockwell, Ia., U.S.	B4	92
Rockwell, N.C., U.S.	B2	110
Rockwell City, Ia., U.S.	B3	92
Rockwell Park, N.C., U.S.	B2	110
Rockwood, Pa., U.S.	G3	115
Rockwood, Tn., U.S.	D9	119
Rocky, stm., N.C., U.S.	B2	110
Rocky, stm., S.C., U.S.	C2	117
Rocky, East Branch, stm., Oh., U.S.	h9	112
Rocky, West Branch, stm., Oh., U.S.	h9	112
Rocky Boys Indian Reservation, Mt., U.S.	B7	103
Rocky Ford, Co., U.S.	C7	83
Rocky Fork Lake, l., Oh., U.S.	C2	112
Rocky Harbour, Newf., Can.	D3	72
Rocky Hill, Ct., U.S.	C5	84
Rocky Lake, l., Me., U.S.	D5	96
Rocky Mount, N.C., U.S.	B5	110
Rocky Mount, Va., U.S.	D3	123
Rocky Mountain, mtn., Mt., U.S.	C4	103
Rocky Mountain House, Alta., Can.	C3	68
Rocky Mountain National Park, Co., U.S.	A5	83
Rocky Mountains, mts., N.A.	E9	61
Rocky Ripple, In., U.S.	k10	91
Rocky River, Oh., U.S.	A4	112
Rocky Top, mtn., Or., U.S.	C4	114
Roddickton, Newf., Can.	C3	72
Roderfield, W.V., U.S.	D3	125
Rodez, Fr.	H9	10
Ródhos (Rhodes), Grc.	M12	16
Ródhos, i., Grc.	M11	16
Rodney, Ont., Can.	E3	73
Rodney, Cape, c., Ak., U.S.	C6	79
Rodney Village, De., U.S.	D3	85
Rodniki, Russia	D24	18
Roebourne, Austl.	D3	50
Roebuck, S.C., U.S.	B4	117
Roeland Park, Ks., U.S.	k16	93
Roeselare, Bel.	E3	8
Roes Welcome Sound, strt., N.W. Ter., Can.	D15	66
Roff, Ok., U.S.	C5	113
Rogagua, Lago, l., Bol.	F5	54
Roger Mills, co., Ok., U.S.	B2	113
Rogers, Ar., U.S.	A1	81
Rogers, Mn., U.S.	E5	100
Rogers, Tx., U.S.	D4	120
Rogers, co., Ok., U.S.	A6	113
Rogers, Mount, mtn., Va., U.S.	f10	123
Rogers City, Mi., U.S.	C7	99
Rogers Lake, res., Ct., U.S.	D6	84
Rogers Pass, Mt., U.S.	C4	103
Rogersville, N.B., Can.	C4	71
Rogersville, Al., U.S.	A2	78
Rogersville, Mo., U.S.	D4	102
Rogersville, Tn., U.S.	C10	119
Roggiano Gravina, Italy	J11	14
Rogue, stm., Or., U.S.	E2	114
Rogue River, Or., U.S.	E3	114
Rohtak, India	F7	38
Roi Et, Thai.	F7	34
Rojo, Cabo, c., Mex.	G11	62
Roland, Ia., U.S.	B4	92
Roland, Ok., U.S.	B7	113
Roland, Lake, res., Md., U.S.	g11	97
Rolândia, Braz.	G3	57
Røldal, Nor.	G6	6
Rolette, N.D., U.S.	A6	111
Rolette, co., N.D., U.S.	A6	111
Rolfe, Ia., U.S.	B3	92
Rolla, Mo., U.S.	D6	102
Rolla, N.D., U.S.	A6	111
Rollingbay, Wa., U.S.	e10	124
Rolling Fork, Ms., U.S.	C3	101
Rolling Fork, stm., Ar., U.S.	C1	81
Rolling Fork, stm., Ky., U.S.	C4	94
Rolling Meadows, Il., U.S.	h8	90
Rollingstone, Mn., U.S.	F7	100
Rollinsford, N.H., U.S.	D5	106
Roma (Rome), Italy	H7	14
Roma, Tx., U.S.	F3	120
Romain, Cape, c., S.C., U.S.	F9	117
Roman, Rom.	C10	16
Romania, ctry., Eur.	F13	4
Roman Nose Mountain, mtn., Or., U.S.	D3	114
Romano, Cape, c., Fl., U.S.	G5	86
Romano, Cayo, i., Cuba	C8	64
Romans [-sur-Isère], Fr.	G12	10
Romanzof, Cape, c., Ak., U.S.	C6	79
Romanzof Mountains, mts., Ak., U.S.	B11	79
Rome, Ga., U.S.	B1	87
Rome, Il., U.S.	C4	90
Rome, N.Y., U.S.	B5	109
Rome City, In., U.S.	B7	91
Romeo, Mi., U.S.	F7	99
Romeoville, Il., U.S.	k8	90
Rome see Roma, Italy	H7	14
Romilly-sur-Seine, Fr.	D10	10
Romney, W.V., U.S.	B6	125
Romorantin-Lanthenay, Fr.	E8	10
Romulus, Mi., U.S.	p15	99
Ron, Mui, c., Viet.	E9	34
Roncador, Serra do, plat., Braz.	F8	54
Roncesvalles, Spain	B10	12
Ronceverte, W.V., U.S.	D4	125
Ronda, Spain	I6	12
Rondônia, Braz.	F6	54
Rondonópolis, Braz.	D1	57
Ronge, Lac la, l., Sask., Can.	B3	75
Rønne, Den.	I10	6
Ronneby, Swe.	H10	6
Ronne Ice Shelf, Ant.	B6	47
Ronse, Bel.	E3	8
Roodhouse, Il., U.S.	D3	90
Rooks, co., Ks., U.S.	C4	93
Roorkee, India	F7	38
Roosendaal, Neth.	D4	8
Roosevelt, Ut., U.S.	C5	121
Roosevelt, co., Mt., U.S.	B11	103
Roosevelt, co., N.M., U.S.	C6	108
Roosevelt, co., stm., Braz.	E6	54
Roosevelt Park, Mi., U.S.	E4	99
Root, stm., Mn., U.S.	G7	100
Root, stm., Wi., U.S.	n12	126
Roper, N.C., U.S.	B6	110
Roquefort, Fr.	H6	10
Roraima, Mount, mtn., S.A.	E12	58
Røros, Nor.	E8	6
Rorschach, Switz.	D8	6
Rørvik, Nor.	E16	10
Rošal', Russia	F22	18
Rosamond, Ca., U.S.	E4	82
Rosamorada, Mex.	F7	62
Rosario, Arg.	C4	56
Rosário, Braz.	D10	54
Rosario, Mex.	F7	62
Rosario, Mex.	B2	62
Rosario, Ven.	B6	58
Rosário Oeste, Braz.	F7	54
Rosarno, Italy	K10	14
Rosas, Golfo de, b., Spain	C15	12
Roscoe, Il., U.S.	A5	90
Roscoe, Tx., U.S.	C2	120
Roscommon, Ire.	H4	7
Roscommon, Mi., U.S.	D6	99
Roscommon, co., Mi., U.S.	D6	99
Roscrea, Ire.	I5	7
Rose, Mount, mtn., Nv., U.S.	D2	105
Roseau, Dom.	G17	64
Roseau, Mn., U.S.	B3	100
Roseau, co., Mn., U.S.	B3	100
Roseau, South Fork, stm., Mn., U.S.	B3	100
Rose-Blanche [-Harbour le Cou], Newf., Can.	E2	72
Roseboro, N.C., U.S.	C4	110
Rosebud, S.D., U.S.	D5	118
Rosebud, Tx., U.S.	D4	120
Rosebud, co., Mt., U.S.	D10	103
Rosebud Indian Reservation, S.D., U.S.	D5	118
Roseburg, Or., U.S.	D3	114
Rosedale, In., U.S.	E3	91
Rosedale, Md., U.S.	g11	97
Rosedale, Ms., U.S.	B2	101
Rose Hill, Ks., U.S.	E6	93
Rose Hill, N.C., U.S.	C4	110
Rose Hill, Va., U.S.	f8	123
Roseland, Fl., U.S.	E6	86
Roseland, In., U.S.	A5	91
Roseland, La., U.S.	D5	95
Roseland, Oh., U.S.	B3	112
Roselle, Il., U.S.	k8	90
Roselle, N.J., U.S.	k7	107
Roselle Park, N.J., U.S.	k7	107
Rosemère, Que., Can.	p19	74
Rosemount, Mn., U.S.	F5	100
Rosenberg, Tx., U.S.	E5	120
Rosendale, Wi., U.S.	E5	126
Rosenheim, Ger.	H12	8
Rose Peak, mtn., Az., U.S.	D6	80
Rosepine, La., U.S.	D2	95
Rose Point, c., B.C., Can.	B2	69
Roseto, Pa., U.S.	E11	115
Roseville, Ca., U.S.	C3	82
Roseville, Il., U.S.	C3	90
Roseville, Mi., U.S.	o16	99
Roseville, Mn., U.S.	m12	100
Roseville, Oh., U.S.	C3	112
Rosewood Heights, Il., U.S.	E3	90
Rosiclare, Il., U.S.	F5	90
Rosignano Marittimo, Italy	F5	14
Roskilde, Den.	I9	6
Roslags-Näsby, Swe.	G12	6
Roslavl', Russia	H15	18
Roslyn, Wa., U.S.	B4	124
Roslyn Heights, N.Y., U.S.	h13	109
Ross, Oh., U.S.	C1	112
Ross, co., Oh., U.S.	C2	112
Rossano, Italy	J11	14
Rossan Point, c., Ire.	G4	7
Ross Barnett Reservoir, res., Ms., U.S.	C3	101
Rossburn, Man., Can.	D1	70
Ross Dam, Wa., U.S.	A4	124
Rossel Island, i., Pap. N. Gui.	B10	50
Rossford, Oh., U.S.	A2	112
Ross Ice Shelf, Ant.	A31	47
Rossignol, Lake, l., N.S., Can.	E4	71
Ross Island, i., Man., Can.	B3	70
Ross Lake National Recreation Area, Wa., U.S.	A5	124
Rossland, B.C., Can.	E9	69
Rosslare, Ire.	I6	7
Rosso, Maur.	E2	42
Ross River, Yukon, Can.	D6	66
Ross Sea, Ant.	B31	47
Rossville, Il., U.S.	C6	90
Rossville, In., U.S.	D4	91
Rossville, Ks., U.S.	C8	93
Rostock, Ger.	A12	8
Rostov, Russia	D22	18
Rostov-na-Donu, Russia	H5	22
Roswell, Ga., U.S.	B2	87
Roswell, N.M., U.S.	D5	108
Rotan, Tx., U.S.	C2	120
Rotenburg, Ger.	B9	8
Rothaargebirge, mts., Ger.	D8	8
Rothenburg ob der Tauber, Ger.	F10	8
Rothesay, N.B., Can.	D4	71
Rothschild, Wi., U.S.	D4	126
Rothsville, Pa., U.S.	F9	115
Roti, Pulau, i., Indon.	H7	32
Rotondella, Italy	I11	14
Rotorua, N.Z.	C6	52
Rotterdam, Neth.	D4	8
Rotterdam, N.Y., U.S.	C6	109
Rottweil, Ger.	G8	8
Roubaix, Fr.	B10	10
Rouen, Fr.	C8	10
Rouge, stm., Que., Can.	D3	74
Rough, stm., Ky., U.S.	C3	94
Rough River Lake, res., Ky., U.S.	C3	94
Roulette, Pa., U.S.	C5	115
Round Island, i., Ms., U.S.	g8	101
Round Lake, Il., U.S.	h8	90
Round Lake Beach, Il., U.S.	h8	90
Round Mountain, Nv., U.S.	E4	105
Round Rock, Tx., U.S.	D4	120
Roundup, Mt., U.S.	D8	103
Round Valley Indian Reservation, Ca., U.S.	C2	82
Round Valley Reservoir, res., N.J., U.S.	B3	107
Rouses Point, N.Y., U.S.	f11	109
Roussillon, hist. reg., Fr.	J9	10
Routt, co., Co., U.S.	A3	83
Rouyn, Que., Can.	k11	74
Rouzerville, Pa., U.S.	G6	115
Rovaniemi, Fin.	C15	6
Rovato, Italy	D4	14
Rovereto, Italy	D6	14
Rovigo, Italy	D6	14
Rovinj, Cro.	D8	14
Rovno, Ukr.	G3	22
Rowan, co., Ky., U.S.	B6	94
Rowan, co., N.C., U.S.	B2	110
Rowland, N.C., U.S.	C3	110
Rowlesburg, W.V., U.S.	B5	125
Rowley Island, i., N.W. Ter., Can.	C17	66
Rowley Shoals, rf., Austl.	C3	50
Roxboro, N.C., U.S.	A4	110
Roxton Falls, Que., Can.	D5	74
Roxton Pond, Que., Can.	D5	74
Roy, Ut., U.S.	B3	121
Royal, stm., Me., U.S.	g7	96
Royal Canal, Ire.	H5	7
Royal Center, In., U.S.	C4	91
Royale, Isle, i., Mi., U.S.	h9	99
Royal Gorge, val., Co., U.S.	C5	83
Royal Oak, Mi., U.S.	F7	99
Royal Pines, N.C., U.S.	f10	110
Royalton, Il., U.S.	F4	90
Royalton, Mn., U.S.	E4	100
Royan, Fr.	G5	10
Royersford, Pa., U.S.	F10	115
Royerton, In., U.S.	D7	91
Royse City, Tx., U.S.	C4	120
Royston, B.C., Can.	E5	69
Royston, Ga., U.S.	B3	87
Rubbestadneset, Nor.	G5	6
Rubcovsk, Russia	G10	24
Rubidoux, Ca., U.S.	n14	82
Rubio, Ven.	D6	58
Ruby Dome, mtn., Nv., U.S.	C6	105
Ruby Lake, l., Nv., U.S.	C6	105
Ruby Mountains, mts., Nv., U.S.	C6	105
Ruby Range, mts., Co., U.S.	C3	83
Ruby Range, mts., Mt., U.S.	E4	103
Rudolf, Lake, l., Afr.	H2	46
Rudolstadt, Ger.	E11	8
Rudyard, Mi., U.S.	B6	99
Rue, Fr.	B8	10
Rufā'ah, Sudan	F12	42
Ruffec, Fr.	F7	10
Rufino, Arg.	C4	56
Rufus Woods Lake, res., Wa., U.S.	A6	124
Rugao, China	C9	28
Rugby, Eng., U.K.	I11	7
Rugby, N.D., U.S.	A6	111
Ruian, China	H9	28
Ruidoso, N.M., U.S.	D4	108
Ruidoso Downs, N.M., U.S.	D4	108
Ruijin, China	F10	26
Ruijin, China	J4	28
Rukwa, Lake, l., Tan.	C6	44
Ruleville, Ms., U.S.	B3	101
Rum, stm., Mn., U.S.	D5	100
Ruma, Yugo.	D3	16
Rumbek, Sudan	G11	42
Rum Cay, i., Bah.	C10	64
Rum Creek, stm., W.V., U.S.	n12	125
Rumford, Me., U.S.	D2	96
Rumia, Pol.	A18	8
Rum Jungle, Austl.	B6	50
Rumoi, Japan	p19	30a
Rumson, N.J., U.S.	C4	107
Rumstick Point, c., R.I., U.S.	D5	116
Ru'nan, China	B3	28
Runanga, N.Z.	E3	52
Runge, Tx., U.S.	E4	120
Rungwa, Tan.	C6	44
Runnels, co., Tx., U.S.	D3	120
Runnemede, N.J., U.S.	D2	107
Ruoqiang, China	D4	26
Rupert, Id., U.S.	G5	89
Rupert, W.V., U.S.	D4	125
Rupert, Rivière de, stm., Que., Can.	h11	74
Rural Hall, N.C., U.S.	A2	110
Rural Retreat, Va., U.S.	D1	123
Rusagonis, N.B., Can.	D3	71
Ruse, Bul.	F9	16
Rush, co., In., U.S.	E6	91
Rush, co., Ks., U.S.	D4	93
Rush, stm., Mn., U.S.	F4	100
Rush, stm., Wi., U.S.	D1	126
Rush City, Mn., U.S.	E6	100
Rush Creek, stm., Oh., U.S.	B2	112
Rush Creek, stm., Ok., U.S.	C4	113
Rushford, Mn., U.S.	G7	100
Rush Lake, l., Mn., U.S.	E5	100
Rush Lake, l., Mn., U.S.	D3	100
Rush Lake, l., Wi., U.S.	E5	126
Rushmere, Va., U.S.	h14	123
Rush Springs, Ok., U.S.	C4	113
Rushville, Il., U.S.	C3	90
Rushville, In., U.S.	E7	91
Rushville, Ne., U.S.	B3	104
Rusk, Tx., U.S.	D5	120
Rusk, co., Tx., U.S.	C5	120
Rusk, co., Wi., U.S.	C2	126
Ruskin, Fl., U.S.	E4	86
Russas, Braz.	D11	54
Russell, Man., Can.	D1	70
Russell, Ont., Can.	B9	73
Russell, Ks., U.S.	D5	93
Russell, Ky., U.S.	B7	94
Russell, Pa., U.S.	C3	115
Russell, co., Al., U.S.	C4	78
Russell, co., Ks., U.S.	D5	93
Russell, co., Ky., U.S.	D4	94
Russell, co., Va., U.S.	f9	123
Russell, Mount, mtn., Ak., U.S.	f16	79
Russell Cave National Monument, Al., U.S.	A4	78
Russell Fork, stm., U.S.	C7	94
Russell Island, i., N.W. Ter., Can.	B13	66
Russell Springs, Ky., U.S.	C4	94
Russellville, Al., U.S.	A2	78
Russellville, Ar., U.S.	B2	81
Russellville, Ky., U.S.	D3	94
Russellville, Mo., U.S.	C5	102
Russellville, Tn., U.S.	C10	119
Rüsselsheim, Ger.	E8	8
Russia, ctry., Eur.	E15	22
Russian, stm., Ca., U.S.	C2	82
Russiaville, In., U.S.	D5	91
Rustavi, Geor.	I7	22
Rustburg, Va., U.S.	C3	123
Rustenburg, S. Afr.	G5	44
Ruston, La., U.S.	B3	95
Ruston, Wa., U.S.	B3	124
Ruth, Nv., U.S.	D6	105
Rutherford, N.J., U.S.	B4	107
Rutherford, Tn., U.S.	A3	119
Rutherford, co., N.C., U.S.	B1	110
Rutherford, co., Tn., U.S.	B5	119
Rutherfordton, N.C., U.S.	B1	110
Ruthven, Ia., U.S.	A3	92
Rutland, Ma., U.S.	B4	98
Rutland, Vt., U.S.	D2	122
Rutland, co., Vt., U.S.	D2	122
Rutledge, Ga., U.S.	C3	87
Rutledge, Tn., U.S.	C10	119
Ruukki, Fin.	D15	6
Ruvuma (Rovuma), stm., Afr.	D7	44
Ružomberok, Czech.	F19	8
Rwanda, ctry., Afr.	B5	44
Ryan, Ok., U.S.	C4	113
Ryan Peak, mtn., Id., U.S.	F4	89
Rybinsk, Russia	C21	18
Rybinskoje Vodochranilišče, res., Russia	C21	18
Rybnik, Pol.	E18	8
Rycroft, Alta., Can.	B1	68
Ryde, Eng., U.K.	K11	7
Rye, N.H., U.S.	D5	106
Rye, N.Y., U.S.	h13	109
Rye Beach, N.H., U.S.	E5	106
Rye Patch Dam, Nv., U.S.	C3	105
Rye Patch Reservoir, res., Nv., U.S.	C3	105
Ryfoss, Nor.	F7	6
Ryōtsu, Japan	D11	30
Rysy, mtn., Eur.	F20	8
Ryukyu Islands see Nansei-shotō, is., Japan	F12	26
Rzeszów, Pol.	E21	8
Ržev, Russia	E17	18

S

Name	Map Ref	Page
Saalfeld, Ger.	E11	8
Saarbrücken, Ger.	F6	8
Saaremaa, i., Est.	C5	18
Saarijärvi, Fin.	E15	6
Saarlouis, Ger.	F6	8
Sab, Tônlé, l., Camb.	H7	34
Saba, i., Neth. Ant.	F16	64
Sabadell, Spain	D14	12
Sabae, Japan	G9	30
Sabana, Archipiélago de, is., Cuba	C8	64
Sabanagrande, Hond.	H4	64
Sabanalarga, Col.	B5	58
Sabang, Indon.	E6	32
Sabanilla, Mex.	E9	62
Sabará, Braz.	E7	57
Sabattus, Me., U.S.	D2	96
Sabetha, Ks., U.S.	C8	93
Sabhah, Libya	C8	42
Sabi (Save), stm., Afr.	F6	44
Sabillasville, Md., U.S.	A3	97
Sabina, Oh., U.S.	C2	112
Sabinal, Tx., U.S.	E3	120
Sabiñánigo, Spain	C11	12
Sabinas, Mex.	D9	62
Sabinas Hidalgo, Mex.	D9	62
Sabine, co., La., U.S.	C2	95
Sabine, co., Tx., U.S.	D6	120
Sabine, stm., U.S.	D6	120
Sabine Lake, l., U.S.	E2	95
Sabine Pass, strt., U.S.	E2	95
Sable, Cape, c., N.S., Can.	H19	66
Sable, Cape, c., Fl., U.S.	G5	86
Sable, Îles de, i., N. Cal.	C11	50
Sable Island, i., N.S., Can.	F10	71
Sabula, Ia., U.S.	B7	92
Sabzevār, Iran	J9	22
Sac, co., Ia., U.S.	B2	92
Sac, stm., Mo., U.S.	D4	102
Sacajawea, Lake, res., Wa., U.S.	C7	124

Name	Map Ref	Page
Sacajawea Peak, mtn., Or., U.S.	B9	114
Sacandaga Lake, l., N.Y., U.S.	B6	109
Sac and Fox Indian Reservation, Ia., U.S.	C5	92
Sacaton, Az., U.S.	D4	80
Sac City, Ia., U.S.	B2	92
Sacedón, Spain	E9	12
Sachalin, Ostrov (Sakhalin), i., Russia	G22	24
Sachalinskij Zaliv, b., Russia	G22	24
Sachigo, stm., Ont., Can.	F14	66
Sachse, Tx., U.S.	n10	120
Sachs Harbour, N.W. Ter., Can.	B8	66
Šachty, Russia	H6	22
Sachuest Point, c., R.I., U.S.	F6	116
Sackville, N.B., Can.	D5	71
Saco, Me., U.S.	E2	96
Saco, stm., U.S.	E2	96
Saco, East Branch, stm., N.H., U.S.	B4	106
Sacramento, Ca., U.S.	C3	82
Sacramento, co., Ca., U.S.	C3	82
Sacramento, stm., Ca., U.S.	C3	82
Sacramento, stm., N.M., U.S.	E4	108
Sacramento Mountains, mts., N.M., U.S.	E4	108
Sacramento Valley, val., Ca., U.S.	C2	82
Sacré-Coeur-Saguenay, Que., Can.	A8	74
Sacred Heart, Mn., U.S.	F3	100
Sádaba, Spain	C10	12
Sa'dah, Yemen	E3	46
Saddle, stm., N.J., U.S.	h8	107
Saddleback Mountain, mtn., Az., U.S.	k8	80
Saddle Brook, N.J., U.S.	h8	107
Saddlebunch Keys, is., Fl., U.S.	H5	86
Saddle Mountain, mtn., Or., U.S.	B3	114
Saddle Mountains, mts., Wa., U.S.	C5	124
Saddle River, N.J., U.S.	A4	107
Sa Dec, Viet.	I8	34
Sādiqābad, Pak.	F4	38
Sado, i., Japan	D11	30
Sado-kaikyō, strt., Japan	E11	30
Saegertown, Pa., U.S.	C1	115
Safety Harbor, Fl., U.S.	E4	86
Säffle, Swe.	G9	6
Safford, Az., U.S.	E6	80
Safi, Mor.	B4	42
Safid, stm., Afg.	B1	38
Säfid Kūh, Selseleh-ye, mts., Afg.	C1	36
Safonovo, Russia	F16	18
Saga, Japan	I3	30
Sagadahoc, co., Me., U.S.	E3	96
Sagaing, Burma	D3	34
Sagamihara, Japan	G12	30
Sagamore Hills, Oh., U.S.	h9	112
Saganaga Lake, l., Mn., U.S.	B7	100
Sägar, India	I3	37
Sägar, India	I8	38
Sag Harbor, N.Y., U.S.	m16	109
Saginaw, Mi., U.S.	E7	99
Saginaw, Tx., U.S.	n9	120
Saginaw, co., Mi., U.S.	E6	99
Saginaw Bay, b., Mi., U.S.	E7	99
Saglek Bay, b., Newf., Can.	f9	72
Sagres, Port.	H3	12
Saguache, co., Co., U.S.	C4	83
Sagua de Tánamo, Cuba	D10	64
Sagua la Grande, Cuba	C7	64
Saguaro Lake, res., Az., U.S.	k10	80
Saguaro National Monument (Tucson Mountain Section), Az., U.S.	E4	80
Saguaro National Monument, Az., U.S.	E5	80
Saguenay, stm., Que., Can.	A7	74
Sagunto, Spain	F11	12
Sahagún, Col.	C5	58
Sahagún, Spain	C6	12
Sahara, des., Afr.	D6	42
Sahāranpur, India	F7	38
Sāhiwāl (Montgomery), Pak.	E5	38
Sahuaripa, Mex.	C5	62
Sahuarita, Az., U.S.	F5	80
Sahuayo, Mex.	G8	62
Saibai, i., Austl.	A8	50
Saïda, Alg.	B6	42
Saidpur, Bngl.	H13	38
Saidu, Pak.	C3	38
Saigō, Japan	F6	30
Saigon see Thanh Pho Ho Chi Minh, Viet.	I9	34
Saijō, Japan	I6	30
Saimaa, l., Fin.	F16	6
Saint Abb's Head, c., Scot., U.K.	F10	7
Saint Adolphe, Man., Can.	E3	70
Saint-Affrique, Fr.	I9	10
Sainte-Agathe, Que., Can.	C6	74
Sainte-Agathe-des-Monts, Que., Can.	C3	74
Saint-Aimé (Massueville), Que., Can.	D5	74
Saint-Alban, Que., Can.	C5	74
Saint Alban's, Newf., Can.	E4	72
Saint Albans, Eng., U.K.	J12	7
Saint Albans, Vt., U.S.	B2	122
Saint Albans, W.V., U.S.	C3	125
Saint Albans Bay, b., Vt., U.S.	B2	122
Saint Albert, Alta., Can.	C4	68
Saint-Amand-Mont-Rond, Fr.	F9	10
Saint-Ambroise, Que., Can.	A6	74
Saint-Ambroix, Fr.	H11	10
Saint-André, Cap, c., Madag.	E8	44
Saint-André-Avellin, Que., Can.	D2	74
Saint-André-Est, Que., Can.	D3	74
Saint-André-les-Alpes, Fr.	I13	10
Saint Andrew Bay, b., Fl., U.S.	u16	86
Saint Andrews, N.B., Can.	D2	71
Saint Andrews, Scot., U.K.	E10	7
Saint Andrews, S.C., U.S.	F7	117
Saint Andrews, S.C., U.S.	C5	117
Saint Anne, Il., U.S.	B6	90
Sainte-Anne-de-Beaupré, Que., Can.	B7	74
Sainte-Anne [-de-Bellevue], Que., Can.	q19	74
Sainte Anne-de-Madawaska, N.B., Can.	B1	71
Sainte Anne-des-Chênes, Man., Can.	E3	70
Saint-Anselme, Que., Can.	C7	74
Saint Ansgar, Ia., U.S.	A5	92
Saint Anthony, Newf., Can.	C4	72
Saint Anthony, Id., U.S.	F7	89
Saint Antoine, N.B., Can.	C5	71
Saint-Apollinaire, Que., Can.	C6	74
Saint Arthur, N.B., Can.	B3	71
Saint-Astier, Fr.	G7	10
Saint-Aubert, Que., Can.	B7	74
Saint Augustin, stm., Can.	C2	72
Saint Augustine, Fl., U.S.	C5	86
Saint Austell, Eng., U.K.	K8	7
Saint-Avold, Fr.	C13	10
Saint-Barthélemy, i., Guad.	F16	64
Saint Basile, N.B., Can.	B1	71
Saint-Basile [-Sud], Que., Can.	C6	74
Saint-Benoît-du-Sault, Fr.	F8	10
Saint-Bernard, Que., Can.	C6	74
Saint Bernard, Al., U.S.	A3	78
Saint Bernard, La., U.S.	E6	95
Saint Bernard, Oh., U.S.	o13	112
Saint Bernard, co., La., U.S.	E6	95
Saint Bernice, In., U.S.	E2	91
Saint Bride, Mount, mtn., Alta., Can.	D3	68
Saint Bride's, Newf., Can.	E4	72
Saint-Brieuc, Fr.	D4	10
Saint-Bruno, Que., Can.	A6	74
Saint-Calais, Fr.	E7	10
Saint-Casimir, Que., Can.	C5	74
Saint Catharines, Ont., Can.	D5	73
Saint Catherine, Lake, l., Vt., U.S.	E2	122
Saint Catherines Island, i., Ga., U.S.	E5	87
Saint-Célestin (Annaville), Que., Can.	C5	74
Saint-Céré, Fr.	H8	10
Saint-Césaire, Que., Can.	D4	74
Saint-Chamond, Fr.	G11	10
Saint-Charles, Que., Can.	C7	74
Saint Charles, Il., U.S.	B5	90
Saint Charles, Mi., U.S.	E6	99
Saint Charles, Mn., U.S.	G6	100
Saint Charles, Mo., U.S.	C7	102
Saint Charles, co., La., U.S.	E5	95
Saint Charles, co., Mo., U.S.	C7	102
Saint-Chély-d'Apcher, Fr.	H10	10
Saint Christopher (Saint Kitts), i., St. K./N.	F16	64
Saint Christopher-Nevis see Saint Kitts and Nevis, ctry., N.A.	F16	64
Saint-Chrysostome, Que., Can.	D4	74
Saint Clair, Mi., U.S.	F8	99
Saint Clair, Mn., U.S.	F5	100
Saint Clair, Mo., U.S.	C6	102
Saint Clair, Pa., U.S.	E9	115
Saint Clair, co., Al., U.S.	B3	78
Saint Clair, co., Il., U.S.	E3	90
Saint Clair, co., Mi., U.S.	F8	99
Saint Clair, co., Mo., U.S.	C4	102
Saint Clair Shores, Mi., U.S.	p16	99
Saint Clairsville, Oh., U.S.	B5	112
Saint Claude, Man., Can.	E2	70
Saint-Claude, Fr.	F12	10
Saint Cloud, Fl., U.S.	D5	86
Saint Cloud, Mn., U.S.	E4	100
Saint-Coeur-de-Marie, Que., Can.	A6	74
Saint-Constant, Que., Can.	q19	74
Sainte-Croix, Que., Can.	C6	74
Saint Croix, co., Wi., U.S.	C1	126
Saint Croix, i., V.I.US.	F15	64
Saint Croix, stm., U.S.	C1	126
Saint Croix, Lake, l., U.S.	D1	126
Saint Croix Falls, Wi., U.S.	C1	126
Saint Croix Stream, stm., Me., U.S.	B4	96
Saint-Damase, Que., Can.	D4	74
Saint David, Az., U.S.	F5	80
Saint-David-de-l'Auberivière, Que., Can.	n17	74
Saint David's, Wales, U.K.	J7	7
Saint-Denis, Que., Can.	D4	74
Saint-Denis, Fr.	D9	10
Saint-Denis, Reu.	F11	44
Saint-Dié, Fr.	D13	10
Saint-Dizier, Fr.	D11	10
Saint-Dominque, Que., Can.	D5	74
Saint Edward, Ne., U.S.	C8	104
Saint Eleanor's, P.E.I., Can.	C6	71
Saint Elias, Cape, c., Ak., U.S.	D11	79
Saint Elmo, Al., U.S.	E1	78
Saint Elmo, Il., U.S.	D5	90
Saint-Éphrem [-de-Tring], Que., Can.	C7	74
Saint Étienne, Fr.	G11	10
Saint-Eustache, Que., Can.	D4	74
Saint-Félicien, Que., Can.	A5	74
Saint-Félix-de-Valois, Que., Can.	C4	74
Saint-Ferdinand (Bernierville), Que., Can.	C6	74
Saint-Ferréol [-les-Neiges], Que., Can.	B7	74
Saint-Flavien, Que., Can.	C6	74
Saint-Florentin, Fr.	D10	10
Saint-Florent-sur-Cher, Fr.	F9	10
Saint-Flour, Fr.	G10	10
Sainte-Foy, Que., Can.	n17	74
Sainte-Foy-la-Grande, Fr.	H7	10
Saint Francis, Ks., U.S.	C2	93
Saint Francis, Mn., U.S.	E5	100
Saint Francis, S.D., U.S.	D5	118
Saint Francis, Wi., U.S.	n12	126
Saint Francis, co., Ar., U.S.	B5	81
Saint Francis, stm., U.S.	A5	81
Saint Francis, Cape, c., Newf., Can.	E5	72
Saint Francisville, Il., U.S.	E6	90
Saint Francisville, La., U.S.	D4	95
Saint-François, co., Mo., U.S.	D7	102
Saint-François, stm., Que., Can.	D5	74
Saint-François, Lac, l., Que., Can.	D6	74
Saint Francois Mountains, hills, Mo., U.S.	D7	102
Saint Froid Lake, l., Me., U.S.	B4	96
Saint-Fulgence, Que., Can.	A7	74
Saint-Gabriel, Que., Can.	C4	74
Saint-Gaudens, Fr.	I7	10
Saint-Gédeon, Que., Can.	D7	74
Sainte Genevieve, Mo., U.S.	D7	102
Sainte Genevieve, co., Mo., U.S.	D7	102
Saint George, Austl.	E9	50
Saint George, N.B., Can.	D3	71
Saint George, Ont., Can.	D4	73
Saint George, S.C., U.S.	E6	117
Saint George, Ut., U.S.	F2	121
Saint George, Cape, c., Newf., Can.	D2	72
Saint George, Cape, c., Fl., U.S.	C1	86
Saint George Island, i., Ak., U.S.	D6	79
Saint George Island, i., Fl., U.S.	C2	86
Saint George's, Newf., Can.	D2	72
Saint-Georges, Que., Can.	C5	74
Saint-Georges, Fr. Gu.	C8	54
Saint Georges, De., U.S.	B3	85
Saint Georges, Gren.	H17	64
Saint George's Bay, b., Newf., Can.	D2	72
Saint George's Bay, b., N.S., Can.	D8	71
Saint George's Channel, strt., Eur.	J6	4
Saint-Georges-Ouest, Que., Can.	C7	74
Saint-Germain, Fr.	D9	10
Saint-Gervais, Que., Can.	C7	74
Saint-Gilles, Que., Can.	C6	74
Saint-Gilles-Croix-de-Vie, Fr.	F5	10
Saint-Girons, Fr.	J8	10
Saint-Grégoire (Larochelle), Que., Can.	C5	74
Saint-Guénolé, Fr.	E2	10
Saint-Guillaume-d'Upton, Que., Can.	D5	74
Saint Helen, Lake, l., Mi., U.S.	D6	99
Saint Helena, Ca., U.S.	C2	82
Saint Helena, co., La., U.S.	D5	95
Saint Helena Bay, b., S. Afr.	H3	44
Saint Helena Island, i., S.C., U.S.	G6	117
Saint Helena Sound, strt., S.C., U.S.	G7	117
Saint Helens, Or., U.S.	B4	114
Saint Helens, Mount, vol., Wa., U.S.	C3	124
Saint Helier, Jersey	C4	10
Saint Henry, Oh., U.S.	B1	112
Saint-Hippolyte, Fr.	E13	10
Saint-Honoré, Que., Can.	D7	74
Saint-Hubert, Que., Can.	q20	74
Saint-Hubert-de-Témiscouata, Que., Can.	B8	74
Saint-Hyacinthe, Que., Can.	D5	74
Saint Ignace, Mi., U.S.	C6	99
Saint Ignace Island, i., Ont., Can.	G15	66
Saint Ignatius, Mt., U.S.	C2	103
Saint Isidore de Prescott, Ont., Can.	B10	73
Saint Jacobs, Ont., Can.	D4	73
Saint Jacques, N.B., Can.	B1	71
Saint-Jacques, Que., Can.	D4	74
Saint James, Mn., U.S.	G4	100
Saint James, Mo., U.S.	D6	102
Saint James, co., La., U.S.	D5	95
Saint James, Cape, c., B.C., Can.	D2	69
Saint James City, Fl., U.S.	F4	86
Saint-Jean, stm., Que., Can.	A7	74
Saint-Jean, Lac, l., Que., Can.	A5	74
Saint Jean Baptiste, Man., Can.	E3	70
Saint-Jean-Chrysostome, Que., Can.	o17	74
Saint-Jean-d'Angély, Fr.	G6	10
Saint-Jean-de-Luz, Fr.	I5	10
Saint-Jean-de-Maurienne, Fr.	G13	10
Saint-Jean-de-Monts, Fr.	F4	10
Saint-Jean-Pied-de-Port, Fr.	I5	10
Saint-Jean-sur-Richelieu, Que., Can.	D4	74
Saint-Jérôme, Que., Can.	D3	74
Saint Jo, Tx., U.S.	C4	120
Saint-Joachim, Que., Can.	B7	74
Saint Joe, stm., Id., U.S.	B3	89
Saint John, N.B., Can.	D3	71
Saint John, In., U.S.	B3	91
Saint John, Ks., U.S.	E5	93
Saint John, i., V.I.U.S.	E15	64
Saint John, stm., N.A.	G19	66
Saint John, Cape, c., Newf., Can.	D4	72
Saint John Bay, b., Newf., Can.	C3	72
Saint Johns, Antig.	F17	64
Saint John's, Newf., Can.	E5	72
Saint Johns, Az., U.S.	C6	80
Saint Johns, Mi., U.S.	F6	99
Saint Johns, co., Fl., U.S.	C5	86
Saint Johns, stm., Fl., U.S.	B5	86
Saint Johnsbury, Vt., U.S.	C4	122
Saint John the Baptist, co., La., U.S.	D5	95
Saint Jones, stm., De., U.S.	D4	85
Saint Joseph, N.B., Can.	D5	71
Saint Joseph, Il., U.S.	C5	90
Saint Joseph, La., U.S.	C4	95
Saint Joseph, Mi., U.S.	F4	99
Saint Joseph, Mo., U.S.	B3	102
Saint Joseph, Tn., U.S.	B4	119
Saint Joseph, co., In., U.S.	A5	91
Saint Joseph, co., Mi., U.S.	G5	99
Saint-Joseph, stm., U.S.	F5	99
Saint-Joseph, Lac, l., Que., Can.	n16	74
Saint Joseph Bay, b., Fl., U.S.	C1	86
Saint-Joseph-de-Beauce, Que., Can.	C7	74
Saint Joseph Point, c., Fl., U.S.	v16	86
Saint Joseph Sound, strt., Fl., U.S.	o10	86
Saint-Jovite, Que., Can.	C3	74
Saint-Julien-en-Born, Fr.	H5	10
Saint-Junien, Fr.	G7	10
Saint-Just-en-Chaussée, Fr.	C9	10
Saint Kilda, i., Scot., U.K.	D4	7
Saint Kitts-Nevis, ctry., N.A.	F16	64
Saint-Lambert, Que., Can.	p19	74
Saint Landry, co., La., U.S.	D3	95
Saint-Laurent, Que., Can.	p19	74
Saint Lawrence, Newf., Can.	E4	72
Saint Lawrence, co., N.Y., U.S.	A5	109
Saint Lawrence, stm., N.A.	G19	66
Saint Lawrence, Cape, c., N.S., Can.	B9	71
Saint Lawrence, Gulf of, b., Can.	G20	66
Saint Lawrence Island, i., Ak., U.S.	C5	79
Saint Lawrence Islands National Park, Ont., Can.	C9	73
Saint Léonard, N.B., Can.	B2	71
Saint-Léonard [-d'Aston], Que., Can.	C5	74
Saint-Liboire, Que., Can.	D5	74
Saint-Lô, Fr.	C5	10
Saint-Louis, Sen.	E2	42
Saint Louis, Mi., U.S.	E6	99
Saint Louis, Mo., U.S.	C7	102
Saint Louis, co., Mn., U.S.	C6	100
Saint Louis, co., Mo., U.S.	C7	102
Saint Louis, stm., U.S.	D6	100
Saint Louis Park, Mn., U.S.	n12	100
Saint Louis-de-Gonzague, Que., Can.	D3	74
Saint Louis-de-Kent, N.B., Can.	C5	71
Saint-Louis-du-Ha! Ha!, Que., Can.	B8	74
Saint Louis Park, Mn., U.S.	n12	100
Saintes, Fr.	G6	10
Saint Lucia, ctry., N.A.	H17	64
Saint Lucia Channel, strt., N.A.	G17	64
Saint Lucie, co., Fl., U.S.	E6	86
Saint Lucie Canal, Fl., U.S.	F6	86
Saint Lucie Inlet, b., Fl., U.S.	E6	86
Sainte-Madeleine, Que., Can.	D4	74
Saint Malo, Man., Can.	E3	70
Saint-Malo, Fr.	D4	10
Saint-Malo, Golfe de, b., Fr.	D4	10
Saint-Marc, Haiti	E11	64
Saint-Marc [-des-Carrières], Que., Can.	C5	74
Saint-Marcellin, Fr.	G12	10
Saint Margaret Bay, b., Newf., Can.	C3	72
Sainte-Marguerite, stm., Que., Can.	A7	74
Sainte-Marie, Que., Can.	C6	74
Sainte-Marie, Cap, c., Madag.	G9	44
Saint Maries, Id., U.S.	B2	89
Sainte-Marthe, Que., Can.	D3	74
Saint Martin, co., La., U.S.	D4	95
Saint-Martin (Sint Maarten), i., N.A.	E16	64
Saint Martin, Lake, l., Man., Can.	D2	70
Saint Martin Island, i., Mi., U.S.	C4	99
Saint Martinville, La., U.S.	D4	95
Saint Mary, co., La., U.S.	E4	95
Saint Mary-of-the-Woods, In., U.S.	F7	91
Saint Mary Peak, mtn., Austl.	H9	50
Saint Marys, Austl.	H9	50
Saint Marys, Newf., Can.	E5	72
Saint Mary's, Ont., Can.	D3	73
Saint Marys, Ak., U.S.	C7	79
Saint Marys, Ga., U.S.	F5	87
Saint Marys, In., U.S.	A5	91
Saint Marys, Ks., U.S.	C7	93
Saint Marys, Oh., U.S.	B1	112
Saint Marys, Pa., U.S.	D4	115
Saint Marys, W.V., U.S.	B3	125
Saint Marys, co., Md., U.S.	D4	97
Saint Marys, stm., N.S., Can.	D8	71
Saint Marys, stm., Fl., U.S.	F5	87
Saint Marys, stm., U.S.	C8	91
Saint Marys, stm., Md., U.S.	D5	97
Saint Mary's, Cape, c., Newf., Can.	E4	72
Saint Mary's Bay, b., Newf., Can.	E5	72
Saint Marys Bay, b., N.S., Can.	E3	71
Saint Marys City, Md., U.S.	D5	97
Saint-Mathieu, Pointe de, c., Fr.	D2	10
Saint Matthew Island, i., Ak., U.S.	C5	79
Saint Matthews, Ky., U.S.	B4	94
Saint Matthews, S.C., U.S.	D6	117
Sainte-Maure-de-Touraine, Fr.	E7	10
Saint-Maurice, stm., Que., Can.	C5	74
Sainte-Maxime, Fr.	I13	10
Sainte-Méen-le-Grand, Fr.	D4	10
Sainte-Menehould, Fr.	C11	10
Sainte-Mère-Église, Fr.	C5	10
Saint Michael, Mn., U.S.	E5	100
Saint Michaels, Md., U.S.	C5	97
Saint-Michel [-de-Bellechasse], Que., Can.	C7	74
Saint-Mihiel, Fr.	D12	10
Saint-Moritz see Sankt Moritz, Switz.	F16	10
Saint-Nazaire, Fr.	E4	10
Saint-Nicolas, Que., Can.	o17	74
Saint-Odilon, Que., Can.	C7	74
Saint-Omer, Fr.	B9	10
Saint-Ours, Que., Can.	D4	74
Saint-Pacôme, Que., Can.	B8	74
Saint-Pamphile, Que., Can.	C8	74
Saint Paris, Oh., U.S.	B2	112
Saint-Pascal, Que., Can.	B8	74
Saint Paul, Alta., Can.	B5	68
Saint Paul, Ak., U.S.	D5	79
Saint Paul, In., U.S.	F6	91
Saint Paul, Ks., U.S.	E8	93
Saint Paul, Mn., U.S.	f12	100
Saint Paul, Mo., U.S.	f12	102
Saint Paul, Va., U.S.	f9	123
Saint Paul Island, i., Ak., U.S.	D5	79
Saint Paul Park, Mn., U.S.	n12	100
Saint Pauls, N.C., U.S.	C4	110
Sainte-Perpétue-de-L'Islet, Que., Can.	B8	74
Saint Peter, Mn., U.S.	F5	100
Saint Peter Port, Guernsey	C4	10
Saint Peters, N.S., Can.	D9	71
Saint Peters, Mo., U.S.	C7	102
Saint Petersburg, Fl., U.S.	E4	86
Saint Petersburg Beach, Fl., U.S.	p10	86
Saint Petersburg see Sankt-Peterburg, Russia	B13	18
Saint Phillips Island, i., S.C., U.S.	G6	117
Saint-Pie, Que., Can.	D5	74
Saint-Pierre, Reu.	F11	44
Saint-Pierre, St. P./M.	E3	72
Saint-Pierre, Lac, l., Que., Can.	C5	74
Saint Pierre and Miquelon, dep., N.A.	G21	66
Saint Pierre Island, i., Sey.	C10	44
Saint-Pierre-Jolys, Man., Can.	E3	70
Saint-Pierre-le-Moûtier, Fr.	F10	10
Saint-Pol-de-Léon, Fr.	D3	10
Saint-Pons, Fr.	I9	10
Saint-Pourçain-sur-Sioule, Fr.	F10	10
Saint-Prime, Que., Can.	A5	74
Saint Quentin, N.B., Can.	B2	71
Saint-Quentin, Fr.	C10	10
Saint-Raphaël, Que., Can.	C7	74
Saint-Raphaël, Fr.	I13	10
Saint-Raymond, Que., Can.	C6	74
Saint-Rédempteur, Que., Can.	o17	74
Saint Regis, Mt., U.S.	C1	103
Saint Regis, West Branch, stm., N.Y., U.S.	f10	109
Saint-Rémi, Que., Can.	D4	74
Saint-Romuald, Que., Can.	C6	74
Saint Rose, La., U.S.	k11	95
Sainte Rose du Lac, Man., Can.	D2	70
Saintes, Fr.	G6	10
Saint Sauveur, N.B., Can.	B4	71
Saint-Sauveur-des-Monts, Que., Can.	D3	74
Saint-Sébastien, Cap, c., Madag.	D9	44
Saint Siméon, Que., Can.	B8	74
Saint Simons Island, Ga., U.S.	E5	87
Saint Simons Island, i., Ga., U.S.	E5	87
Saint Stephen, N.B., Can.	D2	71
Saint Stephen, S.C., U.S.	E8	117
Saint Tammany, co., La., U.S.	D5	95
Sainte-Thècle, Que., Can.	C5	74
Sainte-Thérèse, Que., Can.	D4	74
Saint Thomas, Ont., Can.	E3	73
Saint Thomas, i., V.I.U.S.	E15	64
Saint Timothée, Que., Can.	q18	74
Saint-Tite, Que., Can.	C5	74
Saint-Tropez, Fr.	I13	10
Saint-Valéry-en-Caux, Fr.	C7	10
Saint-Varent, Fr.	F6	10
Sainte-Véronique, Que., Can.	C3	74
Saint-Victor, Que., Can.	C7	74
Saint-Vincent, Cap, c., Madag.	F8	44
Saint Vincent, Gulf, b., Austl.	F7	50
Saint Vincent and the Grenadines, ctry., N.A.	H17	64
Saint Vincent Island, i., Fl., U.S.	C1	86
Saint Vincent Passage, strt., N.A.	H17	64
Saint Vincent's [-Saint Stephens-Peter's River], Newf., Can.	E5	72
Saint-Vith, Bel.	E6	8
Saint Walburg, Sask., Can.	D1	75
Saint-Zacharie, Que., Can.	C7	74
Sairecábur, Cerro, mtn., S.A.	A3	56
Saito, Japan	J4	30
Saitula, China	B8	38
Sajama, Nevado, mtn., Bol.	G5	54
Sajia, China	F13	38
Sajnšand, Mong.	C9	26
Sakai, Japan	H8	30
Sakaide, Japan	H6	30
Sakai-minato, Japan	G6	30
Sakakawea, Lake, res., N.D., U.S.	B3	111
Sakami, Lac, l., Que., Can.	F17	66
Sakata, Japan	D12	30
Sakhalin see Sachalin, Ostrov, i., Russia	G22	24
Sākhar, Afg.	D1	38
Sakishima-shotō, is., Japan	G11	26
Sakon Nakhon, Thai.	F8	34
Sakonnet, stm., R.I., U.S.	E6	116
Sakonnet Point, c., R.I., U.S.	F6	116
Saku, Japan	F11	30
Sakurai, Japan	H8	30
Sal, Point, c., Ca., U.S.	E3	82
Sala, Swe.	G11	6
Salaberry-de-Valleyfield, Que., Can.	D3	74
Sala Consilina, Italy	I10	14
Salado, stm., Arg.	C4	56
Salado, Rio, stm., N.M., U.S.	C2	108
Šalālah, Oman	E5	46
Salamanca, Mex.	G9	62
Salamanca, Spain	E6	12
Salamanca, N.Y., U.S.	C2	109
Salamina, Col.	E5	58
Salamonie, stm., In., U.S.	C6	91
Salamonie Lake, res., In., U.S.	C6	91
Salatiga, Indon.	m15	33a
Salavat, Russia	G9	22
Salawati, i., Indon.	F9	32
Saldanha, S. Afr.	H3	44
Sale, Austl.	G9	50
Sale Creek, Tn., U.S.	D8	119
Salem, India	G5	37
Salem, Ar., U.S.	A4	81
Salem, Il., U.S.	E5	90
Salem, In., U.S.	G5	91
Salem, Ky., U.S.	e9	94
Salem, Ma., U.S.	A6	98
Salem, Mo., U.S.	D6	102
Salem, N.H., U.S.	E4	106
Salem, N.J., U.S.	D2	107
Salem, Oh., U.S.	B5	112
Salem, Or., U.S.	C4	114
Salem, S.D., U.S.	D8	118
Salem, Ut., U.S.	C4	121

Name	Map Ref	Page
Salem, Va., U.S.	C2	123
Salem, W.V., U.S.	B4	125
Salem, Wi., U.S.	n11	126
Salem, co., N.J., U.S.	D2	107
Salem, stm., N.J., U.S.	D2	107
Salem, Lake, l., Vt., U.S.	B4	122
Salemi, Italy	L7	14
Sälen, Swe.	F9	6
Salerno, Italy	I9	14
Salford, Eng., U.K.	H10	7
Salgótarján, Hung.	G19	8
Sali, Cro.	F10	14
Salida, Co., U.S.	C5	83
Salies-de-Béarn, Fr.	I6	10
Salihli, Tur.	K12	16
Salina, Ks., U.S.	D6	93
Salina, Ok., U.S.	A6	113
Salina, Ut., U.S.	E4	121
Salina Cruz, Mex.	I12	62
Salinas, Braz.	D7	57
Salinas, Ca., U.S.	D3	82
Salinas, stm., Ca., U.S.	D3	82
Salinas de Hidalgo, Mex.	F9	62
Salinas Peak, mtn., N.M., U.S.	D3	108
Salinas Pueblo Missions National Monument, N.M., U.S.	C3	108
Saline, Mi., U.S.	F7	99
Saline, co., Ar., U.S.	C3	81
Saline, co., Il., U.S.	F5	90
Saline, co., Ks., U.S.	D6	93
Saline, co., Mo., U.S.	B4	102
Saline, co., Ne., U.S.	D8	104
Saline, stm., Ar., U.S.	D4	81
Saline, stm., Ar., U.S.	C1	81
Saline, stm., Ks., U.S.	C3	93
Saline, North Fork, stm., Il., U.S.	F5	90
Saline Lake, res., La., U.S.	C3	95
Salineville, Oh., U.S.	B5	112
Salisbury, N.B., Can.	C4	71
Salisbury, Eng., U.K.	J11	7
Salisbury, Ct., U.S.	B2	84
Salisbury, Md., U.S.	D6	97
Salisbury, Ma., U.S.	A6	98
Salisbury, Mo., U.S.	B5	102
Salisbury, N.C., U.S.	B2	110
Salisbury see Harare, Zimb.	E6	44
Salisbury Island, i., N.W. Ter., Can.	D17	66
Salisbury Plain, pl., Eng., U.K.	J11	7
Salish Mountains, mts., Mt., U.S.	B2	103
Salkehatchie, stm., S.C., U.S.	E5	117
Salkhad, Syria	C5	40
Salles-Curan, Fr.	H9	10
Sallisaw, Ok., U.S.	B7	113
Salluit, Que., Can.	f11	74
Salmo, B.C., Can.	E9	69
Salmon, Id., U.S.	D5	89
Salmon, stm., N.B., Can.	C4	71
Salmon, stm., Id., U.S.	D3	89
Salmon Creek, Wa., U.S.	D3	124
Salmon Creek Reservoir, res., Id., U.S.	G4	89
Salmon Falls, stm., U.S.	D5	106
Salmon Falls Creek, stm., U.S.	G4	89
Salmon Mountains, mts., Ca., U.S.	B2	82
Salmon Point, c., Ont., Can.	D7	73
Salmon River Mountains, mts., Id., U.S.	E3	89
Salmon River Reservoir, res., N.Y., U.S.	B5	109
Salo, Fin.	F14	6
Salome, Az., U.S.	D2	80
Salon-De-Provence, Fr.	I12	10
Salonika see Thessaloníki, Grc.	I6	16
Salsomaggiore Terme, Italy	E4	14
Salt, stm., Az., U.S.	D4	80
Salt, stm., Ky., U.S.	C4	94
Salt, stm., Mo., U.S.	B6	102
Salta, Arg.	A3	56
Salt Creek, stm., N.M., U.S.	D5	108
Salt Creek, stm., Oh., U.S.	C3	112
Salt Creek, stm., Wy., U.S.	C6	127
Salter Path, N.C., U.S.	C6	110
Salt Fork Lake, res., Oh., U.S.	B4	112
Saltillo, Mex.	E9	62
Saltillo, Ms., U.S.	A5	101
Salt Lake, co., Ut., U.S.	C3	121
Salt Lake, l., Hi., U.S.	g10	88
Salt Lake, l., N.M., U.S.	E6	108
Salt Lake City, Ut., U.S.	C4	121
Salto, Ur.	C5	56
Salton Sea, l., Ca., U.S.	F5	82
Saltonstall, Lake, l., Ct., U.S.	D4	84
Salt Point, c., Ca., U.S.	C2	82
Salt River Indian Reservation, Az., U.S.	k9	80
Salt River Range, mts., Wy., U.S.	D2	127
Saltsburg, Pa., U.S.	F3	115
Salt Springs, Fl., U.S.	C5	86
Saltville, Va., U.S.	f10	123
Salt Wells Creek, stm., Wy., U.S.	E4	127
Saluda, S.C., U.S.	C4	117
Saluda, co., S.C., U.S.	C4	117
Saluda, stm., S.C., U.S.	C4	117
Saluda Dam, S.C., U.S.	C7	117
Sälür, India	C7	37
Saluzzo, Italy	E2	14
Salvador, Braz.	B9	57
Salvador, Lake, l., La., U.S.	E5	95
Salvatierra, Mex.	G9	62
Salween (Nu) (Thanlwin), stm., Asia	D5	34
Salyersville, Ky., U.S.	C6	94
Salzburg, Aus.	H13	8
Salzgitter, Ger.	C10	8
Salzwedel, Ger.	C11	8
Sama [de Langreo], Spain	B6	12
Samaná, Bahía de la, Dom. Rep.	E13	64
Samana Cay, i., Bah.	C11	64
Samandağı, Tur.	A4	40
Samar, i., Phil.	C8	32
Samara, Russia	G8	22
Samarai, Pap. N. Gui.	n17	50a
Samariapo, Ven.	E9	58
Samarinda, Indon.	F6	32
Samarkand, Uzb.	J11	22
Sämarrä', Iraq	B3	46
Samästipur, India	H11	38
Sambalpur, India	J10	38
Sambas, Indon.	E4	32
Sambava, Madag.	D10	44
Sambhal, India	F8	38
Sämbhar, India	G6	38
Samborondón, Ec.	H3	58
Sammamish Lake, l., Wa., U.S.	e11	124
Samneua, Laos	D8	34
Samobor, Cro.	D10	14
Sámos, i., Grc.	L10	16
Samoset, Fl., U.S.	q10	86
Sampit, Indon.	F5	32
Sampit, stm., S.C., U.S.	E9	117
Sampson, co., N.C., U.S.	B4	110
Sam Rayburn Reservoir, res., Tx., U.S.	D5	120
Samson, Al., U.S.	D3	78
Samsun, Tur.	G15	4
Samuels, Id., U.S.	A2	89
Samui, Ko, i., Thai.	J6	34
Samut Prakan, Thai.	H6	34
Samut Sakhon, Thai.	H6	34
San, Mali	F5	42
San, stm., Eur.	E22	8
San'ā', Yemen	E3	46
Sanaga, stm., Cam.	H7	42
San Agustín, Col.	G4	58
San Agustin, Cape, c., Phil.	D8	32
San Agustin, Plains of, pl., N.M., U.S.	C2	108
Sanak Islands, is., Ak., U.S.	E7	79
Sanana, Pulau, i., Indon.	F8	32
Sanandaj, Iran	A4	46
San Andreas, Ca., U.S.	C3	82
San Andrés, Isla de, i., Col.	H7	64
San Andres Mountains, mts., N.M., U.S.	E3	108
San Andres Peak, mtn., N.M., U.S.	E3	108
San Andrés Tuxtla, Mex.	H12	62
San Angelo, Tx., U.S.	D2	120
San Anselmo, Ca., U.S.	h7	82
San Antonio, Tx., U.S.	E3	120
San Antonio, Cabo, c., Arg.	D5	56
San Antonio, Cabo, c., Cuba	D5	64
San Antonio Abad, Spain	G13	12
San Antonio Bay, b., Tx., U.S.	E4	120
San Antonio de Bravo, Mex.	B7	62
San Antonio de los Cobres, Arg.	A3	56
San Antonio del Táchira, Ven.	D6	58
San Antonio Mountain, mtn., N.M., U.S.	A3	108
San Antonio Oeste, Arg.	E4	56
San Augustine, Tx., U.S.	D5	120
San Augustine, co., Tx., U.S.	D5	120
San Benedetto del Tronto, Italy	G8	14
San Benedicto, Isla, i., Mex.	H4	62
San Benito, Guat.	F3	64
San Benito, Tx., U.S.	F4	120
San Benito, co., Ca., U.S.	D3	82
San Benito Mountain, mtn., Ca., U.S.	D3	82
San Bernardino, Ca., U.S.	E5	82
San Bernardino, co., Ca., U.S.	E5	82
San Bernardo, Chile	C2	56
San Blas, Mex.	G7	62
San Blas, Mex.	D5	62
San Blas, Cape, c., Fl., U.S.	v16	86
San Borja, Bol.	F5	54
Sanborn, Ia., U.S.	A2	92
Sanborn, co., S.D., U.S.	D7	118
Sanbornville, N.H., U.S.	C4	106
San Bruno, Ca., U.S.	D2	82
San Carlos, Nic.	I5	64
San Carlos, Az., U.S.	D5	80
San Carlos, Ca., U.S.	k8	82
San Carlos, Ven.	C8	58
San Carlos de Bariloche, Arg.	E2	56
San Carlos de Guaroa, Col.	F6	58
San Carlos de la Rápita, Spain	E12	12
San Carlos del Zulia, Ven.	C7	58
San Carlos de Río Negro, Ven.	G9	58
San Carlos Indian Reservation, Az., U.S.	D5	80
San Carlos Lake, res., Az., U.S.	D5	80
San Cataldo, Italy	L9	14
Sancerre, Fr.	E9	10
Sánchez, Mex.	D10	62
San Clemente, Ca., U.S.	F5	82
San Clemente Island, i., Ca., U.S.	F4	82
Sancoins, Fr.	F9	10
San Cristóbal, Arg.	C4	56
San Cristóbal, Ven.	D6	58
San Cristóbal, Volcán, vol., Nic.	H4	64
San Cristóbal las Casas, Mex.	I13	62
Sancti-Spíritus, Cuba	D8	64
Sand, Nor.	G6	6
Sandakan, Malay.	D6	32
Sanday, i., Scot., U.K.	B10	7
Sand Creek, stm., Wy., U.S.	C7	127
Sanders, Az., U.S.	B6	80
Sanders, co., Mt., U.S.	C1	103
Sanderson, Tx., U.S.	D1	120
Sandersville, Ga., U.S.	D4	87
Sandersville, Ms., U.S.	D4	101
Sand Hill, Ma., U.S.	h13	98
Sand Hill, stm., Mn., U.S.	C2	100
Sandia, Peru	F5	54
Sandia Crest, mtn., N.M., U.S.	k8	108
Sandia Indian Reservation, N.M., U.S.	k7	108
Sandia Mountains, mts., N.M., U.S.	k8	108
San Diego, Ca., U.S.	F5	82
San Diego, co., Ca., U.S.	F5	82
San Diego Naval Station, mil., Ca., U.S.	o15	82
San Diego Naval Training Center, mil., Ca., U.S.	o15	82
Sand Island, i., Hi., U.S.	g10	88
Sand Island, i., Wi., U.S.	B3	126
Sand Key, i., Fl., U.S.	E4	86
Sandlick Creek, stm., W.V., U.S.	n13	125
Sandnes, Nor.	G5	6
Sandoa, Zaire	C4	44
San Donà di Piave, Italy	D7	14
Sandoval, Il., U.S.	E4	90
Sandoval, co., N.M., U.S.	B2	108
Sandoway, Burma	E3	34
Sandpoint, c., U.S.	D7	79
Sandpoint, Id., U.S.	A2	89
Sands Key, i., Fl., U.S.	s3	86
Sand Springs, Ok., U.S.	A5	113
Sandston, Va., U.S.	m18	123
Sandstone, Austl.	E3	50
Sandstone, Mn., U.S.	D6	100
Sandusky, Mi., U.S.	E8	99
Sandusky, Oh., U.S.	A3	112
Sandusky, co., Oh., U.S.	A2	112
Sandusky, stm., Oh., U.S.	B2	112
Sandviken, Swe.	F11	6
Sandwich, Il., U.S.	B5	90
Sandwich, Ma., U.S.	C7	98
Sandwich Bay, b., Newf., Can.	B3	72
Sandy, Or., U.S.	B4	114
Sandy, Ut., U.S.	C4	121
Sandy, stm., Me., U.S.	D2	96
Sandy Creek, stm., Oh., U.S.	B4	112
Sandy Creek, stm., Ok., U.S.	C2	113
Sandy Hook, Ct., U.S.	D2	84
Sandy Hook, spit, N.J., U.S.	C5	107
Sandy Island, i., S.C., U.S.	D9	117
Sandy Lake, l., Ont., Can.	n16	73
Sandy Lake, l., Ont., Can.	D3	72
Sandy Neck, pen., Ma., U.S.	C7	98
Sandy Point, c., R.I., U.S.	h7	116
Sandy Springs, Ga., U.S.	h8	87
Sandy Springs, S.C., U.S.	B2	117
Sandyville, Md., U.S.	A4	97
San Felipe, Ven.	B8	58
San Felipe Indian Reservation, N.M., U.S.	k8	108
San Felipe Pueblo, N.M., U.S.	B3	108
San Felíu de Guixols, Spain	D15	12
San Fernando, Chile	C2	56
San Fernando, Mex.	E10	62
San Fernando, Phil.	q19	32
San Fernando, Phil.	B7	32
San Fernando, Spain	I5	12
San Fernando, Trin.	I17	64
San Fernando, Ca., U.S.	m12	82
San Fernando de Apure, Ven.	D9	58
San Fernando de Atabapo, Ven.	E9	58
Sanford, Co., U.S.	D5	83
Sanford, Fl., U.S.	D5	86
Sanford, Me., U.S.	E2	96
Sanford, Mi., U.S.	E6	99
Sanford, N.C., U.S.	B3	110
Sanford, Mount, mtn., Ak., U.S.	C11	79
San Francisco, Arg.	C4	56
San Francisco, Ca., U.S.	D2	82
San Francisco, co., Ca., U.S.	D2	82
San Francisco, stm., U.S.	D6	80
San Francisco Bay, b., Ca., U.S.	h8	82
San Francisco de Borja, Mex.	D6	62
San Francisco del Oro, Mex.	D7	62
San Francisco del Rincón, Mex.	G9	62
San Francisco de Macorís, Dom. Rep.	E12	64
San Fratello, Italy	K9	14
San Gabriel, Ec.	G4	58
San Gabriel, Ca., U.S.	*m12	82
San Gabriel Mountains, mts., Ca., U.S.	m12	82
Sangamner, India	C3	37
Sangamon, co., Il., U.S.	D4	90
Sangamon, stm., Il., U.S.	C3	90
San Gavino Monreale, Italy	J3	14
Sangay, Volcán, vol., Ec.	H3	58
Sang-e Mäsheh, Afg.	D2	38
Sanger, Ca., U.S.	D4	82
Sanger, Tx., U.S.	C4	120
Sangerhausen, Ger.	D11	8
Sangha, stm., Afr.	B3	44
Sanghar, Pak.	G3	38
Sangihe, Kepulauan, is., Indon.	E8	32
Sangihe, Pulau, i., Indon.	E8	32
San Gil, Col.	D6	58
San Giovanni in Fiore, Italy	J11	14
San Giovanni in Persiceto, Italy	E6	14
San Giovanni Valdarno, Italy	F6	14
Sängli, India	D3	37
Sangolquí, Ec.	H3	58
San Gorgonio Mountain, mtn., Ca., U.S.	E5	82
San Gregorio, Ur.	C5	56
Sangrür, India	E6	38
Sangüesa, Spain	C10	12
Sanibel, Fl., U.S.	F4	86
Sanibel Island, i., Fl., U.S.	F4	86
San Ignacio, Arg.	B5	56
San Ignacio, Hond.	G4	64
Sanilac, co., Mi., U.S.	E8	99
San Isidro, Arg.	C5	56
San Isidro, C.R.	J6	64
San Jacinto, Col.	C5	58
San Jacinto, Ca., U.S.	F5	82
San Jacinto, co., Tx., U.S.	D5	120
San Jacinto, stm., Tx., U.S.	r14	120
Sanjō, Japan	E11	30
San Joaquin, co., Ca., U.S.	D3	82
San Joaquin, stm., Ca., U.S.	D3	82
San Joaquin Valley, val., Ca., U.S.	D3	82
San Jorge, Golfo, b., Arg.	F3	56
San Jorge, Golfo de, b., Spain	E12	12
San José, C.R.	J5	64
San Jose, Ca., U.S.	D3	82
San José, Isla, i., Mex.	E4	62
San José de Chiquitos, Bol.	G6	54
San José de Guanipa, Ven.	C10	58
San José del Cabo, Mex.	F5	62
San José del Guaviare, Col.	F6	58
San José de Mayo, Ur.	C5	56
San José de Ocuné, Col.	E7	58
San José de Raíces, Mex.	E9	62
San Jose Island, i., Tx., U.S.	E4	120
San Juan, Arg.	C3	56
San Juan, Mex.	D8	62
San Juan, P.R.	E14	64
San Juan, Tx., U.S.	F3	120
San Juan, co., Co., U.S.	D3	83
San Juan, co., N.M., U.S.	A1	108
San Juan, co., Ut., U.S.	F5	121
San Juan, co., Wa., U.S.	A2	124
San Juan, stm., N.A.	I6	64
San Juan Capistrano, Ca., U.S.	F5	82
San Juan de Colón, Ven.	C6	58
San Juan [de la Maguana], Dom. Rep.	E12	64
San Juan del Norte, Nic.	I6	64
San Juan de los Cayos, Ven.	B8	58
San Juan de los Morros, Ven.	C9	58
San Juan del Río, Mex.	G9	62
San Juan del Sur, Nic.	I5	64
San Juan Island, i., Wa., U.S.	A2	124
San Juan Mountains, mts., Co., U.S.	D3	83
San Julián, Arg.	F3	56
San Justo, Arg.	C4	56
Sankt Gallen, Aus.	H14	8
Sankt Gallen, Switz.	E16	10
Sankt Johann im Pongau, Aus.	H13	8
Sankt Moritz, Switz.	F16	10
Sankt-Peterburg (Saint Petersburg), Russia	B13	18
Sankt Pölten, Aus.	G15	8
Sankt Veit an der Glan, Aus.	I14	8
Sankt Wendel, Ger.	F7	8
Sankuru, stm., Zaire	B4	44
San Lázaro, Cabo, c., Mex.	E3	62
San Leandro, Ca., U.S.	h8	82
San Lope, Col.	D7	58
San Lorenzo, Arg.	C4	56
San Lorenzo, Ec.	G3	58
San Lorenzo, Isla, i., Peru	F3	54
San Lorenzo de El Escorial, Spain	E7	12
San Lorenzo de la Parrilla, Spain	F9	12
Sanlúcar de Barrameda, Spain	I5	12
San Lucas, Ec.	I3	58
San Lucas, Cabo, c., Mex.	F5	62
San Luis, Arg.	C3	56
San Luis, Cuba	D10	64
San Luis, Guat.	F3	64
San Luis, Az., U.S.	E1	80
San Luis, Co., U.S.	D5	83
San Luis, Ven.	B8	58
San Luis, Lago de, l., Bol.	F6	54
San Luis, Point, c., Ca., U.S.	E3	82
San Luis de la Paz, Mex.	G9	62
San Luis Obispo, Ca., U.S.	E3	82
San Luis Obispo, co., Ca., U.S.	E3	82
San Luis Pass, strt., Tx., U.S.	r14	120
San Luis Peak, mtn., Co., U.S.	D4	83
San Luis Potosí, Mex.	F9	62
San Luis Río Colorado, Mex.	A2	62
San Luis Valley, val., Co., U.S.	D4	83
San Manuel, Az., U.S.	E5	80
San Marcos, Col.	C5	58
San Marcos, Mex.	I10	62
San Marcos, Tx., U.S.	E4	120
San Marcos, stm., Tx., U.S.	h8	120
San Marino, Ca., U.S.	m12	82
San Marino, ctry., Eur.	G10	4
San Martín de Valdeiglesias, Spain	E7	12
San Mateo, Spain	E12	12
San Mateo, Ca., U.S.	D2	82
San Mateo, co., Ca., U.S.	D2	82
San Mateo Mountains, mts., N.M., U.S.	D2	108
San Mateo Mountains, mts., N.M., U.S.	B2	108
San Matías, Golfo, b., Arg.	E4	56
San Miguel, El Sal.	H3	64
San Miguel, co., Co., U.S.	D2	83
San Miguel, co., N.M., U.S.	B5	108
San Miguel, stm., Bol.	F6	54
San Miguel, stm., Co., U.S.	C2	83
San Miguel de Allende, Mex.	G9	62
San Miguel del Monte, Arg.	D5	56
San Miguel de Tucumán, Arg.	B3	56
San Miguel el Alto, Mex.	G8	62
San Miguel Island, i., Ca., U.S.	E3	82
San Miguel Mountains, mts., Co., U.S.	D2	83
Sannär, Sudan	F12	42
Sannicandro Garganico, Italy	H10	14
San Nicolas, Col.	o19	33b
San Nicolás de los Arroyos, Arg.	C4	56
San Nicolas Island, i., Ca., U.S.	F4	82
Sannikova, Proliv, strt., Russia	C21	24
Sanniquellie, Lib.	G4	42
Sano, Japan	F12	30
Sanok, Pol.	F22	8
San Onofre, Col.	C5	58
San Pablo, Col.	G4	58
San Pablo, Phil.	q19	32
San Pablo Balleza, Mex.	D6	62
San Pablo Bay, b., Ca., U.S.	g8	82
San Patricio, co., Tx., U.S.	E4	120
San Pedro, stm., Az., U.S.	E5	80
San Pedro, Punta, c., Chile	B2	56
San Pedro, Volcán, vol., Chile	A3	56
San Pedro Bay, b., Ca., U.S.	n12	82
San Pedro Carchá, Guat.	G2	64
San Pedro de las Colonias, Mex.	E8	62
San Pedro de Macorís, Dom. Rep.	E13	64
San Pedro Mártir, Sierra, mts., Mex.	B2	62
San Pedro Peaks, mts., N.M., U.S.	A3	108
San Pedro Sula, Hond.	G4	64
Sanpete, co., Ut., U.S.	D4	121
Sanpoil, stm., Wa., U.S.	A7	124
San Quintín, Cabo, c., Mex.	B1	62
San Rafael, Arg.	C3	56
San Rafael, Mex.	E9	62
San Rafael, Ca., U.S.	D2	82
San Rafael, N.M., U.S.	B2	108
San Rafael, stm., Ut., U.S.	D5	121
San Rafael Knob, mtn., Ut., U.S.	E5	121
San Rafael Mountains, mts., Ca., U.S.	E4	82
San Ramón, Nic.	G5	64
San Ramon, Ca., U.S.	h9	82
San Remo, Italy	F2	14
San Saba, Tx., U.S.	D3	120
San Saba, co., Tx., U.S.	D3	120
San Salvador, El Sal.	H3	64
San Salvador (Watling Island), i., Bah.	B10	64
San Salvador de Jujuy, Arg.	A3	56
Sansanné-Mango, Togo	F6	42
Sansepolcro, Italy	F7	14
San Sebastián, Spain	B10	12
San Severo, Italy	H10	14
San Simon, stm., Az., U.S.	E6	80
Sanski Most, Bos.	E11	14
Santa Ana, Bol.	F5	54
Santa Ana, Bol.	G5	54
Santa Ana, El Sal.	H3	64
Santa Ana, Mex.	E9	62
Santa Ana, Mex.	B4	62
Santa Ana, Ca., U.S.	F5	82
Santa Ana, Ca., U.S.	n13	82
Santa Ana Indian Reservation, N.M., U.S.	h7	108
Santa Ana Mountains, mts., Ca., U.S.	n13	82
Santa Anna, Tx., U.S.	D3	120
Santa Bárbara, Mex.	D7	62
Santa Barbara, Ca., U.S.	E4	82
Santa Barbara, co., Ca., U.S.	E3	82
Santa Barbara Channel, strt., Ca., U.S.	E3	82
Santa Barbara Island, i., Ca., U.S.	F4	82
Santa Catalina, Gulf of, b., Ca., U.S.	F5	82
Santa Catalina Island, i., Ca., U.S.	F4	82
Santa Catalina Mountains, mts., Az., U.S.	E5	80
Santa Catarina, Ilha de, i., Braz.	B7	56
Santa Clara, Cuba	C8	64
Santa Clara, Ca., U.S.	D2	82
Santa Clara, Ut., U.S.	F2	121
Santa Clara, co., Ca., U.S.	D3	82
Santa Clara, stm., Ca., U.S.	E4	82
Santa Claus, In., U.S.	H4	91
Santa Coloma de Farnés, Spain	D14	12
Santa Comba Dão, Port.	E3	12
Santa Cruz, Arg.	F3	56
Santa Cruz, Bol.	G6	54
Santa Cruz, C.R.	I5	64
Santa Cruz, Phil.	q19	33b
Santa Cruz, Ca., U.S.	D2	82
Santa Cruz, N.M., U.S.	B3	108
Santa Cruz, co., Az., U.S.	F5	80
Santa Cruz, co., Ca., U.S.	D2	82
Santa Cruz, stm., Az., U.S.	E4	80
Santa Cruz del Quiché, Guat.	G2	64
Santa Cruz de Tenerife, Spain	C2	42
Santa Cruz do Rio Pardo, Braz.	G4	57
Santa Cruz Island, i., Ca., U.S.	F4	82
Santa Elena, Ec.	I2	58
Santa Elena, Punta, c., Ec.	I2	58
Santa Eugenia, Spain	C2	12
Santa Eulalia, Spain	E10	12
Santa Eulalia del Río, Spain	G13	12
Santa Fé, Arg.	C4	56
Santa Fé, Braz.	C3	57
Santa Fe, N.M., U.S.	B3	108
Santa Fe, Tx., U.S.	r14	120
Santa Fe, co., N.M., U.S.	B3	108
Santa Fe, stm., N.M., U.S.	h8	108
Santa Fe Baldy, mtn., N.M., U.S.	B4	108
Santa Fe de Bogotá, Col.	E5	58
Santa Inés, Isla, i., Chile	G2	56
Santa Isabel, Ec.	I3	58
Santa Isabel, i., Sol.Is.	A11	50
Santa Isabel see Malabo, Eq. Gui.	H7	42
Santa Lucia Range, mts., Ca., U.S.	E3	82
Santa Magdalena, Isla, i., Mex.	E3	62
Santa Maria, Braz.	B6	56
Santa Maria, Ca., U.S.	E3	82
Santa Maria, stm., Az., U.S.	C2	80
Santa Maria, Cabo de, c., Ang.	D2	44
Santa Maria do Suaçuí, Braz.	E7	57
Santa Maria Mountains, mts., Az., U.S.	C3	80
Santa Marta, Col.	B5	58
Santa Monica, Ca., U.S.	m12	82
Santana do Livramento, Braz.	C5	56
Santander, Col.	F4	58
Santander, Spain	B8	12
Sant' Antioco, Italy	J3	14
Santa Paula, Ca., U.S.	E4	82
Santaquin, Ut., U.S.	D4	121
Sant'Arcangelo, Italy	I11	14
Santarém, Braz.	D8	54
Santarém, Port.	F3	12
Santa Rita, Col.	G8	58
Santa Rita, Hond.	G4	64
Santa Rosa, Arg.	D4	56
Santa Rosa, Bol.	F5	54
Santa Rosa, Ec.	I3	58
Santa Rosa, Ca., U.S.	C2	82
Santa Rosa, N.M., U.S.	C5	108
Santa Rosa, co., Fl., U.S.	u14	86
Santa Rosa de Cabal, Col.	E5	58
Santa Rosa de Copán, Hond.	G3	64
Santa Rosa Island, i., Ca., U.S.	F3	82
Santa Rosa Island, i., Fl., U.S.	u14	86
Santa Rosa Range, mts., Nv., U.S.	B4	105
Santarskije Ostrova, is., Russia	F21	24
Santa Teresa Gallura, Italy	H4	14
Santa Vitória do Palmar, Braz.	C6	56
Santa Ynez, Ca., U.S.	E3	82

Name	Map Ref	Page
Santee, Ca., U.S.	o16	82
Santee, stm., S.C., U.S.	E8	117
Santee Dam, S.C., U.S.	E7	117
Santee Indian Reservation, Ne., U.S.	B8	104
Santhià, Italy	D3	14
Santiago, Chile	C2	56
Santiago, Dom. Rep.	E12	64
Santiago, Pan.	J7	64
Santiago de Compostela, Spain	C3	12
Santiago de Cuba, Cuba	D10	64
Santiago del Estero, Arg.	B4	56
Santiago do Cacém, Port.	G3	12
Santiago Ixcuintla, Mex.	G7	62
Santiago Papasquiaro, Mex.	E7	62
Santiago Peak, mtn., Ca., U.S.	n13	82
Santiago Reservoir, res., Ca., U.S.	n13	82
Santiaguillo, Laguna de, l., Mex.	E7	62
Santiam Pass, Or., U.S.	C4	114
Santipur, India	I13	38
Santisteban del Puerto, Spain	G8	12
Santo Amaro, Braz.	B9	57
Santo Anastácio, Braz.	F3	57
Santo André, Braz.	G5	57
Santo Ângelo, Braz.	B6	56
Santo Antônio de Jesus, Braz.	B9	57
Santo Antônio do Içá, Braz.	D5	54
Santo Domingo, Dom. Rep.	E13	64
Santo Domingo, Nic.	H5	64
Santo Domingo de la Calzada, Spain	C9	12
Santo Domingo de los Colorados, Ec.	H3	58
Santo Domingo Indian Reservation, N.M., U.S.	h8	108
Santo Domingo Pueblo, N.M., U.S.	B3	108
Santoña, Spain	B8	12
Santos, Braz.	G5	57
Santos Dumont, Braz.	F7	57
Santo Tomás, Mex.	B1	62
Santo Tomé, Arg.	B5	56
San Valentín, Monte, mtn., Chile	F2	56
San Vicente, El Sal.	H3	64
San Vicente, Mex.	B1	62
San Vicente de Baracaldo, Spain	B9	12
San Vicente de la Barquera, Spain	B7	12
San Vicente del Caguán, Col.	F5	58
San Vicente Reservoir, res., Ca., U.S.	o16	82
San Xavier Indian Reservation, Az., U.S.	E4	80
Sanzao Dao, i., China	M2	28
Sanza Pombo, Ang.	C3	44
São Bento, Braz.	D10	54
São Borja, Braz.	B5	56
São Caetano do Sul, Braz.	G5	57
São Carlos, Braz.	G5	57
São Domingos, Braz.	B5	57
São Francisco, stm., Braz.	E11	54
São Francisco do Sul, Braz.	B7	56
São Gabriel, Braz.	E8	57
São João da Boa Vista, Braz.	F5	57
São João da Madeira, Port.	E3	12
São João del Rei, Braz.	F6	57
São Joaquim da Barra, Braz.	F5	57
São José do Rio Prêto, Braz.	F4	57
São José dos Campos, Braz.	G6	57
São Leopoldo, Braz.	B6	56
São Lourenço, Braz.	G6	57
São Lourenço, Pantanal de, sw., Braz.	G7	54
São Luís, Braz.	D10	54
São Manuel, Braz.	G4	57
São Mateus, Braz.	E9	57
Saona, Isla, i., Dom. Rep.	E13	64
Saône, stm., Fr.	F11	10
São Paulo, Braz.	G5	57
São Pedro do Ivaí, Braz.	G3	57
São Pedro do Sul, Port.	E3	12
São Romão, Braz.	D6	57
São Roque, Cabo de, c., Braz.	E11	54
São Sebastião, Ponta, c., Moz.	F7	44
São Sebastião do Paraíso, Braz.	F5	57
São Tomé, S. Tom./P.	A1	44
São Tomé, i., S. Tom./P.	A1	44
São Tomé, Cabo de, c., Braz.	F8	57
Sao Tome and Principe, ctry., Afr.	A1	44
São Vicente, Braz.	G5	57
São Vicente, Cabo de, c., Port.	H2	12
Sapé, Braz.	E11	54
Sapele, Nig.	G7	42
Sapelo Island, i., Ga., U.S.	E5	87
Sapitwa, mtn., Mwi.	E7	44
Sappa Creek, stm., U.S.	E5	104
Sapphire Mountains, mts., Mt., U.S.	D3	103
Sappington, Mo., U.S.	f13	102
Sapporo, Japan	p19	30a
Sapri, Italy	I10	14
Sapulpa, Ok., U.S.	B5	113
Sara Buri, Thai.	G6	34
Sarajevo, Bos.	F2	16
Saraland, Al., U.S.	E1	78
Saranac, Mi., U.S.	F5	99
Saranac, stm., N.Y., U.S.	F11	109
Saranac Lake, N.Y., U.S.	f10	109
Saranac Lakes, l., N.Y., U.S.	f10	109
Sarangani Islands, is., Phil.	D8	32
Saransk, Russia	G7	22
Sarapul, Russia	F8	22
Sarasota, Fl., U.S.	E4	86
Sarasota, co., Fl., U.S.	E4	86
Sarasota Bay, b., Fl., U.S.	E4	86
Saratoga, Ca., U.S.	k8	82
Saratoga, Tx., U.S.	D5	120
Saratoga, Wy., U.S.	E6	127
Saratoga, co., N.Y., U.S.	B7	109
Saratoga Lake, l., N.Y., U.S.	C7	109
Saratoga National Historical Park, N.Y., U.S.	B7	109
Saratoga Springs, N.Y., U.S.	B7	109
Saratov, Russia	G7	22
Saravane, Laos	G9	34
Sarcoxie, Mo., U.S.	D3	102
Sardalas, Libya	C8	42
Sardārshahr, India	F6	38
Sardegna, i., Italy	I3	14
Sardinia see Sardegna, i., Italy	I3	14
Sardis, Ga., U.S.	D5	87
Sardis, Ms., U.S.	A4	101
Sardis Lake, res., Ms., U.S.	A4	101
Sar-e Pol, Afg.	B1	38
Sarepta, La., U.S.	B2	95
Sargent, Ga., U.S.	C2	87
Sargent, Ne., U.S.	C6	104
Sargent, co., N.D., U.S.	C8	111
Sargodha, Pak.	D5	38
Sarh, Chad	G9	42
Sariñena, Spain	D11	12
Şarköy, Tur.	I11	16
Sarlat-la-Canéda, Fr.	H8	10
Sarmi, Indon.	F10	32
Sarmiento, Arg.	F3	56
Särna, Swe.	F9	6
Sarnia, Ont., Can.	E2	73
Sarpy, co., Ne., U.S.	C9	104
Sarralbe, Fr.	C14	10
Sarrebourg, Fr.	D14	10
Sarreguemines, Fr.	C14	10
Sarria, Spain	C4	12
Sartang, stm., Russia	D20	24
Sartell, Mn., U.S.	E4	100
Sarthe, stm., Fr.	E6	10
Sarufutsu, Japan	n20	30a
Sarzeau, Fr.	E4	10
Sasarām, India	H11	38
Sasebo, Japan	I2	30
Saskatchewan, prov., Can.	E3	75
Saskatchewan, stm., Can.	F12	66
Saskatoon, Sask., Can.	C16	24
Saskylach, Russia	G24	18
Sasovo, Russia	B5	97
Sassafras, stm., Md., U.S.	B5	97
Sassafras Mountain, mtn., U.S.	A2	117
Sassandra, I.C.	H4	42
Sassandra, stm., I.C.	G4	42
Sassari, Italy	I3	14
Sassnitz, Ger.	A13	8
Sassuolo, Italy	E5	14
Sastown, Lib.	H4	42
Satah Mountain, mtn., B.C., Can.	C5	69
Sata-misaki, c., Japan	L3	30
Satanta, Ks., U.S.	E3	93
Sātāra, India	D2	37
Satilla, stm., Ga., U.S.	E5	87
Satkānia, Bngl.	I15	38
Satna, India	H9	38
Sātpura Range, mts., India	B4	37
Satsuma, Al., U.S.	E1	78
Satsuma, i., Japan	v29	31b
Satsunan-shotō, is., Japan	v29	31b
Satu Mare, Rom.	B6	16
Satura, Russia	F22	18
Satus Creek, stm., Wa., U.S.	C5	124
Sauceda Mountains, mts., Az., U.S.	E3	80
Sauda, Nor.	G6	6
Saudi Arabia, ctry., Asia	D4	46
Saufley Field Naval Air Station, mil., Fl., U.S.	u14	86
Saugatuck, Mi., U.S.	F4	99
Saugatuck, stm., Ct., U.S.	D2	84
Saugatucket, stm., R.I., U.S.	F4	116
Saugatuck Reservoir, res., Ct., U.S.	D2	84
Saugerties, N.Y., U.S.	C7	109
Saugus, Ma., U.S.	B5	98
Saugus, stm., Ma., U.S.	g11	98
Sauk, co., Wi., U.S.	E4	126
Sauk, stm., Mn., U.S.	E4	100
Sauk, stm., Wa., U.S.	A4	124
Sauk Centre, Mn., U.S.	E4	100
Sauk City, Wi., U.S.	E4	126
Sauk Rapids, Mn., U.S.	E4	100
Saukville, Wi., U.S.	E6	126
Saulgau, Ger.	G9	8
Saulnierville, N.S., Can.	E3	71
Sault-au-Mouton, Que., Can.	A8	74
Sault Sainte Marie, Ont., Can.	p18	73
Sault Sainte Marie, Mi., U.S.	B6	99
Saumarez Reef, rf., Austl.	D10	50
Saumur, Fr.	E6	10
Saunders, co., Ne., U.S.	C9	104
Saunderstown, R.I., U.S.	E4	116
Saurimo, Ang.	C4	44
Sausalito, Ca., U.S.	D2	82
Sava, Italy	I12	14
Sava, stm., Eur.	E3	16
Savage, Md., U.S.	B4	97
Savage, stm., Md., U.S.	k12	97
Savage River Reservoir, res., Md., U.S.	k12	97
Savanna, Il., U.S.	A3	90
Savanna, Ok., U.S.	C6	113
Savannah, Ga., U.S.	D5	87
Savannah, Mo., U.S.	B3	102
Savannah, Tn., U.S.	B3	119
Savannah, stm., U.S.	F5	117
Savannah River Plant, sci., S.C., U.S.	E4	117
Savannakhet, Laos	F8	34
Savanna Lake, l., Md., U.S.	D6	97
Savanna-la-Mar, Jam.	E5	64
Savaştepe, Tur.	J11	16
Save (Sabi), stm., Afr.	F6	44
Savenay, Fr.	E5	10
Saverdun, Fr.	I8	10
Saverne, Fr.	D14	10
Savigliano, Italy	E2	14
Saville Dam, Ct., U.S.	B4	84
Savona, Italy	E3	14
Savonlinna, Fin.	F17	6
Savonranta, Fin.	E17	6
Savoonga, Ak., U.S.	C5	79
Savoy, Il., U.S.	C5	90
Savu Sea see Sawu, Laut, Indon.	G7	32
Sawai Mādhopur, India	G7	38
Sawākin, Sudan	E13	42
Sawang, Indon.	N7	34
Sawatch Range, mts., Co., U.S.	B4	83
Sawdā', Qurnat as-, mtn., Leb.	B5	40
Sawel Mountain, mtn., N. Ire., U.K.	G5	7
Sawhāj, Egypt	C12	42
Sawknah, Libya	C9	42
Sawnee Mountain, mtn., Ga., U.S.	B2	87
Sawtooth Mountains, mts., Id., U.S.	F4	89
Sawtooth National Recreation Area, Id., U.S.	E3	89
Sawu, Laut (Savu Sea), Indon.	G7	32
Sawu, Pulau, i., Indon.	H7	32
Sawwān, Ard as-, pl., Jord.	D5	40
Sawyer, co., Wi., U.S.	C2	126
Sawyerville, Que., Can.	D6	74
Saxmundham, Eng., U.K.	I14	7
Saxonburg, Pa., U.S.	E2	115
Saxons, stm., Vt., U.S.	E3	122
Saxtons River, Vt., U.S.	E3	122
Sayaboury, Laos	E6	34
Sayan Mountains (Sajany), mts., Asia	G12	18
Sayaxché, Guat.	F2	64
Saybrook, Il., U.S.	C5	90
Saybrook Manor, Ct., U.S.	D6	84
Saydā (Sidon), Leb.	C4	40
Saydel, Ia., U.S.	e8	92
Sayhūt, Yemen	E5	46
Saylesville, R.I., U.S.	B4	116
Saylorsburg, Pa., U.S.	E11	115
Saylorville, Ia., U.S.	e8	92
Saylorville Lake, res., Ia., U.S.	C4	92
Sayre, Al., U.S.	B3	78
Sayre, Ok., U.S.	B2	113
Sayre, Pa., U.S.	C8	115
Sayreville, N.J., U.S.	C4	107
Sayula, Mex.	H8	62
Say'ūn, Yemen	E4	46
Sayville, N.Y., U.S.	n15	109
Scafell Pikes, mtn., Eng., U.K.	G9	7
Scalp Level, Pa., U.S.	F4	115
Scanlon, Mn., U.S.	D6	100
Scapegoat Mountain, mtn., Mt., U.S.	C3	103
Ščapino, Russia	F25	24
Scappoose, Or., U.S.	B4	114
Scarborough, Ont., Can.	m15	73
Scarborough, Trin.	I17	64
Scarborough, Me., U.S.	E2	96
Scarbro, W.V., U.S.	n13	125
Scarsdale, N.Y., U.S.	h13	109
Ščelkovo, Russia	F21	18
Ščerbakovo, Russia	D26	24
Schaefferstown, Pa., U.S.	F9	115
Schaffhausen, Switz.	E15	10
Schaller, Ia., U.S.	B2	92
Schaumburg, Il., U.S.	h8	90
Schell Creek Range, mts., Nv., U.S.	D7	105
Schenectady, N.Y., U.S.	C7	109
Schenectady, co., N.Y., U.S.	C6	109
Schererville, In., U.S.	B3	91
Schertz, Tx., U.S.	h7	120
Schiller Park, Il., U.S.	k9	90
Schio, Italy	D6	14
Schladming, Aus.	H13	8
Schleicher, co., Tx., U.S.	D2	120
Schleiden, Ger.	E6	8
Schleswig, Ger.	A9	8
Schleswig, Ia., U.S.	B2	92
Schley, co., Ga., U.S.	D2	87
Schneverdingen, Ger.	B9	8
Schofield, Wi., U.S.	D4	126
Schofield Barracks, mil., Hi., U.S.	g9	88
Schoharie, co., N.Y., U.S.	C6	109
Schoharie Creek, stm., N.Y., U.S.	C6	109
Schönebeck, Ger.	B13	8
Schongau, Ger.	H10	8
Schoodic Lake, l., Me., U.S.	C4	96
Schoolcraft, Mi., U.S.	F5	99
Schoolcraft, co., Mi., U.S.	B4	99
Schramberg, Ger.	G8	8
Schrobenhausen, Ger.	G11	8
Schroon Lake, l., N.Y., U.S.	B7	109
Schulenburg, Tx., U.S.	E4	120
Schulter, Ok., U.S.	B6	113
Schurz, Nv., U.S.	E3	105
Schuyler, Ne., U.S.	C8	104
Schuyler, co., Il., U.S.	C3	90
Schuyler, co., Mo., U.S.	A5	102
Schuyler, co., N.Y., U.S.	C4	109
Schuylkill, co., Pa., U.S.	E9	115
Schuylkill, stm., Pa., U.S.	F10	115
Schuylkill Haven, Pa., U.S.	E9	115
Schwabach, Ger.	F11	8
Schwaben, hist. reg., Ger.	G10	8
Schwäbische Alb, mts., Ger.	G9	8
Schwäbisch Gmünd, Ger.	G9	8
Schwäbisch Hall, Ger.	F9	8
Schwandorf in Bayern, Ger.	F12	8
Schwaner, Pegunungan, mts., Indon.	F5	32
Schwarzwald, mts., Ger.	G8	8
Schwaz, Aus.	H11	8
Schwechat, Aus.	G16	8
Schwedt, Ger.	B14	8
Schweinfurt, Ger.	E10	8
Schwerin, Ger.	B11	8
Schwyz, Switz.	E15	10
Sciacca, Italy	L8	14
Scicli, Italy	M9	14
Science Hill, Ky., U.S.	C5	94
Scilly, Isles of, is., Eng., U.K.	L6	7
Scio, Or., U.S.	C4	114
Scioto, co., Oh., U.S.	D3	112
Scioto, stm., Oh., U.S.	B2	112
Scituate, Ma., U.S.	B6	98
Scituate Reservoir, res., R.I., U.S.	C3	116
Scobey, Mt., U.S.	B11	103
Scofield Reservoir, res., Ut., U.S.	D4	121
Ščokino, Russia	G20	18
Scotch Plains, N.J., U.S.	B4	107
Scotia, Ca., U.S.	B1	82
Scotia, N.Y., U.S.	C7	109
Scotland, Ont., Can.	D4	73
Scotland, S.D., U.S.	D8	118
Scotland, co., Mo., U.S.	A5	102
Scotland, co., N.C., U.S.	C3	110
Scotland, ter., U.K.	D8	7
Scotland Neck, N.C., U.S.	A5	110
Scotlandville, La., U.S.	D4	95
Scotrun, Pa., U.S.	D11	115
Scotstown, Que., Can.	D6	74
Scott, La., U.S.	D3	95
Scott, co., Ar., U.S.	C1	81
Scott, co., Il., U.S.	D3	90
Scott, co., In., U.S.	G6	91
Scott, co., Ia., U.S.	C7	92
Scott, co., Ks., U.S.	D3	93
Scott, co., Ky., U.S.	B5	94
Scott, co., Mn., U.S.	F5	100
Scott, co., Ms., U.S.	C4	101
Scott, co., Mo., U.S.	D8	102
Scott, co., Tn., U.S.	C9	119
Scott, co., Va., U.S.	f9	123
Scott, Cape, c., B.C., Can.	D3	69
Scott, Mount, mtn., Or., U.S.	E4	114
Scott Air Force Base, mil., Il., U.S.	E4	90
Scott City, Ks., U.S.	D3	93
Scott City, Mo., U.S.	D8	102
Scottdale, Ga., U.S.	h8	87
Scottdale, Pa., U.S.	F2	115
Scott Islands, is., B.C., Can.	F7	66
Scott Mountain, mtn., Id., U.S.	E3	89
Scott Peak, mtn., Id., U.S.	E6	89
Scott Reef, rf., Austl.	B4	50
Scott Reservoir, res., N.C., U.S.	A1	110
Scottsbluff, Ne., U.S.	C2	104
Scotts Bluff, co., Ne., U.S.	C2	104
Scotts Bluff National Monument, Ne., U.S.	C2	104
Scottsboro, Al., U.S.	A3	78
Scottsburg, In., U.S.	G6	91
Scottsdale, Austl.	H9	50
Scottsdale, Az., U.S.	D4	80
Scottsville, Ky., U.S.	D3	94
Scottsville, N.Y., U.S.	B3	109
Scottville, Mi., U.S.	E4	99
Scourie, Scot., U.K.	C7	7
Scraggly Lake, l., Me., U.S.	B4	96
Scranton, Ks., U.S.	D8	93
Scranton, Pa., U.S.	D10	115
Scranton, S.C., U.S.	D8	117
Screven, Ga., U.S.	E4	87
Screven, co., Ga., U.S.	D5	87
Scribner, Ne., U.S.	C9	104
Scugog, Lake, l., Ont., Can.	C6	73
Scurry, co., Tx., U.S.	C2	120
Scutari, Lake, l., Eur.	G3	16
Seaboard, N.C., U.S.	A5	110
Seabreeze, De., U.S.	F5	85
Seabrook, N.H., U.S.	E5	106
Seabrook, Tx., U.S.	r14	120
Seabrook Island, i., S.C., U.S.	F7	117
Seadrift, Tx., U.S.	E4	120
Seaford, De., U.S.	F3	85
Seaford, Va., U.S.	h15	123
Seaforth, Ont., Can.	D3	73
Seagoville, Tx., U.S.	n10	120
Seagraves, Tx., U.S.	C1	120
Seaham, Eng., U.K.	G11	7
Sea Isle City, N.J., U.S.	E3	107
Seal, Man., Can.	E13	66
Seal Cove, Newf., Can.	D3	72
Seal Point, c., P.E.I., Can.	C5	71
Seal Rock, Or., U.S.	C2	114
Sealy, Tx., U.S.	E4	120
Seaman, Oh., U.S.	D2	112
Seaman Range, mts., Nv., U.S.	F6	105
Searchlight, Nv., U.S.	H7	105
Searcy, Ar., U.S.	B4	81
Searcy, co., Ar., U.S.	B3	81
Searles Lake, l., Ca., U.S.	E5	82
Searsport, Me., U.S.	D4	96
Seaside, Ca., U.S.	D3	82
Seaside, Or., U.S.	A3	114
Seat Pleasant, Md., U.S.	C4	97
Seattle, Wa., U.S.	B3	124
Seattle-Tacoma International Airport, Wa., U.S.	f11	124
Seaview, Wa., U.S.	C1	124
Sebago Lake, Me., U.S.	E2	96
Šebalino, Russia	G11	24
Sebastian, Fl., U.S.	E6	86
Sebastian, co., Ar., U.S.	B1	81
Sebastian, Cape, c., Or., U.S.	E2	114
Sebastian Inlet, b., Fl., U.S.	E6	86
Sebastián Vizcaíno, Bahía, b., Mex.	C2	62
Sebasticook Lake, l., Me., U.S.	D3	96
Sebec Lake, l., Me., U.S.	C3	96
Sebeka, Mn., U.S.	D3	100
Sebewaing, Mi., U.S.	E7	99
Seboeis, stm., Me., U.S.	B4	96
Seboeis Lake, l., Me., U.S.	C4	96
Seboomook Lake, l., Me., U.S.	C3	96
Sebree, Ky., U.S.	C2	94
Sebring, Fl., U.S.	E5	86
Sebring, Oh., U.S.	B4	112
Secaucus, N.J., U.S.	h8	107
Sechelt, B.C., Can.	E6	69
Second Lake, l., N.H., U.S.	f7	106
Second Mesa, Az., U.S.	B5	80
Secret Lake, l., R.I., U.S.	E4	116
Section, Al., U.S.	A4	78
Security, Co., U.S.	C6	83
Sedalia, Mo., U.S.	C4	102
Sedan, Fr.	C11	10
Sedan, Ks., U.S.	E7	93
Sedano, Spain	C8	12
Sedgewick, Alta., Can.	C5	68
Sedgwick, Ks., U.S.	E6	93
Sedgwick, Mount, mtn., N.M., U.S.	B1	108
Sedgwick, co., Co., U.S.	A8	83
Sedgwick, co., Ks., U.S.	E6	93
Sedley, Va., U.S.	D6	123
Sedona, Az., U.S.	C4	80
Sedro Woolley, Wa., U.S.	A3	124
Seeheim, Nmb.	G3	44
Seekonk, Ma., U.S.	C5	98
Seekonk, stm., R.I., U.S.	C4	116
Seeley, Ca., U.S.	F6	82
Seeley Lake, Mt., U.S.	C3	103
Seelyville, In., U.S.	F3	91
Sées, Fr.	D7	10
Segamat, Malay.	M7	34
Ségou, Mali	F4	42
Segovia, Col.	D5	58
Segovia, Spain	E7	12
Segré, Fr.	E6	10
Seguam Island, i., Ak., U.S.	E5	79
Seguam Pass, strt., Ak., U.S.	E5	79
Séguédine, Niger	D8	42
Seguin, Tx., U.S.	E4	120
Sehore, India	I7	38
Seia, Port.	E4	12
Seiling, Ok., U.S.	A3	113
Seinäjoki, Fin.	E14	6
Seine, stm., Fr.	C7	10
Seki, Tur.	M13	16
Sekiu, Wa., U.S.	A1	124
Sekondi-Takoradi, Ghana	H5	42
Šelagskij, Mys, c., Russia	C28	24
Selah, Wa., U.S.	C5	124
Selaru, Pulau, i., Indon.	G9	32
Selatan, Tanjung, c., Indon.	F5	32
Selawik, Ak., U.S.	B7	79
Selawik Lake, l., Ak., U.S.	B7	79
Selayar, Pulau, i., Indon.	G7	32
Selb, Ger.	E12	8
Selby, S.D., U.S.	B5	118
Selbyville, De., U.S.	G5	85
Selçuk, Tur.	L11	16
Seldovia, Ak., U.S.	D9	79
Selemdža, stm., Russia	G20	24
Selenn'ach, stm., Russia	D21	24
Sélestat, Fr.	D14	10
Sélibaby, Maur.	E3	42
Šelichova, Zaliv, b., Russia	E25	24
Seligman, Az., U.S.	B3	80
Selinsgrove, Pa., U.S.	E8	115
Selkirk, Man., Can.	D3	70
Selkirk, Scot., U.K.	F10	7
Selkirk Mountains, mts., N.A.	F9	66
Sellersburg, In., U.S.	H6	91
Sellersville, Pa., U.S.	F11	115
Selles-sur-Cher, Fr.	E8	10
Sells, Az., U.S.	E4	80
Selma, Al., U.S.	C2	78
Selma, Ca., U.S.	D4	82
Selma, In., U.S.	D7	91
Selma, N.C., U.S.	B4	110
Selmer, Tn., U.S.	B3	119
Selva, Arg.	B4	56
Selvas, for., Braz.	E6	54
Selway, stm., Id., U.S.	C3	89
Selwyn Mountains, mts., Can.	D6	66
Semara, W. Sah.	C3	42
Semarang, Indon.	m15	32
Semeru, Gunung, vol., Indon.	n16	33a
Seminoe Mountains, mts., Wy., U.S.	D6	127
Seminoe Reservoir, res., Wy., U.S.	D6	127
Seminole, Ok., U.S.	B5	113
Seminole, Tx., U.S.	C1	120
Seminole, co., Fl., U.S.	D5	86
Seminole, co., Ga., U.S.	F2	87
Seminole, co., Ok., U.S.	B5	113
Seminole, Lake, res., U.S.	F2	87
Semipalatinsk, Kaz.	G10	24
Semisopochnoi Island, i., Ak., U.S.	E3	79
Semmes, Al., U.S.	E1	78
Šemonaicha, Kaz.	G10	24
Semur-en-Auxois, Fr.	E11	10
Sên, stm., Camb.	H8	34
Sena, Moz.	E6	44
Senachwine Lake, l., Il., U.S.	B4	90
Senador Pompeu, Braz.	E11	54
Sena Madureira, Braz.	E5	54
Senanga, Zam.	E4	44
Senath, Mo., U.S.	E7	102
Senatobia, Ms., U.S.	A4	101
Sendai, Japan	K3	30
Sendai, Japan	D13	30
Seneca, Il., U.S.	B5	90
Seneca, Ks., U.S.	C7	93
Seneca, Mo., U.S.	E3	102
Seneca, Pa., U.S.	D2	115
Seneca, S.C., U.S.	B2	117
Seneca, co., N.Y., U.S.	C4	109
Seneca, co., Oh., U.S.	A2	112
Seneca Falls, N.Y., U.S.	C4	109
Seneca Lake, l., N.Y., U.S.	C4	109
Senecaville Lake, res., Oh., U.S.	C4	112
Senegal (Sénégal), ctry., Afr.	F3	42
Sénégal, stm., Afr.	E3	42
Senekal, S. Afr.	G5	44
Senftenberg, Ger.	D13	8
Senigallia, Italy	F8	14
Senise, Italy	I11	14
Senmonorom, Camb.	H9	34
Sennelerre, Que., Can.	k11	74
Sennori, Italy	I3	14
Senoia, Ga., U.S.	C2	87
Sens, Fr.	D10	10
Senta, Yugo.	D4	16
Sentinel, Az., U.S.	B2	113
Seo de Urgel, Spain	C13	12
Seoni, India	I8	38
Seoul see Sŏul, S. Kor.	D12	26
Sept-Îles (Seven Islands), Que., Can.	h13	74
Sepulga, stm., Al., U.S.	D3	78
Sepúlveda, Spain	D8	12
Sequatchie, co., Tn., U.S.	D8	119
Sequatchie, stm., Tn., U.S.	D8	119
Sequim, Wa., U.S.	A2	124
Sequoia National Park, Ca., U.S.	D4	82
Sequoyah, co., Ok., U.S.	B7	113
Seraing, Bel.	E5	8
Seram, i., Indon.	F8	32
Seram, Laut (Ceram Sea), Indon.	F8	32
Serang, Indon.	m13	33a
Serbia, state, Yugo.	F5	16
Seremban, Malay.	M6	34
Serengeti Plain, pl., Tan.	B6	44

Name	Map Ref	Page
Serenje, Zam.	D6	44
Sergeant Bluff, Ia., U.S.	B1	92
Sergeja Kirova, Ostrova, is., Russia	B11	24
Sergijev Podad, Russia	E21	18
Serowe, Bots.	F5	44
Serpa, Port.	H4	12
Serpuchov, Russia	G20	18
Sérrai, Grc.	H7	16
Serra San Bruno, Italy	K11	14
Serra Talhada, Braz.	E11	54
Serres, Fr.	H12	10
Serrezuela, Arg.	C3	56
Serri, Italy	J4	42
Serrinha, Braz.	F11	54
Sertã, Port.	F3	12
Sesfontein, Nmb.	E2	44
Sesheke, Zam.	E4	44
Sessa Aurunca, Italy	H8	14
Sesser, Il., U.S.	E4	90
Sestri Levante, Italy	E4	14
Sète, Fr.	I10	10
Sete Lagoas, Braz.	E6	57
Seth, W.V., U.S.	C3	125
Sétif, Alg.	A7	42
Seto, Japan	G10	30
Seto-naikai, Japan	H6	30
Setúbal, Port.	G3	12
Seul, Lac, l., Ont., Can.	o16	73
Seul Choix Point, c., Mi., U.S.	C5	99
Sevan, ozero, l., Arm.	I7	22
Sevastopol', Ukr.	I4	22
Ševčenko, Kaz.	I8	22
Seven Devils Lake, res., Id., U.S.	D4	81
Seven Devils Mountains, mts., Id., U.S.	D2	89
Seven Hills, Oh., U.S.	h9	112
Seven Mile Beach, N.J., U.S.	E3	107
Sévérac-le-Château, Fr.	H10	10
Severn, Md., U.S.	B4	97
Severn, stm., Ont., Can.	n17	73
Severn, stm., Eng., U.K.	J10	7
Severnaja Dvina, stm., Russia	E6	22
Severnaja Zeml'a, is., Russia	B13	24
Severna Park, Md., U.S.	B4	97
Severn River, b., Md., U.S.	B4	97
Severodvinsk, Russia	E5	22
Severo-Kuril'sk, Russia	G25	24
Severo-Sibirskaja Nizmennost', pl., Russia	C13	24
Severo-Zadonsk, Russia	G21	18
Sevettijärvi, Fin.	B17	6
Sevier, co., Ar., U.S.	D1	81
Sevier, co., Tn., U.S.	D10	119
Sevier, co., Ut., U.S.	E4	121
Sevier, stm., Ut., U.S.	D3	121
Sevier Bridge Reservoir, res., Ut., U.S.	D4	121
Sevier Lake, l., Ut., U.S.	E2	121
Sevierville, Tn., U.S.	D10	119
Sevilla, Col.	E5	58
Sevilla, Spain	H6	12
Seville, Oh., U.S.	A4	112
Seville see Sevilla, Spain	H6	12
Sewanee, Tn., U.S.	D8	119
Seward, Ak., U.S.	C10	79
Seward, Ne., U.S.	D8	104
Seward, co., Ks., U.S.	E3	93
Seward, co., Ne., U.S.	D8	104
Seward Peninsula, pen., Ak., U.S.	B7	79
Sewickley, Pa., U.S.	E1	115
Sexsmith, Alta., Can.	B1	68
Seychelles, ctry., Afr.	B11	44
Seydisfjördur, Ice.	B5	4
Seymour, Ct., U.S.	D3	84
Seymour, In., U.S.	G6	91
Seymour, Ia., U.S.	D4	92
Seymour, Mo., U.S.	D5	102
Seymour, Tx., U.S.	C3	120
Seymour, Wi., U.S.	D5	126
Seymour Inlet, b., B.C., Can.	D4	69
Seymour Johnson Air Force Base, mil., N.C., U.S.	B5	110
Seymour Lake, l., Vt., U.S.	B4	122
Seymourville, La., U.S.	h9	95
Seyne, Fr.	H13	10
Seyssel, Fr.	G12	10
Sézanne, Fr.	D10	10
Sezze, Italy	H8	14
Sfax, Tun.	B8	42
's-Gravenhage (The Hague), Neth.	B5	8
Shabbona, Il., U.S.	B5	90
Shache, China	A7	38
Shackelford, co., Tx., U.S.	C3	120
Shackleton Ice Shelf, Ant.	C22	47
Shaddādī, Syria	A7	40
Shadehill Dam, S.D., U.S.	B3	118
Shadehill Reservoir, res., S.D., U.S.	B3	118
Shadow Mountain National Recreation Area, Co., U.S.	A4	83
Shady Cove, Or., U.S.	E4	114
Shady Side, Md., U.S.	C4	97
Shadyside, Oh., U.S.	C5	112
Shady Spring, W.V., U.S.	D3	125
Shafer, Lake, l., In., U.S.	C4	91
Shafer Butte, mtn., Id., U.S.	F2	89
Shafter, Ca., U.S.	E4	82
Shaftsbury, Vt., U.S.	E2	122
Shāhdādkot, Pak.	G2	38
Shahdol, India	I9	38
Shāhjahānpur, India	G8	38
Shāh Jūy, Afg.	D2	38
Shahrak, Afg.	C1	38
Shahrak, Afg.	I7	38
Shājāpur, India	I7	38
Shakawe, Bots.	E4	44
Shaker Heights, Oh., U.S.	A4	112
Shakhty see Šachty, Russia	H6	22
Shaki, Nig.	G6	42
Shakopee, Mn., U.S.	F5	100
Shaler Mountains, mts., N.W. Ter., Can.	B10	66
Shallotte, N.C., U.S.	D4	110
Shallotte Inlet, b., N.C., U.S.	D4	110
Shallowater, Tx., U.S.	C2	120
Shām, Bādiyat ash-, des., Asia	C6	40
Shām, Jabal ash-, mtn., Oman	D6	46
Shamokin, Pa., U.S.	E8	115
Shamokin Dam, Pa., U.S.	E8	115
Shamrock, Tx., U.S.	B2	120
Shandī, Sudan	E12	42
Shandong, prov., China	D10	26
Shandong Bandao, pen., China	D11	26
Shanghai, China	D10	26
Shanghai Shih, China	E11	26
Shangqiu, China	A4	28
Shangrao, China	G6	28
Shangshui, China	B3	28
Shangzhi, China	B12	26
Shannock, R.I., U.S.	F2	116
Shannon, Ga., U.S.	B1	87
Shannon, Il., U.S.	A4	90
Shannon, Ms., U.S.	A5	101
Shannon, co., Mo., U.S.	D6	102
Shannon, co., S.D., U.S.	D3	118
Shannon, stm., Ire.	I3	7
Shannon, Lake, l., Wa., U.S.	A4	124
Shannontown, S.C., U.S.	D7	117
Shantou (Swatow), China	L5	28
Shantung Peninsula see Shandong Bandao, pen., China	D11	26
Shānxī, prov., China	D8	26
Shānxī, prov., China	D9	26
Shanyin, China	D9	26
Shaoguan, China	K2	28
Shaowu, China	H6	28
Shaoxing, China	E9	28
Shaoyang, China	F9	26
Shark Bay, b., Austl.	E2	50
Sharkey, co., Ms., U.S.	C3	101
Shark Point, c., Fl., U.S.	H5	86
Sharktooth Mountain, mtn., B.C., Can.	E7	66
Sharon, Ct., U.S.	B2	84
Sharon, Ma., U.S.	B5	98
Sharon, Pa., U.S.	D1	115
Sharon, Tn., U.S.	A3	119
Sharon, Wi., U.S.	F5	126
Sharon Hill, Pa., U.S.	p20	115
Sharon Park, Oh., U.S.	n12	112
Sharon Springs, Ks., U.S.	D2	93
Sharonville, Oh., U.S.	n13	112
Sharp, co., Ar., U.S.	A4	81
Sharpe, Lake, res., S.D., U.S.	C6	118
Sharpes, Fl., U.S.	D6	86
Sharpley, De., U.S.	h7	85
Sharpsburg, Md., U.S.	B2	97
Sharpsburg, N.C., U.S.	B5	110
Sharpsburg, Pa., U.S.	k14	115
Sharpsville, In., U.S.	D5	91
Sharpsville, Pa., U.S.	D1	115
Sharptown, Md., U.S.	C6	97
Sharqīyah, As-Sahrā' ash- (Arabian Desert), des., Egypt	C12	42
Shashi, China	E9	26
Shashi, stm., Afr.	F5	44
Shasta, co., Ca., U.S.	B3	82
Shasta, Mount, vol., Ca., U.S.	B2	82
Shasta Lake, res., Ca., U.S.	B2	82
Shattuck, Ok., U.S.	A2	113
Shaw, Ms., U.S.	B3	101
Shaw Air Force Base, mil., S.C., U.S.	D7	117
Shawano, Wi., U.S.	D5	126
Shawano, co., Wi., U.S.	D5	126
Shawano Lake, l., Wi., U.S.	D5	126
Shawinigan, Que., Can.	C5	74
Shawinigan-Sud, Que., Can.	C5	74
Shawnee, Ks., U.S.	k16	93
Shawnee, Ok., U.S.	B5	113
Shawnee, co., Ks., U.S.	D8	93
Shawneetown, Il., U.S.	F5	90
Shawsheen, stm., Ma., U.S.	f11	98
Shaybārā, i., Sau. Ar.	C2	46
Shebele (Shebelle), stm., Afr.	G3	46
Sheberghān, Afg.	B1	38
Sheboygan, Wi., U.S.	E6	126
Sheboygan, co., Wi., U.S.	E6	126
Sheboygan, stm., Wi., U.S.	k10	126
Sheboygan Falls, Wi., U.S.	E6	126
Shediac, N.B., Can.	C5	71
Sheenjek, stm., Ak., U.S.	B11	79
Sheep Mountain, mtn., Az., U.S.	E1	80
Sheep Mountain, mtn., Wy., U.S.	B5	127
Sheep Mountain, mtn., Wy., U.S.	C2	127
Sheep Peak, mtn., Nv., U.S.	G6	105
Sheep Range, mts., Nv., U.S.	G6	105
Sheet Harbour, N.S., Can.	E7	71
Sheffield, Eng., U.K.	H11	7
Sheffield, Al., U.S.	A2	78
Sheffield, Il., U.S.	B4	90
Sheffield, Ia., U.S.	B4	92
Sheffield, Pa., U.S.	C3	115
Sheffield Lake, Oh., U.S.	A3	112
Sheila, N.B., Can.	B5	71
Shēkhābād, Afg.	C3	38
Shekhūpura, Pak.	E5	38
Shelagyote Peak, mtn., B.C., Can.	B4	69
Shelbiana, Ky., U.S.	C7	94
Shelbina, Mo., U.S.	B5	102
Shelburn, In., U.S.	F3	91
Shelburne, Ont., Can.	C4	73
Shelburne Falls, Ma., U.S.	A2	98
Shelburne Pond, l., Vt., U.S.	C2	122
Shelby, Al., U.S.	B3	78
Shelby, In., U.S.	B3	91
Shelby, Ia., U.S.	C2	92
Shelby, Mi., U.S.	E4	99
Shelby, Ms., U.S.	B3	101
Shelby, Mt., U.S.	B5	103
Shelby, Ne., U.S.	C8	104
Shelby, N.C., U.S.	B1	110
Shelby, Oh., U.S.	B3	112
Shelby, co., Al., U.S.	B3	78
Shelby, co., Il., U.S.	D5	90
Shelby, co., In., U.S.	E6	91
Shelby, co., Ia., U.S.	C2	92
Shelby, co., Ky., U.S.	B4	94
Shelby, co., Mo., U.S.	B5	102
Shelby, co., Oh., U.S.	B1	112
Shelby, co., Tn., U.S.	B2	119
Shelby, co., Tx., U.S.	D5	120
Shelbyville, Il., U.S.	D5	90
Shelbyville, In., U.S.	F6	91
Shelbyville, Ky., U.S.	B4	94
Shelbyville, Tn., U.S.	B5	119
Shelbyville, Lake, res., Il., U.S.	C6	90
Sheldon, Il., U.S.	A2	92
Sheldon, Ia., U.S.	r14	120
Sheldon, Tx., U.S.	D7	79
Shelikof Strait, strt., Ak., U.S.	A2	83
Shell Creek, stm., Ak., U.S.	A2	83
Shell Creek, stm., Wy., U.S.	B5	127
Shelley, Id., U.S.	F6	89
Shell Lake, Wi., U.S.	C2	126
Shell Lake, l., Mn., U.S.	D3	100
Shell Lake, l., Wi., U.S.	C2	126
Shellman, Ga., U.S.	E2	87
Shell Rock, Ia., U.S.	B5	92
Shell Rock, stm., Ia., U.S.	B5	92
Shellsburg, Ia., U.S.	B6	92
Shelly Mountain, mtn., Id., U.S.	F5	89
Shelter Island, N.Y., U.S.	m16	109
Shelton, Ct., U.S.	D3	84
Shelton, Ne., U.S.	D7	104
Shelton, Wa., U.S.	B2	124
Shemya Air Force Base, mil., Ak., U.S.	E2	79
Shenandoah, Ia., U.S.	D2	92
Shenandoah, Pa., U.S.	E9	115
Shenandoah, Va., U.S.	B4	123
Shenandoah, co., Va., U.S.	B4	123
Shenandoah, stm., U.S.	A5	123
Shenandoah, North Fork, stm., Va., U.S.	B4	123
Shenandoah, South Fork, stm., Va., U.S.	B4	123
Shenandoah Mountain, mtn., U.S.	B3	123
Shenandoah National Park, Va., U.S.	B4	123
Shenango River Lake, res., U.S.	D1	115
Shengfang, China	D10	26
Shengze, China	E9	28
Shenipsit Lake, l., Ct., U.S.	B6	84
Shenyang (Mukden), China	C11	26
Shenzha, China	E13	38
Shepaug, stm., Ct., U.S.	C2	84
Shepaug Dam, Ct., U.S.	D2	84
Shepaug Reservoir, res., Ct., U.S.	C2	84
Shepherd, Mi., U.S.	E6	99
Shepherd, Tx., U.S.	D5	120
Shepherdstown, W.V., U.S.	B7	125
Shepherdsville, Ky., U.S.	C4	94
Sheppard Air Force Base, mil., Tx., U.S.	C3	120
Shepparton, Austl.	G9	50
Sherborn, Ma., U.S.	h10	98
Sherbro Island, i., S.L.	G3	42
Sherbrooke, Que., Can.	D6	74
Sherburn, Mn., U.S.	G4	100
Sherburne, co., Mn., U.S.	E5	100
Sheridan, Ar., U.S.	C3	81
Sheridan, Il., U.S.	B5	90
Sheridan, In., U.S.	D5	91
Sheridan, Mi., U.S.	E5	99
Sheridan, Mt., U.S.	E4	103
Sheridan, Or., U.S.	B3	114
Sheridan, Wy., U.S.	B6	127
Sheridan, co., Ks., U.S.	C3	93
Sheridan, co., Mt., U.S.	B12	103
Sheridan, co., Ne., U.S.	B3	104
Sheridan, co., N.D., U.S.	B5	111
Sheridan, co., Wy., U.S.	B5	127
Sheridan, Mount, mtn., Wy., U.S.	B2	127
Sherman, Tx., U.S.	C4	120
Sherman, co., Ks., U.S.	C2	93
Sherman, co., Ne., U.S.	C6	104
Sherman, co., Or., U.S.	B6	114
Sherman, co., Tx., U.S.	A2	120
Sherman Reservoir, res., Ne., U.S.	C7	104
Sherrelwood, Co., U.S.	*B6	83
Sherrill, N.Y., U.S.	B5	109
's-Hertogenbosch, Neth.	D5	8
Sherwood, P.E.I., Can.	C6	71
Sherwood, Ar., U.S.	C3	81
Sherwood, Or., U.S.	h12	114
Sherwood, Wi., U.S.	h9	126
Sherwood Manor, Ct., U.S.	A5	84
Sherwood Park, De., U.S.	i7	85
Shetek, Lake, l., Mn., U.S.	G3	100
Shetland Islands, is., Scot., U.K.	A11	7
Shetucket, stm., Ct., U.S.	C7	84
Sheyenne, stm., N.D., U.S.	C8	111
Sheyenne Lake, res., N.D., U.S.	B5	111
Shiawassee, co., Mi., U.S.	F6	99
Shibata, Japan	E12	30
Shibetsu, Japan	p23	30a
Shibukawa, Japan	F11	30
Shickshinny, Pa., U.S.	D9	115
Shijiazhuang, China	D8	26
Shijushan, China	D8	26
Shikārpur, Pak.	G3	38
Shikohābād, India	G8	38
Shikoku, i., Japan	I6	30
Shikoku-sanchi, mts., Japan	I6	30
Shikotsu-ko, l., Japan	q19	30a
Shillington, Pa., U.S.	F10	115
Shillong, India	H14	38
Shiloh National Military Park, Tn., U.S.	B3	119
Shilong, China	L2	28
Shimabara, Japan	J3	30
Shimada, Japan	H11	30
Shimbiris, mtn., Som.	F4	46
Shimizu, Japan	G11	30
Shimminato, Japan	F10	30
Shimodate, Japan	F12	30
Shimoga, India	F3	37
Shimonoseki, Japan	I4	30
Shinano, stm., Japan	E11	30
Shindand, Afg.	C1	36
Shiner, Tx., U.S.	E4	120
Shelby, co., Mo., U.S.	B5	102
Shelby, co., Oh., U.S.	B1	30
Shelby, co., Tn., U.S.	B2	119
Shelby, co., Tx., U.S.	D5	120
Shelby, Oh., U.S.	B3	112
Shelbyville, Il., U.S.	D5	90
Shelbyville, Ky., U.S.	B4	94
Shelbyville, Tn., U.S.	B5	119
Shinglehouse, Pa., U.S.	C5	115
Shingū, Japan	I8	30
Shinjō, Japan	D13	30
Shinnston, W.V., U.S.	B4	125
Shinshār, Syria	B5	40
Shinyanga, Tan.	B6	44
Shiocton, Wi., U.S.	D5	126
Shiogama, Japan	D14	30
Shiojiri, Japan	F10	30
Shiping, China	C7	34
Ship Island, i., Ms., U.S.	E5	101
Ship Island Pass, strt., Ms., U.S.	g7	101
Shippegan, N.B., Can.	B5	71
Shippensburg, Pa., U.S.	F6	115
Shiprock, N.M., U.S.	A1	108
Ship Rock, mtn., N.M., U.S.	A1	108
Shirakawa, Japan	E13	30
Shīrāz, Iran	C5	46
Shire, stm., Afr.	E6	44
Shiretoko-misaki, c., Japan	o23	30a
Shirley, In., U.S.	E6	91
Shirley, Ma., U.S.	A4	98
Shirley Mountains, mts., Wy., U.S.	D6	127
Shirpur, India	B3	37
Shishaldin Volcano, vol., Ak., U.S.	E7	79
Shishmaref, Ak., U.S.	B6	79
Shively, Ky., U.S.	B4	94
Shivpuri, India	H7	38
Shizuoka, Japan	H11	30
Shkodër, Alb.	G3	16
Shoal Creek, stm., U.S.	B4	119
Shoal Harbour, Newf., Can.	D4	72
Shoal Lake, Man., Can.	D1	70
Shoals, In., U.S.	G4	91
Shoals, Isles of, is., Me., U.S.	E2	96
Shoalwater, Cape, c., Wa., U.S.	C1	124
Shōdo-shima, i., Japan	H7	30
Shoemakersville, Pa., U.S.	F10	115
Sholāpur, India	D3	37
Shongopovi, Az., U.S.	B5	80
Shonto, Az., U.S.	A5	80
Shoreview, Mn., U.S.	m12	100
Shorewood, Il., U.S.	k8	90
Shorewood, Mn., U.S.	n11	100
Shorewood, Wi., U.S.	E6	126
Short Beach, Ct., U.S.	D4	84
Shoshone, Id., U.S.	G4	89
Shoshone, co., Id., U.S.	B2	89
Shoshone, stm., Wy., U.S.	B4	127
Shoshone Falls, wtfl, Id., U.S.	G4	89
Shoshone Lake, l., Wy., U.S.	B2	127
Shoshone Mountains, mts., Nv., U.S.	E4	105
Shoshone Peak, mtn., Nv., U.S.	G5	105
Shoshone Range, mts., Nv., U.S.	C5	105
Shoshong, Bots.	F5	44
Shoshoni, Wy., U.S.	C4	127
Shoup, Id., U.S.	D4	89
Shouxian, China	C5	28
Show Low, Az., U.S.	C5	80
Shreve, Oh., U.S.	B3	112
Shreveport, La., U.S.	B2	95
Shrewsbury, Eng., U.K.	I10	7
Shrewsbury, Ma., U.S.	B4	98
Shrewsbury, N.J., U.S.	C4	107
Shrewsbury, Pa., U.S.	G8	115
Shuajingsi, China	E7	26
Shuangcheng, China	B12	26
Shuangyashan, China	B13	26
Shubenacadie, N.S., Can.	D6	71
Shuksan, Mount, mtn., Wa., U.S.	A4	124
Shullsburg, Wi., U.S.	F3	126
Shumagin Islands, is., Ak., U.S.	E7	79
Shunde, China	M2	28
Shungnak, Ak., U.S.	B8	79
Shuqrā', Yemen	F4	46
Shūshtar, Iran	B4	46
Shuswap Lake, l., B.C., Can.	D8	69
Shwebo, Burma	C3	34
Siak see Xi'an, China	D8	32
Sian see Xi'an, China	D8	32
Siargao Island, i., Phil.	D8	32
Šiaškotan, Ostrov, i., Russia	H24	24
Šiauliai, Lith.	F6	18
Šibenik, Cro.	F10	14
Siberia see Sibir', reg., Russia	D16	24
Siberut, Pulau, i., Indon.	F2	32
Sibi, Pak.	E2	38
Sibir' (Siberia), reg., Russia	D16	24
Sibir'akova, Ostrov, i., Russia	C9	24
Sibiti, Congo	B2	44
Sibiu, Rom.	D8	16
Sibley, Ia., U.S.	A2	92
Sibley, La., U.S.	B3	95
Sibley, co., Mn., U.S.	F4	100
Sibolga, Indon.	E2	32
Sibsāgar, India	G16	38
Sibu, Malay.	E5	32
Sibutu Island, i., Phil.	E6	32
Sibuyan Island, i., Phil.	C7	32
Sibuyan Sea, Phil.	C7	32
Sicamous, B.C., Can.	D8	69
Sichote-Alin', mts., Russia	H21	24
Sichuan, prov., China	E7	26
Sicié, Cap, c., Fr.	I12	10
Sicilia, i., Italy	L9	14
Sicily see Sicilia, i., Italy	L9	14
Sicily, Strait of, strt.	L7	14
Sico, stm., Hond.	G5	64
Sicuani, Peru	F4	54
Siddipet, India	J3	30
Siderno, Italy	K11	14
Sidhpur, India	I5	38
Sidi bel Abbès, Alg.	A5	42
Sidi Ifni, Mor.	B3	42
Sidmouth, Eng., U.K.	K9	7
Sidney, B.C., Can.	E6	69
Sidney, Il., U.S.	C5	90
Sidney, Ia., U.S.	D2	92
Sidney, Mt., U.S.	C12	103
Sidney, Ne., U.S.	C3	104
Sidney, N.Y., U.S.	C5	109
Sidney, Oh., U.S.	B1	112
Sidney Lanier, Lake, res., Ga., U.S.	B2	87
Sidon see Şaydā, Leb.	C4	40
Sidra, Gulf of see Surt, Khalīj, b., Libya	B9	42
Siedlce, Pol.	C22	8
Siegburg, Ger.	E7	8
Siegen, Ger.	E8	8
Siĕmréab, Camb.	H7	34
Siena, Italy	F6	14
Sierra, co., Ca., U.S.	C3	82
Sierra, co., N.M., U.S.	D2	108
Sierra Blanca Peak, mtn., N.M., U.S.	D4	108
Sierra Colorada, Arg.	E3	56
Sierra Estrella, mts., Az., U.S.	m8	80
Sierra Leone, ctry., Afr.	G3	42
Sierra Madre, Ca., U.S.	m12	82
Sierra Vista, Az., U.S.	F5	80
Sierre, Switz.	F14	10
Siesta Key, i., Fl., U.S.	E4	86
Sighetul Marmaţiei, Rom.	B7	16
Sighişoara, Rom.	C8	16
Siglufjördur, Ice.	B4	4
Signal Mountain, Tn., U.S.	D8	119
Signal Peak, mtn., Az., U.S.	D1	80
Signal Peak, mtn., Ut., U.S.	F2	121
Signy-l'Abbaye, Fr.	C11	10
Sigourney, Ia., U.S.	C5	92
Sigüenza, Spain	D9	12
Sigües, Spain	C10	12
Siguiri, Gui.	F4	42
Siilinjärvi, Fin.	E16	6
Si-Kacha, Thai.	H6	34
Sīkar, India	G6	38
Sikasso, Mali	F4	42
Sikeston, Mo., U.S.	E8	102
Sikiá, Grc.	I7	16
Sikinos, Grc.	M9	16
Sikkim, state, India	G13	38
Šikotan, Ostrov (Shikotan-tō), i., Russia	I23	24
Sikt'ach, Russia	D19	24
Silandro, Italy	C5	14
Silao, Mex.	G9	62
Silay, Phil.	C7	32
Silba, Cro.	E9	14
Silchar, India	H15	38
Siler City, N.C., U.S.	B3	110
Silesia, hist. reg., Pol.	E16	8
Siletz, Or., U.S.	C3	114
Silifke, Tur.	A3	40
Siliguri, India	G13	38
Siling Co, l., China	E13	38
Silistra, Bul.	E11	16
Šilka, Russia	G18	24
Šilka, stm., Russia	G17	24
Silkeborg, Den.	H7	6
Sillamäe, Est.	B10	18
Sillé-le-Guillaume, Fr.	D6	10
Sillery, Que., Can.	n17	74
Sillon de Talbert, pen., Fr.	D3	10
Siloam Springs, Ar., U.S.	A1	81
Silsbee, Tx., U.S.	D5	120
Silt, Co., U.S.	B3	83
Silvânia, Braz.	B2	37
Silvassa, India	C7	100
Silver Bay, Mn., U.S.	E4	103
Silver Bow, co., Mt., U.S.	D2	105
Silver City, Nv., U.S.	E1	108
Silver City, N.M., U.S.	C8	104
Silver Creek, Ne., U.S.	C1	109
Silver Creek, N.Y., U.S.	D7	114
Silver Creek, stm., Or., U.S.	B3	124
Silverdale, Wa., U.S.	h14	94
Silver Grove, Ky., U.S.	f9	97
Silver Hill, Md., U.S.	C8	93
Silver Lake, Ks., U.S.	f11	98
Silver Lake, Ma., U.S.	F4	100
Silver Lake, Mn., U.S.	F5	126
Silver Lake, Wi., U.S.	D3	85
Silver Lake, l., De., U.S.	A3	92
Silver Lake, l., Ia., U.S.	C3	96
Silver Lake, l., Me., U.S.	E2	106
Silver Lake, l., N.H., U.S.	C4	106
Silver Lake, l., Or., U.S.	D7	114
Silver Lake, l., Wa., U.S.	g13	124
Silverpeak, Nv., U.S.	F4	105
Silver Peak Range, mts., Nv., U.S.	F4	105
Silver Spring, Md., U.S.	C3	97
Silver Springs, Nv., U.S.	D2	105
Silver Star Mountain, mtn., Wa., U.S.	A5	124
Silverthrone Mountain, mtn., B.C., Can.	D4	69
Silvertip Mountain, mtn., Mt., U.S.	C3	103
Silverton, Co., U.S.	D3	83
Silverton, Id., U.S.	B3	89
Silverton, N.J., U.S.	C4	107
Silverton, Oh., U.S.	o13	112
Silverton, Or., U.S.	C4	114
Silvi, Italy	G9	14
Silvies, stm., Or., U.S.	D7	114
Silview, De., U.S.	B3	85
Silvis, Il., U.S.	B3	90
Simanggang, Malay.	E5	32
Šimanovsk, Russia	G19	24
Simav, Tur.	J12	16
Simcoe, Ont., Can.	E4	73
Simcoe, Lake, l., Ont., Can.	C5	73
Simeulue, Pulau, i., Indon.	M3	34
Simferopol', Ukr.	I4	22
Simi Valley, Ca., U.S.	E4	82
Simla, India	E7	38
Simmesport, La., U.S.	D4	95
Simms Stream, stm., N.H., U.S.	g7	106
Simojovel [de Allende], Mex.	I13	62
Simonette, stm., Alta., Can.	B1	68
Simplon Pass, Switz.	F15	10
Simpson, Pa., U.S.	C11	115
Simpson, co., Ky., U.S.	D3	94
Simpson, co., Ms., U.S.	D4	101
Simpson Creek, stm., W.V., U.S.	k10	125

Name	Map Ref	Page
Simpson Desert, des., Austl.	D7	50
Simpson Peninsula, pen., N.W. Ter., Can.	C15	66
Simpsonville, Ky., U.S.	B4	94
Simpsonville, S.C., U.S.	B3	117
Simsboro, La., U.S.	B3	95
Simsbury, Ct., U.S.	B4	84
Simušir, Ostrov, i., Russia	H24	24
Sīnā', Shibh Jazīrat (Sinai Peninsula), pen., Egypt	C12	42
Sinabang, Indon.	M4	34
Sinai Peninsula see Sīnā', Shibh Jazīrat, pen., Egypt	C12	42
Sin'aja, stm., Russia	E18	24
Sinaloa, stm., Mex.	E5	62
Sīnāwan, Libya	B8	42
Sincé, Col.	C5	58
Sincé, Col.	J10	64
Sincelejo, Col.	C5	58
Sinclair, stm., U.S.	E5	127
Sindri, India	I12	38
Sines, Port.	H3	12
Sinfães, Port.	D3	12
Singānallūr, India	G4	37
Singapore, Sing.	N7	34
Singapore, ctry., Asia	E3	32
Singapore Strait, strt., Asia	N7	34
Singen [Hohentwiel], Ger.	H8	8
Singida, Tan.	B6	44
Singkang, Indon.	F7	32
Singkawang, Indon.	E4	32
Siniscola, Italy	I4	14
Sinj, Cro.	F11	14
Sinjah, Sudan	F12	42
Sinkāt, Sudan	E13	42
Sinnamary, Fr. Gu.	B8	54
Sinnemahoning Creek, stm., Pa., U.S.	D5	115
Sinop, Tur.	G15	4
Sinskoje, Russia	E19	24
Sintang, Indon.	E5	32
Sint Eustatius, i., Neth. Ant.	F16	64
Sint Marten (Saint-Martin), i., N.A.	E16	64
Sint-Niklaas, Bel.	D4	8
Sinton, Tx., U.S.	E4	120
Sintra, Port.	G2	12
Sinūiju, N. Kor.	C11	26
Sion, Switz.	F14	8
Sioux, co., Ia., U.S.	A1	92
Sioux, co., Ne., U.S.	B2	104
Sioux, co., N.D., U.S.	C4	111
Sioux Center, Ia., U.S.	A1	92
Sioux City, Ia., U.S.	B1	92
Sioux Falls, S.D., U.S.	D9	118
Sioux Lookout, Ont., Can.	o17	73
Sioux Rapids, Ia., U.S.	B2	92
Siping, China	C11	26
Sipiwesk Lake, l., Man., Can.	B3	70
Sipsey, stm., Al., U.S.	B2	78
Sipsey Fork, stm., Al., U.S.	A2	78
Siracusa, Italy	L10	14
Sirājganj, Bngl.	H13	38
Sir Douglas, Mount, mtn., Can.	D3	68
Sir Edward Pellew Group, is., Austl.	C7	50
Siren, Wi., U.S.	C1	126
Siret, stm., Eur.	C11	16
Sirevåg, Nor.	G5	6
Sir James MacBrien, Mount, mtn., N.W. Ter., Can.	D7	66
Sirohi, India	H5	38
Sirsa, India	F6	38
Sir Sandford, Mount, mtn., B.C., Can.	D9	69
Sirsi, India	E3	37
Sir Wilfrid Laurier, Mount, mtn., B.C., Can.	C8	69
Sisak, Cro.	D11	14
Siskiyou, co., Ca., U.S.	B2	82
Siskiyou Mountains, mts., U.S.	F3	114
Siskiyou Pass, Or., U.S.	E4	114
Sisseton, S.D., U.S.	B8	118
Sisseton Indian Reservation, U.S.	B8	118
Sissiboo, stm., N.S., Can.	E4	71
Sisson Branch Reservoir, res., N.B., Can.	B2	71
Sissonville, W.V., U.S.	C3	125
Sisteron, Fr.	H12	10
Sisters, Or., U.S.	C5	114
Sistersville, W.V., U.S.	B4	125
Sitāpur, India	G9	38
Sitka, Ak., U.S.	D12	79
Sitka National Historical Park, Ak., U.S.	m22	79
Sitka Sound, strt., Ak., U.S.	m22	79
Sittard, Neth.	D5	8
Sittoung, stm., Burma	E4	34
Sittwe (Akyab), Burma	D2	34
Situbondo, Indon.	m16	33a
Sivas, Tur.	H15	4
Sīwah, Egypt	C11	42
Siwān, India	G11	38
Sjælland, i., Den.	I8	6
Skagen, Den.	H8	6
Skagerrak, strt., Eur.	H7	6
Skagit, co., Wa., U.S.	A4	124
Skagway, Ak., U.S.	D12	79
Skaidi, Nor.	A15	6
Skamania, co., Wa., U.S.	D3	124
Skaneateles, N.Y., U.S.	C4	109
Skaneateles Lake, l., N.Y., U.S.	C4	109
Skärdu, Pak.	C6	38
Skarżysko-Kamienna, Pol.	D20	8
Skeena Mountains, mts., B.C., Can.	E7	66
Skegness, Eng., U.K.	H13	7
Skeleton Lake, l., Ont., Can.	B5	73
Skellefteå, Swe.	D13	6
Skelleftehamn, Swe.	D13	6
Skiatook, Ok., U.S.	A5	113
Skiatook Reservoir, res., Ok., U.S.	A5	113
Skibotn, Nor.	B13	6
Skiddaw, mtn., Eng., U.K.	G9	7
Skien, Nor.	G7	6
Skierniewice, Pol.	D20	8
Skikda, Alg.	A7	42
Skillet Fork, stm., Il., U.S.	E5	90
Skillingaryd, Swe.	H10	6
Škofja Loka, Slo.	C9	14
Skokie, Il., U.S.	A6	90
Skokomish Indian Reservation, Wa., U.S.	B2	124
Skopje, Mac.	H5	16
Skövde, Swe.	G9	6
Skovorodino, Russia	G18	24
Skowhegan, Me., U.S.	D3	96
Skull Valley, val., Ut., U.S.	C3	121
Skull Valley Indian Reservation, Ut., U.S.	C3	121
Skuna, stm., Ms., U.S.	B4	101
Skunk, stm., Ia., U.S.	D6	92
Skwentna, stm., Ak., U.S.	g15	79
Skye, Island of, i., Scot., U.K.	D6	7
Skykomish, stm., Wa., U.S.	B4	124
Skyland, Nv., U.S.	D2	105
Skyland, N.C., U.S.	f10	110
Skyline, Al., U.S.	A3	78
Slagnäs, Swe.	D12	6
Slamet, Gunung, vol., Indon.	m14	33a
Slancy, Russia	B11	18
Slano, Cro.	G12	14
Slater, Ia., U.S.	C4	92
Slater, Mo., U.S.	B4	102
Slater, S.C., U.S.	A3	117
Slatersville, R.I., U.S.	A3	116
Slatersville Reservoir, res., R.I., U.S.	B3	116
Slatington, Pa., U.S.	E10	115
Slaton, Tx., U.S.	C2	120
Slaughter, La., U.S.	D4	95
Slave, stm., Can.	D10	66
Slave Lake, Alta., Can.	B3	68
Slavonia see Slavonija, reg., Cro.	D12	14
Slavonija, reg., Cro.	D12	14
Slavonska Požega, Cro.	D12	14
Slavonski Brod, Cro.	D2	16
Slayton, Mn., U.S.	G3	100
Sleeping Bear Dunes National Lakeshore, Mi., U.S.	D4	99
Sleeping Bear Point, c., Mi., U.S.	D4	99
Sleepy Eye, Mn., U.S.	F4	100
Slickville, Pa., U.S.	F2	115
Slidell, La., U.S.	D6	95
Sliderock Mountain, mtn., Mt., U.S.	D3	103
Sligo, Ire.	G4	7
Slinger, Wi., U.S.	E5	126
Slippery Rock, Pa., U.S.	D1	115
Sliven, Bul.	G10	16
Sloan, Ia., U.S.	B1	92
Sloan, N.Y., U.S.	C2	109
Slocomb, Al., U.S.	D4	78
Slonim, Bela.	H8	18
Slope, co., N.D., U.S.	C2	111
Slovakia see Slovensko, hist. reg., Czech.	G19	8
Slovenia, ctry., Eur.	C9	14
Slovenjgradec, Slo.	C10	14
Slovenska Bistrica, Slo.	C10	14
Slovensko, hist. reg., Czech.	G19	8
Sluck, Bela.	H10	18
Słupsk (Stolp), Pol.	A17	8
Sl'ud'anka, Russia	G14	24
Smackover, Ar., U.S.	D3	81
Small Point, c., Me., U.S.	g8	96
Smallwood Reservoir, res., Newf., Can.	g8	72
Smederevo, Yugo.	E4	16
Smethport, Pa., U.S.	C5	115
Šmidovič, Russia	H20	24
Šmidta, Ostrov, i., Russia	A12	24
Smith, co., Ks., U.S.	C5	93
Smith, co., Ms., U.S.	C4	101
Smith, co., Tn., U.S.	A5	119
Smith, co., Tx., U.S.	C5	120
Smith, stm., U.S.	D3	123
Smith, stm., Mt., U.S.	D5	103
Smith and Sayles Reservoir, res., R.I., U.S.	B2	116
Smith Bay, b., Ak., U.S.	A9	79
Smith Canyon, val., Co., U.S.	D7	83
Smith Center, Ks., U.S.	C5	93
Smithers, B.C., Can.	B4	69
Smithers, W.V., U.S.	C3	125
Smithfield, N.C., U.S.	B4	110
Smithfield, Pa., U.S.	G2	115
Smithfield, Ut., U.S.	B4	121
Smithfield, Va., U.S.	D6	123
Smith Island, i., U.S.	D5	97
Smith Island, i., Va., U.S.	C7	123
Smith Mountain Lake, res., Va., U.S.	C3	123
Smith Peak, mtn., Id., U.S.	A2	89
Smith Point, c., Ma., U.S.	D7	98
Smith Point, c., Va., U.S.	C6	123
Smiths, Al., U.S.	C4	78
Smithsburg, Md., U.S.	A2	97
Smiths Falls, Ont., Can.	C8	73
Smiths Grove, Ky., U.S.	C3	94
Smithton, Austl.	H9	50
Smithton, Il., U.S.	E4	90
Smithtown, N.Y., U.S.	n15	109
Smithville, Ga., U.S.	E2	87
Smithville, Ms., U.S.	A5	101
Smithville, Mo., U.S.	B3	102
Smithville, Oh., U.S.	B4	112
Smithville, Tn., U.S.	D8	119
Smithville, Tx., U.S.	D4	120
Smithville Lake, res., Mo., U.S.	B3	102
Smoke Creek Desert, des., Nv., U.S.	C2	105
Smokey, Cape, c., N.S., Can.	C9	71
Smokey Dome, mtn., Id., U.S.	F4	89
Smoky, stm., Alta., Can.	B1	68
Smoky Hill, stm., U.S.	D5	93
Smoky Lake, Alta., Can.	B4	68
Smoky Mountains, mts., Id., U.S.	F4	89
Smolensk, Russia	G15	18
Smooth Rock Falls, Ont., Can.	o19	73
Smoothstone Lake, l., Sask., Can.	C2	75
Smyrna, De., U.S.	C3	85
Smyrna, Ga., U.S.	C2	87
Smyrna, Tn., U.S.	B5	119
Smyrna, stm., De., U.S.	C3	85
Smyth, co., Va., U.S.	f10	123
Smythe, Mount, mtn., B.C., Can.	E8	66
Snake, stm., U.S.	B5	100
Snake, stm., Mn., U.S.	B1	100
Snake, stm., Ne., U.S.	B4	104
Snake Range, mts., Nv., U.S.	E7	105
Snake River Plain, pl., Id., U.S.	F2	89
Snake River Range, mts., U.S.	C2	127
Sneads, Fl., U.S.	B2	86
Sneedville, Tn., U.S.	C10	119
Sneek, Neth.	B5	8
Snipe Keys, is., Fl., U.S.	H5	86
Snohomish, Wa., U.S.	B3	124
Snohomish, co., Wa., U.S.	A4	124
Snoqualmie, Wa., U.S.	B4	124
Snoqualmie, stm., Wa., U.S.	B4	124
Snoqualmie Pass, Wa., U.S.	B4	124
Snowbank Lake, l., Mn., U.S.	B7	100
Snowdon, mtn., Wales, U.K.	H8	7
Snowdonia National Park, Wales, U.K.	I9	7
Snowdrift, N.W. Ter., Can.	D10	66
Snowflake, Az., U.S.	C5	80
Snow Hill, Md., U.S.	D7	97
Snow Hill, N.C., U.S.	B5	110
Snowking Mountain, mtn., Wa., U.S.	A4	124
Snow Lake, Man., Can.	B1	70
Snowmass Mountain, mtn., Co., U.S.	B3	83
Snow Peak, mtn., Wa., U.S.	A7	124
Snowshoe Lake, l., Me., U.S.	B4	96
Snowshoe Peak, mtn., Mt., U.S.	B1	103
Snow Water Lake, l., Nv., U.S.	C7	105
Snowyside Peak, mtn., Id., U.S.	F4	89
Snyder, Ok., U.S.	C3	113
Snyder, Tx., U.S.	C2	120
Snyder, co., Pa., U.S.	E7	115
Soacha, Col.	E5	58
Soalala, Madag.	E9	44
Soap Lake, Wa., U.S.	B6	124
Sobat, stm., Sudan	G12	42
Sobinka, Russia	F23	18
Sobral, Braz.	D10	54
Socastee, S.C., U.S.	D9	117
Sochi see Soči, Russia	I5	22
Soči, Russia	I5	22
Social Circle, Ga., U.S.	C3	87
Society Hill, S.C., U.S.	B8	117
Socorro, Col.	D6	58
Socorro, N.M., U.S.	C3	108
Socorro, co., N.M., U.S.	D2	108
Socorro, Isla, i., Mex.	H4	62
Socotra see Suqutrā, i., Yemen	F5	46
Soc Trang, Viet.	J8	34
Socuéllamos, Spain	F9	12
Sodankylä, Fin.	C16	6
Soda Springs, Id., U.S.	G7	89
Soddy-Daisy, Tn., U.S.	D8	119
Söderhamn, Swe.	F11	6
Södertälje, Swe.	G11	6
Sodo, Eth.	G2	46
Sodus, N.Y., U.S.	B3	109
Soest, Ger.	D8	8
Sofia, stm., Madag.	E9	44
Sofia see Sofija, Bul.	G7	16
Sofija (Sofia), Bul.	G7	16
Sogamoso, Col.	E6	58
Sognafjorden, Nor.	F5	6
Søgne, Nor.	G6	6
Soignies, Bel.	E4	8
Sointula, B.C., Can.	D4	69
Soissons, Fr.	C10	10
Sökal'skogo, Proliv, strt., Russia	B14	24
Söke, Tur.	L11	16
Sokodé, Togo	G6	42
Sokol, Russia	C19	24
Sokol, Russia	B23	18
Sokoto, Nig.	F7	42
Sol, Costa del, Spain	I7	12
Solana, Fl., U.S.	F5	86
Solano, Phil.	p19	33b
Solano, co., Ca., U.S.	C3	82
Solbad Hall in Tirol, Aus.	H11	8
Soldier, stm., Ia., U.S.	C2	92
Soldier Key, i., Fl., U.S.	s3	86
Soldotna, Ak., U.S.	g16	79
Soledad, Col.	B5	58
Soledad, Ca., U.S.	D3	82
Soledad, Ven.	C11	58
Soleduck, stm., Wa., U.S.	B1	124
Solingen, Ger.	D7	8
Sollefteå, Swe.	E11	6
Sollentuna, Swe.	G11	6
Sóller, Spain	F14	12
Solnečnogorsk, Russia	E19	18
Sologoncy, Russia	D16	24
Solok, Indon.	O6	34
Solomon, Ks., U.S.	D6	93
Solomon, stm., Ks., U.S.	C6	93
Solomon Islands, ctry., Oc.	G23	2
Solomons, Md., U.S.	D5	97
Solomon Sea, Oc.	A10	50
Solon, Ia., U.S.	C6	92
Solon, Oh., U.S.	A4	112
Solothurn, Switz.	E14	10
Solsona, Spain	D13	12
Soltau, Ger.	C9	8
Solvay, N.Y., U.S.	B4	109
Solwezi, Zam.	D5	44
Soma, Tur.	J11	16
Somalia, ctry., Afr.	G4	46
Sombor, Yugo.	D3	16
Sombrerete, Mex.	F8	62
Somerdale, N.J., U.S.	D2	107
Somers, Ct., U.S.	B6	84
Somers, Mt., U.S.	B2	103
Somerset, Man., Can.	E2	70
Somerset, Ky., U.S.	C5	94
Somerset, Ma., U.S.	C5	98
Somerset, N.J., U.S.	B3	107
Somerset, Oh., U.S.	C3	112
Somerset, Pa., U.S.	F3	115
Somerset, Tx., U.S.	k7	120
Somerset, Wi., U.S.	C1	126
Somerset, co., Me., U.S.	C2	96
Somerset, co., Md., U.S.	D6	97
Somerset, co., N.J., U.S.	B3	107
Somerset, co., Pa., U.S.	G3	115
Somerset Island, i., N.W. Ter., Can.	B14	66
Somerset Reservoir, res., Vt., U.S.	E3	122
Somers Point, N.J., U.S.	E3	107
Somersville, Ct., U.S.	B6	84
Somersworth, N.H., U.S.	D5	106
Somerton, Az., U.S.	E1	80
Somervell, co., Tx., U.S.	C4	120
Somerville, Ma., U.S.	B5	98
Somerville, N.J., U.S.	B3	107
Somerville, Tn., U.S.	B2	119
Somerville, Tx., U.S.	D4	120
Somerville Lake, res., Tx., U.S.	D4	120
Someş (Szamos), stm., Eur.	B6	16
Sömmerda, Ger.	D11	8
Somonauk, Il., U.S.	B5	90
Somoto, Nic.	H4	64
Son, stm., India	H10	38
Sønderborg, Den.	I7	6
Sondershausen, Ger.	D10	8
Søndre Strømfjord, Grnld.	C22	66
Sondrio, Italy	C4	14
Song Cau, Viet.	H10	34
Songhua, stm., China	B12	26
Songjiang, China	D10	28
Songkhla, Thai.	K6	34
Songnim, N. Kor.	D12	26
Sonīpat, India	F7	38
Son La, Viet.	D7	34
Sonmiāni Bay, b., Pak.	H2	38
Sonneberg, Ger.	E11	8
Sonoita, Mex.	B3	62
Sonoma, Ca., U.S.	C2	82
Sonoma, co., Ca., U.S.	C2	82
Sonoma Peak, mtn., Nv., U.S.	C4	105
Sonoma Range, mts., Nv., U.S.	C4	105
Sonora, Ca., U.S.	D3	82
Sonora, Tx., U.S.	D2	120
Sonora, stm., Mex.	C4	62
Sonseca, Spain	F8	12
Sonsón, Col.	E5	58
Sonsonate, El Sal.	H3	64
Sonsorol Islands, is., T.T.P.I.	D9	32
Son Tay, Viet.	D8	34
Sonthofen, Ger.	H10	8
Soochow see Suzhou, China	D9	28
Soperton, Ga., U.S.	D4	87
Sophia, W.V., U.S.	D3	125
Sopot, Pol.	A18	8
Sopron, Hung.	H16	8
Sopur, India	C6	38
Sora, Italy	H8	14
Sore, Fr.	H6	10
Sorel, Que., Can.	C4	74
Sorgono, Italy	I4	14
Sorgues, Fr.	H11	10
Soria, Spain	D9	12
Sorocaba, Braz.	G5	57
Sorong, Indon.	F9	32
Soroti, Ug.	H12	42
Sorrento, Italy	I9	14
Sorrento, La., U.S.	D4	95
Sorsele, Swe.	D11	6
Sorsogon, Phil.	C7	32
Sort, Spain	C13	12
Sorūbī, Afg.	C3	38
Sos del Rey Católico, Spain	C10	12
Sosnovo-Oz'orskoje, Russia	G16	24
Sosnowiec, Pol.	E19	8
Šoštanj, Slo.	C10	14
Sotkamo, Fin.	D17	6
Soto la Marina, Mex.	F10	62
Sotteville, Fr.	C8	10
Soucook, stm., N.H., U.S.	D4	106
Soudan, Mn., U.S.	C6	100
Souderton, Pa., U.S.	F11	115
Souhegan, stm., N.H., U.S.	E3	106
Souillac, Fr.	H8	10
Soŭl (Seoul), S. Kor.	D12	26
Soulac-sur-Mer, Fr.	G5	10
Souris, Man., Can.	E1	70
Souris, P.E.I., Can.	C7	71
Sousa, Braz.	E11	54
Sousse, Tun.	N5	14
South, stm., N.C., U.S.	C4	110
South Acton, Ma., U.S.	g9	98
South Africa, ctry., Afr.	G5	44
South America	E4	53
South Amherst, Ma., U.S.	B2	98
South Amherst, Oh., U.S.	A3	112
South Amboy, N.J., U.S.	C4	107
South Andaman, i., India	I2	34
South Anna, stm., Va., U.S.	C5	123
South Aulatsivik Island, i., Newf., Can.	E20	66
South Australia, state, Austl.	F7	50
Southaven, Ms., U.S.	A3	101
South Bald Mountain, mtn., Co., U.S.	A5	83
South Baldy, mtn., N.M., U.S.	D2	108
South Barre, Vt., U.S.	C3	122
South Bay, Fl., U.S.	F6	86
South Beloit, Il., U.S.	A4	90
South Bend, In., U.S.	A5	91
South Bend, Wa., U.S.	C2	124
South Berwick, Me., U.S.	E2	96
South Bloomfield, Oh., U.S.	C3	112
South Boston, Va., U.S.	D4	123
South Bound Brook, N.J., U.S.	B3	107
South Branch Lake, l., Me., U.S.	C4	96
Southbridge, Ma., U.S.	B3	98
South Bristol, Me., U.S.	E3	96
South Britain, Ct., U.S.	D3	84
South Broadway, Wa., U.S.	C5	124
South Bruny, i., Austl.	H9	50
South Burlington, Vt., U.S.	C2	122
Southbury, Ct., U.S.	D3	84
South Carolina, state, U.S.	D6	117
South Charleston, Oh., U.S.	C2	112
South Charleston, W.V., U.S.	C3	125
South Chicago Heights, Il., U.S.	m9	90
South China Sea, Asia	C5	32
South Coffeyville, Ok., U.S.	A6	113
South Congaree, S.C., U.S.	D5	117
South Connellsville, Pa., U.S.	G2	115
South Dakota, state, U.S.	C5	118
South Dartmouth, Ma., U.S.	C6	98
South Daytona, Fl., U.S.	C5	86
South Deerfield, Ma., U.S.	B2	98
South Dennis, Ma., U.S.	C7	98
South Duxbury, Ma., U.S.	B6	98
South East Cape, c., Austl.	H9	50
Southeast Cape, c., Ak., U.S.	C6	79
South Easton, Ma., U.S.	B5	98
Southeast Pass, strt., La., U.S.	E7	95
Southeast Point, c., R.I., U.S.	h7	116
South Elgin, Il., U.S.	B5	90
Southend-on-Sea, Eng., U.K.	J13	7
Southern Alps, mts., N.Z.	E3	52
Southern Cross, Austl.	F3	50
Southern Indian Lake, l., Man., Can.	f8	70
Southern Pines, N.C., U.S.	B3	110
Southern Ute Indian Reservation, Co., U.S.	D2	83
South Euclid, Oh., U.S.	g9	112
Southey, Sask., Can.	G3	75
South Fabius, stm., Mo., U.S.	A5	102
South Fallsburg, N.Y., U.S.	D6	109
Southfield, Mi., U.S.	o15	99
South Fork, Pa., U.S.	F4	115
South Fox Island, i., Mi., U.S.	C5	99
South Fulton, Tn., U.S.	A3	119
South Gastonia, N.C., U.S.	B1	110
South Gate, Ca., U.S.	n12	82
Southgate, Ky., U.S.	h14	94
Southgate, Mi., U.S.	p15	99
South Georgia, i., Falk. Is.	G9	56
South Glastonbury, Ct., U.S.	C5	84
South Glens Falls, N.Y., U.S.	B7	109
South Grafton, Ma., U.S.	B4	98
South Grand, stm., Mo., U.S.	C3	102
South Hadley, Ma., U.S.	B2	98
South Hadley Falls, Ma., U.S.	B2	98
South Hamilton, Ma., U.S.	A6	98
South Haven, In., U.S.	A3	91
South Haven, Mi., U.S.	F4	99
South Henik Lake, l., N.W. Ter., Can.	D13	66
South Hero Island, i., Vt., U.S.	B2	122
South Hill, Va., U.S.	D4	123
South Hingham, Ma., U.S.	h12	98
South Holland, Il., U.S.	k9	90
South Holston Lake, res., U.S.	A9	119
South Hooksett, N.H., U.S.	D4	106
South Hopkinton, R.I., U.S.	F1	116
South Houston, Tx., U.S.	r14	120
South Hutchinson, Ks., U.S.	f11	93
South Indian Lake, Man., Can.	A2	70
Southington, Ct., U.S.	C4	84
South International Falls, Mn., U.S.	B5	100
South Island, i., N.Z.	E3	52
South Island, i., S.C., U.S.	E9	117
South Jacksonville, Il., U.S.	D3	90
South Jordan, Ut., U.S.	C3	121
South Kenosha, Wi., U.S.	F6	126
South Lake Tahoe, Ca., U.S.	C4	82
South Lancaster, Ma., U.S.	B4	98
South Laurel, Md., U.S.	*B4	97
South Lebanon, Oh., U.S.	C1	112
South Lyon, Mi., U.S.	F7	99
South Magnetic Pole	C26	47
South Manitou Island, i., Mi., U.S.	C4	99
South Marsh Island, i., Md., U.S.	D5	97
South Miami, Fl., U.S.	G6	86
South Miami Heights, Fl., U.S.	s13	86
South Mills, N.C., U.S.	A6	110
South Milwaukee, Wi., U.S.	F6	126
Southmont, N.C., U.S.	B2	110
South Moose Lake, l., Man., Can.	C1	70
South Mountain, mtn., Id., U.S.	G2	89
South Mountain, mtn., N.M., U.S.	k8	108
South Mountains, mts., Az., U.S.	m8	80
South Mountains, mts., N.C., U.S.	B1	110
South Nahanni, stm., N.W. Ter., Can.	D7	66
South New River Canal, Fl., U.S.	r3	86
South Ogden, Ut., U.S.	B4	121
Southold, N.Y., U.S.	m16	109
South Orange, N.J., U.S.	B4	107
South Orkney Islands, is., B.A.T.	C8	47
South Paris, Me., U.S.	D2	96
South Park, val., Co., U.S.	B5	83
South Pass, Wy., U.S.	D4	127
South Pass, strt., La., U.S.	F6	95
South Patrick Shores, Fl., U.S.	D6	86
South Pekin, Il., U.S.	C4	90
South Pittsburg, Tn., U.S.	D8	119
South Plainfield, N.J., U.S.	B4	107
South Platte, stm., U.S.	C6	76
South Point, c., Mi., U.S.	D7	99
South Pole, Ant.	A12	47
Southport, Eng., U.K.	H9	7
Southport, Fl., U.S.	u16	86
Southport, In., U.S.	E5	91
Southport, N.Y., U.S.	C4	109
Southport, N.C., U.S.	D4	110
South Portland, Me., U.S.	E2	96
South Portsmouth, Ky., U.S.	B6	94
South Range, Mi., U.S.	A2	99
South River, Ont., Can.	B5	73

Name	Map Ref	Page
South River, N.J., U.S.	C4	107
South River, b., Md., U.S.	C4	97
South Ronaldsay, i., Scot., U.K.	C10	7
South Royalton, Vt., U.S.	D3	122
South Saint Paul, Mn., U.S.	n12	100
South Sandwich Islands, is., Falk. Is.	D10	47
South San Francisco, Ca., U.S.	h8	82
South Saskatchewan, stm., Can.	F11	66
South Shetland Islands, is., B.A.T.	C7	47
South Shields, Eng., U.K.	F11	7
Southside, Al., U.S.	B3	78
Southside Place, Tx., U.S.	r14	120
South Sioux City, Ne., U.S.	B9	104
South Skunk, stm., Ia., U.S.	C4	92
South Streator, Il., U.S.	B5	90
South Toms River, N.J., U.S.	D4	107
South Torrington, Wy., U.S.	D8	127
South Tucson, Az., U.S.	E5	80
South Valley Stream, N.Y., U.S.	*n15	109
South Venice, Fl., U.S.	E4	86
South Ventana Cone, vol., Ca., U.S.	D3	82
South Waverly, Pa., U.S.	C8	115
South Wellfleet, Ma., U.S.	C8	98
South Wellington, B.C., Can.	f12	69
South West Africa see Namibia, ctry., Afr.	F3	44
South Westbury, N.Y., U.S.	*n15	109
South West Cape, c., Austl.	H9	50
Southwest Channel, strt., Fl., U.S.	E4	86
Southwest City, Mo., U.S.	E3	102
Southwest Harbor, Me., U.S.	D4	96
Southwest Head, c., N.B., Can.	E3	71
Southwest Miramichi, stm., N.B., Can.	C3	71
Southwest Pass, strt., La., U.S.	E3	95
Southwest Pass, strt., La., U.S.	F6	95
Southwest Point, c., R.I., U.S.	h7	116
South Weymouth Naval Air Station, mil., Ma., U.S.	h12	98
South Whitley, In., U.S.	B6	91
South Williamson, Ky., U.S.	C7	94
South Williamsport, Pa., U.S.	D7	115
South Windham, Ct., U.S.	C7	84
South Windham, Me., U.S.	E2	96
South Windsor, Ct., U.S.	B5	84
Southwood, Co., U.S.	*B6	83
Southwood Acres, Ct., U.S.	A5	84
South Woodstock, Ct., U.S.	B8	84
South Yarmouth, Ma., U.S.	C7	98
South Zanesville, Oh., U.S.	C3	112
Sovetsk (Tilsit), Russia	F4	18
Sovetskaja Gavan', Russia	H22	24
Spa, Bel.	E5	8
Spain, ctry., Eur.	G7	4
Spalding, co., Ga., U.S.	C2	87
Spanaway, Wa., U.S.	B3	124
Spangler, Pa., U.S.	E4	115
Spaniard's Bay, Newf., Can.	E5	72
Spanish Fork, Ut., U.S.	C4	121
Spanish Fort, Al., U.S.	E2	78
Spanish Lake, Mo., U.S.	f13	102
Spanish North Africa, dep., Afr.	A4	42
Spanish Peak, mtn., Or., U.S.	C7	114
Spanish Sahara see Western Sahara, dep., Afr.	D3	42
Spanish Town, Jam.	E9	64
Sparks, Ga., U.S.	E3	87
Sparks, Nv., U.S.	D2	105
Sparta, Ga., U.S.	C4	87
Sparta, Il., U.S.	E4	90
Sparta, Mi., U.S.	E5	99
Sparta, Mo., U.S.	D4	102
Sparta (Lake Mohawk), N.J., U.S.	A3	107
Sparta, N.C., U.S.	A1	110
Sparta, Tn., U.S.	D8	119
Sparta, Wi., U.S.	E3	126
Spartanburg, S.C., U.S.	B4	117
Spartanburg, co., S.C., U.S.	B3	117
Sparta see Spárti, Grc.	L6	16
Spartel, Cap, c., Mor.	L6	16
Spárti (Sparta), Grc.	L6	16
Spartivento, Capo, c., Italy	K3	14
Sparwood, B.C., Can.	E10	69
Spassk-Dal'nij, Russia	I20	24
Spavinaw Creek, stm., Ok., U.S.	A7	113
Spear, Cape, c., Newf., Can.	E5	72
Spearfish, S.D., U.S.	C2	118
Spearman, Tx., U.S.	A2	120
Spearville, Ks., U.S.	E4	93
Speed, In., U.S.	H6	91
Speedway, In., U.S.	E5	91
Spence Bay, N.W. Ter., Can.	C14	66
Spencer, In., U.S.	F4	91
Spencer, Ia., U.S.	A2	92
Spencer, Ma., U.S.	B4	98
Spencer, N.C., U.S.	B2	110
Spencer, Tn., U.S.	D8	119
Spencer, W.V., U.S.	C3	125
Spencer, Wi., U.S.	D3	126
Spencer, co., In., U.S.	H4	91
Spencer, co., Ky., U.S.	B4	94
Spencer, Cape, c., Ak., U.S.	k21	79
Spencer Gulf, b., Austl.	F7	50
Spencer Lake, l., Me., U.S.	C2	96
Spencerport, N.Y., U.S.	B3	109
Spencerville, Md., U.S.	B4	97
Spencerville, Oh., U.S.	B1	112
Sperry, Ok., U.S.	A6	113
Spesutie Island, i., Md., U.S.	B5	97
Spey, stm., Scot., U.K.	D9	7
Speyer, Ger.	F8	8
Spiceland, In., U.S.	E7	91
Spicer, Mn., U.S.	E4	100
Spider Lake, l., Wi., U.S.	B2	126
Spindale, N.C., U.S.	B1	110
Spink, co., S.D., U.S.	C7	118
Spirit Lake, Id., U.S.	B2	89
Spirit Lake, Ia., U.S.	A2	92
Spirit Lake, l., Ia., U.S.	A2	92
Spirit Lake, l., Wa., U.S.	C3	124
Spirit River, Alta., Can.	B1	68
Spirit River Flowage, res., Wi., U.S.	C4	126
Spiro, Ok., U.S.	B7	113
Spittal an der Drau, Aus.	I13	8
Spitz, Aus.	G15	8
Split, Cro.	F11	14
Split, Cape, c., N.S., Can.	D5	71
Split Lake, l., Man., Can.	A4	70
Split Rock Creek, stm., U.S.	G2	100
Splügen, Switz.	F16	10
Spofford Lake, l., N.H., U.S.	E2	106
Spokane, Wa., U.S.	B8	124
Spokane, co., Wa., U.S.	B8	124
Spokane, stm., U.S.	B8	124
Spokane, Mount, mtn., Wa., U.S.	B8	124
Spokane Indian Reservation, Wa., U.S.	B8	124
Spoleto, Italy	G7	14
Spoon, stm., Il., U.S.	C3	90
Spooner, Wi., U.S.	C2	126
Spooner Lake, l., Wi., U.S.	C2	127
Spornoje, Russia	E24	24
Spotswood, N.J., U.S.	C4	107
Spotsylvania, co., Va., U.S.	B5	123
Sprague, W.V., U.S.	n13	125
Sprague, stm., Or., U.S.	E5	114
Sprague Lake, l., Wa., U.S.	B7	124
Spratly Island, i., Asia	D5	32
Spremberg, Ger.	A4	81
Spring, stm., Ar., U.S.	A4	81
Spring Arbor, Mi., U.S.	F6	99
Spring Bay, b., Ut., U.S.	B3	121
Springbok, S. Afr.	G3	44
Spring Brook, stm., Pa., U.S.	n18	115
Spring City, Pa., U.S.	F10	115
Spring City, Tn., U.S.	D9	119
Spring City, Ut., U.S.	D4	121
Spring Creek, stm., U.S.	D4	104
Spring Creek, stm., Nv., U.S.	C4	105
Spring Creek, stm., N.D., U.S.	B3	111
Springdale, Ar., U.S.	A1	81
Springdale, Oh., U.S.	n13	112
Springdale, Pa., U.S.	E2	115
Springdale, Pa., U.S.	D5	117
Springdale, S.C., U.S.	A5	108
Springer, N.M., U.S.	A5	108
Springerville, Az., U.S.	C6	80
Springfield, Co., U.S.	D8	83
Springfield, Fl., U.S.	u16	86
Springfield, Ga., U.S.	D5	87
Springfield, Il., U.S.	D4	90
Springfield, Ky., U.S.	C4	94
Springfield, Ma., U.S.	B2	98
Springfield, Mn., U.S.	F4	100
Springfield, Mo., U.S.	D4	102
Springfield, Ne., U.S.	C9	104
Springfield, N.J., U.S.	B4	107
Springfield, Oh., U.S.	C2	112
Springfield, Or., U.S.	C4	114
Springfield, Pa., U.S.	p20	115
Springfield, S.D., U.S.	E8	118
Springfield, Tn., U.S.	A5	119
Springfield, Vt., U.S.	E4	122
Springfield, W.V., U.S.	g12	125
Springfield, Lake, res., Il., U.S.	D4	90
Springfontein, S. Afr.	H5	44
Spring Garden, Guy.	D13	58
Spring Glen, Ut., U.S.	D5	121
Spring Green, Wi., U.S.	E3	126
Spring Grove, Il., U.S.	h8	90
Spring Grove, Mn., U.S.	G7	100
Spring Grove, Pa., U.S.	G8	115
Spring Hill, Fl., U.S.	D4	86
Spring Hill, Ks., U.S.	D9	93
Springhill, La., U.S.	A2	95
Spring Hill, Tn., U.S.	B5	119
Spring Hope, N.C., U.S.	B4	110
Spring Island, i., S.C., U.S.	G6	117
Spring Lake, Mi., U.S.	E4	99
Spring Lake, N.J., U.S.	C4	107
Spring Lake, N.C., U.S.	B4	110
Spring Lake, res., U.S.	B3	90
Spring Lake, l., Me., U.S.	C2	96
Spring Lake Heights, N.J., U.S.	C4	107
Spring Mountains, mts., Nv., U.S.	G6	105
Springport, Mi., U.S.	F6	99
Springs, S. Afr.	G5	44
Springside, Sask., Can.	F4	75
Springvale, Me., U.S.	E2	96
Springville, Ca., U.S.	o16	82
Springville, Ia., U.S.	B6	92
Springville, N.Y., U.S.	C2	109
Springville, Ut., U.S.	C4	121
Spruce Fork, stm., W.V., U.S.	m12	125
Spruce Grove, Alta., Can.	C4	68
Spruce Knob, mtn., W.V., U.S.	C6	125
Spruce Knob-Seneca Rocks National Recreation Area, W.V., U.S.	C5	125
Spruce Mountain, mtn., Az., U.S.	C3	80
Spruce Mountain, mtn., Nv., U.S.	C7	105
Spruce Pine, N.C., U.S.	f10	110
Spruce Run Reservoir, res., N.J., U.S.	B3	107
Spur, Tx., U.S.	C2	120
Spurr, Mount, mtn., Ak., U.S.	g15	79
Squam Lake, l., N.H., U.S.	C4	106
Squapan Lake, l., Me., U.S.	B4	96
Square Lake, l., Me., U.S.	A4	96
Squatec, Que., Can.	B9	74
Squaw Cap Mountain, mtn., N.B., Can.	B3	71
Squaw Hill, mtn., Wy., U.S.	E7	127
Squaw Peak, mtn., Ut., U.S.	C2	103
Squibnocket Point, c., Ma., U.S.	D6	98
Squinzano, Italy	I13	14
Squire, W.V., U.S.	D3	125
Sragen, Indon.	m15	33a
Sredninyj Chrebet, mts., Russia	F26	24
Srednekolymsk, Russia	D24	24
Srednerusskaja Vozvyšennost', plat., Russia	H20	18
Srednesibirskoje Ploskogorje, plat., Russia	D14	24
Sremska Mitrovica, Yugo.	E3	16
Sri Gangānagar, India	F5	38
Srīkākulam, India	C7	37
Sri Lanka, ctry., Asia	H5	36
Srīnagar, India	C6	38
Srīrampur, India	C3	37
Stack Reservoir, res., R.I., U.S.	C3	116
Stade, Ger.	B9	8
Stadthagen, Ger.	C9	8
Stafford, Eng., U.K.	I10	7
Stafford, Ks., U.S.	E5	93
Stafford, Tx., U.S.	r14	120
Stafford, Va., U.S.	B5	123
Stafford, co., Ks., U.S.	D5	93
Stafford, co., Va., U.S.	B5	123
Stafford Pond, l., R.I., U.S.	D6	116
Stafford Springs, Ct., U.S.	B6	84
Staked Plain see Estacado, Llano, pl., U.S.	E6	76
Stalheim, Nor.	F6	6
Stalingrad see Volgograd, Russia	H6	22
Stalowa Wola, Pol.	E22	8
Stambaugh, Mi., U.S.	B2	99
Stamford, Ct., U.S.	E1	84
Stamford, Tx., U.S.	C3	120
Stamford, Vt., U.S.	F2	122
Stamford, Lake, res., Tx., U.S.	C3	120
Stamping Ground, Ky., U.S.	B5	94
Stamps, Ar., U.S.	D2	81
Stanaford, W.V., U.S.	D3	125
Stanberry, Mo., U.S.	A3	102
Standerton, S. Afr.	G5	44
Standing Rock Indian Reservation, U.S.	B4	118
Standish, Mi., U.S.	E7	99
Stanfield, Az., U.S.	E3	80
Stanfield, Or., U.S.	B7	114
Stanford, Ky., U.S.	C5	94
Stanhope, N.J., U.S.	B3	107
Stanislaus, co., Ca., U.S.	D3	82
Stanke Dimitrov, Bul.	G7	16
Stanley, Falk. Is.	G5	56
Stanley, N.C., U.S.	B1	110
Stanley, N.D., U.S.	A3	111
Stanley, Va., U.S.	B4	123
Stanley, Wi., U.S.	D3	126
Stanley, co., S.D., U.S.	C5	118
Stanley Falls, wtfl, Zaire	A5	44
Stanleytown, Va., U.S.	D3	123
Stanleyville, N.C., U.S.	A2	110
Stanleyville see Kisangani, Zaire	A5	44
Stanly, co., N.C., U.S.	B2	110
Stann Creek, Belize	F3	64
Stanovoj Chrebet, mts., Russia	F19	24
Stanovoje Nagorje (Stanovoy Mountains), mts., Russia	F16	24
Stanstead, Que., Can.	D5	74
Stanton, Ia., U.S.	D2	92
Stanton, Ky., U.S.	C6	94
Stanton, Mi., U.S.	E5	99
Stanton, Ne., U.S.	C8	104
Stanton, Tx., U.S.	C2	120
Stanton, co., Ks., U.S.	E2	93
Stanton, co., Ne., U.S.	C8	104
Stantonsburg, N.C., U.S.	B5	110
Stanwood, Ia., U.S.	C6	92
Stanwood, Wa., U.S.	A3	124
Staples, Mn., U.S.	D4	100
Stapleton, Al., U.S.	E2	78
Star, Id., U.S.	F2	89
Star, N.C., U.S.	B3	110
Starachowice, Pol.	C14	18
Staraja Russa, Russia	D21	8
Stara Planina (Balkan Mountains), mts., Eur.	G8	16
Stara Zagora, Bul.	G9	16
Starbuck, Mn., U.S.	E3	100
Star City, Ar., U.S.	D4	81
Star City, W.V., U.S.	B5	125
Stargard Szczeciński (Stargard in Pommern), Pol.	B15	8
Stargo, Az., U.S.	D6	80
Stark, co., Il., U.S.	B4	90
Stark, co., N.D., U.S.	C3	111
Stark, co., Oh., U.S.	B4	112
Starke, Fl., U.S.	C4	86
Starke, co., In., U.S.	B4	91
Starks, La., U.S.	D2	95
Starkville, Ms., U.S.	B5	101
Star Lake, l., Mn., U.S.	D3	100
Starnberg, Ger.	G11	8
Starogard Gdański, Pol.	B18	8
Star Peak, mtn., Nv., U.S.	C3	105
Starr, co., Tx., U.S.	F3	120
Startex, S.C., U.S.	B3	117
Start Point, c., Eng., U.K.	K9	7
Startup, Wa., U.S.	B4	124
State Center, Ia., U.S.	B4	92
State College, Pa., U.S.	E6	115
Stateline, Nv., U.S.	E2	105
State Line, Pa., U.S.	G6	115
Staten Island, i., N.Y., U.S.	k12	109
Statenville, Ga., U.S.	F4	87
Statesboro, Ga., U.S.	D5	87
Statesville, N.C., U.S.	B2	110
Statham, Ga., U.S.	C3	87
Statue of Liberty National Monument, N.J., U.S.	k8	107
Staunton, Il., U.S.	D4	90
Staunton, Va., U.S.	B3	123
Stavanger, Nor.	G5	6
Stavropol', Russia	H6	22
Stayner, Ont., Can.	C4	73
Stayton, Or., U.S.	C4	114
Steamboat Mountain, mtn., Mt., U.S.	D2	105
Steamboat Mountain, mtn., Wy., U.S.	C4	103
Steamboat Springs, Co., U.S.	E4	127
Stearns, Ky., U.S.	A4	83
Stearns, co., Mn., U.S.	D5	94
	E4	100
Stearns Brook, stm., N.H., U.S.	A4	106
Stebbins, Ak., U.S.	C7	79
Steele, Mo., U.S.	B3	78
Steele, N.D., U.S.	E8	102
Steele, co., Mn., U.S.	C6	111
Steele, co., N.D., U.S.	F5	100
Steele, Mount, mtn., Wy., U.S.	B8	111
Steeleville, Il., U.S.	E6	127
Steelton, Pa., U.S.	E4	90
Steelville, Mo., U.S.	F8	115
Steenkool, Indon.	D6	102
Steens Mountain, mts., Or., U.S.	F9	32
Stefansson Island, i., N.W. Ter., Can.	E8	114
	B11	66
Steger, Il., U.S.	B6	90
Steilacoom, Wa., U.S.	f10	124
Steinbach, Man., Can.	E3	70
Steinhatchee, stm., Fl., U.S.	C3	86
Steinkjer, Nor.	D8	6
Stellenbosch, S. Afr.	H3	44
Stenay, Fr.	C12	10
Stendal, Ger.	C11	8
Stephen, Mn., U.S.	B2	100
Stephens, Ar., U.S.	D2	81
Stephens, co., Ga., U.S.	B3	87
Stephens, co., Ok., U.S.	C4	113
Stephens, co., Tx., U.S.	C3	120
Stephens City, Va., U.S.	A4	123
Stephens Lake, res., Man., Can.	A4	70
Stephenson, Mi., U.S.	C3	99
Stephenson, co., Il., U.S.	A4	90
Stephens Passage, strt., Ak., U.S.	m23	79
Stephenville, Newf., Can.	D2	72
Stephenville, Tx., U.S.	C3	120
Stephenville Crossing, Newf., Can.	D2	72
Sterling, Ak., U.S.	g16	79
Sterling, Co., U.S.	A7	83
Sterling, Il., U.S.	B4	90
Sterling, Ks., U.S.	D5	93
Sterling, Ok., U.S.	C3	113
Sterling, Va., U.S.	A5	123
Sterling, co., Tx., U.S.	D2	120
Sterling City, Tx., U.S.	D2	120
Sterling Heights, Mi., U.S.	o15	99
Sterling Reservoir, res., Co., U.S.	A7	83
Sterlington, La., U.S.	B3	95
Sterlitamak, Russia	G9	22
Stettin see Szczecin, Pol.	B14	8
Stettler, Alta., Can.	C4	68
Steuben, co., In., U.S.	A7	91
Steuben, co., N.Y., U.S.	C3	109
Steubenville, Oh., U.S.	B5	112
Stevenage, Eng., U.K.	J12	7
Stevens, co., Ks., U.S.	E3	100
Stevens, co., Mn., U.S.	E3	100
Stevens, co., Wa., U.S.	A7	124
Stevens Creek Dam, U.S.	C4	87
Stevenson, Al., U.S.	A4	78
Stevenson, Ct., U.S.	D3	84
Stevenson, Wa., U.S.	D4	124
Stevenson Lake, l., Man., Can.	C4	70
Stevens Pass, Wa., U.S.	B4	124
Stevens Peak, mtn., Id., U.S.	B3	89
Stevens Point, Wi., U.S.	D4	126
Stevensville, Md., U.S.	C5	97
Stevensville, Mi., U.S.	F4	99
Stevensville, Mt., U.S.	D2	103
Stewart, co., Ga., U.S.	D2	87
Stewart, co., Tn., U.S.	A4	119
Stewart Island, i., N.Z.	G1	52
Stewart Mountain, mtn., Az., U.S.	k9	80
Stewartstown, Pa., U.S.	G8	115
Stewartsville, Mo., U.S.	B3	102
Stewartville, Mn., U.S.	G6	100
Stewiacke, N.S., Can.	D6	71
Steyr, Aus.	G14	8
Stigler, Ok., U.S.	B6	113
Stigliano, Italy	I11	14
Stikine, stm., B.C., Can.	E7	66
Stikine, stm., Ak., U.S.	D13	79
Stikine Ranges, mts., B.C., Can.	E6	66
Still, stm., Ct., U.S.	B3	84
Stillaguamish, North Fork, stm., Wa., U.S.	A4	124
Stillaguamish, South Fork, stm., Wa., U.S.	A4	124
Stillhouse Hollow Lake, res., Tx., U.S.	D4	120
Stillman Valley, Il., U.S.	A4	90
Stillmore, Ga., U.S.	D4	87
Stillwater, Mn., U.S.	E6	100
Stillwater, Ok., U.S.	A4	113
Stillwater, co., Mt., U.S.	E7	103
Stillwater Range, mts., Nv., U.S.	D3	105
Stillwater Reservoir, res., N.Y., U.S.	B5	109
Stillwater Reservoir, res., R.I., U.S.	B3	116
Stilwell, Ok., U.S.	B7	113
Stimson, Mount, mtn., Mt., U.S.	B3	103
Stine Mountain, mtn., Mt., U.S.	E3	103
Stinking Lake, l., N.M., U.S.	A3	108
Stinnett, Tx., U.S.	B2	120
Štip, Mac.	H6	16
Stirling, Alta., Can.	E4	68
Stirling, Ont., Can.	C7	73
Stirling, Scot., U.K.	E9	7
Stjørdalshalsen, Nor.	E8	6
Stockbridge, Ga., U.S.	C2	87
Stockbridge, Mi., U.S.	F6	99
Stockbridge-Munsee Indian Reservation, Wi., U.S.	D5	126
Stockdale, Tx., U.S.	E4	120
Stockerau, Aus.	G16	8
Stockholm, Swe.	G12	6
Stockton, Ca., U.S.	D3	82
Stockton, Il., U.S.	A3	90
Stockton, Ks., U.S.	C4	93
Stockton, Md., U.S.	D7	97
Stockton, Mo., U.S.	D4	102
Stockton Island, i., Wi., U.S.	B3	126
Stockton Lake, res., Mo., U.S.	D4	102
Stoddard, Wi., U.S.	E2	126
Stoddard, co., Mo., U.S.	E8	102
Stoke-on-Trent, Eng., U.K.	H10	7
Stokes, co., N.C., U.S.	A2	110
Stokesdale, N.C., U.S.	A3	110
Stolbovoj, Ostrov, i., Russia	C21	24
Stollings, W.V., U.S.	n12	125
Ston, Cro.	G12	14
Stone, co., Ar., U.S.	B3	81
Stone, co., Ms., U.S.	E4	101
Stone, co., Mo., U.S.	E4	102
Stoneboro, Pa., U.S.	D1	115
Stone Corral Lake, l., Or., U.S.	C7	114
Stoneham, Ma., U.S.	g11	98
Stonehaven, Scot., U.K.	E10	7
Stone Mountain, Ga., U.S.	C2	87
Stone Mountain, mtn., Ga., U.S.	C2	87
Stones River National Battlefield, hist., Tn., U.S.	B4	119
Stoneville, N.C., U.S.	A3	110
Stonewall, Man., Can.	D3	70
Stonewall, La., U.S.	B2	95
Stonewall, Ms., U.S.	C5	101
Stonewall, co., Tx., U.S.	C2	120
Stonewood, W.V., U.S.	k10	125
Stoney Creek, Ont., Can.	D5	73
Stonington, Ct., U.S.	D8	84
Stonington, Il., U.S.	D4	90
Stonington, Me., U.S.	D4	96
Stono, stm., S.C., U.S.	k11	117
Stono Inlet, b., S.C., U.S.	F8	117
Stony Brook, N.Y., U.S.	n15	109
Stony Brook, stm., N.J., U.S.	C3	107
Stony Creek, stm., Va., U.S.	C5	123
Stony Island, i., N.Y., U.S.	B4	109
Stony Plain, Alta., Can.	C3	68
Stony Point, N.C., U.S.	B1	110
Storby, Fin.	E8	6
Støren, Nor.	E8	6
Storey, co., Nv., U.S.	D2	105
Storfors, Swe.	G10	6
Storkerson Peninsula, pen., N.W. Ter., Can.	B11	66
Storlien, Swe.	E9	6
Storm Lake, Ia., U.S.	B2	92
Storm Lake, l., Ia., U.S.	B2	92
Storm Mountain, mtn., Ak., U.S.	h16	79
Stornoway, Scot., U.K.	C6	7
Storrs, Ct., U.S.	B7	84
Storuman, Swe.	D11	6
Storvreta, Swe.	G11	6
Story, Wy., U.S.	B6	127
Story, co., Ia., U.S.	B4	92
Story City, Ia., U.S.	B4	92
Stoughton, Sask., Can.	H4	75
Stoughton, Ma., U.S.	B5	98
Stoughton, Wi., U.S.	F4	126
Stover, Mo., U.S.	C5	102
Stow, Oh., U.S.	A4	112
Stow Creek, stm., N.J., U.S.	E2	107
Stowe, Pa., U.S.	F10	115
Stowe, Vt., U.S.	C3	122
Stoyoma Mountain, mtn., B.C., Can.	E7	69
Strabane, Pa., U.S.	F1	115
Strafford, Mo., U.S.	D4	102
Strafford, co., N.H., U.S.	D4	106
Straffordville, Ont., Can.	E4	73
Strahan, Austl.	H9	50
Strakonice, Czech.	F13	8
Stralsund, Ger.	A13	8
Stranraer, Scot., U.K.	G7	7
Strasbourg, Fr.	D14	10
Strasburg, Co., U.S.	B6	83
Strasburg, Oh., U.S.	B4	112
Strasburg, Pa., U.S.	G9	115
Strasburg, Va., U.S.	B4	123
Stratford, Ont., Can.	D3	73
Stratford, Ct., U.S.	E3	84
Stratford, Ia., U.S.	B4	92
Stratford, N.J., U.S.	D2	107
Stratford, Ok., U.S.	C5	113
Stratford, Tx., U.S.	A1	120
Stratford, Wi., U.S.	D3	126
Stratford Point, c., Ct., U.S.	E3	84
Stratford-upon-Avon, Eng., U.K.	I11	7
Stratham, N.H., U.S.	D5	106
Strathmore, Alta., Can.	D4	68
Strathmore, Ca., U.S.	D4	82
Strathroy, Ont., Can.	E3	73
Stratton, Co., U.S.	B8	83
Straubing, Ger.	G12	8
Strausberg, Ger.	C13	8
Strawberry, stm., Ar., U.S.	A4	81
Strawberry, stm., Ut., U.S.	C5	121
Strawberry Mountain, mtn., Or., U.S.	C8	114
Strawberry Point, Ia., U.S.	B6	92
Strawberry Point, c., Ma., U.S.	B6	98
Strawberry Range, mts., Or., U.S.	C8	114
Strawberry Reservoir, res., Ut., U.S.	C4	121
Streator, Il., U.S.	B5	90
Stretensk, Russia	G17	24
Strickland, stm., Pap. N. Gui.	m15	50a
Strimón (Struma), stm., Eur.	I7	16
Strmec (Struma), stm., Eur.	C9	7
Stromness, Scot., U.K.	C8	104
Stromsburg, Ne., U.S.	G8	6
Strömstad, Swe.	E10	6
Strömsund, Swe.	D3	81
Strong, Ar., U.S.	D2	96
Strong, Me., U.S.	C4	101
Strong, stm., Ms., U.S.	D7	93
Strong City, Ks., U.S.	C3	90
Stronghurst, Il., U.S.	A4	112
Strongsville, Oh., U.S.	B10	7
Stronsay, i., Scot., U.K.	B5	113
Stroud, Ok., U.S.	E11	115
Stroudsburg, Pa., U.S.	g7	96
Stroudwater, stm., Me., U.S.	D2	126
Strum, Wi., U.S.	H7	16
Struma (Strimón), stm., Eur.	I7	7
Strumble Head, c., Wales, U.K.	H6	16
Strumica, Mac.	E21	8
Strunino, Russia	A5	112
Struthers, Oh., U.S.	A1	112
Stryker, Oh., U.S.	E6	86
Stuart, Fl., U.S.		

Name	Map Ref	Page
Stuart, Ia., U.S.	C3	92
Stuart, Ne., U.S.	B6	104
Stuart, Va., U.S.	D2	123
Stuart, Mount, mtn., Wa., U.S.	B5	124
Stuart Lake, l., B.C., Can.	B5	69
Stuarts Draft, Va., U.S.	B3	123
Stull, stm., Can.	B5	70
Stump Lake, l., N.D., U.S.	B7	111
Stump Pond, res., R.I., U.S.	D2	116
Stung Treng, Camb.	H8	34
Stupino, Russia	G21	18
Sturbridge, Ma., U.S.	B3	98
Sturgeon, Mo., U.S.	B5	102
Sturgeon, stm., Mi., U.S.	B4	99
Sturgeon Bay, Wi., U.S.	D6	126
Sturgeon Bay, b., Man., Can.	C3	70
Sturgeon Falls, Ont., Can.	A5	73
Sturgeon Lake, l., Ont., Can.	C6	73
Sturgis, Sask., Can.	F4	75
Sturgis, Ky., U.S.	e10	94
Sturgis, Mi., U.S.	G5	99
Sturgis, S.D., U.S.	C2	118
Sturtevant, Wi., U.S.	F6	126
Stutsman, co., N.D., U.S.	B6	111
Stuttgart, Ger.	G9	8
Stuttgart, Ar., U.S.	C4	81
Suaita, Col.	D6	58
Subang, Indon.	m13	33a
Subansiri, stm., Asia	G16	38
Subiaco, Italy	H8	14
Sublette, Ks., U.S.	E3	93
Sublette, co., Wy., U.S.	D2	127
Sublett Range, mts., Id., U.S.	G6	89
Sublimity, Or., U.S.	C4	114
Subotica, Yugo.	C3	16
Sučan, Russia	I20	24
Sucarnoochee, stm., Al., U.S.	C1	78
Succasunna, N.J., U.S.	B3	107
Suceava, Rom.	B10	16
Süchbaatar, Mong.	A8	26
Suchumi, Geor.	I6	22
Sucre, Bol.	G5	54
Sucuaro, Col.	E8	58
Sudan, ctry., Afr.	F12	42
Sudan, reg., Afr.	F7	42
Sudbury, Ont., Can.	A4	73
Sudbury, Ma., U.S.	B5	98
Sudbury, stm., Ma., U.S.	B5	98
Sudbury Center, Ma., U.S.	g10	98
Sudbury Reservoir, res., Ma., U.S.	g10	98
Sudeten see Sudety, mts., Eur.	E15	8
Sudety, mts., Eur.	E15	8
Sue, stm., Sudan	G11	42
Sueca, Spain	F11	12
Suez see As-Suways, Egypt	C12	42
Suez Canal see Suways, Qanāt as-, Egypt	D3	40
Suffern, N.Y., U.S.	D6	109
Suffield, Ct., U.S.	B5	84
Suffolk, Va., U.S.	D6	123
Suffolk, co., Ma., U.S.	B5	98
Suffolk, co., N.Y., U.S.	n15	109
Sugar, stm., U.S.	F4	126
Sugar, stm., N.H., U.S.	D2	106
Sugar City, Id., U.S.	F7	89
Sugar Creek, Mo., U.S.	h11	102
Sugarcreek, Pa., U.S.	D2	115
Sugar Creek, stm., Oh., U.S.	C2	112
Sugar Creek, stm., Pa., U.S.	C8	115
Sugar Grove, Va., U.S.	D1	123
Sugar Hill, Ga., U.S.	B2	87
Sugar Island, i., Mi., U.S.	B6	99
Sugar Land, Tx., U.S.	E5	120
Sugarland Run, Va., U.S.	*A5	123
Sugar Loaf, Va., U.S.	C3	123
Sugarloaf Mountain, mtn., Mt., U.S.	C4	103
Sugar Notch, Pa., U.S.	n17	115
Suggi Lake, l., Sask., Can.	C4	75
Sugoj, stm., Russia	E25	24
Sūhār, Oman	D6	46
Suhl, Ger.	E10	8
Suiattle, stm., Wa., U.S.	A4	124
Suide, China	D9	26
Suihua, China	B12	26
Suining, China	E8	26
Suiping, China	B2	28
Suitland, Md., U.S.	C4	97
Suizhong, China	C11	26
Suja, Russia	E24	18
Sukabumi, Indon.	m13	32
Sukagawa, Japan	E13	30
Sukhumi see Suchumi, Geor.	I6	22
Sukkertoppen, Grnld.	C22	66
Sukkur, Pak.	G3	38
Sukumo, Japan	J5	30
Sula, Kepulauan, is., Indon.	F8	32
Sulaimān Range, mts., Pak.	F3	38
Sulawesi (Celebes), i., Indon.	F7	32
Sullana, Peru	D2	54
Sulligent, Al., U.S.	B1	78
Sullivan, Il., U.S.	D5	90
Sullivan, In., U.S.	F3	91
Sullivan, Mo., U.S.	C6	102
Sullivan, co., In., U.S.	F3	91
Sullivan, co., Mo., U.S.	A4	102
Sullivan, co., N.H., U.S.	D2	106
Sullivan, co., N.Y., U.S.	D6	109
Sullivan, co., Pa., U.S.	D9	115
Sullivan, co., Tn., U.S.	C11	119
Sullivan Lake, l., Alta., Can.	D5	68
Sullivans Island, S.C., U.S.	k12	117
Sully, Fr.	E9	10
Sully, Ia., U.S.	C5	92
Sully, co., S.D., U.S.	C5	118
Sulmona, Italy	G8	14
Sulphur, La., U.S.	D2	95
Sulphur, Ok., U.S.	C5	113
Sulphur, stm., U.S.	D2	81
Sulphur Spring Range, mts., Nv., U.S.	C5	105
Sulphur Springs, Tx., U.S.	C5	120
Sultan, Wa., U.S.	B4	124
Sultānpur, India	G10	38
Sulu Archipelago, is., Phil.	D7	32
Sulu Sea, Asia	D6	32
Sulzbach-Rosenberg, Ger.	F11	8
Sumas, Wa., U.S.	A3	124
Sumatera (Sumatra), i., Indon.	F3	32
Sumatra see Sumatera, i., Indon.	F3	32
Sumba, i., Indon.	G7	32
Sumbawa, i., Indon.	G6	32
Sumbawanga, Tan.	C6	44
Sumedang, Indon.	m13	33a
Sumen, Bul.	F10	16
Sumenep, Indon.	m16	33a
Sumgait, Azer.	I7	22
Sumiton, Al., U.S.	B2	78
Summerfield, N.C., U.S.	A3	110
Summerford, Newf., Can.	D4	72
Summer Island, i., Mi., U.S.	C4	99
Summer Lake, l., Or., U.S.	E6	114
Summerland, B.C., Can.	E8	69
Summers, co., W.V., U.S.	D4	125
Summersville, W.V., U.S.	C4	125
Summersville Lake, res., W.V., U.S.	C4	125
Summerton, S.C., U.S.	D7	117
Summertown, Tn., U.S.	B4	119
Summerville, Ga., U.S.	B1	87
Summerville, S.C., U.S.	E7	117
Summit, Il., U.S.	k9	90
Summit, Ms., U.S.	D3	101
Summit, N.J., U.S.	B4	107
Summit, Tn., U.S.	h11	119
Summit, co., Co., U.S.	B4	83
Summit, co., Oh., U.S.	A4	112
Summit, co., Ut., U.S.	C5	121
Summit Hill, Pa., U.S.	E10	115
Summit Lake, l., Ia., U.S.	C3	92
Summit Lake Indian Reservation, Nv., U.S.	B2	105
Summit Mountain, mtn., Nv., U.S.	D5	105
Summit Peak, mtn., Mi., U.S.	D4	83
Summitville, In., U.S.	D6	91
Sumner, Il., U.S.	E6	90
Sumner, Ia., U.S.	B5	92
Sumner, Wa., U.S.	B3	124
Sumner, co., Ks., U.S.	E6	93
Sumner, co., Tn., U.S.	A5	119
Sumner Lake, res., N.M., U.S.	C5	108
Sumner Dam, N.M., U.S.	C5	108
Sumner Strait, strt., Ak., U.S.	m23	79
Sumoto, Japan	H7	30
Šumperk, Czech.	F16	8
Sumrall, Ms., U.S.	D4	101
Šumšu, Ostrov, i., Russia	G25	24
Sumter, S.C., U.S.	D7	117
Sumter, co., Al., U.S.	C1	78
Sumter, co., Fl., U.S.	D4	86
Sumter, co., Ga., U.S.	D2	87
Sumter, co., S.C., U.S.	D7	117
Sumy, Ukr.	G4	22
Sun, stm., Mt., U.S.	C4	103
Sunagawa, Japan	p19	30a
Sunapee, N.H., U.S.	D2	106
Sunapee Lake, l., N.H., U.S.	D2	106
Sunbright, Tn., U.S.	C9	119
Sunbury, Oh., U.S.	B3	112
Sunbury, Pa., U.S.	E8	115
Sunchales, Arg.	C4	56
Sun City, Az., U.S.	k8	80
Suncook, N.H., U.S.	D4	106
Suncook, stm., N.H., U.S.	D4	106
Suncook Lakes, l., N.H., U.S.	D4	106
Sunda, Selat, strt., Indon.	G4	32
Sundance, Wy., U.S.	B8	127
Sundance Mountain, mtn., Wy., U.S.	B8	127
Sundarbans, reg., Asia	J13	38
Sunderland, Ont., Can.	C5	73
Sunderland, Eng., U.K.	G11	7
Sundown, Tx., U.S.	C1	120
Sundre, Alta., Can.	D3	68
Sundridge, Ont., Can.	B5	73
Sundsvall, Swe.	E11	6
Sunflower, Ms., U.S.	B3	101
Sunflower, co., Ms., U.S.	B3	101
Sunflower, Mount, mtn., Ks., U.S.	C2	93
Sungaidareh, Indon.	O6	34
Sungei Patani, Malay.	L6	34
Suniteyouqi, China	C9	26
Sunland Park, N.M., U.S.	F3	108
Sunlight Creek, stm., Wy., U.S.	B3	127
Sunman, In., U.S.	F7	91
Sunndalsøra, Nor.	E7	6
Sunnyside, Newf., Can.	E5	72
Sunnyside, Ut., U.S.	C5	124
Sunnyvale, Ca., U.S.	k8	82
Sun Prairie, Wi., U.S.	E4	126
Sunray, Tx., U.S.	A2	120
Sunrise Manor, Nv., U.S.	*G6	105
Sunset, La., U.S.	D3	95
Sunset, Ut., U.S.	B4	121
Sunset Beach, Hi., U.S.	f9	88
Sunset Crater National Monument, Az., U.S.	B4	80
Sunset Lake, l., Vt., U.S.	D2	122
Suntar, Russia	E17	24
Suntar-Chajata, Chrebet, mts., Russia	E22	24
Suntaug Lake, l., Ma., U.S.	f11	98
Sun Valley, Id., U.S.	F4	89
Sun Valley, Nv., U.S.	D2	105
Sunyani, Ghana	G5	42
Suō-nada, Japan	I4	30
Suonenjoki, Fin.	E16	6
Suordach, Russia	D20	24
Superior, Az., U.S.	D4	80
Superior, Mt., U.S.	C2	103
Superior, Ne., U.S.	D7	104
Superior, Wi., U.S.	B1	126
Superior, Wy., U.S.	E4	127
Superior, Lake, l., N.A.	B9	76
Superstition Mountains, mts., Az., U.S.	m10	80
Supetar, Cro.	F11	14
Suphan Buri, Thai.	G6	34
Suqian, China	B7	28
Suquamish, Wa., U.S.	B3	124
Suqutrā (Socotra), i., Yemen	F5	46
Sūr (Tyre), Leb.	C4	40
Sūr, Oman	D6	46
Sur, Point, c., Ca., U.S.	D3	82
Surabaya, Indon.	m16	32
Surakarta, Indon.	m15	32
Sūrān, Syria	B5	40
Surat, India	B2	37
Surat Thani (Ban Don), Thai.	J5	34
Surendranagar, India	I4	38
Surfside, Fl., U.S.	s13	86
Surfside Beach, S.C., U.S.	D10	117
Surgoinsville, Tn., U.S.	C11	119
Süri, India	I12	38
Surigao, Phil.	D8	32
Surin, Thai.	G7	34
Suriname, ctry., S.A.	C7	54
Surprise, Az., U.S.	k8	80
Surrey, N.D., U.S.	A4	111
Surry, co., N.C., U.S.	A2	110
Surry, co., Va., U.S.	C6	123
Surry Mountain Lake, res., N.H., U.S.	D2	106
Surt, Libya	B9	42
Surt, Khalīj, b., Libya	B9	42
Sürüç, Tur.	A6	40
Suruga-wan, b., Japan	H11	30
Susa, Italy	D2	14
Susanville, Ca., U.S.	B3	82
Susitna, stm., Ak., U.S.	C10	79
Susquehanna, Pa., U.S.	C10	115
Susquehanna, co., Pa., U.S.	C10	115
Susquehanna, stm., U.S.	A5	97
Susquehanna, West Branch, stm., Pa., U.S.	D5	115
Sussex, N.B., Can.	D4	71
Sussex, N.J., U.S.	A3	107
Sussex, Wi., U.S.	m11	126
Sussex, co., De., U.S.	F4	85
Sussex, co., N.J., U.S.	A3	107
Sussex, co., Va., U.S.	D5	123
Susurluk, Tur.	J12	16
Sutherland, S. Afr.	H4	44
Sutherland, Ia., U.S.	B2	92
Sutherland, Ne., U.S.	C4	104
Sutherlin, Or., U.S.	D3	114
Sutlej (Satluj) (Langqên), stm., Asia	F4	38
Sutter, co., Ca., U.S.	C3	82
Sutter Creek, Ca., U.S.	C3	82
Sutton, Que., Can.	D5	74
Sutton, Ne., U.S.	D8	104
Sutton, W.V., U.S.	C4	125
Sutton, co., Tx., U.S.	D2	120
Sutton Lake, res., W.V., U.S.	C4	125
Sutwik Island, i., Ak., U.S.	D8	79
Suur Munamägi, hill, Est.	D10	18
Suwa, Japan	F11	30
Suwałki, Pol.	A22	8
Suwanee, Ga., U.S.	B2	87
Suwannee, co., Fl., U.S.	B3	86
Suwannee, stm., U.S.	C4	86
Suwannee Sound, strt., Fl., U.S.	C3	86
Suways, Qanāt as- (Suez Canal), Egypt	D3	40
Suwŏn, S. Kor.	D12	26
Suxian, China	B5	28
Suzaka, Japan	F11	30
Suzhou (Soochow), China	D9	28
Suzuka, Japan	H9	30
Suzu-misaki, c., Japan	E10	30
Suzzara, Italy	D5	14
Svappavaara, Swe.	C13	6
Svartenhuk, pen., Grnld.	B22	66
Sv'atoj Nos, Mys, c., Russia	C22	24
Sveg, Swe.	E10	6
Svenljunga, Swe.	H9	6
Svensen, Or., U.S.	A3	114
Sverdlovsk see Jekaterinburg, Russia	F10	22
Svetlaja, Russia	H21	24
Svetlyj, Russia	F17	24
Svištov, Bul.	F9	16
Svobodnyj, Russia	G19	24
Svolvær, Nor.	B10	6
Swain, co., N.C., U.S.	f9	110
Swainsboro, Ga., U.S.	D4	87
Swakopmund, Nmb.	F2	44
Swampscott, Ma., U.S.	B6	98
Swan, stm., Can.	C1	70
Swan Creek, stm., Oh., U.S.	e6	112
Swan Falls, wtfl, Id., U.S.	F2	89
Swan Hill, Austl.	G8	50
Swan Hills, Alta., Can.	B3	68
Swan Islands, is., Hond.	F6	64
Swan Lake, l., Man., Can.	C1	70
Swan Lake, l., Me., U.S.	D4	96
Swan Lake, l., Ne., U.S.	C3	104
Swan Peak, mtn., Mt., U.S.	C3	103
Swan Range, mts., Mt., U.S.	C3	103
Swan River, Man., Can.	C1	70
Swansboro, N.C., U.S.	C5	110
Swansea, Wales, U.K.	J9	7
Swansea, Il., U.S.	E4	90
Swanson Lake, res., Ne., U.S.	D4	104
Swanton, Oh., U.S.	A2	112
Swanton, Vt., U.S.	B2	122
Swanzey Center, N.H., U.S.	E2	106
Swarthmore, Pa., U.S.	p20	115
Swartswood Lake, l., N.J., U.S.	A3	107
Swartz Creek, Mi., U.S.	F7	99
Swayzee, In., U.S.	C6	91
Swaziland, ctry., Afr.	G6	44
Swea City, Ia., U.S.	A3	92
Sweden, ctry., Eur.	C10	4
Sweeny, Tx., U.S.	r14	120
Sweet Grass, co., Mt., U.S.	E7	103
Sweet Home, Or., U.S.	C4	114
Sweetser, In., U.S.	C6	91
Sweet Springs, Mo., U.S.	C4	102
Sweetwater, Tn., U.S.	D9	119
Sweetwater, Tx., U.S.	C2	120
Sweetwater, co., Wy., U.S.	E3	127
Sweetwater, stm., Wy., U.S.	D4	127
Sweetwater Creek, Fl., U.S.	p10	86
Sweetwater Creek, stm., Ok., U.S.	B1	113
Swellendam, S. Afr.	H4	44
Swepsonville, N.C., U.S.	A3	110
Świdnica (Schweidnitz), Pol.	E16	8
Swift, co., Mn., U.S.	E3	100
Swift, stm., N.H., U.S.	B4	106
Swift Creek, stm., N.C., U.S.	B5	110
Swift Creek, stm., Va., U.S.	n17	123
Swift Creek Reservoir, res., Wa., U.S.	C3	124
Swift Diamond, stm., N.H., U.S.	g7	106
Swifton, Ar., U.S.	B4	81
Swinburne, Cape, c., N.W. Ter., Can.	B13	66
Swindon, Eng., U.K.	J11	7
Swinford, Ire.	H4	7
Swinomish Indian Reservation, Wa., U.S.	A3	124
Świnoujście (Swinemünde), Pol.	B14	8
Swisher, Ia., U.S.	C6	92
Swisher, co., Tx., U.S.	B2	120
Swissvale, Pa., U.S.	k14	115
Switzer, W.V., U.S.	D3	125
Switzerland, co., In., U.S.	G7	91
Switzerland, ctry., Eur.	F9	4
Swoyerville, Pa., U.S.	D10	115
Syalach, Russia	D18	24
Sycamore, Al., U.S.	B3	78
Sycamore, Il., U.S.	B5	90
Sycamore, Oh., U.S.	B2	112
Sycamore Creek, stm., W.V., U.S.	m13	125
Sydenham, Ont., Can.	C8	73
Sydney, Austl.	F10	50
Syke, Ger.	C8	8
Sykesville, Md., U.S.	B4	97
Sykesville, Pa., U.S.	D4	115
Sykkylven, Nor.	E6	6
Syktyvkar, Russia	E8	22
Sylacauga, Al., U.S.	B3	78
Sylhet, Bngl.	H14	38
Sylva, N.C., U.S.	f9	110
Sylvania, Al., U.S.	A4	78
Sylvania, Ga., U.S.	D5	87
Sylvania, Oh., U.S.	A2	112
Sylvan Lake, Alta., Can.	C3	68
Sylvan Lake, Mi., U.S.	o15	99
Sylvan Lake, l., In., U.S.	B7	91
Sylvan Pass, Wy., U.S.	B2	127
Sylvester, Ga., U.S.	E3	87
Sym, Russia	E11	24
Symmes Creek, stm., Oh., U.S.	D3	112
Symsonia, Ky., U.S.	f9	94
Syracuse, In., U.S.	B6	91
Syracuse, Ks., U.S.	E2	93
Syracuse, Ne., U.S.	D9	104
Syracuse, N.Y., U.S.	B4	109
Syracuse, Ut., U.S.	B3	121
Syrdarja (Syr Darya), stm., Asia	I11	22
Syria, ctry., Asia	B5	40
Syriam, Burma	F4	34
Syrian Desert see Shām, Bādiyat ash-, des., Asia	C6	40
Sysladobsis Lake, l., Me., U.S.	C4	96
Syzran', Russia	G7	22
Szamos (Someş), stm., Eur.	B6	16
Szczecin (Stettin), Pol.	B14	8
Szczecinek (Neustettin), Pol.	B16	8
Szeged, Hung.	I20	8
Székesfehérvár, Hung.	H18	8
Szentes, Hung.	I20	8
Szolnok, Hung.	H20	8
Szombathely, Hung.	H16	8

T

Name	Map Ref	Page
Taal, Lake, l., Phil.	r19	33b
Tabaco, Phil.	r20	33b
Tabarka, Tun.	M3	14
Tabatinga, Serra da, hills, Braz.	F10	54
Tabbys Peak, mtn., Ut., U.S.	C3	121
Tabelbala, Alg.	C5	42
Taber, Alta., Can.	E4	68
Tabernes de Valldigna, Spain	F11	12
Tablas Island, i., Phil.	C7	32
Table Head, c., Newf., Can.	B4	72
Table Mountain, mtn., Az., U.S.	E5	80
Table Rock Lake, res., U.S.	E4	102
Table Top, mtn., Az., U.S.	E3	80
Tabor, Russia	C24	24
Tabor, Ia., U.S.	D2	92
Tabora, Tan.	C6	44
Tabor City, N.C., U.S.	C4	110
Tabou, I.C.	H4	42
Tabrīz, Iran	J7	22
Tabūk, Sau. Ar.	C2	46
Tacámbaro de Codallos, Mex.	H9	62
Tachikawa, Japan	G12	30
Tacna, Peru	G4	54
Tacoma, Wa., U.S.	B3	124
Taconic Range, mts., U.S.	A1	98
Tacuarembó, Ur.	C5	56
Tacubaya, Mex.	C7	62
Tadjerouine, Tun.	N3	14
Tadoule Lake, l., Man., Can.	E13	66
Tadoussac, Que., Can.	A8	74
Tādpatri, India	E5	37
Taegu, S. Kor.	D12	26
Taejŏn, S. Kor.	D12	26
Tafalla, Spain	C10	12
Taft, Ca., U.S.	E4	82
Taft, Tx., U.S.	F4	120
Tagajō, Japan	D13	30
Taganrog, Russia	H5	22
Taglio di Po, Italy	D7	14
Taguatinga, Braz.	B5	57
Taguke, China	D11	38
Tagula Island, i., Pap. N. Gui.	B10	50
Tagus (Tejo) (Tajo), stm., Eur.	F3	12
Tahan, Gunong, mtn., Malay.	L7	34
Tahat, mtn., Alg.	D7	42
Tahlequah, Ok., U.S.	B7	113
Tahoe, Lake, l., U.S.	E1	105
Tahoe City, Ca., U.S.	C3	82
Tahoka, Tx., U.S.	C2	120
Taholah, Wa., U.S.	B1	124
Tahoua, Niger	F7	42
Tahquamenon, stm., Mi., U.S.	B5	99
Tahsis, B.C., Can.	E4	69
Tahtsa Peak, mtn., B.C., Can.	C4	69
T'aichung, Tai.	K9	28
T'aichunghsien, Tai.	K9	28
Taihape, N.Z.	C5	52
Tai Hu, l., China	D9	28
Tailai, China	B11	26
Tain, Scot., U.K.	D8	7
T'ainan, Tai.	L9	28
T'aipei, Tai.	J10	28
T'aipeihsien, Tai.	J10	28
Taiping, Malay.	L6	34
Taishun, China	H8	28
Taitao, Península de, pen., Chile	F2	56
T'aitung, Tai.	M10	28
Taivalkoski, Fin.	D17	6
Taiwan (T'aiwan), ctry., Asia	G11	26
Taiwan Strait, strt., Asia	K8	28
Taixian, China	C9	28
Taixing, China	C9	28
Taiyuan, China	D9	26
Taizhou, China	C8	28
Ta'izz, Yemen	F3	46
Tajikistan, ctry., Asia	J12	22
Tajitos, Mex.	B3	62
Tajmyr, Ozero, l., Russia	C14	24
Tajmyr, Poluostrov, pen., Russia	B14	24
Tajšet, Russia	F13	24
Tajumulco, Volcán, vol., Guat.	G2	64
Tak, Thai.	F5	34
Takada, Japan	E11	30
Takalar, Indon.	G6	32
Takamatsu, Japan	H7	30
Takaoka, Japan	F10	30
Takapuna, N.Z.	B5	52
Takasaki, Japan	F12	30
Takatsuki, Japan	H8	30
Takawa, Japan	I3	30
Takayama, Japan	F10	30
Takefu, Japan	G9	30
Takêv, Camb.	I8	34
Takijuq Lake, l., N.W. Ter., Can.	C10	66
Takikawa, Japan	p19	30a
Takla Lake, l., B.C., Can.	B5	69
Taklimakan Shamo, des., China	D3	26
Takoma Park, Md., U.S.	f8	97
Taku Glacier, Ak., U.S.	k22	79
Tala, Mex.	G8	62
Talagang, Pak.	D5	38
Talaimannar, Sri L.	H5	37
Talara, Peru	D2	54
Talarrubias, Spain	F6	12
Talasea, Pap. N. Gui.	m17	50a
Talaud, Kepulauan, is., Indon.	E8	32
Talavera de la Reina, Spain	F7	12
Talawdī, Sudan	F12	42
Talbot, co., Ga., U.S.	D2	87
Talbot, co., Md., U.S.	C5	97
Talbot Island, i., Fl., U.S.	B5	86
Talbot Lake, l., Man., Can.	B2	70
Talbotton, Ga., U.S.	D2	87
Talca, Chile	D2	56
Talcahuano, Chile	D2	56
Talent, Or., U.S.	E4	114
Taliabu, Pulau, i., Indon.	F7	32
Taliaferro, co., Ga., U.S.	C4	87
Talihina, Ok., U.S.	C6	113
Talkeetna Mountains, mts., Ak., U.S.	f17	79
Talladega, Al., U.S.	B3	78
Talladega, co., Al., U.S.	B3	78
Tallahassee, Fl., U.S.	B2	86
Tallahatchie, co., Ms., U.S.	B3	101
Tallahatchie, stm., Ms., U.S.	B3	101
Tallapoosa, Ga., U.S.	C1	87
Tallapoosa, co., Al., U.S.	C4	78
Tallapoosa, stm., Al., U.S.	C3	78
Tallassee, Al., U.S.	C4	78
Talleyville, De., U.S.	A3	85
Tallinn, Est.	B7	18
Tall Kalakh, Syria	B5	40
Tallmadge, Oh., U.S.	A4	112
Tall Tamir, Syria	A7	40
Tallulah, La., U.S.	B4	95
Tal'menka, Russia	G10	24
Talo, mtn., Eth.	F2	46
Tālogān, Afg.	B3	38
Talquin, Lake, res., Fl., U.S.	B2	86
Talu, Indon.	N5	34
Taluk, Indon.	O6	34
Tama, Ia., U.S.	C5	92
Tama, co., Ia., U.S.	B5	92
Tamale, Ghana	G5	42
Tamalpais, Mount, mtn., Ca., U.S.	h7	82
Tamana, Japan	J3	30
Tamanrasset, Alg.	D7	42
Tamaqua, Pa., U.S.	E10	115
Tamaroa, Il., U.S.	E4	90
Tamazula de Gordiano, Mex.	H8	62
Tamazunchale, Mex.	G10	62
Tambacounda, Sen.	F3	42
Tambohorano, Madag.	E8	44
Tambov, Russia	I24	18
Tambura, Sudan	G11	42
Tamchaket, Maur.	E3	42
Tamel Aike, Arg.	F2	56
Tamiahua, Laguna de, b., Mex.	G11	62
Tamiami Canal, Fl., U.S.	G6	86
Tamil Nadu, state, India	G5	37
Tam Ky, Viet.	G10	34
Tampa, Fl., U.S.	E4	86
Tampa Bay, b., Fl., U.S.	E4	86
Tampere, Fin.	F14	6
Tampico, Mex.	F11	62
Tampico, Il., U.S.	B4	90
Tamrida, Yemen	F5	46
Tamsagbulag, Mong.	B10	26
Tamworth, Austl.	F10	50

Name	Map Ref	Page
Tana, Nor.	A17	6
Tana, stm., Eur.	A16	6
Tana, stm., Kenya	B7	44
Tana, Lake, l., Eth.	F2	46
Tanabe, Japan	I8	30
Tanaga Island, i., Ak., U.S.	E4	79
Tanahjampea, Pulau, i., Indon.	G7	32
Tanami Desert, des., Austl.	C5	50
Tanana, Ak., U.S.	B9	79
Tanana, stm., Ak., U.S.	C10	79
Tananarive see Antananarivo, Madag.	E9	44
Tānda, India	G10	38
Tandil, Arg.	D5	56
Tando Ādam, Pak.	H3	38
Tando Muhammad Khān, Pak.	H3	38
Tanega-shima, i., Japan	u30	31b
Taney, co., Mo., U.S.	E4	102
Taneycomo, Lake, res., Mo., U.S.	E4	102
Taneytown, Md., U.S.	A3	97
Tanezrouft, des., Afr.	D5	42
Tanga, Tan.	C7	44
Tangail, Bngl.	H13	38
Tanganyika, Lake, l., Afr.	C5	44
Tanger (Tangier), Mor.	A4	42
Tangerang, Indon.	m13	33a
Tangermünde, Ger.	C11	8
Tanggula Shan, mts., China	D13	38
Tangier, Va., U.S.	C7	123
Tangier Island, i., Va., U.S.	C6	123
Tangier Sound, strt., Md., U.S.	D6	97
Tangier see Tanger, Mor.	A4	42
Tangipahoa, co., La., U.S.	D5	95
Tangipahoa, stm., La., U.S.	D5	95
Tangra Yumco, l., China	E12	38
Tangshan, China	D10	26
Tanimbar, Kepulauan, is., Indon.	G9	32
Tanjungbalai, Indon.	M5	34
Tanjungkarang-Telukbetung, Indon.	k12	32
Tanjungpinang, Indon.	N8	34
Tanjungselor, Indon.	E6	32
Tānk, Pak.	D4	38
Tännäs, Swe.	E9	6
Tanner, Al., U.S.	A3	78
Tânout, Niger	F7	42
Tanshui, Tai.	J10	28
Tantā, Egypt	B12	42
Tanuku, India	D6	37
Tanzania, ctry., Afr.	C6	44
Taos, Mo., U.S.	C5	102
Taos, N.M., U.S.	A4	108
Taos, co., N.M., U.S.	A4	108
Taos Pueblo, N.M., U.S.	A4	108
Taoudenni, Mali	D5	42
Tapachula, Mex.	J13	62
Tapah, Malay.	L6	34
Tapajós, stm., Braz.	E7	54
Taphan Hin, Thai.	F6	34
Tāpi, stm., India	B2	37
Tappahannock, Va., U.S.	C6	123
Tappan, N.Y., U.S.	g13	109
Tappan, Lake, res., N.J., U.S.	g9	107
Tappan Lake, res., Oh., U.S.	B4	112
Taqātu' Hayyā, Sudan	E13	42
Taquaritinga, Braz.	F4	57
Tar, stm., N.C., U.S.	B5	110
Tara, Ont., Can.	C3	73
Tarābulus (Tripoli), Leb.	B4	40
Tarābulus (Tripoli), Libya	B8	42
Tarābulus (Tripolitania), reg., Libya	B8	42
Tarakan, Indon.	E6	32
Tarancón, Spain	E8	12
Taranto, Italy	I12	14
Taranto, Golfo di b., Italy	I12	14
Tarapacá, Col.	I8	58
Tarare, Fr.	G11	10
Tarascon, Fr.	J8	10
Tarata, Bol.	G5	54
Tarazona, Spain	D10	12
Tarazona de la Mancha, Spain	F10	12
Tarbert, Scot., U.K.	F7	7
Tarbert, Scot., U.K.	D6	7
Tarbes, Fr.	I7	10
Tarboro, N.C., U.S.	B5	110
Tarcento, Italy	C8	14
Taree, Austl.	F10	50
Tareja, Russia	C12	24
Tarentum, Pa., U.S.	E2	115
Tarfaya, Mor.	C3	42
Targhee Pass, U.S.	E7	89
Tarifa, Punta de, c., Spain	I6	12
Tariffville, Ct., U.S.	B4	84
Tarija, Bol.	H6	54
Tarim, stm., China	C3	26
Tarīn Kowt, Afg.	D1	38
Tarkio, Mo., U.S.	A2	102
Tarkwa, Ghana	G5	42
Tarlac, Phil.	q19	32
Tarn, stm., Fr.	I8	10
Tärnaby, Swe.	D10	6
Tarnak, stm., Afg.	D2	38
Tarnów, Pol.	E20	8
Tarnowskie Góry, Pol.	E18	8
Tarpey, Ca., U.S.	D4	82
Tarpon, Lake, l., Fl., U.S.	o10	86
Tarpon Springs, Fl., U.S.	D4	86
Tarquinia, Italy	G6	14
Tarragona, Spain	D13	12
Tarrant, Al., U.S.	B3	78
Tarrant, co., Tx., U.S.	C4	120
Tarrasa, Spain	D14	12
Tarryall Mountains, mts., Co., U.S.	B5	83
Tarrytown, N.Y., U.S.	D7	109
Tarsus, Tur.	A4	40
Tartagal, Arg.	A4	56
Tartas, Fr.	I6	10
Tartu, Est.	C9	18
Tarṭūs, Syria	B4	40
Tarutung, Indon.	M5	34
Tarusa, Turk.	I9	22
Tasejeva, stm., Russia	F12	24
Tasejevo, Russia	F12	24
Taseko Mountain, mtn., B.C., Can.	D6	69
Tashi Gang Dzong, Bhu.	G14	38
Tashkent see Taškent, Uzb.	I11	22
Tasikmalaya, Indon.	m14	32
Taškent, Uzb.	I11	22
Tasmania, state, Austl.	H9	50
Tasman Sea, Oc.	G11	50
Tasso, Tn., U.S.	D9	119
Taštagol, Russia	G11	24
Tatabánya, Hung.	H18	8
Tate, Ga., U.S.	B2	87
Tate, co., Ms., U.S.	A4	101
Tateville, Ky., U.S.	D5	94
Tateyama, Japan	H12	30
Tathlina Lake, l., N.W. Ter., Can.	D9	66
Tatnam, Cape, c., Man., Can.	f9	70
Tatta, Pak.	H2	38
Tattnall, co., Ga., U.S.	D4	87
Tatum, N.M., U.S.	D6	108
Tatvan, Tur.	H16	4
Tau, Nor.	G5	6
Taubaté, Braz.	G6	57
Tauberbischofsheim, Ger.	F9	8
Taujskaja Guba, b., Russia	F24	24
Taumarunui, N.Z.	C5	52
Taum Sauk Mountain, mtn., Mo., U.S.	D6	102
Taungdwingyi, Burma	D3	34
Taunggyi, Burma	D4	34
Taungup Pass, Burma	E3	34
Taunton, Eng., U.K.	J9	7
Taunton, Ma., U.S.	C5	98
Taunton, stm., Ma., U.S.	C5	98
Taupo, Lake, l., N.Z.	C5	52
Tauranga, N.Z.	B6	52
Taureau, Réservoir, res., Que., Can.	C4	74
Taurus Mountains see Toros Dağları, mts., Tur.	H14	4
Tauste, Spain	D10	12
Tavares, Fl., U.S.	D5	86
Tavernier, Fl., U.S.	G6	86
Tavira, Port.	H4	12
Tavoy Point, c., Burma	H5	34
Tavşanlı, Tur.	J13	16
Tawakoni, Lake, res., Tx., U.S.	C4	120
Tawas City, Mi., U.S.	D7	99
Tawas Lake, l., Mi., U.S.	D7	99
Tawau, Malay.	E6	32
Tawitawi Island, i., Phil.	D6	32
Tawkar, Sudan	E13	42
Taxco de Alarcón, Mex.	H10	62
Tay, Loch, l., Scot., U.K.	E8	7
Taylor, B.C., Can.	A7	69
Taylor, Az., U.S.	C5	80
Taylor, Ar., U.S.	D2	81
Taylor, Mi., U.S.	p15	99
Taylor, Pa., U.S.	D10	115
Taylor, Tx., U.S.	D4	120
Taylor, co., Fl., U.S.	B3	86
Taylor, co., Ga., U.S.	D2	87
Taylor, co., Ia., U.S.	D3	92
Taylor, co., Ky., U.S.	C4	94
Taylor, co., Tx., U.S.	C3	120
Taylor, co., W.V., U.S.	B4	125
Taylor, co., Wi., U.S.	C3	126
Taylor, Mount, mtn., N.M., U.S.	B2	108
Taylor Mill, Ky., U.S.	k14	94
Taylor Mountain, mtn., Id., U.S.	E4	89
Taylor Park Reservoir, res., Co., U.S.	C4	83
Taylors, S.C., U.S.	B3	117
Taylors Falls, Mn., U.S.	E6	100
Taylors Island, i., Md., U.S.	D5	97
Taylorsville, In., U.S.	F6	91
Taylorsville, Ky., U.S.	B4	94
Taylorsville, Ms., U.S.	D4	101
Taylorsville, N.C., U.S.	B1	110
Taylorville, Il., U.S.	D4	90
Taymā', Sau. Ar.	C2	46
Tay Ninh, Viet.	I9	34
Tayoltita, Mex.	E7	62
Taytay, Phil.	C6	32
Taz, stm., Russia	D10	24
Taza, Mor.	B5	42
Tazewell, Tn., U.S.	C10	119
Tazewell, Va., U.S.	e10	123
Tazewell, co., Il., U.S.	C4	90
Tazewell, co., Va., U.S.	e10	123
Tazin Lake, l., Sask., Can.	E11	66
Tbessa, Alg.	A7	42
Tbilisi, Geor.	I6	22
Tbong, Camb.	H8	34
Tchefuncta, stm., La., U.S.	D5	95
Tchibanga, Gabon	B2	44
Tchien, Lib.	G4	42
Tchula, Ms., U.S.	B3	101
Tczew, Pol.	A18	8
Tea, S.D., U.S.	D9	118
Teacapán, Mex.	F7	62
Teague, Tx., U.S.	D4	120
Te Anau, Lake, l., N.Z.	F1	52
Teaneck, N.J., U.S.	h8	107
Teano, Italy	H9	14
Teaticket, Ma., U.S.	C6	98
Tebingtinggi, Indon.	M5	34
Téboursouk, Tun.	M4	14
Tecate, Mex.	A1	62
Tecolotlan, Mex.	G7	62
Tecomán, Mex.	H8	62
Tecpan de Galeana, Mex.	I9	62
Tecuala, Mex.	F7	62
Tecuci, Rom.	D11	16
Tecumseh, Ont., Can.	E2	73
Tecumseh, Ks., U.S.	k14	93
Tecumseh, Mi., U.S.	G7	99
Tecumseh, Ne., U.S.	D9	104
Tecumseh, Ok., U.S.	B5	113
Tedžen (Harīrūd), stm., Asia	J10	22
Teeswater, Ont., Can.	C3	73
Tefé, Braz.	D6	54
Tegal, Indon.	m14	32
Tegucigalpa, Hond.	G4	64
Tehachapi, Ca., U.S.	E4	82
Tehachapi Mountains, mts., Ca., U.S.	E4	82
Tehama, co., Ca., U.S.	B2	82
Tehuacán, Mex.	H11	62
Tehuantepec, Mex.	I12	62
Tehuantepec, Golfo de, b., Mex.	J12	62
Tehuantepec, Istmo de, Mex.	I12	62
Teide, Pico de, mtn., Spain	C2	42
Tejamén, Mex.	E7	62
Tejkovo, Russia	E23	18
Tejupan, Punta, c., Mex.	H8	62
Tekamah, Ne., U.S.	C9	104
Tekirdağ, Tur.	I11	16
Tekoa, Wa., U.S.	B8	124
Tekonsha, Mi., U.S.	F5	99
Tela, Hond.	G4	64
Telavåg, Nor.	F5	6
Tel Aviv-Yafo, Isr.	C4	40
Teleckoje, Ozero, l., Russia	G11	24
Telén, Arg.	D3	56
Telescope Peak, mtn., Ca., U.S.	D5	82
Teles Pires, stm., Braz.	E7	54
Telfair, co., Ga., U.S.	E4	87
Telford, Pa., U.S.	F11	115
Teli, Russia	G12	24
Telkwa, B.C., Can.	B4	69
Tell City, In., U.S.	I4	91
Teller, co., Co., U.S.	C5	83
Tellicherry, India	G3	37
Tellico Plains, Tn., U.S.	D9	119
Telluride, Co., U.S.	D3	83
Telok Anson, Malay.	L6	34
Telos Lake, l., Me., U.S.	B3	96
Temagami, Lake, l., Ont., Can.	G16	66
Tembeling, stm., Malay.	L7	34
Tembenči, stm., Russia	D13	24
Temecula, Ca., U.S.	F5	82
Temerloh, Malay.	M7	34
Teminabuan, Indon.	F9	32
Temósachic, Mex.	C6	62
Tempe, Az., U.S.	D4	80
Temperance, Mi., U.S.	G7	99
Temperance, stm., Mn., U.S.	C8	100
Tempio Pausania, Italy	I4	14
Temple, Ga., U.S.	C1	87
Temple, Ok., U.S.	C3	113
Temple, Pa., U.S.	F10	115
Temple, Tx., U.S.	D4	120
Temple Terrace, Fl., U.S.	o11	86
Templin, Ger.	B13	8
Temuco, Chile	D2	56
Tena, Ec.	H4	58
Tenafly, N.J., U.S.	B5	107
Tenaha, Tx., U.S.	D5	120
Tenāli, India	D6	37
Tendaho, Eth.	F3	46
Tende, Col de, Eur.	H14	10
Ten Degree Channel, strt., India	J2	34
Ténéré, des., Niger	E8	42
Tenerife, i., Spain	C2	42
Tengchong, China	B5	34
Tenino, Wa., U.S.	C3	124
Tenkāsi, India	H4	37
Tenkiller Ferry Lake, res., Ok., U.S.	B6	113
Tenkodogo, Burkina	F5	42
Tenmile, stm., U.S.	B5	116
Tenmile Creek, stm., W.V., U.S.	k10	125
Tenmile Lake, l., Mn., U.S.	D4	100
Tennant Creek, Austl.	C6	50
Tennessee, state, U.S.	B5	119
Tennessee, stm., U.S.	D9	76
Tennessee Pass, Co., U.S.	B4	83
Tennessee Ridge, Tn., U.S.	A4	119
Tennille, Ga., U.S.	D4	87
Tenom, Malay.	D6	32
Tenryū, stm., Japan	G10	30
Tensas, co., La., U.S.	B4	95
Tensas, stm., La., U.S.	B4	95
Tensaw, stm., Al., U.S.	E2	78
Ten Sleep, Wy., U.S.	B5	127
Tenterfield, Austl.	E10	50
Ten Thousand Islands, is., Fl., U.S.	G5	86
Teocaltiche, Mex.	G8	62
Teófilo Otoni, Braz.	D8	57
Tepa, Indon.	G8	32
Tepatitlán [de Morelos], Mex.	G8	62
Tepic, Mex.	G7	62
Teplice, Czech.	E13	8
Teramo, Italy	G8	14
Teresina, Braz.	E10	54
Teresópolis, Braz.	G7	57
Termez, Uzb.	B2	38
Termini Imerese, Italy	L8	14
Términos, Laguna de, b., Mex.	H14	62
Termoli, Italy	H9	14
Ternej, Russia	H21	24
Terni, Italy	G7	14
Ternopol', Ukr.	H3	22
Terpenija, Mys, c., Russia	H22	24
Terpenija, Zaliv, b., Russia	H22	24
Terra Alta, W.V., U.S.	B5	125
Terrace, B.C., Can.	B3	69
Terracina, Italy	H8	14
Terralba, Italy	J3	14
Terra Nova National Park, Newf., Can.	D4	72
Terrebonne, Que., Can.	D4	74
Terrebonne, co., La., U.S.	E5	95
Terrebonne Bay, b., La., U.S.	E5	95
Terre Haute, In., U.S.	F3	91
Terrell, Tx., U.S.	C4	120
Terrell, co., Ga., U.S.	E2	87
Terrell, co., Tx., U.S.	D1	120
Terrell Hills, Tx., U.S.	k7	120
Terrenceville, Newf., Can.	E4	72
Terry, Ms., U.S.	C3	101
Terry, Mt., U.S.	D11	103
Terry, co., Tx., U.S.	C1	120
Terrytown, Ne., U.S.	C2	104
Terryville, Ct., U.S.	C3	84
Teruel, Spain	E10	12
Tervola, Fin.	C15	6
Teseney, Eth.	E2	46
Teshekpuk Lake, l., Ak., U.S.	A9	79
Teshio, Japan	o19	30a
Teslin, Yukon, Can.	D6	66
Teslin, stm., Can.	D6	66
Tesouro, Braz.	D2	57
Tessalit, Mali	D6	42
Tesuque, N.M., U.S.	B4	108
Tete, Moz.	E6	44
Teterow, Ger.	B12	8
Teton, co., Id., U.S.	F7	89
Teton, co., Mt., U.S.	C4	103
Teton, co., Wy., U.S.	C2	127
Teton, stm., Mt., U.S.	C5	103
Teton Pass, Wy., U.S.	C2	127
Teton Range, mts., Wy., U.S.	C2	127
Teton Village, Wy., U.S.	C2	127
Tétouan, Mor.	A4	42
Tetovo, Mac.	G4	16
Tet'uche, Russia	I21	24
Teulada, Italy	K3	14
Teulon, Man., Can.	D3	70
Teutopolis, Il., U.S.	D5	90
Teuva, Fin.	E13	6
Tevere (Tiber), stm., Italy	G7	14
Teverya, Isr.	C4	40
Tewksbury, Ma., U.S.	A5	98
Texada Island, i., B.C., Can.	E5	69
Texarkana, Ar., U.S.	D1	81
Texarkana, Tx., U.S.	C5	120
Texas, co., Mo., U.S.	D5	102
Texas, co., Ok., U.S.	e9	113
Texas, state, U.S.	D3	120
Texas City, Tx., U.S.	E5	120
Texhoma, Ok., U.S.	e9	113
Texoma, Lake, res., U.S.	D5	113
Teyvareh, Afg.	D1	38
Teziutlán, Mex.	H11	62
Tezpur, India	G15	38
Thabazimbi, S. Afr.	F5	44
Thai Binh, Viet.	D9	34
Thailand, ctry., Asia	B3	32
Thailand, Gulf of, b., Asia	J6	34
Thai Nguyen, Viet.	D8	34
Thal, Pak.	D4	38
Thames, stm., Ont., Can.	E3	73
Thames, stm., Eng., U.K.	J14	7
Thames, stm., Ct., U.S.	D7	84
Thamesville, Ont., Can.	E3	73
Thāna, India	C2	37
Thanh Hoa, Viet.	E8	34
Thanh Pho Ho Chi Minh (Saigon), Viet.	I9	34
Thanjāvūr, India	G5	37
Thar Desert (Great Indian Desert), des., Asia	G3	38
Thargomindah, Austl.	E8	50
Thatcher, Az., U.S.	E6	80
Thaton, Burma	F4	34
Thayer, Mo., U.S.	E6	102
Thayer, co., Ne., U.S.	D8	104
Thayetmyo, Burma	E3	34
Thayne, Wy., U.S.	D1	127
Thealka, Ky., U.S.	C7	94
The Barrens, plat., Tn., U.S.	B5	119
The Bight, Bah.	B10	64
The Cheviot, mtn., Eng., U.K.	F10	7
The Colony, Tx., U.S.	*C4	120
The Dalles, Or., U.S.	B5	114
The Dells, val., Wi., U.S.	E4	126
Thedford, Ont., Can.	D3	73
The English Company's Islands, is., Austl.	B7	50
The Everglades, sw., Fl., U.S.	G6	86
The Fens, sw., Eng., U.K.	I12	7
The Flat Tops, mts., Co., U.S.	B3	83
The Flume, wtfl, N.H., U.S.	B3	106
The Graves, is., Ma., U.S.	g12	98
The Hague see 's-Gravenhage, Neth.	C4	8
The Heads, c., Or., U.S.	E2	114
Thelon, stm., N.W. Ter., Can.	D12	66
The Narrows, strt., Wa., U.S.	f10	124
Theodore, Austl.	D10	50
Theodore, Al., U.S.	E1	78
Theodore Roosevelt Lake, res., Az., U.S.	D4	80
Theodore Roosevelt National Park (South Unit), N.D., U.S.	C2	111
Theodore Roosevelt National Park (North Unit), N.D., U.S.	B2	111
The Pas, Man., Can.	C1	70
The Plains, Oh., U.S.	C3	112
Theresa, Wi., U.S.	E5	126
Thermopolis, Wy., U.S.	C4	127
The Rockies, mts., Wa., U.S.	C5	124
Thessalon, Ont., Can.	p19	73
Thessaloniki (Salonika), Grc.	I6	16
Thetford Mines, Que., Can.	C6	74
The Thimbles, is., Ct., U.S.	E5	84
The Village, Ok., U.S.	B4	113
The Warburton, stm., Austl.	E7	50
The Wash, b., Eng., U.K.	I13	7
The Weald, reg., Eng., U.K.	J13	7
Thibodaux, La., U.S.	E5	95
Thief, stm., Mn., U.S.	B2	100
Thief Lake, l., Mn., U.S.	B2	100
Thief River Falls, Mn., U.S.	B2	100
Thielsen, Mount, mtn., Or., U.S.	D4	114
Thiene, Italy	D6	14
Thiensville, Wi., U.S.	E6	126
Thiers, Fr.	G10	10
Thiès, Sen.	F2	42
Thika, Kenya	B7	44
Thimphu, Bhu.	G13	38
Thingangyun, Burma	F4	34
Thionville, Fr.	C13	10
Thíra, i., Grc.	M9	16
Third Lake, l., N.H., U.S.	f7	106
Thirsk, Eng., U.K.	G11	7
Thisted, Den.	H7	6
Thívai (Thebes), Grc.	K7	16
Thiviers, Fr.	G7	10
Thomas, Ok., U.S.	B3	113
Thomas, co., Ga., U.S.	F3	87
Thomas, co., Ks., U.S.	C2	93
Thomas, co., Ne., U.S.	C5	104
Thomasboro, Il., U.S.	C5	90
Thomaston, Ct., U.S.	C3	84
Thomaston, Ga., U.S.	D2	87
Thomaston, Me., U.S.	D3	96
Thomaston Reservoir, res., Ct., U.S.	C3	84
Thomastown, Ire.	I5	7
Thomasville, Al., U.S.	D2	78
Thomasville, Ga., U.S.	F3	87
Thomasville, N.C., U.S.	B2	110
Thompson, Man., Can.	B3	70
Thompson, Ct., U.S.	B8	84
Thompson, N.D., U.S.	B8	111
Thompson, stm., U.S.	A4	102
Thompson Falls, Mt., U.S.	C1	103
Thompson Island, i., Ma., U.S.	g11	98
Thompson Lake, l., U.S.	D2	96
Thompson Peak, mtn., Ca., U.S.	B2	82
Thompson Peak, mtn., N.M., U.S.	h9	108
Thompson Reservoir, res., Or., U.S.	E5	114
Thomsen, stm., N.W. Ter., Can.	B9	66
Thomson, Ga., U.S.	C4	87
Thon Buri, Thai.	H6	34
Thongwa, Burma	F4	34
Thonon-les-Bains, Fr.	F13	10
Thonotosassa, Fl., U.S.	D4	86
Thonze, Burma	F3	34
Thorburn, N.S., Can.	D7	71
Thoreau, N.M., U.S.	B1	108
Thornbury, Ont., Can.	C4	73
Thorndale, Tx., U.S.	D4	120
Thornton, Ont., Can.	C5	73
Thorntown, In., U.S.	D4	91
Thorold, Ont., Can.	D5	73
Thorp, Wi., U.S.	D3	126
Thorsby, Al., U.S.	C3	78
Thouars, Fr.	F6	10
Thousand Islands, is., N.Y., U.S.	A4	109
Thousand Lake Mountain, mtn., Ut., U.S.	E4	121
Thousand Springs Creek, stm., U.S.	B7	105
Thrace, hist. reg., Eur.	G13	4
Thrakikón Pélagos, Grc.	I8	16
Three Fingered Jack, mtn., Or., U.S.	C5	114
Three Forks, Mt., U.S.	E5	103
Three Hills, Alta., Can.	D4	68
Three Lakes, Wi., U.S.	C4	126
Three Mile Plains, N.S., Can.	E5	71
Three Oaks, Mi., U.S.	G4	99
Three Pagodas Pass, Asia	G5	34
Three Points, Cape, c., Ghana	H5	42
Three Rivers, Ma., U.S.	B3	98
Three Rivers, Mi., U.S.	G5	99
Three Rivers, Tx., U.S.	E3	120
Three Sisters, mtn., Or., U.S.	C5	114
Three Springs, Austl.	E3	50
Throckmorton, co., Tx., U.S.	C3	120
Throop, Pa., U.S.	m18	115
Throssell Range, mts., Austl.	D4	50
Thu Dao Mot, Viet.	I9	34
Thule, Grnld.	B19	128
Thun, Switz.	F14	10
Thunder Bay, Ont., Can.	o17	73
Thunder Bay, b., Mi., U.S.	D7	99
Thunder Bay, stm., Mi., U.S.	D6	99
Thunderbird, Lake, res., Ok., U.S.	B4	113
Thunderbolt, Ga., U.S.	D5	87
Thunder Butte Creek, stm., S.D., U.S.	B3	118
Thunersee, l., Switz.	F14	10
Thüringen, hist. reg., Ger.	D11	8
Thurles, Ire.	I5	7
Thurmont, Md., U.S.	A3	97
Thurso, Que., Can.	D2	74
Thurso, Scot., U.K.	C9	7
Thurston, co., Ne., U.S.	B9	104
Thurston, co., Wa., U.S.	C2	124
Tiancang, China	C7	26
Tiandong, China	C9	34
Tianjin (Tientsin), China	D10	26
Tianjun, China	D6	26
Tianmen, China	E2	28
Tianshui, China	E8	26
Tiaret, Alg.	A6	42
Tibagi, Braz.	A6	56
Tibasti, Sarīr, des., Libya	D9	42
Tibesti, mts., Chad	D9	42
Tibet, hist. reg., China	E12	38
Tiburón, Isla, i., Mex.	C3	62
Tice, Fl., U.S.	F5	86
Tichît, Maur.	E3	42
Tichvin, Russia	B16	18
Tickfaw, stm., La., U.S.	D5	95
Ticonderoga, N.Y., U.S.	B7	109
Ticul, Mex.	G15	62
Tide Head, N.B., Can.	B3	71
Tidjikdja, Maur.	E3	42
Tieling, China	C11	26
Tienen, Bel.	E4	8
Tien Shan, mts., Asia	C2	26
Tientsin see Tianjin, China	D10	26
Tierra Amarilla, N.M., U.S.	A3	108
Tierra Blanca, Mex.	H11	62
Tierra del Fuego, Isla Grande de, i., S.A.	G3	56
Tierralta, Col.	C4	58
Tietê, stm., Braz.	F3	57
Tieton, Wa., U.S.	C5	124
Tieton, stm., Wa., U.S.	C4	124
Tieton Dam, Wa., U.S.	C4	124
Tiffany Mountain, mtn., Wa., U.S.	A6	124
Tiffin, Oh., U.S.	A2	112

Name	Map Ref	Page
Tiffin, stm., Oh., U.S.	A1	112
Tift, co., Ga., U.S.	E3	87
Tifton, Ga., U.S.	E3	87
Tigard, Or., U.S.	h12	114
Tigerton, Wi., U.S.	D4	126
Tigil', Russia	F25	24
Tignall, Ga., U.S.	C4	87
Tignish, P.E.I., Can.	C5	71
Tigre, stm., Peru	D3	54
Tigris (Dijlah), stm., Asia	A3	46
Tiguentourine, Alg.	C7	42
Tijesno, Cro.	F10	14
Tijuana, Mex.	A1	62
Tikamgarh, India	H8	38
Tikrīt, Iraq	B3	46
Tilburg, Neth.	D5	8
Tilbury, Ont., Can.	E2	73
Tilden, Il., U.S.	E4	90
Tilden, Ne., U.S.	B8	104
Tilghman, Md., U.S.	C5	97
Tilghman Island, i., Md., U.S.	C5	97
Tilhar, India	G8	38
Tillabéry, Niger	F6	42
Tillamook, Or., U.S.	B3	114
Tillamook, co., Or., U.S.	B3	114
Tillanchong Island, i., India	J2	34
Tillery, Lake, res., N.C., U.S.	B2	110
Tillman, co., Ok., U.S.	C2	113
Tillmans Corner, Al., U.S.	E1	78
Tillsonburg, Ont., Can.	E4	73
Tilton, Il., U.S.	C6	90
Tilton, N.H., U.S.	D3	106
Tiltonsville, Oh., U.S.	B5	112
Timaru, N.Z.	F3	52
Timbalier Island, i., La., U.S.	E5	95
Timberlake, Va., U.S.	C3	123
Timberville, Va., U.S.	B4	123
Timbuktu see Tombouctou, Mali	E5	42
Timimoun, Alg.	C6	42
Timiris, Cap, c., Maur.	E2	42
Timişoara, Rom.	D5	16
Timmins, Ont., Can.	o19	73
Timmonsville, S.C., U.S.	C8	117
Timms Hill, hill, Wi., U.S.	C3	126
Timor, i., Indon.	G8	32
Timor Sea	B5	50
Timotes, Ven.	C7	58
Timpanogos Cave National Monument, Ut., U.S.	C4	121
Timpton, stm., Russia	F19	24
Tims Ford Lake, res., Tn., U.S.	B5	119
Tinaquillo, Ven.	C8	58
Tindivanam, India	F5	37
Tindouf, Alg.	C4	42
Tingmerkpuk Mountain, mtn., Ak., U.S.	B7	79
Tingo María, Peru	E3	54
Tingvoll, Nor.	E7	6
Tinharé, Ilha de, i., Braz.	F11	54
Tinker Air Force Base, mil., Ok., U.S.	B4	113
Tinley Park, Il., U.S.	k9	90
Tinniswood, Mount, mtn., B.C., Can.	D6	69
Tinogasta, Arg.	B3	56
Tinsukia, India	G16	38
Tinton Falls, N.J., U.S.	C4	107
Tioga, La., U.S.	C3	95
Tioga, N.D., U.S.	A3	111
Tioga, co., N.Y., U.S.	C4	109
Tioga, co., Pa., U.S.	C7	115
Tioga, stm., Pa., U.S.	B7	115
Tiogue Lake, res., R.I., U.S.	D3	116
Tioman, Pulau, i., Malay.	M8	34
Tionesta Creek, stm., Pa., U.S.	C3	115
Tionesta Lake, res., Pa., U.S.	D3	115
Tioughnioga, stm., N.Y., U.S.	C4	109
Tippah, co., Ms., U.S.	A5	101
Tippah, stm., Ms., U.S.	A4	101
Tipp City, Oh., U.S.	C1	112
Tippecanoe, co., In., U.S.	D4	91
Tippecanoe, stm., In., U.S.	C4	91
Tipperary, Ire.	I4	7
Tipton, Ca., U.S.	D4	82
Tipton, In., U.S.	D5	91
Tipton, Ia., U.S.	C6	92
Tipton, Mo., U.S.	C5	102
Tipton, co., In., U.S.	D5	91
Tipton, co., Tn., U.S.	B2	119
Tipton, Mount, mtn., Az., U.S.	B1	80
Tiptonville, Tn., U.S.	A2	119
Tiquisate, Guat.	G2	64
Tiracambu, Serra do, plat., Braz.	D9	54
Tīrān, Maḍīq, strt.	F4	40
Tiran, Strait of see Tīrān, Maḍīq, strt.	F4	40
Tiranë, Alb.	H3	16
Tirano, Italy	C5	14
Tiraspol', Mol.	H3	22
Tirat Karmel, Isr.	C4	40
Tire, Tur.	K11	16
Tiree, i., Scot., U.K.	E6	7
Tîrgovişte, Rom.	E9	16
Tîrgu-Jiu, Rom.	D7	16
Tîrgu Mureş, Rom.	C10	16
Tîrgu-Ocna, Rom.	C10	16
Tîrnavos, Grc.	J6	16
Tirschenreuth, Ger.	F12	8
Tiruchchirāppalli, India	G5	37
Tirunelveli, India	H4	37
Tirupati, India	F5	37
Tiruppattūr, India	F5	37
Tiruppur, India	G4	37
Tiruvannāmalai, India	F5	37
Tishomingo, Ok., U.S.	C5	113
Tishomingo, co., Ms., U.S.	A5	101
Tiskilwa, Il., U.S.	B4	90
Tit-Ary, Russia	C19	24
Titicaca, Lago, l., S.A.	G5	54
Titograd, Yugo.	G3	16
Titonka, Ia., U.S.	A3	92
Titovo Užice, Yugo.	F3	16
Titov Veles, Mac.	H5	16
Titule, Zaire	H11	42
Titus, co., Tx., U.S.	C5	120
Titusville, Fl., U.S.	D6	86
Titusville, Pa., U.S.	C2	115
Tiverton, Ont., Can.	C3	73
Tiverton, Eng., U.K.	K9	7
Tiverton, R.I., U.S.	D6	116
Tivoli, Italy	H7	14
Tizimín, Mex.	G15	62
Tizi-Ouzou, Alg.	A6	42
Tlahualilo de Zaragoza, Mex.	D8	62
Tlaltenango de Sánchez Román, Mex.	G8	62
Tlaxiaco, Mex.	I11	62
Tlemcen, Alg.	B5	42
Tlētē Ouāte Gharbī, Jabal, mtn., Syria	B6	40
Toamasina, Madag.	E9	44
Toano, Va., U.S.	C6	123
Toano Range, mts., Nv., U.S.	C7	105
Toast, N.C., U.S.	A2	110
Toba, Japan	H9	30
Toba, Danau, l., Indon.	M5	34
Tobacco Root Mountains, mts., Mt., U.S.	E5	103
Tobago, i., Trin.	I17	64
Toba Inlet, b., B.C., Can.	D5	69
Toba Kākar Range, mts., Pak.	E2	38
Tobarra, Spain	G10	12
Tobermory, Scot., U.K.	E6	7
Tobin, Mount, mtn., Nv., U.S.	C4	105
Tobin Lake, l., Sask., Can.	D4	75
Tobin Range, mts., Nv., U.S.	C4	105
Tobique, stm., N.B., Can.	B2	71
Tobol'sk, Russia	F7	24
Tobruk see Tubruq, Libya	B10	42
Tobyhanna, Pa., U.S.	D11	115
Tocantínia, Braz.	E9	54
Tocantinópolis, Braz.	E9	54
Tocantins, stm., Braz.	D9	54
Toccoa, Ga., U.S.	B3	87
Toccoa, stm., Ga., U.S.	B2	87
Toccoa Falls, Ga., U.S.	B3	87
Tochigi, Japan	F12	30
Töcksfors, Swe.	G8	6
Toco, Chile	A3	56
Tocopilla, Chile	A2	56
Todd, co., Ky., U.S.	D2	94
Todd, co., Mn., U.S.	D4	100
Todd, co., S.D., U.S.	D5	118
Todi, Italy	G7	14
Todos Santos, Mex.	F4	62
Todtnau, Ger.	H7	8
Tofield, Alta., Can.	C4	68
Tofino, B.C., Can.	E5	69
Togiak, Ak., U.S.	D7	79
Togian, Kepulauan, is., Indon.	F7	32
Togo, ctry., Afr.	G6	42
Togwotee Pass, Wy., U.S.	C2	127
Tohakum Peak, mtn., Nv., U.S.	C2	105
Tohatchi, N.M., U.S.	B1	108
Tohopekaliga, Lake, l., Fl., U.S.	D5	86
Toiyabe Range, mts., Nv., U.S.	D4	105
Tok, Ak., U.S.	C11	79
Tōkamachi, Japan	E11	30
Tokara-kaikyō, strt., Japan	u30	31b
Tokara-rettō, is., Japan	v29	31b
Tokat, Tur.	G15	4
Tokelau Islands, dep., Oc.	G1	2
Toki, Japan	G10	30
Tokuno-shima, i., Japan	x28	31b
Tokushima, Japan	H7	30
Tokuyama, Japan	H4	30
Tōkyō, Japan	G12	30
Tokzār, Afg.	C1	38
Toleak Point, c., Wa., U.S.	B1	124
Toledo, Spain	F7	12
Toledo, Il., U.S.	D5	90
Toledo, Ia., U.S.	B5	92
Toledo, Oh., U.S.	A2	112
Toledo, Or., U.S.	C3	114
Toledo Bend Reservoir, res., U.S.	C2	95
Tolentino, Italy	F8	14
Toler, Ky., U.S.	C7	94
Toliara, Madag.	F8	44
Toljatti, Russia	G7	22
Tol'ka, Russia	E10	24
Tolland, Ct., U.S.	B6	84
Tolland, co., Ct., U.S.	B6	84
Tollesboro, Ky., U.S.	B6	94
Tolleson, Az., U.S.	m8	80
Tolmezzo, Italy	C8	14
Tolmin, Slo.	C8	14
Tolo, Teluk, b., Indon.	F7	32
Tolono, Il., U.S.	D5	90
Tolosa, Spain	B9	12
Tolt Reservoir, res., Wa., U.S.	B4	124
Toluca, Il., U.S.	C4	90
Toluca, Nevado de, vol., Mex.	H10	62
Toluca [de Lerdo], Mex.	H10	62
Tom', stm., Russia	F11	24
Tomah, Wi., U.S.	E3	126
Tomahawk, Wi., U.S.	C4	126
Tomahawk Lake, l., Wi., U.S.	C4	126
Tomakomai, Japan	q19	30a
Tomar, Port.	F3	12
Tomaszów Mazowiecki, Pol.	D20	8
Tomatlán, Mex.	H7	62
Tomball, Tx., U.S.	D5	120
Tombigbee, stm., U.S.	D1	78
Tombouctou (Timbuktu), Mali	E5	42
Tombstone, Az., U.S.	F5	80
Tombua, Ang.	E2	44
Tomelloso, Spain	F9	12
Tom Green, co., Tx., U.S.	D2	120
Tomini, Teluk, b., Indon.	F7	32
Tomo, stm., Col.	E8	58
Tom Nevers Head, c., Ma., U.S.	D8	98
Tompkins, co., N.Y., U.S.	C4	109
Tompkinsville, Ky., U.S.	D4	94
Tomptokan, Russia	F20	24
Tomra, Nor.	E6	6
Toms, stm., N.J., U.S.	C4	107
Tomsk, Russia	F10	24
Toms River, N.J., U.S.	D4	107
Tonalá, Mex.	I13	62
Tonasket, Wa., U.S.	A6	124
Tonawanda Indian Reservation, N.Y., U.S.	B2	109
Tondabayashi, Japan	H8	30
Tone, stm., Japan	F12	30
Tonga, ctry., Oc.	H1	2
Tonganoxie, Ks., U.S.	C8	93
Tongbai, China	C2	28
Tongchuan, China	D8	26
Tongeren, Bel.	E5	8
Tonggu, China	E9	26
Tonghai, China	B7	34
Tonghua, China	C12	26
Tongliao, China	C11	26
Tongling, China	E6	28
Tongsa Dzong, Bhu.	G14	38
Tongtianheyan, China	D15	38
Tongue, Scot., U.K.	C8	7
Tongue, stm., Mt., U.S.	E10	103
Tongue, stm., Tx., U.S.	p13	120
Tongzi, China	F8	26
Tonk, India	G6	38
Tonkawa, Ok., U.S.	A4	113
Tonkin, Gulf of, b., Asia	E9	34
Tonle Sap see Sab, Tônlé, l., Camb.	H7	34
Tonneins, Fr.	H7	10
Tonnerre, Fr.	E10	10
Tonopah, Nv., U.S.	E4	105
Tønsberg, Nor.	G8	6
Tonstad, Nor.	G6	6
Tonto National Monument, Az., U.S.	D4	80
Tonto Natural Bridge, Az., U.S.	C4	80
Tooele, Ut., U.S.	C3	121
Tooele, co., Ut., U.S.	C2	121
Toole, co., Mt., U.S.	B5	103
Toombs, co., Ga., U.S.	D4	87
Toomsboro, Ga., U.S.	D3	87
Toowoomba, Austl.	E10	50
Topeka, In., U.S.	A6	91
Topeka, Ks., U.S.	C8	93
Topia, Mex.	E6	62
Topock, Az., U.S.	C1	80
Toppenish, Wa., U.S.	C5	124
Topsfield, Ma., U.S.	A6	98
Topsham, Me., U.S.	E3	96
Topton, Pa., U.S.	F10	115
Toquima Range, mts., Nv., U.S.	E5	105
Torbay, Newf., Can.	E5	72
Torbert, Mount, mtn., Ak., U.S.	g15	79
Torch Lake, l., Mi., U.S.	D5	99
Tordesillas, Spain	D6	12
Töre, Swe.	D14	6
Torgau, Ger.	D12	8
Torhout, Bel.	D3	8
Torino (Turin), Italy	D2	14
Torit, Sudan	H12	42
Torkestān, Band-e, mts., Afg.	C2	38
Tornealven, stm., Eur.	B12	4
Torngat Mountains, mts., Can.	f8	72
Toro, Spain	D6	12
Toronto, Ont., Can.	D5	73
Toronto, Oh., U.S.	B5	112
Toronto Lake, res., Ks., U.S.	E7	93
Toro Peak, mtn., Ca., U.S.	F5	82
Tororo, Ug.	A6	44
Torquay (Torbay), Eng., U.K.	K9	7
Torquemada, Spain	C7	12
Torrance, Ca., U.S.	n12	82
Torrance, co., N.M., U.S.	C3	108
Torrão, Port.	G3	12
Torre Annunziata, Italy	I9	14
Torre Baja, Spain	E10	12
Torreblanca, Spain	E12	12
Torrecilla en Cameros, Spain	C9	12
Torre de Moncorvo, Port.	D4	12
Torredonjimeno, Spain	H8	12
Torrelaguna, Spain	E8	12
Torrelavega, Spain	B7	12
Torremaggiore, Italy	H10	14
Torremolinos, Spain	I7	12
Torrens, Lake, l., Austl.	F7	50
Torrente, Spain	F11	12
Torreón, Mex.	E8	62
Torres Novas, Port.	F3	12
Torres Strait, strt., Oc.	B8	50
Torres Vedras, Port.	F2	12
Torrevieja, Spain	H11	12
Torridon, Scot., U.K.	D7	7
Torriglia, Italy	E4	14
Torrijos, Spain	F7	12
Torrington, Ct., U.S.	B3	84
Torrington, Wy., U.S.	D8	127
Torrox, Spain	I8	12
Torsby, Swe.	F9	6
Tórshavn, Faer. Is.	C6	4
Tortola, i., Br. Vir. Is.	E15	64
Tortoli, Italy	J4	14
Tortona, Italy	E3	14
Tortosa, Spain	E12	12
Tortue, Île de la, i., Haiti	D11	64
Toruń, Pol.	B18	8
Toržok, Russia	D17	18
Tosa-shimizu, Japan	J5	30
Tosa-wan, b., Japan	I6	30
Tostado, Arg.	B4	56
Totagatic, stm., Wi., U.S.	B2	126
Totana, Spain	H10	12
Toteng, Bots.	F4	44
Tôtes, Fr.	C8	10
Tot'ma, Russia	B25	18
Totowa, N.J., U.S.	B4	107
Totson Mountain, mtn., Ak., U.S.	C8	79
Tottenham, Ont., Can.	C5	73
Tottori, Japan	G7	30
Toubkal, Jbel, mtn., Mor.	B4	42
Touchet, stm., Wa., U.S.	C7	124
Touggourt, Alg.	B7	42
Touisset, Ma., U.S.	C5	98
Toul, Fr.	D12	10
Toulon, Fr.	I12	10
Toulon, Il., U.S.	B4	90
Toulouse, Fr.	I8	10
Tounan, Tai.	L9	28
Toungoo, Burma	E4	34
Tourcoing, Fr.	B10	10
Tournai, Bel.	E3	8
Tournon, Fr.	G11	10
Tournus, Fr.	F11	10
Tours, Fr.	E7	10
Touside, Pic, mtn., Chad	D9	42
Toussaint Creek, stm., Oh., U.S.	f7	112
Toutle, North Fork, stm., Wa., U.S.	C3	124
Tovar, Ven.	C7	58
Towanda, Il., U.S.	C5	90
Towanda, Ks., U.S.	E7	93
Towanda, Pa., U.S.	C9	115
Towanda Creek, stm., Pa., U.S.	C8	115
Tower City, Pa., U.S.	E8	115
Town Creek, Al., U.S.	A2	78
Towner, N.D., U.S.	A5	111
Towner, co., N.D., U.S.	A6	111
Towns, co., Ga., U.S.	B3	87
Townsend, De., U.S.	C3	85
Townsend, Mt., U.S.	D5	103
Townshend Reservoir, res., Vt., U.S.	E3	122
Townsville, Austl.	C9	50
Towson, Md., U.S.	B4	97
Toyama, Japan	F10	30
Toyohashi, Japan	H10	30
Toyokawa, Japan	H10	30
Toyonaka, Japan	H8	30
Toyooka, Japan	G7	30
Toyota, Japan	G10	30
Tozeur, Tun.	B7	42
Trabzon, Tur.	G15	4
Tracadie, N.B., Can.	B5	71
Tracy, N.B., Can.	D3	71
Tracy, Que., Can.	C4	74
Tracy, Ca., U.S.	D3	82
Tracy, Mn., U.S.	F3	100
Tracy City, Tn., U.S.	D8	119
Tracyton, Wa., U.S.	e10	124
Tradewater, stm., Ky., U.S.	C2	94
Traer, Ia., U.S.	B5	92
Trafford, Pa., U.S.	k14	115
Trafford, Lake, l., Fl., U.S.	F5	86
Trail, B.C., Can.	E9	69
Trail Creek, In., U.S.	A4	91
Traill, co., N.D., U.S.	B8	111
Trail Ridge, mtn., U.S.	F4	87
Tralee, Ire.	I3	7
Tranås, Swe.	G10	6
Trancas, Arg.	B3	56
Trang, Thai.	K5	34
Trangan, Pulau, i., Indon.	G9	32
Trani, Italy	H11	14
Transylvania, co., N.C., U.S.	f10	110
Transylvania, hist. reg., Rom.	C7	16
Transylvanian Alps see Carpaţii Meridionali, mts., Rom.	D8	16
Trapani, Italy	K7	14
Trappe, Md., U.S.	C5	97
Trapper Peak, mtn., Mt., U.S.	E2	103
Traun, Aus.	G14	8
Traunstein, Ger.	H12	8
Travelers Rest, S.C., U.S.	B3	117
Traverse, co., Mn., U.S.	E2	100
Traverse, Lake, l., U.S.	B9	118
Traverse City, Mi., U.S.	D5	99
Tra Vinh, Viet.	J9	34
Travis, co., Tx., U.S.	D4	120
Travis Air Force Base, mil., Ca., U.S.	h8	82
Travnik, Bos.	E12	14
Tray Mountain, mtn., Ga., U.S.	B3	87
Treasure, co., Mt., U.S.	D9	103
Treasure Island Naval Station, mil., Ca., U.S.	h8	82
Trecate, Italy	D3	14
Trego, co., Ks., U.S.	D4	93
Tregosse Islets, is., Austl.	C10	50
Tréguier, Fr.	D3	10
Treherne, Man., Can.	E2	70
Treinta y Tres, Ur.	C6	56
Trélazé, Fr.	E6	10
Trelew, Arg.	E3	56
Trelleborg, Swe.	I9	6
Tremblant, Mont, mtn., Que., Can.	C3	74
Tremont, Il., U.S.	C4	90
Tremont, Pa., U.S.	E9	115
Tremonton, Ut., U.S.	B3	121
Tremp, Spain	C12	12
Trempealeau, Wi., U.S.	D2	126
Trempealeau, co., Wi., U.S.	D2	126
Trempealeau, stm., Wi., U.S.	D2	126
Trenche, stm., Que., Can.	B5	74
Trenčín, Czech.	G18	8
Trent, stm., N.C., U.S.	B5	110
Trente et un Milles, Lac des, l., Que., Can.	C2	74
Trento, Italy	C6	14
Trenton, Ont., Can.	C7	73
Trenton, Fl., U.S.	C4	86
Trenton, Ga., U.S.	B1	87
Trenton, Il., U.S.	E4	90
Trenton, Mi., U.S.	F7	99
Trenton, Mo., U.S.	A4	102
Trenton, Ne., U.S.	D4	104
Trenton, N.J., U.S.	C3	107
Trenton, Oh., U.S.	C1	112
Trenton, Tn., U.S.	B3	119
Trepassey, Newf., Can.	E5	72
Trepassey Bay, b., Newf., Can.	E5	72
Tres Arroyos, Arg.	D4	56
Trescow, Pa., U.S.	E10	115
Três Corações, Braz.	F6	57
Tres Esquinas, Col.	G5	58
Três Lagoas, Braz.	F3	57
Três Marias, Reprêsa, res., Braz.	E6	57
Tres Picos, Cerro, mtn., Arg.	D4	56
Três Pontas, Braz.	F6	57
Tres Puntas, Cabo, c., Arg.	F3	56
Três Rios, Braz.	G7	57
Treutlen, co., Ga., U.S.	D4	87
Treviglio, Italy	D4	14
Treviso, Italy	D7	14
Trevor, Wi., U.S.	n11	126
Trevorton, Pa., U.S.	E8	115
Treynor, Ia., U.S.	C2	92
Trezevant, Tn., U.S.	A3	119
Triadelphia, W.V., U.S.	A4	125
Triadelphia Reservoir, res., Md., U.S.	B3	97
Triangle, Va., U.S.	B5	123
Tribune, Ks., U.S.	D2	93
Trichūr, India	G4	37
Tri City, Or., U.S.	E3	114
Trident Peak, mtn., Nv., U.S.	B3	105
Trieben, Aus.	H14	8
Trier, Ger.	F6	8
Trieste, Italy	D8	14
Trigg, co., Ky., U.S.	D2	94
Triglav, mtn., Slo.	C8	14
Trigo Mountains, mts., Az., U.S.	D1	80
Trikala, Grc.	J5	16
Trikora, Puncak, mtn., Indon.	F10	32
Tri Lakes, In., U.S.	B7	91
Trim, Ire.	H6	7
Trimble, Tn., U.S.	A2	119
Trimble, co., Ky., U.S.	B4	94
Trimont, Mn., U.S.	G4	100
Trincheras, Mex.	B4	62
Trincomalee, Sri L.	H6	37
Třinec, Czech.	F18	8
Tring Jonction, Que., Can.	C6	74
Trinidad, Bol.	F6	54
Trinidad, Col.	E7	58
Trinidad, Cuba	D8	64
Trinidad, Co., U.S.	D6	83
Trinidad, i., Trin.	I17	64
Trinidad and Tobago, ctry., N.A.	I17	64
Trinidad Head, c., Ca., U.S.	B1	82
Trinity, Al., U.S.	A2	78
Trinity, Tx., U.S.	D5	120
Trinity, co., Ca., U.S.	B2	82
Trinity, co., Tx., U.S.	D5	120
Trinity, stm., Ca., U.S.	B2	82
Trinity, stm., Tx., U.S.	D5	120
Trinity Bay, b., Newf., Can.	D5	72
Trinity Islands, is., Ak., U.S.	D9	79
Trinity Mountain, mtn., Id., U.S.	F3	89
Trinity Mountains, mts., Ca., U.S.	B2	82
Trinity Peak, mtn., Nv., U.S.	C3	105
Trinity Range, mts., Nv., U.S.	C3	105
Trion, Ga., U.S.	B1	87
Tripoli, Ia., U.S.	B5	92
Tripoli see Tarābulus, Leb.	B4	40
Tripoli see Tarābulus, Libya	B8	42
Tripp, S.D., U.S.	D8	118
Tripp, co., S.D., U.S.	D6	118
Triumph, La., U.S.	E6	95
Trivandrum, India	H4	37
Trnava, Czech.	G17	8
Troarn, Fr.	C6	10
Trobriand Islands, is., Pap. N. Gui.	A10	50
Trochu, Alta., Can.	D4	68
Trogir, Cro.	F11	14
Trois-Pistoles, Que., Can.	A8	74
Trois-Rivières, Que., Can.	C5	74
Trois-Rivières-Ouest, Que., Can.	C5	74
Trojan, Bul.	G8	16
Trollhättan, Swe.	G9	6
Trombetas, stm., Braz.	C7	54
Tromelin, i., Afr.	C10	44
Tromsø, Nor.	B12	6
Trona, Ca., U.S.	E5	82
Tronador, Monte, mtn., S.A.	E2	56
Trondheim, Nor.	E8	6
Trondheimsfjorden, Nor.	E8	6
Tropea, Italy	K10	14
Trophy Mountain, mtn., B.C., Can.	D8	69
Trotwood, Oh., U.S.	C1	112
Troup, co., Ga., U.S.	C1	87
Trousdale, co., Tn., U.S.	A5	119
Trout, stm., Fl., U.S.	m8	86
Trout, stm., Vt., U.S.	B3	122
Trout Creek, Ont., Can.	B5	73
Trout Creek Pass, Co., U.S.	C5	83
Trout Lake, Wa., U.S.	D4	124
Trout Lake, l., N.W. Ter., Can.	D8	66
Trout Lake, l., Ont., Can.	o16	73
Trout Lake, l., Mn., U.S.	B6	100
Trout Lake, l., Wi., U.S.	B4	126
Troutman, N.C., U.S.	B2	110
Trout Peak, mtn., Wy., U.S.	B3	127
Trout River, Newf., Can.	D2	72
Trouville [-sur-Mer], Fr.	C7	10
Troy, Al., U.S.	D4	78
Troy, Id., U.S.	C2	89
Troy, Il., U.S.	E4	90
Troy, Ks., U.S.	C8	93
Troy, Mi., U.S.	o15	99
Troy, Mo., U.S.	C7	102
Troy, Mt., U.S.	B1	103
Troy, N.H., U.S.	E2	106
Troy, N.Y., U.S.	C7	109
Troy, N.C., U.S.	B3	110
Troy, Oh., U.S.	B1	112
Troy, Pa., U.S.	C8	115
Troy, Tn., U.S.	A2	119
Troyes, Fr.	D11	10
Troy Peak, mtn., Nv., U.S.	E6	105
Truchas Peak, mtn., N.M., U.S.	B4	108
Trucial States see United Arab Emirates, ctry., Asia	D5	46
Truckee, Ca., U.S.	C3	82
Truckee, stm., U.S.	D2	105
Trujillo, Hond.	G4	64
Trujillo, Peru	E3	54
Trujillo, Spain	F6	12
Trujillo, Ven.	C7	58
Truman, Mn., U.S.	G4	100
Trumann, Ar., U.S.	B5	81
Trumansburg, N.Y., U.S.	C4	109
Trumbull, Ct., U.S.	E3	84
Trumbull, co., Oh., U.S.	A5	112

Name	Map Ref	Page
Trumbull, Mount, mtn., Az., U.S.	A2	80
Truro, Eng., U.K.	K7	7
Trussville, Al., U.S.	B3	78
Trustom Pond, l., R.I., U.S.	G3	116
Truth or Consequences (Hot Springs), N.M., U.S.	D2	108
Trutnov, Czech.	E15	8
Tryon, N.C., U.S.	f10	110
Tržič, Slo.	C9	14
Tsala Apopka Lake, l., Fl., U.S.	D4	86
Tsaratanana, Madag.	E9	44
Tsaratanana, Massif du, mts., Madag.	D9	44
Tschida, Lake, res., N.D., U.S.	C4	111
Tshabong, Bots.	G4	44
Tshangalele, Lac, l., Zaire	D5	44
Tshikapa, Zaire	C4	44
Tshofa, Zaire	C5	44
Tshuapa, stm., Zaire	C4	44
Tsoying, Tai.	M9	28
Tsu, Japan	H9	30
Tsubame, Japan	E11	30
Tsuchiura, Japan	F13	30
Tsugaru-kaikyō, strt., Japan	A13	30
Tsukumi, Japan	I4	30
Tsukushi-sanchi, mts., Japan	I3	30
Tsumeb, Nmb.	E3	44
Tsuruga, Japan	G9	30
Tsuruoka, Japan	D12	30
Tsushima, is., Japan	H2	30
Tsushima-kaikyō, strt., Japan	I2	30
Tsuyama, Japan	G7	30
Tual, Indon.	G9	32
Tualatin, stm., Or., U.S.	h11	114
Tuba City, Az., U.S.	A4	80
Tuban, Indon.	m16	33a
Tubarão, Braz.	B7	56
Tubruq, Libya	B10	42
Tucannon, stm., Wa., U.S.	C8	124
Tucano, Braz.	F11	54
Tuckahoe, N.Y., U.S.	h13	109
Tuckahoe, stm., N.J., U.S.	E3	107
Tucker, Ga., U.S.	h8	87
Tucker, co., W.V., U.S.	B5	125
Tucker Island, i., N.J., U.S.	E4	107
Tuckerman, Ar., U.S.	B4	81
Tuckernuck Island, i., Ma., U.S.	D7	98
Tuckerton, N.J., U.S.	D4	107
Tucson, Az., U.S.	E5	80
Tucumcari, N.M., U.S.	B6	108
Tucumcari Mountain, mtn., N.M., U.S.	B6	108
Tucupita, Ven.	C11	58
Tucuruí, Braz.	D9	54
Tudela, Spain	C10	12
Tudmur (Palmyra), Syria	B6	40
Tugaloo Lake, res., U.S.	B1	117
Tug Fork, stm., U.S.	C2	125
Tuguegarao, Phil.	p19	32
Tugur, Russia	G21	24
Tukangbesi, Kepulauan, is., Indon.	G7	32
Tuktoyaktuk, N.W. Ter., Can.	C6	66
Tukwila, Wa., U.S.	f11	124
Tula, Russia	F10	62
Tula, Russia	G20	18
Tulalip Indian Reservation, Wa., U.S.	A3	124
Tulancingo, Mex.	G10	62
Tulare, Ca., U.S.	D4	82
Tulare, co., Ca., U.S.	D4	82
Tulare Lake, l., Ca., U.S.	D4	82
Tularosa, N.M., U.S.	D3	108
Tularosa Mountains, mts., N.M., U.S.	D1	108
Tularosa Valley, val., N.M., U.S.	E3	108
Tulcán, Ec.	G4	58
Tulcea, Rom.	D12	16
Tule Lake, sw., Ca., U.S.	B3	82
Tule River Indian Reservation, Ca., U.S.	E4	82
Tule Valley, val., Ut., U.S.	D2	121
Tulia, Tx., U.S.	B2	120
Tūlkarm, Jord.	C4	40
Tullahoma, Tn., U.S.	B5	119
Tullamore, Ire.	H5	7
Tulle, Fr.	G8	10
Tullins, Fr.	G12	10
Tulsa, Ok., U.S.	A6	113
Tulsa, co., Ok., U.S.	B6	113
Tuluá, Col.	E4	58
Tulum, Mex.	G16	62
Tulun, Russia	G14	24
Tulungagung, Indon.	n15	33a
Tuma, stm., Nic.	H5	64
Tumacácori National Monument, Az., U.S.	F4	80
Tumaco, Col.	G3	58
Tuman-gang, stm., Asia	C12	26
Tumany, Russia	E25	24
Tumatumari, Guy.	E13	58
Tumba, Lac, l., Zaire	B3	44
Tumbes, Peru	D2	54
Tumble Mountain, mtn., Mt., U.S.	E4	103
Tumbler Ridge, B.C., Can.	B7	69
Tumen, China	C12	26
Tumiritinga, Braz.	E8	57
Tumkūr, India	F4	37
Tummo, Libya	D8	42
Tumsar, India	B5	37
Tumuc-Humac Mountains, mts., S.A.	C8	54
Tumwater, Wa., U.S.	B3	124
Tunbridge Wells, Eng., U.K.	J13	7
Tunduru, Tan.	D7	44
Tundža, stm., Eur.	G10	16
T'ung, stm., Russia	D17	24
Tungabhadra, stm., India	E4	37
Tungabhadra Reservoir, res., India	E4	37
Tungchiang, Tai.	M9	28
Tungsha Tao (Pratas Islands), is., Tai.	G10	26
Tungshih, Tai.	K9	28
Tunica, Ms., U.S.	A3	101
Tunica, co., Ms., U.S.	A3	101
Tunis, Tun.	M5	14
Tunisia, ctry., Afr.	B7	42
Tunja, Col.	E6	58
Tunkhannock, Pa., U.S.	C10	115
Tunk Lake, l., Me., U.S.	D4	96
Tunnel Hill, Ga., U.S.	B1	87
Tununak, Ak., U.S.	C6	79
Tunxi, China	F7	28
Tuobuja, Russia	E18	24
Tuolumne, Ca., U.S.	D3	82
Tuolumne, co., Ca., U.S.	C4	82
Tuolumne, stm., Ca., U.S.	D3	82
Tupã, Braz.	F3	57
Tupaciguara, Braz.	E4	57
Tupanciretã, Braz.	B6	56
Tupelo, Ms., U.S.	A5	101
Tupiza, Bol.	H5	54
Tupper Lake, N.Y., U.S.	A6	109
Tupper Lake, l., N.Y., U.S.	A6	109
Túquerres, Col.	G4	58
Tura, India	H14	38
Tura, Russia	E14	24
Turan, Russia	G12	24
Turbat, Pak.	D1	36
Turbeville, S.C., U.S.	D7	117
Turbo, Col.	C4	58
Turda, Rom.	C7	16
Turgutlu, Tur.	K11	16
Turimiquire, Cerro, mtn., Ven.	B11	58
Turin see Torino, Italy	D2	14
Turkey, ctry., Asia	H14	4
Turkey, stm., Ia., U.S.	B6	92
Turkey Creek, stm., Ok., U.S.	A3	113
Turkey Point, c., Md., U.S.	B5	97
Turkmenistan, ctry., Asia	I9	22
Turks and Caicos Islands, dep., N.A.	D12	64
Turks Islands, is., T./C. Is.	D12	64
Turku (Åbo), Fin.	F14	6
Turley, Ok., U.S.	A6	113
Turlock, Ca., U.S.	D3	82
Turnbull, Mount, mtn., Az., U.S.	D5	80
Turneffe Islands, is., Belize	F4	64
Turner, Or., U.S.	C4	114
Turner, co., Ga., U.S.	E3	87
Turner, co., S.D., U.S.	D8	118
Turners Falls, Ma., U.S.	A2	98
Turner Valley, Alta., Can.	D3	68
Turnhout, Bel.	D4	8
Turnor Lake, l., Sask., Can.	m7	75
Turnu-Măgurele, Rom.	F8	16
Turpan, China	C4	26
Turquino, Pico, mtn., Cuba	E9	64
Turret Peak, mtn., Az., U.S.	C4	80
Turtle Creek, Pa., U.S.	k14	115
Turtle Flambeau Flowage, res., Wi., U.S.	B3	126
Turtle Lake, N.D., U.S.	B5	111
Turtle Lake, Wi., U.S.	C1	126
Turtle Lake, l., Sask., Can.	D1	75
Turtle Mountain Indian Reservation, N.D., U.S.	A6	111
Turu, stm., Russia	D14	24
Turuchan, stm., Russia	D11	24
Turukhansk, Russia	D11	24
Tuscaloosa, Al., U.S.	B2	78
Tuscaloosa, co., Al., U.S.	B2	78
Tuscarawas, co., Oh., U.S.	B4	112
Tuscarawas, stm., Oh., U.S.	B4	112
Tuscarora Indian Reservation, N.Y., U.S.	B2	109
Tuscarora Mountain, mtn., Pa., U.S.	F6	115
Tuscarora Mountains, mts., Nv., U.S.	B5	105
Tuscola, Il., U.S.	D5	90
Tuscola, co., Mi., U.S.	E7	99
Tuscumbia, Al., U.S.	A2	78
Tuskegee, Al., U.S.	C4	78
Tusket, stm., N.S., Can.	E4	71
Tustumena Lake, l., Ak., U.S.	g16	79
Tuticorin, India	H5	37
Tutóia, Braz.	D10	54
Tuttle, Ok., U.S.	B4	113
Tuttle Creek Lake, res., Ks., U.S.	C7	93
Tututalak Mountain, mtn., Ak., U.S.	B7	79
Tutwiler, Ms., U.S.	A3	101
Tuvalu, ctry., Oc.	G24	2
Tuwayq, Jabal, mts., Sau. Ar.	D4	46
Tuxedo, N.C., U.S.	f10	110
Tuxedo Park, De., U.S.	i7	85
Tuxpan, Mex.	G11	62
Tuxpan de Rodríguez Cano, Mex.	G11	62
Tuxtla Gutiérrez, Mex.	I13	62
Túy, Spain	C3	12
Tuy Hoa, Viet.	H10	34
Tuz Gölü, l., Tur.	H14	4
Tuzigoot National Monument, Az., U.S.	C4	80
Tuzla, Bos.	E2	16
Tveitsund, Nor.	G7	6
Tver', Russia	E18	18
Tweed, Ont., Can.	C7	73
Tweedsmuir Provincial Park, B.C., Can.	C4	69
Tweedy Mountain, mtn., Mt., U.S.	E4	103
Twelvepole Creek, stm., W.V., U.S.	C2	125
Twentymile Creek, stm., W.V., U.S.	C3	125
Twentynine Palms, Ca., U.S.	E5	82
Twentynine Palms Marine Corps Base, mil., Ca., U.S.	E5	82
Twiggs, co., Ga., U.S.	D3	87
Twillingate, Newf., Can.	D4	72
Twin Buttes, mtn., Or., U.S.	C4	114
Twin Buttes Reservoir, res., Tx., U.S.	D2	120
Twin City, Ga., U.S.	D4	87
Twin Creek, stm., Oh., U.S.	C1	112
Twin Falls, Id., U.S.	G4	89
Twin Falls, co., Id., U.S.	G4	89
Twin Knolls, Az., U.S.	m9	80
Twin Lakes, Ga., U.S.	F3	87
Twin Lakes, Wi., U.S.	F5	126
Twin Lakes, l., Ct., U.S.	A2	84
Twin Lakes, l., Ia., U.S.	B3	92
Twin Lakes, l., Me., U.S.	C4	96
Twin Mountains, mtn., Wy., U.S.	E7	127
Twin Peaks, mts., Id., U.S.	E4	89
Twin Rivers, N.J., U.S.	C4	107
Twinsburg, Oh., U.S.	A4	112
Twin Valley, Mn., U.S.	C2	100
Twisp, Wa., U.S.	A5	124
Two Harbors, Mn., U.S.	C7	100
Two Hills, Alta., Can.	C5	68
Two Mile Beach, N.J., U.S.	F3	107
Two Rivers, Wi., U.S.	D6	126
Two Rivers, North Branch, stm., Mn., U.S.	B2	100
Two Rivers, South Branch, stm., Mn., U.S.	B2	100
Tybee Island, Ga., U.S.	D6	87
Tychy, Pol.	E18	8
Tygart Lake, res., W.V., U.S.	B5	125
Tygart River, Falls of the, wtfl, W.V., U.S.	k10	125
Tygart Valley, stm., W.V., U.S.	B4	125
Tyger, stm., S.C., U.S.	B4	117
Tyler, Mn., U.S.	F2	100
Tyler, Tx., U.S.	C5	120
Tyler, co., Tx., U.S.	D5	120
Tyler, co., W.V., U.S.	B4	125
Tyler, Lake, res., Tx., U.S.	C5	120
Tyler Branch, stm., Vt., U.S.	B3	122
Tyler Heights, W.V., U.S.	C3	125
Tylertown, Ms., U.S.	D3	101
Tymochtee Creek, stm., Oh., U.S.	B2	112
Tyndall, S.D., U.S.	E8	118
Tyndall Air Force Base, mil., Fl., U.S.	u16	86
Tyonek, Ak., U.S.	C9	79
Tyre see Şūr, Leb.	C4	40
Tyrma, Russia	G20	24
Tyrone, N.M., U.S.	E1	108
Tyrone, Ok., U.S.	e9	113
Tyrone, Pa., U.S.	E5	115
Tyronza, Ar., U.S.	B5	81
Tyrrell, co., N.C., U.S.	B6	110
Tyrrhenian Sea (Mare Tirreno), Eur.	I6	14
Tysse, Nor.	F5	6
Tzaneen, S. Afr.	F6	44

U

Name	Map Ref	Page
Uatumã, stm., Braz.	D7	54
Uaupés, Braz.	D5	54
Ubá, Braz.	F7	57
Ubangi (Oubangui), stm., Afr.	H9	42
Ube, Japan	I4	30
Úbeda, Spain	G8	12
Uberaba, Braz.	E5	57
Uberlândia, Braz.	E4	57
Ubly, Mi., U.S.	E8	99
Ubon Ratchathani, Thai.	G8	34
Ubundi, Zaire	B5	44
Učami, Russia	E13	24
Ucayali, stm., Peru	E4	54
Uchiura-wan, b., Japan	q18	30a
Ucluelet, B.C., Can.	E5	69
Ucon, Id., U.S.	F7	89
Uda, stm., Russia	G13	24
Uda, stm., Russia	G20	24
Udaipur, India	H5	38
Udall, Ks., U.S.	E6	93
Uddevalla, Swe.	G8	6
Udgīr, India	C4	37
Udine, Italy	C8	14
Udipi, India	F3	37
Udon Thani, Thai.	F7	34
Udskaja Guba, b., Russia	G21	24
Udža, Russia	C17	24
Ueckermünde, Ger.	B14	8
Ueda, Japan	F11	30
Uele, stm., Zaire	H10	42
Uelen, Russia	D31	24
Uelzen, Ger.	C10	8
Ueno, Japan	H9	30
Uere, stm., Zaire	H11	42
Ufa, Russia	G9	22
Uganda, ctry., Afr.	A6	44
Ugashik Lakes, l., Ak., U.S.	D8	79
Ugine, Fr.	G13	10
Uglegorsk, Russia	H22	24
Uglič, Russia	D21	18
Uhrichsville, Oh., U.S.	B4	112
Uige, Ang.	C3	44
Uijõngbu, S. Kor.	D12	26
Uil, stm., Kaz.	I9	22
Uinta, co., Wy., U.S.	E2	127
Uinta, stm., Ut., U.S.	C5	121
Uintah, co., Ut., U.S.	D6	121
Uintah and Ouray Indian Reservation, Ut., U.S.	C5	121
Uinta Mountains, mts., Ut., U.S.	C5	121
Uitenhage, S. Afr.	H5	44
Uivak, Cape, c., Newf., Can.	f9	72
Ujandina, stm., Russia	D22	24
Uji, Japan	H8	30
Ujiji, Tan.	B5	44
Ujjain, India	I6	38
Ujungpandang, Indon.	G6	32
Uka, Russia	F26	24
Ukiah, Ca., U.S.	C2	82
Ukraine, ctry., Eur.	H4	22
Ulaanbaatar (Ulan Bator), Mong.	B8	26
Ulaangom, Mong.	B5	26
Ulak Island, i., Ak., U.S.	E4	79
Ulan Bator see Ulaanbaatar, Mong.	B8	26
Ulan-Ude, Russia	G15	24
Ulhāsnagar, India	C2	37
Uliastaj, Mong.	B6	26
Ulindi, stm., Zaire	B5	44
Ulja, Russia	F21	24
Uljanovsk, Russia	G7	22
Ullapool, Scot., U.K.	D7	7
Ullŭng-do, i., S. Kor.	D13	26
Ulm, Ger.	G10	8
Ulsan, S. Kor.	D12	26
Ulster, co., N.Y., U.S.	D6	109
Ulster, hist. reg., Eur.	G5	7
Ulu, Russia	E19	24
Ulubat Gölü, l., Tur.	I12	16
Ulungur Hu, l., China	B4	26
Ulysses, Ks., U.S.	E2	93
Umag, Cro.	C8	14
Umanak, Grnld.	B22	66
Umanak Fjord, Grnld.	B22	66
Umatilla, Fl., U.S.	D5	86
Umatilla, Or., U.S.	B7	114
Umatilla, co., Or., U.S.	B8	114
Umatilla, stm., Or., U.S.	B7	114
Umatilla Indian Reservation, Or., U.S.	B8	114
Umbagog Lake, l., U.S.	A4	106
Umboi Island, i., Ak., U.S.	D11	6
Umeå, Swe.	E13	6
Umm Durmān (Omdurman), Sudan	E12	42
Umnak Island, i., Ak., U.S.	E6	79
Umnäs, Swe.	D11	6
Umpqua, stm., Or., U.S.	D3	114
Umsaskis Lake, l., Me., U.S.	B3	96
Umtata, S. Afr.	H5	44
Umzinto, S. Afr.	H6	44
Unadilla, Ga., U.S.	D3	87
Unadilla, stm., N.Y., U.S.	C5	109
Unalakleet, Ak., U.S.	C7	79
Unalaska Island, i., Ak., U.S.	E6	79
'Unayzah, Sau. Ar.	C3	46
Uncasville, Ct., U.S.	D7	84
Uncompahgre, stm., Co., U.S.	C3	83
Uncompahgre Mountains, mts., Co., U.S.	C3	83
Uncompahgre Peak, mtn., Co., U.S.	C3	83
Underwood, Al., U.S.	B3	78
Underwood, N.D., U.S.	B4	111
Ungava, Péninsule d', pen., Que., Can.	g12	71
Ungava Bay, b., Can.	E19	66
União dos Palmares, Braz.	E11	54
Unicoi, Tn., U.S.	C11	119
Unicoi, co., Tn., U.S.	C11	119
Unicoi Mountains, mts., U.S.	D9	119
Unimak Island, i., Ak., U.S.	D7	79
Unimak Pass, strt., Ak., U.S.	E6	79
Union, Ky., U.S.	k13	94
Union, Ms., U.S.	C4	101
Union, Mo., U.S.	C6	102
Union, Or., U.S.	B9	114
Union, S.C., U.S.	B4	117
Union, Wa., U.S.	B2	124
Union, co., Ar., U.S.	D3	81
Union, co., Fl., U.S.	B4	86
Union, co., Ga., U.S.	B2	87
Union, co., Il., U.S.	F4	90
Union, co., In., U.S.	E8	91
Union, co., Ia., U.S.	C3	92
Union, co., Ky., U.S.	C2	94
Union, co., La., U.S.	B3	95
Union, co., Ms., U.S.	A4	101
Union, co., N.J., U.S.	B4	107
Union, co., N.M., U.S.	A6	108
Union, co., N.C., U.S.	B2	110
Union, co., Oh., U.S.	B2	112
Union, co., Or., U.S.	B8	114
Union, co., Pa., U.S.	E7	115
Union, co., S.C., U.S.	B4	117
Union, co., S.D., U.S.	E9	118
Union, co., Tn., U.S.	C10	119
Union, West Branch, stm., Me., U.S.	D4	96
Union Beach, N.J., U.S.	C4	107
Union Bridge, Md., U.S.	A3	97
Union City, Ca., U.S.	h8	82
Union City, Ga., U.S.	C2	87
Union City, In., U.S.	D8	91
Union City, Mi., U.S.	F5	99
Union City, N.J., U.S.	h8	107
Union City, Oh., U.S.	B1	112
Union City, Ok., U.S.	B4	113
Union City, Pa., U.S.	C2	115
Union City, Tn., U.S.	A2	119
Union Flat Creek, stm., Wa., U.S.	C8	124
Union Gap, Wa., U.S.	C5	124
Union Grove, Wi., U.S.	F5	126
Union Lake, l., N.J., U.S.	E2	107
Union Pier, Mi., U.S.	G4	99
Union Point, Ga., U.S.	C3	87
Union Springs, Al., U.S.	C4	78
Uniontown, Al., U.S.	C2	78
Uniontown, Ky., U.S.	C2	94
Uniontown, Oh., U.S.	B4	112
Uniontown, Pa., U.S.	G2	115
Union Village, R.I., U.S.	B3	116
Union Village Reservoir, res., Vt., U.S.	D4	122
Unionville, Mo., U.S.	A4	102
United Arab Emirates, ctry., Asia	D5	46
United Kingdom, ctry., Eur.	E7	4
United Nations Headquarters, N.Y., U.S.	h12	109
United States, ctry., N.A.	D7	76
United States Air Force Academy, mil., Co., U.S.	B6	83
United States Military Academy, mil., N.Y., U.S.	C6	109
United States Naval Academy, mil., Md., U.S.	C4	97
Unity Reservoir, res., Or., U.S.	C8	114
University City, Mo., U.S.	C7	102
University Heights, Ia., U.S.	C6	92
University Heights, Oh., U.S.	h9	112
University Park, Ia., U.S.	C5	92
University Park, N.M., U.S.	E3	108
University Park, Tx., U.S.	n10	120
University Place, Wa., U.S.	f10	124
Unnão, India	G9	38
Uozu, Japan	F10	30
Upata, Ven.	C11	58
Upemba, Lac, l., Zaire	C5	44
Upernavik, Grnld.	B21	66
Upington, S. Afr.	G4	44
Upland, Ca., U.S.	E5	82
Upland, In., U.S.	D7	91
Upleta, India	J4	38
Upolu Point, c., Hi., U.S.	C6	88
Upper Ammonoosuc, stm., N.H., U.S.	A4	106
Upper Arlington, Oh., U.S.	B2	112
Upper Arrow Lake, l., B.C., Can.	F9	66
Upper Arrow Lake, res., B.C., Can.	D9	69
Upperco, Md., U.S.	A4	97
Upper Darby, Pa., U.S.	G11	115
Upper Greenwood Lake, N.J., U.S.	A4	107
Upper Humber, stm., Newf., Can.	D3	72
Upper Iowa, stm., Ia., U.S.	A5	92
Upper Island Cove, Newf., Can.	E5	72
Upper Kapuas Mountains, mts., Asia	E5	32
Upper Klamath Lake, l., Or., U.S.	E4	114
Upper Marlboro, Md., U.S.	C4	97
Upper New York Bay, b., U.S.	k8	107
Upper Red Lake, l., Mn., U.S.	B4	100
Upper Saddle River, N.J., U.S.	A4	107
Upper Sandusky, Oh., U.S.	B2	112
Upper Sheila, N.B., Can.	B5	71
Upper Volta see Burkina Faso, ctry., Afr.	F5	42
Uppsala, Swe.	G11	6
Upright, Cape, c., Ak., U.S.	C5	79
Upshur, co., Tx., U.S.	C5	120
Upshur, co., W.V., U.S.	C4	125
Upson, co., Ga., U.S.	D2	87
Upton, Que., Can.	D5	74
Upton, Ky., U.S.	C4	94
Upton, Ma., U.S.	B4	98
Upton, Wy., U.S.	B8	127
Upton, co., Tx., U.S.	D2	120
Uquía, Cerro, mtn., Ven.	E11	58
Urabá, Golfo de, b., Col.	C4	58
Ural, stm., Asia	H8	22
Ural Mountains see Ural'skije gory, mts., Russia	F9	22
Ural'sk, Kaz.	G8	22
Ural'skije gory (Ural Mountains), mts., Russia	F9	22
Urania, La., U.S.	C3	95
Urbana, Il., U.S.	C5	90
Urbana, Oh., U.S.	B2	112
Urbancrest, Oh., U.S.	m10	112
Urbandale, Ia., U.S.	C4	92
Urbino, Italy	F7	14
Urfa, Tur.	H15	4
Urgenč, Uzb.	I10	22
Uribe, Col.	F5	58
Uribia, Col.	B6	58
Urla, Tur.	K10	16
Uruapan [del Progreso], Mex.	H8	62
Urubamba, stm., Peru	F4	54
Urucuia, stm., Braz.	D6	57
Uruguaiana, Braz.	B5	56
Uruguay, ctry., S.A.	C5	56
Uruguay (Uruguai), stm., S.A.	C5	56
Ürümqi, China	C4	26
Ur'ung-Chaja, Russia	C16	24
Urun-Islāmpur, India	D3	37
Urup, Ostrov, i., Russia	H23	24
Usa, Japan	I4	30
Uşak, Tur.	K13	16
Usedom, i., Eur.	B14	8
Ushibuka, Japan	J3	30
Ushuaia, Arg.	G3	56
Usolje-Sibirskoje, Russia	G14	24
Usquepaug, R.I., U.S.	F3	116
Ussel, Fr.	G9	10
Ussuri (Wusuli), stm., Asia	B14	26
Ussurijsk, Russia	I20	24
Ust'-Barguzin, Russia	G15	24
Ust'-Belaja, Russia	D28	24
Ust'Čaun, Russia	D28	24
Ústí nad Labem, Czech.	E14	8
Ust'-Kamčatsk, Russia	F26	24
Ust'-Kamenogorsk, Kaz.	H10	24
Ust'-Kut, Russia	F15	24
Ust'-Maja, Russia	E20	24
Ust'-Nera, Russia	E22	24
Usu, China	C3	26
Usuki, Japan	I4	30
Usulután, El Sal.	H3	64
Usumacinta, stm., N.A.	I14	62
Utah, co., Ut., U.S.	C4	121
Utah, state, U.S.	D4	121
Utah Lake, l., Ut., U.S.	C4	121
Utashinai, Japan	p20	30a
Ute Creek, stm., N.M., U.S.	A6	108
Ute Mountain Indian Reservation, U.S.	D2	83
Ute Reservoir, res., N.M., U.S.	B6	108
Utete, Tan.	C7	44
Uthai Thani, Thai.	G6	34
Utiariti, Braz.	F7	54
Utica, Il., U.S.	B5	90
Utica, Mi., U.S.	F7	99
Utica, Ms., U.S.	C3	101
Utica, Ne., U.S.	D8	104
Utica, N.Y., U.S.	B5	109
Utica, Oh., U.S.	B3	112
Utiel, Spain	F10	12
Utikuma Lake, l., Alta., Can.	B3	68
Utrecht, Neth.	C5	8
Utrera, Spain	H6	12
Utsunomiya, Japan	F12	30
Uttar Pradesh, state, India	G8	38
Uusikaupunki (Nystad), Fin.	F13	6
Uvá, stm., Col.	F8	58
Uvalde, Tx., U.S.	E3	120
Uvalde, co., Tx., U.S.	E3	120
Uvdal, Nor.	F7	6
Uvinza, Tan.	C6	44
Uvs Nuur, l., Asia	A5	26
Uwajima, Japan	I5	30
'Uwaynāt, Jabal al-, mtn., Afr.	D10	42
Uwharrie, stm., N.C., U.S.	B3	110

Name	Map Ref	Page
Uxbridge, Ma., U.S.	B4	98
Uyuni, Bol.	H5	54
Uyuni, Salar de, pl., Bol.	H5	54
Uzbekistan, state, Asia	I10	22
Uzerche, Fr.	G8	10
Uzès, Fr.	H11	10
Uzlovaja, Russia	H21	18
Uzunköprü, Tur.	H10	16
Užur, Russia	F11	24

V

Name	Map Ref	Page
Vaala, Fin.	D16	6
Vaasa (Vasa), Fin.	E13	6
Vác, Hung.	H19	8
Vaca Key, i., Fl., U.S.	H5	86
Vacaville, Ca., U.S.	C3	82
Vaccarès, Étang de, b., Fr.	I11	10
Vach, stm., Russia	E9	24
Vacherie, La., U.S.	h10	95
Vadsø, Nor.	A17	6
Vaduz, Liech.	H9	8
Váh, stm., Czech.	G18	8
Vaiden, Ms., U.S.	B4	101
Vail, Co., U.S.	B4	83
Väkhän, stm., Afg.	B5	38
Väkhän, reg., Afg.	B5	38
Våládalen, Swe.	E9	6
Val-Bélair, Que., Can.	n17	74
Valcheta, Arg.	E3	56
Valcourt, Que., Can.	D5	74
Val-David, Que., Can.	C3	74
Valdecañas, Embalse de, res., Spain	F6	12
Valdemarsvik, Swe.	G11	6
Valdepeñas, Spain	G8	12
Valderrobres, Spain	E12	12
Valders, Wi., U.S.	D6	126
Valdés, Península, pen., Arg.	E4	56
Valdese, N.C., U.S.	B1	110
Valdez, Ak., U.S.	C10	79
Val-d'Isère, Fr.	G13	10
Valdivia, Chile	D2	56
Valdivia, Col.	D5	58
Val-d'Or, Que., Can.	k11	74
Valdosta, Ga., U.S.	F3	87
Vale, Or., U.S.	D9	114
Valemount, B.C., Can.	C8	69
Valença, Braz.	B9	57
Valença, Port.	C3	12
Valençay, Fr.	E8	10
Valence, Fr.	H11	10
Valencia, Spain	F11	12
Valencia, Az., U.S.	m7	80
Valencia, Ven.	C8	58
Valencia, co., N.M., U.S.	C3	108
Valencia, Golfo de, b., Spain	F12	12
Valencia de Alcántara, Spain	F4	12
Valencia de Don Juan, Spain	C6	12
Valencia Heights, S.C., U.S.	D6	117
Valenciennes, Fr.	B10	10
Valentine, Ne., U.S.	B5	104
Valenza, Italy	D3	14
Valera, Ven.	C7	58
Valga, Est.	D9	18
Valhalla, N.Y., U.S.	D7	109
Valhermoso Springs, Al., U.S.	A3	78
Valjevo, Yugo.	E3	16
Valkeakoski, Fin.	F15	6
Valkenswaard, Neth.	D5	8
Valladolid, Mex.	G15	62
Valladolid, Spain	D7	12
Vall de Uxó, Spain	F11	12
Vallecito Reservoir, res., Co., U.S.	D3	83
Valle de Guanape, Ven.	C10	58
Valle de la Pascua, Ven.	C9	58
Valle de Santiago, Mex.	G9	62
Valle de Zaragoza, Mex.	D7	62
Valledupar, Col.	B6	58
Vallée-Jonction, Que., Can.	C7	74
Valle Hermoso, Mex.	E11	62
Vallejo, Ca., U.S.	C2	82
Vallelunga Pratameno, Italy	L8	14
Vallenar, Chile	B2	56
Valletta, Malta	N9	14
Valley, Ne., U.S.	C9	104
Valley, co., Id., U.S.	E3	89
Valley, co., Mt., U.S.	B10	103
Valley, co., Ne., U.S.	C6	104
Valley, stm., Man., Can.	D1	70
Valley Center, Ks., U.S.	E6	93
Valley City, N.D., U.S.	C8	111
Valley Cottage, N.Y., U.S.	g13	109
Valley East, Ont., Can.	p19	73
Valley Falls, Ks., U.S.	C8	93
Valley Falls, R.I., U.S.	B4	116
Valley Forge, Pa., U.S.	o20	115
Valley Mills, Tx., U.S.	D4	120
Valley Park, Mo., U.S.	f12	102
Valley Springs, S.D., U.S.	D9	118
Valley Station, Ky., U.S.	g11	94
Valley Stream, N.Y., U.S.	n15	109
Valleyview, Alta., Can.	B2	68
Valley View, Pa., U.S.	E8	115
Valliant, Ok., U.S.	D6	113
Vallo della Lucania, Italy	I10	14
Valls, Spain	D13	12
Vallscreek, W.V., U.S.	D3	125
Valmeyer, Il., U.S.	E3	90
Valognes, Fr.	C5	10
Valparai, India	G4	37
Valparaíso, Chile	C2	56
Valparaíso, Mex.	F8	62
Valparaiso, Fl., U.S.	u15	86
Valparaiso, In., U.S.	B3	91
Valréas, Fr.	H11	10
Vals, Tanjung, c., Indon.	G10	32
Valtimo, Fin.	E17	6
Val Verde, Ut., U.S.	C4	121
Valverde, Dom. Rep.	E12	64
Val Verde, co., Tx., U.S.	E2	120
Valverde del Camino, Spain	H5	12
Van, Tur.	H16	4
Van, Tx., U.S.	C5	120
Van, W.V., U.S.	n12	125
Van Alstyne, Tx., U.S.	C4	120
Vanavara, Russia	E14	24
Van Buren, Ar., U.S.	B1	81
Van Buren, In., U.S.	C6	91
Van Buren, Me., U.S.	A5	96
Van Buren, Mo., U.S.	E6	102
Van Buren, co., Ar., U.S.	B3	81
Van Buren, co., Ia., U.S.	D6	92
Van Buren, co., Mi., U.S.	F4	99
Van Buren, co., Tn., U.S.	D8	119
Vance, co., N.C., U.S.	A4	110
Vance Air Force Base, mil., Ok., U.S.	A3	113
Vanceboro, N.C., U.S.	B5	110
Vanceburg, Ky., U.S.	B6	94
Vancleave, Ms., U.S.	E5	101
Vancouver, B.C., Can.	E6	69
Vancouver, Wa., U.S.	D3	124
Vancouver, Cape, c., Austl.	G3	50
Vancouver Island, i., B.C., Can.	E4	69
Vancouver Island Ranges, mts., B.C., Can.	D4	69
Vandalia, Il., U.S.	E4	90
Vandalia, Mo., U.S.	B6	102
Vandenberg Air Force Base, mil., Ca., U.S.	E3	82
Vander, N.C., U.S.	B4	110
Vanderbilt Peak, mtn., N.M., U.S.	E1	108
Vanderburgh, co., In., U.S.	H2	91
Vandergrift, Pa., U.S.	E2	115
Vanderhoof, B.C., Can.	C5	69
Van Diemen Gulf, b., Austl.	B6	50
Vänern, l., Swe.	G9	6
Vänersborg, Swe.	G9	6
Vangaindrano, Madag.	F9	44
Van Gölü, l., Tur.	H16	4
Vangunu, i., Sol.Is.	A11	50
Van Horn, Tx., U.S.	o12	120
Van Horne, Ia., U.S.	B5	92
Vanier, Ont., Can.	h12	73
Väniyambädi, India	F5	37
Vankarem, Russia	D30	24
Vankleek Hill, Ont., Can.	B10	73
Van Kull, Kill, stm., N.J., U.S.	k8	107
Van Lear, Ky., U.S.	C7	94
Van Meter, Ia., U.S.	C4	92
Vännäs, Swe.	E12	6
Vannes, Fr.	E4	10
Van Rees, Pegunungan, mts., Indon.	F10	32
Vanrhynsdorp, S. Afr.	H3	44
Vansant, Va., U.S.	e9	123
Vansbro, Swe.	F10	6
Vansittart Island, i., N.W. Ter., Can.	C16	66
Vanuatu, ctry., Oc.	H24	2
Van Vleck, Tx., U.S.	r14	120
Van Wert, Oh., U.S.	B1	112
Van Wert, co., Oh., U.S.	B1	112
Van Zandt, co., Tx., U.S.	C5	120
Varades, Fr.	E5	10
Väränasi (Benares), India	H10	38
Varaždin, Cro.	C11	14
Varazze, Italy	E3	14
Varberg, Swe.	H9	6
Vardaman, Ms., U.S.	B4	101
Vardar (Axiós), stm., Eur.	H6	16
Vardø, Nor.	A18	6
Varennes, Que., Can.	D4	74
Varennes-sur-Allier, Fr.	F10	10
Varese, Italy	D3	14
Varginha, Braz.	F6	57
Varina, Ia., U.S.	B3	92
Varkaus, Fin.	E16	6
Varkhān, stm., Afg.	F11	16
Varna, Bul.	F11	16
Värnamo, Swe.	H10	6
Varnville, S.C., U.S.	F5	117
Varzy, Fr.	E10	10
Vasai (Bassein), India	C2	37
Vashon, Point, c., Wa., U.S.	e11	124
Vashon Island, i., Wa., U.S.	f11	124
Vass, N.C., U.S.	B3	110
Vassar, Mi., U.S.	E7	99
Västerås, Swe.	G11	6
Västervik, Swe.	H11	6
Vasto, Italy	G9	14
Vas'ugan, stm., Russia	F9	24
Vatican City (Città del Vaticano), ctry., Eur.	H7	14
Vatnajökull, Ice.	C4	4
Vättern, l., Swe.	G10	6
Vaucouleurs, Fr.	D12	10
Vaudreuil, Que., Can.	D3	74
Vaughan, Ont., Can.	D5	73
Vaughn, Mt., U.S.	C5	103
Vaughn, N.M., U.S.	C4	108
Vaupés (Uaupés), stm., S.A.	G7	58
Vauxhall, Alta., Can.	D4	68
Växjö, Swe.	H10	6
Vazante, Braz.	D5	57
V'azemskij, Russia	H20	24
V'az'ma, Russia	F17	18
V'azniki, Russia	E25	18
Veazie, Me., U.S.	D4	96
Vechta, Ger.	C8	8
Veedersburg, In., U.S.	D3	91
Veendam, Neth.	B6	8
Vegreville, Alta., Can.	C4	68
Vejer de la Frontera, Spain	I6	12
Vejle, Den.	I7	6
Vela Luka, Cro.	G11	14
Velda Rose Estates, Az., U.S.	*D4	80
Velenje, Slo.	C10	14
Vélez-Málaga, Spain	I7	12
Vélez Rubio, Spain	H9	12
Velhas, Rio das, stm., Braz.	D6	57
Velike Lašče, Slo.	D9	14
Velikije Luki, Russia	E13	18
Veliko Târnovo, Bul.	F9	16
Vella Lavella, i., Sol.Is.	A11	50
Velletri, Italy	H7	14
Vellore, India	F5	37
Velma, Ok., U.S.	C4	113
Velva, N.D., U.S.	A5	111
Venado Tuerto, Arg.	C4	56
Venango, co., Pa., U.S.	D2	115
Venda Nova, Braz.	E7	57
Vendeuvre-sur-Barse, Fr.	D11	10
Vendôme, Fr.	E8	10
Veneta, Or., U.S.	C3	114
Venezia (Venice), Italy	D7	14
Venezuela, ctry., S.A.	B5	54
Venezuela, Golfo de, b., S.A.	B7	58
Veniaminof, Mount, mtn., Ak., U.S.	D8	79
Venice, Fl., U.S.	E4	86
Venice, Il., U.S.	E3	90
Venice, Gulf of, b., Eur.	D7	14
Venice see Venezia, Italy	D7	14
Vénissieux, Fr.	G11	10
Venlo, Neth.	D6	8
Venosa, Italy	I10	14
Ventanas, Ec.	H3	58
Ventnor City, N.J., U.S.	E4	107
Ventspils, Lat.	D4	18
Ventuari, stm., Ven.	E9	58
Ventura (San Buenaventura), Ca., U.S.	E4	82
Ventura, co., Ca., U.S.	E4	82
Venustiano Carranza, Mex.	I13	62
Vera, Arg.	B5	56
Veracruz [Llave], Mex.	H11	62
Veräval, India	J4	38
Verbania, Italy	D3	14
Vercelli, Italy	D3	14
Verchères, Que., Can.	D4	74
Verchn'aja Amga, Russia	F19	24
Verchneimbatskoje, Russia	E11	24
Verchojansk, Russia	D20	24
Verchojanskij Chrebet, mts., Russia	D19	24
Verda, Ky., U.S.	D6	94
Verde, stm., Az., U.S.	C4	80
Verden, Ger.	C9	8
Verdi, Nv., U.S.	D2	105
Verdigre, Ne., U.S.	B7	104
Verdigris, Ok., U.S.	A6	113
Verdigris, stm., U.S.	A6	113
Verdi Peak, mtn., Nv., U.S.	C6	105
Verdun, Que., Can.	q19	74
Verdun, Fr.	C12	10
Vereeniging, S. Afr.	G5	44
Vergara, Spain	B9	12
Vergennes, Vt., U.S.	C2	122
Vergne, Fr.	G11	10
Veríssimo, Braz.	E4	57
Vermilion, Alta., Can.	C5	68
Vermilion, Oh., U.S.	A3	112
Vermilion, co., Il., U.S.	C6	90
Vermilion, co., La., U.S.	E3	95
Vermilion, stm., Alta., Can.	C5	68
Vermilion, stm., Il., U.S.	C5	90
Vermilion, stm., La., U.S.	E3	95
Vermilion, stm., Mn., U.S.	B6	100
Vermilion, stm., Oh., U.S.	A3	112
Vermilion Bay, b., La., U.S.	E3	95
Vermilion Lake, l., Mn., U.S.	C6	100
Vermilion Pass, Can.	D2	68
Vermillion, S.D., U.S.	E9	118
Vermillion, co., In., U.S.	E2	91
Vermillion, East Fork, stm., S.D., U.S.	C8	118
Vermillon, stm., Que., Can.	B4	74
Vermont, Il., U.S.	C3	90
Vermont, state, U.S.	D3	122
Vermontville, Mi., U.S.	F5	99
Vernal, Ut., U.S.	C6	121
Verneuil-sur-Avre, Fr.	D7	10
Vernon, B.C., Can.	D8	69
Vernon, Fr.	C8	10
Vernon, Al., U.S.	B1	78
Vernon, Tx., U.S.	B3	120
Vernon, co., La., U.S.	C2	95
Vernon, co., Mo., U.S.	D3	102
Vernon, co., Wi., U.S.	E3	126
Vernon Hills, Il., U.S.	h9	90
Vernonia, Or., U.S.	B3	114
Vero Beach, Fl., U.S.	E6	86
Véroia, Grc.	I6	16
Verona, Ont., Can.	C8	73
Verona, Italy	D5	14
Verona, Ms., U.S.	A5	101
Verona, N.J., U.S.	B4	107
Verona, Pa., U.S.	k14	115
Verona, Wi., U.S.	E4	126
Verret, Lake, l., La., U.S.	E4	95
Versailles, Fr.	D9	10
Versailles, In., U.S.	F7	91
Versailles, Ky., U.S.	B5	94
Versailles, Mo., U.S.	C5	102
Versailles, Oh., U.S.	B1	112
Vert, Cap, c., Sen.	F2	42
Vertientes, Cuba	D8	64
Vertou, Fr.	E5	10
Verviers, Bel.	E5	8
Vesoul, Fr.	E13	10
Vestal, N.Y., U.S.	C4	109
Vestavia Hills, Al., U.S.	g7	78
Vestmannaeyjar, Ice.	C3	4
Vesuvio, vol., Italy	I9	14
Vesuvius see Vesuvio, vol., Italy	I9	14
Veszprém, Hung.	H17	8
Vetlanda, Swe.	H10	6
Vevay, In., U.S.	G7	91
Vevey, Switz.	F13	10
Veynes, Fr.	H12	10
Viadana, Italy	E5	14
Viana, Ok., U.S.	B7	113
Viana del Bollo, Spain	C4	12
Viana do Alentejo, Port.	G3	12
Viana do Castelo, Port.	D3	12
Viangchan, Laos	F7	34
Viareggio, Italy	F5	14
Viborg, Den.	H7	6
Viborg, S.D., U.S.	D8	118
Vibo Valentia, Italy	K11	14
Viburnum, Mo., U.S.	D6	102
Vic-en-Bigorre, Fr.	I7	10
Vicente, Point, c., Ca., U.S.	n12	82
Vicenza, Italy	D6	14
Vich, Spain	D14	12
Vichada, stm., Col.	E8	58
Vichy, Fr.	F10	10
Vici, Ok., U.S.	A2	113
Vicksburg, Mi., U.S.	F5	99
Vicksburg, Ms., U.S.	C3	101
Vicksburg National Military Park, Ms., U.S.	C3	101
Viçosa, Braz.	F7	57
Victor, Ia., U.S.	C5	92
Victor, N.Y., U.S.	C3	109
Victoria, B.C., Can.	E6	69
Victoria, Newf., Can.	E5	72
Victoria (Xianggang), H.K.	M3	28
Victoria, Sey.	B11	44
Victoria, Ks., U.S.	D4	93
Victoria, Tx., U.S.	E4	120
Victoria, Va., U.S.	*C4	123
Victoria, state, Austl.	G9	50
Victoria, co., Tx., U.S.	E4	120
Victoria, Lake, l., Afr.	B6	44
Victoria, Mount, mtn., Burma	D2	34
Victoria de las Tunas, Cuba	D9	64
Victoria Falls, wtfl, Afr.	E5	44
Victoria Harbour, Ont., Can.	C5	73
Victoria Island, i., N.W. Ter., Can.	B10	66
Victoria Lake, res., Newf., Can.	D3	72
Victoria Land, reg., Ant.	B28	47
Victoria Nile, stm., Ug.	H12	42
Victoria Peak, mtn., Belize	F3	64
Victoria Strait, strt., N.W. Ter., Can.	C12	66
Victoriaville, Que., Can.	C6	74
Victoria West, S. Afr.	H4	44
Victorville, Ca., U.S.	E5	82
Vičuga, Russia	D24	18
Vidalia, Ga., U.S.	D4	87
Vidalia, La., U.S.	C4	95
Vidisha, India	I7	38
Vidor, Tx., U.S.	D5	120
Viechtach, Ger.	F12	8
Viedma, Arg.	E4	56
Viedma, Lago, l., Arg.	F2	56
Viella, Spain	C12	12
Vienna, Ga., U.S.	D3	87
Vienna, Il., U.S.	F5	90
Vienna, Mo., U.S.	C6	102
Vienna, Va., U.S.	B5	123
Vienna, W.V., U.S.	B3	125
Vienna see Wien, Aus.	G16	8
Vienne, Fr.	G11	10
Vientiane see Viangchan, Laos	F7	34
Vieques, Isla de, i., P.R.	E15	64
Vieremä, Fin.	E16	6
Vierwaldstätter See, l., Switz.	F15	10
Vierzon, Fr.	E9	10
Vieste, Italy	H11	14
Vietnam, ctry., Asia	B4	32
Vieux Desert, Lac, l., Wi., U.S.	B4	126
Vigan, Phil.	p19	33b
Vigevano, Italy	D3	14
Vignola, Italy	E5	14
Vigo, Spain	C3	12
Vigo, co., In., U.S.	F3	91
Vihti, Fin.	F15	6
Vijayawāda, India	D6	37
Vijose (Aóös), stm., Eur.	I3	16
Vikajärvi, Fin.	C16	6
Viking, Alta., Can.	C5	68
Vila Coutinho, Moz.	D6	44
Vila do Conde, Port.	D3	12
Vila Fontes, Moz.	E7	44
Vilafranca del Panadés, Spain	D13	12
Vilafranca de Xira, Port.	G3	12
Vilanculos, Moz.	F7	44
Vila Nova de Famalicão, Port.	D3	12
Vila Nova de Foz Côa, Port.	D4	12
Vila Nova de Gaia, Port.	D3	12
Vila Pery, Moz.	E6	44
Vila Real, Port.	D4	12
Vilas, co., Wi., U.S.	B4	126
Vila Velha, Braz.	F8	57
Vila Velha de Ródão, Port.	F4	12
Vilhelmina, Swe.	D11	6
Vilhena, Braz.	F6	54
Vil'kickogo, Proliv, strt., Russia	B14	24
Villa Ahumada, Mex.	B6	62
Villa Bella, Bol.	F5	54
Villablino, Spain	C5	12
Villa Bruzual, Ven.	C8	58
Villacañas, Spain	F8	12
Villacarriedo, Spain	B8	12
Villacarrillo, Spain	G8	12
Villach, Aus.	I13	8
Villacidro, Italy	J3	14
Villa Colón (Caucete), Arg.	C3	56
Villa del Rosario, Ven.	I11	64
Villa de Méndez, Mex.	E10	62
Villadiego, Spain	C7	12
Villafranca del Bierzo, Spain	C5	12
Villafranca de los Barros, Spain	G5	12
Villafranca di Verona, Italy	D5	14
Villa Frontera, Mex.	D9	62
Villagarcia, Spain	C3	12
Villa Grove, Il., U.S.	D5	90
Villaguay, Arg.	C5	56
Villa Hayes, Para.	B5	56
Villahermosa, Mex.	I13	62
Villajoyosa, Spain	G11	12
Villalón de Campos, Spain	C6	12
Villalonga, Arg.	D4	56
Villalpando, Spain	D6	12
Villa Maria, Arg.	C4	56
Villamartín, Spain	I6	12
Villa Montes, Bol.	H6	54
Villanova Monteleone, Italy	I3	14
Villanueva, Col.	B6	58
Villanueva de Córdoba, Spain	G7	12
Villanueva de la Serena, Spain	G6	12
Villanueva de los Infantes, Spain	G9	12
Villanueva del Río y Minas, Spain	H6	12
Villanueva y Geltrú, Spain	D13	12
Villa Park, Il., U.S.	k8	90
Villa Pedro Montoya, Mex.	G10	62
Villarcayo, Spain	C8	12
Villa Rica, Ga., U.S.	C2	87
Villarreal, Spain	F11	12
Villarrica, Chile	D2	56
Villarrobledo, Spain	F9	12
Villas, N.J., U.S.	E3	107
Villa San Giovanni, Italy	K10	14
Villasayas, Spain	D9	12
Villa Unión, Arg.	B4	56
Villavicencio, Col.	E6	58
Villaviciosa de Córdoba, Spain	G6	12
Villedieu, Fr.	D5	10
Villefort, Fr.	H10	10
Villefranche, Fr.	G11	10
Villefranche-de-Rouergue, Fr.	H9	10
Villena, Spain	G11	12
Villeneuve-de-Berg, Fr.	H11	10
Villeneuve-Saint-Georges, Fr.	D9	10
Villeneuve-sur-Lot, Fr.	H7	10
Ville Platte, La., U.S.	D3	95
Villers-Bocage, Fr.	C6	10
Villers-Cotterêts, Fr.	C10	10
Ville Saint-Georges, Que., Can.	C7	74
Villeurbanne, Fr.	G11	10
Villingen-Schwenningen, Ger.	G8	8
Villisca, Ia., U.S.	D2	92
Villupuram, India	G5	37
Vilnius, Lith.	G8	18
Vilonia, Ar., U.S.	B3	81
Vilsbiburg, Ger.	G12	8
Vil'uj, stm., Russia	E18	24
Vil'ujsk, Russia	E18	24
Vimianzo, Spain	B2	12
Vimoutiers, Fr.	D7	10
Vina, stm., Cam.	G8	42
Viña del Mar, Chile	C2	56
Vinalhaven, Me., U.S.	D4	96
Vinalhaven Island, i., Me., U.S.	D4	96
Vinaroz, Spain	E12	12
Vincennes, In., U.S.	G2	91
Vincent, Al., U.S.	B3	78
Vinces, Ec.	H3	58
Vindeln, Swe.	D12	6
Vindhya Range, mts., India	I7	38
Vine Brook, stm., Ma., U.S.	g11	98
Vinegar Hill, mtn., Or., U.S.	C8	114
Vine Grove, Ky., U.S.	C4	94
Vineland, N.J., U.S.	E2	107
Vineyard Haven, Ma., U.S.	D6	98
Vineyard Sound, strt., Ma., U.S.	D6	98
Vinh, Viet.	E8	34
Vinhais, Port.	D4	12
Vinh Long, Viet.	I8	34
Vinita, Ok., U.S.	A6	113
Vinkovci, Cro.	D2	16
Vinnica, Ukr.	H3	22
Vinnitsa see Vinnica, Ukr.	H3	22
Vinson Massif, mtn., Ant.	B4	47
Vinton, Ia., U.S.	B5	92
Vinton, La., U.S.	D2	95
Vinton, Va., U.S.	C3	123
Vinton, co., Oh., U.S.	C3	112
Viola, Il., U.S.	B3	90
Violet, La., U.S.	k12	95
Vipava, Slo.	D8	14
Vipiteno, Italy	C6	14
Virac, Phil.	C7	32
Viramgām, India	I5	38
Viranşehir, Tur.	A6	40
Virden, Man., Can.	E1	70
Virden, Il., U.S.	D4	90
Vire, Fr.	D6	10
Virgin, stm., U.S.	G8	105
Virginia, S. Afr.	G5	44
Virginia, Al., U.S.	g6	78
Virginia, Il., U.S.	D3	90
Virginia, Mn., U.S.	C6	100
Virginia, state, U.S.	C4	123
Virginia Beach, Va., U.S.	D7	123
Virginia City, Nv., U.S.	D2	105
Virginia Peak, mtn., Nv., U.S.	D2	105
Virgin Islands, dep., N.A.	E15	64
Virje, Cro.	C11	14
Virkie, Scot., U.K.	B11	7
Viroqua, Wi., U.S.	E3	126
Virovitica, Cro.	D12	14
Virtaniemi, Fin.	B17	6
Virudunagar, India	H4	37
Vis, Cro.	F11	14
Visalia, Ca., U.S.	D4	82
Visby, Swe.	H12	6
Viscount Melville Sound, strt., N.W. Ter., Can.	B10	66
Viseu, Port.	E4	12
Vishākhapatnam, India	D7	37
Vislinskij Zaliv, b., Eur.	A19	8
Visnagar, India	I5	38
Vista, Ca., U.S.	F5	82
Vistula see Wisła, stm., Pol.	A18	8
Vitarte, Peru	F3	54
Vitebsk, Bela.	F13	18
Viterbo, Italy	G7	14
Vitigudino, Spain	D5	12
Vitim, Russia	F16	24
Vitim, stm., Russia	F16	24
Vitória, Braz.	F8	57
Vitoria, Spain	C9	12
Vitória da Conquista, Braz.	C8	57
Vitré, Fr.	D5	10
Vitry-le-François, Fr.	D11	10
Vitteaux, Fr.	E11	10
Vittel, Fr.	D12	10
Vittoria, Italy	M9	14
Vittorio Veneto, Italy	D7	14
Viver, Spain	F11	12
Vivero, Spain	B4	12
Vivian, La., U.S.	B2	95
Viviers, Fr.	H11	10
Vivonne, Fr.	F7	10
Vizcachas, Meseta de las, plat., Arg.	G2	56
Vizcaíno, Desierto de, des., Mex.	D3	62
Vizianagaram, India	C7	37
Vizille, Fr.	G12	10
Vladikavkaz, Russia	I6	22

Name	Map Ref	Page
Vladimir, Russia	E23	18
Vladivostok, Russia	E35	128
Vlissingen (Flushing), Neth.	D3	8
Vlorë, Alb.	I3	16
Vltava, stm., Czech.	F14	8
Vöcklabruck, Aus.	G13	8
Vodnjan, Cro.	E8	14
Vogelsberg, mts., Ger.	E9	8
Voghera, Italy	E4	14
Vohenstrauss, Ger.	F12	8
Vohibinany, Madag.	E9	44
Vohimarina, Madag.	D10	44
Voi, Kenya	B7	44
Voinjama, Lib.	G4	42
Voiron, Fr.	G12	10
Voitsberg, Aus.	H15	8
Volcano, Hi., U.S.	D6	88
Volchov, Russia	B15	18
Volda, Nor.	E6	6
Volga, S.D., U.S.	C9	118
Volga, stm., Russia	H7	22
Volgograd (Stalingrad), Russia	H6	22
Volkovysk, Bela.	H7	18
Voločanka, Russia	C12	24
Vologda, Russia	B22	18
Volokolamsk, Russia	E18	18
Vólos, Grc.	J6	16
Volta, Lake, res., Ghana	G5	42
Volta Blanche (White Volta), stm., Afr.	F5	42
Volta Noire (Black Volta), stm., Afr.	F6	42
Volta Redonda, Braz.	G6	57
Volterra, Italy	F5	14
Volusia, co., Fl., U.S.	C5	86
Volžskij, Russia	H6	22
Von Frank Mountain, mtn., Ak., U.S.	C9	79
Vonore, Tn., U.S.	D9	119
Voríai Sporádhes, is., Grc.	J7	16
Voronec, Russia	G5	22
Voronezh see Voronež, Russia	G5	22
Voronež, Russia	G5	22
Vosges, mts., Fr.	D14	10
Voskresensk, Russia	F21	18
Voss, Nor.	F6	6
Vostočno-Sibirskoje More (East Siberian Sea), Russia	C25	24
Vostočnyj Sajan, mts., Russia	G13	24
Votkinsk, Russia	F8	22
Votuporanga, Braz.	F4	57
Vouziers, Fr.	C11	10
Voyageurs National Park, Mn., U.S.	B5	100
Vraca, Bul.	F7	16
Vrangel'a, Ostrov, i., Russia	C29	24
Vranje, Yugo.	G5	16
Vrhnika, Slo.	D9	14
Vryburg, S. Afr.	G4	44
Vryheid, S. Afr.	G6	44
Vsevidof, Mount, mtn., Ak., U.S.	E6	79
Vsevoložsk, Russia	A13	18
Vukovar, Cro.	D2	16
Vulcan, Alta., Can.	D4	68
Vung Tau (Cap-St.-Jacques), Viet.	I9	34
Vuoggatjålme, Swe.	C11	6
Vuoksenniska, Fin.	F17	6
Vyborg, Russia	A11	18
Vyška, Russia	D18	18
Vysokogornyj, Russia	G21	24
Vyšnij Voloček, Russia	D17	18

W

Name	Map Ref	Page
Wa, Ghana	F5	42
Waawaa, Puu, mtn., Hi., U.S.	D6	88
Wabana (Bell Island), Newf., Can.	E5	72
Wabasca, Alta., Can.	B4	68
Wabasca, stm., Alta., Can.	f1	68
Wabash, In., U.S.	C6	91
Wabash, co., Il., U.S.	E6	90
Wabash, co., In., U.S.	C6	91
Wabash, stm., U.S.	H2	91
Wabasha, Mn., U.S.	F6	100
Wabasha, co., Mn., U.S.	F6	100
Wabasso, Fl., U.S.	E6	86
Wabasso, Mn., U.S.	F3	100
Wabaunsee, co., Ks., U.S.	D7	93
Wabeno, Wi., U.S.	C5	126
Wabowden, Man., Can.	B2	70
Wabush, Newf., Can.	h8	72
Waccamaw, stm., U.S.	D9	117
Waccamaw, Lake, l., N.C., U.S.	C4	110
Waccasassa, Bay, Fl., U.S.	C4	86
Wachusett Mountain, mtn., Ma., U.S.	B4	98
Wachusett Reservoir, res., Ma., U.S.	B4	98
Waco, Tx., U.S.	D4	120
Waco Lake, res., Tx., U.S.	D4	120
Waconda Lake, res., Ks., U.S.	C5	93
Waconia, Mn., U.S.	F5	100
Waddeneilanden, is., Neth.	B5	8
Waddenzee, Neth.	B5	8
Waddi, Chappal, mtn., Nig.	G8	42
Waddington, Mount, mtn., B.C., Can.	D5	69
Wadena, Mn., U.S.	D3	100
Wadena, co., Mn., U.S.	D4	100
Wädenswil, Switz.	E15	10
Wadesboro, N.C., U.S.	C2	110
Wādī Ḥalfā', Sudan	D12	42
Wading, stm., N.J., U.S.	D3	107
Wadley, Ga., U.S.	D4	87
Wad Madanī, Sudan	F12	42
Wadmalaw Island, i., S.C., U.S.	F7	117
Wadsworth, Il., U.S.	h9	90
Wadsworth, Nv., U.S.	D2	105
Wadsworth, Oh., U.S.	A4	112
Wagener, S.C., U.S.	D5	117
Wageningen, Neth.		
Wager Bay, b., N.W. Ter., Can.	C15	66
Wagga Wagga, Austl.	G9	50
Wagin, Austl.	F3	50
Wagner, S.D., U.S.	D7	118
Wagoner, Ok., U.S.	B6	113
Wagoner, co., Ok., U.S.	B6	113
Wagontire Mountain, mtn., Or., U.S.	D7	114
Wagrowiec, Pol.	C17	8
Wah, Pak.	D5	38
Waha, Libya	C9	42
Wahiawa, Hi., U.S.	B3	88
Wahiawa Reservoir, res., Hi., U.S.	g9	88
Wahkiakum, co., Wa., U.S.	C2	124
Wahoo, Ne., U.S.	C9	104
Wahpeton, N.D., U.S.	C9	111
Wahweap Creek, stm., Ut., U.S.	F4	121
Waialua, Hi., U.S.	B3	88
Waialua Bay, b., Hi., U.S.	B3	88
Waianae, Hi., U.S.	B3	88
Waianae Range, mts., Hi., U.S.	f9	88
Waidhofen an der Ybbs, Aus.	H14	8
Waigeo, Pulau, i., Indon.	F9	32
Waihi, N.Z.	B5	52
Waikapu, Hi., U.S.	C5	88
Waikiki Beach, Hi., U.S.	g10	88
Wailua, Hi., U.S.	A2	88
Wailuku, Hi., U.S.	C5	88
Waimanalo, Hi., U.S.	B4	88
Waimanalo Bay, b., Hi., U.S.	g11	88
Waimea, Hi., U.S.	B2	88
Waimea, Hi., U.S.	f9	88
Wainwright, Alta., Can.	C5	68
Wainwright, Ak., U.S.	A8	79
Waipahu, Hi., U.S.	B3	88
Waipio Acres, Hi., U.S.	g9	88
Waipio Peninsula, pen., Hi., U.S.	g10	88
Waipukurau, N.Z.	D6	52
Waite Park, Mn., U.S.	E4	100
Waits, stm., Vt., U.S.	C4	122
Waitsburg, Wa., U.S.	C7	124
Wajir, Kenya	H3	46
Wakarusa, In., U.S.	A5	91
Wakarusa, stm., Ks., U.S.	D8	93
Wakasa-wan, b., Japan	G8	30
Wakatomika Creek, stm., Oh., U.S.	B3	112
Wakayama, Japan	H8	30
Wake, co., N.C., U.S.	B4	110
WaKeeney, Ks., U.S.	C4	93
Wakefield, Que., Can.	D2	74
Wakefield, Ks., U.S.	C6	93
Wakefield, Ma., U.S.	B5	98
Wakefield, Mi., U.S.	n12	99
Wakefield, Ne., U.S.	B9	104
Wakefield, R.I., U.S.	F3	116
Wakefield, Va., U.S.	D6	123
Wake Forest, N.C., U.S.	B4	110
Wake Island, dep., Oc.	E24	2
Wakema, Burma	F3	34
Wakeman, Oh., U.S.	A3	112
Wakkanai, Japan	n19	30a
Wakulla, co., Fl., U.S.	B2	86
Walbridge, Oh., U.S.	e6	112
Wałbrzych (Waldenburg), Pol.	E16	8
Walcott, Ia., U.S.	C7	92
Walcott, Lake, res., Id., U.S.	G5	89
Walden, Ont., Can.	A3	73
Walden, Co., U.S.	A4	83
Walden, N.Y., U.S.	D6	109
Walden Ridge, mtn., Tn., U.S.	D8	119
Waldheim, Sask., Can.	E2	75
Waldo, Ar., U.S.	D2	81
Waldo, co., Me., U.S.	D3	96
Waldoboro, Me., U.S.	D3	96
Waldo Lake, l., Ma., U.S.	h11	98
Waldo Lake, l., Or., U.S.	D4	114
Waldport, Or., U.S.	C2	114
Waldron, Ar., U.S.	C1	81
Waldron, In., U.S.	F6	91
Waldshut, Ger.	H8	8
Waldwick, N.J., U.S.	A4	107
Wales, ter., U.K.	I9	7
Wales Island, i., N.W. Ter., Can.	C15	66
Waleska, Ga., U.S.	B2	87
Walgett, Austl.	E9	50
Walhalla, N.D., U.S.	A8	111
Walhalla, S.C., U.S.	B1	117
Walhonding, stm., Oh., U.S.	B3	112
Walker, Ia., U.S.	B6	92
Walker, La., U.S.	g10	95
Walker, Mi., U.S.	E5	99
Walker, Mn., U.S.	C4	100
Walker, co., Al., U.S.	B2	78
Walker, co., Ga., U.S.	B1	87
Walker, co., Tx., U.S.	D5	120
Walker, stm., Nv., U.S.	D3	105
Walker Lake, l., Nv., U.S.	E3	105
Walker River Indian Reservation, Nv., U.S.	D3	105
Walkersville, Md., U.S.	B3	97
Walkerton, Ont., Can.	C3	73
Walkerton, In., U.S.	B5	91
Walkertown, N.C., U.S.	A2	110
Walkerville, Mt., U.S.	D4	103
Wall, S.D., U.S.	D3	118
Wallace, Id., U.S.	B3	89
Wallace, N.C., U.S.	B4	110
Wallace, co., Ks., U.S.	D2	93
Wallaceburg, Ont., Can.	E2	73
Wallace Lake, res., La., U.S.	B2	95
Walla Walla, Wa., U.S.	C7	124
Walla Walla, co., Wa., U.S.	C7	124
Walla Walla, stm., U.S.	C7	124
Walled Lake, Mi., U.S.	o15	99
Wallen, In., U.S.	B7	91
Wallenpaupack, Lake, l., Pa., U.S.	D11	115
Waller, Tx., U.S.	q14	120
Waller, co., Tx., U.S.	E4	120
Wallingford, Ct., U.S.	D4	84
Wallingford, Vt., U.S.	E3	122
Wallington, N.J., U.S.	h8	107
Wallis and Futuna, dep., Oc.	G1	2
Wallkill, N.Y., U.S.	D6	109
Wallkill, stm., N.Y., U.S.	D6	109
Wall Lake, Ia., U.S.	B2	92
Wall Lake, l., Ia., U.S.	B4	92
Walloomsac, stm., U.S.	F2	122
Walloon Lake, l., Mi., U.S.	C6	99
Wallowa, Or., U.S.	B9	114
Wallowa, co., Or., U.S.	B9	114
Wallowa Mountains, mts., Or., U.S.	B9	114
Wallula, Lake, res., U.S.	C7	124
Wallum Lake, l., U.S.	A1	116
Walnut, Il., U.S.	B4	90
Walnut, Ia., U.S.	C2	92
Walnut, stm., Ks., U.S.	E6	93
Walnut Canyon National Monument, Az., U.S.	B4	80
Walnut Cove, N.C., U.S.	A2	110
Walnut Creek, Ca., U.S.	h8	82
Walnut Creek, stm., Ks., U.S.	D4	93
Walnut Grove, Al., U.S.	A3	78
Walnut Grove, Mn., U.S.	F3	100
Walnutport, Pa., U.S.	E10	115
Walnut Ridge, Ar., U.S.	A5	81
Walpole, Ma., U.S.	B5	98
Walpole, N.H., U.S.	D2	106
Walsall, Eng., U.K.	I11	7
Walsenburg, Co., U.S.	D6	83
Walsh, Co., U.S.	D8	83
Walsh, co., N.D., U.S.	A8	111
Walsrode, Ger.	C9	8
Walterboro, S.C., U.S.	F6	117
Walter F. George Dam, U.S.	D4	78
Walter F. George Lake, res., U.S.	D4	78
Walters, Ok., U.S.	C3	113
Walthall, co., Ms., U.S.	D3	101
Waltham, Ma., U.S.	B5	98
Walthill, Ne., U.S.	B9	104
Walthourville, Ga., U.S.	E5	87
Walton, In., U.S.	C5	91
Walton, Ky., U.S.	B5	94
Walton, N.Y., U.S.	C5	109
Walton, co., Fl., U.S.	u15	86
Walton, co., Ga., U.S.	C3	87
Walvisbaai (Walvis Bay), S. Afr.	F2	44
Walworth, Wi., U.S.	F5	126
Walworth, co., S.D., U.S.	B5	118
Walworth, co., Wi., U.S.	F5	126
Wamac, Il., U.S.	E4	90
Wamba, stm., Afr.	C3	44
Wamego, Ks., U.S.	C7	93
Wamesit, Ma., U.S.	A5	98
Wamsutter, Wy., U.S.	E5	127
Wanaka, N.Z.	F2	52
Wanamingo, Mn., U.S.	F6	100
Wanapum Dam, Wa., U.S.	C6	124
Wanapum Lake, res., Wa., U.S.	B6	124
Wanaque, N.J., U.S.	A4	107
Wanaque Reservoir, res., N.J., U.S.	A4	107
Wanatah, In., U.S.	B4	91
Wanchese, N.C., U.S.	B7	110
Wando, stm., S.C., U.S.	F8	117
Wando Woods, S.C., U.S.	k11	117
Wanganui, N.Z.	C5	52
Wanganui, stm., N.Z.	C5	52
Wangaratta, Austl.	G9	50
Wangen [im Allgäu], Ger.	H9	8
Wangpan Yang, b., China	E10	28
Wänkäner, India	I4	38
Wanxian, China	E8	26
Wapakoneta, Oh., U.S.	B1	112
Wapato, Wa., U.S.	C5	124
Wapawekka Lake, l., Sask., Can.	C3	75
Wapello, Ia., U.S.	C6	92
Wapello, co., Ia., U.S.	C5	92
Wapiti, stm., Can.	B1	68
Wappapello, Lake, res., Mo., U.S.	D7	102
Wappingers Falls, N.Y., U.S.	D7	109
Wapsipinicon, stm., Ia., U.S.	B6	92
War, W.V., U.S.	D3	125
Waramaug, Lake, l., Ct., U.S.	C2	84
Warangal, India	C5	37
Ward, Ar., U.S.	B4	81
Ward, co., N.D., U.S.	A4	111
Ward, co., Tx., U.S.	D1	120
Warden, Wa., U.S.	C6	124
Wardha, India	B5	37
Ward Mountain, mtn., Mt., U.S.	D2	103
Ware, Ma., U.S.	B3	98
Ware, co., Ga., U.S.	E4	87
Ware, stm., Ma., U.S.	B3	98
War Eagle Mountain, mtn., Id., U.S.	G2	89
Wareham, Ma., U.S.	C6	98
Warehouse Point, Ct., U.S.	B5	84
Waren, Ger.	B12	8
Warendorf, Ger.	D7	8
Ware Shoals, S.C., U.S.	C3	117
Warfield, B.C., Can.	E9	69
Warminster, Eng., U.K.	J10	7
Warminster, Pa., U.S.	F11	115
Warm Springs Indian Reservation, Or., U.S.	C5	114
Warm Springs Reservoir, res., Or., U.S.	D8	114
Warnemünde, Ger.	A12	8
Warner, N.H., U.S.	D3	106
Warner, Ok., U.S.	B6	113
Warner, stm., N.H., U.S.	D3	106
Warner Mountains, mts., Ca., U.S.	B3	82
Warner Peak, mtn., Or., U.S.	E7	114
Warner Robins, Ga., U.S.	D3	87
Warr Acres, Ok., U.S.	B4	113
Warren, Ar., U.S.	D3	81
Warren, Il., U.S.	A4	90
Warren, In., U.S.	C7	91
Warren, Mi., U.S.	F7	99
Warren, Mn., U.S.	B2	100
Warren, Oh., U.S.	A5	112
Warren, Or., U.S.	B4	114
Warren, Pa., U.S.	C3	115
Warren, R.I., U.S.	D5	116
Warren, Vt., U.S.	C3	122
Warren, co., Ga., U.S.	C4	87
Warren, co., Il., U.S.	C3	90
Warren, co., In., U.S.	D3	91
Warren, co., Ky., U.S.	C3	94
Warren, co., Ms., U.S.	C3	101
Warren, co., Mo., U.S.	C6	102
Warren, co., N.J., U.S.	B3	107
Warren, co., N.Y., U.S.	B7	109
Warren, co., N.C., U.S.	A4	110
Warren, co., Oh., U.S.	C1	112
Warren, co., Pa., U.S.	C3	115
Warren, co., Tn., U.S.	D8	119
Warren, co., Va., U.S.	B4	123
Warren, co., U.S.	E6	93
Warren Park, In., U.S.	k10	91
Warren Peaks, mts., Wy., U.S.	B8	127
Warrensburg, Il., U.S.	D4	90
Warrensburg, Mo., U.S.	C4	102
Warrensburg, N.Y., U.S.	B7	109
Warrensville Heights, Oh., U.S.	h9	112
Warrenton, S. Afr.	G4	44
Warrenton, Ga., U.S.	C4	87
Warrenton, Mo., U.S.	C6	102
Warrenton, N.C., U.S.	A4	110
Warrenton, Or., U.S.	A3	114
Warrenton, Va., U.S.	B5	123
Warrenville, Il., U.S.	k8	90
Warrenville, S.C., U.S.	D4	117
Warri, Nig.	G7	42
Warrick, co., In., U.S.	H3	91
Warrington, Eng., U.K.	H10	7
Warrington, Fl., U.S.	u14	86
Warrior, Al., U.S.	B3	78
Warrior Lake, res., Al., U.S.	C2	78
Warrnambool, Austl.	G8	50
Warroad, Mn., U.S.	B3	100
Warsaw, Il., U.S.	C2	90
Warsaw, In., U.S.	B6	91
Warsaw, Ky., U.S.	B5	94
Warsaw, Mo., U.S.	C4	102
Warsaw, N.Y., U.S.	C2	109
Warsaw, N.C., U.S.	B4	110
Warsaw, Va., U.S.	C6	123
Warsaw see Warszawa, Pol.	C21	8
Warszawa (Warsaw), Pol.	C21	8
Warta, stm., Pol.	C15	8
Warthe see Warta, stm., Pol.	C15	8
Wartburg, Tn., U.S.	C9	119
Warwick, Austl.	E10	50
Warwick, Que., Can.	D6	74
Warwick, Md., U.S.	B6	97
Warwick, N.Y., U.S.	D6	109
Warwick, R.I., U.S.	D4	116
Warwick, Eng., U.K.	I11	7
Wasatch, co., Ut., U.S.	C4	121
Wasco, Ca., U.S.	E4	82
Wasco, co., Or., U.S.	B5	114
Waseca, Mn., U.S.	F5	100
Waseca, co., Mn., U.S.	F5	100
Washakie, co., Wy., U.S.	C5	127
Washakie Needles, mts., Wy., U.S.	C3	127
Washburn, Il., U.S.	C4	90
Washburn, Ia., U.S.	B5	92
Washburn, Me., U.S.	B4	96
Washburn, N.D., U.S.	B5	111
Washburn, Wi., U.S.	B3	126
Washburn, co., Wi., U.S.	C2	126
Washburn, Mount, mtn., Wy., U.S.	B2	127
Washington, D.C., U.S.	C3	97
Washington, Ga., U.S.	C4	87
Washington, Il., U.S.	C4	90
Washington, In., U.S.	G3	91
Washington, Ia., U.S.	C6	92
Washington, Ks., U.S.	C6	93
Washington, Ky., U.S.	B6	94
Washington, La., U.S.	D3	95
Washington, Mo., U.S.	C6	102
Washington, N.J., U.S.	B3	107
Washington, N.C., U.S.	B5	110
Washington, Pa., U.S.	F1	115
Washington, Ut., U.S.	F2	121
Washington, co., Al., U.S.	D1	78
Washington, co., Ar., U.S.	A1	81
Washington, co., Co., U.S.	B7	83
Washington, co., Fl., U.S.	u16	86
Washington, co., Ga., U.S.	C4	87
Washington, co., Id., U.S.	E2	89
Washington, co., Il., U.S.	E4	90
Washington, co., In., U.S.	G5	91
Washington, co., Ia., U.S.	C6	92
Washington, co., Ks., U.S.	C6	93
Washington, co., Ky., U.S.	C4	94
Washington, co., La., U.S.	D5	95
Washington, co., Me., U.S.	D5	96
Washington, co., Md., U.S.	A2	97
Washington, co., Mn., U.S.	E6	100
Washington, co., Ms., U.S.	B3	101
Washington, co., Mo., U.S.	D7	102
Washington, co., Ne., U.S.	C9	104
Washington, co., N.Y., U.S.	B7	109
Washington, co., N.C., U.S.	B6	110
Washington, co., Oh., U.S.	C4	112
Washington, co., Ok., U.S.	A6	113
Washington, co., Or., U.S.	B3	114
Washington, co., Pa., U.S.	F1	115
Washington, co., R.I., U.S.	E2	116
Washington, co., Tn., U.S.	C11	119
Washington, co., Tx., U.S.	D4	120
Washington, co., Ut., U.S.	F2	121
Washington, co., Vt., U.S.	C3	122
Washington, co., Va., U.S.	f9	123
Washington, state, U.S.	C5	124
Washington, Lake, l., Fl., U.S.	D6	86
Washington, Lake, l., Mn., U.S.	E4	100
Washington, Lake, l., Ms., U.S.	B3	101
Washington, Lake, l., Wa., U.S.	e11	124
Washington, Mount, mtn., N.H., U.S.	B4	106
Washington Court House, Oh., U.S.	C2	112
Washington Island, i., Wi., U.S.	C7	126
Washington Park, Il., U.S.	E3	90
Washington Terrace, Ut., U.S.	B4	121
Washita, Ok., U.S.	B3	113
Washita, co., Ok., U.S.	B2	113
Washita, stm., Ok., U.S.	C4	113
Washoe, co., Nv., U.S.	C2	105
Washoe City, Nv., U.S.	D2	105
Washougal, Wa., U.S.	D3	124
Washow Bay, b., Man., Can.	D3	70
Washtenaw, co., Mi., U.S.	F7	99
Wasilla, Ak., U.S.	C10	79
Wasior, Indon.	F9	32
Waskom, Tx., U.S.	C5	120
Waspán, Nic.	G5	64
Wasque Point, c., Ma., U.S.	D7	98
Wassen, Switz.	F15	10
Wassookeag, Lake, l., Me., U.S.	C3	96
Wassuk Range, mts., Nv., U.S.	E3	105
Wataga, Il., U.S.	B3	90
Watauga, co., N.C., U.S.	A1	110
Watauga, stm., Tn., U.S.	C12	119
Watauga Lake, res., Tn., U.S.	C12	119
Watchaug Pond, l., R.I., U.S.	F2	116
Watch Hill Point, c., R.I., U.S.	G1	116
Watchung, N.J., U.S.	B4	107
Waterbury, Ct., U.S.	C3	84
Waterbury, Vt., U.S.	C3	122
Waterbury Center, Vt., U.S.	C3	122
Waterbury Reservoir, res., Vt., U.S.	C3	122
Wateree, stm., S.C., U.S.	D6	117
Wateree Lake, res., S.C., U.S.	C6	117
Waterford, Ire.	I5	7
Waterford, Ct., U.S.	D7	84
Waterford, N.Y., U.S.	C7	109
Waterford, Pa., U.S.	C2	115
Waterford, Wi., U.S.	F5	126
Waterhen Lake, l., Man., Can.	C2	70
Waterloo, Bel.	E4	8
Waterloo, Ont., Can.	D4	73
Waterloo, Que., Can.	D5	74
Waterloo, Il., U.S.	E3	90
Waterloo, In., U.S.	B7	91
Waterloo, Ia., U.S.	B5	92
Waterloo, N.Y., U.S.	C4	109
Waterloo, Wi., U.S.	E5	126
Waterman, Il., U.S.	B5	90
Waterman Reservoir, res., R.I., U.S.	B3	116
Waterproof, La., U.S.	C4	95
Watersmeet, Mi., U.S.	n12	99
Waterton Lakes National Park, Alta., Can.	E3	68
Watertown, Ct., U.S.	C3	84
Watertown, Ma., U.S.	g11	98
Watertown, N.Y., U.S.	B5	109
Watertown, S.D., U.S.	C8	118
Watertown, Tn., U.S.	A5	119
Watertown, Wi., U.S.	E5	126
Water Valley, Ms., U.S.	A4	101
Waterville, Ks., U.S.	C7	93
Waterville, Me., U.S.	D3	96
Waterville, Mn., U.S.	F5	100
Waterville, N.Y., U.S.	C5	109
Waterville, Oh., U.S.	A2	112
Waterville, Wa., U.S.	B5	124
Watervliet, Mi., U.S.	F4	99
Watervliet, N.Y., U.S.	C7	109
Watford, Ont., Can.	E3	73
Watford City, N.D., U.S.	B2	111
Wathena, Ks., U.S.	C9	93
Watkins, Mn., U.S.	E4	100
Watkins Glen, N.Y., U.S.	C4	109
Watkinsville, Ga., U.S.	C3	87
Watonga, Ok., U.S.	B3	113
Watonwan, co., Mn., U.S.	F4	100
Watonwan, stm., Mn., U.S.	G4	100
Watseka, Il., U.S.	C6	90
Watson Lake, Yukon, Can.	D7	66
Watsontown, Pa., U.S.	D8	115
Watsonville, Ca., U.S.	D3	82
Watts Bar Dam, Tn., U.S.	D9	119
Watts Bar Lake, res., Tn., U.S.	D9	119
Wattsville, S.C., U.S.	B4	117
Wattwil, Switz.	E16	10
Watubela, Kepulauan, is., Indon.	F9	32
Waubaushene, Ont., Can.	C5	73
Waubay, S.D., U.S.	B8	118
Waubay Lake, l., S.D., U.S.	B8	118
Wauchula, Fl., U.S.	E5	86
Wauconda, Il., U.S.	h8	90
Waugh Mountain, mtn., Id., U.S.	D4	89
Waukee, Ia., U.S.	C4	92
Waukegan, Il., U.S.	A6	90
Waukesha, Wi., U.S.	F5	126
Waukesha, co., Wi., U.S.	E5	126
Waukewan, Lake, l., N.H., U.S.	C3	106
Waukomis, Ok., U.S.	A4	113
Waukon, Ia., U.S.	A6	92
Waunakee, Wi., U.S.	E4	126
Wauneta, Ne., U.S.	D4	104
Waupaca, Wi., U.S.	D5	126
Waupaca, co., Wi., U.S.	D5	126
Waupun, Wi., U.S.	E5	126
Wauregan, Ct., U.S.	C8	84
Waurika, Ok., U.S.	C4	113
Waurika Lake, res., Ok., U.S.	C3	113
Wausau, Wi., U.S.	D4	126
Wausau, Lake, res., Wi., U.S.	D4	126
Wauseon, Oh., U.S.	A1	112
Waushara, co., Wi., U.S.	D4	126
Wautoma, Wi., U.S.	D4	126
Wauwatosa, Wi., U.S.	m12	126
Wave Hill, Austl.	C6	50
Waveland, Ms., U.S.	E4	101
Waverley, N.S., Can.	E6	71
Waverly, Il., U.S.	D4	90
Waverly, Ia., U.S.	B5	92
Waverly, Ks., U.S.	D8	93
Waverly, Mn., U.S.	E5	100
Waverly, Mo., U.S.	B4	102
Waverly, Ne., U.S.	D9	104
Waverly, N.Y., U.S.	C4	109
Waverly, Oh., U.S.	C3	112
Waverly, Tn., U.S.	A4	119
Waverly, Va., U.S.	C5	123
Waverly Hall, Ga., U.S.	D2	87
Wāw, Sudan	G11	42
Wawanesa, Man., Can.	E2	70
Wawasee, Lake, l., In., U.S.	B6	91

Name	Map Ref	Page
Wawayanda Lake, l., N.J., U.S.	A4	107
Wawota, Sask., Can.	H4	75
Waxahachie, Tx., U.S.	C4	120
Waxhaw, N.C., U.S.	A5	110
Waycross, Ga., U.S.	E4	87
Wayland, Ia., U.S.	C6	92
Wayland, Ma., U.S.	g10	98
Wayland, Mi., U.S.	F5	99
Wayland, N.Y., U.S.	C3	109
Waylyn, S.C., U.S.	k12	117
Waymart, Pa., U.S.	C11	115
Wayne, Mi., U.S.	p15	99
Wayne, Ne., U.S.	B8	104
Wayne, N.J., U.S.	B4	107
Wayne, W.V., U.S.	C2	125
Wayne, co., Ga., U.S.	E5	87
Wayne, co., Il., U.S.	E5	90
Wayne, co., In., U.S.	E7	91
Wayne, co., Ia., U.S.	D4	92
Wayne, co., Ky., U.S.	D5	94
Wayne, co., Mi., U.S.	F7	99
Wayne, co., Ms., U.S.	D5	101
Wayne, co., Mo., U.S.	D7	102
Wayne, co., Ne., U.S.	B8	104
Wayne, co., N.Y., U.S.	B3	109
Wayne, co., N.C., U.S.	B4	110
Wayne, co., Oh., U.S.	B4	112
Wayne, co., Pa., U.S.	C11	115
Wayne, co., Tn., U.S.	B4	119
Wayne, co., Ut., U.S.	E4	121
Wayne, co., W.V., U.S.	C2	125
Wayne City, Il., U.S.	E5	90
Waynesboro, Ga., U.S.	C4	87
Waynesboro, Ms., U.S.	D5	101
Waynesboro, Pa., U.S.	G6	115
Waynesboro, Tn., U.S.	B4	119
Waynesboro, Va., U.S.	B4	123
Waynesburg, Oh., U.S.	B4	112
Waynesburg, Pa., U.S.	G1	115
Waynesville, Mo., U.S.	D5	102
Waynesville, N.C., U.S.	f10	110
Waynesville, Oh., U.S.	C1	112
Waynetown, In., U.S.	D3	91
Waynewood, Va., U.S.	g12	123
Waynoka, Ok., U.S.	A3	113
Wayzata, Mn., U.S.	n11	100
Wazīrābād, Pak.	D6	38
Weakley, co., Tn., U.S.	A3	119
Weatherford, Ok., U.S.	B3	113
Weatherford, Tx., U.S.	C4	120
Weatherly, Pa., U.S.	E10	115
Weatogue, Ct., U.S.	B4	84
Weaver, Al., U.S.	B4	78
Weaver Mountains, mts., Az., U.S.	C3	80
Weaverville, Ca., U.S.	B2	82
Weaverville, N.C., U.S.	f10	110
Webb, Al., U.S.	D4	78
Webb, Ms., U.S.	B3	101
Webb, co., Tx., U.S.	F3	120
Webb City, Mo., U.S.	D3	102
Webbers Falls, Ok., U.S.	B6	113
Webberville, Mi., U.S.	F6	99
Webb Lake, l., Me., U.S.	D2	96
Weber, co., Ut., U.S.	B4	121
Weber City, Va., U.S.	f9	123
Webster, Ma., U.S.	B4	98
Webster, N.Y., U.S.	B3	109
Webster, Pa., U.S.	F2	115
Webster, S.D., U.S.	B8	118
Webster, co., Ga., U.S.	D2	87
Webster, co., Ia., U.S.	B3	92
Webster, co., Ky., U.S.	C2	94
Webster, co., La., U.S.	B2	95
Webster, co., Ms., U.S.	B4	101
Webster, co., Mo., U.S.	D5	102
Webster, co., Ne., U.S.	D7	104
Webster, co., W.V., U.S.	C4	125
Webster City, Ia., U.S.	B4	92
Webster Groves, Mo., U.S.	f13	102
Webster Reservoir, res., Ks., U.S.	C4	93
Webster Springs, W.V., U.S.	C4	125
Websterville, Vt., U.S.	C4	122
Weddell Sea, Ant.	B8	47
Wedgeport, N.S., Can.	F4	71
Wedgewood, Mo., U.S.	f13	102
Wedowee, Al., U.S.	B4	78
Weed, Ca., U.S.	B2	82
Weed Heights, Nv., U.S.	E2	105
Weedon, Que., Can.	D6	74
Weedsport, N.Y., U.S.	B4	109
Weedville, Pa., U.S.	D5	115
Weehawken, N.J., U.S.	h8	107
Weeksbury, Ky., U.S.	C7	94
Weeping Water, Ne., U.S.	D9	104
Wegscheid, Ger.	G13	8
Weiden in der Oberpfalz, Ger.	F12	8
Weifang, China	D10	26
Weihai, China	D11	26
Weilburg, Ger.	E8	8
Weilheim, Ger.	H11	8
Weimar, Ger.	E11	8
Weimar, Tx., U.S.	E4	120
Weiner, Ar., U.S.	B5	81
Weinheim, Ger.	F8	8
Weipa, Austl.	B8	50
Weippe, Id., U.S.	C3	89
Weir, Ks., U.S.	E9	93
Weir, Lake, l., Fl., U.S.	C5	86
Weirsdale, Fl., U.S.	D5	86
Weirton, W.V., U.S.	A4	125
Weiser, Id., U.S.	E2	89
Weiser, stm., Id., U.S.	E2	89
Weishi, China	A3	28
Weissenburg in Bayern, Ger.	F10	8
Weissenfels, Ger.	D11	8
Weiss Lake, res., U.S.	A4	78
Weisswasser, Ger.	D14	8
Weiz, Aus.	H15	8
Wejherowo, Pol.	A18	8
Welch, W.V., U.S.	D3	125
Welcome, Mn., U.S.	G4	100
Welcome, S.C., U.S.	B3	117
Weld, co., Co., U.S.	A6	83
Weldon, N.C., U.S.	A5	110
Weldon Spring, Mo., U.S.	f12	102
Weleetka, Ok., U.S.	B5	113
Welkom, S. Afr.	G5	44
Welland, Ont., Can.	E5	73
Wellesley, Ont., Can.	D4	73
Wellesley, Ma., U.S.	B5	98
Wellesley Islands, is., Austl.	C7	50
Wellford, S.C., U.S.	B3	117
Wellington, Ont., Can.	D7	73
Wellington, N.Z.	D5	52
Wellington, Co., U.S.	A5	83
Wellington, Ks., U.S.	E6	93
Wellington, Mo., U.S.	B4	102
Wellington, Nv., U.S.	E2	105
Wellington, Oh., U.S.	A3	112
Wellington, Tx., U.S.	B2	120
Wellington, Ut., U.S.	D5	121
Wellington, Isla, i., Chile	F2	56
Wellington Channel, strt., N.W. Ter., Can.	A14	66
Wellman, Ia., U.S.	C6	92
Wells, Me., U.S.	E2	96
Wells, Mi., U.S.	C3	99
Wells, Mn., U.S.	G5	100
Wells, Nv., U.S.	B7	105
Wells, co., In., U.S.	C7	91
Wells, co., N.D., U.S.	B6	111
Wells, stm., Vt., U.S.	C4	122
Wellsboro, Pa., U.S.	C7	115
Wellsburg, Ia., U.S.	B5	92
Wellsburg, W.V., U.S.	A4	125
Wellston, Oh., U.S.	C3	112
Wellston, Ok., U.S.	B4	113
Wellsville, Ks., U.S.	D8	93
Wellsville, Mo., U.S.	B6	102
Wellsville, N.Y., U.S.	C3	109
Wellsville, Oh., U.S.	B5	112
Wellsville, Ut., U.S.	B4	121
Wellton, Az., U.S.	E1	80
Wels, Aus.	G14	8
Welsh, La., U.S.	D3	95
Welshpool, Wales, U.K.	I9	7
Wembley, Alta., Can.	B1	68
Wenatchee, Wa., U.S.	B5	124
Wenatchee, stm., Wa., U.S.	B5	124
Wenatchee Lake, l., Wa., U.S.	B5	124
Wenatchee Mountains, mts., Wa., U.S.	B5	124
Wendell, Id., U.S.	G4	89
Wendell, N.C., U.S.	B4	110
Wendover, Ut., U.S.	C1	121
Wenham, Ma., U.S.	A6	98
Wenham Lake, l., Ma., U.S.	f12	98
Wenona, Il., U.S.	B4	90
Wenshan, China	C4	106
Wentworth, Lake, l., N.H., U.S.	C4	106
Wentzville, Mo., U.S.	C7	102
Wenzhou, China	G9	28
Weohyakapka, Lake, l., Fl., U.S.	E5	86
Wernigerode, Ger.	D10	8
Wertheim, Ger.	F9	8
Wesel, Ger.	D6	8
Weser, stm., Ger.	B8	8
Weslaco, Tx., U.S.	F4	120
Wesleyville, Newf., Can.	D5	72
Wesleyville, Pa., U.S.	B2	115
Wessel Islands, is., Austl.	B7	50
Wesserunsett Lake, l., Me., U.S.	D3	96
Wessington Springs, S.D., U.S.	C7	118
Wesson, Ms., U.S.	D3	101
West, Tx., U.S.	D4	120
West, stm., Ct., U.S.	D5	84
West, stm., Ma., U.S.	h9	98
West, stm., Vt., U.S.	E3	122
West Acton, Ma., U.S.	g10	98
West Alexandria, Oh., U.S.	C1	112
West Allis, Wi., U.S.	m11	126
West Alton, Mo., U.S.	f13	102
West Andover, Ma., U.S.	A5	98
West Baden Springs, In., U.S.	G4	91
West Baton Rouge, co., La., U.S.	D4	95
West Bay, b., Fl., U.S.	u16	86
West Bay, b., N.C., U.S.	B6	110
West Bay, b., Tx., U.S.	r15	120
West Bend, Ia., U.S.	B3	92
West Bend, Wi., U.S.	E5	126
West Bengal, state, India	I12	38
West Berlin, N.J., U.S.	D3	107
West Billerica, Ma., U.S.	f10	98
West Blocton, Al., U.S.	B2	78
Westborough, Ma., U.S.	B4	98
West Bountiful, Ut., U.S.	C4	121
West Boylston, Ma., U.S.	B4	98
West Branch, Ia., U.S.	C6	92
West Branch, Mi., U.S.	D6	99
West Branch Reservoir, res., Ct., U.S.	B3	84
West Bridgewater, Ma., U.S.	B5	98
Westbrook, Ct., U.S.	D6	84
Westbrook, Me., U.S.	E2	96
Westbrook, Mn., U.S.	F3	100
West Burlington, Ia., U.S.	D6	92
West Butte, mtn., Mt., U.S.	B5	103
Westby, Wi., U.S.	E3	126
West Cache Creek, stm., Ok., U.S.	C3	113
West Caldwell, N.J., U.S.	B4	107
West Canada Creek, stm., N.Y., U.S.	B6	109
West Carroll, co., La., U.S.	B4	95
West Carrollton, Oh., U.S.	C1	112
West Carthage, N.Y., U.S.	B5	109
Westchester, Il., U.S.	k9	90
West Chester, Pa., U.S.	G10	115
Westchester, co., N.Y., U.S.	D7	109
West Chicago, Il., U.S.	k8	90
West Chop, c., Ma., U.S.	D6	98
West College Corner, In., U.S.	E8	91
West Columbia, S.C., U.S.	D5	117
West Columbia, Tx., U.S.	E5	120
West Concord, Ma., U.S.	B5	98
West Concord, Mn., U.S.	F6	100
West Concord, N.C., U.S.	B2	110
Westconnaug Reservoir, res., R.I., U.S.	C2	116
West Cote Blanche Bay, b., La., U.S.	E4	95
West Covina, Ca., U.S.	m13	82
West Crossett, Ar., U.S.	D4	81
West Cumberland, Me., U.S.	E2	96
West Dennis, Ma., U.S.	C7	98
West Des Moines, Ia., U.S.	C4	92
West Elk Mountains, mts., Co., U.S.	C3	83
West Elk Peak, mtn., Co., U.S.	C3	83
Westerly, R.I., U.S.	F1	116
Western Australia, state, Austl.	D4	50
Western Desert see Gharbīyah, Aṣ-Ṣaḥrā' al-, des., Egypt	C11	42
Western Ghāts, mts., India	E3	37
Westernport, Md., U.S.	m12	97
Western Sahara, dep., Afr.	D3	42
Western Samoa, ctry., Oc.	G1	2
Western Springs, Il., U.S.	k9	90
Westerstede, Ger.	B7	8
Westerville, Oh., U.S.	B3	112
West Falkland, i., Falk. Is.	G4	56
West Falmouth, Ma., U.S.	C6	98
West Fargo, N.D., U.S.	C9	111
West Feliciana, co., La., U.S.	D4	95
Westfield, N.B., Can.	D3	71
Westfield, In., U.S.	D5	91
Westfield, Ma., U.S.	B2	98
Westfield, N.J., U.S.	B4	107
Westfield, N.Y., U.S.	C1	109
Westfield, Pa., U.S.	C6	115
Westfield, Wi., U.S.	E4	126
Westfield, stm., Ma., U.S.	B2	98
West Fork, Ar., U.S.	B1	81
West Fork, stm., W.V., U.S.	B4	125
West Frankfort, Il., U.S.	F5	90
West Freehold, N.J., U.S.	C4	107
West Friendship, Md., U.S.	B4	97
Westgate, Fl., U.S.	F6	86
West Grand Lake, l., Me., U.S.	C5	96
West Grove, Pa., U.S.	G10	115
West Hanover, Ma., U.S.	h12	98
West Hartford, Ct., U.S.	B4	84
West Haven, Ct., U.S.	D4	84
West Hazleton, Pa., U.S.	E9	115
West Helena, Ar., U.S.	C5	81
West Hill Reservoir, res., Ma., U.S.	B4	98
Westhope, N.D., U.S.	A4	111
West Indies, is.	E12	64
West Island, i., Ma., U.S.	C6	98
West Jefferson, N.C., U.S.	A1	110
West Jefferson, Oh., U.S.	C2	112
West Jordan, Ut., U.S.	C3	121
West Kingston, R.I., U.S.	F3	116
West Lafayette, In., U.S.	D4	91
West Lafayette, Oh., U.S.	B4	112
Westlake, La., U.S.	D2	95
Westlake, Oh., U.S.	h9	112
West Lake, l., Me., U.S.	C4	96
Westland, Mi., U.S.	F7	99
West Laramie, Wy., U.S.	E7	127
West Lawn, Pa., U.S.	F10	115
West Lebanon, In., U.S.	D3	91
West Liberty, Ia., U.S.	C6	92
West Liberty, Ky., U.S.	C6	94
West Liberty, Oh., U.S.	B2	112
West Liberty, W.V., U.S.	f8	125
West Linn, Or., U.S.	B4	114
Westlock, Alta., Can.	B4	68
West Long Branch, N.J., U.S.	C4	107
West Lorne, Ont., Can.	E3	73
West Marion, N.C., U.S.	f10	110
West Medway, Ma., U.S.	B5	98
West Memphis, Ar., U.S.	B5	81
West Miami, Fl., U.S.	s13	86
West Middlesex, Pa., U.S.	D1	115
West Mifflin, Pa., U.S.	F2	115
West Milton, Oh., U.S.	C1	112
West Milwaukee, Wi., U.S.	m12	126
Westminster, Ca., U.S.	n12	82
Westminster, Co., U.S.	B5	83
Westminster, Md., U.S.	A4	97
Westminster, S.C., U.S.	B1	117
West Monroe, La., U.S.	B3	95
Westmont, Ca., U.S.	*n12	82
Westmont, Il., U.S.	k9	90
Westmont, N.J., U.S.	D2	107
Westmont, Pa., U.S.	F4	115
Westmoreland, Tn., U.S.	A5	119
Westmoreland, co., Pa., U.S.	F2	115
Westmoreland, co., Va., U.S.	B6	123
Westmorland, Ca., U.S.	F6	82
West Musquash Lake, l., Me., U.S.	C5	96
West Mystic, Ct., U.S.	D8	84
West Newton, Pa., U.S.	F2	115
West New York, N.J., U.S.	h8	107
West Nishnabotna, stm., Ia., U.S.	C2	92
West Norriton, Pa., U.S.	o20	115
Weston, Ct., U.S.	E2	84
Weston, Ma., U.S.	g10	98
Weston, Mo., U.S.	B3	102
Weston, Oh., U.S.	A2	112
Weston, Or., U.S.	B8	114
Weston, W.V., U.S.	B4	125
Weston, Wi., U.S.	*D4	126
Weston, co., Wy., U.S.	C8	127
Weston-super-Mare, Eng., U.K.	J10	7
West Orange, N.J., U.S.	B4	107
Westover, Md., U.S.	D6	97
Westover, W.V., U.S.	B5	125
Westover Air Force Base, mil., Ma., U.S.	B2	98
West Palm Beach, Fl., U.S.	F6	86
West Pawlet, Vt., U.S.	E2	122
West Pearl, stm., La., U.S.	D6	95
West Pelzer, S.C., U.S.	B3	117
West Pensacola, Fl., U.S.	u14	86
West Peoria, Il., U.S.	C4	90
Westphalia, Mi., U.S.	F6	99
West Pittsburg, Pa., U.S.	E1	115
West Pittston, Pa., U.S.	m17	115
West Plains, Mo., U.S.	E6	102
West Point, Ca., U.S.	C3	82
West Point, Ga., U.S.	D1	87
West Point, Ia., U.S.	D6	92
West Point, Ky., U.S.	C4	94
West Point, Ms., U.S.	B5	101
West Point, Ne., U.S.	C9	104
West Point, N.Y., U.S.	D7	109
West Point, Va., U.S.	C6	123
West Point, mtn., Ak., U.S.	C11	79
West Point Lake, res., U.S.	C1	87
Westport, Ont., Can.	C8	73
Westport, N.Z.	D3	52
Westport, Ct., U.S.	E2	84
Westport, In., U.S.	F6	91
Westport, Wa., U.S.	C1	124
West Portsmouth, Oh., U.S.	D2	112
West Quoddy Head, c., Me., U.S.	D6	96
Westray, i., Scot., U.K.	B10	7
Westray Firth, strt., Scot., U.K.	B9	7
West Reading, Pa., U.S.	F10	115
West Rutland, Vt., U.S.	D2	122
West Saint Paul, Mn., U.S.	n12	100
West Salem, Il., U.S.	E5	90
West Salem, Oh., U.S.	B3	112
West Salem, Wi., U.S.	E2	126
West Scarborough, Me., U.S.	E2	96
West Seneca, N.Y., U.S.	C2	109
West Simsbury, Ct., U.S.	B4	84
West Slope, Or., U.S.	g12	114
West Spanish Peak, mtn., Co., U.S.	D6	83
West Springfield, Ma., U.S.	B2	98
West Springfield, Va., U.S.	g12	123
West Swanzey, N.H., U.S.	E2	106
West Terre Haute, In., U.S.	F3	91
West Thompson Lake, res., Ct., U.S.	B8	84
West Union, Ia., U.S.	B6	92
West Union, Oh., U.S.	D2	112
West Union, W.V., U.S.	B4	125
West Unity, Oh., U.S.	A1	112
West University Place, Tx., U.S.	r14	120
West Valley City, Ut., U.S.	C4	121
West Vancouver, B.C., Can.	f12	69
West Van Lear, Ky., U.S.	C7	94
West View, Pa., U.S.	h13	115
Westville, Il., U.S.	C6	90
Westville, In., U.S.	A4	91
Westville, N.H., U.S.	E4	106
Westville, N.J., U.S.	D2	107
Westville, Ok., U.S.	A7	113
Westville Lake, res., Ma., U.S.	B3	98
West Virginia, state, U.S.	C4	125
West Walker, stm., U.S.	E2	105
West Wareham, Ma., U.S.	C6	98
West Warwick, R.I., U.S.	D3	116
Westwego, La., U.S.	k11	95
Westwood, Ca., U.S.	B3	82
Westwood, Ks., U.S.	k16	93
Westwood, Ky., U.S.	B7	94
Westwood, Ma., U.S.	B5	98
Westwood, N.J., U.S.	B4	107
Westwood Lakes, Fl., U.S.	s13	86
West Wyoming, Pa., U.S.	n17	115
West Yarmouth, Ma., U.S.	C7	98
West Yellowstone, Mt., U.S.	F5	103
West York, Pa., U.S.	G8	115
Wetar, Pulau, i., Indon.	G8	32
Wetaskiwin, Alta., Can.	C4	68
Wethersfield, Ct., U.S.	C5	84
Wet Mountains, mts., Co., U.S.	C5	83
Wetumka, Ok., U.S.	B5	113
Wetumpka, Al., U.S.	C3	78
Wetzel, co., W.V., U.S.	B4	125
Wetzlar, Ger.	E8	8
Wewahitchka, Fl., U.S.	k15	86
Wewak, Pap. N. Gui.	k15	50a
Wewoka, Ok., U.S.	B5	113
Wexford, Ire.	I6	7
Wexford, co., Mi., U.S.	D5	99
Weyauwega, Wi., U.S.	D5	126
Weymouth, Eng., U.K.	K10	7
Weymouth, Ma., U.S.	B6	98
Whaleyville, Md., U.S.	D7	97
Whalsay, i., Scot., U.K.	A12	7
Whangarei, N.Z.	A5	52
Wharton, N.J., U.S.	B3	107
Wharton, Tx., U.S.	E4	120
Wharton, co., Tx., U.S.	E4	120
What Cheer, Ia., U.S.	C5	92
Whatcom, co., Wa., U.S.	A4	124
Whatcom, Lake, l., Wa., U.S.	A3	124
Wheatfield, In., U.S.	B3	91
Wheatland, Ca., U.S.	C3	82
Wheatland, Ia., U.S.	C7	92
Wheatland, Wy., U.S.	D8	127
Wheatland, co., Mt., U.S.	D7	103
Wheatland Reservoir, res., Wy., U.S.	E7	127
Wheatley, Ont., Can.	E2	73
Wheaton, Il., U.S.	B5	90
Wheaton, Md., U.S.	B3	97
Wheaton, Mn., U.S.	E2	100
Wheaton, Mo., U.S.	E3	102
Wheat Ridge, Co., U.S.	B5	83
Wheelbarrow Peak, mtn., Nv., U.S.	F5	105
Wheeler, Ms., U.S.	A5	101
Wheeler, Tx., U.S.	B2	120
Wheeler, co., Ga., U.S.	D4	87
Wheeler, co., Ne., U.S.	C7	104
Wheeler, co., Or., U.S.	C6	114
Wheeler, co., Tx., U.S.	B2	120
Wheeler Air Force Base, mil., Hi., U.S.	g9	88
Wheeler Lake, res., Al., U.S.	A2	78
Wheeler Peak, mtn., Ca., U.S.	C4	82
Wheeler Peak, mtn., Nv., U.S.	E7	105
Wheeler Peak, mtn., N.M., U.S.	A4	108
Wheelersburg, Oh., U.S.	D3	112
Wheeling, Il., U.S.	h9	90
Wheeling, W.V., U.S.	A4	125
Wheeling Creek, stm., W.V., U.S.	f8	125
Wheelwright, Ky., U.S.	C7	94
Whetstone, stm., U.S.	E2	100
Whidbey Island, i., Wa., U.S.	A3	124
Whidbey Island Naval Air Station, mil., Wa., U.S.	A3	124
Whigham, Ga., U.S.	F2	87
Whiskey Peak, mtn., Wy., U.S.	D5	127
Whiskeytown-Shasta-Trinity National Recreation Area, Ca., U.S.	B2	82
Whistler, B.C., Can.	D6	69
Whitacres, Ct., U.S.	A5	84
Whitakers, N.C., U.S.	A5	110
Whitbourne, Newf., Can.	E5	72
Whitby, Ont., Can.	D6	73
Whitchurch-Stouffville, Ont., Can.	D5	73
White, co., Ar., U.S.	B4	81
White, co., Ga., U.S.	B3	87
White, co., Il., U.S.	E5	90
White, co., In., U.S.	C4	91
White, co., Tn., U.S.	D8	119
White, stm., N.A.	D4	66
White, stm., U.S.	C4	81
White, stm., U.S.	D5	118
White, stm., U.S.	C7	121
White, stm., Az., U.S.	D5	80
White, stm., In., U.S.	H2	91
White, stm., Mi., U.S.	E4	99
White, stm., Nv., U.S.	E6	105
White, stm., Tx., U.S.	C2	120
White, stm., Vt., U.S.	D4	122
White, stm., Wa., U.S.	B5	124
White, stm., Wa., U.S.	B4	124
White, Lake, l., Austl.	D5	50
White Bay, b., Newf., Can.	D3	72
White Bear, stm., Newf., Can.	E3	72
White Bear Lake, Mn., U.S.	E5	100
White Bluff, Tn., U.S.	A4	119
White Butte, mtn., N.D., U.S.	C2	111
White Castle, La., U.S.	D4	95
White Center, Wa., U.S.	e11	124
White City, Or., U.S.	E4	114
White Clay Creek, stm., U.S.	A3	104
White Cloud, Mi., U.S.	E5	99
Whitecourt, Alta., Can.	B3	68
White Creek, stm., U.S.	E2	122
Whiteday, stm., W.V., U.S.	h10	125
White Deer, Tx., U.S.	B2	120
White Earth Indian Reservation, Mn., U.S.	C3	100
White Earth Lake, l., Mn., U.S.	C3	100
Whiteface, stm., Mn., U.S.	C6	100
Whiteface Mountain, mtn., N.Y., U.S.	f11	109
Whitefield, N.H., U.S.	B3	106
Whitefish, Mt., U.S.	B2	103
Whitefish Bay, Wi., U.S.	m12	126
Whitefish Bay, b., Mi., U.S.	B6	99
Whitefish Lake, l., Mn., U.S.	D4	100
Whitefish Range, mts., Mt., U.S.	B2	103
Whiteford, Md., U.S.	A5	97
White Hall, Al., U.S.	C3	78
White Hall, Ar., U.S.	C3	81
White Hall, Il., U.S.	D3	90
Whitehall, Mi., U.S.	E4	99
Whitehall, Mt., U.S.	E4	103
Whitehall, N.Y., U.S.	B7	109
Whitehall, Oh., U.S.	m11	112
Whitehall, Wi., U.S.	D2	126
Whitehall Reservoir, res., Ma., U.S.	h9	98
Whitehaven, Eng., U.K.	G9	7
White Haven, Pa., U.S.	D10	115
Whitehorn, Point, c., Wa., U.S.	A3	124
Whitehorse, Yukon, Can.	D5	66
White Horse, N.J., U.S.	C3	107
Whitehouse, Oh., U.S.	A2	112
White House, Tn., U.S.	A5	119
White Island Shores, Ma., U.S.	C6	98
White Knob Mountains, mts., Id., U.S.	F5	89
White Lake, l., La., U.S.	E3	95
Whiteman Air Force Base, mil., Mo., U.S.	C4	102
White Meadow Lake, N.J., U.S.	*B3	107
White Mesa Natural Bridge, Az., U.S.	A4	80
White Mountain Peak, mtn., Ca., U.S.	D4	82
White Mountains, mts., U.S.	D4	82
White Mountains, mts., N.H., U.S.	B3	106
Whitemouth, stm., Man., Can.	E4	70
Whitemouth Lake, l., Man., Can.	E4	70
White Nile (Al-Bahr al-Abyaḍ), stm., Sudan	F12	42
White Oak, Oh., U.S.	o12	112
White Oak Creek, stm., Oh., U.S.	D2	112
Whiteoak Creek, stm., Tn., U.S.	A4	119
White Oak Lake, res., Ar., U.S.	D2	81
White Pigeon, Mi., U.S.	G5	99
White Pine, Mi., U.S.	m12	99
White Pine, Tn., U.S.	C10	119
White Pine, co., Nv., U.S.	D6	105
White Plains, Md., U.S.	C4	97
White Plains, N.Y., U.S.	D7	109
Whiteriver, Az., U.S.	D6	80
White River Junction, Vt., U.S.	D4	122
White Rock, B.C., Can.	E6	69
White Russia see Belarus, ctry., Eur.	G3	18
White Salmon, Wa., U.S.	D4	124
White Salmon, stm., Wa., U.S.	D4	124
White Sands Missile Range, mil., N.M., U.S.	E3	108
White Sands National Monument, N.M., U.S.	E3	108
Whitesboro, N.Y., U.S.	B5	109
Whitesboro, Tx., U.S.	C4	120
Whitesburg, Ga., U.S.	C2	87
Whitesburg, Ky., U.S.	C7	94
Whites Creek, stm., Tn., U.S.	g10	119
White Sea see Beloje more, Russia	D5	22
Whiteside, co., Il., U.S.	B3	90
White Sulphur Springs, Mt., U.S.	D6	103
White Sulphur Springs, W.V., U.S.	D4	125
Whitesville, Ky., U.S.	C3	94
White Swan, Wa., U.S.	C5	124

Name	Map Ref	Page
White Tank Mountains, mts., Az., U.S.	k7	80
Whiteville, N.C., U.S.	C4	110
Whiteville, Tn., U.S.	B2	119
White Volta (Volta Blanche), stm., Afr.	F5	42
Whitewater, Ks., U.S.	E6	93
Whitewater, Wi., U.S.	F5	126
Whitewater, stm., U.S.	F7	91
Whitewater, stm., Ks., U.S.	E6	93
Whitewater Baldy, mtn., N.M., U.S.	D1	108
Whitewater Bay, b., Fl., U.S.	G6	86
Whitewood, S.D., U.S.	C2	118
Whitewright, Tx., U.S.	C4	120
Whitfield, co., Ga., U.S.	B2	87
Whitfield Estates, Fl., U.S.	q10	86
Whiting, In., U.S.	A3	91
Whiting, Ia., U.S.	B1	92
Whiting, Wi., U.S.	D4	126
Whiting Field Naval Air Station, mil., Fl., U.S.	u14	86
Whitinsville, Ma., U.S.	B4	98
Whitley, co., In., U.S.	B6	91
Whitley, co., Ky., U.S.	D5	94
Whitley City, Ky., U.S.	D5	94
Whitman, Ma., U.S.	B6	98
Whitman, W.V., U.S.	D2	125
Whitman, co., Wa., U.S.	B8	124
Whitman Square, N.J., U.S.	D2	107
Whitmire, S.C., U.S.	B4	117
Whitmore Lake, Mi., U.S.	p14	99
Whitmore Village, Hi., U.S.	f9	88
Whitney, S.C., U.S.	B4	117
Whitney, Tx., U.S.	D4	120
Whitney, Lake, res., Tx., U.S.	D4	120
Whitney, Mount, mtn., Ca., U.S.	D4	82
Whitney Point Lake, res., N.Y., U.S.	C5	109
Whittier, Ak., U.S.	C10	79
Whittier, Ca., U.S.	F4	82
Whitwell, Tn., U.S.	D8	119
Wholdaia Lake, l., N.W. Ter., Can.	D12	66
Whyalla, Austl.	F7	50
Wiarton, Ont., Can.	C3	73
Wibaux, Mt., U.S.	D12	103
Wibaux, co., Mt., U.S.	D12	103
Wichita, Ks., U.S.	E6	93
Wichita, co., Ks., U.S.	D2	93
Wichita, co., Tx., U.S.	B3	120
Wichita Falls, Tx., U.S.	C3	120
Wichita Mountains, mts., Ok., U.S.	C3	113
Wick, Scot., U.K.	C9	7
Wickenburg, Az., U.S.	D3	80
Wickiup Reservoir, res., Or., U.S.	E5	114
Wickliffe, Ky., U.S.	f8	94
Wickliffe, Oh., U.S.	A4	112
Wicklow, Ire.	I6	7
Wicklow Head, c., Ire.	I6	7
Wicklow Mountains, mts., Ire.	H6	7
Wicomico, co., Md., U.S.	D6	97
Wicomico, stm., Md., U.S.	D6	97
Wiconisco, Pa., U.S.	E8	115
Widefield, Co., U.S.	C6	83
Wielkopolska, reg., Pol.	D17	8
Wien (Vienna), Aus.	G16	8
Wiener Neustadt, Aus.	H16	8
Wiesbaden, Ger.	E8	8
Wiesloch, Ger.	F8	8
Wiggins, Ms., U.S.	E4	101
Wiggins Peak, mtn., Wy., U.S.	C3	127
Wikwemikong, Ont., Can.	B3	73
Wilbarger, co., Tx., U.S.	B3	120
Wilber, Ne., U.S.	D9	104
Wilberforce, Oh., U.S.	C2	112
Wilbraham, Ma., U.S.	B3	98
Wilbur, Wa., U.S.	B7	124
Wilburton, Ok., U.S.	C6	113
Wilcannia, Austl.	F8	50
Wilcox, Pa., U.S.	C4	115
Wilcox, co., Al., U.S.	D2	78
Wilcox, co., Ga., U.S.	E3	87
Wild, stm., U.S.	B4	106
Wild Ammonoosuc, stm., N.H., U.S.	B3	106
Wild Branch, stm., Vt., U.S.	B4	122
Wilder, Id., U.S.	F2	89
Wilder, Vt., U.S.	D4	122
Wilder Dam, U.S.	C2	106
Wildhorse Creek, stm., Ok., U.S.	C4	113
Wild Horse Reservoir, res., Nv., U.S.	B6	105
Wildorado, Tx., U.S.	B1	120
Wild Rice, stm., Mn., U.S.	C2	100
Wild Rice, stm., N.D., U.S.	C8	111
Wildwood, Fl., U.S.	D4	86
Wildwood, N.J., U.S.	F3	107
Wildwood Crest, N.J., U.S.	F3	107
Wilhelm, Mount, mtn., Pap. N. Gui.	m16	50a
Wilhelmina Gebergte, mts., Sur.	C7	54
Wilhelmina Peak see Trikora, Puntjak, mtn., Indon.	F10	32
Wilhelmshaven, Ger.	B8	8
Wilkes, co., Ga., U.S.	C4	87
Wilkes, co., N.C., U.S.	A1	110
Wilkes-Barre, Pa., U.S.	D10	115
Wilkesboro, N.C., U.S.	A1	110
Wilkes Land, reg., Ant.	C24	47
Wilkin, co., Mn., U.S.	D2	100
Wilkinsburg, Pa., U.S.	F2	115
Wilkinson, W.V., U.S.	D3	125
Wilkinson, co., Ga., U.S.	D3	87
Wilkinson, co., Ms., U.S.	D2	101
Will, co., Il., U.S.	B6	90
Willacoochee, Ga., U.S.	E3	87
Willacy, co., Tx., U.S.	F4	120
Willamette, stm., Or., U.S.	C3	114
Willamette Pass, Or., U.S.	D4	114
Willamina, Or., U.S.	B3	114
Willapa Bay, b., Wa., U.S.	C1	124
Willard, Mo., U.S.	D4	102
Willard, Oh., U.S.	A3	112
Willard, Ut., U.S.	B3	121
Willard Bay, b., Ut., U.S.	B3	121
Willards, Md., U.S.	D7	97
Willard Stream, stm., Vt., U.S.	B5	122
Willcox, Az., U.S.	E6	80
Willcox Playa, l., Az., U.S.	E5	80
Willemstad, Neth. Ant.	H13	64
William "Bill" Dannelly Reservoir, res., Al., U.S.	C2	78
Williams, Az., U.S.	B3	80
Williams, Ca., U.S.	C2	82
Williams, co., N.D., U.S.	A2	111
Williams, co., Oh., U.S.	A1	112
Williams, stm., Vt., U.S.	E3	122
Williams, stm., W.V., U.S.	C4	125
Williams Air Force Base, mil., Az., U.S.	D4	80
Williams Bay, Wi., U.S.	F5	126
Williamsburg, In., U.S.	E8	91
Williamsburg, Ia., U.S.	C5	92
Williamsburg, Ky., U.S.	D5	94
Williamsburg, Oh., U.S.	C1	112
Williamsburg, Pa., U.S.	F5	115
Williamsburg, Va., U.S.	C6	123
Williamsburg, co., S.C., U.S.	D8	117
Williams Fork, stm., Co., U.S.	A3	83
Williams Lake, B.C., Can.	C6	69
Williamson, N.Y., U.S.	B3	109
Williamson, W.V., U.S.	D2	125
Williamson, co., Il., U.S.	F4	90
Williamson, co., Tn., U.S.	B5	119
Williamson, co., Tx., U.S.	D4	120
Williamsport, In., U.S.	D3	91
Williamsport, Md., U.S.	A2	97
Williamsport, Pa., U.S.	D7	115
Williamston, Mi., U.S.	F6	99
Williamston, N.C., U.S.	B5	110
Williamston, S.C., U.S.	B3	117
Williamstown, Ky., U.S.	B5	94
Williamstown, Ma., U.S.	A1	98
Williamstown, N.J., U.S.	D3	107
Williamstown, Pa., U.S.	E8	115
Williamstown, Vt., U.S.	C3	122
Williamstown, W.V., U.S.	B3	125
Williamsville, Il., U.S.	D4	90
Williamsville, N.Y., U.S.	C2	109
Willimantic, Ct., U.S.	C7	84
Willimantic, stm., Ct., U.S.	B6	84
Willimantic Reservoir, res., Ct., U.S.	C7	84
Willingboro, N.J., U.S.	C3	107
Willis, Tx., U.S.	D5	120
Willis Islets, is., Austl.	C9	50
Williston, Fl., U.S.	C4	86
Williston, N.D., U.S.	A2	111
Williston, S.C., U.S.	E5	117
Williston Lake, res., B.C., Can.	B6	69
Willits, Ca., U.S.	C2	82
Willmar, Mn., U.S.	E3	100
Willoughby, Oh., U.S.	A4	112
Willoughby, Lake, l., Vt., U.S.	B4	122
Willoughby Hills, Oh., U.S.	A4	112
Willow, Ak., U.S.	g17	79
Willow Creek, stm., Nv., U.S.	E5	105
Willow Creek, stm., Ut., U.S.	D6	121
Willow Creek, stm., Wy., U.S.	C6	127
Willow Grove Naval Air Station, mil., Pa., U.S.	F11	115
Willowick, Oh., U.S.	A4	112
Willowmore, S. Afr.	H4	44
Willow Reservoir, res., Wi., U.S.	C3	126
Willow Run, De., U.S.	i7	85
Willow Run, Mi., U.S.	p14	99
Willows, Ca., U.S.	C2	82
Willow Springs, Il., U.S.	k9	90
Willow Springs, Mo., U.S.	E6	102
Willston, Va., U.S.	*B5	123
Wilmar, Ar., U.S.	D4	81
Wilmerding, Pa., U.S.	k14	115
Wilmette, Il., U.S.	A6	90
Wilmington, De., U.S.	B3	85
Wilmington, Il., U.S.	B5	90
Wilmington, Ma., U.S.	A5	98
Wilmington, N.C., U.S.	C5	110
Wilmington, Oh., U.S.	C2	112
Wilmington, Vt., U.S.	F3	122
Wilmington Manor, De., U.S.	i7	85
Wilmore, Ky., U.S.	C5	94
Wilmot, Ar., U.S.	D4	81
Wilson, Ar., U.S.	B5	81
Wilson, Ks., U.S.	D5	93
Wilson, La., U.S.	D4	95
Wilson, N.C., U.S.	B5	110
Wilson, Ok., U.S.	C4	113
Wilson, Pa., U.S.	E11	115
Wilson, Wy., U.S.	C2	127
Wilson, co., Ks., U.S.	E8	93
Wilson, co., N.C., U.S.	B5	110
Wilson, co., Tn., U.S.	A5	119
Wilson, co., Tx., U.S.	E3	120
Wilson, Cape, c., N.W. Ter., Can.	C16	66
Wilson, Mount, mtn., Az., U.S.	B1	80
Wilson, Mount, mtn., Ca., U.S.	m12	82
Wilson, Mount, mtn., Co., U.S.	D2	83
Wilson, Mount, mtn., Nv., U.S.	E7	105
Wilson, Mount, mtn., Or., U.S.	B5	114
Wilson Creek, stm., Wa., U.S.	B5	124
Wilson Creek, stm., Wa., U.S.	B6	124
Wilson Lake, res., Al., U.S.	A2	78
Wilson Lake, res., Ks., U.S.	D4	93
Wilsons Beach, N.B., Can.	E3	71
Wilsonville, Al., U.S.	B3	78
Wilsonville, Or., U.S.	h12	114
Wilton, Al., U.S.	B3	78
Wilton, Ct., U.S.	E2	84
Wilton, Ia., U.S.	C6	92
Wilton, Me., U.S.	D2	96
Wilton, N.H., U.S.	E3	106
Wilton, N.D., U.S.	B5	111
Wiluna, Austl.	E4	50
Wimauma, Fl., U.S.	E4	86
Wimico, Lake, l., Fl., U.S.	C1	86
Winamac, In., U.S.	B4	91
Wincheck Pond, l., R.I., U.S.	E1	116
Winchendon, Ma., U.S.	A3	98
Winchester, Ont., Can.	B9	73
Winchester, Eng., U.K.	J11	7
Winchester, Il., U.S.	D3	90
Winchester, In., U.S.	D8	91
Winchester, Ks., U.S.	k15	93
Winchester, Ky., U.S.	C5	94
Winchester, Ma., U.S.	g11	98
Winchester, Nv., U.S.	G6	105
Winchester, N.H., U.S.	E2	106
Winchester, Oh., U.S.	D2	112
Winchester, Tn., U.S.	B5	119
Winchester, Va., U.S.	A4	123
Winchester Bay, Or., U.S.	D2	114
Wind, stm., Wa., U.S.	D4	124
Wind, stm., Wy., U.S.	C4	127
Windber, Pa., U.S.	F4	115
Wind Cave National Park, S.D., U.S.	D2	118
Winder, Ga., U.S.	C3	87
Windermere, Eng., U.K.	G10	7
Windfall, In., U.S.	D6	91
Windgap, Pa., U.S.	E11	115
Windham, Ct., U.S.	C7	84
Windham, Oh., U.S.	A4	112
Windham, co., Ct., U.S.	B7	84
Windham, co., Vt., U.S.	F3	122
Windhoek, Nmb.	F3	44
Wind Lake, Wi., U.S.	F5	126
Wind Lake, l., Wi., U.S.	n11	126
Windmill Point, c., Va., U.S.	C6	123
Windom, Mn., U.S.	G3	100
Windom Peak, mtn., Co., U.S.	D3	83
Windorah, Austl.	E8	50
Window Rock, Az., U.S.	B6	80
Wind Point, Wi., U.S.	n12	126
Wind River Indian Reservation, Wy., U.S.	C4	127
Wind River Peak, mtn., Wy., U.S.	D3	127
Wind River Range, mts., Wy., U.S.	C3	127
Windsor, Newf., Can.	D4	72
Windsor, Ont., Can.	E1	73
Windsor, Que., Can.	D5	74
Windsor, Eng., U.K.	J12	7
Windsor, Co., U.S.	A6	83
Windsor, Ct., U.S.	B5	84
Windsor, Il., U.S.	D5	90
Windsor, Mo., U.S.	C4	102
Windsor, N.C., U.S.	A6	110
Windsor, Pa., U.S.	G8	115
Windsor, Vt., U.S.	E4	122
Windsor, Va., U.S.	D6	123
Windsor, co., Vt., U.S.	D3	122
Windsor Heights, Ia., U.S.	e8	92
Windsor Locks, Ct., U.S.	B5	84
Windward Islands, is., N.A.	H17	64
Windward Passage, strt., N.A.	E10	64
Windy Hill, S.C., U.S.	C8	117
Windy Peak, mtn., Wa., U.S.	A6	124
Winefred Lake, l., Alta., Can.	B5	68
Winfield, Al., U.S.	B2	78
Winfield, Ia., U.S.	C6	92
Winfield, Ks., U.S.	E7	93
Winfield, Mo., U.S.	C7	102
Winfield, W.V., U.S.	C3	125
Wing, stm., Mn., U.S.	D3	100
Wingate, N.C., U.S.	C2	110
Wingham, Ont., Can.	D3	73
Winifrede, W.V., U.S.	m12	125
Winisk, stm., Ont., Can.	n18	73
Winisk Lake, l., Ont., Can.	F15	66
Wink, Tx., U.S.	D1	120
Winkelman, Az., U.S.	E5	80
Winkler, Man., Can.	E3	70
Winkler, co., Tx., U.S.	D1	120
Winlock, Wa., U.S.	C3	124
Winn, co., La., U.S.	C3	95
Winnebago, Il., U.S.	A4	90
Winnebago, Mn., U.S.	G4	100
Winnebago, Ne., U.S.	B9	104
Winnebago, Wi., U.S.	h8	126
Winnebago, co., Il., U.S.	A4	90
Winnebago, co., Ia., U.S.	A4	92
Winnebago, co., Wi., U.S.	D5	126
Winnebago, stm., Ia., U.S.	A4	92
Winnebago, Lake, l., Wi., U.S.	E5	126
Winnebago Indian Reservation, Ne., U.S.	B9	104
Winneconne, Wi., U.S.	D5	126
Winnemucca, Nv., U.S.	C4	105
Winnemucca Lake, l., Nv., U.S.	C2	105
Winner, S.D., U.S.	D6	118
Winneshiek, co., Ia., U.S.	A6	92
Winnetka, Il., U.S.	A6	90
Winnfield, La., U.S.	C3	95
Winnibigoshish, Lake, l., Mn., U.S.	C4	100
Winnipeg, Man., Can.	E3	70
Winnipeg, stm., Can.	D4	70
Winnipeg, Lake, l., Man., Can.	C3	70
Winnipeg Beach, Man., Can.	D3	70
Winnipegosis, Man., Can.	D2	70
Winnipegosis, Lake, l., Man., Can.	C2	70
Winnipesaukee, Lake, l., N.H., U.S.	C4	106
Winnisquam, N.H., U.S.	C3	106
Winnisquam Lake, l., N.H., U.S.	C3	106
Winnsboro, La., U.S.	B4	95
Winnsboro, S.C., U.S.	C5	117
Winnsboro, Tx., U.S.	C5	120
Winnsboro Mills, S.C., U.S.	C5	117
Winona, Mn., U.S.	F7	100
Winona, Ms., U.S.	B4	101
Winona, Mo., U.S.	D6	102
Winona, co., Mn., U.S.	F7	100
Winona Lake, In., U.S.	B6	91
Winona Lake, l., Vt., U.S.	C2	122
Winooski, Vt., U.S.	C2	122
Winooski, stm., Vt., U.S.	C3	122
Winslow, Az., U.S.	C5	80
Winslow, In., U.S.	H3	91
Winslow, Me., U.S.	D3	96
Winsted, Ct., U.S.	B3	84
Winsted, Mn., U.S.	F4	100
Winston, Fl., U.S.	D4	86
Winston, Or., U.S.	D3	114
Winston, co., Al., U.S.	A2	78
Winston, co., Ms., U.S.	B4	101
Winston-Salem, N.C., U.S.	A2	110
Winter Garden, Fl., U.S.	D5	86
Winter Harbor, Me., U.S.	D4	96
Winter Haven, Fl., U.S.	D5	86
Winter Park, Fl., U.S.	D5	86
Winter Park, N.C., U.S.	C5	110
Winterport, Me., U.S.	D4	96
Winter Ridge, mtn., Or., U.S.	E6	114
Winters, Ca., U.S.	C2	82
Winters, Tx., U.S.	D3	120
Winterset, Ia., U.S.	C4	92
Wintersville, Oh., U.S.	B5	112
Winterswijk, Neth.	D6	8
Winterthur, Switz.	E15	10
Winterton, Newf., Can.	E5	72
Winterville, Ga., U.S.	C3	87
Winterville, N.C., U.S.	B5	110
Winthrop, Ia., U.S.	B6	92
Winthrop, Me., U.S.	D3	96
Winthrop, Ma., U.S.	B6	98
Winthrop, Mn., U.S.	F4	100
Winthrop, Lake, l., Ma., U.S.	h10	98
Winthrop Harbor, Il., U.S.	A6	90
Winton, Austl.	D8	50
Winton, N.C., U.S.	A6	110
Winton Lake, res., Oh., U.S.	o12	113
Winyah Bay, b., S.C., U.S.	E9	117
Wirt, co., W.V., U.S.	B3	125
Wiscasset, Me., U.S.	D3	96
Wisconsin, state, U.S.	D4	126
Wisconsin, stm., Wi., U.S.	E3	126
Wisconsin, Lake, res., Wi., U.S.	E4	126
Wisconsin Dells, Wi., U.S.	E4	126
Wisconsin Rapids, Wi., U.S.	D4	126
Wise, Va., U.S.	f9	123
Wise, co., Tx., U.S.	C4	120
Wise, co., Va., U.S.	e9	123
Wishek, N.D., U.S.	C6	111
Wishram, Wa., U.S.	D4	124
Wisła, stm., Pol.	A18	8
Wismar, Ger.	B11	8
Wisner, La., U.S.	C4	95
Wisner, Ne., U.S.	C9	104
Wissota, Lake, res., Wi., U.S.	D2	126
Wister, Ok., U.S.	C7	113
Wister Lake, res., Ok., U.S.	C7	113
Witbank, S. Afr.	G5	44
Withamsville, Oh., U.S.	C1	112
Witherspoon, Mount, mtn., Ak., U.S.	g18	79
Withlacoochee, stm., U.S.	B3	86
Withlacoochee, stm., Fl., U.S.	C4	86
Witless Bay, Newf., Can.	E5	72
Witt, Il., U.S.	D4	90
Wittenberg, Ger.	D12	8
Wittenberg, Wi., U.S.	D4	126
Wittenberge, Ger.	B11	8
Wittlich, Ger.	F6	8
Wittman, Md., U.S.	C5	97
Wittmann, Az., U.S.	D3	80
Wittstock, Ger.	B12	8
Wixom, Mi., U.S.	o14	99
Wixom Lake, res., Mi., U.S.	E6	99
Włocławek, Pol.	C19	8
Woburn, Ma., U.S.	B5	98
Wokam, Pulau, i., Indon.	G9	32
Woking, Eng., U.K.	J12	7
Wolcott, Ct., U.S.	C4	84
Wolcott, In., U.S.	C3	91
Wolcottville, In., U.S.	A7	91
Wolf, stm., Ms., U.S.	E4	101
Wolf, stm., Tn., U.S.	e9	119
Wolf, stm., Wi., U.S.	C5	126
Wolf Creek, Or., U.S.	E3	114
Wolf Creek, stm., U.S.	A2	113
Wolf Creek, stm., W.V., U.S.	m13	125
Wolf Creek Pass, Co., U.S.	D3	83
Wolfe, co., Ky., U.S.	C6	94
Wolfeboro, N.H., U.S.	C4	106
Wolfeboro Falls, N.H., U.S.	C4	106
Wolfe City, Tx., U.S.	C4	120
Wolfen, Ger.	D12	8
Wolfenbüttel, Ger.	C10	8
Wolf Lake, Mi., U.S.	E4	99
Wolf Lake, l., Il., U.S.	k9	90
Wolf Mountain, mtn., Ak., U.S.	B9	79
Wolf Point, Mt., U.S.	B11	103
Wolfsberg, Aus.	I14	8
Wolfsburg, Ger.	C10	8
Wolf Swamp, sw., N.C., U.S.	C5	110
Wolgast, Ger.	A13	8
Wollaston, Cape, c., N.W. Ter., Can.	B9	66
Wollaston, Islas, is., Chile	H3	56
Wollaston Lake, l., Sask., Can.	m8	75
Wollaston Peninsula, pen., N.W. Ter., Can.	C10	66
Wollongong, Austl.	F10	50
Wolverhampton, Eng., U.K.	I10	7
Woman Lake, l., Mn., U.S.	D4	100
Womelsdorf, Pa., U.S.	F9	115
Wonder Lake, Il., U.S.	A5	90
Wonewoc, Wi., U.S.	E3	126
Wŏnsan, N. Kor.	D12	26
Wood, co., Oh., U.S.	A2	112
Wood, co., Tx., U.S.	C5	120
Wood, co., W.V., U.S.	B3	125
Wood, co., Wi., U.S.	D3	126
Wood, stm., Sask., Can.	H2	75
Wood, stm., R.I., U.S.	F2	116
Wood, stm., Wy., U.S.	C3	127
Wood, Mount, mtn., Mt., U.S.	E7	103
Woodall Mountain, mtn., Ms., U.S.	A5	101
Woodbine, Ga., U.S.	F5	87
Woodbine, Ia., U.S.	C2	92
Woodbine, Ky., U.S.	D5	94
Woodbine, N.J., U.S.	E3	107
Woodbridge, Ct., U.S.	D3	84
Woodbridge, Va., U.S.	B5	123
Woodbridge [Township], N.J., U.S.	B4	107
Woodburn, In., U.S.	B8	91
Woodburn, Or., U.S.	B4	114
Woodbury, Ct., U.S.	C3	84
Woodbury, Ga., U.S.	D2	87
Woodbury, Mn., U.S.	F6	100
Woodbury, N.J., U.S.	D2	107
Woodbury, Tn., U.S.	B5	119
Woodbury, co., Ia., U.S.	B1	92
Woodcliff Lake, N.J., U.S.	g8	107
Woodcliff Lake, l., N.J., U.S.	g8	107
Wood Dale, Il., U.S.	k9	90
Wood End, spit, Ma., U.S.	B7	98
Woodfield, S.C., U.S.	C6	117
Woodford, co., Il., U.S.	C4	90
Woodford, co., Ky., U.S.	B5	94
Woodhull, Il., U.S.	B3	90
Woodlake, Ca., U.S.	D4	82
Woodland, Ca., U.S.	C3	82
Woodland, Me., U.S.	C5	96
Woodland, N.C., U.S.	A5	110
Woodland, Wa., U.S.	D3	124
Woodland Acres, Co., U.S.	D6	83
Woodland Park, Co., U.S.	C5	83
Woodlark Island, i., Pap. N. Gui.	A10	50
Woodlawn, Ky., U.S.	e9	94
Woodlawn, Md., U.S.	g10	97
Woodlawn, Oh., U.S.	n13	112
Woodlawn, Va., U.S.	D2	123
Woodmont, Ct., U.S.	E4	84
Woodmoor, Md., U.S.	B4	97
Woodridge, Il., U.S.	k8	90
Wood-Ridge, N.J., U.S.	h8	107
Wood River, Il., U.S.	E3	90
Wood River, Ne., U.S.	D7	104
Woodroffe, Mount, mtn., Austl.	E6	50
Woodruff, S.C., U.S.	B3	117
Woodruff, Wi., U.S.	C4	126
Woodruff, co., Ar., U.S.	B4	81
Woods, co., Ok., U.S.	A3	113
Woods, Lake, res., Tn., U.S.	B5	119
Woods, Lake of the, l., N.A.	G14	66
Woodsboro, Tx., U.S.	E4	120
Woods Cross, Ut., U.S.	C4	121
Woodsfield, Oh., U.S.	C4	112
Woods Hole, Ma., U.S.	C6	98
Woodson, Ar., U.S.	C3	81
Woodson, co., Ks., U.S.	E8	93
Woodstock, N.B., Can.	C2	71
Woodstock, Ont., Can.	D4	73
Woodstock, Ga., U.S.	B2	87
Woodstock, Il., U.S.	A5	90
Woodstock, Md., U.S.	B4	97
Woodstock, N.Y., U.S.	C6	109
Woodstock, Vt., U.S.	D3	122
Woodstock, Va., U.S.	B4	123
Woodstown, N.J., U.S.	D2	107
Woodsville, N.H., U.S.	B2	106
Woodville, N.Z.	D5	52
Woodville, Fl., U.S.	B2	86
Woodville, Ms., U.S.	D2	101
Woodville, Oh., U.S.	A2	112
Woodville, Tx., U.S.	D5	120
Woodville, Wi., U.S.	D1	126
Woodward, Ia., U.S.	C4	92
Woodward, Ok., U.S.	A2	113
Woodward, co., Ok., U.S.	A2	113
Woodworth, La., U.S.	C3	95
Woolmarket, Ms., U.S.	E5	101
Woolrich, Pa., U.S.	D7	115
Woolsey Peak, mtn., Az., U.S.	D3	80
Woomera, Austl.	F7	50
Woonsocket, R.I., U.S.	A3	116
Woonsocket, S.D., U.S.	C7	118
Woonsocket Reservoir Number Three, res., R.I., U.S.	B3	116
Wooramel, Austl.	E2	50
Wooster, Oh., U.S.	B4	112
Worcester, S. Afr.	H3	44
Worcester, Eng., U.K.	I10	7
Worcester, Ma., U.S.	B4	98
Worcester, co., Md., U.S.	D7	97
Worcester, co., Ma., U.S.	A3	98
Worden, Il., U.S.	E4	90
Worden Pond, l., R.I., U.S.	F3	116
Workington, Eng., U.K.	G9	7
Worland, Wy., U.S.	B5	127
Worms, Ger.	F8	8
Worth, Il., U.S.	k9	90
Worth, co., Ga., U.S.	E3	87
Worth, co., Ia., U.S.	A4	92
Worth, co., Mo., U.S.	A3	102
Worthing, Eng., U.K.	K12	7
Worthington, In., U.S.	F4	91
Worthington, Ky., U.S.	B7	94
Worthington, Mn., U.S.	G3	100
Worthington, Oh., U.S.	B2	112
Worthington Peak, mtn., Nv., U.S.	F6	105
Wowoni, Pulau, i., Indon.	F7	32
Wrangell, Ak., U.S.	D13	79
Wrangell, Cape, c., Ak., U.S.	E2	79
Wrangell, Mount, mtn., Ak., U.S.	f19	79
Wrangell Island, i., Ak., U.S.	m24	79
Wrangell Mountains, mts., Ak., U.S.	C11	79
Wrangell-Saint Elias National Park, Ak., U.S.	C11	79
Wrath, Cape, c., Scot., U.K.	C7	7
Wray, Co., U.S.	A8	83
Wreck Reefs, rf., Austl.	D11	50
Wrens, Ga., U.S.	C4	87
Wrentham, Ma., U.S.	B5	98
Wrexham, Wales, U.K.	H9	7
Wright, co., Ia., U.S.	B4	92
Wright, co., Mn., U.S.	E4	100
Wright, co., Mo., U.S.	D5	102
Wright, Mount, mtn., Mt., U.S.	C4	103
Wright Brothers National Memorial, hist., N.C., U.S.	A7	110
Wright City, Mo., U.S.	C8	102
Wright City, Ok., U.S.	C6	113
Wright-Patterson Air Force Base, mil., Oh., U.S.	C1	112
Wrightson, Mount, mtn., Az., U.S.	F5	80
Wrightstown, N.J., U.S.	C3	107
Wrightstown, Wi., U.S.	D5	126
Wrightsville, Ar., U.S.	C3	81
Wrightsville, Ga., U.S.	D4	87
Wrightsville, Pa., U.S.	F8	115
Wrightsville Beach, N.C., U.S.	C5	110

Name	Map Ref	Page
Wrightsville Reservoir, res., Vt., U.S.	C3	122
Wrigley, N.W. Ter., Can.	D8	66
Wrocław (Breslau), Pol.	D17	8
Wuchuan, China	D11	34
Wudu, China	E7	26
Wugang, China	F9	26
Wuhan, China	E3	28
Wuhu, China	D7	28
Wunstorf, Ger.	C9	8
Wupatki National Monument, Az., U.S.	B4	80
Wuppertal, Ger.	D7	8
Wurtsmith Air Force Base, mil., Mi., U.S.	D7	99
Würzburg, Ger.	F9	8
Wurzen, Ger.	D12	8
Wushan, China	E8	26
Wushenqi, China	D8	26
Wusong, China	D10	28
Wutongqiao, China	F7	26
Wuwei, China	D7	26
Wuwei, China	D6	26
Wuxi (Wuhsi), China	D9	28
Wuyi Shan, mts., China	I5	28
Wuyuan, China	C8	26
Wuzhong, China	D8	26
Wuzhou (Wuchow), China	C11	34
Wyaconda, stm., Mo., U.S.	A6	102
Wyandot, co., Oh., U.S.	B2	112
Wyandotte, Mi., U.S.	F7	99
Wyandotte, co., Ks., U.S.	C9	93
Wyanet, Il., U.S.	B4	90
Wyk, Ger.	A8	8
Wylie, Lake, res., U.S.	A5	117
Wyman Lake, res., Me., U.S.	C3	96
Wymore, Ne., U.S.	D9	104
Wyndham, Austl.	C5	50
Wynndel, B.C., Can.	E9	69
Wynne, Ar., U.S.	B5	81
Wynnewood, Ok., U.S.	C4	113
Wynoochee, stm., Wa., U.S.	B2	124
Wyoming, Ont., Can.	E2	73
Wyoming, De., U.S.	D3	85
Wyoming, Il., U.S.	B4	90
Wyoming, Ia., U.S.	B6	92
Wyoming, Mi., U.S.	F5	99
Wyoming, Mn., U.S.	E6	100
Wyoming, Oh., U.S.	o13	112
Wyoming, Pa., U.S.	n17	115
Wyoming, R.I., U.S.	E2	116
Wyoming, co., N.Y., U.S.	C2	109
Wyoming, co., Pa., U.S.	D9	115
Wyoming, co., W.V., U.S.	D3	125
Wyoming, state, U.S.	C5	127
Wyoming Peak, mtn., Wy., U.S.	D2	127
Wyoming Range, mts., Wy., U.S.	D2	127
Wyomissing, Pa., U.S.	F10	115
Wysocking Bay, b., N.C., U.S.	B7	110
Wythe, co., Va., U.S.	D1	123
Wytheville, Va., U.S.	D1	123

X

Xai-Xai, Moz.	G6	44
Xangongo, Ang.	E3	44
Xánthi, Grc.	H8	16
Xapuri, Braz.	F5	54
Xenia, Oh., U.S.	C2	112
Xertigny, Fr.	D13	10
Xi, stm., China	G9	26
Xiaguan, China	E9	26
Xiahe, China	D7	26
Xiamen (Amoy), China	K7	28
Xi'an (Sian), China	E8	26
Xiangcheng, China	B2	28
Xiangfan, China	E9	26
Xiangkhoang, Laos	E7	34
Xiangride, China	D6	26
Xiangtan, China	H1	28
Xianyou, China	J7	28
Xiaogan, China	E2	28
Xiaolan, China	M2	28
Xiashi, China	E9	28
Xichang, China	F7	26
Xiegeer, China	F12	38
Xigazê, China	F13	38
Xihua, China	B3	28
Xilinhaote, China	C10	26
Xinavane, Moz.	G6	44
Xingtai, China	D9	26
Xingu, stm., Braz.	D8	54
Xingyi, China	B8	34
Xinhui, China	M2	28
Xining, China	D7	26
Xinjiang Uygur Zizhiqu, prov., China	B9	38
Xinxiang, China	D9	26
Xinyang, China	C3	28
Xiping, China	B3	28
Xique-Xique, Braz.	F10	54
Xizang Zizhiqu, prov., China	D12	38
Xuancheng, China	E7	28
Xuanhua, China	C10	28
Xuchang, China	A2	28
Xuwen, China	D11	34
Xuyong, China	F8	26
Xuzhou (Süchow), China	A6	28

Y

Yaan, China	E7	26

Yacolt, Wa., U.S.	D3	124
Yacuiba, Bol.	H6	54
Yadgir, India	D4	37
Yadkin, co., N.C., U.S.	A2	110
Yadkin, stm., N.C., U.S.	B2	110
Yadkinville, N.C., U.S.	A2	110
Yainax Butte, mtn., Or., U.S.	E5	114
Yaizu, Japan	H11	30
Yakima, Wa., U.S.	C5	124
Yakima, co., Wa., U.S.	C4	124
Yakima, stm., Wa., U.S.	C6	124
Yakima Indian Reservation, Wa., U.S.	C5	124
Yakobi Island, i., Ak., U.S.	m21	79
Yakumo, Japan	q18	30a
Yaku-shima, i., Japan	u30	31b
Yakutat, Ak., U.S.	D12	79
Yakutat Bay, b., Ak., U.S.	D11	79
Yala, Thai.	K6	34
Yale, Mi., U.S.	E8	99
Yale, Ok., U.S.	A5	113
Yale, Mount, mtn., Co., U.S.	C5	83
Yale Lake, res., Wa., U.S.	D3	124
Yalobusha, co., Ms., U.S.	A4	101
Yalobusha, stm., Ms., U.S.	B4	101
Yalu (Amnok-kang), stm., Asia	C12	28
Yamachiche, Que., Can.	C5	74
Yamagata, Japan	D13	30
Yamaguchi, Japan	H4	30
Yamato-takada, Japan	H8	30
Yambio, Sudan	H11	42
Yamdena, Pulau, i., Indon.	G9	32
Yamethin, Burma	D4	34
Yamhill, Or., U.S.	h11	114
Yamhill, co., Or., U.S.	B3	114
Yamoussoukro, I.C.	G4	42
Yampa, stm., Co., U.S.	A2	83
Yamsay Mountain, mtn., Or., U.S.	E5	114
Yamuna, stm., India	H9	38
Yanbu', Sau. Ar.	D2	46
Yancey, co., N.C., U.S.	f10	110
Yanceyville, N.C., U.S.	A3	110
Yanchang, China	D9	26
Yancheng, China	B9	28
Yandoon, Burma	F3	34
Yangjiang, China	G9	26
Yangon (Rangoon), Burma	B2	32
Yangquan, China	D9	26
Yangzhou, China	C8	28
Yangtze see Chang, stm., China	E10	26
Yanji, China	C12	26
Yankton, S.D., U.S.	E8	118
Yankton, co., S.D., U.S.	D8	118
Yanqi, China	C4	26
Yantai (Chefoo), China	D11	26
Yantic, stm., Ct., U.S.	C7	84
Yaoundé, Cam.	H8	42
Yapen, Pulau, i., Indon.	F10	32
Yaqui, stm., Mex.	C5	62
Yaraka, Austl.	D8	50
Yardley, Pa., U.S.	F12	115
Yardville, N.J., U.S.	C3	107
Yaritagua, Ven.	B8	58
Yarmouth, Me., U.S.	E2	96
Yarnell, Az., U.S.	C3	80
Yarumal, Col.	D5	58
Yashiro-jima, i., Japan	I5	30
Yates, co., N.Y., U.S.	C3	109
Yates Center, Ks., U.S.	E8	93
Yates City, Il., U.S.	C3	90
Yathkyed Lake, l., N.W. Ter., Can.	D13	66
Yatsushiro, Japan	J3	30
Yatta Plateau, plat., Kenya	B7	44
Yaupi, Ec.	I4	58
Yavapai, co., Az., U.S.	C3	80
Yavarí (Javarí), stm., S.A.	D4	54
Yavatmāl, India	B5	37
Yaví, Cerro, mtn., Ven.	E10	58
Yaviza, Pan.	J9	64
Yawatahama, Japan	I5	30
Yawgoog Pond, l., R.I., U.S.	E1	116
Yaxian, China	E10	34
Yazd, Iran	B5	46
Yazoo, co., Ms., U.S.	C3	101
Yazoo, stm., Ms., U.S.	C3	101
Yazoo City, Ms., U.S.	C3	101
Ye, Burma	G4	34
Yeadon, Pa., U.S.	p21	115
Yeagertown, Pa., U.S.	E6	115
Yecheng, China	B7	38
Yecla, Spain	G10	12
Yei, stm., Sudan	G12	42
Yell, co., Ar., U.S.	B2	81
Yell, i., Scot., U.K.	A11	7
Yellow, stm., U.S.	u15	86
Yellow, stm., In., U.S.	B4	91
Yellow, stm., Wi., U.S.	D3	126
Yellow, stm., Wi., U.S.	C3	126
Yellow Creek, stm., Tn., U.S.	A4	119
Yellowhead Pass, Can.	C1	68
Yellow see Huang, stm., China	D10	26
Yellowjacket Mountains, mts., Id., U.S.	D4	89
Yellowknife, N.W. Ter., Can.	D10	66
Yellow Lake, l., Wi., U.S.	C1	126
Yellow Medicine, co., Mn., U.S.	F2	100
Yellow Sea, Asia	D11	26
Yellow Springs, Oh., U.S.	C2	112
Yellowstone, co., Mt., U.S.	D8	103
Yellowstone, stm., U.S.	D10	103
Yellowstone Lake, l., Wy., U.S.	B2	127
Yellowstone National Park, co., Mt., U.S.	E6	103
Yellowstone National Park, U.S.	B2	127

Yellville, Ar., U.S.	A3	81
Yelm, Wa., U.S.	C3	124
Yemassee, S.C., U.S.	F6	117
Yemen, ctry., Asia	E4	46
Yenangyaung, Burma	D3	34
Yen Bai, Viet.	D8	34
Yendéré, Burkina	F5	42
Yendi, Ghana	G5	42
Yenisey see Jenisej, stm., Russia		
Yenshui, Tai.	L9	28
Yeovil, Eng., U.K.	K10	7
Yerevan see Jerevan, Arm.	I6	22
Yerington, Nv., U.S.	E2	105
Yerington Indian Reservation, Nv., U.S.	D2	105
Yermasóyia, Cyp.	B3	40
Yermo, Ca., U.S.	E5	82
Yerupajá, Nevado, mtn., Peru	F3	54
Yerushalayim (Jerusalem), Isr.	D4	40
Yeste, Spain	G9	12
Yexian, China	B2	28
Yibin, China	F9	26
Yichang, China	E9	26
Yichun, China	B12	26
Yichun, China	H3	28
Yilan, China	B12	26
Yiliang, China	B7	34
Yinchuan, China	D8	26
Yingde, China	K2	28
Yingkou, China	C11	26
Yining, China	C3	26
Yirga Alem, Eth.	G2	46
Yishan, China	B10	34
Yíthion, Grc.	M6	16
Yitulihe, China	A11	26
Yiyang, China	F9	26
Ylivieska, Fin.	E13	6
Ynykčanskij, Russia	E21	24
Yoakum, Tx., U.S.	E4	120
Yoakum, co., Tx., U.S.	C1	120
Yockanookany, stm., Ms., U.S.	C4	101
Yocona, stm., Ms., U.S.	A4	101
Yogyakarta, Indon.	m15	32
Yoho National Park, B.C., Can.	D9	69
Yokkaichi, Japan	H9	30
Yokohama, Japan	G12	30
Yokosuka, Japan	G12	30
Yokote, Japan	C13	30
Yola, Nig.	G8	42
Yolo, co., Ca., U.S.	C2	82
Yolombó, Col.	D5	58
Yomba Indian Reservation, Nv., U.S.	D4	105
Yonago, Japan	G6	30
Yoncalla, Or., U.S.	D3	114
Yonezawa, Japan	E13	30
Yongdeng, China	D7	26
Yongdingzhen, China	A6	34
Yongfeng, China	H4	28
Yonkers, N.Y., U.S.	E7	109
Yopal, Col.	E6	58
York, Ont., Can.	D5	73
York, Eng., U.K.	H11	7
York, Al., U.S.	C1	78
York, Me., U.S.	E2	96
York, Ne., U.S.	D8	104
York, Pa., U.S.	G8	115
York, S.C., U.S.	B5	117
York, co., Me., U.S.	E2	96
York, co., Ne., U.S.	D8	104
York, co., Pa., U.S.	G8	115
York, co., S.C., U.S.	A5	117
York, co., Va., U.S.	C6	123
York, stm., Ont., Can.	B7	73
York, stm., Va., U.S.	C6	123
York, Cape, c., Austl.	B8	50
York Beach, Me., U.S.	E2	96
York Harbor, Me., U.S.	E2	96
Yorklyn, De., U.S.	A3	85
Yorktown, In., U.S.	D7	91
Yorktown, Tx., U.S.	E4	120
Yorktown, Va., U.S.	C6	123
Yorktown Manor, R.I., U.S.	E4	116
Yorkville, Il., U.S.	B5	90
Yorkville, N.Y., U.S.	B5	109
Yorkville, Oh., U.S.	B5	112
Yoro, Hond.	G4	64
Yoron-jima, i., Japan	x28	31b
Yosemite National Park, Ca., U.S.	D4	82
Yosu, S. Kor.	E12	26
Youbou, B.C., Can.	g11	69
Youghal, Ire.	J5	7
Youghiogheny, stm., U.S.	F2	115
Youghiogheny River Lake, res., U.S.	G3	115
Young, Az., U.S.	C5	80
Young, co., Tx., U.S.	C3	120
Young Harris, Ga., U.S.	B3	87
Youngs, Lake, l., Wa., U.S.	f11	124
Youngstown, N.Y., U.S.	B1	109
Youngstown, Oh., U.S.	A5	112
Youngsville, La., U.S.	D3	95
Youngsville, Pa., U.S.	C3	115
Youngtown, Az., U.S.	k8	80
Youngwood, Pa., U.S.	F2	115
Youyang, China	F8	26
Ypres see Ieper, Bel.	E2	8
Ypsilanti, Mi., U.S.	F7	99
Yreka, Ca., U.S.	B2	82
Yssingeaux, Fr.	G11	10
Ystad, Swe.	I9	6
Yu, stm., China	C10	34

Yuanling, China	F9	26
Yuba, co., Ca., U.S.	C3	82
Yuba, stm., Ca., U.S.	C3	82
Yuba City, Ca., U.S.	C3	82
Yūbari, Japan	p19	30a
Yucatan Channel, strt., N.A.	C4	64
Yucatan Peninsula, pen., N.A.	H15	62
Yucca Lake, l., Nv., U.S.	F5	105
Yucca Mountain, mtn., Nv., U.S.	G5	105
Yuci, China	D9	26
Yueyang, China	F2	28
Yugoslavia, ctry., Eur.	G11	4
Yukon, Ok., U.S.	B4	113
Yukon, prov., Can.	D6	66
Yukon, stm., N.A.	m19	76a
Yukuhashi, Japan	I3	30
Yulee, Fl., U.S.	B5	86
Yulin, China	D8	26
Yulin, China	C11	34
Yuma, Az., U.S.	E1	80
Yuma, Co., U.S.	A8	83
Yuma, co., Az., U.S.	E1	80
Yuma, co., Co., U.S.	A8	83
Yuma Marine Corps Air Station, mil., Az., U.S.	E1	80
Yumen, China	D6	26
Yuncheng, China	D9	26
Yunnan, prov., China	F7	26
Yurimaguas, Peru	E3	54
Yuriria, Mex.	G9	62
Yü Shan, mtn., Tai.	L9	28
Yushu, China	E6	26
Yutan, Ne., U.S.	C9	104
Yutian, China	B9	38
Yuty, Para.	B5	56
Yuxian, China	A2	28
Yuyao, China	E10	28
Yverdon, Switz.	F13	10
Yvetot, Fr.	C7	10

Z

Zaandam, Neth.	C4	8
Zabīd, Yemen	F3	46
Zabrze, Pol.	E18	8
Zacapa, Guat.	G3	64
Zacapu, Mex.	H9	62
Zacatecas, Mex.	F8	62
Zachary, La., U.S.	D4	95
Zacualtipán, Mex.	G10	62
Zadar, Cro.	E10	14
Zadetkyi Kyun, i., Burma	J5	34
Zafer Burnu, c., N. Cyp.	B4	40
Zafra, Spain	G5	12
Zagreb, Cro.	D10	14
Zágros, Kūhhā-ye, mts., Iran	B5	46
Zāhedān, Iran	C7	46
Zahlah, Leb.	C4	40
Zaire, ctry., Afr.	B4	44
Zajsan, Kaz.	H10	24
Zajsan, Ozero, l., Kaz.	H10	24
Zákinthos, i., Grc.	L4	16
Zakopane, Pol.	F19	8
Zalaegerszeg, Hung.	I16	8
Zambezi (Zambeze), stm., Afr.	E6	44
Zambia, ctry., Afr.	D5	44
Zamboanga, Phil.	D7	32
Zamfara, stm., Nig.	F7	42
Zamora, Ec.	J3	58
Zamora, Spain	D6	12
Zamora de Hidalgo, Mex.	H8	62
Zamość, Pol.	E23	8
Zanesville, Oh., U.S.	C4	112
Zanjān, Iran	J7	22
Zanzibar, Tan.	C7	44
Zanzibar, i., Tan.	C7	44
Zaouia el Kahla, Alg.	C7	42
Zaouiet el Mgaïz, Tun.	M5	14
Zaoz'ornyj, Russia	F12	24
Zapadnyj Sajan, mts., Russia	G12	24
Zapala, Arg.	D2	56
Zapata, Tx., U.S.	F3	120
Zapata, co., Tx., U.S.	F3	120
Zapata, Península de, pen., Cuba	C7	64
Zaporozh'ye see Zaporožje, Ukr.	H5	22
Zaporožje, Ukr.	H5	22
Zaragoza, Spain	D11	12
Zarajsk, Russia	G21	18
Zárate, Arg.	C5	56
Zaraza, Ven.	C10	58
Zard Kūh, mtn., Iran	B5	46
Zarembo Island, i., Ak., U.S.	m23	79
Zarghūn Shahr, Afg.	D3	38
Zaria, Nig.	F7	42
Zarzal, Col.	E4	58
Žary (Sorau), Pol.	D15	8
Zāskār, stm., India	D7	38
Zāskār Mountains, mts., Asia	C4	36
Zavala, co., Tx., U.S.	E3	120
Zavolžje, Russia	E26	18
Zavolžsk, Russia	D25	18
Zawiercie, Pol.	E19	8
Zduńska Wola, Pol.	D18	8
Zearing, Ia., U.S.	B4	92
Zebulon, Ga., U.S.	C2	87
Zebulon, N.C., U.S.	B4	110
Zeehan, Austl.	H9	50
Zeeland, Mi., U.S.	F5	99
Zeerust, S. Afr.	G5	44
Zehdenick, Ger.	C13	8
Zeigler, Il., U.S.	F4	90

Zeila, Som.	F3	46
Zeitz, Ger.	D12	8
Zeja, Russia	G19	24
Zeja, stm., Russia	G19	24
Železnogorsk-Ilimskij, Russia	F14	24
Zelienople, Pa., U.S.	E1	115
Zelina, Cro.	D11	14
Zell, Ger.	E7	8
Zell am See, Aus.	H12	8
Zemio, Cen. Afr. Rep.	G11	42
Zenica, Bos.	E12	14
Zenith, Wa., U.S.	f11	124
Zenobia Peak, mtn., Co., U.S.	A2	83
Zephyr Cove, Nv., U.S.	E2	105
Zephyrhills, Fl., U.S.	D4	86
Zerbst, Ger.	D12	8
Zereh, Gowd-e, l., Afg.	D1	36
Zermatt, Switz.	F14	10
Zeytindağ, Tur.	K11	16
Zgierz, Pol.	D19	8
Zhalutegi, China	C11	26
Zhangjiakou (Kalgan), China	C9	26
Zhangzhou (Longxi), China	K6	28
Zhanjiang, China	D11	34
Zhaoan, China	L6	28
Zhaotong, China	F7	26
Zhaxigang, China	D8	38
Zhejiang, prov., China	F10	28
Zhengzhou, China	E9	26
Zhenjiang, China	C8	28
Zhenyuan, China	F8	26
Zhitomir see Žitomir, Ukr.	G3	22
Zhob, stm., Pak.	E3	38
Zhongba, China	F10	38
Zhongshan, China	M2	28
Zhoushan Dao, i., China	E11	28
Zhoushan Qundao, is., China	E10	28
Zhujiangkou, stm., Asia	M2	28
Zhumadian, China	C3	28
Zhungeerqi, China	D9	26
Zhuoxian, China	D10	26
Zhuzhou, China	H2	28
Zia Indian Reservation, N.M., U.S.	h7	108
Zibo, China	D10	26
Ziebach, co., S.D., U.S.	C4	118
Ziel, Mount, mtn., Austl.	D6	50
Zielona Góra (Grünberg), Pol.	D15	8
Žigalovo, Russia	G15	24
Žigansk, Russia	D18	24
Zigong, China	F7	26
Ziguinchor, Sen.	F2	42
Zihuatanejo, Mex.	I9	62
Žilina, Czech.	F18	8
Zillah, Wa., U.S.	C5	124
Zillertaler Alpen, mts., Eur.	B6	14
Zilwaukee, Mi., U.S.	E7	99
Zima, Russia	G14	24
Zimbabwe, ctry., Afr.	E5	44
Zimmerman, Mn., U.S.	E5	100
Zinder, Niger	F7	42
Zion, Il., U.S.	A6	90
Zion National Park, Ut., U.S.	F3	121
Zion Reservoir, res., Az., U.S.	C6	80
Zionsville, In., U.S.	E5	91
Zipaquirá, Col.	E5	58
Zirkel, Mount, mtn., Co., U.S.	A4	83
Ziro, India	G15	38
Zitácuaro, Mex.	H9	62
Žitomir, Ukr.	G3	22
Zittau, Ger.	E14	8
Žiway, Lake, l., Eth.	G2	46
Žižickoje, Ozero, l., Russia	E14	18
Zlarin, Cro.	F10	14
Zlín, Czech.	F17	8
Žlobin, Bela.	I13	18
Zmeinogorsk, Russia	G10	24
Znojmo, Czech.	G16	8
Zolfo Springs, Fl., U.S.	E5	86
Zomba, Mwi.	E7	44
Zonguldak, Tur.	G14	4
Zorita, Spain	F6	12
Zouar, Chad	D9	42
Zrenjanin, Yugo.	D4	16
Zuckerhütl, mtn., Aus.	I11	8
Zudañez, Bol.	G6	54
Zuera, Spain	D11	12
Zug, Switz.	E15	10
Zugspitze, mtn., Eur.	H10	8
Zuiderzee see IJsselmeer, Neth.	C5	8
Zumba, Ec.	J3	58
Zumbo, Moz.	E6	44
Zumbro, stm., Mn., U.S.	F6	100
Zumbrota, Mn., U.S.	F6	100
Zuni (Zuni Pueblo), N.M., U.S.	B1	108
Zuni, stm., U.S.	C6	80
Zuni Indian Reservation, N.M., U.S.	B1	108
Zuni Mountains, mts., N.M., U.S.	B1	108
Zunyi, China	F8	26
Zuqar, Jazīrat, i., Yemen	F3	46
Zurich, Ont., Can.	D3	73
Zürich, Switz.	E15	10
Zürichsee, l., Switz.	E15	10
Zutphen, Neth.	C6	8
Zvishavane, Zimb.	F6	44
Zvolen, Czech.	G19	8
Zwettl, Aus.	G15	8
Zwickau, Ger.	E12	8
Zwolle, Neth.	C6	8
Zwolle, La., U.S.	C2	95
Zyr'anka, Russia	D24	24
Żyrardów, Pol.	C20	8